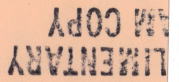

HUMAN

SEXUALITY

Bryan Strong

University of California, Santa Cruz

Christine DeVault

MAYFIELD PUBLISHING COMPANY

Mountain View, California

London • Toronto

TO OUR GOOD FRIENDS,
FRANK GRAHAM AND MARGARET BOND

Library of Congress Cataloging-in-Publication Data

Strong, Bryan.
   Human sexuality / Bryan Strong, Christine DeVault.
      p.   cm.
   Includes index.
   ISBN 1-55934-104-1
   1. Sex. 2. Sex customs. 3. Hygiene, Sexual. I. DeVault,
Christine. II. Title.
HQ12.S74 1994
306.7--dc20   93-32037
                                                                             CIP

Manufactured in the United States of America
10 9 8 7 6 5 4 3 2 1

Mayfield Publishing Company
1280 Villa Street
Mountain View, California 94041

Sponsoring editor, Franklin C. Graham; production editor, Sharon Montooth; manuscript editor, Betsy Dilernia; art director, Jeanne M. Schreiber; text and cover designer, Donna Davis; art editor, Susan Breitbard; illustrators, Jennifer Hagerman, Natalie Hill, Marilyn Krieger, and Kevin Somerville; photo researcher, Melissa Kreischer; manufacturing manager, Martha Branch. The text was set in 10.5/12 Goudy by GTS Graphics, Inc. and printed on 45# Mead Pub Matte by R.R. Donnelley & Sons.

Photo credits appear immediately following the bibliography.
Cover photo: © True Redd.

Brief Contents

Contents

Preface

Were this textbook to make the study and teaching of human sexuality a meaningful and rewarding experience for both students and instructors. We present the study of human sexuality in such a manner as to enlarge both the student's personal and intellectual understanding. A personal approach does not exclude scholarship; nor does scholarship exclude personal understanding. Instead, scholarship allows the student to see beyond his or her own experience; and personal exploration breathes life into academic research.

The primary goal of this textbook is to integrate the personal and intellectual foundations of human sexuality. This goal led us to ask two fundamental questions. First, what would we, as college students, want and need to know and understand about human sexuality? Second, what do we, as instructors and researchers, believe is important for an educated person to know about human sexuality? With these questions in mind, we formulated the structure and direction of this textbook. There are six important aspects to this textbook, described below.

Popular Culture. As we thought about the context in which students would read this textbook, we were struck by how powerful popular culture is in shaping attitudes, beliefs, and ideas about sexuality. In contemporary America, Dr. Ruth, Abigail van Buren, Oprah, Donahue, Geraldo, as well as Sharon Stone, Sylvester Stallone, Dana Carvey, RuPaul, and Madonna, are among the most significant sources of sexual information, ideas, stereotypes, and values. It is important that students think about the depictions of sexuality in popular culture and critically evaluate their impact on our lives. Just as any research finding on human sexuality is subject to critical thought, so too is every image given to us by our popular culture.

Integration of Gay/Lesbian/Bisexuality Research. As we considered the subject of sexual orientation, we decided that it is important to integrate gay/lesbian/bisexual research into the text rather than segregate them into a separate chapter. There are no compelling intellectual reasons to segregate research on gay, lesbian, and bisexual men and women from general discussions per se of communication, love, cohabitation, sexual expression, and so on. Such segregation implies differences where none may exist. It distorts our common humanity and relegates gay men, lesbians, and bisexuals to a "special" category. Such segregation, we believe, unintentionally encourages continued stigmatization.

Ethnic Diversity. As we looked at the demographic composition of our classes, colleges, and universities, we were struck by their increasing ethnic diversity. This diversity reflects the diversity of our nation in which over 20% of Americans are from African American, Latino, Asian America, Native American, or other ethnic descent. To reflect this diversity, we have integrated scholarship on ethnicity and sexuality as much as posssible. This scholarship, however, is limited; and much of it is problem-oriented. But we believe it is important in our ethnically-diverse society to expand the study of human sexuality to include all distinct ethnic groups.

HIV/AIDS Crisis. We are acutely aware of the HIV/AIDS epidemic. Because of its severity, we have devoted a chapter to examining its various aspects, including not only the biological and health aspects but also the personal, social, and psychological aspects.

Research Based. We are deeply committed to scholarship and to presenting cutting-edge research in the field of human sexuality. In writing this book we carefully evaluated the current literature, using bibliographic databases and communicating with scholars around the country. We include what we believe to be the most up-to-date, important, and interesting research findings available. Our own research on love and sexuality continues to remind us of the joys (and limits) of research.

Teaching Support. We want to provide as much support as we can to the instructor teaching human sexuality. We believe a textbook's effectiveness as a teaching tool is dramatically increased when the text is systematically integrated with supplementary instructional material. We have developed a comprehensive, integrated teaching package that dovetails with the text and with classroom needs. Included in this package (described in detail below) are an instructor's resource book, two printed test banks, corresponding computerized test banks, a student study guide, supplemental videos and audiocassettes, and a newsletter.

PEDAGOGICAL AIDS

Human Sexuality is written in an accessible style at a level appropriate for most undergraduates. To support both teaching and learning, we have incorporated several learning aids in the text. Each chapter begins with a **chapter preview,** a self-quiz that challenges students' preconceptions about the topic presented in that chapter. The preview is followed by a **chapter outline,** designed to give the student an overview of topics discussed in the chapter. Reinforcing these two aids is an **"In this chapter"** paragraph, describing the chapter's contents.

Providing students with greater understanding of particular high-interest topics in every chapter are **perspectives** boxes. Each chapter contains at least one of these boxes. Titles include "Carnival: Sexual Transgression in Contemporary Brazil," "Masturbation: From Sin to Insanity," "The Tuskegee Syphilis Study," and "The Unkindest Cut? Female Circumcision." Also found in many chapters are **self-assessments,** which give students the opportunity to reflect on their own attitudes, beliefs, and behaviors. The assessments are actual research instruments or adaptations closely resembling the original versions.

Important **key terms** are printed in boldface type in every chapter and defined in context. A list of key terms appears at the end of each chapter for review purposes. Also appearing at the end of chapters are **chapter summaries,** designed to assist students in understanding main ideas and in reviewing chapter material. An annotated listing of **suggestions for further reading** is included at the end of every chapter as well, providing the student with sources of additional information and resources for research projects. Together, these pedagogical aids support and facilitate effective teaching and successful learning.

INTEGRATED TEACHING PACKAGE

As noted above, *Human Sexuality* includes an integrated package of materials designed to increase its effectiveness as a teaching tool. At the heart of this package is the **The Resource Book: A Teacher's Tool Kit,** which we have developed using a new approach. The resource book begins with course planning material, such as reference tools and resources; suggestions for background reading; bibliographies of materials on human sexuality and ethnicity; and suggested films, videos, transparency masters, and student worksheets. Material for each chapter follows: chapter outlines, selected bibliographies, discussion questions, activities, and sample test questions.

Two **computerized test banks** of close to 3,800 test items have been prepared by Grace Galliano, Kennesaw State College, and Kina Leitner, New York University. Together they bring substantial experience in teaching and in testing and measurement to this element of the package. Each chapter contains approximately 200 test items, including multiple choice questions, true-false questions, fill-in questions tied to key terms, short-answer questions, and essay questions. The test bank can be used with either IBM or Macintosh computers. These two test banks are also printed and bound into one volume.

A student **study guide** has been prepared by Bobbi Mitzenmacher, Long Beach State University, and Barbara Sayed, San Jose State University. The study guide contains detailed chapter outlines, learning objectives, practice tests, activities, and personal involvement assessments.

Our selection of **videotapes** gives instructors the opportunity to illustrate and extend coverage of the most current and compelling topics treated in the text. For information about the videos, instructors should contact their Mayfield representative or call 1-800-433-1279.

Finally, a biannual **newsletter** provides updates to the text, information on new research and relevant current events, suggestions for lectures and activities, and perspectives on the latest issues in human sexuality.

ACKNOWLEDGMENTS

Many people contributed to the creation and development of this book. We are grateful, first of all, for the kind assistance of the reference staff at the Dean McHenry Library at the University of California, Santa Cruz. Reference librarians Alan Ritch, Deborah Murphy, Paul Machlis, and Jaquelyn Maria were very helpful in compiling bibliographies, answering questions, verifying citations, obtaining books and journals through interlibrary loans, and assisting us in the use of on-line and CD-ROM bibliographic systems. The reference staff at the Santa Cruz Public Library also provided much-appreciated assistance.

Ruth Gunn Mota, Director of Education, Santa Cruz AIDS Project (SCAP), provided valuable information about HIV and AIDS. She is deeply committed to increasing AIDS awareness among students and members of the community, as are the SCAP staff and a number of people living with AIDS in our community. We applaud their work.

Our friend and colleague Art Aron, one of the leading researchers in the social psychology of love, assisted us in developing Chapter 9, Communicating about Sex. Terence Crowley, professor of library science at San Jose State University, continues to assist us—and entertain us—when we have difficult questions to research. Pepper Schwartz at the University of Washington has shared her ideas with us about the relationship between sex research and its popularization in the media. Fran Bussard, formerly of California State University, Chico, is an ever-thoughtful friend who provides ongoing insight into human relationships. Herb Colston and Michael Santos contributed greatly to the development of the instructor's manual. Special thanks to William Yarber of Indiana University for allowing us to use his health assessment instruments. We also thank James Barbour of the University of Maine for allowing us to reprint in the Resource Book his essay on human sexuality discussion groups. Zoe Sodja, Nona William, and Cheryl VanDeVeer patiently and cheerfully helped us input the text. To all, we express our deep appreciation.

Of those at Mayfield Publishing Company, we particulary wish to acknowledge Frank Graham, our editor, and thank him for his inspiration, knowledge, and hard work. We also want to thank our production editor, Sharon Montooth, for her dedication and persistence in producing a complex textbook. Editorial assistant Andrea Sarros was always there when we needed her, making things run smoothly. Melissa Kreischer did outstanding work in developing our photo program, Susan Breitbard skillfully managed the art program, and Pamela Trainer competently managed the permissions. Linda Toy, vice president and director of production, has been a constant source of encouragement in producing the book and especially in developing the art program. Dick Greenberg, president of Mayfield, has offered support and encouragement; it has been a pleasure working with him.

We also thank our children—Gabe, Willy, Maria, and Kristin—whose continued development from toddlerhood to young adulthood is an ever-rich source of challenge, delight, and insight.

Finally, we wish to thank the instructors and researchers, listed here alphabetically, whose ideas and feedback contributed to the final shape of this book: Michael J. Bayly, University of Charleston; Katherine Bruce, University of North Carolina at Wilmington; Linda Devillers, Chaffey College; Richard Elliott, Sierra College; David A. Gershaw, Arizona Western College; James A. Johnson, Sam Houston State University; Peter F. Manino, Normandale Community College; Marcia L. McCoy, University of Kansas; David Myers, Hope College; Joanne Smyth, Mendocino Community College; and Donald M. Stanley, North Harris College.

Prologue

Being sexual is an essential part of being human. Through our sexuality, we are able to connect with others on the most intimate levels, revealing ourselves and creating strong bonds. Sexuality is a source of great pleasure and profound satisfaction. It is the means by which we reproduce—bringing new life into the world, and transforming ourselves into mothers and fathers. Paradoxically, sexuality can also be a source of guilt and confusion, a pathway to infection, and a means of exploitation and aggression. Examining the multiple aspects of human sexuality will help you understand your own sexuality and that of others. It will provide the basis for enriching your relationships.

Throughout our lives, we make sexual choices based on our experience, attitudes, values, and knowledge. The decisions many of us may face include whether to become or keep on being sexually active; whether to establish, continue, or end an intimate relationship; whether to practice safer sex consistently; and how to resolve conflicts, if they exist, between our values and our sexual desires, feelings, and behaviors. The choices we make may vary at different times in our lives. Our sexuality changes and evolves as we ourselves change.

STUDYING HUMAN SEXUALITY

Students begin studying sexuality for many reasons: to gain insight into their sexuality and relationships, to explore personal sexual issues, to dispel anxieties and doubts, to resolve traumatic sexual experiences, to prepare for the helping professions, or to increase their general knowledge. Many students find the study of sexuality empowering. They discover their ability to make intelligent sexual choices based on their own needs, desires, and values rather than on guilt, ignorance, pressure, fear, or conformity.

The study of human sexuality differs from the study of accounting, plant biology, and medieval history because human sexuality is surrounded by a vast array of taboos, fears, prejudices, and hypocrisy. For many Americans, sexuality creates feelings of stress. It is linked not only with intimacy and pleasure, but also with stress, guilt, and discomfort. As a result, you may find yourself confronted with society's mixed feelings about sexuality as you study it. You may find, for example, that others perceive you as somehow "different" for taking a course in human sexuality. Some may feel threatened in a vague, undefined way. Parents, partners, or spouses (not to mention your own children, if you are a parent) may wonder why you want to take a "sex class"; they may want to know why you don't take something more "seri-

WHAT STUDENTS WANT TO LEARN IN A HUMAN SEXUALITY COURSE: THE PERSONAL DIMENSION

Students begin the study of human sexuality for a multitude of reasons. When we asked our students to tell us what they wanted to learn in our class, their answers emphasized the personal dimension of learning. The student responses below are representative.

My biggest issue is setting my own sexual guidelines, rather than accepting those of others, such as my friends, society, etc. —a 20-year-old woman

I want to know the difference between sex and love. When I have sex with a woman, I think I'm in love with her, or at least want to be. Am I kidding myself? —a 21-year-old man

I have a hard time telling my boyfriend what I want him to do. I get embarrassed and end up not getting what I need. —a 19-year-old woman

I lost my virginity last week. What do you do when you sleep with someone for the first time? —an 18-year-old man

I recently separated from my husband and am beginning to date again. I'd like to know what the proper sexual etiquette is today. Such as, do you kiss or have sex on the first date . . . or what? —a 37-year-old woman

I'm gay, but my family would disown me if they found out. What can I do to make my parents understand that it's OK to be gay? —a 20-year-old man

My parents continue to hassle me about sex. They want me to be a virgin when I marry (which is next to impossible, since I lost my virginity when I was 16).

Any suggestions on how to raise parents? —a 19-year-old woman

Is it wrong to masturbate if you have a regular partner? —a 22-year-old man

Why do women get called "sluts" if they have more than one partner, and it doesn't matter for guys? In fact, the more women they "have," the more points they get. —an 18-year-old woman

How do I know if I'm normal? What is normal? And why do I care? —a 21-year-old man

I'm a sexy 70-year-old. How come young people think sex stops when you're over 40? We don't spend all day just knitting, you know. —a 70-year-old woman

Some of these questions relate to facts, some concern attitudes or relationships, and still others concern values. But all of them are within the domain of human sexuality. As you study human sexuality, you may find answers to many of these questions, as well as those of your own. You will also find that your class will raise questions the textbook or instructor cannot answer. Part of the reason we cannot answer all your questions is that there is insufficient research available to give an adquate response. But part of the reason also may be that it is not the domain of social science to answer questions of value. As social scientists, it is our role to provide you with knowledge, analytical skills, and insights for making your own moral evaluations. It is you who is ultimately responsible for determining your sexual value system.

ous"—as if sexuality were not one of the most important issues we face as individuals and as a society. Sometimes this uneasiness manifests itself in humor, one of the ways in which we deal with ambivalent feelings: "You mean you have to take a *class* on sex?" "Are there labs?" "Why don't you let me show you?"

Ironically, despite societal ambivalance, you may quickly find that your human sexuality textbook becomes the most popular book in your dormitory or apartment. "I can never find my textbook when I need it," one of our student's complained. "My roommates are always reading it. And they're not even taking the course!" Another student observed: "My friends used to kid me about taking the class, but now the first thing they ask when they see me is what we discussed in class." "People borrow my book so often without asking," wrote one student, "that I hide it now."

What these responses signify is simple: Despite their ambivalence, people *want* to learn about human sexuality. On some level, they understand that what they have learned may have been haphazard, unreliable, stereotypical, incomplete, unrealistic, irrelevant—or dishonest. As adults, they are ready to move beyond "sperm meets egg" stories.

As you study human sexuality, you will discover yourself exploring areas not ordinarily discussed in other classes. Sometimes they are rarely talked about even among friends. They may be prohibited by parental or religious teaching. The more an area is judged to be in some way "bad" or "immoral," the less likely it is to be discussed. Ordinary behaviors such as masturbation and sexual fantasies are often the source of considerable guilt. But in your human sexuality course, they will be examined objectively. You may be surprised to discover, in fact, that part of your learning consists in *unlearning* myths, half-truths, factual errors, and distortions you learned earlier.

You may feel uncomfortable when you go to the first class meetings. That's not at all uncommon. When I (Bryan Strong) went to the first day of my human sexuality class as a student in 1970, I felt embarrassed, out of place. The class was in a darkened auditorium, which gave me the uncomfortable sense I was in an adult movie house. Because I was nervous, I went with a friend; I slouched low in my seat. In retrospect, these feelings are not surprising. Sexuality may be the most tabooed subject we study as undergraduates. (Highly respected sex researchers have been investigated by the FBI because of their research.) Your comfort level in class will probably increase as you recognize that you and your fellow students have a common purpose in learning about sexuality. Your sense of ease may also increase as you and your classmates get to know each other and discuss sexuality, both inside and outside class.

You may find that as you become used to using the accepted sexual vocabulary, the more comfortable in discussing various topics you will become. Perhaps you may find that you have never before used the words "masturbation," "sexual intercourse," "vulva," "penis," "heterosexuality," or "homosexuality" in a class setting (or any kind of setting, for that matter). But after a while, they may become second nature to you. You may discover that discussing sex academically becomes as easy as discussing geography, accounting, or literature. You may even find youself, as many students do, telling your friends what you learned in class while on a bus or in a restaurant, as other passengers or diners gasp in shock or lean toward you to hear better!

Studying sexuality requires respect for your fellow students. You'll discover that the experienes and values of your classmates vary greatly. Some students have little sexual experience, while others have substantial experience; some students hold liberal sexual values, while others hold conservative ones. Some students are gay, lesbian, or bisexual, while the majority are heterosexual. Most students are young, others middle-aged, some old—each in a different stage of life and with different development tasks before them. Furthermore, the presence of students from any of the more than 124 ethnic groups in the United States remind us that there is no single behavioral, attitudinal, value, or belief system that encompasses sexuality in contemporary America.

Because of America's diversity in terms of experience, values, orientation, age, and ethnicity, the study of sexuality calls for us to be open-minded: to be receptive to new ideas and to differentness; to seek to understand what we have not understood before; to reexamine old assumptions, ideas, and beliefs; to encompass the humanity in each of us. In our quest for knowledge and understanding, we need to be intellectually curious. As writer Joan Nestle observes, "Curiosity builds bridges. . . . Curiosity is not trivial; it is the respect one life pays to another."

THE AUTHORS' PERSPECTIVE

We developed this textbook along several themes, which we believe will help you better understand your sexuality and that of others.

Psychosocial Orientation

Although we are creatures rooted in biology, hormones and the desire to reproduce are not the most important factors shaping our sexuality. We believe that the most significant factor is the interplay between our individual personality and social factors. As a result, we use a psychosocial perspective in explaining human sexuality. A psychosocial perspective emphasizes the role of psychological factors (such as motivation, emotions, and attitudes) and social learning (the process of learning from others and society). We look at how sexuality is shaped in our culture; we examine how it differs in different historical periods and between different ethnic groups in our culture. We also examine how sexuality takes different forms in other cultures throughout the world.

Sex as Intimacy

We believe that sex in our culture is basically an expressive and intimate activity. It is a vehicle for expressing feelings, whether positive or negative. It is also a means for establishing and maintaining intimacy. Sex is also important as a means of reproduction, but because of the widespread use of birth control, reproduction has become increasingly a matter of choice.

Gender Roles

Gender roles are societal expectations of how women and men are expected to behave in a particular culture. Among other things, gender roles tell us how we are to act sexually. While women and men differ, we believe most differences are rooted more in social learning than in biology.

Traditionally, our gender roles have viewed men and women as "opposite" sexes. Men were active, women passive; men were sexually aggressive, women sexually receptive; men sought sex, women sought love. Research, however, suggests that we are more alike than different as men and women. To reflect our commonalities rather than differences, we refer not to the "opposite" sex, but to the "other" sex.

Sexuality and Popular Culture

Much of what we learn about sexuality from popular culture and the media—from so-called sex experts, magazine articles, how-to-do it books, and TV and the movies—is wrong, half-true, or stereotypical. Prejudice may masquerade as fact. Scholarly research may also be flawed for various reasons. Throughout the textbook, we look at how we can evaluate what we read and see, both in popular culture and in scholarly research. We compare scholarly findings to sexual myths and beliefs, including research about gay men and lesbians and ethnic groups.

Homosexuality as a Normal Sexual Variation

We recognize the normality of gay and lesbian sexual orientations. Gay men and lesbians have been subjected to discrimination, prejudice, and injustice for centuries because of their orientation. But as society has become more enlightened, it has discovered that lesbians and gay men do not differ from heterosexuals in any significant aspect except in their choice of sexual partners. In 1972, the American Psychiatric Association removed homosexuality from its list of mental disorders. Today, the major professional psychological, sociological, and health associations in the United States regard homosexuality as a normal sexual variation. For this reason, we have integrated discussions of lesbians and gay men throughout the book.

The Significance of Ethnicity

Until recently, Americans have ignored ethnicity as a factor in studying human sexuality. We have acted as if being white, African American, Latino, Asian American, or Native American made no difference in terms of sexual attitudes, behaviors, and values. But there are important differences that we discuss throughout the textbook. It is important to examine these differences within their cultural context. Ethnic differences, therefore, should not be interpreted as "good" or "bad," "healthy" or "deficient," but as reflections of culture. Our understanding of the role of ethnicity, however, is limited because ethnic research is only now beginning to emerge.

Over the years, we have asked our students to briefly state what they learned or gained in our human sexuality class. Here are some of their answers.

> I learned to value the exploration of my sexuality much more. I learned that sexuality comes in many forms, and I'm one of them. The class gave me a forum or safe place to explore sexuality, especially since I have not yet had a fully sexual relationship.

> I found the psychological, historical, and anthropological elements of sexuality we discussed to be very valuable. I see homosexuality in a totally new light.

I learned that being sexual is OK, that basically we are all sexual beings and that it is normal to want to have sex. I am no longer afraid to talk about sex with my boyfriend.

The information about AIDS cleared up many misconceptions and fears I had. I will always practice safer sex from now on.

The class has helped me come to terms with things that have happened over the last few months that are disturbing to me.

I have paid more attention to the erotic nature of things, not just the physical aspects of sex.

We believe that the knowledge you gain from studying human sexuality will be something you will carry with you the rest of your life. We hope it will help you understand and appreciate not only yourself but those who differ from you, and that it will enrich, expand, and enliven your experiences and your relationships.

Chapter One

PERSPECTIVES ON HUMAN SEXUALITY

P R E V I E W : S E L F - Q U I Z

1. The division of sexual behavior into natural and unnatural acts is based on the biological sciences. True or false?

2. Sexual themes often run through family-oriented situation comedies. True or false?

3. Value judgments, such as "good" and "bad," are useful tools for scientifically describing sexual behavior. True or false?

4. High levels of sexual desire are found in all cultures. True or false?

5. All cultures divide human beings into only two genders, male and female. True or false?

6. The media increasingly depicts sexuality as it exists in the real world. True or false?

7. Sexual relationships between men are universally condemned. True or false?

8. College students' sexual ideas tend to reflect popular culture. True or false?

9. Using sexual images in advertising is an effective device for all products. True or false?

10. The most explicit TV sex is usually found on crime shows. True or false?

ANSWERS 1. F, 2. T, 3. F, 4. F, 5. F, 6. F, 7. F, 8. T, 9. F, 10. F

Chapter Outline

Sexuality was once hidden from view in our culture: Fig leaves covered the "private parts" of nudes; poultry breasts were renamed "white meat"; censors prohibited the publication of the works of D. H. Lawrence, James Joyce, and Henry Miller; and homosexuality was called "the love that dares not speak its name." But over the last few generations, sexuality has become more open. In recent years, popular culture and the media have transformed what we "know" about sexuality. Not only is sexuality *not* hidden from view, it often seems to surround us.

In this chapter, we examine popular culture and the media to see how they shape our ideas about sexuality. Then we look at how sexuality has been treated in different cultures and at different times in history. Finally, we examine how society defines various aspects of our sexuality as natural or normal.

The first flower that blossomed on this earth was an invitation to the unborn song.
Rabindranath Tagore

SEXUALITY, POPULAR CULTURE, AND THE MEDIA

Much of our sexuality is influenced and shaped by popular culture, especially the mass media. Popular culture presents us with myriad images of what it means to be sexual. But what kind of sexuality is portrayed by the media—and consumed by us? What are media messages about sex to children, adolescents, adults, and the aged? To men? To women? To whites, African

Americans, Latinos, Asian Americans, and other ethnic groups? Perhaps as important as what the media portrays sexually is what is not portrayed—for example, masturbation, condom use, and erotic marital interactions.

Media Portrayals of Sexuality

Media depictions of sexuality are not as obvious and straightforward as we may initially think. On television, for example, we are usually presented with visual images that suggest but do not show sexual activities other than kissing. In the movies, a wider range of sexual behaviors are shown more explicitly. "Steamy" sex scenes and female nudity (often combined with violence) are part of the Hollywood formula for success. ("How can we put more tits and c— [sic] into this movie?" the director of *Basic Instinct* reportedly asked, upon walking onto the set [Zevin, 1992].)

The music industry is awash with sexual images. Contemporary pop music, from rock 'n' roll to hip hop, bursts with lyrics about sexuality mixed with love, rejection, violence, and loneliness. Heavy metal often reinforces negative attitudes toward women (St. Lawrence & Joyner, 1991). Popular music is transmitted through CD or cassette players or through television and radio. MTV, VH1, and music video programs televise videos filled with sexually suggestive lyrics, images, and dance. Because of censorship issues, the most overtly sexual music is not played on radio, except for some college stations. Disk jockeys, "shock jocks" such as Howard Stern (who was recently fined by the FCC for sexually offensive and racist remarks), weather reporters, and sportscasters make numerous sexual references. They also reinforce conformist gender roles by calling men "guys," "mister," or "sir," while referring to women in terms of family roles, such as "wife," "mother," "daughter," "sister," or "ladies" (Lont, 1990). (For a general discussion of the portrayal of women in popular culture, see Cantor, 1987.)

Magazines, tabloids, and books contribute to the sexualization of our environment. Sexual references (measured as the ratio of references per page) tripled between 1950 and 1980 in such magazines as *Reader's Digest*,

Shock jocks such as Howard Stern are popular radio personalities whose programs are filled with sexual references and innuendos. What messages do they suggest about sexuality? Men? Women? Homosexuality?

Women's magazines, such as Cosmopolitan, Redbook, and Mademoiselle, use sex to sell their publications. How do these magazines differ from men's magazines, such as Playboy and Penthouse, in their treatment of sexuality?

Time, and *Newsweek* (Scott, 1986). Popular novels, romances, and self-help books, such as *The ESO Ecstasy Program* (Brauer, Brauer, & Rhodes, 1991) and *Women, Sex, and Addiction* (Kasl, 1989) help disseminate popular ideas and values about sexuality. Supermarket tabloid headlines exploit the unusual ("Woman with Two Vaginas Has Multiple Lovers") or sensational ("Televangelist's Love Tryst Exposed").

Men's magazines have been singled out for their sexual sell. *Playboy* and *Penthouse,* with their Playmates of the Month, Pets of the Month, and other nude pictorials, are among the most popular magazines in the world (Wolf & Kielwasser, 1991). Playboy sells about 10 million issues monthly, including 2 million to women (Martin, 1992). (One-quarter of the top 40 best-selling videocassettes are usually produced by *Playboy* and *Penthouse.*) *Sports Illustrated's* annual swimsuit edition sells over 5 million copies, twice as many as its other issues. But it would be a mistake to think that only male-oriented magazines focus on sex.

Women's magazines, such as *Cosmopolitan* and *Redbook,* have their own sexual content (McMahon, 1990). These magazines feature romantically staged photographs of lovers to illustrate stories with such titles as "Sizzling Sex Secrets of the World's Sexiest Women," "Making Love Last: If Your Partner Is a Premature Ejaculator," and "Turn on Your Man with Your Breasts (Even If They Are Small)." Katherine McMahon (1990) writes:

> *Cosmopolitan* magazine, with its familiar cover, has been an icon of feminine sexuality since the mid-1960s. The cover "Cosmo girl," dressed in costumes signifying leisure and sexual availability, levels a gaze suggesting at least pique if not downright hostility. . . . Sex sells not only to males but also to a female mass market. The question becomes, what kind of sex is being marketed. . . ? Which desires are defined as permissible and which are relegated to the status of the impossible?

McMahon found that almost all the articles she surveyed over a 12-year period in the magazine dealt directly or indirectly with sex.

Advertising in all media uses the sexual sell, promising sex, romance, popularity, and fulfillment provided the consumer purchases the right soap, perfume, cigarettes, alcohol, toothpaste, jeans, or automobile. An advertisement for Infiniti, for example, claims: "It's not a car. It's an aphrodisiac." In reality, not only does one *not* become "sexy" or popular by consuming a certain product, the product may actually be detrimental to one's sexual well-being. It is ironic, in fact, to link cigarettes and alcohol with sex. Heavy smoking, for example, is associated with erectile dysfunction, the inability of the penis to become erect, and with lowered fertility in both men and women (Rosen et al., 1991). Alcohol consumption is linked to both male and female sexual problems and severe birth defects in the children of heavy drinkers (see Chapter 13).

In magazine advertising, the figure representing the subject, or "self," the model with whom we are expected to identify, is self-absorbed, emotionally distant, and unresponsive. Others are attracted to this "self" because of what he or she is wearing, driving, drinking, consuming, or owning. The magazine "self" is attractive to others by virtue of what he or she owns or consumes, not because of *who* he or she is (Masse & Rosenblum, 1988). Over the last generation, the degree of nudity has increased in magazine advertising. The level of sexually provocative attire is greater for female models than for

Television is one of the most pervasive media affecting our views of sexuality. What ideas and images about sexuality do your favorite programs convey?

Sexual images are used to sell products. What ideas are conveyed by this advertisement? How does its appeal differ according to whether one is male or female?

males; the level of provocation has also been increasing (Soley & Reid, 1986).

Media images of sexuality permeate all areas of life. They are more important than family in influencing the sexual attitudes and behavior of adolescents and college students. Studies indicate that movies are one of the leading sources of sex information for Anglo, Latino, and Native American male adolescents. They appear to learn more from movies than from their female peers (Davis & Harris, 1982). Half of the college men (but fewer women) in a recent study reported that pornography had been a source of information for them on masturbation, oral-genital sex, and anal intercourse (Duncan, 1990). Overall, only peers are as important as the media in transmitting sexual knowledge (Courtright & Baran, 1980; Moffatt, 1989).

To study the social life of college students, anthropologist Michael Moffatt (1989) lived for several years in a campus dormitory. He discovered that media images have an overwhelming impact on college students. Moffatt writes:

> The direct sources of students' sexual ideas were located almost entirely in mass consumer culture: the late-adolescent/young adult exemplars displayed in movies, popular music, advertising, and on TV; Dr. Ruth, sex manuals, *Playboy, Penthouse, Cosmopolitan, Playgirl*, etc.; Harlequins and other pulp romances (females only); the occasional piece of real literature; sex education and popular psychology as it had filtered through these sources, as well as through public schools as it continued to filter through the student-life infrastructure of the college; classic soft-core and hard-core pornographic movies; books; and . . . videocassettes.

Mass-media depictions of sexuality are meant to entertain, not to inform. As a result, the media do not present us with "real" depictions of sexuality. Sexual activities, for example, are usually not explicitly acted out or described in mainstream media. The various media present the social *context* of sexuality (C. Smith, 1991); that is, the programs, plots, movies, stories, articles, newscasts, and vignettes tell us *what* behaviors are appropriate (e.g., kissing or sexual intercourse), *with whom* they are appropriate (e.g., girlfriend/boyfriend, partner, among heterosexuals), and *why* they are appropriate (e.g., attraction, love, loneliness, exploitation).

Television

Television is the most pervasive and influential medium affecting our views of sexuality. The visual depiction of explicit sexual behavior on network television, however, is limited. We generally see nothing more than kissing and occasional fondling and only between heterosexuals. (It was not until 1991 that C.J. and Abby on "L.A. Law" shared prime time's first lesbian kiss; there has been no comparable kissing between men.) Other sexual behaviors, such as coitus or oral sex, may be suggested through words ("Oh, it feels so good") or visual or sound cues (closeups of faces tensing during orgasm or music from Ravel's *Bolero* playing on the soundtrack). Sexual behavior is never overtly depicted as it is in sexually oriented films. References to masturbation are rarely made; when they are, they are usually negative and consigned to an adolescent context, suggesting that such behavior is "immature." Female breasts may be shown, but usually in tight garments, with suggestive cleavages or nipples outlined through clothing; nipples themselves are taboo.

Subscriber cable television, however, offers more sexually oriented programs than network programs. The Playboy Channel offers explicit films. But most cable stations do not show X-rated films. One hard-core cable company, The Exxxtasy Channel, was forced out of business as a result of government obscenity prosecutions. Because of concern about community reaction, sexually oriented films are generally R-rated (no penetration, ejaculation, or gay/lesbian sex). But some media are seeking new ways of exploiting the TV sex market. MCA Universal has hired Jaron Lanier, who coined the term "virtual reality," to develop VR technology that will allow cable subscribers to use goggles, gloves, and body sensors to create their own virtual sexual reality. Lanier says (quoted in Kaplan, 1992):

> If you think of Virtual Reality sex as a really creative, dynamic way to change the perception of your body and your lover's body and do wild, surreal, erotic explorations, then you have something really interesting. The stranger your fantasy is, the more effective Virtual Reality will be.

While virtual reality lies in the future, today television helps form our sexual perceptions through its depiction of stereotypes and its reinforcement of **norms,** which are cultural rules or standards. Television shapes our perceptions differently, however, depending on the TV genre (the type of program). There are five major TV genres in which sexual stereotyping and norms are especially influential: situation comedies, soap operas, crime/ action-adventure programs, made-for-TV movies, and music videos. In addition, TV commercials can be considered a genre.

TV—chewing gum for the eyes.
Frank Lloyd Wright
(1869–1959)

Televison situation comedies, such as "Married with Children," frequently use sexual themes. What are some of the sexual themes or ideas of the most popular sitcoms? Do they differ according to ethnicity?

Each genre has a different formula for what is sexually permissible and how to depict sex. The formulas are influenced by network censors and conservative advocacy groups, such as Donald Wildmon's American Family Association (Montgomery, 1989). These groups exert pressure on networks and advertisers to present morally correct programming. Positive references to birth control, abortion, and gays and lesbians, for example, are considered to be promoting immorality. The effectiveness of pressure groups can be seen if you think of the last time you saw a condom advertisement or heard the word "condom" on any of the major networks.

Situation Comedies Sex in situation comedies? When asked, most people think there is none. After all, sitcoms usually deal with families or familylike relationships; children are often the major characters. Because they are family-oriented, sitcoms do not deal with explicit depictions of sex (C. Smith, 1991; Taylor, 1989). Instead, they deal with sexuality in the form of taboos centering around marital or family issues. The taboos are mild, such as the taboo against a married person flirting with another man or woman. If a sitcom dealt with a major taboo, such as incest, the program would go beyond the sitcom's normal boundaries; it would not be funny.

In sitcoms, the formula is to put a character in a situation in which he or she unknowingly violates a conventional social rule, thereby creating chaos. The chaos, however, is resolved by the show's end, and everyone "lives happily ever after" until the next episode. Thus, a married man can be getting an eyelash out of his sister-in-law's eye when his wife comes home early and becomes jealous, suspecting her husband and sister of kissing. While the laugh track plays, the husband tries to explain that "she had something in her eye."

Sitcoms are sexually stereotypical. Their range of sexual standards and implied behaviors is limited, although the sexual references have increased considerably since the days of "I Love Lucy" (Cantor, 1991). Despite the increase in sexual references, sitcoms barely touch on the variety of values and behaviors found in the real world. Billy Crystal's breakthrough gay character in "Soap" and Martin Mull's in "Roseanne" are examples of sympathetic gay characters in mainstream sitcoms, but they remain the exception. Conservative advocacy groups continue to oppose depictions of gay men and lesbians as normal (Montgomery, 1989). While sitcoms have a limited range, they are nevertheless affirming of connectedness and family values. They provide a context of intimacy for sexuality. Whatever transgression occurs, it is forgotten by the next episode.

Soap Operas Soap operas are one of the most popular TV genres. One soap, "Days of Our Lives," is among the top ten most-watched television programs among college students (Cary, 1992). While sexual transgressions are soon forgotten in sitcoms, they are never forgotten in soap operas. Transgressions are the lifeblood of soaps: jealousy and revenge are ever-present. Most characters are now, or once were, involved with each other. The ghosts of past loves haunt the mansions and townhouses; each relationship carries a heavy history with it. Infidelity, pregnancy alarms, wild affairs, betrayals, and jealousy punctuate every episode. Depictions of sexual behavior are fairly frequent. One study of soaps found one reference to sexual intercourse every 40 minutes; scenes of sexual intercourse were depicted every 90 minutes (Greenberg & D'Alessio, 1985).

There are very definite rules governing soap sex, although they vary from soap to soap. Linda Gottlieb, the executive producer of "One Life to Live," says of the rules governing her soap: "You cannot show the moment of penetration. And you're not supposed to show unbuttoning, either" (Van Buskirk, 1992). In a comic sadomasochism scene between Alex and Carlo, Gottlieb says, "She was allowed to wear very revealing clothes and to torture him. But [network censors] wouldn't allow us to use handcuffs. . . . They did allow him to tie her to the bed with scarves, just not with handcuffs" (Van Buskirk, 1992). "Days of Our Lives" prohibits women from lying on their backs on their beds and kissing the man on top of them; the man must be sitting upright on the bed. Gottlieb says of daytime soaps: "I don't believe women want to see graphic sex . . ." (Van Buskirk, 1992). And the producer of "Another World" says: "If you go too far visually, you've stepped beyond the bounds of romance. It gets too personal and embarrassing and the fantasy goes away" (Van Buskirk, 1992).

Gender roles tend to be stereotypical, with men generally more dominant and aggressive than women. Few characters over age 40 are depicted as sexually active (Greenberg & D'Alessio, 1985). African Americans have been notably absent in soaps. When a black does appear, it is generally as a single character in the context of dealing with racial issues, such as discrimination. African American characters often are engaged in interracial affairs. These affairs do not last long, and the characters generally find other black men or women to be partners (Geraghty, 1990). No major American soap incorporates representative numbers of African Americans, Latinos, Asian Americans, or other ethnic groups. Only "EastEnders," the popular English soap opera shown on many PBS stations, thoroughly integrates ethnic characters and families into its story lines.

In recent years, *telenovelas*, Spanish-speaking soaps such as "La Fuerza del Amor" ("The Force of Love"), "Destino" ("Destiny"), and "Muchachitas" ("Girls") from Latin America, have become increasingly popular in the Latino population. The content and messages of Latino soaps, however, do not differ significantly from soaps produced in the United States. They differ mainly in presenting fewer scenes suggestive of sexual activities, such as characters in bed (Raisbaum, 1986).

The most explicit nudity is seen on the soaps: frontal shots of nude male

torsos (genitals are not shown) and back shots of nude female torsos (to avoid the taboo naked female breast). Characters lounge in bed, wrapped in sheets; they are either about to engage in sex or basking in its pleasurable aftermath. At the same time, no one seems to use contraception or take measures to prevent sexually transmitted diseases (STDs). By the odds, one would expect many pregnancies and an epidemic of STDs (Lowry & Towles, 1989). Corliss Smith (1991) observes:

> Sex is made very hot, too hot in many cases, but irresistible, so the characters seem to fall into sexual relations almost against their wills. . . . Yet paradoxically, the characters also flee to sexual interludes as brief respites, as islands of pleasure in the otherwise inexorable confrontations the soap opera format demands. . . . They have to forget the inevitable consequences since sex is their only relief. Also, they must be constantly tempted so as to continue the soap's ongoing creation of suspense.

Although there is also intimacy in the world of soaps, it is intense, unstable, and desperate. Relationships are usually stormy and short-lived, setting the scene for jealousy and revenge in subsequent episodes. There is no satisfaction or fulfillment in most soap relationships.

Crime/Action-Adventure Programs In crime and action-adventure programs, there are few intimate relationships. Instead, relationships are fundamentally sexual, based on attraction. They are the backdrop to crime and adventure, which form the main plot of the story. The basic theme of a crime program is disorder (a crime) that must be resolved so that order can be restored. Often the disorder is caused by a sexual act or a sexually related issue, such as prostitution, pornography, rape, cross-dressing, sexual blackmail, or seduction for criminal purposes. As such, we see the underside of sex. Plots involve police searching for female killers who turn out to be cross-dressers, prostitutes who are murdered by sociopaths, runaways lured into pornography, and so on. Detectives and police go under cover, leading the audience into the underworld of prostitutes, pimps, and johns.

The detectives live remote emotional lives. Their involvements are ephemeral, usually not lasting beyond a single episode. Often their love interests are murdered; other times, the women themselves prove to be criminals. Detectives are portrayed as loners. They find intimacy with their detective partners or with secretaries, even in such a nontraditional series as "Cagney and Lacey," in which the primary bonding remains between the two women (Clark, 1992).

Made-for-TV Movies Made-for-TV movies focus on "problem" themes. In contrast to most series, TV movies revolve around more controversial topics. When plots center on sexuality, they generally focus on sex as a social issue rather than sex as intimacy. Their plots feature such issues as adolescent pregnancy, extramarital affairs, rape, sexual harassment, and AIDS. (TV movies about AIDS have introduced, for the first time, nonstereotypical gay and lesbian characters who display a fuller range of human emotions.) But because TV seeks to entertain rather than inform, most sexual topics lend easily to sensationalism, which TV often exploits.

TV movies in which rape occurs often place rape within the context of entertainment. Such movies may use gratuitous sexual aggression as a means of "hooking" an audience. In the process, these movies may distort the seriousness of rape (Wilson, 1988). Rape movies may present misleading stereotypes, such as a woman being sexually provocative, "deserving" to be raped, or "leading the man on." By using a certain type of music, they make rape seem titillating (Pfaus, Myronuk, & Jacobs, 1986). While most rapists are known to the victim, TV films generally depict rapists as strangers. And although most rapes take place between members of the same ethnic group, rape movies on TV disproportionately depict African American men preying on white women (South & Felson, 1990; Wilson, 1988).

Music Videos: MTV and VH1 MTV, VH1, and music-video programs such as "Friday Night Videos" and "Night Track" are some of the most popular programs among adolescents and young adults. Most viewers, however, do not watch them for longer than 15 minutes at a time, because the videos are repetitive.

Unlike audio-recorded music, music videos play upon the eye as well as the ear. Some productions, such as those of Michael Jackson and Madonna, are exceptionally artistic. Cindy Lauper's "Girls Just Want to Have Fun" was a breakthrough video with its affirmation of female freedom (Lewis, 1992).

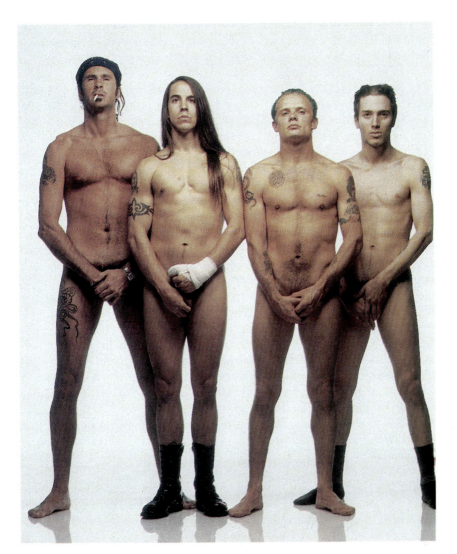

More recently, Madonna's blending of musical and visual components, especially dance, brings an erotic female presence to music videos. In fact, according to one critic, Madonna's videos represent powerful affirmations of female sexuality and power (Lewis, 1992; McClary, 1990).

But most videos are of average quality, relying on flashing visual images to sustain audience interest. Since TV prohibits the explicit depiction of sexual acts, music videos use sexual innuendos and suggestiveness to impart sexual meaning (Baxter et al., 1985; Sherman & Dominck, 1987). There is considerable aggression against both men and women. But contrary to popular images, in music videos women are more likely to initiate aggression against men (Kalis & Neuendorf, 1989). Women are often portrayed condescendingly; they are usually provocatively dressed. A study of 110 music videos aired on MTV revealed that 57% of the videos depicted women as sexual objects; another 17% showed women being "kept in place." Only

My sexual image is looming out there in front of me. Everyone probably thinks I'm a raving nymphomaniac, that I have an insatiable appetite, when the truth is, I'd rather read a book.

Madonna

14% portrayed women as the equal of men (Vincent et al., 1987). In contrast to videos featuring whites, those featuring African Americans are more likely to depict blacks in caring roles (Brown & Campbell, 1986).

TV Commercials Commercials form a unique genre of TV programming. Although they are not part of a television program per se, because they are inserted before, after, and during the program, they become a free-floating part of the program. In commercials, television advertisers may manipulate sexual images to sell products. The most sexually explicit commercials generally advertise jeans, beer, and perfume.

These commercials present a story told visually through a series of brief scenes or images. They do not pretend to explain the practical benefits of their product, such as cost or effectiveness. Instead, they offer the consumer an image or attitude. Directed especially toward adolescents and young adults, these commercials play upon fantasies of attractiveness, sexual success, and fun. The consumer will supposedly acquire these attributes as a result of using a particular product.

While sexual images get our attention, they are not especially effective in advertising. There is some evidence, in fact, that sexual stimuli can distract us from a commercial's product message. We are more likely to remember a sexy scene than the product's name (Bello, Pitts, & Etzel, 1983; Severn, Belch, & Belch, 1990). Sexual images tend to be effective only when they promote products associated with sex or sexual attractiveness, such as condoms, perfume, and lingerie. In fact, women tend to have a negative attitude toward nudity in advertising (Alexander & Judd, 1986). Despite their lack of effectiveness, the belief that sex sells *anything* is so strong that advertising agencies continue to sexualize their advertisements and commercials.

Other TV Genres Sex is present in other TV genres, too. Game shows often play on sexual themes, either suggestively ("The Dating Game") or explicitly ("Studs"). Among the staples of daytime talk shows, such as "Donahue," "Oprah," "Sally Jesse Raphael," "Geraldo," and "Cristina," are unconventional guests and topics, such as women married to gay men or transsexuals, so-called sex addicts, and polygamists. Such talk shows use unconventional sexuality to provoke viewer interest. While their prime purpose remains entertainment, talk shows can provide first-hand accounts of atypical sexual behavior that differs from the more common forms of sexual expression. These shows reveal the diversity of human sexuality, as well as give its participants a human face. As critic Walter Goodman (1992) observes: "They carry a gospel of tolerance, preaching openness for the unusual and encouraging greater acceptance of groups and behavior that have long been the objects of ignorance and fear." A few syndicated programs, such as Ruth (Dr. Ruth) Westheimer's "Good Sex," offer more thoughtful (though still entertaining) discussions of sexuality from a therapeutic perspective (Buxton, 1991).

News programs continuously report rapes, child sexual abuse, pornography, sex therapies, and opinion polls on sexuality. TV news magazines examine various sexual issues in more "depth" (i.e., they devote more time, not thought). Both types of news programs usually deal with atypical or controversial aspects of sexuality. Corliss Smith (1991) notes: "The news eye por-

The vast wasteland of TV is not interested in producing a better mousetrap but in producing a worse mouse.

Laurence Coughlin

I find television very educating. Every time somebody turns on the set I go into the other room and read a book.

Groucho Marx

Most American television stations reproduce all night what only a Roman could have seen in the Coliseum during the reign of Nero.

George Faludy

trays its gaze as a dispassionate one which, because of its objectivity, may delve prurience and bring it into the living room."

In addition to mainstream television broadcasting, there are religious television networks and programs that have wide-scale appeal. Religious programming, such as "The 700 Club," broadcasts Christian fundamentalist visions of sex, sin, and morality (Shepard, 1989; Wills, 1989, 1990). These programs stress conservative family themes, such as adolescent chastity, opposition to sex education based on choice rather than abstinence, pro-life appeals, and homophobia. Of the most important televangelists during the 1980s, only Pat Robertson, who ran for the Republican presidential nomination in 1988, and Jerry Falwell remain active. The other powerful televangelists, Jim Bakker and Jimmy Swaggart, lost their ministries because of sexual improprieties.

Hollywood Films

American motion pictures follow different rules from those of television regarding sexuality. Movies generally are permitted greater license in graphically depicting sexual behavior. But films are still limited by censorship. Like television, films tend to depict sexual stereotypes and to adhere to mainstream sexual norms.

Mainstream Films From their very inception, motion pictures have dealt with sexuality. In 1896, a film entitled *The Kiss* outraged moral guardians when it showed a couple stealing a quick kiss. "Absolutely disgusting," complained one critic. "The performance comes near being indecent in its emphasized indecency. Such things call for police action" (quoted in Webb, 1983). Today, by contrast, film critics use "sexy," a word independent of artistic value, to praise a film. "Sexy" films are movies in which the requisite "sex scenes" are sufficiently titillating to overcome their lack of aesthetic merit. *Basic Instinct*, for example, was most noted for its "hot" sex scenes played by Sharon Stone, who subsequently achieved stardom based on her "sexiness" rather than her acting ability. Interestingly, sex scenes do not create equally famous male stars.

Nudity and overt eroticism were absent from American films until the late 1950s and early 1960s. Instead, Hollywood dealt with sex as "the war between the sexes." In these films, playboys tried (unsuccessfully) to seduce virgins, as in Doris Day sex farces, such as *That Touch of Mink* (1962). The underlying message was that premarital and extramarital sex were immoral; sex was permitted only in marriage. In these comedies, virtue triumphed; only when the man married the virgin would she permit him to "take" her virginity on the wedding night (although the camera faded as newlyweds approached the bedroom). Today, because of changes in social customs, such films seem as dated as the corset.

In Hollywood films of the 1990s, there is considerable female nudity, especially above the waist. But men are never filmed nude in the same manner as women. Men are generally clothed or partially covered; if they are fully nude, the scene takes place at night, the scene is blurred, or we see only his backside. Except on rare occasions, the penis is never visible; if it is visible, it is limp, not erect, according to one film director (Toback, 1992). In *Basic Instinct*, the director reported that the motion picture ratings board

Filming a love scene is very much like shooting a fight scene.
Sharon Stone

permitted him to show the penis of a murdered man "because it was dead" (Andrews, 1992). (In the more liberal European version of the film, however, a scene reveals Michael Douglas's penis in a frontal nude shot; the shot was cut for the American release.) A film psychologist notes: "People have gotten accustomed to wanting to see women nude. They don't think a nude woman looks vulnerable anymore. When a man is uncovered . . . the reaction is that he is extremely vulnerable" (Andrews, 1992).

While there is more naked flesh, the old war-between-the-sexes theme continues with a significant variation. In today's film comedies and dramas, men pursue women and women resist, as they did before. What is new, however, is that the man's persistence awakens the woman's sexual desire. They fall in love, make love (or vice versa), and have passionate sex happily ever after. In these films, sex takes place outside of marriage (usually premaritally), reflecting the widespread acceptance of nonmarital intercourse. Such scenarios reflect traditional male/female stereotypes of the active man and passive woman. At the same time, however, they validate premarital sexual intercourse as a social norm.

Shots suggesting sexual intercourse and oral sex are commonplace in today's films. But scenes of sexual intercourse are generally filmed from a male perspective; the camera explores the woman's body and her reaction (Andrews, 1992). Even family-centered films have scenes intimating oral sex (such as *Parenthood* [1990] when Steve Martin's screen wife performs fellatio on him, causing a car crash). But other common forms of sexual behavior, such as masturbation, are virtually absent from contemporary films. Director Richard Benjamin's acting career came to a virtual halt after he played a comic masturbation scene in *Portnoy's Complaint* (1972).

In films, dangerous men and dangerous women are depicted differently. As film critic Jerome Weeks (1993) notes:

> Masculine menace on screen and stage is usually seen as a generalized threat: Anyone would fear this particular male because he's a master of violence or dangerously out of control. But if female performers are dangerous, they're dangerous only "to men." It's practically unheard of for a female character to be intimidating in any terms that are not sexual. If they're killers, they kill their husbands, lovers, or the patsies they need and therefore seduce.

There are only a few female stars, such as Linda Hamilton in *The Terminator* movies and Sigourney Weaver in the *Alien* movies, who dispense violence with the ease of a Clint Eastwood, Arnold Schwartzenegger, or Jean-Claude van Damme.

Gay Men and Lesbians in Film Gay men and lesbians are generally absent from mainstream films. When gay men and lesbians do appear, they are consistently defined in terms of their sexual orientation, as if there was nothing more to their lives than sexuality. Gay men are generally stereotyped as effeminate, flighty, or "arty." Lesbians are often stereotyped as humorless, mannish, or "butch." (The popular *Fried Green Tomatoes* [1992] muted the lesbian relationship between the central female characters found in the novel.)

If gay men and lesbians are not seen as effeminate or butch, they are portrayed as sinister beings. Their sexual orientation is symptomatic of a dangerous pathology. In *The Silence of the Lambs*, the best of the recent

psycho-thrillers, the killer is a gay cross-dresser (Tharp, 1991). Film director Tom Kalin notes that films about obsessive love and murder between men and women, such as *Double Indemnity* (1944) and *Body Heat* (1981), never "argue that heterosexuals are inherently pathological, driven to crime by their sexuality" (Kalin, 1992). And one film critic (Weir, 1992) notes:

> In Hollywood movies, heterosexuals are never defined as evil or irrelevant simply *because* of their sexuality. Whether they act nobly or ignominiously, other aspects of their personalities are brought to bear. Gay men and lesbians, on the other hand, are consistently characterized solely in terms of their homosexuality—when they are depicted at all. What's more, in American movies, homosexuality seems invariably to signal that a character is either sinister or irrelevant.

Recently, gay and lesbian films have been increasingly integrating their characters' gayness into a wider focus. The poignant *Torch Song Trilogy* (1989), based on the Tony award-winning play about a gay female impersonator, and *Desert Hearts* (1986), an insightful love story about two women, are not as much films about being gay or lesbian as they are about being human. Foreign films, by contrast, often treat gay men and lesbians more realistically than American films do. *My Beautiful Laundrette* (1985), *Maurice* (1986), and *The Crying Game* (1992) all include gay themes, but the films are not about homosexuality per se. Instead, they touch on universal themes, such as love, loyalty, and self-discovery. Film historian Vito Russo (1987) observed:

> The fact they are movies about self-identified gays often confuses people into thinking that they are films by gays about homosexuality. This confusion will end when gayness is no longer a controversial topic. As Quentin Crisp has said, "Homosexuality won't be accepted until it is completely seen as boring—a mundane, inconsequential part of everyday life."

There is no more need to identify *Desert Hearts* as being about lesbians than there is to identify *Pretty Woman* as being about heterosexuals.

Romance Novels

While we tend to focus on television and film depictions of sexuality, we often overlook other media portrayals. Romance novels, which account for 40% of all paperback book sales, are important vehicles for conveying sexual meanings. They are directed primarily at women. Novels by such romance writers as Barbara Taylor Bradford (who recently received a $24-million advance for three novels) head the best-seller lists. Like television, where they often form the basis of miniseries, romance novels have limited formulas in what they depict. These formulas both reflect and create the tastes and fantasies of their audience (Cantor, 1987; Christian-Smith, 1990).

Because it appeals to different fantasies, the romance book industry generally publishes its books in categories, such as Desire, Ecstasy, Loveswept, and Rapture. (Harlequin numbers its books so that its readers can request them by number rather than title.) Each category has its own particular formula of how much sex to allow and in what circumstances. Whatever amount of sex is permitted, however, the formula follows a set of rules known as the "Cinderella legend." One romance writer, Kathyrn Falk (1984), describes the basic formula as follows:

> Female meets devastating man, sparks fly, lovers meld, lovers are torn apart, get back together, resolve their problems, and commit themselves, usually, to marriage.... Romance falls into the sensual mode, but even at its most steamy a romance is never soft-core pornography. A romance is sex with commitment, pornography is sex without commitment.

Romance readers do not like to encounter words like "penis" or "vulva," notes Falk. Because their audience wants sexuality veiled, she continues, "many romance writers collect pretty ways of describing anatomical parts, the clichés now being *temple of love, creamy thighs, Mound of Venus,* etc." Sexual references become acceptable by disguising them, using euphemisms.

Love, marriage, and sex are the heroine's goals in romance novels. The plot often reinforces traditional norms, such as those prohibiting premarital or extramarital sexual intercourse, while at the same time titillating its readers with "creamy thighs." (More recently, reflecting contemporary sexual norms, some novels permit the heroine to engage in premarital sex if it is with the "right" man who has committed himself to marriage.) But because traditional norms are upheld, readers can both identify with the heroine's "throbbing heart" and reassure themselves of their own morality. In fact, some researchers argue that "romances are essentially pornography for people ashamed to read pornography" (Snitow, 1983).

The romance heroine is sensual, but her sensuality is dormant, waiting to be awakened. The awakening of her sexuality creates dramatic tension as the heroine tries to resolve the conflict between her sexual passion and her conventional morality. In the end, honor triumphs over desire.

The threat of moral transgression weaves through romance plots. Temptation and seduction are major themes. Seducers and lovers alike ache for the heroine's "temple of love," but she resists, then wavers, flushed with desire. At the last minute, she reasserts her moral values; she resists temptation or repulses seduction. Morality is upheld. She saves her virginity for marriage, for "Mr. Right" who commits to her, thereby reaffirming the power of love. Like the fairy-tale Cinderella, the heroine, who yields her virginity in holy matrimony (or, if she is liberal, after marriage is promised), lives with her husband/prince happily ever after (Cantor, 1987).

While such morality tales are stereotypical, there are also more disturbing themes of rape and incest underlying many romance novels. This is particularly true in gothic romance novels, which generally take place in former times, especially in the early nineteenth century. Male aggression is often an important element in romances. (Because of aggressive sexual themes, romance novels are also known as "bodice rippers.") Aggression frequently takes the form of seduction. By linking female sexuality to seduction, romances relieve their heroines of sexual responsibility and initiative. Seduction reaffirms the belief that moral women are sexually passive.

Often these so-called seductions are really rapes made pretty by romance novelists. In such seductions/rapes, the heroine resists the man's desires; he ignores her constant refusals and takes her into his arms, kissing her passionately. She may continue to refuse, but already the kiss begins to awaken her slumbering sexuality. After token resistance, she surrenders to his willful masculinity and is grateful. The archetypal image of rape as seduction is Rhett Butler's taking of the fiercely independent Scarlett O'Hara in Margaret Mitchell's novel *Gone with the Wind* (and in the movie starring Clark Gable and Vivian Leigh) (Haskell, 1987). Scarlett resists Rhett as he tries to kiss her, but her resistance is half-hearted. Against her continued protests, he lifts her into his arms and carries her up the great staircase into her bedroom. The next morning she awakens, radiant, for Rhett has also awakened the woman in her. Such seduction scenes validate the stereotype that women really mean "yes" or "coax me" when they say "no" and discredit the experience of women who have been raped.

Incest is a persistent theme in gothic romances, which are set in dark, crumbling mansions or castles. But incest in romance novels bears little relationship to real incest (see Chapter 18). Gothic incest is often the result of mistaken identity. Brothers and sisters, separated at birth, fall in love with each other but discover their blood relationship at the last minute, prior to consummating their romance. This type of incest does not include sexual assault on young children or adolescents, as often occurs in reality.

A particularly disturbing trend is found in the plantation romance. The modern plantation novel mixes violence, sexual passion, and racism. An analysis of over 200 plantation novels found several themes (Geist, 1980). These include the dominance of white men, the exalted status of white women, the inferiority of African Americans, interracial sex (often between a slave and his plantation mistress), and interactions featuring hostility, violence, and sexuality. The planter and his family frequently have slaves as lovers who, because of their relationship with their owners, may exercise significant power. Alternatively, the planter may discover that his wife is his slave's lover, which leads to a jealous rage, resulting in beating the slave. The plantation novel exploits stereotypes of African American sexual prowess that date back to the sixteenth century (Jordan, 1968).

In romance novels, masturbation is virtually nonexistent. If cross-dressing or transsexuality are introduced, it is generally to imply danger or humor. Gay men and lesbians are generally absent unless they, too, are presented humorously or menacingly. It was not until 1980 that the first gay romance novel, *Gaywyck* (Virga, 1980), was introduced. Its gothic cover depicts a dark garden, a shadowy mansion, and an angry sea, against which is poised a dark man in a cape resting his hand on the fragile-looking shoulder of another man. The cover has typical gothic copy: "He was innocent . . . until he fell captive to the brooding master and sinister secrets of *Gaywyck*." Because of its immense success, publishers have since introduced numerous gay and lesbian romances. In addition, gay and lesbian mystery novels, such as Michael Nava's *How Town* (Nava, 1990) and Claire Kensington's *Elise* (Kensington, 1991), have been published as well.

While most readers read romances as "escapist" books, the novels nevertheless reinforce conventional norms. They perpetuate stereotypes of women as sexually passive; most disturbingly, they perpetuate dangerous misconceptions about rape and incest. At the same time, writes Ann Snitow (1983): "The ubiquity of the books indicates a central truth: romance is a primary category of the female imagination." For its audience, often hardworking, poorly paid single women, wives, and mothers, romance novels provide an escape into a fictional world. In this imaginative world, their need to be loved and valued can be met in a way that is not possible in the real world (Jensen, 1984; Radway, 1984).

SEXUALITY ACROSS CULTURES AND TIMES

What we have learned to call "natural" in our culture may be viewed as unnatural in other cultures. Few Americans would disagree about the erotic potential of kissing. But other cultures perceive kissing as the exchange of saliva. To the Mehinaku of the Amazonian rain forests, for example, "kissing" is a disgusting sexual abnormality. No Mehinaku engages in it (Gregor, 1985). The fact that whites press their lips against each other, salivate, *and* become sexually excited merely confirms their "strangeness" to the Mehinaku. And the Nigerians had a last laugh on the English colonizers who tried to "civilize" them. In contemporary Nigeria, the obscene words relating to sex in Nigeria are "sexual intercourse," "penis," and "vagina." John Money (1980) explains how this occurred:

> The moral taboos were taught by missionaries and administrators who used only clean words. The dirty words used by sailors, traders, and the like, became part of Nigerian vernacular English, with no taboos attached. In consequence, today it is as forbidden to say sexual intercourse, penis, and vagina on Nigerian television as it is to say fuck, cock, and cunt on the national networks in the United States. In Nigeria, the latter terms are considered normal and respectable. . . . To say that a young woman has a vagina or that she [had] sexual intercourse is . . . not tolerated. The correct and expected reference is to her cunt and to fucking.

The sensual movements of Latin American dancing have become popular in American culture, evidenced in films featuring the "Lambada," and by the thousands enrolled in Latin American dance classes. These dancers are celebrating their culture in a Latin American Heritage festival.

Culture takes our **sexual impulses**—our incitements or inclinations to act sexually—and molds and shapes them, sometimes celebrating sexuality, other times condemning it. Sexuality can be viewed as a means of spiritual enlightenment, as in the Hindu tradition, where the gods themselves engage in sexual activities; or it can be at war with the divine, as in the Judeo-Christian tradition, where the flesh is the snare of the devil (Parrinder, 1980).

Culture is the most powerful force shaping how we feel and behave sexually. A brief exploration of sexual themes across cultures and times will give you a sense of the diverse shapes and meanings human beings have given to sexuality.

Sexual Impulse

All cultures assume that adults have the *potential* for becoming sexually aroused and for engaging in sexual intercourse for the purpose of reproduction (Davenport, 1987). But cultures differ considerably in terms of how strong they believe sexual impulses are. These beliefs, in turn, affect the level of desire expressed in each culture.

The Mangaia Among the Mangaia in Polynesia, both sexes, beginning in early adolescence, experience high levels of sexual desire (Marshall, 1971). Around age 13 or 14, following a circumcision ritual, boys are given instruction in the ways of pleasing a girl: erotic kissing, cunnilingus, breast fondling and sucking, and techniques for bringing a partner to multiple orgasm. After two weeks, an older, sexually experienced woman has sexual

Self-Assessment

EXPLORING YOUR SEXUAL ATTITUDES

As you study human sexuality, you may find yourself reassessing or changing some of your attitudes or beliefs as a result of what you learn. To get a sense of how you change, answer the questions below on a separate sheet of paper. Save your responses. At the end of the course, answer the questions again and compare your responses.

The abridged Eysenck Inventory of Sexual Attitudes reprinted below has been widely used by researchers to study sexual attitudes. It will take 5–10 minutes to complete.

Read each statement carefully, then circle Yes or No, depending on your views. If you cannot decide, circle the question mark. There are no right or wrong answers. Don't think too long over each question; try to give an immediate answer that represents your feeling on each issue. Some questions are similar to others; there are good reasons for getting at the same attitude in slightly different ways.

1.	Members of the opposite sex will respect you more if you are not too familiar with them.	Yes	?	No
2.	Sex without love ("impersonal sex") is highly unsatisfactory.	Agree	?	Disagree
3.	Conditions have to be just right to get me excited sexually.	Yes	?	No
4.	All in all I am satisfied with my sex life.	Yes	?	No
5.	Virginity is a girl's most valuable possession.	Yes	?	No
6.	I think only rarely of sex.	Agree	?	Disagree
7.	Sometimes it has been a problem to control my sex feelings.	Yes	?	No
8.	Masturbation is unhealthy.	Yes	?	No
9.	If I love a person I could do anything with him or her.	Yes	?	No
10.	I get pleasant feelings from touching my sexual parts.	Yes	?	No
11.	I have been deprived sexually.	Yes	?	No
12.	I am sexually rather unattractive.	Yes	?	No
13.	Sex contacts have never been a problem to me.	True	?	False
14.	It is disturbing to see necking in public.	Yes	?	No
15.	Sexual feelings are sometimes unpleasant to me.	Yes	?	No
16.	Something is lacking in my sex life.	Yes	?	No
17.	My sexual behavior has never caused me any problems.	True	?	False
18.	My love life has been disappointing.	Yes	?	No
19.	I never had many dates.	True	?	False
20.	I consciously try to keep sexual thoughts out of my mind.	Yes	?	No
21.	It wouldn't bother me if the person I married were not a virgin.	True	?	False
22.	At times I have been afraid of myself for what I might do sexually.	Yes	?	No
23.	I have had conflicts about my sexual feelings toward a person of my own sex.	Yes	?	No

24.	I have many friends of the opposite sex.	Yes	?	No
25.	I have strong sex feelings, but when I get a chance I can't seem to express myself.	Yes	?	No
26.	My parents' influence has inhibited me sexually.	Yes	?	No
27.	People of my own sex frequently attract me.	Yes	?	No
28.	There are some things I would not want to do with anyone.	True	?	False
29.	Children should be taught about sex.	Yes	?	No
30.	I think about sex almost every day.	Yes	?	No
31.	I get excited sexually very easily.	Yes	?	No
32.	It is better not to have sexual relations until you are married.	True	?	False
33.	I like to look at sexy pictures.	Yes	?	No
34.	My conscience bothers me too much.	Yes	?	No
35.	My religious beliefs are against sex.	Yes	?	No
36.	Sometimes sexual feelings overpower me.	Yes	?	No
37.	I feel nervous with members of the opposite sex.	Yes	?	No
38.	When I get excited I can think of nothing else but satisfaction.	Yes	?	No
39.	I feel ill at ease with people of the opposite sex.	Yes	?	No
40.	It is hard to talk with people of the opposite sex.	Yes	?	No
41.	I feel more comfortable when I am with members of my own sex.	Yes	?	No
42.	I enjoy petting.	Yes	?	No
43.	I worry a lot about sex.	Yes	?	No
44.	Seeing a person nude doesn't interest me.	True	?	False
45.	Sometimes thinking about sex makes me very nervous.	Yes	?	No
46.	I am embarrassed to talk about sex.	Yes	?	No
47.	Young people should learn about sex through their own experience.	Yes	?	No
48.	A person should learn about sex gradually by experimenting with it.	Yes	?	No
49.	I have sometimes felt like humiliating my sex partner.	Yes	?	No
50.	(M) I get very excited when touching a woman's breast. (F) I get very excited when men touch my breasts.	Yes	?	No
51.	I have been involved with more than one sexual affair at the same time.	Yes	?	No
52.	Homosexuality is normal for some people.	Yes	?	No
53.	I have sometimes felt hostile toward my sex partner.	Yes	?	No
54.	I like to look at pictures of nudes.	Yes	?	No
55.	If I had a chance to see people making love, without being seen, I would like it.	Yes	?	No
56.	Prostitution should be legally permitted.	Yes	?	No

(continued)

EXPLORING YOUR SEXUAL ATTITUDES *(continued)*

57.	Decisions about abortion should be the concern of no one but the woman concerned.	Yes ? No
58.	The dual standard of morality, allowing men greater freedom, is natural, and should be continued.	Yes ? No
59.	Sex is far and away my greatest pleasure.	Yes ? No
60.	Sexual permissiveness threatens to undermine the entire foundation of civilized society.	Yes ? No
61.	Sex should be used for the purpose of reproduction, not for personal pleasure.	True ? False
62.	It is all right for children to see their parents naked.	Yes ? No
63.	Women who get raped are partly responsible themselves.	Yes ? No
64.	Buttocks excite me.	Yes ? No
65.	Men marry to have intercourse; women have intercourse for the sake of marriage.	Yes ? No

Source: Adapted from Eysenck, H. J. *Sex and Personality*. London: Open Books, 1976.

intercourse with the boy to instruct him further on how to sexually satisfy a woman. Girls the same age are instructed by older women on how to be orgasmic: how to thrust their hips and rhythmically move their vulvas in order to have multiple orgasms. A girl finally learns to be orgasmic through the efforts of a "good man." If the woman's partner fails to satisfy her, she is likely to leave him; she may also ruin his reputation with other women by denouncing his lack of skill. Young men and women are expected to have many sexual experiences prior to marriage.

This adolescent paradise, however, does not last forever. Mangaian culture believes sexuality is strongest during youth. As a result, when they leave young adulthood, youths experience a rapid decline in sexual desire and activity. They cease to be aroused as passionately as they once were. They attribute this swift decline to the workings of nature and settle into a sexually contented adulthood.

The Dani In contrast to the Mangaia, the New Guinean Dani show little interest in sexuality. To them, sex is a relatively unimportant aspect of life. The Dani express no concern about sexual techniques or enhancing erotic pleasure. Sexual affairs and jealousy are rare. As their only sexual concern is reproduction, sexual intercourse is performed quickly, ending with male orgasm. Female orgasm appears to be unknown to them. Following childbirth, both mothers and fathers go through five years of sexual abstinence. When anthropologist Karl Heider (1979) first reported this long period of abstinence, most anthropologists believed that he was wrong. His critics insisted that the Dani had other sexual activities that ordinarily lead to orgasm. But, as Heider noted, "a five-year period of sexual abstinence seems unlikely [to us] because of certain assumptions we make about human nature.... [T]hese assumptions hold that all people have a high level of sexual drive." As the Dani live in a fertile valley and have adequate nutrition, they have no environmental reasons for limiting sexual intercourse as a means of spacing or reducing the number of births. (The average woman has one or two children.) Heider concluded that the Dani are an extreme example in which culture rather than biology shapes sexual impulses.

Victorian Americans In the nineteenth century, white middle-class Americans believed that women had little sexual desire. If they experienced desire at all, it was "reproductive desire," the wish to have children. Reproduction entailed the unfortunate "necessity" of engaging in sexual intercourse. A leading reformer (Alcott, 1868) wrote that in her "natural state" a woman never makes advances based on sexual desires, for the "very plain reason that she does not feel them." Those women who did feel desire were "a few exceptions amounting in all probability to diseased cases." Such women were classified by a prominent physician as suffering from "Nymphomania, or Furor Uterinus" (Bostwick, 1860).

While women were viewed as asexual, men were believed to be driven by raging sexual appetites. Men, driven by lust, sought to satisfy their desires on innocent women. Both men and women believed that male sexuality was dangerous, uncontrolled, and animal-like. It was part of a woman's duty to tame unruly male sexual impulses.

The polar beliefs about the nature of male and female sexuality created destructive antagonisms between angelic women and demonic men. These beliefs provided the rationale for a "war between the sexes." They also led to the separation of sex from love. Intimacy and love had nothing to do with male sexuality. In fact, male lust always lingered in the background of married life, threatening to destroy love by its overbearing demands.

Although almost 100 years have passed since the end of the Victorian era, many Victorian sexual beliefs and attitudes continue to influence us. Some of these include the belief that men are "naturally" sexually aggressive and women sexually passive, the sexual double standard, and the value placed on women being sexually "inexperienced."

Sexual Orientation

Sexual orientation is the pattern of sexual and emotional attraction based on the gender of one's partner. **Heterosexuality** refers to sexual relationships between men and women. **Homosexuality** refers to same-sex sexual relationships. In contemporary American culture, heterosexuality is the only sexual orientation receiving full social legitimacy. While same-sex relationships are relatively common, they do not receive general social acceptance. Many other cultures, however, view same-sex relationships as normal, acceptable, or preferable. Marriage between members of the same sex is recognized in 15 to 20 cultures throughout the world (Gregersen, 1986).

In ancient Greece, the highest form of love was that expressed between males.

Ancient Greece In ancient Greece, the birthplace of European culture, the Greeks accepted same-sex relationships as naturally as Americans today accept heterosexuality. For the Greeks, same-sex relationships between men represented the highest form of love. In *Protagoras* (Hamilton & Cairns, 1961), one of the great works in Western philosophy, Plato (427?–347? B.C.) described a scene in which a friend greeted Socrates:

FRIEND: Where have you come from, Socrates? No doubt from pursuit of the captivating Alcibiades. Certainly when I saw him only a day or two ago, he seemed still to be a handsome man, but between ourselves, Socrates, "man" is the word. He's actually growing a beard.

SOCRATES: What of it? Aren't you an enthusiast of Homer, who says that the most charming age is that of the youth with his first beard, just the age of Alcibiades now?

Socrates was in love with Alcibiades. Socrates' friend was chiding him because, by Athenian standards, Alcibiades was growing too old to be Socrates' lover. It never occurred to either man that a love relationship between two males was improper, especially between an adult and an older adolescent. Indeed, it was superior to a male-female relationship because the low status of women made them unacceptable companions for men.

The male-male relationship was based on love and reciprocity; sexuality was only one component of it. In this relationship, the code of conduct called for the older man to initiate the relationship. The youth initially resisted; only after the older man courted the young man with gifts and words of love would the youth reciprocate. The two men formed a close, emotional bond. The older man was also the youth's mentor as well as his lover. He introduced the youth to men who would be useful for his advancement later; he assisted him in learning his duties as a citizen. As the youth entered adulthood, the erotic bond between the two evolved into a deep friendship. After the youth became an adult, he married a woman and later initiated a relationship with an adolescent boy.

Greek male-male relationships, however, were not substitutes for male-female marriage. The Greeks discouraged exclusive male-male relationships because marriage and children were required to continue the family. Men regarded their wives primarily as domestics and the bearers of children (Keuls, 1985). (The Greek word for woman, *gyne,* literally translates as "childbearer.") Husbands did not turn to their wives for sexual pleasure but to **hetaerae** (*hi-TIR-ee*), highly regarded courtesans who were usually educated slaves. The great Athenian orator Demosthenes affirmed this by writing: "We keep hetaerae for pleasure, concubines for the daily care of our body, and wives for the bearing of legitimate children and to keep watch over the house" (quoted in Keuls, 1985).

The Sambians of New Guinea Among Sambian males of New Guinea, sexual orientation is very malleable (Herdt, 1981). Young boys begin sexual activities with older boys, move to sexual activities with both sexes during adolescence, and engage in exclusively male-female activities in adulthood. Sambians believe that a boy can grow into a man only by the ingestion of semen, which is, they say, like mother's milk. At age 7 or 8, boys begin their sexual activities with older boys; as they get older, they seek multiple partners to accelerate their growth into manhood. At adolescence, their role changes, and they must provide semen to boys to enable them to develop. At first they worry about their own loss of semen, but they are taught to drink tree sap, which magically replenishes their semen. During adolescence, boys are betrothed to preadolescent girls with whom they engage in sexual activities. When the girls mature, the boys give up their sexual involvement with other males. They become fully involved with adult women, losing their desire for men. They become sexually interested only in women from then on.

Gender

While sexual impulses and orientation may be influenced by culture, it is difficult to imagine that culture has anything to do with **gender,** the characteristics associated with being male or female. There are, after all, only two sexes: male and female. These appear solidly rooted in our biological nature. But is being male or female *really* biological? The answer is yes *and* no. Having male or female genitalia is anatomical. But the possession of a penis does not *always* make a person a man, nor does the possession of a vulva and vagina *always* make a person a woman. Men who consider themselves women, "women with penises," are accepted or honored in many cultures throughout the world (Bullough, 1991).

Transsexuals Within the United States there are approximately 15,000 **transsexuals,** people whose genitalia and identities as men or women are discordant. In transsexuality, a person with a penis, for example, identifies as a woman, or a person with a vulva and vagina identifies as a man. In the psychiatric literature, transsexuals are considered psychologically impaired.

In order to make their genitalia congruent with their gender identity, many transsexuals have their genitalia surgically altered. If being male or female depends on genitalia, then postsurgical transsexuals have changed their sex—men become women and women become men. But defining sex in terms of genitalia presents problems, as has been shown in the world of sports (see Perspective 1). In the 1970s, Renee Richards, whose genitalia had been surgically transformed from male to female, began competing on the women's professional tennis circuit. Protests began immediately. Although Ms. Richards's genitalia were female, her body and musculature were male. Despite the surgery, she remained genetically male because her sex chromosomes were male. Her critics insisted that genetics, not genitalia, defined one's sex; anatomy could be changed, but chromosomes could not. Richards, however, maintained that she was a woman by any common definition of the word. (Issues of sex, gender, and biology are discussed in Chapter 5.)

Berdache Most Americans consider transsexuality problematical at best. But this is not necessarily true in all cultures. In some cultures, an anatomical man identifying as a woman might be considered a "man-woman" and accorded high status and special privileges. He would be identified as a berdache. A **berdache** (*ber-DASH*) is a man who assumes female dress, gender role, and status. Berdache is regarded as a third gender (Callendar et al., 1983). It is neither transsexuality, transvestism (wearing the clothes, or passing as a member, of the other sex), nor a form of same-sex relationship (Callendar & Kochems, 1985; Forgey, 1975; Roscoe, 1991). Berdache is found in numerous cultures throughout the world, including Native American, Filipino, Lapp, and East Indian cultures. It is almost always men who become berdaches, although there are a few cases of women assuming male roles in a similar fashion (Blackwood, 1984). Berdaches are often considered shamans, individuals who possess great spiritual power.

Among the Zuni of New Mexico, berdaches are considered a third sex (Roscoe, 1991). Despite the existence of transsexuals and pseudohermaphrodites, Western beliefs about gender focus on gender as biological. The Zuni, by contrast, believe that gender is socially acquired. In his description of We'wha (1849–1896), a famous Zuni man-woman, Will Roscoe (1991) writes:

> Berdaches . . . were considered an affirmation of humanity's original, pre-gendered unity—representatives of a form of solidarity and wholeness that transcended the division of humans into men and women. The third gender role of the berdache was one of native North America's most striking social inventions.

Berdaches were suppressed by missionaries and the government as "unnatural" or "perverts." Their ruthless repression led anthropologists to believe that berdaches had been driven out of existence in Native American cultures. But there is evidence that berdaches continue to hold ceremonial

In some cultures, men who dress or identify as women are considered shamans. We'wha was a Zuni man-woman who lived in the nineteenth century.

THE OLYMPIC OFFICE OF GENDER VERIFICATION

Defining a person's sex genetically rather than anatomically is not necessarily a solution to the problem of identifying a person as being male or female. There are numerous hormonal and chromosomal "errors" that may cause people to have the reproductive organs and physical characteristics of both sexes or the sex other than their genetic sex (see Chapter 5). As many as one out of every 1500 people has such a hormonal condition, and as many as one out of 500 has a chromosomal problem (Nielsen & Wohlert, 1991; Shah et al., 1992). Sometimes individuals can have the chromosomes of one sex but the genitalia (usually only partially developed) of the other, as in the case of *pseudohermaphrodites*. Stella Walsh, for example, set a world's record for the women's 100-meter dash in the 1932 Olympics and won the U.S. women's pentathlon in 1954. But when she died in 1980, it was discovered that she possessed nonfunctional male genitalia. Genetically, some of her cells contained XX (female) sex chromosomes, while others contained XY (male) sex chromosomes. On a chromosomal level, she was both male and female; anatomically, she had undeveloped male genitalia. She identified herself as a woman and was at least partially female genetically.

Because the Olympic Committee feared that men would compete as women, it established the sinister-sounding Olympic Office of Gender Verification. The committee believed that transsexuals and pseudohermaphrodites would have an unfair advantage over other women in female sporting events. (Only in 1936, when a Nazi male competed in the female high jump and lost to three women, has a man passed as a woman in the Olympic Games [Grady, 1992].) The Office of Gender Verification requires that a woman be female by chromosomal, hormonal, anatomical, and psychological definitions. The Olympics consider female genitalia and gender identity to be insufficient criteria for establishing a claim to be female (De La Chapelle, 1986). After Maria Patiño, a Spanish hurdler, failed to pass a female chromosomal test for the 1985 World University Games, the question of chromosomal and hormonal testing in sports created a storm of controversy. (A new test currently used by the Olympic Committee may misidentify a woman as male if male cells, including dandruff cells, are floating in the air.) Many geneticists as well as athletes argue that there should be no gender checking at all, including anatomical checking. Women athletes cite the embarrassment of random genital inspections by some sports associations (Grady, 1992). Furthermore, as one sports physician points out, "There's such a broad spectrum in human beings that it would be hard to disqualify somebody" (Grady, 1992).

and social roles in some tribes, such as the Lakota Sioux. Understandably, berdache activities are kept secret from outsiders for fear of reprisals (Williams, 1985). Among gay and lesbian Native Americans, the berdache provides historical continuity with their traditions (Roscoe, 1991).

SOCIETAL NORMS AND SEXUALITY

The immense diversity across cultures and times immediately calls into question the appropriateness of labeling sexual behaviors as *inherently* natural or unnatural, normal or abnormal. Too often we give such labels to sexual behaviors without thinking about the basis on which we make those judgments. Such categories discourage knowledge and understanding because they are value judgments, evaluations of right and wrong. As such, they are not objective descriptions about behaviors but statements of how we feel about those behaviors.

Natural Sex

How do we decide if a sexual behavior is natural or unnatural? To make this decision, we must have some standard of nature against which to compare the behavior. But what is "nature"? On the abstract level, nature is the essence of all things in the universe. Or, personified as Nature, it is the force regulating the universe. These definitions, however, do not give us much information for deciding what is natural or unnatural.

When we asked our students to identify their criteria for determining which sexual behaviors they considered "natural" or "unnatural," there was a variety of responses. These included the following:

If a person feels something instinctive, I believe it is a natural feeling.

I feel that certain acts are natural and certain ones are not.

I don't really know how I decide.

Natural and unnatural have to do with the laws of nature. What these parts were intended for.

I decide by my gut instincts.

I think all sexual activity is natural as long as it doesn't hurt yourself or anyone else.

I feel natural/unnatural behavior can be defined by how safe emotionally it is for a person. If it is not an emotionally or physically safe sex activity, it is not natural.

Everything possible is natural. Everything natural is normal. If it is natural and normal, it is moral.

Students were unable to find common ground. Richard W. Smith (1979) found that when he questioned people about what they believed was sexually "natural" and "unnatural," they also gave conflicting or contradictory explanations. Smith writes:

Natural and unnatural sex, it seems, are supposed to be self-evident to all people, and it is threatening to find inconsistencies between *your* version of "nature" and those of *other* people. It is even more threatening to detect inconsistencies *inside* your own strongly held value judgments—especially when there is no place to localize the causality . . . except in your basic "nature."

Reviewing the variety of explanations, one researcher (Weeks, 1985) concludes, "There are . . . as many natures as there are conflicting values." This should not be surprising. Another definition of natural is what is regarded as normal or acceptable. What we call natural is, in fact, a confused mixture of biological and religious explanations used to justify our culture's norms (Gagnon, 1977; Weeks, 1985).

When we label sexual behavior as "natural" or "unnatural," we are actually indicating whether the behavior conforms to our culture's sexual norms. Our sexual norms appear natural because we have internalized them since infancy. These norms are part of the cultural air we breathe, and, like the air, they are invisible. We have learned our culture's rules so well that they have become a "natural" part of our personality, a "second nature" to us. They seem "instinctive."

Normal Sex

Closely related to the idea that sexual behavior is natural or unnatural is the belief that sexuality is either normal or abnormal. More often than not, describing behavior as "normal" or "abnormal" is merely another way of making value judgments. The relationship between "nature" and "normal" occurred when biology and psychology merged in the early twentieth century. John Gagnon (1977) writes:

> This merging between the biological and psychological produced such distinctions as *normal* and *abnormal, healthy* and *perverse* or *pathological.* As the psychological tradition emancipated itself from the biological, it retained such distinctions as *mental health* and *mental illness,* and opposed "healthy" with a range of terms—*neurotic, immature* and *aberrant*—as labels for bad sex.

While "normal" has often been used to imply "healthy" or "moral" behavior, among social scientists it is used strictly as a statistical term. For them, **normal sexual behavior** is behavior that conforms to a group's average or median patterns of behavior. Normality has nothing to do with moral or psychological deviance.

Ironically, while we may feel pressure to behave like the average person (the statistical norm), most of us don't actually know how others behave sexually. People don't ordinarily reveal much about their sexual activities. If they do, they generally reveal only their most conformist sexual behaviors, such as sexual intercourse. They rarely disclose their masturbatory activities, their sexual fantasies, their anxieties or feelings of guilt. All that most people present of themselves—unless you know them well—is the conventional self that masks their actual sexual feelings, attitudes, and behaviors.

The only guidelines most of us have for determining our normality are given to us by our friends, partners, and parents (who usually present conventional sexual images of themselves) through stereotypes, media images, religious teachings, customs, and cultural norms. None of these, however, tells you much about how people *actually* behave. Since we don't know how people really behave, it is easy for us to imagine that we are abnormal if we differ from our cultural norms and stereotypes. We wonder if our desires, fantasies, and activities are normal: Is it normal to fantasize? To masturbate? To enjoy erotica? To be attracted to someone of the same sex? Some of us believe that everyone else is "normal" and that only we are "sick" or "abnormal."

As the great American sex researcher Alfred Kinsey (1948) pointed out almost half a century ago, "normal" sexual behavior is the sexual behavior

Morality is the custom of one's country and the current feeling of one's peers. Cannibalism is moral in a cannibal country.
Samuel Butler (1612–1680)

a culture defines as normal. He wrote: "The similarity of distinctions between the terms normal and abnormal, and the terms right and wrong, amply demonstrates the philosophic, religious, and cultural origins of these concepts." Because culture determines what is normal, there is a vast range of normal behaviors across different cultures. What is considered the normal sexual urge for the Dani would send most of us into therapy for treatment of low sexual desire. And the idea of teaching sexual skills to early adolescents, as the Mangaia do, would horrify most American parents.

We commonly use several criteria in deciding whether to label different sexual behaviors "normal" or "abnormal." These criteria are conventional, biological, psychological, and moral. Regardless of what criteria we use, they ultimately reflect societal norms.

Sin is geographical.
Bertrand Russell (1872–1970)

- *Conventionally "normal" behavior.* People engage in certain forms of sexual behavior more than others because cultural norms, customs, and laws encourage them to do so. The fact that a behavior is not widely practiced does not make it abnormal except in a statistical sense. **Fellatio** *(fel-AY-she-o)* (oral stimulation of the penis) and **cunnilingus** *(cun-i-LIN-gus)* (oral stimulation of the female genitalia), for example, are widely practiced today because they have become "acceptable" behaviors. But a generation ago, oral sex was tabooed as something "dirty" or "shameful." As a result, only a minority engaged in it (Kinsey, Pomeroy, & Martin, 1948; Kinsey, Pomeroy, Martin, & Gebhard, 1953; Rubin, 1990; Simon & Gagnon, 1986).

- *Biologically "normal" behavior.* Human beings have sexual impulses that are rooted in our biological makeup. But simply having sexual impulses does not mean that these impulses have to be expressed through a specific type of behavior. The idea that the "natural" purpose of sex is reproduction reflects religious dogma rather than biology. If our sexuality could only be expressed legitimately in sexual intercourse, erotic kissing would be considered biologically abnormal. For men and women alike, sexual intercourse with a woman who has gone through menopause would similarly be considered abnormal because conception is not possible. When it comes to specific behaviors, what is biologically normal is what culture defines as normal.

- *Psychologically "normal" behavior.* Sexual behavior that enhances our satisfaction or sense of psychological well-being is often identified as normal or healthy. Behavior that creates feelings of guilt, shame, anxiety, tension, or frustration is often regarded as abnormal. But such "psychologically healthy" sexual behavior makes us feel good because we have learned to feel satisfied when we act in socially approved ways. If we feel guilty about masturbating, it is because we have been taught to feel guilty about masturbation, not because masturbation is intrinsically unhealthy. In the nineteenth century, when women were expected to be asexual, so-called "furor uterinus," excessive female desire, was diagnosed as a pathological condition. Not surprisingly, women who experienced strong sexual desires complained to physicians about their desires being unnatural—and the physicians agreed (Strong, 1973).

- *Morally "normal" behavior.* If "normal" sexual behavior is "moral" sexual behavior, the morality of any act depends on *whose* morality we choose to use—yours, mine, or someone else's. Morality is culturally relative; there are no universal moral absolutes regarding sexuality. Even within contemporary Judeo-Christian traditions, unanimity about sexual matters does not exist.

Kissing is "natural" and "normal" in our culture. It is an expression of intimacy, love, and passion for young and old, heterosexuals, gay men, and lesbians.

Catholics, for example, condemn birth control as a sin, while Protestants do not. Many American religious groups regard same-sex relations as sinful, while some Lutheran churches and Reformed Jewish synagogues ordain gay men and lesbians as ministers or rabbis. All find justification for their beliefs in their scriptures but interpret the passages differently; they emphasize some passages and ignore others.

These four criteria form the basis of what we usually consider normal behavior. Often the different interpretations of "normal" conflict with each other. How does a person determine whether he or she is normal if conventionally "normal" behavior, such as oral sex, is condemned as immoral by one's religion? Such dilemmas are commonplace and lead many people to question their normality. They should not question, however, their normality as much as their *concept* of normality.

Typical and Atypical Sexual Behavior

Sex researchers have generally rejected the traditional sexual dichotomies of natural/unnatural, normal/abnormal, moral/immoral, and good/bad. Regarding the word "abnormal," Ira Reiss (1989) writes:

> We need to be aware that people will use those labels to put distance between themselves and others they dislike. In doing so, these people are not making a scientific diagnosis but are simply affirming their support of certain shared concepts of proper sexuality.

Instead of classifying behavior into what are essentially moralistic normal/abnormal and natural/unnatural categories, researchers view human sexuality as characterized by **sexual variation**—that is, sexual variety and diversity. As human beings, we vary enormously in terms of our sexual orientation, our desires, our fantasies, our attitudes, and our behaviors. Kinsey (1948) succinctly stated the matter like this: "The world is not to be divided into sheep and goats."

To understand our sexual diversity, researchers believe that the best way to examine sexual behavior is to view our activities as existing on a continuum. On this continuum, the frequency with which individuals engage in different sexual activities, such as sexual intercourse, masturbation, and oral sex, ranges from "Never" to "Always." Significantly, there is no point on the continuum that marks normal or abnormal behavior. In fact, the difference between one individual and the next on the continuum is minimal (Kinsey et al., 1948, 1953). The most that can be said of a person is that his or her behaviors are more or less typical or atypical of the group average. Furthermore, nothing can be inferred about an individual whose behavior differs significantly from the group average except that his or her behavior is atypical. The individual who differs is not sick, abnormal, or perverse; rather, he or she is a sexual nonconformist (Reiss, 1986, 1989). Except for engaging in sexually atypical behavior, a person may be indistinguishable from any other person.

Many activities that are usually thought of as **deviant sexual behavior**—activities diverging from the norm, such as exhibitionism, voyeurism, and fetishism—exist in most of us to some degree or another. We may delight in displaying our bodies on the beach or "dirty dancing" in crowded clubs (exhibitionism). We may like watching ourselves make love, viewing erotic videos, or seeing our partner undress (voyeurism). Or we may enjoy kissing our lover's photograph, keeping a lock of hair, or sleeping with an article of his or her clothing (fetishism). Most of the time these feelings or activities are only one aspect of our sexual selves; they are not especially significant in our overall sexuality. Such atypical behaviors represent nothing more than sexual nonconformity when they occur between mutually consenting adults and do not cause distress (Reiss, 1989).

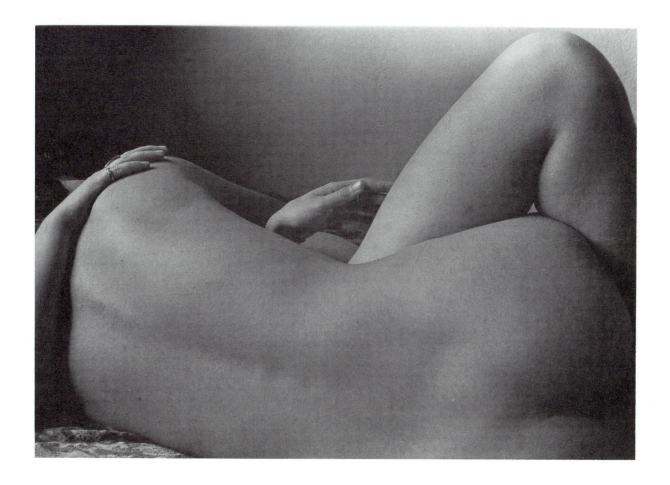

The rejection of natural/unnatural, normal/abnormal, and moral/immoral categories by sex researchers does not mean that standards for evaluating sexual behavior do not exist. There are many sexual behaviors that are harmful to oneself (e.g., masturbatory asphyxia, suffocating or hanging oneself during masturbation to increase sexual arousal) and to others (e.g., rape, child molestation, exhibitionism, and obscene phone calling). Current psychological standards for determining the harmfulness of sexual behaviors center around the issues of coercion, grave potential for inflicting harm on oneself or others, or personal distress. (These issues are discussed in greater detail in Chapter 11.)

As social scientists, the role of sex researchers is to *describe* sexual behavior, not evaluate it as good or bad, moral or immoral. It is up to the individual to evaluate the ethical or moral aspect of sexual behavior in accordance with his or her ethical or religious values. At the same time, however, understanding diverse sexual attitudes, motives, behaviors, and values will help deepen the individual's own value system.

Curiosity builds bridges. . . . Judgment builds the power of some over others.

Joan Nestle

Popular culture both encourages and discourages sexuality. It promotes stereotypical sexual interactions between men and women that fail to touch on the deeper significance sexuality holds for us. Marital love and sexuality are infrequently depicted in contrast to casual or nonmarital sex. (By ignoring marital sex, popular culture implies that marriage is a sexual wasteland. Yet it is within marriage that the overwhelming majority of sexual interactions between men and women take place.) The media ignore or disparage the wide array of sexual behaviors and choices, from masturbation to gay and lesbian relationships, that are significant in many people's lives. It discourages the linking of sex and intimacy, contraceptive responsibility, and the acknowledgment of STD risks.

What is clear from examining other cultures is that sexual behaviors and norms vary from culture to culture and, within our own society, from one time to another. The variety of sexual behaviors even within our own culture testifies to diversity not only between cultures but within cultures as well. Understanding diversity allows us to acknowledge that there is no such thing as inherently "normal" or "natural" sexual behavior. Rather, sexual behavior is strongly influenced by culture—including our own.

SUMMARY

Sexuality, Popular Culture, and the Media

• Popular culture, especially the media, strongly influences our sexuality through the depiction of sexual stereotypes and *norms*. Mainstream media do not explicitly depict sexual behavior.

• Each television genre depicts sexuality according to its formula. Situation comedies focus on the violation of minor taboos centering on marital and family issues. Soap operas deal with sexual transgressions, jealousy, and power linked to sex. Crime/action-adventure programs depict relationships that are based on attraction and are short-lived; detective heroes form close relationships primarily with their detective partners or secretaries. Made-for-TV movies focus on "problem" themes, such as rape or adolescent pregnancy. Music videos rely on suggestiveness and innuendo to depict sexuality; women are usually portrayed as sex objects. TV commercials may promote a product by suggesting that consuming the product will lead to attractiveness or sexual success.

• Although Hollywood films depict sexual behavior more graphically than television does, sex scenes are often gratuitous. Sexuality tends to be stereotypical. Gay men and lesbians have generally been absent from films except in stereotypical roles. More recently, a few nonstereotypical gay and lesbian characters have been introduced.

• Romance novels are directed primarily at women. They emphasize romance, sensuality, seduction, and morality. The dramatic tension results from the conflict between the heroine's powerful sexuality and her sense of morality. Usually morality triumphs, reinforcing conventional norms.

Sexuality Across Cultures and Times

• The most powerful force shaping human sexuality is culture. Culture molds and shapes our *sexual impulses*.

• In terms of sexual impulse, the Mangaia of Polynesia believe that beginning in early adolescence, boys and girls have high levels of sexual desire. Adolescents, especially boys, are trained to please members of each sex. As they leave young adulthood, however, Mangaians experience a rapid decline in sexual desire and activity, which they believe is natural.

• The Dani of New Guinea, by contrast, believe that neither men nor women have strong sexual drives; the female orgasm is unknown. They rarely engage in sexual activities and believe that sex is for reproduction. Following childbirth, they undergo five years of abstinence.

• Middle-class Americans in the nineteenth century believed that men had strong sexual drives while women had little sexual desire. Since sexuality was considered animalistic, the Victorians separated sex and love.

• In ancient Greece, same-sex relationships between men represented the highest form of love. The preferred relationship was between a youth and an older man. Love between men and women was inferior to male-male love because women's low status rendered them unworthy of male love. Among the Sambians of New Guinea, boys have sexual relations with older boys, believing that the ingestion of semen is required for growth. When the girls to whom they are betrothed reach puberty, adolescent boys cease sexual relations with other boys; they then have sexual activity only with females.

• A *transsexual* has the genitalia of one sex but identifies as a member of the other sex. A *pseudohermaphrodite* may identify as one sex with the genitalia of that sex but has the chromosomes of the other sex. In our culture, transsexuality is considered a psychological disorder, but such individuals may be highly regarded in other cultures.

• A *berdache* is a person of one sex who identifies with the other sex; in some cultures, such as the Zuni, a berdache is considered a third gender and is believed to possess great spiritual power.

Societal Norms and Sexuality

• Sexuality tends to be evaluated according to categories of natural/unnatural, normal/abnormal, and moral/immoral. These terms are value judgments, reflecting social norms rather than any quality inherent in the behavior itself.

• There is no commonly accepted definition of natural sexual behavior. *Normal sexual behavior* is what a culture defines as normal. We commonly use four criteria to categorize sexual behavior as normal or abnormal: conventionally normal, biologically normal, psychologically normal, and morally normal.

• Human sexuality is characterized by *sexual variation*. Researchers believe that the best way to examine sexual behavior is by using a continuum. On the continuum, the frequency with which people engage in different sexual activities ranges from "Never" to "Always." Most people fall somewhere in between these two extremes. There is no point on the continuum that marks normal or abnormal behavior; the difference between one individual and the next on the continuum is minimal. Many activities that are considered *deviant sexual behavior* exist in most of us to some degree or another. These include exhibitionism, voyeurism, and fetishism.

• Behaviors are not abnormal or unnatural; rather they are more or less typical or atypical of the group average. Those whose behaviors are atypical may be regarded as sexual nonconformists rather than abnormal or perverse.

KEY TERMS

norm

sexual impulse

sexual orientation

heterosexuality

homosexuality

hetaera

gender

transsexual

berdache

normal sexual
    behavior

fellatio

cunnilingus

sexual variation

deviant sexual
    behavior

SUGGESTIONS FOR FURTHER READING

Bullough, Vern. *Sexual Variance in Society and History*. New York: Wiley, 1976. A thorough examination of attitudes toward sexuality in Western and non-Western cultures.

Chapple, Steve, and David Talbot. *Burning Desires: Sex in America. A Report from the Field*. New York: Doubleday, 1989. An entertaining and informative work on contemporary sexuality and popular culture by two journalists.

D'Emilio, John, and Estelle Freedman. *Intimate Matters: A History of Sexuality in America*. New York: Harper & Row, 1988. An important study of American sexuality, especially in the nineteenth century.

Gregor, Thomas. *Anxious Pleasures: The Sexual Lives of an Amazonian People*. Chicago: University of Chicago Press, 1985. An excellent study of how an Amazonian culture perceives sexuality.

Haskell, Molly. *From Reverence to Rape: The Treatment of Women in the Movies*, 2nd ed. Chicago: University of Chicago Press, 1987. A thoughtful work on changing attitudes toward women and sexuality in films.

Russo, Vito. *The Celluloid Closet*. New York: Harper & Row, 1987. A history of gay men and lesbians in the cinema, as directors, actors, and actresses, how they are depicted, and the evolution of gay and lesbian filmmaking.

Suggs, David N., and Andrew Miracle, eds. *Culture and Human Sexuality*. Pacific Grove, CA: Brooks/Cole, 1993. A collection of essays on sexuality in diverse cultures throughout the world.

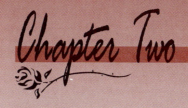

Chapter Two

STUDYING HUMAN SEXUALITY

PREVIEW: SELF-QUIZ

1. "College students should engage in premarital sexual intercourse to gain experience" is an example of a value judgment. True or false?

2. Attitudes accurately predict behaviors. True or false?

3. Research on the role of ethnicity has been generally limited to problem areas, such as adolescent pregnancy. True or false?

4. Because of ethical considerations, it is impossible to conduct experimental studies in human sexuality. True or false?

5. Sexual stereotypes usually reflect basic truths about various groups. True or false?

6. The sexual values of inner-city and middle-class African Americans are quite similar. True or false?

7. "Latino men are macho" is an example of a stereotypical statement. True or false?

8. Because they place a high value on children, African Americans of all classes tend to believe there is no such thing as an "illegitimate" or "illegally born" child. True or false?

9. Since the turn of the century, the most influential sex researchers have considered masturbation normal. True or false?

10. Gay and lesbian studies tend to focus on the causes of homosexuality. True or false?

ANSWERS 1. T, 2. F, 3. T, 4. F, 5. F, 6. F, 7. T, 8. T, 9. T, 10. F

Chapter Outline

"An important discovery about orgasm was announced today by Harvard researchers. . . . But first, a message from. . . ." So begins a commercial lead-in on the ten o'clock news report, reminding us that sex research is often part of both news and entertainment. In fact, most of us learn about the results of sex research from TV and magazines rather than from scholarly journals and books. After all, the mass media are more entertaining than most scholarly research. And unless we are studying human sexuality, few of us have the time to read the scholarly journals in which scientific research is regularly published.

But how accurate is what the mass media tell us about sex and sex research? In this chapter, we discuss the dissemination of sex information by the various media. Then we look at the critical-thinking skills that help us evaluate how we discuss and think about sexuality. When are we making objective statements? When are we reflecting biases or opinions? Next, we examine sex research methods, as they are critical to the scientific study of human sexuality. Then, we look at the leading sex researchers to see how they have influenced our understanding of sexuality. Finally, we examine feminist, gay/lesbian, and ethnic sex research to see how they enrich our knowledge of sexuality.

SEX, ADVICE COLUMNISTS, AND POP PSYCHOLOGY

As we saw in Chapter 1, the mass media convey seemingly endless sexual images. But in addition to the various television, film, and advertising genres, there is another genre that we might call the sex information/advice genre, which transmits *information* rather than images. The **sex information/advice genre** is a media genre that transmits information and norms about sexuality to a mass audience to both inform and entertain in a simplified manner. For most college students, as well as many others, the sex information/advice genre is a major source of their sexual knowledge (Moffatt, 1989).

A veritable industry exists to support the sex information/advice genre. It produces sex manuals, self-help books, advice columns, radio and television shows, as well as numerous articles in magazines and newspapers. Sex information comes in torrents. But what do we really learn about sexuality from the sex information/advice genre?

This genre is ostensibly concerned with transmitting information that is factual and accurate. In newspapers, it is represented by such popular national columnists as Abigail Van Buren (whose column "Dear Abby" is now written by a man), Ann Landers, Beth Winship, and Pat Califia. Sexual self-help and pop sex books written by "experts" frequent the best-seller lists, ranging from David Reuben's *Everything You Ever Wanted to Know About Sex—But Were Afraid to Ask* (1969) to Naura Hayden's recent *How to Satisfy a Woman Every Time* (1991). On radio and television, Ruth Westheimer, a professional therapist, has hosted shows dispensing sex information and advice.

Pop Sex Information and Advice as Entertainment

Newspaper columns, magazine articles, and TV programs share several features. First, their primary purpose is to sell newspapers and magazines or to raise program ratings. This goal is in marked contrast to scholarly research, whose primary purpose is to pursue knowledge. Even the inclusion of survey questionnaires in magazines asking readers to respond about their sexual attitudes or behaviors is ultimately designed to promote sales. We fill out the questionnaires for fun, much as we would crossword puzzles or anagrams. Then we buy the subsequent issue or watch a later program to see how we compare to others.

Popular advice columnists and sex experts, such as Dr. Ruth, moralize as well as dispense information that is often oversimplified and sometimes erroneous.

Yo persigo una forma que no encuentra mi estilo,
boton de pensamiento que busca ser la rosa.

I pursue a form my pen cannot discover,
a bud of thought that seeks to be a rose.

Rubén Darío

SEX AND POP PSYCHOLOGY: CAVEAT EMPTOR

As this book went to press, P. Thaddeus ("Thad") Barnum, M.D., Ph.D., had become a familiar face on the television talk-show circuit and in the media. Following publication of his sensational best-selling book, *Erotosexophilia: The Silent Epidemic* (Popular Psychology Press, 1994), Dr. Barnum became known as Dr. Sex. Oprah Winfrey applauded him for his courage and insight, while Phil Donahue praised him for following the tradition of the great eighteenth-century Swiss physician Simon Tissot. Dr. Barnum's photograph has appeared on the covers of such diverse publications as *Popular Psychology Today, Time, Soap Opera Digest* (following a cameo role in "Days of Our Lives"), and even the *National Enquirer*. A short time ago, he began hosting his own syndicated cable television program, "Dr. Sex Knows." He is an outgoing man, whose distinguished appearance and graying beard inspire confidence and remind one of Sigmund Freud ("My idol," Dr. Barnum confesses).

Erotosexophilia is a psychological disorder discovered by Dr. Barnum, first described in an article published in *Cosmopolitan* and then reprinted a few months later in *Reader's Digest*. According to Dr. Barnum's research, the victims of erotosexophilia exhibit one or more of the following symptoms:

- *Intrusive sexual thoughts.* The individual finds himself or herself constantly thinking about sex.

- *Poor impulse control.* Erotosexophiles indicate that they often feel their sexual impulses control them.

- *Sexual secrets.* They keep many parts of their sexual selves secret from others, including sexual fantasies and masturbation.

- *Excessive masturbation.* Erotosexophiles masturbate too much.

- *Inability to make permanent commitments.* Sufferers go from one relationship to another, unable to settle down. Married erotosexophiles find themselves attracted to others.

Based on his clinical practice in New York's Upper East Side (where his patients pay $175 an hour for his services), Dr. Barnum estimates that 20–25% of Americans suffer from erotosexophilia. "That is a conservative estimate," he explains. "I suspect the numbers are larger, but I do not want to appear as an alarmist." Sufferers do not talk about their affliction. "Because they feel intense doubt or shame about their sexual feelings," Dr. Barnum notes, "they do not share their concerns with others. Which is why I call erotosexophilia the 'Silent Epidemic.' It is everywhere, but it is shamed into silence." Many sufferers, the psychiatrist suggests, are in denial. "Despite overwhelming evidence, they refuse to accept the fact that they are erotosexophiles. Such denial," Dr. Barnum says,

Second, the media must entertain while disseminating information about sexuality. The success of media personalities such as Ruth Westheimer does not rest as much on their expertise as it does on their ability to present information as entertainment (Buxton, 1991). (See Perspective 1.) Because the genre seeks to entertain, sex information and advice must be simplified. Complex explanations and analyses must be avoided because they would interfere with the entertainment purpose. Furthermore, the genre relies on high-interest or bizarre material to attract readers or viewers. Consequently, we are more likely to read or view stories about increasing sexual attractiveness or unusual sexual practices than stories about new research methods or the process of sexual stereotyping.

"may be construed as further evidence of their affliction."

Dr. Barnum explains the origins of erotosexophilia. "Its etiology is found in early childhood, although the symptoms don't emerge until around college age." The trauma seems to center in the parents' relationship with the child. "Paradoxically, the mother and father may be overinvolved or underinvolved, sometimes both simultaneously."

Dr. Barnum's treatment program, known as anhedonic therapy, has been over 90% successful in treating sufferers of erotosexophilia. It is somewhat unconventional, but, he assures us, less dramatic means routinely fail. Dr. Barnum treats the disorder by utilizing penile rings and chastity belts, devices whose history can be traced back to the Middle Ages. His aversive behavioral techniques, applied over a three-month period, have been overwhelmingly successful. "Not only have my patients' unruly sexual impulses been tamed, in some instances they have disappeared," Dr. Barnum reports approvingly.

As you may have guessed, what you read above is satirical. There is no such thing as erotosexophilia, but by coining a Latin/Greek-sounding word, the term is given a certain medico-scientific legitimacy. P. T. Barnum was a famous nineteenth-century showman/fraud best remembered today for the Barnum & Bailey Circus. (P. T. Barnum was also the one who said, "There's a sucker born every minute.") By giving today's Barnum the title of Dr., we give him an air of authority.

The *Barnum effect*, however, is real. It refers to people's tendency to mistakenly believe that general statements, which apply more or less to everyone, apply specifically to them. It is known as the Barnum effect because fortune tellers, Tarot card readers, and psychics traveling in circuses used such general statements to make their customers believe they possessed special powers.

The fact that erotosexophilia and Dr. Barnum initially may have appeared convincing is due to several factors: (1) Our culture treats much sexual behavior as pathological, making people anxious about their sexual normality and susceptible to manipulation; (2) the so-called symptoms are feelings and behaviors shared by many people; (3) erotosexophilia is presented as scientific and based on the work of a "doctor"; and (4) erotosexophilia is defined as a problem that can be cured, offering the "sufferer" hope.

Much of the information presented in popular psychology books, articles, and programs is useful. Most writers, psychologists, therapists, and physicians present their information in an interesting, intelligent manner that not only entertains but also informs. Self-help books and programs have helped millions better understand themselves and their relationships. But it is important not to accept them uncritically. Though they appear to be scientific or based on sound psychological principles, they may be oversimplified to the point of error. As Mark Twain once warned: "Don't read medical advice. You might die of a misprint."

Third, the genre focuses on how-to information or on morality. The how-to material advises us on how to improve our sex lives. Westheimer's book, *Dr. Ruth's Guide to Good Sex* (1983), for example, advises its readers on oral sex:

> Not everybody has to be engaging in oral sex. So after saying that, if your husband likes it a lot and really craves for that, then one of the ways you might try... eat an ice-cream cone.... Then when you do perform oral sex, think of that ice-cream cone. Don't tell your husband. Just put an ice-cream cone in your head.

Advice columnists often give advice on issues of sexual morality. "Is it alright to have sex without commitment?" "Yes, if you love him/her" or "No, casual sex is empty," and so on. Advice columnists act as moral arbiters, much as ministers, priests, and rabbis.

The line between media sex experts and advice columnists is often blurred. Ruth Westheimer, for example, mixes information and normative judgments. In her discussion of oral sex and ice cream cones, for example, not only does Westheimer suggest ways to engage in oral sex, she also implies two contradictory norms: (1) Oral sex is a matter of individual choice, and (2) a woman should do what a man wants. The use of the word "good" in the title of her book (as well as in her radio and television programs) is significant. "Good" can be interpreted in two ways: good as sexually satisfying or good as virtuous.

Fourth, the genre uses the trappings of social science and psychiatry without their substance. Writers and columnists interview social scientists and therapists to give an aura of scientific authority to their material. They rely especially heavily on therapists whose background is clinical rather than academic. Because clinicians tend to deal with people with problems, they often see sexuality as problematical.

In order to reinforce their authority, the media also incorporate statistics, which are key features of social science research. But as Susan Faludi (1991) notes:

> The statistics that the popular culture chooses to promote most heavily are the very statistics we should view with the most caution. They may well be in wide circulation not because they are true but because they support widely held media preconceptions.

Even such renowned sex researchers as William Masters and Virginia Johnson could sometimes be guilty of "statistical excess." Without a shred of evidence, for example, they made the oft-quoted claim that "half of American marriages are sexual disaster areas" (Masters & Johnson, 1974). The media unquestioningly repeated this statistic for years because it reinforced the popular conception that sex and marriage don't mix. In the 1980s, the media also popularized the G spot, a supposedly highly erotic area within the vagina, supported by questionable scientific evidence. The media publicized the G spot as an incontrovertible fact, while its existence and significance continue to be disputed among sex researchers (Tavris, 1992). (The G spot is discussed further in Chapter 3.) A few years later, the media promoted the idea of an infertility "epidemic" occurring because women delayed childbearing until their thirties. While there was an increase in infertility, it was due not as much to aging as to STDs going undetected and untreated (Faludi, 1991).

The media frequently quote or describe social science research, but they may do so in an oversimplified or distorted manner. Scholars tend to qualify their findings as tentative or limited to a certain group. They are very cautious about making generalizations. By contrast, the media tend to make results sound more certain and generalizable. The media may report, for example, a study finding that premarital sexual intercourse generally results in feelings of guilt, while a later study finds no relationship between the two. On what basis do you decide which study to believe? Many of us think all studies are equal, that one is as good as another as long as they are conducted by experts who presumably know what they are doing. But all studies

Every truth is true only up to a point. Beyond that, by way of counterpoint, it becomes untruth.
Søren Kierkegaard (1813–1855)

are not necessarily comparable or equally well done. One study may have drawn its sample from the fundamentalist Bob Jones University, while the other drew its sample from the more liberal Harvard University. In one case, information may have been drawn from a clinical study of students being treated for depression, while the other may have been based on a cross section of nondepressed students. Often such critical information about studies is missing in media research accounts.

Professor Pepper Schwartz, who is simultaneously a sex researcher, TV commentator, and columnist for *Glamour* magazine, describes the different requirements of each role. As a scholar and researcher, she says, her work consists of asking "questions that matter in people's lives and then doing a fairly fastidious examination so that you have every chance to prove yourself wrong" (Schwartz, 1992). She continues:

> You're guarded in how much you can say from what you did. You know all the limitations of your work. In the media, if you're that guarded nobody will believe you know anything. So you have to be more of a generalist.

In her TV commentary, Schwartz gets "a minute twenty to make a point, support it, and get out of there." She is further constrained by the language she is allowed to use—to talk about sex without uttering words like "penis," "clitoris," "cunnilingus," or "fellatio."

In Schwartz's *Glamour* column, she answers on the first page questions sent in by readers, trying to give "a tight answer that's based on research as much as I can." On the second page, she boils down data to give the readers accurate information. The information is only the essence, without the "ifs, buts, this social class group, that age group" that characterize research findings. For Schwartz, the challenge is to accurately disseminate research to the general public within the limits of each medium.

Evaluating Pop Sex

After you have read several sex books and watched several sex experts on television, you discover that they tend to be repetitive. There are two main reasons for their repetitiveness. First, the media repeatedly report more-or-less the same stories because there is relatively little new in the world of sex or sexual science. Scientific research is painstakingly slow, and the results are tedious to produce. Research results rarely change the way we view a topic; usually they flesh out what we already know. While research is seldom revolutionary, the media must nevertheless continually produce new stories to fill their pages and programs. Consequently, they report similar material in different guises: as interviews, survey results, and first-person stories, for example.

Second, the media are repetitive because their scope is narrow. There are only so many ways how-to books can tell you how to do it. Similarly, the personal and moral dilemmas most of us face are remarkably similar to each other: Am I normal? Should I have an affair? Is sex without love moral?

With the media awash with sex information and advice, how can we evaluate what is presented to us? Here are some important guidelines:

- *Be skeptical.* Remember, much of what you read or see is meant to entertain you. If it seems superficial, it probably is.

- *Search for biases, stereotypes, and lack of objectivity.* Information is often distorted by points of view. What conflicting information may have been omitted? How are women and ethnicity portrayed?

- *Look for moralizing.* Many times what passes as fact is really disguised moral judgment. What are the underlying values of the article or program?

- *Go to the original source or sources.* The media always simplify. Find out for yourself what the studies really reported. How valid were their methodologies? What were their strengths and limitations?

- *Seek additional information.* The whole story is probably not told. Look for additional information in scholarly books and journals, reference books, or textbooks.

Next, we will discuss critical-thinking skills. Using critical thinking will help you analyze media presentations on sex.

THINKING (CRITICALLY) ABOUT SEX

Although each of us has his or her own perspective, values, and beliefs regarding sexuality, as students, instructors, and researchers, we are committed to the scientific study of sexuality. Basic to any scientific study is a fundamental commitment to **objectivity,** the observation of things as they exist in reality as opposed to our feelings or beliefs about them. Objectivity calls for us to suspend the beliefs, biases, or prejudices we have about a subject in order to understand it (Reiss, 1980).

Objectivity is not always easy, for sexuality is the focal point of powerful emotions, moral ambivalence, anxiety, and fear. As one researcher (Weeks, 1986) noted:

The strong emotions it undoubtedly arouses gives to the world of sexuality a seismic sensitivity, making it a transmission belt for a wide variety of needs and desires: for love and anger, tenderness and aggression, empathy and power.

We experience sex very subjectively. But whether we find it easy or difficult to be objective, objectivity is the prerequisite for studying sexuality.

Most of us think about sex, but thinking about it critically requires us to think with logic and objectivity. We make common errors when discussing sexuality that inhibit our understanding and comprehension. Some of these mistakes are discussed below.

Value Judgments Versus Objectivity

For many of us, objectivity about sex is difficult because our culture has traditionally viewed sexuality in moral terms: Sex is moral or immoral, right or wrong, good or bad. When examining sexuality, we tend, therefore, to make **value judgments,** evaluations based on moral or ethical standards rather than objective ones. Unfortunately, value judgments are often blinders to understanding. They do not tell us about motivations, how frequently a behavior is practiced, or how its participants feel. Value judgments do not tell us anything about sexuality except how we ourselves feel. In studying human sexuality, then, we need to put aside value judgments as incompatible with the pursuit of knowledge.

How does one tell the difference between a value judgment and an objective statement? Examine the two statements below. Which is a value judgment? Which is an objective statement?

1. College students should not engage in premarital sexual intercourse.
2. The majority of students engage in premarital sexual intercourse sometime during their college careers.

The first is a value judgment; the second is an objective statement. There is a simple rule of thumb for telling the difference between the two: Value judgments imply how a person *ought* to behave, whereas objective statements describe how people *actually* behave. The first statement is a value judgment because it makes a judgment about premarital sexual behavior. The second is an objective statement because it describes how people act.

There is a second difference between value judgments and objective statements: Value judgments cannot be empirically validated, while objective statements can be validated. The truth or accuracy of an objective statement can be measured and tested. Researchers can conduct studies, such as surveys, to determine whether it is true that the majority of college students engage in premarital intercourse. Value judgments, by contrast, can never be tested because they are based on an individual's beliefs. Their validity rests on ethical, moral, or religious standards that can never be proved or disproved empirically. Despite claims of universality, these standards are generally regarded by social scientists as culturally relative. (**Cultural relativity** is an important anthropological concept meaning that the positive or negative appropriateness of any custom or activity must be evaluated in terms of how it fits in with the culture as a whole.)

There is no truth that a blockhead could not turn into an error.
Luc de Vauvenargues

Opinions, Biases, and Stereotypes

Value judgments obscure our search for understanding. They substitute judgment for objective description of the world as it exists. Opinions, biases, and stereotypes also interfere with the pursuit of knowledge.

Ignorance is like a delicate exotic fruit; touch it and the bloom is gone.
Oscar Wilde

Opinions An **opinion** is an unsubstantiated belief or conclusion about what seems to be true according to an individual's personal thoughts. Opinions are not based on positive knowledge or concrete evidence. Because opinions are unsubstantiated, they often reflect the individual's personal values or biases.

Biases A **bias** is a personal leaning or inclination. Biases lead to selecting information that supports our views or beliefs while ignoring information that does not. We need not be victims, however, of our biases. We can make a concerted effort to discover what they are and overcome them. Indeed, as William Simon (1992) writes of scientific research:

> Science as an enduring institution is essentially an ethical posture. It is a pledge that while we cannot control or ever be fully aware of our biases, we will not knowingly lie, we will not fudge the data.

To avoid personal bias, scholars apply the objective methods of social science research.

Stereotypes A **stereotype** is a set of simplistic, rigidly held, overgeneralized beliefs about an individual, a group of people, an idea, and so on. Stereotypical beliefs are resistant to change. While we may think our perceptions of women have changed, research indicates that we continue to hold the same stereotypical beliefs about women today as we did 20 years ago (Bergen & Williams, 1991). Furthermore, stereotypes—especially sexual ones—are often negative.

Common sexual stereotypes include the following:

- Men are "animals."
- "Nice" women are not interested in sex.
- Virgins are uptight and asexual.
- Gay men are child molesters.
- Lesbians hate men.
- African Americans are sexually uninhibited.
- Latino men are macho.

Most of us know that these are stereotypical statements, and as such they are either exaggerations or untrue. Without much effort, we can usually find examples (which may include ourselves or friends) that contradict a stereotype, yet stereotypes persist. Why? There are two important reasons: (1) Stereotypes structure knowledge, and (2) stereotypes justify discrimination.

Psychologists believe that stereotypes structure knowledge. They affect the ways in which we process information: what we see, what we notice, what we remember, and how we explain things (Hamilton, 1979). Or, as humorist Ashleigh Brilliant said, "Seeing is believing. I wouldn't have seen it if I hadn't believed it." A stereotype is a type of **schema,** a way in which we organize knowledge in our thought processes. Schemas help us channel or filter the mass of information we receive in order for us to make sense of it. They determine what we will regard as important. Although these mental plans are useful, they can also create blind spots. With stereotypes we see what we expect to see and ignore what we don't expect to see. For example, suppose we accept the traditional stereotype that "nice" women aren't interested in sex. Then, if a woman is sexual, she is, by definition, not nice. Or we may say she is "the exception that proves the rule." In either case, contradictory evidence is ignored.

Sociologists point out that sexual stereotyping is often used to justify discrimination. Targets of stereotypes are usually members of subordinate social groups, such as women, low-income groups, and members of ethnic groups. "Two frequent elements in stereotyping," note Eligio Padilla and Kevin O'Grady (1987), "suggest that members of the designated group are by nature intellectually less capable and are by choice immoral, as evidenced most clearly in promiscuous sexual behavior" (Padilla & O'Grady, 1987). As we will see, sexual stereotyping is especially powerful in stigmatizing African Americans, Latinos, and gay men and lesbians.

We all have opinions and biases; most of us to varying degrees think stereotypically. But the commitment to objectivity requires us to become aware of these opinions, biases, and stereotypes and to put them aside in the pursuit of knowledge.

Confusing Attitudes and Behavior

An **attitude** is a predisposition a person has to act, think, or feel in certain ways toward particular things. A **behavior** is the way a person acts. There are two problems we commonly experience when discussing sexual attitudes and behavior: (1) We fail to identify whether we are discussing attitudes or behavior, and (2) we assume attitudes reflect behavior and vice versa.

Failure to identify whether we are discussing attitudes or behavior can lead to confusion and an endless round of disagreement. Imagine, for example, two friends discussing premarital sex without either specifying whether he or she is talking about attitudes or behavior. One says, "Everyone I know accepts premarital sex." The other disagrees: "That's not so. Almost all our friends are virgins." The fact is, both may be correct. But the first person is talking about premarital sexual *attitudes* while the second is talking about actual premarital sexual *behavior*. The two may never be able to find agreement because they are both talking about different things.

There is often a discrepancy between attitudes and behavior. As a result, we cannot infer a person's behavior from his or her attitudes about sexuality, or vice versa. A person may disapprove of premarital sexual intercourse, for example, but nevertheless engage in it. A woman may oppose abortion but may terminate her own pregnancy.

Common Fallacies: Egocentric and Ethnocentric Thinking

A **fallacy** is an error in reasoning that affects our understanding of a subject. Fallacies distort our thinking, leading us to come to false or erroneous conclusions. In the field of sexuality, egocentric and ethnocentric fallacies are common.

The Egocentric Fallacy The **egocentric fallacy** is the mistaken belief that one's own personal experience and values are held by others in general. As a result of this false consensus, we use our own beliefs and values to explain the attitudes, motivations, and behaviors of others. Of course, our

Enlightenment is man's release from his self-imposed tutelage. Tutelage is man's inability to make use of his understanding without direction from another. . . . Have courage to use your own reason.

Immanuel Kant (1724–1804)

own experiences and values are important; they are the source of personal strength and knowledge. They are often valuable in giving us insight into others. But we cannot necessarily generalize from our own experience to that of others. Our own personal experiences are limited and may be unrepresentative; sometimes they are merely opinions or disguised value judgments.

Let's suppose, for example, that you have several married friends, none of whom masturbate, as far as you know. Does that mean that married men and women do not masturbate? Or should not masturbate? No. It only means that as far as you know, your married friends do not masturbate (and they may not be telling you the truth). Imagine that you enjoy erotica (or do not), or that your friends do (or do not). What can you say about how most people feel about erotica? Nothing, really, because your knowledge is limited to your own experience and that of your friends (who again may not be telling the truth).

The Ethnocentric Fallacy The **ethnocentric fallacy,** also known as **ethnocentrism,** is the belief that one's own ethnic group, nation, or culture is innately superior to others. Ethnocentrism is reinforced by opinions, biases, and stereotypes about other groups and cultures. As members of a group, we tend to share similar values and attitudes with other group members. But the mere fact that we share these beliefs with others is not sufficient proof of their truth.

Ethnocentrism has been increasingly evident as a reaction to the increased awareness of **ethnicity,** ethnic affiliation or identity. For many Americans, a significant part of their sense of self comes from identification with their ethnic group. An **ethnic group** is a group of people distinct from other groups because of cultural characteristics, such as language, religion, and customs that are transmitted from one generation to another. Contemporary American ethnic groups include African Americans, Latinos (Hispanics), Native Americans, Japanese Americans, and Chinese Americans.

Although there has been little research on ethnicity and sexuality until recently, evidence suggests that there is significant ethnic variation in terms of sexual attitudes and behavior (Cortese, 1989; Staples, 1991; Staples & Johnson, 1993). For example, it appears that whites are less sexually permissive than African Americans, and Latinos are less permissive than either whites or African Americans. From a white ethnocentric viewpoint, the greater acceptance of premarital sex among African Americans may be evidence that blacks are "promiscuous." From an African American point of view, whites may be viewed as sexually "uptight." Latinos may see both groups as "immoral."

Ethnocentrism is also expressed in stereotyping other cultures as "primitive," "innocent," "inferior," or "not as advanced." We may view the behavior of other peoples as strange, exotic, unusual, or bizarre, but to them it is normal. Their attitudes, behaviors, values, and beliefs form a unified sexual system, which makes sense within their culture. In fact, we engage in many activities that appear peculiar to those outside our culture, as already discussed in Chapter 1. For example, Amazonian people do not understand why young men or women would masturbate. As a Mehinaku youth asked incredulously: "Having sex with the hand? Why would anyone bother? There are plenty of women around" (Gregor, 1985). Many liken

America to a tribal society that practices a form of male genital mutilation. Instead of calling it genital mutilation, however, we call it circumcision and justify it on grounds of religion, health, or appearance.

SEX RESEARCH METHODS

One of the key factors that distinguishes the findings of social science from beliefs, prejudice, bias—and pop psychology—is its commitment to the scientific method. The **scientific method** is the method by which a hypothesis is formed from impartially gathered data and tested empirically. The scientific method relies on **induction,** that is, forming arguments whose premises are intended to provide some support, but not conclusive support, for their conclusions. The scientific method seeks to describe the world rather than evaluate or judge it.

Although sex researchers use the same methodology as other social scientists, they are constrained by ethical concerns and taboos that those in other fields do not experience. Because of the taboos surrounding sexuality, some traditional research methods are inappropriate. Imagine, for example, that in our culture eating was subject to the same taboos as sexuality. A researcher wishing to study American eating behaviors in a natural setting, such as the kitchen, would face the same obstacles observing people eat as he or she currently faces observing people engaged in sexual behavior in their bedrooms. A researcher's colleagues and friends might think he or she was suffering from a food fetish or an unfortunate gastronomic obsession. Watching people eat at McDonald's would be considered voyeurism. "May I observe you masticating your Big Mac?" would be greeted as a shocking display of prurience.

Ethnocentrism views one's own culture or ethnic group as superior to that of others. While child marriage is prohibited in our society, it is acceptable in many cultures throughout the world, including India. Such marriages generally do not include cohabitation or sexual relations until the couple is old enough in the eyes of their society.

All universal judgments are weak, loose, and dangerous.
Michel de Montaigne
(1533–1595)

Sex research, like most social science research, uses different methodological approaches. These include the following:

- Clinical research
- Survey research: questionnaires and interviews
- Observational research
- Experimental research

Research Concerns

There are two general concerns researchers face in conducting their work. The first concern is ethical, centering around the use of human beings as subjects. The second concern is methodological, regarding sampling techniques and their accuracy. Without a representative sample, the conclusions drawn by these methodologies are limited.

Ethical Issues Ethics are important in any scientific endeavor. They are especially important in such an emotional and value-laden subject as sexuality. Among the most important ethical issues are (1) informed consent, (2) protection from harm, (3) confidentiality, and (4) the use of deception.

Informed consent is the full disclosure to an individual of the purpose, potential risks, and benefits of participating in a research project. The individual must be over age 18 and without mental impairment. Under informed consent, people are free to decide whether to participate in a project without coercion or deceit. Once a study begins, a person has the right to withdraw at any time without penalty.

Each research participant is entitled to protection from harm. Some sex research, such as the viewing of explicit films to measure physiological responses, may cause some people psychological distress. Other experimental studies may require the subject to administer or receive an electrical shock. Research must be designed to avoid serious discomfort, stress, or harm.

The identity of research subjects is to be confidential. Because of the highly charged nature of sexuality, participants need to be guaranteed anonymity. Anonymity is often required to protect subjects from embarrassment, ridicule, or potential harmful effects on their relationships. Some people might be embarrassed if others knew that they masturbated; others may fear their relationships could be destroyed if their partner knew they were involved in sexual activities outside the relationship. In other instances, because much sexual behavior (such as oral-genital sex) is illegal in many states, participants need protection from possible legal intrusion.

Of all the ethical issues surrounding research, the use of deception is the most problematic. Sometimes it is necessary to deceive subjects in order for the experiment to work. If participants in a study on the role of attractiveness at first meetings knew they were being studied in terms of their response to attractive people rather than, say, opening lines, their responses might be different. Few people want to admit that they are swayed by such "superficial" qualities as the way a person looks. Such deceptions are relatively benign. But other deceptions, such as a person's being led to believe he or she is administering painful (but actually simulated) electrical shocks, can be very disturbing. The issue of deception is generally resolved by requiring the researcher to debrief an individual following the experiment. During the debriefing, the deception is revealed and its necessity explained. The participant is given the opportunity to ask questions. He or she may also request that their data be removed from the study and destroyed.

Most colleges and universities have review boards or human subject committees to make sure that research follows ethical guidelines. Proposed research is submitted to the committee prior to the project's beginning. If the committee believes the research poses ethical problems, the project will not be approved until the problems are corrected.

Sampling In each research approach, the choice of a sample—a portion of a larger group of people observed or studied—is critical. To be useful, a sample should be a **random sample,** that is, collected in an unbiased way. Further, the sample should be a **representative sample,** a small group representing the larger group in terms of age, sex, ethnicity, social class, orientation, and so on. Samples that are not representative of the larger group are known as **biased samples.** Using samples is important. It would be impossible, for example, to study the sexual behaviors of all college students in the United States. But we can select a representative sample of college students from various schools and infer from their behavior how other college students behave. Using the same sample to infer the sexual behavior of Americans in general, however, would be a biased sample. We cannot infer the sexual activities of Americans from studying college students because the sample would be biased in terms of age (young), education (college), socioeconomic status (middle class), and ethnicity (white).

Most samples in sex research are limited for several reasons:

1. They depend on volunteers or clients. Since these samples are generally self-selected, we cannot assume that they are representative of the population as a whole (Morokoff, 1986; Harry, 1986). Volunteers for sex research are generally more sexually experienced, more liberal, and less religious than the population as a whole. They are more likely, for example, to be tolerant of premarital sex than those who do not participate.

2. Most sex research takes place in a university or college setting with student volunteers. ("The college student and white rat have been our greatest sources of knowledge," researcher John Gagnon [1977] observes.) College students, however, are generally in late adolescence or early adulthood and are single; they are at the beginning of their sexual lives. Is the value they place on sexuality in marriage, for example, likely to be the same as older, married adults?

3. Ethnic groups are generally underrepresented. Representative samples of African Americans, Latinos, Native Americans, and some Asian Americans are not easily found because they are underrepresented in colleges and universities where subjects are generally recruited.

4. The study of gay men and lesbians presents unique sampling problems. Are gay men and lesbians who have come out (publicly identified themselves as gay or lesbian) different from those who have not? How does one find and recruit subjects who have not come out?

Because the above factors limit most studies, one must be careful in making generalizations from them.

Clinical Research

Clinical research is the in-depth examination of an individual or group who come to a psychiatrist, psychologist, or social worker for assistance with psychological or medical problems or disorders. Clinical research is descriptive. Inferences of cause and effect cannot be drawn from it. The individual is interviewed and treated for a specific problem. At the same time the person is being treated, he or she is being studied. In their evaluations, clinicians attempt to determine the causes of a disorder and how it may be treated. They may also try to infer from dysfunctional people how healthy people develop.

Clinical research focuses largely on what is considered deviant, abnormal, inadequate, or unhealthy sexual behavior, such as transsexuality (individuals who feel they are trapped in bodies of the wrong sex) and sexual dysfunctions (such as lack of desire, premature ejaculation, erectile difficulties, or lack of orgasm).

A major limitation of clinical research is its emphasis on unhealthy or **pathological behavior** (diseased behavior). Such an emphasis makes clinical research dependent on cultural definitions of what is "unhealthy" or "pathological." These definitions, however, change. In the nineteenth century, for example, masturbation was considered pathological. Physicians and clinicians went to great lengths to root it out. In the case of women, surgeons sometimes removed the clitoris.

In evaluating clinical research, there are several questions to ask (Gagnon, 1977). First, on what basis is a condition defined as healthy or unhealthy? For example, are the bases for classifying homosexuality and masturbation as healthy or unhealthy behaviors scientific, cultural, or moral? Second, can inferences gathered from the behavior of patients be applied to others? For example, if we learn that male-to-female transsexuals tended to play with dolls when they were young, should we discourage male children from playing with dolls? Third, how do we know that the people we are studying are representative of that group? Most of what we know about the psychological makeup of rapists comes from the study of imprisoned rapists. But are imprisoned rapists representative of all rapists?

Survey Research

Survey research is a method used to gather information from a small group and to make inferences for a larger group. The survey method uses questionnaires or interviews to gather information. Questionnaires offer anonymity, may be completed fairly quickly, and are relatively inexpensive to administer; however, they usually do not allow an in-depth response. A person must respond with a short answer or a limited choice. Interview techniques avoid some of the shortcomings of questionnaires, as interviewers are able to probe in greater depth and follow paths suggested by the subject.

While the survey method is an important source of information, it has several limitations. First, people tend to be poor reporters of their own sexual behavior. Men may exaggerate their number of sexual partners, while women may minimize their casual encounters. Members of both sexes generally underreport experiences considered deviant or immoral, such as same-sex experiences, bondage, and so on. Second, interviewers may allow their

Self-Assessment

THE KINSEY INSTITUTE/ROPER
ORGANIZATION NATIONAL SEX KNOWLEDGE TEST

This self-assessment was given to a representative sample of Americans in 1990.

Circle one answer after reading each question carefully.

1. **Nowadays, what do you think is the age at which the** *average* **or** *typical* **American** *first* **has sexual intercourse?**

a. 11 or younger	d. 14	g. 17	j. 20
b. 12	e. 15	h. 18	k. 21 or older
c. 13	f. 16	i. 19	l. Don't know

2. **Out of every ten married American men, how many would you estimate have had an extramarital affair—that is, have been sexually unfaithful to their wives?**

a. Less than one out of ten	e. Four out of ten (40%)	i. Eight out of ten (80%)
b. One out of ten (10%)	f. Five out of ten (50%)	j. Nine out of ten (90%)
c. Two out of ten (20%)	g. Six out of ten (60%)	k. More than nine out of ten
d. Three out of ten (30%)	h. Seven out of ten (70%)	l. Don't know

3. **Out of every ten American women, how many would you estimate have had anal (rectal) intercourse?**

a. Less than one out of ten	e. Four out of ten (40%)	i. Eight out of ten (80%)
b. One out of ten (10%)	f. Five out of ten (50%)	j. Nine out of ten (90%)
c. Two out of ten (20%)	g. Six out of ten (60%)	k. More than nine out of ten
d. Three out of ten (30%)	h. Seven out of ten (70%)	l. Don't know

4. **A person can get AIDS by having anal (rectal) intercourse even if neither partner is infected with the AIDS virus.**

   True   False   Don't know

5. **There are over-the-counter spermicides people can buy at the drugstore that will kill the AIDS virus.**

   True   False   Don't know

6. **Petroleum jelly, Vaseline Intensive Care, baby oil, and Nivea are** *not* **good lubricants to use with a condom or diaphragm.**

   True   False   Don't know

7. **More than one out of four (25 percent) of American men have had a sexual experience with another male during either their teens or adult years.**

   True   False   Don't know

(continued)

THE SEX KNOWLEDGE TEST *(continued)*

8. It is usually difficult to tell whether people *are* or *are not* homosexual just by their appearance or gestures.

   True   False   Don't know

9. A woman or teenage girl can get pregnant during her menstrual flow (her "period").

   True   False   Don't know

10. A woman or teenage girl can get pregnant even if the man withdraws his penis before he ejaculates (before he "comes").

    True   False   Don't know

11. Unless they are having sex, women do not need to have regular gynecological examinations.

    True   False   Don't know

12. Teenage boys should examine their testicles ("balls") regularly just as women self-examine their breasts for lumps.

    True   False   Don't know

13. Problems with erection are most often started by a physical problem.

    True   False   Don't know

14. Almost all erection problems can be successfully treated.

    True   False   Don't know

15. Menopause, or change of life as it is often called, does *not* cause most women to lose interest in having sex.

    True   False   Don't know

16. Out of every ten American women, how many would you estimate have masturbated either as children or after they were grown up?

    a. Less than one out of ten
    b. One out of ten (10%)
    c. Two out of ten (20%)
    d. Three out of ten (30%)
    e. Four out of ten (40%)
    f. Five out of ten (50%)
    g. Six out of ten (60%)
    h. Seven out of ten (70%)
    i. Eight out of ten (80%)
    j. Nine out of ten (90%)
    k. More than nine out of ten
    l. Don't know

own preconceptions to influence the way in which they frame questions and to bias their interpretations of responses as well. Third, some respondents may feel uncomfortable about revealing information—such as masturbation or incestuous experiences—in a face-to-face interview. Fourth, the interviewer's gender may also influence how comfortable respondents are in disclosing information about themselves. Finally, some ethnic groups, because of their cultural values, may be reluctant to reveal sexual information about themselves. Recent findings suggest, however, that African Americans and Latinos are willing to participate in research and to answer sensitive questions (Jackson, 1991; Marin & Marin, 1989, 1991).

17. What do you think is the length of the average man's *erect* penis?

a. 2 inches	d. 5 inches	g. 8 inches	j. 10 inches
b. 3 inches	e. 6 inches	h. 9 inches	k. 12 inches
c. 4 inches	f. 7 inches	i. 10 inches	l. Don't know

18. Most women prefer a sexual partner with a larger-than-average penis.

True   False   Don't know

Scoring the Test

Each question is worth one point. So, the total possible number of points you can get is 18. Using this chart, score each item and then add up your total number of points. When a range of possible answers is correct, according to currently available research data, all respondents choosing one of the answers in the correct range are given a point.

Question number	Give yourself a point if you circled any of the following answers	Circle the number of points you received	Question number	Give yourself a point if you circled any of the following answers	Circle the number of points you received
1	f,g	0 1	11	False	0 1
2	d,e	0 1	12	True	0 1
3	d,e	0 1	13	True	0 1
4	False	0 1	14	True	0 1
5	(any answer, everyone gets a point as explained in discussion of question)	1	15	True	0 1
6	True	0 1	16	g,h,i	0 1
7	True	0 1	17	d,e,f	0 1
8	True	0 1	18	False	0 1
9	True	0 1			
10	True	0 1			

Total Number of Points: _____

Source: Reinisch, J. *The New Kinsey Report*. New York: St. Martin's Press, 1990, pp. 3–5.

Observational Research

Observational research is the method by which a researcher unobtrusively observes and makes systematic notes about people's behavior without trying to manipulate it. The observer does not want to affect the subject's behavior by his or her presence. But because sexual behavior is regarded as significantly different from other behaviors, there are serious ethical concerns involved in observing people's sexual behavior without their knowledge and consent. (Even with their knowledge and consent, such observation may be considered voyeuristic and subject to criminal prosecution.) Since research-

Discovery consists of seeing what everybody has seen and thinking what nobody has thought.
Albert Szent-Gyorgyi

ers cannot observe sexual behavior as they might observe flirting at a party, dance, or bar, such observations usually take place in a laboratory setting. In such instances, the setting is not a natural environment; participants are aware that their behavior is under observation.

Probably the largest observational study in human sexuality was William Masters and Virginia Johnson's work on sexual response in which they observed and measured more than 10,000 orgasms in a hospital's soundproof laboratory. (The soundproofing was necessary to prevent physicians and nurses from eavesdropping; some even placed stethoscopes against the walls in an attempt to listen.) In such studies, volunteer bias may be a particularly critical issue. Are individuals who participate in such studies exhibitionistic? How does awareness that they are being observed affect their behavior? Masters and Johnson tried to eliminate bias by extensive interviews with their volunteers. They allowed their participants practice sessions in the laboratories to familiarize them with the setting.

One way of avoiding such volunteer bias is through participant observation, in which the researcher participates in the behaviors he or she is studying. A researcher may study prostitution by becoming a customer (Snyder, 1974); swinging, by exchanging partners in a group of swingers (Bartell, 1970); anonymous sex between men in public restrooms by posing as a lookout (Humphreys, 1975). There are several questions raised by such participant observation. First of all, how does the observer's participation affect the interactions being studied? For example, does a prostitute respond differently to a researcher as he tries to obtain information? Second, if the observer participates, how does this affect his or her objectivity? If observers are involved in swinging, for example, are they more likely to report favorably on swinging? Third, what are the researcher's ethical responsibilities regarding informing those he or she is studying?

Experimental Research

Experimental research is the systematic manipulation of the environment to learn the effect of such manipulation on behavior. It enables researchers to isolate a single factor under controlled circumstances to determine its influence. Researchers are able to control their experiments by using **variables,** aspects or factors that can be manipulated in experiments. There are two types of variables: independent variables and dependent variables. **Independent variables** are factors that can be manipulated or changed by the experimenter; **dependent variables** are factors that are affected by changes in the independent variable.

Because it controls variables, experimental research differs from the previous methods we have examined. Clinical studies, surveys, and observational research are correlational in natural. **Correlational studies** measure two or more naturally occurring variables to determine their relationship to each other. Because they do not manipulate the variables, they cannot tell us which variable *causes* the other to change. But because experimental studies manipulate the independent variables, researchers *can* reasonably determine what variables cause the other variables to change.

Much experimental research on sexuality depends on measuring physiological responses. These responses are usually measured by **plethysmographs,** devices attached to the genitals to measure physiological response.

Researchers use either a penile plethysmograph or **strain gauge** (a rubber-bandlike device) for men and a vaginal plethysmograph for women. Both the penile plethysmograph and strain gauge are placed around the penis; they measure changes in the circumference of the penis that accompany sexual arousal. The vaginal plethysmograph is about the size of a menstrual tampon and is inserted into the vagina like a tampon. The vaginal plethysmograph measures the amount of blood within the vaginal walls, which increases as a woman becomes aroused.

Imagine that researchers want to study the influence of alcohol on sexual response. They would use a plethysmograph to measure sexual response, the dependent variable. In this study, the independent variables would be the levels of alcohol consumption: no alcohol consumption, moderate alcohol consumption, and high alcohol consumption. In such experiments, subjects may view an erotic film. To get a baseline measurement, researchers measure the genitals' physiological patterns in an unaroused state prior to viewing the film or drinking. Then they measure sexual arousal (dependent variable) to erotica as they increase the levels of alcohol consumption (independent variables).

Good experiments are difficult to design because the experimental situation must resemble the real world. There are four important concerns about experimental research. (1) To what degree does the experiment replicate the complexities and settings of real-life sexuality? Does a laboratory setting radically alter responses? (2) Do the devices used to measure sexual response affect the subject's sexual responsiveness? (3) The measuring devices measure only genital response, while the overall sexual response includes increased heart rate, muscle tension, changed brain-wave patterns, sexual fantasies and thoughts, and so on. (4) Can the results from the experiment be generalized to nonlaboratory conditions? Because there are so many variables outside controlled laboratory conditions, many researchers believe that experimental findings are highly limited when applied to the real world.

Differences in sampling and methodological techniques help explain why scientific studies of the same phenomenon may result in different conclusions. They also help explain a common misperception about scientific studies. Many of us believe that because studies have different conclusions, none is valid. What conflicting studies really mean, however, is that researchers are constantly exploring issues from different perspectives in an attempt to achieve consensus.

Sometimes researchers discover errors or problems in sampling or methodology that lead to new conclusions. As William Simon (1992) notes:

> Science is more than a set of specific methods, these change over time.... We pledge to accurately describe our methods, our answers to the question, "How do you know?" In other words, we pledge to do our thinking in public. This does not protect us from error; it does provide the optimum conditions for discovering error.

Improvements are constantly being made in sampling and methodologies that enable researchers to elaborate on or disprove earlier studies. In fact, the word "research" is derived from the prefix *re-*, meaning "over again," and *search*, meaning "to examine closely." And that is the essence of the scientific endeavor: searching and re-searching for knowledge.

THE SEX RESEARCHERS

It was not until the nineteenth century that Western sexuality began to be studied using a scientific framework. Prior to that time, sexuality was claimed by religion rather than science; sex was the subject of moral rather than scientific scrutiny. From the earliest Christian era, treatises, canon law, papal bulls, as well as sermons and confessions catalogued the sins of the flesh. Reflecting this Christian tradition, the early students of sexuality were concerned with the excesses and deviances of sexuality rather than its healthy functioning. They were fascinated by what they considered the pathologies of sex, such as fetishism, sadism, masturbation, and homosexuality—the very behaviors that religion condemned as sinful. Alfred Kinsey ironically noted that nineteenth-century researchers created "scientific classifications . . . nearly identical with theological classifications and with moral pronouncements . . . of the fifteenth century" (Kinsey et al., 1948).

But as we will see, there has been a liberalizing trend in our thinking about sexuality. Both Richard von Krafft-Ebing and Sigmund Freud viewed sexuality as inherently dangerous and needing repression. But Havelock Ellis, Alfred Kinsey, William Masters and Virginia Johnson, and a number of more recent researchers have viewed sexuality more positively; in fact, historian Paul Robinson (1976) regards these later researchers as modernists ("sexual enthusiasts," he calls them). Three themes are evident in their work. First, they believed that sexual expression was essential to an individual's well-being. Second, they sought to broaden the range of legitimate sexual activity, including homosexuality. Third, they believed that female sexuality was the equal of male sexuality.

As much as possible, sex researchers attempt to examine sexuality objectively. But, like all of us, many of their views are intertwined with the beliefs and values of their times. This is especially apparent among the early sex researchers.

Richard von Krafft-Ebing (1840–1902) viewed most sexual behavior other than marital coitus as a sign of pathology.

Richard von Krafft-Ebing (1840–1902)

As the nineteenth century progressed, there was increasing scientific interest in human sexuality. Physicians and psychiatrists in particular began to probe what they believed were the mysterious and dangerous realms of sexuality. Richard von Krafft-Ebing, a Viennese professor of psychiatry, was probably the most influential of the early researchers. In 1886, he published his most famous work, *Psychopathia Sexualis*, a collection of case histories of fetishists, sadists, masochists, and homosexuals. (He invented the words "sadomasochism" and "transvestite.") The title of his book indicated the fundamental belief that straying from the Victorian standard was by its very nature deranged and pathological (Gay, 1986). Krafft-Ebing's studies of men enamored of handkerchiefs, psychotic child murderers, women with whips, and transvestites dressed as nuns provided the material for his theories.

Krafft-Ebing traced variations in Victorian sexuality to "hereditary taint," "moral degeneracy," and, in particular, to masturbation. He intermingled descriptions of fetishists who became sexually excited by kid gloves with those of sadists who disemboweled their victims. For Krafft-Ebing, the origins of fetishism and murderous sadism, as well as most variations, lay in masturbation, the sexual sin of the nineteenth century. Fetishists and sadists, homosexuals and transvestites, masochists and transsexuals—all were basically indistinguishable from each other, and each represented an aspect of sexual degeneracy. They were cut from the same cloth, he believed. They differed only in degree, not in kind.

In our time, Krafft-Ebing's theories on the origins, nature, and dangers of sexual aberrations are little more than amusing stories or strange curiosities. Much of what he considered degeneracy, such as masturbation, is today considered normal sexual behavior. Ironically, his greatest contribution was quite different from what he had hoped. He expressed great concern that his studies not be read by what he considered an ignorant and prurient public. His *Psychopathia Sexualis*, however, brought to public attention and discussion an immense range of sexual behaviors that had never before been documented in a dispassionate, if erroneous, manner. A darkened region of sexual behavior was brought into the open for public examination (Bullough, 1976).

Sigmund Freud (1856–1939)

Few people have had as dramatic an impact on the way we think about the world as the Viennese physician Sigmund Freud. In his attempt to understand the **neuroses,** psychological disorders characterized by anxiety or tension, plaguing his patients, Freud explored the unknown territory of the unconscious, "the dark, inaccessible part of our personality . . . a chaos, a cauldron of seething excitation" (quoted in Rieff, 1979). If unconscious motives were brought to consciousness, a person could change his or her behavior. But, he believed, **repression,** a psychological mechanism that keeps people from becoming aware of hidden memories and motives because they arouse guilt, prevents such knowledge.

To explore the unconscious, Freud used various techniques; in particular, he analyzed the meaning of dreams. His journeys into the mind led to the development of **psychoanalysis,** a psychological system that traces behavior to unconscious desires. He fled Vienna when Hitler annexed Austria in 1938 and died a year later in England.

Sigmund Freud (1856–1939) was the founder of psychoanalysis and one of the most influential European thinkers of the first half of the twentieth century. Freud viewed sexuality with suspicion.

The Theory of Personality His clinical work led Freud to develop a theory of personality in which sexuality played a critical role. (For the best concise discussion of Freudian psychology, see Hall, 1979.) According to Freud's theory, personality consists of three parts: the id, the ego, and the superego. The **id** represents the instincts and is driven by the **libido,** which seeks pleasure, especially sexual pleasure. The libido, or sexual drive, pursues pleasure regardless of the cost; it followed what Freud called the **pleasure principle,** the idea that organisms seek pleasure and avoid pain. The **ego,** however, deals with reality. It acts as an intermediary between the demands of the id and those of society. It is governed by the **reality principle,** the control the external world exerts on the organism, which postpones pleasure. The **superego** acts as the individual's conscience. It is an internalization of society's demands, which the individual learns from birth. These various elements are in constant conflict with each other. The id is constantly seeking gratification; the superego is constantly seeking to repress it. The repression of instinctive desires often leads to neurosis.

The Theory of Psychosexual Development

Freud believed that sexuality begins at birth. His belief in infant and child sexuality set him apart from other researchers. Freud described five stages in psychosexual development. The first stage is the **oral stage,** lasting from birth to age 1. During this time, the infant's eroticism is focused on the mouth; thumb-sucking produces an erotic pleasure. Freud believed the "most striking character of this sexual activity . . . is that the child gratifies himself on his own body; . . . he is autoerotic" (Freud, 1938). The second stage, between ages 1 and 3, is the **anal stage.** The erotic activities continue to be autoerotic, but the region of pleasure shifts to the anus. From age 3 through 5, the child is in the **phallic stage,** in which he or she exhibits interest in the genitals. At age 6, children enter a **latency stage,** in which their sexual impulses are no longer active. At puberty, they enter the **genital stage,** at which point the adolescent becomes interested in genital sexual activities, especially sexual intercourse.

The phallic stage is the critical stage in both male and female development. The boy develops sexual desires for his mother, leading to the **Oedipal complex.** He simultaneously desires his mother and fears his father. This fear leads to **castration anxiety,** the belief that the father will cut off his penis because of jealousy. Girls follow a more complex development, according to Freud. A girl develops an **Electra complex,** desiring her father while fearing her mother. Upon discovering that she does not have a penis, she feels deprived and develops **penis envy.** By age 6, both boys and girls resolve their Oedipal and Electra complexes by relinquishing their desires for the parent of the other sex and identifying with their same-sex parent. In this manner, they develop their masculine and feminine identities. But because girls never acquire their "lost penis," Freud believed they fail to develop an independent character like that of boys.

Critique

In many ways, such as in his commitment to science and his explorations of the unconscious, Freud seems the embodiment of twentieth-century thought. But over the last generation, his influence among American sex researchers has dwindled. Two of the most important reasons are (1) his lack of empiricism and (2) his inadequate description of female development.

American sex researchers follow an empirical tradition that emphasizes the scientific collection and analysis of data. They are reluctant to speculate or make generalizations without empirical evidence. By contrast, Freud in many ways was a philosopher who was given to constant speculation.

Freud's conception of female development reflected his strong nineteenth-century traditionalism. Most obvious was his belief that women were biologically "destined" to be mothers. He argued, for example, against women attending universities: "Intellectual training may make them deprecate the feminine role for which they were intended" (quoted in Rieff, 1979). Because he believed that the model for psychosexual development was fundamentally male, with special emphasis on the penis, he was unable to develop an adequate model of female development (Lips, 1992). He believed that women experienced themselves as "defective" males who envied the penis. Such ideas were without empirical evidence.

Because of its limitations, Freud's work has become mostly of historical interest to mainstream sex researchers. It continues to exert influence in

Oedipus, schmedipus, as long as he loves his mother.

Anonymous

The great question . . . which I have not been able to answer, despite my thirty years of research into the feminine soul, is "What does a woman want?"

Sigmund Freud

some fields of psychology but has been greatly modified by others. Even among contemporary psychoanalysts, his work has been radically revised. "Psychoanalysis has been turned upside down," Janet Sayers (1991) writes. "Once patriarchal and phallocentric, it is now almost entirely mother-centered." Research has turned from studying sex, repression, and castration to interpersonal issues of maternal care and child development.

[Psychoanalysis] is not the only way to resolve inner conflicts. Life itself still remains a very effective therapist.
Karen Horney (1885–1952)

Havelock Ellis (1859–1939)

Havelock Ellis, who became one of the most influential sexual thinkers and reformers in the twentieth century, was a child of the Victorian era. A native of England, his boyhood and youth were marked by the sexual repression and fears of that time. It was against these sexual inhibitions that he set himself in order to free humanity from ignorance. He was among the first modern affirmers of sexuality. "Sex lies at the root of life," he wrote, "and we can never learn to reverence life until we know how to understand sex" (Ellis, 1900). He believed that the negators of sexuality used morality and religion to twist and deform sex until it became little more than sin and degradation. He was a radical thinker who sought radical change in the name of enlightenment.

Ellis was the earliest important modern sexual thinker. His *Studies in the Psychology of Sex* (the first six volumes of which were published between 1897 and 1910) consisted of case studies, autobiographies, and personal letters. According to Paul Robinson (1976), Ellis's *Studies* "established the basic moral categories for nearly all subsequent sexual theorizing." These included the relativity of sexual values, the normality of masturbation, women as the sexual equals of men, the expansion of "normal" sexual behavior, homosexuality as a sexual variation, and toleration of sexual diversity.

Relativity of Sexual Values In the nineteenth century, Americans and Europeans alike believed that their society's dominant sexual beliefs were the only morally and naturally correct standards. But Ellis demonstrated that Western sexual standards were not the only moral standards and that they were not necessarily rooted in nature. In doing so, he was among the first researchers to appeal to studies in animal behavior, anthropology, and history. If homosexuality—what Ellis called "sexual inversion"—was unnatural, for example, then it would not exist in nature. But he cited numerous incidences of same-sex behavior in primates to show that homosexuality was practiced among animals. Using anthropological studies, he found numerous examples of homosexuality in other cultures; many cultures, he stated, revered homosexuals. He found historical examples, such as ancient Greece, where homosexuality was treated as superior to heterosexuality.

Normality of Masturbation Masturbation was the scourge of the nineteenth century. Ellis, however, challenged that view. He argued that masturbation was widespread and that there was no evidence linking it with any serious mental or physical problems. He recorded countless men and women who masturbated without ill effect. In fact, he argued, masturbation provided a positive function: It relieved tension. His major objection to masturbation was neither medical nor moral. He felt that its primary limitation was that it was a solitary rather than an interpersonal expression of sexuality.

In his study of masturbation, Ellis argued that it was part of a larger category of sexual behavior for which he coined the term *autoeroticism*, self-stimulation or erotic behavior involving only the self. Since his time, autoeroticism, which includes masturbation, erotic dreams, sexual fantasies, and nocturnal orgasms, has become a basic category of sexual behaviors.

Women as the Sexual Equals of Men The nineteenth century viewed women as essentially "pure beings" who possessed reproductive rather than sexual desires. Men, by contrast, were driven by such strong sexual passions that their sexuality had to be severely controlled and repressed. In countless case studies, Ellis documented that women possessed sexual desires no less intense than those of men.

His studies indicated that female sexuality, however, was more diffuse than male sexuality. While male sexuality was centered in the genitals, female sexuality spread beyond the genitals to include much of the body, especially the breasts. In describing nongenital areas of the body as erotically sensitive, Ellis helped formulate the concept of *erogenous zones*, areas or parts of the body that are especially receptive to erotic stimulation.

Redefinition of Normal Sexual Behavior Normality was never discussed, Ellis noted, because "every one was supposed to know instinctively" (Ellis, 1938). He questioned this assumption:

> As soon as we inquire into the actual and intimate facts of the sexual life, we see that this ancient and traditional assumption is mistaken. So far from there being only one pattern of sex life, it would be nearer the truth to say that there are as many patterns as there are individuals.

A wide range of behaviors, he argued, was normal, including much behavior that the Victorians considered abnormal. He argued that both masturbation and female sexuality were normal behaviors and that even the so-called abnormal elements of sexual behavior were simply exaggerations of the normal. He argued that sadomasochism, for example, existed on a continuum, where the biting and scratching of couples in passionate intercourse represented one end and violence the other. "Every normal man in matters of sex, when we examine him carefully enough," Ellis wrote, "is found to show some abnormal elements, and the abnormal man is merely manifesting in a disordered or extravagant shape some phase of the normal man." The normal and abnormal were different more in degree than in kind.

Reevaluation of Homosexuality The nineteenth century viewed homosexuality as the essence of sin and perversion. It was dangerous, lurid, and criminal. Ellis, however, reevaluated homosexuality. It was not a disease or vice, he insisted, but a congenital condition: A person was born homosexual; one did not *become* homosexual. By insisting that homosexuality was congenital, Ellis denied that it could be considered a vice or a form of moral degeneracy because a person did not *choose* it. If homosexuality was both congenital and harmless, then, Ellis reasoned, it should not be considered immoral or criminal.

Ellis considered homosexuality abnormal primarily in its choice of sexual objects: the object of some men's desires being other men and some women's desires being women. But homosexuality, wrote Ellis, "possesses all the attributes which in other respects appeal to human affection" (Ellis, 1938). Homosexuals possessed the same abilities as heterosexuals to love, to be loyal, and to be faithful—all of which constitute moral goodness.

Toleration of Differences Ellis possessed a generous spirit, seeking compassionate understanding rather than condemnation and persecution. "We must aim not only to be just," he wrote, "but also to be sympathetic" (Ellis, 1938). His broadening of the definition of normality and his passionate defense of homosexuality are but two examples of such sympathy. He argued that it was hopeless to try to deal with sexual variations as crimes if there were no victims. Furthermore, such attempts discredited the legal system by their lack of justice and ineffectiveness. Similar arguments ultimately became the justification for the decriminalization of private sexual behavior in much of the United States.

Alfred Kinsey (1894–1956)

Prior to 1948, most middle-class Americans continued to congratulate themselves on their standards of sexual propriety. They publicly proclaimed their virtue as something that set them apart from the decadent Europeans, who took a careless if not immoral attitude toward sexuality. Americans found comfort in their moral superiority. Conformity was a virtue and nonconformity often a crime.

In 1948, Alfred A. Kinsey, a biologist at Indiana University and America's leading authority on gall wasps, destroyed forever the belief in American sexual innocence and virtue. He accomplished this through two books, *Sexual Behavior in the Human Male* (1948) and *Sexual Behavior in the Human Female* (1953). These two volumes statistically documented the actual sex-

Alfred Kinsey (1894–1956) shocked Americans by revealing how they actually behaved sexually. His scientific efforts led to the termination of his research funding because of political pressure.

ual behavior of Americans. In massive detail, they demonstrated the great discrepancy between *public* standards of sexual behavior and *actual* sexual behavior. In the firestorm that accompanied the publication of Kinsey's books (popularly known as the *Kinsey Reports*), many Americans protested the destruction of their cherished ideals and illusions.

Statistical Study of Sexuality Kinsey began his research in 1938 when he was asked to teach a course on the role of sex in marriage at Indiana University. When he went to the university library, he discovered that there was no systematic study of how people behave sexually. As a biological scientist, he was disturbed by this lack of reliable information (Pomeroy, 1972).

Because there were no significant statistical studies of sexual behavior of the general population, Kinsey undertook what remains—more than two generations later—the most important survey of American sexual behavior. Between 1938 and 1956, Kinsey and his colleagues collected detailed information on the sex lives of almost 17,000 people. He himself conducted 8000 interviews. Because of the sensitive nature of his questions, Kinsey took care to guard the privacy of his respondents; he recorded his notes in code.

Sexual Diversity and Variation What Kinsey discovered in his research was an extraordinary diversity in individual sexual behaviors. Among men, he found individuals who had orgasms daily and others who went months without orgasms. Among women, he found those who had never had orgasms and those who had them several times a day. He discovered one male who had ejaculated only once in 30 years and another who climaxed 30 times a week on average. "This is the order of variation," he commented dryly, "which may occur between two individuals who live in the same town and who are neighbors, meeting in the same place of business and coming together in common social activities" (Kinsey et al., 1948).

Reevaluation of Masturbation Kinsey's work aimed at a reevaluation of the role of masturbation in a person's sexual adjustment. His treatment of masturbation, observed Robinson (1976), made Kinsey "unquestionably . . . among the foremost modern defenders of autoeroticism." Kinsey made three points about masturbation: (1) It is harmless, (2) it is not a substitute for sexual intercourse but a distinct form of sexual behavior that provides sexual pleasure, and (3) it plays an important role in women's sexuality because it is a more reliable source of orgasm than heterosexual intercourse, and because its practice seems to facilitate women's ability to become orgasmic during intercourse. Indeed, Kinsey believed that masturbation was the best way to measure a woman's inherent sexual responsiveness because it did not rely on another person.

Same-Sex Behavior Prior to Kinsey's work, an individual was identified as homosexual if he or she engaged in a single sexual act with a member of the same sex. Kinsey found, however, that many people had sexual experiences with members of both sexes. He reported that 50% of the men and 28% of the women in his studies had same-sex experiences; 38% of the men and 13% of the women had orgasms during these experiences (Kinsey, 1948,

I hardly see him at night anymore since he took up sex.

Clara Kinsey

The fact will one day flower into a truth.

Henry David Thoreau
(1817–1862)

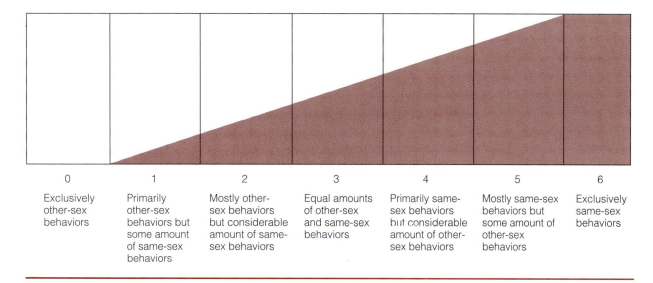

0	1	2	3	4	5	6
Exclusively other-sex behaviors	Primarily other-sex behaviors but some amount of same-sex behaviors	Mostly other-sex behaviors but considerable amount of same-sex behaviors	Equal amounts of other-sex and same-sex behaviors	Primarily same-sex behaviors but considerable amount of other-sex behaviors	Mostly same-sex behaviors but some amount of other-sex behaviors	Exclusively same-sex behaviors

FIGURE 2.1 The Kinsey scale focused on the degree to which a person engaged in other-sex and same-sex sexual behaviors.

1953). Furthermore, he discovered that sexual preferences could change over the course of a person's lifetime. Kinsey's research led him to believe that it was erroneous to classify people as either heterosexual or homosexual. A person's sexuality was significantly more complex and fluid.

Kinsey wanted to eliminate the concept of heterosexual and homosexual *identities*. He did not believe that homosexuality, any more than heterosexuality, existed as a fixed psychological identity. Instead, he argued, there were only sexual acts, and acts alone did not make a person gay, lesbian, or heterosexual. It was more important to determine what proportion of behaviors were same-sex and other-sex than to label a person as gay, lesbian, or heterosexual.

He devised the Kinsey scale to represent the proportion of an individual's sexual behaviors with the same or other sex (Figure 2.1). This scale charted behaviors from no behaviors with the same sex to behaviors exclusively with members of the same sex. These behaviors existed on a continuum. His scale radicalized the categorization of human sexual behavior (McWhirter, 1990). It continues to be valuable as an expression of the fact that "dichotomous categories, such as heterosexual and homosexual, fail to reflect adequately the complex realities of sexual orientation, and human sexuality in general" (Sanders, Reinisch, & McWhirter, 1990).

Rejection of Normal/Abnormal Dichotomy

As a result of his research, Kinsey insisted that the distinction between normal and abnormal was meaningless. Like Ellis, he argued that sexual differences were a matter of degree, not kind. Almost any sexual behavior could be placed alongside another that differed from it only slightly. He argued:

> It is not possible to insist that any departure from the sexual mores [customs], or any participation in socially taboo activities, always, or even usually, involves a neurosis or psychosis, for the case histories abundantly demonstrate that most individuals who engage in taboo activities make satisfactory social adjustments.

The only unnatural sex act is the one that can't be performed.
Alfred Kinsey

His observations led him to be a leading advocate of the toleration of sexual differences.

Critique While Kinsey's statistical methodology has been criticized, the two most important criticisms of his work are (1) his emphasis on the quantification of sexual behavior, and (2) his rejection of the psychological dimension.

Because Kinsey wanted to quantify behaviors, he studied only those behaviors that could be objectively measured. Thus, he defined sexual behaviors as those that lead to orgasm. By defining sexuality in this way, Kinsey reduced sexual behavior to genital activity. Because sexual activities, such as kissing and erotic fantasies, did not ordinarily lead to orgasm, Kinsey excluded them from his research.

He also neglected the psychological dimension of sexuality. Motivation and attitudes did not interest him because he did not believe they could be objectively measured. As a consequence, the role of emotions, such as love, did not enter into his discussion of sexuality. Nor did it matter whether a person experienced an intensely satisfying orgasm or one that was hardly worth mentioning. Kinsey wanted simply to know *if* the person experienced an orgasm. For him, a "cosmic" orgasm was the equal of a "ho-hum" one.

Kinsey's lack of interest in the psychological dimension of human sexuality led him to reject homosexual/heterosexual *identities* as meaningless. While a person's sexual behaviors may not correspond to his or her identity as homosexual or heterosexual, this identity is nevertheless a critical aspect of self-concept. By ignoring these elements, Kinsey seriously limited his understanding of human sexuality.

William Masters and Virginia Johnson

In the 1950s, William Masters, a St. Louis physician, became interested in treating sexual inadequacy, such problems as premature ejaculation and erection difficulties in men, and lack of orgasm in women. As a physician, he felt that a systematic study of human sexual response was necessary, but none existed. To fill this void, he decided to conduct his own research. Masters was joined several years later by Virginia Johnson. Later they married, and in 1992 they divorced.

Masters and Johnson detailed the sexual response cycles of 382 men and 312 women during over 10,000 acts of sexual behavior, including masturbation and sexual intercourse. The researchers combined observation with direct measurement of changes in male and female genitals using electronic devices.

Human Sexual Response (1966), their first book, became an immediate success among both researchers and the public at large. What made their work significant was not only the detailed description of physiological responses, but the articulation of several key ideas. First, Masters and Johnson discovered that, physiologically, male and female sexual responses were very similar. Second, they demonstrated that women achieved orgasm primarily through clitoral stimulation. Penetration of the vagina was not needed for orgasm to occur. By demonstrating the primacy of the clitoris, Masters and Johnson destroyed once and for all the Freudian distinction between vaginal and clitoral orgasms. (Freud believed that a woman's orgasm experienced through masturbation was somehow physically and psychologically inferior to one experienced through sexual intercourse. He made no such distinction for men.) By destroying the myth of the vaginal orgasm, Masters and Johnson legitimized female masturbation.

In 1970, Masters and Johnson published *Human Sexual Inadequacy,* which revolutionized sex therapy by treating sexual problems as simply difficulties that could be easily treated using behavioral therapy. They argued that sexual problems were not the result of underlying neuroses or personality disorders. More often than not, problems resulted from a lack of information, poor communication between couples, or marital conflict. Their behavioral approach, which included "homework" exercises such as clitoral or penile stimulation, led to an astounding increase in the successful treatment of sexual problems. Their work made them pioneers in modern sex therapy.

William Masters and Virginia Johnson detailed the sexual response cycle in the 1960s and revolutionized sex therapy in the 1970s.

Critique While Masters and Johnson continued to publish work on sexuality, their later books have not been as well received as their early pioneering efforts. In fact, some of their subsequent work has been highly criticized as unscientific. Their work on homosexuality, for example, advocated methods for "reversing" homosexuality (Masters & Johnson, 1979). Critics pointed out that mainstream psychologists reject the idea of reversing homosexuality; instead, the customary treatment is directed toward healthy adjustment and acceptance. Their book on AIDS (Masters, Johnson, & Kolodny, 1988) was rejected by sex researchers and public-health authorities alike (Irvine, 1990; Randolph, 1988; Specter, 1988). Among other things, it erroneously claimed that HIV could be contracted through casual contact. A review in the *Journal of Sex Research* dismissed Masters and Johnson's conclusions as "contradicted by their own data" (Kaplan, 1988).

Mainstream sex research follows many of the lines first drawn by Ellis, Kinsey, and Masters and Johnson. Some of the areas that continue to interest sex researchers include premarital sexuality, sexual response, sexual dysfunction, sexual orientation, male and female differences, erotica, sexual aggression, paraphilias, and transsexuality. We'll examine all these areas in later chapters.

EMERGING RESEARCH PERSPECTIVES

While sex research continues to explore diverse aspects of human sexuality, some scholars have felt their particular interests have been given insufficient attention. Feminists and gay and lesbian scholars have focused their research on issues that mainstream scholars have largely ignored. And ethnic research, only now beginning to be undertaken, points to the lack of knowledge about the sexuality of African Americans, Latinos, Asian Americans, and other ethnic Americans. These emerging research perspectives enrich our knowledge of sexuality.

Feminist Scholarship

The initial feminist research generated an immense amount of groundbreaking work on women in almost every field of the social sciences and humanities. Feminists made gender and gender-related issues significant research questions in a multitude of academic disciplines. In the field of sexuality, feminism expanded the scope of research to include the subjective experience and meaning of sexuality for women, sex and power, pornography, and issues of female victimization, such as rape, the sexual abuse of children, and sexual harassment.

There is no single feminist perspective; instead, there are several feminist perspectives. Nevertheless, feminist research shares certain characteristics. As Carol Pollis (1988) notes, "The preeminent concern of feminist scholarship has centered on understanding female experience in cultural and historical context—the social construction of gender and gender asymmetry." (**Social construction** means the construction or development of social categories, such as masculinity, femininity, and homosexuality, by society.) Feminists believe that:

- *Gender is significant in all aspects of social life.* Like class and ethnicity, gender determines a person's social status or position in society.

- *The female experience of sex has been devalued.* By emphasizing genital sex, such as frequency of sexual intercourse and number of orgasms, both researchers and society ignore important aspects of female sexuality, such as kissing, caressing, love, commitment, and communication. Female sexuality is even more devalued in lesbian relationships. Until the 1980s, most research on homosexuality centered on men, making lesbians invisible.

- *Power is a critical element in male-female relationships.* Because women are subordinated to men as a result of our cultural beliefs about gender, women have less power than men. As a result, feminists believe men have defined female sexuality to benefit themselves. Not only do men decide when to initiate sex, but the man's orgasm takes precedence over the woman's orgasm. The most brutal form of the male expression of sexual power is rape.

- *Traditional empirical research needs to be combined with qualitative research and interpretive studies to provide a full understanding of human sexuality.* Because social science emphasizes objectivity and quantification, its methodology thwarts us from fully exploring the complexity of what sex "means" and how it is personally experienced.

- *Ethnic diversity must be addressed.* Ethnic women, feminists point out, face a double stigma: being female *and* being from a minority-status group. Although very few studies exist on ethnicity and sexuality, feminists are committed to examining the role of ethnicity in female sexuality.

Despite its contributions, Pollis contends, feminist research "continues to be suspect in much of academia because of its commitment to work which will contribute to social change and its insistence on the value-laden nature of all scholarship" (Pollis, 1988). As a result, in 1986 a group of women formed a feminist caucus in the Society for the Scientific Study of Sexuality, the major professional organization of sex researchers, because they were "concerned that feminism and feminist work on sexuality were relatively invisible within sexology and that sexologists defined science [too] narrowly" (Vance & Pollis, 1990).

Gay and Lesbian Research

During the nineteenth century, sexuality became increasingly perceived as the domain of science, especially medicine. Physicians competed with ministers, priests, and rabbis in defining what was "correct" sexual behavior. But medicine's so-called scientific conclusions were not scientific; rather, they were morality disguised as science. "Scientific" definitions of healthy sex closely resembled religious definitions of moral sex. In studying sexual activities between men, they "invented" and popularized the distinction between heterosexuality and homosexuality (Gay, 1986; Weeks, 1986).

Early Researchers and Reformers While most physician-moralists condemned same-sex relationships as pathological as well as immoral, a few individuals stand out in their attempt to understand same-sex sexuality.

Karl Heinrich Ulrichs (1825–1895) Karl Ulrichs was a German poet and political activist who developed the first scientific theory about homosexuality in the 1860s (Kennedy, 1988). As a rationalist, he believed reason was superior to religious belief, and therefore rejected religion as superstition. He argued from logic and inference and collected case studies from numerous men to buttress his beliefs. Ulrichs maintained that men who were attracted to other men represented a third sex, whom he called "Urnings." (The word is derived from Greek mythology, referring to the mother of Aphrodite, known as Aphrodite Uranus, whose male children were repelled by women and inspired by the love of men.) Urnings were born as Urnings; their sexuality was not the result of immorality or pathology. Ulrichs believed that Urnings had a distinctive feminine quality about them that distinguished them from men who loved women. He fought for Urning rights and the liberalization of sex laws; he attempted to publish an uranian periodical and develop uranian literature. Ulrichs called for Urnings to become active in changing their condition. "The greater mass of Urnings," he complained, "unfortunately show little understanding for the efforts that have been made to gain freedom, justice, and a position in human society" (quoted in Kennedy, 1988).

Karl Maria Kertbeny (1824–1882) Karl Kertbeny, a Hungarian physician, created the terms "heterosexuality" and "homosexuality" in his attempt to understand same-sex relationships (Feray & Herzer, 1990). Kertbeny believed that "homosexualists" were as "manly" as "heterosexualists." For this reason, he broke with Ulrichs' conceptualization of Urnings as inherently "feminine" (Herzer, 1985).

Kertbeny's study of homosexuality seems to have been life-long. He records that when he was 16 years old, a close friend committed suicide because he was being threatened with imprisonment for his "vice." Kertbeny argued that homosexuality was inborn and thus not immoral. He also maintained "the rights of man" (quoted in Herzer, 1985):

> The rights of man begin . . . with man himself. And that which is most immediate to man is his own body, with which he can undertake fully and freely, to his advantage or disadvantage, that which he pleases, insofar as in so doing he does not disturb the rights of others.

Magnus Hirschfeld (1868–1935) was a leading European sex reformer who championed homosexual rights. He founded the first institute for the study of sexuality. The institute was burned when the Nazis took power in Germany; he fled for his life.

According to Kertbeny, it was but a "riddle of nature" that led men to be attracted to other men. To demonstrate their manliness, he compiled a list of famous homosexuals from history, beginning with Plato.

Magnus Hirschfeld (1868–1935) In the first few decades of the twentieth century, there was a great ferment of reform in England and parts of Europe. While Ellis was the leading reformer in England, Magnus Hirschfeld was the leading crusader in Germany, especially for homosexual rights.

Hirschfeld was both a homosexual and possibly a transvestite. He eloquently presented the case for the humanity of transvestites (Hirschfeld, 1991). And in defense of homosexual rights, he argued that homosexuality was not a perversion but the result of the hormonal development of inborn traits. His defense of homosexuality led to the popularization of the word "homosexual." Hirschfeld's importance, however, lies not so much in his theory of homosexuality as in his sexual reform efforts (Bullough, 1976). In Berlin in 1897, he helped found the first organization for homosexual rights. He began the first journal devoted to the study of sexuality. In addition, he founded the first Institute of Sexual Science, where he gathered a library of more than 20,000 volumes. He helped convene the first International Congress for Sex Reform in Berlin in 1921, from which came the World League for Sexual Reform. Both he and Havelock Ellis became presidents of the league.

When Hitler took power in Germany, the Nazis attacked the sex reform movement and destroyed Hirschfeld's institute. In fear of his life, Hirschfeld fled into exile and died several years later (Bullough, 1976; see Wolff, 1986, for Hirschfeld's biography).

Evelyn Hooker As a result of Kinsey's research, Americans learned that same-sex sexual relationships were widespread among both men and women. A few years later, psychologist Evelyn Hooker startled her colleagues by demonstrating that homosexuality in itself was not a psychological disorder. She found that ordinary gay men did not differ significantly in personality characteristics from similar heterosexual men (Hooker, 1957). The reverberations of her work continue to this day (McWhirter, 1990).

Earlier studies had erroneously found psychopathology among gay men and lesbians for two reasons. First, as most researchers were clinicians, their samples consisted mainly of gay men and lesbians who were seeking treatment. The researchers failed to compare their results against a control group of similar heterosexuals. (A **control group** is a group that is not being treated or experimented on. It controls for any variables that are introduced as a result of the treatment.) Second, researchers were predisposed to believing homosexuality was in itself a sickness, reflecting traditional beliefs about homosexuality. Consequently, emotional problems were automatically attributed to the client's homosexuality rather than to other sources. Hooker's work was initially ignored or rejected, but ten years later, she was appointed chairperson of the National Institute of Mental Health's task force on homosexuality.

Contemporary Research By the mid-1960s, political activism and a growing body of scientific literature, based on the work of Ellis, Kinsey, and Hooker, began challenging the traditional psychopathological model of homosexuality (Bayer, 1981). In 1973, the American Psychiatric Association (APA) removed homosexuality from its list of psychological disorders in its *Diagnostic and Statistical Manual of Mental Disorders (DSM-II)*. The APA decision was reinforced by similar resolutions by the American Psychological Association and the American Sociological Association.

As a result of the rejection of the psychopathological model, social and behavioral research on gay men and lesbians has moved in a new direction (Herek, 1984). Research no longer focuses primarily on the causes and cures of homosexuality. (See Schwanberg, 1985, for a review of the impact of the "demedicalization" of homosexuality on health sciences literature.) Most of the new research approaches homosexuality in a neutral manner. (See Herek, 1985, for a brief discussion of the social origins of the new scholarship. The only major exception to the shift in perspective is found in psychoanalytic literature [see Cornett & Hudson, 1985].)

The new approach allows researchers to ask three new types of questions. Such questions were unheard-of a generation ago.

1. *What is the experience of being gay and lesbian in America?* What, for example, is the process through which individuals define themselves as gay or lesbian? What are gay and lesbian relationships like?

2. *What are the origins and nature of prejudice against homosexuality on both an individual and a societal level?* What are the forces, for example, that create negative or hostile feelings toward people based on their sexual orientation? In religion, how and why do some groups choose biblical interpretations that foster prejudice, while others choose interpretations that encourage acceptance? Is prejudice against gay men and lesbians similar to racism or sexism (Heyl, 1989)?

3. *How is homosexuality constructed?* How does being gay or lesbian differ across groups, cultures, and historical periods? How do heterosexual as well as homosexual orientations develop (McWhirter et al., 1990)?

Ethnicity and Sexuality

Over the last few years, researchers have begun to recognize the significance of ethnicity in various aspects of American life, including sexuality. Although there is little research available, we will attempt to provide some background to assist an understanding of sexuality and ethnicity.

It is difficult to overestimate the significance of ethnicity in American society. According to the 1990 census, there are over 130 ethnic groups in America, accounting for approximately one-fifth of the American population. The largest ethnic groups are African Americans (31 million), Latinos (19.4 million), Asian Americans (6 million), and Native Americans (1.5 million). Between 16 and 18 million Americans are foreign-born.

While many descendants of European immigrants continue to cherish their ethnic heritage, their ethnic identity is declining in significance as they leave their ethnic neighborhoods, increase their economic status, and marry outside their group. A major study (Lieberson & Waters, 1988) on contemporary American ethnic groups concluded:

> White ethnics, while different from one another on a variety of measures, are still much more similar to each other than they are to blacks, Hispanics, Amer-

ican Indians, and Asians. . . . For whatever cause(s), a European–non-European distinction remains a central division of our society.

Sexuality cannot be fully understood without considering ethnic variation. Groups of people differ in their attitudes, values, and behaviors along ethnic lines. Unfortunately, research on sex and ethnicity has been slow to emerge. While ethnicity is an important force in American life, the vast majority of studies on sexuality have focused on young white, middle-class men and women, mostly college students. As a result, our concepts of sexuality have frequently, if unintentionally, excluded ethnicity.

The overwhelming majority of existing ethnic research focuses on African Americans and Latinos. Studies about Asian Americans, Native Americans, Caribbean Islanders, and Pacific Islanders are virtually nonexistent. Only three studies have been published in 20 years on Japanese American sexuality. Only one has been published on Vietnamese Americans (Carrier, Nguyen, & Su, 1992). None exists on Korean Americans or Filipino Americans. The only studies on contemporary Native American sexuality are undertaken from an anthropological or health-problem perspective.

Until the last few years, sex research on African Americans and Latinos has generally approached these groups from a problem perspective. Most research on sexuality and ethnicity has focused on adolescent sexuality, especially fertility issues such as birth control and pregnancy, and has been funded by the federal government. Government agencies view fertility and disease as social problems because of their social and economic costs, especially in terms of public funding. But because research has centered on adolescent fertility and disease, we know very little about the sexual attitudes, values, and behaviors of the majority of adult African Americans and Latinos.

African Americans African Americans represent the largest ethnic group in America. While white stereotypes may depict African Americans negatively, as promiscuous or "oversexed," it is important to remember that those terms are not value-free; they are negative terms used to describe ethnic differences. While there are black/white differences in terms of adolescent sexual activity and childbirth, those differences need to be placed within a sociocultural framework. Furthermore, it is important for those who are not black to remember that African Americans have a strong sense of family, value children, and live in a vital network of kin, friends, and community (Hunter & Davis, 1992; Staples & Johnson, 1993; Taylor, Chatters, Tucker, & Lewis, 1991). Many of the black/white differences in adolescent sexual activity and births to unmarried women are more closely associated with poverty and unemployment than ethnicity.

Historical Background Slavery ripped native Africans from their tribes and placed them in a brutal system that exploited and worked them to death by the millions throughout the Americas. It dramatically altered their sexual customs. Sexual morality and behavior in African tribal society was traditionally regulated by kinship groups composed of numerous related families. As with the ancient Greeks, religion did not concern itself with sexual behavior and morality. Violations of the sexual code were not religious offenses but individual or community offenses (Diop, 1987).

African Americans have a strong sense of family; they value children, and live in a vital network of family and friends.

Slavery also altered African families and family traditions. During the eighteenth century and later, West African family systems were severely repressed throughout the New World (Gutman, 1976). At first, some of those who were enslaved tried unsuccessfully to continue polygamy, the practice of having more than one spouse, which was strongly rooted in many African cultures. Although blacks who were enslaved were legally prohibited from marrying, they created their own marriages. Enduring great hardship, African Americans developed strong emotional bonds and family ties. The emerging slave culture discouraged casual sexual relationships and placed a high value on marital stability. On the large plantations, most slaves lived in two-parent families with their children. As time went on, the developing African American family blended West African and English family traditions (Gutman, 1976).

In the nineteenth century, images of African American women's sexuality provided a stark contrast to those of white women. While white women were believed to be sexually pure, black women were viewed by whites as sexually promiscuous. Such misperceptions encouraged white men to sexually exploit black women while remaining sexually restrained with their "chaste" wives. Enslaved blacks were also subject to sexual abuse by their masters without recourse; resistance was punishable by whippings (McLaurin, 1991).

When freedom came, despite generations of bondage and degradation, the formerly enslaved African Americans had strong emotional ties and traditions forged from slavery and from their West African heritage (Gutman, 1976; Lantz, 1980). Because they were now legally able to marry, thousands of former slaves who had "jumped the broomstick" in slave marriage now formally renewed their vows. At the same time, African Americans continued a more permissive attitude toward sex. Further, blacks did not classify women as good or bad based on whether they were virgins prior to marriage (Staples & Johnson, 1993).

Factors in the Study of African American Sexuality In studying African American sexuality, there are several factors to consider: (1) sexual stereotypes, (2) socioeconomic status, (3) black subculture, and (4) number of single adults.

Sexual stereotypes greatly distort our understanding of black sexuality. One of the most common stereotypes is the depiction of African Americans as sexually driven (Murry, 1991). Although this is an age-old stereotype dating back to the fifteenth century, it continues to hold considerable strength among nonblacks. Discussing African American men, Robert Staples (1991) writes: "Black men are saddled with a number of stereotypes that label them as irresponsible, criminalistic, hypersexual, and lacking in masculine traits."

Socioeconomic status is a person's ranking in society based on a combination of occupational, educational, and income levels. It is an important element in African American sexual values and behaviors (Staples & Johnson, 1993). While stereotypes suggest that *all* blacks have a low income, at least 37% are middle class in lifestyle and income (Staples, 1988). Middle-class blacks share many sexual attitudes and values with middle-class whites (Howard, 1988; Staples, 1988). For example, the overwhelming majority of births to single mothers are among low-income African Americans. But as income level increases among blacks, births to single mothers decrease significantly (Staples, 1988).

Values and behaviors are shaped by culture and social class. The subculture of blacks of low socioeconomic status is deeply influenced by poverty, discrimination, and structural subordination. In contrast to middle-class whites and blacks, low-income blacks are more likely to engage in sexual intercourse at an earlier age and to have children outside of marriage. Because of the poverty, violence, and prejudice of inner-city life, low-income black children do not experience a prolonged or "innocent" childhood. They are forced to become adults at an early age. As one mother living in the Chicago projects says, "There are no children here. They've seen too much to be children" (Kotlowitz, 1991). In this fierce, dangerous environment, survival is a paramount issue. (Homicide is a leading cause of death among young inner-city black males.) Peer groups, which are especially important, encourage both boys and girls to become sexually active.

Premarital sexual activity is not considered immoral or stigmatized, as it is in middle-class communities. Because sexual activity is regarded as natural, premarital sex is considered appropriate as relationships become more involved. Furthermore, as mere survival is not even guaranteed, adolescents may see no reason to wait for a future they may never have. In the inner-city subculture, boys tend to use sex exploitively and competitively. For

Ethnic variation and socioeconomic status must be considered to understand the diverse aspects of human sexuality. Many of our values are related more to our socioeconomic status than to our cultural or ethnic background.

them, sex is not so much a means of achieving intimacy with partners as it is a way of achieving status among their male peers. For girls, sex is a means of demonstrating their maturity; it is a sign of their womanhood.

For inner-city black adolescents, one becomes a woman by becoming a mother (Zinn & Eitzen, 1990). The black community, which values children highly, generally does not stigmatize the unmarried mother. For blacks of all classes, there is no such thing as an "illegitimate" or "illegally born" child. All children are considered valuable (Collins, 1991; Stack, 1974).

While socioeconomic status is significant in understanding patterns of black sexuality, it is important to note that African Americans form a distinct subculture. Generally speaking, black sexual behavior *is* more permissive than white or Latino sexual behavior. Martin Weinberg and Colin Williams (1988) attribute this difference to several factors. First, aspects of West African heritage continue to influence contemporary black sexuality. West Africans viewed sex as natural and valued it for the pleasure it gave men and women alike. African Americans continue to reflect similar views. Second, because of their subculture, blacks were not subject to the same restrictive moral pressures that shaped white culture during much of the nineteenth and twentieth centuries. Third, black families exert fewer controls to restrict sexual activities. These factors combine, assert Weinberg and Williams, to override black class differences. Subculture, they believe, is more important than socioeconomic status.

A high proportion of African American women are single (Staples & Johnson, 1993). There are 1.5 million more African American women than men. This gender imbalance is the result of high death rates, incarceration, and drug use among black men, often attributable to the effects of discrimination (see Chapter 7). If they wish to have children, many African American women are likely to be unmarried single parents. Furthermore, the single lifestyle, whether white or black, is associated with more sexual partners, a lack of contraceptive responsibility, and a greater likelihood of contracting STDs.

While there has been a significant increase in African American research over the last decade, much still needs to be done (Bryant & Coleman, 1988; Taylor, Chatters, Tucker, & Lewis, 1991). For example, we need to (1) explore the sexual attitudes and behaviors of the general African American population, not merely adolescents; (2) examine black sexuality from an African American cultural context; and (3) utilize a cultural equivalency perspective that rejects differences between blacks and whites as signs of inherent deviance. (The **cultural equivalency perspective** is the view that the attitudes, values, and behaviors of one ethnic group are similar to those of another ethnic group.) From this perspective, differences between African Americans and whites are viewed as the result of black adaptation to historical and social forces, including their African heritage, slave legacy, discrimination, and resulting poverty.

Por our mothers somos Mexican
por destiny, americanos
comprendemos el English
and we speak el castellaño
we're bilingües to the bone
we're purititos chicanos
Jose B. Cuéllar (aka Dr. Loco of the Rockin' Jalapeños)

Latinos Latinos are the fastest-growing and second-largest ethnic group in the United States. Between 1980 and 1990, the Latino population increased by 35%, mostly as a result of immigration from Mexico. There is very little research, however, about Latino sexuality.

Historical Background Latino culture began with the conquest and settlement of the New World by Spain and Portugal. The conquest required Europeans to interact with Native Americans, such as the Aztecs, Mayans, and Incas, whose cultures differed radically from their own. This contact created unique cultural adaptations in sexuality and marriage. Because in the early years there were small numbers of Spanish women in the New World, Spaniards formed unions with Native American or enslaved African women. The few Spanish women (and their descendants) were held in high social esteem because of their "Europeanness" or whiteness. By the mid-fifteenth century, the crown and church overcame the rule of the conquistadors. Together the church and state worked at establishing European sexual and social standards for the conquered peoples. Using the Inquisition as an instrument of forced acculturation, Spain attempted to root out indigenous customs, such as polygamy, condemning them as Satanic practices (Behar, 1989; Twinam, 1989). Catholic beliefs were superimposed on native ones. Over the next 500 years, Latino culture emerged from the interplay of European and indigenous cultures.

Sexual Stereotypes Two common stereotypes depict Latinos as sexually permissive and Latino males as pathologically *macho,* or hypermasculine (Becerra, 1988; Espín, 1984). Like African Americans, Latino males are stereotyped as being promiscuous, engaging in excessive and indiscriminate sexual activities. No research, however, validates this stereotype. In fact, one study concludes that in contrast to the dominant stereotype, they are significantly less experienced sexually than their Anglo peers (Padilla & O'Grady, 1987).

The macho stereotype paints Latino males as hypermasculine—swaggering and domineering. But the stereotype of machismo distorts its cultural meaning among Latinos. (The Spanish word was originally incorporated into English in the 1960s as a slang term to describe any male who was sexist.) Within its cultural context, however, **machismo** is a positive concept, characterized by a man's courage, strength, generosity, politeness, and

In studying Latino sexuality, it is important to remember that Latinos come from diverse ethnic groups, including Mexican American, Cuban American, and Puerto Rican, each with its own unique background and set of cultural values.

respect for others. And in day-to-day functioning, relations between Latino men and women are significantly more egalitarian than the macho stereotype suggests. This is especially true among Latinos who are more acculturated (Becerra, 1988; Griswold del Castillo, 1984). (**Acculturation** is the process of adaptation of an ethnic group to the values, attitudes, and behaviors of the dominant culture.)

Factors in Studying Latino Sexuality   There are three important factors to consider when studying Latinos: (1) diversity of ethnic groups, (2) significance of socioeconomic status, and (3) degree of acculturation.

Latinos are comprised of numerous ethnic subgroups, the largest of which are Mexican American, Puerto Rican, and Cuban (Vega, 1991). Each group has its own unique background and set of cultural traditions that affect sexual attitudes and behaviors. For example, Latino adolescents differ in their contraceptive use according to their ethnic background (Durant, Pendergast, & Seymore, 1990). Fertility rates also differ between groups. The fertility rate of Mexican Americans, for example, is almost one-third higher than that of Anglos; by contrast, the fertility rate for Cuban Americans is lower than that of Anglos (Staples, 1988).

Socioeconomic status is important, as middle-class Latino values appear to differ from those of low-income Latinos. The birth rate for single women, for example, is significantly higher among low-income Latinas than among middle-class Latinas (Bean & Tienda, 1987). Furthermore, Latino ethnic groups rank differently on the socioeconomic scale. The middle class is largest among Cuban Americans, followed by Puerto Ricans, and then Mexican Americans.

The degree of acculturation may be the most important factor affecting sexual attitudes and behavior among Latinos. This can be viewed on a continuum: traditional at one pole, bicultural in the middle, and acculturated at the other pole (Guerrero Pavich, 1986). (This same continuum may also be used with other ethnic groups, such as Europeans, Asian Americans, and Caribbean and Pacific Islanders.) *Traditional Latinos* were born and raised in Latin America; they adhere to the norms, customs, and values of their original homeland, speak mostly Spanish, and have strong religious ties. Foreign-born Latinos, who may number as many as 7 million, hold the most traditional values. *Bicultural Latinos* may have been born in either Latin America or the United States; they speak both Spanish and English, are able to function well in both Latino and Anglo cultures, and have moderate religious ties. *Acculturated Latinos* do not identify with their Latino heritage; they speak only English and have (at most) moderate religious ties.

Traditional Latinos tend to place a high value on female virginity while encouraging males, beginning in adolescence, to be sexually active (Guerrero Pavich, 1986). Females are regarded according to a virgin/whore dichotomy—"good" girls are virgins, "bad" girls are sexual (Espín, 1984). Females are taught to put the needs of others, especially males, before their own. Among traditional Latinos, fears about American "sexual immorality" produce their own stereotypes of Anglos. One researcher (Espín, 1984) notes:

> One of the most prevalent myths encountered by immigrant Hispanic women is that all American women are very free with sex. For the parents and young women alike, "to become Americanized" is equated with becoming sexually promiscuous. Thus, in some cases, sexuality may become the focus of the parents' fears and the girl's desires during the acculturation process.

Adolescent boys learn about masturbation from peers, while girls rarely learn about it because of its tabooed nature. There is little acceptance of gay men and lesbians, whose relationships are often regarded as "unnatural" or sinful (Bonilla & Porter, 1990).

In traditional Latino culture, Catholicism plays an important role, especially in the realm of sexuality. The Church teaches premarital virginity and prohibits both contraception and abortion. For traditional Latinas, using contraception may lead to "considerable guilt and confusion on the part of the individual woman who feels she is alone in violating the cultural taboos against contraception" (Guerrero Pavich, 1986). Traditional Latinas are more negative toward birth control and are less likely to use it than more acculturated women (Ortiz & Casas, 1990). Abortion is out of the question. Only the most acculturated Latinas view abortion as an option.

Among bicultural Latinos, there may be gender-role conflict (Salgado de Snyder, 1990). Emma Guerrero Pavich describes the conflicts some Latinas experience: "She observes the freedom and sexual expression 'Americanas' have. At first she may condemn them as 'bad women'; later she may envy their freedom. Still later she may begin to want those freedoms for herself" (Guerrero Pavich, 1987).

For bicultural Latinos, sexual values and attitudes appear to lie at different points along the continuum, depending on the degree of acculturation. Research, however, is lacking.

There is significantly greater flux among Latinos as a result of continuing high rates of immigration and the acculturation process. Much current research on Latinos focuses on the acculturation of new immigrants. We know less, however, about bicultural Latinos and even less about acculturated Latinos. But we know next to nothing about the sexuality of all these groups.

It is difficult to forecast the direction sex research will take in regard to ethnicity and sex. To date, we know little. We trust, however, that serious research will soon begin in this area.

Popular culture surrounds us with sexual images disseminated through advertising, music, television, and film that form a backdrop to our daily living. Much of what is conveyed is simplified, stereotypical, shallow—and entertaining. But through sex research, we can gain tools for evaluating the mass of sex information disseminated through the media. Studying sex research enables us to understand how research is conducted and to be aware of its strengths and its limitations. Traditional sex research has been expanded in recent years by feminist and gay and lesbian research which provides fresh insights and perspectives. While the study of sexuality and ethnicity is only now beginning to emerge, it promises to enlarge our understanding of the diversity of attitudes, behaviors, and values in contemporary America.

SUMMARY

Sex, Advice Columnists, and Pop Psychology

• The *sex information/advice genre* transmits information to both entertain and inform; the information is generally oversimplified so that it does not interfere with the genre's primary entertainment purpose. Much of the information or advice conveys social norms. While it uses the social science framework, it tends to overgeneralize and distort.

Thinking (Critically) About Sex

• *Value judgments* are evaluations based on moral or ethical standards. *Objective* statements are based on observations of things as they exist in themselves. *Opinions* are unsubstantiated beliefs based on an individual's personal thoughts. *Biases* are personal leanings or inclinations. *Stereotypes*, rigidly held beliefs about the personal characteristics of a group of people, are a type of *schema*, the organization of knowledge through thought processes.

• *Attitudes* are predispositions to acting, thinking, or feeling certain ways toward things. *Behaviors* are the ways people act. Behaviors cannot necessarily be inferred from attitudes, or vice versa.

• *Fallacies* are errors in reasoning. The *egocentric fallacy* is the belief that others necessarily share one's own values, beliefs, and attitudes. The *ethnocentric fallacy* is the belief that one's own ethnic group, nation, or culture is inherently superior to any other.

Sex Research Methods

• Ethical issues are important concerns in sex research. The most important issues are *informed consent*, protection from harm, confidentiality, and the use of deception.

• In sex research, sampling is a particularly acute problem. To be meaningful, samples should be representative of the larger group from which they are drawn. But most samples are limited by volunteer bias, dependence on college students, underrepresentation of ethnic groups, and difficulties in sampling gay men and lesbians.

• The most important methods in sex research are clinical, survey, observational, and experimental. *Clinical research* relies on in-depth examinations of individuals or groups who come to the clinician seeking treatment for psychological or medical problems. *Survey research* uses questionnaires or interviews to gather information from a small representative sample of people. *Observational research* requires the researcher to observe interactions carefully in as unobtrusive a manner as possible. *Experimental research* presents subjects with various stimuli under controlled conditions in which their responses can be measured.

• Experiments are controlled through the use of *independent variables* (which can be changed by the experimenter) and *dependent variables* (which are changes dependent on changes in the independent variable). Clinical, survey, and observational research efforts, by contrast, are *correlational studies* that infer relationships between variables without manipulating them. In experimental research, physiological responses are often measured by *plethysmographs* or *strain gauges*.

The Sex Researchers

• Richard von Krafft-Ebing, who published his *Psychopathia Sexualis* in 1886, was one of the earliest sex researchers. His work emphasized the pathological aspects of sexuality. Although his theories are now out of date, he documented a vast range of sexual behaviors and brought them into public discussion.

• Sigmund Freud was one of the most influential thinkers in Western civilization. According to Freud's theory, personality consisted of three parts: the id, ego, and superego. The *id* represented the instincts, the *ego* represented the part of the personality dealing with the real world, and the *superego* represented the conscience. Freud believed there were five stages in psychosexual development: the *oral stage, anal stage, phallic stage, latency stage*, and *genital stage*. The phallic stage is the critical stage in development: Boys develops an *Oedipal complex*, leading to *castration anxiety*; girls develop an *Electra complex*, leading to *penis envy*.

• Havelock Ellis developed the concepts of autoeroticism and erogenous zones. His ideas included the relativity of sexual values, the normality of masturbation, a belief in the sexual equality of men and women, the redefinition of "normal," a reevaluation of homosexuality, and tolerance of sexual differences.

• Alfred Kinsey applied statistical techniques to the study of human sexuality. His work documented enormous diversity in sexual behavior, emphasized the role of masturbation in sexual development, and argued that the distinction between normal and abnormal behavior was meaningless. The Kinsey scale charts sexual activities along a continuum ranging from exclusive heterosexual behaviors to exclusive same-sex behaviors.

- William Masters and Virginia Johnson detailed the physiology of the human sexual response cycle. Their physiological studies demonstrated the similarity between male and female sexual responses; they demonstrated that women achieved orgasms through clitoral stimulation. Their work on sexual inadequacy revolutionized sex therapy through the use of behavioral techniques.

Emerging Research Perspectives

- There is no single feminist perspective in sex research. Most feminist research, however, focuses on gender issues, assumes that the female experience of sex has been devalued, believes power is a critical element in male-female relationships, argues that empirical research must be supplemented by qualitative research to capture the personal experience and meaning of sexuality, and explores ethnic diversity.

- Research on homosexuality has rejected the moralistic-pathological approach. The pioneers of gay/lesbian research included Karl Ulrichs, Karl Kertbeny, Magnus Hirschfeld, and Evelyn Hooker. Contemporary gay/lesbian research focuses on the psychological and social experience of being gay or lesbian, and the origins of prejudice against homosexuals.

- The role of ethnicity in human sexuality has been largely overlooked until recently. Most studies on sex and ethnicity have focused on such problems as adolescent pregnancy among African Americans and Latinos. As a result, we know very little about ethnic sexuality in general.

- Slavery destroyed much traditional African culture among those enslaved. Under slavery, sexual images of black women contrasted with those of "pure" white women, encouraging sexual exploitation of slaves by their masters. Slave culture emphasized family and discouraged casual sexual relationships.

- *Socioeconomic status* is important in the study of African American sexuality. Other factors include stereotyping of blacks as hypersexual and promiscuous, the importance of the African American subculture, and the large number of single adults.

- Latino culture was created by the interaction of Native American and Spanish and Portuguese cultures. Two common stereotypes are that Latinos are sexually permissive and that males are pathologically *macho*. Factors in studying Latino sexuality include the diversity of ethnic groups, such as Mexican American, Cuban American, and Puerto Rican; the role of socioeconomic status; and the degree of acculturation.

KEY TERMS

sex information/ advice genre	schema	ethnic group
objectivity	attitude	scientific method
value judgment	behavior	induction
cultural relativity	fallacy	informed consent
opinion	egocentric fallacy	random sample
bias	ethnocentric fallacy	representative sample
stereotype	ethnocentrism	biased sample
	ethnicity	clinical research

pathological behavior	psychoanalysis	Oedipal complex
survey research	id	castration anxiety
observational research	libido	Electra complex
experimental research	pleasure principle	penis envy
variable	ego	social construction
independent variable	reality principle	control group
dependent variable	superego	socioeconomic status
correlational study	oral stage	cultural equivalency perspective
plethysmograph	anal stage	
strain gauge	phallic stage	machismo
neurosis	latency stage	acculturation
repression	genital stage	

SUGGESTIONS FOR FURTHER READING

Geer, James, and William O'Donohue, eds. *Theories of Human Sexuality*. New York: Plenum Press, 1987. A collection of essays briefly describing various theories of human sexuality.

Haberstein, Charles, and Robert Mindel. *Ethnic Families in America: Patterns and Variations*, 3rd ed. New York: Elsevier North Holland, 1988. An important collection of essays on different ethnic groups, including historical background and current status. Excellent background for understanding sexual values and the dynamics of diverse groups.

Irvine, Janice. *Disorders of Desire: Sex and Gender in Modern American Sexology*. Philadelphia: Temple University Press, 1990. A critical examination, from a feminist perspective, of sexology, including the Kinsey studies, the work of Masters and Johnson, sex therapy, and gender research, especially gay/lesbian sexuality and transsexuality.

McKinney, Kathleen, and Susan Sprecher, eds. *Human Sexuality: The Societal and Interpersonal Context*. New York: Ablex, 1989. Sociologically oriented essays on human sexuality.

Minton, Henry, ed. *Gay and Lesbian Studies: Emergence of a Discipline*. Binghamton, NY: Harrington Press, 1992. A collection of essays on the development of gay/lesbian studies.

Vance, Carole. *Pleasure and Danger: Exploring Female Sexuality*. Boston: Routledge & Kegan Paul, 1984. A provocative collection of essays dealing with female sexuality from a feminist perspective.

Weeks, Jeffrey. *Sexuality and Its Discontents: Meanings, Myths, and Modern Sexualities*. London: Routledge & Kegan Paul, 1985. An excellent study on the changing meanings of sexuality.

Chapter Three

FEMALE SEXUAL ANATOMY, PHYSIOLOGY, AND RESPONSE

P R E V I E W : S E L F - Q U I Z

1. Sexual reproduction is more wasteful than asexual reproduction, from a genetic point of view. True or false?

2. The female reproductive organs are collectively known as the vagina. True or false?

3. The center of sexual arousal in women is the clitoris. True or false?

4. Many women can tell when they are ovulating by the consistency of the mucus secreted by the cervix. True or false?

5. At birth, the ovaries of the human female contain about 25,000 immature eggs. True or false?

6. Women's ovaries produce estrogen and testosterone. True or false?

7. Menstrual cramps are often psychosomatic (induced by the mind or by emotions). True or false?

8. A common cause of a missed menstrual period is pregnancy. True or false?

9. For women, orgasms from intercourse are generally more physically intense than orgasms from masturbation. True or false?

10. Studies have found that some women ejaculate from the urethra upon orgasm. True or false?

ANSWERS 1. T; 2. F; 3. T; 4. T; 5. F; 6. T; 7. F; 8. T; 9. F; 10. T

Chapter Outline

Although women and men are similar in many more ways than they are different, we tend to focus on the differences rather than the similarities. Various cultures hold diverse ideas about exactly what it means to be female or male, but just about the only differences that are consistent are actual physical differences, most of which relate to sexual structure and function. In this chapter and the following one, we discuss both the similarities and differences in the anatomy (body structures), physiology (body functions), and sexual response of males and females. This chapter introduces the sexual structures and functions of women's bodies, including the influence of hormones and the menstrual cycle. We also look at models of sexual arousal and response, the relationship of these to women's experiences of sex, and the role of orgasm. In Chapter 4, we discuss male anatomy and physiology, and in Chapter 5, we move beyond biology to look at gender and the meanings we ascribe to being male and female.

WHY TWO SEXES?

Most of us have learned the basics of human anatomy and physiology in life science or biology classes. We know the fundamentals of reproduction: asexual, practiced by simple organisms such as amoebae and bacteria, and by some types of plants, insects, fish, and reptiles; and sexual, practiced by all other organisms, including humans. Most sexual reproduction requires two types of the particular organism; we refer to the types as "sexes." (Some plants and animals, such as starfish, snails, sea slugs, and many kinds of plants, are undifferentiated and can play either role; some can even fertilize themselves if necessary.) Sexual reproduction has turned out to be the most successful way for species to assure their ability to survive, even though it is a relatively time-consuming and wasteful process: Sexually reproducing organisms pass on only half their genes and "toss" the rest. About 99.9% of higher organisms reproduce sexually (Gutin, 1992).

Scientists have many theories (but no proof) about how sexual reproduction came to be. They do know, however, that it appears to have significant advantages over asexual reproduction: Sexual reproduction confers genetic variety on members of a species and gives them the ability to take advantage of adaptive variations, ensuring greater possibilities of survival. It also apparently allows species to genetically "outrun" pathogens, disease-causing organisms (Gutin, 1992). "Pathogens," writes anthropologist JoAnn Gutin,

> can reproduce (usually asexually) in seconds and mutate many times while their hosts are held to slower reproductive timetables. The genetic variability afforded by sex gives us hosts at least a fighting chance against our various nemeses, and the breathing room it provides is what makes sex worth the trouble.

Organisms that reproduce asexually pass an exact copy of their genetic material to the next generation. They do it on their own, without needing to be in contact with other like organisms. Organisms that reproduce sexually pass only half their genetic material to their offspring. The other half must come from a sexual partner. As discussed above, most organisms that reproduce sexually have two variations, each with a different reproductive function. We call these variations "female" and "male." Some organisms are hermaphroditic, able to play the male or female role as the situation warrants.

Anatomically speaking, all embryos appear as females when their reproductive organs begin to develop (Figure 3.1). If it does not receive certain genetic and hormonal signals, the fetus will continue to develop as a female. In humans and most other mammals, the female, in addition to providing half the genetic instructions for the offspring, provides the environment in which it can develop until it becomes capable of surviving as a separate entity. She also nourishes the offspring, both during gestation (the period of carrying the young in the uterus) via the placenta and following birth via the breasts through lactation (milk production).

FEMALE SEX ORGANS: WHAT ARE THEY FOR?

It is clear that the sex organs serve a reproductive function. But they perform other functions as well. Some sexual parts serve to bring pleasure to their owners; they may also serve to attract potential sexual partners. Because of the mutual pleasure partners give each other, we can see that sexual structures also serve an important role in human relationships. People demonstrate their affection for one another by sharing sexual pleasure and

Rose is a rose is a rose.
Gertrude Stein

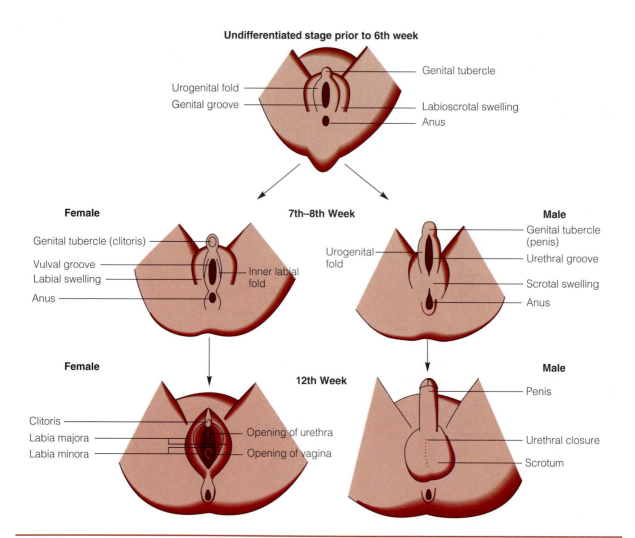

FIGURE 3.1 Embryonic-Fetal Differentiation of the External Reproductive Organs. Female and male reproductive organs are formed from the same embryonic tissues. An embryo's external genitals are female in appearance until certain genetic and hormonal instructions signal the development of male organs. Without such instructions, the genitals continue to develop as female.

The head Sublime, the heart Pathos, the genitals Beauty, the hands and feet Proportion.
William Blake (1757–1827)

generally form enduring partnerships at least partially on the basis of mutual sexual sharing. Let's look at the features of human female anatomy and physiology that provide pleasure to women and their partners and enable them to conceive and give birth.

External Structures (The Vulva)

The sexual and reproductive organs of both men and women are also called **genitals,** or genitalia, from the Latin *genere,* to beget. The external female genitals are the mons pubis, the clitoris, the labia majora, and the labia minora, collectively known as the **vulva** (Figure 3.2). (People often use the word "vagina" when they are actually referring to the vulva. The vagina is an internal structure.) Researcher Mildred Ash calls the vulva "the misnamed female sex organ" (Ash, 1980). The word "vulva," she writes,

remains unknown and unheard, unspoken in polite society, while the word *vagina* passes with almost as much ease as the word *penis* into common use. The word

Sharing sensual and sexual pleasure helps strengthen the affectionate bonds of enduring relationships.

FIGURE 3.2 External Female Sexual Structures (Vulva).

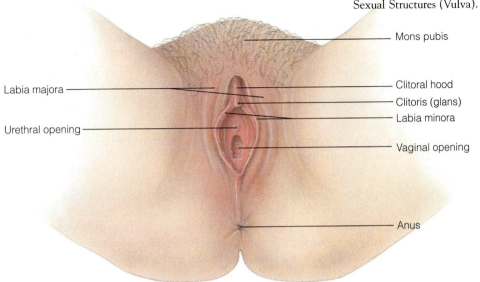

Labia majora

Urethral opening

Mons pubis

Clitoral hood

Clitoris (glans)

Labia minora

Vaginal opening

Anus

vulva is not being taught to children early in life, so it cannot be as acceptable as the word *penis* is.

The Mons Pubis The **mons pubis** (pubic mound) or **mons veneris** (mound of Venus) is a pad of fatty tissue that covers the area of the pubic bone about 6 inches below the navel. Beginning in puberty, the mons is covered with pubic hair. This area is sensitive to sexual stimulation in some women.

The Clitoris The **clitoris** is the center of sexual arousal in the female. It contains a high concentration of nerve endings and is exquisitely sensitive to stimulation, especially at the tip of its shaft, the **glans clitoridis.** A fold of skin called the **clitoral hood** covers the glans when the clitoris is not engorged. Although the clitoris is structurally analogous to the penis (it is formed from the same embryonic tissue), its sole function is sexual arousal. (The penis serves the additional functions of urine excretion and semen ejaculation.) The shaft of the clitoris is both an external and an internal structure. The external portion is about 0.25–1.0 inch long. Internally, the shaft is divided into two branches called **crura** (singular, *crus*), each of which is about 3 inches long. The crura contain two *corpora cavernosa*, hollow chambers that fill with blood and swell during arousal. When stimulated, the clitoris enlarges initially, then retracts beneath the hood just before and during orgasm. With repeated orgasms, it follows the same pattern of engorgement and retraction, although its swellings may not be as pronounced after the initial orgasm.

In a controversial exhibit called "The Dinner Party," artist Judy Chicago created a series of plates representing the vulvas of famous women. Virginia Woolf (top) and Sappho (bottom) are shown here.

The Labia Majora and Labia Minora The **labia majora,** major lips, are two folds of spongy flesh extending from the mons pubis and enclosing the labia minora, clitoris, urethral opening, and vaginal entrance. The **labia minora,** minor lips, are smaller folds within the labia majora that meet above the clitoris to form the clitoral hood. They are smooth, hairless, and vary quite a bit in appearance from woman to woman. They are sensitive to the touch and swell during sexual arousal, doubling or tripling in size. The area enclosed by the labia minora is referred to as the **vestibule.** Within the vestibule, on either side of the vaginal opening, are two small ducts from the **Bartholin's glands** (or vestibular glands), which secrete a small amount of moisture during sexual arousal.

Internal Structures

The internal female sexual structures and reproductive organs include the vagina; the uterus and its lower opening, the cervix; the fallopian tubes; and the ovaries (Figure 3.3).

The Vagina The **vagina,** from the Latin word for sheath, is a flexible, muscular structure that begins between the legs and extends diagonally toward the small of the back. The vagina serves two reproductive functions: It encompasses the penis during **coitus** (sexual intercourse) so that sperm will be deposited near the entrance of the uterus, and it is the **birth canal**

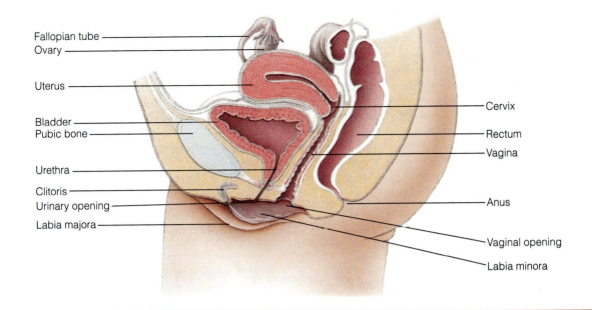

Fallopian tube
Ovary
Uterus
Bladder
Pubic bone
Urethra
Clitoris
Urinary opening
Labia majora

Cervix
Rectum
Vagina
Anus
Vaginal opening
Labia minora

FIGURE 3.3 Internal Female
Sexual Structures.

through which an infant is born. In women who have not given birth, the
vagina is about 3 inches long at its back wall and 2.5 inches at the front;
after childbirth, it may be somewhat larger. Normally the walls of the vagina
are relaxed and collapsed together, but during sexual arousal, the inner two-
thirds of the vagina expand. Mucous membranes line the vagina, providing
lubrication during arousal. The opening of the vagina is known as the **introitus.** Prior to first intercourse or other intrusion, the introitus is partially
covered by a thin membrane, the **hymen** (named for the Roman god of
marriage). (Maintaining good vaginal health is discussed in Chapter 14.)

The Hymen The hymen typically has one or several perforations, allowing
menstrual blood and mucous secretions to flow out of the vagina (and generally allowing for tampon insertion). In many cultures, it is (or was) important for a woman's hymen to be intact on her wedding night. Blood on the
nuptial sheets is taken as proof of her virginity. (Even in some developed
countries today, plastic surgeons do a brisk trade reconstructing the hymens
of brides-to-be.) The stretching or tearing of the hymen may or may not be
painful. According to one study of first intercourse, 25% of women experienced no pain, 40% had moderate pain, and 33% felt severe pain (Weis,
1985). The women who experienced pain tended to be younger than those
who did not; they held more conservative sexual values, had more negative
feelings toward their partners and toward intercourse with them, and more
often expected intercourse to be painful. Prior to first intercourse, the
hymen may be stretched somewhat by tampon insertion, by the woman's
self-manipulation, or by a partner during noncoital sexual activity.

The Grafenberg Spot Fairly recently, controversial research has asserted
that an erotically sensitive area, the **Grafenberg spot,** is located on the front
wall of the vagina midway between the introitus and the cervix (on the
vaginal side of the urethra). This area, also known as the **G spot,** is

described as being about the size of a small bean during its unaroused state and growing to the size of a dime during arousal (Ladas, Whipple, & Perry, 1982). Stimulation of the G spot is said to lead to orgasm, and, in some women, the ejaculation of a clear fluid from the urethra. Masters and Johnson noted, however, in a study of 100 women, that fewer than 10% experienced any special sensitivity in that area (Masters, Johnson, & Kolodny, 1992). They suggest that additional research is necessary. Reviewing the G spot controversy, social psychologist Carol Tavris writes that it "nicely highlights the unfortunate consequences of trying to explain sexuality in terms of the right anatomical configuration and a single paradigm of normal response" (Tavris, 1992). It is interesting to note that Ernest Grafenberg, the gynecologist who described the area as an erogenous zone, did not name it, nor did he refer to it as a specific anatomical structure, in his 1950 journal article, "The Role of Urethra in Female Orgasm" (Grafenberg, 1950). (Female ejaculation will be discussed later in the chapter.)

Vaginal Secretions and Lubrication The mucous membranes lining the walls of the vagina normally produce clear, white, or pale-yellow secretions. In addition, secretions from the cervix pass through the vagina. A woman's vaginal secretions will vary in color, consistency, odor, and quantity depending on the phase of her menstrual cycle, her health, and her unique physical characteristics. Although the vagina's walls are generally moist, sexual excitement causes lubrication to increase substantially. This lubrication serves two biological purposes. First, it increases the possibility of conception by alkalizing the normally acidic chemical balance in the vagina, thus making it more hospitable to sperm, which die faster in acid environments. Second, it makes coitus easier and more pleasurable for both the woman and the man, as friction between the vaginal walls and penis is reduced.

Myths About the Vagina Although we have many popular myths about the penis, there are relatively few where the vagina is concerned. What myths there are tend to reflect male anxieties rather than female concerns. Perhaps the most prevalent myth is that the penis may become trapped in a constricting vagina. (Perhaps this fear is based on the fact that copulating dogs sometimes get "stuck," but this phenomenon has to do with the anatomical peculiarities of both male and female dogs.) Women are able to constrict the muscles of the vagina during intercourse, generally increasing their pleasure as well as that of their partner, but they cannot prevent the penis from withdrawing. Vaginismus, an involuntary constriction of the vagina, is experienced by some women, but these contractions have the effect of keeping the penis out of the vagina rather than inside it (see Chapter 15). Another myth that reflects men's fears concerns what Freud called the *vagina dentata*, or "toothed vagina" (Carrera, 1981). Tales both ancient and modern cite instances of evil women (prostitutes, perhaps) who hide within their vaginas sharp objects such as broken glass or razor blades.

The Uterus and Cervix The **uterus,** or womb, is a hollow, thick-walled, muscular organ held in the pelvic cavity by a number of flexible ligaments and supported by several muscles. It is pear-shaped, with the tapered end, the **cervix,** extending down and opening into the vagina. If a woman has not given birth, the uterus is about 3 inches long and 3 inches wide at the top; it is somewhat larger in women who have given birth. The uterus expands during pregnancy to the size of a volleyball or larger, to accommodate the developing fetus. The lining of the uterine walls, the **endometrium,** is filled with tiny blood vessels. During the menstrual cycle, this tissue is built up, then shed and expelled through the cervical **os** (opening), unless fertilization has occurred. In the event of pregnancy, the pre-embryo is embedded in the nourishing endometrium.

In addition to the more-or-less monthly menstrual discharge, mucous secretions from the cervix also flow out through the vagina. These secretions tend to be somewhat white, thick, and sticky following menstruation, becoming thinner as ovulation approaches. At ovulation, the mucous flow tends to increase and to be clear, slippery, and stretchy, somewhat like egg white. (Birth control using cervical mucus to determine the time of ovulation is discussed in Chapter 12.)

The Ovaries   On each side of the uterus, held in place by several ligaments, is one of a pair of ovaries. The **ovary** is a **gonad,** an organ that produces **gametes,** the sex cells containing the genetic material necessary for reproduction. Female gametes are called **oocytes,** from the Greek words for egg and cell. (Oocytes are commonly referred to as eggs or **ova** [singular, **ovum**]. Technically, however, the cell does not become an egg until it completes its final stages of division following fertilization.) The ovaries are the size and shape of large almonds. In addition to producing oocytes, they serve the important function of hormone production. The basic female hormones, estrogen and progesterone, are discussed later in this chapter.

At birth the human female's ovaries contain 400,000–700,000 oocytes (Marieb, 1992; Masters, Johnson, & Kolodny, 1992). During childhood, many of these will degenerate; then, beginning in puberty and ending after menopause, a total of about 400 oocytes will mature and be released on a more-or-less monthly basis. The release of an oocyte is called **ovulation.** The immature oocytes are embedded in saclike structures called **ovarian follicles.** The fully ripened follicle is called a **vesicular** or **Graffian follicle.** At maturation, the follicle ruptures, releasing the oocyte to begin its journey. After the oocyte emerges, the ruptured follicle becomes the **corpus luteum** (from Latin for yellow body), a producer of important hormones; it eventually degenerates.

The Fallopian Tubes   At the top of the uterus, one on each side, are two tubes known as **fallopian tubes,** uterine tubes, or oviducts. The tubes are about 4 inches long. They extend toward the ovaries but are not attached to them. Instead, the funnel-shaped end of each tube (the **infundibulum**) fans out into fingerlike **fimbriae,** which drape over the ovary but may not actually touch it. Tiny, hairlike **cilia** on the fimbriae become active during ovulation. Their waving motion conducts the oocyte that has been released from the ovary into the fallopian tube. Just within the infundibulum is the **ampulla,** the widened part of the tube in which fertilization normally occurs if sperm and oocyte are there at the same time. (The process of ovulation and the events leading to fertilization are discussed later in this chapter; fertilization is covered in Chapter 13.)

Other Structures

There are several other important anatomical structures in the genital areas of both men and women. Although they may not serve reproductive functions, they may be involved in sexual activities. Some of these areas may also be affected by sexually transmitted diseases. In women, these structures include the urethra, anus, and perineum. The **urethra** is the tube through which urine passes; the **urethral opening** is located between the clitoris and the vaginal opening. Between the vulva and the **anus**—the opening of the rectum, through which excrement passes—is a diamond-shaped region called the **perineum.** This area of soft tissue covers the muscles and ligaments of the **pelvic floor,** the underside of the pelvic area extending from the top of the pubic bone (above the clitoris) to the anus. The anus consists of two sphincters, circular muscles that open and close like valves. The tissue that rings the opening is tender and is erotically sensitive for some people.

In sex play or intercourse involving the anus or rectum, care must be taken not to rupture the delicate tissues. Anal sex, insertion of the penis into the rectum, is not considered safe, because abrasions of the tissue provide easy access for pathogens, such as HIV (the virus that causes AIDS), into the bloodstream (see Chapter 17).

The Breasts

Both women and men have breasts. At puberty, the female breasts begin to develop in response to hormonal stimuli (Figure 3.4). At maturity, the left breast is often slightly larger than the right (Rome, 1992).

Reproductive Function The reproductive function of the breasts is to nourish the offspring through **lactation,** or milk production. A mature female breast, also known as a **mammary gland,** is composed of fatty tissue and 15–25 lobes that radiate around a central protruding nipple. Around the nipple is a ring of darkened skin called the **areola.** Tiny muscles at the base of the nipple cause it to become erect in response to touch, cold, or sexual arousal.

When a woman is pregnant, the structures within the breast undergo further development. Directly following childbirth, in response to hormonal signals, small glands within the lobes called **alveoli** begin producing milk. The milk passes into ducts, each of which has a dilated region for storage; the ducts open to the outside at the nipple. (Breast-feeding is discussed in detail in Chapter 13.) During lactation, a woman's breasts increase in size from enlarged glandular tissues and stored milk. In women who are not lactating, however, breast size is dependent mainly on fat content, often determined by hereditary factors.

Erotic Function In our culture, breasts also serve an erotic function. Many, but not all, women find breast stimulation intensely pleasurable, whether it occurs during breast-feeding or sexual contact. Men tend to be aroused by both the sight and touch of women's breasts. Although it has no basis in reality, they may believe that large breasts denote greater sexual responsiveness than small breasts. Whereas in other cultures breasts may be

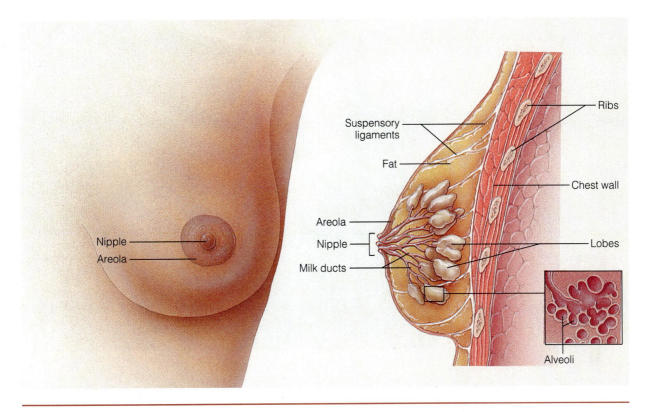

Nipple
Areola

Suspensory
ligaments
Fat
Areola
Nipple
Milk ducts

Ribs
Chest wall
Lobes
Alveoli

FIGURE 3.4 The Female Breast.

regarded simply as utilitarian baby-feeders, in Western society we tend to be quite ambivalent where breasts, especially women's breasts, are concerned. Husbands often feel confused or even jealous when their wives are nursing. A man may feel the woman's breasts are *his* property and for his pleasure. Some people are offended by the sight of a breast-feeding woman; they see something vaguely sexual and shameful in the act. And women themselves may feel this ambivalence; they sometimes wonder if it's "wrong" to feel sensual pleasure from nursing a child.

In magazine ads, in movies, and on TV, we can see our cultural ideals for breasts and body types. Currently the ideal is "a hybrid form that is all but impossible for most women: big-breasted but narrow hipped" (Tavris, 1992). But voluptuous breasts are not always the sexual ideal. In the 1920s and again in the late 1960s and 1970s, small breasts were "in." Tavris suggests that we associate large breasts with femininity and nurturing and small breasts (which are more "masculine") with intelligence and competence. (Body image is discussed at greater length in Chapter 14; also see Chapter 14 for material on breast care and diseases of the breast.)

FEMALE SEXUAL PHYSIOLOGY

The female reproductive cycle can be viewed as having two components (although, of course, there are multiple biological processes involved): the ovarian cycle, in which eggs develop, and the menstrual or uterine cycle,

Western culture tends to be ambivalent about breasts and nudity.
Most people are probably comfortable with artistic portrayals of the
nude female body, as in this photograph by Imogen Cunningham
entitled Triangles.

in which the womb is prepared for pregnancy. These cycles repeat approximately every month for about 40 or 50 years. The task of directing these
processes belongs to a class of chemicals called hormones.

Reproductive Hormones

Hormones are chemical substances that serve as messengers, traveling
within the body through the bloodstream. Most hormones are composed of
either amino acids (building blocks of proteins) or steroids (derived from
cholesterol). They are produced by the ovaries and the endocrine glands—
the adrenals, pituitary, and hypothalamus. Hormones assist in a variety of
tasks, including development of the reproductive organs and secondary sex
characteristics during puberty, regulation of the menstrual cycle, maintenance of pregnancy, initiation and regulation of childbirth, and initiation
of lactation. Hormones that act directly on the gonads are known as **gonadotropins.** Among the most important of the female hormones is **estrogen,**
which affects the maturation of the reproductive organs, menstruation, and
pregnancy. The principal hormones involved in a woman's reproductive and
sexual life and their functions are described in Table 3.1.

Oogenesis and the Ovarian Cycle

The development of female gametes is a complex process that begins even
before a woman is born. In infancy and childhood, the cells that will
develop into ova (eggs) undergo no further development. During puberty,
hormones trigger the completion of the process of **oogenesis** (*oh-uh-JEN-uh-
sis*), literally, "egg beginning." This process (Figure 3.5), called the ovarian
cycle, continues until a woman reaches menopause.

TABLE 3.1 Female Reproductive Hormones

Hormone	Where Produced	Functions
Estrogen (including estradiol, estrone, estriol)	Ovaries, adrenal glands, placenta (during pregnancy)	Promotes maturation of reproductive organs, development of secondary sex characteristics and growth spurt at puberty, regulates menstrual cycle, sustains pregnancy
Progesterone	Ovaries, adrenal glands	Promotes breast development, maintains uterine lining, regulates menstrual cycle, sustains pregnancy
Gonadotropin-releasing hormone (GnRH)	Hypothalamus	Promotes maturation of gonads, regulates menstrual cycle
Follicle-stimulating hormone (FSH)	Pituitary	Regulates ovarian function and maturation of ovarian follicles
Luteinizing hormone (LH)	Pituitary	Assists in production of estrogen and progesterone, regulates maturation of ovarian follicles, triggers ovulation
Human chorionic gonadotropin (HCG)	Embryo and placenta	Helps sustain pregnancy
Testosterone	Ovaries, adrenal glands	Helps stimulate sexual interest
Oxytocin	Hypothalamus	Stimulates uterine contractions during childbirth
Prolactin	Pituitary	Stimulates milk production
Prostaglandins	All body cells	Mediate hormone response, stimulate muscle contractions

Oocyte Development As mentioned earlier, at birth a female infant's ovaries contain 400,000–700,000 immature eggs, called primary oocytes. At puberty, a small number of oocytes begin further development. About once a month, one of the oocytes completes the stage of cell division known as meiosis I.

Meiosis is the form of cell division in which the cell's nucleus undergoes two consecutive divisions (Figure 3.6). In the first division, meiosis I, the chromosomes replicate (copy themselves) and are then divided, with half of them going to each new cell. In the next division, meiosis II, the cells divide without replicating, with the result that each of the four "daughter" cells contains half the chromosomes of the original cell. Since the normal number of chromosomes in human cells is 46 (in 23 pairs), the number of chromosomes in cells that have gone through meiosis is 23. Gametes are

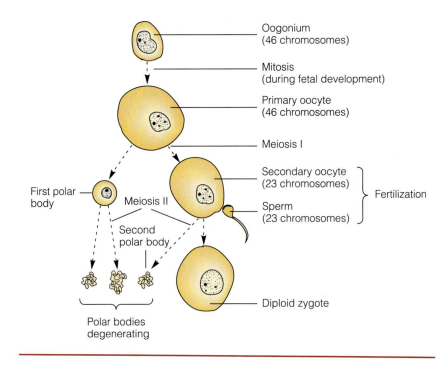

FIGURE 3.5 Oogenesis. This diagram charts the development of an ovum, beginning with embryonic development of the oogonium and ending with fertilization of the secondary oocyte, which then becomes the diploid zygote. Primary oocytes are present in a female at birth; at puberty, hormones stimulate the oocyte to undergo meiosis.

Oogonium
(46 chromosomes)

Mitosis
(during fetal development)

Primary oocyte
(46 chromosomes)

Meiosis I

Secondary oocyte
(23 chromosomes)

Sperm
(23 chromosomes)

Fertilization

First polar body

Meiosis II

Second polar body

Polar bodies degenerating

Diploid zygote

called **haploid cells** because they contain *half* of the set of chromosomes needed for fertilization to occur; they must unite with another gamete, forming a **diploid cell** with *twice* as many chromosomes. One of these pairs of chromosomes determines the genetic sex of the offspring; in females, each chromosome pair is identical; they are labeled XX. Males have both X and Y sex chromosomes. Because the chromosome from the mother is always an X chromosome but the one from the father may be either an X or a Y, in order for a male to develop, a Y chromosome must be contributed by the sperm. In order for a female to develop, an X chromosome must be contributed. (The role of sperm in sex selection is discussed in more detail in Chapter 4.)

In oogenesis, the two cells produced during meiosis I are quite dissimilar. The smaller cell, called a *polar body,* usually undergoes meiosis II, producing two more polar bodies, which degenerate. The larger cell, however, continues to mature, but it does not complete division (meiosis II) until it has united with a sperm. The mature oocyte is a tiny sphere about $1/175$ of an inch in diameter, barely visible to the naked eye. It is surrounded by three layers: a cell membrane, a gel-like membrane called the *zona pellucida,* and an outer layer of cells called the *corona radiata.* Inside these membranes are cellular fluid (cytoplasm), a nucleus containing chromosomes, and a polar body. Once a sperm is drawn inside, the oocyte casts out its polar body and becomes a true ovum (egg).

The Ovarian Cycle The activities of the ovaries and the development of oocytes for ovulation are described as the three-phase **ovarian cycle.** The

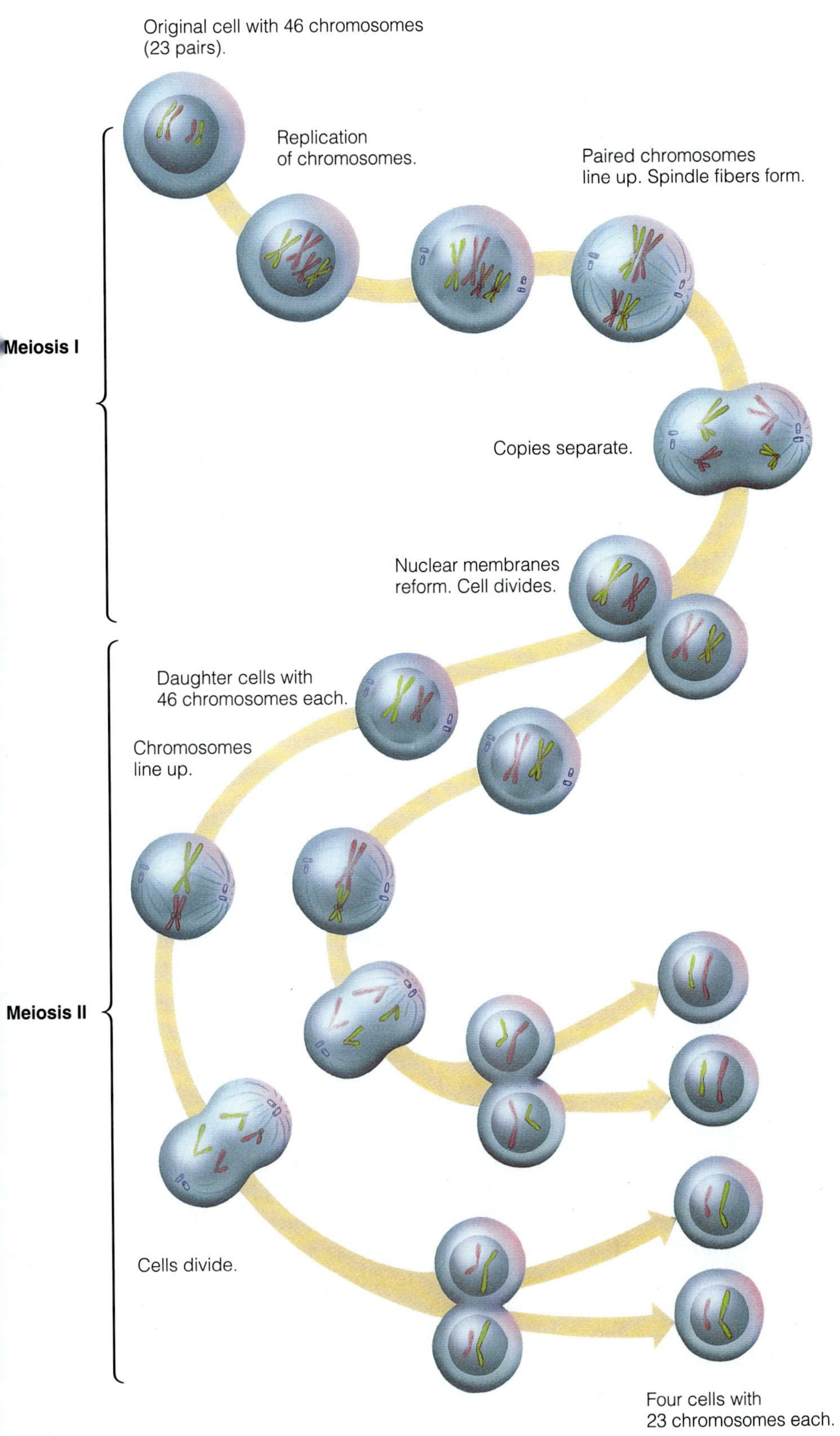

Original cell with 46 chromosomes
(23 pairs).

Replication
of chromosomes.

Paired chromosomes
line up. Spindle fibers form.

Meiosis I

Copies separate.

Nuclear membranes
reform. Cell divides.

Daughter cells with
46 chromosomes each.

Chromosomes
line up.

Meiosis II

Cells divide.

Four cells with
23 chromosomes each.

FIGURE 3.6 Meiosis. Through the process of meiosis, a single cell undergoes two consecutive divisions to become four haploid cells, each with half the number of chromosomes of the original cell. During the first division, meiosis I, the cell's chromosomes replicate prior to division. In the second division, meiosis II, the two cells divide without replicating their chromosomes. In sperm development, this results in four complete sperm cells. In oocyte development, only one oocyte matures; the other three cells (polar bodies) degenerate.

FIGURE 3.7 Ovarian and Menstrual Cycles. The ovarian cycle consists of the activities within the ovaries and the development of oocytes; it includes the follicular, ovulatory, and luteal phases. The menstrual cycle consists of events in the uterus. Hormones regulate these cycles.

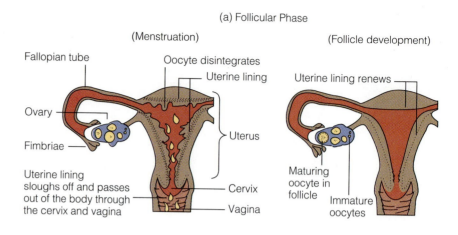

(a) Follicular Phase

(Menstruation)

(Follicle development)

Fallopian tube
Oocyte disintegrates
Uterine lining
Uterine lining renews
Ovary
Fimbriae
Uterus
Maturing oocyte in follicle
Immature oocytes
Uterine lining sloughs off and passes out of the body through the cervix and vagina
Cervix
Vagina

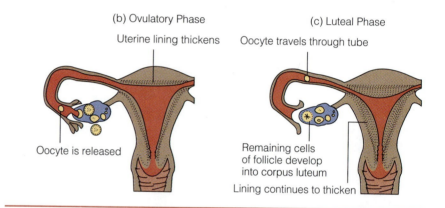

(b) Ovulatory Phase
Uterine lining thickens

Oocyte is released

(c) Luteal Phase
Oocyte travels through tube

Remaining cells of follicle develop into corpus luteum
Lining continues to thicken

cycle averages 28 days in length, although there is considerable variation among women, ranging from 21 to 40 days; most women, however, experience little variation in their own particular cycle length after puberty. Generally ovulation occurs in only one ovary each month, alternating between the right and left sides with each successive cycle. If a single ovary is removed, the remaining one begins to ovulate every month (Fox, 1987). The ovarian phases are called follicular, ovulatory, and luteal (Figure 3.7). As an ovary undergoes its changes, there are corresponding changes in the uterus. These changes, called the uterine, or menstrual, cycle are discussed after the ovarian cycle.

Follicular Phase On the first day of the cycle, **gonadotropin-releasing hormone (GnRH)** is released from the hypothalamus. GnRH begins to stimulate the pituitary to release **follicle-stimulating hormone (FSH)** and **luteinizing hormone (LH),** initiating the **follicular phase.** During the first ten days, 10 to 20 ovarian follicles begin to grow, stimulated by FSH and LH. In 98–99% of cases, just one of the follicles will mature completely during this period. (The maturation of more than one oocyte is one factor in multiple births.) All the developing follicles begin secreting estrogen. Under the influence of FSH and estrogen, the oocyte matures; it begins to bulge from the surface of the ovary.

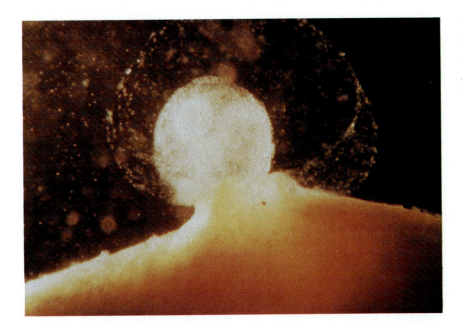

During ovulation, the ovarian follicle swells and ruptures, releasing the mature oocyte to begin its journey through the fallopian tube.

Ovulatory Phase The **ovulatory phase** begins at about day 11 and culminates with ovulation at about day 14. Stimulated by an increase of LH from the pituitary, the primary oocyte completes meiosis I and is ready for ovulation. The ballooning follicle wall thins and ruptures, and the oocyte enters the abdominal cavity near the beckoning fimbriae. Ovulation is now complete. Some women experience a sharp twinge on one side of the lower abdomen during ovulation. This twinge is known as **mittelshmerz** (German for middle pain) and is probably a result of the swelling or rupturing of the ovary wall. A very slight, bloody discharge from the vagina may also occur.

Luteal Phase Following ovulation, estrogen levels drop rapidly, and the ruptured follicle, still under the influence of increased LH, becomes a corpus luteum, which secretes **progesterone** and small amounts of estrogen. Increasing levels of these hormones serve to inhibit pituitary release of FSH and LH. Unless fertilization has occurred, the corpus luteum deteriorates, becoming a mass of scar tissue called the *corpus albicans* (Latin for white body). In the event of pregnancy, the corpus luteum maintains its hormonal output, helping to sustain the pregnancy. The hormone human chorionic gonadotropin (HCG)—similar to LH—is secreted by the embryo and signals the corpus luteum to continue until the placenta has developed sufficiently to take over hormone production.

The **luteal phase** typically lasts from day 14 (immediately after ovulation) through day 28 of the ovarian cycle. Even when cycles are more or less than 28 days, the duration of the luteal phase remains the same; the time between ovulation and the end of the cycle is always 14 days. At this point, the ovarian hormone levels are at their lowest, GnRH is released, and FSH and LH levels begin to rise.

FIGURE 3.8 The Menstrual Cycle, Ovarian Cycle, and Hormone Levels. This chart compares the activities of the ovaries and uterus and shows the relationship of hormone levels to these activities.

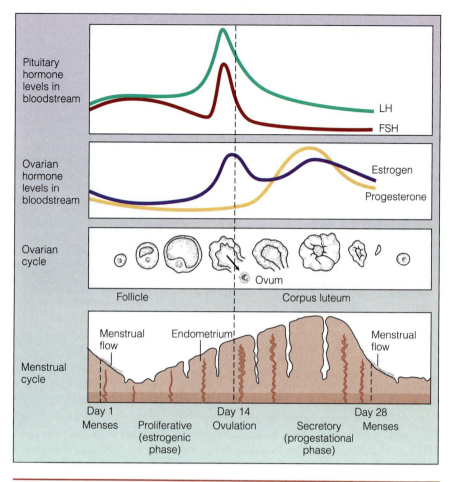

The Menstrual Cycle

As estrogen levels fall following the degeneration of the corpus luteum, the uterine lining (endometrium) is shed because it will not be needed to help sustain a fertilized ovum. The shedding of endometrial tissue and the bleeding that accompanies it are, collectively, a monthly event in the lives of women from puberty through menopause. Cultural and religious attitudes as well as personal experience influence our feelings about this phenomenon. (The physical and emotional effects of menstruation are discussed later in this section. The onset of menstruation and its effect on a woman's psychosexual development is discussed in Chapter 6. Menopause is discussed in Chapter 14.)

Phases of the Menstrual Cycle The **menstrual cycle** (or uterine cycle), like the ovarian cycle, is divided into three phases. What occurs within the uterus is inextricably related to what is happening in the ovaries, but only in their final phases do the two cycles actually coincide (Figure 3.8). The menstrual cycle consists of the menstrual, proliferative, and secretory phases.

Menstrual Phase With hormone levels low because of the degeneration of the corpus luteum, the outer layer of the endometrium becomes detached from the uterine wall. The shedding of the endometrium marks the beginning of the **menstrual phase.** This endometrial tissue, along with mucus, other cervical and vaginal secretions, and a small amount of blood (2–5 oz per cycle) is expelled through the vagina. The menstrual flow, or **menses,** generally occurs over a period of 3–5 days. FSH and LH begin increasing around day 5, marking the end of this phase.

Proliferative Phase The **proliferative phase** lasts about 9 days. During this time, the endometrium builds up in response to increased estrogen. The mucous membranes of the cervix secrete a clear, thin mucus with a crystalline structure that facilitates the passage of sperm. The proliferative phase ends with ovulation.

Secretory Phase During the first part of the **secretory phase,** with the help of progesterone, the endometrium begins to prepare for the arrival of a fertilized ovum. Glands within the uterus enlarge and begin secreting glycogen, a cell nutrient. The cervical mucus thickens and starts forming a plug to seal off the uterus, in the event of pregnancy. If fertilization does not occur, the corpus luteum begins to degenerate, as LH levels decline. Progesterone levels then fall, and the endometrial cells begin to die. The secretory phase lasts 14 days, corresponding with the luteal phase of the ovarian cycle. It ends with the shedding of the endometrium.

Cultural Considerations Some societies view menstruation as problematic. They may isolate menstruating women or view menstrual blood as darkly powerful; others may simply view menstruating women as being slightly "off," overly emotional, unpredictable, or untrustworthy. The origins of fears and taboos regarding menstruation undoubtedly have their roots in the "mysterious" nature of the process: It occurs in regular cycles, perhaps tied to those of the moon; it involves blood, the mainstay of life, which normally stays inside the body unless there is an injury (a menstruating woman may, in fact, be equated with a man whose penis has been cut off); and it has something to do with pregnancy (since it ceases at that time), another mysterious process. Women as well as men may have viewed menstruation as a sign of special power. Among the native Ohlone of California, for example, a girl's first menstruation, or **menarche,** was considered a major event such as birth and death, "an incontrovertible message that the world of power had begun to take notice of her" (Margolin, 1978). According to Malcolm Margolin:

> She knew that from now until she was past childbearing age she would, at the first sign of menstruation, withdraw once more into a corner of the dwelling to re-establish a relationship with the spirit world in a monthly ritual that would become one of the most dominant parts of her adult life.

American society today tends to treat menstruation as a problem, an illness, or a shameful (or, at the very least, tasteless) activity. While it is true that at some time or other many women experience significant discomfort or pain associated with their periods and that changing hormonal levels can

And if a woman shall have an issue, and her issue in her flesh be blood, she shall be separated seven days; and whatsoever touches her shall be unclean.

Leviticus 15:19

Menstrual Period Slang
that time of month
monthlies
the curse
female troubles
a visit from my friend
a visit from Aunt Sally (or other woman's name)
a visit from George (or other man's name)
on the rag
on a losing streak
falling off the roof

affect mood, there is nothing inherent in the menstrual process that makes women any less capable or reliable than men. Esther Rome (1992) writes:

> In the belief that the whole menstrual cycle makes women unstable or less capable, some people deny jobs to women and treat us as inferior. Both women and men experience mood swings, but for women the changes are seen as a sign of inherent instability. . . . Men, however, who are much more prone to seriously incapacitating and unpredictable diseases, such as heart problems, continue in highly responsible positions (the presidency of the country, for example).

There is much that is not understood concerning such areas as the interplay of hormones and the emotions, the role of hereditary factors, and other physiological phenomena that relate to a woman's reproductive cycle.

Menstrual Effects   For some women, menstruation is a problem. For others, it is simply a fact of life that creates little disruption. For individual women, the problems associated with their menstrual period may be physiological, emotional, or practical. Various studies report that about 70% of menstruating women notice at least one emotional, physical, or behavioral change in the week or so prior to menstruation (Hopson & Rosenfeld, 1984). Most women describe the changes negatively: breast tenderness and swelling, abdominal bloating, irritability, cramping, depression, or fatigue. Some women also report positive changes, such as increased energy, heightened sexual arousal, or a general feeling of well-being. These changes are usually mild to moderate; they appear to have little impact on most women's lives. (Toxic shock syndrome, a blood infection associated with menstruation, is discussed in Chapter 14.) The most common problems associated with menstruation are discussed below.

Premenstrual Syndrome   More severe menstrual problems have been attributed to what is commonly called **premenstrual syndrome (PMS),** a term coined by Katherina Dalton in the late 1960s to describe the most commonly reported cluster of severe physical and emotional symptoms. About 3–12% of menstruating women report a dozen or more negative changes that severely affect their lives (Hopson & Rosenfeld, 1984). Some studies, however, suggest that the number of seriously affected women may be as high as 30% (Laube, 1985). But because of the variety of symptoms and the difficulty involved in evaluating them, studies on PMS are contradictory and inconclusive (Reid, 1986). In 1994 the American Psychiatric Association included "premenstrual dysphoric disorder" in the fourth edition of its *Diagnostic and Statistical Manual of Mental Disorders* (DSM-IV), which is used for psychiatric diagnosis. The most common symptoms leading to a diagnosis of premenstrual syndrome include (Hatcher et al., 1990):

Dysphoria (depression, nervousness, irritability, anxiety)

Fluid retention (bloating, swelling, weight gain)

Breast tenderness

Headache

Fatigue

Food cravings (especially for salt, sugar, chocolate)

If men could menstruate, they would probably find a way to brag about it. Most likely they would record it as a spontaneous ejaculation, an excess of vital spirits. Their cup runneth over. Their sexuality superogates. . . . All that is turned around when it is a woman who bleeds. Bleeding is interpreted as a sign of infirmity, inferiority, uncleanliness and irrationality.

Nancy Friday

The greatest difficulty in understanding PMS is how to separate information that clearly indicates premenstrual symptoms from other aspects of a woman's physical and emotional health (González, 1981). Certain questions need to be answered before firm conclusions can be drawn. For instance, do women who report severe premenstrual (luteal/secretory phase) headaches also have them during the other phases of their cycle? Are the women who report intense symptoms suffering from general stress, disease, nutritional deficiencies, or other health problems? Are some women biochemically disposed to premenstrual syndrome? To what degree do cultural expectations and sexual attitudes affect symptoms? There is no conclusive information to answer these questions.

Researchers generally agree that studies have been insufficiently controlled. There is little research on the "normal" female population. Most studies have been conducted on small groups of women for short periods of time. Often the women studied have not been in good health. Some studies on attitudes have indicated that the expectation among both men and women that there will be negative physical or behavioral changes may actually create the symptoms; in other words, people tend to conform to expectations (Lips, 1992; Ruble, 1977).

Dysmenorrhea Some women experience pelvic cramping and pain during the menstrual cycle; this condition is called **dysmenorrhea.** There are two basic types. *Primary dysmenorrhea* is characterized by pain that begins with uterine shedding (or just before) and by the absence of pain at other times in the cycle. It can be very severe and may be accompanied by nausea, weakness, or other physical symptoms. In *secondary dysmenorrhea*, the symptoms may be the same, but there is an underlying condition or disease causing them; pain may not be limited to the menstrual phase alone. Secondary dysmenorrhea may be caused by pelvic inflammatory disease (PID), endometriosis, endometrial cancer, or other conditions (see Chapters 14 and 16).

The effects of dysmenorrhea can totally incapacitate a woman for several hours or even days. Primary dysmenorrhea is often caused by high levels of **prostaglandins,** a type of hormone with a fatty-acid base that is found throughout the body. One type of prostaglandin is synthesized in the uterus and stimulates uterine contractions; excessive amounts cause tighter and longer contractions and keep oxygen from reaching the uterus and abdominal muscles (Rome, 1992). The discovery of a hormonal basis for dysmenorrhea has resulted in gynecologists taking menstrual pain more seriously in recent years (González, 1980). Previously, (male) physicians had often dismissed menstrual pain as being in the head, not the body (although women, of course, had a different opinion). (See Perspective 1.)

Amenorrhea When women do not menstruate for reasons other than aging, the condition is called **amenorrhea.** A principal cause of amenorrhea is pregnancy. Lack of menstruation, if not a result of pregnancy, is categorized as either primary or secondary amenorrhea. Women who have passed the age of 16 and never menstruated are diagnosed as having *primary amenorrhea*. It may be that they have not yet reached their critical weight (when an increased ratio of body fat triggers menstrual cycle-inducing hormones), or that they are hereditarily late maturers. But it can also signal hormonal

Perspective 1

RELIEVING MENSTRUAL SYMPTOMS

For women, recognizing their menstrual patterns, learning about their bodies, and recognizing and dealing with existing difficulties can be useful in heading off or easing potential problems. Different remedies work for different women. We suggest you try varying combinations of them and keep a record of your response to each. Below are suggestions for relieving the more common premenstrual and menstrual symptoms; both self-help and medical treatments are included.

For Premenstrual Symptoms

- *Diet.* Moderate amounts of protein and substantial amounts of carbohydrates (such as fresh fruits and vegetables, whole grain breads and cereals, beans, rice, and pasta) are recommended. Reduce or avoid salt, sugar, and caffeine products such as coffee and colas (Rossignol, Zhang, Chen, & Xiang, 1989). Even though you may crave chocolate, it may have a negative effect on you; try fruit or popcorn instead, and see how you feel. Frequent small meals may be better than two or three large meals.
- *Alcohol and tobacco.* Avoid them.

- *Exercise.* Moderate exercise is suggested, but be sure to include about 30 minutes of aerobic movement three or four times per week (Hatcher et al., 1990). Aerobic exercise brings oxygen to body tissues and stimulates the production of endorphins, chemical substances that help promote feelings of well-being. Yoga may also be helpful, especially the "cobra" position.

- *Medical treatments.* For severe PMS, progesterone therapy is sometimes recommended (Dalton, 1984). There is much controversy within the medical profession about its actual effectiveness, however. Vitamin and mineral supplements may be helpful, but they should be taken under medical supervision, because some can cause severe reactions if the quantity is too large. Hormonal contraceptives are sometimes prescribed to relieve premenstrual (and menstrual) distress. Prostaglandin inhibitors, discussed below, may help relieve premenstrual headaches and cramping. If eliminating salt from the diet does not work to reduce fluid retention, diuretics may be prescribed.

deficiencies, abnormal body structure, or hermaphroditism. Most primary amenorrhea can be treated with hormone therapy.

Secondary amenorrhea exists when a previously menstruating woman stops menstruating for several months. If it is not due to pregnancy, breast-feeding, or the use of hormonal contraceptives, the source of secondary amenorrhea may be found in stress, lowered body fat, heavy athletic training, or hormonal irregularities. Anorexia (discussed in Chapter 14) is a frequent cause of amenorrhea (Benson, 1980). If a woman is not pregnant, is not breast-feeding, and can rule out hormonal contraceptives as a cause, she should see her health practitioner if she has gone six months without menstruating.

Sexuality and the Menstrual Cycle Although studies have tried to determine whether there is a biologically based cycle of sexual interest and activity in women that correlates with the menstrual cycle (such as higher interest around ovulation), the results have been conflicting. Researchers have found everything from no significant correlation (Bancroft, 1984;

For Cramps

- *Relaxation.* Rest, sleep, and relaxation exercises can help reduce pain from uterine and abdominal cramping, especially in combination with one or more of the remedies listed below.

- *Heat.* A heating pad, hot-water bottle (or, in a pinch, a cat) applied to the abdominal area may help relieve cramps; a warm bath may also help.

- *Massage.* Lower back massage, or other forms of massage, such as acupressure, Shiatsu, or polarity therapy, are quite helpful for many women. See *The New Our Bodies, Ourselves* (Boston Women's Health Book Collective, 1992) for guidelines for menstrual massage.

- *Herbal remedies.* Herbal teas, especially raspberry leaf, are helpful for some women. Health food stores carry a variety of teas, tablets, and other preparations. Use them as directed, and stop using them if you experience additional discomfort or problems.

- *Prostaglandin inhibitors.* Antiprostaglandins reduce cramping of the uterine and abdominal muscles. Aspirin is a mild prostaglandin inhibitor. Ibuprophen, a highly effective prostaglandin inhibitor, was often prescribed for menstrual cramps (as Motrin) before it became available over the counter. Aspirin increases menstrual flow slightly, whereas ibuprophen reduces it (Speroff, Glass, & Kase, 1989). Stronger antiprostaglandins may be prescribed: naproxen (Naprosyn), naproxen sodium (Anaprox), or mefenamic acid (Ponstel). Taking medication at the first sign of cramping increases its effectiveness greatly, as opposed to waiting until the pain is severe before starting treatment.

- *Orgasm.* Some women report relief of menstrual congestion and cramping from orgasm (with or without a partner).

If pain cannot be controlled with the above methods, further medical evaluation is needed. The symptoms may indicate an underlying problem such as endometriosis or pelvic inflammatory disease (PID).

Meuwissen & Over, 1992) to significantly higher correlations at different phases (Bancroft et al., 1983; Harvey, 1987; Matteo & Rissman, 1984). There is apparently a great deal of individual variation.

There is also variation in how people feel about sexual activity during different phases. If a woman believes she is ovulating, and if she and her partner do not want a pregnancy, they may feel negative or ambivalent about intercourse. (See Chapter 12 for a discussion about the psychology of contraceptive risk taking.) If a woman is menstruating, she, her partner, or both of them may not wish to engage in intercourse or cunnilingus. There are a number of reasons.

First of all, there is a general taboo in our culture, as in many others, against sexual intercourse during menstruation. This taboo may be based on religious beliefs. Among Orthodox Jews, for example, women are required to refrain from intercourse for seven days following the end of menstruation. They may then resume sexual activity after a ritual bath, the *mikvah*. Contact with blood may make some people squeamish. A man may view men-

It is an extraordinary jump for women to accept the idea that bleeding means health.

Judith Bardwick

strual blood as "somehow dangerous, magical, and apparently not something he wants to get on his penis" (Delaney, Lupton, & Toth, 1977). Many women, especially at the beginning of their period, feel bloated or uncomfortable; they may experience breast tenderness or a general feeling of not wanting to be touched. Others may find that lovemaking helps relieve menstrual discomfort.

For some couples, just dealing with the logistics of bloodstains, bathing, and laundry may be enough to discourage them from intercourse at this time. For many people, however, menstrual blood holds no special connotation; some find they enjoy intercourse more because of the relatively low risk of pregnancy (although women with short or irregular cycles may ovulate during or very soon after menstruation). Some women find that a diaphragm holds back the flow and facilitates lovemaking. While it is not recommended that women engage in intercourse while a tampon is inserted because of possible injury to the cervix, cunnilingus is a possibility. And inventive lovers can, of course, find many ways to give each other pleasure that do not require putting the penis into the vagina.

Sexual intercourse during menstruation may carry health risks for women who have multiple sexual partners or whose partners may have been exposed to a sexually transmitted disease. Organisms, including HIV, have an easy pathway into a woman's bloodstream through the uterine walls exposed by endometrial shedding. Moreover, a woman with a pathogen in her blood, such as the hepatitis virus or HIV, could pass it to a partner in her menstrual blood. Therefore, during menstruation, as well as at other times, safer sex practices, including condom use, are strongly recommended. (See Chapter 16 for safer sex guidelines.)

FEMALE SEXUAL RESPONSE

Scientific research has contributed much to our understanding of sexual arousal and response. Masters and Johnson, for example, did women (and men) a great service by helping demystify the female orgasm and validating the role of the clitoris (although even they made a number of assumptions that are currently being challenged). One way in which researchers investigate and describe phenomena is through the creation of models, hypothetical descriptions used to study or explain something. While models are useful as tools for general understanding or for assisting in the treatment of specific clinical problems (lack of arousal, for example), we should remember that they are only models. They are not reality and may not reflect our own subjective experiences. Being human, we tend to compare ourselves to others to find out if we're OK. The danger here is that we may create a problem where none existed. Regarding the material in this chapter, as well as others, we encourage you to use the text as a guide, but to chart your own course. Although it's important to know the "nuts and bolts," much of the joy in sexuality comes from our personal explorations and discoveries.

Much of what follows applies to sexual response in both women and men. Because this chapter focuses on women, we pay particular attention to the aspects of sexual response that apply mainly or exclusively to women. (In Chapter 4, we discuss men's sexual response in the areas that it differs from that of women.)

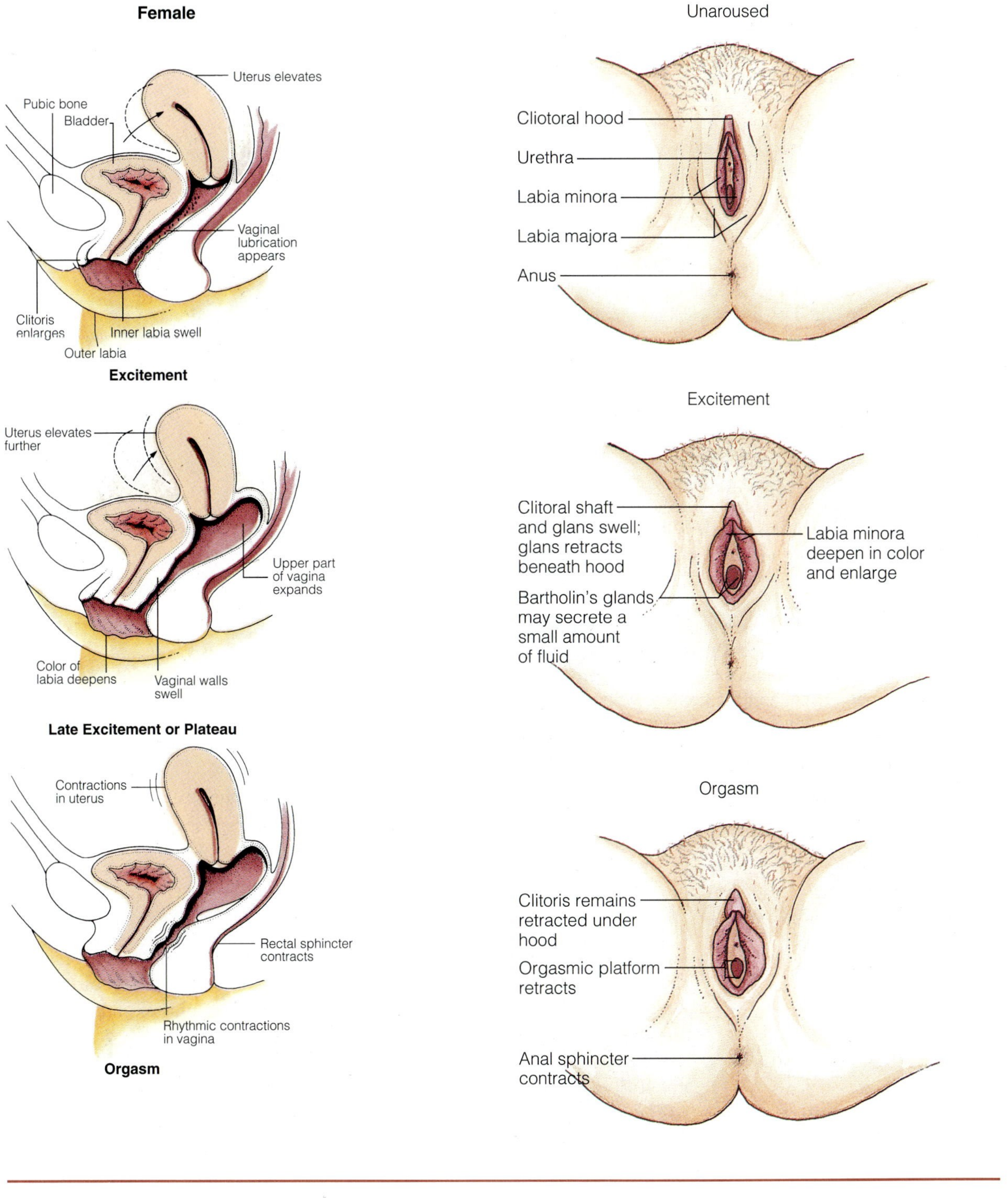

Female

- Uterus elevates
- Pubic bone
- Bladder
- Vaginal lubrication appears
- Clitoris enlarges
- Inner labia swell
- Outer labia

Excitement

- Uterus elevates further
- Upper part of vagina expands
- Color of labia deepens
- Vaginal walls swell

Late Excitement or Plateau

- Contractions in uterus
- Rectal sphincter contracts
- Rhythmic contractions in vagina

Orgasm

Unaroused

- Cliotoral hood
- Urethra
- Labia minora
- Labia majora
- Anus

Excitement

- Clitoral shaft and glans swell; glans retracts beneath hood
- Labia minora deepen in color and enlarge
- Bartholin's glands may secrete a small amount of fluid

Orgasm

- Clitoris remains retracted under hood
- Orgasmic platform retracts
- Anal sphincter contracts

FIGURE 3.9 Stages of Female Sexual Response (internal, left; and external, right).

Sexual Response Models

The **Masters and Johnson Four-Phase Model of Sexual Response** identifies the significant stages of response as excitement, plateau, orgasm, and resolution (Figure 3.9). Helen Singer Kaplan collapses the excitement and pla-

TABLE 3.2 Sexual Response Models Compared: Masters/Johnson and Kaplan

Psychological/Physiological Process	Name of Phase	
Some form of thought, fantasy, or erotic feeling causes us to seek sexual gratification. (An inability to become sexually aroused may be due to a lack of desire, which can have a variety of causes.)	Desire (Kaplan)	
Physical and/or psychological stimulation produces characteristic physical changes. In men, increased amounts of blood flow to the genitals produces erection of the penis; the scrotal skin begins to smooth out, and the testicles draw up toward the body. Later in this phase, the testes increase slightly in size. In women, vaginal lubrication begins, the upper vagina expands, the uterus is pulled upward, and the clitoris becomes engorged. In both women and men, the breasts enlarge slightly, and the nipples may become erect. Both men and women experience increasing muscular contractions.	Excitement (Masters/Johnson)	Excitement (Kaplan)
Sexual tension levels off. In men, the testes swell and continue to elevate. The diameter of the head of the penis swells slightly and may deepen in color. In women, the outer third of the vagina swells, lubrication may slow down, and the clitoris pulls back. Coloring and swelling of the labia increase. In both men and women, muscular tension, breathing, and heart rate increase.	Plateau (Masters/Johnson)	
Increased tension peaks and discharges, affecting the whole body. Rhythmic muscular contractions affect the uterus and outer vagina in women. In men, there are contractions of the tubes that produce and carry semen, the prostate gland, and the urethral bulb, resulting in the expulsion of semen (ejaculation).	Orgasm (Masters/Johnson and Kaplan)	
The body returns to its unaroused state. In women, this phase may not occur until after multiple orgasms.	Resolution (Masters/Johnson)	

teau phases into one, eliminates the resolution phase, and adds a phase to the beginning of the process. **Kaplan's Tri-Phasic Model of Sexual Response** includes the desire, excitement, and orgasm phases. These models are described and compared in Table 3.2.

Criticism of the Masters and Johnson model centers around three points. (1) It does not account for the role of desire in sexual arousal. According to Helen Singer Kaplan (1977), "Sexual desire is an appetite or drive which is produced by the activation of a specific neural system in the brain, while the excitement and orgasm phases involve the genital organs." The idea that "the brain is the sexiest organ in the body" underscores the importance of desire as the psychological component of sexual arousal and response. (2) Critics of the Masters and Johnson model point out that the responses described as the plateau phase are not clinically distinguishable from the excitement phase (Robinson, 1976). Excitement is actually experienced as a process rather than a set of separate events. The only part of sexual response that can be described as an event in itself is orgasm; for most people who experience it, it's very clear when it begins and when it ends. (3) Resolution should not be included as a phase of response. The reasoning behind using a model to understand sexual response is that it may prove useful for identifying problem areas experienced by an individual or a couple. But resolution is not a problem (as far as we know, no one sees a sex therapist for difficulties with their resolution phase).

Kaplan's model has been criticized for overemphasizing the role of desire. At times, the physiological processes of sexual arousal seem to precede the psychological. Our bodies may respond automatically, even before we have become aware of erotic thoughts, emotions, or feelings. We should keep in mind that while models are useful for identifying and treating problems, they are not necessarily guides to behavior. Each individual responds sexually in his or her own unique way.

Desire: Mind or Matter?

Desire is the psychological component of sexual arousal. Although we can experience desire without becoming aroused, and in some cases become aroused without feeling desire, some form of erotic thought or feeling is usually involved in our sexual behavior. The physical manifestations of sexual arousal involve a complex interaction of thoughts and feelings, sensory organs, neural responses, and hormonal reactions involving various parts of the body, including the cerebral cortex and limbic system of the brain, the nervous system, the circulatory system, the endocrine glands—as well as the genitals.

The Neural System and Sexual Stimuli   The brain is crucial to sexual response, yet relatively little is known about the manner in which the brain functions to create these responses. Through the neural system, the brain receives stimuli from the five senses plus one: sight, smell, touch, hearing, taste, *and* the imagination.

The Brain   The brain, of course, plays a major role in all of our body's functions. Nowhere is its role more apparent than in our sexual functioning. The relationship between our thoughts and feelings and our actual behavior is not well understood (and what is known would require a course in neurophysiology to satisfactorily explain it). Cultural influences, as well as expectations, fantasies, hopes, and fears, combine with sensory inputs and hormonal messages to bring us to where we are ready, willing, and able to be sexual. Even then, potentially erotic messages may be short-circuited by the brain itself, which may inhibit as well as excite sexual responses. It is not known how the inhibitory mechanism works, but guilt, anxiety, fear, and negative conditioning will prevent the brain from sending messages to the genitals. In fact, the reason moderate amounts of alcohol and marijuana appear to enhance sexuality is because they reduce the control mechanisms of the brain that act as inhibitors (Kaplan, 1974).

Anatomically speaking, the areas of the brain that appear to be involved most in sexual behaviors of both men and women are the cerebral cortex and the limbic system (Figure 3.10). The cerebral cortex is the convoluted covering of most of the brain area. It is the area that is associated with

Magic . . . can be controlled—by a magician. A magician is a transmitter just as a mystic is rather strictly a receiver. Just as love can be made, using materials no more ethereal than an erect penis, a moist vagina and a warm heart, so, too, can magic be made, wholly and willfully, from the most obvious and mundane. Magic does not seep from within of its own volition (or appear unannounced to someone in a state of heightened awareness); it is a matter of cause and effect. The seemingly unrealistic or supernatural ("magic") act occurs through the acting of one thing upon another through a secret link.

Tom Robbins

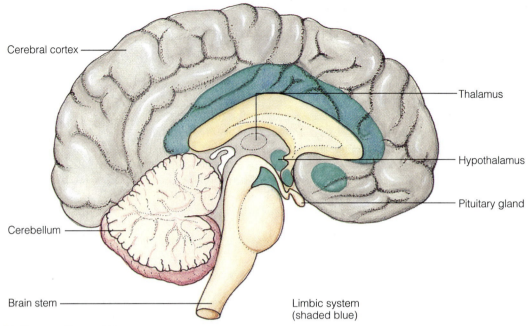

Cerebral cortex

Thalamus

Hypothalamus

Pituitary gland

Cerebellum

Brain stem

Limbic system
(shaded blue)

The Limbic System. Deep within the brain, a group of structures, collectively known as the limbic system, is involved with emotions and motivation. Parts of the limbic system involved in sexual arousal may be referred to as "pleasure centers."

To our bodies turn we
  then, that so
Weak men on love
  revealed may look;
Love's mysteries in souls
  do grow,
But yet the body is his book.
    John Donne (1573–1631)

conscious behavior such as perception, memory, communication, understanding, and voluntary movement. Beneath the cortex, the **limbic system,** which consists of several separate parts, is involved with emotions and feelings. There are extensive connections between the limbic system and the cerebral cortex, explaining perhaps why "emotions sometimes override logic and, conversely, why reason can stop us from expressing our emotions in inappropriate situations" (Marieb, 1992). Some parts of the limbic system have been dubbed "pleasure centers" (Olds, 1956) because their stimulation produces sexual arousal (Heath, 1972).

The Senses An attractive person (sight), a body fragrance or odor (smell), a lick or kiss (taste), a loving caress (touch), and erotic whispers (hearing) are all capable of sending sexual signals to the brain. Many of the connections we experience between sensory data and emotional responses are probably products of the limbic system. Some sensory inputs may evoke sexual arousal without a lot of conscious thought or emotion. Certain areas of the skin, called **erogenous zones,** are highly sensitive to touch. These areas may include the genitals, breasts, mouth, ears, neck, inner thighs, and buttocks; erotic associations with these areas vary from culture to culture and individual to individual. Our olfactory sense (smell) may bring us sexual messages below the level of our conscious awareness. Scientists have isolated chemical substances, called **pheromones,** that are secreted into the air by many kinds of animals including ants, moths, pigs, dogs, and monkeys. One function of pheromones, in animals at least, appears to be to arouse sexual interest. Definitive research on human pheromones, however, has yet to be developed.

The Role of Hormones The sex drive, or *libido*, in both men and women is biologically influenced by the hormone *testosterone*. In men, testosterone is produced mainly in the testes. In women, it is produced in the ovaries and adrenal glands. Although women produce much less testosterone than men, this does not mean they have less sexual interest; apparently, women are much more sensitive than men to its effects (Persky et al., 1982). The relationship between testosterone level and sexual interest is not well understood. Although a drop in testosterone often reduces sexual interest or functioning, this is not always the case. Estrogen also plays a role in sexual functioning. In women, estrogens help maintain the vaginal lining; it is not clear how much of a role, if any, estrogen plays in maintaining the libido. Men also produce small amounts of estrogen, but its particular function is not known. Too much estrogen, however, can induce erection difficulties.

Experiencing Sexual Arousal

For both males and females, physiological changes during sexual excitement depend on two processes: vasocongestion and myotonia. **Vasocongestion** is the concentration of blood in body tissues. For example, blood fills the genital regions of both males and females, causing the penis to become erect and the clitoris to swell. **Myotonia** is increased muscle tension accompanying the approach of orgasm; upon orgasm, the body undergoes involuntary muscle contractions and then relaxes. The sexual response pattern remains the same for all forms of sexual behavior, whether autoerotic or coital experiences, heterosexual or homosexual (Masters & Johnson, 1966, 1979).

Sexual Excitement For women, the first sign of sexual excitement is the moistening of the vaginal walls through a process called **sweating.** These secretions lubricate the vagina, enabling it to encompass the penis easily. The inner two-thirds of the vagina expands in a process called **tenting;** the vagina expands about an inch in length and doubles its width. Vasocongestion affects the labia differently depending on whether the woman has borne children. The major lips of women who have not given birth (nulliparous women) open slightly and become flatter and thinner. In women who have given birth (parous women), the major lips tend to be larger and may double or triple in size as a result of being engorged with blood. The minor lips begin to protrude outside the major lips during sexual excitement. Breathing and heart rate increase. These signs do not occur on a specific timetable; each woman has her own pattern of arousal, which may vary under different conditions, with different partners, and so on.

Contractions raise the uterus, but the clitoris remains virtually unchanged during this early phase. Although the clitoris responds more slowly than the penis to vasocongestion, it is, nevertheless, affected. The initial changes, however, are minor. Clitoral tumescence (swelling) occurs simultaneously with engorgement of the minor lips. During masturbation and oral sex, the clitoris is generally stimulated directly. During intercourse, clitoral stimulation is mostly indirect, caused by the clitoral hood being pulled over the clitoris or pressure in the general clitoral area. At the same time that these changes are occurring in the genitals, the breasts are also responding. The

The use of medical language mystifies human experience, increasing dependence on professionals and experts. If sexuality becomes fundamentally a matter of vasocongestion and myotonia. . . , personal experience requires expert interpretation and explanation.

Leonore Tiefer

Sensory inputs such as the sight, touch, or smell of someone we love, or the sound of his or her voice, may evoke desire and sexual arousal.

nipples become erect, and the breasts may enlarge somewhat because of the engorgement of blood vessels; the areolae may also enlarge. About 25% of women experience a **sex flush,** a rash that temporarily appears as a result of blood rushing to the skin's surface during sexual excitement.

As excitement increases, the clitoris retracts beneath the clitoral hood and virtually disappears. The major lips of nulliparous women do not show additional changes; those of parous women continue to swell. The minor lips become progressively larger until they double or triple in size. They deepen in color, becoming pink, bright red, or a deep wine-red color. This intense coloring is sometimes referred to as the "sex skin." When it appears, orgasm is imminent. Meanwhile, the vaginal opening decreases by about one-third. Its outer third becomes more congested with blood; the congested walls are known as the **orgasmic platform.** The vagina expands further, but lubrication decreases or may even stop. The uterus becomes fully elevated through muscular contractions.

Changes in the breasts continue. The areolae become larger, while, in contrast, the nipples decrease in relative size. If the woman has not breast-fed, her breasts may increase by up to 25% of their unaroused size; women who have breast-fed may have little change in size. An additional 75% of women experience a sex flush during this stage of response.

Orgasm Continued stimulation brings **orgasm,** rhythmic contractions of the vagina, uterus, and pelvic muscles, accompanied by intensely pleasurable sensations. Orgasm is most apparent in the orgasmic platform of the vagina, where there is a series of 3 to 15 contractions. Initially, these contractions are 0.8 second apart, but after a few contractions, the movements become weaker and occur at wider intervals. The inner two-thirds of the vagina does not contract; instead, it continues its tenting effect. The labia do not change during orgasm. The breasts also remain unchanged. (The role of orgasm in our culture is discussed in Perspective 2 on the following page.)

What is the earth? What are the body and soul without satisfaction?
Walt Whitman (1819–1892)

After orgasm, the orgasmic platform rapidly subsides. The clitoris re-emerges from beneath the clitoral hood within 5–10 seconds, although it does not return to its unaroused state for another 5–10 minutes. (If the woman has not had an orgasm, the clitoris may remain engorged for several hours, possibly creating a feeling of frustration.) The labia slowly return to their unaroused state, and the sex flush gradually disappears. About 30–40% of women perspire as the body begins to cool.

Multiple Orgasm Following orgasm, men experience a refractory period, in which they are unable to become aroused. By contrast, women are often physiologically able to be orgasmic immediately following the previous orgasm. As a result, women can have multiple orgasms if they continue to be stimulated. Kinsey (1953) estimated that 13% of the women in his study experienced multiple orgasms. It is not at all uncommon for a woman to desire to continue erotic activity and orgasm while her partner is in his refractory period. Since the man is unable to continue intercourse during this time, a woman may stimulate herself, or he may continue to stimulate her manually or orally.

Female Ejaculation Upon orgasm, some women ejaculate a clear fluid from the urethra. This ejaculation has been associated with stimulation of the G spot. Studies of female ejaculation report that 10–40% of women ejaculate a fluid that is not urine, although it may contain traces of urine (Darling, Davidson, & Conway, 1990; Ladas, Whipple, & Perry, 1983; Perry & Whipple, 1981). Researchers suggest that this fluid may come from a "female prostate," glandular tissue near the bladder that is derived from the same embryonic tissue as the male prostrate gland (Heath, 1984). It is said to bear a similarity to semen (Zaviacic, Zaviacicova, Holoman, & Molcan, 1988). More research needs to be done before we can make definitive statements regarding female ejaculation. For now, it should be noted that this, like many other aspects of our sexuality, is subject to individual variation.

In the next chapter, we discuss the anatomical features and physiological functions that characterize men's sexuality and sexual response. The information in these two chapters should serve as a comprehensive basis for understanding the material that follows.

THE ROLE OF THE ORGASM

Many of us measure both our sexuality and ourselves in terms of orgasm: Did we have one? Did our partner have one? Was it good? When we measure our sexuality by orgasm, however, we discount activities that do not necessarily lead to orgasm, such as touching, caressing, and kissing. We discount erotic pleasure as an end in itself. Our culture tends to identify sex with sexual intercourse, and the end of sexual intercourse is literally orgasm (especially male orgasm).

An Anthropological Perspective

A fundamental, biological fact about orgasm is that the male orgasm and ejaculation are required for reproduction, while the female orgasm is not. Whereas the male orgasm is universal in both animal and human species, sociobiologists and anthropologists have found immense variation in the experience of female orgasm. Anthropologists such as Margaret Mead (1967) found that some societies, such as the Mundugumor, emphasize the female orgasm, while it is virtually nonexistent in other societies, such as the Arapesh.

In our culture, women most consistently experience orgasm through clitoral stimulation; penile thrusting during intercourse is not always sufficient for clitoral stimulation. In cultures that cultivate female orgasm, according to sociobiologist Donald Symons (1979), there is, in addition to an absence of sexual repression, an emphasis placed on men's skill in arousing women. Among the Mangaians, for example, as boys enter adolescence, they are given expert advice on kissing and stimulating a woman's breasts, cunnilingus, and how to bring their partners to multiple orgasm before they themselves ejaculate (Marshall, 1971). In our own culture, among men who consider themselves (and are considered) good lovers, great emphasis is placed on their abilities to arouse and bring their partners to orgasm. These skills include not only penile penetration but, often more important, clitoral stimulation. The woman, of course, may also stimulate her own clitoris to experience orgasm.

The Tyranny of the Orgasm

Sociologist Philip Slater (1974) suggests that our preoccupation with orgasm is an extension of the Protestant work ethic, in which nothing is enjoyed for its own sake; everything is work, including sex. Thus, we "achieve" orgasm much as we achieve success. Those who achieve orgasm are the "successful workers" of sex; those who do not are the "failures."

As we look at our sexuality, we can see pressure to be successful lovers. Men talk of performance anxiety.

SUMMARY

Why Two Sexes?

• Sexual reproduction confers genetic variety on members of a species. Most organisms that reproduce sexually have two variations: female and male.

Female Sex Organs: What Are They For?

• Sex organs serve a reproductive purpose, but they perform other functions also: giving pleasure, attracting sex partners, and bonding in relationships.

• The external female *genitals* are known collectively as the *vulva*. The *mons pubis* is a pad of fatty tissue that covers the area of the pubic bone and is covered with pubic hair. The *clitoris* is the center of sexual arousal in the female. The *labia majora* are two folds of spongy flesh extending from the mons pubis and

We tend to evaluate a woman's sexual self-worth in terms of being orgasmic (able to have orgasms). For men, the significant question about women's sexuality has recently shifted from "Is she a virgin?" to "Is she orgasmic?"

Faking Orgasm

Although during sexual intercourse women are not as consistently orgasmic as men, there is considerable pressure on them to be so. In one study of almost 750 orgasmic women, 58% had faked orgasm at least once (Darling & Davidson, 1986). But the reason these women faked orgasm was not to protect themselves as much as to protect their partners. The most frequent reason given is the woman's desire to please her partner and to avoid hurting or disappointing him. Other reasons include fear of her own sexual inadequacy, to prevent her partner from seeking another partner, and to end boring or painful intercourse (Darling & Davidson, 1986).

"Was It Good for You?"

A question that women are often asked following intercourse is, "Was it good for you?" or its variation, "Did you have an orgasm?"

Such questions are usually asked by men rather than women, and women tend to resent them (Dar-

ling & Davidson, 1986). (In fact, Zilbergeld [1992] describes the question "Didjacome?" as a surefire turn-off.) Part of the pressure to pretend having an orgasm is caused by these questions. What is really being asked? If the woman experienced orgasm? If she enjoyed intercourse? If the man is a good lover? Or is the question just a signal that the lovemaking is over?

If a partner cares about the other's enjoyment and wants to improve the couple's erotic pleasures, the appropriate time to inquire about their lovemaking is not during or immediately following intercourse. Researchers Carol Darling and Kenneth Davidson (1986) advise that such discussion be initiated at a neutral time and place. Moreover, both women *and* men need to be free to inquire about their partner's satisfaction. The goal should be to increase a couple's fulfillment, rather than to complain about "performance" or soothe a ruffled ego. Even among lesbians, who undoubtedly are more acquainted with the ins and outs of female anatomy than most men are, partners need to be aware of making assumptions about what is sexually arousing. One woman comments (cited in Boston Women's Health Book Collective, 1992): "The more women I sleep with, the more I realize you can't assume what you like is what she likes. There are tremendous differences. All kinds of stuff needs to be talked about and often isn't."

enclosing the other external genitals. The *labia minora* are smooth, hairless folds within the labia majora that meet above the clitoris.

- The internal female sexual structures and reproductive organs include the vagina, the uterus, the cervix, the fallopian tubes, and the ovaries. The *vagina* is a flexible muscular organ that encompasses the penis during sexual intercourse and is the *birth canal* through which an infant is born. The mucous membranes lining the walls of the vagina produce secretions, which vary in color, consistency, odor, and quantity depending on the phase of a woman's menstrual cycle, her health, and her unique physical characteristics. The opening of the vagina, the *introitus*, is partially covered by a thin, perforated membrane, the *hymen*, prior to first intercourse or other intrusion.

- Controversial research has posited the existence of an erotically sensitive area, the *Grafenberg spot (G spot)*, on the front wall of the vagina midway between the introitus and the cervix. Stimulation of the G spot is said to lead to orgasm and, in some women, the ejaculation of a clear fluid from the urethra.

• The *uterus*, or womb, is a hollow, thick-walled, muscular organ; the tapered end, the *cervix*, extends downward and opens into the vagina. The lining of the uterine walls, the *endometrium*, is built up, then shed and expelled through the cervical *os* (opening) during menstruation. In the event of pregnancy, the pre-embryo is embedded in the nourishing endometrium. On each side of the uterus is one of a pair of *ovaries*, the female *gonads* (organs that produces *gametes*, sex cells containing the genetic material necessary for reproduction). At the top of the uterus are the *fallopian tubes* or uterine tubes. They extend toward the ovaries but are not attached to them. The funnel-shaped end of each tube (the *infundibulum*) fans out into fingerlike *fimbriae*, which drape over the ovary. Hair-like *cilia* on the fimbriae conduct the ovulated oocyte into the fallopian tube. The *ampulla* is the widened part of the tube in which fertilization normally occurs. Other important structures in the area of the genitals include the *urethra*, *anus*, and *perineum*.

• The reproductive function of the female breasts, or *mammary glands*, is to nourish the offspring through *lactation*, milk production. A breast is composed of fatty tissue and 15–25 lobes that radiate around a central protruding nipple. *Alveoli* within the lobes produce milk. Around the nipple is a ring of darkened skin called the *areola*. In our culture, breasts also serve an erotic function.

Female Sexual Physiology

• *Hormones* are chemical substances that serve as messengers, traveling through the bloodstream. Important hormones that act directly on the gonads *(gonadotropins)* are *follicle-stimulating hormone (FSH)* and *luteinizing hormone (LH)*. Hormones produced in the ovaries are *estrogen*, which helps regulate the menstrual cycle, and *progesterone*, which helps maintain the uterine lining.

• At birth the human female's ovaries contain 400,000–700,000 *oocytes*, female gametes. During childhood, many of these degenerate. In a woman's lifetime, about 400 oocytes will mature and be released, beginning in puberty when hormones trigger the completion of *oogenesis*, the production of oocytes, commonly called eggs or *ova*. About once a month, an oocyte completes meiosis I. *Meiosis* is the form of cell division in which a cell's nucleus undergoes two divisions, resulting in each of four "daughter" cells containing half the chromosomes of the original cell. Gametes are called *haploid cells* because they contain half the set of chromosomes needed for fertilization to occur; they must unite with another gamete, forming a *diploid cell* with twice as many chromosomes.

• The activities of the ovaries and the development of oocytes for *ovulation*, the expulsion of the oocyte, are described as the three-phase *ovarian cycle*. The phases are *follicular* (maturation of the oocyte), *ovulatory* (expulsion of the oocyte), and *luteal* (hormone production by the *corpus luteum*). The cycle averages 28 days in length.

• The *menstrual cycle* (or uterine cycle), like the ovarian cycle, is divided into three phases. The shedding of the endometrium marks the beginning of the *menstrual phase*. With other cervical and vaginal secretions, a small amount of blood is expelled through the vagina. The menstrual flow, or *menses*, generally occurs over a period of 2–5 days. Endometrial tissue builds up during the *proliferative phase*; it produces nutrients to sustain an embryo in the *secretory phase*.

- Some societies view menstruation as problematic. They may isolate menstruating women or view menstrual blood as darkly powerful; others (such as ours) may simply view menstruating women as being overly emotional or unpredictable. The most severe menstrual problems have been attributed to *premenstrual syndrome (PMS)*, a cluster of severe physical and emotional symptoms, which are not agreed upon because of contradictory studies. The most common symptoms include dysphoria (depression, nervousness, irritability, anxiety), fluid retention, breast tenderness, headache, fatigue, and food cravings. Some women experience pelvic cramping and pain during the menstrual cycle (*dysmenorrhea*). When women do not menstruate for reasons other than aging, the condition is called *amenorrhea*. A principal cause of amenorrhea is pregnancy.

Female Sexual Response

- The *Masters and Johnson Four-Phase Model of Sexual Response* identifies the significant stages of response as excitement, plateau, orgasm, and resolution. *Kaplan's Tri-Phasic Model of Sexual Response* consists of three phases: desire, excitement, and orgasm.

- The physical manifestations of sexual arousal involve a complex interaction of thoughts and feelings, sensory organs, neural responses, and hormonal reactions occurring in many parts of the body, including the cerebral cortex and *limbic system* of the brain, the nervous system, the circulatory system, the endocrine glands, and the genitals. The sex drive, or libido, in both men and women is biologically influenced by the hormone testosterone. For both males and females, physiological changes during sexual excitement depend on two processes: *vasocongestion*, the concentration of blood in body tissues, such as the penis, clitoris, labia, or breasts; and *myotonia*, increased muscle tension with approaching orgasm. For women, the first sign of sexual excitement is the moistening of the vaginal walls, or *sweating*. The inner two-thirds of the vagina expands in a process called *tenting*; the labia may enlarge or flatten and separate; the clitoris swells. Breathing and heart rate increase. The nipples become erect, and the breasts may enlarge somewhat. The uterus elevates. As excitement increases, the clitoris retracts beneath the clitoral hood. The vaginal opening decreases by about one-third, and its outer third becomes more congested, forming the *orgasmic platform*.

- Continued stimulation brings *orgasm*, rhythmic contractions of the vagina, uterus, and pelvic muscles, accompanied by very pleasurable sensations. Women are often able to be orgasmic following a previous orgasm if they continue to be stimulated. The role of the female orgasm is largely determined by culture.

KEY TERMS

genitals	labia majora	hymen
vulva	labia minora	Grafenberg spot
mons pubis	vestibule	uterus
mons veneris	Bartholin's glands	cervix
clitoris	vagina	endometrium
glans clitoridis	coitus	os
clitoral hood	birth canal	ovary
crura	introitus	gonad

gamete

oocyte

ovum

ovulation

ovarian follicle

vesicular follicle

Graffian follicle

corpus luteum

fallopian tube

infundibulum

fimbriae

cilia

ampulla

urethra

urethral opening

anus

perineum

pelvic floor

lactation

mammary gland

areola

alveoli

hormone

gonadotropin

estrogen

oogenesis

meiosis

haploid cell

diploid cell

ovarian cycle

gonadotropin-releasing hormone (GnRH)

follicle-stimulating hormone (FSH)

luteinizing hormone (LH)

follicular phase

ovulatory phase

mittelshmerz

progesterone

luteal phase

menstrual cycle

menstrual phase

menses

proliferative phase

secretory phase

menarche

premenstrual syndrome (PMS)

dysmenorrhea

prostaglandins

amenorrhea

Masters and Johnson Four-Phase Model of Sexual Response

Kaplan Tri-Phasic Model of Sexual Response

limbic system

erogenous zone

pheromone

vasocongestion

myotonia

sweating

tenting

sex flush

orgasmic platform

orgasm

SUGGESTIONS FOR FURTHER READING

Ackerman, Diane. *A Natural History of the Senses*. New York: Random House, 1990. A sensual (and surprising) exploration of our experiences in the physical world.

Buckley, Thomas, and Alma Gottlieb, eds. *Blood Magic: The Anthropology of Menstruation*. Berkeley: University of California Press, 1988. Studies of menstruation in a variety of cultures.

Dan, Alice J., and Linda L. Lewis. *Menstrual Health in Women's Lives*. Urbana/Chicago: University of Illinois Press, 1992. A practical, positive self-help guide.

Ladas, Alice Kahn, Beverly Whipple, and John D. Perry. *The G Spot and Other Recent Discoveries About Human Sexuality*. New York: Dell, 1983. Controversial studies of the Grafenberg spot and female ejaculation.

Lark, Susan. *Premenstrual Syndrome Self-Help Book: A Woman's Guide to Feeling Good All Month*. Berkeley, CA: Celestial Arts, 1989. Helpful information and advice for women who experience PMS or other menstruation-related discomfort.

Madaras, Lynda, and Jane Patterson. *Womancare: A Gynecological Guide to Your Body*. New York: Avon Books, 1984. A thorough, very readable guide to women's gynecological health.

Sloane, Ethel. *Biology of Women*. Albany, NY: Delmar, 1985. A feminist perspective on female anatomy and physiology.

Chapter Four

MALE SEXUAL ANATOMY, PHYSIOLOGY, AND RESPONSE

PREVIEW: SELF-QUIZ

1. Erection of the penis is caused by muscle contractions. True or false?

2. An erection is not always a sign of sexual interest. True or false?

3. Semen is produced within the testicles. True or false?

4. Male breasts basically consist of the same structures as females breasts. True or false?

5. It has been scientifically proven that the hormone testosterone causes aggression. True or false?

6. Men as well as women experience mood cycles. True or false?

7. It takes about a day for a sperm to be created. True or false?

8. An important function of semen is to provide nourishment for sperm. True or false?

9. Men may experience orgasm without ejaculation and vice versa. True or false?

10. The average number of sperm expelled in an ejaculation is around one million. True or false?

ANSWERS 1. F, 2. T, 3. F, 4. T, 5. F, 6. T, 7. F, 8. T, 9. T, 10. F

Chapter Outline

It's clear that male sexual structures and functions differ in many ways from those of females. What may not be as apparent, however, is that there are also a number of similarities in the functions of the sex organs and the sexual response patterns of both men and women. In the previous chapter, we learned that the sexual structures of both females and males derive from the same embryonic tissue (see Figure 3.1). But when it receives the signals to begin differentiation into a male, the embryonic reproductive organs begin to change their appearance dramatically.

MALE SEX ORGANS: WHAT ARE THEY FOR?

Where you tend a rose, my lad, a thistle cannot grow.
Frances Hodgson Burnett

Like female sex organs, male sex organs serve several functions. In their reproductive role, a man's sex organs manufacture and store gametes and deliver them to a woman's reproductive tract. Some of the organs, especially the penis, provide a source of physical pleasure for both their owners and their owners' partners.

External Structures

The external male sexual structures are the penis and the scrotum.

The Penis The **penis** (from the Latin word for tail) is the organ through which both sperm and urine pass. It is attached to the male perineum, the

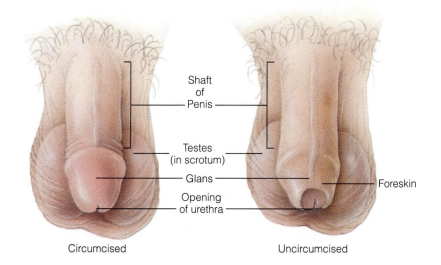

FIGURE 4.1 External Sexual Structures.

Shaft
of
Penis

Testes
(in scrotum)

Glans

Opening
of urethra

Foreskin

Circumcised

Uncircumcised

diamond-shaped region extending from the pubic bone to the coccyx (the tail bone).

Structure of the Penis The penis consists of three main sections: the root, the shaft, and the head (Figure 4.1). The **root** attaches the penis within the pelvic cavity, while the body of the penis, the **shaft,** hangs free. At the end of the shaft is the enlarged head of the penis, the **glans penis,** and at its tip is the urethral opening. The rim at the base of the glans is known as the **corona.** On the underside of the penis is a triangular area of sensitive skin called the **frenulum,** which attaches the glans to the foreskin. The glans penis is particularly important in sexual arousal because it contains a relatively high concentration of nerve endings, making it especially responsive to stimulation.

A loose skin covers the shaft of the penis and extends to cover the glans penis; the sleevelike covering of the glans is known as the **foreskin** or **prepuce.** It can be pulled back easily to expose the glans. In the United States, the foreskins of male infants are often surgically removed by an operation called **circumcision.** As a result of this operation, the glans penis is left exposed. The reasons for circumcision seem to be rooted more in tradition, hospital profits, and religious beliefs (it is an important ritual in Judaism and Islam) than in any firmly established health principles (see Chapter 13). Beneath the foreskin are several small glands that produce an oily substance called **smegma.** If smegma accumulates, it thickens and produces a foul odor. It is important for uncircumcised adult men to observe good hygiene by periodically retracting the skin and washing the glans to remove the smegma. Lack of proper hygiene may be associated with sexually transmitted diseases, urinary infections, and penile cancer (McAninch, 1989; Rotolo & Lynch, 1991).

The shaft of the penis contains three parallel columns of erectile tissue. The two that extend along the front surface are known as the **corpora cavernosa** (cavernous bodies), and the third, which runs beneath them, is called the **corpus spongiosum** (spongy body). At the root of the penis, the corpora cavernosa form the **crura,** which are anchored by muscle to the

The clitoris, hidden by a hoodlike fold of the labia, is so tiny and insignificant in size that various thinkers have referred to it, darkly, as the missing penis. Freud thought the phrase "the missing penis" was a good description of the difference between men and women. However, this is no more reasonable than to assume that the difference between men and women is "the missing clitoris"—in men.

Ruth Herschberger

pubic bone. The **urethra,** a tube that transports both urine and semen, runs from the bladder (where it expands to form the **urethral bulb**), through the spongy body, to the tip of the penis, where it opens to the outside. Inside the three chambers are a large number of blood vessels through which blood freely circulates when the penis is flaccid (relaxed). During sexual arousal, these vessels fill with blood and expand, causing the penis to become erect. (Sexual arousal, including erection, is discussed in greater detail later in the chapter.)

In an unaroused state, the *average* penis is slightly under 4 inches long, although there is a great deal of individual variation. When erect, penises become more uniform in size, as the percentage of volume increase is greater with smaller penises than with larger ones. But even in an unaroused state, penis size may vary. Cold air, water, fear, or anxiety, for example, often cause the penis to be pulled closer to the body and decrease its size. When the penis is erect, the urinary duct is temporarily blocked, allowing for the ejaculation of semen. But erection does not necessarily mean sexual excitement. A man may have erections at night during REM sleep, the phase of the sleep cycle when dreaming occurs (Chung & Choi, 1990; Marshall, Surridge, & Delva, 1981) or when he is anxious, for example.

Myths About the Penis Myths about the penis, which appear to be believed more by men than by women, equate its size with masculinity, aggressiveness, sexual ability, and sexual attractiveness. Men may also mistakenly believe that the penis will shrink or atrophy if they don't have frequent sexual relations ("Use it or lose it"). People may also believe—or at least joke about—the relationship of a man's hand, foot, thumb, or nose size to that of his penis. Some penis myths are racist, implying that members of a particular race have particularly large or small organs and that their sexual abilities are directly proportional.

It is fairly common for men to worry about their penis size, especially in adolescence, since the growth of the penis is one of the marks of puberty. But apparently a significant number of adult men are also quite convinced that everyone else's penis is larger than theirs (Strage, 1980). Popular novels do little to reassure the average man; they often feature penises so big, so hard, and so rambunctious that women weep, wail, or faint dead away. Men's magazines frequently exploit male anxieties with advertisements of penis enlargers; regrettably for the men who send in their $25, the devices work no better than spaghetti stretchers (Glenn, 1981). A 28-year-old man expressed this feeling (quoted in Zilbergeld, 1992):

> You would think I'd know better. I mean, I'm well educated and have read a lot about sex. But I still believe that I'd be more attractive to women and a better lover if my penis was an inch or two longer and an inch wider.

The size of the penis, whether unaroused or erect, is not specifically related to a man's body size, weight, muscular structure, race, masculinity, or sexual orientation. Its size is determined by individual hereditary factors. Furthermore, there is no relationship between the size of a man's penis and his ability to have sexual intercourse or to excite his partner. A large penis will not make a woman have an orgasm any more than a small one will (Masters & Johnson, 1966) (see Perspective 1).

It is a Freudian thesis, with which I am inclined to agree, that the pistol, whether in the hands of an amateur or a professional gunman, has significance for the owner as a symbol of virility, an extension of the male organ, and that excessive interest in guns is a form of fetishism.

Ian Fleming

Nowhere does one read of a penis that quietly moseyed out for a look at what was going on before springing and crashing into action.

Bernie Zilbergeld

It can be safely said that the adult male population suffers an almost universal anxiety in regard to penile size.

James F. Glenn, MD

THE PENIS: MORE THAN MEETS THE EYE

Man's preoccupation with his "generative organ" extends far back into history and appears in diverse cultures in every part of the world. The penis is an almost universal symbol of power and fertility. It may also be a source of considerable anxiety for the individual human who happens to possess one.

Power to the Penis

Earthenware figurines from ancient Peru, ink drawings from medieval Japan, painted walls in the villas of Pompeii—in the art and artifacts from every corner of the world, we find a common theme: penises! And not just any old penises, but organs of such length, girth, and weight that they can barely be supported by their possessors. Whether as an object of worship or an object of jest, the giant penis has been (and continues to be) a symbol that holds deep cultural significance, especially in societies where men are dominant over women (Strage, 1980). While it seems reasonable for the erect penis to be used as a symbol of love or at least lust, many of its associations seem to be as an instrument of aggression and power. In New Guinea, Kiwai hunters pressed their penises against the trees from which they would make their harpoons, thereby assuring the strength and straightness of their weapons. Maori warriors in New Zealand crawled under the legs of their chief so that the power of his penis would descend onto them (Strage, 1980).

In classical Greece, stone columns called *hermae* each sported a carved male head on top and sprouted a prominent *phallos* (penis) from the front. These columns were erected throughout city and countryside as signposts, markers, and milestones. When, on the eve of a military expedition planned by the Athenians, hundreds of *hermae* were "unmanned" by persons unknown, the army was thrown into a panic, and the battle plans had to be temporarily scrapped (Keuls, 1985).

Even today, there are many people who would argue that men are deeply attached to symbolic images of their potency—cars, motorcycles, missiles, and especially guns. Lest they become confused as to which is the symbol and which the reality, young grunts in Marine bootcamp are instructed in the following drill (to be shouted with appropriate gestures):

> This is my rifle! This is my gun!
> This is for fighting! This is for fun!

To take away a man's gun is to threaten him with impotence. (The word "potent" is from the Latin *potens*, meaning ability or power; the word "impotent," in addition to meaning powerless, also implies the inability to get an erection.)

In many cultures, the penis has also represented fertility and prosperity. In India, large stone phalluses (*lingams*), associated with the Hindu god Siva, are adorned with flowers and propitiated with offerings. Ancient peoples as diverse as the Maya in Central America and the Egyptians in Africa believed that the blood from the penises of their rulers was especially powerful. Mayan kings ceremonially pierced their penises with sting-ray spines, and the pharaohs and high priests of Egypt underwent ritual circumcision. In other places, men have ritually offered their semen to assure a plentiful harvest. According to the legends of some Amazonian peoples, the Milky Way is actually the "seminal flow that fertilizes all of . . . the underlying biosphere" (Reichel-Dolmatoff, 1971).

"Phallic Phallacies"

It is interesting (but perhaps not surprising) that the responsibility of owning an instrument of great power can carry with it an equally great burden of anxiety. In some ways, the choice of the penis as a symbol of domination seems rather unwise. Any man (and a good many women) can tell you that a penis can be disturbingly unreliable and appear to have a mind of its own.

(continued)

THE PENIS: MORE THAN MEETS THE EYE (continued)

For men who are already insecure or lacking in confidence about their abilities on the job or in the bedroom, the penis can take on meanings quite beyond those of simple procreation, elimination, or sensual pleasure. How can a man be expected to control his employees, his wife, his children, or even his dog when he can't control the behavior of his own penis?

As discussed already in Chapter 2, according to Sigmund Freud, women were unconsciously jealous of men's penises and felt deeply inadequate for not having one (penis envy). While women may feel inadequate (or depressed, or just plain mad), it may well be due to lack of status rather than lack of penis. Those who most appear to suffer from penis envy are men, who although they indeed possess a penis, often seem to long for a bigger one. The idea that "the larger the penis the more effective the male in coital connection" is referred to by Masters and Johnson as a "phallic phallacy" (Masters & Johnson, 1966). Another manifestation of penile anxiety, also named by Freud, is castration anxiety (see Chapter 2). Mark Strage points out that this term is misleading, for it does not describe what the actual fear is about. Castration is the removal of the testes, but castration anxiety is fear of losing the penis. Strage (1980) writes: "The most pervasive evidence for the existence and intensity of male anxiety regarding the penis may be that . . . we cannot even bring ourselves to utter its correct name." In China and other parts of Asia and Africa, there have been documented epidemics of *koro* (a Japanese term), the conviction that one's penis is shrinking and is going to disappear. A doctor in Singapore in 1968 reported 4500 cases of *koro*, which appears to have no physiological basis but to grow in the psyches of anxiety-prone men (Yap, 1993).

Rising Anxiety

Mark Strage (1980) makes the case that penile anxiety has resulted in men's efforts "to segregate women, to impute them with sinister intentions, and to persecute and punish them." Moreover, he goes on, "the level of this male anxiety rises as women, through no action or fault of their own, are perceived in a context of increased femaleness or sexuality." Finally, he states, men have devised ways "to resolve, or at least attenuate their anxiety—thereby inflicting harm on women, on the world, and, perhaps most grievously, on themselves." On the subject of performance anxiety, therapist Bernie Zilbergeld (1992) says:

> It's not easy to always have to perform and succeed, whether on the athletic field, in the boardroom, or in the bedroom. . . . It's not unusual for athletes to throw up in locker rooms before competition . . . and to get themselves in a murderous rage that under any other circumstances would rightfully be considered psychotic. This process, by the way, is often called "getting it up." . . . Being a male is like living in a suit of armor, ready for battle to prove himself. The armor may offer protection (although it's not clear against what), but it's horribly confining and not much fun.

For his own psyche's sake, as well as the sake of his partner and that of society, a man would do well to consider how his feelings about his penis and his masculinity affect his well-being. At this point, we can only speculate, but perhaps there will come a time when men will allow themselves to focus less on the size and performance of their equipment—both sexual and martial—and more on acceptance, communication, and the mutual sharing of pleasure.

The penis is a prominent symbol in both ancient and modern art. Here we see a contemporary phallic sculpture in Frogner Park, Oslo, Norway, and a pair of well-endowed ceremonial figures from Nigeria.

The Scrotum Hanging loosely at the root of the penis is the **scrotum,** a pouch of skin that holds the two testicles. The skin of the scrotum is more heavily pigmented than the skin elsewhere on the body; it is sparsely covered with hair and divided in the middle by a ridge of skin. The skin of the scrotum varies in appearance under different conditions. When a man is sexually aroused, for example, or when he is cold, the testicles are pulled close to the body, causing the skin to wrinkle and become more compact. The changes in the surface of the scrotum help maintain a fairly constant temperature within the testicles (about 93°F). Two sets of muscles control these changes: the **dartos muscle,** a smooth muscle under the skin, contracts and causes the surface to wrinkle; the fibrous **cremaster muscle** within the scrotal sac causes the testes to elevate.

Internal Structures

Male internal reproductive organs and structures include the testes (testicles), seminiferous tubules, epididymis, vas deferens, ejaculatory ducts, seminal vesicles, prostate gland, and Cowper's (bulbourethral) glands (Figure 4.2).

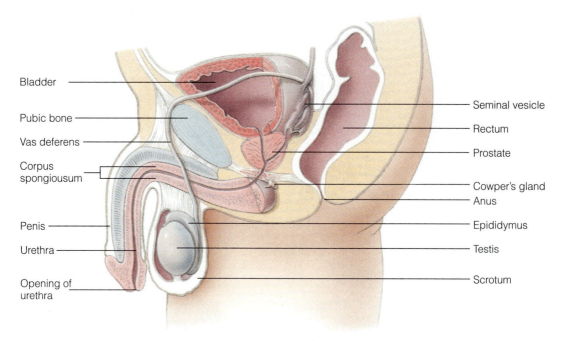

Bladder

Pubic bone

Vas deferens

Corpus spongiousum

Penis

Urethra

Opening of urethra

Seminal vesicle

Rectum

Prostate

Cowper's gland

Anus

Epididymus

Testis

Scrotum

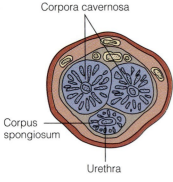

Corpora cavernosa

Corpus spongiosum

Urethra

Underside of penis (cross section)

FIGURE 4.2 Internal Male Sexual Structures.

The Testes Inside the scrotum are the male reproductive glands or gonads, which are called **testicles** or **testes** (singular, *testis*). The testes have two major functions: sperm production and hormone production. Each olive-shaped testis is about 1.5 inches long and 1 inch in diameter and weighs about 1 ounce; as a male ages, the testis decreases in size and weight. The testicles are usually not symmetrical; the left testicle generally hangs slightly lower than the right one. Within the scrotal sac, each testicle is suspended by a **spermatic cord** containing nerves, blood vessels, and a vas deferens, the tube that carries sperm from the testicle (Figure 4.3). Within each testicle are around 1000 **seminiferous tubules,** tiny, tightly compressed tubes 1–3 feet long (they would extend several hundred yards if laid end to end). Within these tubes, the process of spermatogenesis, the production of sperm, takes place.

As a male fetus grows, the testes develop within the pelvic cavity; toward the end of the gestation period, the testes usually descend into the scrotum. In about 3–4% of cases, however, one or both of the testes fail to descend (McClure, 1988). In premature births, the incidence is much higher— around 30%. This condition, known as **cryptorchidism,** usually corrects itself within a year or two. If the testes have not descended by this time, medical advice should be sought. Treatment such as hormone therapy or surgery may be advised, as the warmer temperature within the body cavity can inhibit normal sperm production and lead to infertility. Cryptorchidism is also associated with increased risk of testicular cancer.

The Epididymis and Vas Deferens The epididymis and vas deferens (or ductus deferens) are the ducts that carry sperm from the testicles to the urethra for ejaculation. The seminiferous tubules merge to form the **epididymis,** a comma-shaped structure consisting of a coiled tube about 20 feet

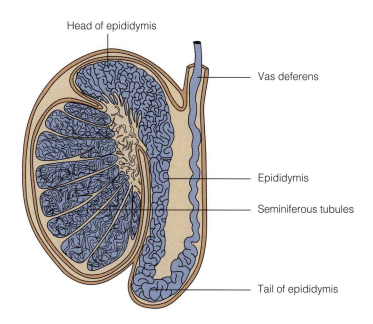

Head of epididymis

Vas deferens

Epididymis

Seminiferous tubules

Tail of epididymis

FIGURE 4.3 Cross Section of a Testicle.

long, where the sperm finally mature. Each epididymis merges into a **vas deferens** (plural, *vasa deferentia*), a tube about 18 inches long, extending into the abdominal cavity, over the bladder, and then downward, widening into the flask-shaped **ampulla.** The vas deferens joins the **ejaculatory duct** within the prostate gland. The vas deferens can be felt easily in the scrotal sac. Since it is easily accessible and is crucial for sperm transport, it is usually the point of sterilization for men. The operation is called a vasectomy (it is discussed fully in Chapter 12). A vasectomy does not affect the ability to ejaculate since only the sperm are transported through the vas deferens. Most of the semen that is ejaculated comes from the prostate gland and the seminal vesicles.

The Seminal Vesicles, Prostate Gland, and Cowper's Glands At the back of the bladder lie two glands, each about the size and shape of a finger. These **seminal vesicles** secrete a fluid that makes up about 60% of the seminal fluid. The tube from each seminal vesicle forms the ejaculatory duct where it joins the tubes that exit the ampullae of the vasa deferentia. Encircling the urethra just below the bladder is a small muscular gland about the size and shape of a chestnut. The **prostate gland** produces about 30–35% of the seminal fluid that makes up the ejaculated semen. These secretions flow into the urethra through a system of tiny ducts. Some men who enjoy receiving anal sex experience erotic sensations when the prostate is gently stroked; others find that contact with the prostate is uncomfortable (Morin, 1986). Men, especially if they are older, may be troubled by a variety of prostate problems, ranging from relatively benign conditions to more serious inflammations and prostate cancer. (Problems and diseases of the prostate are covered in Chapter 14.)

Below the prostate gland are two pea-sized glands connected to the urethra by tiny ducts. These are **Cowper's glands** or **bulbourethral glands,** which secrete a thick, clear mucus prior to ejaculation. This fluid may appear at the tip of the erect penis; its alkaline content may help buffer the acidity within the urethra and provide a more hospitable environment for sperm. Fluid from the Cowper's glands may contain sperm that have remained in the urethra since a previous ejaculation or that have leaked in from the ampullae.

The Breasts and Other Structures

Male anatomical structures that do not serve a reproductive function but may be involved in or affected by sexual activities include the breasts, urethra, buttocks, rectum, and anus.

Breasts While the male breast contains the same basic structures as the female breast—nipple, areola, fat, and glandular tissue—the amounts of underlying fatty and glandular tissues are much smaller in men. Our culture appears to be ambivalent about the erotic function of a man's breasts. We usually do not even call them breasts, but refer to the general area as the chest. Some men find stimulation of their breasts to be sexually arousing, while others do not. Heterosexual women and gay men may find the sight and/or feel of a man's breast to be erotically pleasing. Society in general, however, does not acknowledge this potential eroticism, as witnessed by the freedom with which men are allowed to expose their naked chests. (But prior to the 1930s, it was considered indecent for a man to show his breasts in public.) **Gynecomastia,** the swelling or enlargement of the male breast, can occur during adolescence or adulthood. In puberty, gynecomastia is a normal response to hormonal changes, as we discuss in Chapter 6. In adulthood, its causes may include alcoholism, liver or thyroid disease, or cancer.

Evolutionary biologist Stephen Jay Gould, who writes a column for *Natural History* magazine, says that the subject that evokes the most confusion among those who write to him is male nipples. What are they for? They're not "for" anything, Gould explains, but they develop from the same embryonic structures as female nipples. In other words, men have nipples because women have them (Why Gal, 1992).

Other Structures In men, the urethra serves as the passageway for both urine and semen. Because the urinary opening is at the tip of the penis, it is vulnerable to injury and infection. The sensitive mucous membranes around the opening may be subject to abrasion and can provide an entrance into the body for infectious organisms. Condoms, properly used, provide an effective barrier between this vulnerable area and potentially infectious secretions or other substances. Men's buttocks may be a source of sexual attraction. For both women and men, the buttocks, anus, and rectum may be erotically sensitive. Both men and women may enjoy oral stimulation of the anus ("rimming"); the insertion of fingers, a hand ("fisting"), a dildo, or a penis into the rectum may bring erotic pleasure to both the receiver and the giver. (Anal sex is discussed more fully in Chapter 10; safer sex guidelines appear in Chapter 16.)

If I worship any particular thing it shall be some of the spread of my body;

Translucent mould of me it shall be you,

Shaded ledges and rests, firm masculine coulter, it shall be you,

Whatever goes to the tilth of me it shall be you,

You my rich blood, your milky stream pale strippings of my life;

Breast that presses against other breasts it shall be you.

My brain it shall be your occult convolutions,

Root of washed sweet-flag, timorous pond-snipe, nest of guarded duplicate eggs, it shall be you . . .
                                    Walt Whitman

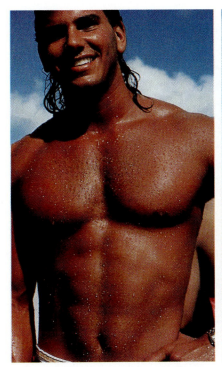

MALE SEXUAL PHYSIOLOGY

The reproductive processes of the male body include the production of hormones and the production and delivery of sperm, the male gametes. Although men do not have a monthly reproductive cycle comparable to that of women, they do experience regular fluctuations of hormone levels; there is also some evidence that men's moods follow a cyclical pattern.

Sex Hormones

Within the connective tissues of a man's testes are **Leydig cells** (also called interstitial cells), which secrete **androgens** (male hormones). The most important of these is testosterone, which triggers sperm production and regulates the sex drive. Other important hormones in male reproductive physiology are GnRH, FSH, and LH (also known as ICSH), which were discussed in Chapter 3 in regard to their influence on the female reproductive cycle. In addition, men produce the protein hormone *inhibin* and small amounts of estrogen (see Table 4.1).

Testosterone As discussed in Chapter 3, **testosterone** is a steroid hormone synthesized from cholesterol. In men, it is produced principally within the testes; small amounts are also secreted by the adrenal glands. During puberty, besides acting on the seminiferous tubules to produce sperm, testosterone targets other areas of the body. It causes the penis, testicles, and other reproductive organs to grow and is responsible for the development of

TABLE 4.1 Male Reproductive Hormones

Hormone	Where Produced	Functions
Testosterone	Testes, adrenal glands	Stimulates sperm production in testes, triggers development of secondary sex characteristics, regulates sex drive
GnRH	Hypothalamus	Stimulates pituitary during sperm production
FSH	Pituitary	Stimulates sperm production in testes
ICSH (LH)	Pituitary	Stimulates testosterone production in interstitial cells within testes
Inhibin	Testes	Regulates sperm production by inhibiting release of FSH
Relaxin	Prostate	Increases sperm motility

secondary sex characteristics, such as pubic, facial, and underarm hair, and for the deepening of the voice. It also influences the growth of bones and increase of muscle mass and causes the skin to thicken and become oilier (leading to acne in many teenage boys). In addition to stimulating sexual interest, testosterone may also play a role in aggressiveness, according to some studies. Researcher Hilary Lips suggests, however, that these studies need to be carefully interpreted. While there is some evidence that prenatal exposure to excess testosterone leads to increased rough-and-tumble play among children of both sexes (Hines, 1982; Reinisch, 1991), the connection between such play and actual aggressive behavior has not been adequately demonstrated (Lips, 1992).

The Brain-Testicular Axis Before discussing sperm production, it is useful to understand the influence of hormones on the process. A complex feedback system involving the hypothalamus, the pituitary gland, and the testes regulates the events of spermatogenesis; this system is called the **brain-testicular axis** (Marieb, 1992) (Figure 4.4). The events in this process, which bears a number of similarities to the female ovarian cycle, are as follows:

1. Falling testosterone levels cause the hypothalamus to release gonadotropin-releasing hormone (GnRH), which then stimulates the pituitary to release follicle-stimulating hormone (FSH) and luteinizing hormone (LH).

2. FSH stimulates sperm production in the testes. First, it stimulates the release of androgen-binding protein (ABP). Then, the ABP causes the sperm-producing cells to accumulate testosterone, which stimulates sperm growth.

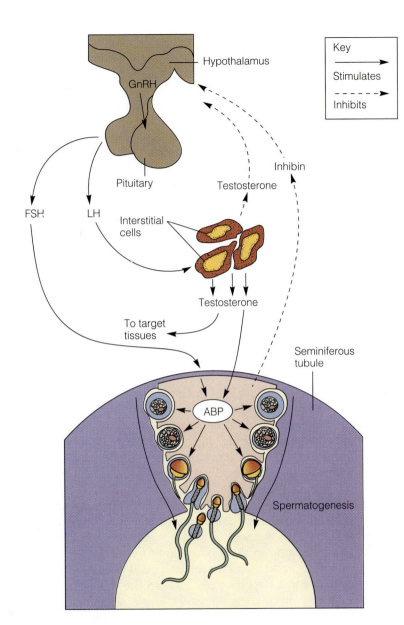

Key
→ Stimulates
- - -▶ Inhibits

Hypothalamus
GnRH
Pituitary
FSH
LH
Interstitial cells
Testosterone
Inhibin
Testosterone
To target tissues
Seminiferous tubule
ABP
Spermatogenesis

FIGURE 4.4 The Brain-Testicular Axis. The process of sperm production is regulated by a feedback system referred to as the brain-testicular axis. Hormones produced by the hypothalamus, pituitary, and testes are involved.

3. LH binds to the cells (interstitial cells) that secrete testosterone within the testes, stimulating its production. For this reason, LH is often referred to as interstitial cell-stimulating hormone, or ICSH, in men. The seminiferous tubules are then bathed in high concentrations of testosterone, which is also dispersed through other parts of the body in the bloodstream.

4. Testosterone inhibits the release of GnRH by the hypothalamus. The hormone **inhibin,** which increases as the sperm count rises, inhibits the release of FSH from the pituitary (and probably also inhibits the release of GnRH from the hypothalamus). Then, as the sperm count decreases, inhibin decreases, testosterone decreases, and the cycle begins again.

Male Cycles Studies comparing men and women have found that both sexes are subject to changes in mood and behavior patterns (Lips, 1992). Whereas such changes in women are often attributed (rightly or wrongly) to menstrual cycle fluctuations, it is not clear that male changes are related to levels of testosterone or other hormones, although there may well be a connection. Men do appear to undergo cyclic changes, although their testosterone levels do not fluctuate as dramatically as do women's estrogen and progesterone levels. On a daily basis, men's testosterone levels appear to be lowest around 8:00 P.M. and highest around 4:00 A.M. (Gorman, 1992). Moreover, their overall levels appear to be relatively lower in the spring and higher in the fall. While the effects of higher or lower testosterone levels on the emotions or mental processes are not well understood, a study did find that on tests involving the mental rotation of objects, men performed better in the spring than in the fall (Gouchie & Kimura, 1991). Other studies found evidence of men's mood patterns repeating in periodic cycles ranging from four to nine weeks (Ramey, 1972). As researchers pay more attention to the phenomenon of male cycles, they "begin to see that the menstrual cycle in women is not unique among human cycles in the magnitude of its effects" (Lips, 1992).

Spermatogenesis

Within the testes, from puberty on, **spermatogenesis,** the production of sperm, is an ongoing process. Every day, a healthy, fertile man produces several hundred million sperm within the seminiferous tubules of his testicles (Figure 4.5). The cause of infertility in some men may be the result of a hormone deficiency or a physical impairment that inhibits one or more of the stages of spermatogenesis. (Infertility is discussed further in Chapter 13.)

Meiosis Like oogenesis, spermatogenesis involves the type of cell division known as meiosis. In meiosis, as discussed in Chapter 3, a cell undergoes two consecutive divisions without a second replication of chromosomes between divisions, resulting in the production of four daughter cells, each with half the number of chromosomes as the original cell. Prior to puberty, cells called **spermatogonia** ("sperm seeds") within the seminiferous tubules of the testes divide by mitosis, the process of simple replication. With the onset of puberty, however, the spermatogonia begin to produce two distinct types of cells. The "type A" cell remains within the membrane, but the "type B" cell becomes a **primary spermatocyte,** which will divide during meiosis II to become four spherical **spermatids.**

Spermiogenesis The spermatid is destined to become a **spermatozoon** (*sper-mat-o-ZO-un*) or **sperm,** but it must first undergo **spermiogenesis,** giving up its excess cytoplasm (cellular material) and developing a whiplike tail. The sperm consists of three sections: the *head,* containing the gamete's nucleus with its DNA; the *midpiece,* containing tightly coiled cell structures called mitochondria, which provide energy to the sperm; and the **flagellum,** or tail, which propels the sperm in a jerky, more-or-less forward motion. The flattened head of the sperm is encased in a helmetlike **acrosome** containing enzymes that will assist in the penetration of an oocyte's wall, should the sperm ever get that far. After they are formed in the seminiferous tubules,

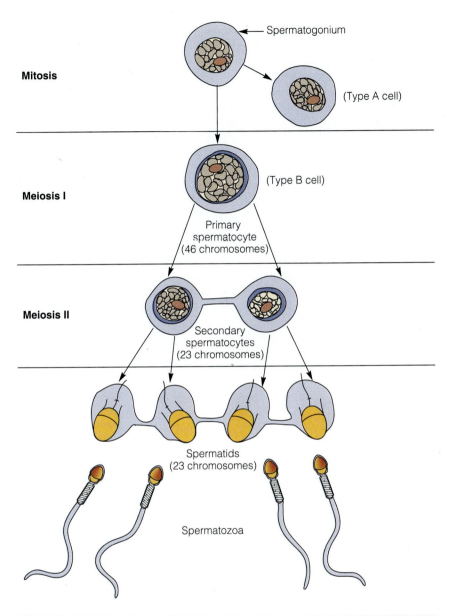

Mitosis

Spermatogonium

(Type A cell)

Meiosis I

(Type B cell)

Primary
spermatocyte
(46 chromosomes)

Meiosis II

Secondary
spermatocytes
(23 chromosomes)

Spermatids
(23 chromosomes)

Spermatozoa

FIGURE 4.5 Spermatogenesis. This diagram shows the development of spermatozoa, beginning with a single spermatogonium and ending with four complete sperm cells. Spermatogenesis is an ongoing process that begins in puberty. Several hundred million sperm are produced every day within the seminiferous tubules of a healthy man.

which takes 64–72 days, immature sperm are stored in the epididymis. It then takes about 20 days for the sperm to travel the length of the epididymis, during which time they become fertile and motile (able to move). Upon ejaculation, sperm in the tail section of the epididymis are expelled by muscular contractions of its walls into the vas deferens; similar contractions within the ampulla of the vas deferens propel the sperm into the urethra, where they are mixed with semen and then expelled from the urethral opening.

Blood-Testis Barrier Because sperm are formed from cells that have undergone meiosis II, they are genetically different from other body cells

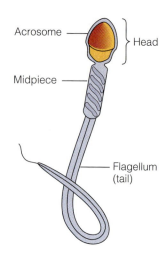

Acrosome — Head

Midpiece —

Flagellum (tail) —

The human spermatozoon (sperm) consists of three sections: head, midpiece, and whiplike tail (flagellum). The head contains the sperm's nucleus, including the chromosomes, and is encased in a helmetlike acrosome. Between 100 million and 600 million sperm are present in the semen from a single ejaculation. Typically, following ejaculation during intercourse, less than 100 will get as far as a fallopian tube, where an ovulated oocyte is present. (It takes just one sperm, however, to ultimately achieve fertilization.)

(containing only half the genetic material of the other kinds of cells). Normally, the immune system will attack cells it does not recognize as "self." If sperm were so attacked, sterility would result. Sperm, however, are protected by the **blood-testis barrier,** which prevents antigens from the developing sperm from getting into the bloodstream and provoking an immune response. (See Chapter 17 for a discussion of the immune system.) Developing sperm may be affected, however, by radiation and environmental toxins such as lead, pesticides, and chemical solvents. Alcohol, marijuana, and a number of commonly prescribed drugs can also influence spermatogenesis, causing the formation of abnormal sperm or lowering a man's fertility.

Sex Determination   As discussed in Chapter 3, the sex of the zygote produced by the union of egg and sperm is determined by the chromosomes of the sperm. The ovum always contributes a female sex chromosome (X), whereas the sperm may contribute either a female or a male sex chromosome (Y). The combination of two X chromosomes (XX) means that the zygote will develop as a female; with an X and a Y chromosome (XY) it will develop as a male. In some cases, combinations of sex chromosomes other than XX or XY occur, causing sexual development to proceed differently; these variations are discussed in Chapter 5. X-bearing sperm and Y-bearing sperm are somewhat different from each other in appearance and behavior. X-bearing sperm swim more slowly and live longer than Y-bearing sperm. Y-bearing sperm are slimmer and longer, they swim faster, and they are more delicate and therefore more easily damaged by the normally acidic vaginal environment. Researchers have suggested ways of preselecting a baby's sex based on the differences in sperm types (Hewitt, 1987; Whelan, 1986). Their suggestions are often contradictory, however, and the results appear to be quite inconclusive. It is possible to separate X- and Y-bearing sperm from ejaculated semen in a laboratory and then inseminate the mother-to-be with the desired type. This practice raises ethical questions, however.

Semen Production

Semen, or seminal fluid, is the ejaculated liquid that contains sperm. The function of semen is to nourish sperm and provide them a hospitable environment and means of transport when they are deposited within the vagina. It is mainly made up of secretions from the seminal vesicles and prostate gland, which mix together in the urethra during ejaculation. Immediately after ejaculation, the semen is somewhat thick and sticky from clotting factors in the fluid. This consistency keeps the sperm together initially; then the semen becomes liquefied, allowing the sperm to swim out. The seminal fluid is made up of a number of ingredients. The carbohydrate fructose, produced in the seminal vesicles, provides fuel for the sperm. Prostaglandins help reduce the viscosity of cervical mucus. The hormone *relaxin* and other enzymes, produced by the prostate, increase sperm motility. A chemical called seminalplasmin helps keep bacteria from growing in the semen. Semen is relatively alkaline and helps neutralize the vagina's normal acidity, enhancing sperm motility. Semen ranges in color from opalescent or milky white to yellowish or grayish tones upon ejaculation, but it becomes clearer as it liquefies. Normally, about 2–6 milliliters (about 1 teaspoonful) of semen are ejaculated at one time; this amount of semen generally contains between 100 million and 600 million sperm.

MALE SEXUAL RESPONSE

At this point, it might be useful to review the material on sexual arousal and response in Chapter 3, including the models of Masters and Johnson and of Kaplan. Even though their sexual anatomy is quite different, women and men follow roughly the same pattern of excitement and orgasm, with two exceptions: (1) Generally (but certainly not always), men become fully aroused and ready for penetration in a shorter amount of time than women do; and (2) once men experience orgasm, they usually cannot have another one for some time, whereas women may experience multiple orgasms.

Sexual arousal in men includes the processes of myotonia (increased muscle tension) and vasocongestion (engorgement of the tissues with blood). Vasocongestion in men is most apparent in the erection of the penis.

Erection

When a male becomes aroused, the blood circulation within the penis changes dramatically (Figure 4.6). During the process of **erection,** the blood vessels expand, increasing the volume of blood, especially within the corpora cavernosa. At the same time, expansion of the penis compresses the veins that normally carry blood out, so the penis becomes further engorged. (There are no muscles in the penis that make it erect, nor is there a bone

What is it men in women do require?
The lineaments of Gratified Desire.

What is it women do in men require?
The lineaments of Gratified Desire.
William Blake

FIGURE 4.6 Stages of Male Sexual Response.

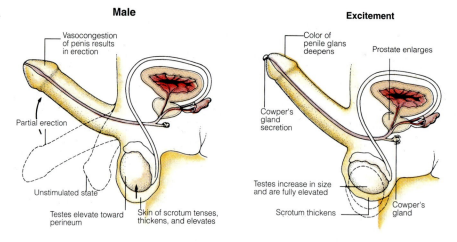

Male

Vasocongestion of penis results in erection

Partial erection

Unstimulated state

Testes elevate toward perineum

Skin of scrotum tenses, thickens, and elevates

Excitement

Color of penile glans deepens

Prostate enlarges

Cowper's gland secretion

Testes increase in size and are fully elevated

Scrotum thickens

Cowper's gland

Late Excitement or Plateau

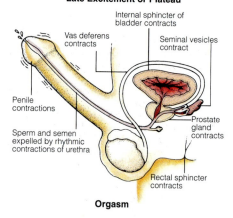

Internal sphincter of bladder contracts

Vas deferens contracts

Seminal vesicles contract

Penile contractions

Sperm and semen expelled by rhythmic contractions of urethra

Prostate gland contracts

Rectal sphincter contracts

Orgasm

When the appetite arises in the liver, the heart generates a spirit which descends through the arteries, fills the hollow of the penis and makes it hard and stiff. The delightful movements of intercourse give warmth to all the members, and hence to the humor which is in the brain; this liquid is drawn through the veins which lead from behind the ears to the testicles and from them it is squirted by the penis into the vulva.

Constantinus Africanus (c. 1070)

in it.) Secretions from the Cowper's glands appear at the tip of the penis during erection.

The **erection reflex** may be triggered by various sexual and nonsexual stimuli, including the tactile stimulation (touching) of the penis or other erogenous areas; sights, smells, or sounds (usually words or sexual vocalizations); and emotions or thoughts. Even negative emotions, such as fear, can produce an erection. Conversely, emotions and thoughts can also inhibit erection, as can unpleasant or painful physical sensations. The length of time an erection lasts varies greatly from individual to individual and situation to situation. With experience, most men are able to gauge the amount of stimulation that will either maintain the erection without reaching orgasm or cause orgasm to occur soon. Failure to attain erection even though one is desired is something most men experience at one time or another. If this condition is persistent, the man should see a medical practitioner because the cause may be physical, not emotional as many people believe. (Erectile difficulties are discussed further in Chapter 15.)

Ejaculation and Orgasm

Increasing stimulation of the penis generally leads to **ejaculation,** the process by which semen is forcefully expelled from a man's body. When the impulses that cause erection reach a critical point, a spinal reflex sets off a massive discharge of nerve impulses to the ducts, glands, and muscles of the reproductive system. Ejaculation then occurs in two stages.

Emission   In the first stage, **emission,** contractions of the walls of the tail portion of the epididymis send sperm into the vas deferens. Rhythmic contractions also occur in the vasa deferentia, ampullae, seminal vesicles, and ejaculatory ducts, which spill their contents into the urethra. The bladder's sphincter muscle closes to prevent urine from mixing with the semen and semen from entering the bladder, and another sphincter below the prostate also closes, trapping the semen in the expanded urethral bulb. At this point, the man feels a distinct sensation of **ejaculatory inevitability,** the point at which ejaculation *must* occur (Masters & Johnson, 1966). These events are accompanied by increased heart rate and respiration, elevated blood pressure, and general muscular tension. About 25% of men experience a sex flush.

Expulsion   In the second stage of ejaculation, **expulsion,** there are rapid, rhythmic contractions of the urethra, the prostate, and the muscles at the base of the penis, occurring initially at 0.8-second intervals. (The same interval occurs with women's orgasmic contractions.) The first few contractions are the most forceful, causing semen to spurt from the urethral opening. Gradually, the intensity of the contractions decreases and the interval between them lengthens. The average length of the expulsion stage is 3–10 seconds. Breathing rate and heart rate may reach their peak at expulsion.

Some men experience **retrograde ejaculation,** the "backward" expulsion of semen into the bladder rather than out of the urethral opening. This malfunctioning of the urethral sphincters may be temporary (induced by tranquilizers, for example), but if it persists, the man should seek medical counsel to determine if there is an underlying problem. Retrograde ejaculation is not normally harmful; the semen is simply collected in the bladder and eliminated during urination.

> *Tumescence is the piling on of the fuel; detumescence is the leaping out of the devouring flame whence is lighted the torch of life to be handed from generation to generation.*
>
> Havelock Ellis

Orgasm   The intensely pleasurable physical sensations and general release of tension that accompany ejaculation constitute the experience of **orgasm.** Orgasm does not always occur with ejaculation, however. It is possible to ejaculate without having an orgasm and to experience orgasm without ejaculating. (The relationship of orgasm to sexual fulfillment was discussed in Chapter 3.) Following orgasm, men experience a **refractory period,** during which they are not capable of becoming erect or having an orgasm again. Refractory periods vary greatly in length, ranging from a few minutes to many hours (or even days, in the cases of some older men). Other changes occur immediately following orgasm. Erection diminishes as blood flow returns to normal, the sex flush (if there was one) disappears, and fairly heavy perspiration may occur. Men who experience intense sexual arousal without orgasm may feel some heaviness or discomfort in the testicles; this is generally not as painful as the common term "blue balls" implies. If dis-

> *Bring me my bow of burning gold. Bring me my arrows of desire.*
> William Blake

comfort persists, it may be relieved by a period of rest or by ejaculation through manual stimulation (by either the man or his partner).

I n this chapter and the previous one, we have looked at the *physical* characteristics that designate us as female or male. But, as we will discover in the following chapter, there's more to gender than mere chromosomes or reproductive organs. How we feel about our male or female anatomy and how we act (our gender roles) also determine our identities as men or women.

SUMMARY

Male Sex Organs: What Are They For?

- In their reproductive role, a man's sex organs produce and store gametes and deliver them to a woman's reproductive tract. The *penis* is the organ through which both sperm and urine pass. The shaft of the penis contains two *corpora cavernosa* and a *corpus spongiosum*, which fill with blood during arousal, causing an erection. The head is called the *glans penis*; it is normally covered by the *foreskin*. Myths about the penis equate its size with masculinity and sexual prowess. The *scrotum* is a pouch of skin that hangs at the root of the penis. It holds the testes.

- The paired *testes* or *testicles* have two major functions: sperm production and hormone production. Within each testicle are about 1000 *seminiferous tubules*, where the production of sperm takes place. The seminiferous tubules merge to form the *epididymis*, a coiled tube where the sperm finally mature, and each epididymis merges into a *vas deferens*, which joins the *ejaculatory duct* within the prostate gland. The *seminal vesicles* and *prostate gland* produce semen, which nourishes and transports the sperm. Two tiny glands called *Cowper's* or *bulbourethral glands* secrete a thick, clear mucus prior to ejaculation.

- Male anatomical structures that do not serve a reproductive function but that may be involved in or affected by sexual activities include the breasts, urethra, buttocks, rectum, and anus.

Male Sexual Physiology

- The reproductive processes of the male body include the production of hormones and the production and delivery of *sperm*, the male gametes. Although men do not have a monthly reproductive cycle comparable to that of women, they do experience regular fluctuations of hormone levels; there is also some evidence that men's moods follow a cyclical pattern. The most important male hormone is *testosterone*, which triggers sperm production and regulates the sex drive. Other important hormones in male reproductive physiology are GnRH, FSH, LH (also known as ICSH), and inhibin.

- A feedback system called the *brain-testicular axis* involves the hypothalamus, the pituitary gland, and the testes in regulating the events of *spermatogenesis*, sperm production. From puberty on, a man produces several hundred million sperm daily. Within the seminiferous tubules *spermatids* are created through meiosis; these undergo *spermiogenesis*, which transforms them into sperm. The sperm consists of three sections: the head, containing the gamete's nucleus with its

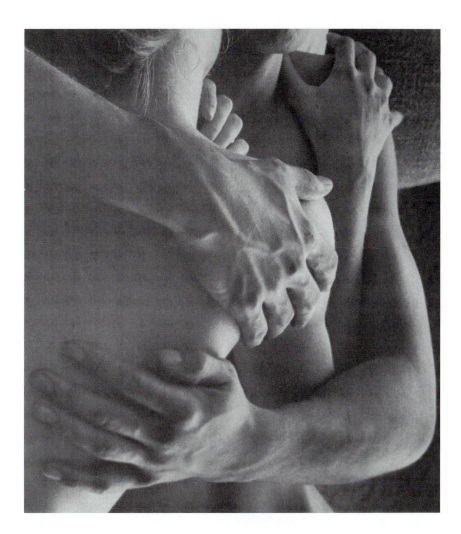

Sexual fulfillment is related to a variety of factors, both physiological and psychological.

DNA; the midpiece, containing mitochondria, which provide energy to the sperm; and the tail, which propels the sperm. Immature sperm are stored in the epididymis where they become mature, motile, and fertile. Sperm carry either an X chromosome, which will produce a female zygote, or a Y chromosome, which will produce a male.

• *Semen*, or seminal fluid, is the ejaculated liquid that contains sperm. The function of the semen is to nourish sperm and provide them a hospitable environment and means of transport when they are deposited within the vagina. It is mainly made up of secretions from the seminal vesicles and prostate gland. The semen from a single ejaculation generally contains between 100 million and 600 million sperm.

Male Sexual Response

• Male sexual response, like that of females, involves the processes of vasocongestion and myotonia. *Erection* of the penis occurs when sexual or tactile stimuli cause its chambers to become engorged with blood. Continuing stimulation leads to *ejaculation*, which occurs in two stages. In the first stage, *emission*, semen mixes with sperm in the urethral bulb. In the second stage, *expulsion*, semen is forcibly expelled from the penis, generally resulting in orgasm.

KEY TERMS

penis	dartos muscle	Cowper's gland	spermiogenesis
root	cremaster muscle	bulbourethral gland	flagellum
shaft	testicle		acrosome
glans penis	testes (sing.: testis)	gynecomastia	blood-testis barrier
corona		Leydig cell	
frenulum	spermatic cord	androgen	semen
foreskin	seminiferous tubule	testosterone	erection
prepuce	cryptorchidism	brain-testicular axis	erection reflex
circumcision	epididymis	inhibin	ejaculation
smegma	vas deferens (pl., vasa deferentia)	spermatogenesis	emission
corpora cavernosa		spermatogonia	ejaculatory inevitability
corpus spongiosum		primary spermatocyte	expulsion
crura	ampulla	spermatid	retrograde ejaculation
urethra	ejaculatory duct	spermatozoon	refractory period
urethral bulb	seminal vesicle	sperm	
scrotum	prostate gland		

SUGGESTIONS FOR FURTHER READING

Castleman, Michael. *Sexual Solutions: A Guide for Men and Women Who Love Them.* New York: Touchstone Books, 1989. For heterosexual men (and women), the ins and outs of lovemaking; includes a reassuring section on penis size.

Diagram Group Staff. *Man's Body.* New York: Bantam Books, 1983. Good drawings and diagrams of male anatomy.

Masters, William H., and Virginia E. Johnson. *Human Sexual Response.* Boston: Little, Brown, 1966. The ground-breaking (if sometimes flawed) work, based on observational studies of men and women, that describes in detail the physiological processes involved in sexual arousal and response.

Strage, Mark. *The Durable Fig Leaf: A Historical, Cultural, Medical, Social, Literary, and Iconographic Account of Man's Relations with His Penis.* New York: William Morrow, 1980. An entertaining book, well-rooted in scholarship.

Zilbergeld, Bernie. *The New Male Sexuality.* New York: Bantam Books, 1992. Explains both male and female anatomy and sexual response, plus communication, sexual problem solving, and much more. Authoritative, interesting, and readable; written for men (but recommended for women as well).

Chapter Five

GENDER AND
GENDER ROLES

PREVIEW: SELF-QUIZ

1. Gender roles reflect the inherent natures of women and men. True or false?

2. Psychologists believe the increasing similarity of male and female gender roles reflects a decline in mental health. True or false?

3. A person's femininity or masculinity is independent of his or her sexual orientation. True or false?

4. Males and females are opposites in terms of aggression and nurturance. True or false?

5. One's gender identity as female or male is inborn. True or false?

6. Transsexuality and homosexuality are distinctly different phenomena. True or false?

7. In adulthood, men and women tend to become more similar in their gender roles. True or false?

8. Being independent has traditionally been a component of the female gender role among African American women. True or false?

9. It is next to impossible to tell an infant's gender by behavior alone. True or false?

10. Latinos place a high value on female virginity. True or false?

ANSWERS 1. F, 2. F, 3. T, 4. F, 5. F, 6. T, 7. T, 8. T, 9. T, 10. T

Chapter Outline

What's in a name? That which we call a rose
By any other name would smell as sweet.

William Shakespeare

ow can you tell the difference between a man and a woman? Everyone knows that women and men are very basically distinguished by their genitals. But accurate as this answer may be academically, it is not particularly useful in social situations. In most social situations—except in nudist colonies and hot tubs, and while sunbathing *au naturel*—one's genitals are usually not visible to the casual observer. One does not expose himself or herself (or ask another to do so) for gender verification. We are more likely to rely on secondary sex characteristics, such as breasts and body hair, or on bone structure, musculature, and height. But even these characteristics are not always reliable, given the great variety of shapes and sizes we come in as human beings. And farther away than a few yards, we

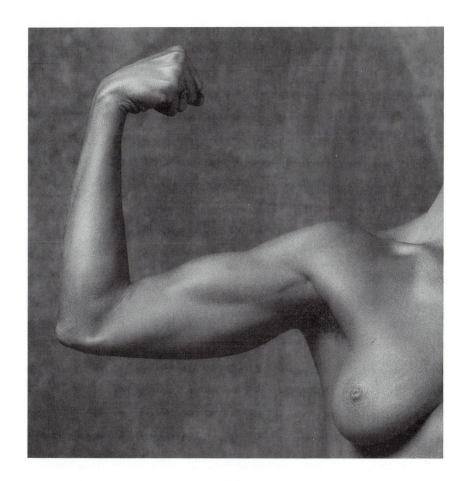

cannot always distinguish these characteristics. Instead of relying entirely on physical characteristics to identify males and females, we often look for other clues.

Culture provides us with an important clue for recognizing whether a person is female or male in most situations: dress. In almost all cultures, male and female clothing differs to varying degrees so that we can easily identify a person's gender (Bullough, 1991). Some cultures, such as our own, may accentuate secondary sex characteristics, especially for females. One study found that of the different types of male/female differences, both men and women found appearance to be the greatest (Martin et al., 1991). Traditional feminine clothing, for example, emphasizes a woman's gender: dress or skirt, a form-fitting or low-cut top revealing the breasts (a secondary sex characteristic), high heels, and so on. For adventuresome women, lacy bustiers, garter belts, and brassieres, once considered undergarments, may be worn as outerwear, emphasizing "femaleness." Most clothing, in fact, that emphasizes or exaggerates secondary sex characteristics is female. Makeup (red lipstick, rouge, eyeliner) and hairstyle also serve to mark or exaggerate the differences between females and males. Even smells (perfume and aftershave cologne) and colors (blue for boys, pink for girls) help distinguish females and males.

Clothing and other aspects of appearance exaggerate the physical differences between women and men. And culture encourages us to accentuate (or invent) psychological, emotional, mental, and behavioral differences. But are men and women as different as we ordinarily think?

In this chapter, we examine some of the critical ways being male or female affects us both as human beings and as sexual beings. We look at the connection between our genitals, our identity as female or male, and our feelings of being feminine or masculine. We also examine the relationship between femininity, masculinity, and sexual orientation. Then we look at whether masculine and feminine traits are the result of biology or socialization. Because we believe socialization is the most significant factor, we next focus on theories of socialization and how we learn to act masculine and feminine in our culture. Then we look at traditional, contemporary, and androgynous gender roles. Finally, we examine hermaphroditism and transsexuality, two phenomena that raise complex issues pertaining to gender and gender identity.

STUDYING GENDER AND GENDER ROLES

Sex, Gender, and Gender Roles: What's the Difference?

Let's define some key terms, to provide us with a common terminology. If we keep these definitions in mind, it will make our discussion clearer. The word **sex** refers to whether we are biologically female or male, based on our genetic and anatomical sex. Our **genetic sex** refers to our chromosomal and hormonal sex characteristics, such as whether our chromosomes are XY or XX, and whether estrogens or testosterone dominate our hormonal system. **Anatomical sex** refers to our physical sex, such as our gonads, uterus, vulva, vagina, or penis.

Although "sex" and "gender" have often been used interchangeably, gender is not the same as biological sex (Unger, 1991). **Gender** is our femininity or masculinity, the social and cultural characteristics associated with our biological sex. While sex is rooted in biology, gender is rooted in culture. Our **assigned gender** is the gender given us by others, usually at birth. When we are born, someone looks at our genitals and exclaims, "It's a boy!" or "It's a girl!" With that single utterance, we are transformed from an "it" into a "male" or a "female." Our **gender identity** is the gender we *feel* ourselves to be.

Gender roles are the roles that a person is expected to perform as a result of being female or male in a particular culture. The term "gender role" is gradually replacing the traditional term "sex role," because sex role continues to suggest a connection between biological sex and behavior (Unger, 1991). Biological males are expected to act out masculine gender roles; biological females are expected to act out feminine gender roles. A **gender-role stereotype** is a rigidly held, oversimplified, and overgeneralized belief that all males and all females possess distinct psychological and behavioral traits. Stereotypes tend to be false or misleading not only for the group as a whole ("women are more interested in relationships than sex") but for any individual in the group (Jane may be more interested in sex than relationships). Even if a generalization is statistically valid in describing a group average

Roles came with costumes and speeches and stage directions. In a role, we don't have to think.

Ellen Goodman

(males are generally taller than females), such generalizations do not necessarily predict whether Roberto will be taller than Tanya. **Gender-role attitude** refers to the beliefs we have of ourselves and others regarding appropriate female and male personality traits and activities. **Gender-role behavior** refers to the actual activities or behaviors we engage in as females and males. When we discuss gender roles, it is important not to confuse stereotypes with reality and attitudes with behavior.

There are three central aspects of our identity as men or women: biological sex, gender identity, and gender role. Together they form our identity as female or male. For most of us, the three are in agreement. Our male or female anatomy usually coincides with our belief that we are male or female. And as male or female, we more or less act out the masculine or feminine gender role dictated by our culture.

Sex and Gender Identity

We develop our gender through the interaction of its biological and psychosocial components. The biological component includes genetic and anatomical sex, while the psychosocial component includes assigned gender and gender identity.

Assigned Gender   When we were born, based on anatomical appearance, we were given our assigned gender. We had no sense of ourselves as females or males. Assigned gender is significant because it tells *others* how to respond to us. After all, one of the first questions an older child or adult asks upon seeing an infant is whether it's a girl or boy. We *learned* that we were girls and boys from the verbal responses of others. "What a pretty *girl*" or "What a good *boy*," our parents and others would say. We are constantly given signals about our gender. Your birth certificate states your sex; your name, such as Paul or Paula, is most likely gender-coded. Your clothes, even in infancy, reveal your gender.

By the time we were 2 years old, we were probably able to identify ourselves as a girl or a boy based on what we had internalized from what others told us. But we didn't really know *why* we were a girl or a boy. We didn't associate our gender with our genitals. In fact, until the age of 3 or so, most children identify girls or boys by hairstyles, clothing, or other nonanatomical signs. At around age 3, children begin to learn that the genitals are what makes a person male or female. It still takes them a while to understand that they are *permanently* a boy or a girl. They often believe that they can become the other sex later.

Gender Identity   By about 24 months, we internalize and identify with our gender. We *feel* we are a girl or a boy. This feeling of our femaleness or maleness is our gender identity. Once a child's gender identity is established, he or she will often react strongly if someone mistakes that identity. For most people, gender identity is permanent and is congruent with their sexual anatomy and assigned gender. Furthermore, it is virtually impossible to develop a personal identity without a gender identity as a female or a male (Money & Tucker, 1976). Our sense of femaleness or maleness is a core component of our identity.

Some cultures, however, defer instilling gender identity in males until

He is playing masculine. She is playing feminine.

He is playing masculine because she is playing feminine. She is playing feminine because he is playing masculine.

He is playing the kind of man that she thinks the kind of woman she is playing ought to admire. She is playing the kind of woman that he thinks the kind of man he is playing ought to desire.

Betty Roszak and
Theodore Roszak

The moment we are born, we are identified as male or female and are socialized to fulfill masculine and feminine gender roles.

later. They believe in a latent or dormant femaleness in males. As a consequence, such cultures institute rituals or ceremonies in childhood to ensure that males will identify themselves as males (Whiting, 1979). In some East African societies, for example, male children are referred to as "woman-child"; there appear to be few social differences between boys and girls. Around age 7, the boy undergoes male initiation rites, such as circumcision, whose avowed purpose is to "make" the child into a man. Such ceremonies "may act as a form of therapeutic 'brainwashing,' helping the young male make the transition to a new gender identity with new role expectations" (Whiting, 1979). Other cultures allow older males to act out a latent female identity with such practices as the couvade, in which husbands mimic their wives giving birth. And in our own society, into the early years of this century, boys were dressed in gowns and wore their hair in long curls until age 2. At age 2 or 3, their dresses were replaced by pants and their hair cut. From then on, masculine socialization was stressed (Garber, 1991).

Masculinity and Femininity: Opposites or Similar?

One half of the world cannot understand the pleasures of the other.
Jane Austen (1775–1817)

The traditional view of masculinity and femininity sees men and women as polar opposites. Our popular terminology, in fact, reflects this view. Women and men refer to each other as the "opposite sex." But this implies that women and men are opposites, that we have little in common with each other. Our gender stereotypes fit this pattern of polar differences: Men are aggressive, women are passive; men embody **instrumentality** and are task-oriented; women embody **expressiveness** and are emotion-oriented; men are rational, women are irrational; men want sex, women want love; and so on.

This view of women and men has several implications. First, if one differs

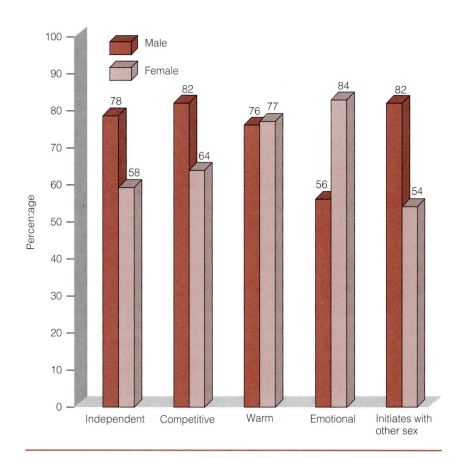

FIGURE 5.1 Gender-Role Stereotypes. Gender-role stereotypes are probabilities that a female or male will have certain characteristics based on her or his gender.

from the male or female stereotype, he or she becomes more like the other gender. If a woman is sexually assertive, for example, not only is she less feminine, she is also more masculine. Similarly, if a man is nurturing, not only is he less masculine, he is also more feminine. A "real man" possesses exclusively masculine traits and behaviors, and a "real woman" possesses exclusively feminine traits and behaviors. Second, because they are opposites, they cannot share the same traits or qualities. A man is assertive, a woman is receptive; in reality, women and men are both assertive *and* receptive. Third, because they are opposites, they have little in common with each other; a "war between the sexes" is the norm. Women and men can't understand each other, nor can they expect to. Difficulties in their relationships is attributed to their "oppositeness."

It is important to recognize that gender stereotypes, despite their depiction of men and women as opposites, are usually not all-or-nothing notions. Most of us do not think that only men are assertive or only women nurturing. As individuals, along with our friends and family, we probably disprove of this all-or-nothing notion. Stereotypes reflect *probabilities* that a woman or man will have a certain characteristic based on his or her gender, as Figure 5.1 indicates. As the graph shows, when we say that men are more independent than women, we mean there is a greater probability that a man will be more independent than a woman (Deaux, 1984).

The war between the sexes is the only one in which both sides regularly sleep with the enemy.
Quentin Crisp

Unwittingly, the feuding experts and conflicting experiments testify to the truth: we will never have a Sears catalogue of sex differences because human beings are too diverse for labels and measurements. For every trait studied, the differences within each sex are greater than the average differences between the two sexes.
Letty Cottin Pogrebin

An analysis of the literature on gender differences in social behavior concluded that differences attributable to gender are generally below 10%; more typically, they are around 5% (Eagly, 1987). Nevertheless, a review of gender stereotypes between 1972 and 1988 found little change among Americans (Bergen & Williams, 1991). Females and males continue to be viewed as significantly different in their personalities and behaviors: Men should be men, and women should be girls (only larger).

The fundamental problem with the view of women and men as opposites is that it is not true. Men and women are significantly more alike than they are different. But our culture encourages us to look for differences and, when we find them, to exaggerate their degree and significance. It teaches us to ignore the single most important fact about males and females: that we are both human. As human beings, we are significantly more alike biologically and psychologically than we are different. As women and men, we share similar respiratory, circulatory, neurological, skeletal, and muscular systems. (Even the penis and the clitoris evolved from the same undifferentiated embryonic structure, as discussed in Chapter 3.) Hormonally, both produce androgens and estrogens (but in different amounts). Where men and women biologically differ most significantly is in terms of their reproductive functions: Men impregnate, while women gestate and nurse. Beyond these reproductive differences, biological differences are not great.

A review of gender differences in social behavior and experiences found very little difference between males and females that was inherent (Lips, 1992). In terms of social behavior, studies suggest that men are more aggressive both physically and verbally than women; the gender difference, however, is not large. The most common form of male aggression is physical, while female aggression is more often verbal. Where differences in levels of aggression occur, much of it can be attributed to greater social tolerance of male aggression. Neither men nor women were found to be more likely to dominate or to be more or less susceptible to influence, nurturing, altruistic, or empathetic. Hilary Lips (1992) writes: "Despite the fact that women and men are often referred to as opposites, psychological research finds gender differences relatively small in size or inconsistent in many areas of social behavior." Most differences can be traced to gender-role expectations, male/female status, and gender stereotyping.

The *perception* of female/male differences is far greater than findings on the differences themselves (Hare-Mustin & Marecek, 1990b). It is not even clear what constitutes a "difference." Rachel Hare-Mustin and Jeanne Marecek (1990c) write:

> The very criteria for deciding what should constitute a difference as opposed to a similarity are disputed. How much difference makes a difference? Even the anatomical differences between men and women seem trivial when humans are compared to daffodils or ducks.

Each of us possess to one degree or another most of the traits assigned to the other sex. Although we possess traits of both sexes, most of us feel either feminine or masculine; we do not doubt our gender (Heilbrun, 1982). Unfortunately, when people believe that individuals should *not* have the attributes of the other sex, males suppress their expressiveness and females suppress their instrumentality. As a result, the range of human behaviors is limited by a person's gender role. As psychologist Sandra Bem (1975) point-

The perpetual obstacle to human advancement is custom.
John Stuart Mill (1806–1873)

The fact that we are all human beings is infinitely more important than all the peculiarities that distinguish humans from one another.
Simone de Beauvoir

The perception of male/female psychological differences is far greater than they are in fact.

edly wrote: "Our current system of sex role differentiation has long since outlived its usefulness, and . . . now serves only to prevent both men and women from developing as full and complete human beings."

Gender and Sexual Orientation

Gender, gender identity, and gender role are conceptually independent of sexual orientation (Lips, 1992). But, in many people's minds, these concepts are closely related to sexual orientation, discussed at greater length in Chapters 6 and 7. Our traditional notion of gender roles assumes that heterosexuality is a critical component of masculinity and femininity (Riseden & Hort, 1992). A "masculine" man is attracted to women and a "feminine" woman is attracted to men. From this assumption follow two beliefs about homosexuality: (1) If a man is gay, he cannot be masculine, and if a woman is lesbian, she cannot be feminine; and (2) if a man is gay, he must have some feminine characteristics, and if a woman is lesbian, she must have some masculine characteristics (Ross, 1983a). What these beliefs imply is that homosexuality is somehow associated with a failure to fulfill traditional gender roles (DeCecco & Elia, 1993). A "real" man is not gay; therefore, gay men are not "real" men. Similarly, a "real" woman is not a lesbian; therefore, lesbians are not "real" women.

Stereotypes of gay men often link them with "feminine" characteristics such as weakness, emotionality, and submissiveness. Such stereotypes can be traced back to the turn of the century, when both Havelock Ellis and Sigmund Freud (discussed in Chapter 2) believed that homosexuality was the result of inversion, reversed gender roles. Inside the gay male dwelled the soul of a woman, they thought (Ross, 1983a, 1983b). Many heterosexual men and women currently accept that view. In a study that showed a videotaped interview to 20 students, half the students were told that the man

Stereotypes fall in the face of humanity . . . this is how the world will change for gay men and lesbians.

Anna Quindlen

being interviewed was gay. Those who believed he was gay thought that he possessed a number of female characteristics (Weissbach & Zagon, 1975).

Some evidence suggests that gay men may have more feminine traits than heterosexual men. But the evidence is not conclusive because such studies often rest on gender-role stereotypes (Ross, 1983b; Tuttle & Pillard, 1991). There is no scientific evidence, for example, to support the belief that gay men are more artistic than heterosexual men (Demb, 1992). In fact, if gay men are (or were) more creatively expressive than heterosexual men, such traits may reflect the gay male's beliefs in "how" gays are supposed to act rather than an innate characteristic. Such supposedly "gay" characteristics were more prominent prior to the 1970s, after which time gay male roles began to emphasize masculinity or role flexibility (Altman, 1982; Bell & Weinberg, 1978; Garber, 1991). Some writers argue that prior to the 1970s, the only way a man could be openly gay was to act effeminate and therefore appear "ridiculous" and nonthreatening to society at large (Garber, 1991).

As with some gay men who assumed effeminate styles as a form of self-defense, some lesbians assumed a masculine style for the same reason. From the turn of the century on, the most visible lesbians were those who assumed masculine attire and attitudes. The butch role, a superficially masculinelike lesbian role, subjected lesbians to ridicule but also protected them by making them "pathetic." Questions continue, however, as to whether lesbians and heterosexual women are similar or different in terms of gender-role characteristics (apart from sexual orientation). One study suggested that lesbians are more androgynous in their gender roles than are heterosexual women (LaTorre & Wendenburg, 1984). Another study found no relationship between instrumental/expressive traits and sexual orientation in women (Dancey, 1992). (See Perspective 1 for a discussion of effeminate gay males and butch lesbians.)

There are no conclusive findings on the relationship between sexual orientation and gender roles (Paul, 1993). Gay and lesbian roles may emphasize certain personality traits or behaviors during one time period and different ones at another time. These traits and behaviors are not necessarily inherent to being gay or lesbian. Like gender roles, gay and lesbian roles may reflect views on how people are expected to act.

Lesbian and gay gender stereotypes are also applied to heterosexuals who do not fit stereotypical female and male gender and gender roles. A study of gender stereotypes found that when an individual engaged in a behavior not typical for his or her gender, the person was suspected of being lesbian or gay. When a male engaged in nursing or secretarial work, students believed there was a 40% chance that he was gay (Deaux & Lewis, 1983). Another study found that when men had "feminine" faces and women had "masculine" faces, they were thought likely to be gay or lesbian (Dunkle & Francis, 1990). Divergences from traditional gender stereotypes are linked with prejudice against gay men and lesbians. Men or women whose body shape, facial structure, mannerisms, dress, behaviors, or values do not match gender stereotypes may be derided as "queers" or "dykes."

Studies on attitudes toward gay men and lesbians indicate a relationship between negative attitudes and gender roles (Herek, 1984; Kite, 1984). A comparison between individuals who hold negative attitudes toward gay men and lesbians and those who hold neutral or positive attitudes found some evidence of differences. Those holding negative attitudes were more

DON'T JUDGE A MAN BY HIS LIPSTICK OR A WOMAN BY HER MOTORCYCLE BOOTS

A group of adolescent boys passed a lesbian with short hair, wearing a blue workshirt, a pair of old Levis, and motorcycle boots. One of the boys taunted her: "Are you a man or a woman?" She looked him straight in the eye: "I'm more man than you'll ever be and more woman than you'll ever be able to handle." The boy slunk away with his friends (Wolf, 1980).

While the overwhelming majority of gay men and lesbians are as masculine or feminine as heterosexuals, some purposely act out effeminate or butch roles. (*Effeminacy* is the possession of femalelike qualities. Effeminate men or masculine-appearing women are not necessarily gay or lesbian; nor are they transvestites or cross-dressers.) In the gay/lesbian subculture, *butch* women are lesbians who dress and act in a stylized masculine manner; effeminate gay men are men who, without denying their maleness, mimic feminine characteristics in their dress and mannerisms. Many gay men and lesbians feel ambivalent or hostile toward such men and women. They believe effeminate gay men and butch lesbians reinforce negative stereotypes about homosexuality.

Some elements of contemporary gay culture regard effeminate gay men as self-hating. The witty Quentin Crisp, who prides himself on his hennaed hair, makeup, red fingernails, and jewelry, however, views himself as both confrontational *and* self-protective. He does not want to pass as a woman, but to present himself as an "image of homosexuality that is outrageously effeminate" (Crisp, 1982). The effeminate gay man parodies masculinity and, like the cross-dresser, provokes confrontation because of his visibility. This arouses homophobia among some heterosexuals because they believe the men are flaunting their effeminacy. It arouses "transvestophobia" among some gay men because they believe effeminate dressing presents a distorted or stereotypical image of homosexuality as somehow "female" (Garber, 1991).

Since at least the 1890s, with the "invert" balls in

New York, where lesbians dressed in tuxedos and danced with others wearing gowns, butch-femme relationships have been an important element of the lesbian subculture in America and England (Faderman, 1991). (A *femme* is a feminine lesbian known by her butch partner choice; a butch is also referred to nonpejoratively in butch-femme culture as a *dyke* [Nestle, 1983].)

During the 1950s, butch and femme were the dominant role models for young and working class lesbians. (Middle-class and upper-class lesbians generally preferred to remain invisible during this time and lived their lives outside the lesbian subculture.) Butches assumed traditional masculine heterosexual roles, such as being the dominant partner and controlling of emotions, while femmes assumed feminine heterosexual roles, such as being submissive, supportive, and caring (Faderman, 1991). These "heterosexual" roles, however, did not translate erotically. Writer Joan Nestle (1983) notes: "Butch-femme relationships . . . were complex erotic and social statements, *(continued)*

DON'T JUDGE A MAN BY HIS LIPSTICK OR A WOMAN BY HER MOTORCYCLE BOOTS *(continued)*

not phony heterosexual replicas. They were filled with a deeply lesbian language of stance, dress, gesture, love, courage and autonomy."

While the butch role may appear to be a male imitation, for women of the 1950s and earlier, it was empowering in contrast to the submissiveness of the traditional heterosexual female role. And unlike middle-class and wealthy lesbians, butches made themselves visible as lesbians. Femmes were not typical '50s females, either; they "were attracted to a rebel sexuality" and permitted themselves to be seen with butches whose outlaw status was clearly visible by their appearance (Faderman, 1991).

Beginning in the late 1960s, however, lesbian roles shifted in response to the challenges of women's liberation. Lesbian feminists rejected butch and femme as being heterosexual models. Instead, they sought a unique lesbian identity. Lesbians were to be strong women as women, not as lesbian imitations of men. The femme role was rejected as an imitation of a male-defined passive heterosexual female.

In the 1980s, butch-femme relationships re-emerged in the lesbian subculture. But the new butch-femme relationship took on a distinctive sexual meaning that had been absent earlier: It was now mixed with erotic power, in which control and passivity became part of lesbian sex play. Seduction became an important element. "The goal was for women to use those roles for their own pleasurable ends," wrote historian Lillian Faderman (1991), "to demand freedom and sexual excitement as lesbians seldom dared before."

But just as many gay men feel uncomfortable with effeminacy, many lesbians also feel uncomfortable with butch and femme roles. They continue to view them as repressive relationships that mock the possibility of equality and strength in female-female relationships. What Faderman calls "the lesbian sex wars" continues today as lesbian-feminists and sexual radicals debate the "correctness" of butch-femme relationships.

likely to (1) adhere to traditional gender roles, (2) stereotype men and women, and (3) support the sexual double standard, granting men greater sexual freedom than women. Males tended to be more negative than women toward gay men and lesbians. And heterosexual men tended to be more negative toward gay men than toward lesbians; heterosexual women were more negative toward lesbians than toward gay men.

EXPLAINING GENDER ROLES: WHAT'S SEX GOT TO DO WITH IT?

What is the relationship between our biological sex as male or female to our gender role as masculine or feminine? Do we act the way we act because it is inbred in us or because of socialization? There is no universally accepted consensus.

Sociobiology

Until this century, differences in male and female behavior were usually explained as a result of inherent nature or natural selection. This approach was challenged by psychologists, sociologists, and anthropologists as unscientific and as a rationalization for the status quo. More recently, biological explanations of gender differences focusing on genes and hormones have found increasing support. Genetic and hormonal explanations, however, continue to view sex differences as natural. Nature, not nurture (socialization), is viewed as the primary factor determining differences between males and females.

Sociobiology is a theory based in evolutionary biology asserting that nature has structured us with an inborn desire to pass on our individual genes to future generations, and that this desire motivates much, if not all, of our behavior. Sociobiologists base their view on Charles Darwin's theory of evolution. According to Darwin's theory, evolution favors certain physical traits that enable the species to survive, such as the ability to walk. Sociobiologists believe that evolution also favors certain genetically based psychological traits that enhance an individual's ability to pass on his or her genes. They find biological justifications for male dominance, the sexual double standard, and maternal behavior.

Sociobiologists explain the different attitudes males and females hold toward sex and love, for example, as a result of reproductive strategies rather than cultural conditioning (see Symons, 1979, for a sociobiological approach to human sexuality). Sociobiologists are not very romantic about sex and love. In the sociobiological perspective, males, who are constantly fertile from early adolescence on, seek to impregnate as many partners as possible in order to ensure genetic success. For males, sex is important. Females, however, ovulate only once a month; a single act of intercourse can result in pregnancy, childbirth, and years of child rearing. For women, it is important to be selective about choosing a partner with whom they will pass on their genes. Women want partners on whom they can rely for child rearing and support. As a result, love is important for females. Love is their guarantee that males will remain with them to share the obligations of child rearing. Females trade sex for love, and males trade love for sex.

There are several difficulties with sociobiological explanations, however (Tavris & Wade, 1984). First, most sociobiological studies rely on animal studies or inferences drawn from animal studies. There is not much empirical data to back them up in terms of human behavior. Many assumptions about human behavior, such as males wanting sex and females wanting love, may represent cultural stereotypes rather than actual behavior. Second, direct genetic evidence is difficult, if not impossible, to obtain. Genetic evolution occurs over thousands of years, and breeding experiments such as those done with insects and animals cannot be ethically conducted with human beings. Third, there is no way to test the theories empirically because they rely on logic, inference, and internal consistency. Fourth, the explanations are so abstract and general that they do little to elucidate individual behavior. It is difficult for us to think that when we are attracted to someone, our primary motivation is to pass on our genes.

Finally, sociobiological theories generally reinforce traditional gender-role

Love is just a system for getting someone to call you darling after sex.

Julian Barnes

I have a brain and a uterus, and I use both.

Patricia Schroeder

MACHIHEMBRA: ROOSTER NOW, HEN BEFORE

There is some evidence that hormones influence gender identity. The evidence comes from 18 males born in a small village in the Dominican Republic (Imperato-McGinley et al., 1974, 1979). Because they were DHT-deficient, having been born with a hormonal disorder that prevents genetic males from developing normal genitals, the children were identified as girls because their underdeveloped penises resembled clitorises. They led typical lives as girls, but when they reached adolescence, the DHT deficiency reversed, and their bodies were able to develop normal male characteristics. Their testes descended, and their "clitorises" matured into penises.

If socialization were the most important factor in developing gender identities and gender roles, then one would expect the children to remain psychologically female. Of the 18 children, however, only one chose to remain female. The others adopted male gender roles. The child who remained female married and became a transsexual; another child who adopted the male gender identity and gender role cross-dressed.

The research was provocative because it suggested

(1) that gender identity was biologically determined rather than learned, and (2) that gender identity can be changed without severe emotional trauma. The study has been criticized, however, on several counts. First, the genitals were ambiguous rather than completely female in appearance; it is unlikely that the children would have been treated as "normal" girls. Second, after the children developed penises, others may have encouraged them to act as males. In fact, villagers ridiculed them as "penis-at-twelve." Third, because DHT deficiency was relatively common for the village (the condition was known locally as *machihembra*, "rooster now, hen before"), the transition from female to male may have been institutionalized. Finally, other studies conflict with the Dominican Republic studies. Studies of American children afflicted with congenital adrenal hyperplasia show that they usually remain female after their bodies are masculinized (Rubin, Reinisch, & Haskett, 1981). If there is a hormonal contribution, it may be considerably weaker than the Dominican study suggests. More research needs to be conducted on this complex subject.

---

stereotypes, which suggests a possible conservative bias. When sociobiologists illustrate their ideas with examples from the animal kingdom, they generally choose species in which the males are dominant and aggressive and ignore other species in which females are the dominant and assertive ones (Fausto-Sterling, 1985).

The biological perspective of gender identity and roles indicates that biology probably influences us as men and women. The question is, how much? Biologically men and women *are* different, and there may be a relationship between our biology and our psychology. But there is certainly no *direct* relationship between our genetic or hormonal makeup and our specific actions and behaviors. Culture intervenes too powerfully. As Tavris and Wade (1984) point out:

> Cultural variability shows that our bodies are not straitjackets for personality. . . .
> And research reveals that experience and learning can override biological factors

to a remarkable degree: Hermaphrodites with the same physical condition can successfully be assigned to different genders. High testosterone does not make all men violent and sex-mad, nor do low estrogen and progesterone make all menstruating or menopausal women anxious and depressed. Bodily changes interact with social ones; people interpret and label—or ignore—the feelings caused by changing hormone levels according to cues provided by the social context.

Gender Theory

Each culture determines the content of gender roles in its own way. Among the Arapesh of New Guinea, both sexes possess what we consider feminine traits. Both men and women tend to be passive, cooperative, peaceful, and nurturing. The father is said to "bear a child" as well as the mother; only the father's continual care can make a child grow healthily, both in the womb and in childhood. Eighty miles away, the Mundugumor live in remarkable contrast to the peaceful Arapesh. "Both men and women," Margaret Mead (1975) observed, "are expected to be violent, competitive, aggressively sexed, jealous, and ready to see and avenge insult, delighting in display, in action, in fighting." She concluded:

> Many, if not all, of the personality traits which we have called masculine or feminine are as lightly linked to sex as are the clothing, the manners, and the form of head-dress that a society at a given period assigned to either sex. . . . The evidence is overwhelmingly in favor of social conditioning.

Biology creates males and females, but culture creates masculinity and femininity.

The social sciences have not paid much attention to *why* culture develops its particular gender roles. They have been more interested in such topics as the process of socialization and male/female differences. In the 1980s, however, gender theory developed to explore the role of gender in society. **Gender theory** argues that society may be best understood by how it is organized according to gender. Gender is viewed as a basic element in social relationships, based on the socially perceived differences between the sexes that justify unequal power relationships (Scott, 1986). Imagine, for example, an infant crying in the night. In the mother/father parenting relationship, which parent gets up to take care of the baby? In most cases, the mother does because women are socially perceived to be nurturing, and it is the woman's "responsibility" as mother (even if she hasn't fully slept in four nights and is employed full-time). Yet the father could just as easily care for the crying infant. He doesn't, because caregiving is socially perceived as "natural" to women.

In psychology, gender theory focuses on (1) how gender is created and what its purposes are, and (2) how specific traits, behaviors, or roles are defined as male or female and how they create advantages for males and disadvantages for females. Gender theorists reject the idea that biology creates male/female differences. Gender differences are largely, if not entirely, created by society (Hare-Mustin & Marecek, 1991; Lott, 1991).

The key to the creation of gender inequality lies in the belief that men and women are, indeed, "opposite" sexes; that they are opposite each other in personalities, abilities, skills, and traits. Furthermore, the differences between the sexes are unequally valued: Reason and aggression (defined as

Wives, submit yourselves unto your own husbands, as unto the Lord.
Paul of Tarsus
(Ephesians 5:22)

male traits) are considered to be more valuable than emotion and passivity (defined as female traits). In reality, however, males and females are more like each other than they are different. Both are reasonable and emotional, aggressive and passive (Ferree, 1991).

Gender is socially constructed (Lott, 1991). In other words, it is neither innate nor instinctive; it is the result of the exercise of social power. Making the sexes appear to be opposite and of unequal value requires the suppression of natural similarities by the use of social power. The exercise of social power might take the form of greater societal value being placed on appearance over achievement for women, sexual harassment of women in the workplace or school, patronizing attitudes toward women, and so on.

There are several problems with gender theory, which derives many of its ideas and assumptions from social constructionism and conflict theory. Social constructionism discounts the role of biology rather than examining how biology and society may interact to create gender differences. Furthermore, it often overstates its case: Does the fact that a few cultures do not divide people into two genders *prove* that gender is entirely socially constructed? Perhaps ignoring the existence of gender is itself socially constructed. Conflict theory reduces interactions to issues of power and dominance, which, on the abstract level, may appear to be correct. But when applied to any specific male-female relationship, such a description may not be accurate. Furthermore, gender theory underestimates altruism, love as an antidote to power, and the actual amount of cooperation between men and women in day-to-day interactions. Finally, gender theory makes several erroneous assumptions about human beings: (1) women and men are passive recipients of gender roles, (2) they are unable to form their own views and interpretations of society, and (3) they are unable to change the roles and society in which they partake.

GENDER-ROLE LEARNING

Theories of Socialization

Although there are a number of ways of examining how we acquire our gender roles, two of the most prominent are cognitive social learning theory and cognitive development theory.

Cognitive Social Learning Theory **Cognitive social learning theory** is derived from behaviorist psychology. In explaining our actions, behaviorists emphasize observable events and their consequences, rather than internal feelings and drives. According to behaviorists, we learn attitudes and behaviors as a result of social interactions with others (hence the term "social learning").

The cornerstone of cognitive social learning theory is the belief that consequences control behavior. Acts that are regularly followed by a reward are likely to occur again; acts that are regularly followed by a punishment are less likely to recur. Girls are rewarded for playing with dolls ("What a nice mommy!"), but boys are not ("What a sissy!").

This behaviorist approach has been modified recently to include **cognition**—mental processes that intervene between stimulus and response, such as evaluation and reflection. The cognitive processes involved in social learning include our ability to (1) use language, (2) anticipate consequences, and (3) make observations. By using language, we can tell our daughter that we like it when she does well in school and that we don't like it when she hits someone. A person's ability to anticipate consequences affects behavior. A boy doesn't need to wear lace stockings in public to know that such dressing will lead to negative consequences. Finally, children observe what others do. A girl may learn that she "shouldn't" play video games by seeing that the players in video arcades are mostly boys.

We also learn gender roles by imitation. Learning through imitation is called **modeling.** Most of us are not even aware of the many subtle behaviors that make up gender roles—the ways in which men and women use different mannerisms and gestures, speak differently, use different body language, and so on. We don't "teach" these behaviors by reinforcement. Children tend to model friendly, warm, and nurturing adults; they also tend to imitate adults who are powerful in their eyes—that is, adults who control access to food, toys, or privileges. Initially, the most powerful models that children have are their parents. As children grow older and their social world expands, so do the number of people who may act as their role models: siblings, friends, teachers, media figures. Children sift through the various demands and expectations associated with the different models to create their own unique selves.

Cognitive Development Theory In contrast to social learning theory, **cognitive development theory** focuses on the child's active interpretation of the messages he or she receives from the environment. Whereas social learning assumes that children and adults learn in fundamentally the same way, cognitive development theory stresses that we learn differently depending on our age. Swiss psychologist Jean Piaget showed that children's ability to reason and understand changes as they grow older (Santrock, 1983). Lawrence Kohlberg (1969) took Piaget's findings and applied them to how children assimilate gender-role information at different ages. At age 2, children can correctly identify themselves and others as boys or girls, but they tend to base this identification on superficial features such as hair and clothing. Girls have long hair and wear dresses; boys have short hair and never wear dresses. Some children even believe they can change their gender by changing their clothes or hair length. They don't identify gender in terms of genitalia, as older children and adults do. No amount of reinforcement will alter their view, because their ideas are limited by their developmental stage.

When children are 6 or 7, they begin to understand that gender is permanent; it is not something you can alter like you can change your clothes. They acquire this understanding because they are capable of grasping the idea that basic characteristics do not change. A woman can be a woman even if she has short hair and wears pants. Oddly enough, although children can understand the permanence of gender, they tend to insist on rigid adherence to gender-role stereotypes. Even though boys can play with dolls, children believe they shouldn't because dolls are for girls. Researchers speculate that children exaggerate gender roles to make the roles "cognitively clear."

According to cognitive social learning theory, boys and girls learn appropriate gender-role behavior through reinforcement and modeling. But, according to cognitive development theory, once children learn that gender is permanent, they independently strive to act like "proper" girls or boys. They do this on their own because of an internal need for congruence, the agreement between what they know and how they act. Also, children find performing the appropriate gender-role activities rewarding in itself. Models and reinforcement help show them how well they are doing, but the primary motivation is internal.

Gender-Role Learning in Childhood and Adolescence

It is difficult to analyze the relationship between biology and personality, for learning begins at birth. Evidence shows, for example, that infant females are more sensitive than infant males to pain and to sudden changes of environment. Such responses may be encouraged by learning that begins immediately after birth.

In our culture, infant girls are usually held more gently and treated more tenderly than boys, who are ordinarily subjected to rougher forms of play. The first day after birth, parents characterize their daughters as soft, fine-featured, and small, and their sons as hard, large-featured, big, and attentive. Fathers tend to stereotype their sons more extremely than mothers do (Fagot & Leinbach, 1987; Rubin, Provanzano, & Luria, 1974). Although it is impossible for strangers to know the sex of a diapered baby, once they learn the baby's sex, they respond accordingly.

Children are taught the significance of gender differences. They learn that "the dichotomy between male and female has intensive and extensive relevance to virtually every domain of human experience" (Bem, 1985). Thus, children learn very early that it is important whether someone is female or male.

Parents as Socializing Agents During infancy and early childhood, a child's most important source of learning is the primary caretaker, whether the mother, father, grandmother, or someone else. Most parents are not aware that their words and actions contribute to their children's gender-role socialization (Culp, Cook, & Housely, 1983). Nor are they aware that they treat their daughters and sons differently because of their gender. Although parents may recognize that they respond differently to sons than to daughters, they usually have a ready explanation: the "natural" differences in the temperament and behavior of girls and boys. Parents may also believe they adjust their responses to each particular child's personality. In everyday living situations that involve changing diapers, feeding babies, stopping fights, and providing entertainment, it is difficult for busy parents to recognize that their own actions may be largely responsible for the differences they attribute to nature.

Children are socialized in gender roles through four very subtle processes: manipulation, channeling, verbal appellation, and activity exposure (Oakley, 1985).

- *Manipulation.* Parents manipulate their children from infancy onward. They treat a daughter gently, tell her she is pretty, and advise her that nice girls do not fight. They treat a son roughly, tell him he is strong, and advise him that big boys do not cry. Eventually, children incorporate their parents' views in such matters as integral parts of their personalities.

- *Channeling.* Children are channeled by directing their attention to specific objects. Toys, for example, are differentiated by sex. Dolls are considered appropriate for girls, cars for boys.

- *Verbal appellation.* Parents use different words with boys and girls to describe the same behavior. A boy who pushes others may be described as "active," whereas a girl who does the same is usually called "aggressive."

- *Activity exposure.* The activity exposure of girls and boys differs markedly. Although both are usually exposed to feminine activities early in life, boys are discouraged from imitating their mothers, whereas girls are encouraged to be "mother's little helper." Even the chores children do are categorized by gender. Girls may wash dishes, make beds, and set the table; boys are assigned to carry out trash, rake the yard, and sweep the walk. The boy's domestic chores take him outside the house, whereas the girl's keep her in it—another rehearsal for traditional adult life.

It is generally accepted that parents socialize their children differently according to gender (Block, 1983; Fagot & Leinbach, 1987). Fathers, more than mothers, pressure their children to behave in gender-appropriate ways. Fathers set higher standards of achievement for their sons than for their daughters; for their daughters, fathers emphasize the interpersonal aspect of their relationship. But mothers also reinforce the interpersonal aspect of the parent-daughter relationship (Block, 1983).

By adolescence, both parents and their teenage children believe that parents treat girls and boys differently. It is not clear, however, whether parents are reacting to differences or creating them (Fagot & Leinbach, 1987). It is probably both, although by that age, gender differences are fairly well established in the minds of adolescents. Although awareness of differences may be related to parents' and adolescents' both recognizing the visible changes accompanying puberty—the development of breasts among girls and change in musculature among boys—for parents, most of the change is probably cumulative. That is, interactions with their children reflect long-held traditional beliefs about the differences between males and females. One researcher concluded that parental gender-role attitudes toward their 4-year-old children predicted their attitudes toward their children when they were 15 years old (Block, 1983).

Various studies have indicated that ethnicity and class are important in influencing gender roles (Zinn, 1990; see Wilkinson, Chow, & Zinn, 1992, for new scholarship on the intersection of ethnicity, class, and gender). Working-class families tend to differentiate more sharply between boys and girls in terms of appropriate behavior than middle-class families; they tend to place more restrictions on girls. In contrast to white families, African American families tend to socialize their daughters to be more independent (Gump, 1980; E. Smith, 1982). Indeed, among African Americans, the "traditional" female role model may never have existed. The African American female role model in which the woman is both wage-earner and homemaker is more typical and more accurately reflects African American experience (Basow, 1986).

As children grow older, their social world expands, and so do their sources of learning. Around the time children enter day care or kindergarten, teachers and peers become important influences.

Nobody was born a man; you earned your manhood, provided you were good enough.

Norman Mailer

Similarity in the exposure to activities among girls and boys helps break down the belief that females and males are opposites.

Teachers as Socializing Agents Day-care centers, nursery schools, and kindergartens are often the child's first experience in the wider world outside the family. Teachers become important role models for their students. Because most day-care, kindergarten, and elementary school teachers are women, children tend to think of child-adult interactions as primarily the province of women. In this sense, schools reinforce the idea that women are concerned with children, whereas men are not (Koblinsky & Sugawara, 1984).

Teachers tend to be conventional in the gender-role messages they convey to children (Wynn & Fletcher, 1987). They tend to encourage different activities and abilities in boys and girls. They give children messages about appropriate activities, such as contact sports for boys and gymnastics or dance for girls. Academically, teachers tend to encourage boys more than girls in math and science and girls more than boys in language skills.

Peers as Socializing Agents Peers, a person's age-mates, become especially important when children enter school. By granting or withholding approval, friends and playmates influence what games children play, what they wear, what music they listen to, what television programs they watch, and even what cereal they eat. Peers provide standards for gender-role behavior in several ways (Absismaan, Crombie, & Freeman, 1993; Carter, 1987b; Moller, Hymel, & Rubin, 1992):

1. Peers provide information about gender-role norms through play activities and toys. Girls play with dolls that cry and wet or glamorous dolls with well-developed figures and expensive tastes. Boys play with dolls known as "action figures," such as GI-Joe and Ninja Turtles with guns, numchuks, and bigger-than-life biceps.

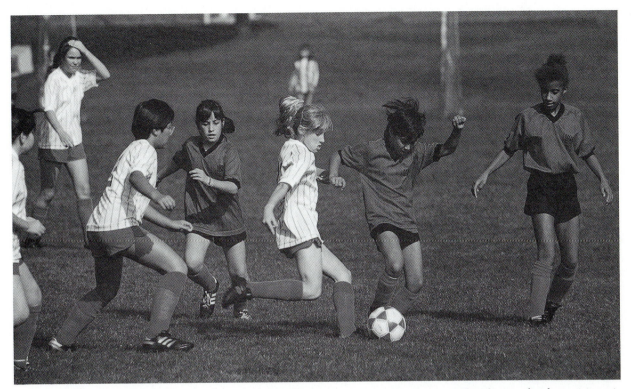

When boys and girls participate in sports together, they develop comparable athletic skills. Segregation of boys and girls encourages the development of differences that otherwise might not occur.

2. Peers influence the adoption of gender-role norms through verbal approval or disapproval. "That's for boys!" or "Only girls do that!" is a severe negative message when a girl plays with a football or a boy wears an earring.

3. Children's perceptions of their friends' gender-role attitudes, behaviors, and beliefs encourage them to adopt similar ones in order to be accepted. If a girl's friends play soccer, she is more likely to play soccer. If a boy's same-sex friends display feelings, he is more likely to display feelings.

Even though parents tend to fear the worst from peers, peers provide important positive influences. It is within their peer groups, for example, that adolescents learn to develop intimate relationships (Gecas & Seff, 1991). Adolescents in peer groups tend to be more egalitarian than parents, especially fathers (Thornton, 1989).

Media Influences Much of television programming promotes or condones negative stereotypes about gender, ethnicity, age, and gay men and lesbians. Images of women have improved somewhat in recent years, but television continues to depict rigid gender-role stereotypes. Ninety percent of the narrators in commercials are men. Males are overrepresented, and both men and women are portrayed stereotypically. Male characters are shown as aggressive and constructive; they rescue others from danger. Female characters, by contrast, are passive and submissive; they are irrational and are depicted primarily as housewives, mothers, or sex objects.

Women typically are under age 40, well-groomed, attractive, and excessively concerned with their appearance. Furthermore, ethnic stereotypes continue to be standard fare in television—"the Native American in full headdress, the black man as villain and Hispanics with lots of children" (Wardle, 1989/1990).

Not surprisingly, research indicates that heavy TV viewers, in contrast to light viewers, hold more stereotypical gender-role views (Lips, 1992). Parents need to supervise their children's TV watching, limiting their access and teaching them how to recognize stereotypes. It is especially important to lay the groundwork during childhood because once a child reaches adolescence, such supervision is next to impossible.

Gender-Role Learning in Adulthood

Researchers have generally neglected gender-role learning in adulthood (Losh-Hesselbart, 1987; Sinnott, 1986). Several scholars, however, have formulated a life-span perspective for gender-role development known as role transcendence (Hefner, Rebecca, & Oleshansky, 1975).

The role-transcendence approach argues that there are three stages an individual goes through in developing his or her gender-role identity: an undifferentiated stage, a polarized stage, and a transcendent stage. Young children have not clearly differentiated their activities into those considered appropriate for males or females. As the children enter school, however, they begin to identify behaviors as masculine and feminine. They tend to polarize masculinity and femininity as they test the appropriate roles for themselves. As they enter young adulthood, they begin slowly to shed the rigid male/female polarization as they are confronted with the realities of relationships. As they mature and grow older, women and men transcend traditional femininity and masculinity. They combine femininity and masculinity into a more complex transcendent role.

GENDER SCHEMA: EXAGGERATING DIFFERENCES

Actual differences between females and males are minimal or nonexistent, except in levels of aggression, verbal skills, and visual/spatial skills. Yet culture exaggerates these differences or creates differences where none otherwise exist (Carter, 1987c). One way that culture does this is by creating schema (Figure 5.2). As you recall from Chapter 2, a schema is a set of interrelated ideas that helps us process information by categorizing it in useful ways. We may often categorize people by age, ethnicity, nationality, physical characteristics, and so on. Gender is one such way of categorizing.

Sandra Bem (1983) observes that although gender is not inherent in inanimate objects or in behaviors, we treat many objects and behaviors as if they were masculine or feminine. These gender divisions form a complex structure of associations that affect our perceptions of reality. Bem refers to this cognitive organization of the world according to gender as **gender schema.**

Children begin thinking in terms of gender schema relatively early (Liben & Signorella, 1993). Knowledge about different aspects of gender is usually completed between ages 2 and 4. One study found that the more

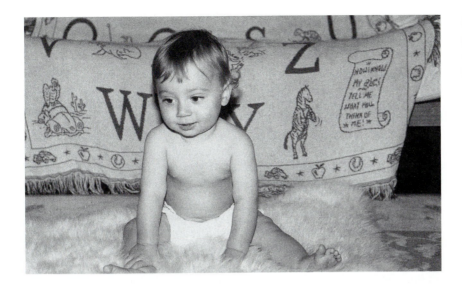

important gender was for children, the earlier they had learned it (Hort, Leinbach, & Fagot, 1991). Adults who have strong gender schemas quickly categorize people's behavior, personality characteristics, objects, and so on into masculine/feminine categories. They disregard information that does not fit their gender schema.

Our gender schema views the earth, for example, as feminine, as "Mother Earth." Humanity is collectively known as "mankind," even though there are more females than males. Some languages, such as Spanish and other Romance languages, divide nouns into masculine and feminine. We regard dogs as masculine, cats as feminine. Activities (nurturing, fighting), feelings (compassion, anger), behavior (playing with dolls or Ninja Turtles), clothing (dresses or pants), and even colors (pink or blue) are considered appropriate for one gender but not the other. But these are arbitrary associations.

When we initially meet a person, we unconsciously note whether the individual is female or male and respond accordingly (Skita & Maslach, 1990). But what happens if we can't immediately classify a person as male or female? Many of us feel uncomfortable because we don't know how to act if we don't know the gender. This is true even if gender is irrelevant, as in a bank transaction, walking past someone on the street, or answering a query about the time. ("Was that a man or woman?" a person may ask in frustration, although it makes no difference.) An inability to tell a person's gender may provoke a hostile response. As Lips (1992) writes:

> It is unnerving to be unsure of the sex of the person on the other end of the conversation. The labels *female* and *male* carry powerful associations about what to expect from the person to whom they are applied. We use the information the labels provide to guide our behavior toward other people and to interpret their behavior toward us.

Our need to classify people as female or male and its significance is demonstrated in the well-known Baby X experiment (Condry & Condry, 1976). In this experiment, three groups played with an infant known as Baby X. The first group was told that the baby was a girl, the second group was told that the baby was a boy, and the third group was not told what sex the baby was. The group that did not know what sex Baby X was felt extremely uncomfortable, but the group participants then made a decision based on whether the baby was "strong" or "soft." When the baby was labeled a boy, its fussing behavior was called "angry"; if the baby was labeled a girl, the same behavior was called "frustrated." Once the baby's gender was determined (whether correctly or not), a train of responses followed that would have profound consequences in his or her socialization. The study was replicated numerous times with the same general results. A review of studies on infant labeling found that gender stereotyping is strongest among children, adolescents, and college students (Stern & Karraker, 1989). Stereotyping diminishes with adults, especially among infants' mothers (Vogel, Lake, Evans, & Karraker, 1992).

Processing information by gender is important in cultures such as ours. First, gender-schema cultures make multiple associations between gender and other non-sex-linked qualities, such as affection and strength. Our culture regards affection as a feminine trait and strength as a masculine one. Second, such cultures make gender distinctions important, using them as a basis for norms, status, taboos, and privileges. Men are assigned leadership positions, for example, while women are placed in the rank and file (if not kept in the home); men are sexually assertive, while women are sexually passive.

"Gender has come to have cognitive primacy over many other social categories," writes Bem (1985), "because the culture has made it so." She suggests doing away with the concept of masculine and feminine altogether. Gender schemas, she argues, are not inevitable. In many cultures, the masculine/feminine division is not as important as it is in ours.

CHANGING GENDER ROLES

Within the past generation, there has been a significant shift from traditional toward more egalitarian gender roles. While women have changed more than men, men are also changing. These changes seem to affect all socioeconomic classes. Those from conservative religious groups, such as Mormons, Catholics, and fundamentalist and evangelical Protestants, adhere most strongly to traditional gender roles (Spence et al., 1985). Despite the continuing disagreement, it is likely that the egalitarian trend will continue (Mason & Lu, 1988; Thornton, 1989).

Traditional Gender Roles

One's only real life is the life one never leads.

Oscar Wilde (1854–1900)

Most gender-role studies have focused on the white middle class. Very little is known about gender roles among African Americans, Latinos, Asian Americans, and other ethnic groups (Binion, 1990; Reid & Comas-Diaz, 1990; True, 1990; see *Sex Roles* 22: 7–8 [April 1990] for a special issue on gender roles and ethnicity). As a result, white middle-class students and researchers need to be careful not to project gender-role concepts or aspirations based on their values onto other groups. Too often such projections can lead to distortions or moral judgments. There is evidence, for example, that the feelings of low self-esteem and dependence often associated with traditional female roles do not apply to African American women. In con-

Despite traditional gender-role stereotypes that depict men as instrumental, men can be nurturing as well.

trast to middle-class whites, African Americans have traditionally valued strong, independent women (Gump, 1980; E. Smith, 1982). And among Latinos, "machismo" has a positive meaning.

The Traditional Male Gender Role

What is it to be a "real" man in America? Bruce Feirstein (1982) parodied him in his book, *Real Men Don't Eat Quiche*:

Question: How many Real Men does it take to change a light bulb?

Answer: None. Real Men aren't afraid of the dark.

Question: Why did the Real Man cross the road?

Answer: It's none of your damn business.

Central personality traits associated with the traditional male role— whether white, African American, Latino, or Asian American—include aggressiveness, emotional toughness, independence, feelings of superiority, and decisiveness. Males are generally regarded as being more power-oriented than females. Men demonstrate higher degrees of aggression, especially violent aggression (such as assault, homicide, and rape), dominance, and competitiveness. While these tough, aggressive traits may be useful in the cor-

In every real man a child is hidden that wants to play.
Friedrich Nietzsche (1844–1900)

porate world, politics, and the military (or in hunting sabre-toothed tigers), such characteristics are rarely helpful to a man in his intimate relationships, which require understanding, cooperation, communication, and nurturing.

Males from ethnic groups must move between dominant and ethnic cultures with different role requirements. They are expected to conform not only to the gender-role norms of the dominant group but to those of their own group as well. Black males, for example, must conform to dominant stereotype expectations (success, competition, and aggression) as well as expectations of the African American community, most notably cooperation and the promotion of ethnic survival (Hunter & Davis, 1992). They must also confront negative stereotypes about black masculinity, such as hypersexuality and violence.

Male Sexual Scripts While considerable research exists on masculine personality traits, little work has been done on the sexual traits associated with masculinity. A preliminary study by Riseden and Hort (1992) indicates that there are eight traits regarding sexuality associated with the traditional male stereotype: (1) sexual competence, (2) the ability to give a partner orgasm(s), (3) a strong sexual desire, (4) prolonged erection, (5) reliable erection, (6) being a good lover, (7) fertility, (8) heterosexuality. The researchers suggest that sexual components of the male stereotype are more central than personality traits. They observe that their results "offer the rather sad suggestion that men's gender [role] identity may be heavily dependent on the vagaries of a capricious physiological event" (Riseden & Hort, 1992). A study of African American men found that the sexual component of their sense of manhood ranked significantly lower than other components, such as sense of self, responsibility, parenting and family, and provider (Hunter & Davis, 1992).

In sociology, a **script** refers to the acts, rules, and expectations associated with a particular role. It is like the script handed out to an actor. Unlike dramatic scripts, social scripts allow considerable improvisation within their general boundaries. We are given many scripts in life according to the various roles we play. Among them are sexual scripts that outline how we are to behave sexually when acting out our gender roles. See Chapter 10 for further discussion on sexual scripts.

Bernie Zilbergeld (1992) suggests that the male sexual script includes the following:

- *Men should not have (or at least should not express) certain feelings.* Men should not express doubts; they should be assertive, confident, and aggressive. Tenderness and compassion are not masculine feelings.

- *Performance is the thing that counts.* Sex is something to be achieved, to win at. Feelings only get in the way of the job to be done. Sex is not for intimacy but for orgasm.

- *The man is in charge.* As in other things, the man is the leader, the person who knows what is best. The man initiates sex and gives the woman her orgasm. A real man doesn't need a woman to tell him what women like; he already knows.

- *A man always wants sex and is ready for it.* It doesn't matter what else is going on, a man wants sex; he is always able to become erect. He is a machine.

- *All physical contact leads to sex.* Since men are basically sexual machines, any physical contact is a sign for sex. Touching is seen as the first step toward sexual intercourse, not an end in itself. There is no physical pleasure except sexual pleasure.

- *Sex equals intercourse.* All erotic contact leads to sexual intercourse. Foreplay is just that: warming up, getting your partner excited for penetration. Kissing, hugging, erotic touching, and oral sex are only preliminaries to intercourse.

- *Sexual intercourse leads to orgasm.* The orgasm is the proof the pudding. The more orgasms, the better the sex. If a woman does not have an orgasm, she is not sexual. The male feels that he is a failure because he was not good enough to give her an orgasm. If she requires clitoral stimulation to have an orgasm, she has a problem.

Common to all these myths is a separation of sex from love and attachment. Sex is seen as performance.

The Traditional Female Gender Role

The Traditional Female Gender Role Although many of the features of the traditional male gender role are the same across ethnic lines, such as being in control, there are striking ethnic differences in the female role.

Whites The traditional white female gender role centers around women as wives and mothers. When a woman leaves adolescence, she is expected to get married and have children. Although a traditional woman may work prior to marriage, she is not expected to defer marriage for work goals. And soon after marriage, she is expected to be "expecting." Once married, she is expected to devote her energies to her husband and family and to find her meaning as a woman by fulfilling her roles as wife and mother. Within the household, she is expected to subordinate herself to her husband. Often this subordination is sanctioned by religious teachings.

In recent years, the traditional role has been modified to include work and marriage. Work roles, however, are clearly subordinated to marital and family roles. Upon the birth of the first child, the woman is expected to remain home, if economically feasible, to become a full-time mother.

African Americans The traditional white female gender role does not extend to African American women. This may be attributed to a combination of the African heritage, slavery, which subjugated women to the same labor and hardships as men, and economic discrimination, which forced women into the labor force (Hatchett, 1991). Karen Drugger (1988) notes:

> A primary cleavage in the life experiences of Black and White women is their past and present relationship to the labor process. In consequence, Black women's conceptions of womanhood emphasize self-reliance, strength, resourcefulness, autonomy, and the responsibility of providing for the material as well as [the] emotional needs of family members. Black women do not see labor-force participation and being a wife and mother as mutually exclusive; rather, in Black culture, employment is an integral, normative, and traditional component of the roles of wife and mother.

African American men are generally more supportive than white or Latino men of more egalitarian gender roles for both women and men.

What are little girls made of?
Sugar and spice
And everything nice.
That's what little girls are made of.
What are little boys made of?
Snips and snails
And puppy dog's tails.
That's what little boys are made of.
    Nursery Rhyme

Women have served all these centuries, as looking glasses possessing the magic and delicious power of reflecting the figure of man at twice its natural size.
    Virginia Woolf (1882–1941)

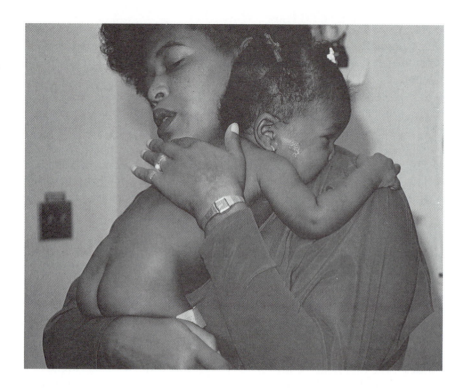

Among African Americans, the traditional female gender role includes strength and independence.

Man's love is of man's life a part; it is woman's whole existence.
Lord Byron (1788–1824)

The beautiful bird gets caged.
Chinese proverb

Latinas In traditional Latina gender roles, women subordinate themselves to males (Vasquez-Nuthall, Romero-Garcia, & DeLeon, 1987). But this subordination is based more on respect for the man's role as provider than on dominance (Becerra, 1988). Unlike in the Anglo culture, gender roles are strongly affected by age roles, in which the young subordinate themselves to the old. In this dual arrangement, notes Rosina Becerra (1988), "females are viewed as submissive, naive, and somewhat childlike. Elders are viewed as wise, knowledgeable, and deserving of respect." As a result of this intersection of gender and age roles, older women are treated with greater deference than younger women.

Female Sexual Scripts Whereas the traditional male sexual script focuses on sex over feelings, the traditional female sexual script focuses on feelings over sex, on love over passion. The traditional female sexual script cited by Lonnie Barbach (1982) includes the following ideas:

- *Sex is good and bad.* Women are taught that sex is both good and bad. What makes sex good? Sex in marriage or a committed relationship. What makes sex bad? Sex in a casual or uncommitted relationship. Sex is "so good" that you need to save it for your husband (or for someone with whom you are deeply in love). Sex is bad; if it is not sanctioned by love or marriage, you'll get a bad reputation.
- *Don't touch me "down there."* Girls are taught not to look at their genitals, not to touch them, especially not to explore them. As a result, women know very little about their genitals. They are often concerned about vaginal odors, making them uncomfortable about cunnilingus.

- *Sex is for men.* Men want sex, women want love. Women are sexually passive, waiting to be aroused. Sex is not a pleasurable activity as an end in itself; it is something performed by women *for* men.

- *Men should know what women want.* This script tells women that men know what they want, even if women don't tell them. Women are supposed to remain pure and sexually innocent. It is up to the man to arouse the woman, even if he doesn't know what a particular woman finds arousing. To keep her image of sexual innocence, she does not tell him what she wants.

- *Women shouldn't talk about sex.* Many women cannot talk about sex easily because they are not expected to have strong sexual feelings. Some women may know their partners well enough to have sex with them but not well enough to communicate their needs to them.

- *Women should look like "Playmates."* The media present ideally attractive women as beautiful models with slender hips, supple breasts, no fat; they are always young, with never a pimple, wrinkle, or gray hair in sight. As a result of these cultural images, many women are self-conscious about their physical appearance. They worry that they are too fat, too plain, too old. They often feel awkward without their clothes on to hide their imagined flaws.

- *Women are nurturers.* Women give, men receive. Women give themselves, their bodies, their pleasures to men. Everyone else's needs come first; his desire over hers, his orgasm over hers. If a woman always puts her partner's enjoyment first, she may be depriving herself of her own enjoyment. As Barbach (1982) points out, "If our attention is so totally riveted on another person, or on external events rather than on ourselves, it is impossible to experience the full pleasure and sensation of the sexual event."

- *There is only one right way to have an orgasm.* Women often "learn" that there is only one "right" way to have an orgasm: during sexual intercourse as a result of penile stimulation. But there are many ways to have an orgasm: through oral sex; manual stimulation before, during, or after intercourse; masturbation; and so on. For women who rarely or never have an orgasm during heterosexual intercourse to believe that this is the only legitimate way to have one deprives them of expressing themselves sexually in other ways.

Contemporary Gender Roles

Until recently, most Americans tended to look at women and men as if they were each a distinct species that shared few traits, behaviors, and attitudes. Males traditionally suppressed "feminine" traits in themselves, and females suppressed "masculine" traits. What is apparently happening today, especially among women, is that gender roles are becoming more androgynous—that is, incorporating both masculine and feminine traits. There is a considerable body of evidence suggesting that androgynous gender roles help us have more flexible and fulfilling relationships and lives.

Contemporary gender roles are evolving from traditional hierarchical gender roles (in which one sex is subordinate to the other) to more egali-

Everybody wants to be somebody; nobody wants to grow.
Johann Goethe (1749–1832)

Some of us are becoming the men we wanted to marry.
Gloria Steinem

tarian roles (in which both sexes are treated equally) and androgynous roles (in which both sexes display the instrumental and expressive traits previously associated with one sex). Thus, contemporary gender roles often display traditional elements as well as egalitarian and androgynous ones.

Questioning Motherhood Changes in women's roles profoundly reinforce the contemporary trend to separate sex from reproduction. Record numbers of women are rejecting motherhood because of the conflicts child rearing creates with marriage and work. It is estimated that 20–25% of female "baby boomers" are choosing to remain childfree to maximize work opportunities and time with their husbands (Nock, 1987). This contrasts with an approximately 10% childlessness rate of the previous generation.

Similarly, women are having fewer children than ever before. Stephen Nock (1987) suggests that women are limiting their fertility or remaining childfree because childbearing symbolizes the acceptance and limitations of traditional gender roles. As such, the erotic and intimate aspects of sex become even more important than the reproductive aspect in their lives. And the decision not to have children makes effective, safe birth control an even more central issue in these women's lives.

Women from ethnic and minority status groups, however, are less likely to view motherhood as an impediment. African American women and Latinas tend to place greater value on motherhood than the white (Anglo) majority. For African Americans, the tradition has generally combined work and motherhood; the two are not viewed as necessarily antithetical (Basow, 1986). For Latinas, the cultural and religious emphasis on family, the higher status conferred on motherhood, and their own familial attitudes have contributed to high fertility rates (Jorgensen & Adams, 1988).

I don't know why people are afraid
of new ideas. I am terrified of the
old ones.

John Cage (1912–1992)

The Breakdown of the Instrumental/Expressive Dichotomy The identification of masculinity with instrumentality and femininity with expressiveness appears to be breaking down. In part, this is because the instrumental/expressive dichotomy was a false dichotomy to begin with. This division of traits, developed by sociologist Talcott Parsons (1955), was more theoretical than real. Parsons believed that the more an individual was instrumental, the less he or she was expressive, and vice versa. In reality, instrumentality and expressiveness exist independently of each other (Spence et al., 1985).

While women and men may identify themselves as feminine or masculine, they generally view themselves as possessing both expressive and instrumental traits. As a group, however, men perceive themselves to be more instrumental than women do, and women perceive themselves as being more expressive than men do. A substantial minority of both sexes is relatively high in both instrumentality and expressiveness, or low in both. Interestingly, the instrumental/expressiveness ratings men and women give each other have very little to do with how they rate themselves as masculine or feminine (Spence & Sawin, 1985).

Contemporary Sexual Scripts As gender roles change, so do sexual scripts. Traditional sexual scripts have been challenged by more liberal and egalitarian ones. Sexual attitudes and behaviors have become increasingly liberal for both white and African American males and females, although

While attitudes toward motherhood are changing, especially among middle-class whites, it continues to be highly valued in our culture.

African American attitudes and behaviors continue to be somewhat more liberal than those of whites (Belcastro, 1985; Gutherie, 1988; Peters & Wyatt, 1988; Weinberg & Wilson, 1988; Wilson, 1986). Many college-age women have made an explicit break with the more traditional scripts, especially the good girl/bad girl dichotomy and the older belief that "nice" girls don't enjoy sex (Moffatt, 1989). Older professional women who are single also appear to reject the old images (Davidson & Darling, 1988). We do not know how Latino sexuality and Asian American sexuality have changed, as there is almost no research on their sexual scripts, values, and behaviors.

Contemporary sexual scripts include the following elements for both sexes (Gagnon & Simon, 1987; Reed & Weinberg, 1984; Rubin, 1990; Seidman, 1989):

- Sexual expression is a positive good.
- Sexual activities are a mutual exchange of erotic pleasure.
- Sexuality is equally involving, and both partners are equally responsible.
- Legitimate sexual activities are not limited to sexual intercourse but also include masturbation and oral-genital sex.

If sex is a war, I am a conscientious objector; I will not play.
Marge Piercy

Androgyny encourages men and women to express both instrumental and expressive qualities.

- Sexual activities may be initiated by either partner.
- Both partners have a right to experience orgasm, whether through intercourse, oral-genital sex, or manual stimulation.
- Premarital sex is acceptable within a relationship context.

These contemporary scripts give increasing recognition to female sexuality. They are increasingly relationship-centered rather than male-centered. Women, however, are still not granted full sexual equality with males (Williams & Jacoby, 1989).

All men are animals, but some make nice pets.

Mia Vogue

Throughout history the more complex activities have been defined and redefined, now as male, now as female—sometimes as drawing equally on the gifts of both sexes. When an activity to which each sex could have contributed is limited to one sex, a rich, differentiated quality is lost from the activity itself.

Margaret Mead (1901–1978)

Androgyny

Some scholars have challenged the traditional masculine/feminine gender-role dichotomy, arguing that such models are unhealthy and fail to reflect the real world. Instead of looking at gender roles in terms of polarized opposites they suggest examining them in terms of androgyny (Roopnarine & Mounts, 1987). **Androgyny** refers to flexibility in gender roles and the unique combination of instrumental and expressive traits as influenced by individual differences, situations, and stages in the life cycle (Bem, 1976; Kaplan, 1979). (The term "androgyny" is derived from the Greek *andros*,

MASCULINITY, FEMININITY, AND ANDROGYNY

Increased interest in androgynous gender roles has led to the development of a number of instruments to measure masculinity, femininity, and androgyny in individuals. The one below is patterned after the Bem Sex Role Inventory (BSRI), which is one of the most widely used tests (Bem, 1974, 1981).

To get a rough idea of how androgynous you are, examine the 21 personality traits below. Use a scale of 1 to 5 to indicate how well a personality trait describes you.

1	2	3	4	5
NOT AT ALL	SLIGHTLY	SOMEWHAT	QUITE A BIT	VERY MUCH

1. Aggressive
2. Understanding
3. Helpful
4. Decisive
5. Nurturing
6. Happy
7. Risk-taker
8. Shy
9. Unsystematic
10. Strong
11. Affectionate
12. Cordial
13. Assertive
14. Tender
15. Moody
16. Dominating
17. Warm
18. Unpredictable
19. Independent-minded
20. Compassionate
21. Reliable

Scoring

Your masculinity, femininity, and androgyny scores may be determined as follows:

1. To determine your masculinity score, add up your answers for numbers 1, 4, 7, 10, 13, 16, and 19, and divide the sum by seven.
2. To determine your femininity score, add up your answers for numbers 2, 5, 8, 11, 14, 17, and 20, and divide the sum by seven.
3. To determine your androgyny score, subtract the femininity score from the masculinity score.

The closer your score is to zero, the more androgynous you are. A high positive score indicates masculinity; a high negative score indicates femininity. A high masculine score not only indicates masculine attributes but also a rejection of feminine attributes. Similarly, a high feminine score indicates not only feminine characteristics, but a rejection of masculine attributes.

Source: Strong, Bryan, and Christine DeVault. *The Marriage and Family Experience*. St. Paul, MN: West Publishing, 1992.

man, and *gyne*, woman.) An androgynous person combines both the instrumental traits previously associated with masculinity and the expressive traits associated with traditional femininity. An androgynous lifestyle allows men and women to choose from the full range of emotions and behaviors, according to their temperament, situation, and common humanity, rather than their gender. Men are permitted to cry and display tenderness; they can touch, feel, and nurture without being considered effeminate. Women can be aggressive or career-oriented; they can seek leadership and can be mechanical or physical.

Flexibility and integration are important aspects of androgyny. Individuals who are rigidly instrumental or expressive, despite the situation, are not considered androgynous. A woman who is always aggressive at work and passive at home, for example, would not be considered androgynous, as work may call for compassion and home life for assertion.

There is considerable evidence that androgynous individuals and couples have a greater ability to form and sustain intimate relationships and adopt a wider range of behaviors and values. Androgynous college students and older people tend to have greater confidence in social situations than individuals who are **sex-typed,** following gender-role stereotypes (Puglisi & Jackson, 1981). Androgynous people have shown greater resilience to stress (Roos & Cohen, 1987). They are more aware of feelings of love and more expressive of them (Ganong & Coleman, 1987). The characteristics women often describe their ideal partner as having are those associated with androgyny (Cramer, Dragna, Cupp, & Stewart, 1991). Also, androgynous couples may have greater satisfaction in their relationships than sex-typed couples. One study found that androgynous couples felt more commitment and satisfaction in their relationships than sex-typed couples (Stephen & Harrison, 1985). Another study found that androgynous couples expressed greater sexual satisfaction than couples with stereotypical sex roles (Rozenweig & Dailey, 1989). Even those couples who generally believed themselves to be stereotypical experienced more satisfaction if they considered their behavior "feminine" in sexual situations, such as being sexually responsive, expressive, and tender. Transcending traditional female and male behaviors and values, the androgynous couples were more flexible in their responses to each other and to the environment.

It is not clear what proportion of individuals may be identified as androgynous or traditional. Although it has been suggested that androgyny is a white middle-class concept, one study (Binion, 1990) of African American women indicated that 37% identified themselves as androgynous, 18% as feminine, and 24% as masculine. (The remaining women did not identify themselves.) That such a large percentage were androgynous or masculine, the study argues, is not surprising, given the demanding family responsibilities and cultural expectations that require instrumental and active traits. Another study of college students from India indicated a high degree of androgyny, suggesting cross-cultural validity (Ravinder, 1987).

Androgyny, like other personality theories, assumes that masculinity and femininity are basic aspects of an individual's personality. It assumes that when we are active, we are expressing our masculine side, and when we are sensitive, we are expressing the feminine side of our personality. Androgyny retains the concept of masculinity and femininity, and thus it retains some of the categories of bipolar gender role thinking (Willemsen, 1993).

Living up to an androgynous gender role may be just as stultifying to an individual as trying to be traditionally feminine or masculine. In advocating the expression of both feminine and masculine traits, perhaps we are imposing a new form of gender-role rigidity on ourselves. Bem, one of the leading proponents of androgyny, has become increasingly critical of the idea. She believes now that androgyny replaces "a prescription to be masculine or feminine with the doubly incarcerating prescription to be masculine *and* feminine. The individual now has not one but two potential sources of inadequacy to contend with" (Bem, 1983).

Some researchers have hypothesized that instrumental traits in general, rather than androgyny, may lead to higher self-esteem for both women and men (Orlofsky & O'Heron, 1987). It is not always clear whether androgyny or instrumentality is the most important factor accounting for higher rates of self-esteem, adjustment, and flexibility (Basow, 1985). There is evidence that traditional feminine traits, such as passivity, are associated with depression among the elderly (Krames, England, & Flett, 1988). It will probably be some time before these factors can be tested to everyone's satisfaction.

GENDER PROBLEMS: HERMAPHRODITISM AND TRANSSEXUALITY

For most of us, there is no question about our gender: We *know* we are female or male. We may question our femininity or masculinity, but rarely do we question being female or male. For hermaphrodites and transsexuals, however, "What sex am I?" is a real and painful question. Their dilemma, however, reinforces the fact that our gender identity as male or female is not "natural" but learned.

Hermaphroditism: Chromosomal and Hormonal Errors

Unusual genital or physical development can make a person's sex unclear. Usually such ambiguity is caused by chromosomal or hormonal errors during prenatal development. Sometimes a child is born with an underdeveloped penis or an enlarged clitoris, making it unclear whether the child is male or female. The most common chromosomal and hormonal errors in prenatal development are discussed below. They are summarized in Table 5.1.

Many of these individuals are **hermaphrodites,** males or females possessing the sex characteristics of both sexes, as mentioned in Chapter 1. (The term is derived from Hermaphroditus in Greek mythology; the son of Hermes and Aphrodite, he and the nymph Salmacis merged into a single body that possessed both male and female genitals.) A *true hermaphrodite* develops both male and female gonads: either one of each, two of each, or two ovotestes (gonads that have both ovarian and testicular tissue in the same gland). The external appearance of a true hermaphrodite is ambiguous, with genital and other physical characteristics of both sexes. *Pseudohermaphrodites*, as we saw in Chapter 1, have two testes or two ovaries but an ambiguous genital appearance. (While rare among humans, hermaphroditism is fairly common in the animal world, where snails, for example, possess the reproductive organs of both sexes, changing "genders" for the purpose of copulation.)

TABLE 5.1 Abnormalities in Prenatal Development

	Chromosomal Sex*	Gonads	Internal Reproductive Structures	External Reproductive Structures	Secondary Sex Characteristics	Gender Identity
Chromosomal Errors						
Turner syndrome	Female (45, XO)	Nonfunctioning or absent ovaries	Normal female except for ovaries	Underdeveloped genitals	No breast development or menstruation at puberty	Female
Klinefelter syndrome	Male (47, XXY)	Testes	Normal male	Small penis and testes	Female secondary sex characteristics develop at puberty	Male, but frequent gender confusion at puberty
Hormonal Errors						
Androgen-insensitivity syndrome	Male (46, XY)	Testes, but body unable to utilize androgen (testosterone)	Shallow vagina, lacks normal male structures	Labia	Female secondary sex characteristics develop at puberty; no menstruation	Female
Congenital adrenal hyperplasia (pseudo-hermaphroditism)	Female (46, XX)	Ovaries	Normal female	Ambiguous, tending toward male appearance; fused vagina and enlarged clitoris may be mistaken for empty scrotal sac and micropenis	Female secondary sex characteristics develop at puberty	Usually male unless condition discovered at birth and rectified by hormonal therapy
DHT deficiency	Male (46, XY)	Testes undescended until puberty	Partially formed internal structures but no prostate	Ambiguous; clitoral-appearing micropenis; penis enlarges and testes descend at puberty	Male secondary sex characteristics develop at puberty	Female identity until puberty; majority assume male identity later

* Chromosomal sex refers to 46, XX (female) or 46, XY (male). Sometimes a chromosome will be missing, as in 45, XO, or there will be an extra chromosome, as in 47, XXY. In these notations, the number refers to the number of chromosomes (46, in 23 pairs, is normal); the letters X and Y refer to chromosomes and O refers to a missing chromosome.

Because society does not accept sex ambiguity, when an infant is born with ambiguous genitalia, both parents and physician give the newborn a gender assignment as soon as possible. (In some cultures, ambiguous genitalia result in the child's being killed [Jacobs & Cromwell, 1992].) Sometimes the assignment is arbitrary. To make the gender assignment more definitive, the physician may tell the parents that the newborn is "really" a girl or a boy and merely needs hormonal or surgical treatment to correct the infant's anatomy. The physician examines the infant and, based on the physical characteristics and possibility for treatment, decides whether to pronounce the newborn a boy or a girl.

Interestingly, the basis for this decision reflects cultural beliefs as much as it does the infant's "real" sex. For instance, during the nineteenth century, when a woman's role as mother was considered basic to her identity, the determining factor for a newborn's gender assignment was whether ovaries were present. If they were, the infant was generally pronounced a girl; if they were absent, the infant was pronounced a boy. In contemporary America, however, sexuality is emphasized more than reproduction. As a result, external reproductive organs are more important than internal ones in assigning gender. Thus, a newborn with an enlarged clitoris and fused vagina would be reared as male, even if the internal female organs were normal (Costlier, 1990).

Sometimes a child may develop as one sex, but upon puberty begins to develop the physical characteristics of the other sex. And as the child matures, he or she may be confronted with genitals or other physical characteristics that fail to conform to cultural definitions of maleness or femaleness. As one can imagine, such situations create great turmoil and confusion. What most of us take for granted—our femaleness or maleness—is for them problematical.

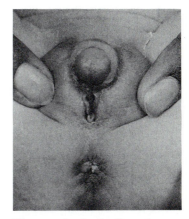

The genitals of a fetally androgenized female may resemble those of a male.

Chromosomal Errors Chromosomal errors are common. One study of 35,000 Danish newborns found that the incidence of sex chromosome errors was 1 in 426 children, or 2.34 in 1000 (Nielsen & Wohlert, 1991). Chromosomal errors occur when an individual has fewer or more X or Y chromosomes than normal. Abnormally elevated levels of human chorionic gonadotropin (HCG) during pregnancy may indicate the infant is at risk for a sex chromosome error (Barnes-Kedar, Amiel, Maor, & Fejgin, 1993). There are two syndromes resulting from erroneous chromosomal patterns that may result in gender confusion: Turner syndrome and Klinefelter syndrome. In both of these, the body develops with some marked physical characteristics of the other sex.

Turner Syndrome Females with **Turner syndrome** are born lacking an X chromosome (notated as 45, XO). It is one of the most common chromosomal errors among females, occurring about once in 2500 live births (Mullins, Lynch, Orten, & Youll, 1991). (About 95% of embryos and fetuses with Turner syndrome are spontaneously aborted [Kelly, Ferguson, & Golden, 1992].) Mothers are twice as likely as fathers to be the carrier of the error; there is no firm evidence that it is linked to maternal age (Hassold, Arnovitz, Jacobs, May, & Robinson, 1990; Mathur, Stekol, Schatz, Macharen, Scott, & Lippe, 1991).

Infants and young girls with Turner syndrome appear normal externally, but they have no ovaries. At puberty, changes initiated by ovarian hormones cannot take place. The body does not gain a mature look or height, and menstruation cannot occur. School-age children often experience academic and social-adjustment problems (Downy, Elkin, Ehrhard, Meyer-Balburg, Bell, & Morishima, 1991; Williams, 1992; Williams, Richman, & Yarbrough, 1992). The adolescent girl may question her femaleness because she does not menstruate or develop breasts like her peers. Hormonal therapy, including estrogen therapy and human growth hormone (HGH) therapy, can replace the hormones necessary to produce normal adolescent changes, such as growth and menstruation (LaFranchi, 1992; Rongen-Westerlaken, Vanes, Wit, Otten, & Demuink, 1992; Rosenfeld, Frane, Altic, Brasel, Bursten, & Clara, 1992). In some cases without hormonal treatment, the pubertal growth spurt will occur two or three years after the normal time (Massa, Maes, Heinrichs, Vandewegke, Craen, & Vanderschueren-Lodeweyckx, 1993; Pelz, Sager, Hinkel, Kirchner, Kruger, & Verroy, 1991).

Even with hormonal therapy, women with Turner syndrome will likely remain infertile; there are only 13 known cases of fertile women with Turner syndrome. Often the syndrome is first discovered when women come into fertility centers. Despite their syndrome, they may successfully give birth through embryo transfer following in vitro fertilization with donated ova (Rogers, Murphy, Leeton, Hoise, & Beaton, 1992). (For a review essay on Turner syndrome, see Verschraegen-Spae, Dypere, Speleman, Dhondt, & De Paepe, 1992).

Klinefelter Syndrome   Males with **Klinefelter syndrome** have one or more extra X chromosomes (47, XXY; 48, XXXY; or 49, XXXXY). One study estimated the incidence as 1 in 576 boys (Nielsen & Wohlert, 1991). The presence of the Y chromosome designates a person as male. It causes the formation of testes and ensures a masculine physical appearance. However, the presence of a double X chromosome pattern, which is a female trait, adds some female physical traits. At puberty, female secondary sex characteristics such as breasts and hips will develop, and male characteristics tend to be weak: small penis and testes; scanty, soft body hair. XXY boys often experience a lag in neurological development, have academic difficulties, and are prone to psychological distress (Mandoki, Hoffman, & Riconda, 1991). The XXY male is often confused about his gender identity. He may be subject to teasing or ridicule by others. If the condition is identified early, many of the problems associated with it will respond to hormonal treatment (Mandoki & Sumner, 1991). Because of low testosterone levels, the vast majority of males with the syndrome are unable to experience erections; virtually all are sterile.

Hormonal Errors   As discussed in Chapters 3 and 4, men and women both produce androgens (masculinizing hormones) and estrogens (feminizing hormones). The natural trend of the body is to develop as female. Furthermore, it is not the level of androgens or estrogens in the body that affects development as much as the ratio of one to the other (Ledwitz-Rigby, 1980). Hormonal imbalances may result in males and females developing physical characteristics associated with the other sex.

Androgen-Insensitivity Syndrome **Androgen-insensitivity syndrome** or **testicular feminization** is a hereditary condition passed through X chromosomes (Williams, Patterson, & Hughes, 1993; see Kaplan & Owett, 1993, for female androgen-deficiency syndrome.) A genetic male is born with testes, but because of his body's inability to absorb testosterone, the estrogen influence prevails. From the earliest stages, therefore, his body tends toward a female appearance, failing to develop male internal and external reproductive structures. Externally the infant is female, with labia and vagina, but the internal female structures are not present. At puberty, the body develops breasts, hips, and other secondary female sex characteristics. The testes remain in the abdomen and are sterile. People with androgen insensitivity are usually assigned female gender status at birth (Gooren & Cohen-Kettenis, 1991; Shah, Wooley, & Costin, 1992).

Physically, individuals with androgen-insensitivity syndrome develop as typical females, except for their inability to menstruate. They appear to have more or less the same cognitive abilities as others (Imperato-McGinley, Pichardo, Gautier, Voyer, & Bryden, 1991). It is often not until puberty that the physical anomaly is discovered. Usually the person is comfortable about her female gender identity. She can enjoy sex and orgasm (Money & Tucker, 1975).

Congenital Adrenal Hyperplasia In **congenital adrenal hyperplasia** (formerly known as adrenogenital syndrome), a genetic female with ovaries and vagina develops externally as a male, the result of a malfunctioning adrenal gland. The adrenal gland produces androgen instead of androgen-inhibiting cortisone. An individual afflicted with congenital adrenal hyperplasia is sometimes known as a pseudohermaphrodite.

At birth, the child appears to be a male with a penis and an empty scrotum. The appearance, however, may be ambiguous. Some have only an enlarged clitoris, with or without a vaginal opening, some a micropenis, and some a complete penis and scrotum. When the situation is discovered at birth, the child is usually assigned female status, and treatment is given to promote female development. The child develops as a female. If the condition is discovered after the child establishes a male gender identity, a decision must be made to support the male gender identity or to initiate a sex change.

DHT Deficiency Because of a genetic disorder, some males are unable to convert testosterone into the hormone dihydrotestosterone (DHT). This disorder is known as **DHT deficiency.** DHT is required for the normal development of external male genitalia. At birth, children with DHT deficiency have internal male organs but clitorislike penises, undescended testes, labialike scrotums, and closed vaginal cavities. They are usually identified as girls. At puberty, however, their testes descend and their clitorises begin to resemble penises.

Transsexuality

Gender dysphoria is the state of dissatisfaction individuals experience when they feel they are trapped in the body of the "wrong" sex (Freund & Watson, 1993; Pauly, 1990). They feel they are not *really* the gender to which their genitals have "condemned" them. Gender dysphoric people who wish to have, or have had, their genitals surgically altered to conform to their gender identity are known as **transsexuals.** Transsexuals are classified as preoperative transsexuals and postoperative transsexuals.

Many people are confused about the transsexual phenomenon. They often wonder whether a person is *really* a man or woman following transsexual surgery. But as John Money and Patricia Tucker (Money & Tucker, 1975) point out:

> When you see a transsexual . . . it's no use asking, "Is she *really* still a man, or was he *really* a woman all those years?" The question is meaningless. All you can say is that this is a person whose sex organs differentiated as male and whose gender identity differentiated as female. Medical science has found ways to reduce the incompatibility by modifying anatomy to help that person achieve unity as a member of a sex, . . . but medical science has not yet found a way to modify a fully differentiated gender identity.

I wish I could change my sex as I change my shirt.

André Breton (1896–1966)

In transsexuality, the individual's gender identity and sexual anatomy are at war. Transsexuals are convinced that by some strange quirk of fate they have been given the body of the wrong sex. They generally want to change their sex, not their personality. Many have little interest in sexual relationships. It is more important for them to acquire the anatomy of the desired gender than to have greater sexual satisfaction (Arndt, 1991; Braunthal, 1981).

As transsexuality revolves around issues of gender identity, it is a distinctly different phenomenon from cross-dressing, transvestism, or homosexuality. Transvestites, cross-dressers, gay men, and lesbians are not transsexuals (Garber, 1991). In contrast to transsexuals, they feel confident of their female or male identity. Being lesbian or gay reflects sexual orientation rather than gender questioning. A study of female-to-male transsexuals and lesbians, for example, revealed that most members of both groups had sexual experiences with males, but the female-to-male transsexuals fantasized being males, while the lesbians completely identified with being female (McCauley & Ehrhardt, 1980). Furthermore, postoperative transsexuals may or may not change their sexual orientation, whether it is toward members of the same, the other, or both sexes.

In Western culture, because of the equations penis = male and vulva = female, transsexuals often seek surgery to bring their genitals in line with their gender identity (Hausman, 1992). A few transsexuals, however, are able to successfully "change" their gender without surgery. They identify themselves as women who happen to have male genitals. Various forms of therapy help transsexuals sort out the different lifestyle options, including transsexual surgery, changing one's gender identity to conform with anatomical sex, or accepting one's gender identity despite conflicting genitalia by prioritizing gender identity over anatomy (Edelman, 1986; Stermac, Blanchard, Clemmensen, & Ray, 1991). Currently, the most popular alternative is surgery, distantly followed by changing gender identity. Relatively few choose to accept a gender identity that conflicts with their anatomical sex. (For a review of the clinical treatment of gender dysphoria, see Brown, 1990.)

Estimates of the prevalence of transsexuality vary greatly, ranging from 1 in 100,000 to 1 in 37,000 for males and from 1 in 400,000 to 1 in 100,000 for females. In countries where there is greater tolerance of transsexuality, such as the Netherlands, estimates of male transsexuals range from 1 in 29,000 to 1 in 18,000 (Arndt, 1991). Some cultures, however, accept a gender identity that is not congruent with sexual anatomy and create an alternative third sex, as we saw in Chapter 1. "Men-women"—Native American berdaches, Indian *hijas*, and Burmese *acaults*—are considered a third gender (Bullough, 1991; Coleman, Colgan, & Gooren, 1992; Roscoe, 1991). Members of these third genders are often believed to possess spiritual powers because of their "specialness." Our culture, however, provides no similar category, and such discordance in gender identity is considered pathological.

Causes of Transsexuality There are no known definitive causes of transsexuality (Arndt, 1991; Bullough, 1991; Money, 1980). Among those known as *primary transsexuals*, transsexuality may begin in childhood; it is detectable sometimes in the first two years after birth. *Secondary transsexuals* experience gender dysphoria later, usually in adulthood. Parents of primary transsexuals often remark that their male children, who by age 4 or 5 identified themselves psychologically as girls, had acted as girls from the very beginning. Throughout childhood, these children engaged in girls' activities, play, and dress; they moved, walked, and ran as girls. Their playmates were girls. By the time the transsexual child reaches late adolescence, he may request an operation to change his genitals to those of a woman's; male to female operations vastly outnumber female to male by a ratio of three to one. By this time, the adolescent has usually learned the roles associated with femininity so well that he can easily pass as a woman in most situations.

Because primary transsexuals have lived much of their lives in their preferred gender (despite their genitals), they are often able to move into their "new" gender with relative ease. Secondary transsexuals, however, who have lived most of their lives in their assigned gender, have more difficulty in making the transition to the behaviors associated with their preferred gender (Leavitt & Burger, 1990).

Preoperative transsexuals vary in their interest in sexual activity. One study of preoperative male-to-female transsexuals who were attracted to males found that 44% abstained from sexual activity, 19% were sexually active but avoided using their penises, and 37% were sexually active with their penises and enjoyed their experiences (Leavitt & Berger, 1990).

Transsexual Surgery Many transsexuals do not view their dilemma as a psychological problem but as a medical one. As a result, they tend to seek surgeons who may change their genitalia rather than psychiatrists who can change their gender identity (Pauly & Edgerton, 1986).

Gender dysphoric individuals seeking **sex reassignment surgery (SRS),** the surgical process by which the reproductive organs are surgically altered from one sex to the other, go through a comprehensive treatment program prior to their operation. There are four basic steps:

1. *Gender dysphoria therapy*. The client meets with a therapist or group of other gender dysphoric individuals regularly for a period of six months. The client must demonstrate to the therapist that a persistent desire has existed for at least two years to be rid of his or her assigned gender and

The genitals of a postoperative female-to-male transsexual, left, and the genitals of a postoperative male-to-female transsexual, right.

 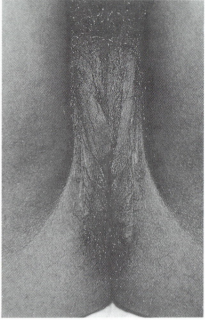

genitals prior to hormonal treatment (Chong, 1990). One study reported that 23% of those attending a gender dysphoria clinic eventually were referred for sex reassignment surgery (Burns, Farrell, & Christie-Brown, 1990).

2. *Hormonal treatment.* Preoperative males-to-females receive estrogen therapy and females-to-males receive testosterone therapy. These therapies induce the appropriate secondary sex characteristics, such as breasts for male-to-female transsexuals, and facial and body hair and penises (enlarged clitorises) for female-to-male transsexuals.

3. *Living as a member of the preferred gender.* The client must live successfully for a year as a member of the preferred gender. This is not an easy task, for such subtle gender clues as mannerisms, voice inflections, and body movement, learned in childhood, must be altered.

4. *Sex reassignment surgery (SRS).* For former males, SRS involves the removal of the penis and testes and the construction of a clitoris from the former penis, vaginal lips from excess skin and tissue, and an artificial vagina (Hage, Bout, Bloem, & Negens, 1993). For former females, the clitoris is refashioned into a penis, removable penile implants are used for erections, and a scrotum is built with artificial testes (Eldh, 1993; Fang, Chen, & Ma, 1992). Some are able to experience orgasm (Lief & Hubschman, 1993). Because the surgery is considered necessary rather than cosmetic, Medicaid will fund it (Gordon, 1991).

Of the estimated 10,000–15,000 transsexuals in the United States, about 3000–4000 have undergone surgery to correct nature's anatomical "mistake." Unfortunately, there have been few long-term studies of the impact of SRS on adjustment. A longitudinal study (Lindemalm, 1986) of thirteen male-to-female transsexuals found that about one-third felt the surgery was a mistake. Other studies are not as pessimistic. Several factors appear to affect the satisfaction of postoperative transsexuals. First, the surgery must be skillfully done so that the transsexual will have a positive body image (Ross & Need, 1989). Second, gay men and lesbians are generally more satisfied with their transsexual status than are heterosexuals (Blanchard, Steiner, Clemmensen, & Dickey, 1989). Third, female-to-male transsexuals appear to be more satisfied than males to females in terms of sexual satisfaction and intimate relationships (both preoperatively and postoperatively) (Kockott & Fahrner, 1988). Fourth, primary transsexuals have an easier adjustment than secondary transsexuals because of their greater amount of experience in their preferred gender (Leavitt & Burger, 1990).

We ordinarily take our gender as female or male for granted. The making of gender, however, is a complex process involving both biological and psychological elements. Biologically, we are male or female in terms of genetic and anatomical makeup. Psychologically, we are male or female in terms of our assigned gender and our gender identity. Only in rare cases, as with chromosomal and hormonal errors or gender dysphoria, is our gender identity problematical. For most of us, gender identity is rarely a source of concern. More often, what concerns us is related to our gender roles: Am I sufficiently masculine? Feminine? What it means to be feminine or masculine differs from culture to culture. While femininity and masculinity are regarded as opposites in our culture, there are relatively few significant inherent differences aside from males impregnating and females giving birth and lactating. The majority of social and psychological differences are exaggerated or culturally encouraged. All in all, women and men are more similar than different.

SUMMARY

Studying Gender and Gender Roles

- *Sex* is the biological aspect of being female or male. *Gender* is the social and cultural characteristics associated with biological sex. Normal gender development depends on both biological and psychological factors. Psychological factors include *assigned gender* and *gender identity*. *Gender roles* are the roles that tell us how we are to act as men and women.

- While our culture encourages us to think that men and women are "opposite" sexes, they are more similar than dissimilar. Innate gender differences are generally minimal; differences are encouraged by socialization.

- Masculine and feminine stereotypes assume heterosexuality. If men or women do not fit the stereotypes, they are likely to be considered gay or lesbian. Gay men and lesbians, however, are as likely as heterosexuals to be masculine or feminine.

Explaining Gender Roles: What's Sex Got to Do With It?

- *Sociobiology* is based on an evolutionary theory asserting that nature has structured us with an inborn desire to pass on our individual genes; this desire motivates much of our behavior. According to sociobiology, males want to impregnate as many females as possible; females want partners who will assist in child rearing and support. Accordingly, for males, sex is important; for females, love is important. Limitations of this theory include primary reliance on animal rather than human studies, the fact that direct genetic evidence is difficult or impossible to obtain, the fact that theories cannot be empirically tested, and explanations that are too abstract to apply to individual behavior.

• *Gender theory* examines gender as a basic element in society and social arrangements. It focuses on how gender is created and how and why specific traits, behaviors, and roles benefit or cost women and men. In general, gender theorists believe gender differences are socially created to the benefit of men. Limitations of this theory include the discounting of biology, a commitment to conflict theory, an underestimation of altruism and love in male-female relationships, and erroneous assumptions about the passivity of individuals in changing and creating roles.

Gender-Role Learning

• The two most important socialization theories are cognitive social learning theory and cognitive development theory. *Cognitive social learning theory* emphasizes learning behaviors from others through *cognition* and *modeling*. *Cognitive development theory* asserts that once children learn gender is permanent, they independently strive to act like "proper" girls and boys because of an internal need for congruence.

• Children learn their gender roles from parents through manipulation, channeling, verbal appellation, and activity exposure. Parents, teachers, peers, and the media are the most important agents of socialization during childhood and adolescence.

• A life-span perspective of gender roles views individuals as going through three stages: undifferentiated, polarized, and transcendent.

Gender Schema: Exaggerating Differences

• *Gender schema* is the cognitive organization of the world according to gender. Children to whom gender is most important have learned about it earlier than those to whom it is relatively unimportant. Gender schema classifies many non-gender related objects, behaviors and activities as male or female. Classifying a person as male/female is very important in our culture, as the Baby X experiment suggests.

Changing Gender Roles

• The traditional male gender role emphasizes aggression, independence, instrumentality, and sexual prowess. Traditional male sexual scripts include the denial of the expression of feelings, an emphasis on performance and being in charge, the belief that men always want sex and that all physical contact leads to sex, and assumptions that sex equals intercourse and that sexual intercourse always leads to orgasm.

• Traditional female roles emphasize passivity, compliance, physical attractiveness, and being a wife and mother. Among African Americans, women are expected to be instrumental; there is no conflict between work and motherhood. Among Latinos, women are deferential to men generally from respect rather than subservience; elders, regardless of gender, are afforded respect.

• Female sexual scripts suggest that sex is good and bad (depending on the context); genitals should not be touched; sex is for men; men should know what women want; women shouldn't talk about sex; women should look like "Playmates"; women are nurturers; and there is only one right way to experience an orgasm.

• Contemporary gender roles are more egalitarian. Important changes affecting today's gender roles include increasing questioning, especially among white women, of motherhood as a core female identity; and the breakdown of the instrumental/expressive dichotomy.

• Contemporary sexual scripts are more egalitarian and include the belief that sex is a positive good, that it involves a mutual exchange, and that it may be initiated by either partner.

• *Androgyny* combines traditional female and male characteristics into a more flexible pattern of behavior, rather than seeing them as opposites. Evidence suggests that androgyny contributes to psychological and emotional health.

Gender Problems: Hermaphroditism and Transsexuality

• A number of hormonal and chromosomal errors can affect gender development. Some of these errors can result in people who are known as *hermaphrodites* or *pseudohermaphrodites*. Chromosomal errors include *Turner syndrome* and *Klinefelter syndrome*. Hormonal errors include *androgen-insensitivity syndrome, congenital adrenal hyperplasia*, and *DHT deficiency*.

• *Gender dysphoria* is the state of dissatisfaction individuals may experience about their gender. People who have (or plan to have) surgery to construct the "appropriate" gender are known as *transsexuals*. This surgery is known as *sex reassignment surgery (SRS)*. Transsexuals are not gay or lesbian. The causes of transsexuality are not known.

KEY TERMS

sex

genetic sex

anatomical sex

gender

assigned gender

gender identity

gender role

gender-role stereotype

gender-role attitude

gender-role behavior

instrumentality

expressiveness

sociobiology

gender theory

cognitive social learning theory

cognition

modeling

cognitive development theory

peer

gender schema

script

androgyny

sex-typed

hermaphrodite

Turner syndrome

Klinefelter syndrome

androgen-insensitivity syndrome

testicular feminization

congenital adrenal hyperplasia

DHT deficiency

gender dysphoria

transsexual

sex reassignment surgery (SRS)

SUGGESTIONS FOR FURTHER READING

Ehrenreich, Barbara. *The Hearts of Men: American Dreams and the Flight from Commitment*. Garden City, NY: Doubleday, 1984. A provocative analysis of contemporary male-female relationships, in which men reject commitment because it forces them into stifling, traditional roles.

Fausto-Sterling, Anne. *Myths of Gender: Biological Theories About Women and Men*. New York: Basic Books, 1985. A well-written book by a developmental geneticist arguing that most biological explanations of gender differences are unscientific justifications for traditional gender roles that subordinate women to men.

Kimmel, Michael S., and Michael A. Messner. *Men's Lives*, 2nd ed. New York: Macmillan, 1992. A collection of essays on contemporary multiethnic masculinity.

Rodgers-Rose, La Frances, ed. *The Black Woman*. Beverly Hills, CA: Sage Publications, 1980. Essays on various aspects of being black and female in America.

Rubin, Lillian. *Intimate Strangers: Men and Women Together*. New York: Harper & Row, 1983. A sensitive discussion of the sources of male-female misunderstandings—the female need for union and the male need for separation—which turn husbands and wives into "intimate strangers."

Tavris, Carol. *The Mismeasure of Woman*. New York: Simon & Schuster, 1992. An examination of various misconceptions and biases that affect our understanding of women; includes critiques of sociobiology, the G spot, premenstrual and postmenstrual syndromes, and the codependency and addiction movements.

Wainrib, Barbara Rubin, ed. *Gender Issues Across the Life Cycle*. New York: Springer Publishing Company, 1992. Clinically oriented essays on developmental issues facing men and women from adolescence through old age.

Chapter Six

SEXUALITY FROM CHILDHOOD THROUGH ADOLESCENCE

PREVIEW: SELF-QUIZ

1. Our education about what's "right" and "wrong" sexually begins in infancy. True or false?

2. Masturbation is not healthy, and children should be discouraged from engaging in it. True or false?

3. Peer pressure does not actually have as much influence on teenagers as is commonly believed. True or false?

4. Many gay and lesbian teenagers are aware of their sexual orientation but are very fearful of revealing it. True or false?

5. Oral sex is one of the least common sexual behaviors among teenagers. True or false?

6. By age 19, over two-thirds of young women and young men have engaged in sexual intercourse. True or false?

7. Most teenagers do not use contraceptives when they begin having intercourse. True or false?

8. Risk taking is a normal and healthy part of growing up. True or false?

9. The United States has the highest teenage pregnancy rate among developed countries. True or false?

10. Studies show that most teenage fathers want to provide for their children. True or false?

ANSWERS 1. T, 2. F, 3. F, 4. T, 5. F, 6. T, 7. T, 8. T, 9. T, 10. T

Chapter Outline

Although we are reproductive beings for part of our life, we are sexual beings for our whole life. Infants and young children are capable of sexual arousal and orgasm (Kinsey, Pomeroy, Martin, & Gebhard, 1953; Montauk and Clasen, 1989). Sonograms reveal that male fetuses have erections (Calderone, 1983a). But sexuality is more than genital activity, body parts, and their functions. Culture gives meaning to sexuality on many levels—spiritual, emotional, intellectual, and social—that influence us from birth to death. Thus, the dimensions of our sexuality include how we feel about our bodies, how we acquire gender and social roles, and how we achieve love and intimacy. These dimensions develop continuously throughout infancy, childhood, and adolescence; they form the basis of our adult sexual self.

In this chapter, we discuss both the innate and the learned aspects of sexuality from infancy through adolescence. We discuss both physical development and **psychosexual development,** which involves the psychological aspects of sexuality. We see how culture, the family, the media, and other factors affect children's feelings about their bodies and influence their sexual

I only know that summer sang in me . . .
    Edna St. Vincent Millay

Kissing and cuddling are essential to an infant's healthy psychosexual development.

feelings and activities. We look at how the physical changes experienced by teenagers affect their sexual awareness and sexual identity as heterosexual, gay, or lesbian. We also discuss adolescent sexual behaviors, sex education, teenage pregnancy, and teenage parenthood.

Most studies about children and sex deal exclusively with areas such as sexual abuse, teenage risk taking, and adolescent pregnancy. The danger of such a problem-oriented approach is that it misleads us into thinking that problems are the norm. While there are many challenges faced by young people, and many stresses for their parents as well, growing up is a process that includes exploration, self-discovery, and relationship building. In addition to frustration and tears, it offers the possibilities of fulfillment and joy.

INFANT SEXUALITY

Infants cannot talk to us about their lives, and most of us don't remember what happened or how we felt when we were babies. Our understanding of infant sexuality is based on observation and inference. It is obvious that babies derive sensual pleasure from stroking, cuddling, bathing, and other tactile stimulation. Ernest Borneman, a researcher of children's sexuality since the 1950s, suggests that the first phase of sexual development be called the cutaneous phase (from the Greek *kytos*, skin). During this period, an infant's skin can be considered a "single erogenous zone" (Borneman, 1983).

The young child's healthy psychosexual development lays the foundation for further stages of growth (Constantine & Martinson, 1981). Psychosexual maturity, including the ability to love, begins to develop in infancy when babies are lovingly touched all over their appealing little bodies (which appear to be designed to attract the caresses of their elders).

Infants and very young children communicate by smiling, gesturing, crying, and so on. Before they understand our words, they learn to interpret our movements, facial expressions, body language, and tone of voice. Our earliest lessons are conveyed in these ways. During infancy, we begin to learn how we "should" feel about our bodies. If a parent frowns, speaks sharply, or spanks an exploring hand, the infant quickly learns that a particular activity—touching the genitals, for example—is not right. The infant may or may not continue the activity, but if he or she does, it will be in secret, probably accompanied by the beginnings of guilt and shame (Renshaw, 1988).

Infants also learn about the gender role they are expected to fulfill. In our culture, baby girls are often handled more gently than baby boys. They are dressed up more and given soft toys and dolls to play with. Baby boys are expected to be "tough." Their dads may roughhouse with them and speak more loudly to them than to their sisters. They will be given "boy toys"—blocks, cars, and tiny plastic "superheroes." This gender-role learning is reinforced as the child grows older (see Chapter 5).

Learning about sex in our society is learning about guilt.

John Gagnon and
William Simon

CHILDHOOD SEXUALITY

Children become aware of sex and sexuality much earlier than many people realize. They generally learn to disguise their interest rather than risk the disapproval of their elders, but they continue as small scientists—collecting data, performing experiments, and attending conferences with their colleagues.

Curiosity and Sex Play

Oh, what a tangled web parents weave
When they think their children are naive.

Ogden Nash

Starting as early as age 3, when they begin playful interaction with their peers, children begin to explore their bodies together. They may play "mommy and daddy" and hug and kiss and lie on top of each other; they may play "doctor" so that they can look at each other's genitals (Golden, 1989). Letty Cottin Pogrebin (1983) suggests that we think of children as "students" rather than "voyeurs." It is important for them to know what others look like in order to feel comfortable about themselves. Pogrebin advises:

Create opportunities for comparative anatomy lessons. Let girls and boys peek at one another, have sleep-over dates, and bathe together when they are small. Arrange visits so they can watch a baby being changed or watch their friends going to the toilet or getting undressed.

Dr. Mary Calderone (1983b) stresses that children's sexual interest should never be labeled "bad," but that it may be called inappropriate for certain times, places, or persons. According to Calderone, "the attitude of the parents should be to socialize for privacy rather than to punish or forbid."

Children who participate in sex play generally do so with members of their own sex. Most go on to develop heterosexual orientations; some do not. But whatever a person's sexual orientation, it seems clear that childhood sex play does not create the orientation. The origins of homosexuality are not well understood; in some cases, there may indeed be a biological

Children are naturally curious about bodies. Although the playground may not be considered the appropriate place to satisfy such curiosity, it is important that these kinds of explorations not be labeled "bad." Many sex educators advise parents to allow young children to observe each other naked in such settings as the bathroom or the beach.

basis, but at this point there is more speculation than hard evidence (see Perspective 1). Many gay men and lesbians say they first became aware of their attraction to members of the same sex during childhood, but many heterosexuals also report these feelings. Such feelings and behaviors appear to be quite common and congruent with healthy psychological development in heterosexuals, lesbians, and gays (Van Wyk & Geist, 1984).

If children's natural curiosity about their sexuality is satisfied, they are likely to feel comfortable with their own bodies as adults (Renshaw, 1988). This is especially important for little girls, whose parents rarely discuss their daughters' genitals or teach the proper names for them (vulva, vagina, clitoris, urethra). Girls may learn to devalue their sexuality not because of the "mysterious and concealed nature" of their anatomy but because of the "mysterious and concealed nature of [their parents'] communication about it" (Lerner, 1975; Pogrebin, 1983).

The secrecy that shrouds sexual matters leads children to develop their

THE "ORIGINS" OF HOMOSEXUALITY

What causes homosexuality? What causes heterosexuality? While many have asked the first question, few have asked the second. Although researchers don't understand the origins of sexual orientation in general, they have nevertheless focused almost exclusively on homosexuality. Their explanations generally fall into either biological or psychological categories.

Biological Theories

The earliest researchers, including Ulrichs, Kertbeny, Krafft-Ebing, Hirschfeld, and Ellis, believed that homosexuality was something hereditary. The biological perspective, however, lost influence over the years; it was replaced by psychological theories, most notably psychoanalytic theories. Recently there has been some renewed interest in the biological perspective. Today, many researchers, as well as many gay men and lesbians, believe that homosexuality is innate—people are "born" homosexual. Researchers point to possible genetic or hormonal factors.

In the first controlled genetic study of homosexuality in 40 years, researchers found a strong genetic link to male homosexuality (Bailey & Pillard, 1991). The researchers matched 157 identical and fraternal twin brothers and adopted brothers the same age to determine if there was a genetic connection. (Identical twins are genetic clones, having developed from a single egg that split after fertilization. Fraternal twins develop simultaneously from two separate eggs.) The study found that 52% of the identical twin brothers were gay, compared to 22% of fraternal twins, and 11% of genetically unrelated (adopted) brothers. The researchers estimated that the genetic contribution to male homosexuality could range from 30–70%. Next they conducted a study of lesbian and heterosexual twins that came to similar conclusions. They found that if one identical twin was lesbian, there was about a 50% chance that her sister was also lesbian (Bailey, Pillard, Neale, & Agyei, 1993). For those genetically predisposed to homosexuality, social learning remains an important factor in their sexual expression.

Other researchers have explored the possibility that homosexuality could have a hormonal basis. As hormonal levels are sensitive to such factors as general health, diet, smoking, and stress, it is very difficult to control studies measuring sexual orientation. A review by researcher John Money (1988) of controlled studies comparing hormone levels of adult gay men, lesbians, and heterosexuals found no difference in circulating hormones.

It has also been hypothesized that prenatal hormonal levels may affect fetal brain development. Animal experiments have found that prenatally manipulating hormones can cause ewes (female sheep) to

---

Friends misrepresent sex. Parents repress sex. The culture exploits sex. How can children make sense of their bodies?

Letty Cottin Pogrebin

own sexual subculture. They have songs, rhymes, jokes, and riddles that reveal that they are not quite as innocent as their parents may suppose. While their information may be a bit sketchy, their enthusiasm is boundless: "Where's the beef?" "In Wendy's buns." This may not get a big laugh from mom and dad, but it's guaranteed to crack up 7- to 11-year-olds (see Borneman, 1983, for a discussion of children's sexuality, including rhymes and songs).

Children's sexual exploration is part of their search for identity. A child who is secure and comfortable with his or her body, including the genitals, will have higher self-esteem than a child who is confused or frightened, and

engage in the mounting behavior associated with rams (Money, 1988). As there is a critical prenatal period for brain development in human fetuses, it is possible that the fetus may be affected by changes in the mother's hormonal levels.

Because it is unethical to experiment with living fetuses, we cannot make any meaningful conclusions about the effect of hormones on fetal brain development. There are some relevant studies, however. An analysis of maternal stress found no correlation between stress, hormonal fluctuation, and sexual orientation (Bailey, Willerman, & Parks, 1991). But in a study conducted by Simon LeVay (1991) on gay men and heterosexual men and women, LeVay found that the brain's anterior hypothalamus, which influences sexual behavior, was smaller among gay men than among those he assumed were heterosexuals. But as the study was conducted on the cadavers of gay men who had died from AIDS, the smaller hypothalamic size may have resulted from the disease. It may also have resulted from their behavior.

Psychological Theories

Psychoanalysis provided the earliest psychological theory accounting for the development of homosexuality. Freud believed that human beings were initially bisexual but gradually developed heterosexuality. But if children did not successfully resolve their Oedipus or Electra complex, their development would be ar-

rested. In the 1960s, psychoanalyst Irving Bieber (1962), reflecting popular stereotypes, proposed that men became homosexual because they were afraid of women. In a study of 200 heterosexual and gay men, Bieber found that gay men tended to have overprotective, dominant mothers and passive or absent fathers in contrast to heterosexuals. A review of Bieber's and similar studies found that there was some evidence to support the view that males from such families are slightly more likely to be gay (Marmor, 1980). But one woman (Price, 1993) asks, tongue-in-cheek: "If having a dominant mother and a weak or absent father were truly a recipe for homosexuality, wouldn't most Americans be gay?" Most gay men and lesbians appear to come from families no different from those of heterosexuals. Their siblings (except for identical twins) are not especially likely to be gay (Gagnon, 1977; Masters & Johnson, 1979).

Because research on the origins of sexual orientation examines homosexuality and not heterosexuality as well, there tends to be an underlying bias that homosexuality is not an acceptable or normal sexual variation. This bias has skewed research studies, especially psychoanalytic studies. As homosexuality has become increasingly accepted by researchers as a normal sexual variation, scholars have shifted their research from determining the "causes" of homosexuality to understanding the nature of gay and lesbian relationships.

will also be less vulnerable to manipulation and victimization (see Pogrebin, 1983).

Masturbation and Permission to Feel Pleasure

It is a safe bet to say that most of us masturbate; it is also safe to say that most of us were raised to feel guilty about it. Research shows that although most parents accept that their children masturbate, many of them still respond negatively when confronted with it (Gagnon, 1985). The message "If it feels good, it's bad" is often internalized at an early age, leading to

Conscience is the inner voice which warns us that someone may be looking.

H. L. Mencken

psychological and sexual disorders in later life. Virtually all sex researchers and therapists advise that masturbation is not harmful. Some also suggest that there are physically harmful effects from "early sexual deprivation" (Money, 1980; Pogrebin, 1983; Vaughter, 1976). (Masturbation is discussed further in Chapter 10.)

Children need to understand that pleasure from self-stimulation is normal and acceptable (Feitel, 1990). They also should know that it is something we do in private, something that some people are uncomfortable with. It is important for young children to know the proper names of their genitals and what they are for (pleasure, elimination, future reproduction). Thus, according to Calderone (1983b), children can be given a "time dimensional understanding of the acceptability of the genital organs and of their powerful feelings, and an understanding of their present and future roles in relation to these and to reproductive functioning." Such acceptance by parents is essential to assure a sense of self-esteem in children.

The Family Context

Family styles of physical expression and feelings about modesty and privacy vary considerably.

Parents should be taught to bless, honor, dignify, conserve, and celebrate their children's sexuality.
Committee report to SIECUS by interfaith group of clergy

Family Nudity Some families are comfortable with nudity in a variety of contexts: bathing, swimming, sunbathing, dressing, undressing. Others are comfortable with partial nudity from time to time: when sharing the bathroom, changing clothes, and so on. Still others are more modest and carefully guard their privacy. Most researchers and therapists would allow that all these styles can be compatible with the creation of sexually well-adjusted children, as long as some basic guidelines are observed. For example:

1. The child's body (and nudity) is accepted and respected. If 4-year-old Katie runs naked into her parents' dinner party, she should be greeted with friendliness, not horror or harsh words. If her parents are truly uncomfortable, they can help her get dressed matter-of-factly, without recrimination.

2. The child is not punished or humiliated for seeing the parent naked, going to the bathroom, or making love. If the parent screams or lunges for a towel, little Robbie will think he has witnessed something wicked or frightening. He can be gently reminded that mommy or daddy wants privacy at the moment.

3. The child's need for privacy is respected. Many children, especially as they approach puberty, become quite modest. It is a violation of the child's developing sense of self not to respect his or her need for privacy. If 9-year-old Mark starts meticulously locking the bathroom door or 11-year-old Sarah covers her chest when a parent interrupts her while dressing, it is most likely a sign of normal development. Children whose privacy and modesty are respected will learn to respect those of others.

Expressing Affection Families also vary in the amount and type of physical contact in which they participate. Some families hug and kiss, give back rubs, sit and lean on each other, and generally maintain a high degree of physical closeness. Some parents extend this closeness to their sleeping habits, allowing their infants and small children in their beds each night. (In many cultures, this is the rule rather than the exception.) Other families limit their contact to hugs and tickles. Variations of this kind are normal. Concerning children's needs for physical contact, we can make the following generalizations:

1. All children (and adults) need a certain amount of freely given physical affection from those they love. Although there is no prescription for the right amount or form of such expression, its quantity and quality both affect children's emotional well-being and the emotional and sexual health of the adults they will become (Kagan, 1976; Montauk & Clasen, 1989).

2. Children should be told, in a nonthreatening way, what kind of touching by adults is "good" and what is "bad." They need to feel that they are in charge of their own bodies, that parts of their bodies are "private property," and that no adult has the right to touch them with sexual intent.

3. It is not necessary to frighten a child by going into great detail about the kinds of things that might happen. A better strategy is to instill a sense of self-worth and confidence in children, so they will not allow themselves to be victimized (Pogrebin, 1983).

4. We should also learn to listen to children and trust them. They need to know that if they are sexually abused, it is not their fault. They need to feel that they can tell about it and still be worthy of love.

ADOLESCENT PSYCHOSEXUAL DEVELOPMENT

Puberty is the stage of human development when the body becomes capable of reproduction. For legal purposes (laws relating to child abuse, for example), puberty is considered to begin at age 12 for girls and age 14 for boys. **Adolescence** is the social and psychological state that occurs during puberty.

The concept of adolescence is a relatively recent historical phenomenon. Psychologist G. Stanley Hall coined the word in 1904 to describe the period between childhood and adulthood. ("Adolescent" previously was used only as a synonym for growing or maturing.) In many traditional, nonindustrial cultures, adulthood is considered to begin at puberty. The traits of adolescence, such as dependency, identity crisis, and role anxiety, are determined by our culture. Adolescents are sexually mature (or close to it) in a physical sense, but they are still learning their gender roles and social roles, and they still have much to learn about their sexual scripts (see Chapter 5). They may also be struggling to understand the meaning of their sexual feelings for others and their sexual orientation.

Physical Changes During Puberty

The physical changes of puberty are centered around the development of secondary sex characteristics (in both sexes) and the onset of menstruation (in girls) and ejaculation (in boys). (See Chapters 3 and 4.) During this time, the adolescent's body becomes to him or her a source of interest, wonder, and bewilderment (Maddock, 1973):

In addition to biological factors, social forces strongly influence young teenagers. Peers are very important, especially for boys, whose self-esteem and social status may be linked to evaluations from their friends. Because certain types of violence and aggression are considered "manly" by our society, the boys in this photograph take great pleasure in an arcade game featuring simulated warfare.

For adolescent girls, the physical and hormonal changes of puberty often result in a great deal of interest (some would say obsession) with personal appearance. Cultural norms and media influences emphasizing female beauty reinforce this interest.

The pressure to conform to sex role behavior stereotypes becomes especially intense. There is an intensification of body awareness . . . based upon the fact that the body is a primary "symbol of self" in which feelings of personal worth, security, and competence are rooted.

Adolescents must leave behind their childhood image and begin to see themselves and their bodies as sexual. Generally, their body development is surging ahead of their feelings, experience, and maturity. A crucial task for them is to develop a new identity that includes the sexual component of their being.

Female Changes   Physical changes in girls usually begin between ages 9 and 14. These include a rapid increase in height (called the growth spurt), the beginnings of breast development, the growth of pubic and underarm hair, and the onset of vaginal mucous secretions. Menarche, the onset of menstruation, follows within a year or two (see Chapter 3). The average age of menstruation is 12 or 13, although girls may begin menstruating as early as age 9 or as late as age 17 (Calderone & Johnson, 1981; Zacharias et al., 1976). Although menstruation is a basic part of female maturation, a study by the manufacturers of Tampax tampons, conducted in the early 1980s, revealed that one-third of the girls and women polled did not know what was happening to them when they got their first menstrual period (Sarrel & Sarrel, 1984).

The experience of using tampons can be highly significant in a girl's life. One survey of college women showed that 80% had begun using tampons within one year following menarche and 90% used them within two years (Sarrel & Sarrel, 1984). Often the insertion of a tampon will be a girl's first experience with vaginal penetration. If hymenal tissue blocks the vagina (and causes pain when tampon insertion is attempted), or if a girl experiences physical and psychological pain during a gynecological examination, she may experience fear and pain later on when she begins to have intercourse (Reinisch, 1986; Sarrel & Sarrel, 1984).

Breast development is a visible symbol of approaching womanhood. Some girls who develop early may feel awkward and embarrassed. Those who develop slowly may feel anxious and insecure. Nora Ephron (1975) recalled:

> I started out with a 28AA bra. I don't think they made them any smaller in those days.... I went to the store alone, shaking, positive they would look me over and smile and tell me to come back next year.... "Lean over," said the fitter.... I leaned over, with the fleeting hope that my breasts would miraculously fall out of my body.... Nothing.
>
> "Don't worry about it," said my friend Libby.... "When you get married your husband will touch your breasts and rub them and kiss them and they'll grow."
>
> That was the killer. Necking I could deal with. Intercourse I could deal with. But it had never crossed my mind that a man was going to touch my breasts.... I became dizzy.... And I knew no one would ever want to marry me. I had no breasts. I would never have breasts.

Male Changes   Some boys reach puberty around the time they enter junior high school (about age 12); others, not until their later teens. Generally, however, they lag about two years behind girls in pubertal development. Changes in boys include a growth spurt, hand and foot growth, muscle-mass growth, voice deepening, and hair growth on the face, the underarms, the pubic area, and sometimes other parts of the body.

A boy's penis and testicles also develop, often to the consternation of the youth. Writer Julius Lester (1973) recalled:

> God, how I envied girls.... Whatever it was on them, it didn't dangle between their legs like an elephant's trunk. No wonder boys talked about nothing but sex. That thing was always there. Every time we went to the john, there it was, twitching around like a fat little worm on a fishing hook. When we took baths, it floated in the water like a lazy fish and God forbid we should touch it! It sprang

to life like lightning leaping from a cloud. . . . I was helpless. It was there, with a life and mind of its own, having no other function than to embarrass me.

Boys also begin to ejaculate semen, which accompanies the experience of orgasm they may have been having for some time. Just as girls often do not know what is happening when they begin to menstruate, many boys are unnerved by the first appearance of semen as a result of masturbation, or by nocturnal emissions during sleep ("wet dreams"). Like menstruation for girls, the onset of ejaculation is a sexual milestone for boys. It is the beginning of their fertility. Kinsey called first ejaculation the most important psychosexual event in male adolescence (Kinsey et al., 1948).

Other possible physical changes boys may experience in puberty are severe acne and gynecomastia. Both conditions are temporary. Acne occurs when the skin begins to secrete an excess amount of oil which clogs the pores, especially on the face. **Gynecomastia** is an enlargement of the breasts that occurs to some extent in about 80% of boys (Calderone & Johnson, 1989). As hormone levels adjust to the changes of adolescence, gynecomastia disappears.

Influences on Psychosexual Development

Besides biological forces, many other influences are involved in adolescent psychosexual development. Peer pressure, the perceived attitudes and opinions of their friends, is the single most powerful social influence on adolescents. One educator (De Armand, 1983) found that ninth-graders ranked "Friends/Peer Group" and "Everybody's Doing It" as their leading influences. Parents were ranked fifth or sixth by most. Other research has found the media, especially television, to be highly influential in shaping adolescent values, attitudes, and behavior (see Chapter 1).

Parental Influence Children learn a great deal about sexuality from their parents. For the most part, however, they don't learn because their parents set out to teach them but because they are avid observers of their parents' behavior. Much of what they learn concerns the hidden nature of sexuality (Roberts, 1983):

> Children create their own notion of what it means to be male or female by watching their parents and other important people in their lives or on television. They learn what activities, what attitudes, and what values are appropriate for one sex and not the other. They observe how feelings and affections are expressed, or not, and by whom. . . . However, the silence that surrounds sexuality in most families and in most communities carries its own important messages. It communicates that some of the most important dimensions of life are secretive, off limits, bad to talk about or think about.

As they enter adolescence, young people are especially concerned about their own sexuality, but they are often too embarrassed to ask their parents directly about these "secret" matters. And most parents are ambivalent about their children's developing sexual nature. They are often fearful that their children (daughters especially) will become sexually active if they have "too much" information. They tend to indulge in wishful thinking: "I'm sure Jenny's not really interested in boys yet"; "I know Joey would never do any-

I'm half-inclined to think we're all ghosts. It's not only what we've inherited from our fathers and mothers that exists again in us, but all sorts of old ideas and opinions. They aren't actually alive in us; but they hang on all the same, and we can never rid ourselves of them.
Henrik Ibsen

thing like that." Parents may put off talking seriously with their children about sex, waiting for the "right time." Or they may bring up the subject once, make their points, breathe a sigh of relief, and never mention it again. Sociologist John Gagnon calls this the "inoculation" theory of sex education: "Once is enough" (Roberts, 1983). But children need frequent "boosters" where sexual knowledge is concerned. When a parent does undertake to educate a child about sex, it is usually the mother. Thus, most children grow up believing that sexuality is an issue that men don't deal with unless they have a specific problem (Roberts, 1983).

Recent research indicates that parental concern and involvement with sons and daughters is a key factor in preventing teenage pregnancy (Hanson, Myers, & Ginsburg, 1987). Parental influence in instilling values, such as respect for others and responsibility for one's actions, provides a context in which young people can use their knowledge about sex. A strong bond with parents appears to lessen teenagers' dependence on the approval of their peers and their need for interpersonal bonding, which may lead to sexual relationships (DiBlasio & Benda, 1992; Miller & Fox, 1987). But parents also need to be aware of the importance of friends in their teenagers' lives. Families that stress familial loyalty and togetherness over interactions with others outside the family may set the stage for rebellion. Traditional Latino families, for example, may expect that daughters will spend most of their time at home, often caring for their siblings. This can lead to conflict, as the "mainstream culture" expects teenagers of both sexes to be socially active (Guerrero Pavich, 1986).

Parents can also contribute to their children's feelings of self-worth by their ongoing demonstrations of acceptance and affection. Adolescents need to know that their sexuality is OK and that they are loved in spite of the changes they are going through (Gecas & Seff, 1991). While low self-esteem increases vulnerability to peer pressure, high self-esteem increases adolescents' confidence and can enhance their sense of responsibility regarding their sexual behavior.

Peer Influence

Adolescents garner a wealth of misinformation from each other about sex. They also put pressure on each other to carry out traditional sex roles. Boys encourage other boys to be sexually active even if they are unprepared or uninterested. They must camouflage their inexperience with bravado, which increases misinformation; they cannot reveal sexual ignorance. Bill Cosby (1968) recalled the pressure to have sexual intercourse as an adolescent: "But how do you find out how to do it without blowin' the fact that you don't know how to do it?" On his way to his first sexual encounter, he realized that he didn't have the faintest idea of how to proceed:

> So now I'm walkin', and I'm trying to figure out what to do. And when I get there, the most embarrassing thing is gonna be when I have to take my pants down. See, right away, then, I'm buck naked . . . buck naked in front of this girl. Now, what happens then? Do . . . do you just . . . I don't even know what to do . . . I'm gonna just stand there and she's gonna say, "You don't know how to do it." And I'm gonna say, "Yes, I do, but I forgot." I never thought of her showing me, because I'm a man and I don't want her to show me. I don't want nobody to show me, but I wish somebody would kinda slip me a note.

Most mothers think that to keep young people from love making it is enough not to speak of it in their presence.

Marie Madeline de la Fayette (1678)

One reason sex education is not being taught at home today is that parents have very good and very bad memories. They forget what they were like when they were young except when kids come in late from a date. And then parents have memories like elephants, and in Technicolor.

James Merrill

Even though many teenagers find their early sexual experiences less than satisfying, they still seem to feel a great deal of pressure to conform, which means continuing to be sexually active (DiBlasio & Benda, 1992). The following are typical statements from a group of teenagers in a study by Children's Home Society (De Armand, 1983): "I had to do it. I was the only virgin" (from a 15-year-old girl); "If you want a boyfriend, you have to put out" (from a 13-year-old girl); "You do what your friends do or you will be bugged about it" (from a 12-year-old boy). The students interviewed also said that "everyone" has to make the decision about having sexual intercourse by age 14. Researcher Charlotte De Armand comments that although, of course, "not 'everyone' is involved, certainly a large number of young people are making this decision at 14 or younger."

A recent study found that friendships among girls influenced their sexual experience. Girls whose best friends were sexually active were twelve times more likely to become active also than those whose best friends were virgins. The researchers also found that although these adolescents did not drop friends whose sexual experience differed from their own, they tended to acquire new friends with levels of sexual experience similar to theirs (Billy & Udry, 1985, 1986).

For boys, especially those with working-class backgrounds, adolescence is characterized by **homosociality,** relationships in which self-esteem and status are more closely linked to evaluations from people of the same sex than of the other sex. Homosociality has important consequences in terms of relationships with girls. A girlfriend's importance may lie in giving a boy status among other boys, his relationship with her being secondary. The generalized role expectations of males—that they must be competitive, aggressive, and achievement-oriented—carry over into sexual activities. They receive recognition for "scoring" with a girl, much as they would for scoring a touchdown or home run.

Sexual encounters, as opposed to sexual relationships, function in large part to confer status among peers (Levin, 1975; Zelnik & Kantner, 1972). Boys who have experienced rigidly homosocial activities during adolescence are often limited in the range of their later heterosexual relations. In adolescence, they may learn to relate to women in terms of their own status needs, rather than as people. As a result, some men find it difficult to develop **heterosociality,** friendships with members of the other sex, or relationships in which sexual activities involve respect or love for a woman. Hetersocial relationships bind boys and girls and men and women together, in striking contrast to homosocial relationships, in which girls or women are used to bind boys or men together. Some researchers have noted increasing levels of heterosocial relationships among adolescents in recent years (Borneman, 1983).

The Media Extensive, controlled research on the effects of sexual portrayals in the mass media has not been done. We can speculate with some degree of certainty, however, that unrealistic, stereotypical presentations of the roles of men and women have a negative effect on the attitudes and understanding of those who view them, especially if the viewers are young and impressionable. As discussed in Chapter 1, we know that erotic portrayals—nudity, sexually provocative language, and displays of sexual passion—are of great interest to the American viewing public. This public includes many curious and malleable children and adolescents. To the extent that these erotic images or actions outside a real-life context are mistaken for reality, they are potentially confusing at best and dangerously misleading at worst. A survey of 391 adolescents found a strong correlation between sexual activity and watching TV shows with high sexual content. It did not determine, however, if the viewing led to sexual activity, or whether the sexual activity led to increased interest in viewing such programs (Brown & Newcomer, 1991).

Although some would choose to protect young viewers by censoring what is shown on television or played on the radio, a more viable solution to sexual hype in the media is to balance it with information about real life. Parents can help their children understand that sexuality occurs in a context, that it is complex, and that it entails a great deal of personal responsibility. Themes from television can be used by parents to initiate discussions about sex, love, and desire (including the desire of advertisers to sell their products). Parents can also get involved in changing TV programming by writing to the networks to express their views, or by joining an activist group such as A.C.T. (Action for Children's Television). Or they can simply push the "off" button, pull the plug, or throw the whole contraption out the window. (To our knowledge, there is no research indicating any harmful effect from television deprivation.)

Most important of all, perhaps, parents can encourage their children to think for themselves. Because adolescents generally feel a strong need to conform to the ideals of their subculture, it can be especially hard for them to discriminate between what they think they should do and what they actually feel comfortable doing. Much of the process of becoming a mature adult involves the rejection of these images and the discovery and embracing of one's own unique identity.

Gay and Lesbian Adolescents

During adolescence and early adulthood, sexual orientation may become an issue. Many young people experience sexual fantasies involving others of their own sex; some engage in same-sex play. For most, these feelings of sexual attraction are transitory, but for 4–10% of the population the realization of a romantic attraction to members of their own sex will begin to grow. Some gay men and lesbians report that they began to be aware of their "difference" in middle or late childhood. Some, but not all, gay men report "feminine" behaviors or occurrences, such as a preference for girls' games, playing with dolls, imagining themselves as a model or dancer, or being called a sissy. (A number of heterosexual men also report these childhood behaviors, however.) More predictive of adult gay orientation is a lack of "masculine" behaviors, such as a preference for boys' games, rough-and-tumble play, a desire to grow up like one's father, and imagining oneself to be a sports figure (Hockenberry & Billingham, 1987; Phillips & Over, 1992; Whitam, 1977). Gay and lesbian adolescents usually have heterosexual dating experiences during their teens, but they report ambivalent feelings about them. They may not feel like kissing their date or pursuing the relationship beyond simple friendship (Bell, Weinberg, & Hammersmith, 1981).

"I can't tell you just now what the moral of that is, but I shall remember it in a bit."
"Perhaps it hasn't one," Alice ventured to remark.
"Tut, tut, child!" said the Duchess. "Everything's got a moral, if only you can find it."

Lewis Carroll

Lesbian and gay teenagers often have an especially difficult time coming to terms with their sexuality because society generally disapproves of their orientation. The young people in this photograph may be more fortunate than most, as they attend a school specifically for gay and lesbian youth. They have teachers who understand them and friends for mutual support.

Nowadays the polite form of homophobia is expressed in safeguarding the family, as if homosexuals somehow came into existence independent of families and without family ties. . . . The estrangement between individual homosexuals and their families is a direct result of homophobia.

Dennis Altman

Society in general has difficulty dealing with the fact of adolescent sexuality. The fact of gay and lesbian (or bisexual) adolescent sexuality has been virtually impossible for society to deal with. The "assumed heterosexuality" of society, which includes social scientists, educators, health-care providers, and so on, has resulted in the virtual invisibility of gay, lesbian, and bisexual youth (Savin-Williams & Rodriguez, 1993).

National concern about AIDS has brought the existence of people with homosexual orientations into public focus. One effect of this is that it is "more difficult for a homoerotically inclined youth to ignore the reality of his or her attractions, impulses and desires than in previous generations" (Savin-Williams & Rodriguez, 1993). Consequently, many gay and lesbian teenagers are able to correctly identify their feelings and identify themselves (at least to themselves) as gay or lesbian. According to researchers Ritch Savin-Williams and Richard Rodriguez, this realization may be "a bolt of lightning or, more likely, a series of small realizations sandwiched around efforts to deny or conceal them from one's consciousness."

For virtually all gay and lesbian teens, the process of coming to terms with their sexuality and with the expectations of their parents and peers is confusing and painful. Suicide rates may be especially high among this group. A 1985 study of 29 young gay males by the University of Minnesota Adolescent Health Care Program found that ten of them had attempted suicide and all except one had considered it (Behr, 1986). Although there is more understanding of homosexuality now than in decades past, and more counseling and support services are available in some areas, young gays and lesbians are still subject to ridicule and rejection. Very few feel they can talk to their parents about their sexual orientation. Many (especially boys) leave home or are "kicked out" because their parents cannot accept their sexuality. It is sobering to think that a significant number of our children are forced into secrecy and suffering because of society's reluctance to openly acknowledge the existence of homosexual orientations.

ADOLESCENT SEXUAL BEHAVIOR

Hormonal changes during puberty, which serve the human species by preparing each member for his or her reproductive function, bring about a dramatic increase in sexual interest.

Learning to Be Sexual

Brent Miller and colleagues take a "biosocial approach" to the study of adolescent development. They state that (Miller, Christopherson, & King, 1993):

> Hormonal changes early in adolescence have both a direct biological influence on sexual interest and motivation and an indirect influence on sexual involvement by altering the adolescent's physical appearance and . . . attractiveness. In addition, social processes are recognized as facilitating or inhibiting sexual involvement, altering forms of sexual expression, and defining appropriate sexual partners.

Masturbation If children have not begun masturbating before adolescence, the chances are good that they will begin once the hormonal and physical changes of puberty start. Masturbation is less common among African Americans and Latinos, however, than among whites (Belcastro, 1985; Cortese, 1989). By the time they enter college, about 5 out of 6 males and 7 or 8 out of 10 females masturbate (Sarrel & Sarrel, 1984). In addition to providing release from sexual tension, masturbation gives us the opportunity to learn about our own sexual functioning, knowledge that can later be shared with a sexual partner. Despite these positive aspects, adolescents, especially girls, often feel very concerned and guilty about their autoerotic activities. Novelist Philip Roth (1968) described a boy's anxiety:

> It was at the end of my freshman year of high school—and freshman year of masturbating—that I discovered on the underside of my penis, just where the shaft met the head, a little discolored dot that has since been diagnosed as a freckle. Cancer. I had given myself cancer. All that pulling and tugging at my own flesh, all that friction, had given me an incurable disease. And not yet fourteen! In bed at night the tears rolled from my eyes. "No!" I sobbed. "I don't want to die. Please—no." But then, because I would shortly be a corpse anyway, I went ahead as usual and jerked off.

The other side of the masturbation issue involves what some young people experience as the pressure to masturbate. This "side effect" of the liberalization of attitudes toward sexual conduct causes some young people to feel inadequate if they don't masturbate. They may fail at reaching orgasm as a result of "spectatoring," watching themselves so closely that they are unable to let go. It is important to know that "a person doesn't have to masturbate in order to be fully sexual" (Sarrel & Sarrel, 1984). (Masturbation is discussed further in Chapter 10.)

First Base, Second Base: A Normative Sequence of Behaviors

Most heterosexual adolescent couples follow a normative pattern in the sequence of their sexual behaviors: hand-holding, embracing, kissing, fon-

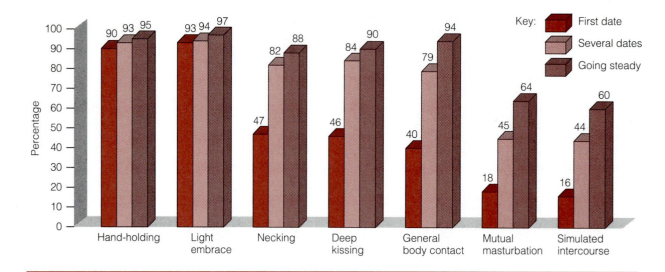

FIGURE 6.1 Percentage of Adolescents Engaging in Heterosexual Behaviors at Various Stages of Dating.

dling and petting, and (for some) intercourse (Miller et al., 1993). A study of Australian adolescents (McCabe & Collins, 1984) measured the frequency of twelve sexual behaviors, seven of which are shown in Figure 6.1. Hand-holding and embracing were the most common behaviors on first dates; as relationships became more serious, sexual activity increased. Boys expressed a desire for greater sexual intimacy than girls on first dates, but girls' desire for intimacy increased as the relationships progressed. Older female adolescents also expressed an increased desire for sexual intimacy. (It is interesting to note that the literature on adolescent sexual behavior rarely mentions the role of love in sexuality. "Commitment" and "emotional involvement" may be cited as reasons for sexual intimacy, but the word "love" is almost never used.)

A study in the United States showed a normative behavior sequence for white adolescents (Smith & Udry, 1985). The normal progression was necking, feeling breasts through clothing, feelings breasts directly, feeling female genitals, feeling penis directly, and intercourse (occurring least often). The sequence was not predictable, however, for young blacks. For example, more African American adolescents had experienced intercourse than had engaged in unclothed petting involving either the breasts or the genitals. For most teens, both white and black, however, increasing commitment to the relationship brought an increased desire for sexual intimacy. Emotional involvement expands the range of sexual behavior that is normatively acceptable (Thornton, 1990).

Kissing is an important activity for teenage couples. An adolescent's first erotic kiss often proves to be an unforgettable experience, "a milestone, a rite of passage, the beginning of adult sexuality" (Alapack, 1991). It is largely through kissing that we learn to be sexually intimate, to be comfortable with physical closeness, and to give and take sexual pleasure. Young couples may spend hours alternately kissing and gazing into each other's eyes.

Oral sex among teenagers, including heterosexuals, lesbians, and gays, has apparently become increasingly frequent in recent years, paralleling its growing acceptability in the culture at large (Wilson & Medora, 1990). In a study

Among teenagers, increased commitment to a relationship generally brings increased sexual intimacy.

of junior high school students, cunnilingus was the most commonly reported form of oral sex. Among the girls surveyed, more had given or received oral sex than had engaged in intercourse; among the boys, more had engaged in intercourse than had given or received oral sex (Newcomer & Udry, 1985). (See Miller & Dyk, 1990, for a review of empirical studies on "fertility-related" behaviors of adolescents.)

First Intercourse and Virginity With the advent of the "sexual revolution" in the late 1960s, adolescent sexual behavior began to change. The average age for first intercourse has dropped sharply, and almost as many girls as boys are engaging in it. By age 15 or 16, about 1 out of every 4 white girls and boys have started having intercourse, as have 5 out of 10 African American girls and 9 out of 10 African American boys (Beyette, 1986). A recent study of 13,454 Native American adolescents (in Alaska, Arizona, California, Minnesota, Montana, New Mexico, South Dakota, and Tennessee) found that by the twelfth grade, 58% of the girls and 65% of the boys had had intercourse (Blum et al., 1992). Altogether, by age 19, 7 out of 10 girls and 8 out of 10 boys have had intercourse (Beyette, 1986).

African American teenagers generally initiate sexual intercourse earlier than white or Latino teenagers. A recent study showed that 20% of black adolescent boys experienced first intercourse prior to 13 years of age, compared to 3% of whites and 4% of Latinos (Sonenstein et al., 1991). Among Native Americans in grades 7 through 9, 22% of boys and 15% of girls had had intercourse (Blum et al., 1992). White female adolescents of all ages show increasing sexual activity. While black teenage girls generally begin sexual activity sooner, white girls narrow the gap considerably by the later teens (Centers for Disease Control, 1991).

In the past, peer pressure among girls was an important factor in limiting their sexual behavior. Today, girls' peers seem to exert the opposite effect. Teenagers told columnist Anna Quindlen that "virgin" was shorthand for "geek, nerd, weirdo, somebody who was so incredibly out of it that they were in high school and still hadn't had sex" (Quindlen, 1986). However, teenagers may feel compelled to act more sexually sophisticated than they actually are; they may lie to protect themselves from being thought of as immature. The context in which she "gives up" her virginity is still important for many girls; most feel that they are doing it for love (Hass, 1979).

In spite of increased social pressure to engage in intercourse, there are "significant fractions of Americans who experience first coitus after marriage" (Thornton, 1990). Among older teens and young adults who have experienced intercourse, many say they wish they had postponed first intercourse until they were more emotionally mature. In a study from Rutgers University (Weis, in Sarrel & Sarrel, 1984), one-third of the responding women reported feeling exploited during first intercourse. Two-thirds felt pleasure, but half of these reported high levels of anxiety and guilt nevertheless. One-third of the total felt no pleasure whatsoever. According to Sarrel and Sarrel (1984), this study showed:

> . . . what every mother knows and wishes her daughter knew. If you are older (at least 17), if you haven't rushed into intercourse but have built up to it gradually, and if your partner is loving, tender, and considerate, you are more likely to enjoy it and less likely to feel anxious and guilty.

Adolescents and Contraception

Most teenagers, especially younger ones, do not take measures to protect themselves against pregnancy or sexually transmitted diseases (STDs) when they begin having sexual intercourse. Teenage clients of family planning clinics have their first clinic visit an average of 13.2 months after their first intercourse (Kisker, 1984). Those who begin having sex at age 18 or 19 are much more likely to use contraception (Zelnik, Kantner, & Ford, 1981). (Adolescents and STDs are discussed in Chapters 16 and 17.)

Prior to the late 1960s, boys were generally the ones who initiated sexual activity and provided contraception (a condom), if it was used. Then contraceptive technology shifted, giving the woman the burden of responsibility for protection. "Condom consciousness" was no longer an important aspect of a boy's sexual life. This trend may be changing once again, due to the

It is now vitally important that we find a way of making the condom a cult object of youth.

Germaine Greer

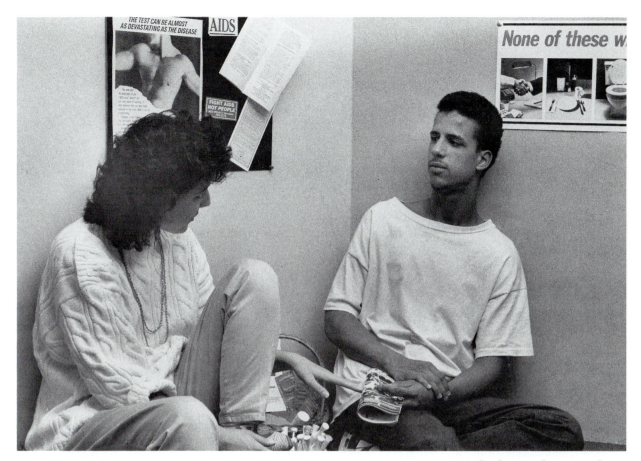

Family planning clinics provide young people with information about contraception and STD prevention. They also provide physical exams and health care related to sexuality, usually free of charge.

recent increasing popularity of condoms engendered by concern about HIV and AIDS (Voydanoff & Donnelly, 1990). Condoms are popular among teens who do use contraception, especially in casual relationships or the early stages of more serious ones (Kisker, 1985). A recent study showed that 57% of 15- to 19-year-old males had used a condom at last intercourse (Sonenstein, Pleck, & Ku, 1989). Along with condoms, withdrawal (an unreliable method) is the method most frequently practiced by teenagers who use contraception, although it may be less common now than a decade ago (Blum & Resnick, 1982; Sonenstein et al., 1989).

Young women involved in serious relationships are more likely to use a reliable contraceptive method, such as the pill, than are those who are just beginning to have intercourse. Freya Sonenstein and colleagues (1989) found that 20% of adolescents reported using the pill at last intercourse. Hormonal implants (Norplant) may prove to be a popular method for teenagers, although they are relatively new on the market and at present require the outlay of several hundred dollars for implantation. Implants do protect against pregnancy for five years, however. (See Chapter 12 for information on contraception and birth control.)

Erotophobia: Fear of Sexuality
Although she is supposed to look alluring and arouse the desire of her partner, she is not expected to have erotic

Sin is whatever obscures the soul.
André Gide

There are more than a million teenage pregnancies every year in the United States; about 60% are carried to term. Most of these births occur outside of marriage to young girls who are ill-prepared for the responsibilities of parenthood.

feelings herself. She believes that sex is something that "happens" to you. Her dilemma gives her two choices: (1) to acknowledge erotic feelings, plan for intercourse, and risk being thought of (or thinking of herself) as promiscuous; or (2) to be passive and "swept off her feet" and run the risk of pregnancy or a sexually transmitted disease (Kisker, 1986; Roberts, 1980). Psychologist William A. Fisher explains this dilemma in terms of **erotophobia,** fear of sexuality. As he observes (Fisher, 1983):

> It seems likely that the teenagers who get pregnant without planning to are the relatively erotophobic ones; young people whose fear of sex is too great to allow them to plan for intercourse but not great enough to keep them from having it.

(See Chapter 10 for more detail; also see Byrne & Fisher, 1983.)

Research indicates that among sexually active teenage girls, those who regularly attend religious services are less likely to use an effective medical method of contraception (such as the pill) than those who do not attend religious services. Because of their religion's attitudes toward sexuality, these girls appear to have substantial difficulty acknowledging this aspect of themselves (Singh, 1986; Studer & Thornton, 1987).

A side effect of sex education in the form it is currently taught (see Perspective 2) may be that it fosters a fear of intimacy (Adelman, 1992; Hochhauser, 1991). In general, sexuality is associated with violence, victimization, and individual morality but not desire. As one researcher asserts, "The naming of desire, pleasure, or sexual entitlement, particularly for females, barely exists in the formal agenda of public schooling on sexuality" (Fine, 1988). "Fear-based" education, designed to scare young people into not having sexual relations, may backfire. Adolescents may be so reluctant to acknowledge their sexual behaviors that they avoid using any kind of contraception. To do so would only serve to remind them that they are, indeed, sexual and, not only that, but that they *planned* to be sexual (it didn't just "happen") (Hafner, 1992).

Lack of Information   Another factor that contributes to the lack of contraceptive use among teenagers is the notoriously inaccurate information they share with one another ("You can't get pregnant the first time," "You can't get pregnant if you do it standing up," and so on). One teenage father told an interviewer, "I didn't think she'd get pregnant because she had such little breasts" (Robinson, 1987). Adolescents apparently drastically underestimate the ability of teenage girls to get pregnant. One study found that only 36% of sexually active teens believed they could easily get pregnant (Peacock, 1982). Others rely heavily on unreliable methods such as withdrawal and "rhythm." Furthermore, many teenagers perceive the health risks of oral contraception, the method recommended by many family planning practitioners for most sexually active girls, to be much greater than they are (Kisker, 1986). Although knowledge alone is not sufficient to ensure consistent contraceptive use among sexually active adolescents, having accurate information gives them a solid basis for making responsible decisions when they are emotionally and developmentally capable of doing so.

Risk Taking and Role Testing   Teenagers are generally perceived to be risk takers, but they may not view themselves as such. Adolescence is often thought of as a perilous journey, at least by adults: pregnancy, sexually transmitted diseases (especially AIDS), alcohol, drugs, gang violence, car crashes, and so on. What's a poor parent (or teacher or social worker) to do? Most teenagers, however, seem relatively unconcerned about such potential threats. They feel these things may happen to other people, but not to them. This "magical thinking" helps teenagers convince themselves that they are "somehow special and exempt" from the conditions that apply to the rest of the world (Robinson, 1987).

Another view of adolescent risk taking sees it as a normal and essential part of psychological development (Hochhauser, 1991). One study of 161 16-year-olds found that those who had done some experimentation with marijuana were better adjusted than those who had never experimented (Shedler & Block, 1990). AIDS consultant Mark Hochhauser (1991) feels that "this conclusion may be extended to sexual experimentation . . . and challenges the wisdom of defining abstinence as the only goal of [AIDS] prevention programs." He feels that the goal of prevention should be to help young people learn about "inappropriate and appropriate" risks. Adult life holds many risks, and those who have experience in evaluating them will be best able to cope.

An important psychological task of adolescence is to answer the question, "Who am I?" One of the ways we discover who we are is by **role testing,** trying out different roles. We incorporate what we like about these roles into our identity. Sexual experimentation is one way of testing roles. Part of finding one's own identity involves differentiating oneself from others. For adolescents, this often entails a certain amount of rebellion against authority in general and against parents in particular. Some teenagers may engage in sexual activity as a way of rebelling against parental authority. It may be that allowing teenagers "acceptable" forms of rebellion—through music, clothing, hairstyles, or speaking out on their beliefs, for example—lessens their need to rebel sexually (Elkind, 1984; Hochhauser, 1991).

Parents who fail to provide contraceptive information to both girls and boys are guilty of child abuse. Having a child while she is a child abuses a girl's body and ruins her life.

Letty Cottin Pogrebin

Adam was but human—this explains it all. He did not want the apple for the apple's sake, he wanted it only because it was forbidden.

Mark Twain

Perspective 2

SEX EDUCATION TODAY

Sex education is not a new idea in the United States. Its origins can be traced to the 1880s when the YMCA and other groups sponsored lectures on sex-related topics. In the 1890s, the National Educational Association and the National Congress of Parents and Teachers began to discuss the addition of sex education to school curricula. In 1905, the American Society for Sanitary and Moral Prophylaxis instituted classes in schools to educate about venereal disease. They called for a return to Victorian values, emphasizing the "pure" nature of women and the importance of sexual restraint in men (Strong, 1973). This led, however, to the development of broader programs that included discussions of biology, reproduction, and birth. Teacher training in "sex hygiene" began in the 1920s (Carrera, 1980). The 1950s witnessed a broadening of the sex education movement. Mary Calderone founded SIECUS (Sex Information and Education Council of the United States), and other organizations and programs were developed that provided guidance for sex education in schools.

Today, most students receive some type of sex education before graduating from high school. Most of these classes, however, can hardly be called comprehensive; some are referred to merely as "organ recitals." Yet a poll by Yankelovich, Clancy, and Shulman showed that 86% of the respondents were in favor of sex education in the schools ("How the Public Feels," 1986). Most of those polled also thought that information about birth control, sexually transmitted diseases (including HIV infection and AIDS), sexual intercourse, premarital sex, abortion, and homosexuality should be given to 12-year-olds in school. Sex educators say that teenagers have pressing concerns about such subjects as contraception, abortion, masturbation, and homosexuality, yet these subjects are often considered taboo by schools. What's going on here?

The Relentless Pursuit of the Fallopian Tubes

Among parents, teachers, and school administrators, there is substantial disagreement about what a "comprehensive" course in sex education should include. Some feel that only basic reproductive biology should be taught. One critic of this approach calls it the "relentless pursuit of the fallopian tubes" (Gordon, 1986). Others see the prevention (or at least the reduction) of STDs as legitimate goals of sex education. Still others would like the emphasis to be on the prevention of sexual activity among adolescents. Most sex educators seem to feel that *all* of these goals are worthy of pursuit. Some feel it's also important to address more controversial issues, such as gay and lesbian identities and the role of pleasure and desire in sexuality. Most also feel that young people need to develop the skills necessary to make healthful, responsible decisions regarding their sexual behavior. Strict prohibitions and threats are not at all effective in regulating teenage sexual activities (Brody, 1986; Elkind, 1984).

Although the opposition to comprehensive sex education may be small, it is very vocal. Many school administrators are simply afraid of provoking controversy. Those opposed to sex education fear that knowledge about sexuality will lead to increased sexual activity.

HIV/AIDS Education

The alarming spread of sexually transmitted diseases, especially HIV and AIDS, has also sparked controversy. Former U.S. Surgeon General C. Everett Koop recommended that instruction about HIV begin in the third grade. He said, "We have to be as explicit as necessary to get the message across. You can't talk of the dangers of snake poisoning and not mention snakes" (quoted in Leo, 1986). A poll by Yankelovich, Clancy, and Shulman showed that 95% of the respondents were in favor of HIV education for 12-year-olds; only 23%, however, thought it appropriate for 8-year-olds ("How the Public Feels," 1986). The quality of HIV education is also an important issue. Misinformation or incomplete information can cause unnecessary anxiety and fears among the young.

Teaching About Homosexuality

Lessons about AIDS have brought the subject of homosexuality into the classroom. This is a highly controversial subject; some parents fear their children will "catch" it if they learn about it. Nevertheless, it is important for young people to understand that same-sex orientations are normal, for two principal reasons. One is that gay and lesbian teenagers need to have their identities validated; the other is that bias-related violence against gays and lesbians is largely perpetrated by teenage boys. Some school districts are taking steps to eliminate prejudice against gays and lesbians. In 1992, the New York City Board of Education mandated that all curricula be revised to reflect diversity, including diversity in sexual orientation. (Parent opposition, however, forced cancellation of the curriculum.) In Los Angeles, a program called Project 10 offers counseling to gay and lesbian teens in the schools. In San Francisco, each school has a "gay sensitive" staff member to work with gay and lesbian students (Humm, 1992; Uribe & Harbeck, 1991).

Too Little, Too Late

One reason sex education doesn't succeed better at reducing sexual activity, disease, and pregnancy may be that it is too little, too late. One study showed that 52% of girls who began intercourse at age 15 had not had a sex education course prior to that time. The proportion of sexually active but "sexually uneducated" younger girls was even greater. Boys were still less likely to have taken a sex education class prior to beginning intercourse. Seventy-four percent of sexually active 15-year-old boys had not had a prior sex education course (Marsiglio & Mott, 1986).

The earlier children are introduced to sexual topics appropriate for their age, the easier it is for them to discuss such matters later on without self-consciousness and embarrassment (Uslander, 1973).

Secondary Virginity and Abstinence-Based Curricula

One kind of sex education curriculum that is increasing in popularity, often with the help of federal funds, stresses abstinence (chastity) for teens as the only form of birth control. Some educators teach the concept of "secondary virginity" (Smith, 1986). Its message is that even though someone has begun having intercourse, he or she doesn't have to continue. This message is true as far as it goes. Most teenagers, younger teens in particular, aren't mature enough to handle the emotional or physiological consequences of intercourse. Many can benefit by learning that it's all right to say "no" to sex. But the fact remains that the majority of teens continue to say "yes." Abstinence-based programs turn many teenagers off because of their emphasis on morality and "saving yourself for marriage." While younger adolescents may be willing and able to postpone sexual involvement, most of them expect to have intercourse by their late teens. Most adults expect this also. With people now tending to marry in their mid-twenties or later, it is simply unrealistic to expect all but the most religious or conservative of teenagers to adopt a "marriage-only" standard. For most young people, the issue is not "if" but "when."

Double Message

According to veteran sex educator Sol Gordon (1984), what "works" with young people is the "double message." Adolescents should know that their parents think they're too young for serious sexual involvement. (They can also learn what forms of sexual behavior are more appropriate, such as petting or masturbation.) But if they decide to have intercourse anyway, teenagers must be prepared with knowledge—and contraceptives. Gordon (1984) writes that parents should work toward being "askable": "If children know that they are always welcome to ask, parents are in the best position to educate as their own values dictate." Sociologist Frank Furstenberg's study of 400 15- and 16-year-olds showed that among those who had sex education in school and discussions with parents at home, only 16% engaged in sexual intercourse (Furstenberg, Herceg-Baron, Shea, & Webb, 1984).

(continued)

SEX EDUCATION TODAY (continued)

Does Education Lead to Sex?

Does talking about sex lead to having sex? Several studies indicate that this is not the case. Furstenberg and colleagues showed that 17% of the 15- and 16-year-olds who had taken sex education courses had intercourse, but 26% of those who had *not* taken such courses also had intercourse (Furstenberg et al., 1985). Other studies showed no apparent correlation between taking sex education courses and engaging in sexual activity (Dawson, 1986; Zelnik & Kim, 1982). No study that we know of indicates a positive correlation between sex education and sexual intercourse.

Studies have shown that when information about birth control is included in sex education courses, contraceptive use has increased accordingly (Dawson, 1986; Marsiglio & Mott, 1986; Zabin, Hirsch, Smith, Strett, & Hardy, 1986). A study by Susheela Singh (1986) showed a significantly lower pregnancy rate among white high school seniors who had received sex education than among those who had not. In Cal-ifornia, a study of 13 high schools featuring a curriculum emphasizing both abstinence and contraception showed a 40% drop in the frequency of unprotected sexual intercourse among students who had not previously begun having sex (Kirby, Barth, Leland, & Fettro, 1991). There was little change in contraceptive use, however, among those who were already sexually active at the time of the program. These results indicate that sex education and prevention skills should be initiated well before the age when students are likely to begin having intercourse.

One thing seems clear: Talking about sex does not cause it to happen. Learning about sex in age-appropriate increments, at home and at school, and having access to contraception and protection from STDs, seem to be the best defenses against the unhappy consequences of "too much, too soon." Young people guided by their parents and armed with knowledge and self-confidence can make informed decisions and direct their own sexual destinies.

For many teenagers, the impetus to begin using contraception is a pregnancy scare of their own or of one of their friends (Kisker, 1986; Zabin & Clark, 1981). Then the myth of their invulnerability is shattered, and they must deal with a reality that cannot be denied.

ADOLESCENT PREGNANCY

The vast majority of births to teenage girls are unplanned. Between 1983 and 1988, 87% of births to unmarried 15- to 18-year-olds were reported by them to be unwanted or mistimed. A study by Susheela Singh (1986) of the Alan Guttmacher Institute, which researches family planning, indicated that about 11% of teenage girls between 15 and 19 become pregnant every year in this country. Nevada, California, and Texas had the highest rates (about 140 pregnancies per 1000 girls), while North Dakota had the lowest (74.8 per 1000). Every year, more than a million American teenagers (including about 30,000 under age 15) become pregnant.

Although the birthrate among teens was actually higher 30 years ago than it is today, it was accounted for by early marriage; nearly 25% of 18- and 19-year-old young women were married. Most teenage births were to girls 17 and older, within the context of marriage. Today, most of the births to teenagers occur outside of marriage (more than 75% of births in some parts of the country) (Wallis, 1985). Melvin Zelnik and colleagues found that pregnant white girls were six or seven times more likely to marry than African American girls (Zelnik et al., 1981). Among sexually active 15- to 19-year-olds, Latinas are more than twice as likely as non-Latina white girls to be married. Adolescent Latinas are more than five times as likely to be married as adolescent African American girls (Torres & Singh, 1986).

About 42% of pregnant teenagers choose abortion over childbirth (Henshaw & Van Vort, 1989). Although teenage motherhood poses many hardships, for some, abortion may also have physical and emotional consequences. Poor girls are more likely than their more well-to-do counterparts to have their babies (the reasons are discussed later in the chapter). Less than 5% of teenage mothers give up their infants for adoption (Voydanoff & Donnelly, 1990).

According to the Center for Population Options (1992), teen pregnancies and births cost the U.S. more than $25 billion a year in medical, welfare, and related expenses, trapping most of the young mothers and fathers and their children in a downward spiral of lowered expectations and poverty. Because of poor nutrition and inadequate medical care during pregnancy, babies born to teenagers have twice the normal risk of low birth weight, which is responsible for numerous physical and developmental problems. Also, many of these children will have disrupted family lives, absent fathers, and the attendant problems of poverty, such as poor diet, violent neighborhoods, limited health care, and limited access to education. They are also at higher risk of being abused than children born to older parents. The Center estimates that the federal government would have saved 40% of its expenditures for Medicaid, food stamps, and Aid to Families with Dependent Children (AFDC) in 1990 if all births to teenage mothers had been delayed until the mother was in her twenties.

In 1985, to mitigate the effects of poverty on children of unmarried teens, the state of Wisconsin instituted a law obligating the parents of teenage mothers and fathers to provide financial support for their grandchildren to the extent that the teen parents are unable to do so. This "grandparents liability law" has provoked a great deal of controversy, but a number of other states are considering similar legislation (Shipp, 1985).

Why Teenagers Get Pregnant

Why do teenagers begin intercourse as early as they do, and why do they rarely use contraception? As discussed earlier in the chapter, the forces of their hormones, combined with pressure from peers and the media, tend to propel teenagers into sexual activity before they are emotionally prepared for it. They often don't use contraception because they are afraid to acknowledge their sexuality; or they may have difficulties in obtaining it, be too embarrassed to ask for it, not know how to use it properly, or not have it readily available. They may underestimate the risks or not fully understand their implications. Adolescent contraceptive use is discussed in greater detail later in the chapter.

But not all teen pregnancies are accidental. About 10–20% of them are planned (DeSalvo, 1985; Thompson, 1986; Wattleton, in Beyette, 1986). Some teenage girls or couples see having a baby as a way to escape from an oppressive home environment. One 17-year-old girl said (quoted in De Salvo, 1985):

> I wanted to get pregnant. My stepfather and I never got along, and I wanted to get away from him and have my own life. . . . I've always been the kind of person who wants to stay home and have a family.

The pull of having someone to love them exclusively and unconditionally is strong for some girls. A young woman who had her first child at 17 said (quoted in De Salvo, 1985):

> I had broken up with my boyfriend, and I wanted someone to care for me when I felt depressed. Even though it didn't understand me, I could talk to it. My baby would always be there.

Both girls and boys may see parenthood as a way to enhance their status, to give them an aura of maturity, or to enhance their masculinity or femininity. A 17-year-old boy, whose girlfriend was 14, said (quoted in De Salvo, 1985):

> I figured it would help us stay together. Her parents were threatening me with statutory rape charges and I figured that if I fathered their grandchild, they'd drop the charges and let me marry her.

Some believe a baby will cement a shaky relationship. (Many adult women and men choose to have babies for these same less-than-sensible reasons.) Unfortunately, for many teens, parenthood may turn out to be as much a disaster as a blessing.

Teenage Mothers

Most teenage mothers feel that they are "good" girls and that they became pregnant in a moment of unguarded passion. Apparently, most also say they would "do it again," although they would counsel other girls to use birth control in similar situations (Thompson, 1986). The reality of the *boy + girl = baby* equation often doesn't sink in until pregnancy is well advanced. This lack of realism makes it difficult (emotionally and physically) or impossible to have an abortion for those who might otherwise choose one. Teenage mothers are far more likely than other mothers to live below the poverty level and to receive welfare. Only about half of them finish high school, compared to 96% of girls who are not mothers (Wallis, 1985). Planned Parenthood identifies teenage girls at greatest risk of becoming pregnant as those from single-parent homes, those whose mothers or sisters became pregnant in their teens, and those who do not do well in school (Beyette, 1986).

African American Teenage Mothers African American teenage girls have by far the highest fertility rate of any teenage population group in the world (Jones et al., 1985). This is partly explained by the way in which the forces of racism and poverty combine to limit the options of young people of color (Singh, 1986). (Poor whites also have disproportionately high teenage birthrates.) But there are additional factors that contribute to pregnancy and childbirth among black teens. For one thing, African American communities are far more accepting of out-of-wedlock births than their white counterparts; three-generation families are much more common, with the result that grandparents often have an active role in child rearing. (This is also true of Latino communities.) For another, there is often a great deal of pressure among young African American men (especially in communities with lower socioeconomic status) to prove their masculinity by engaging in sexual activity (Staples & Johnson, 1993). Another reason may be related to a lack of role models for African American girls to identify with (Janice Anderson in Wallis, 1985). Strategies for dealing with these issues are discussed at the end of this chapter.

Images of the adolescent African American mother as "unemployed, uneducated, and living on welfare with three or more unkempt, poorly motivated and socialized children" represent a minority of cases (Staples & Johnson, 1993; also see Franklin, 1988; Furstenberg, Brooks-Gunn, & Morgan, 1987). While many black teenage mothers drop out of school, a decade later, nearly 70% have received a high school diploma, 30% take courses after high school, and at least 5% graduate from college. Those most likely to be on welfare, live in poverty, and "produce children who fail academically and socially" are the 25–30% of teen mothers who have not completed high school (Staples & Johnson, 1993).

Strengths of Teenage Motherhood   On the brighter side, some studies have shown positive outcomes to teen pregnancies if certain criteria are met. One study found that teenage mothers and their infants did well in families that gave them financial support and help with child care (Furstenberg, 1981). The adolescent mothers often gained higher status in the family, and the infants were "universally esteemed." With this in mind, it has been suggested that "awareness of the young mother's potential and accomplishments is imperative for planning treatment and parent education programs that will maximize the positive behavior shown by many of these teenagers" (Buchholz & Gol, 1986). Furthermore, teenagers with family support are more likely to have had adequate health care during pregnancy, thereby reducing the risks to their children's health.

Needs of Teenage Mothers   The most pressing needs of teenage mothers that can be provided within the community are health care and education (Voydanoff & Donnelly, 1990). Regular prenatal care (before the birth) is essential to monitor fetal growth and the mother's health, including diet, possible sexually transmitted disease, and possible alcohol or drug use. After the birth, both mother and child need continuing care. The mother may need contraceptive counseling and services, and the child needs regular physical checkups and immunizations. Graduation from high school is an important goal of education programs for teenage mothers, as it directly influences their employability and ability to support (or help support) themselves and their children. Other goals of education include developing parenting and life-management skills, and job training. Mentoring programs, which connect the mother with a woman from her community who serves as a role model and a special friend, have proved beneficial (Wallis, 1985). Many teenage mothers need financial assistance, at least until they complete their education. Programs such as AFDC, food stamps, Medicaid, and WIC

(Women, Infants, and Children, a program that provides coupons for essential foods) are often crucial to the survival of young mothers and their children. These government programs are underfunded, however, and most families need additional income to survive.

The coordination of health, educational, and social services is important because it reduces costs and provides the most comprehensive support (Voydanoff & Donnelly, 1990). School-based health clinics, which provide prenatal and postnatal care, contraception, and counseling, and teenage mother education programs, which provide general education, job skills, and life skills, are examples of coordinated care (Stevens-Simon & Beach, 1992). Such programs may be costly, but the costs of not providing these services are far greater.

Teenage Fathers

The incidence of teenage fatherhood is lower than that of teenage motherhood because almost half the fathers of infants born to teenage mothers are age 20 or older (Sonenstein, 1986). About 5–10% of adolescent boys are likely to be responsible for a teen pregnancy (Elster & Panzarine, 1983). It is often assumed that teenage fathers are irresponsible, selfish, and uninterested in their partners and children. Many times this is not the case, as indicated by a 1985 study conducted by the Bank Street College of Education (Stengel, 1985; "Teen-Age Fathers," 1986). This study, as well as others, found teenage fathers to be a seriously neglected group who face numerous hardships.

Researcher Bryan Robinson (1988) suggests that there are five myths or stereotypes commonly believed about teenage fathers:

1. *The Super Stud Myth.* He is "worldly wise" and knows more than most teenagers about sex.
2. *The Don Juan Myth.* He exploits unsuspecting and helpless girls by taking advantage of them.
3. *The Macho Myth.* He feels inadequate and has an unnatural need to prove his masculinity.
4. *The Mr. Cool Myth.* He has a casual relationship with the mother of his child and few feelings about the pregnancy.
5. *The Phantom Father Myth.* He is basically absent and leaves mother and child to fend for themselves.

What studies show, however, is that adolescent fathers typically remain physically or psychologically involved throughout the pregnancy and have "intimate feelings toward both mother and baby" (Robinson, 1988). Most continue to be involved with the mother during the pregnancy and for at least some period of time after the birth. About 10% of pregnant teenage couples marry, but the chances of the marriage working out are very slim (Robinson, 1988). It is usually difficult for teenage fathers to contribute much to the support of their children, although most express the intention of doing so during the pregnancy. Most have lower incomes, less education, and more children than men who postpone having children until age 20 or more. They may feel overwhelmed at the responsibility and may doubt their ability to be good providers. Teenage fathers are often the sons of absent

Studies show that many teenage fathers continue to be involved with the mother during pregnancy and for at least some time following the birth. Most express interest in supporting their children, although in reality it often proves to be very difficult.

fathers; they may not have a male parent role model and may in fact have numerous models of pregnancy outside of marriage. But most do want to learn to be fathers.

Programs to assist teenage fathers are few, but the number is growing. These programs generally provide young fathers with jobs or job training, the opportunity to finish high school, classes in parenting, and counseling. Robinson (1988) suggests a "holistic approach to health care and a variety of measures to meet the multiple needs" of young fathers. If they are given hope and the opportunity to be successful providers, they generally demonstrate high aspirations for their children. One former teenage father said, "My father was a parent when he was a teenager. My mother and grandmother were. It didn't stop with me or my brothers. I know it will stop with my son" (quoted in Stengel, 1985).

Reducing Adolescent Pregnancy

According to the Alan Guttmacher Institute's extensive study of teenage pregnancy in 37 countries, the United States has an astonishingly high birthrate (AGI, 1986; Jones et al., 1985). When compared to similarly developed countries (Canada, England, France, Sweden, and the Netherlands), it is nearly twice as great as that of the next highest country (England) and more than six times greater than that of the Netherlands. The U.S. also leads these countries in abortion rates by a wide margin. These countries have similar levels of sexual activity among teenagers. What is the reason for this huge birthrate discrepancy? In a word, contraception.

A multifaceted approach to reducing teen pregnancy is suggested by family planning experts, sociologists, demographers, and others who have studied these issues:

1. The underlying issues of poverty and the racism that often reinforces it must be dealt with. There must be a more equitable distribution of income so that all children can have a true variety of educational, occupational, social, and personal options in their future.

2. Contraception must be made available, along with practical information and a climate of openness about sexuality. This is one of the lessons to be learned from developed countries that have low teenage birthrates. Both sex education and tolerance of teenage sexual activity prevail in Western Europe. The U.S. appears prudish and hypocritical by comparison.

3. At the same time, schools, health-care agencies, and welfare agencies "have to be marching in the same direction, all at the same time" (Dryfoos, 1985). A concerted effort to educate young people and to help them combat feelings of worthlessness and despair must be made. Programs such as Reach for the Stars, which pairs black teenage girls with successful black role models, and Family Life in New York, which fosters self-esteem in "dead-end kids," seem to be remarkably effective in both raising the aspirations of the young people they serve and dramatically reducing the pregnancies among them (Wallis, 1985).

Psychosexual development should be viewed as a continuum rather than a series of discrete stages. Each person develops in his or her own way, according to personal and social circumstances and the dictates of biology. As adolescents grow toward sexual maturity, the gap between their physiological development and their psychological development begins to narrow; their emotional and intellectual capabilities begin to "grow into" their bodies. Nearing adulthood, young people become less dependent on their elders and more capable of developing intimacy on a new level.

SUMMARY

Infant Sexuality

• *Psychosexual development* begins in infancy, when we begin to learn how we "should" feel about our bodies and our gender roles. Infants need stroking and cuddling to ensure healthy psychosexual development.

Childhood Sexuality

• Children learn about their bodies and those of their siblings and friends through various forms of sex play. Their sexual interest should not be labeled "bad" but may be called inappropriate for certain times, places, or persons. Children need to know that masturbation is normal and acceptable but private.

• In families, children should know that their bodies (and nudity) are accepted, not be punished or humiliated for seeing a parent naked or making love, and have their privacy respected. They also need expressions of physical affection and to be told nonthreateningly about "good" and "bad" touching by adults.

Adolescent Psychosexual Development

- *Puberty* is the biological stage when reproduction becomes possible. The psychological state of puberty is *adolescence*, a time of growth and often confusion as the body matures faster than the emotional and intellectual abilities. The traits of adolescence are culturally determined.

- Pubertal changes in girls begin between ages 9 and 14. They include a growth spurt, breast development, pubic and underarm hair, vaginal secretions, and menarche (first menstruation).

- Pubertal changes in boys generally begin about two years later than in girls. They include a growth spurt; voice deepening; hair growth on the face, the underarms, the pubic area, and sometimes other parts of the body; development of external genitals; and the ejaculation of semen. Boys may experience acne, a skin condition, and *gynecomastia*, temporary breast enlargement.

- Children and adolescents often learn from their parents that sex is secretive, off limits, and bad to talk about or think about. Parents are often reluctant to talk to their children about sex. A strong bond between parent and child reduces the risk of early sexual involvement and pregnancy. Parents can be significant builders of self-esteem.

- Peers are the strongest influence on the values, attitudes, and behavior of adolescents. They are also a source of much misinformation regarding sex. Boys, especially, are subject to the pressures of *homosociality*. For boys, a girl's importance may lie in giving the boy status among his peers. Both boys and girls may exert pressure on their friends to be sexually active.

- The media present highly charged images of sexuality that are often out of context. Parents can counteract media distortions by discussing the context of sexuality with their children and controlling access to television. They can encourage children to think for themselves.

- Young gays and lesbians are largely invisible because of society's assumption of heterosexuality. Gays and lesbians may begin to come to terms with their homosexuality during their teenage years. They usually have heterosexual dating experiences but may feel ambivalent about them. Because of society's reluctance to acknowledge homosexuality openly, most gay and lesbian teens suffer a great deal of emotional pain.

Adolescent Sexual Behavior

- A "biosocial" approach to adolescent sexuality suggests that an interplay of hormonal and social forces are involved. Most adolescents engage in masturbation. White adolescent heterosexual couples generally follow a normative sequence of adolescent behaviors, from hand-holding to intercourse. African American teens do not necessarily follow such a sequence. For most teenagers, increased emotional involvement leads to increased sexual activity. Kissing is an important activity for adolescents. Oral sex appears to be increasingly practiced.

- The average age of first intercourse has dropped sharply in the last two decades. By age 15 or 16, 1 in 4 white girls and boys have started intercourse, as have 5 in 10 black girls and 9 in 10 black boys. Altogether, by age 19, 7 out of 10 girls and 8 out of 10 boys have had intercourse.

• Most teenagers do not consistently protect themselves against sexually transmitted diseases and pregnancy. Those that do rely mainly on condoms or withdrawal (an unreliable method). About 20% of teenage girls in serious relationships use the pill. Adolescents may not use contraception because of *erotophobia*, the fear of sexuality, or because of not having correct information on contraception. Teenagers' feelings of invulnerability, risk-taking behaviors, and *role testing* are also factors contributing to lack of contraception.

Adolescent Pregnancy

• The U.S. leads the world's developed nations in teen pregnancies, births, and abortions. The results of teenage pregnancy are often poverty, dropping out of school, poor infant health, and disrupted family life. Adolescents get pregnant mainly because they do not use contraception or use it improperly; some get pregnant intentionally.

• Black communities are more accepting of births outside of marriage than are white communities. Teenage mothers' principal needs are for health care, including prenatal care, and education, including parenting and life skills and job training.

• Recent studies and programs find that teenage fathers are a "seriously neglected population." Many are willing or eager to help support the families they've created. They need assistance in building self-esteem, finishing their education, getting jobs, and learning to be parents.

• Part of the solution to reducing teenage pregnancy is to work toward eliminating the poverty and racism that limit the options and lower the self-esteem of many adolescents. Contraception should be readily available for teenagers who choose to be sexually active.

KEY TERMS

psychosexual development
puberty

adolescence
gynecomastia

homosociality
heterosociality

erotophobia
role testing

RESOURCES

Action for Children's Television (A.C.T.)
20 University Road
Cambridge, MA 02138
(617) 876-6620
A consumer organization that influences the TV networks and government on behalf of quality programming for children and limits to advertising on children's programs; also funds studies of the effects of TV on children.

Sex Information and Education Council of the United States (SIECUS)
130 W. 42nd Street, Suite 2500
New York, NY 10036
(212) 819-9770
Provides information to individuals, organizations, and schools on many aspects of sexuality; extensive library and computer database, numerous publications.

Planned Parenthood Federation of America
810 Seventh Avenue
New York, NY 10019
(212) 541-7800
Provides information, counseling, and medical services related to reproduction and sexual health to anyone, regardless of age, social group, or ability to pay. Many cities have Planned Parenthood offices; check your phone directory.

The Hetrick-Martin Institute
401 West Street
New York, NY 10014
(212) 633-8920
A multiservice agency for lesbian and gay youth and their families; provides counseling, advocacy, and education.

Search Institute
122 West Franklin Avenue, Suite 525
Minneapolis, MN 55404
(612) 870-9511; (800) 888-7328
Researches and evaluates mentor programs throughout the country.

SUGGESTIONS FOR FURTHER READING

The following journals contain articles on adolescent psychosexual development, sexuality education, and other issues concerning teenagers: SIECUS Reports, Family Planning Perspectives, *published by the Alan Guttmacher Institute, and* Journal of Adolescence.

Blume, Judy. *Letters to Judy: What Your Kids Wish They Could Tell You*. New York: Putnam, 1986. Letters to the popular children's book author from children who didn't think their parents would understand.

Brown, Rita Mae. *Rubyfruit Jungle*. New York: Bantam, 1973. The classic, comic novel about growing up as a lesbian in the South.

Calderone, Mary S., and Eric W. Johnson. *The Family Book About Sexuality*, rev. ed. New York: Harper & Row, 1989. An excellent guide for parents who want to transmit humanistic values about sexuality to their children.

Gullotta, Thomas P., Gerald R Adams, and Raymond Montemayor, eds. *Adolescent Sexuality*. Newbury Park, CA: Sage Publications, 1993. Current research in many areas of adolescent sexuality, including sexual behavior, gay and lesbian teenagers, teenage pregnancy, and promoting sexual responsibility.

Heron, Ann, ed. *One Teenager in Ten: Writings by Gay and Lesbian Youth*. Boston: Alyson Publications, 1983. Writings by 26 lesbian and gay young people from varied ethnic, religious, and socioeconomic backgrounds.

Klein, Marty. *Ask Me Anything*. New York: Simon & Schuster, 1992. A book for adults (teachers, parents, therapists) who want to be prepared to give straightforward, knowledgeable answers to any question a child may ask about sex, concerning, for example, homosexuality, love, masturbation, or orgasm.

Voydanoff, Patricia, and Brenda W. Donnelly. *Adolescent Sexuality and Pregnancy*. Newbury Park, CA: Sage Publications, 1990. Up-to-date information about many aspects of teenage pregnancy: factors associated with teenage sexual activity and pregnancy, pregnancy resolution, consequences, and intervention strategies.

Chapter Seven

SEXUALITY IN ADULTHOOD

PREVIEW: SELF-QUIZ

1. Overall, there are significantly more unmarried young adult men than women. True or false?

2. Cohabitation has become part of the marital selection process in contemporary America. True or false?

3. Among college students, premarital sexual intercourse generally is considered acceptable even if it takes place outside a loving context. True or false?

4. For middle-class African Americans, churches are important places for unmarried blacks to meet socially. True or false?

5. The frequency of marital sex tends to decline over time but is not considered especially problematical if the overall relationship is judged good. True or false?

6. Among the aged, good health is a key factor in continuing sexual activity. True or false?

7. Cohabiting gay men and lesbians tend to divide labor along age lines. True or false?

8. Despite stereotypes, extramarital affairs tend to be more emotional than sexual. True or false?

9. Sexually nonexclusive marriages are more likely to end in divorce than monogamous ones. True or false?

10. As a result of high divorce rates, the largest number of single adults are those who have been married previously. True or false?

ANSWERS 1. T, 2. T, 3. F, 4. T, 5. T, 6. T, 7. F, 8. F, 9. F, 10. F

Chapter Outline

As we consider the human life cycle from birth to death, we cannot help but be struck by how profoundly sexuality weaves its way through our lives. From the moment we are born, we are rich in sexual and erotic potential, which begins to take shape in our sexual experimentations of childhood. As children, we were still unformed, but the world around us helped shape our sexuality. In adolescence, our education continued as a random mixture of learning and yearning. But as we enter adulthood, with greater experience and understanding, we develop a potentially mature sexuality. We establish our sexual orientation as heterosexual, gay, or lesbian; we integrate love and sexuality; we forge intimate connections and make commitments; we make decisions regarding our fertility; we develop a coherent sexual philosophy. Then, in our middle years, we redefine sex in our intimate relationships, accept our aging, and reevaluate our sexual philosophy. Finally, as we become elderly, we reinterpret the meaning of sexuality in accordance with the erotic capabilities of our bodies. We come to terms with the possible loss of our partner and our own eventual decline. In all these stages, sexuality weaves its bright and dark threads through our lives.

In this chapter, we look at sexuality in early, middle, and late adulthood. In early adulthood, we examine developmental concerns, premarital sexuality, the establishment of sexual orientation, being single, and cohabitation. Next, we turn to middle adulthood, where we look at developmental concerns, marital and extramarital sexuality, and divorce and sexuality. Finally, we look at sexuality in late adulthood, examining developmental issues, age stereotypes, differences in aging between men and women, and the role of the partner in sustaining health.

And I will make thee beds of roses,
And a thousand fragrant
    posies. . . .
            Christopher Marlowe

SEXUALITY IN EARLY ADULTHOOD

Developmental Concerns

There are several tasks that challenge us as we develop our sexuality as young adults (Gagnon & Simon, 1973).

- *Establishing sexual orientation.* As we saw in the previous chapter, children and adolescents may engage in sexual experimentation, such as playing doctor, kissing, and fondling, with members of both sexes. They do not necessarily associate these activities with sexual orientation (Gagnon & Simon, 1973). Instead, their orientation as heterosexual, gay, or lesbian is emerging. Most develop a heterosexual orientation. Others find themselves attracted to members of the same sex and begin to develop gay or lesbian identities.

- *Integrating love and sex.* Traditional gender roles call for men to be sex-oriented and women to be love-oriented. In adulthood, the sex-versus-love opposition needs to be addressed. Instead of polarizing love and sex, we need to develop ways of uniting them.

- *Forging intimacy and making commitments.* Young adulthood is characterized by increasing sexual experience. Through dating, courtship, and cohabitation, we gain knowledge of ourselves and others as potential partners. As our relationships become more meaningful, the degree of intimacy and interdependence increases. Sexuality can be a means of enhancing intimacy and self-disclosure as well as a means of physical pleasure. As we become more intimate, we need to develop our ability to make commitments. A commitment requires us to value the other as much as ourselves, to stay together through the good and the bad, and to give meaning to the changing nature of long-term sexual relationships. There may be different levels of commitment during young adulthood, symbolized by dating, long-term, cohabiting, or marital relationships.

- *Making fertility/childbearing decisions.* Childbearing is socially discouraged during adolescence, but it becomes increasingly legitimate in our twenties, especially if we are married. Fertility issues are often critical but unacknowledged, especially for single young adults. If they are sexually active, how important is it to prevent or defer pregnancy? What will they do if the woman gets unintentionally pregnant? If a single woman wants to have a child on her own, what will she do? If a couple is cohabiting

For everything there is a season,
and a time to every purpose
under heaven:
a time to be born and a time to
die;
a time to plant, and a time to pluck
up what is planted;
a time to kill, and a time to heal;
a time to break down, and a time
to build up;
a time to weep, and a time to
laugh;
a time to mourn, and a time to
dance;
a time to cast away stones and a
time to gather stones together;
a time to embrace, and a time to
refrain from embracing;
a time to seek, and a time to lose;
a time to keep, and a time to cast
away;
a time to rend, and a time to sew;
a time to keep silence, and a time
to speak;
a time to love, and a time to hate;
a time for war, and a time for
peace.

Ecclesiastes 3:1–8

or married, do they plan to have a child? When? If they are lesbian or gay, how will they deal with the desire to have a child?

- *Evolving a sexual philosophy.* As we move from adolescence to adulthood, we reevaluate our moral standards, moving from moral decision making based on authority to standards based on our own personal principles of right and wrong, of caring and responsibility (Gilligan, 1982; Kohlberg, 1969). We become responsible for developing our own moral code, which includes sexual issues. In doing so, we need to evolve a personal philosophical perspective to give coherence to our sexual attitudes, behaviors, beliefs, and values. We need to place sexuality within the larger framework of our lives and relationships. We need to integrate our personal, religious, spiritual, or humanistic values with our sexuality (Kupersmid & Wonderly, 1980).

Premarital Sexuality

Premarital sex refers to sexual activities, especially sexual intercourse, that take place prior to marriage. Using "premarital sex" to describe sexual behavior among all unmarried adults is becoming increasingly questioned for two reasons. (1) At least 10% of adult Americans will never marry, and 30% of divorced men and women will not remarry. It is misleading to describe their sexual activities as "premarital." (2) As increasing numbers of never-married adults are over age 30, "premarital sex" does not adequately describe the nature of their sexual activities. To distinguish between the sexual activities of younger never-married adults (under age 30) and other singles, we use "premarital," as it remains the commonly accepted term. We use **nonmarital sex** to refer to the sexual activities occurring primarily among adults over 30 and divorced or widowed men and women. Although this guideline is not absolute, it will help clarify the differences between these groups.

Premarital Sex: From Sin to Acceptance

A little more than a generation ago, virginity was the norm regarding premarital sex. Sex outside of marriage was considered sinful and immoral. In 1969, according to a Gallup survey, only 32% of the American population believed that premarital sex was acceptable (Lord, 1985). Today, however, values have shifted. Premarital intercourse among young adults (but not adolescents) in a relational context has become the norm (Sprecher & McKinney, 1993; Tanfer & Schoorl, 1992). Because young adults have greater control over their lives and are more capable of making informed choices than adolescents, most research studying young adult sexual behavior rejects a problem approach (Tanfer & Cubbins, 1992). Only some older Americans and groups with conservative religious backgrounds, such as Catholics and fundamentalist Protestants, continue to believe all nonmarital sex is morally wrong (Beck, Cole, & Hammond, 1991; Cochran & Beeghley, 1991; Thornton & Camburn, 1987). But religious conviction does not eliminate premarital sex. A survey of 1000 readers of the conservative *Christianity Today*, for example, found that 40% had engaged in premarital intercourse (Robinson, 1992).

The shift from sin to acceptance is the result of several factors. The advent of effective contraception, legal abortion, and changing gender roles

Among the most important factors associated with premarital sex for both men and women are their liking and loving each other, physical arousal and willingness, preplanning, and sexual arousal prior to their encounter.

legitimizing female sexuality have played major roles in this change. But one of the most significant factors may be traced to demography. Over the last 20 years, there has been a dramatic increase in unmarried men and women over age 18 (Cate & Lloyd, 1992). It is this group that has traditionally looked the most favorably on premarital intercourse. Consider some of the recent demographic changes (U.S. Bureau of the Census, 1992):

- In 1991, the median age for first marriage for men was 26.3 years compared to 23.5 years in 1975. For women, the median age in 1991 was 24.1 years, compared to 21.1 years in 1975. On average, men and women have three additional years in which they may become sexually active prior to marriage.

- The proportion of unmarried adults has risen from 28% of the population in 1971 to 39% in 1991. They represent one of the fastest-growing segments of the American population, nearly 41.5 million in 1991, almost twice the number found in 1971 (21.4 million).

- Most of this growth in the numbers of unmarried men and women has been with individuals in their twenties and early thirties. The proportion of never-married women age 20–24 rose from 36% in 1970 to 64% in 1991. Almost 80% of men in the same age group have never married, compared to 55% in 1970 (U.S. Bureau of the Census, 1992).

- The ratio of single men to single women is unequal and differs by race and ethnicity. Among Anglos and Latinos, there are "too many men" and "too few women" in their twenties and thirties. Among African Americans, however, there are significantly more single women than men. This imbalance means that many heterosexual men and women will be unable to find a marital partner more or less their same age.

The demographic shift in unmarried adults was seismic in proportion. Their numbers, coupled with access to birth control and the emergence of egalitarian gender roles, submerged the old norms in a tidal wave of change.

Factors Leading to Premarital Sexual Involvement What factors lead individual women and men to have premarital sexual intercourse? One study indicated that among women and men who had premarital sex, the most important factors were their love (or liking) for each other, physical arousal and willingness of both partners, and preplanning and arousal prior to the encounter (Christopher & Cate, 1985). Among nonvirgins, as with virgins, love or liking between the partners was extremely important (Christopher & Cate, 1984), but feelings of obligation or pressure were about as important as actual physical arousal. Women reported affection as being slightly more important than did men. An interesting finding is that men perceived slightly more pressure or obligation to engage in intercourse than women.

Examining the sexual decision-making process more closely, researcher Susan Sprecher identifies individual, relationship, and environmental factors affecting the decision to have premarital intercourse (Sprecher, 1989; Sprecher & McKinney, 1993).

Individual Factors There are a number of individual factors influencing the decision to have premarital intercourse. These include previous sexual experience, sexual attitudes, personality characteristics, and gender. The more premarital sexual experience a man or woman has had in the past, the more likely he or she is to engage in sexual activities in the present. Once the psychological barrier against premarital sex is broken, sex appears to become less taboo. This seems to be especially true if the earlier sexual experiences were rewarding in terms of pleasure and intimacy. Those with liberal sexual attitudes are more likely to engage in sexual activity than those with restrictive attitudes. In terms of personality characteristics, men and women who do not feel high levels of guilt about sexuality are more likely to engage in sex, as are those who value erotic pleasure.

Relationship Factors Two of the most important factors determining sexual activity in a relationship are the level of intimacy in the relationship and the length of time the couple has been together (Figure 7.1). Even those who are less permissive in their sexual attitudes accept sexual involvement if the relationship is emotionally intimate and long-standing. People who are less committed (or not committed) to a relationship are less likely to be sexually involved. Finally, people in relationships that share power equally are more likely to be sexually involved than those in inequitable ones.

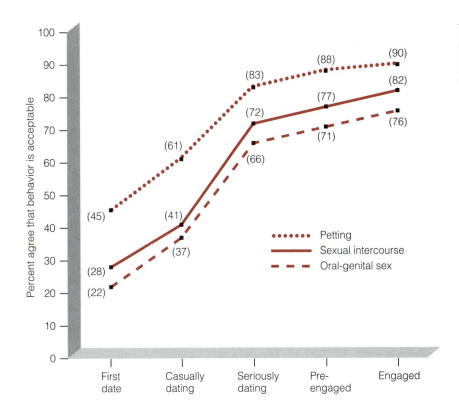

FIGURE 7.1 Acceptance of Sexual Activity by Stage in the Relationship. (Source: Sprecher & McKinney, 1993.)

Petting legend values on chart: (45), (61), (83), (88), (90)
Sexual intercourse values: (28), (41), (72), (77), (82)
Oral-genital sex values: (22), (37), (66), (71), (76)

Environmental Factors   In the most basic sense, the physical environment affects the opportunity for sex. Since sex is a private activity, the opportunity for it may be precluded by the presence of parents, friends, roommates, or children (Tanfer & Cubbins, 1992). The cultural environment also affects premarital sex. The values of one's parents or peers may encourage or discourage sexual involvement. A person's ethnic group also affects premarital involvement: generally, African Americans are more permissive than whites; Latinos are less permissive than Anglos (Baldwin, Whitely, & Baldwin, 1992). Furthermore, a person's subculture—such as the university or church environment, the singles world, the gay and lesbian community—exerts an important influence on sexual decision making.

Establishing Sexual Orientation

A critical task of adulthood is establishing one's sexual orientation as heterosexual, gay, or lesbian. In childhood and early adolescence, there is considerable sex play or sexual experimentation with members of the other sex and same sex (see Chapter 6). These exploratory experiences are tentative in terms of sexual orientation (Van Wyk & Geist, 1984). But in late adolescence and young adulthood, men and women are confronted with the important developmental task of establishing intimacy. And part of the task of establishing intimate relationships is solidifying one's sexual orientation as heterosexual, gay, or lesbian. A relatively small minority of individuals identify themselves as bisexual. **Bisexuality** refers to being sexually involved or attracted to members of both sexes (see Perspective 1).

Most people develop a heterosexual identity by adolescence or young adulthood. Their task is simplified because their development as heterosexuals is approved by society (Wilkinson & Kitzinger, 1993). But for those who are lesbian, gay, or unsure, development is filled with more doubt and anxiety. Because those who are attracted to members of the same sex are aware that they are violating deep societal taboos, confirming their sexual orientation takes longer.

The Gay/Lesbian Identity Process We do not know the numbers of men and women who are heterosexual, gay, lesbian, or bisexual. In large part, this is because homosexuality is stigmatized. Gay men and lesbians are often reluctant to reveal their identities in random surveys, and large-scale national surveys have been blocked because of conservative opposition.

Studies suggest that as many as 10% of Americans are lesbian or gay. Among women, about 13% have had orgasms with other women, but only 1–3% identify themselves as lesbian (Fay et al., 1989; Kinsey et al., 1948, 1953; Marmor, 1980). Among males, including adolescents, as many as 20–37% have had orgasms with other males, according to Kinsey's studies. Ten percent were predominantly gay for at least 3 years; 4% were exclusively gay throughout their entire lives (Kinsey et al., 1948). A review of studies on male same-sex behavior between 1970 and 1990 estimated that a minimum of 5–7% of adult men had had sexual contact with other men in adulthood. Based on their review, the researchers suggest that about 4.5% of men are exclusively gay (Rogers & Turner, 1991). A more recent large-scale study of 3300 men age 20–39 reported that 2% had engaged in same-sex sexual activities and 1% considered themselves gay (Billy, Tanfer, Grady, & Klepinger, 1993).

What are we to make of these differences between studies? In part, the variances may be explained by different methodologies, interviewing techniques, sampling, or definitions of homosexuality. Furthermore, sexuality is more than simply sexual behaviors; it also includes attraction and desire. One can be a virgin or celibate and still be gay or heterosexual. Finally, because sexuality is varied and changes over time, its expression at any one time is not necessarily its expression at another time or for all time.

Identifying oneself as lesbian or gay takes considerable time and includes several phases, usually beginning in late childhood or early adolescence (Blumenfeld & Raymond, 1989; Troiden, 1988). Homoerotic feelings—that is, feelings of sexual attraction to members of the same sex—almost always precede lesbian or gay activity by several years (Bell et al., 1981). With increasing societal awareness of homosexuality, gay and lesbian adolescents are beginning to recognize their orientation earlier than men and women did in the 1970s (Savin-Williams & Rodriguez, 1993).

The first phase of acquiring a lesbian or gay identity is marked by fear and suspicion that somehow one's desires are different. At first, the person finds it difficult to label these emotional and physical desires for the same sex. His or her initial reactions often include fear, confusion, or denial (Herdt & Boxer, 1992).

BISEXUALITY

Heterosexuality and homosexuality are terms used to categorize people according to the sex of their sexual partners. But as we noted in discussing Kinsey's work in Chapter 2, such categories do not always adequately reflect the complexity of sexual orientation, nor do they reflect the complexity of human sexuality in general. Stephanie Sanders and colleagues note that believing that the labels "heterosexual" and "homosexual" reflect "actual sexual behavior patterns . . . leads to gross underestimates of the prevalence of behavioral bisexuality" (Sanders, Reinisch, & McWhirter, 1990).

Although they may be sexually involved with members of both sexes, relatively few people identify themselves as bisexual. Bisexual people may be sexually involved with both sexes or with one sex while continuing to experience feelings for the other sex as well (MacDonald, 1981). A recent study, however, found that more people identified themselves as bisexual than gay or lesbian: 5% of the men and 3% of the women said they were bisexual, while only 4% identified themselves as gay and 2% as lesbian (Janus & Janus, 1993).

There is a general negativity toward bisexuals among many heterosexuals, gay men, and lesbians (Herdt, 1984; Paul, 1984). There are several reasons for this attitude. First, we tend to categorize men and women as heterosexual or homosexual. The bisexual categorization confounds our tendency to polarize traits. It suggests that our sexual orientations are more fluid than we usually think they are (Cass, 1983, 1984). Second, our culture places a high value on monogamy. If someone is involved with a bisexual man or woman, there is a fear that the bisexual partner will turn to another sexual partner to satisfy the unfulfilled part of his or her desires. Third, along with heterosexual male intravenous drug users, bisexual males are the people who are most likely to sexually transmit HIV to women.

Adolescent Same-Sex Experimentation

How is it that most people who have had same-sex experiences identify themselves as heterosexuals rather than bisexuals or homosexuals? The reason is simple: Most of these same-sex experiences took place during adolescent sexual experimentation and in situations where males and females are segregated according to sex. Most of the people in Kinsey's studies had their same-sex experience during early or middle adolescence. This behavior is much closer to childhood sex play than to adult sexuality because it lacks the commitment to a heterosexual, homosexual, or bisexual orientation. As the young adolescent gets older, however, same-sex experimentation is discouraged by peers and adults. The adolescent begins to make a sexual commitment to either heterosexuality or homosexuality. Few adolescents make a commitment to bisexuality.

Situational Homosexuality

A major source of same-sex experiences for heterosexuals is in situations in which they are isolated from the other sex. This is usually referred to as *situational homosexuality*. It is most frequently found in prisons, the military, and sexually segregated schools and colleges. In prisons, about 25% of the males are involved in homosexual activities (Bundy, 1981), most of which are not linked to affection. Rather, dominance, power, violence, and status tend to be its motivating force. For some, it is merely a form of sexual release.

Impersonal Same-Sex Activity by Heterosexuals

Some people seek occasional same-sex contacts to supplement their heterosexual activity. These people, usually men, often have families and desire to have impersonal same-sex contacts away from home. They tend to have a high level of guilt about their desires, are fearful of discovery, and reject a gay label. A classic study (Humphreys, 1970) of the "tearoom trade"

(continued)

Perspective I

BISEXUALITY *(continued)*

(anonymous sex in public restrooms) found that participants were often middle-class, conservative, respectable citizens in their communities.

Sequential Sexual Orientation

Some people identify themselves as being heterosexual and then after many years change their orientation to homosexual. It is not that rare for married couples to separate after many years when one of the partners announces his or her homosexual orientation. Within marriage, the discovery of a gay or lesbian self often leads to intense emotional turmoil. The person acknowledging or changing his or her sexual orientation frequently finds it difficult to fulfill these new emotional and sexual desires within marriage. Such people must either try to repress those needs or separate. Some may have entered marriage in order to ward off fears of being gay or lesbian; others because it was expected of them and they did not realize it would fail to meet their deepest emotional and sexual needs.

Bisexual Orientation

Finally, there are those people who define themselves as bisexual. They have partners of both sexes, and they reject either a heterosexual or a homosexual identity. Sometimes they have had only one or two same-sex experiences, but they identify themselves as bisexual. They believe they can love and enjoy sex with both women and men. In other instances, those with predominantly homosexual experience and only limited heterosexual experience consider themselves bisexual. In most cases, bisexual people do not have sex with men one night and women the next. Their bisexuality is sequential. They are involved in heterosexual relationships for certain periods, ranging from a few weeks to years; later, they are involved in same-sex relations for another period of time.

Little is known about bisexuality, but it challenges the belief that we are either heterosexual or homosexual. Bisexuality points to the fact that human sexual behavior cannot be easily categorized.

In the second phase, the person actually labels these feelings of attraction, love, or desire as **homoerotic,** that is, gay or lesbian. The third phase includes the person's self-definition as gay. This may be difficult, for it entails accepting a label that society generally regards as deviant. Questions then arise about whether to tell parents or friends, whether to hide one's identity ("stay in the closet"), or make it known ("come out of the closet").

Some or most gay men or lesbians may go through two additional phases. The next phase begins with a person's first gay or lesbian love affair (Troiden, 1988). This marks the commitment to unifying sexuality and affection. Most lesbians and gay men have had such love affairs. Alan Bell and Martin Weinberg (1978) found that virtually every gay male and lesbian they interviewed had experienced at least one long-term relationship. The first love affair usually took place between the ages of 20 and 23. Almost all their respondents reported that the affair was important and meaningful to them. One gay man said: "I got a feeling of being loved and having my love accepted. It was a great feeling—companionship and mutual dependence." Another wrote of love's affirming effect: "It made me capable of loving others. I used to withdraw and be afraid of people, but now my main orientation is toward people." A lesbian commented on her first love affair: "I got a deeper understanding of the meaning of love, of myself, and what I was capable of, an understanding of another person's capacity for feeling." Another recalled: "There was a great deal of respect, a very close feeling—consideration, enjoyment. Usually there were other roommates, but the two of us shared a bed. We both knew and said we loved each other. We took care of each other. We're still very close."

The last phase a lesbian or gay man may enter is becoming involved in the gay subculture (see further discussion later in the chapter). A gay man or lesbian may begin acquiring exclusively gay friends, going to gay bars and clubs, or joining gay activist groups. In the gay/lesbian world, gay and lesbian identities incorporate a way of being in which sexual orientation is a major part of one's identity as a person. As Michael Denneny, a prominent editor of gay fiction, said: "I find my identity as a gay man as basic as any other identity I can lay claim to. Being gay is a more elemental aspect of who I am than my profession, my class, or my race" (quoted in Altman, 1982). Similarly, author and activist Pat Califia said: "Knowing I was a lesbian transformed the way I saw, heard, perceived the whole world. I became aware of a network of sensations and reactions that I had ignored all my life" (quoted in Weeks, 1985).

Coming Out For many, being lesbian or gay is associated with a total lifestyle and way of thinking (Conrad & Schneider, 1980). In making gay or lesbian orientation a lifestyle, **coming out,** publicly acknowledging one's homosexuality, has become especially important as an affirmation of one's sexual orientation (Richardson, 1984). Coming out is a major decision, because it may jeopardize many relationships, but it is also an important means of self-validation. By publicly acknowledging one's lesbian or gay orientation, a person begins to reject the stigma and condemnation associated with it (Friend, 1980). Generally, coming out to heterosexuals occurs in stages, first involving family members, especially the mother and siblings, and later the father. Coming out to the family often creates a crisis, but generally the family accepts the situation and gradually adjusts (Holtzen & Agresti, 1990). Misinformation about gay and lesbian sexuality, religious beliefs, and prejudice against homosexuality, however, often interfere with parental response, initially making adjustment difficult (Borhek, 1988; Cramer & Roach, 1987). After the family, friends may be told, and, in fewer cases, employers and co-workers.

Lesbians and gay men are often "out" to varying degrees. Some may be out to no one, not even themselves. Some are out only to their lovers, others to close friends and lovers but not to their families, employers, associates, or fellow students. Others may be out to everyone. Because of fear of reprisal, dismissal, or public reaction, gay and lesbian school teachers, police officers, members of the military, politicians, and members of other such professions are rarely out to their employers, co-workers, or the public.

Being Single

Over the last 20 years, there has been a staggering increase in the numbers of unmarried adults (never married, divorced, or widowed). Most of this increase has been the result of men and women, especially young adults, marrying later.

The New Social Context of Singlehood Some of the results of this dramatic shift affecting unmarried young adults include:

- *Greater premarital sexual experience.* As men and women are marrying later, they are more likely to have more premarital experience and sexual partners than earlier generations. Premarital sex is becoming the norm among adults.

- *Widespread acceptance of cohabitation.* As young adults are deferring marriage longer, cohabitation has become an integral part of young adult life. Some scholars suggest cohabitation is becoming part of the normal mate-selection process (Gwartney-Gibbs, 1986; Surra, 1990). Because gay men and lesbians are not legally permitted to marry, cohabitation has become for many of them a form of marriage.

- *Increased unintended pregnancies.* Because greater numbers of women are single and sexually active, more single women are likely to become unintentionally pregnant as a result of unprotected sexual intercourse or contraceptive failure.

- *Increased numbers of abortions and births to single women.* The increased numbers of unintended pregnancies has led to more abortions and births to single mothers. (About 20% of marriages take place with the woman being pregnant.) In 1989, for example, single women age 20–24 accounted for approximately 30% of all abortions. During the same period, over one-third of all births were to unmarried women in the same age group (U.S. Bureau of the Census, 1992).

- *Greater numbers of separated and divorced men and women.* In 1991, over 13% of the young adults from 20 to 28 were separated or divorced; the figure rises to 29% if we include 30- to 34-year-olds (U.S. Bureau of the Census, 1992). Because of their previous marital experience, separated and divorced men and women tend to have different expectations about relationships than never-married young adults. Forty percent of all marriages are now remarriages for at least one partner (Surra, 1990).

- *Rise of single-parent families.* The rise of divorce and births to single women has led to a 61% increase of single-parent families between 1970 and 1989 (U.S. Bureau of the Census, 1991). Today, there are 6.8 million single-parent families, representing 29% of all families in 1991 (U.S. Bureau of the Census, 1992). Eighty-seven percent of single-parent families are headed by women.

The world that unmarried young adults enter is one in which greater opportunities than ever before exist for exploring intimate relationships.

The College Environment The college environment is important not only for intellectual development but also for social development. The social aspects of the college setting—classes, dormitories, fraternities and sororities, parties, mixers, and sports events—provide opportunities for meeting others. For many of us, college is where we search for or find mates.

Dating in college is similar to high school dating in many ways. It may be formal or informal ("getting together"); it may be for recreation or to find a mate. Some of the features that distinguish college dating from high school dating, however, are the more independent setting (away from home,

diminished parental influence, and so on), the increased maturity of each partner, more role flexibility, and the increased legitimacy of sexual interactions.

There appears to be a general expectation among students that they will engage in sexual intercourse at some point during their college career (Komarovsky, 1985; Sprecher & McKinney, 1993) and that sexual involvement will occur within a loving relationship. When Mirra Komarovsky asked students, "Who, in your opinion, is more on the defensive in this college—a virgin or a sexually experienced student?" the common response was the former. The exceptions are those who, because of their religious beliefs, are committed to virginity until marriage.

Sociologist Ira Reiss (1967) described four moral standards of premarital sexuality among college students. The first is the *abstinence standard*, which was the official sexual ideology in American culture until the 1950s and early 1960s. This belief held that it was wrong for either men or women to engage in sexual intercourse before marriage regardless of the circumstances or their feelings for each other. The second is the *double standard*, widely practiced but rarely approved publicly, which permitted men to engage in premarital intercourse. Women, however, were considered immoral if they had premarital intercourse. *Permissiveness with affection* represents a third standard. It describes sex between men and women who have an affectionate, stable, and loving relationship. This standard is widely held today (Sprecher, McKinney, Walsh, & Anderson, 1988; Sprecher & McKinney, 1993). *Permissiveness without affection* is the fourth standard. It holds that

THE AFRICAN AMERICAN MALE SHORTAGE

An important factor affecting both singlehood and marriage is the ratio of men to women. In *Too Many Women* (Guttentag & Secord, 1983), researchers argue that whenever there is a shortage of women in society, marriage and monogamy are valued; when there is an excess of women, marriage and monogamy are devalued. The scarcer sex is able to weight the rules in its favor.

Consider the following: Among whites age 25–29, there are 136 single men per 100 women; among Latinos, there are 141 men per 100 women. Among whites age 30–34, there are 133 single men per 100 single women; among Latinos, the ratio is 125 single men for 100 women. By the simple law of supply and demand, white and Latina women can be more selective about their partners because the pool of single men is large. The percentage of married individuals was 64% among whites and 61% among Latinos.

But the story is different for African Americans: Single African American men are in short supply. Among blacks age 25–29, there are 98 single men per 100 women; among those age 30–34, there are 77 men per 100 women. By age 40–44, there are only 65 single men per 100 women. There are an estimated 1.5 million more African American women than men (Staples & Johnson, 1993).

There are several important consequences resulting from this. First, the percentage of married African Americans has declined significantly, from 64% in 1971 to 44% in 1991 (U.S. Bureau of the Census, 1992). Second, single African American women have sex less often than single white women (Tanfer & Cubbins, 1992). Third, many black women give birth while single and raise their children with the assistance of their extended family and the biological father (Staples, 1988). Births to single mothers are associated with enduring poverty.

Inner-city African Americans have higher rates of singlehood than middle-class blacks. Among college-educated African Americans, the gender ratio is more extreme as people tend to marry those with similar educational backgrounds. Overall, the ratio of single college-educated black women is 2 to 1. For divorced black women over 35 with more than 5 years of college, the ratio of comparable men is 38 to 1 (Staples, 1991). Furthermore, significantly fewer African Americans marry because of the lack of eligible men. Not only are there fewer males because of the gender ratio, but because of lack of jobs or skills, they are often unemployed. Marriage among blacks is often a function of the male's being employed (Tucker & Taylor, 1989). More African Americans than whites are single because of social problems, such as the gender ratio and high unemployment, rather than a rejection of marriage (Tucker & Taylor, 1989).

The proportion of single black males to females decreased sharply between 1971 and 1991, while it rose among both whites and Latinos (U.S. Bureau of the Census, 1992). Why the decline in African American males? Sociologist Robert Staples (1988) points to the

people may have sexual relationships with each other even if there is no affection or commitment (see Jacoby & Williams, 1985).

While acceptance of premarital sex is widespread among college students, there are limits. If a woman has sexual intercourse, it should take place in the context of a committed relationship. Women who "sleep around" are morally censured. Reflecting the continuing double standard, men are not

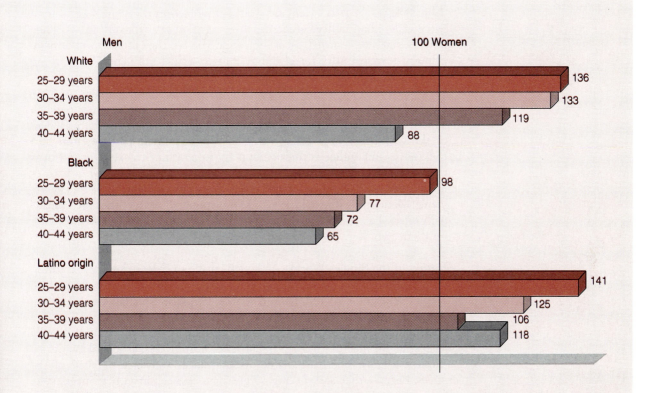

effects of institutional racism: high infant mortality, premature death, devastating homicide rates, poor healthcare access, HIV/AIDS, and illegal drugs. High unemployment, disproportionate incarceration rates, increasing school dropout rates, and drug abuse further make affected young African American men less desirable as mates. As Staples (1988) writes: "Due to the operational effects of institutional racism, large num-

bers of Black males are incarcerated, unemployed, narcotized, or fall prey to early death. . . ."

It is important to establish social policies to reverse the devastation visited upon African Americans by discrimination and poverty. Such policies are important in reversing the gender imbalance and the consequences that have developed over the last 20 years.

usually condemned as harshly as women for having sex without commitment (Komarovsky, 1985).

For gay men and lesbians, the college environment is often liberating because many campuses are more accepting of sexual diversity than society at large is. College campuses often have lesbian and gay organizations that sponsor social events, dances, and get-togethers. There they can freely meet others in open circumstances that permit meaningful relationships to develop and mature. While prejudice against gay men and lesbians continues to exist in colleges and universities, college life has been an important safe haven for many.

The Singles World　Men and women involved in the singles world tend to be older than college students; they range in age from 25 to 40. They have never been married, or, if they are divorced, they usually do not have primary responsibility for children. Single adults are generally working rather than attending school (Cargan & Melko, 1982).

While young adults are remaining unmarried in record numbers, in 1991 the majority of unmarried young adults under 30 lived with their parents. Thirty-one percent of young adults age 25–29 live at home (U.S. Bureau of the Census, 1992). Young adults living with their parents often find themselves in conflict as their parents try to continue to exert control over their sexuality. They find themselves restricted from bringing a partner home over night or spending the night at a girlfriend's or boyfriend's apartment (Mancini & Bliexner, 1990). Many young adults feel they are continually treated as children and lack the freedom of their peers who are living on their own.

Dating in the Singles World　Although dating in the singles world is somewhat different from dating in high school and college, there are similarities. Singles, like their counterparts in school, emphasize recreation and entertainment, sociability, and physical attractiveness.

The problem of meeting other single people is very often central. In college, students meet each other in classes or dormitories, at school events, or through friends. There are many meeting places and large numbers of eligibles. Because they are working, singles have less opportunity to meet available people. For single adults, friends, common interests, parties, work, or talking to a stranger are the most frequent means of meeting others (Shostak, 1987).

To fill the demand for meeting other singles, the singles world has spawned a multibillion-dollar industry—bars, resorts, clubs, and housing (Shostak, 1987). The bar has become the symbol of the singles scene, but most singles reject such bars as "meat markets," even though they may occasionally go to one. Single bars never developed among African Americans, however; instead, they may attend a happy hour at a favorite restaurant or bar (Staples, 1991).

Singles increasingly rely on personal classified ads where men advertise themselves as "success objects" and women advertise themselves as "sex objects" (Davis, 1990). Their ads tend to reflect stereotypical gender roles. Men advertise for women who are attractive, deemphasizing intellectual, professional, and financial aspects. Women advertise for men who hold jobs and who are financially secure, intelligent, emotionally expressive, and interested in commitment. Men are twice as likely as women to place ads. Additional forms of meeting others include video dating services, introduction services, computer bulletin boards, and 900 party-line phone services.

Single men and women often rely on their churches and church activities to meet other singles. Black churches are especially important for middle-class African Americans as they have less chance of meeting other African

Americans in integrated work and neighborhood settings. African Americans also attend black-oriented concerts, plays, film festivals, and other social gatherings (Staples, 1991). For black women, the situation is complicated by a dearth of eligible single black men (see Perspective 2).

Singles and Sexuality As a result of the growing acceptance of sexuality outside marriage, singles are presented with various sexual options. Some choose celibacy for religious or moral reasons. Others choose celibacy over casual sex; when they are involved in a committed nommarital relationship, they may become sexually intimate. Some are temporarily celibate; they are taking "a vacation from sex." They utilize their celibacy to clarify the meaning of sexuality in their relationships (Brown, 1980).

Sexual experimentation is important for many. Peter Stein (1983) observes:

> For many singles, sexual experimentation is a part of their single identity, enjoyed for itself or used as a stage leading to marriage or choice of a single sexual partner. Those who try a variety of relationships can learn much about the world and about themselves. They may avoid commitments in order to work on a career or on personal growth, or to recover from a painful past relationship. Some set up a hierarchy of relationships involving special obligations to a primary partner and lesser responsibilities to others.

While an individual may derive personal satisfaction from sexual experimentation, he or she must also manage the stress of conflicting commitments, loneliness, and a lack of connectedness.

Many single women reject the idea of casual sex (Stein, 1983). Instead, they feel that sex must take place within the context of a relationship. In relationship sex, intercourse becomes a symbol of the degree of caring between two persons. Such relationships are expected to be "leading somewhere," such as to commitment, love, cohabitation, or marriage. As men and women get older, marriage becomes an increasingly important goal of a relationship.

Gay and Lesbian Singlehood

As a result of the stigmatization of homosexuality, in the late nineteenth century groups of gay men and lesbians began congregating in their own secretive clubs and bars. (See Perspective 3 for a discussion of myths about homosexuality.) There, in relative safety, they could find acceptance and support, meet others, and socialize. By the 1960s, some neighborhoods in the largest cities (such as Christopher Street in New York and the Castro district in San Francisco) became identified with gay men and lesbians. These neighborhoods feature not only openly gay or lesbian bookstores, restaurants, coffeehouses, and bars but also clothing stores, physicians, lawyers, hair salons—even driving schools. They have gay churches, such as the Metropolitan Community Church, where gay men and lesbians worship freely; they have their own political organizations, newspapers, and magazines (such as *The Advocate*). They have family and child-care services oriented to the needs of the gay and lesbian communities; they have gay and lesbian youth counseling programs.

Gay and lesbian businesses, institutions, and neighborhoods are important for affirming positive identities; they enable gay men and lesbians to interact beyond a sexual context. They help make being lesbian or gay a complex social identity consisting of many parts—student, parent, worker, professional, churchgoer—rather than simply a sexual role (Altman, 1982).

In these neighborhoods, men and women are free to express their affection as openly as heterosexuals. They experience little discrimination or intolerance and are involved in gay and lesbian social and political organizations (Weinberg & Williams, 1974). More recently, with increasing acceptance in some areas, many middle-class gay men and lesbians are moving to suburban areas. In the suburbs, however, they remain more discreet than in large cities (Lynch, 1992).

The Gay Male Subculture The urban gay male subculture that emerged in the 1970s emphasized sexuality. While relationships were important, sexual experiences and variety were even more important. Despite the emphasis on sex over relationships, two researchers found that most gay men in their study had at least one exclusive relationship (Weinberg & Williams, 1974). In fact, involvement in the gay subculture enhanced the likelihood of lasting relationships. The researchers speculated that closeted gay men were more likely than open gay men to avoid attachments for fear of discovery.

With the rise of the HIV/AIDS epidemic in the 1980s and 1990s, the gay subculture has placed an increased emphasis on the relationship context of sex (Carl, 1986; Isensee, 1990). Relational sex has become the norm among large segments of the gay population (Levine, 1992). Most gay men have sex within dating or love relationships. (In fact, some AIDS organizations are giving classes on gay dating in order to encourage safe sex.) One researcher (Levine, 1992) said of the men in his study: "The relational ethos fostered new erotic attitudes. Most men now perceived coupling, monogamy, and celibacy as healthy and socially acceptable." This is a dramatic reversal from 15 years earlier.

African American gay men often experience a conflict between their black and gay identities (Petersen, 1992). African Americans are less likely to disclose their gay identity because the black community is less accepting of homosexuality than the white community. At the same time, African Americans may experience racial discrimination in the predominantly white gay community. Gay African Americans whose primary identity is racial tend to socialize in the black community where they are tolerated only as long as they are closeted. As a result, there are no gay institutions available to them as there are in the gay white community. They must rely on discreet friendship circles or clandestine bars to meet other gay black men.

African Americans whose primary identity is gay rather than black usually socialize in the mainstream gay subculture where they become involved with gay white groups and organizations. They may work for greater inclusion of blacks in the gay community. A large proportion develop friendships and love relationships with white men because of the relatively smaller number of available gay African Americans.

Among gay Latinos in cities with large Latino populations, there is usually at least one gay bar. They usually specialize in dancing or female imper-

COMMON MISCONCEPTIONS ABOUT HOMOSEXUALITY

There are numerous misconceptions about being gay or lesbian. They nevertheless continue to circulate, adding to the fires of prejudice. These misconceptions include:

• *Misconception No. 1: Men and women are gay or lesbian because they can't get a heterosexual partner.* This belief is reflected in such remarks about lesbians as "All she needs is a good lay" (implying a man). Similar remarks about men include "He just needs to meet the right woman." Research indicates that lesbians and gay men have about as much heterosexual high school dating experience as their peers. Furthermore, the majority of lesbians had sexual experiences with men; many of those experiences were pleasurable (Bell et al., 1981).

• *Misconception No. 2: Lesbians and gay men "recruit" heterosexuals to become gay.* People are not recruited or seduced into being gay anymore than they are recruited into being heterosexual. Most gay men and lesbians have their first gay experience with a peer, either a friend or an acquaintance. They report having had homosexual feelings prior to their first experience (Bell et al., 1981).

• *Misconception No. 3: Gay men are child molesters.* This is a corollary to the recruitment misconception above. The overwhelming majority of child molesters are heterosexual males who molest girls; these men include fathers, stepfathers, uncles, and brothers. A large percentage of men who molest boys identify themselves as heterosexual (Arndt, 1991).

• *Misconception No. 4: Homosexuality can be caught.* Homosexuality is not the flu. Some parents express fear about having their children taught by homosexual teachers. They fear their children will model themselves after the teacher or be seduced by him or her. But a child's sexual orientation is well-estab-

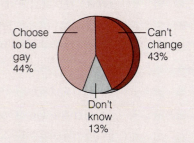

Percentage of Adults Who Believe Homosexuality Is Chosen or Can't Be Changed

lished by the time he or she enters school, and a teacher would not have an impact on that child's orientation (Marmor, 1980).

• *Misconception No. 5: Gay men and lesbians could change if they wanted.* There is no evidence that gay men and lesbians can change their sexual orientation. The belief that they should reflects assumptions that homosexuality is abnormal or sinful. Most psychotherapy with gay men and lesbians who are unhappy about their orientation aims at helping them adjust to it.

• *Misconception No. 6: Homosexuality is condemned in the Bible.* The Bible condemned same-sex sexual activities between men, not homosexuality. Some biblical scholars believe that the rejection of same-sex sexual activities was based on historical factors, including the lack of the concept of sexual orientation, the exploitative and abusive nature of much same-sex activity in ancient times, the belief that the purpose of sex was procreation, and purity or holiness concerns that such acts were impure (there were similar concerns about sexual intercourse with a menstruating woman). There is increasing debate among religious groups as to whether same-sex relationships are inherently sinful.

sonation. The extent to which a gay Latino participates in the Anglo or Latino gay world depends on the individual's degree of acculturation (Carrier, 1992).

The Lesbian Community Beginning in the 1950s and 1960s, young and working-class lesbians developed their own institutions, especially women's softball teams and exclusively female gay bars as places to socialize. Historian Lillian Faderman (1991) notes of lesbian bars:

> They represented the one public place where those who had accepted a lesbian sociosexual identity did not have to hide who they were. They offered companionship and the possibilities of romantic contacts. They often bristled with the excitement of women together, defying their outlaw status and creating their own rules and their own worlds.

During the late 1960s and 1970s, **lesbian separatists,** lesbians who wanted to create a separate "womyn's" culture distinct from heterosexual *and* gay men, rose to prominence. They developed their own music, literature, and erotica; they had their own clubs and bars. But by the middle of the 1980s, according to Faderman, the lesbian community underwent a "shift to moderation." It became more diverse and included Latinas, African American women, Asian American women, and older women. It has developed closer ties with the gay male community. Lesbians now view gay men as sharing much in common with them because of the common prejudice directed against both groups.

In contrast to the gay male subculture, the lesbian community centers its activities around couples. Lesbian therapist JoAnn Loulan (1984) writes:

> Being single is suspect. Single women may be seen as a loser no one wants. Or there's the "swinging single" no one trusts. The lesbian community is as guilty of these prejudices as the world at large.

Lesbians tend to value the emotional quality of relationships more than the sexual component. Lesbians usually form longer-lasting relationships than gay men (Tuller, 1988). Lesbians' emphasis on emotions over sex and the more enduring quality of their relationships reflects their socialization as women. Being female influences a lesbian more than being gay.

Cohabitation

In 1990, more than 2.9 million heterosexual couples and 1.5 million gay or lesbian couples were living together in the United States (U.S. Bureau of the Census, 1991). In contrast, only 523,000 heterosexual couples were cohabiting in 1970. Delaying marriage has increased the number of men and women cohabiting (Tanfer & Cubbins, 1992). For census purposes, heterosexuals who cohabit are called **POSSLQs** *(possel-kews)*, people of the other sex sharing living quarters.

A New Norm Cohabitation is increasingly accepted at almost every level of society. By age 30, about 40–50% of all young adult women will have cohabited (Surra, 1990). Currently, 4% are cohabiting (Bumpass & Sweet, 1988). Some scholars, in fact, believe that cohabitation is becoming institutionalized as part of the normal mate-selection process (Gwartney-Gibbs, 1986). The concept of **domestic partnership** has led to laws granting some of the protections of marriage to men and women, including gay men and lesbians, who cohabit in committed relationships. In 1989, New York state granted limited rights to committed gay and lesbian couples, such as insurance and pension coverage. Several cities, including San Francisco, as well as some universities, such as Stanford University, recognize domestic partnerships. In Europe, both Sweden and Denmark legally recognize domestic partnerships. The Danish accord to gay men and lesbians the same rights and responsibilities in domestic partnerships as in marriage, except for the adoption of children and child custody.

Today, the only difference between those who cohabit and those who don't lies not in social adjustment, family background, or social class but in degree of religiousness. Those who have a high degree of religiosity and regular church attendance tend not to live together before marriage. For the religious, living together is still often considered "living in sin" (Newcomb, 1979).

Living together has become more widespread and accepted in recent years for several reasons. First, the general climate regarding sexuality is more liberal than it was a generation ago. Sexuality is more widely considered to be an important part of a person's life, whether or not he or she is married. The moral criterion for judging sexual intercourse has shifted; love rather than marriage is now widely regarded as making a sexual act moral. Second, the meaning of marriage is changing. Because of the dramatic increase in divorce rates over the last two decades, marriage is no longer thought of necessarily as a permanent commitment. Permanence is increasingly replaced by **serial monogamy,** a succession of marriages. Since the average marriage now lasts only seven years, the distinction between marriage and living together is losing its clarity. Third, young adults are continuing to defer marriage. At the same time, they want the companionship found by living intimately with another person.

For young adults, there are a number of advantages to cohabitation. First, because their lives are often in transition—as they finish school, establish careers, or become more secure financially—cohabitation represents a "tentatively" committed relationship. Second, in cohabiting relationships, partners tend to be more egalitarian. They do not have to deal with the more structured roles of husband and wife. They are freer to develop their own individuality independent of marital roles. Third, the couple knows they are together because they want to be, not because of the pressure of marital obligations.

While there are a number of advantages, there may also be disadvantages. Parents may refuse to provide support for school as long as their child is living with someone; they may not welcome their child's partner into their home. Cohabiting couples also may find they cannot easily buy houses together as banks may not count their income as joint; they usually don't qualify for insurance benefits. If one partner has children, the other partner is usually not as involved as if they were married. Cohabiting couples who live together often find themselves socially stigmatized if they have a child. Finally, cohabiting relationships generally don't last more than two years; couples either break up or get married.

When two people live together, their primary commitment is to each other. As long as they feel they love each other, they will stay together. In marriage, the couple makes a commitment not only to each other but to their marriage as well. Marriage often seems to become a third party that enters the relationship between a man and a woman. Each partner will do things to save a marriage; they may give up dreams, work, ambitions, and extramarital relationships to make a marriage work. A man and a woman who are living together may not work as hard to save their relationship. Although society encourages married couples to make sacrifices to save their marriage, unmarried couples rarely receive the same support. Parents may even urge their "living together" children to split up rather than give up plans for work, school, or career. If the couple is beginning to encounter sexual difficulties, it is more likely that they will split up if they are cohabiting than if they are married. It may be easier to abandon a problematic relationship than to change it.

There is no consensus about whether cohabitation significantly increases or decreases later marital stability (Teachman & Polonko, 1990). Although couples who are living together often argue that cohabitation helps prepare them for marriage, such couples are statistically as likely to divorce as those who do not live together before marriage. In one study (Newcomb & Bentler, 1980), researchers interviewed 159 couples applying for marriage licenses. About half were living together at the time; the other half had not lived together. Four years later, the researchers were able to interview 77 of these couples. Thirty-one percent had divorced. Those who had lived together were no less likely to have divorced than those who had not lived together. Other studies have found that those who had cohabited before marriage were no more or less satisfied with their marriages than other couples (Jacques & Chason, 1979; Watson, 1983).

Gay and Lesbian Cohabitation In 1990, there were over 1.5 million gay male or lesbian couples living together. The relationships of gay men and lesbians have been stereotyped as less committed than heterosexual couples because (1) lesbians and gay men cannot legally marry, (2) they may not appear to emphasize sexual exclusiveness, and (3) heterosexuals misperceive love between lesbian and gay couples as being somehow less real than love between heterosexuals. Numerous similarities, however, exist between gay and heterosexual couples, according to Letitia Peplau (1981, 1988). Regardless of their sexual orientation, most people want a close, loving relationship with another person. For gay men, lesbians, and heterosexuals, intimate relationships provide love, romance, satisfaction, and security. There is one important difference, however. Heterosexual couples tend to adopt a traditional marriage model, whereas gay couples tend to have a "best-friend" model. Peplau (1988) observes:

> A friendship model promotes equality in love relationships. As children, we learn that the husband should be the "boss" at home, but friends "share and share alike." Same-sex friends often have similar interests, skills, and resources—in part because they are exposed to the same gender-role socialization in growing up. It is easier to share responsibilities in a relationship when both partners are equally skilled or inept at cooking, making money, and disclosing feelings.

Two women register as domestic partners. Domestic partnerships provide committed, cohabiting heterosexuals, gay men, and lesbians some of the legal protection and rights previously associated only with marriage, such as health benefits. The evolution of domestic partnership laws increases the legitimacy of cohabitation.

In this model, tasks and chores are often shared, alternated, or performed by the person who has more time. Usually, both members of the couple support themselves; rarely does one financially support the other (Peplau & Gordon, 1982).

Few lesbian and gay relationships are divided into the traditional heterosexual provider/homemaker roles. Among heterosexuals, these divisions are gender-linked as male or female. But in cases in which the couple consists of two men or two women, these traditional gender divisions make no sense. As one gay male remarked, "Whenever I am asked who is the husband and who is the wife, I say, 'We're just a couple of happily married husbands.'" Tasks are often divided pragmatically, according to considerations such as who likes cooking more (or dislikes it less) and work schedules (Marecek, Finn, & Cardell, 1988). Most gay couples are dual-worker couples; neither partner supports or depends on the other economically. And because gay and lesbian couples are the same sex, the economic discrepancies based on greater male earning power are absent. One partner does not necessarily have greater power than the other based on income. Although gay couples emphasize egalitarianism, if there are differences in power, they are attributed to personality; if there is an age difference, the older partner is usually more powerful (Harry, 1988).

Because they confront societal hostility, lesbians and gay men fail to receive the general social support given heterosexuals in maintaining relationships. One rarely finds parents, for example, urging their gay male or lesbian children to make a commitment to a stable same-sex relationship or, if the relationship is rocky, to stick it out.

SEXUALITY IN MIDDLE ADULTHOOD

In our middle years, family and work become especially important. Our personal time is spent increasingly on marital and family matters, especially if we have children. Sexual expression often decreases in frequency, intensity, and significance, replaced by family and work concerns. Sometimes the change reflects a higher value placed on family intimacy. At other times, it may reflect habit, boredom, or conflict.

Developmental Concerns

In the middle adult years, some of the psychosexual developmental tasks begun in young adulthood may be continuing. These tasks may have been deferred or only partly completed in young adulthood, such as intimacy issues or childbearing decisions. Because of separation or divorce, we may find ourselves facing the same intimacy and commitment tasks at age 40 we thought we completed 15 years earlier (Cate & Lloyd, 1992). But life does not stand still; it moves steadily forward, ready or not. Other developmental issues appear, including the ones below.

- *Redefining sex in marital or other long-term relationships.* In new relationships, sex is often passionate, intense; it may be the central focus. But in long-term marital or cohabiting relationships, habit, competing parental and work obligations, fatigue, and unresolved conflicts often erode the passionate intensity associated with sex. Sex may need to be redefined as a form of intimacy and caring. Individuals may also need to decide how to deal with the possibility, reality, and meaning of extramarital or extra-relational affairs.

- *Reevaluating one's sexuality.* Single women and men may need to weigh the costs and benefits of sex in casual or lightly committed relationships. In long-term relationships, sexuality often becomes less than central to relationship satisfaction. Nonsexual elements, such as communication, intimacy, and shared interests and activities, become increasingly important to relationships. Women who have deferred their childbearing begin to reappraise their decision: Should they remain child-free, race against their biological clock, or adopt a child? Some people may redefine their sexual orientation. One's sexual philosophy continues to evolve.

- *Accepting the biological aging process.* As we age, our skin wrinkles, our flesh sags, our hair turns gray (or falls out), our vision blurs—and we become, in the eyes of society, less attractive and less sexual. By our forties, our physiological responses have begun to slow noticeably. By our fifties, society begins to "neuter" us, especially women who have been through menopause. The challenge of aging is to accept its biological mandate.

Marital Sexuality

When people marry, they may discover that their sexual lives are very different than before marriage. Sex is now morally and socially sanctioned. It is in marriage that the great majority of heterosexual interactions take place. Yet as a culture, we feel ambivalent about marital sex. On the one hand,

It is better to marry than to burn.
Paul of Tarsus, I Corinthians 7:9

You can only hold your stomach in for so many years.
Burt Reynolds

All tragedies are finished by a death.
All comedies are ended by a marriage.
Lord Byron (1788–1824)

Although stereotypes among the young desexualize middle-aged and older couples, they may be as affectionate and sexual as younger couples—or even more so.

marriage is the only relationship in which sexuality is legitimized. On the other hand, marital sex is the endless source of humor and ridicule.

In popular culture, marital sex is often considered an oxymoron, a contradiction in terms. Polly Frost (1992), for example, gives women the following humorous (but typical) advice: "You don't have to love the man you're having sex with. In fact, if you wait until you love a man to have sex with him, it may not happen very often, especially if you and he are married." And married men joke: "Marital sex? What's that?"

If we were to judge by the media, little sex occurs within marriages. On television, five times as much sex takes place between unmarried partners as between married ones. Men have sex more often with prostitutes than with their wives. Erotic activity is often linked with violence (Roberts, 1982). Sex research is not much different from popular culture. In 1993, we conducted a computer search through the PsychLit database for scholarly articles published between 1987 and 1992 on marital sexuality. There was only a single article indexed under marital sexuality. By contrast, there were 45 on premarital sex, 38 on extramarital sex, and 469 on sexual dysfunctions (Figure 7.2)!

The Frequency of Sexual Interactions

Sexual intercourse tends to diminish in frequency the longer a couple is married (Figure 7.3). For newly married couples, the average rate of sexual intercourse is about three times a week. As they get older, the frequency drops. In early middle age, married couples make love an average of one-and-a-half to two times a week. After age 50, the rate is about once a week or less. This decreased frequency, however, does not necessarily mean that sex is no longer important or that the marriage is unsatisfactory. It often means simply that one or both members are too tired. For dual-worker families and families with children, fatigue

Marriage has many pains but celibacy has no pleasures.
Samuel Johnson (1709–1784)

FIGURE 7.2 Percentages of 553 scholarly articles published between 1988 and 1992 on selected human sexuality topics. (Source: Data from PsycLit database search, 1993.)

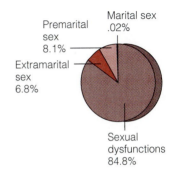

Premarital sex 8.1%

Marital sex .02%

Extramarital sex 6.8%

Sexual dysfunctions 84.8%

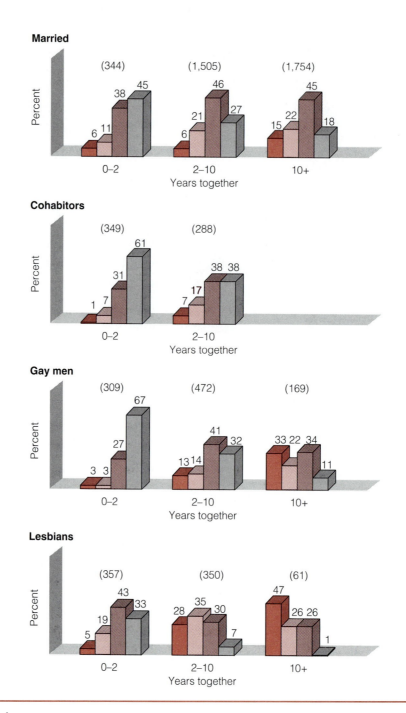

Married

(344)   (1,505)   (1,754)

0–2   2–10   10+
Years together

Cohabitors

(349)   (288)

0–2   2–10
Years together

Gay men

(309)   (472)   (169)

0–2   2–10   10+
Years together

Lesbians

(357)   (350)   (61)

0–2   2–10   10+
Years together

Sex once a month or less

Sex between once a month and once a week

Sex between one and three times a week

Sex three times a week or more

Numbers in parentheses are the number of couples on which the percentages are based.

FIGURE 7.3 Frequency of Sexual Interactions by Duration of Relationship, Relationship Status, and Gay or Lesbian Sexual Orientation. (Source: Blumstein & Schwartz, 1983.)

and lack of private time may be the most significant factors in the decline of frequency (Blumstein & Schwartz, 1983; Olds, 1985). Philip Blumstein and Pepper Schwartz (1983) found that most people attributed the decline in sexual intercourse to lack of time or physical energy or to "being accustomed" to each other. In addition, other activities and interests engage them besides sex.

Most married couples don't seem to feel that declining frequency is a major problem if their overall relationship is good (Cupach & Comstock, 1990; Sprecher & McKinney, 1993). Sexual intercourse is only one erotic bond among many in marriage. There are also kissing, caressing, nibbling, stroking, massaging, candlelight dinners, walking hand-in-hand, looking into each other's eyes, and intimate words.

Giving New Meaning to Sex

Sexuality within marriage is significantly different from premarital sex in at least three ways. First, sex in marriage is expected to be monogamous. Second, procreation is a legitimate goal. Third, sex takes place in the everyday world. These differences present each person with important tasks.

Monogamy One of the most significant factors shaping marital sexuality is the expectation of monogamy. Before marriage or following divorce, a person may have various sexual partners, but within marriage, all sexual interactions are expected to take place between the spouses. This expectation of monogamy lasts a lifetime; a person marrying at 20 commits himself or herself to 40–60 years of sex with the same person. Within a monogamous relationship, each partner must decide how to handle fantasies, desires, and opportunities for extramarital sexuality. Do you tell your spouse that you have fantasies about other people? That you masturbate? Do you flirt with others? Do you have an extramarital relationship? If you do, do you tell your spouse? How do you handle sexual conflicts or difficulties with your partner? How do you deal with sexual boredom or monotony?

Socially Sanctioned Reproduction Sex also takes on a procreative meaning within marriage. Although it is obviously possible to get pregnant before marriage, marriage is the only socially sanctioned setting for having children. In marriage, partners are confronted with the task of deciding whether or when to have children. It is one of the most crucial decisions they will make, for having children profoundly alters a relationship. If the couple decides to have a child, the nature of their lovemaking may change from simply an erotic activity to an intentionally reproductive act as well.

Changed Sexual Context The sexual context changes with marriage. Because married life takes place in a day-to-day living situation, sex must also be expressed in the day-to-day world. Sexual intercourse must be arranged around working hours and at times when the children are at school or asleep. One or the other partner may be tired, frustrated, or angry. The emotions associated with premarital sex may disappear. Some of the passion of romantic love eventually disappears as well, to be replaced with a love based on intimacy, caring, and commitment. Although we may tend to believe that good sex depends on good techniques, it really depends more on the quality of the marriage.

Lesbians, Gay Men, and Bisexuals in Heterosexual Marriages

Although there are no reliable studies, it is estimated that about 20% of gay men and 33% of lesbians have been married (Bell & Weinberg, 1978). Estimates run into the millions for married bisexual men and women (Gochros, 1989; Hill, 1987). Relatively few men and women are consciously aware of their homosexuality or bisexuality at the time they marry. Those who are

Fidelity is part of every human relationship. It is the strain toward permanence and toward public commitment to permanence that is involved in any relationship beyond the most superficial. Fidelity is a longing for love that does not end.
Andrew Greeley

Seldom, or perhaps never, does a marriage develop into an individual relationship smoothly and without crisis; there is no coming to consciousness without pain.
Carl Jung (1875–1961)

The long course of marriage is a long event of perpetual change, in which a man and a woman mutually build up their souls and make themselves whole. It is like rivers flowing on, through new country, always unknown.
D. H. Lawrence (1885–1930)

aware rarely disclose their feelings to their prospective partner (Gochros, 1989). Like heterosexuals, lesbians and gay men marry because of pressure from family, friends, and girlfriend/boyfriend, genuine love for one's heterosexual partner, the wish for companionship, and the desire to have children (Bozett, 1987).

When husbands or wives discover their partner's homosexuality or bisexuality, they initially experience shock, then they feel deceived or stupid. Many feel shame (Hays & Samuels, 1987). "His coming out of the closet in some ways put the family in the closet," recalled one woman who felt ashamed to tell anyone of her situation (Hill, 1987). At the same time, homosexual or bisexual spouses often feel deeply saddened for hurting loved ones. If they have children, they fear losing them (Voeller, 1980).

When gay men, lesbians, or bisexuals disclose their orientation to their spouse, separation and divorce is the usual outcome. Many gay men and lesbians are also parents at the time they separate from their spouse. It is generally important for them to affirm their identities both as lesbian or gay *and* as parents (Bozett, 1989c). This is especially important because negative stereotypes portray gay men and lesbians as "anti-family." Men and women begin to fuse their identities as lesbian or gay with their parental role.

Extramarital Sexuality

To be faithful to one is to be cruel to all others.

Wolfgang Amadeus Mozart, (1756–1791) *Don Giovanni*

A fundamental assumption in our culture is that marriages are monogamous. Each person remains the other's exclusive intimate partner, in terms of both emotional and sexual intimacy. Extramarital relationships violate that assumption.

While we tend to think of extramarital involvements as being sexual, they actually assume several forms (Thompson, 1983). They may be (1) sexual but not emotional, (2) sexual and emotional, or (3) emotional but not sexual (Thompson, 1984). Very little research has been done on extramarital relationships in which both people are emotionally but not sexually involved. Thompson's study, however, found that of 378 married and cohabiting people, the three types of extrarelational involvement were about equally represented. Twenty-one percent had been in relationships that were primarily sexual, 19% in relationships that were sexual and emotional, and 18% in relationships that were emotional but not sexual. All told, 43% had been in some form of extramarital relationship.

Extrarelational Sex in Dating and Cohabiting Relationships You don't have to be married to have sex outside a relationship (Blumstein & Schwartz, 1983; Hansen, 1987). Both cohabiting couples and those in committed relationships usually have expectations of sexual exclusiveness. But, like some married men and women who take vows of fidelity, they do not always remain sexually exclusive. Blumstein and Schwartz (1983) found that those involved in cohabiting relationships had similar rates of extrarelational involvement as married couples, except that cohabiting males had somewhat fewer partners than husbands did. Gay men had more partners than cohabiting and married men. And lesbians had fewer partners than any other group.

Large numbers of both women and men have sexual involvements outside dating relationships that are considered exclusive. One study of college students (Hansen, 1987) indicated that over 60% of the men and 40% of the women had been involved in erotic kissing outside the relationship; 35% of the men and 11% of the women had had sexual intercourse with someone else. Of those who knew of their partner's affair, a large majority felt that it had hurt their own relationship. When both partners had engaged in affairs, each believed that their partner's affair had harmed the relationship more than their own had. Both women and men seem to be unable to acknowledge the negative impact of their own outside relationships. It is not known whether those who tend to have outside involvement in dating relationships are also more likely to have extramarital relationships after they marry.

Extramarital Sex in Exclusive Marriages

In marriages that assume emotional and sexual exclusivity, mutuality and sharing are emphasized. Extramarital sexual relationships are assumed to be destructive of the relationship; nonsexual heterosexual relationships may also be judged threatening. The possibility of infecting one's husband or wife with an STD must also be considered.

As a result of marital assumptions, both sexual and nonsexual extramarital relationships take place without the knowledge or permission of the other partner. If the marital assumptions are violated, David Weiss (1983) points out that we have been given "guidelines" on how to handle the violation:

> These guidelines encourage the "adulterer" to be secretive and discreet, suggest that guilt will be a consequence, and maintain that the spouse will react with feelings of jealousy and rejection if the [extramarital sex] is discovered.

If the extramarital relationship is discovered, a marital crisis ensues. Many married people feel that the spouse who is unfaithful has broken a basic trust (Weiss, 1975). Sexual accessibility implies emotional accessibility. When a person learns that his or her spouse is having an affair, the emotional commitment of that spouse is brought into question. How can you prove that you still have a commitment? You cannot; commitment is assumed, it can never be proved. Furthermore, the extramarital relationship may imply to the partner (rightly or wrongly) that he or she is sexually inadequate or uninteresting.

Extramarital Sex in Nonexclusive Marriages

There are several types of nonexclusive marriage (Weiss, 1983): (1) open marriage in which intimate but nonsexual friendships with others are encouraged, (2) open marriage in which outside sexual relationships are allowed, (3) swinging, and (4) group marriage/multiple relationships. The marriage relationship is considered the primary relationship in both nonconsensual extramarital relationships and in open marriages and swinging relationships. Only the group marriage/multiple relationships model rejects the primacy of the married relationship. Group marriage is the equal sharing of partners, as in polygamy; it may consist of one man and two women, one woman and two men, or two couples. The two most common types of consensual extramarital sex are swinging and sexually open marriages.

The secret is surrounded by the possibility and temptation of betrayal, and the external danger of being discovered is interwoven with the internal danger, which is like the fascination of the abyss, of giving oneself away. The secret creates a barrier between men but, at the same time, it creates the tempting challenge to break through it, by gossip or confession—and the challenge accompanies its psychology like a constant overtone.

George Simmel

Swinging Swinging (also called mate sharing or wife swapping) is a form of consensual extramarital sex in which couples engage in sexual activities with others in a social context clearly defined as recreational sex. These contexts may include swinging parties or commercial clubs. Married swingers swing together (Weiss, 1983). Forming an intimate relationship with an extramarital partner is prohibited. In terms of health, swinging may be an especially risky form of behavior.

Most sex research on consensual extramarital sex has been done on swinging (Weiss, 1983). It has been estimated that 2% of adult Americans have engaged in swinging. Although swingers are popularly perceived to be deviant, radical, or psychologically troubled, they tend not to differ significantly from most Americans. They tend to be white, overwhelmingly middle class, politically conservative, and quite "normal" except for their swinging. They tend to be less religious than nonswingers (Jenks, 1985; Weiss, 1983).

Open Marriage In **open marriage** partners may mutually agree to allow sexual relationships with others. There has been little research on open marriages. Blumstein and Schwartz (1983) found that 15–26% of the couples in their sample had "an understanding" that permitted extramarital relations in certain circumstances, such as the affair's occurring only out of town, never seeing the same person twice, never having sex with a mutual friend, and so on.

Two researchers found that successful sexually open marriages required: (1) a commitment to the primacy of the marriage, (2) a high degree of affection and trust between the spouses, (3) good interpersonal skills to manage complex relationships, and (4) nonmarital partners who did not compete with the married partner (Knapp & Whitehurst, 1977).

A study attempted to measure the impact of sexually open marriages on marital stability (Rubin & Adams, 1986). It matched 82 couples in 1978 and was able to do a follow-up study of 74 of the couples 5 years later. It found that there was no significant difference in marital stability related to whether the couples were sexually open or monogamous in their marriages. Among those marriages that broke up, the reasons given were not related to extramarital sex. No appreciable differences were found in terms of marital happiness or jealousy.

While considerable numbers of Americans engage in extramarital sexual activity, it does not appear that they will reject the monogamous norm. Extramarital relationships will probably continue for the most part as secretive affairs.

Motivation for Extramarital Sex People who engage in extramarital affairs have a number of different motivations, and affairs satisfy a number of different needs (Moultrup, 1990). John Gagnon (1977) describes the attraction extramarital affairs have for the people involved:

> Most people find their extramarital relationships highly exciting, especially in the early stages. This is a result of psychological compression: the couple gets together; they are both very aroused (desire, guilt, expectation); they have only three hours to be together. . . . Another source of attraction is that the other person is always seen when he or she looks good and is on best behavior, never

when feeling tired or grubby, or when taking care of children, or when cooking dinner. . . . Each time, all the minutes that the couples has together are special because they have been stolen from all these other relationships. The resulting combination of guilt and excitement has a heightening effect, which tends to explain why people may claim that extramarital sex and orgasms are more intense.

Research by Ira Reiss and colleagues (1980) suggests that extramarital affairs appear to be related to two variables: unhappiness of the marriage and/or extramarital sexual permissiveness. Generally speaking, in happy marriages, a partner is less likely to seek outside sexual relationships. If a person had premarital sex, he or she is more likely to have extramarital sex. Once the first prohibition is broken, the second holds less power.

Characteristics of Extramarital Sex The majority of extramarital sexual involvements are sporadic. Most people in such relationships probably do not have extramarital sexual intercourse more than five times a year (Gagnon, 1977). It is not clear how many people become involved in extramarital sex. Most of the large-scale nationwide surveys have been nonrepresentative samples of their readers by *Redbook, Playboy,* and *Cosmopolitan* magazines. These studies suggest that about 50% of men have extramarital affairs (Petersen et al., 1983; Rubenstein & Tavris, 1987; Tavris & Sadd, 1977; Wolfe, 1982). The 1977 *Redbook* study found that among women age 20–25, 25% had had extramarital sex (Tavris & Sadd, 1977). The *Cosmopolitan* survey found among female respondents 18 to 34 years old, 50% had had affairs (Wolfe, 1982). A 1987 *Redbook* survey found that 26% of its respondents of all ages had had at least one extramarital involvement, down from 29% in 1984 (Rubenstein & Tavris, 1987). But how many of these women had meaningful involvements as opposed to one-time-only experiments is not known.

Men are more likely to have extramarital sex when they are younger, women when they are older. Women in their late thirties tend to be more interested in sex than they were when younger. This difference between male and female sexual life cycles may account for women's increasing involvement in extramarital sex as they get older. The *Playboy* survey, however, found that among young marrieds, significantly more women than men had affairs (Peterson et al., 1983).

Most extramarital sex is not a love affair; it is generally self-contained and more sexual than emotional (Gagnon, 1977). Affairs that are both emotional and sexual appear to detract most from the marital relationship, whereas affairs that are only sexual or only emotional seem to detract least (Thompson, 1984). More women than men have emotional affairs; almost twice as many men as women have affairs that are only sexual. About equal percentages of men and women are involved in affairs that are both sexual and emotional.

Emotionally significant extramarital relationships form a complex system of relationships between three people (Moultrup, 1990). Long-lasting relationships can form a second but secret "marriage." In some ways, these relationships resemble polygamy, in which the third person is a "junior" partner with limited access to the other. Such relationships form a triangular system. The two involved in the affair continually negotiate their relationship with each other and with the uninvolved partner (whose needs, demands, or possible presence or suspicions must always be considered). Meanwhile, the uninvolved person mistakenly believes his or her partner is monogamous. As a result, he or she misinterprets situations. The partner's absence, for example, is believed to be the result of working late rather than an affair. Meanwhile, the involved pair, who know their system consists of *three* people, must try to meet each other's needs for time, affection, intimacy, and sex while taking the uninvolved partner into consideration. Such extramarital systems are considerably stressful and demanding. Most people find great difficulty in sustaining them.

Studies have found little significant correlation between social background characteristics and extramarital sexuality (Thompson, 1983). One study (Weiss & Jurich, 1985) did find that the size of a community was directly related to extramarital attitudes; the smaller the community, the greater the disapproval. Personal characteristics and the quality of the marriage appear to be more important, and of the two, personal characteristics—social alienation, need for intimacy, emotional independence, and egalitarian gender roles—were stronger correlates of extramarital sex than the quality of the marriage (Thompson, 1984). Generally, the lower the marital satisfaction and the frequency and quality of marital intercourse, the greater the likelihood of extramarital sexual relationships. Most people become involved in extramarital sex because they feel something is missing in their marriage. They have judged it defective, although not defective enough to consider divorce. Extramarital relationships are a compensation or substitute for these deficiencies (Cuber, 1969). They help maintain the status quo by giving emotional satisfaction to the unhappy partner.

Divorce and After

Don't leave in a huff. Leave in a minute and a huff. If you can't leave in a minute and a huff, leave in a taxi.

Groucho Marx

Divorce has become a major force in American life. Today, 50–60% of all new marriages are likely to end in divorce (Martin & Bumpass, 1989). In 1991, 15.8 million Americans (8.1%) were divorced. Most Americans who divorce, however, do not stay divorced for long. They usually remarry within 3 to 4 years (Coleman & Ganong, 1991).

Scholars suggest that divorce does not represent a devaluation of marriage but, oddly enough, an idealization of it. We would not divorce if we did not have so much hope about marriage's ability to fulfill various needs (Furstenberg & Cherlin, 1991; Furstenberg & Spanier, 1987). Our high divorce rate further tells us that we may no longer believe in the permanence of marriage. Instead, we remain married only as long as we are in love or a potentially better partner comes along (Glenn, 1991).

Dating Again A first date after years of marriage and subsequent months of singlehood evokes some of the same emotions felt by inexperienced adolescents. Separated or divorced men and women who are beginning to date again may be excited, nervous, worry about how they look, and wonder whether or not it's OK to hold hands, kiss, or make love. They may feel that dating is incongruous with their former selves or be annoyed with themselves for feeling excited and awkward. Furthermore, they have little idea of the norms of postmarital dating (Spanier & Thompson, 1987).

Dating serves several important functions for separated and divorced people. First, it is a statement to both the former spouse and the world at large that the person is available to become someone else's partner (Vaughan, 1986). Second, dating is an opportunity to enhance one's self-esteem (Spanier & Thompson, 1987). Free from the stress of an unhappy marriage, people may discover, for example, that they are more interesting and charming than either they or (especially) their former spouses had imagined. Third, dating initiates people into the singles subculture, where they can experiment with the freedom about which they may have fantasized when they were married.

Several features of dating following marital separation and divorce differ from premarital dating. First, dating does not seem to be a leisurely matter. Divorced people "are too pressed for time, too desperately in search of the 'right' person to waste time on a first date that might not go well" (Hunt & Hunt, 1977). Second, dating may be less spontaneous if the divorced woman or man has primary responsibility for children. The parent must make arrangements about child care; he or she may wish not to involve the children in the dates. Third, finances may be strained; divorced mothers may have income only from low-paying or part-time jobs, or AFDC benefits, while having many child-care expenses. In some cases, a father's finances may be strained by paying alimony or child support. Finally, separated and divorced men and women often have a changed sexual ethic based on the simple fact that there are few (if any) divorced virgins (Spanier & Thompson, 1987).

Sexual activity is an important component in the lives of separated and divorced men and women. Engaging in sexual relations for the first time following separation assists people in accepting their newly acquired single status. Because sexual fidelity is usually an important element in marriage, becoming sexually active with someone other than one's spouse is a dramatic symbol that the old marriage vows are no longer valid (Spanier & Thompson, 1987). Men initially tend to enjoy their sexual freedom following divorce, but women generally do not find it as meaningful. For men, sexual experience following separation is linked with their well-being. Sex seems to reassure men and bolster their self-confidence. Sexual activity is not as strongly connected to women's well-being (Spanier & Thompson, 1987). After a while, sex becomes a secondary consideration in dating, as people look for a deeper, more intimate relationship (Kohen et al., 1979).

There is little known about the sexual behavior of divorced men and women. Early nationwide studies by Alfred Kinsey (1953) and Morton Hunt (1974) found high levels of sexual activity, but these studies were either small or unrepresentative. A recent study using national data on 340 divorced people found that the level of sexual activity for the divorced was much smaller than earlier studies and popular mythology suggest (Stack & Gundlach, 1992). Over a year, the study found that 74% had either a single partner or none. Sixteen percent of the men and 34% of the women had no sexual partner.

Single Parenting In 1989, there were over 6 million single-parent families, representing 24% of all families. While over a quarter of all children live in single-parent families, close to 60% of African American families live in such families. Thirty-five percent of single-parent families were formed

Although we tend to think of single parents as women, about 10% of them are men. But whether they are women or men, because of their child-rearing responsibilities, single parents are usually not part of the singles world.

by divorce, and 33% by births to single mothers. Ninety percent of all single parents are women.

Single parents are not often a part of the singles world, which involves more than simply not being married. It requires leisure and money, both of which single parents generally lack because of their parenting responsibilities. Because of stereotypes of single women being sexually "loose," single mothers are often cautious about developing new relationships (Kissman & Allen, 1993).

The presence of children affects a divorced woman's sexual activity. Single divorced parents are less likely than divorced women without children to be sexually active (Stack & Gundlach, 1992). Children enormously complicate a single parent's sexual decision making. A single mother must decide, for example, whether to permit a man to spend the night with her when her children are present. This is often an important symbolic act for a woman, for several reasons. First, it involves her children in her romantic relationships. Women are often hesitant to again expose their children to the distress associated with the memory of the initial parental separation and divorce, often painfully seared into everyone's mind. Second, it reveals to her children that their mother is sexual, which may make her feel uncomfortable. Third, it opens her up to receiving moral judgments from her children regarding her sexuality. Single parents are often fearful that their children will lose respect for them, which may happen sometimes when children reach middle childhood. Fourth, having someone sleep over may trigger the resentment and anger that the children feel toward their parents for splitting up. They may feel deeply threatened and act out.

SEXUALITY IN LATE ADULTHOOD

Developmental Concerns

Many of the psychosexual tasks older Americans must undertake are directly related to the aging process.

- *Changing sexuality.* As older men's and women's physical abilities change with age, their sexual responses change as well. A 70-year-old, though still sexual, is not sexual in the same manner as an 18-year-old. As men and women continue to age, their sexuality tends to be more diffuse, less genital, and less insistent. Chronic illness and increasing frailty understandably result in diminished sexual activity. These considerations contribute to the ongoing evolution of the individual's sexual philosophy.

- *Loss of a partner.* One of the most critical life events is the loss of a partner. After age 60, there is a significant increase in spousal deaths. As having a partner is the single most important factor determining an older person's sexual interactions, his or her death signals a dramatic change in the survivor's sexual interactions.

These tasks are accomplished within the context of continuing aging. Their resolution helps prepare us for acceptance of our own eventual death.

Stereotypes of Aging

Our society stereotypes aging as a lonely and depressing time, but most studies of the aged find that they express relatively high levels of satisfaction and well-being. It is poverty and poor health that make old age difficult. But even so, the aged have lower levels of poverty than most Americans, including young adults, women, and children. More important, until their mid-seventies, most older people report few if any restrictions on their activities because of health.

The sexuality of older Americans tends to be invisible. Society tends to discount their sexuality (Libman, 1989). In fact, one review of the aging literature concludes that the decline in sexual activity among aging men and women is more cultural than biological in origin (Kellett, 1991). Several factors account for this in our culture (Barrow & Smith, 1992). First, we associate sexuality with the young, assuming that sexual attraction exists only between those with youthful bodies. Interest in sex is considered normal and virile in 25-year-old men, but in 75-year-old men, it is considered lecherous (Corby & Sarit, 1983). Second, we associate the idea of romance and love with the young; many of us find it difficult to believe that the aged can fall in love or love intensely. Third, we continue to associate sex with procreation, measuring a woman's femininity by her childbearing and mater-

Anyone who fails to go along with life remains suspended, stiff, and rigid in mid-air. That is why so many people get wooden in their old age; they look back and cling to the past with a secret fear of death in their hearts. From the middle of life onward, only he remains vitally alive who is ready to die with life, for in the secret hour of life's midday the parabola is reversed, death is born. We grant goal and purpose to the ascent of life, why not to the descent?

Carl Jung

When we look at the image of our own future provided by the old we do not believe it: an absurd inner voice whispers that that will never happen to us—when that happens it will no longer be ourselves that it happens to. Until the moment it is upon us, old age is something that only affects other people. So it is understandable that society prevents us from seeing our own kind, or fellowmen, when we look at the old.

Simone de Beauvoir

One of the most famous twentieth-century sculptures is Auguste Rodin's The Kiss, *which depicts young lovers embracing. Here, the aging model Antoni Nordone sits before the statue that immortalized his youth.*

nal role and a man's masculinity by the children he sires. Finally, the aged do not have as strong sexual desires as the young, and they are not expressed as openly. Intimacy is especially valued and important for an older person's well-being (Mancini & Blieszner, 1992).

Sexuality is one of the least understood aspects of life in old age (Weg, 1983a). Many older people continue to adhere to the standards of activity or physical attraction they held when they were young (Creti & Libman, 1989). They need to become aware of the taboos and aging stereotypes they held when they were younger so that they can enjoy their sexuality in their later years (Kellett, 1991).

Aging gay men and lesbians face a double stereotype: They are old *and* gay. But like other stereotypes of aging Americans, this one reflects myths rather than realities. A study of gay men over 60 found that over 80% felt accepting of their homosexuality; about half worried about growing old (Berger, 1982). And a study of aging lesbians found 71% were satisfied with being lesbian; about half were concerned about aging (Kehoe, 1988). (For a review of gay and lesbian aging studies, see Cruikshank, 1990.)

Not only do stereotypes and myths of aging affect the sexuality of the aged. The narrow definition of sexuality contributes to the problem. Sexual behavior is defined by researchers and the general population in terms of masturbation, sexual intercourse, and orgasm. Ruth Weg (1983b), a gerontologist (one who studies the aged and the aging process), notes that these definitions have

> overshadowed the emotional, sensual, and relationship qualities that give meaning, beyond release, to sexual expression. . . . What has been ignored are the walking hand-in-hand or arm-in-arm; the caring for one another; the touching and holding, with or without intercourse.

Male and Female Differences

Aged women and men face different problems sexually (Robinson, 1983). Physiologically, men are less responsive. The decreasing frequency of intercourse and the increasing time required to attain an erection produce anxieties in many older men about erectile dysfunction (impotence)—anxieties that may very well lead to such dysfunctions. When the natural slowing down of sexual responses is interpreted as the beginning of erectile dysfunction, this self-diagnosis triggers a vicious spiral of fears and even greater difficulty in having or maintaining an erection. One study (Weitzman & Hart, 1987) found that about 31% of elderly male respondents were unable to have an erection. But, as Masters and Johnson (1966) have pointed out:

> Inevitably all physical responses are slowed down. . . . A man can't run around the block as fast as he could 20 or 30 years previously. Yet the simple fact that sexual functioning is but one more element in his total physiologic functioning has never occurred to him.

Among older adults, fantasies become more diffuse, turning from those that are obviously sexual to those centering more on pleasurable experiences in general (Barclay, 1980). As some men get older, their erotic performance becomes more dependent on fantasies; they are less responsive to simple tactile stimulation of the genitals. Some men also tend to have fewer inhibitions in acting out their sexual fantasies, which accounts for the change in behavior as they age. It is not uncommon for some men to abandon the puritanical outlook of their youth and become more sexually overt as they grow older (Money, 1980).

Women, who are sexually capable throughout their lives, have different concerns. They face greater social constraints than men (Robinson, 1983). Women are confronted with an unfavorable sex ratio (27 unmarried men per 100 unmarried women over age 65), a greater likelihood of widowhood, and norms against marrying younger men. Grieving over the death of a partner, isolation, and depression also affect their sexuality (Rice, 1989). Finally, there is a double standard of aging. In our culture, as men age, they become distinguished; as women age, they simply get older. Femininity is connected with youth and beauty. But as women age, they tend to be regarded as more

Epitaph on His Wife

*Here lies my wife; here let her lie!
Now she's at rest. And so am I.*
        John Dryden (1631–1700)

masculine. A young woman, for example, is "beautiful," but an older woman is "handsome," a term ordinarily used for men of any age.

Partner Availability and Health

The greatest determinants of an aged person's sexual activity are the availability of a partner and health. A major study of older people found only 7% of those who were single or widowed to be sexually active, in contrast to 54% of those living with a partner (Verwoerdt et al., 1969). Frequency of sexual intercourse for the latter group, with an average age of 70, ranged from three times a week to once every two months. Those who described their sexual feelings as having been weak or moderate in their youth stated that they were without sexual feelings. More recently, researchers studied over 800 married whites and African Americans over age 60 (Marisiglio & Donnelly, 1991). They found that over half the sample (and 24% of those older than 76) had sexual intercourse within the previous month. Those who had sex during the month had it an average of four times. Among the sexually active older people, there were no differences by gender or race. Those who do not have partners may turn to masturbation as an alternative to sexual intercourse (Pratt & Schmall, 1989).

After age 75, a significant decrease in sexual activity takes place. This seems to be related to health problems, such as heart disease, arthritis, and diabetes. Often older people indicate that they continue to feel sexual desires; they simply lack the ability to express them because of their health (Verwoerdt et al., 1969). In a study of men and women in nursing homes, whose ages averaged 82, 91% reported no sexual activity immediately prior to their interviews (White, 1982). Seventeen percent of these men and women, however, expressed a desire for sexual activity. Unfortunately, most nursing homes make no provision for the sexuality of the aged. Instead, they actively discourage sexual expression—not only sexual intercourse but also masturbation—or try to sublimate their clients' erotic interests into crafts or television. Such manipulations, however, do little to satisfy the erotic needs of the elderly.

For some of the very old, noted Erik Erikson (1986), "memories seem to evoke an immediate, sensual reinvolvement in their earliest adulthood commitments to intimacy." Erikson related the story of one elderly woman, who vibrantly recalled meeting her husband:

> I was crazy about him. We went out together for three months, but he never touched me. Finally I told him, "Something better happen tonight or else." I wouldn't explain any more. So he kissed me that night and he kissed me until the day he died.

"Reminiscing about the sensuality of early love," Erikson (1986) wrote, "enables her to view with life-span perspective the unwelcome extent to which she now remains largely apart. Perhaps, in eliciting the feelings of an earlier time, it also helps fill this current void." Many older widows do not miss the sexual aspect of their lives, however, as much as they do the social aspects of their married lives. It is the companionship, the activity, the pleasure found in their partners that these older women most acutely miss (Malatesta, Chambless, Pollock, & Cantor, 1989).

Love and affection cross age and ethnic boundaries.

As we leave adolescence and enter adulthood, we begin to engage in many tasks that define our adult sexuality. In young adulthood, these include establishing our sexual orientation, making commitments, entering long-term intimate relationships, and making childbearing decisions. None of these tasks is accomplished overnight. Many are ongoing processes that continue, in fact, throughout one's lifetime. A certain task, such as making a commitment, may be seemingly resolved forever, only to reappear later when one's life changes as a result of separation or divorce. Nor does a task necessarily end as we move into a new stage of our lives: We need, for example, to continuously nurture, care for, and renew our intimate relationships.

In middle adulthood, we have new tasks involving the nature of our long-term relationships. Often these tasks involve reevaluating our relationships. In some cases, the reevaluation results in ending relationships and beginning new ones. As we enter late adulthood, we need to adjust to the aging process: our changed sexual responses and needs, declining physical health, the loss of a partner, and our own eventual death. Each stage is filled with its own unique meaning, which gives shape and significance to our lives and sexuality.

SUMMARY

Sexuality in Early Adulthood

- There are several tasks to undertake in developing sexuality in young adulthood, including establishing sexual orientation, integrating love and sex, forging intimacy and making commitments, making fertility/childbearing decisions, and evolving a sexual philosophy.

- *Premarital sex* among young adults (but not adolescents) in a relational context has become the norm. An important factor in this shift is the surge in numbers of unmarried men and women who represent 39% of the adult population.

- Factors leading to premarital sexual involvement include individual factors (prior experience, personality, and gender); relationship factors (intimacy level and relationship duration); and environmental factors (privacy, values). Ethnicity also affects premarital involvement. Generally, African Americans are more permissive than whites; Latinos are less permissive than Anglos.

- A critical task of adulthood is establishing one's sexual identity as heterosexual, gay, lesbian, or bisexual. As many as 10% of Americans have had a significant amount of same-sex sexual contact. Various studies suggest that 4.5–7% of men identify themselves as gay during some point in their adult lives. About 1–3% of women identify themselves as lesbian. Identifying oneself as a lesbian or a gay male, however, is complex and includes several phases: fear and confusion about desires that society stigmatizes; labeling feelings as *homoerotic*; self-definition as gay or lesbian; first gay or lesbian affair, unifying sexuality and affection; involvement in the gay or lesbian subculture. *Coming out* is publicly acknowledging one's homosexuality.

- The changes in the nature of singlehood include greater premarital sexual experience, widespread acceptance of cohabitation, increased unintended pregnancies, increased numbers of abortions and births to single women, greater numbers of separated and divorced men and women, and the rise of single-parent families.

- The two most widely held standards regarding premarital sexual intercourse are permissiveness with affection and the double standard. For gay men and lesbians, the college environment is often liberating because of greater acceptance.

- Among noncollege single men and women, meeting others is often an important problem. Singles often meet at work, clubs, resorts, and housing complexes. Churches are also important, especially among middle-class African Americans who have less chance of meeting other African Americans in integrated work and neighborhood settings.

- Gay neighborhoods are found in the largest cities. They are important in enabling lesbians and gay men to interact outside a sexual context. Relational sex has become the norm among large segments of the gay population. African American gay men often experience a conflict between their black and gay identities. Gay Latino bars are found in most large cities with major Latino populations.

- The contemporary lesbian community is currently more moderate and diverse than in prior years. It has closer ties with the gay community. Lesbians' emphasis on emotions over sex and the more enduring quality of their relationships reflects their socialization as women.

- Cohabitation is part of the courtship process. Living together has become more widespread and accepted in recent years for several reasons, including delayed marriage, a more liberal sexual climate, and the changed meaning of marriage. Over 1.5 million gay or lesbian couples and 2.9 million heterosexual couples cohabit. Heterosexual couples tend to adopt a traditional marriage model, whereas lesbian or gay male couples tend to have a "best-friend" model. *Domestic partnerships* provide some legal protection for cohabitating couples in committed relationships.

Sexuality in Middle Adulthood

- Developmental issues of sexuality in middle adulthood include redefining sex in long-term relationships, reevaluating one's sexuality, and accepting the biological aging process.

- In marriage, sex tends to diminish in frequency the longer a couple is married. Most married couples don't feel that declining frequency is a major problem if their overall relationship is good. Significant factors shaping marital sexuality include the expectation of monogamy, socially sanctioned reproduction, and changed sexual context.

- Many lesbians and gay men have been married and are parents. Except for denying or hoping to "cure" their homosexuality, their motivations to marry are no different from heterosexuals. When they disclose their orientation to their spouse, separation and divorce are the usual outcome. Gay men and lesbians who are also parents need to affirm both their gay and their parental identities.

- Extrarelational sexual involvement exists in dating, cohabiting, and marital relationships. In monogamous marriages, extramarital sexual relationships are assumed to be destructive of the relationship and are kept secret. If the extramarital relationship is discovered, a marital crisis often ensues. In addition, there are nonexclusive marriages that permit extramarital sex. These types are nonsexually open marriages, sexually open marriages, swinging, and group marriage/multiple relationships. Successful sexually open marriages require commitment to the primacy of the marriage, a high degree of affection and trust, good interpersonal skills, and partners who do not compete with the married partner.

- Extramarital affairs appear to be related to two variables: unhappiness of the marriage and/or premarital sexual permissiveness. The majority of extramarital sexual involvements are sporadic. Men are more likely to have extramarital sex when they are younger, women when they are older. Personal characteristics, such as alienation, need for intimacy, emotional independence, and egalitarian gender roles, are stronger correlates of extramarital sex than the quality of the marriage.

- Today, 50–60% of all new marriages are likely to end in divorce. Following divorce, dating is both a statement that the individual is available and an opportunity to enhance one's self-esteem. Sexual experiences following divorce are linked to well-being, especially for men. Single parents are not often a part of the singles world because the presence of children constrains their freedom. Single divorced parents are less likely than divorced women without children to be sexually active.

Sexuality in Late Adulthood

- Many of the psychosexual tasks older Americans must undertake are directly related to the aging process, including changing sexuality and the loss of a partner. Most studies of the aged find that they express relatively high levels of satisfaction and well-being. Sexuality of the aged tends to be invisible because we associate sexuality and romance with youth, link sex to procreation, and are used to greater demonstrativeness.

- Aging lesbians and gay men face a double stereotype: They are old *and* gay. Most aging gay men and lesbians are accepting of their homosexuality; about half worry about growing older.

- Sexual behavior in late adulthood often becomes more intimacy-based, involving touching and holding rather than genital activity. Physiologically, men are less responsive. Women's concerns are more social than physical, as they have an unfavorable sex ratio, a greater likelihood of widowhood, and the double standard of aging.

- The greatest determinants of an aged individual's sexual activity are the availability of a partner and health. Among sexually active older people, there are no differences by gender or race. Those who do not have partners may turn to masturbation as an alternative. After age 75, a significant decrease in sexual activity takes place due to health problems.

KEY TERMS

premarital sex	coming out	domestic partnership
nonmarital sex	lesbian separatist	serial monogamy
homoeroticism	POSSLQ	open marriage
bisexuality		

SUGGESTIONS FOR FURTHER READING

Blumstein, Philip, and Pepper Schwartz. *American Couples: Money, Work, Sex.* New York: William Morrow, 1983. A classic work examining power as expressed in money, work, and sex in cohabiting, married, gay, and lesbian relationships.

Hutchins, Loraine, and Lani Kaahumanu, eds. *Bi Any Other Name: Bisexual People Speak Out.* Boston: Alyson Publications, 1991. A collection of essays, poems, and stories about bisexuality.

Gochros, Jean S. *When Husbands Come Out of the Closet.* New York: Harrington Park Press, 1989. A study of heterosexual women who married gay or bisexual men.

Moffatt, Michael. *Coming of Age in New Jersey.* New Brunswick, NJ: Rutgers University Press, 1989. An anthropologist living among college students for several years studies their social, sexual, and academic lives.

Rubin, Lillian. *Erotic Wars: What Happened to the Sexual Revolution?* New York: Harper & Row, 1991. An examination of changing sexual mores among young adults and married couples.

Sprecher, Susan, and Kathleen McKinney. *Sexuality.* Newbury Park, CA: Sage Publications, 1993. A comprehensive examination of sexuality within the context of close relationships, such as dating, cohabitation, and marriage.

Staples, Robert. *The World of Black Singles: Changing Patterns of Male/Female Relationships.* Westport, CT: Greenwood Press, 1981. An analysis of the characteristics of African American singles, how they deal with singlehood, and their lifestyles.

Weg, Ruth, ed. *Sexuality in the Later Years: Roles and Behavior.* New York: Academic Press, 1983. An excellent, multidisciplinary approach to aging and sexuality.

Chapter Eight

LOVE, INTIMACY, AND SEX

PREVIEW: SELF-QUIZ

1. Researchers tend to believe that whatever form of love they value most is "true" love. True or false?

2. People tend to think that love and commitment overlap in important aspects. True or false?

3. Love relationships are similar in many ways to parent/infant relationships. True or false?

4. In romantic relationships, caring is less important than physical attraction. True or false?

5. Males and females, whites, African Americans, Latinos, Asians, heterosexuals, gay men and lesbians, old and young are equally as likely to fall in love. True or false?

6. In many ways, love is like the attachment an infant experiences for his or her caregiver. True or false?

7. The love that lesbians and gay men experience is similar in quality to that experienced by heterosexuals. True or false?

8. Infatuation is usually equally intense for both parties. True or false?

9. Not telling the person you like that you like him or her is important in getting that person to fall in love with you. True or false?

10. A high degree of jealousy is a sign of true love. True or false?

ANSWERS 1. T, 2. T, 3. T, 4. F, 5. T, 6. T, 7. T, 8. F, 9. F, 10. F

Chapter Outline

It is at the edge of the petal that love waits.
    William Carlos Williams

The head is always the dupe of the heart.
    François de la Rochefoucauld

Love is one of the most profound human emotions, and it manifests itself in various forms across all cultures. In our culture, love binds us together as partners, parents, children, and friends. It is a powerful force in the intimate relationships of heterosexuals, gay men, and lesbians; it crosses all ethnic boundaries (Aron & Aron, 1991). We make major life decisions, such as whom we marry, based on love (Simpson, Campbell, & Berscheid, 1986). We make sacrifices for it, sometimes sacrificing even our lives for those we love.

But how do we know if what we feel is love? Perhaps it is merely infatuation, or lust disguising itself as love. It is not unusual to torture ourselves with the question, "Is this *really* love?" Many of us have gone through frustrating scenes such as the following (Greenburg & Jacobs, 1966):

At the beginning of a relationship, it is often impossible to tell whether one's feelings are infatuation or the beginning of love.

YOU: "Do you love me?"

MATE: "Yes, of course I love you."

YOU: "Do you really love me?"

MATE: "Yes, I really love you."

YOU: "You are sure you love me—you are absolutely sure?"

MATE: "Yes, I'm absolutely sure."

YOU: "Do you know the meaning of love?"

MATE: "I don't know."

YOU: "Then how can you be sure you love me?"

MATE: "I don't know. Perhaps I can't."

YOU: "You can't, eh? I see. Well, since you can't even be sure you love me, I can't really see much point in our remaining together. Can you?"

MATE: "I don't know. Perhaps not."

YOU: "You've been leading up to this for a pretty long time, haven't you?"

Love is both a feeling and an activity. A person feels love for someone and acts in a loving manner. But we can also be angry with the person we love, frustrated, bored, or indifferent. This is the paradox of love: It encompasses opposites. A loving relationship includes affection and anger, excitement and boredom, stability and change, bonds and freedom. Its paradoxical quality makes some ask whether they are really in love when they are not feeling "perfectly" in love or when their relationship is not going smoothly. Love does not give us perfection, however; it gives us meaning. In fact, as sociologist Ira Reiss (1980) suggests, a more important question to ask is not if one is feeling love, but, "Is the love I feel the kind of love on which I can build a lasting relationship or marriage?"

Whereas love was once the province of lovers, poets, and philosophers, social scientists have begun to appear on the scene. But studying love is no guarantee of finding it. As researcher John A. Lee (1988) explains, "I have studied love because it is my life's most difficult problem. Although I have made much progress, the 'impossible dream' of a truly fulfilling mutual love remains one I have yet to achieve." The study of romantic love is still in its infancy. In the 34 years between 1949 and 1983, only 27 articles on love appeared in sociology and psychology journals (Baron, 1983); since 1983, there have been well over 100.

In this chapter, we examine the relationship between sex and love. We look at the always perplexing question of the nature of love. Then we examine the ways that social scientists study love to gain new insights into it. We then turn to the darker side of love—jealousy—to understand its dynamics. Finally, we see how love transforms itself from passion to intimacy, providing the basis for long-lasting relationships.

LOVE AND SEXUALITY

Love and sexuality are intimately intertwined (Aron & Aron, 1991). While marriage was once the only acceptable context for sexual intercourse, for most people today, love legitimizes premarital sex. With the "sex with affection" standard of premarital intercourse, we use individualistic rather than social norms to legitimize sexual relations. Our sexual standards have become personal rather than institutional. This shift to personal responsibility makes love even more important in sexual relationships.

We can even see this connection between love and sex in our everyday use of words. Think of the words we use to describe sexual interactions. When we say that we "make love," are "lovers," or are "intimate" with someone, we generally mean that we are sexually involved. But this sexual involvement carries overtones of relationship, caring, or love. Such potential meanings are absent in such technically correct words as "sexual intercourse," "fellatio," or "cunnilingus," as well as in such obscene words as "fuck" or "screw."

Men, Sex, and Love

Men and women who are not in an established relationship have different expectations. Men are more likely than women to separate sex from affection. Studies consistently demonstrate that for the majority of men, sex and love can be easily separated (Blumstein & Schwartz, 1983; Carroll et al., 1985).

Although men are more likely than women to separate sex and love, Linda Levine and Lonnie Barbach (1985) found in their interviews that men indicated that their most erotic sexual experiences took place in a relational context. The researchers quoted one man:

> Emotions are everything when it comes to sex. There's no greater feeling than having an emotional attachment with the person you're making love to. If those emotions are there, it's going to be fabulous. . . . They don't call it "making love" for nothing.

Most men in the study responded that it was primarily the emotional quality of the relationship that made their sexual experiences special.

Women, Sex, and Love

Women generally view sex from a relational perspective. In the decision to have sexual intercourse, the quality and degree of intimacy of a relationship were more important for women than men (Christopher & Cate, 1984). Women were more likely to report feelings of love if they were sexually involved with their partners than if they were not sexually involved (Peplau, Rubin, & Hill, 1977). For women, love is also more closely related to feelings of self-esteem (Walsh & Balazs, 1990).

While women generally seek emotional relationships, some men initially seek physical relationships. This difference in intentions can place women in a bind. Carole Cassell (1984) suggests that today's women face a "damned if you do, damned if you don't" dilemma in their sexual relationships. If a woman has sexual intercourse with a man, he says goodbye; if she doesn't, he says he respects her and still says goodbye. A young woman Cassell interviewed related the following:

Absence makes the heart grow fonder; then you forget.
Floyd Zimmerman

> I really hate the idea that, because I'm having sex with a man whom I haven't known for a long, long time, he'll think I don't value myself. But it's hard to know what to do. If you meet a man and date him two or three times and don't have sex, he begins to feel you are either rejecting him or you have serious sex problems. . . . But I really dread feeling that I could turn into, in his eyes, an easy lay, a good-time girl. I want men to see me as a grown-up woman who has the same right as they do to make sexual choices.

Traditionally, women were labeled "good" or "bad" based on their sexual experience and values. "Good" women were virgins, sexually naive, or passive, whereas "bad" women were sexually experienced, independent, and passionate. According to Lillian Rubin (1990), this attitude has not entirely changed. Rather, we are ambivalent about sexually experienced women. One exasperated woman leaped out of her chair and began to pace the floor, exclaiming to Rubin, "I sometimes think what men really want is a sexually experienced virgin. They want you to know the tricks, but they don't like to think you did those things with anyone else."

Gay Men, Lesbians, and Love

Love is equally important for heterosexuals, gay men, lesbians, and bisexuals (Aron & Aron, 1991; Keller & Rosen, 1988; Kurdek, 1988; Peplau & Coch-

For lesbians, gay men, and bisexuals, love is an important component in the formation and acceptance of their sexual orientation. The public declaration of love and commitment is a milestone in the lives of many couples.

We two boys together clinging
One the other never leaving.
Walt Whitman

ran, 1981). Many heterosexuals, however, perceive lesbian and gay love relationships as less satisfying and less loving than heterosexual ones. In a study of 360 heterosexual undergraduates (Testa, Kinder, & Aronson, 1987), students were presented with identical information about a couple that was variously described as heterosexual, gay, and lesbian. When the couple was identified as heterosexual, it ranked high on love and satisfaction; when it was identified as lesbian or gay, students ranked the levels of love and satisfaction significantly lower. Because the couple was identical except for sexual orientation, the researchers concluded that there was a heterosexual bias in the perception of gay and lesbian love relationships. It is well documented that love is important for gay men and lesbians; their relationships have multiple emotional dimensions and are not based solely on sex, as others might believe (Adler, Hendrick, & Hendrick, 1989).

While men in general are more likely to separate love and sex than women, gay men are especially likely to make this separation. Although gay men value love, they also value sex as an end in itself. Furthermore, they place less emphasis on sexual exclusiveness in their relationships. Researchers suggest, however, that heterosexual men are not as different from gay men in terms of their acceptance of casual sex. Heterosexual men, they maintain, would be as likely as gay men to engage in casual sex if women were equally interested. Women, however, are not as interested in casual sex; as a result, heterosexual men do not have as many willing partners as gay men do (Foa, Anderson, Converse, & Urbansky, 1987; Symmons, 1979).

For lesbians, gay men, and bisexuals, love has special significance in the formation and acceptance of their identities. While significant numbers of men and women have had sexual experiences with members of the same sex or both sexes, relatively few identify themselves as gay or lesbian. As we saw in Chapter 7, same-sex sexual interactions are not in themselves sufficient to acquiring a gay or lesbian identity. An important element in solidifying such an identity is loving someone of the same sex. Love signifies a commitment to being lesbian or gay by unifying the emotional and physical dimensions of a person's sexuality (Troiden, 1988). For the gay man or lesbian, it marks the beginning of sexual wholeness and acceptance. In fact, some researchers believe that the ability to love someone of the same sex, rather than having sex with him or her, is the critical element that distinguishes being gay or lesbian from being heterosexual (Money, 1980).

Sex Without Love

Is love necessary for sex? We assume that it is, but that assumption is based on motives and values. It cannot be answered by reference to empirical or statistical data (Crosby, 1985). The question becomes a more fundamental one: Is sexual activity legitimate in itself, or does it require justification? Researcher John Crosby (1985) observes:

> Sexual pleasure is a value in itself and hence capable of being inherently meaningful and rewarding. The search for extrinsic justification and rationalization simply belies our reluctance to believe that sex is a pleasurable activity in and of itself.

To believe that sex does not require love as a justification, argues Crosby, does not deny the significance of love and affection in sexual relations. In fact, love and affection are important and desirable for enduring relationships. They are simply not necessary, Crosby believes, for affairs in which erotic pleasure is the central feature.

Ironically, while sex without love violates our overt beliefs about sexuality, it is the least threatening form of extrarelational sex. Even those who accept their partner's having sex outside the relationship find it especially difficult to accept their partner's having a meaningful affair. "They believe that two intense romantic relationships cannot co-exist and that one would have to go" (Blumstein & Schwartz, 1983).

THIS THING CALLED LOVE: THE PHENOMENA OF LOVE, SEX, AND COMMITMENT

For most of us, love, sex, and commitment are closely linked ideals in our intimate relationships. Love reflects the positive factors—such as caring—that draw people together and sustain them in a relationship. Sex reflects both emotional and physical elements in a relationship, such as closeness and sexual excitement, that differentiate romantic love from other forms of love, such as parental love or the love between friends. **Commitment,** the determination to continue, reflects the stable factors—including love but also obligations and social pressure—that help maintain the relationship

I beg you, Gongyla,
To take your harp and sing to us
For again the aura of desire
Surrounds your beauty
And your dress excites all who see
*   you.*
My heart quickens in my breast.
Once I scorned Aphrodite, the god-
*   dess of love,*
But now I pray for you to soon
*   come*
And for us never to be apart.
*   Sappho (7th century B.C.)*

Annie Hall: Sex without love is an
empty experience.
Alvie Singer: Yes, but as empty
experiences go, it's one of the best.
*   Woody Allen*

Upon my bed by night
I sought him, but found him not;
I called him, but he gave no
*   answer.*
In the streets and in the squares,
*   I will seek him whom my soul*
*   loves.*
The watchmen found me as they
*   went about in the city.*
"Have you seen him whom my
*   soul loves?"*
Scarcely had I passed them,
When I found him whom my soul
*   loves.*
I held him, and would not let him
*   go until I had brought him into*
*   my mother's house and into the*
*   chamber of her that conceived*
*   me.*
I adjure you, O daughters of Jeru-
*   salem, by the gazelles or the*
*   hinds of the field,*
That you stir not up nor awaken
*   love until it pleases.*
*   Song of Solomon*

"for better or for worse." Although the three are related, they are not necessarily connected. One can exist without the others. It is possible to love someone without being committed or sexually involved. It is also possible to be sexually involved and in love with someone but not committed. The combinations go on and on (in fact, there are 27 possible combinations). Despite the various permutations of love, sex, and commitment, most of us long for a special relationship that contains all three.

Prototypes of Love, Sex, and Commitment

Despite centuries of discussion, debate, and complaint by philosophers and lovers, no one has succeeded in finding definitions of love on which all can agree. Ironically, such discussions seem to engender conflict and disagreement rather than love and harmony.

Because of the unending confusion surrounding definitions of love, some researchers wonder whether such definitions are even possible (Fehr, 1988; Kelley, 1983). In the everyday world, however, we do seem to have something in mind when we declare our love for someone. We may not have formal definitions of love, but we do have **prototypes,** or models, of what we mean by love stored in the backs of our minds. Researchers suggest that instead of looking for formal definitions of love, sex, and commitment, we examine people's prototypes; in some ways, these prototypes may be more important than formal definitions. For example, when we say "I love you," we are referring to our prototype of love rather than its definition. By thinking in terms of prototypes, we can study how people actually use the words love, sex, and commitment in real life and how the meanings attached to these words help define the progress of their intimate relationships.

Prototypes of Love To discover people's prototypes, researcher Beverly Fehr (1988) asked 172 respondents to rate the central features of love. The twelve central attributes of love they listed are:

1. Trust
2. Caring
3. Honesty
4. Friendship
5. Respect
6. Concern for the other's well-being
7. Commitment
8. Loyalty
9. Acceptance of the other the way he or she is
10. Supportiveness
11. Wanting to be with the other
12. Interest in the other

Prototypes of Sex Utilizing Fehr's prototypical approach, two researchers asked several hundred students to rank the attributes they associate with sex (Aron & Strong, 1993). The attributes fell into three general categories: (1) emotional, such as caring and closeness; (2) physical, such as intensity and

excitement; and (3) consequential, such as pregnancy and pain. The most important attributes associated with sex were emotional. The attributes for the different categories are:

Emotional	Physical	Consequential
1. Caring	1. Intensity	1. Pregnancy
2. Closeness	2. Excitement	2. Pain
3. Expression of feelings	3. Pleasure	3. Violence
4. Specialness	4. Desire	4. Danger
5. Communication	5. Hot/sweaty	5. Diseases
6. Love	6. Sensuality	
7. Relationship	7. Lust	
8. Happiness	8. Satisfaction	
9. Commitment	9. Enjoyment	
10. Emotions	10. Different positions	

We can see that there is a close connection between sex and love, as the central emotional aspects of sex are very similar to the attributes we associate with love. Sex differs from love primarily in terms of its physical qualities and consequences. The physical aspects, however, are generally positive, while the consequential ones are perceived as negative. (Students regard pregnancy negatively because it occurs most often for them in the context of premarital sexuality. We suspect that when they desire children, reproduction would become more central.) The negative consequences, however, are rarely mentioned. They may be peripheral to our thinking about sex. But the fact that pregnancy and disease are peripheral may suggest why people tend to be sexual risk takers rather than routine users of birth control or condoms to protect themselves and others.

Prototypes of Commitment Commitment is the element that gives stability to a relationship or marriage. According to Fehr (1988), the twelve central attributes of commitment are:

1. Loyalty
2. Responsibility
3. Living up to your word
4. Faithfulness
5. Trust
6. Being there for the other in good and bad times
7. Devotion
8. Reliability
9. Giving your best effort
10. Supportiveness
11. Perseverance
12. Concern about the other's well-being

Beauty stands
in the admiration of weak minds
Led captive.
John Milton (1608–1674)

Nonperipheral Aspects of Love, Sex, and Commitment There are many other characteristics identified as features of love (euphoria, thinking about the other all the time, butterflies in the stomach), sex (nudity, unfulfillment), or commitment (putting the other first, contentment). These, however, tend to be peripheral. As relationships progress, the central aspects of love and commitment become more characteristic of the relationship than the peripheral ones. The central features, observes Fehr (1988), "act as true barometers of a move toward increased love or commitment in a relationship." Similarly, violations of central features of love and commitment were considered to be more serious than violations of peripheral ones. A loss of caring, trust, honesty, or respect threatens love, while the disappearance of butterflies in the stomach does not. Similarly, lack of responsibility or faithfulness endangers commitment, whereas discontent is not perceived as threatening. Researchers have found that love and commitment were correlated to satisfaction in romantic relationships (Hendrick & Hendrick, 1988b).

I am not one of those who do not
believe in love at first sight, but I
do believe in taking a second look.
Henry Vincent (1813–1878)

While research indicates that people regard the physical aspects of sex as less important than the emotional aspects, it is in the physical realm that sex occurs. This raises several questions. What is the relationship between the emotional and physical dimensions of sex? How secondary is the physical? Within the physical realm, which aspects are central and which are peripheral? We know that over time, physical intensity and excitement tend to diminish but pleasure and satisfaction can increase. How will people interpret these changes? What does low intensity but high satisfaction indicate? What if the emotional level is high but the physical level moderate or low? How does one evaluate the overall sexual level?

Attitudes and Behaviors Associated with Love

A review of the research finds a number of attitudes, feelings, and behaviors associated with love (Kelley, 1983). Notice how some of these are also associated with sex.

In terms of attitudes and feelings, positive attitudes and feelings toward the other bring people together. Zick Rubin (1970, 1973) found that there were four feelings identifying love. These feelings, which correspond fairly well to the prototypical characteristics identified with love, are:

- *Caring for the other*, wanting to help him or her.
- *Needing the other*, having a strong desire to be in the other's presence and to have the other care for you.
- *Trusting the other*, mutually exchanging confidences.
- *Tolerating the other*, including his or her faults.

Of these, caring appears to be the most important, followed by needing, trusting, and tolerating (Steck, Levitan, McLane, & Kelley, 1982). J. R. Davitz (1969) identified similar feelings associated with love but noted, in addition, that respondents reported feeling an inner glow, optimism, and cheerfulness. They felt harmony and unity with the person they loved. They were intensely aware of the other person, feeling that they were fully concentrated on him or her.

Love is also expressed in certain behaviors. One study found that romantic love was expressed in several ways (Swensen, 1972). Notice that the expression of love often overlaps thoughts of love:

- *Verbally expressing affection*, such as saying, "I love you."
- *Self-disclosing*, such as revealing intimate facts about yourself.
- *Giving nonmaterial evidence*, such as emotional and moral support in times of need, and respecting the other's opinion.
- *Expressing nonverbal feelings*, such as feeling happier, more content, more secure when the other is present.
- *Giving material evidence*, such as gifts, flowers, small favors, or doing more than your share of something.
- *Physically expressing love*, such as hugging, kissing, making love.
- *Tolerating the other*, such as accepting his or her idiosyncrasies, peculiar routines, or forgetfulness about putting the cap on the toothpaste.

These behavioral expressions of love are consistent with the prototypical characteristics of love. In addition, recent research supports the belief that people "walk on air" when they are in love. Researchers have found that those in love view the world more positively than those who are not in love (Hendrick & Hendrick, 1988a).

There is no love apart from the deeds of love; no potentiality of love than that which is manifested in loving. . . .

Jean-Paul Sartre

The meeting of two personalities is like the contact of two chemical substances; if there is any reaction, both are transformed.

Carl Jung

According to sociologist John Lee, there are six styles of love: eros, mania, ludus, storge, agape, and pragma. What style do you believe this couple illustrates. Why?

HOW DO I LOVE THEE? APPROACHES TO THE STUDY OF LOVE

Researchers have developed a number of ways of studying love (Hendrick & Hendrick, 1987). Each approach looks at love from different perspectives. Although no single perspective wholly accounts for the experience of love, together they provide considerable insight.

Styles of Love

Sociologist John Lee describes six basic styles of love (Borrello & Thompson, 1990; Lee, 1973, 1988). These styles of love, he cautions, describe relationship styles, not individual styles. The style of love may change as the relationship changes or when individuals enter different relationships. (See the Self-Assessment for determining your style of love.)

1. **Eros:** Love of beauty.
2. **Mania:** Obsessive love.
3. **Ludus:** Playful love.
4. **Storge:** Companionate love.
5. **Agape:** Altruistic love.
6. **Pragma:** Practical love.

In addition to these pure forms, there are mixtures of the basic types: Storgic-Eros, Ludic-Eros, and Storgic-Ludus.

Are the man and woman in this photograph friends or lovers? What clues do you find to support your answer?

Eros Eros was the ancient Greek god of love, the son of Aphrodite. (The Romans called him Cupid.) Erotic lovers delight in the tactile, the sensual, the immediate; they are attracted to beauty (though beauty is in the eye of the beholder). They love the lines of the body, its feel and touch. They are fascinated by every detail of their beloved. Their love burns brightly but soon flickers and dies.

Mania The word "mania" comes from the Greek word for madness. The Russian poet Mikhail Lermontov aptly described a manic lover:

He in his madness prays for storms,
And dreams that storms will bring him peace.

For manic lovers, nights are marked by sleeplessness and days by pain and anxiety. The slightest sign of affection brings ecstasy for a short while, only to disappear. Satisfactions last but a moment before they must be renewed. Manic love is roller-coaster love. The French ballad "Plaisir d'Amour" is the manic lover's anthem:

The pleasures of love are but a moment long
But the pain of love endures the whole life through.

Ludus "Ludus" is the Latin word for play. For ludic lovers, love is a game, something to play at rather than to become deeply involved in. Love is ultimately *ludic*rous. Love is for fun; encounters are casual, carefree, and often careless. "Nothing serious" is the motto of ludic lovers.

It is only with the heart that one can see rightly; what is essential is invisible to the eye.
Antoine de Saint-Exupéry
(1900–1944)

Self-Assessment

YOUR STYLE OF LOVE

John Lee, who developed the idea of styles of love, also developed a questionnaire that allows men and women to identify their style of love. Complete the questionnaire to identify your style of love. Then ask yourself to which style of love you find yourself drawn in others. Is it the same as your own or different?

Discover Your Own Style of Loving

Consider each characteristic as it applies to a current relationship that you define as love, or to a previous one if that is more applicable. For each, note whether the trait is *almost always* true (AA), *usually* true (U), *rarely* true (R), or *almost never* true (AN).

	Eros	Ludus	Storge	Mania	Ludic Eros	Storgic Eros	Storgic Ludus	Pragma
1. You consider your childhood less happy than the average of peers.	R		AN	U				
2. You were discontented with life (work, etc.) at time your encounter began.	R		AN	U	R			
3. You have never been in love before this relationship.					U	R	AN	R
4. You want to be in love or have love as security.	R	AN		AA		AN	AN	U
5. You have a clearly defined ideal image of your desired partner.	AA	AN	AN	AN	U	AN	R	AA
6. You felt a strong gut attraction to your beloved on the first encounter.	AA	R	AN	R		AN		
7. You are preoccupied with thoughts about the beloved.	AA	AN	AN	AA			R	
8. You believe your partner's interest is at least as great as yours.		U	R	AN			R	U
9. You are eager to see your beloved almost every day; this was true from the beginning.	AA	AN	R	AA		R	AN	R
10. You soon believed this could become a permanent relationship.	AA	AN	R	AN	R	AA	AN	U
11. You see "warning signs" of trouble but ignore them.	R	R		AA		AN	R	R
12. You deliberately restrain frequency of contact with partner.	AN	AA	R	R	R	R	U	
13. You restrict discussion of your feelings with beloved.	R	AA	U	U	R		U	U
14. You restrict display of your feelings with beloved.	R	AA	R	U	R		U	U
15. You discuss future plans with beloved.	AA	R	R				AN	AA
16. You discuss wide range of topics, experiences with partner.	AA	R				U	R	AA

17.	You try to control relationship, but feel you've lost control.	AN	AN	AN	AA	AN	AN		
18.	You lose ability to be first to terminate relationship.	AN	AN		AA	R	U	R	R
19.	You try to force beloved to show more feeling, commitment.	AN	AN		AA		AN	R	
20.	You analyze the relationship, weigh it in your mind.			AN	U		R	R	AA
21.	You believe in the sincerity of your partner.	AA			U	R	U	AA	
22.	You blame partner for difficulties of your relationship.	R	U	R	U	R	AN		
23.	You are jealous and possessive but not to the point of angry conflict.	U	AN	R		R	AN		
24.	You are jealous to the point of conflict, scenes, threats, etc.	AN	AN	AN	AA	R	AN	AN	AN
25.	Tactile, sensual contact is very important to you.	AA		AN		U	AN		R
26.	Sexual intimacy was achieved early, rapidly in the relationship.	AA		AN	AN	U	R	U	
27.	You take the quality of sexual rapport as a test of love.	AA	U	AN		U	AN	U	R
28.	You are willing to work out sex problems, improve technique.	U	R		R	U		R	U
29.	You have a continued high rate of sex, tactile contact throughout the relationship.	U		R	R	U	R		R
30.	You declare your love first, well ahead of partner.		AN	R	AA		AA		
31.	You consider love life your most important activity, even essential.	AA	AN	R	AA		AA	R	R
32.	You are prepared to "give all" for love once under way.	U	AN	U	AA	R	AA	R	R
33.	You are willing to suffer abuse, even ridicule from partner.		AN	R	AA			R	AN
34.	Your relationship is marked by frequent differences of opinion, anxiety.	R	AA	R	AA	R	R		R
35.	The relationship ends with lasting bitterness, trauma for you.	AN	R	R	AA	R	AN	R	R

To diagnose your style of love, look for patterns across characteristics. If you consider your childhood less happy than that of your friends, were discontent with life when you fell in love, and very much want to be in love, you have "symptoms" that are rarely typical of eros and almost never true of storge, but which do suggest mania. Where a trait did not especially apply to a type of love, the space in that column is blank. Storge, for instance, is not the *presence* of many symptoms of love, but precisely their absence; it is cool, abiding affection rather than *Sturm und Drang*.

The patron saint of ludic lovers is the poet Sir John Suckling (1609–1642), a favorite of the English court (and the inventor of cribbage), who, when banished, committed suicide. His poem "The Constant Lover" sums up the philosophy of the ludic lover:

Out upon it, I have loved
Three whole days together!
And am like to love three more,
If it prove fair weather.

Storge Storge (STOR-gay), from the Greek word for natural affection, is the love between companions. It is, wrote Lee, "love without fever, tumult, or folly, a peaceful and enchanting affection." It begins usually as friendship and then gradually deepens into love. If the love ends, it also occurs gradually, and the couple often become friends once again. Of such love Theophile Gautier wrote, "To love is to admire with the heart; to admire is to love with the mind."

Agape Agape (AH-ga-pay), from the Greek word for brotherly love, is the traditional Christian love that is chaste, patient, and undemanding; it does not expect to be reciprocated. It is the love of saints and martyrs. Agape is more abstract and ideal than concrete and real. It is easier to love all of humankind than an individual in this way.

Pragma "Pragma" is derived from the Greek word meaning business. Pragmatic lovers are, first and foremost, businesslike in their approach to looking for someone who meets their needs. They use logic in their search for a partner, seeking background, education, personality, religion, and interests that are compatible with their own. If they meet a person who satisfies their criteria, erotic, manic, or other feelings may develop. But, as Samuel Butler warned, "Logic is like the sword—those who appeal to it shall perish by it."

Two researchers (Hendrick & Hendrick, 1988a) found that college students in love were more erotic and agapic and less ludic than those not in love. In another study, researchers found that heterosexual and gay men have similar attitudes toward eros, ludus, storge, and mania.

Romantic Love and Adrenaline: The Two-Component Theory

The contradictory nature of romantic love has confused lovers (and those who theorize about love) for centuries. Is passionate love pleasure or pain—or both? The scientific explanation of romantic love was given a boost by Stanley Schachter's two-component theory of human emotions. According to his theory, for a person to experience an emotion, two factors must be present: physiological arousal and an appropriate emotional explanation for the arousal. By recognizing that love is accompanied by physiological arousal, psychologists are able to explain why both intensely positive and intensely negative experiences can lead to love. Stimuli that generate attraction, sexual arousal, jealousy, loneliness, rejection, relief, confusion, and gratitude, for example, can all produce intense physiological arousal. "Thus, these positive and negative experiences may all have the potential for deepening an individual's passion for another" (Berscheid & Walster, 1974).

Love is patient and kind; love is not jealous or boastful; it is not arrogant or rude. Love does not insist on its own way; it is not irritable or resentful; it does not rejoice at wrong, but rejoices in the right. Love bears all things, believes all things, hopes all things, endures all things.

I Corinthians 13:4–7

*Love looks not with the eyes
But with the mind.*

William Shakespeare

*My love is like to ice, and I to fire:
How comes it then that this her
  cold so great
Is not dissolved through my so hot
  desire,
But harder grows the more I her
  entreat?
Or how comes it that my exceeding
  heat
Is not allayed by her heart-frozen
  cold,
But that I burn much more in boil-
  ing sweat,
And feel my flames augmented
  manifold?
What more miraculous thing may
  be told
That fire, which all things melts,
  should harden ice,
And ice, which is congeal'd with
  senseless cold,
Should kindle fire by wonderful
  device?
  Such is the power of love in
    gentle mind,
  That it can alter all the course
    of kind.*

Edmund Spenser
(1552–1599)

In William Shakespeare's A Midsummer Night's Dream, *Titania*, *Queen of the Fairies*, has fallen in love with Bottom, who has been transformed into an ass. We all make mistakes sometimes when it comes to love. (In this production, the role of Titania is played by a man, highlighting the use of cross-dressing in contemporary culture and the arts, as discussed further in Chapter 11. In Shakespeare's time, all women's roles were performed by men.)

The way people label their physiological responses is important in determining the way they feel. In a situation in which those feelings may reasonably be labeled "love," the person may indeed experience love. We learn to label our physiological responses as we grow up. An adolescent may ask, "When I see Maria come into class, my heart leaps. Does that mean I am in love?" The response is crucial. If the answer is yes, the adolescent is going to identify the feeling with love. If a boy gets nervous every time he talks to another student, he may label the nervousness "love" and fall in love. If he labels the nervousness "fear," he may not fall in love and may even avoid the other person.

A number of unpleasant situations may generate physiological arousal, including fear, rejection, frustration, and challenge. Similarly, pleasant experiences—attraction, sexual arousal, satisfaction of needs, excitement—may facilitate passion. There are few of us who have not fallen in love or had infatuations as a result of these strange, mysterious, and wonderful physiological arousal mechanisms.

We can turn to Shakespeare for an illustration of the two-component theory. In *A Midsummer Night's Dream*, Titania, Queen of the Fairies, is given a potion that will make her fall in love with the first being she sees when she wakes from her sleep. The love potion is a stimulant that, like certain drugs, induces intense physiological responses. This stimulation is the basis for all love potions and spells, real or imagined. In this aroused state, Titania awakens and her eyes fall on Bottom, who has just been transformed into a donkey:

TITANIA: What angel wakes me from my flowery bed? . . .
  Thy fair virtue's force perforce doth move
  On the first view to say, to swear, I love thee.

BOTTOM: Methinks, mistress, you should have little reason for that:
  and yet to say the truth, reason and love keep little company
  together now-a-days.

Love reckons hours for months, and days for years; and every little absence is an age.

John Dryden

I hate and I love.
You ask how that can be.
Yet I do not know.
But I feel it.
And it torments me.
  Catullus (84?–54? B.C.)

Of course, Bottom is neither wise nor beautiful; he is a donkey. But love aroused keeps no company with reason—although in a comedy about love, it is reasonable that Titania believes she is in love with an ass. (We may all make that mistake sometimes!) When the spell induced by the potion is broken (that is, when the physiological stimuli stop), Titania sees Bottom as the donkey he truly is. So it is with all romantic love, according to Schacter's theory. It does not endure; indeed, it cannot endure. People cannot sustain the high degree of physiological stimulation. J. K. Folsom (quoted in Hatfield & Walster, 1981) writes:

> Love grows less exciting with time for the same biological reasons that the second run on a fast toboggan slide is less exciting than the first. The diminished excitement, however, may increase the real pleasure. Extreme excitement is practically the same as fear, and is unpleasant. After the excitement has diminished below a certain point, however, pleasure will again diminish, unless new kinds of pleasure have meanwhile arisen.

Because of the physiological arousal that accompanies sexual arousal, we can mistake sexual attraction for love, especially since we are expected to be sexually attracted to those we love. As Erich Fromm (1974) points out:

> Because sexual desire is in the minds of most people coupled with the idea of love, they are easily misled to conclude that they love each other when they want each other physically.... Sexual attraction creates, for the moment, the illusion of union.

Without love, however, the illusion of oneness soon disappears, and people are left as far apart as before. In some ways, remarks Fromm (1974), they become even more distant, "because when the illusion has gone they feel their estrangement even more markedly than before."

The Triangular Theory of Love

The triangular theory of love, developed by Robert Sternberg (1986), emphasizes the dynamic quality of love relationships. This theory sees love as composed of three elements, as in the points of a triangle. These elements are intimacy, passion, and decision/commitment (see Figure 8.1). Each can be enlarged or diminished in the course of a love relationship, which will affect the quality of the relationship. They can also be combined in different ways. Each combination gives us a different type of love, such as romantic love, infatuation, empty love, liking, and so on. We may combine the components differently at different times in the same love relationship.

The Components of Love According to Robert Sternberg, there are three components to love: intimacy, passion, and decision/commitment. These components may combine in different proportions.

The Intimacy Component Intimacy refers to the warm, close, bonding feelings we get when we love someone. According to Sternberg and Grajek (1984), there are ten signs of intimacy:

1. Wanting to promote your partner's welfare.
2. Feeling happiness with your partner.

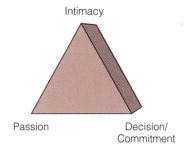

FIGURE 8.1 According to Robert Sternberg's triangle theory of love, the three triangle points are intimacy, passion, and decision/commitment.

3. Holding your partner in high regard.

4. Being able to count on your partner in time of need.

5. Being able to understand each other.

6. Sharing yourself and your possessions with your partner.

7. Receiving emotional support from your partner.

8. Giving emotional support to your partner.

9. Being able to communicate with your partner about intimate things.

10. Valuing your partner's presence in your life.

The Passion Component The passion component refers to the elements of romance, attraction, and sexuality in your relationship. These may be fueled by desires to increase self-esteem, to be sexually active or fulfilled, to affiliate with others, to dominate, or to subordinate.

The Decision/Commitment Component This component consists of two separate parts, a short-term part and a long-term part. The short-term part refers to your decision that you love someone. You may or may not make the decision consciously. But it usually occurs before you decide to make a commitment to that person. The commitment represents the long-term part; it is the maintenance of love. But a decision to love someone does not necessarily entail a commitment to maintaining that love.

Kinds of Love The intimacy, passion, and decision/commitment components can be combined in eight basic ways, according to Sternberg. These combinations form the basis for classifying love:

1. Liking (intimacy only)

2. Infatuation (passion only)

3. Romantic love (intimacy and passion)

4. Companionate love (intimacy and commitment)

5. Fatuous love (passion and commitment)

6. Consummate love (intimacy, passion, and commitment)

7. Empty love (decision/commitment only)

8. Nonlove (absence of intimacy, passion, and commitment)

These types represent extremes which probably few of us experience. Not many of us, for example, experience infatuation in its purest form, in which there is absolutely *no* intimacy. (Empty love, in fact, is not really love at all.) These categories are nevertheless useful for examining the nature of love.

Liking: Intimacy Only Liking represents the intimacy component alone. It forms the basis for close friendships but is neither passionate nor committed. As such, liking is often an enduring kind of love. Boyfriends and girlfriends may come and go, but good friends remain.

No disguise can long conceal love where it exists, nor long feign it where it is lacking.
François de la Rochefoucauld

The physiological sensations accompanying sexual arousal are often identified as feelings of love.

Intimacy

Passion

Decision/
Commit-
ment

a. Perfectly matched
involvements

b. Closely matched
involvements

c. Moderately mismatched
involvements

d. Severely mismatched
involvements

Self   Other

FIGURE 8.2 According to the
triangle theory of love, the shape
and size of each person's triangle
indicates how well each is
matched to the other.

Infatuation: Passion Only Infatuation is "love at first sight." It is the kind of love that idealizes its object; it rarely sees the other as a "real" person who sometimes has bad breath (but is worthy of being loved nonetheless). Infatuation is marked by sudden passion and a high degree of physical and emotional arousal. It tends to be obsessive and all-consuming; one has no time, energy, or desire for anything or anyone but the beloved (or thoughts of him or her). To the dismay of the infatuated individual, infatuations are usually asymmetrical: One's passion (or obsession) is rarely returned equally. And the greater the asymmetry, the greater the distress in the relationship (Sternberg & Barnes, 1985).

Romantic Love: Intimacy and Passion Romantic love combines intimacy and passion. It is similar to liking except it is more intense as a result of physical or emotional attraction. It may begin with an immediate union of the two components, with friendship that intensifies with passion, or with passion that also develops intimacy. Although commitment is not an essential element of romantic love, it may develop.

Companionate Love: Intimacy and Commitment Companionate love is essential to a committed friendship. It often begins as romantic love, but as the passion diminishes and the intimacy increases, it is transformed into companionate love. Some couples are satisfied with such love, while others are not. Those who are dissatisfied in companionate love relationships may seek extrarelational affairs to maintain passion in their lives. They may also end the relationship to seek a new romantic relationship in the hope that it will remain romantic.

Fatuous Love: Passion and Commitment Fatuous or deceptive love is whirlwind love; it begins the day a couple meet, quickly results in cohabitation or engagement, then marriage. It goes so fast one hardly knows what happened. Often enough, nothing much really did happen that will permit the relationship to endure. As Sternberg (1989) observes, "It is fatuous in the sense that a commitment is made on the basis of passion without the stabilizing element of intimate involvement—which takes time to develop." Passion fades soon enough, and all that remains is commitment. But commitment that has had relatively little time to deepen is a poor foundation on which to build an enduring relationship. With neither passion nor intimacy, the commitment wanes.

Consummate Love: Intimacy, Passion, and Commitment Consummate love is born when intimacy, passion, and commitment combine to form their unique constellation. It is the kind of love we dream about but do not expect in all our love relationships. Many of us can achieve it, but it is difficult to sustain over time. To sustain it, we must nourish its different components, for each is subject to the stress of time.

The Geometry of Love The shape of the love triangle depends on the intensity of the love and the balance of the parts. Intense love relationships create triangles with greater area; such triangles occupy more of one's life. Just as love relationships can be balanced or unbalanced, so can love triangles. The balance determines the shape of the triangle (Figure 8.2). A relationship in which the intimacy, passion, and commitment components are equal forms an equilateral triangle. But if the components are not equal, unbalanced triangles form. The size and shape of a person's triangle gives a good pictorial sense of how that person feels about another. The greater the match between each person's triangle in a relationship, the more each is likely to experience satisfaction in the relationship (Sternberg & Barnes, 1985).

Love as Attachment

Attachment theory, the most prominent new approach to the study of love, examines love as a form of **attachment,** a close, enduring emotional bond that finds its roots in infancy (Hazan & Shaver, 1987; Shaver, Hazan, & Bradshaw, 1984, 1988). Research suggests that romantic love and infant/caregiver attachment have similar emotional dynamics. Philip Shaver and colleagues (1988) suggest that "all important love relationships—especially the first ones with parents and later ones with lovers and spouses—are attachments." Based on infant/caregiver work by John Bowlby (1969, 1973, 1980), some love researchers suggest numerous similarities between attachment and romantic love (Shaver et al., 1988). These include the following:

Attachment

- Attachment bond's formation and quality depend on attachment object's (AO) responsiveness and sensitivity.
- When AO is present, infant is happier.
- Infant shares toys, discoveries, objects with AO.
- Infant coos, talks baby talk, "sings."
- Feelings of oneness with AO.

Romantic love

- Feelings of love are related to lover's interest and reciprocation.
- When lover is present, person feels happier.
- Lovers share experience and goods; give gifts.
- Lovers coo, sing, and talk baby talk.
- Feelings of oneness with lover.

Studies conducted by Mary Ainsworth and colleagues (1978, cited in Shaver et al., 1988) indicate that there are three styles of infant attachment: secure, anxious/ambivalent, and avoidant. In **secure attachment,** the infant feels secure when the mother is out of sight. He or she is confident that the mother will offer protection and care. In **anxious/ambivalent attachment,** the infant shows separation anxiety when the mother leaves. He or she feels insecure when the mother is not present. In **avoidant attachment,** the infant senses the mother's detachment and rejection when he or she desires close bodily contact. The infant shows avoidance behavior with the mother as a means of defense. In the study, 66% of the infants were secure, 19% were anxious/ambivalent, and 21% were avoidant.

Shaver and colleagues (1988) hypothesized that the styles of attachment developed during infancy continue through adulthood. They conducted several surveys with adults, which revealed similar styles of attachment.

According to attachment theory, the holding and cuddling behaviors between parents and babies resemble those of adult lovers.

Secure Adults Secure adults found it relatively easy to get close to others. They felt comfortable depending on others and having others depend on them. They didn't frequently worry about being abandoned or having someone get too close to them. More than avoidant and anxious/ambivalent adults, they felt that others generally liked them; they believed that people were generally well intentioned and good-hearted. In contrast to the other styles, secure adults were less likely to believe in media images of love and

The cuddling, cooing, and "baby-talk" between lovers mimics parent-infant communication.

believe that romantic love can last. Their love experiences tended to be happy, friendly, and trusting. They accepted and supported their partners. On average, their relationships lasted ten years. About 56% of the adults in the study were secure.

Anxious/Ambivalent Adults   Anxious/ambivalent adults felt that others did not get as close as they themselves wanted. They worried that their partners didn't really love them or would leave them. They also wanted to merge completely with another, which sometimes scared others away. More than others, they felt that it is easy to fall in love. Their experiences in love were often obsessive and marked by desire for union, high degrees of sexual attraction and jealousy, and emotional highs and lows. Their love relationships lasted an average of five years. Between 19 and 20% of the adults were identified as anxious/ambivalent.

Avoidant Adults   Avoidant adults felt discomfort in being close to others; they were distrustful and fearful of becoming dependent. More than others, they believed that romance seldom lasted, but that at times it could be as intense as it was at the beginning. Their partners wanted more closeness than they did. Avoidant lovers feared intimacy and experienced emotional highs and lows and jealousy. Their relationships lasted an average of six years. Twenty-three to 25% of the adults in the study were avoidant.

In adulthood, the attachment style developed in infancy combines with sexual desire and caring behaviors to give rise to romantic love.

Never seek to tell thy love
*   Love that never told can be;*
For the gentle wind does move
*   Silently, invisibly.*
I told my love, I told my love,
*   I told her all my heart;*
Trembling, cold, in ghastly fears,
*   Ah! She did depart!*
Soon as she was gone from me,
*   A traveler came by,*
Silently, invisibly,
*   He took her with a sigh.*
             William Blake

Many of us think that the existence of jealousy proves the existence of love. We may try to test someone's interest or affection by attempting to make him or her jealous by flirting with another person. If our date or partner becomes jealous, the jealousy is taken as a sign of love (Salovey & Rodin, 1991; White, 1980a). But provoking jealousy proves nothing except that the other person can be made jealous. Making jealousy a litmus test of love is dangerous, for jealousy and love are not necessary companions. Jealousy may be a more accurate yardstick for measuring insecurity or possessiveness than love. In William Shakespeare's *Othello*, for example, the jealous Othello murders his devoted wife because he is misled into believing she was unfaithful. Upon discovering her innocence, he cries out that "he loved not wisely but too well." But did Othello love too well? Or was he a victim of his overweening pride and possessiveness?

It's important to understand jealousy for several reasons. First, jealousy is a painful emotion filled with anger and hurt. Its churning emotions can turn us inside out, making us feel out of control. If we can understand jealousy, especially when it is irrational, then we can eliminate some of its pain. Second, jealousy can help cement or destroy a relationship. Jealousy helps maintain a relationship by guarding its exclusiveness. But in its irrational or extreme forms, it can destroy a relationship by its insistent demands and attempts at control. We need to understand when and how jealousy is functional and when it is not. Third, jealousy is often linked to violence (Follingstad, Rutledge, Berg, & Hause, 1990; Laner, 1990). It is a factor in precipitating violence in dating relationships among both high school and college students (Burcky, 1988; Stets & Pirog-Good, 1987). Marital violence and rape are often provoked by jealousy (Russell, 1990). It is often used by abusive spouses to justify their violence (Adams, 1990).

Jealousy in Cross-Cultural Perspective

Jealousy appears to be present in all cultures; however, it differs from culture to culture in its level of intensity and what evokes jealous responses. Researcher Ralph Hupka (1981) divides cultures into low-jealousy and high-jealousy cultures. Low-jealousy cultures are characterized by sharing attitudes, positive attitudes toward sexual pleasure, and the prizing of children regardless of paternity. High-jealousy cultures, by contrast, are possessive of goods and people, have restrictive attitudes toward sexuality, and require the legitimizing of children through marriage. They place high value on romantic love and marriage as a source of intimacy.

The United States is a relatively high-jealousy society. In a study of 103 men and women, half described themselves as a "jealous person" (Pines & Aronson, 1983). In high-jealousy cultures, the husband is permitted to physically assault his wife if she is found having sexual intercourse with another man. In the United States, some states once excused "a crime of passion" as justifiable homicide if the killing was committed by a husband in a fit of jealous rage. Such laws, however, did not ordinarily extend to women in similar situations.

Behavior that causes jealousy differs across cultures. A study of seven countries, including the United States and Mexico, found that flirting, kissing, and sexual relationships evoked jealous responses among all respondents

---

Beware, my Lord, of jealousy. It is the green-eyed monster that mocks the meat it feeds on.

William Shakespeare

A man was jealous of his wife, who, despite his jealousies, was always faithful. She gave him no reason to be jealous, but it did not matter; he tormented her with his constant tirades. Finally, one evening she left and was never seen again. But outside the camp, her sons discovered a great rock which resembled their mother. Their father's jealousy, they said, had turned her to stone.

Plains Indian tale

Here lies the body of Mannie They put him here to stay; He lived the life of Riley While Riley was away.

Boot Hill epitaph

Cultures can be divided into high-jealousy and low-jealousy cultures. American culture is a high-jealousy culture, while various Native American tribes differ in their jealousy levels.

(Buunk & Hupka, 1987). The most intense response was provoked by their partner having sexual intercourse with someone else. Dancing, hugging, and having sexual fantasies about another person were more neutral. There were not many differences between men and women, except that women were generally more jealous if their partners kissed someone else; men were more upset if their partners had sexual fantasies about someone else.

What Is Jealousy?

Jealousy is an aversive response that occurs because of a partner's real, imagined, or likely involvement with a third person (Bringle & Buunk, 1985). Jealousy sets boundaries for the behaviors that are acceptable in relationships; the boundaries cannot be crossed without evoking jealousy (Reiss, 1986).

The Psychological Dimension As most of us know, jealousy is a painful emotion. It is an agonizing compound of hurt, anger, depression, fear, and doubt. We feel less attractive and acceptable to our partner (Bush, Bush, & Jennings, 1988). Jealous responses are most intense in committed or marital relationships because both assume "specialness." This specialness occurs because one's intimate partner is different from everyone else. With him or her, you are most confiding, revealing, vulnerable, caring, and trusting. There is a sense of exclusiveness. To have sex outside the relationship violates that sense of exclusiveness because sex symbolizes specialness. Words such as "disloyalty," "cheating," and "infidelity" reflect the sense that an unspoken pledge has been broken. This unspoken pledge is the normative expectation that serious relationships, whether dating or marital, will be sexually exclusive (Lieberman, 1988).

As our lives become more and more intertwined, we become less and less independent. For some, this loss of independence increases the fear of losing the partner. But it takes more than simple dependency to make a person jealous. To be jealous, we also need to lack self-esteem and have a feeling of insecurity, either about ourselves or about our relationships (Berscheid &

Frei, 1977; McIntosh, 1989). Insecure people tend to feel jealous in their relationships (McIntosh & Tate, 1990). This is true for both whites and African Americans (McIntosh, 1989).

Jealous responses are most intense when they involve sexuality, as Americans tend to be particularly insecure and competitive in this realm (Bringle & Buunk, 1991). Consider, for example, the different responses you might feel if you believe your partner is talking to, holding hands with, kissing, or having sexual intercourse with a potential or real rival. Which activities do you find most threatening? Least? If you are like most people, the more sexual the interaction, the higher the level of jealousy.

Types of Jealousy Social psychologists suggest that there are two types of jealousy: suspicious and reactive (Bringle & Buunk, 1991). **Suspicious jealousy** occurs when there is no reason to be suspicious, or only ambiguous evidence to suspect that a partner is involved with a third person. **Reactive jealousy** occurs when a partner is involved in a current, past, or anticipated relationship with another person.

Suspicious Jealousy Suspicious jealousy tends to occur most often when a relationship is in its early stages. The relationship is not firmly established, and the couple is unsure about its future. The smallest distraction, imagined slight, or inattention can be taken as evidence of interest in another person. Even without *any* evidence, a jealous partner may worry ("Is he or she seeing someone else but not telling me?"). The partner may engage in vigilance, watching his or her partner's every move ("I'd like to audit your human sexuality class"). He or she may snoop, unexpectedly appearing in the middle of the night to see if someone else is there ("I was just passing by and thought I'd say hello"). The partner may try to control the other's behavior ("If you go to your friend's party without me, we're through").

Sometimes, however, suspicions are valid. That's the terrible thing about suspicions: Sometimes they *are* legitimate. Suspicious jealousy, in fact, may be a reasonable response to circumstantial evidence. (If both partners are nonsmokers, for example, the cigarette butt next to the bed may provoke some questions. "The maid must have left the cigarette. How messy of her!" is not a convincing response in such a situation.) Robert Bringle and Bram Buunk, in fact, believe that a certain amount of suspicious jealousy may be functional. They observe that "emotional reactions to these [circumstantial] events may forewarn the partner of what will happen if there are serious transgressions and thereby serve the role of *preventing* extradyadic involvements" (Bringle and Buunk, 1991).

At the same time, suspicious jealousy may be wholly unfounded. It can be self-defeating. The jealous man or woman may feel out of control and, as a result, his or her self-esteem suffers. "I can't help it. I know it is irrational, and I hate myself for it. I am a terrible person. But every time you are out of my sight, I think you are seeing someone else." Such jealousy may undermine the relationship. A jealous partner may try to control the other's feelings, activities, and movements until the partner feels suffocated. Such irrational jealousy can destroy the very relationship it is trying to preserve.

Reactive Jealousy Reactive jealousy occurs when one learns of a partner's present, past, or anticipated sexual involvement with another person. This usually provokes the most intense jealousy. If the affair occurred during the current relationship, the discovering partner may feel that the entire relationship has been based on a lie. Trust is questioned. Every word and event must be reevaluated: "If you slept with each other when you said you were going to the library, did you also sleep with him/her when you said you were going to the laundromat?" Or, "How could you say you loved me when you were seeing him/her?" The damage can be irreparable.

If the affair is currently going on, similar questions arise but with an important difference. If the affair is over, it is clear that the partner involved in the affair has chosen to remain. But if the affair is continuing, the involved partner may be confronted with a choice: With whom will he or she remain? Sometimes, however, there is no choice. Because of the affair, the offended partner breaks off the relationship or marriage.

Boundary Markers   As we noted earlier, jealousy represents a boundary marker. It points out what the boundaries are in a particular relationship. It determines how, to what extent, and in what manner others can interact with members of the relationship. It also shows the limits to which the members of the relationship can interact with those outside the relationship. Culture prescribes the general boundaries of what evokes jealousy, but individuals adjust them to the dynamics of their own relationship.

Boundaries may vary depending on the type of relationship, gender, sexual orientation, and ethnicity. While the majority of people believe sexual exclusiveness to be important in serious dating relationships and cohabitation, it is virtually mandatory in marriage (Blumstein & Schwartz, 1983; Buunk & van Driel, 1989; Hansen, 1985; Lieberman, 1988). Men are generally more restrictive than women; heterosexuals are more restrictive than gay men and lesbians. Although we know very little about jealousy and ethnicity, traditional Latinos and new Latino and Asian immigrants tend to be more restrictive than Anglos or African Americans (Mindel, Habenstein, & Roosevelt, 1988). Despite variations in where the boundary lines are drawn, jealousy functions to guard those lines.

While our culture sets down the general marital boundaries, each couple evolves its own relationship boundaries. For some, it is permissible to carve out an area of individual privacy. A person may have a few or many separate friends (of the same or other sex), activities, and interests apart from the couple. Others have no separate spheres, because of either jealousy or a lack of interest. But wherever a married couple draws its boundaries, each member usually understands where the lines are drawn. Each implicitly or explicitly knows what behavior will evoke a jealous response from the partner (Bringle & Buunk, 1991). For some, it is having lunch with a member of the other sex (or same sex, if they are lesbian or gay); for others, it is having dinner; for others, it is having dinner and seeing a movie. For one married partner to pretend to the other that he or she doesn't "know" that a particular action (a flirtatious suggestion, lingering kiss, or dinner alone) will provoke a jealous response is often hypocritical.

Gender and Orientation Differences

While women and men both experience jealousy, it differs along both gender and orientation lines.

But jealous souls will not be answer'd so;
They are not ever jealous for the cause;
But jealous for they are jealous; 'tis a monster
Begot upon itself, born on itself.
       William Shakespeare

He who is not jealous is not in love.
       Augustine of Hippo

Gender Differences Both women and men fear their partner may be attracted to someone else because of dissatisfaction or the desire for sexual variety; women, however, feel especially vulnerable to losing their partner to an attractive rival (White, 1981). Men and women tend to become jealous about different matters. Men tend to experience jealousy when they feel their partners are sexually involved with other men. Women, by contrast, tend to experience jealousy over intimacy issues. They feel the most jealousy when they believe their partners are physically *and* emotionally involved with other women (White, 1981).

Men tend to react to jealousy by expressing anger. Women more often react with depression. Ira Reiss suggests that this difference is consistent with cultural restraints prohibiting women from expressing anger (Reiss, 1986). At the same time, it reflects their greater powerlessness vis-à-vis men. As a result, women turn their anger inward, transforming it into depression. In this manner, they are able to avoid direct confrontation.

There may be some truth to the belief that women are more jealous than men. But such jealousy is not inherent in being female. It is more likely related to the greater sexual freedom that men are permitted. (Even in marriage, it is more acceptable for men to "roam" because they are believed to be "naturally" more sexual than women.) If women appear to be more jealous than men, it may be because men, granted greater autonomy than women, have more opportunities to evoke jealous responses from women (Reiss, 1986).

Orientation Differences Gay men and lesbians appear to be less prone to jealousy than heterosexuals. There are two factors accounting for this. First, heterosexual norms place a higher value on sexual exclusiveness than do gay and lesbian norms (Hawkins, 1990). (The higher normative value placed on heterosexual monogamy, however, does not prevent heterosexual men and women from having affairs.) In lesbian and gay culture, the model for relationships is not marriage but a "best-friends" model, discussed in Chapter 7 (Peplau, 1988). In the marital model, sexual fidelity is normative, while in the gay/lesbian best-friends model, it is negotiable (Kurdek, 1991). Monogamy is not necessarily the norm among gay men and lesbians. As a consequence, many gay men and lesbians are more able to have sexual relationships outside the primary relationship without provoking the same high degree of jealousy.

Second, sex does not necessarily symbolize love. In exclusive heterosexual relationships, sex and love are equated. Sex and love are intertwined for lesbians as well, perhaps reflecting their socialization as women (Nichols, 1987). For lesbians, however, there appears to be an emphasis on intimacy over sex. Among lesbian feminists, there is a strong commitment to *not* be jealous. Jealousy is perceived as a patriarchal emotion used to repress female freedom. While jealousy continues to exist, the jealous lesbian feminist bears a double burden: jealousy *and* guilt for feeling jealous (Wolf, 1980).

For gay men, as for heterosexual men, sex and love may be more easily separated. For them, sex can be more closely related to pleasure than to expressions of intimacy. Unlike heterosexual couples, gay male couples are more able to consciously choose to make their relationship exclusive (closed) or nonexclusive (open). While extramarital relationships are often symptomatic of problems among married couples, they are not necessarily symptomatic among gay couples. Rather, nonexclusiveness among gay couples may reflect different norms (Kurdek, 1991; Kurdek & Schmitt, 1988). Nevertheless, the potential for jealousy exists in open as well as closed gay relationships. To minimize jealousy in open relationships, extrarelational sex is generally allowed only in certain agreed-upon circumstances so as not to threaten the primary relationship.

For bisexual men and women, the issue of jealousy is compounded, especially for the jealous partner (Isensee, 1990). If a bisexual woman is involved in a primary relationship with a man, for example, the man may feel his partner's involvement with another woman is more threatening than her potential involvement with another man. In such cases, not only is the relationship threatened, but the man may feel inadequate as a male. Further, the man may feel he cannot compete sexually with another woman because of physical and emotional differences. Finally, he may fear his partner is neither heterosexual nor bisexual, but lesbian, and therefore, as a male, he may have little that would appeal to her. A woman with a bisexual male partner may experience similar anxieties.

There is no greater glory than love nor greater punishment than jealousy.

Lope de Vega

Managing Jealousy

Jealousy can be unreasonable, based on fears and fantasies, or realistic, reacting to genuine threats or events. Unreasonable jealousy can become a problem when it interferes with an individual's well-being or that of the relationship. Dealing with irrational suspicions can often be very difficult, for such feelings touch deep recesses in ourselves. As we noted earlier, jealousy is often related to personal feelings of insecurity and inadequacy. The source of such jealousy lies within ourselves, not within the relationship.

If we can work on the underlying causes of our insecurity, then we can deal effectively with our irrational jealousy. Excessively jealous people may need considerable reassurance, but at some point they must also confront their own irrationality and insecurity. If they do not, they emotionally imprison their partner. Their jealousy may destroy the very relationship they have been desperately trying to preserve.

But jealousy is not always irrational. Sometimes there are real reasons, such as the relationship boundaries being violated. In this case, the cause lies not within ourselves but within the relationship. Gordon Clanton and Lynn Smith (1977) write:

> Jealousy cannot be treated in isolation. *Your* jealousy is not *your* problem alone. It is also a problem for your partner and for the person whose interest in your partner sparks your jealousy. Similarly, when your partner feels jealous, you ought not to dismiss the matter by pointing a finger and saying "That's your problem." Typically, three or more persons are involved in the production of jealous feelings and behaviors. Ideally, all three should take a part of the responsibility for minimizing the negative consequences.

If the jealousy is well founded, the partner may need to modify or end the relationship with the third party whose presence initiated the jealousy. Modifying the third-party relationship reduces the jealous response and, more important, symbolizes the partner's commitment to the primary relationship. If the partner is unwilling to do this, because of a lack of commitment, unsatisfied personal needs, or problems in the primary relationship, the relationship is likely to reach a crisis. In such cases, jealousy may be the agent for profound change.

There are no set rules for dealing with jealousy. Each person must deal with it using his or her own understanding and insights. As with most of life's puzzling problems, jealousy has no simple answers.

THE TRANSFORMATION OF LOVE: FROM PASSION TO INTIMACY

Ultimately, romantic love may be transformed or replaced by a quieter, more lasting love. Otherwise, the relationship will likely break up, and each person will search for another who will once again ignite his or her passion.

The Instability of Passionate Love

According to Sternberg (1988), time affects our levels of intimacy, passion, and commitment.

Intimacy Over Time When we first meet someone, intimacy increases rapidly as we make discoveries about each other, ranging from our preference for strawberry or chocolate ice cream to our innermost thoughts about life and death. As the relationship continues, the rate of growth decreases and then levels off. After the growth levels off, the couple no longer "consciously" feels as close to each other. This may be because they actually are beginning to drift apart, or it may be because they are continuing to grow intimate at a different, less conscious, but deeper level. It is the kind of intimacy that is not easily observed. Instead, it is a latent intimacy that nevertheless is forging stronger, more enduring bonds between them.

Passion Over Time Passion is subject to habituation: What was once thrilling, whether it be love, sex, or roller coasters, becomes less so the more we get used to it. Once we become habituated, more time with a person (or more sex or more roller-coaster rides) does not increase our arousal or satisfaction.

If the person leaves, however, we experience withdrawal symptoms (fatigue, depression, anxiety), just as if we were addicted. In becoming habituated, we have also become dependent. We fall beneath the emotional baseline we were at when we met our partner. Over time, however, we begin to return to that original level.

Commitment Over Time Unlike intimacy and passion, time does not necessarily diminish, erode, or alter a commitment. Our commitments are most affected by how successful our relationship is. Initially, commitment grows more slowly than intimacy or passion. As the relationship becomes long term, commitment growth levels off. Our commitment will remain high as long as we judge the relationship to be successful. If the relationship begins to deteriorate, after a time the commitment will probably decrease as well. Eventually, it may disappear, and an alternative relationship may be sought.

The Disappearance of Romance as Crisis

The disappearance (or transformation) of passionate love is often experienced as a crisis in a relationship. A study of college students found that half would seek divorce if passion disappeared from their marriage (Berscheid, 1983). But intensity of feeling does not necessarily measure depth of love. Intensity, like the excitement of toboggan runs, diminishes over time. It is then that we begin to discover if the love we experience for each other is one that will endure.

Our search for enduring love is complicated by our contradictory needs. Elaine Hatfield and William Walster (1981) write:

> What we really want is the impossible—a perfect mixture of security and danger. We want someone who understands and cares for us, someone who will be around through thick and thin, until we are old. At the same time, we long for sexual excitement, novelty, and danger. The individual who offers just the right combination of both ultimately wins our love. The problem, of course, is that, in time, we get more and more security—and less and less excitement—than we bargained for.

The disappearance of passionate love, however, allows people to refocus their relationship. They are given the opportunity to move from an intense, one-on-one togetherness that excludes others to one that includes family, friends, and external goals. They can look outward on the world together.

Perspective

MAKING LOVE LAST: THE ROLE OF COMMITMENT

Although we generally make commitments because we love someone, love alone is not sufficient to make a commitment last. Our commitments seem to be affected by several factors that can strengthen or weaken the relationship. Ira Reiss (1980) believes that there are three important factors: the balance of costs to benefits, normative inputs, and structural constraints.

The Balance of Costs to Benefits

Whether we like it or not, human beings have a tendency to look at romantic, marital, and sexual relationships from a cost-benefit perspective. Most of the time, when we are satisfied, we are unaware that we may judge our relationships in this manner. But when there is stress or conflict, we often ask ourselves, "What am I getting out of this relationship?" Then we add up the pluses and minuses. If the result is on the plus side, we are encouraged to continue the relationship; if the result is negative, we are more likely to discontinue it, especially if the negativity continues over a long period of time. By this system, sexual in-

teractions can have a positive or negative value. But while sex is important, it is generally not the only factor; it is not even necessarily the most important factor.

Normative Inputs

Normative inputs for relationships are the values that you, your partner, and society hold about love, relationships, marriage, and family. These values can either sustain or detract from a commitment. How do you feel about a love commitment? If you are heterosexual, a marital commitment? Do you believe that marriage is for life? If you are gay, lesbian, or bisexual, what are the values you and your partner bring to your relationship in terms of commitment? How do you create your own positive norms in the face of negative societal norms?

Structural Constraints

The structure of a relationship will add to or detract from commitment. Depending on the type of relationship—whether it is dating, living together, or mar-

---

Intimate Love: Commitment, Caring, and Self-Disclosure

The opposite of loneliness is not togetherness. It is intimacy.

Richard Bach

There is only one serious question. And that is, who knows how to make love stay?

Tom Robbins

Although love is one of the most important elements of our humanity, it seems to come and go. The kind of love that stays is what we might call intimate love. In intimate love, each person knows he or she can count on the other. The excitement comes from the achievement of other goals—from creativity, from work, from child rearing, from friendships—as well as from the relationship. Hatfield and Walster (1981) write:

> A husband and wife often enjoy being able to count on the fact that, while their friends must contend with one emotional upheaval after another, their lives drift on in a serene, unruffled flow. They enjoy the fact that they can share day-to-day pleasures and that, in old age, they'll be together to reminisce and savor their lives. This portrait is very alluring.

The key to making love stay does not seem to be in love's passionate inten-

riage—there are different structural roles and expectations. In marital relationships, there are partner roles (husband/wife) and economic roles (employed worker/homemaker). There may also be parental roles (mother/father). There is the expectation of monogamy. In gay and lesbian relationships, the marital relationship model is replaced by the best-friends model, in which sexual exclusiveness is generally negotiable.

These different factors interact to increase or decrease commitment in a relationship. Commitments are more likely to endure in marriage than in cohabiting or dating relationships, which tend to be relatively short-lived. They are more likely to last in heterosexual relationships than in gay or lesbian relationships (Testa et al., 1987). The reason commitments tend to endure in marriage may or may not have anything to do with a couple's being happy. Marital commitments tend to last because of norms, and structural constraints may compensate for the lack of personal satisfaction.

For most people, love seems to include commitment and commitment includes love. The two seem to overlap considerably. Beverly Fehr (1988) found that if a person violated a central attribute of love, such as caring, that person was also seen as violating his or her commitment. And if a person violated a central attribute of commitment, such as loyalty, it called love into question. Because love and sex share many of the same emotional attributes, sexuality is closely tied to love (Aron & Strong, 1993). If sexual satisfaction diminishes, it is likely that it will also affect love. But as love increases, the emotional aspects of sexual satisfaction may also increase. Because of the overlap between love and commitment, we can mistakenly assume that if someone loves us, he or she is also committed to us. As one researcher pointed out, "Expressions of love can easily be confused with expressions of commitment.... Misunderstandings about a person's love versus commitment can be based on honest errors of communication, on failures of self-understanding" (Kelley, 1983). Or a person can intentionally mislead his or her partner to believe that there is a greater commitment than there actually is. Even if a person is committed, it is not always clear what the commitment means: Is it a commitment to the person or to the relationship? For a short time or for a long time? Is it for better and for worse?

sity but in transforming it into intimate love. Intimate love is based on commitment, caring, and self-disclosure.

Commitment Commitment is an important component of intimate love. It is a determination to continue a relationship or marriage in the face of bad times as well as good (Reiss, 1986). It is based on conscious choice rather than on feelings, which, by their very nature, are transitory. Commitment is a promise of a shared future, a promise to be together, come what may. (See Perspective 1 for a discussion of commitment.)

Commitment has become an important concept in recent years. We seem to be as much in search of commitment as we are in search of love or marriage. We speak of "making a commitment" to someone or to a relationship. (Among singles, commitment is sometimes referred to as the unutterable "C word.") A "committed" relationship has become almost a stage of courtship, somewhere between dating and being engaged or living together.

Caring Caring is the making of another's needs as important as your own. It requires what the philosopher Martin Buber called an "I-Thou" relationship. Buber described two fundamental ways of relating to people: I-Thou and I-It. In an I-Thou relationship, each person is treated as a Thou—that is, as a person whose life is valued as an end in itself. In an I-It relationship, each person is treated as an It; the person has worth only as someone who can be used. When a person is treated as a Thou, his or her humanity and uniqueness are paramount.

Self-Disclosure **Self-disclosure** is the revelation of personal information that others would not ordinarily know because of its riskiness. When we self-disclose, we reveal ourselves—our hopes, our fears, our everyday thoughts—to others. Self-disclosure deepens others' understanding of us. It also deepens our own understanding, for we discover unknown aspects as we open ourselves to others.

Without self-disclosure, we remain opaque and hidden. If others love us, such love leaves us with anxiety: Are we loved for ourselves, or for the image we present to the world?

Together, these elements help transform love. But in the final analysis, perhaps the most important means of sustaining love are our words and actions; caring words and deeds provide the setting for maintaining and expanding love (Byrne & Murnen, 1988).

The study of love is only beginning, but it is already helping us to understand the various components that make up this complex emotion. Although there is something to be said for the mystery of love, understanding how it works in the day-to-day world may help us keep our love vital and growing.

SUMMARY

Love and Sexuality

• Sexuality and love are intimately related in our culture. Sex is most highly valued in loving relationships. Sex with affection rivals marriage as an acceptable moral standard for intercourse. Love is valued by heterosexual men and women, gay men, lesbians, and bisexuals.

• Men are more likely than women to separate sex from love; women tend to view sex within a relational context. Gay men are more likely than heterosexual men to be involved in purely sexual relationships. Researchers suggest, however, that heterosexual males would have more sex-centered relationships if there were more willing women; they are constrained, however, by the availability of consenting women.

This Thing Called Love: The Phenomena of Love, Sex, and Commitment

• *Prototypes* of love, sex, and commitment are models of how people define these ideas in everyday life. The central aspects of the love prototype include trust, caring, honesty, friendship, respect, and concern for the other. Sexual aspects are divided into three categories: emotional, physical, and consequential. The central aspects of sex belong to the emotional dimension, which include caring, closeness, expression of feelings, and specialness. Central aspects of the commitment prototype include loyalty, responsibility, living up to one's word, faithfulness, and trust.

- Attitudes and feelings associated with love include caring, needing, trusting, and tolerating. Behaviors associated with love include verbal, nonverbal, and physical expression of affection, self-disclosure, giving of nonmaterial and material evidence, and tolerance.

How Do I Love Thee? Approaches to the Study of Love

- According to John Lee, there are six basic styles of love: *eros*, *mania*, *ludus*, *storge*, *agape*, and *pragma*.

- The two-component theory of human emotions suggests that physiological arousal and an appropriate emotional explanation for the arousal must be present for love to occur.

- The triangular theory of love views love as consisting of three components: intimacy, passion, and decision/commitment.

- The attachment theory of love views love as being similar in nature to the attachments we form as infants. The *attachment* (or love) styles of both infants and adults are *secure*, *anxious/ambivalent*, and *avoidant*.

Jealousy

- Jealousy is present in all cultures, which can be divided into low-jealousy and high-jealousy cultures. Extramarital sexual relations evoke the most intense jealous responses in most cultures.

- Jealous responses are most likely in committed or marital relationships because of presumed "specialness" of the relationship. Specialness is symbolized by sexual exclusiveness.

- *Jealousy* is an aversive response to a partner's real, imagined, or likely involvement with a third person. As individuals become more interdependent, there is a greater fear of loss. Fear of loss, coupled with insecurity of self or the relationship, increases the likelihood of jealousy.

- There are two types of jealousy: suspicious and reactive. *Suspicious jealousy* occurs when there is no reason to be suspicious or only ambiguous evidence. *Reactive jealousy* occurs when a partner reveals a current, past, or anticipated relationship with another.

- Jealousy acts as a boundary marker for relationships. Boundaries vary according to type of relationship, gender, sexual orientation, and ethnicity.

- Gender differences exist in the type of behavior that evokes jealousy. Women feel most vulnerable to losing their partner to attractive rivals. Men feel most jealous when their partners are sexually involved; women tend to experience the most jealousy over intimacy issues. Men express jealousy through anger, women through depression. Women may be more jealous than men because men have greater autonomy and more opportunities than women.

- There are some differences between gay men, lesbians, and bisexuals, and heterosexuals in terms of jealousy. First, heterosexuals place a higher value on sexual exclusiveness as a norm than do others. Second, sex does not necessarily symbolize love for gay men. Third, for many lesbians, especially feminist lesbians, jealousy is perceived as a patriarchal emotion to be avoided. Men and women may feel especially threatened by their bisexual partners if the third person is a different sex from themselves.

The Transformation of Love: From Passion to Intimacy

• Time affects romantic relationships. The rapid growth of intimacy tends to level off, and we become habituated to passion. Commitment tends to increase, provided that the relationship is judged to be rewarding.

• Romantic love tends to diminish. It may either end or be replaced by intimate love. Many people experience the disappearance of romantic love as a crisis. Intimate love is based on commitment, caring, and *self-disclosure*—the revelation of information not normally known by others.

KEY TERMS

commitment	agape	avoidant attachment
prototype	pragma	jealousy
eros	attachment	suspicious jealousy
mania	secure attachment	reactive jealousy
ludus	anxious/ambivalent attachment	self-disclosure
storge		

SUGGESTIONS FOR FURTHER READING

Buscaglia, Leo. *Loving Each Other.* New York: Ballantine Books, 1984. America's most popular proponent of love in a series of thoughtful essays about relationships.

Hatfield, Elaine, and William Walster. *A New Look at Love.* Reading, MA: Addison-Wesley, 1981. A breezy but serious examination of love from a sociological perspective.

Hendrick, Susan, and Clyde Hendrick. *Romantic Love.* Newbury Park, CA: Sage Publications, 1991. A concise review of social science research on romantic love.

Peck, M. Scott. *The Road Less Traveled: A New Psychology of Love, Traditional Values, and Spiritual Growth.* New York: Simon & Schuster, 1978. A psychological/spiritual approach to love that sees love's goal as spiritual growth.

Sternberg, Robert, and Michael Barnes, eds. *The Psychology of Love.* New Haven: Yale University Press, 1988. An excellent collection of essays by some of the leading researchers in the area of love.

White, Greg, and Paul Mullen. *Jealousy: A Clinical and Multidisciplinary Approach.* New York: Guilford, 1989. A comprehensive examination of what we know about jealousy (and its treatment).

Chapter Nine

COMMUNICATING
ABOUT SEX

P R E V I E W : S E L F - Q U I Z

1. Most people verbally indicate their interest in initiating a sexual interaction. True or false?

2. Women often covertly signal their interest in beginning a conversation with someone. True or false?

3. Studies suggest that those couples with the highest marital satisfaction tend to disclose more than those who are unsatisfied. True or false?

4. Overall, men and women tend to touch about the same amount. True or false?

5. Conflict and intimacy go hand in hand in intimate relationships. True or false?

6. Good communication is primarily the ability to offer reasonable advice to your partner to help him or her change. True or false?

7. In ongoing relationships, women respond positively to sexual invitations at about the same rate as men. True or false?

8. The party with the least interest in continuing a relationship generally has the most power in it. True or false?

9. There is a considerable difference between white and African American sexual slang. True or false?

10. The most effective way of expressing your desire not to have sex is by directly stating so. True or false?

ANSWERS 1. F, 2. T, 3. T, 4. T, 5. T, 6. F, 7. T, 8. T, 9. T, 10. T

Chapter Outline

Communication is the thread that connects sexuality and intimacy. The quality of the communication affects the quality of the relationship, and the quality of the relationship affects the quality of the sex (Cupach & Metts, 1991). Good relationships tend to have good sex, while bad relationships often have bad sex. Sex, in fact, frequently serves as a barometer for the quality of the relationship. The ability to communicate about sex is important in developing and maintaining both sexual and relationship satisfaction (Cupach & Comstock, 1990; Metts & Cupach, 1989). People who are satisfied with their sexual communication also tend to be satisfied with their relationship as a whole (Wheeless, Wheeless, & Baus, 1984).

Most of the time, we don't think about our ability to communicate. Only

If love were what the rose is,
And I were like the leaf,
Our lives would grow together
In sad or singing weather.
Algernon Swinburne

when problems arise do we consciously think about it. Then we become aware of our limitations in communicating, or more often, what we believe are the limitations of others: "You just don't get it, do you?" "You're not listening to me." And as we know, communication failures are marked by frustration.

There are generally two types of communication problems in relationships. The first problem is the failure to self-disclose. The second is poor communication skills. Although much of what we discuss here refers to interpersonal communication in general, such knowledge will enrich your ability to communicate about sexual issues as well.

It's important to realize, however, that not all of a relationship's problems are communication problems. Often we understand each other very clearly; the problem is that we are unable or unwilling to change or compromise. Good communication will not salvage a bad relationship or the "wrong" relationship. But good communication will allow us to see our differences. It will allow us to see the consequence of our actions or inactions, and it will provide us with the ability to make informed decisions.

In this chapter, we examine the characteristics of communication and how different contexts affect it. Next, we look at forms of nonverbal communication, such as touch, which are especially important in sexual relationships. Then we examine the different ways we communicate about sex in intimate relationships. Afterward, we explore ways we can develop our communication skills in order to enhance our relationships. Finally, we look at the different types of conflicts in intimate relationships and how to resolve them.

THE NATURE OF COMMUNICATION

Communication is a transactional process by which we convey symbols, such as words, gestures, and movements, to establish human contact, exchange information, and reinforce or change our attitudes and behaviors and those of others. In order to understand how communication works, we need to understand its different elements.

Characteristics of Communication

There are three key concepts in the nature of communication: transaction, process, and symbols.

- *Communication is a transaction.* It takes place within a relational context in which two (or more) people interact with each other. What we communicate affects the other, whose response (even silence) in turn affects us. The type of relationship affects the transaction. If a relationship is egalitarian, both partners are more likely to listen and change, but if a relationship is inegalitarian, the more powerful person is less likely to listen and change.

- *Communication is a process.* As a process, it is continuous, ongoing, and complex. Because it is a process, communication between people in a relationship does not have a point where it really begins or ends. Our conversations, actions, and interactions blend into and influence each

Whenever a feeling is voiced with truth and frankness . . . a mysterious and far-reaching influence is exerted. At first it acts on those who are inwardly receptive. But the circle grows larger and larger. . . . The effect is but the reflection of something that emanates from one's own heart.

I Ching

other. In a sense, communication never begins or ends because it *always* exists in a relationship. Furthermore, it is complex because we bring to each interaction our own unique personality, our relationship's past, present, and future, our current mood or state of mind (happy/unhappy, satisfied/dissatisfied), and our physical environment (pleasant/unpleasant, quiet/noisy, alone/with others).

Words are given to man to enable him to conceal his true feelings.
François Voltaire (1694–1778)

- *Communication is symbolic.* When we communicate, we use **symbols,** such as words or gestures, that stand for something else. Language is symbolic. When we say "sex," for example, the word "sex" is not sexual behavior but a linguistic symbol for it. But symbolic communication is not limited to verbal or written language. Much symbolic communication is expressed through nonverbal behaviors. For example, moving closer to someone may symbolize sexual interest. But not all nonverbal behaviors are symbolic. Your partner may be moving closer to you because he or she is cold. In that case, the nonverbal behavior is not symbolic. In nonverbal communication, we utilize various contextual clues, such as setting, relationship, and previous interactions, to interpret the meaning of an action.

Communication Contexts

Our communication takes place simultaneously within cultural, social, and psychological contexts. These contexts affect our ability to communicate clearly by prescribing rules (usually unwritten or unconscious) for communicating about various subjects, including sexuality.

The Cultural Context The cultural context refers to the language, values, beliefs, and customs in which communication takes place. On the whole, reflecting our Judeo-Christian heritage, our culture has viewed sexuality negatively. Sexual topics are often tabooed. Children and adolescents are discouraged from obtaining sexual knowledge; they learn they are not supposed to talk about sex. Censorship abounds in the media, with the ever-present "beep" on television or the "f--k" in newspapers and magazines to indicate a "forbidden" sexual word. Our language has few words for describing "the sex act" except scientific or impersonal ones ("sexual intercourse," "coitus," or "copulation"), moralistic ones ("fornication"), euphemistic ones ("doing it," "being intimate," or "sleeping with"), and tabooed ones ("fucking"). There are a few terms that place sexual interactions in a relational category, such as "making love." But love is not always involved—as in, for example, a single encounter between strangers—and the term does not capture the erotic quality of sex. Furthermore, the gay and lesbian subculture has developed its own sexual argot or slang, because society prohibits the open discussion or expression of homosexuality.

Different ethnic groups within our culture also have different language patterns that affect the way they communicate about sexuality. African American culture creates distinct communication patterns (Hecht, Collier, & Ribeau, 1993). Among African Americans, for example, language and expressive patterns are characterized by, among other things, emotional vitality, realness, and valuing direct experience (White & Parham, 1990). Emotional vitality is expressed in the animated, expressive use of words. Realness refers to "telling it like it is," using concrete, nonabstract words.

Nonverbal communication conveys interpersonal attitudes, expresses emotions, and handles the ongoing interaction.

Direct experience is valued because "there is no substitute in the Black ethos for actual experience gained in the course of living" (White & Parham, 1990). In sexual (and other) matters, "mother wit," practical or experiential knowledge, may be valued over knowledge gained from books or lectures. African American sexual vernacular often differs from that of whites. African American males may refer to masturbation as "chokin' the chicken," while white males may refer to it as "stroking" (Mays, Cochran, Bellinger, & Smith, 1992).

Among Latinos, especially traditional Latinos, there is the assumption that sexual matters will not be discussed openly (Guerrero Pavich, 1986). One researcher writes of Mexican Americans: "Ideally, there should be a certain formality in the relationship between spouses. No deep intimacy or intense conflict is expected. Respect, consideration, and curtailment of anger or hostility are highly valued" (Falicov, 1982). Confrontations are to be avoided; negative feelings are not to be expressed. As a consequence, nonverbal communication is especially important. Women are expected to read men's behavior for clues to their feelings and for discovering what is acceptable. Because confrontations are unacceptable and sex cannot be openly discussed, secrets are important. They are shared between friends but not between partners. Sometimes secrets are hinted at; at times of crisis, they may be revealed through anger.

Asian Americans tend to be less individualistic than other Americans in general. Whereas mainstream American culture views the individual as self-reliant and self-sufficient, Asian American subcultures are more relationally oriented. Researchers Steve Shon and Davis Ja note of Asian American thinking (Shon & Ja, 1982):

> They emphasize that individuals are the products of their relationship to nature and other people. Thus, heavy emphasis is placed on their relationship with other people, generally with the aim of maintaining harmony through proper conduct and attitudes.

Asian Americans are less verbal and expressive in their interactions than white Americans. They rely to a great degree on indirection and nonverbal communication, such as silence and the avoidance of eye contact as signs of respect (Del Carmen, 1990).

Because harmonious relationships are highly valued, Asian Americans have a greater tendency to avoid direct confrontation if possible. Japanese Americans, for example, "value implicit, nonverbal, intuitive communication over explicit, verbal, the rational exchange of information" (Del Carmen, 1990). In order to avoid conflict, verbal communication is often indirect or ambiguous; it skirts around issues rather than confronting them. As a consequence, Asian Americans rely on each other to interpret the meaning of a conversation or nonverbal clues.

The Social Context The social context of communication refers to the roles we play in society. These roles are derived from being members of different groups. As men and women, we play out masculine and feminine roles. As members of marital units, we act out roles of husband and wife. As members of cohabiting units, we perform heterosexual, gay, or lesbian cohabiting roles.

As we saw in Chapter 5, the two most important roles affecting our sexual interactions are those relating to gender and sexual orientation. We are given sexual scripts in accordance with both our gender and our orientation roles. These scripts include, among other things, scripts for communicating about sexual matters. Males are instrumental, females are expressive; males seek independence, females seek connectedness. Men don't talk about their sexual feelings; women do. Traditional feminine and masculine roles have an enormous impact on our ability to communicate with each other. When we consider gender role *and* sexual orientation, we find that lesbian relationships are likely to be most communicative, heterosexual relationships moderately communicative, and gay male relationships less communicative (Blumstein & Schwartz, 1983).

Roles exist in relationship to other people. Without a female role, there would be no male role; without a wife role, there would be no husband role. Because roles exist in relationship to others, **status,** a person's position in a group, is important. In traditional gender roles, men are accorded higher status than women; in traditional marital roles, husbands are superior in status to wives. And in terms of orientation, society awards higher status to heterosexuals than to gay men, lesbians, and bisexuals. Because of this male/female disparity, heterosexual relationships tend to have a greater power imbalance than gay and lesbian couples (Lips, 1992).

Whether individuals have equal or unequal status profoundly affects communication. We are more likely to speak our minds to those of equal status than to those of superior status. We are more likely to persuade an equal than a superior to change. In large part this is because the person with higher status often has, at least in theory, greater power. And whether we like to admit it or not, power, the ability to effect change, is an important element in interpersonal relationships, as we will see later in this chapter.

The Psychological Context While the cultural and social contexts are important factors in communication, they do not *determine* how people communicate. We are not prisoners of culture and society, but unique individuals. We may accept some cultural or social aspects, such as language taboos, but reject, ignore, or modify others, such as traditional gender roles. Because we have distinct personalities, we express our uniqueness by the way we communicate: We may be assertive or submissive, rigid or flexible, sensitive or insensitive; we may exhibit high self-esteem or low self-esteem.

Our personality characteristics affect our ability to communicate, change, or manage conflict. Rigid people, for example, are less likely to change than flexible ones, regardless of the quality of communication. People with high self-esteem may be more open to change because they do not necessarily take conflict as an attack on themselves. Personality characteristics relating to sexuality, such as being erotophobic or erotophilic (having negative or positive feelings about sex), affect our sexual communication more directly. Most obviously, erotophobic people are less likely to communicate about sex than erotophilic men and women. Erotophobes find it difficult to discuss sex because they feel sex is "dirty"; talking about it arouses anxiety or feelings of guilt. Because of their negative feelings about sex, they are not likely to express their needs, fantasies, or desires. If their partners are similarly erotophobic, their verbal communication is likely to be minimal or indirect; if their partners are erotophilic, a positive discussion of sex may make them feel uncomfortable. (See Self-Assessment to examine your satisfaction with sexual communication.)

NONVERBAL COMMUNICATION

There is no such thing as not communicating. Even when you are not talking, you are communicating by your silence (an awkward silence, a hostile silence, a tender silence). You are communicating by the way you position your body and tilt your head, through your facial expressions, your physical distance from another person, and so on. Look around you. How are the people in your presence communicating nonverbally?

Much of our communication of feeling is nonverbal. We radiate our moods: a happy mood invites companionship; a solemn mood pushes people away. Joy infects; depression distances—all without a word being said. Nonverbal expressions of love are particularly effective—a gentle touch, a loving glance, or the gift of a flower.

One of the problems with nonverbal communication, however, is the imprecision of its messages. Is a person frowning or squinting? Does the smile indicate friendliness or nervousness? A person may be in reflective silence, but we may interpret the silence as disapproval or distance.

Married couples who love each other tell each other a thousand things without talking.

Chinese proverb

SEXUAL COMMUNICATION SATISFACTION QUESTIONNAIRE

This questionnaire assesses your satisfaction with your sexual communication with your partner. Use the following scale to indicate how strongly you agree or disagree with each statement:

1 = Strongly agree   **4** = Disagree
2 = Agree   **5** = Strongly disagree
3 = Neither agree nor disagree

_____   1. I tell my partner when I am especially sexually satisfied.

_____   2. I am satisfied with my partner's ability to communicate his/her sexual desires to me.

_____   3. I do not let my partner know things that I find pleasing during sex.

_____   4. I am very satisfied with the quality of our sexual interactions.

_____   5. I do not hesitate to let my partner know when I want to have sex with him/her.

_____   6. I do not tell my partner whether or not I am sexually satisfied.

_____   7. I am dissatisfied over the degree to which my partner and I discuss our sexual relationship.

_____   8. I am not afraid to show my partner what kind of sexual behavior I find satisfying

_____   9. I would not hesitate to show my partner what is a sexual turn-on to me.

_____ 10. My partner does not show me when he/she is sexually satisfied.

_____ 11. I show my partner what pleases me during sex.

_____ 12. I am displeased with the manner in which my partner and I communicate with each other during sex.

_____ 13. My partner does not show me things he/she finds pleasing during sex.

_____ 14. I show my partner when I am sexually satisfied.

_____ 15. My partner does not let me know whether sex has been satisfying or not.

_____ 16. I do not show my partner when I am sexually satisfied.

_____ 17. I am satisifed concerning my ability to communicate about sexual matters with my partner.

_____ 18. My partner shows me by the way he/she touches me if he/she is satisfied.

_____ 19. I am dissatisfied with my partner's ability to communicate his/her sexual desire to me.

_____ 20. I have no way of knowing when my partner is sexually satisifed.

_____ 21. I am not satisfied in the majority of our sexual interactions.

_____ 22. I am pleased with the manner in which my partner and I communicate with each other after sex.

Source: Wheeless, Lawrence R., Virginia Eman Wheeless, and Raymond Baus. "Sexual Communication, Communication Satisfaction, and Solidarity in the Developmental Stages of Intimate Relationships," _Western Journal of Speech Communication,_ 48(3), p. 224, copyright © 1984 by the Western Speech Communication Association. Reprinted by permission of the Western Speech Communication Association.

Functions of Nonverbal Communication

An important study of nonverbal communication and marital interaction found that nonverbal communication has three important functions in close relationships (Noller, 1984): conveying interpersonal attitudes, expressing emotion, and handling the ongoing interaction.

Conveying Interpersonal Attitudes Nonverbal messages are used to convey attitudes. Anthropologist Gregory Bateson described nonverbal communication as revealing "the nuances and intricacies of how two people are getting along" (quoted in Noller, 1984). Holding hands suggests intimacy; sitting on opposite sides of the couch suggests distance. Not looking at each other in conversation may suggest awkwardness or a lack of intimacy. Repeatedly ignoring sexual cues may well indicate a troubled relationship.

Expressing Emotion Our emotional states are expressed through our bodies. A depressed person walks slowly; a happy person walks with a spring. Smiles, frowns, furrowed brows, tight jaws, tapping fingers—all these express emotion. A lingering kiss expresses desire; a cursory one may connote emotional indifference. Expressing emotion is important because it lets our partner know how we are feeling so that he or she can respond appropriately. It also allows our partner to share our feeling, to laugh or weep with us, to feel the flush of desire or the coldness of distance.

Handling the Ongoing Interaction Nonverbal communication helps us handle the ongoing interaction by indicating interest and attention. An intent look indicates our interest in the conversation; a yawn indicates boredom. Posture and eye contact are especially important. Are we leaning toward the person with interest, or slumping back, thinking about something else? Do we look at the person who is talking, or are we distracted, glancing at other people as they walk by, watching the clock? In sexual interactions, nonverbal cues tell us whether our partner is sexually interested. Does he or she touch or kiss us in response to our touch or kiss? If he or she responds, our partner is giving us nonverbal cues to continue with the sexual interaction. If not, then he or she is discouraging us. In either case, we rely on nonverbal communication to direct the ongoing interaction.

Verbal and Nonverbal Agreement The messages that we send and receive contain verbal and nonverbal components. The verbal part expresses the basic content of the message, whereas the nonverbal part expresses what is known as the relationship or command part of the message. The relationship part of the message tells the attitude of the speaker (friendly, neutral, hostile) and indicates how the words are to be interpreted (as a joke, request, or command). The full content of any message has to be understood according to both the verbal and the nonverbal parts.

For a message to be most effective, both verbal and nonverbal components must be in agreement. If you are feeling loving, say "I love you," and your facial expression and voice both show tenderness; your message is clear. But if you say, "I love you" in a neutral tone of voice without facial expres-

Silence is the one great art of conversation.
William Hazlitt (1778–1830)

The cruelest lies are often told in silence.
Robert Louis Stevenson (1850–1890)

Words must be supported by one's entire conduct. If words and conduct are not in accord and not consistent, they will have no effect.
I Ching

sion, your message is ambiguous. If you say, "I love you" but clench your teeth and use an angry voice, your message is also unclear. Which takes precedence: the verbal or nonverbal message?

Proximity, Eye Contact, and Touching

Three of the most important forms of nonverbal communication are proximity, eye contact, and touching.

Proximity Proximity is nearness in physical space and time. Where we sit or stand in relation to another person signifies a level of intimacy or relationship. Many of our words that convey emotion relate to proximity, such as feeling "distant" or "close," or being "moved" by someone. We also "make the first move," "move in" on someone else's partner, or "move in together."

In a social gathering, the face-to-face distances between people when starting a conversation are clues to how the individuals wish to define the relationship. All cultures have an intermediate distance in face-to-face interactions that are neutral. In most cultures, decreasing the distance signifies an invitation to greater intimacy or a threat. (The expression "in your face" suggests aggressiveness.) Moving away denotes the desire to terminate the interaction. When you stand at an intermediate distance from someone at a party, you send the message, "intimacy is not encouraged." If you want to move closer, however, you risk the chance of rejection. Therefore, you must exchange clues, such as laughter and small talk, before moving closer in order to avoid facing direct rejection. If the person moves farther away during this exchange ("Excuse me, I think I see a friend"), he or she is signaling disinterest. But if the person moves closer, then there is the "proposal" for greater intimacy. As relationships develop, there is close gazing into each other's eyes, holding hands, walking with arms around each other—all of which require close proximity.

But because of cultural differences, there can be misunderstandings. The neutral intermediate distance for Latinos, for example, is much closer than for Anglos, who may misinterpret the same distance as "too close for comfort." In social settings, this can lead to problems. As Carlos Sluzki (1982) points out, "A person raised in a non-Latino culture will define as seductive behavior the same behavior that a person raised in a Latin culture defines as socially neutral." An Anglo may interpret the behavior as an invitation for intimacy, while the Latino may interpret it as neutral. Because of the miscue, the Anglo may withdraw or flirt, depending on his or her feelings. If the Anglo flirts, the Latino may respond to what he or she believes is the other's initiation. Additionally, among people whose culture features greater intermediate distances and less overt touching, such as Asian Americans, neutral responses may be misinterpreted negatively by those outside the culture.

The ability to correctly interpret nonverbal communication appears to be an important ingredient in successful relationships. "I can tell when something is bothering him/her" reveals the ability to read nonverbal clues, such as body language. This ability is especially important in ethnic groups and cultures that rely on nonverbal expression of feelings, such as Latino and Asian cultures. While the value placed on nonverbal expression may vary among groups and across cultures, the ability to communicate and

The physical distance between individuals connotes levels of intimacy or the type of relationship. The appropriate distance in face-to-face interactions may differ according to ethnicity.

understand nonverbally remains important in all cultures. A comparative study of Chinese and American romantic relationships, for example, found that shared nonverbal meanings were important for the success of relationships in both cultures (Gao, 1991).

Eye Contact   Much can be discovered about a relationship by watching how people look at each other. Making eye contact with another person, if only for a split second longer than usual, is a signal of interest. Brief and extended glances, in fact, play a significant role in women's expression of initial interest (Moore, 1985). (The word "flirting" is derived from the old English word "flitting," which means darting back and forth, as so often occurs when one flirts with his or her eyes.) When you can't take your eyes off another person, you probably have a strong attraction to him or her. In fact, you can easily distinguish people in love by their prolonged looking into each other's eyes. In addition to eye contact, dilated pupils may be an indication of sexual interest.

Research suggests that the amount of eye contact between a couple in conversation can distinguish between those who have high levels of conflict and those who don't. Those with the greatest degree of agreement have the greatest eye contact with each other (Beier & Sternberg, 1977). Those in conflict tend to avoid eye contact (unless it is a daggerlike stare). As we saw earlier, however, the level of eye contact may differ by culture.

Touching   It is difficult to overestimate the significance of touch. It is the most basic of all senses. Skin contains receptors for pleasure and pain, heat and cold, roughness and smoothness. "Touch is the mother sense and out of it, all the other senses have been derived," writes anthropologist Ashley Montagu (1986). Touch is a life-giving force for infants. If babies are not

The union and interaction of individuals is based upon mutual glances. This is perhaps the purest and most direct reciprocity that exists anywhere. . . . So tenacious and subtle is this union that it can only be maintained by the shortest and straightest line between the eyes, and the smallest deviation from it, the slightest glance aside, completely destroys the unique character of this union.

Georg Simmel

touched, they may fail to thrive and may even die. We hold hands with small children and those we love. Many of our words relating to emotions are derived from words referring to physical contact: "attraction," "attachment," and "feeling," for example. When we are moved by someone or something, we speak of being "touched."

But touch can also be a violation. Strangers or acquaintances may touch as if they were more familiar than they are. Your date or partner may touch you in a manner you don't like or want. And sexual harassment includes unwelcomed touching (see Chapter 18).

As with eye contact, touching is a form of communication. The amount of contact, from almost imperceptible touches to "hanging all over each other," helps differentiate lovers from strangers. How and where a person is touched can suggest friendship, intimacy, love, or sexual interest. Levels of touching differ between cultures and ethnic groups. Members of Latin cultures—Mexican Americans, Puerto Ricans, and Italians—as well as Jews, touch more than Americans of English or European descent, while Asian Americans touch less (Henley, 1977). Touching is important among African Americans. Writes prominent sex educator June Dobbs Butts (1981):

> Perhaps it is in the touching and the enjoyment of contact with human bodies that black culture is most alive, and is introduced into the life of the growing child. The fondness for touch permeates black culture from cradle to grave.

American men hugging each other in greeting has provoked controversy, as President Bill Clinton's publicly hugging men attests. Some consider male hugging unmanly, while others view it as a sign of openness. French men, however, often kiss each other on the cheeks as a greeting.

Despite stereotypes of women touching and men avoiding touch, studies suggest that there are no consistent differences between the sexes in the amount of overall touching (Andersen et al., 1987). Men do not seem to initiate touch with women any more than women do with men. Women are markedly unenthusiastic, however, about receiving touches from strangers and express greater concern in general about being touched. For women, there is greater touch avoidance unless there is a relational context with the man (Heslin & Alper, 1983). However, in situations with sexual overtones, men, regardless of their marital status, initiate more touching than women (Blumstein & Schwartz, 1983).

Growing research on touching indicates that it often signals intimacy, immediacy, and emotional closeness (Thayer, 1986). In fact, touch may very well be the *closest* form of nonverbal communication. One researcher writes: "If intimacy is proximity, then nothing comes closer than touch, the most intimate knowledge of another" (Thayer, 1986). And touching seems to go hand-in-hand with self-disclosure. Those who touch appear to self-disclose more; in fact, touch seems to be an important factor in prompting others to talk more about themselves (Heslin & Alper, 1983; Norton, 1983).

Sexual behavior relies above all else on touch: the touching of self and others; the touching of hands, faces, chests, arms, necks, legs, and genitals. (Sex is a contact sport, some say, with more truth than they realize.) In sexual interactions, touch takes precedence over sight, as we often close our eyes to caress, kiss, and make love. In fact, we close our eyes to better focus on the sensations aroused by touch; we shut out visual distractions to intensify the tactile experience of sexuality.

Science writer Diane Ackerman (1990) describes sex as "the ultimate touching." Of kissing, she writes:

> Setting out on a kiss caravan of the other's body, we map the new terrain with our fingertips and lips, pausing at the oasis of a nipple, the hillock of a thigh, the backbone's meandering riverbed. It is a kind of pilgrimage of touch, which leads us to the temple of our desire.

Erotic touching transforms our bodies into what the poet Walt Whitman called "the body electric." Our genitals, especially the clitoris and glans penis, have a high concentration of nerve endings that make them exquisitely sensitive to touch. But our body's erotic sensitivity does not end there. Erogenous zones, which include lips, mouth, and tongue; male and female nipples and breasts; ears, neck, anus, and buttocks—are all potentially sensitive to erotic touch.

SEXUAL COMMUNICATION

Communication is important in understanding, developing, and maintaining sexual relationships. In childhood and adolescence, communication is critical for transmitting sexual knowledge and values and in forming our sexual identities. As we establish our relationships, communication enables us to signal sexual interest and initiate sexual interactions. In developed relationships, communication allows us to explore and maintain our sexuality as a couple. (Perspective 1 discusses how *not* to communicate.)

Men and women use the same words but speak a different language.

Deborah Tannen

TEN RULES FOR AVOIDING INTIMACY

If you want to avoid intimacy, here are ten rules that have proved effective in nationwide testing with lovers, husbands and wives, parents, and children. Follow these guidelines, and we guarantee you'll never have an intimate relationship.

1. *Don't talk.* This is the basic rule for avoiding intimacy. If you follow this one rule, you will never have to worry about being intimate again. Sometimes, however, you may be forced to talk. But don't talk about anything meaningful. Talk about the weather, baseball, class, the stock market—anything but feelings.

2. *Never show your feelings.* Showing your feelings is almost as bad as talking, because feelings are ways of communicating. If you cry or show anger, sadness, or joy, you are giving yourself away. You might as well talk, and if you talk you could become intimate. So the best thing to do is remain expressionless (which, we admit, is a form of communication, but at least it's sending the message that you don't want to be intimate).

3. *Always be pleasant.* Always smile, always be friendly, especially if something's bothering you.

You'll be surprised at how effective hiding negative feelings from your partner is in preventing intimacy. It may even fool your partner into believing that everything's OK in your relationship.

4. *Always win.* If you can't be pleasant, try this one. Never compromise, never admit that your partner's point of view may be as good as yours. If you start compromising, it's an admission that you care about your partner's feelings, which is a dangerous step toward intimacy.

5. *Always keep busy.* Keeping busy at school or work will take you away from your partner, and you won't have to be intimate. Your partner may never figure out that you're using work to avoid intimacy. Because our culture values hard work, he or she will feel unjustified in complaining. Devoting yourself to your work will give your partner the message that he or she is not as important as your work. You can make your partner feel unimportant in your life without even talking!

6. *Always be right.* There is nothing worse than being wrong, because it is an indication that you are human. If you admit you're wrong, you might

Sexual Communication in Beginning Relationships

As we saw in Chapter 5, our interpersonal sexual scripts provide us with "instructions" on how to behave sexually, including the initiation of potentially sexual relationships. Because as a culture we share our interpersonal sexual scripts, we know how we are supposed to act at the beginning of a relationship. The very process of acting out interpersonal scripts, in fact, communicates sexual meanings (Simon & Gagnon, 1987). But how do we begin relationships? What is it that attracts us to someone?

It is human nature to think wisely and act foolishly.
Anatole France (1844–1924)

The Halo Effect   Imagine yourself unattached at a party. You notice someone standing next to you as you reach for some chips. In a split second, you decide whether you are interested in him or her. On what basis do you

have to admit your partner's right, and that will make him or her as good as you. If he or she is as good as you, then you might have to consider your partner, and before you know it, you will be intimate!

7. *Never argue.* If you can't always be right, don't argue at all. If you argue, you might discover that you and your partner are different. If you're different, you may have to talk about the differences in order to make adjustments. And if you begin making adjustments, you may have to tell your partner who you really are, what you really feel. Naturally, these revelations may lead to intimacy.

8. *Make your partner guess what you want.* Never tell your partner what you want. That way, when your partner tries to guess and is wrong (as he or she often will be), you can tell your partner that he or she doesn't really understand or love you. If your partner did love you, he or she would know what you want without asking. Not only will this prevent intimacy, but it will drive your partner crazy as well.

9. *Always look out for number one.* Remember, you are number one. All relationships exist to fulfill your needs, no one else's. Whatever you feel like doing is just fine. You're OK; your partner's not OK. If your partner can't satisfy your needs, he or she is narcissistic; after all, you are the one making all the sacrifices in the relationship.

10. *Keep the television on.* Keep the television turned on at all times: during dinner, while you're reading, when you're in bed, and while you're talking (especially if you're talking about something important). This rule may seem petty compared with the others, but it is good preventive action. Watching television keeps you and your partner from talking to each other. Best of all, it will keep you both from even noticing that you don't communicate. If you're cornered and have to talk, you can both be distracted by a commercial, a seduction scene, or the sound of gunfire. And when you actually think about it, wouldn't you rather be watching "The Simpsons" or "In Living Color" anyway?

This list is not complete. Everyone knows additional ways for avoiding intimacy. These may be your own inventions or techniques you have learned from your boyfriend or girlfriend, husband or wife, friends, or parents. To round out this compilation, list additional rules for avoiding intimacy on a separate sheet of paper. The person with the best list wins—and never has to be intimate again.

make that decision? Is it looks, personality, style, sensitivity, intelligence, or what?

If you're like most people, you base this decision consciously or unconsciously on appearance. If you decide to talk to the person, you probably formed a positive opinion on him or her based on appearance. In other words, he or she looked "cute," like a "fun person," gave a "good first impression," or seemed "interesting." As Elaine Hatfield and Susan Sprecher (1986) point out:

> Appearance is the sole characteristic apparent in every social interaction. Other information may be more meaningful but far harder to ferret out. People do not have their IQs tattooed on their foreheads, nor do they display their diplomas prominently about their persons. Their financial status is a private matter between themselves, their bankers, and the Internal Revenue Service.

Physical attractiveness is particularly important during the initial meeting and early stages of a relationship. If you don't know anything else about a person, you tend to judge him or her on appearance.

Most people would deny that they are attracted to others just because of their looks. We like to think we are deeper than that. But looks are important unconsciously. We tend to infer qualities based on looks. This inference is based on what is known as the **halo effect,** the assumption that attractive people possess more desirable social characteristics than unattractive people. In one well-known experiment, students were shown pictures of attractive people and asked to describe what they thought these people were like (Dion, Berscheid, & Walster, 1972). Attractive men and women were assumed to be more sensitive, kind, warm, sexually responsive, strong, poised, and outgoing than others; they were assumed to be more exciting and to have better characters than "ordinary" people. Research indicates that, overall, the differences in perceptions between very attractive and average people are minimal. It is when attractive and average people are compared to those considered to be unattractive that there are pronounced differences; those perceived as unattractive are rated more negatively (Hatfield & Sprecher, 1986).

Interest and Opening Lines

After we have sized someone up based on his or her appearance, what happens next in interactions between men and women? (Gay and lesbian beginning relationships are discussed later.) Does the man initiate the encounter? On the surface yes, but in reality, the woman often "covertly initiates . . . by sending nonverbal signals of availability and interest" (Metts & Cupach, 1989). The woman will "glance" at him once or twice and "catch" his eye; she may smile or flip her hair. If the man moves into her physical space, the woman then relies on nodding, leaning close, smiling, or laughing (Moore, 1985).

If the man believes the woman is interested, he then initiates a conversation using an "opening line." The opening line tests the woman's interest and availability. There are an array of opening lines that men use. According to women, the most effective are innocuous, such as "I feel a little embarrassed, but I'd like to meet you" or "Are you a student here?" The least effective are sexually blunt, such as "You really turn me on." Women more than men prefer direct but innocuous opening lines over cute-flippant ones, such as "What's a good-looking babe like you doing in a college like this?"

The First Move

After we first meet someone, we weigh each others' attitudes, values, and philosophy to see if we are compatible. We evaluate their sense of humor, their intelligence, their "partner" potential, their ability to function in a relationship, their sex appeal, and so on. Based on our overall judgment, we may continue the relationship. If the relationship continues in a romantic vein, we may move into one that includes some kind of physical intimacy. To signal this transition from nonphysical to physical intimacy, one of us must "make the first move." Making the first move marks the transition from a potentially sexual relationship to an actual one.

If the relationship develops along traditional gender-role patterns, one of the partners, usually the male, will make the first move to initiate sexual intimacy, whether it is kissing, petting, or engaging in sexual intercourse

(O'Sullivan & Byers, 1992). The point at which this occurs generally depends on two factors: the level of intimacy and the length of the relationship (Sprecher, 1989). The more emotionally involved the couple, the more likely they will be sexually involved as well. The duration of the relationship also affects the likelihood of sexual involvement.

Initial sexual involvement can occur as early as the first meeting or later, as part of a well-established relationship. While some people become sexually involved immediately ("lust at first sight"), the majority begin their sexual involvements in the context of an ongoing relationship. Strategies for "making the first move" vary depending on the motives of each person and the nature of the relationship. If neither person knows the other well, both are likely to rely on traditional sexual scripts, with the man making the first overt move. If the motive for both partners is sexual pleasure, both may acknowledge their desire for noninvolvement. But if one desires pleasure and the other commitment, different strategies may be used. The pleasure-oriented partner, for example, may cease his or her overtures, feign commitment, or utilize sexual pressure. The other partner may withhold sex unless a commitment is made.

In new or developing relationships, communication is generally indirect and ambiguous about sexuality. As one communication scholar notes about developing relationships, "The typical relationship process is not dominated by open, direct communication, but rather involves the construction of a web of ambiguity by which parties signal their relationship indirectly" (Baxter, 1987). Direct strategies are sometimes used to initiate sexual involvement, but these usually occur when the person is confident in the other's interest or is not concerned about being rejected. A study of sexual initiation among college students found that males and females used similar strategies to initiate sex (O'Sullivan & Byers, 1992).

In new relationships, we communicate *indirectly* about sex because while we want to become sexually involved with the other person, we also want to avoid rejection. By using indirect strategies, such as turning down the lights, moving closer, touching the other's face or hair, we may test the other's interest in sexual involvement. If the other person responds positively to our cues, we can initiate a sexual encounter. At the same time, if the other turns the lights up, moves farther away, or does not respond to our touching, he or she gives the message of disinterest. Because we have not made direct overtures, we can save face. The sexual cues, innuendos, and signals can pass unacknowledged. Consequently, a direct refusal does not occur. We can breathe a sigh of relief because we have avoided rejection.

Because so much of our sexual communication is indirect, ambiguous, or nonverbal, there is a high risk of misinterpretation between women and men. There are four basic reasons for this (Cupach & Metts, 1991). First, men and women tend to disagree about *when* sexual activities should take place in a relationship. Men more than women tend to want sexual involvement earlier and with a lower level of intimacy. Second, men may be skeptical about women's refusals. Men often misinterpret women's cues, such as misinterpreting a woman's friendly touch as a sexual cue. Men also believe that women often say "no" when they actually mean "coax me." Men believe that women say "no" as token resistance.

Third, because we are indirect, women may be unclear in signaling their disinterest. They may turn their face aside, move a man's hand back to its

It was fortunate that love did not need words, or else it would be full of misunderstandings and foolishness.
Hermann Hesse (1877–1962)

proper place, say that it's getting late, or try to change the subject. Research indicates that women are most effective by making strong, direct verbal refusals; men become more compliant if women are persistent in such refusals (Christopher & Frandsen, 1990; Murnen, Perot, & Byrne, 1989). Fourth, men are more likely than women to interpret nonsexual behavior or cues as sexual. As William Cupach and Sandra Metts (1991) write, "Men may wear sex-colored glasses." While both men and women flirt for fun, men are more likely to flirt with a sexual purpose. Reflecting their own tendencies, men are more likely to interpret a woman's flirtation as sexual.

Directing Sexual Activity   As we begin a sexual involvement, we have several tasks to accomplish. First, we need to practice safer sex (see Chapter 16). We should gather information about our partner's sexual history, determine whether he or she knows how to practice safer sex, and use condoms. Unlike much of our sexual communication, which is nonverbal or ambiguous, practicing safer sex requires direct verbal discussion. Second, we must discuss birth control (unless both partners have agreed to try for pregnancy). Contraceptive responsibility, like safer sex, requires verbal communication (see Chapter 12).

In addition to communicating about safer sex and contraception, we also need to communicate about what we like and what we need sexually. What kind of foreplay do we like? Afterplay? Do we like to be orally or manually stimulated during intercourse? If so, how? What does each partner need to be orgasmic? Many of our needs and desires can be communicated nonverbally by movements or by giving our partner physical cues. But if our partner does not pick up our nonverbal signals or cues, we need to discuss them directly and clearly to avoid ambiguity.

Gay and Lesbian Relationships Gay men and lesbians, like heterosexuals, rely on both nonverbal and verbal communication in expressing sexual interest in others. Unlike heterosexuals, however, they cannot necessarily assume that the person in whom they are interested is of the same sexual orientation. Instead, they must rely on specific identifying factors, such as meeting at a gay or lesbian bar, wearing a gay/lesbian pride button, participating in gay/lesbian events, or being introduced by friends to others identified as lesbian or gay (Tessina, 1989). In situations where sexual orientation is not clear, gay men and lesbians use "gaydar," gay radar, in which they look for clues as to orientation. They give ambiguous cues as to their own orientation while looking for cues from the other. These cues can include mannerisms, speech patterns, slang usage, or lingering glances. They may also include the mention of specific places for entertainment or recreation that are frequented mainly by lesbians or gay men, music or songs that can be interpreted to have "gay" meanings, such as "Strangers in the Night" or "Secret Love," or movies with gay or lesbian themes, such as *Maurice* or *Desert Hearts*. Tina Tessina (1989) writes:

> Drop a hint about your Holly Near records, or say, "I just came from the Rodeo in San Francisco." If you get a naive response, such as "Oh, who is that?" or "Are you a cowboy?" you can easily step back.

Gay men and lesbians, like heterosexuals, prefer innocuous opening lines. To prevent awkwardness, the opening line usually does not make an overt reference to orientation unless the other person is clearly lesbian or gay. "Go slowly," Tessina suggests. "What you need to know will find its way into the conversation before too long" (Tessina, 1989).

Once a like orientation is established, lesbians and gay men engage in nonverbal processes to express interest. There are mutual glances, smiles, subtle body movements; someone initiates a conversation with an opening line. In these beginning interactions, physical appearance is important, especially for gay males.

Because of their socialization as males, gay men are more likely than lesbians to initiate sexual activity earlier in the relationship. In large part, this is because both partners are free to initiate and because men are not expected to refuse sex as women are. But this same sexual socialization makes it difficult for some gay men to refuse sexual activity. As therapist Rik Isensee (1990) writes:

> As men we've been socialized to be "ready and willing" at any moment and this can create unrealistic expectations about our availability for sexual relations. We may find it easier to have sex, for example, than to admit our desire for attention or comfort.

Lesbians do not initiate sex as often as do gay or heterosexual men. In contrast to men, they often feel uncomfortable because women have not been socialized to sexually initiate. Philip Blumstein and Pepper Schwartz (1983) write that "many lesbians are not comfortable in the role of sexual aggressor and it is a major reason why they have sex less often than other kinds of couples."

Sexual Communication in Established Relationships

As a relationship develops and becomes established, the partners begin modifying their individual sexual scripts as they interact with each other. The scripts become less rigid and conventional as each adapts to the uniqueness of their partner. The couple develops a shared sexual script. Through their sexual interactions, they learn what each other likes, dislikes, wants, or needs. Much of this learning takes place nonverbally as partners in established relationships, like those in emerging relationships, tend to be indirect and ambiguous in their sexual communication. The reason that partners are indirect in established relationships is the same as for those in new relationships: They want to avoid rejection. Indirection allows them to express sexual interest while at the same time protecting themselves from loss of face.

Initiating Sexual Activity Within established relationships, men continue to overtly initiate sexual encounters more frequently than women. But women continue to signal their willingness. They pace the frequency of intercourse by showing their interest with nonverbal cues, such as giving a "certain look" or lighting candles by the bed. They may also overtly suggest "doing the wild thing." Their partners pick up on the cues and "initiate" sexual interactions. In marital relationships, many women feel more comfortable with overtly initiating sex. In part this may be related to the decreasing significance of the double standard as relationships continue. In a new relationship, the woman initiating intercourse may be viewed negatively, as a sign of promiscuity. But in an established relationship, the woman's initiation may be viewed positively, as an expression of love. The increase may also be the result of couples becoming more egalitarian in their gender-role attitudes.

Not surprisingly, sexual initiations are more often successful in marital relationships than in new or dating relationships. There are several reasons for this. First, long-term partners know each other's sexual feelings and routines and can evaluate their partner's likely interest. If they don't sense their partner's potential interest, they won't initiate. Second, people may engage in sex even if they are not in the mood because they want to satisfy their partner (either as a gift of love or as placating behavior), because they would feel guilty otherwise, because it is "no big deal," or because they don't want to hurt their partner's feelings. Positive responses to initiation are usually nonverbal, such as beginning or continuing the sexual interaction by kissing or touching erotically.

Unlike new relationships, sexual disinterest is communicated verbally in established relationships (Byers & Heinlein, 1989). In established relationships, a direct refusal is not viewed as much of a threat to the relationship as it is in new relationships. In an established relationship, refusals are usually accompanied by a face-saving explanation, "I would like to but am too tired." "You are pretty sexy, but I have to finish studying for my human sexuality exam." "Let's wait until after the kids go over to their friend's." Such direct refusals are also more effective than indirect ones.

Partners in established relationships tend to develop a shared sexual script. Touching and sharing feelings (by smiling or laughing, for example) are two forms of nonverbal communication that help people learn about each other.

In most cases, when a partner refuses sexual initiation, the couple agrees not to have sex. They generally agree to have sex at a different time or "agree to disagree," in which case disagreement is acceptable and not a threat. Partners are most satisfied in the way the disagreement is resolved if the initiation is made verbally, such as, "Do you want to make love?" than if the initiation is made physically, such as by erotic touching or kissing. Partners find it easier to say or accept "no" to a verbal request than to a physical one.

Although women are more likely to refuse sexual initiation more frequently than men, it is because men overtly initiate more frequently than women. Women are also more likely than men to respond positively to sexual initiation. If we consider the ratio of initiations to refusals rather than total numbers (because women initiate less frequently), the ratio of acceptances to refusals is similar for men and women. Contrary to the common stereotype, women do not restrict sexual activities any more than men (Byers & Heinlein, 1989; O'Sullivan & Byers, 1992).

Lesbian and Gay Interactions In both lesbian and gay relationships, the more emotionally expressive partner is likely to initiate sexual interaction (Blumstein & Schwartz, 1983). The gay or lesbian partner who talks more about feelings, who spontaneously gives his or her partner hugs or kisses, is the one who most often begins sexual activity.

One of the key differences between heterosexuals and gay males and lesbians, however, is how they handle extrarelational sex. In marriage and committed heterosexual relationships, both partners are expected to be sexually exclusive; when heterosexual men and women engage in affairs, they ordinarily keep such matters secret. In gay and lesbian culture, by contrast, sexual exclusivity is often negotiable. Sexual exclusiveness is not necessarily equated with commitment or fidelity. It is acceptable, sometimes expected, to be open with one's partner about extrarelational sex.

As a result of these differing norms, lesbians and gay men must decide early in the relationship whether they will be sexually exclusive (Isensee, 1990). If they choose to have a nonexclusive relationship, they need to discuss how outside sexual interests will be handled. They must decide whether to tell each other, whether to have affairs with friends; they should discuss what degree of emotional involvement is acceptable, and how to deal with jealousy. They need to deal with STD and HIV risks resulting from a third person's being in the relationship.

Communication Patterns in Intimate Relationships

Communication Patterns and Satisfaction Researchers studying marital satisfaction have found a number of communication patterns that offer clues to enhancing our intimate relationships (Hendrick, 1981; Noller & Fitzpatrick, 1991; Schaap, Buunk & Kerkstra, 1988). They found that men and women in satisfied relationships tended to have the following common characteristics regarding communication:

- *The ability to disclose or reveal private thoughts and feelings, especially positive ones, to each other.* Dissatisfied spouses tend to disclose mostly negative thoughts to their partners. Satisfied couples say such things as "I love you," "You're sexy," or "I feel vulnerable, please hold me." Unhappy couples may also say they love each other, but more often they say things like "Don't touch me; I can't stand you," "You turn me off," or "This relationship makes me miserable and frustrated."

- *The expression by both partners of more-or-less equal levels of affective disclosures.* Both are likely to say such words as "You make me feel happy," "I love you more than I can ever say," or "I love the way you touch me."

- *More time spent talking, discussing personal topics, and expressing feelings in positive ways.* They talk about their sexual feelings, the fun they have in bed together.

- *A willingness to accept conflict but to engage in conflict in nondestructive ways.* They view conflict as a natural part of intimate relationships. When they have sexual disagreements, they do not accuse or blame; instead, they seek common ground and are willing to compromise.

- *Less frequent conflict and less time spent in conflict.* Both satisfied and unsatisfied couples, however, experience conflicts about the same topics, especially about communication, sex, and personality characteristics.

- *The ability to accurately encode (send) verbal and nonverbal messages and accurately decode (understand) such messages from their spouses.* This is especially important for men. In satisfied couples, for example, if a man wants his partner to initiate sex more often, he can say, "I'd like you to initiate sex more often," and his partner will understand the message correctly.

In dissatisfied couples, the man may stop initiating sex, hoping his partner will be forced to initiate more often in order to have sex. Or he may ask his partner to initiate sex more often, but his partner may mistakenly interpret it as a personal attack.

Many of these communication patterns appear to hold true for gay and lesbian relationships as well. One study of gay couples reported that, in contrast to dissatisfied couples, highly satisfied couples had less conflict, more positive feelings of love, and appreciated the partner and relationship (Jones & Bates, 1988).

Gender Differences in Marital Communication For some time, researchers have been aware of gender differences in general communication patterns. More recently, they have discovered specific gender differences in marital communication (Noller & Fitzpatrick, 1991; Thompson & Walker, 1989).

- *Wives send clearer messages to their husbands than their husbands send to them.* Wives tend to be more sensitive and responsive to their husbands' messages, both during conversation and during conflict. They are more likely to reply to either positive messages ("You look yummy") or negative messages ("You look awful") than are their husbands, who may not reply at all to such statements.

- *Husbands more than wives tend to give neutral messages.* An example would be, "It doesn't matter to me." Wives give more positive or negative messages. Because women tend to smile or laugh when they send messages, however, they send fewer clearly neutral messages. The neutral responses of husbands make it more difficult for wives to decode what their partners are really trying to say. Imagine a wife responding to her husband's sexual overture by saying, "Let's do it later, when I'm not so tired." Her husband gives a neutral response: "Whatever." But the response is unclear: Does the husband really not care, or is he pretending he doesn't to avoid possible conflict?

- *Wives tend to set the emotional tone of an argument.* Although communication differences in arguments between husbands and wives are usually small, wives escalate conflict with negative verbal and nonverbal messages ("Don't give me that!") or deescalate arguments by setting an atmosphere of agreement ("I understand your feelings"). Husbands' inputs are less important in setting the climate for resolving or escalating conflicts. Wives tend to use emotional appeals and threats more than husbands, who tend to reason, seek conciliation, and try to postpone or end an argument. A wife is more likely to say, "If you loved me, you would try to understand my needs," while a husband is more likely to say, "Be rational. Let's analyze the problem like reasonable human beings."

DEVELOPING COMMUNICATION SKILLS

Studies suggest that poor communication skills precede the outset of marital problems (Markman, 1981; Markman et al., 1987). The material that follows will assist you in understanding and developing your skills in communicating about sexual matters.

Love can be angry . . . with a kind of anger in which there is no gall, like the dove's and not the raven's.
Augustine, Bishop of Hippo
(354–430)

Anger causes a man to be far from the truth.

Hasidic saying

Developing Self-Awareness

Before we can communicate with others, we must first know how we feel ourselves. Yet we often place obstacles in the way. First, we suppress "unacceptable" feelings, especially anger, hurt, frustration, and jealousy. After a while, we don't even consciously experience them. Second, we deny our feelings. If we are feeling hurt and our partner looks at our pained expression and asks us what we're feeling, we may reply, "Nothing." We may feel nothing because we have anesthetized our feelings. Third, we displace our feelings. Instead of recognizing that we are jealous, we may accuse our partner of being jealous; instead of feeling hurt, we may say our partner is hurt.

Becoming aware of ourselves requires us to become aware of our feelings. Perhaps the first step toward this self-awareness is realizing that feelings are simply emotional states—they are neither good nor bad in themselves. As feelings, however, they need to be felt, whether they are warm or cold, pleasurable or painful. They do not necessarily need to be acted out or expressed. We do not need to censor our feelings or deny them. It is the acting out that holds the potential for problems or hurt.

Feelings are valuable guides for action. If we feel irritated at our partner, the irritation is a signal that something is wrong, and we can work toward change. But if we suppress or deny our feeling, perhaps because we are fearful of conflict, we do not have the impetus for change. The cause remains, and the irritation increases until it is blown out of proportion; a minor annoyance becomes a major source of anger. If we are bothered by our partner's bad breath, we can say so and he or she has the option of brushing his or her teeth. But if we suppress or deny our irritation, the bad breath may continue; we may alternately feel alienated or repulsed without giving our partner the opportunity to change. We may altogether avoid being in intimate situations with him or her; our sexual ardor may disappear.

Talking About Sex

Obstacles to Sexual Discussions
The process of articulating our feelings about sex can be very difficult. There are several reasons for this. First, we rarely have models for talking about sex. As children and adolescents, we probably never spoke with our parents about sex. If we talked about sex in their presence, they probably discouraged it or felt uncomfortable. We learned that sex is not an appropriate subject of conversation in "polite" company.

Second, talking about sexual matters defines us as being interested in sex, and interest in sex is often identified with being sexually obsessive, immoral, prurient, or "bad." If the sexual topic is tabooed, we risk further danger of being labeled "bad." While we can sometimes talk about such things as heterosexual intercourse or oral sex, other behaviors may be culturally or personally tabooed. We may feel uncomfortable about discussing masturbation, attraction to others, homoerotic feelings, curiosity about bondage, sexual fantasies, and so on.

Third, we may feel that talking about sex will threaten our relationship. We don't talk about tabooed sexual feelings, fantasies, or desires because we fear our partner may be repelled or disgusted. We also are reluctant to talk about sexual difficulties or problems because of their inherent riskiness.

Since sexuality is central to our identities, we are fearful that discussing problems will damage the other's self-esteem; we may feel our partner will respond angrily or reject us.

Sexual Vocabulary We shift our sexual vocabulary depending on the context or to whom we are talking. Some words are uncomfortable or inappropriate in different contexts. To describe sexuality, we have medical terms that objectify and deeroticize it: "penis," "vulva," "vagina," "sexual intercourse." These are the words we use in formal situations, as in medical or academic settings or when talking with our parents or our children; they are the acceptable terms for the printed page and for talk shows. This noneritic language arose in the nineteenth century to replace the commonplace sexual language that is now considered slang or obscene (Foucault, 1980). The fact that we generally use these terms when (and if) we discuss our sexuality with others reveals the degree to which we wish to hide our eroticism.

Slang words retain their sexual connotations: "cock," "cunt," "screw." These are the "dirty" words of our language. They are most often used in informal settings, among friends or peers. Gay men and lesbians have developed their own colloquial or slang terms. Among lesbians and gay men, "husband" refers to the dominant member of a couple; gay men refer to nipples as "tits." Among the terms gay whites use to refer to the penis are "dick," "tool," and "rod," while gay African Americans prefer terms such as "pole," "junior," and "spermin' Herman" (Mays et al., 1992).

Colloquial and slang words have powerful connotations. To modify their power, we have euphemisms, terms such as "making love" and "sleeping together," whose emotional impact stands somewhere between medical and slang terms. And, finally, we have our own private vocabulary of "pet names" for sexual body parts, such as "Miss Muff" or "Wilbur," that may develop within a relationship and be shared only with our partner (Cornog, 1986).

Obscene and slang words tend to be part of a male language. Men can use them among themselves and sometimes with women and not lose status. In fact, such words often confer status among men, demonstrating masculinity, daring, and contempt for convention. Obscenities and slang are not as frequently used among women. Most studies reveal that men have a far larger, more varied, slang vocabulary than women in virtually every field of sexuality except for menstrual slang expressions (Ernster, 1975). Although both males and females tend to use medico-scientific language when talking with parents and members of the other sex, men are more likely to use slang in these contexts than women. Furthermore, men change their terms less frequently in varying context than women do (Sanders & Robinson, 1979). Women tend to use medico-scientific terms in most contexts; when they do not, they use euphemisms.

Because a man and a woman tend to use a different sexual vocabulary, it can be difficult for them to communicate with each other about sexual matters. A woman may be offended by the vocabulary her boyfriend uses among his friends; the man may think his girlfriend is unduly reticent because she uses euphemisms to describe sexuality. A couple must often negotiate the language they will use in order not to offend each other. Sometimes this problem will be resolved into open, acceptable communication; at other times, it may result in silence.

Four-letter words (itself a euphemistic expression to skirt having to use the words) are more strictly taboo than any others in the English language. . . . The sexual act described in fuck *refers to standard sexual behavior, and so there is nothing intrinsically "bad" or "dirty" in this word. Any word is an innocent collection of sounds until a community surrounds it with connotations and then decrees that it cannot be used in certain speech situations; this is what happened when the English speech community relegated* fuck *to forbidden status around 1650.*

Peter Farb

The Keys to Good Communication

Self-Disclosure Self-disclosure creates the environment for mutual understanding (Derlega, Metts, Potronio, & Margulis, 1993). Most people know us only through the conventional roles we play as female/male, wife/husband, parent/child. These roles, however, do not necessarily reflect our deepest selves. If we act as if we are nothing more than our roles, we may reach a point at which we no longer know who we are. Almost 150 years ago, Nathaniel Hawthorne cautioned, "No man, for any considerable period, can wear one face to himself, and another to the multitude, without finally getting bewildered as to which may be true."

Through the process of self-disclosure we not only reveal ourselves to others, we also discover who we are. We discover the depths of feeling we have hidden, repressed, or ignored. We nurture forgotten aspects of ourselves by bringing them to the surface. Moreover, self-disclosure is reciprocal. In the process of our sharing, others share themselves with us. Men are less likely than women, however, to disclose intimate aspects of themselves. Because they have been taught to be strong, they are more reluctant to express tenderness or feelings of vulnerability. Women find it easier to disclose their feelings because they have been taught from childhood to express themselves (Notarius & Johnson, 1982). These differences can drive wedges between men and women. Even when people live together or are married, they feel lonely because there is no contact. And the worst kind of loneliness is feeling alone when we are with someone with whom we want to feel close.

Trust When we talk about intimate relationships, the two words that most frequently pop up are "love" and "trust." And as we saw in our discussion of the prototypes of love in Chapter 8, trust is the primary characteristic we associate with love. But what, exactly, is trust? **Trust** is the belief in the reliability and integrity of a person.

When a person says, "Trust me," he or she is asking for something that does not easily occur. For trust to develop, three conditions must exist. First, a relationship has to exist with the likelihood of continuing. We generally do not trust strangers or people we have just met with information that makes us vulnerable, such as our sexual anxieties. We trust people with whom we have a significant relationship. Second, we must be able to predict how a person is likely to behave. If we are married or in a committed relationship, we trust that our partner will not do something that will hurt us, such as have an affair. In fact, if we discover that our partner is involved in an affair, we often speak of our trust being violated or destroyed. If trust is destroyed, it is because the predictability of sexual exclusiveness is no longer there. Third, the other person must also have acceptable options available to him or her. If we were marooned on a desert island alone with our partner, he or she would have no choice but to be sexually monogamous. But if a third person, sexually attractive to our partner, swam ashore a year later, our partner would have an alternative. Our partner would then have a choice of being sexually exclusive or nonexclusive; his or her behavior would then be evidence of trustworthiness—or the lack of it.

Trust is critical in close relationships for two reasons. First, self-disclosure requires trust because it makes you vulnerable. A person will not self-dis-

CHAPTER 9 COMMUNICATING ABOUT SEX

Good communication requires trust, self-disclosure, and feedback.

close if he or she believes the information may be misused, by mocking or revealing a secret, for example. Second, the degree to which you trust a person influences the way you are likely to interpret ambiguous or unexpected messages from him or her. If your partner says he or she wants to study alone tonight, you are likely to take the statement at face value if you have a high level of trust. But if you have a low level of trust, you may believe he or she is going to be meeting someone else.

Trust in personal relationships has both a behavioral and motivational component. The behavioral component has to do with the probability that a person will act in a trustworthy manner. The motivational component consists of the reasons a person engages in trustworthy actions. While the behavioral element is important in all types of relationships, the motivational element is important in close relationships. One has to be trustworthy for the "right" reasons. As long as you trust your mechanic to charge you fairly for rebuilding your car's engine, you don't care *why* he or she is trustworthy. But you *do* care why your partner is trustworthy. For example, you want your partner to be sexually exclusive because he or she loves you or is attracted to you. Being faithful because of duty or not being able to find anyone better is the wrong motivation. Disagreements about the motivational bases for trust are often a source of conflict. "I want to be with you because you love me, not because you need me," or "You don't really love me; you're just saying that because you want sex," are typical examples of conflict about motivation.

When my love swears that she is made of truth I do believe her, though I know she lies.
William Shakespeare

Ninety-nine lies may save you, but the hundredth will give you away.
West African proverb

Feedback   Self-disclosure is reciprocal. If we self-disclose, we expect our partner to self-disclose as well. As we self-disclose, we build trust; as we withhold self-disclosure, we erode trust. To withhold ourselves is to imply that we don't trust the other person, and if we don't, he or she will not trust us.

A critical element in communication is **feedback,** the ongoing process in which participants and their messages create a given result and are subsequently modified by that result. If my partner self-discloses to me, my response to that self-disclosure is my feedback. My partner's response is feedback to my feedback. It is a continuous process. The most important form of feedback for improving relationships is *constructive* feedback. Constructive feedback focuses on self-disclosing information that will help your partner understand the consequences of his or her actions on you and on the relationship. For example, if your partner discloses his or her doubts about the relationship, you can respond in a number of ways. Among these are remaining silent, venting anger, expressing indifference, or giving constructive feedback. Of these responses, constructive feedback is the most likely to encourage positive change.

Remaining silent is usually a negative response, perhaps as powerful as saying outright that you do not want your partner to self-disclose this type of information. If you respond angrily, you may convey the message to your partner that self-disclosing will lead to arguments rather than understanding and possible change. If you remain indifferent, responding neither negatively nor positively, you show your partner there is no point in making a self-disclosure. But you can also acknowledge your partner's feelings as valid (rather than right or wrong) and disclose how you feel in response to his or her statement. This acknowledgment and response are constructive feedback. Constructive feedback may or may not remove your partner's doubts, but it opens up the possibility for change, whereas silence, anger, and indifference do not. (See Perspective 2 for guidelines on giving effective feedback.)

CONFLICT AND INTIMACY

Conflict is a special type of communication. **Conflict** is the communication process in which people perceive interference from others in achieving their goals.

We expect love to unify us, but sometimes it doesn't. Two people do not become one when they love each other, although at first they may have this feeling. While their love may not be an illusion, their sense of ultimate oneness is. In reality, we retain our individual identities, needs, wants, and pasts—even while loving one another. It is a paradox that the more intimate two people become, the more likely they may be to experience conflict. But it is not conflict itself that is dangerous to intimate relationships; it is the manner in which the conflict is handled. The presence of conflict does not necessarily indicate that love is going or has gone. It may mean that love is *growing*.

Conflict in relationships is expressed differently by different ethnic groups. Non-Latino whites tend to seek either dominance, which is confrontational and controlling, or integration, which is solution-oriented.

Conflict is natural in intimate re-lationships because each person has her or his own unique iden-tity, values, needs, and history.

They seem to believe that conflict is more natural and expected in a rela-tionship, perhaps because of the high value placed on individualism. Both African Americans and Mexican Americans view conflict less positively; they believe that conflict has both short-term and long-term negative effects. A comparison between whites and African Americans found that whites tend to be more solution-oriented than blacks, who tend to be more controlling. In interpersonal relationships, both groups tend to identify con-flict in terms of issues and goals. By contrast, Mexican Americans view con-flict more in relationship terms; conflict occurs when a relationship is out of balance or harmony (Collier, 1991).

These differing views of conflicts and conflict resolution affect each group's willingness to deal with sexual conflicts. Understanding these dif-ferences will assist in resolving sexual problems and issues.

Keep thy eyes wide open before marriage, and half shut afterwards.
Benjamin Franklin (1706–1790)

Types of Conflict

Basic Versus Nonbasic Conflicts Two types of conflict—basic and nonbasic—affect the stability of a relationship. Basic conflicts challenge the fundamental assumptions or rules of a relationship, whereas nonbasic con-flicts do not.

Argument is the worst sort of conversation.
Jonathan Swift (1667–1745)

GUIDELINES FOR EFFECTIVE FEEDBACK

Some guidelines (developed by David Johnston for the Minnesota Peer Program) will help you engage in dialogue and feedback with your partner:

1. *Focus on "I" statements.* An "I" statement is a statement about *your* feelings: "I feel unloved." By contrast, "You" statements tell another person how *he* or *she* is, feels, or thinks: "You don't love me." "You" statements are often blaming or accusatory. Because "I" messages don't carry blame, the recipient is less likely to be defensive or resentful.

2. *Focus on behavior rather than on the person.* If you focus on a person's behavior rather than on the person, you are more likely to secure change, because a person can change behaviors, but not himself or herself. If you want your partner to stimulate your clitoris during intercourse, say, "I'd like you to touch my clitoris while we're making love because it would help me have an orgasm." This statement focuses on behavior that can be changed. If you say, "You're not a particularly hot lover," you are attacking the person, and he is likely to respond defensively: "Talk about crummy lovers, how come you need my help to have an orgasm? What's wrong with you?"

3. *Focus feedback on observations rather than on inferences or judgments.* Focus your feedback on what you actually observe rather than what you think the behavior means. "I don't receive enough stimulation during intercourse to have an orgasm" is an observation. "You don't really care about how I feel because you never try to help me have an orgasm" is an inference that our partner's sexual interactions indicate a lack of regard. The inference moves the discussion from sexual stimulation to the partner's caring.

4. *Focus feedback on observations based on a more-or-less continuum.* Behaviors fall on a continuum. Your partner doesn't *always* do or not do a particular thing. When you say your partner does something sometimes, or even most of the time, you are *measuring* behavior. "The last three times you wanted to make love I didn't want to because of the way you smelled" is a measuring statement; its accuracy can be tested. But if you say your partner *always* (or *never*) does something, you are probably distorting reality. "You *always* smell when you come to bed" or "You *never* take a shower before sex" are probably exaggerations that may provoke hostile responses. "What do you mean? I showered last month. You got some kind of hang-up?"

Basic relationship conflicts revolve around carrying out marital or partner roles and obligations in a relationship. In marriage, for example, being monogamous, providing companionship, working, and rearing children are some of these roles. It is assumed that partners will be sexually exclusive. But if one partner decides, against the wishes of the other, to have a sexually open relationship, a basic conflict is likely to occur because it breaks a fundamental marital premise. No room for compromise exists in such a matter. If one partner cannot convince the other to change his or her beliefs, the conflict is likely to destroy the relationship.

Nonbasic conflicts do not strike at the heart of a relationship. If a couple

The return of understanding after estrangement: Everything must be treated with tenderness at the beginning so that the return may lead to understanding.

I Ching

5. *Focus feedback on sharing ideas or offering alternatives rather than giving advice*. No one likes being told what to do. Unsolicited advice often produces anger or resentment, because advice implies that you know more about what a person needs to do than he or she does. Advice implies a lack of respect. But by sharing ideas and offering alternatives, you give the other person the freedom to decide based on his or her own perceptions and goals. "What you need to do is pay attention to some of my needs" is advice. "I wish I could be more orgasmic in intercourse. Let's try some other things. If I had more clitoral stimulation, like your rubbing my clitoris when we are making love. . . . something like that would be great. . . . Or I could stimulate myself. What do you think?" Such responses offer alternatives.

6. *Focus feedback according to its value for the recipient.* If your partner says something that upsets you, your initial response may be to lash back. A cathartic response may make you feel better for the time being, but it may not be useful for your partner. For example, your partner says that he or she has been faking orgasms. You can respond with anger or accusations, or you can express concern and try to find out why he or she felt it was necessary.

7. *Focus feedback on the amount the recipient can process.* Don't overload your partner with your response. Your partner's disclosure may touch deep, pent-up feelings in you, but he or she may not be able to comprehend all that you say. If you respond to your partner's revelation of doubts about your relationship with a listing of all the doubts you have *ever* experienced about it, you may overwhelm your partner.

8. *Focus feedback at the appropriate time and place.* When you discuss anything of importance, choose an appropriate time and place so that nothing will distract you. Choose a time when you are not likely to be interrupted. Turn the television off, and put the answering machine on. Also, choose a time that is relatively stress-free. Talking about something of great personal importance just before an exam or a business meeting is likely to sabotage any attempt at communication. Finally, choose a place that will provide privacy; don't start an important conversation if you are worried about people overhearing or interrupting you. A crowded dormitory lounge during "Ren and Stimpy," a kitchen filled with kids, a football stadium during a big game, or a car full of people on the way to the beach are inappropriate places.

disagree about the frequency of sex, the conflict may be serious but not basic, because both agree on the desirability of sex in the relationship. In such cases, resolution is possible.

Situational Versus Personality Conflicts

Some conflicts occur because of a situation and others occur because of the personality of one (or both) of the partners.

Situational conflicts are conflicts arising from a specific situation. They may occur when at least one partner needs to make changes in a relationship. Such conflicts are also known as realistic conflicts. They are based on

> *A number of porcupines huddled together for warmth on a cold day in winter; but because they began to prick each other with their quills, they were obliged to disperse. However, the cold drove them together again, when just the same thing happened. At last, after many turns of huddling and dispersing, they discovered that they would be best off by remaining at a little distance from each other.*
>
> Arthur Schopenhauer
> (1788–1860)

specific demands, like showering before having sex, waiting until the children are asleep, sharing sexual initiation more equitably, and so on. Conflict arises when one person tries to change the situation about the showering, children, or initiation.

Personality conflicts arise from differing personality characteristics. They do not occur because of situations that need to be changed but because of personality. Such conflicts may pit an erotophobic person against an erotophilic one or a sloppy person against a fastidious one. These conflicts are essentially unrealistic; they are not directed toward making changes in the relationship but simply toward releasing pent-up frustration. This sometimes takes the form of violence: slapping, hitting, pushing, and shoving. Whereas situational conflicts can be resolved through compromise, bargaining, or mediation, personality conflicts often require a therapeutic approach.

Power Conflicts

The politics of relationships—who has the power, who makes the decisions, who has which responsibilities—can be every bit as complex and explosive as politics at the national level. **Power** is the ability or potential ability to influence another person or group (Scanzoni, 1979). Most of the time, we are not aware of the power aspects of our relationships. One reason is that we tend to believe intimate relationships are based on love alone. Another reason is that the exercise of power is often subtle. When we think of power, we tend to think of coercion or force, but as we will see, power takes many forms in relationships. A final reason is that power is not constantly exercised. It comes into play only when an issue is important to both people and they have conflicting goals.

Because men generally have more power and status than women in the larger world, it would seem reasonable to infer that they also do in intimate relationships. They do, more or less—but not always.

Power as Multidimensional

Power is not a simple phenomenon. It is generally agreed among researchers that power in relationships is a dynamic, multidimensional process (Szinovacz, 1987). Generally speaking, no single individual is always the most powerful person in every aspect of the relationship. Nor is power necessarily always based on gender, role, or age. Power often shifts from person to person, depending on the issue. In the classic study of power in marital relationships, J. P. French and Bertram Raven (1959) found six bases of power:

1. *Reward power, based on the belief that the other person will do something in return.* If your partner attempts to understand your sexual feelings and desires, he or she expects you to do the same.

2. *Expert power, based on the belief that the other has greater knowledge.* If you believe your partner has greater knowledge regarding contraceptive use and effectiveness, you are more likely to defer to him or her.

3. *Legitimate power, based on the right to demand compliance.* Gender roles are an important source of legitimacy, as they give an aura of "rights" based on gender. Gender roles, for example, legitimize male initiation and female refusal of sexual activities. Law is also important. A woman

Changes in male-female relation-ships have led to men participating more in child care and other household responsibilities.

has the legal right to determine whether to continue or terminate a pregnancy during the first trimester.

4. *Referent power, based on identifying with the partner and receiving satisfaction by acting similarly.* If your partner is a good lover, sensitive to your feelings and needs, you are more likely to model yourself after him or her.

5. *Informational power, based on the partner's persuasive explanation.* If your partner does not want to wear a condom because he thinks it's like wearing an inner tube, you can provide information about the erotic sensitivity of thin latex condoms and the dangers of HIV and STDs.

6. *Coercive power, based on the fear that the partner will punish the other.* Coercion can be emotional or physical. A pattern of shouting, belittling, degrading, threatening, or throwing or destroying objects can intimidate and terrify a partner into sexual submission. Although coercive power is the least used form of power, it can be manifested in date or marital rape (see Chapter 18).

Men generally have access to more power bases or a relatively greater share of a power base than do women. Economic power results in men's having greater reward power; traditional gender roles, such as the male as the head of the family, provide men with greater legitimate power; men's

In the old days we both agreed
That I was you and you were me.
But now what has happened
That makes you, you
And me, me?

Ancient Sanskrit poem

greater physical strength gives them a clear coercive advantage (attested to by the startling number of abused women).

A study of power in heterosexual, gay, and lesbian relationships examined power strategies on two dimensions: directiveness and interactiveness (Falbo & Peplau, 1980). The directiveness dimension refers to how direct (ordering) or indirect (manipulating) a person is in attempting to influence change. The interactiveness dimension refers to whether requests are unilateral (giving an order) or bilateral (subject to give and take). "Do you want to make love?" is a direct-influence attempt, while turning down the lights, playing a romantic CD, and moving closer represents an indirect-influence attempt. "You must have sex with me now" is unilateral, while "Would you like to make love with me now?" is a bilateral attempt, the beginning of a two-way dialogue. The researchers found that influence strategies varied among all three groups according to perceptions of who had more power. Those who believed they had more power used more direct and bilateral strategies. Those who believed they had less power used more indirect and unilateral strategies. Finally, gender differences between heterosexuals, gay men, and lesbians influenced perceptions of power. In contrast to lesbians and gay men, heterosexuals either viewed themselves at a disadvantage with their partners or wanted more power than their partners. Both heterosexual women and lesbians preferred egalitarian power relationships more than did heterosexual and gay men.

Another study of heterosexual and gay relationships had surprising results regarding the use of tactics associated with strength and weakness (Howard et al., 1986). The researchers expected women to use weak strategies, such as supplication (pleading, acting ill, or begging) and manipulation (flattering, flirting, or seducing) and men to use strong strategies, such as bullying (threatening, insulting, or using violence) or autocracy (demanding or acting in an authoritarian manner). The study found that both women and some gay men were likely to use "weak strategies." The researchers note: "The power associated with being male thus appears to be expressed in behavior that elicits weak strategies from one's partner."

The Power of Love The complexity of intimate relationships can be seen in how love is used as a power resource. As anyone who has been in love realizes, love is a *powerful* force.

Nothing is so much to be feared as fear.

Henry David Thoreau

Relative Love and Need Power is explained in the **relative love and need theory** in terms of a person's involvement and needs in a relationship. Each partner brings certain resources, feelings, and needs to the relationship. Each may be seen as exchanging love, companionship, money, help, and status with the other. What each gives and receives, however, may not be equal. One partner may be gaining more from the relationship than the other. The person gaining the most from the relationship is the one who is most dependent. Constantina Safilios-Rothschild (1970) observes:

> The relative degree to which the one spouse loves and needs the other may be the most crucial variable in explaining the total power structure. The spouse who has relatively less feeling for the other may be the one in the best position to control and manipulate all the "resources" that he has in his command in order to effectively influence the outcome of decisions.

Love is a major power resource in a relationship. Those who love equally are likely to share power equally (Safilios-Rothschild, 1976). Such couples are likely to make decisions according to referent, expert, and legitimate power.

The Principle of Least Interest Akin to relative love and need as a way of looking at power is the **principle of least interest.** Sociologist Willard Waller coined this term to describe the curious (and often unpleasant) situation in which the partner with the least interest in continuing a relationship has the most power in it (Waller & Hill, 1951). At its most extreme form, it is the stuff of melodrama. "I will do anything you want, Charles," Laura says pleadingly, throwing herself at his feet. "Just don't leave me." "Anything, Laura?" he replies with a leer. "Then yield me your virginity."

Quarreling couples may unconsciously use the principle of least interest to their advantage. The less-involved partner may use threatening to leave as leverage in an argument: "All right, if you don't do it my way, I'm going." The threat may be extremely powerful in coercing a dependent partner, while it may have little effect if it comes from the dependent partner, because he or she has too much to lose to be persuasive. The less-involved partner can easily call the bluff.

Sexual Conflicts

Fighting About Sex Fighting and sex can be intertwined in several different ways. A couple may have a specific disagreement about sex that leads to a fight. One person wants to have sexual intercourse and the other does not, so they fight. A couple may also have an indirect fight about sex. The woman does not have an orgasm, and after intercourse, her partner rolls over and starts to snore. She lies in bed feeling angry and frustrated. In the morning, she begins to fight with her partner because he never does his share of the housework. The housework issues obscures why she is really angry.

Sex can also be used as a scapegoat for nonsexual problems. A man is angry because his wife calls him a lousy provider. He takes it out on her sexually by calling her a lousy lover. They fight about their lovemaking rather than about the real issue, his provider role. A couple may also fight about the wrong sexual issue. A woman berates her partner for being too quick in sex, but what she is really frustrated about is that he is not interested in oral sex with her. She, however, feels ambivalent about oral sex ("Maybe I smell bad"), so she cannot confront her partner with the real issue.

Finally, a fight can be a cover-up. If a man feels sexually inadequate and does not want to have sex as often as his partner, he may pick a fight and make his partner so angry that the last thing she would want to do is to be sexual with him.

It's hard to tell during a fight if there are deeper causes than the one about which a couple is currently fighting. If you repeatedly fight about sexual issues without getting anywhere, the ostensible cause may not be the real one. If fighting does not clear the air and make intimacy possible again, you should look for other reasons for the fights. It may be useful to talk with

Hatred does not cease by hatred at any time. Hatred ceases by love. This is an unalterable law.
Siddartha Gautama, the Buddha (c. 563–483 B.C.)

If we had no faults, we should not take so much pleasure in noting them in others.
François de la Rochefoucauld

The mind is its own place, and in itself can make a heaven of Hell, a hell of Heaven.
John Milton (1608–1674)

Excuses are always mixed with lies.
Arabic proverb

your partner about why the fights do not seem to accomplish anything. Step back and look at the circumstances of the fight, what patterns occur, and how each of you feels before, during, and after a fight.

Sex and Power Conflicts

In power struggles, sexuality can be used as a weapon, but this is generally a destructive tactic (Szinovacz, 1987). A classic strategy for the weaker person in a relationship is to withhold something that the more powerful one wants. In male-female struggles, this is often sex. By withholding sex, a woman gains a certain degree of power (Kaplan, 1979). Men also use sex in its most violent form: They use rape (including date rape and marital rape) to overpower and subordinate women (see Chapter 18).

In long-term gay male relationships, refusing sex can take on symbolic meaning. Refusing sex is sometimes associated with power struggles occurring as a result of having two sexual initiators (Blumstein & Schwartz, 1983). Because initiating sex is associated with power and dominance, two men being sexually assertive can become a form of competition. The man who feels himself less powerful can try to reassert his power by refusing his partner's sexual advances. In many lesbian relationships, power issues are often disguised because of each partner's commitment to equality. In these cases, power struggles are often indirect and obscure (Burch, 1987). Sexual rejection or lack of interest may hide issues of power.

Power Versus Intimacy

The problem with power imbalances or the blatant use of power is the negative effect on intimacy. As Ronald Sampson (1966) observed in his study of the psychology of power, "to the extent that power is the prevailing force in a relationship—whether between husband and wife or parent and child, between friends or between colleagues—to that extent love is diminished." If partners are not equal, self-disclosure may be inhibited, especially if the powerful person believes his or her power will be lessened by sharing feelings (Glazer-Malbin, 1975). Genuine intimacy appears to require equality in power relationships. Decision making in the happiest marriages seems to be based not on coercion or "tit for tat" but on caring, mutuality, and respect for the other person. Women who feel vulnerable to their mates may withhold feelings or pretend to feel what they do not. Unequal power in marriage may encourage power politics, as each partner struggles to keep or gain power.

It is not easy to change unequal power relationships after they become embedded in the overall structure of a relationship, yet they can be changed. Talking, trying to understand, and negotiating are the best approaches. Still, in attempting changes, a person may risk estrangement or the breakup of a relationship. He or she must weigh the possible gains against the possible losses in deciding whether change is worth the risk.

Conflict Resolution

The way in which a couple deals with conflict resolution reflects and perhaps contributes to their marital happiness (Boland & Follingstad, 1987).

Marriage is one long conversation, chequered by disputes.
Robert Louis Stevenson
(1850–1894)

To say what we think to our superiors would be inexpedient; to say what we think to our equals would be ill-mannered; to say what we think to our inferiors is unkind. Good manners occupy the terrain between fear and pity.
Quentin Crisp

Kindness in words creates confidence. Kindness in thinking creates profoundness. Kindness in giving creates love.
Lao-Tse (sixth century B.C.)

Conflict Resolution and Relationship Satisfaction Happy couples tend to act in positive ways to resolve conflicts, such as changing behaviors (putting the cap on the toothpaste rather than denying responsibility) and presenting reasonable alternatives (purchasing toothpaste in a pump dispenser). Unhappy or distressed couples, in contrast, use more negative strategies in attempting to resolve conflicts ("If the cap off the toothpaste bothers you, then you put it on."). A study of happily and unhappily married couples found distinctive communication traits as these couples tried to resolve their conflicts (Ting-Toomey, 1983). The communication behaviors of happily married couples displayed the following traits:

- *Summarizing.* Each person summarized what the other said. "Let me see if I can repeat the different points you were making."

- *Paraphrasing.* Each put what the other said into his or her own words. "What you are saying is that you feel badly when I don't acknowledge your feelings."

- *Validation.* Each affirmed the other's feelings. "I can understand how you feel."

- *Clarification.* Each asked for further information to make sure that he or she understood what the other was saying. "Can you explain what you mean a little bit more to make sure that I understand you?"

In contrast, unhappily married couples displayed the following reciprocal patterns:

- *Confrontation.* Each member of the couple confronted. "You're frigid!" "Not me, buddy. It's you who can't get it up."

- *Confrontation and defensiveness.* One confronted, while the other defended himself or herself. "You're a lousy lover! I did what you told me you wanted and you still can't come."

- *Complaining and defensiveness.* One complained, while the other was defensive. "I try to please you but it still does no good!" "I am too tired and distracted."

Strategies for Resolving Conflicts There are a number of ways to end conflicts. You can give in, but unless you believe that the conflict ended fairly, you are likely to feel resentful. You can try to impose your will through the use of power, force, or the threat of force. But using power to end conflict leaves your partner with the bitter taste of injustice. Or you can end the conflict through negotiation. In negotiations, both partners sit down and work out their differences until they can come to a mutually acceptable agreement.

Sometimes, even if we sincerely commit ourselves to working out our problems, it is difficult to see our own role in sustaining a pattern of interaction. If a couple is unable to resolve their conflicts, they should consider entering relationship counseling. A therapist or other professional can often help identify underlying problems, as well as help a couple develop negotiating skills.

Conflicts can be solved through negotiation in three major ways: agreement as a gift, bargaining, and coexistence.

The only way to speak the truth is to speak lovingly.
Henry David Thoreau

A little sincerity is a dangerous thing, and a great deal of it is absolutely fatal.
Oscar Wilde

Pass no judgment, and you will not be judged; do not condemn, and you will not be condemned; acquit, and you will be acquitted; give and gifts will be given to you . . . for whatever measure you deal out to others will be dealt to you in return.
Luke 6:37–38

Be to her virtues very kind.
Be to her faults a little blind.
Matthew Prior (1664–1721)

Agreement as a Gift   If you and your partner disagree on an issue, you can freely agree with your partner as a gift. If a woman wants her partner to stimulate her clitoris, and he doesn't want to because he feels it reflects badly on him, he can agree to try it because he cares about his partner. Similarly, a woman who does not want to try oral sex can try as a gift of caring. (Neither the man nor the woman, however, needs to continue if the activity continues to be objectionable.)

Agreement as a gift is different from giving in. When you give in, you do something you don't want to do. But when you agree without coercion or threats, the agreement is a gift of love. As in all exchanges of gifts, there will be reciprocation. Your partner will be more likely to give you a gift of agreement in return.

Bargaining   Bargaining means making compromises. But bargaining in relationships is different from bargaining in the marketplace or in politics. In relationships, you don't want to get the best deal for yourself, but the most equitable deal for both you *and* your partner. At all points during the bargaining process, you need to keep in mind what is best for the relationship, as well as for yourself, and trust your partner to do the same. In a relationship, both partners need to win. The purpose of conflict resolution in a relationship is to solidify the relationship, not to make one partner the winner and the other the loser. Achieving your end by exercising coercive power or withholding love, affection, or sex is a destructive form of bargaining. If you get what you want, how will that affect your partner and the relationship? Will your partner feel you're being unfair and become resentful? A solution has to be fair to both of you, or it won't enhance the relationship.

Coexistence   Sometimes differences can't be resolved, but they can be lived with. If a relationship is sound, differences can be absorbed without undermining the basic ties. All too often we regard differences as threatening rather than as the unique expression of two personalities. If one person likes to masturbate, the partner can accept it as an expression of his or her unique sexuality.

If you can't talk about what you like and what you want, there is a good chance you won't get either one. Communication is the basis for good sex and good relationships. Communication and intimacy are reciprocal: Communication creates intimacy, and intimacy, in turn, creates good communication.

If we fail to communicate, we are likely to turn our relationships into empty facades. Each person acts according to a role rather than revealing his or her deepest self. But communication is learned behavior. If we have learned *not* to communicate, we can learn *how* to communicate. Communication allows us to expand ourselves and to maintain our relationships.

SUMMARY

The Nature of Communication

- The ability to communicate is important in developing and maintaining ongoing relationships. Couples satisfied with their sexual communication tend to be satisfied about their relationships as a whole.

• *Communication* is a transactional process by which we convey *symbols*, such as words, gestures, and movements, to establish human contact, exchange information, and reinforce or change the attitudes and behaviors of ourselves and others.

• Communication takes place within cultural, social, and psychological contexts. The cultural context refers to the language, values, beliefs, and customs in which communication takes place. Ethnic groups communicate about sex differently, depending on their language patterns and values. The social context refers to the roles we play in society that influence our communication. The most important roles affecting sexuality are those relating to gender and sexual orientation. The psychological context refers to our personality characteristics, such as erotophilia or erotophobia.

Nonverbal Communication

• Communication includes both verbal and nonverbal communication. The functions of nonverbal communication are to convey interpersonal attitudes, express emotion, and handle the ongoing interaction. For communication to be unambiguous, verbal and nonverbal messages must agree. *Proximity*, eye contact, and touching are especially important forms of nonverbal communication. The ability to correctly interpret nonverbal messages is important in successful relationships.

Sexual Communication

• In initial encounters, physical appearance is especially important. Because of the *halo effect*, we infer positive qualities about people based on their appearance. Women send nonverbal cues to men indicating interest; men then begin a conversation with an "opening line."

• The "first move" marks the transition to physical intimacy; the male generally initiates. In initiating the first sexual interaction, communication is generally nonverbal, ambiguous, and indirect. Sexual disinterest is usually communicated nonverbally. With sexual involvement, the couple must communicate verbally about contraception, STD prevention, and sexual likes and dislikes.

• Unless there are definite clues as to orientation, gay men and lesbians try to determine through nonverbal cues whether others are appropriate partners. Because of male gender roles, gay men initiate sex earlier than heterosexuals; for parallel reasons, lesbians initiate sex later.

• In established relationships, many women feel more comfortable in initiating sexual interactions. Sexual initiations are more likely to be accepted in established relationships; sexual disinterest is communicated verbally. Women do not restrict sexual activities any more than men.

• Research indicates that happily married couples disclose private thoughts and feelings to partners, express equal levels of affective disclosure, spend more time together talking or expressing feelings in positive ways, are willing to engage in conflict in nondestructive ways, have less frequent conflict and spend less time in conflict, and accurately encode and decode messages.

- There are gender differences in marital communication. Wives send clearer messages; husbands tend to give neutral messages, whereas wives tend to give more positive or negative messages; and wives tend to set the emotional tone and escalate arguments more than husbands.

Developing Communication Skills

- Obstacles to talking about sex include a lack of role models, fear of being identified as "bad," cultural and personal taboos on unacceptable sexual subjects, and a lack of adequate vocabulary. Sexual vocabulary shifts according to context. Sexual vocabulary exists as medico-scientific terms, euphemisms, slang, and a private vocabulary.

- The keys to effective communication are self-disclosure, trust, and feedback. *Self-disclosure* is the revelation of intimate information about ourselves. *Trust* is the belief in the reliability and integrity of another person. *Feedback* is a constructive response to another's self-disclosure.

Conflict and Intimacy

- *Conflict* is natural in intimate relationships. Types of conflict include basic versus nonbasic conflict, and situational versus personality conflict. Basic conflicts may threaten the foundation of a relationship because they challenge fundamental roles; nonbasic conflicts do not threaten basic assumptions and may be negotiable. Situational conflicts are realistic conflicts based on specific issues; personality conflicts are unrealistic conflicts based on a couple's fundamental personality differences or on the need of one partner or both partners to release pent-up feelings.

- *Power* is the ability or potential ability to influence another person or group. The six bases of marital power are reward, expert, legitimate, referent, informational, and coercive. These bases of power shift in different domains. Other theories of power include the *relative love and need theory* and the *principle of least interest.*

- Conflicts about sex can be specific disagreements about sex, indirect disagreements in which a partner feels frustrated or angry and takes it out in sexual ways, arguments that are ostensibly about sex but that are really about nonsexual issues, or disagreements about the wrong sexual issue.

- In resolving conflicts, happily married couples communicate by summarizing, paraphrasing, and clarifying. Unhappily married couples use confrontation, confrontation and defensiveness, or complaining and defensiveness. Conflict resolution may be achieved through negotiation in three ways: agreement as a freely given gift, bargaining, or coexistence. Counseling is often helpful in improving a couple's conflict resolution skills.

KEY TERMS

communication	trust	relative love and need theory
symbol	feedback	
status	conflict	principle of least interest
proximity	power	
halo effect		

SUGGESTIONS FOR FURTHER READING

Derlega, Valerian, Sandra Metts, Sandra Petronio, and Steven Margulis. *Self-Disclosure*. Newbury Park, CA: Sage Publications, 1993. How self-disclosure affects intimate relationships in terms of closeness, privacy, feelings of vulnerability, and love.

Gottman, John, et al. *A Couple's Guide to Communication*. Champaign, IL: Research Press, 1976. A book that focuses on the couple as the communication unit.

Hecht, Michelle, Mary Jane Collier, and Sidney Ribeau. *African American Communication*. Newbury Park, CA: Sage Publications, 1993. A synthesis of research on African American communication and culture, including effective and ineffective communication patterns.

Henley, Nancy. *Body Politics: Power, Sex, and Nonverbal Communication*. Englewood Cliffs, NJ: Prentice-Hall, 1977. An insightful analysis of how power is exerted nonverbally in male-female interactions.

Satir, Virginia. *The New Peoplemaking*, rev. ed. Palo Alto, CA: Science and Behavior Books, 1988. One of the most influential (and easy to read) books of the last 25 years on communication and family relationships.

Tannen, Deborah. *You Just Don't Understand: Women and Men in Conversation*. New York: William Morrow, 1990. A best-selling, intelligent, and lively discussion of how women use communication to achieve intimacy and men use communication to achieve independence.

Ting-Toomey, Stella, and Felipe Korzenny, eds. *Cross-Cultural Interpersonal Communication*. Newbury Park, CA: Sage Publications, 1991. A ground-breaking collection of scholarly essays on communication and relationships among different ethnic and cultural groups, including African American, Latino, Korean, and Chinese ethnic groups and cultures.

Chapter Ten

SEXUAL EXPRESSION

P REVIEW: SELF-QUIZ

1. Americans believe that attractive people are more sexually permissive and responsive than unattractive people. True or false?

2. Women and gay men share many of the same ideas about ideal male body types. True or false?

3. Whites, African Americans, Latinos, and Asian Americans hold more or less the same attitudes toward oral sex. True or false?

4. Fantasies about others during sexual intercourse generally indicate a lack of sexual interest in one's partner. True or false?

5. Sexual behaviors may be defined as heterosexual, gay, or lesbian. True or false?

6. Rape fantasies do not indicate an underlying desire to be raped. True or false?

7. Oral-genital sex is more widely practiced by whites than by African Americans. True or false?

8. About the same percentage of males and females masturbate. True or false?

9. Nineteenth-century physicians believed that masturbation and sexual intercourse could both lead to death. True or false?

10. Both men and women rank buttocks as the body's most sexually attractive feature. True or false?

ANSWERS 1. T, 2. T, 3. F, 4. F, 5. F, 6. T, 7. T, 8. F, 9. T, 10. T

Chapter Outline

What is a kiss but the rosy dot above the "i" of loving?
Edmond Rostand

Sexual expression is a complex process through which we reveal our sexual selves. Sexual expression involves more than simply sexual behaviors. It involves our feelings as well. "Behavior can never be un-emotional," one scholar observed (Blechman, 1990). As human beings, we do not separate feelings from behavior, including sexual behavior. Our sexual behaviors are rich with emotions, ranging from love to anxiety, desire to antipathy.

To fully understand our sexuality, we need to examine our sexual behaviors *and* the emotions we experience along with them. If we studied sexual activities apart from our emotions, we would distort the human meaning of sexuality. It would make them appear mechanistic, nothing more than genitals rubbing against each other.

In this chapter, we first discuss sexual attraction and desire, for they motivate our sexual behaviors. Next, we turn to sexual scripts that give form to our sexual drives. Then we examine the most common sexual behaviors, both autoerotic behaviors, such as fantasies and masturbation, and interpersonal behaviors, such as oral-genital sex, sexual intercourse, and anal eroticism.

SEXUAL ATTRACTION AND DESIRE

Of all the sexual emotions we experience, desire may be the most important because it motivates us to be sexual. As we saw in our discussion of the triphasic model of sexual response in Chapter 3, it is the initial stage. Without desire, few of us would engage in sexual behaviors. But desire is not a simple psychological state: It requires an object, either real or imaginary. Desire is associated with sexual attraction. Before we discuss desire, we'll turn to its ever-present partner, attraction.

In the beginning there was desire, which was the primal germ of the mind:
The sages searching in their hearts with wisdom,
found in non-existence the king of existence.
   The Vedas (Hindu scriptures)

Sexual Attractiveness

Sexual attraction is an important element in desire. But what constitutes sexual attractiveness?

Aspects of Sexual Attractiveness In a landmark cross-cultural study of sexuality, Cleland Ford and Frank Beach (1972) demonstrated that there is no universal standard of sexual attractiveness. In fact, the study found that there was considerable variation from culture to culture as to what parts of the body were considered erotic. In some cultures, the eyes were the key to sexual attraction; in others, height and weight; and in still others, the size and shape of the genitals. In our culture, breasts are considered erotic; in others, they are not.

Cultures that agree on which body parts are erotic may still disagree on what constitutes attractiveness. In terms of female beauty, American culture considers the slim body attractive. But worldwide, Americans are in the minority, for the type of female body most desired cross-culturally is plump. Similarly, we prefer slim hips, but the majority of cultures in Ford and Beach's study found wide hips most attractive. In our culture, large breasts are ideal, but others prefer small breasts, and still others, long and pendulous breasts. In the last decade, well-defined pectoral and arm muscles have become part of the ideal male body.

What is it that men and women find attractive in each other? One survey found that women regarded men's most attractive features as small and sexy buttocks (39%), slimness (15%), flat stomach (13%), and expressive eyes (11%) (cited in Gagnon, 1977). Interestingly, men misperceived what women found attractive about them. Men believed that women thought the most sexually attractive parts of men's bodies were, in descending order, muscular chest and shoulders (21%), muscular arms (18%), and large penis (15% [only 2% of the women indicated that a large penis was important]).

An informal classroom survey found that men were most interested in women's buttocks (25%), faces (20%), and breasts (17%) (cited in Luria et al., 1987). Women, however, misperceived men's interests. Forty-nine percent felt that men were most interested in breasts, and only 7% felt that men were interested in faces. Only the women's perception of male interest in buttocks—17%—approximated actual male interest.

Another study found that gay men and heterosexual women shared many of the same perceptions about what made men sexually attractive (Bell, 1974). Thirty-seven percent of gay men found male buttocks attractive. Where gay men and heterosexual women differed most markedly was that

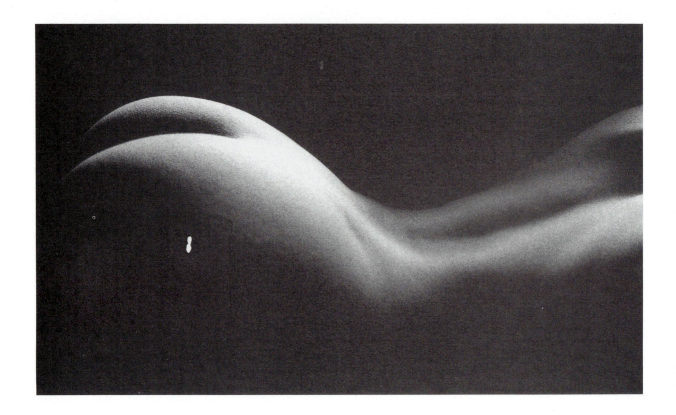

42% of the gay men found a male's naked chest attractive, and 12% thought a large penis was important.

For bisexual men and women, the question of attractiveness is more complex. What is it that attracts bisexuals to certain people? Is a bisexual man, for example, attracted to women in the same manner as heterosexuals and to men in the same way as gay men? There is some evidence that gender is not as important as other physical and personality characteristics (Kaplan & Rogers, 1984). Bisexuals may be attracted to men and women, for example, with similar physical characteristics, such as being slight or heavy-set, dark- or light-skinned. Personality characteristics may also be similar, such as being assertive or passive, traditionally masculine or feminine, or androgynous.

Sex is one of the nine reasons for reincarnation. . . . The other eight are unimportant.

Henry Miller

The Halo Effect Revisited   As discussed in Chapter 9, attractive people are surrounded by a halo effect. The halo effect extends to assumptions about sexuality. A study of men from two universities found that among the various traits attributed to attractive women, the trait most affected by their appearance was their sexual behavior (Tanke, 1982). Attractive women were viewed as more sexually warm, exciting, and permissive than unattractive ones. An unpublished study found that attractive men and women were believed to have a stronger sex drive, to be sexually permissive, to enjoy multiple sexual relationships, and to play a more dominant role in sexual activities (cited in Hatfield & Sprecher, 1986).

While most studies on sexuality and attractiveness relate to beliefs about attractive people, an intriguing study of 100 college women found some evidence indicating a relationship between attractiveness and actual sexual behavior (Stelzer et al., 1987). While there seemed to be no relationship between level of attractiveness and the time when a woman began dating, engaging in sexual intercourse, or contraceptive use, attractive women were significantly more likely to engage in sexual intercourse and oral sex than the other women. This finding suggests that the halo effect may create a self-fulfilling expectation about sexual behavior. Because attractive women are *expected* to be more sexually active, they *become* more sexually active.

Another study found that attractive women are more likely to be on top during sexual intercourse and to engage in cunnilingus and fellatio (Blumstein & Schwartz, 1983). The researchers speculate that attractiveness bestows sexual power on women. Being attractive increases women's self-esteem and permits them to express themselves more freely.

While attractiveness is important, it's good to remember that looks aren't everything. Looks are most important to certain types or groups of people and in certain situations or locations, such as classes, parties, and bars, where people do not interact extensively with each other daily. Looks are less important to those in ongoing relationships and to adults over 30 or so (Hatfield & Sprecher, 1986). Attractiveness remains important, however, in established relationships as well. Blumstein and Schwartz (1983) found that the happiest people in cohabiting and married relationships thought of their partners as attractive. People who found their partners attractive had the best sex lives. Another study found that as husbands and wives aged, changes in the wife's physical appearance seemed to have a greater impact on the quality of marital sexuality than changes in the husband's appearance (Margolin & White, 1987). These changes led to greater sexual disinterest, a decline in sexual satisfaction, and, to a lesser extent, unfaithfulness, especially on the part of the husband.

Sexual Desire

Desire can exist separately from overtly physical sexual expression. As discussed in Chapter 3, it is the psychological component that motivates sexual behavior. But almost no scientific research exists on sexual desire. One of the most important reasons researchers have avoided studying it is that desire is difficult to define and quantify.

The only way to get rid of temptation is to yield to it.
Oscar Wilde

The Nature of Desire   According to researcher Stephen Levine (1987), sexual desire is highly variable, and its source is a mystery to most of us. He suggests that we can understand both its variability and origin if we divide sexual desire into three components: sexual drive, sexual wishes, and sexual motivation. Sexual drive is basically biological, rooted in our brain's neuroendocrine system. The sexual drive may be low, moderate, or high. It manifests itself in spontaneous tumescence or lubrication, sexual fantasies and dreams, a heightened significance of physical attractiveness in others, and sexual activities. As a result of aging, health, interpersonal relations, stress,

Abstinence sows sand all over the ruddy limbs and flaming hair.
William Blake

and other environmental factors, an individual's sexual drive is subject to considerable variability.

Sexual wishes and motivation are closely related. A sexual wish is a desire or a "wanting" to be sexual. A person may wish to be sexual because sex makes one feel good physically, valued, loved, masculine or feminine, connected, and so on. Individuals may also wish *not* to be sexual, as they may not feel emotionally ready, not know how to behave sexually, fear pregnancy or STDs, or believe premarital sex is immoral.

Sexual motivation, according to Levine, depends on four intrapsychic/interpersonal contexts: (1) sexual identity, (2) quality of nonsexual relationships, (3) patterns of arousal, and (4) transference from past attachments. Sexual identity includes gender identity and sexual orientation. Conflicting feelings in these areas are likely to inhibit sexual desire. Sexual desire is also closely related to one's nonsexual feelings about a partner. Love, for example, is likely to increase desire, while anger is likely to diminish it.

The way a person regulates his or her sexual arousal also affects motivation. In some cases, sexual drive might lead to a preoccupation with sexual fantasies. The person may wait until the arousal passes, try to divert his or her interest, masturbate, or engage in sexual activities with a partner. He or she may choose to masturbate when single, but when in a relationship, may masturbate as a means of supplementing interpersonal sex. Finally, past experiences with parents and partners may involve lasting issues of intimacy, trust, and love. Transferences of past experiences of hurt to the present relationship may impede sexual desire, while the transference of positive experiences will enhance it.

Levine believes that two important aspects of sexual desire—its fluctuating frequency and intensity, and its obscure source—are the result of changes in sexual drive, wishes, and motivation throughout a person's life. Because each component is complex and interacts with the other two, Levine argues, sexual desire is subject to considerable variation through our lifetime. Its complexity lends to its sense of mystery.

Bliss is unnatural.
Emily Dickinson

There may be some things better than sex, and some things worse, but there is nothing exactly like it.
W. C. Fields

Erotophilia and Erotophobia Desire is affected by erotophilia and erotophobia. **Erotophilia** is a positive emotional response to sex, and erotophobia is a negative emotional response to sex. In recent years, researchers have hypothesized that the place where someone falls on the erotophilic/erotophobic continuum strongly influences his or her overt sexual behavior (Fisher, 1986). In contrast to erotophobic individuals, for example, erotophilic men and women accept and enjoy their sexuality, seek out sexual situations, engage in more autoerotic and interpersonal sexual activities, enjoy talking about sex, and are more likely to obtain and use contraception. Furthermore, erotophilic people are more likely to have positive sexual attitudes, to engage in more involved sexual fantasies, and to have seen more erotica than erotophobic people.

A person's emotional response to sex is also linked to how they evaluate other aspects of sex. Erotophilic individuals, for example, tend to evaluate sexually explicit material more positively. In fact, one study found that erotophilics identified explicit movies as erotic, while erotophobics described the same films as pornographic (Byrne, et al., 1974) (see Chapter 19).

Researchers have found intriguing evidence of a relationship between erotophilia/erotophobia and personality traits. Erotophobic individuals tend to be more authoritarian, believing in rules and order. They experience higher levels of guilt about sexual matters, feeling guilty about masturbation and premarital sex. They are more rigid in their gender roles, believing that men and women are basically different, especially about sexual matters (Fisher, Byrne, White, & Kelley, 1988).

But erotophilic and erotophobic traits are not fixed. Positive experiences can alter erotophobic responses over time. In fact, some therapy programs work on the assumption that consistent positive feelings, such as love, affirmation, caring, touching, and communication, can do much to diminish the fear of sex. Positive sexual experiences can help dissolve much of the anxiety that underlies erotophobia.

SEXUAL SCRIPTS

As you recall from Chapter 5, gender roles have an immense impact on how we behave sexually, for sexual behavior and feelings depend more on learning than on biological drives. Our sexual drives can be molded into almost any form. What is "natural" is what society calls natural; there is very little spontaneous, unlearned behavior (Gagnon & Simon, 1973). Sexual behavior, like all other forms of social behavior (such as courtship, classroom behavior, and sports), relies on scripts. (See Simon & Gagnon, 1986 for a brief introduction to scripting theory and its application to sexual behavior.)

Scripts are like plans that organize and give direction to our behavior. The sexual scripts we receive strongly influence our sexual activities as men and women in our culture. As William Gagnon (1977) writes:

> A script is simpler than the activity we perform. . . . It is like a blueprint or roadmap or recipe, giving directions but not specifying everything that must be done. Regardless of its sketchiness, the script is often more important than the concrete acts. It is our script that we carry from action to action, modified by our concrete acts, but not replaced by them. Scripts do change, as new elements are added and old elements are reworked, but very few people have the desire, energy, or persistence to create highly innovative or novel scripts.

Our sexual scripts have three main components: cultural, intrapersonal, and interpersonal.

- *Cultural component.* The cultural component provides the general pattern that sexual behaviors are expected to take. Our general cultural script, for example, emphasizes heterosexuality, gives primacy to sexual intercourse, discourages masturbation, and so on.

- *Intrapersonal component.* The intrapersonal component deals with the internal and physiological states that lead to, accompany, or identify sexual arousal, such as a pounding heart, erection or vaginal lubrication, and so on.

- *Interpersonal component.* The interpersonal component deals with the shared conventions and signals that enable two people to engage in sexual behaviors, such as body language, words, and erotic touching.

In the beginner's mind there are many possibilities, in the expert's mind there are few.
Shunryo Suzuki

Cultural Scripting

Our culture sets the general contours of our sexual scripts. It tells us which behaviors are acceptable ("moral" or "normal") and which are unacceptable ("immoral" or "abnormal"). Among middle-class white Americans, the norm is a sequence of sexual events consisting of kissing, genital caressing, and sexual intercourse. If large numbers of people did not share these conventions, there would be sexual chaos. Imagine a scenario in which two people from different cultures try to initiate a sexual encounter. The one from our culture follows our culture's sexual sequence, and the other from a different culture follows a sequence beginning with sexual intercourse, moving to genital caressing, and ending with passionate kissing. At least initially, such a couple might experience endless frustration and confusion as one tried to initiate the sexual encounter with kissing and the other with sexual intercourse.

Yet this kind of confusion occurs fairly often because there is not necessarily a direct relation between what our culture calls erotic and what any particular individual calls erotic. Culture sets the general contours, but there is too much diversity in terms of personality, socioeconomic status, and ethnic group for each person to have exactly the same erotic script. Thus, sexual scripts can be highly ambiguous.

We may believe that everyone shares our own particular script, projecting our experiences onto others and assuming that they share our erotic definitions of objects, gestures, and situations. But often, they initially do not. Our partner may have come from a different socioeconomic group or religious background and may have had far different learning experiences. Each has to learn the other's sexual script and be able to complement and adjust to it. If our scripts are to be integrated, we must make our needs known through words, gestures, or movements. This is the reason many people view their first intercourse as somewhat of a comedy or tragedy—or perhaps a little bit of both.

Intrapersonal Scripting

On the intrapersonal level, sexual scripts enable people to give meaning to their physiological responses. The meaning depends largely on the situation. An erection, for example, does not always mean sexual excitement. Young boys sometimes have erections when they are frightened, anxious, or worried. In the morning, men may experience erections that are unaccompanied by arousal. Adolescent girls sometimes experience sexual arousal without knowing what their sensations mean. They report them as funny, weird kinds of feelings; or as anxiety, fear, or an upset stomach. The sensations are not linked to a sexual script until the girl becomes older and physiological states acquire a definite erotic meaning.

The intrapersonal, internal script also determines what physiological events our minds will become aware of. During masturbation or intercourse, for example, an enormous number of physiological events occur simultaneously, but we are aware of only a few of them. These are the events we associate with sexual arousal, such as increasing heartbeat and tensing muscles. Others, such as curling toes, may not filter through to our consciousness.

Finally, internal scripts provide a sequence of body movements by acting as mechanisms that activate biological events and release tension. We learn, for example, that we may create an orgasm by manipulating the penis or clitoris during masturbation.

Interpersonal Scripting

The interpersonal level is the area of shared conventions, which make sexual activities possible. Very little of our public life is sexual. Yet there are signs and gestures—verbal and nonverbal—that define encounters as sexual. We make our sexual motives clear by the way we look at each other, the tone of our voices, the movements of our bodies, and other culturally shared phenomena. A bedroom or a motel room, for example, is a potentially erotic location, while a classroom, office, or factory is not. The movements we use in arousing ourselves or others are erotic activators. Within a culture, there are normative scripts leading to sexual intercourse. People with little experience, especially young adolescents, are often unfamiliar with sexual scripts. What do they do after kissing? Do they embrace? Caress

Very little of our sexual life is displayed in public. When we encounter public displays of passion, we often avert our eyes to avoid acknowledging it. What would you do if you were walking past this couple? Would your response be different if they were gay or lesbian?

above the waist? Below? Eventually, they learn a comfortable sequence based on cultural inputs and personal and partner preferences. For gay men and lesbians, learning the sexual script is more difficult because it is socially stigmatized. The sexual script is also related to age. Older children and young adolescents often limit their scripts to kissing, holding hands, and embracing, and they feel completely satisfied. Kissing for them may be as exciting as sexual intercourse for more experienced people. When the range of their scripts increases, the earlier stages lose some of their sexual intensity.

AUTOEROTICISM

Autoeroticism consists of sexual activities that involve only the self. Autoeroticism is an *intrapersonal* activity rather than an *interpersonal* one. It includes sexual fantasies, masturbation, and erotic dreams. A universal phenomenon in one form or another (Ford & Beach, 1952), autoeroticism is one of our earliest expressions of sexual stirrings. It is also one that traditionally has been condemned in our society. By condemning it, however, our culture sets the stage for the development of deeply negative and inhibitory attitudes toward sexuality.

Sexual Fantasies and Dreams

Sexual Fantasies "A fantasy is a map of desire, mastery, escape, and obscuration," wrote Nancy Friday (1980), "the navigational path we invent to steer ourselves between the reefs and shoals of anxiety, guilt, and inhibition." Erotic fantasy is probably the most universal of all sexual behaviors. Nearly everyone has experienced such fantasies, but because they touch on feelings or desires considered personally or socially unacceptable, they are not widely discussed. They may interfere with an individual's self-image, causing a loss of self-esteem as well as confusion.

Occurring spontaneously or as a result of outside stimuli, fantasies are part of the body's regular healthy functioning, as is the heart's beating or the stomach's digesting. A study of 120 men and women found that the average number of sexual fantasies was eight a day (Schwartz & Masters, 1984). Research indicates that sexual fantasies are related to sexual drives: The higher the sexual drive, the higher the frequency of sexual fantasies (Wilson, 1978). Fantasies help create an equilibrium between our environment and our inner selves, seeking a balance between the two (Wilson, 1978). They usually accompany our masturbatory experiences to enhance them, as well as oral-genital sex, sexual intercourse, and other interpersonal experiences.

Our erotic fantasies develop with our experiences, although, as we will see, there are distinct gender differences. As we enter early adolescence, erotic fantasies usually center on holding hands, kissing, and touching the breasts or genitals. Later in adolescence, fantasies progress to heavy petting, oral-genital sex, and sexual intercourse. The context may be heterosexual, homosexual, with one person or many; the fantasies may involve seduction or rape, sadomasochism or romance, animals or undergarments. The main contours of fantasy generally do not radically alter through adulthood; but as we age and our sexual drives decrease, so do the frequency and intensity of our fantasies. Among older adults, fantasies become more diffuse, turning from those that are obviously sexual to those centering more on pleasurable or pleasant experiences in general (Barclay, 1980). As some men get older, their erotic performance becomes more dependent on fantasies; they are less responsive to simple tactile stimulation of the genitals. Some men also tend to have fewer inhibitions in acting out their sexual fantasies, which accounts for the change in behavior as they age.

The Function of Sexual Fantasies Sexual fantasies have a number of important functions in maintaining our psychic equilibrium. First, fantasies help direct and define our erotic goals. They take our generalized sexual drives and give them concrete images and specific content. These goals are generally conservative insofar as they usually do not greatly exceed idealized models of the type of person we are attracted to; we fantasize about certain types of men or women, and reinforce our attraction through fantasy

Many are saved from sin by being inept at it.

Mignon McLaughlin

Two monks, Tanzan and Ekido, were travelling down the road in a heavy rain. As they turned a bend, they came upon a beautiful young woman in a silk kimono. She was unable to pass because the rain had turned the road to mud.

Tanzan said to her, "Come on," and lifted her in his arms and carried her across the mud. Then he put her down and the monks continued their journey.

The two monks did not speak again until they reached a temple in which to spend the night. Finally, Ekido could no longer hold back his thoughts and he reprimanded Tanzan. "It is not proper for monks to go near women," he said. "Especially young and beautiful ones. It is unwise. Why did you do it?"

"I left the woman behind," replied Tanzan. "Are you still carrying her?"

Zen tale

Erotic fantasies are a healthy part of our sexuality.

involvement. Unfortunately, our fantasy model may be unreasonable or unattainable, which is one of the pitfalls of fantasy; we can imagine perfection, but we can rarely find it in the real world.

Second, sexual fantasies allow us to plan or anticipate situations that may arise. Fantasies provide a form of rehearsal, allowing us to practice in our minds how to act in various situations. Our fantasies of what *might* take place on a date, after a party, or in bed with our partner give us a certain amount of preparation.

Third, erotic fantasies provide escape from a dull or oppressive environment. Routine or repetitive labor often gives rise to fantasies as a way of coping with the boredom in which we are trapped. Fourth, even if our sexual lives are satisfactory, we may indulge in sexual fantasies to bring novelty and excitement into the relationship. Many people fantasize things they would not actually do in real life. Fantasy offers a safe outlet for sexual curiosity. One researcher (Wilson, 1978) notes:

> We all have a need for adventure, but set limits on how far we permit curiosity to determine our actual behavior. This limit varies according to our personality

and stage of development. Imagining an experience is less radical than doing it, so our criterion of what is socially and personally acceptable often falls between the two. The nice thing about fantasy is that it allows us to explore, yet at the same time retain our physical safety and avoid hurting other people.

One study found that fantasies appear to help many married women become sexually aroused and experience orgasm during sexual intercourse (Davidson & Hoffman, 1986).

Fifth, sexual fantasies have an expressive function in somewhat the same manner as dreams do. Our sexual fantasies may offer a clue to our current interests, pleasures, anxieties, fears, or problems. Since fantasies make use of only a few details from the stream of reality, what we select is significant, expressing feelings that often lie beneath the surface of our consciousness (Sue, 1979). Fantasies of extramarital relationships, for example, may signify deep dissatisfaction with a marriage, whereas fantasies centering around impotence may represent fears about sexuality or a particular relationship.

Fantasies During Intercourse A sizable number of people fantasize during sex. The fantasies are usually a continuation of daydreams or masturbation fantasies, transforming one's partner into a Luke Perry or Janet Jackson. Various studies report that 60–90% of the respondents fantasize during sex, depending on gender and ethnicity (Knafo & Jaffe, 1984; Price & Miller, 1984; Sue, 1979). African Americans are somewhat more likely than whites to have experienced fantasies during intercourse (Price & Miller, 1984). In a study of more than 400 college students, 60% reported that they fantasized at least occasionally during sexual intercourse; more than 80% believed that such fantasies were normal, but the remaining 20% felt that sexual fantasies during coitus were a source of shame or uneasiness (Sue, 1979). Thirty-eight percent of males and 46% of females fantasized in order to sexually arouse themselves; 30% of males and 22% of females fantasized to increase their partner's sexual attractiveness. The only significant difference between men and women in this study was that twice as many men as women fantasized from the beginning of a sexual relationship. Another study found that during sexual intercourse, some women fantasized about forced sex, group sex, and sex with an imaginary lover (Hariton & Singer, 1974). Their feelings of guilt were related to the degree to which they believed their fantasies were deviant or abnormal.

Despite their prevalence, fantasies during intercourse provoke guilty feelings in a number of people. A study of college students found that 84% of its respondents reported having such fantasies (Cado & Leitenberg, 1990). Those who felt guilty (about one-quarter) reported significantly fewer fantasies than those who did not feel guilty. The respondents who felt guilty tended to believe that fantasies during intercourse were abnormal, immoral, and uncommon. They also believed that such fantasizing indicated relationship problems. "If something wasn't wrong with our relationship," they seemed to think, "I wouldn't be having these fantasies." The researchers suggest that guilty reactions to such fantasies inhibit sexual satisfaction and adjustment. If fantasizing during intercourse was recognized as a normal, common phenomenon, much of the guilt attending it would be relieved. It is the guilt, rather than the fantasizing itself, that may be harmful to the relationship.

The world of difference between "rape fantasy" and rape can be expressed in one word: control. The point of a fantasy is that a woman . . . orders the reality within it, ordains its terms, and censors it according to her needs. The point of rape is that a woman is violated against her will.

Molly Haskell

FIGURE 10.1 Masturbation is an important form of sexual behavior in which individuals explore their erotic capacities and bring pleasure to themselves.

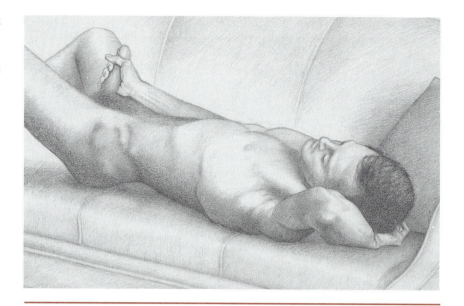

Erotic Dreams Almost all of the men and two-thirds of the women in Kinsey's studies reported having had overtly sexual dreams (Kinsey et al., 1948, 1953). Sexual images in dreams are frequently very intense. Although people tend to feel responsible for fantasies, which occur when awake, they are usually less troubled by sexual dreams.

Overtly sexual dreams are not necessarily exciting, while dreams that are apparently nonsexual may cause arousal. It is not unusual for individuals to awaken in the middle of the night to find their bodies moving as if they were making love. They may also experience nocturnal orgasm. About 2–3% of a woman's orgasms may be nocturnal, while for men the number may be around 8% of their total orgasms (Kinsey et al., 1948, 1953). About 50% of the men interviewed by Kinsey had more than five nocturnal orgasms a year, but less than 10% of the women experienced them that frequently.

Dreams almost always accompany nocturnal orgasm. The dreamer may awaken, and men usually ejaculate. Although the dream content may not be overtly sexual, it is always accompanied by sensual sensations. Erotic dreams run the gamut of sexual possibilities: heterosexual, homosexual, or autoerotic; incestuous, dominance and submission, bestial, fetishistic. Women seem to feel less guilt or fear about nocturnal orgasms than men do, accepting them more easily as pleasurable experiences.

Masturbation

People **masturbate** by rubbing, caressing, or otherwise stimulating their genitals to give themselves sexual pleasure or to release sexual tension (Figures 10.1 and 10.2). They may masturbate during particular periods or throughout their entire lives. Kinsey (1953) reported that 92% of the men and 58% of the women he interviewed said they had masturbated. Today, there appears to be a slight increase in both incidence and frequency. Nevertheless, gender differences continue to be significant (Atwood & Gagnon, 1987; Leitenberg, Detzer, & Srebnik, 1993).

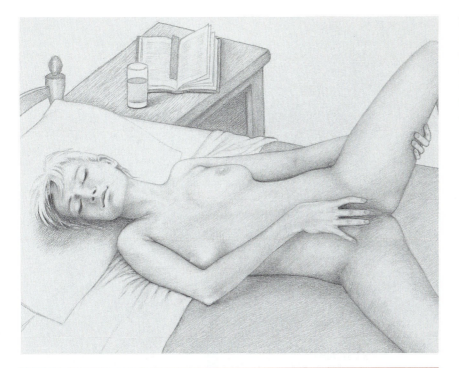

FIGURE 10.2 Many people "discover" their sexual potential through masturbation. Sometimes women learn to be orgasmic through masturbation, then carry this knowledge over into their relationships.

Fantasy often accompanies masturbation as a means of enhancing the erotic pleasure. In fact, Freud (1953) believed that masturbation consists of two elements: the creation of the sexual fantasy, and the physical act of masturbation that produces erotic pleasure. The fantasy and physical components of masturbation are welded together to form a powerful image of an ideal sexual interaction. This image becomes a powerful motivating force in our sexuality. Our fantasy of having sex in a particular fashion, such as in the sand on a moonlit beach as the waves wash against us, is reinforced by the pleasure we obtain from masturbating. In this manner, the ideal image enters our repertoire of sexual wishes. But we do not have a single ideal image. Because we fantasize and masturbate about a multitude of different situations, individuals, and activities, we have multiple ideal sexual scenarios we wish to act out. Many, of course, are never fulfilled outside our masturbatory or fantasy lives.

Men and women may also read erotic stories, look at erotic photographs or magazines, or view X-rated videos to heighten the fantasies accompanying their masturbation. They may use vibrators or apply oils to their genitals to increase their physical sensitivity.

Attitudes toward masturbation and masturbatory behaviors vary along ethnic lines. Whites are the most accepting of masturbation, for example, while African Americans are less so. The differences can be explained culturally. Because whites tend to begin coital activities later than blacks, whites regard masturbation as an acceptable alternative to sexual intercourse. Black culture, by contrast, accepts sexual activity at an earlier age. In this context, blacks may view masturbation as a sign of personal and sexual inadequacy. As a result, many blacks tend to view sexual intercourse as normal and masturbation as deviant (Cortese, 1989; Kinsey et al., 1948;

He who wears his morality as his best garment were better naked.
Kahlil Gibran

You have heard it said, "You shall not commit adultery." But I say to you that all who look at a woman lustfully has already committed adultery in his heart with her. If your right eye causes you to sin, pluck it out, and throw it away. It is better that you lose one of your members than that your entire body be thrown into hell. And if your right hand causes you to sin, cut it off, and throw it away. It is better to lose one of your members than that your whole body goes into hell.
Matthew 5:27–30

Wilson, 1986). Recently, however, masturbation is becoming more accepted within the African American community as a legitimate sexual activity (Wilson, 1986; Wyatt et al., 1989).

Latinos, like African Americans, are more conservative than Anglos in their attitudes about masturbation (Cortese, 1989; Padilla & O'Grady, 1987). In Latino culture, masturbation is not considered an acceptable sexual option for either men or women (Guerrero Pavich, 1986). In part this is because of the cultural emphasis on sexual intercourse and the influence of Catholicism, which regards masturbation as sinful. As with other forms of sexual behavior, acceptance becomes more likely as Latinos become more assimilated. A study of Mexican American college students found their attitudes toward masturbation more liberal than the Mexican American community as a whole (Padilla & O'Grady, 1987).

In general, college appears to make masturbation more acceptable (Atwood & Gagnon, 1987). Among college women, masturbation becomes increasingly accepted as a healthy sexual activity as they progress in their education; this is especially true if they have studied sexuality (Adams, 1986; Davidson & Darling, 1986). Despite these changes among women, another study of college students found that twice as many men as women had ever masturbated. Furthermore, the men masturbated about three times as often as the women. Harold Leitenberg and associates note that this continued gender difference is all the more striking as the double standard in other areas of adolescent and young adult sexuality have narrowed considerably or been eliminated entirely, as in premarital sexual intercourse (Leitenberg, Detzer, & Srebnik, 1993). The researchers point out that their results suggest that "young women in our society simply do not find masturbation as pleasurable or acceptable as do young men." They point out that women, more than men, have been socialized to associate sex with romance, relationships, and emotional intimacy. Their results, they note, suggest that "the recent effort to encourage women to take more responsibility for their own sexuality and the explicit suggestion to masturbate more has not altered this socialization process."

Masturbation is an important means of learning about our bodies (Atwood & Gagnon, 1987). Through masturbation, children and adolescents learn what is sexually pleasing, how to move their bodies, and what their natural rhythms are. The activity has no harmful physical effects. Although masturbation often decreases significantly when individuals make love regularly, it is not necessarily a temporary substitute for sexual intercourse but a legitimate form of sexual activity in its own right. Sex therapists may encourage clients to masturbate as a means of overcoming specific sexual problems and discovering their personal sexual potential. Masturbation, whether practiced alone or mutually with a partner, is also a form of safer sex, because ordinarily there is no exchange of semen, vaginal secretions, or blood, which could transmit HIV or other organisms that cause STDs. (See Chapters 16 and 17 for discussion of STDs, HIV, and safer sex guidelines.)

We are capable of experiencing genital pleasure from birth through old age. Male infants have been observed with erect penises a few hours after birth. A baby boy may laugh in his crib while playing with his erect penis (although he does not ejaculate). Baby girls sometimes move their bodies rhythmically, almost violently, appearing to experience orgasm. And men as old as 102 have reported masturbating. In fact, for the aged, because of the loss of partners, masturbation regains much of the primacy it lost after adolescence as a means of sexual pleasure.

Childhood Children often accidentally discover that playing with their genitals is pleasurable and continue this activity until reprimanded by an adult (see Chapter 6). By the time they are 4 or 5, children have usually been taught that adults consider this form of behavior "nasty." Parents generally react overwhelmingly negatively to masturbation, regardless of the age and gender of the child (Gagnon, 1985). Later, this negative attitude becomes generalized to include the sexual pleasure that accompanies the behavior. Children thus learn to conceal their masturbatory play. (See Perspective 1.)

Adolescence When boys and girls reach adolescence, they no longer regard masturbation as ambiguous play, but know that it is sexual. As discussed in Chapter 6, this is a period of intense change emotionally and biologically. Complex emotions are often involved in adolescent masturbation. Teenagers may feel guilt and shame for engaging in a practice that their parents and other adults indicate is wrong or bad, and they may be fearful of discovery. A girl who feels vaginal lubrication or finds stains on her underpants for the first time may be frightened, as may a boy who sees the

Masturbation is an intrinsically and seriously disordered act.
Vatican Declaration
on Sexual Ethics

Perspective 1

MASTURBATION: FROM SIN TO INSANITY

Masturbation has a long history of being associated with sin or psychopathology. Our traditional aversion to it can be traced to antiquity.

The Judeo-Christian grounding for the prohibition against masturbation is found in the story of Onan (Genesis 38:7–19):

And Er, Judah's first born, was wicked in the sight of the Lord; and the Lord slew him. And Judah said unto Onan, Go in unto thy brother's wife, and marry her, and raise up the seed to thy brother. And Onan knew that the seed should not be his; and it came to pass, when he went in unto his brother's wife, that he spilled it on the ground, lest that he should give seed to his brother. And the thing which he did displeased the Lord; whereupon he slew him also.

Although God struck Onan down, it is not clear why he was slain: Was it because of withdrawal (coitus interruptus) or because he had disobeyed God's command? (The general consensus among biblical scholars is that he was slain for the sin of disobedience [Bullough, 1976]). But the historical significance of the story is that, despite the message's reference to withdrawal, the "sin of Onan" has traditionally been interpreted as masturbation. "Onanism," in fact, has been used interchangeably with "masturbation." And because Onan was slain, masturbation has been viewed as a particularly heinous sexual offense in the eyes of God. In the Talmudic tradition, masturbation was made a capital offense. Christianity identified it as a form of sodomy, which, at different times, was punishable by burning.

In the Judeo-Christian tradition, masturbation was treated as a sin with a high price: damnation. The nineteenth century, however, exacted a new tribute from the sinner: physical debilitation, insanity, or death (Hall, 1992). Under the leadership of physicians, the consequences of masturbation shifted from moral to physical. They believed that semen contained precious nutrients that were absorbed by the body to sustain life and growth. The Swiss physician Tissot had first warned of the physical dangers of masturbation in 1758, asserting that weakness was caused by the loss of semen and the draining of "nervous energy" from the brain. By the middle of the nineteenth century, physicians warned of a masturbatory plague that was enveloping the civilized world (Gay, 1986).

For nineteenth-century Americans, masturbation was *the* sexual evil against which individuals had to struggle. O. S. Fowler urged citizens to form groups aimed at abolishing masturbation. "You must gird yourselves," he wrote, "to this disagreeable but indispensable work for philanthropy and reform, till we drive this common enemy from our midst" (Fowler, 1878). Children were especially susceptible to the practice. Victorians believed that children were not *naturally* sexual but learned to be sexual through exposure to vice and bad examples. External sources were responsible for children's becoming sexually pre-

semen of his first ejaculation. Although open discussion could alleviate fears, frank talk is not always possible in a setting that involves shame.

According to one survey, teenage boys masturbate about five times a week (LoPresto, Sherman, & Sherman, 1985). By the end of adolescence, virtually all males and about three-quarters of females have masturbated to orgasm. These gender differences may be the result of social conditioning

cocious. By refusing to recognize spontaneous childhood sexuality, Victorians were able to sustain the myth of childhood innocence.

Because children learned about masturbation by associating with "vile" playmates or being exposed to suggestive books, songs, or pictures, it became the parents' duty to closely supervise their children's friends and activities. These fears virtually compelled parents to interfere with their children's developing sexuality (Foucault, 1980). Because masturbation was a "secret vice," parents were to be suspicious of everything. Responsible parents, despite their reticence about sex, warned their children against the dangers of "self-abuse." There were patented devices to be attached to the child's penis so that if he touched it, an alarm sounded in his parents' bedroom, alerting them to the danger. Parents and masturbators alike purchased penile rings embedded with sharp prongs, which promised freedom from self-abuse.

Dr. Homer Bostwick (1860) received patients who were suffering from the "damnable effects of masturbation," recording a case history that describes the treatment:

> I advised him to have 25 leeches applied to the perinaeum [base of the penis] immediately, and sit over a bucket of hot water as soon as they should drop off, so that the steam and warm bathing would keep up further bleeding. I ordered the leeches to be followed by a blister, and hot poultices, hot mustard hip baths, etc., etc. I had his bowels opened with a dose of castor oil, and confined him to a light gruel, vegetable, and fruit diet, advising him to scrupulously avoid everything stimulating, to drink nothing but cold water and mucilaginous fluids.

The treatments continued for five weeks, until the man was pronounced "cured" and returned home. ("He was, of course, somewhat weakened and debilitated," Bostwick concluded.)

The almost hysterical fear of masturbation helped sustain the severe sexual restrictions that characterized the nineteenth century. Because masturbation is one of a person's first overtly sexual experiences, the feelings children develop about it will strongly influence their attitudes toward sexuality in general (Heiman, LoPicolo, & LoPicolo, 1988). Masturbatory hysteria instilled sexual fears and anxieties in the children of the nineteenth century. As these children grew into adults, they were vulnerable to believing the myths of sexual danger that would regulate their adult lives.

Fears about masturbation continued in diminished form throughout the first half of the twentieth century. Masturbation was no longer associated with death and insanity, however, but with arrested psychological development in children and neuroses in adults. Today, it continues to be viewed as immoral and a sign of emotional immaturity by many conservative religious denominations, especially by the Roman Catholic Church, which declared masturbation "an intrinsically and seriously disturbed act" (Patton, 1986). Until the late 1970s, *The Boy Scout Handbook* warned against the moral and psychological dangers of masturbation (Rowan, 1989).

and communication. Most boys discuss masturbatory experiences openly, relating different methods and recalling "near misses" when they were almost caught by their parents. Among boys, masturbation is a subject for camaraderie. In contrast, girls usually learn to masturbate through self-discovery. Because "nice girls" are not supposed to be sexual, they seldom talk about their own sexuality but hide it, repress it, or try to forget it. While white males are most likely to have their first ejaculation during masturbation, African American males more often experience their first ejaculation during sexual intercourse (Staples & Johnson, 1993). Comparable information is not available for female black adolescents and young adults.

Adulthood Masturbation continues after adolescence, although the frequency often declines among men and increases among women. A study found that 60% of women between ages 18 and 24 masturbated; they masturbated an average of 37 times a year (Hunt, 1974). About 80% of women reported masturbating by their late twenties or early thirties. Their masturbatory experiences remained stable through middle age and then slowly decreased.

Women who masturbate appear to hold more positive sexual attitudes and are more likely to be orgasmic than women who don't masturbate (Kelly, Strassberg, & Kircher, 1990). Among women who experience multiple orgasms, 26% experience them through masturbation (Darling & Davidson, 1991). Although the majority of women feel that orgasms experienced through masturbation differ from those experienced in sexual intercourse, they felt the same levels of sexual satisfaction (Davidson & Darling, 1989).

Most people continue to masturbate after they marry, although the rate is significantly smaller. Hunt reported that among married men in their late twenties or early thirties, about 72% masturbated, with a median frequency of 24 times a year (Hunt, 1974). Sixty-eight percent of the married women of this age group masturbated according to the median frequency. A *Redbook* survey of 100,000 women indicated that almost 75% masturbated during marriage—20% occasionally, and 20% often (Tavris & Sadd, 1977). The frequency was significantly higher among women who rated their marriages as unsatisfactory, suggesting that they masturbated because their personal and sexual relationships were unfulfilling.

There are many reasons for continuing the activity during marriage: Masturbation is a pleasurable form of sexual excitement, a spouse is away or unwilling, sexual intercourse is not satisfying, the partner(s) fear(s) sexual inadequacy, the individual acts out fantasies, or he or she seeks to release tension. During times of marital conflict, masturbation may act as a distancing device, with the masturbating spouse choosing masturbation over sexual intercourse as a means of emotional protection (Betchen, 1991).

Masturbation becomes an increasingly important means of sexual expression as men and women enter old age. Among older men and women, one researcher (Brecher, 1984) found in a nonrepresentative sample that among 60- to 69-year-old subjects, 50% of the men and 37% of the women reported masturbating; among those older than 70, 43% of the men and 33% of the women reported masturbating. As men aged, the frequency of masturbation increased while that of sexual intercourse declined (Weizman & Hart, 1987). By the time married men and women reached their eighties, the most common overt genital activity was masturbation. Masturbatory rates remained more or less constant between ages 80 and 90. Aged men nevertheless prefer sexual intercourse to masturbation (Mulligan & Palguta, 1991). Socioeconomic status also seems correlated to masturbation rates in old age. One study found that aged blue-collar men had lower rates of mutual masturbation with their wives than aged middle-class men (Cogen & Steinman, 1990).

INTERPERSONAL SEXUALITY

We often think that sex is sexual intercourse and that sexual interactions end with orgasm (usually the male's). But sex is not limited to sexual intercourse. Heterosexuals engage in a wide variety of sexual activities, which may include erotic touching, kissing, and oral and anal sex. Except for sexual intercourse, gay and lesbian couples engage in basically the same sexual activities as do heterosexuals.

One false move and I'm yours.
Groucho Marx

Touching

Where does sex begin for you? Whether it begins with the heart or the genitals, touch is the fire that melds the two into one. Touching is both a sign of caring and a signal for arousal.

Touching is often thought of as merely a prelude to the more overt sexual behaviors that lead to orgasm. Shere Hite (1976), however, argued that touching is a form of sexual behavior in itself. In fact, she titled a chapter in her book on female sexuality "Touching Is Sex, Too." "Women often said," reported Hite, "how much more important body contact and closeness were to them than orgasms per se in sex with a partner." According to one of her respondents, "Sex should be sheer luxuriating in pleasure, enveloped in warmth and touching all over—not a race for orgasm." Hite (1976) writes:

> There is no reason why physical intimacy with men should always consist of "foreplay" followed by intercourse and male orgasm; and there is no reason why intercourse must always be a part of heterosexual sex. Sex is intimate physical contact for pleasure, to share pleasure with another person (or just alone). You can have sex to orgasm, or not to orgasm, genital sex, or just physical intimacy—whatever seems right to you. There is never any reason to think the "goal" must be intercourse, and try to make what you feel fit into that context.

The most exciting thing is not doing it. If you fall in love with someone and never do it, it's much more exciting.

Andy Warhol

Touching does not need to be directed toward genitals or erogenous zones. The entire body is responsive to a touch or a caress; there are at least 50 nerve receptors per 100 square millimeters of skin, and the number of tactile points varies from 7 to 135 per square centimeter (Montagu, 1986). While women appear to be especially responsive to touch, traditional male sex roles give little significance to touching. Men tend to regard touching as a prelude to intercourse. When this occurs, touch is transformed into a demand for intercourse rather than an expression of intimacy or erotic play. The man's partner may become inhibited from touching or showing affection for fear her gestures will be misinterpreted as a sexual invitation (Barbach, 1982).

Masters and Johnson suggest a form of touching they call "pleasuring." **Pleasuring** is nongenital touching and caressing. Neither partner tries to sexually stimulate the other; they simply explore, discovering how their bodies respond to touching. The man guides the woman's hand over his body, telling her what feels good; she takes his hand and moves it over her body, telling him what she likes. Masters and Johnson (1970) write:

> The partner who is pleasuring is committed first to do just that; give pleasure. At a second level in the experience, the giver is to explore his or her own component of personal pleasure in doing the touching—to experience and appreciate

the sensuous dimensions of hard and soft, smooth and rough, warm and cool, qualities of texture and, finally, this somewhat indescribable aura of physical receptivity expressed by the partner being pleasured. After a reasonable length of time . . . the partners are to exchange roles of pleasuring (giving) and being pleasured (getting) and then repeat the procedure.

Such sharing gives each a sense of his or her own responses; it also allows each to discover what the other likes and dislikes. We can't assume we know what a particular person likes, for there is too much variation between people. Pleasuring opens the door to communication; couples discover that the entire body, not just the genitals, is erogenous.

Nude or clothed massages, back rubs, foot rubs, scalp massages—all are soothing and loving forms of touch. The sensuousness of touching may be enhanced by the use of lubricating oils. Such erotic touching is a form of safer sex.

Other forms of touching are more directly sexual, such as caressing, fondling, or rubbing our own or our partner's genitals or breasts. Sucking or licking earlobes, the neck, toes, or the insides of thighs, palms, or arms, can be highly stimulating. Oral stimulation of a woman's or man's breasts or nipples is often exciting. Moving one's genitals or breasts over a partner's face, chest, breasts, or genitals is very erotic for some people.

Stimulating your partner's clitoris or penis with your hand or fingers can increase excitement or lead to orgasm. Inserting a finger or fingers into your partner's wet vagina and rhythmically moving it at the pace your partner likes may be pleasing. Some women like to have their clitoris licked or stimulated with one hand while their vagina is being penetrated with the other. Men like having their penises lubricated so that their partner's hand glides smoothly over the shaft and glans penis. (Be sure to use a water-based lubricant if you plan to use a condom later, because oil-based lubricants may cause the condom to deteriorate.) Masturbating while your partner is holding you can be highly erotic for both people. Mutual masturbation can also be intensely sexual. Some people use sex toys, such as dildos, vibrators, or ben-wah balls to enhance sexual touching. These are discussed in Chapter 15.

As we enter old age, touching becomes increasingly significant as a primary form of erotic expression. Touching in all its myriad forms, ranging from holding hands to caressing, massaging to hugging, walking with arms around each other to fondling, becomes the touchstone of eroticism for the elderly (Weg, 1983b). One study found touching to be the primary form of erotic expression for married couples over age 80 (Bretschneider & McCoy, 1988).

Kissing

Kissing is usually our earliest interpersonal sexual experience, and its primal intensity may be traced back to our suckling as infants. The kiss is magic: Fairy tales keep alive the ancient belief that a kiss can undo spells and bring a prince or princess back to life. Parental kisses show love and often remedy the small hurts and injuries of childhood (Landau, 1989). And, of course, there is the kiss of betrayal: Judas's kiss, the Mafia "kiss of death."

I want a lover with a slow hand.
The Pointer Sisters

. . . I'll smother thee with kisses;
And yet not cloy thy lips with
loathed satiety,
But rather famish them amid their
plenty,
Making them red and pale with
fresh variety;
Ten kisses short as one, one long as
twenty:
A summer's day will seem an hour
but short
Being wasted in such time-beguiling
sport.
William Shakespeare

Pleasuring is the giving and receiving of erotic pleasure for its own sake.

Kissing is often associated with religious themes. The tradition of kissing under mistletoe can be traced to ancient times when mistletoe was revered as the most sacred plant of the Druids, the priestly clan of the Celtics. Throughout pagan Europe, mistletoe was venerated because it retained its green leaves when the oak, another sacred plant, lost its green mantle. Northern Europeans thought that the mistletoe, which was believed to be the oak's genitals, held the oak's spirit during its wintery "death." Kissing under mistletoe during winter, when the plant is rich in berries, was believed to ensure fertility. (Because of its pagan associations, mistletoe is rarely found in churches.) The string of Xs at the end of a love letter, representing kisses, links kissing to Christianity, for the X symbolized the Greek letter *chi*, which during the Middle Ages stood for Christ. Because most medieval men and women were illiterate, they signed their names with an X and kissed the mark to affirm their sincerity; eventually, the kiss and the X became synonymous (Tuleja, 1987).

Kissing is probably the most acceptable of all premarital sexual activities (Jurich & Polson, 1985). The tender lover's kiss symbolizes love, and the erotic lover's kiss, of course, simultaneously represents and *is* passion. Both men and women regard kissing as a romantic act, a symbol of affection as well as desire (Tucker, 1992; Tucker, Marvin, & Vivian, 1991). A cross-cultural study of jealousy found that kissing is also associated with a couple's boundary maintenance. In each culture studied, kissing another person evoked jealousy (Buunk & Hupka, 1987). Although kissing is expected to be confined to a single partner in exclusive dating relationships, a study of college students found that 60% of the men and 40% of the women had been involved in erotic kissing outside the relationship (Hansen, 1987).

The lips and mouth are highly sensitive to touch and are exquisitely erotic parts of our bodies. Kisses discover, explore, and excite the body. They also involve the senses of taste and smell, which are especially important because they activate unconscious memories and associations. Often we are aroused by familiar smells associated with particular sexual memories: a person's body scent, a perfume associated with an erotic experience. In some languages—among the Borneans, for example—the word "kiss" literally translates as smell. In fact, among the Eskimos and Maoris, there is no mouth kissing, only the touching of noses to facilitate smelling.

While kissing may appear innocent, it is in many ways the height of intimacy. The adolescent's first kiss is often regarded as a milestone, a rite of passage, the beginning of adult sexuality (Alapack, 1991). It is an important developmental step, marking the beginning of a young person's sexuality. Blumstein and Schwartz (1983) report that many of their respondents found it unimaginable to engage in sexual intercourse without kissing. In fact, they found that those who have a minimal (or nonexistent) amount of kissing feel distant from their partners but may have intercourse anyway as a physical release. (Interestingly, both female and male prostitutes are more willing to engage in oral sex, sexual intercourse, or other sexual activities than to kiss their clients, specifically *because* kissing symbolizes intimacy.)

The amount of kissing differs according to sexual orientation. Lesbian couples tend to engage in kissing more than heterosexual couples, while gay male couples kiss less than heterosexual couples (Blumstein & Schwartz, 1983).

Ordinary kissing is considered safer sex. French kissing is probably safe, unless the kiss is hard and draws blood, or either partner has sores or cuts in or around the mouth. (See Chapter 17 for further discussion of kissing and HIV.)

Oral-Genital Sex

In recent years, oral sex has become a part of our sexual scripts (Gagnon, 1986). The two types of oral-genital sex are cunnilingus and fellatio. **Cunnilingus** is the erotic stimulation of a woman's vulva by her partner's mouth and tongue. The word is derived from the Latin *cunnus*, vulva, and *lingere*, to lick. **Fellatio** is the oral stimulation of a man's penis by his partner's sucking and licking. It is from the Latin *fellare*, to suck. Cunnilingus and fellatio may be performed singly or simultaneously. When two people orally stimulate each other simultaneously, their activity is sometimes called "sixty-nine" or *"soixante-neuf,"* which means sixty-nine in French. The term comes from the configuration "69," which visually suggests the activity.

For people of every orientation (especially among high school and college students), oral sex is an increasingly important and healthy aspect of their sexual selves (Wilson & Medora, 1990). Psychologist Lilian Rubin reports that young women today express pleasure about oral sex, in contrast to twenty years ago; a minority of middle-aged women, who earlier believed oral sex was "dirty" or immoral, continue to feel some ambivalence (Rubin,

Rufus T. Firefly: *What about your husband?*

Teasdale: *He's dead.*

Firefly: *He's just using that as an excuse.*

Teasdale: *I was with him to the end.*

Firefly: *No wonder he passed away.*

Teasdale: *I held him in my arms and kissed him.*

Firefly: *So—it was murder.*

The Marx Brothers

Whoever named it necking was a poor judge of anatomy.

Groucho Marx

1990). Of the men and women in various studies, 60–90% report that they have engaged in oral sex (Delamater & MacCorquodale, 1979; Petersen et al., 1983). Blumstein and Schwartz (1983) found that 50% of gay couples, 39% of lesbian couples, and 30% of heterosexual couples usually or always had oral sex as part of their lovemaking routine.

While oral-genital sex is increasingly accepted by white middle-class Americans, it remains less permissible among some ethnic groups. African Americans, for example, have lower rates of oral-genital sex than whites, because many blacks consider it immoral (Wilson, 1986). A recent large-scale national study found that 79% of white men had performed oral sex, compared with 43% of African American men and 74.8% of Latino men. Eighty-one percent of white men had received oral sex, compared to 61% of African American men, and 79.3% of Latinos. The higher the education level, the greater the likelihood of having been involved in oral sexual activities (Billy, Tanfer, Grady, & Klepinger, 1993). Oral sex is becoming increasingly accepted, however, among black women (Wyatt, Peters, & Gutherie, 1988). This is especially true if they have a good relationship and communicate well with their partners (Wyatt & Lyons-Rowe, 1990). Among married Latinos, oral sex is relatively uncommon. When oral sex occurs, it is usually at the male's instigation, as women are not expected to be interested in erotic variety (Guerrero Pavich, 1986). Although little is known about older Asian Americans and Asian immigrants, college-age Asian Americans appear to accept oral-genital sex to the same degree as middle-class whites (Cochran, Mays, & Leung, 1991).

Among girls of junior high school age, more have given or received oral sex than have engaged in sexual intercourse; among boys, more have had sexual intercourse than have given or received oral sex. For both sexes, fellatio is less common than either sexual intercourse or cunnilingus (Newcomer & Udry, 1985). A study of university students of both sexes found that oral sex was regarded as an egalitarian, mutual practice (Moffatt, 1989). Students felt less guilty about it than about sexual intercourse because oral sex was not "going all the way." Another study of female undergraduates found that 61% had engaged in oral sex (Herold & Way, 1983). For college students, oral sex is more acceptable after the early stages of a relationship; students are more likely to approve of it for people in general than for their close friends, brothers, or sisters (Sprecher, 1989).

Some (including the Catholic Church) consider oral sex unnatural or sinful because it does not serve reproduction. Others believe it is something in which only gay men or lesbians engage. The right of states to criminalize oral sex as sodomy was upheld by the Supreme Court in 1986 (*Bowers* v. *Hardwick*). Although criminal statutes against oral sex apply to men and women of all sexual orientations, in recent years sodomy laws have been enforced only against gay men and lesbians (Leonard, 1991).

Cunnilingus In cunnilingus, a woman's genitals are stimulated by her partner's tongue and mouth, which gently and rhythmically caress and lick her clitoris and the surrounding area (Figure 10.3). During arousal, the mouth and lips can nibble, lick, and kiss the inner thighs, the stomach, the mons pubis, and then move to the sensitive labia minora. Orgasm may be brought on by rhythmically stimulating the clitoris. Many women find cun-

FIGURE 10.3 Cunnilingus.

nilingus one of the most arousing activities. Hite (1976) reported that 42% of the women in her study had orgasms regularly from cunnilingus. One woman wrote: "A tongue offers gentleness and precision and wetness and is the perfect organ for contact. And, besides, it produces sensational orgasms!"

Until about 20 years ago, cunnilingus was not widely accepted as part of the sexual repertoire of heterosexual couples. Increasing acceptance is due to more liberal sexual attitudes, which encourage sexual experimentation and view the purpose of sex as erotic pleasure rather than reproduction. In addition, the women's movement of the 1960s and 1970s encouraged women to reject the view of their genitals as "pudenda," things of shame. Women began to celebrate the beauty of their bodies and to accept the looks, smell, and wetness of their genitals (Rubin, 1990). In 1987, a survey of 26,000 women reported that 45% of its respondents engaged in cunnilingus at least half the time they had intercourse; 84% reported enjoying it (Rubenstein & Tavris, 1987). Another survey found that the overwhelming majority of men enjoyed giving oral sex to their partners (Petersen et al., 1983).

Some women feel uneasy about receiving oral sex. In part, this may be a continuation of old taboos or negative feelings about their genitals. In part it may also be an issue of reciprocity (Blumstein & Schwartz, 1983). Because many women do not give oral sex as often as they receive it, they may feel uncomfortable about cunnilingus.

Among lesbians, cunnilingus is a common activity for experiencing orgasm. In contrast to heterosexual couples, lesbian couples may be more inventive, less restrained, and more involved (Califia, 1979). This may be partly because, as women, each partner can identify with what the other may enjoy. But as many as 25% of the lesbians in Blumstein and Schwartz's study (1983) engaged in cunnilingus rarely or never. Instead, they relied on

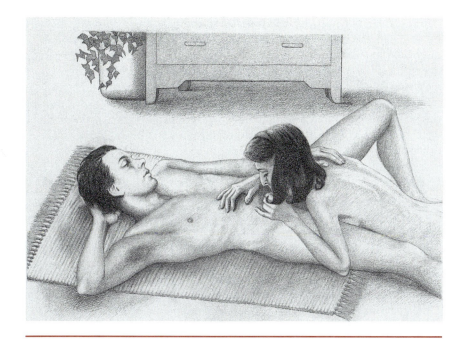

FIGURE 10.4 Fellatio.

holding, kissing, manual stimulation, and pressing themselves erotically against each other. Nevertheless, the more often lesbians in the study had oral sex, the more likely they were to be satisfied with their sex lives and partners.

There are, however, concerns for some women regarding cunnilingus. The most common worries revolve around whether the other person is enjoying it and, especially, whether the vulva has an unpleasant odor (Hite, 1976). Concerns about vaginal odors may be eased by washing. Undeodorized white soap will wash away unpleasant smells without disturbing the vagina's natural erotic scent. If an unpleasant odor arises from the genitals, it may be because the woman has a vaginal infection.

A woman may also worry that her partner is not enjoying the experience because the partner is giving pleasure rather than receiving it. What she may not recognize is that such sexual excitement is often mutual. Because our mouths and tongues are erotically sensitive, the giver finds erotic excitement in arousing his or her partner. As one man explained (Levine & Barbach, 1983):

> I love the softness, the warmth, and the moisture, which is a direct reaction to what I'm doing, so that's terribly exciting. A woman responding to the way I touch her genitals is one of the biggest turn-ons.

Fellatio In fellatio, a man's penis is taken into his partner's mouth. The partner licks the glans penis and gently stimulates the shaft (Figure 10.4). If the penis is not erect, it usually will become erect within a few minutes. The partner sucks more vigorously as excitement increases, down toward the base of the penis and then back up, in a rhythmical motion, being careful not to bite hard or scrape the penis with the teeth. While the man is being stimulated by mouth, his partner can also stroke the shaft of the penis by hand. Gently playing with the testicles is also arousing as long as they are not held too tightly. As in cunnilingus, the couple should experiment to discover what is most stimulating and exciting. The man should be careful not to thrust his penis too deeply into his partner's throat, for that may cause a gagging reflex. He should let his partner control how deeply the penis goes into the mouth. The gag reflex can also be reconditioned by slowly inserting the penis into the mouth at increasing depth over a number of times. Some women feel that fellatio is more intimate than sexual intercourse, whereas others feel that it is less intimate (Petersen et al., 1983). It is the most common form of sexual activity performed on men by prostitutes (Freund, Lee, & Leonard, 1991).

While men are generally enthusiastic about fellatio, women have mixed feelings about it (Blumstein & Schwartz, 1983). Some find it highly arousing, while others feel it is a form of submissiveness, especially if they sense that their partner demands it. If the woman's partner is too demanding or directing, she may feel he is controlling or selfish. If she accedes to his wishes, she may feel psychologically coerced. This sense of coercion may block the pleasure she may otherwise have enjoyed by engaging in fellatio.

For gay men, fellatio is an important component of their sexuality. As with sexual intercourse for heterosexual men, however, fellatio is only one activity in their sexual repertoire. Generally speaking, the more often gay couples engage in giving and receiving oral sex, the more satisfied they are (Blumstein & Schwartz, 1983). Because oral sex often involves power symbolism, reciprocity is important. If one partner always performs oral sex, he may feel he is subordinate to the other. The most satisfied gay couples alternate between giving and receiving oral sex.

A common concern about fellatio centers around ejaculation. Should the male ejaculate into his partner's mouth? Semen may have a slightly bitter taste for some, but others definitely like it. Some people find it exciting to suck even harder on the penis during or following ejaculation; others do not like the idea of semen in the mouth. For many, a key issue is whether to swallow the semen. Some swallow it, others spit it out; many rinse their mouth afterward. It is simply a matter of personal preference, and the man who is receiving fellatio should accept his partner's feelings about it and avoid equating a dislike for swallowing with a personal rejection.

Some partners worry, as they should, about the transmission of HIV through fellatio (see Chapter 17). It is possible to orally contract HIV if there are sores within the mouth. To be safe, a condom should be worn during fellatio.

Sexual Intercourse

The sexual act is in time what the tiger is in space.

Georges Bataille

Sexual intercourse is a very popular activity. Throughout the world, there are over 100 million acts of sexual intercourse daily. It is also a complex activity with a multitude of meanings and consequences. Each day, there are 910,000 conceptions, 150,000 abortions, and 350,000 cases of STDs (World Health Association, 1992). But pregnancy and disease are only some of the consequences. Sexual intercourse has intense personal meaning (Cate, Long, Angera, & Draper, 1993; Schwartz, 1993). It is a source of pleasure, communication, and love. If forced, however, it becomes an instrument of aggression and pain. Its meaning changes depending on the context in which we engage in it (Sprecher & McKinney, 1993). How we feel about it may depend as much (or more) on the feelings and motives we bring to it as on the techniques we use or the orgasms we experience.

While sexual intercourse is important for most sexually involved couples, its significance differs between men and women (Blumstein & Schwartz, 1983; Sprecher & McKinney, 1993). For men, sexual intercourse is only one of several activities that they enjoy. For many heterosexual women, however, intercourse is central to their sexual satisfaction. More than any other heterosexual sexual activity, sexual intercourse involves equal participation by both partners. Both partners equally and simultaneously give and receive. As a result, women feel a greater shared intimacy than they do in other activities.

Meanings of Sexual Intercourse Sexual behaviors, but especially sexual intercourse because of its cultural significance, can be used in a variety of ways: to express love, explore erotic pleasures, to reproduce, to keep a person interested in you, to relieve loneliness, to dominate another, to make yourself or another feel guilty, or to relieve physical tension. A person can make love one day to show affection, the next to gain revenge, the next to pretend love. Other sexual activities may also take on many of the same meanings among gay men and lesbians, as well as heterosexuals. (See Perspective 2 for discussion of nineteenth-century attitudes toward sexual intercourse.)

Sexual positions and activities may also have meanings that vary from person to person and from time to time. A person who wishes to control, for example, may insist on always being in the position above his partner as a symbol of power. Another person may refuse to assume any but the traditional "missionary" position because of embarrassment or shame concerning sex. There are no rules that define a specific meaning for particular acts; meaning changes from context to context and from person to person.

Sexual Positions There are two basic positions in sexual intercourse—face-to-face and rear-entry—although the playfulness of the couple, their movement from one bodily configuration to another, and their ingenuity can provide an infinite variety. The same positions played out in different settings can cause an intensity that transforms the ordinary into the extraordinary.

Face-to-Face, Man Above There are several advantages to the man-above position (Figure 10.5). First, it is the traditional, correct, or "official" position in our culture, which many people find reassuring and validating of their sexuality. (The man-above position is commonly known as the missionary position because it was the position missionaries encouraged people to use.) Second, it can allow the male maximum activity, movement, and control of coitus, validating the traditional gender roles, in which the male controls and the woman responds. Third, it allows the woman freedom to stimulate her clitoris to assist in her orgasm. The primary disadvantages are that it limits the woman's movement and that she may feel too much weight on her if her partner does not raise himself with his arms or elbows.

Our collective fantasies center on mayhem, cruelty, and violent death. Loving images of the human body—especially of bodies seeking pleasure or expressing love—inspire us with the urge to censor.
Barbara Ehrenreich

The sexual act without intimacy retains a separateness that cannot be forgotten by orgasm.
Erich Fromm

It's not the men in my life, it's the life in my men that counts.
Mae West

The conventional position makes me claustrophobic. And the others give me either a stiff neck or lockjaw.
Tallulah Bankhead

FIGURE 10.5 Face-to-Face, Man Above.

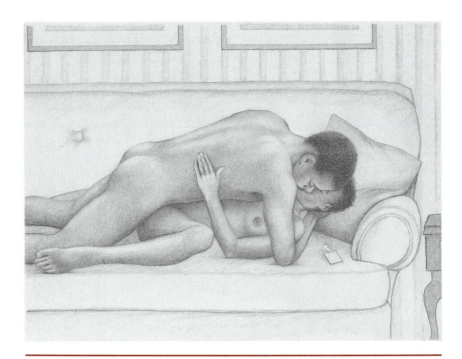

FIGURE 10.6 Face-to-Face, Woman Above.

Face-to-Face, Woman Above The woman either lies above her partner or sits astride him (Figure 10.6). There are several advantages to the woman-above position. First, it allows her maximum activity, movement, and control. She can control the depth to which the penis penetrates. Second, when

NINETEENTH-CENTURY ATTITUDES TOWARD SEXUAL INTERCOURSE

While our culture places a high value on sexual intercourse, it was once viewed as perilous activity. During the nineteenth century, "excessive" sexual intercourse was considered as dangerous as masturbation.

The Fear of Death

Moralists complained that many men assumed that if they had refrained from masturbation as boys they were then free to have intercourse as often as they pleased after marriage. Physicians disabused them of this idea. Sexual intercourse could also lead to death. "But does marriage entitle the party to kill the other or themselves?" Fowler (1878) asked. Coitus, like masturbation, involved the loss of semen, a loss considered dangerous to a man's health. John Cowan, whose *Science of New Life* (1870) was reprinted frequently between 1860 and 1920, warned men:

> It is best to avoid marrying widows, who may have had one or more husbands, whose premature deaths were caused by other than accident, or other plainly unavoidable cause; for . . . they are likely to possess qualities in them, that in their exercise use up their husband's stock of vitality, rapidly weakening the system, and so causing premature death.

Sexual intercourse was believed to be dangerous not only because of the emission of semen but also because of the orgasm. Dr. Trall wrote that "the very intensity of the sexual orgasm, when legitimately exercised (that is, for procreation) is sufficient evidence that it is not to be promiscuously nor too frequently excited with impunity" (Trall, 1853). Dio Lewis, another prominent sexual reformer, cautioned that a married couple should engage in intercourse "with a temperate affection, without violent transporting desires of too sensual applications" (Lewis, 1890). (The sports superstition held today by some male players and coaches about the necessity of avoiding sexual contact with women before games can be traced back to Victorian fears about semen loss.) By the 1920s, however, male fears of death resulting from "excessive" masturbation or intercourse had disappeared from public consciousness.

Female Control of Sexual Intercourse

The nineteenth century witnessed a dramatic improvement in the status of women and a growing consciousness of women as individuals. Despite the celebration of motherhood, women were no longer accepting themselves as simply the bearers of children and the helpmates of men. They were increasingly viewing large families as burdens or obstacles to their greater participation in the world outside the home. In order to improve their status, women sought to free themselves from the burdens of limitless childbearing and familial responsibilities (Degler, 1980). In fact, this period witnessed the most dramatic decline in fertility in American history. Between 1800 and 1900, fertility dropped 50%, falling from an average of seven children per woman to about three and a half.

Almost without exception, feminists in the nineteenth century supported the idea that women possessed less sexuality than men and that women were to be responsible for determining the frequency of sexual intercourse.

According to historian Carl Degler (1980), the ideology of male restraint and female purity served women's desire to limit family size. Women reduced their childbearing by insisting that they, not men, control the frequency of intercourse. In this sense, the Victorian belief in women's sexual purity worked not against women's emancipation but for it. Degler (1980) wrote:

(continued)

she sits astride her partner, either of them can caress or stimulate her vulva and clitoris. The primary disadvantage is that some men or women may feel uneasy about the woman assuming a position that signifies an active role in coitus.

Rear-Entry   There are several variations on the rear-entry position. The woman may kneel supported on her arms and receive the penis in her vagina from behind. The couple may lie on their sides, with the woman's back to her partner (Figure 10.7). This position offers variety and may be particularly suitable during pregnancy. Clitoral stimulation by the woman is facilitated in this position. Generally, it is also possible for the man to stimulate her during intercourse. Some people object to the rear-entry position as being "animal-like." Or they may feel it inhibits intimacy or resembles anal intercourse.

Face-to-Face on Side   In this position, both partners lie on their sides facing each other (Figure 10.8). Each partner has greater freedom to caress and stimulate the other. The major drawback is that some may find it difficult to keep the penis inside the vagina.

Anal Eroticism

Anal eroticism refers to sexual activities involving the anus, whose delicate membranes (as well as tabooed nature) make it erotically sensitive for many people. These activities include **analingus,** the licking of the anal region (colloquially known as "rimming" or "tossing salad"). Anal-manual contact consists of stimulating the anal region with the fingers; sometimes an entire fist may be inserted (known as "fisting" among gay white males and "fingering" by gay African Americans). Many couples engage in this activity along with fellatio or sexual intercourse.

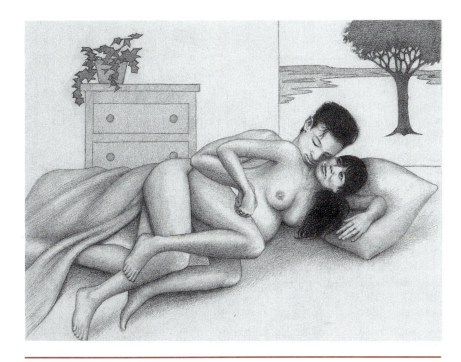

FIGURE 10.7 Rear-Entry.

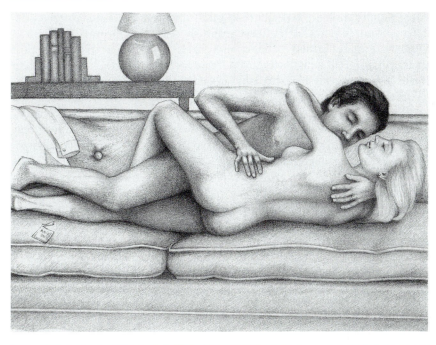

FIGURE 10.8 Face-to-Face on Side.

Anal intercourse refers to the male's inserting his erect penis into his partner's anus. Both heterosexuals and gay men participate in this activity (colloquially known as "butt fucking" by heterosexuals, "Greek" by gay white males, and "georging" by gay African Americans [Mays, Cochran, Belinger, & Smith, 1992]). Anal intercourse is a major mode of sexual interaction for gay men. In fact, there are more colloquial terms for anal eroticism among gay men than any other form of sexual activity (Mays et al., 1992; Mays, Cochran, Smith, & Daniels, 1993). For heterosexual couples, anal intercourse is generally an experiment or occasional activity rather than a common mode of sexual expression. In the 1974 *Redbook* survey, almost 40% of the women had tried anal intercourse; in the 1987 survey, 43% had tried it, but only 12% reported enjoying it, in contrast to 40% in the earlier survey (Rubenstein & Sadd, 1987; Tavris & Sadd, 1977). In the Hunt study (1974), almost half the married men and a quarter of the married women had tried it. A national study of anal sex practices by American men (orientation not stated) found considerable variation by ethnicity (Billy, Tanfer, Grady, & Klepinger, 1993). Among men age 20–39, about 21% of whites, 13.6% of African Americans, and 24% of Latinos have experienced anal intercourse. A review of recent studies found that about 10% of heterosexual couples regularly engage in anal sex (Voeller, 1991).

Among gay men, anal intercourse is less common than oral sex, but it is, nevertheless, an important ingredient to the sexual satisfaction of many gays (Berger, 1991; Blumstein & Schwartz, 1983). While heterosexual imagery portrays the person who penetrates as "masculine" and the penetrated person as "feminine," this imagery does not generally reflect gay reality. For both partners, anal intercourse is regarded as masculine.

While anal sex may heighten eroticism for those who engage in it, from a health perspective it is riskier than most other forms of sexual interaction. The rectum is particularly susceptible to sexually transmitted diseases (Agnew, 1986). Because of HIV, anal intercourse is potentially the most dangerous form of sexual interaction. Anal intercourse is the most prevalent mode of transmitting HIV sexually, among both gay men and heterosexuals (Voeller, 1991). Because the delicate rectal tissues are easily lacerated, the tissues allow the AIDS virus (carried within semen) to enter the bloodstream. If a couple practices anal intercourse, they should engage in it *only* if both are certain that they are free from HIV *and* if they use a condom. As a result of health concerns, the rate of unprotected anal sex between gay men is diminishing (McKusick, Coates, Morin, & Pollack, 1990).

If the penis or a foreign object is inserted in the anus, it must be washed before insertion into the vagina because it may cause a bacterial infection. Other health hazards associated with anal erotic practices include rupturing the rectum with foreign objects, and laceration of the anus or rectal wall through the use of enemas. Licking the anus puts individuals at risk of acquiring HIV, hepatitis, or other sexually transmitted diseases (see Chapter 16).

The degree and kind of a person's sexuality reaches up into the ultimate pinnacle of his spirit.
Friedrich Nietzsche

As we have seen, sexual behaviors cannot be separated from attraction and desire. Our autoerotic activities are as important to our sexuality as our interpersonal ones. Although the sexual behaviors we examined in this chapter are the most common in our society, there are other, less typical activities in which many of us engage. These include cross-dressing and fetishism, as well as such consensual activities as dominance and submission. Still others include nonconsensual behaviors ranging from exhibitionism and voyeurism to child molestation. We discuss these atypical behaviors in Chapter 11.

SUMMARY

Sexual Attraction and Desire

• What constitutes sexual attractiveness varies across cultures. Our culture prefers slender women with large breasts and men with well-defined arm and pectoral muscles. Both men and women are attracted to the buttocks of the other sex. Gay men and heterosexual women share many of the same ideals regarding body shape for men; bisexuals may be attracted to others on the basis of particular physical characteristics rather than on the basis of gender.

• Because of the halo effect, attractive people are assumed to be more sexual and permissive than unattractive people. Attractive college women may be more likely to have engaged in sexual intercourse and oral sex than unattractive women.

• Sexual desire may exist independently of overt sexual responses. Desire is highly variable and consists of three components: sexual drive, sexual wishes, and sexual motivation. Fluctuations in frequency and intensity can be attributed to changes in these components throughout life.

Sexual Scripts

• Sexual scripts organize our sexual impulses. They have three major components: cultural, intrapersonal, and interpersonal. The cultural script provides the general patterns sexual behaviors are expected to take in a particular society. The intrapersonal script interprets our physiological responses as sexual or not. The interpersonal script is the shared conventions and signals that make sexual activities between two people possible.

Autoeroticism

• *Autoeroticism* refers to sexual activities that involve only the self. They include sexual fantasies, erotic dreams, and masturbation.

• Sexual fantasies are probably the most universal of all sexual behaviors; they are normal aspects of our sexuality. Erotic fantasies have several functions: they take our generalized sexual drives and help define and direct them, they allow us to plan or anticipate erotic situations, they provide pleasurable escape from routine, they introduce novelty, and they offer clues to our unconscious.

• Most men and women masturbate. Masturbation may begin as early as infancy and continue throughout old age. Attitudes toward masturbation vary by ethnicity.

Interpersonal Sexuality

• The erotic potential of touching has been undervalued because our culture tends to be orgasm-oriented, especially among males. *Pleasuring* is a means by which couples get to know each other erotically through touching and caressing.

• Erotic kissing is usually our earliest interpersonal sexual experience and is regarded as a rite of passage into adult sexuality.

• Oral-genital sex is becoming increasingly accepted, especially among young adults. *Cunnilingus* is the stimulation of the vulva with the tongue; it is engaged in by both heterosexuals and lesbians. *Fellatio* is the stimulation of the penis with the mouth; it is engaged in by both heterosexuals and gay men.

• Sexual intercourse is a complex interaction between two people. It is both a means of reproduction and a form of communication.

• Anal eroticism refers to sexual activities involving the anus. It is engaged in by heterosexuals, gay men, and lesbians.

KEY TERMS

erotophilia	pleasuring	analingus
autoeroticism	cunnilingus	anal intercourse
masterbation	fellatio	

SUGGESTIONS FOR READING

Barbach, Lonnie. *For Each Other: Sharing Sexual Intimacy*. New York: Bantam, 1984. A best-selling book describing women's sexual activities, attitudes, and feelings.

Comfort, Alex. *The Joy of Sex: A Gourmet Guide to Lovemaking*, 2nd ed. New York: Crown Publishers, 1986. A revised version of the contemporary classic on sex and sexuality.

Dodson, Betty. *Sex for One*. New York: Harmony Publications, 1987. Self-discovery techniques through masturbation for women and men; includes sensitive illustrations.

Janus, Samuel, and Cynthia Janus. *The Janus Report on Sexual Behavior*. New York: John Wiley & Sons, 1993. A large-scale, representative study of contemporary American sexual behavior.

Kennedy, Adele, and Susan Dean. *Touching for Pleasure*. Chatsworth, CA: Chatsworth Press, 1986. An exploration of the varieties of sensual and sexual touch, with soft charcoal drawings.

Kroll, Ken, and Erica Levy Klein. *Enabling Romance: A Guide to Love, Sex, and Relationships for the Disabled*. New York: Harmony Books, 1992. Hundreds of men and women with disabilities discuss stereotypes, different ways of being sexual, the use of sex toys, and strengthening relationships.

Loulan, JoAnn. *Lesbian Sex*. San Francisco: Spinsters Books, 1984. One of the most popular books on lesbian sexuality and sexual enhancement.

Silverstein, Charles, and Felice Picano. *The New Joy of Gay Sex*. New York: HarperCollins, 1992. An illustrated guide to gay male sexuality.

Zilbergeld, Bernie. *The New Male Sexuality Book*. Boston: Little, Brown, 1992. An updated version of the classic work on male sexuality, describing sexual myths, communication, and sexual expression.

Chapter Eleven

ATYPICAL AND PARAPHILIC SEXUAL BEHAVIOR

PREVIEW: SELF-QUIZ

1. Domination and submission activities are generally more secret among heterosexuals than among gay men and lesbians. True or false?

2. Sadomasochism is clinically described as a sexual perversion. True or false?

3. Exhibitionists are usually old men who expose their genitals to children. True or false?

4. Sexual interactions with animals were once believed to be a sign of witchcraft. True or false?

5. In most cases, the best response to receiving an obscene phone call is to say nothing and hang up. True or false?

6. Men who molest boys may identify themselves as gay, bisexual, or heterosexual in their adult sexual relationships. True or false?

7. Voyeurs are often also exhibitionists or obscene phone callers. True or false?

8. The story of Sleeping Beauty contains elements of necrophilia. True or false?

9. As many as 1000 males accidentally hang or asphyxiate themselves each year while engaging in unusual masturbatory activities. True or false?

10. Unusual or bizarre sexual fantasies are experienced at times by most people. True or false?

ANSWERS 1. T, 2. F, 3. F, 4. T, 5. T, 6. T, 7. T, 8. T, 9. T, 10. T

Chapter Outline

In a particularly vicious election campaign, the late Florida senator Claude Pepper was accused of being a "shameless extrovert," whose sister was known to be a New York "thespian." His opponent claimed that the senator "practiced celibacy" prior to marriage and later engaged in "nepotism" with his sister-in-law (Catchpole, 1992). These "accusations," which Pepper's opponent hoped would imply some kind of unnatural or perverted activity, refer simply to the senator's being outgoing (an extrovert), having an actress sister (a thespian), being sexually abstinent prior to marriage (celibacy), and giving his sister-in-law preferential treatment because of their relationship (nepotism). But the use of clinical- or moral-sounding terms points to the power of labeling. Sometimes, labels help us understand behavior; at other times, they interfere. This is especially true as we examine unusual or atypical sexual activities.

In this chapter, we examine atypical sexual behaviors, such as cross-dressing and domination and submission (D/S), which are not within the range of sexual behaviors in which people typically engage. Then we turn to sexual behaviors that are classified by the American Psychiatric Association (1994) as paraphilias. The noncoercive paraphilias include fetishism, transvestism, and zoophilia. The coercive paraphilias include pedophilia, sexual sadism, sexual masochism, and necrophilia. Finally, we examine treatment for paraphilias.

ATYPICAL VERSUS PARAPHILIC BEHAVIOR

The range of human sexual behavior is almost infinite. Yet most of our activities and fantasies, such as coitus, oral-genital sex, masturbation, and our orientation as heterosexual, gay, lesbian, or bisexual, cluster within a general range of behaviors and desires. Those behaviors and fantasies that do not fall in this general range are considered atypical. In this chapter, we will use **atypical sexual behavior** to refer to those consensual behaviors that are not *statistically* typical of American sexual behaviors. It is important to remember, however, that atypical does not necessarily mean abnormal; it simply means that the majority of people do not engage in that particular behavior. Sexual behaviors that are classified as mental disorders are known as paraphilias. Atypical sexual behaviors tend to differ from paraphilic ones in that paraphilic behaviors tend to be compulsive, long-standing, and distressing to the individual.

According to the American Psychiatric Association's newly revised *Diagnostic and Statistical Manual of Mental Disorders IV (DSM-IV)* (1994), a **paraphilia** is characterized by "recurrent intense sexual urges and sexually arousing fantasies" lasting at least 6 months and involving (1) nonhuman objects, (2) the suffering or humiliation of oneself or one's partner (not merely simulated), or (3) children or other nonconsenting people. In addition, "the person has acted upon these urges or is markedly distressed by them" (American Psychiatric Association, 1994).

The distinction between atypical and paraphilic behavior is sometimes more a difference of degree than kind. For example, many men find that certain objects, such as black lingerie, intensify their sexual arousal, while for others, it is a necessity for arousal. In the first case, there is nothing particularly unusual. In fact, a study of almost 200 students found that 16% of the women and 7% of the men had recently worn erotic garments (Person, Terestman, Myers, & Goldberg, 1989). But if a man were unable to become excited without the lingerie and the purpose of sex was to bring him in contact with the panties, the behavior would be considered fetishistic.

It is also important to recognize that seemingly scientific or clinical terms may not be scientific at all. (See Perspective 1 for a discussion of sexual addiction.) Instead, they may be pseudoscientific terms hiding moral judgments, as in the case of nymphomania and satyriasis. **Nymphomania** is a

A rose, bent by the wind and pricked by thorns, yet has its heart turned upwards.

Huna (Babylonian)

Through me forbidden voices.
Voices of sexes and lusts . . .
Voices veiled, and I remove the veil,
Voices indecent by me clarified and transfigured.

Walt Whitman (1819–1892)

Perspective

THE MYTH OF SEXUAL ADDICTION: CAVEAT EMPTOR II

Are you a sex addict? As you read descriptions of sexual addiction, you may begin to think that you are. But don't believe everything you read.

"The moment comes for every addict," writes psychologist Patrick Carnes (1983), who developed and marketed the idea of sexual addiction, "when the consequences are so great or the pain so bad that the addict admits life is out of control because of his or her sexual behavior." Money is spent on pornography, affairs threaten a marriage, masturbation replaces jogging, fantasies interrupt studying. . . . Sex, sex, sex is on the addict's mind. And he or she has no choice but to engage in these activities.

Sex addicts' lives are filled with guilt or remorse. They cannot make a commitment; instead, they move from one affair to another. They make promises to themselves, to their partners, and to God to stop, but they cannot. Like all addicts, they are powerless before their addiction (Carnes, 1983; Martin, 1989). Their addiction is rooted in deep-seated feelings of worthlessness, despair, anxiety, and loneliness. These feelings are temporarily allayed by the "high" obtained from sexual arousal or orgasm. Sex addicts, writes Carnes, go through a four-step cycle.

1. *Preoccupation with sex, an obsessive search for sexual stimulation.* Everything passes through a sexual filter. Sex becomes an intoxication, a high.

2. *Ritualization, or special routines that lead to sex.* The ritual may include body oils and massage, cruising, watching others, candles next to the bed, champagne.

3. *Compulsive sexual behavior,* such as masturbation, bondage, extramarital affairs, exhibitionism, or incest.

4. *Despair: the addicts' realization that they are helpless to change their sexual addiction.* Guilt, feelings of isolation, or suicidal tendencies may be present.

There are several levels of sexual addiction, categorized according to behavior. The first level of behavior includes excessive masturbation, numerous heterosexual relationships, interest in pornography, relations with prostitutes, and homosexuality. The second level includes exhibitionism, voyeurism, and obscene phone calls. The third level includes child molestation, incest, and rape. The addict moves from one level of behavior to the next in search of excitement and satisfaction.

Sexual addiction is viewed in the same light as alcoholism and drug addiction; it is an activity over which the addict has no control. And like alcoholism, Carnes suggests recovery through a version of Alcoholics Anonymous's Twelve-Step Program. The first step is for the addict to admit that he or she is helpless to end the addiction. Subsequent steps include turning to a Higher Power for assistance, listing all moral shortcomings, asking forgiveness from those who have been harmed and making amends to them, and finding a spiritual path to wholeness.

After reading this description of sexual addiction, do you feel a little uneasy? Do some of the signs of sexual addiction seem to apply directly to you? Are you wondering, "Am I a sex addict?" Don't worry; you're probably not. Remember the Barnum effect, discussed in Chapter 2. The reason you might think you're suffering from sexual addiction is that its definition taps into many of the underlying anxieties and uncertainties we feel about sexuality in our culture.

pejorative term, usually referring to "abnormal or excessive" sexual desire in a woman. It is usually applied to sexually active single women. What is "abnormal" or "excessive" is often defined moralistically rather than scientifically. Nymphomania is not recognized as a clinical condition by the

The problem lies not in you but in the concept of sexual addiction.

Although the sexual addiction model has found some adherents among clinical psychologists, they are clearly a minority. There are a few people, it is true, who are compulsive in their sexual behaviors, but compulsion is not addiction. The influence of the sexual addiction model is not due to its impact on therapy, psychology, and social work. Its influence is due mainly to its popularity with the media, where talk-show hosts such as Geraldo Rivera interview so-called sex addicts, and advice columnists such as Ann Landers caution their readers about the signs of sexual addiction. The popularity of an idea is no guarantee of its validity, however.

The sexual addiction model has been rejected by a number of sex researchers as nothing more than pop psychology. These researchers suggest that the idea of sexual addiction is really repressive morality in a new guise. It is a conservative reaction to sexual diversity, eroticism, and sex outside of monogamous relationships. It makes masturbation a sign of addiction, just as in earlier times, masturbation was viewed as a sign of moral degeneracy. According to the sexual addiction model, sex is healthy if it takes place within a relationship; outside a relationship, it is pathological (Levine & Troiden, 1988).

The critiques of the sexual addiction model by sex researchers have undermined its credibility (Barth & Kinder, 1987; Coleman, 1986; Levine & Troiden, 1988). First, the researchers point out, addiction requires physiological dependence on a chemical substance arising from habitual use. Sex is not a substance. Nor is there physiological distress, such as diarrhea, convulsions, or delirium, from withdrawal. Second, research fails to convincingly document sexual addiction as a clinical condition. There is virtually no empirical evidence to support the sexual addiction model. What little evidence there is comes from small clinical samples in which there are no comparable control groups. Indeed, the case studies Carnes describes in his book are not even real. "The stories used in this book," Carnes (1983) writes, "are fictionalized composites." As a result, one study calls the literature on sexual addiction "purely conjecture" (Barth & Kinder, 1987).

Third, there is no sexual hierarchy. Suggesting that masturbation leads to pornography, pornography to exhibitionism, and exhibitionism to rape borders on the irresponsible. Fourth, the sexual addiction model is highly moralistic. The committed, monogamous, heterosexual relationship is the model against which all other behaviors are measured. Nonprocreative sex such as masturbation is viewed as symptomatic. Gay and lesbian sex is also considered symptomatic. Fifth, the characteristics of the addictive process—"preoccupation, ritualization, compulsive sexual behavior"—are subjective and value-laden. Sociologists Martin Levine and Richard Troiden (1988) note: "Each of these characteristics could just as well describe the intense passion of courtship or the sexual routines of conventional couples." Nor is there evidence to support the notion that a person goes through three levels of behavior in search of greater excitement. "Carnes' notion of levels of addiction is a classic instance of moral judgment parading as scientific fact" (Levine & Troiden, 1988).

If your sexual fantasies and activities are distressing to you, or your behaviors are emotionally or physically harmful to yourself or others, you should consult a therapist. The chances are, however, that your sexuality and your unique expression of it are as normal as anyone else's.

DSM-IV (American Psychiatric Association, 1994). Although the term "nymphomania" dates back to the seventeenth century, it was popularized in the nineteenth century by Krafft-Ebing and others. Physicians and psychiatrists used the term to pathologize women's sexual behavior if it deviated from nineteenth-century moral standards. Even today, "nymphomania," "nymphomaniac," and "nympho" retain pathological connotations.

Satyriasis, referring to "abnormal" or "uncontrollable" sexual desire in men, is less commonly used than nymphomania because men are expected to be more sexual than women. For this reason, definitions of satyriasis infrequently include the adjective "excessive." Instead, reflecting ideas of male sexuality as a powerful drive, "uncontrollable" becomes the significant adjective. Satyriasis is not recognized by the American Psychiatric Association (1994).

As you continue this chapter, remember to distinguish clearly between the use of the various terms clinically, judgmentally, or casually. It can be tempting to define a behavior you don't like or approve of as paraphilic. And unless you are clinically trained, you cannot diagnose someone (including yourself) as having a mental disorder.

ATYPICAL SEXUAL BEHAVIORS

Don't do unto others as you would they should do unto you. Their taste may be different.
George Bernard Shaw
(1856–1950)

Atypical sexual behaviors are not rare. They are, in fact, often commonplace. A study of recent sexual behaviors and fantasies among 193 college and graduate students found that 23% of the women and 38% of the men had recently watched their partner masturbate (Person et al., 1989). Fourteen percent of the women and 6% of the men had used sex toys. Eleven percent of the women and 18% of the men had performed sexual acts in front of mirrors. And 5% of the women and 4% of the men had watched others engage in sexual intercourse. In terms of fantasies, 10% of men and of women had imagined themselves members of the other gender. Ten percent of the women and 5% of the men fantasized themselves as prostitutes. One film critic suggests that the popularity of vampire movies and novels may reflect our fascination with forbidden impulses or obsessions about which we may fantasize but never act out (James, 1992).

Two of the most controversial and widespread forms of atypical sexual behaviors are cross-dressing and domination and submission, also known as sadomasochism.

Cross-Dressing

Cross-dressing is wearing clothing of a person of the other sex. Men and women cross-dress for many reasons. Some who cross-dress are considered psychologically disordered, as in transvestism, discussed later. (Transvestites represent a minority of cross-dressers.) Many cross-dress as a way of challenging traditional gender concepts ("gender bending"); others do it as a parody of masculinity. Still others, such as gay drag queens or butch lesbians, cross-dress as a sexual statement. Six percent of men and 3% of women reported cross-dressing according to a large scale study of sexual behavior by Samuel Janus and Cynthia Janus in 1993.

Throughout history, cross-dressing has been both celebrated and condemned. In ancient Greece, male followers of the god Dionysius dressed in female garments for festivals. Roman emperors sometimes wore women's tunics and makeup. But according to Deuteronomy (22:5) in the Judeo-

Dame Edna is a well-known comic cross-dresser who appears on TV. When not dressed as Edna, Barry Humphries is an "ordinary" married man.

Christian Old Testament, cross-dressing was a sin: "Women shall not wear men's garments nor shall a man wear the garments of women, for whomever do so are an abomination to the Lord God." During the Middle Ages, cross-dressing continued in the European countryside, where pagan festivals remained beyond the reach of the Christian church (Bullough & Bullough, 1993). Unlike today, when most cross-dressers are male, during medieval times there were more female than male cross-dressers. In fact, one of the charges for which Joan of Arc was burned was wearing male attire and hair-styles, in violation of biblical injunctions. As Vern Bullough (1991) notes:

> One of the things that appears obvious in a cross-cultural or historical study of sexual behavior is that cross-dressing and impersonation of the opposite sex are ubiquitous. It is no exaggeration to state that genitalia alone have never been either a universal or essential insignia of a lifelong gender. In many societies, gender is an achieved rather than an ascribed characteristic, and is based on tasks performed and the significance of clothing rather than any anatomical character.

Girls will be boys and boys will be girls
It's a mixed up, muddled up, shook up world.
The Kinks, "Lola"

Cross-Dressing in American Culture   Although cross-dressing is relatively common, our society expresses ambivalence about it. It gives rise to both fear and laughter within our culture. In Alfred Hitchcock's movie *Psycho*, Norman Bates revealed his mental derangement when he dressed as his

Ru-Paul is a well-known cross-dresser who appears on MTV. Cross dressing has been an important part of popular culture, especially comedy, since Shakespeare's time.

Sin multiplies the possibilities of desire.
Luis Buñuel (1900–1983)

I don't mind drag—women have been female impersonators for some time.
Gloria Steinem

mother. In *Silence of the Lambs,* Jame Gumb donned a dress before killing his victims (Tharp, 1991). At the same time, we find ourselves roaring with laughter at *Tootsie, Victor/Victoria,* and the classic *Some Like It Hot* (Straayer, 1992).

Cross-dressing is a staple of television sitcoms, such as "Martin" (and the focus in "Bosom Buddies") and of comedy shows such as "Saturday Night Live" and "In Living Color." Dame Edna, an Australian cross-dresser, and MTV's Ru Paul are cable TV staples. Cross-dressing is often an important part of the performances of female pop-culture icons, past and present, from Marlene Dietrich to Madonna, and Greta Garbo to Josephine Baker. Rock culture includes cross-dressed performances by such legends as Little Richard, Alice Cooper, Mick Jagger, David Bowie, and Madonna. Madonna challenges male/female stereotypes in her use of drag (cross-dressing) in music videos and performances. She says her songs are "about sex, but not any specific kind of sex. They're not limited to any gender, they are just about sex. . . . I don't think about boundaries" (Martin, 1992). Critic Peter Ackroyd (1979) writes of the role of cross-dressing in rock performance:

> It suggests a defiance of the established sexual order on a theatrically convincing scale, but it can also represent those infantile and fetishistic longings which have become a noticeable part of contemporary culture. Autoeroticism, narcissism and the acting out of private fantasies play as large a part in rock culture as they do in certain kinds of male transvestism.

But interest in cross-dressing is not restricted to entertainment and popular culture. Vast numbers of ordinary men dress as women during Halloween, Mardi Gras, and Carnival (see Perspective 2), when custom allows men to dress as women and act "outrageously" feminine (Garber, 1991; Parker, 1991). During these times, traditional sexual mores are loosened. Behind masks and costumes, men and women play out fantasies that are forbidden in their daily lives. The holidays, however, are structured, and what was allowed Halloween night is strictly forbidden the next morning.

There are other structured occasions in which men are permitted to cross-dress: during theatrical events and all-male retreats. Men kick up their high heels and lift up their skirts as "females" in cancans and chorus lines in such all-American events as Boy Scout and PTA skits, college revues, and military talent shows. Such "female" shows are an integral part of American life. In fact, Harvard's Hasty Pudding Club has presented its annual drag (cross-dressing) revue since the 1840s. And the prestigious male-only Bohemian Club (whose members include Ronald Reagan as well as governors, senators, and corporate heads), each year presents a drag musical at its retreat. In these instances, dressing as women serves not only as entertainment but also as a form of male bonding, as "the girls" laugh and giggle among themselves about their "silly" behavior. Outside of these structured events or retreats such behavior is tabooed (Garber, 1991).

Cross-Dressing and Gender Comfort   For some men, there is nothing more pleasant than sitting around the house with a cold beer and a pizza on a Saturday afternoon watching football while wearing a comfortable house dress and leisurely applying red fingernail polish. For these men, cross-dressing is a form of gender relaxation. It allows them to get in touch with the softer, more "feminine" side of their personalities.

CARNIVAL: SEXUAL TRANSGRESSION IN CONTEMPORARY BRAZIL

Carnival is an ancient tradition that originated in the Latin countries of medieval Europe. Today, its most famous celebrations are found in Brazil and the Caribbean. The word "carnival" means "farewell to flesh" (derived from the Latin *carne*, flesh, and *vale*, farewell). It is celebrated the three days before Shrove Tuesday announcing the beginning of Lent, a time of fasting and penance. (In Louisiana, carnival is celebrated as Mardi Gras, literally "Fat Tuesday.") As a tug-of-war between pagan sensuality and Christian asceticism, Carnival represents the last triumph of the flesh before its banishment at Lent. For countries celebrating it today, especially Brazil, it is a time apart from all other times of the year. It is the time when inhibitions are relaxed. During Carnival, everyday roles, responsibilities, rules, and work are put aside to celebrate the return of freedom, especially libidinous freedom.

To understand Carnival's erotic freedom, it is important to recognize that during the rest of the year, Brazil practices both a public conventional sexuality and a hidden, unconventional sexuality (Parker, 1991). The unconventional sexuality in which Brazilians engage is known as *sacanagem (sa-ka-NA-shem)*, a word for which there is no English equivalent. *Sacanagem* roughly means playful or tabooed sex; sex that transgresses boundaries or conventions. (In English, the phrases "doing the wild thing" and "down and dirty" give a faint sense of the meaning of *sacanagem*.) In *sacanagem*, sings Caetano Veloso, "it's prohibited to prohibit." While this form of sexuality exists side by side with conventional sexuality, it is ordinarily submerged or hidden.

During Carnival, *sacanagem* emerges from its exile. Carnival becomes a ritualized rebellion against convention and rules. But the activities that take place during Carnival are not regarded as sinful. They are viewed as "play," but play with a double meaning: the innocent play of children but also the play of adults who, having shed their sexual inhibitions, have assumed a childlike innocence.

In Carnival, revelers crowd the streets, pushing, dancing, and merging into a single unruly mass, where they lose their ordinary sense of self. The masks and costumes, which are selected to reflect their fantasies, permit them to act out their fantasy selves. What is most striking about the fantasy selves that emerge during Carnival is the transvestite self. Transvestism, more than any other image, is the one that symbolizes Carnival. Just as Carnival's unrestrained sexuality represents a coming to the surface of the hidden side of sexuality, so does cross-dressing represent a surfacing of the hidden side of gender. Men are women, and women are men. From childhood on, boys and girls learn to cross-dress for Carnival, stuffing pillows in their clothes for make-believe breasts or socks for penises.

Cross-dressing takes many forms during Carnival. There are the comic "dirty ones" who affect an absurd tone in their dress and actions. Poor, adolescent males dress as high-class prostitutes and call themselves *piranhas*. Gay men dress in low-cut gowns, bare their masculine chests, wear heavy makeup, and sprinkle glitter in their beards. But the center of attention focuses on the actual transvestites who ply the streets daily as prostitutes. Whereas ordinarily they are regarded with bemusement or contempt, during Carnival, they are celebrated and feted.

During Carnival, the forbidden becomes the norm, *sacanagem* becomes the conventional. As one Brazilian says (quoted in Parker, 1991):

Everything is permitted. . . . There is no censorship, and the unrestrained exhibitionism and the desire to expose oneself are very common in the carnivalesque atmosphere. During this period, sex is everywhere.

(continued)

CARNIVAL: SEXUAL TRANSGRESSION IN CONTEMPORARY BRAZIL *(continued)*

There is no place where we don't encounter a sexuality linked to the grotesque. . . . The permissiveness of *carnaval* is not interrupted by anything, and bodies, souls, and semen are left at their will, giving to everyone the freedom to do what they really desire. It is a good period for prostitution and the buyers of pleasure. Everything is sold, everything is bought, everything is given, everything is received with a lewd and inviting smile on the face. Beaches, corners, bars, bathrooms, parks, buses, trains, and other places are stages for sensuality and sex. The streets become completely given over to the beat of *samba* and the frenzy of sweaty bodies having sex.

At the end of three days, Brazil settles back again into its daily life. The ordinary roles, privileges, and rules once again become dominant. The transvestite once again becomes an outcast, and *sacanagem* retreats to the secret underbelly of Brazilian life. The utopian vision of freedom fades until the return of summer, when once again Brazilians begin to contemplate Carnival.

Feeling comfortable acting out the female gender role appears to be a primary goal for many cross-dressers. One man writes: "I feel much gender comfort when I cross-dress. I feel at ease—very passive and warm. Actually, I'm a very aggressive person when acting out my male role. When I dress as a woman I feel this offsets the other side of my personality" (Talamini, 1982). And a woman reports similar changes in her husband (Woodhouse, 1985): "When he's dressed up he's so different. . . . He'll say to me, 'Would you like a cup of tea?' which he'd never think of doing. I mean he's a real chauvinist pig when he's not dressed. . . ."

Why does our culture seem disproportionately preoccupied with cross-dressing? Our interest, writes Marjorie Garber (1992), reflects "a crisis in categories." She asserts that the categories of male/female and heterosexual/homosexual are inadequate for describing the full range of human experience. Just as bisexuality challenges the heterosexuality/homosexuality dichotomy, cross-dressing challenges the traditional masculine/feminine dichotomy. Can a man wearing a dress *really* be a man? Can a heterosexual male wearing a dress *really* be heterosexual? Cross-dressing, Garber notes, destroys our usual either/or ways of categorizing people. She believes part of the success of Michael Jackson lies in his ambiguous persona. Garber (1992) writes:

> Michael Jackson as a cultural figure . . . erases and detraumatizes not only the boundaries between male and female, youth and age, but also that between black and white. . . . He seems to internalize these cultural category crises, and internalizing them, to make possible a new fantasy of transcendence.

Cross-Dressing as Camp Although men who cross-dress can have any sexual orientation, in the gay subculture, cross-dressing is a type of **camp,** a form of satire based on the affectionate exaggeration or parody of social conventions. **Drag queens** (gay men who dress "outrageously" as women) and **female impersonators** (drag entertainers) are an integral part of gay life.

Drag, or cross-dressing, is a source of distinct gay humor and parody. But in several ways, drag parody is ambivalent humor. First, while drag expresses admiration for forceful women, it also denigrates them as "men in drag." Second, drag mocks traditional masculinity but trivializes gay men as somehow feminine or effeminate (Altman, 1982). After the rise of gay liberation, with its emphasis on political action, many gay men viewed camp, and especially drag, as passive responses to oppression. In fact, a "transvestophobia" began to develop in the gay liberation movement, as gay men increasingly emphasized masculinity and feared that cross-dressing would lead to all gay men being identified as effeminate or feminine (Altman, 1982; Garber, 1992). In defense of camp, Richard Dyer (1977) writes:

> Fun and wit are their own justification, but camp fun has other merits too: it's a form of self-defense. Particularly in the past, the fact that gay men could so sharply and brightly make fun of themselves meant that the real awfulness of their situation could be kept at bay—they need not take things too seriously, need not let it get them down. Camp kept, and keeps, a lot of gay men going.

Gay men involved in cross-dressing feel that drag is not only an important aspect of their culture but also a form of cultural resistance to masculine values that emphasize power, domination, and aggression.

In recent years, drag has become increasingly admired in the gay subculture as a form of resistance. Some regard drag as "macho" (Garber, 1992). Others simply like the clothes.

Domination and Submission

Domination and submission (D/S) refers to sexual arousal derived from the *consensual* acting out of sexual scenes in which one person dominates and the other submits. The term **sadomasochism (S&M),** which is also used to describe domination and submission, was coined by Krafft-Ebing in 1886 (Moser, 1988). Studies have found few differences between D/S and non-D/S samples. As a consequence, the word "sadomasochism" is no longer used as a clinical term in psychiatry and psychology to describe consensual domination and submission (Breslow, 1989). "Sadomasochism" continues to be used, however, by those involved in the domination and submission subculture as well as the general public.

I'm all for bringing back the birch, but only between consenting adults.
Gore Vidal

Dominion and submission are forms of fantasy sex. The critical element is not pain, but power. The dominant partner is all-powerful and the submissive partner is all-powerless. (In D/S slang, the dominant partner is known as the "top" or "husband," and the submissive partner is known as the "bottom" or "wife.") Significantly, the amount or degree of "pain," which is usually feigned or slight, is controlled by the submissive partner. As such, fantasy plays a central role, especially for the submissive person (Arndt, 1991). (For a review of recent sociological literature on domination and submission, see Weinberg, 1987.)

Bondage and discipline, or B&D, often involves leather, handcuffs, and other restraints as part of its scripting.

A large-scale study of a nonclinical population found that the majority involved in domination and submission did so as "a form of sexual enhancement which they voluntarily and mutually choose to explore" (Weinberg et al., 1984). As such, domination and submission is not paraphilic. To be considered paraphilic, such behavior requires the suffering or humiliation of oneself or one's partner to be real, not merely simulated (American Psychiatric Association, 1994). (Sexual sadism and sexual masochism, which are considered paraphilias, are discussed later in the chapter.)

Types of Domination and Submission

Domination and submission take many forms. The participants generally assume both dominant and submissive roles at different times; few are interested only in being "top" or "bottom" (Moser, 1988). Probably the most widely known form is bondage and discipline. **Bondage and discipline (B&D)** refers to activities in which a person is bound with scarves, leather straps, underwear, handcuffs, chains, or other such devices while another simulates or engages in light to moderate discipline activities, such as spanking, whipping, and so on. The bound person may be blindfolded or gagged. A woman specializing in disciplining a person is known as a **dominatrix**, and her submissive partner is called a slave. A dominatrix describes her technique (Smith & Cox, 1983):

> I love to encase a slave in Saran Wrap from his neck to his feet with the arms by his side so he can't move. I call it "The Wrap." Then I give him a spanking with my hands. It's very effective because the plastic leaves the body real taut.

Sadism by no means involves any love of inflicting pain outside the sphere of sexual emotions, and is even compatible with a high degree of general tender-heartedness.
Havelock Ellis

Bondage and discipline may take place in specialized settings called "dungeons" furnished with restraints, body-suspension devices, racks, whips, and chains (Stoller, 1991). Eleven percent of both men and women have had experience with bondage, according to a recent study (Janus & Janus, 1993).

Another common form of domination and submission is *humiliation,* in which the person is debased or degraded (Arndt, 1991). Five percent of the men and 7% of the women in the Janus study had engaged in verbal humiliation (Janus & Janus, 1993). One-third of the submission respondents in another study received enemas ("water treatment"), were urinated on ("golden showers"), or defecated on ("scat") (Breslow, Evans, & Langley, 1985). In the Janus study, 6% of the men and 4% of the women had participated in golden showers (Janus & Janus, 1993). Humiliation activities may include servilism, babyism, kennelism, and tongue lashing. In *servilism,* the person desires to be treated as a servant or slave. In *babyism,* the person acts in an infantile manner—using baby talk, wearing diapers, being pampered, scolded, or spanked by his or her "mommy" or "daddy." *Kennelism* refers to being treated like a dog, wearing a studded dog collar, and being tied to a leash, or ridden like a horse, while the dominant partner applies whip or spurs. *Tongue lashing* is verbal abuse by a dominant partner who uses language that humiliates and degrades the other.

People engage in D/S in private or as part of an organized subculture complete with clubs and businesses catering to the acting out of D/S fantasies (Stoller, 1991). This subculture is sometimes known as "the velvet underground." There are scores of noncommercial D/S clubs throughout the United States (Arndt, 1991). The clubs are often specialized: lesbian S&M, dominant men/submissive women, submissive men/dominant women, gay men's S&M, and transvestite S&M. Leather sex bars are meeting places for gay men who are interested in D/S. The D/S subculture includes D/S videos, books, and magazines (Houlberg, 1991; Murray, 1989).

The world of D/S is secretive, but the degree of secrecy depends on the different groups involved and the types of activities they undertake. Gay D/S, especially the leathersex culture, where men contact other men in bars, is the most visible (Kamel, 1983a, 1983b). The world of heterosexual D/S is more hidden; their contacts are limited to private, small networks (Weinberg & Kammel, 1983b). One study of heterosexual D/S participants found that most of their friends and families did not know of their involvement (Spengler, 1983). Forty percent of their wives, two-thirds of their parents and siblings, 70% of their colleagues, and 59% of their friends were ignorant of their D/S activities.

D/S as Theater

Pain in itself is not what the submissive partner seeks, nor is it what the dominating partner wishes to give. A submissive partner receives no pleasure from accidentally cutting or burning himself or herself. What the partner seeks is stimulation.

Physiological stimulation is the common thread linking mild pain, anxiety, and fear or other emotional states with heightened sexual arousal (Arndt, 1991). This link between pain and increased sexual excitement can be explained by the two-component theory of emotions discussed in Chapter 8 (see Baumeister, 1988a, 1988b, and 1989 for an alternative theory). The bites, scratches, lashes, or blows increase the body's physiological responses, including muscular tension, respiration, and heart rate. These

Ah beautiful, passionate body,
That never has ached with a heart!
On the mouth though the kisses are
  bloody,
Though they sting till it shudder
  and smart
More kind than the love we adore
  is
They hurt not the heart nor the
  brain
Oh bitter and tender Dolores
Our Lady of Pain.

Algernon Swinburne
(1837–1909)

Betty Page, who has become a cult figure among those interested in domination and submission, was one of the most photographed women in the 1950s.

physiological responses are similar to those accompanying the sexual response cycle. Within the D/S scenario, where painful or other stimulation is expected to be erotic, these responses are interpreted as sexual, augmenting the submissive's erotic intensity.

The pain has to be part of the drama. D/S is theater, in which the play is carefully planned, and each player has a script. The play is either structured or unstructured. Gerald and Caroline Green (1974) describe the scenarios:

> The couple can agree to go into a scene with fairly rigid outlines, even down to dialogue. The submissive can thus work out (and in a sense control) the various stages of the impending punishment, even perhaps deciding at what point to interject intercourse; the couple can agree how much begging off, stalling, imploring, is or is not turning on, how much pain is to be given, and shown (or mimed). . . . In the unstructured . . . the dominant obviously carries the greater onus. He/she must take the initiative, while the submissive follows a lead, sensing perhaps more thrill in the unknown . . . responding in kind to the ordering around, the particular amount of touching and humiliation and punishment allotted and designed.

Fetishism, the sexualization of inanimate objects, may be associated with domination and submission as their participants often utilize leather, boots, uniforms (especially police and military), whips, handcuffs, and chains (Spengler, 1983). These accoutrements heighten the sexual excitement (Arndt, 1991).

THE PARAPHILIAS

We have no reliable estimates as to how many individuals are paraphiliacs. But recent work suggests that many of the activities of convicted sex offenders, such as exhibitionism, voyeurism, and pedophilia may also be present in the general population (Crepault & Couture, 1980; Finkelhor, Hotaling, Lewis, & Smith, 1990; Koss, 1988; Templeman & Stinnett, 1991). A study of 60 college men attempted to find out what percentage of the young male nonoffender, nonclinical population engaged in coercive atypical sexual behaviors (Templeman & Stinnett, 1991). By collecting life histories of the men, the researchers found that 65% had engaged in some form of sexual misconduct, such as voyeurism, obscene phone calling, or sexually rubbing themselves against a woman. The study concluded that young men were easily aroused to diverse stimuli, blurring the distinction between typical and atypical behavior.

Of all the sexual aberrations, the most peculiar is chastity.
Remy de Gourmont
(1858–1915)

Studying Paraphilic Behavior

What we know about paraphilias comes from convicted sex offenders, police records, outpatient clinics, and victims. But such sources are not necessarily representative of paraphiliacs in general. Furthermore, because women are infrequently seen in clinics, almost nothing is known about female paraphilias.

The overwhelming majority of paraphilias occur among men. Paraphilias occur among heterosexuals, gay men, male bisexuals, and transsexuals. It is important to realize that sexual orientation is not related to paraphilia. A gay exhibitionist, for example, is considered paraphilic not because of his attraction to other men but because he exposes his genitals (Levine, Risen, & Althof, 1990).

Characteristics of Paraphiliacs

Males are most likely to engage in paraphilic activities between ages 15 and 25. Individuals with paraphilias, or **paraphiliacs,** generally have the following characteristics: a long-standing, highly arousing, and unusual erotic preoccupation; a need to act out the fantasy; and an inability to have a conventional sexual relationship (Levine et al., 1990).

1. *Long-standing, highly arousing, and unusual erotic preoccupation.* Although they may begin as early as childhood, paraphilic impulses usually manifest themselves in adolescence or early adulthood. Paraphilic people find their erotic fantasies and masturbatory activities centering on unusual activities. These fantasies are usually aggressive ones (such as exhibitionism or molestation) or masochistic, directed against the self (such as being a sexual slave or spanked).

2. *Need to act out the fantasy.* Paraphilic men and women feel a strong need to satisfy their unusual fantasies. They experience intense frustration and sexual dissatisfaction if they are unable to fulfill their fantasies. Given the choice of engaging in normal heterosexual or homosexual behaviors or in acting out their fantasy, paraphiliacs would choose the fantasy behavior. They do not often victimize others, however. They usually relieve the internal pressure by masturbating.

3. *Inability to have a conventional sexual relationship.* Despite high rates of orgasm occurring when involved in unusual fantasies or activities, paraphilic individuals are often dysfunctional with their partners under ordinary sexual conditions. Wives of paraphiliacs typically complain that their husbands are not interested in sex with them, never initiate, are unable to maintain an erection or have an orgasm. They do not seem to enjoy sex unless their wives act out paraphilic fantasies.

Frequently, a person with one paraphilia will have another as well (Fedora, Reddon, Morrison, & Fedora, 1992; Freund, Sher, & Hunkers, 1983). Transvestism, exhibitionism, voyeurism, and sadism most frequently occur with multiple paraphilias. While pedophilia, sexual attraction to children, is usually not associated with other paraphilias, a significant percentage of sexually aggressive men are also exhibitionists and voyeurs (Fedora, Reddon, Morrison, & Fedora, 1992).

The Development of Paraphilias

There are four important factors in the development and maintenance of paraphilias in people: predisposing conditions, instigation of the behavior, commission of the first paraphilic act, and maintenance of the paraphilic behavior.

Predisposing Conditions Most of the behaviors classified as paraphilias exist in many of us to varying degrees. They become paraphilic when they are intense, recurring, and acted out or, if not acted out, when they are distressing to the individual. Why is it, however, that for some of us these behaviors remain only a part of our sexual repertoire, often nothing more than fantasies, while for others, they become paraphilic? Researchers believe there may be predisposing conditions leading to paraphilias, yet there is no consensus as to what those conditions are. They may be biological, such as a hormonal imbalance or distorted brain structure (Flor-Henry, Lang, Koles, & Frenzel, 1991; Langevin, Wright, & Handy, 1988; Wright, Nobregra, Langevin, & Wortzman, 1990), or they may be the result of psychodynamic factors from childhood (Freund, Watson, & Dickey, 1990). There is no clear-cut evidence pointing either way.

Instigation of the Behavior Gene Abel (1989), a leading researcher in the field, suggests several possible instigators that are involved in the development of paraphilias. As we review these instigators, it is important to remember, however, that none of them *causes* paraphilia. Millions have engaged in or experienced similar incidents without ill effects.

First, memories of early experiences, especially shared sexual experiences, from early childhood, may trigger paraphilic interests. Second, modeling the pedophilic acts of others may instigate the first paraphilic activity. Such modeling may occur if the person sees or learns of others (especially older adolescents or adults he admires) engaging in paraphilic activity, such as an older brother peering through a window while someone is undressing.

Third, among those predisposed to paraphilia, imitating the sexual activities portrayed in the media may trigger the initial paraphilic episode. A scene from a slasher movie may encourage a paraphiliac's first sadistic act, or watching "Martin" may provide the initial impetus for cross-dressing.

Fourth, paraphiliacs may recall emotionally laden events from the past. These powerful memories may act as fuel for their own later deviant activities. The childhoods of pedophiles, for example, are disproportionately filled with histories of sexual abuse.

Socialization is important in determining whether people act on their instigators. They evaluate their fantasies according to the beliefs and attitudes they have developed. Because these people probably began their paraphilic fantasies early in life, their fantasies reinforced their urges for a considerable time. And because they probably did not share their fantasies with others, they did not realize their unacceptableness until their paraphilia became well established.

Commission of the First Paraphilic Act Considerable time may pass between the instigating event and the actual acting-out. The person may feel conflict or fear or be consumed with guilt. But once the decision is made, the first paraphilic act may be very simple, depending on the act. If it involves a rubber fetish, for example, the individual need only find the right rubber glove for masturbating. If the person is pedophilic, considerable planning may be involved. He or she may befriend a child or the child's parents or participate in a youth group. If the person is related to the child, he or she may need to wait for an opportunity when the child is unsupervised.

Maintenance of Paraphilic Behavior There are three important factors involved in maintaining paraphilic activities: positive evaluation of its consequences, pairing of paraphilic fantasies with masturbation, and rationalization.

First, after the individual completes the first paraphilic act, he or she evaluates its consequences. Was it pleasurable? Were there negative consequences, such as discovery, punishment, or injury to self or victim? If the act was not pleasurable or there were unacceptable negative consequences, then the behavior is not likely to occur again. If there were no inhibitors, however, then the individual is likely to repeat his or her activity.

Second, the person maintains his or her paraphilia by pairing masturbation with paraphilic fantasies or memories of paraphilic experiences. By masturbating to paraphilic fantasies or recollections, the person increases their erotic appeal. When fantasizing about the initial act, the individual electively represses its negative aspects. For example, he suppresses his fear of discovery and the act's impact on his victim. At the same time, he recalls only its positive aspects, such as the pleasure derived from arousal or orgasm. In such a manner, the fantasies may become more erotic than the actual behavior, which may surprise the person when he or she again engages in the paraphilic act.

Third, paraphiliacs develop the ability to rationalize their acts. While the paraphilia usually develops when the person is young, the activity may be well established by the time he or she is old enough to understand that it is prohibited by society. To justify the paraphilia, the individual develops a distorted belief system that legitimates the behavior. This is especially important when the paraphilia involves victimization. The voyeur explains he was just curious and didn't hurt anyone. The pedophile claims to be the innocent victim of the child's seduction.

NONCOERCIVE PARAPHILIAS

An important aspect of paraphilias is whether they involve coercion. Non-coercive paraphilias are regarded as relatively benign or harmless because they are victimless. Noncoercive paraphilias include fetishism, transvestism, and zoophilia, discussed below in alphabetical order.

Fetishism

We attribute special or magical powers to many things: a lucky number, a saint's relic, an heirloom, a lock of hair, or an automobile. These objects possess a kind of symbolic magic (Belk, 1991). We will carry our boyfriend's or girlfriend's photograph (and sometimes talk to it or kiss it), ask for a keepsake if we part, become nostalgic for an old love when we hear a particular song. All these are normal, but point to the symbolic power of objects, or fetishes.

Fetishism is sexual attraction to objects, which become for the fetishist sexual symbols. Instead of relating to another person, a fetishist gains sexual gratification from kissing a shoe, caressing a glove, drawing a lock of hair against his or her cheek, or masturbating with a piece of underwear. But the person does not necessarily focus on an inanimate object; he may be attracted to a woman's feet, ears, breasts, legs, elbows, or any other part of her body (Cautela, 1986). (According to the *DSM-IV*, exclusive attraction to body parts is known as **partialism.**) Some researchers consider *Playboy*'s centerfold to be fetishistic in its focus on female breasts and genitalia (Rosegrant, 1986). Reports of types of fetishes even include arousal from sneezes (King, 1990). According to a recent study, 11% of the men and 6% of the women had engaged in fetishistic behaviors (Janus & Janus, 1993).

Paul Gebhard views fetishistic behavior as existing on a continuum, moving from a slight preference for an object to a strong preference, to the necessity of the object for arousal, and finally to the object as a substitute for a sexual partner (Gebhard, 1976). Most people have slight fetishistic traits: Men describe themselves as leg men or breast men; they prefer dark-haired or light-haired women. Some women are attracted to muscular men, others to hairy chests, and still others to shapely buttocks.

It is only when a person develops a strong preference for an object that his or her attachment moves outside the range of statistical normality. Classical case histories emphasized parts of the body (hair, breasts, and so forth), clothing (shoes, boots, stockings), materials (leather, satin), body products (urine, blood, sweat, ear wax), or inanimate objects (cigarette holders, doughnuts, liver). (Among some lesbians, there is debate as to whether the

Inanimate objects or parts of the body, such as the foot, may be sexualized by some people.

use of dildos represents a form of fetishism. Most believe dildos are merely a means of enhancing erotic pleasure, not a "penis" fetish [Findlay, 1992].) In recent years, however, there appears to have been a change in target stimuli among fetishists. Today, very few fetishists are aroused by parts of the body or nonclothing objects. Two researchers believe that the decline in fetishistic attachment to the body is due to "society's acceptance of the fact that 'bodies are for touching' " (Gosselin & Wilson, 1980).

How a person develops fetishistic responses is not known with any certainty, but it seems rooted in childhood. In some manner, shoes, panties, or some other object becomes associated in the child's mind with sexual excitement (Freund & Blanchard, 1993). These objects often belong to a person of emotional significance to the young boy, such as a mother or sister. Through powerful symbolic transformation, the object, write Paul Gebhard and colleagues (1965), "is given all the power and reality of the actual thing and the person responds to the symbol just as he would the thing." The object gains erotic significance usually before puberty, during which time the boy tends to have few girls for playmates. By the time fetishistic boys reach adulthood, they have had very little heterosexual experience and use their fetishes as substitutes for genuine sexual encounters with women (Gebhard, Pomeroy, & Christiansen, 1965).

Many researchers believe that fetishism may be associated with both domination and submission and cross-dressing (Arndt, 1991). Participants in D/S often wear leather, boots, and bustiers, and use whips, chains, and handcuffs, all of which may be fetishistic. Cross-dressers may become sexually aroused by wearing fetishistic garments, such as nylons, panties, bustiers, bras, dresses, and the like (Wise et al., 1991). One study found that heterosexual cross-dressers who denied that they found cross-dressing sexually arousing were more aroused while listening to audiotapes about cross-dressing than tapes with neutral subject matter (Blanchard et al., 1986).

Transvestism

Transvestism is the wearing of clothing of a member of the other sex for purposes of sexual arousal. The term, coined by Magnus Hirschfeld, is derived from the Latin *trans*, cross, and *vestire*, to dress. Transvestites differ from cross-dressers in the compulsivity and sexual arousal associated with their behavior.

There are two types of transvestites. **Fetishistic transvestites,** heterosexual men who become sexually excited by wearing women's clothes, and **nonfetishistic transvestites,** men who dress in women's clothes to relieve the tensions associated with being male (Arndt, 1991). (No published research exists on female fetishistic transvestism.) Only fetishistic transvestism is considered paraphilic (American Psychiatric Association, 1994). Fetishistic and nonfetishistic transvestism may coexist in different intensities; their relative importance may change over time. This is especially true for fetishistic transvestites who initially find female clothing sexually arousing. As time passes, however, the erotic element decreases, and the comfort level increases.

Transvestites are usually quite conventional in their masculine dress and attitudes. Dressed as women, they may become sexually aroused and masturbate or make love with a woman. Transvestites have no desire to undertake a sex-change operation. They are rarely attracted to other men (Wise & Meyer, 1980). Transvestites believe they have both masculine and feminine personalities within themselves. Their feminine personality appears when they cross-dress; sometimes they give their female personality a name (Brierly, 1979). Transvestites may even walk around town as women and not be recognized.

Over two-thirds of transvestites are or have been married. In fact, a number of them marry in hopes of "curing" their desire to cross-dress. Of those married, about two-thirds have children. Some voluntarily reveal their cross-dressing after marriage, but the majority have it discovered. Invariably, the transvestites' partners are distressed and blame themselves for somehow "emasculating" their partners. Many transvestites and their wives and families are able to adjust to the cross-dressing. Wives sometimes accompany their cross-dressed husbands in public (Brown & Collier, 1989). Many women have sex with male partners when the men are wearing undergarments, nightgowns, or other feminine attire (Bullough & Weinberg, 1988). But often the stress is too great, and separation follows soon after the transvestism is discovered.

Male transvestites, who may behave conventionally when wearing men's clothing, often find they feel more sensitive when wearing women's clothing. They also may be concerned about their lipstick.

As transvestism is neither dangerous nor reversible, the preferred clinical treatment is to help the transvestite and those close to him accept his cross-dressing. He needs to cope, for example, with feelings of guilt and shame (Peo, 1988).

Zoophilia

Zoophilia, sometimes referred to as "bestiality," involves sexual excitement derived from animals (American Psychiatric Association, 1994). It is a **nonspecific paraphilia,** that is, a paraphilia that does not meet the criteria of the major paraphilias. Although conception is biologically impossible from such matings, classical mythology includes stories of such offspring as satyrs (human/goat), centaurs (human/horse), and minotaurs (human/bull). In Greek mythology, Zeus transformed himself into a bull in order to have intercourse with Europa, into a swan with Leda, and into a serpent with Persephone.

Although sexual activity is not especially common, it is a frequent theme in Greek mythology. In the myth of Leda and the Swan, the Greek god Zeus transforms himself into a swan and "possesses" Leda. The myth was popular among Renaissance painters; this is Michelangelo's rendition. (Leonardo da Vinci's painting depicting the myth was later burned as obscene.)

From medieval times to the end of the eighteenth century, sex with animals was associated with witchcraft. The devil was thought to take the form of a dog and then have sex with witches. In seventeenth-century New England, a boy was hanged for engaging in bestiality. The colony's governor reported (quoted in Strong, 1972):

> A sow . . . among other pigs had one without hair, and some other human resemblances . . . also one eye blemished, just like one eye of a loose fellow in the town, which occasioning him to be suspected, he confessed . . . for which they put him to death.

Whosoever loveth wisdom is righteous but he that keepeth company with fowl is weird.

Woody Allen

Kinsey reported that about 8% of the men and 3% of the women he surveyed had experienced at least one sexual contact with animals. Seventeen percent of the men who had been reared on farms had had such contact, but these activities accounted for less than 1% of their total sexual outlet (Kinsey et al., 1948, 1953). (One study, however, reported a man becoming sexually aroused by ants crawling on his testicles [Dewaraja & Money, 1986].) Sexual contact with animals usually takes place among adolescents and is a transitory phenomenon. Among adults, such contact usually occurs when human partners are not available.

COERCIVE PARAPHILIAS

Few noncoercive paraphilias are brought to public attention because of their private, victimless nature. But coercive paraphilias, which involve victimization, are the subject of concern by society because of the harm they cause others. The majority of adult women have been victimized by some kind or another of these coercive paraphilias.

All of these paraphilias involve some kind of coercive or nonconsensual relationship with another person. A study of over 400 outpatient sex offenders found that they attempted over 239,000 sex crimes, of which the majority were exhibitionism, voyeurism, obscene phone calls, and frotteurism (sexually rubbing against another person). These disorders also appear to be linked to child sexual abuse and rape. As many as 80% of rapists begin their assaultive behavior with "hands-off" sexual behavior, such as exhibitionism, voyeurism, obscene phone calls, and so on. Of exhibitionists, 29.7% were involved in child sexual abuse, and 29.2% were involved in rape. Of voyeurs, 13.8% were involved in child sexual abuse and 20.2% in rape (Knopp, 1984).

Voyeurism

Viewing sexual activities is a commonplace activity. As we saw earlier, relatively large percentages of individuals have used mirrors to view themselves in sex acts, watched their partners masturbate, or watched others having intercourse (Person et al., 1989). Americans' interest in viewing sexual activities, in fact, has spawned a multibillion-dollar sex industry devoted to fulfilling visual desires. Erotic magazines, books, and X-rated videos are available in almost every city, town, and hamlet in America. Topless bars, strip and peep shows, and erotic dancing attest to the attraction of visual erotica.

As Arndt (1991) notes, "Since looking at erotic scenes is so pervasive among males, it is difficult to determine when these acts are pathological." It is generally agreed, however, that the critical difference between casual, consensual viewing and voyeurism is consent.

Voyeurism involves recurring, intense sexual urges and fantasies to secretly observe another person who is nude, disrobing, or engaging in sexual activity (American Psychiatric Association, 1994). In order to become aroused, the man must hide and remain unseen, and the woman or couple must be unaware of his presence. The excitement is intensified by the possibility of being discovered. Sometimes the voyeur will masturbate while he is peering through the window or keyhole.

Very little study has been done of voyeurs, nine out of ten of whom are men. Voyeurs do not seek random females to watch undress or engage in sexual activities; instead, they seek out females they find sexually attractive. What voyeurs consider arousing differs from one voyeur to another. Some require viewing nude bodies, breasts, or vulvas; others desire watching sexual intercourse or lesbian sex. Voyeurism appears to appeal primarily to heterosexual men (Arndt, 1991).

Exhibitionism

Exhibitionism is the recurring, intense urge or fantasy to display one's genitals to an unsuspecting stranger (American Psychiatric Association, 1994). The individual has acted on these urges or is greatly disturbed by them. (Exhibitionism is also known as "indecent exposure.") While exhibitionists derive sexual gratification from the exposure of their genitals, the exposure is not a prelude or invitation to intercourse. Instead, it is an escape from intercourse, for the man never exposes himself to a willing woman—only

Some people like to exhibit their bodies within public settings that are "legitimized," as in this wet T-shirt party. Such displays may be exhibitionistic, but they are not considered exhibitionism in the clinical sense.

to strangers or near strangers. Exhibitionists generally expose themselves to children, adolescents, and young women; they rarely expose themselves to older women. In those few instances in which a woman shows interest, the exhibitionist immediately flees (Stoller, 1977). Usually, there is no physical contact.

Exhibitionism is a fairly common paraphilia; over one-third of all males arrested for sexual offenses are arrested for exhibitionism. Many of the men arrested for exhibitionism also had engaged in voyeurism, frotteurism (sexual touching without consent), obscene phone calling, and attempted rape (Lang et al., 1987). Seven percent of college men in one study expressed interest in exhibiting themselves; 2% actually had (Templeman & Stinnett, 1991). Another study found that exhibitionistic offenders became slightly more aroused by descriptions of exposure than nonoffending men (Marshall, Eccles, & Barabee, 1991). Because of the widespread incidence of exhibitionism, at least half of adult women may have witnessed indecent exposure at least once in their lives (Arndt, 1991).

The stereotype of the exhibitionist as a dirty old man, lurking in parks or building entryways, dressed only in a raincoat and sneakers, is erroneous. (Fewer than 10% of exhibitionists are over 50 years old, although a few may be as old as in their eighties when they first begin [Arndt, 1991; Kenyon, 1989].) Exhibitionists are typically regarded as comic or pathetic characters. Such erroneous stereotypes form the basis for cartoons in *Playboy*, *Penthouse*, and more explicit sex-oriented magazines, as well as television and film.

Exhibitionists appear to find fully clothed women more erotic than nude or partially nude women. For some reason, they misinterpret neutral or nonerotic signals from women as erotic (Fedora, Reddon, & Yeudall, 1986). Most reportedly hope that the women will enjoy the experience (Lang et al., 1987).

Exhibitionistic acts generally occur during two periods: mid-adolescence and young adulthood. For some individuals, these times may be periods of high stress and anxiety. The first period is when the adolescent is simultaneously establishing an identity independent from his family and also developing his sense of masculinity. A study of adolescent exhibitionists found that they had committed numerous sex offenses, were maladjusted, and came from dysfunctional families (Bryant, 1982; Green, 1987; Saunders & Awad, 1991).

During adolescence, not all exhibitionistic exposure is paraphilic. In the male adolescent subculture, for example, peers sometimes encourage "mooning" and "streaking," which are not sexual in origin. Other times, especially among younger adolescents, exposure may be due to poor socialization, bad judgment, antisocial behavior, or faulty impulse control (Bryant, 1982; Green, 1987; Saunders & Awad, 1991).

The second period in which males may expose themselves is during dating, courtship, and the early years of marriage. During this time, the young man may experience frustration and feel threatened by physical and emotional intimacy. Exhibitionism may also occur during middle age, usually in conjunction with an identity crisis or marital disruption (Bryant, 1982).

Exhibitionists are generally introverted, insecure, or sexually inadequate men (Arndt, 1991; Marshall, Eccles, & Barabee, 1991). They feel impotent as men, and their sexual relations with their wives are usually poor. This sense of impotence gives rise to anger and hostility, which they direct toward other women by exhibiting themselves.

Telephone Scatalogia

Telephone scatalogia, the making of obscene phone calls, is a nonspecific paraphilia, a sexual behavior that does not meet the criteria of any of the major paraphilias (American Psychiatric Association, 1994). Because the acts are compulsive and repetitive or their fantasies cause distress to the individual, they are considered to be paraphilias.

Sixty-one percent of the women in one study reported receiving at least one obscene phone call; 45% had received two or more calls (Herold, Mantel, & Zemitis, 1979). Eight percent of the college students in another study reported making such calls at least once (Templeman & Stinnett, 1991). Obscene phone calls are generally made randomly, by chance dialing or phone book listings.

The overwhelming majority of callers are male, but there are some female obscene callers as well (Saunders & Awad, 1991). Male callers frequently make their female victims annoyed, frightened, anxious, upset, or angry. Their victims often feel violated. But female callers have a different effect on male recipients, who generally do not feel violated or who may enjoy the call as titillation (Matek, 1988).

If you receive an obscene telephone call, telephone companies advise that you not respond in any manner, just hang up the telephone. If you say "You're sick," or "Stop this, don't call me again," the caller is receiving the angry response he wants. Blowing a loud whistle into the phone or shouting into the mouthpiece is also ineffective in deterring repeat callers. If the caller persists, the telephone company recommends changing your number. (Many companies will do this at no charge.) In more extreme cases, working with law enforcement departments, the telephone company will trace the calls you receive. Some states permit the individual to purchase and use caller identification technology, which enables you to identify the telephone number of incoming calls.

Frotteurism

Frotteurism (also known as "frottage") involves recurrent, intense urges or fantasies—lasting at least 6 months—to sexually touch another person without consent (American Psychiatric Association, 1994). It is the touching, not the lack of consent, that is sexually arousing. It is not known how many people practice frotteurism, but one study of normal college males found that 21% had engaged in at least one frotteuristic act (Templeman & Stinnett, 1991).

The frotteur usually carries out his touching or rubbing in crowded subways, buses, or large sporting events or rock concerts. When he enters a crowd, his initial rubbing can be disguised by the crush of people. He usually rubs against his victim's buttocks or thighs with his erect penis inside his pants. At other times, he may use his hands to rub a woman's buttocks, pubic region, thighs, or breasts. Generally, he rubs against the woman for 60–90 seconds. If he ejaculates, he stops. If not, he usually moves on to find another victim (Abel, 1989).

Frotteurism often occurs with other paraphilias, especially exhibitionism, voyeurism, pedophilia, and sadism, the sexually arousing infliction of pain. It is also associated with rape.

Necrophilia

Necrophilia is sexual activity with a corpse. As with telephone scatalogia, necrophilia is classified in the *DSM-IV* as a nonspecific paraphilia (American Psychiatric Association, 1994). It is regarded as nonconsensual, since a corpse is obviously unable to give consent. There are relatively few instances of necrophilia, yet it retains a fascination in horror literature, especially vampire stories and legends, and in gothic novels. It is also associated with ritual cannibalism in other cultures. Within our own culture, *Sleeping Beauty* features a necrophilic theme, as does the crypt scene in Shakespeare's *Romeo and Juliet*. Some heavy metal music deals with necrophilia (Rosman & Resnick, 1989).

A review of 122 cases of supposed necrophilia or necrophilic fantasies found only 54 instances of true necrophilia (Rosman & Resnick, 1989). The study found that neither sadism, psychosis, nor mental impairment was inherent in necrophilia. Instead, the most common motive for necrophilia was the possession of a partner who neither resisted nor rejected. As Ernest Jones wrote (quoted in Rosman & Resnick, 1989): "The dead person who loves will love forever and will never be weary of giving and receiving caresses." In order to find such "partners," necrophiliacs often choose occupations giving them access to corpses, such as mortician or morgue attendant. Yet even some who have access to bodies nevertheless commit murder as part of their necrophilic behavior.

Pedophilia

Pedophilia refers to "recurrent intense sexual urges and sexually arousing fantasies involving sexual activity with a prepubescent child or children" that the individual, referred to as a **pedophile,** has acted upon or finds distressing (American Psychiatric Association, 1994). The children are age 13 or younger. A pedophile must be at least 16 and at least 5 years older than the child. (A late adolescent is not considered pedophilic if he or she is involved in an ongoing sexual relationship with a 12-year-old or older child.) A large number of arrested pedophiles currently are or previously have been involved in exhibitionism, voyeurism, or rape. In this section, we will discuss only pedophilia. We will discuss nonpedophilic child sexual abuse and incest, their impact on the victim, and prevention of child sexual abuse in Chapter 18.

Sexual attraction to children is fairly widespread in the nonoffending population. A study of child-focused thoughts and fantasies among 193 male college students found that 21% reported sexual attraction to children, 9% had sexual fantasies of children, and 5% had masturbated to such fantasies (Briere & Runtz, 1989). These individuals tended to have had negative early sexual experiences; they reported dominance attitudes toward women, as well as a likelihood of raping them. An earlier study of the sexual fantasies of 94 men found that during masturbation or sexual intercourse, 61% had experienced pedophilic fantasies, 54% voyeuristic fantasies, and 33% rape fantasies (Crepault & Couture, 1980).

Types of Pedophilia   For most adult men and women, whether they are heterosexual, gay, or lesbian, the gender of their partner is important. But heterosexual/homosexual orientation is less important to pedophiles. For pedophiles, it is more important that the child *is* a child (Freund & Watson, 1993; Freund, Watson, Dickey, & Rienzo, 1991). As a consequence, many heterosexually identified men may molest boys or boys and girls. Homosexually identified men may molest both boys and girls, although they are less likely to molest girls (Arndt, 1991; Freund et al., 1991).

Pedophiles may be divided into two classes: fixated and regressed. A study of sex offenders found pedophiles evenly divided between the two groups (Groth et al., 1982).

Fixated Pedophiles   Fixated pedophiles have arrested psychosexual development. Since adolescence, they have been attracted only to children. If they have had sexual experience with their peers, it has been initiated by the other. They are more childlike than adult. They may take pride in never having grown up and prefer the company of children to adults. Their targets are primarily boys, and they relate to them boy-to-boy rather than man-to-boy. Their primary sexual orientation is toward children rather than adults. They plan their involvement; they become involved with children through neighborliness, sports, or church activities, or other involvements that give them seemingly innocent access.

Regressed Pedophiles   Regressed pedophiles are not generally attracted to children. Their primary sexual interest is in adult women. They live an adult lifestyle and are usually married. But because of stress, marital conflict, or divorce, regressed pedophiles turn to female children as adult substitutes. As they prefer adult women, the pedophile relates to children as if they were adults. They talk to the children as equals, feel that they are accepting or understanding of them. Their initial sexual contact is impulsive.

Cross-Sex Pedophilia Regressed male pedophiles are the most likely to sexually molest female children, the majority of whom are between ages 8 and 9. Adolescent pedophiles, averaging 15 years of age, sexually misuse girls around age 7 (Arndt, 1991). About half the pedophiles report stressful events, such as marital or work conflict, personal loss, or rejection, preceding the molestation. Many are fearful that their sexual abilities are decreasing or that they are impotent. Alcohol consumption, resulting in disinhibition, is involved in 30–50% of the offenses. One-third claim that viewing explicit child pornography led, at least occasionally, to their committing the offense (Marshall, 1988).

Seduction and enticement were used in about one-third of the cases reported (Groth & Birnbaum, 1978). In these instances, the pedophile is known to the girl. The pedophile befriends the girl, talking to her, giving her candy, taking her to the store, going for walks with her, letting her watch TV at his house. Gradually, he initiates tactile contact with her, such as having her sit on his lap, rough-housing with her, or giving her a back rub. Eventually, he will attempt to fondle her (Lang & Frenzel, 1988). If she resists, he will stop and try later. He will try added inducements or pressure but will rarely use force (Groth, Hobson, & Gary, 1982).

Pedophilic acts rarely involve sexual intercourse. The pedophile usually seeks to fondle or touch the child, usually on her genitals, legs, and buttocks. Sometimes the pedophile exposes himself and has the child touch his penis. Occasionally, oral or anal stimulation is involved (Arndt, 1991).

Although a pedophile may have sexual relationships with women, they are not necessarily his preferred partners. About half of pedophiles are or have been married. Most married pedophiles claim their marriages are happy, although they describe their wives as controlling and sexually distant. Their frequency of marital intercourse does not differ from nonoffenders, but many report a low sex drive and erectile difficulties. Few have serious mental disorders, such as psychosis (Arndt, 1991).

When they are apprehended, pedophiles express different reactions. About 25% deny the offense. Others admit the possibility of the offense but can't remember committing it because of drinking. This permits them to admit the offense without taking responsibility for it or acknowledging that they are pedophiles. Still others respond hypocritically, bragging about their religiosity, morality, or uprightness. Having admitted the offense, pedophiles often accuse their victims of initiating the event by "seducing" or arousing them by wearing provocative clothes or makeup (Arndt, 1991; Gudjonsson, 1990).

Same-Sex Pedophilia Same-sex pedophilia is a complicated phenomenon. It does not appear to be as closely linked to homosexuality as cross-sex pedophilia is to heterosexuality. A different kind of psychosexual dynamic seems to be at work for a large number of same-sex pedophiles. While most same-sex pedophiles have little interest in heterosexual relationships, a significant number do not identify themselves as gay. One study of imprisoned offenders, for example, found that over half identified themselves as heterosexual or bisexual. Many reject a gay identity or are homophobic. Although some people believe that pedophilia is the means by which the gay community "recruits" boys into homosexuality, pedophiles are soundly rejected by the gay subculture (Peters, 1992).

Studies measuring penile tumescence of same-sex pedophiles to identify sexual preference found that they were more aroused to male *and* female adolescents than they were to adults of either sex. This is in marked contrast to the majority of gay males for whom their partner's gender was the most important factor (Arndt, 1991; Freund & Watson, 1993; Freund et al., 1991). A male identifying himself as heterosexual told a researcher that ordinary sexual orientation wasn't applicable in describing man-boy relationships. It was as if prepubescent boys were neither male nor female, masculine nor feminine. They were beyond ordinary categories of gender (Arndt, 1991).

The mean age of the molested boy is between 10 and 12. A large number of pedophiles describe feelings of love, friendship, or caring for the boy. Others blatantly entice or exploit their victims. Force is rarely used. Voluntary interviews with 27 same-sex pedophiles reveal four themes to explain their involvement with children: (1) Their pedophilic desire feels "natural" to them, (2) children are appealing because they are gentle and truthful, (3) adult-child sexual involvement can be positive for the child, and (4) the relationship is characterized by romantic love, not casual sex (Li, 1990). Such views, however, are generally regarded as cognitive distortions or rationalizations. Adult-child sexual relationships are by definition exploitive. The majority of children report feelings of victimization (Finkelhor, 1990).

The most common activities are fondling and masturbation, usually the man masturbating the boy. Other acts include oral-genital sex, with the adult fellating the boy, and anal sex, with the adult assuming the active role.

Female Pedophilia Although there are relatively few reports of female pedophiles, there appears to be a small percentage (Arndt, 1991; Rowan, 1988).

Female pedophilia appears to be underreported for two reasons (Rowan, 1988). First, male/female stereotypes disguise female sexual contact with children. Men are viewed as aggressive and sexual, while women are viewed as maternal and nurturing. Because of these stereotypes, women are given greater freedom than men in touching children and expressing feelings for them. As a consequence, when a pedophilic female embraces, kisses, or pets a child, her behavior is viewed as nurturing rather than sexual. But when a nonpedophilic male does the same thing, his behavior may be misinterpreted as sexual.

Second, the majority of male children who have sexual contact with adult women generally view the experience positively rather than negatively (Condy, Templer, Brown, & Veaco, 1987). As a consequence, they do not report the contact. The media also reinforce a belief in the essentially benign nature of female pedophilia in such films as *Rambling Rose,* in which a central comic scene depicts a sexually curious 13-year-old boy petting with Rose, a nonpedophilic but sex-loving young woman. Because of our feelings about female and same-sex molestation, it is impossible to imagine a comparable scene with a 13-year-old girl with a sex-loving young man, or an adult male with a young boy being depicted comically.

Adult female sexual contact with young boys is fairly common. A study of almost 1600 male and female college students and prison inmates found that 16% of male college students and 46% of male prison inmates had sexual contacts with women when they were 12 years old or younger and the women were in their early twenties (Condy, Templer, Brown, & Veaco, 1987). Over half of the men in the study reported having sexual intercourse with the women. The majority of the women were friends, neighbors, baby-sitters, or strangers. Among the women in the study reporting sexual contact with boys, 0.5% were college students, and 7.5% were prisoners.

Over half the college males and two-thirds of the prisoners in the study reported that at the time, they felt their childhood experiences with adult females were positive. Twenty-five percent of the college males and 6% of the male prisoners regarded it as negative. And 12% of the college males and 25% of the prisoners regarded the experience as mixed. Thirty-six percent of the college males and 43% of the male prisoners felt its impact on their adult sex life was positive; 16% and 22%, respectively, felt it was negative; 9% and 10%, respectively, felt it was mixed; and 28% and 22%, respectively, felt it had no effect. The critical factor affecting how they evaluated the experience was whether force was used. Those forced into sex generally regarded the experience as negative.

Female sexual abuse of male children differs from male sexual abuse of female children in several significant ways (Condy Templer, Brown, & Veaco, 1987; Cooper, Swaminath, Baxter, & Poulin, 1990; Fritz, Stall, & Wagner, 1981; Okami, 1991). First, half the female sexual abusers had sexual intercourse with the male children, while relatively few male sexual abusers had sexual intercourse with female children. Second, female abusers forced male children to engage in sexual activities significantly less frequently than male abusers forced female children. Third, male children tend not to be as traumatized by female abusers as female children are by male abusers.

Sexual Sadism and Sexual Masochism

While we tend to think of sadism and masochism as different aspects of a single phenomenon, sadomasochism, sadists are not necessarily masochists, nor are masochists necessarily sadists. Sadism and masochism are separate but sometimes related phenomena. In order to make this distinction clear, the American Psychiatric Association (1994) has created separate categories: sexual sadism and sexual masochism.

There is no clear dividing line between sexual sadism, sexual masochism, and domination and submission. In the case of sadism, coercion separates sexual sadism from domination. But in consensual behaviors, there is no clear distinction. A rule of thumb separating consensual sexual sadism and masochism from domination and submission may be that the activities are extreme, compulsive, and dangerous.

Sexual Sadism According to the *DSM-IV*, a person may be diagnosed with **sexual sadism** if, over a period of at least 6 months, he or she experiences intense, recurring sexual urges or fantasies involving real (not simulated) acts in which physical or psychological harm (including humiliation) is inflicted upon a victim for purposes of sexual arousal. The individual has acted on these urges or finds them extremely distressful (American Psychiatric Association, 1994). Characteristic symptoms include obsessive and compelling sexual thoughts and fantasies involving acts centering on a victim's physical suffering. The victim may be a consenting masochist or someone unknown and abducted by the sadist. The victim may be tortured, raped, mutilated, or killed; often the victim is physically restrained and blindfolded or gagged (Money, 1990).

While most rapes are not committed by sexual sadists, sadistic rapes account for about 5% of all stranger rapes (Groth, 1979). Sadistic rapes are the most brutal. The rapist finds "intentional maltreatment gratifying and takes pleasure in torment, anguish, distress, helplessness, and suffering" (Groth, 1979). There is often bondage and a ritualistic quality to such rapes.

Sexual Masochism For a diagnosis of **sexual masochism** to be made, a person must experience for a period of at least 6 months intense, recurring sexual urges or fantasies involving real (not simulated) acts of being "humiliated, beaten, bound, or otherwise made to suffer." The individual has acted on these urges or is highly distressed by them (American Psychiatric Association, 1994).

Autoerotic asphyxia, a form of sexual masochism linking strangulation with masturbation, causes hundreds of deaths annually. Between 500 and 1000 autoerotic asphyxia deaths may occur each year, but most are mistaken as intentional suicides.

An analysis of over 100 such deaths found that most victims were males, ranging from age 10 and up, who died from hanging, strangulation, or suffocation as they tried to heighten their masturbatory arousal and orgasm by cutting off oxygen to their brain. Many victims, especially those who crossdressed, were playing out erotic bondage rituals and observing themselves with mirrors or recording the activity with video cameras (Blanchard & Hucker, 1991). Researchers, however, know very little about the dynamics of such autoerotic behavior because individuals in therapy rarely disclose such activities (Eber & Wetli, 1985; Saunders, 1989). And, like much atypical sexual activity, friends and relatives are usually unaware that the victim was engaged in such behavior (Garza-Leal & Landron, 1991). (For case histories, see Cosgray, Hanna, Fawley, & Money, 1991; and Garza-Leal & Landron, 1991.)

The birthplace of masochism is fantasy.
Theodore Reik (1888–1969)

TREATING PARAPHILIACS

Paraphiliacs generally come into treatment as the result of arrest. When their exhibitionism, child molestation, or other paraphilic behavior is made public, the stress and humiliation lead to a sudden and dramatic decrease of their previously secret activities. They often believe they are cured. The reduction of paraphilic desire, however, is only temporary. Once the intense crisis stage passes, the desires return. But the paraphiliac believes that he has conquered his deviancy. This belief feeds into the paraphiliac's denial. Once again, he believes he does not need treatment. In fact, one of the first tasks clinicians must undertake is to make their clients recognize that they *do* need treatment.

Psychologists and psychiatrists face unique difficulties in treating men and women with paraphilias (O'Carroll, 1989). Because most clients enter treatment through the criminal justice system, they view the therapist suspiciously. Yet the therapist must rely heavily on self-report, which may be distorted (Freund, Watson, & Reinzo, 1988). For example, paraphiliacs may not tell their therapists of other paraphilias for fear of additional prosecution. In addition, there are few empirically tested treatment guidelines for the psychologist to use in determining the most appropriate therapy. And these problems are further complicated by the difficulty of predicting future behavior: Will the client cease from his offensive behavior when he completes the treatment program? (See O'Carroll, 1989, for an illustrative case study of these problems.)

Decreasing Paraphilic Behavior

The primary task for the clinician and his or her client is to decrease the paraphilic behavior (Abel, 1989).

Disrupting Antecedent Events

Paraphiliacs rarely spontaneously engage in their deviant activities. Most acts are the result of a sequence of behaviors leading up to the paraphilic activity. A paraphiliac fantasizes about the activity, such as how a woman might react if he exposed himself as she approached her car; he may stalk outside an apartment waiting for a woman to undress in front of an open window. If therapists make offenders aware of the role of these antecedent events, the events can serve as alarm bells. If the client interrupts these antecedents, he or she may be successful in overcoming the impulse to act out.

Several techniques may be used to disrupt antecedents. First, therapists use **covert sensitization,** a form of aversion therapy in which negative fantasies are used as punishment for engaging in unacceptable fantasies. It is used for a wide range of paraphilias (Lamontagne & Lesage, 1986; Moergen, 1990; Rangaswamy, 1987). If a pedophile, for example, fantasizes about molesting a child, he creates a negative fantasy to counteract the paraphilic one. To reinforce the negative consequences of his paraphilic fantasy, he may fantasize the sound of sirens, his arrest, the jail door slamming, or his name announced on the evening news. Second, clients learn to associate noxious stimuli, such as ammonia fumes, with their deviant fantasy. When a paraphilic fantasy arises, they break open an ammonia capsule and inhale its fumes. Both techniques interrupt the chain of events leading to paraphilic acts.

Decreasing Paraphilic Arousal

In addition to disrupting antecedent events, clinicians attempt to decrease paraphilic arousal. They believe paraphilic desires cannot be eliminated, only reduced to manageable levels. Therapists have two goals: (1) to teach the offender how to *reduce* his paraphilic interests so that he can control them; and (2) to teach him to self-administer treatment so that if paraphilic fantasies, desires, or interests arise, he can immediately treat them.

In order to accomplish these goals, therapists utilize satiation, signal punishments, and drug therapy. *Satiation* is based on boredom. The paraphiliac masturbates to orgasm utilizing acceptable sexual fantasies, which he verbalizes into a tape recorder. In his postorgasmic state, when he has little, if any, desire, he then repeats his most exciting paraphilic fantasies on audiotape in a boring manner. He repeats this exercise for 30–60 minutes daily. In this manner, he becomes satiated and bored with his paraphilic fantasies; eventually, they lose their erotic capacity. *Signal punishment* uses electrical shocks, biofeedback, and paraphilic stimuli to recondition the patient's responses. With this technique, the client listens to or watches videotapes of deviant behavior. At the same time, his penis is wired to a device measuring his penile tumescence in response to the material. When the device records an erection, indicating the patient is responding to paraphilic stimuli, he receives a shock.

Drug therapy, the use of pharmacological agents to modify emotions or behavior, is used when the client does not respond to behavioral treatment or if he is dangerous, requiring immediate, effective treatment. The use of drugs has been effective in significantly reducing the sexual drives of dangerous individuals, such as pedophiles and sadists. Such drug therapy is known as **chemical castration.** It works by reducing the testosterone level.

Some exhibitionists, voyeurs, frotteurists, and fetishists have responded to fluoxetine drug treatment, which reduces anxiety in obsessive-compulsive disorders. The success of this treatment suggests that paraphiliacs may sexualize their obsessive-compulsiveness (Emmanuel, Lydiard, & Ballinger, 1991; Lorefice, 1991; Perilstein, Lipper, & Friedman, 1991). Treatment with other anti-obsessive-compulsive drugs provides additional support to the sexualization hypothesis (Kruesi, Fine, Valladares, & Philips, 1992).

Teaching Social Skills

Most paraphiliacs are aroused by both normal and paraphilic stimuli. Although they may find people desirable and sexual intercourse erotic, they may lack the skills to begin a conversation or introduce themselves to others. They may feel sexually inadequate or fearful of entering an intimate relationship. Because of these many problems, a key goal in therapy is to teach them skills for interacting in the adult world.

Teaching social skills is an important element because it gives paraphiliacs the ability to relate to people in socially acceptable ways (Marshall, Eccles, & Barabee, 1991). Therapists attempt to teach communication and social skills by modeling appropriate methods, such as demonstrating how to make "I statements," how to introduce oneself to a stranger, and how to carry on a conversation. They role-play with their clients to teach them various points of view and how others perceive or react to them. Finally, they reinforce their clients' development by praise and encouragement.

Stress management is also important, because stress often activates the undesirable behaviors (Levine, Risen, & Althof, 1990; Marshall, Eccles, & Barabee, 1991). By learning to cope with stress through relaxation, exercise, and new response patterns, people are able to reduce their paraphilic urges.

Cognitive training enables the patient to recognize the inappropriateness of his deviant fantasies and desires. This is especially important because paraphiliacs have developed long-standing but distorted belief systems that rationalize their behavior. Pedophiles may justify their molestation on the grounds that the child seduced them, or exhibitionists may rationalize that women secretly enjoy viewing males masturbating.

These treatment programs are not mutually exclusive. Many therapists combine behavioral techniques, social skill enhancement, cognitive training, and drug therapy (Dwyer & Myers, 1990).

Studying atypical and paraphilic sexual behaviors reveals the variety and complexity of sexual behavior. It also underlines the limits of tolerance. Some unconventional sexual behaviors, undertaken in private between consenting adults as the source of erotic pleasure, are of concern only to the people involved. As long as physical or psychological harm is not done to the self or others, it is no one's place to judge.

SUMMARY

Atypical Versus Paraphilic Behavior

• *Atypical sexual behavior* is consensual behavior in which less than the majority of individuals engage. Atypical sexual behavior is not abnormal behavior, the definition of which varies from culture to culture and from one historical period to another.

• Today, sexual behaviors that are classified as mental disorders are known as *paraphilias*. Paraphilias tend to be either coercive or injurious, compulsive, and long-standing. A paraphilia is characterized by recurring, intense sexual urges and sexual fantasies involving nonhuman objects, the suffering or humiliation of oneself or one's partner, or children or other nonconsenting individuals.

Atypical Sexual Behaviors

• *Cross-dressing* is wearing the clothes of a person of the other sex. Cross-dressing themes are found in the media and popular culture; *drag* is important in gay culture. Cross-dressing involves challenging traditional male/female and heterosexual/homosexual dichotomies.

• *Domination and submission (D/S)*, also known as *sadomasochism (S&M)*, is a form of fantasy sex with power the central element. The physiological stimulation accompanying the activities heightens the sexual emotions accompanying D/S.

The Paraphilias

• Although there are no reliable statistics on the number of individuals, paraphilic activities are widespread in the nonoffender population.

• There are four elements in the instigation of paraphilias: memories of early experiences, modeling of paraphilic acts by others, imitating media portrayals, and recalling the emotionally laden events of childhood.

• Paraphiliacs maintain their behavior by positive evaluation of its consequences, pairing of paraphilic fantasies with masturbation, and rationalization.

Noncoercive Paraphilias

• *Fetishism* is sexual attraction to objects. Many researchers believe fetishism is also associated with D/S and transvestism. *Fetishistic transvestism* refers to sexual arousal occurring as a result of heterosexual males wearing female clothing.

• *Zoophilia* involves sexual excitement derived from animals. In the past, zoophilia was believed proof of witchcraft.

Coercive Paraphilias

• *Voyeurism* is the nonconsensual and secret observation of others for the purpose of sexual arousal.

• *Exhibitionism* is the nonconsensual exposure of the genitals to a nonconsenting stranger.

• *Telephone scatalogia* is the nonconsensual telephoning of strangers and using sexually obscene language.

• *Frotteurism* involves recurrent sexual urges, fantasies, and behaviors involving the sexual touching of a nonconsenting stranger.

• *Necrophilia* is sexual activity with a corpse. Although it rarely takes place in reality, it is a recurrent theme in literature, from *Romeo and Juliet* to *Sleeping Beauty* and vampire tales.

• *Pedophilia* refers to sexual arousal and contact with children age 13 or younger by adults, or by adolescents older than age 16 with children age 11 or younger. Only one-third to one-half of child molesters are pedophiles; others engage in sex with children for other reasons. For most pedophiles, the fact that a child is a child is more important than gender. Heterosexuals and gay men may both be pedophilically attracted to boys, while gay pedophiles are less attracted to girls.

• There are two types of pedophilia: fixated pedophiles, with arrested emotional development; and regressed pedophiles, who are ordinarily attracted to adults but may regress to children as a result of stress or crisis. The majority of pedophiles know their victim. About half of pedophiles have been married. The most common activities are fondling and masturbation.

• There are relatively few reported cases of female pedophilia, but it may be underreported for two reasons. Because of stereotypes of female nurturance, pedophilic activities may not be recognized; and the majority of male children apparently view the event positively or neutrally.

• *Sexual sadism* refers to sexual urges or fantasies of intentionally inflicting real physical or psychological pain or suffering on a partner. About 5% of all rapes are sadistic.

• *Sexual masochism* is the recurring sexual urge or fantasy of being humiliated or caused to suffer through real acts, not simulated ones. *Autoerotic asphyxia* is death occurring as a result of masturbatory activities linked with hanging or suffocation.

Treating Paraphiliacs

• Most paraphiliacs come into treatment as a result of arrest.

- Therapists attempt to decrease paraphilic behavior by disrupting antecedent events, decreasing paraphilic arousal, and teaching social skills.

KEY TERMS

atypical sexual behavior

paraphilia

nymphomania

satyriasis

cross-dressing

camp

drag queen

female impersonator

drag

domination and submission (D/S)

sadomasochism (S&M)

bondage and discipline (B&D)

dominatrix

paraphiliac

fetishism

partialism

transvestism

fetishistic transvestite

nonfetishistic transvestite

nonspecific paraphilia

zoophilia

voyeurism

exhibitionism

telephone scatalogia

frotteurism

necrophilia

pedophilia

pedophile

sexual sadism

sexual masochism

autoerotic asphyxia

covert sensitization

chemical castration

SUGGESTIONS FOR FURTHER READING

Arndt, William B., Jr. *Gender Disorders and the Paraphilias*. Madison, CT: International Universities Press, 1991. A comprehensive look at transvestism, transsexuality, and the paraphilias.

Daily, Dennis, ed. *The Sexually Unusual: A Guide to Understanding and Helping*. New York: Harrington Park Press, 1988. A thoughtful and often compassionate examination of what are usually considered paraphilias.

Garber, Marjorie. *Vested Interests: Cross-Dressing and Cultural Anxiety*. New York: Routledge, 1992. A provocative study of the role of cross-dressing in contemporary culture. Cross-dressers, the author argues, call attention to cultural inconsistencies about being male and female in our society.

Maletsky, Barry M. *Treating the Sexual Offender*. Newbury Park, CA: Sage Publications, 1991. An extensive and detailed examination of sex offenders, most of whom were offenders against children.

Money, John, and Margaret Lamacz. *Vandalized Lovemaps*. Buffalo, NY: Prometheus Press, 1987. An exploration of how psychosexual distortions in childhood can lead to paraphilias in adulthood.

Scholder, Amy, and Ira Silverberg, eds. *High Risk: An Anthology of Forbidden Writings*. New York: NAL/Dutton 1991. An anthology of essays, stories, poems, and memoirs by men and women involved in "forbidden" pursuits; includes sadomasochists, fetishists, and cross-dressers.

Weinberg, Thomas, and G. W. Levi Kamel, eds. *S and M: Studies in Sadomasochism*. Buffalo, NY: Prometheus Books, 1983. An outstanding collection of scholarly essays on nonclinical sadomasochism.

Chapter Twelve

CONTRACEPTION AND BIRTH CONTROL

PREVIEW: SELF-QUIZ

1. Recent studies show that most couples use some form of birth control the first time they have intercourse. True or false?

2. The most common forms of birth control in the United States are surgical sterilization and the pill. True or false?

3. Birth control pills do *not* help protect against sexually transmitted diseases. True or false?

4. A condom that is worn by women is currently available. True or false?

5. Spermicides (chemicals toxic to sperm) are also toxic to many organisms that cause sexually transmitted diseases. True or false?

6. Most IUDs (intrauterine devices) were taken off the market because they were proven to be hazardous to women's health. True or false?

7. The most effective reversible form of birth control is probably the hormonal implant (Norplant). True or false?

8. A woman can get pregnant up to 72 hours following ovulation. True or false?

9. In the United States, about 30% of pregnancies are terminated by abortion. True or false?

10. Women in over 80 countries take injections of the hormone DMPA (Depo-Provera) every 3 or 6 months as their method of birth control, but the drug is not available in this country. True or false?

ANSWERS: 1. F, 2. T, 3. T, 4. T, 5. T, 6. F, 7. T, 8. F, 9. T, 10. F

Chapter Outline

To humankind both ancient and modern, the management of fertility has been a primary pursuit. The fertility of people and of the land that sustains them is essential for survival itself. Abundant crops—of grains, produce, animals, and children—are a great boon. In addition, historically and today, people have used fertility as a measure of individual worth. Because of their failure to produce offspring, women in some societies have been abandoned or even killed.

And yet, though greatly desired, animal and human fertility must be controlled. Too many cattle will eat all the grain; too many dogs will roam the streets, half-starved. As for the children, even they can become too much of a good thing when there isn't enough food in the community to sustain them. Fertility is a double-edged sword. It is the object of great struggle and fervent prayer. Yet it often must be suppressed in order to preserve life itself.

Those of us who wish to take charge of our reproductive destinies need to be informed about the methods we have to choose from. But information is only part of the picture. We also need to understand our own personal dynamics so that we can choose methods we will use consistently. In this way, we avoid taking risks. In this chapter, we begin by examining the psychology of risk taking and the role of individual responsibility in contraception. We then describe in detail the numerous contraceptive devices and techniques (including abstinence) that are used today: methods of use, effectiveness rate, advantages, and possible problems. We also take a look at the future of contraceptive research. Finally, we look at the process of abortion and its effect on individuals and society.

Most can raise the flowers now,
For all have got the seed.
Alfred, Lord Tennyson

RISK AND RESPONSIBILITY

A woman has about a 2–4% chance of becoming pregnant during intercourse without contraception. If intercourse occurs the day before ovulation, the chance of pregnancy is about 30%; if it occurs on the day of ovulation, the chance is about 15% (Hatcher et al., 1990). Over a period of a year, a couple that does not use contraception has a 90% chance of pregnancy.

Because the possibility of pregnancy is so high for a sexually active couple, it seems reasonable that sexually active men and women would use contraception to avoid unintended pregnancy. Unfortunately, all too often this is not the case. One major study found that during their first intercourse, fewer than half the couples used contraception (Zelnick & Shaw, 1983). Of those who planned first intercourse (17% of the women and 25% of the men), almost three-quarters of the women used contraception. Another study of 83 adolescent couples found that the majority had discussed birth control, but rarely before their first intercourse (Polit-O'Hara & Kahn, 1985). In recent years, there has been a slight increase in contraceptive use. Jacqueline Forrest and Susheela Singh (1990) found that nearly two-thirds of the adolescent girls they surveyed used contraception. Moreover, as men and women age, they become more consistent contraceptive users. One national study found that twice as many married women as single women (whether never married, separated, or divorced) used contraception (Bachrach, 1984).

Numerous studies have indicated that the most consistent users of contraception are men and women who explicitly communicate about the sub-

A lily pond, so the French riddle goes, contains a single leaf. Each day the number of leaves doubles—two leaves the second day, four the third, eight the fourth, and so on. Question: If the pond is completely full on the thirtieth day, when is it half full? Answer: On the twenty-ninth day. The global lily pond in which four billion of us live may already be half full.

Lester Brown

ject. Those at greatest risk are those in casual dating relationships and those who infrequently discuss contraception with their partners or others. A review of the literature on the interpersonal factors in contraceptive use concluded: "Individuals in stable, serious relationships of long duration who had frequent, predictable patterns of sexual activity were most likely to use contraception" (Milan & Kilmann, 1987).

The Psychology of Risk Taking

How did people decide to get pregnant, I wondered. It was such an awesome decision. To undertake responsibility for a new life when you had no way of knowing what it would be like. I assumed that women got pregnant without thinking about it, because if they ever once considered what it really meant, they would surely be overwhelmed with doubt.

Erica Jong

Most people know they are taking a chance when they don't use contraception. But, as demonstrated in Kristin Luker's classic study (1975) of contraceptive risk taking, the more frequently a person takes chances with unprotected intercourse without resultant pregnancy, the more likely he or she is to take chances again. A subtle psychology develops: Somehow, apparently by will power, "good vibes," or the gods' kindly intervention, the woman will not get pregnant. Eventually, the woman or couple will feel almost magically invulnerable to pregnancy. Each time they are lucky, their risk taking is reinforced.

The consequences of an unintended pregnancy—economic hardships, adoption, or abortion—may be overwhelming. So why do people take chances in the first place? Part of the reason is faulty knowledge. People often underestimate how easy it is to get pregnant. Or, they may not know how to use a contraceptive method correctly.

Additionally, Luker has suggested, we can look at contraceptive use in cost-benefit terms. She observed, "The decision to take a contraceptive risk is typically based on the immediate costs of contraception and the anticipated benefits of pregnancy." But the anticipated benefits often prove illusory. "The potential benefits of pregnancy seldom become real; they vanish with the verdict of a positive pregnancy test or [are] later outweighed by the actual costs of the pregnancy" (Luker, 1975).

Let's examine some of the perceived costs of contraceptive planning versus the anticipated benefits of pregnancy.

Perceived Costs of Contraceptive Planning The reasons people avoid taking steps to prevent pregnancy include acknowledging their sexuality, along with problems in obtaining, planning, and continuing contraception.

Acknowledging Sexuality On the surface, it may seem fairly simple to acknowledge that we are sexual beings, especially if we have conscious sexual desires and engage in sexual intercourse. Yet acknowledging our sexuality is not necessarily easy, for it may be surrounded by feelings of guilt, conflict, and shame. The younger or less experienced we are, the more difficult it is to acknowledge our sexuality.

Planning contraception requires us to admit not only that we are sexual but also that we plan to be sexually active. Without such planning, men and women can pretend that their sexual intercourse "just happens"—in a moment of passion, when they have been drinking, or when the moon is full—even though it happens frequently.

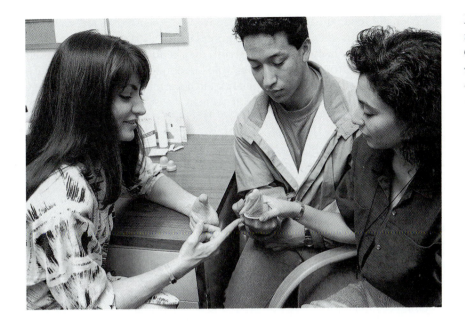

Planning contraception requires us to acknowledge our sexuality. One way a responsible couple can reduce the risk of pregnancy is by visiting a family planning clinic— together.

Obtaining Contraception Difficulty in obtaining contraception may be a deterrent to using it. It is often embarrassing for sexually inexperienced people to be seen in contexts that identify them as sexual beings. The person who sits behind you in your chemistry class may be sitting next to you in the waiting room of the family planning clinic. If you go to the drugstore to buy condoms, who knows if your mother, teacher, or minister might be down the aisle buying toothpaste (or contraceptives, for that matter) and might see you? A friend relates the following story from his youth:

> I went into the drugstore and waited for a long time until no one was around. An old lady was in the pharmacy section, waiting for a prescription to be filled; she reminded me of my grandmother. I thought about maybe buying a bottle of aspirin or hanging around there. So I bought a bottle of aspirin and left. Then I said to myself, "You are really a coward. Go ahead and get your rubbers." I went back inside. The pharmacist was gone but there was another man there by the shelves. So I took a deep breath and went up to him. I wanted to sound like I knew what I was doing, so I decided I would ask for prophylactics. "Rubbers" sounded too crude. I kind of stood behind him, breathing kind of heavy, I thought; he must have sensed me because he turned around toward me. I had to say it. There was no turning back. "Uh . . . excuse me, sir . . . do you have any *properlaxatives* . . . er . . . uh . . . I mean *properphiliacs.* . . ." I was panicked now. I couldn't say the word. . . . "Uh . . . you know . . . rubbers." And he just looked at me and smiled and said, "I'm sorry, son. I don't work here."

Planning and Continuing Contraception Contraceptive developments in the last few decades (especially the pill) shifted responsibility from the man to the woman. Required to more consciously define themselves as sexual, women have had to abandon traditional, passive sexual roles. Some women, however, are reluctant to plan contraceptive use because they fear they will be regarded as sexually aggressive or promiscuous.

Because it is women who get pregnant, men tend to be unaware of their responsibility or to downplay their role in conception and pregnancy, although with the reemerging popularity of the condom, responsibility may become more balanced (especially if women insist on it). Nevertheless, males, especially adolescents, often lack the awareness that supports contraceptive planning (Freeman, 1980). Yet males are more fertile than females. The average male is fertile 24 hours a day for 50 years or more. Females, in contrast, are fertile only a day or two out of the month for 35 or so years.

Many people, especially women using pills, practice birth control consistently and effectively within a steady relationship but give up their contraceptive practices if the relationship breaks up. They define themselves as sexual only within the context of a relationship. When men or women begin a new relationship, they may not use contraception because the relationship has not yet become established. They do not expect to have sexual intercourse or to have it often, so they are willing to take chances.

Using contraceptive devices such as a condom or diaphragm may destroy the feeling of "spontaneity" in sex. For those who justify their sexual behavior by romantic impulsiveness, using these devices seems cold and mechanical. Others do not use them because they feel it would interrupt the passion of the moment.

Anticipated Benefits of Pregnancy Many men and women fantasize that even an "accidental" pregnancy might be beneficial. Ambivalence about pregnancy is a powerful incentive *not* to use contraception (Demb, 1991).

Proof of Womanhood or Manhood Being pregnant proves that a woman is indeed feminine on the most fundamental biological level. Getting a woman pregnant provides similar proof of masculinity for a man. Being a mother is one of the most basic definitions of traditional womanhood. In an era in which there is considerable confusion about women's roles, pregnancy helps, even forces, a woman to define herself in a traditional manner. Adolescent and young men may also find the idea of fatherhood compelling. They may feel that fathering a child will give them a sense of accomplishment and an aura of maturity.

Proof of Fertility Pregnancy also proves beyond any doubt that a person is fertile. Many men and women have lingering doubts about whether they can have children. This is especially true for couples who have used contraception for a long time, but it is also true for those who constantly take chances. If they have taken chances many times without pregnancy resulting, they may begin to have doubts about their fertility.

Defining a Commitment Another anticipated benefit of pregnancy is that it requires a couple to define their relationship and commitment to each other. It is a form of testing, albeit often an unconscious one. It raises many questions that must be answered. How will the partner react? Will it lead to marriage or a breakup? Will it solidify a marriage or a relationship? Will the partner be loving and understanding, or will he or she be angry and rejecting? What is the real nature of the commitment? Many men and women unconsciously expect their partners to be pleased; frequently, however, this is not the case.

Relationship to Parents Pregnancy involves not only the couple but their parents as well (especially the woman's). Pregnancy forces a young person's parents to pay attention and deal with him or her as an adult. Being pregnant puts a female on the very verge of adulthood, for in most cultures, marriage and motherhood are major rites of passage. Similarly, fatherhood is an adult status for a male, transforming him from a boy into a man. Pregnancy may mean many things in regard to the parent-child relationship. It may be a sign of rebellion, a form of punishment for a parental lack of caring, a plea for help and understanding, or an insistence on autonomy, independence, or adulthood.

Women, Men, and Birth Control: Who Is Responsible?

Because women bear children and have most of the responsibility for raising them, they may have a greater interest than their partners in controlling their fertility. Women "want to know they are in charge," says Roberta Synal of Planned Parenthood (cited in Perkins, 1991). Also, it has generally been easier to keep one egg from being fertilized once a month than to stop millions of sperm during each act of intercourse. Nevertheless, it is unfair to assume, as people generally do in our society, that the total responsibility for birth control should lie with women. In some countries, such as Italy and Japan, male methods of contraception (such as withdrawal or condoms) are used more than female methods. Although withdrawal is not considered a reliable method of birth control, the condom is quite effective when used properly, especially in combination with a spermicide.

In addition to using a condom, a man can help take contraceptive responsibility by (1) exploring ways of making love without intercourse; (2) helping pay doctor or clinic bills and sharing the cost of pills, implants, or other birth control supplies; (3) checking on supplies, helping keep track of the woman's menstrual cycle, and helping his partner with her part in the birth control routine; and (4) in a long-term relationship, if no (or no more) children are wanted, having a vasectomy.

PREVENTING SEXUALLY TRANSMITTED DISEASES

Most sexually transmitted diseases (STDs), if treated in their early stages, are not particularly dangerous. AIDS is the notable exception; it is a terminal illness. Because of AIDS, people are much more aware of their vulnerability to STDs. (STDs are discussed in Chapter 16; HIV and AIDS are discussed in Chapter 17.)

Fortunately, there are contraceptive methods that do excellent double duty as prophylactics (disease-preventers). The condom, in fact, was apparently originally devised as such in the sixteenth century by the renowned anatomist Gabriel Fallopius (who first identified the fallopian tube). Fallopius's linen sheaths, however, were designed to be applied *after* the sexual

One of the fallacies that has permeated our minds on the topic of reproduction is the belief, conscious and unconscious, that women are the reproductive units of the species. The fertility of the male is rarely taken into consideration, as if women reproduced by themselves. We forget that we are fertile only during a limited period of our lives, between adolescence and menopause, while males are fertile throughout their lives. Moreover, women are fertile only during a certain portion of the menstrual cycle. If we think in terms of male fertility and focus on the male as the target for birth control, we begin to get a feeling of the exploitative framework on which birth control ideology is based.

Rita Arditti

What is the message of these posters? What myths or stereotypes do they challenge?

act and were first to be treated with a preparation of wine, copper, mercury, gentian root, ivory ash, red coral, and burnt horn of deer, among other ingredients (Quétel, 1990).

Latex rubber condoms provide a barrier against the herpes virus, chlamydia, gonococcus, and HIV (the AIDS virus). They work both ways, protecting the wearer of the condom from a disease carried by his partner, and vice versa. (Animal membrane condoms, however, do not protect against all disease-carrying organisms—notably HIV—and should only be used for contraception by couples in mutually monogamous relationships who know they are free of STDs.)

It is vital to note that condoms (or any other methods) do *not* guarantee absolute protection from STDs, just as they do not guarantee absolute protection from pregnancy. They have been known to leak, break, or slip off. Furthermore, disease may be spread by hands, mouth, and genital areas other than the penis and vagina (if there are herpes lesions on the scrotum or vulva, for example).

Spermicides, chemicals that kill sperm, are toxic to many disease agents, including those responsible for gonorrhea, trichomonas, herpes, chlamydia, and, according to recent laboratory tests, possibly HIV. For this reason, condoms pretreated with spermicide or used with spermicidal foam or film can provide extra protection, although there is no way to be sure that *all* the disease organisms will be killed.

Barrier methods for women—the diaphragm, cervical cap, female condom, and sponge—help protect against diseases of the cervix and uterus. The prophylactic function of these barriers is increased by their use with a spermicide (which the sponge already contains).

There is no absolute guarantee against contracting a sexually transmitted disease except total abstinence from sexual activity. Therefore, the value of caution and sound judgment for sexually active people cannot be overstated.

When you're talking birth control, what blocks it and freezes it out is that it's not a matter of more or fewer babies being argued. That's just on the surface. What's underneath it is a conflict of faith, of faith in empirical social planning versus faith in the authority of God as revealed in the teachings of the Catholic Church. You can prove the practicality of planned parenthood 'til you get tired of listening to yourself and it's going nowhere because your antagonist isn't buying the assumption that anything socially practical is good per se. Goodness for him has other sources which he values as much or more than social practicality.

Robert Pirsig

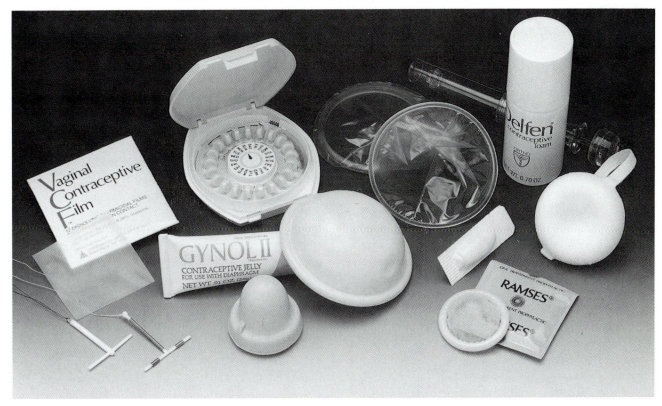

METHODS OF CONTRACEPTION AND BIRTH CONTROL

The methods we use to prevent pregnancy or to keep it from progressing vary widely according to our personal beliefs, tastes, health, and other life circumstances. For many people, especially women, the search for an "ideal" method of birth control is one of ongoing frustration. Some methods pose health risks to certain women, others run counter to religious or moral beliefs, and others are inconvenient or aesthetically displeasing. There are a number of methods and techniques to choose from, however, and scientific research is increasing our options for safe and effective contraception. Most individuals and couples can find a method that they can use with comfort and, most important, with regularity. Popular methods (or nonmethods) that are unreliable or completely ineffective are discussed in Perspective 1.

Today, a wide variety of contraceptive methods and devices is available. It is important for each person to choose the method he or she will use with comfort and consistency.

Birth Control and Contraception

Although the terms "birth control" and "contraception" are often used interchangeably, there is actually a subtle difference in meaning. **Birth control** is any means of preventing a birth from taking place. Thus, methods that prevent a fertilized egg from implanting in the uterine wall (such as the IUD in some instances) and methods that remove the **conceptus**—the fertilized egg, embryo, or fetus—from the uterus (such as "morning-after" pills and surgical abortions) are forms of birth control. These are not, how-

UNRELIABLE AND MYTHICAL METHODS OF CONTRACEPTION

Humans are a very inventive species. In the area of birth control, however, some of our inventions do not deserve to be patented.

"Traditional" birth control techniques such as withdrawal and lactation have some merit in that they work some of the time for some people. Other methods, such as Coca Cola douches or plastic bag condoms, are worse than useless; they may be harmful.

Coitus Interruptus (Withdrawal)

The oldest contraceptive technique known is **coitus interruptus** (also known as *withdrawal*, or "pulling out"), which involves removing the penis from the vagina before ejaculation. This method is widely used throughout the world and can be considered somewhat successful for *some* people. Success may depend on technique, combination with calendar methods, or on the physical characteristics of the partners (such as the tendency toward infertility in one or both partners).

A problem with this method is its riskiness. Secretions from the man's Cowper's glands, urethra, or prostrate, which sometimes seep into the vagina before ejaculation, can carry thousands of healthy sperm. Also, the first few drops of ejaculate carry most of the sperm. If the man is slow to withdraw or allows any ejaculate to spill into (or near the opening of) the vagina, the woman may get pregnant. A man using this method should wipe off any fluid at the tip of the penis before insertion into the vagina. If he has difficulty determining when he is about to ejaculate, he should *not* rely on withdrawal for contraception. The highest observed effectiveness rate using coitus interruptus is 84%. The actual user effectiveness rate is 77%. Although it is generally considered an unreliable method of birth control, coitus interruptus is certainly better than nothing.

Douching

Douching involves flushing the vagina with water or a medicated liquid. As a contraceptive method it is

ever, true contraceptive methods. **Contraception,** the prevention of conception altogether, is the category of birth control in which the sperm and egg are prevented from uniting. This is done in a variety of ways, including barrier methods, such as condoms and diaphragms, which place a physical barrier between sperm and egg; spermicides, which kill the sperm before they can get to the egg; and hormonal methods, such as the pill and implants, which inhibit the release of the oocyte from the ovary.

Choosing a Method

In order to be fully responsible in using birth control, a person must know what options he or she has available, how reliable these methods are, and the advantages and disadvantages (including possible side effects) of each method. How to choose the best form of birth control for yourself and your partner, especially if you have not been practicing contraception, is not easy.

When people feel that technology will show the way, they are misled . . . we must find harmony between the inner person and outer developments.

Isaac Bashevis Singer

faulty, because after ejaculation, douching is already too late. By the time a woman can douche, the sperm may already be swimming through the cervix into the uterus. The douche liquid may even push the sperm into the cervix. Douching with any liquid, especially if done often, tends to upset the normal chemical balance in the vagina and may cause irritation or infection. There is also evidence that frequent douching can result in ectopic pregnancy (Chow et al., 1985).

Lactation

When a woman breast-feeds her child after giving birth, she may not begin to ovulate as long as she continues to nourish her child exclusively by breast-feeding. However, although some women do not ovulate while lactating, others do. Cycles may begin immediately after delivery or in a few months. The woman never knows when she will begin to be fertile. Lactation is considered a contraceptive method in some countries, but the success rate is extremely low.

Mythical Methods

There are many myths among young and old about contraception. The young learn many myths from ru-

mors. Some of the old, who should know better, still believe misconceptions hatched in "the old days," when contraceptive devices were not as easily obtained or as dependable as they are today. (The dependability of condoms, always the most easily purchased device, was greatly improved when the product came under the supervision of the Federal Trade Commission.) Today, when satisfactory methods are so easy to obtain, it is senseless for anyone to use risky ones.

Widely known methods that are *totally* useless include:

1. Standing up during or after intercourse (sperm have no problem swimming "upstream").

2. Taking a friend's pill the day of, or the day after, intercourse (doesn't work, and may even be dangerous).

3. Only having intercourse occasionally (it is when, not how often, that makes a difference; once is enough, if the woman is fertile at that time).

4. Using plastic wrap or plastic bags as condoms (too loose, undependable, and unsanitary).

But knowing the facts about the methods gives you a solid basis from which to make decisions, and more security once a decision is reached. If you need to choose a birth control method for yourself, remember that *the best method is the one you will use consistently*. (The Self-Assessment in this chapter will help you determine which method of birth control will be the most comfortable for you.) When you are having intercourse, a condom left in a purse or wallet, a diaphragm in the bedside drawer, or a forgotten pill in its packet on the other side of town is *not* an effective means of birth control.

In the following discussion of method effectiveness, "theoretical effectiveness" implies perfectly consistent and correct use; "user effectiveness" refers to *actual* use (and misuse) based on studies by health-care organizations, medical practitioners, academic researchers, and pharmaceutical companies. User effectiveness is sometimes significantly lower than theoretical effectiveness because of factors that keep people from using a method properly or consistently. These factors may be inherent in the method or may be the result of a variety of influences on the user, as discussed earlier.

Self-Assessment

AM I GOING TO BE COMFORTABLE AND SUCCEED WITH THIS METHOD OF BIRTH CONTROL?

It is important to choose a method of birth control that works. All the methods offered at a family planning clinic will work well—if you use them properly.

It is also important to choose a method you will like! Ask yourself these questions, in order to make an informed decision: What type of birth control are you thinking about? Have you ever used it before? If yes, how long did you use it?

	Circle Your Answers		
Are you afraid of using this method?	Yes	No	Don't know
Would you rather not use this method?	Yes	No	Don't know
Will you have trouble remembering to use this method?	Yes	No	Don't know
Have you every become pregnant while using this method?	Yes	No	Don't know
Will you have trouble using this method carefully?	Yes	No	Don't know
Do you have unanswered questions about this method?	Yes	No	Don't know
Does this method make menstrual periods longer or more painful?	Yes	No	Don't know
Does this method cost more than you can afford?	Yes	No	Don't know
Does this method ever cause serious health problems?	Yes	No	Don't know
Do you object to this method because of religious beliefs?	Yes	No	Don't know
Have you already had problems using this method?	Yes	No	Don't know
Is your partner opposed to this method?	Yes	No	Don't know
Are you using this method without your partner's knowledge?	Yes	No	Don't know
Will using this method embarrass you?	Yes	No	Don't know
Will using this method embarrass your partner?	Yes	No	Don't know
Will you enjoy intercourse less because of this method	Yes	No	Don't know
Will this method interrupt lovemaking?	Yes	No	Don't know
Has a nurse or doctor ever told you not to use this method?	Yes	No	Don't know

Do you have any "Don't know" answers? If so, ask your clinic counselor to help you with more information.

Do you have any "Yes" answers? "Yes" answers mean you may not like this method. Ask your clinic counselor to talk this over with you. You may need to think about another method.

Source: Adapted from Hatcher, Robert, et al. *Contraceptive Technology*. New York: Irvington Publishers, 1990.

Sexual Abstinence

Before we begin our discussion of devices and techniques for preventing conception, we must acknowledge the oldest and most reliable birth control method of all. **Abstinence**—refraining from sexual intercourse—should be regarded as a legitimate personal choice, yet those who choose not to express their sensuality or sexuality through genital contact risk being stigmatized as uptight, frigid, or weird. The term "celibacy" is sometimes used interchangeably with "abstinence." We use the word "abstinence" because "celibacy" often implies the avoidance of *all* forms of sexual activity and, often, the religious commitment not to marry or to maintain a nonsexual lifestyle.

Individuals who choose not to have intercourse are still free to express affection (and give and receive sexual satisfaction if they so desire) in a variety of ways. Ways to show love without making babies include talking, hugging, massaging, kissing, petting, and manual stimulation of the genitals. Those who choose sexual abstinence as their method of birth control need to communicate this clearly to their dates or partners. They should also be informed about other forms of contraception. And, in the event that someone experiences a change of mind, it can't hurt to have a condom handy. An advantage of abstinence is that refraining from sexual activity allows a couple to get to know and trust each other gradually before they face the emotions and stresses brought about by high degrees of intimacy.

Abstinence sows sand all over the ruddy limbs and flaming hair.
William Blake

Hormonal Methods: The Pill and Implants

In addition to the tried-and-true birth control pill, a number of new forms of hormonal contraception are or soon will be available. These include capsules that are implanted under a woman's skin, and injectable hormones for both women and men.

The Pill **Oral contraceptives,** popularly called "the pill," are used by approximately 13.8 million women in the United States today (Hatcher et al., 1990). In 1988, 18.5% of women (and 24.7% of single women) chose the pill as their method of birth control, making it the most popular method among women ("Sterilization," 1990). The pill is actually a series of pills (20, 21, or 28 to a package) containing synthetic estrogen and/or progesterone, which regulate egg production and the menstrual cycle. When taken for birth control, they accomplish some or all of the following:

- Inhibit ovulation.
- Thicken cervical mucus (preventing sperm entry).
- Inhibit implantation of the fertilized ovum.
- Promote early spontaneous abortion of the fertilized ovum.

The pill produces basically the same chemical conditions that would exist in a woman's body if she were pregnant.

Oral contraceptives must be prescribed by a physician or family planning clinic. There are a number of brands available, containing various amounts of hormones. Most commonly prescribed are the combination pills, which contain a fairly standard amount of estrogen and different doses of progestin according to the pill type. In the triphasic pill, the amount of progestin is altered during the cycle, purportedly to approximate the normal hormonal pattern. (The various manufacturers of the triphasic pills seem to disagree with one another, however, as to what constitutes a normal hormonal pattern [Hatcher et al., 1990].) There is also a "minipill" containing progestin only, but it is generally prescribed only in cases when the woman should not take estrogen. It is considered slightly less effective than the combined pill, and it must be taken with precise, unfailing regularity to be effective.

With the 20- and 21-day pills, one pill is taken each day until they are all used. Two to five days later, the woman should begin her menstrual flow. Commonly, it is quite light. (If the flow does not begin, the woman should start the next series of pills seven days after the end of the last series. If she repeatedly has no flow, she should talk to her health practitioner.) On the fifth day of her menstrual flow, the woman should start the next series of pills.

The 28-day pills are taken continuously. Seven of the pills have no hormones. They are there simply to avoid breaks in the routine; some women prefer them because they find them easier to remember.

The pill is considered the most effective birth control method available (except for sterilization) when used correctly. (We note that when adequate time has passed to study the effects of the hormonal implant, it will likely also be highly rated.) It is not effective when used carelessly. The pill must be taken every day, as close as possible to the same time each day. If one is missed, it should be taken as soon as the woman remembers, and the next one taken on schedule. If two are missed, the method cannot be relied on, and an additional form of contraception should be used for the rest of the cycle. It should be remembered that the pill in no way protects against sexually transmitted diseases. Women on the pill should consider the additional use of a condom to reduce the risk of STDs. A year's supply of birth control pills costs between $180 and $240.

Effectiveness The combined pill is more than 99.5% effective theoretically. User effectiveness (the rate shown by actual studies) is between 95% and 98%. Progestin-only pills are somewhat less effective, especially among younger, presumably more fertile, younger women (Trussell & Kost, 1987; Vessey, Lawless, Yeates, & McPherson, 1985).

Advantages Pills are easy to take. They are dependable. No applications or interruptions are necessary before or during intercourse. Some women experience side effects that please them, such as more regular or reduced menstrual flow, or enlarged breasts.

Possible Problems There are many possible side effects, which may or may not bother the user, that can occur from taking the pill. Those most often reported are:

- Change (usually a decrease) in menstrual flow.
- Breast tenderness.
- Nausea or vomiting.
- Weight gain or loss.

Some of the other side effects are:

- Spotty darkening of the skin.
- Nervousness, dizziness.
- Loss of scalp hair.
- Change in appetite.
- Change (most commonly, a decrease) in sex drive.
- Mood changes.
- Increase in body hair.
- Increase in vaginal discharges and yeast infections.

These side effects can sometimes be eliminated by changing the prescription, but not always. Certain women react unfavorably to the pill because of existing health factors or extra sensitivity to female hormones. Women with heart or kidney diseases, asthma, high blood pressure, diabetes, epilepsy, gall bladder disease, sickle-cell anemia, or those prone to migraine headaches or depression are usually considered poor candidates for the pill. Certain medications may react differently or unfavorably with the pill. The effects of diazepam (Valium), for example, last over 20% longer if a woman is using oral contraceptives.

The pill also creates certain health risks, but to what extent is a matter of controversy. Women taking the pill stand a greater chance of problems with circulatory diseases, blood clotting, heart attack, and certain kinds of liver tumors. There is also an increased risk of contracting chlamydia. The health risks are low for the young (about half the number of risks encountered at childbirth), but they increase with age. The risk for smokers, women over 35, and those with certain other health disorders is about four times as great as childbirth. For women over 40, the risks are considered high. Current literature on the pill especially emphasizes the risks for women who smoke. Definite risks of cardiovascular complications and various forms of cancer exist because of the synergistic action of the ingredients of cigarettes and oral contraceptives. Table 12.1 compares the relative risk of contraceptive-related death to deaths related to pregnancy and activities such as smoking and driving.

A number of studies have linked pill use with certain types of cancer, but they are not conclusive. The risk of some types of cancer, such as ovarian and endometrial, appears to be significantly *reduced* by pill use (Hankinson, Colditz, Hunter, Spencer, Rosner, & Stampfler, 1992). On the other hand, a link between cervical cancer and long-term pill use has been suggested by several studies (Vessey et al., 1983; World Health Organization, 1984). A 1986 study found a slightly increased risk of cervical cancer with the use of pills high in estrogen and with an increased duration of pill use (Brinton et al., 1986). Regular Pap smears (see Chapter 14) are recommended as an excellent defense against cervical cancer, for pill users and nonusers alike.

Findings regarding the pill and breast cancer are conflicting. The largest study, however, involving more than 9300 women, found no increased risk of breast cancer among pill users (Centers for Disease Control, 1986; Schlesselman, 1990).

Certain other factors may need to be taken into account in determining if oral contraceptives are appropriate. Young girls who have not matured

TABLE 12.1 Putting Voluntary Risks into Perspective

Risk	Chance of Death in a Year (U.S.)
Smoking	1 in 200
Motorcycling	1 in 1000
Automobile driving	1 in 6000
Power boating	1 in 6000
Rock climbing	1 in 7500
Playing football	1 in 25,000
Canoeing	1 in 100,000
Using tampons (TSS)	1 in 350,000
Having sexual intercourse (PID)	1 in 50,000
Preventing pregnancy:	
Oral contraceptive, nonsmoker	1 in 63,000
Oral contraceptive, smoker	1 in 16,000
IUD	1 in 100,000
Barrier methods	None
Natural methods	None
Undergoing sterilization:	
Laparoscopic tubal ligation	1 in 20,000
Hysterectomy	1 in 1600
Vasectomy	None
Deciding about pregnancy:	
Continuing pregnancy	1 in 10,000
Terminating pregnancy:	
Illegal abortion	1 in 3000
Legal abortion:	
Before 9 weeks	1 in 400,000
9–12 weeks	1 in 100,000
13–16 weeks	1 in 25,000
After 16 weeks	1 in 10,000

SOURCE: Adapted from Hatcher, Robert, et al. *Contraceptive Technology*. New York: Irvington Publishers, 1990.

physically may have their development slowed by early pill use. Nursing mothers cannot use pills containing estrogen because the hormone inhibits milk production. Some lactating women use the minipill successfully (Hatcher et al., 1990).

Millions of women use the pill with moderate to high degrees of satisfaction. For many women, if personal health or family history does not contraindicate it, the pill is both effective and safe.

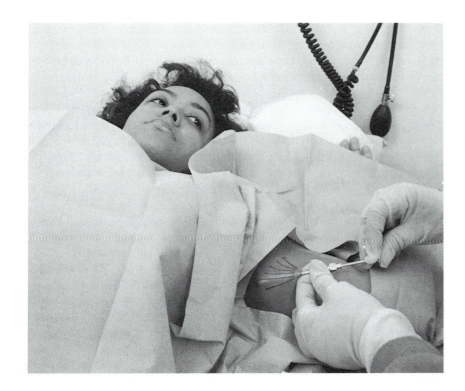

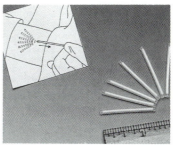

Contraceptive implants are inserted under the skin of a woman's arm in a 10-minute office procedure. One set of implants prevents pregnancy for 5 years.

Implants In December 1990, the FDA approved the contraceptive **implant,** thin, matchstick-sized capsules containing levonorgestrel (a progestin) that are implanted under a woman's skin. Over a period of up to 5 years, the hormone is slowly released. When the implants are removed, which may be done at any time, fertility is restored. A set of soft tubes is surgically implanted under the skin of the upper arm in a simple office procedure with a local anesthetic. Once implanted, the capsules are not visible (or are barely visible) but may be felt under the skin. The implants, under the trade name **Norplant,** are currently on the market in more than 14 countries. The cost of the implant, including the procedure, is between $450 and $700, depending on where it is obtained. It may seem high, but it is probably less expensive than a 5-year supply of birth control pills.

Another type of implant, a biodegradable capsule marketed as Capronor, contains the same type of progestin as Norplant. These capsules are also surgically placed under the skin; they are effective for 18 months. Norethindrone, another progestin, may be administered in a set of four biodegradable pellets that are inserted under the skin. They are effective for 12 months or longer. Norethindrone may also be injected in tiny "microspheres" at 3-month intervals (Hatcher et al., 1990). Capronor and the norethindrone implants are not widely available.

Effectiveness Although Norplant has not been observed or tested to the degree that other contraceptives have, initial reports indicate a failure rate one-tenth to one-twentieth that of the pill. The implants should be removed after 5 years, as their effectiveness drops sharply in the 6th year. New implants may be inserted at that time. Removable progestin implants such as Norplant may be the most effective reversible contraceptive ever marketed (Hatcher et al., 1990).

Advantages   Convenience is clearly a big advantage of the implant. Once the implant is in, there's nothing to remember, buy, do, or take care of. Because implants contain no estrogen, users generally experience fewer side effects than with the pill. Many users report light to nonexistent menstrual flow and a reduction of menstrual cramps and pain. The risk of endometrial cancer may be reduced (Hatcher et al., 1990).

Possible Problems   Side effects of contraceptive implants may be similar to those of oral contraceptives. The chief negative side effect, experienced by about half of implant users, is a change in the pattern of menstrual bleeding, such as lengthened periods or spotting between periods. Progestin implants should not be used by women with acute liver disease, breast cancer, blood clots, or unexplained vaginal bleeding, nor should they be used by women who are breast-feeding or those who may possibly be pregnant. Implant users are advised not to smoke. Possible long-term negative effects are not known at this time.

Depo-Provera (DMPA)   The injectable contraceptive medroxyprogesterone acetate, **Depo-Provera,** or **DMPA,** which provides protection from pregnancy for 3–6 months, is used in over 80 countries throughout the world, and has recently been approved for use in the United States. Generally speaking, DMPA has been shown to be remarkably free of serious side effects and complications. It does cause cessation of the menstrual period while it is being administered, and it may cause delayed fertility (up to a year in some cases) until the effects wear off. Sometimes "breakthrough bleeding" (bleeding not associated with the menstrual period) is a problem. A year's protection with DMPA (given in four injections at 3-month intervals) costs about $120.

Barrier Methods: The Condom, Diaphragm, Cervical Cap, Sponge, and the Female Condom

Barrier methods are designed to keep sperm and egg from getting together. Today's methods are considerably more sophisticated (and presumably at least as effective) as the well-known Puritan barrier device, the bundling board (placed in bed between visiting sweethearts who were bundled up against the cold New England winter). Barrier methods available to women are the diaphragm, the cervical cap, the contraceptive sponge (which also contains a spermicide), and the new female condom. The barrier device worn by men is the condom. The effectiveness of all barrier methods is increased by use with spermicides, which are discussed later in this chapter.

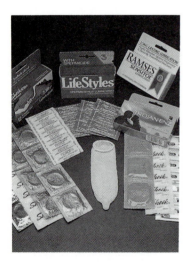

The Condom   A **condom** is a thin sheath of latex rubber (or processed animal tissue) that fits over the erect penis and thus prevents semen from being transmitted (Figure 12.1). Condoms are available in a variety of sizes,

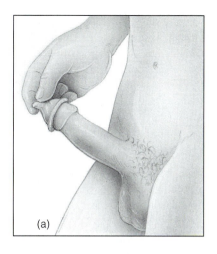

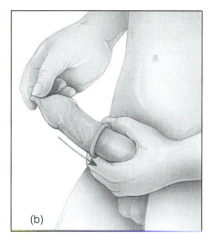

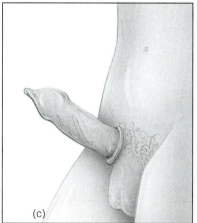

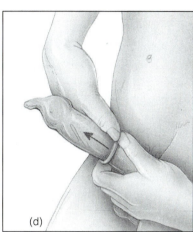

FIGURE 12.1 Using a Condom. (a) Place the rolled condom on the erect penis, leaving about a half-inch of space at the tip (first, squeeze any air out of the condom tip). (b) Roll the condom down, smoothing out any air bubbles. (c) Roll the condom to the base of the penis. (d) After ejaculation, hold the condom base while withdrawing the penis. (See Perspective 2 for further hints on effective condom use.)

shapes, and colors. Some are lubricated, and some are treated with spermicides. They are easily obtainable from drugstores and family planning clinics, and most kinds are relatively inexpensive. Condoms are the third most widely used form of birth control in the United States (after sterilization and the pill). Their use has increased significantly since the late 1980s, due in large part to their effectiveness in helping prevent the spread of STDs. It is estimated that 5 billion condoms are used worldwide annually (Hatcher et al., 1990). A condom costs anywhere from about thirty cents (for "plain") to $1.50 (for "fancy"). They are often available free from family planning clinics and AIDS education programs.

Condoms provide effective contraception when properly used. *Latex* condoms (but not those made of animal tissue) also help guard against the transmission of a number of sexually transmitted diseases such as chlamydia, gonorrhea, genital herpes, and HIV infection. Due to increased publicity regarding the transmissibility of HIV, both heterosexuals and gay men are increasingly using condoms as prophylactic devices. Condom use does not guarantee *total* safety from STDs, however, because sexual partners may also transmit certain diseases by hand, mouth, and genital areas other than the penis or vagina. Condoms may also occasionally tear or leak. As mentioned above, animal tissue (or "lambskin") condoms can be permeated by several kinds of disease-causing organisms such as HIV. Therefore, they should only be used for contraceptive purposes by monogamous couples who understand that such condoms do not protect against STDs.

Today, 40–70% of condoms are purchased by women, and condom advertising and packaging increasingly reflect this trend (Barron, 1987; Hatcher et al., 1990). The authors of *Contraceptive Technology*, a leading reference book for family planning clinics, make four key points in regard to women and condom use (Hatcher et al., 1990):

1. Women have more to lose than men when it comes to sexually transmitted diseases; they can suffer permanent infertility, for example.

2. Men infected with STDs infect two out of three of their female partners, whereas women with STDs transmit the illness to one out of three male partners.

3. Condoms help protect women against unplanned pregnancy, ectopic pregnancy, bacterial infections such as vaginitis and PID, viral infections such as herpes and HIV, cervical cancer, and infections that may harm a fetus or an infant during delivery.

4. A woman has the right to insist on condom use. Even if a woman regularly uses another form of birth control, such as the pill or an IUD, she may want to have the added protection provided by a condom, especially if it has been treated with spermicide (which provides further protection against disease organisms). Contraceptive aerosol foam and contraceptive film (a thin, translucent square of tissue that dissolves into a gel) are the most convenient spermicidal preparations to use with condoms.

Effectiveness Condoms are 98–99% effective theoretically. User effectiveness is about 88%. Failures sometimes occur from mishandling the condom, but they are usually the result of not putting it on until after some semen has leaked into the vagina, or simply not putting it on at all. (For hints on effective condom use, see Perspective 2.)

Advantages Condoms are easy to obtain. They are easy to carry in a wallet or purse. Latex rubber condoms help protect against STDs, including herpes and AIDS.

Possible Problems The chief drawback of a condom is that it must be put on after the man has been aroused but before penetration. This interruption is the major reason for users to neglect or "forget" to put them on. Some men complain that sensation is dulled, and (very rarely) cases of allergy to rubber are reported. Men who experience significant loss of feeling with a condom are advised to try other kinds. Many of the newer condoms are very thin (but also strong); they conduct heat well and allow quite a bit of sensation to be experienced. The condom user (or his partner) must take care to hold the sheath at the base of his penis when he withdraws, in order to avoid leakage. Condoms should be used with water-based lubricants only, as oil-based lubricants such as Vaseline can weaken the rubber. Vaginally

"Hear me, and hear me good, kid. Unroll the condom all the way to the base of the erect penis, taking care to expel the air from the reservoir at the tip by squeezing between the forefinger and thumb . . . "

Reproduced by Special Permission of PLAYBOY Magazine. Copyright © 1989 by PLAYBOY.

applied medications such as Monistat (for yeast infections) and Premarin (an estrogen cream) may also cause condom breakage.

The Diaphragm A **diaphragm,** a rubber cup with a flexible rim, is placed deep inside the vagina, blocking the cervix, to prevent sperm from entering the uterus and fallopian tubes. Different women require different sizes, and a woman may change size, especially after a pregnancy; the size must be determined by an experienced practitioner. Diaphragms are available by prescription from doctors and family planning clinics. Somewhat effective by itself, the diaphragm is highly effective when used with a spermicidal cream or jelly. (Creams and jellies are considered more effective than foam for use with a diaphragm.) Diaphragm users should be sure to use an adequate amount of spermicide and to follow their practitioner's instructions with care. Diaphragms are relatively inexpensive—about $15 plus the cost of spermicide and the initial exam and fitting.

The diaphragm can be put in place up to 2 hours before intercourse. It should be left in place 6 to 8 hours afterward. A woman should not dislodge it or douche before it is time to remove it. If intercourse is repeated within

The Diaphragm.

HINTS FOR EFFECTIVE CONDOM USE

- Use condoms every time you have sexual intercourse; this is the key to successful contraception and disease prevention.

- Use a spermicide with the condom. Foam and film are both easy to apply. Spermicide helps protect against pregnancy and STDs, including chlamydia, gonorrhea, genital herpes, and HIV infection.

- Always put the condom on before the penis touches the vagina. Even if the man has great "control," there is always the possibility of leakage prior to ejaculation.

- Leave about a half-inch of space at the condom tip, and roll the condom all the way down to the base of the penis.

- Soon after ejaculation, the penis should be withdrawn. Make sure someone holds the base of the condom firmly against the penis as it is withdrawn.

- After use, check the condom for possible torn spots. If you are not using a spermicide and you find a tear or hole, immediately insert foam or jelly into the vagina. This may reduce the chance of pregnancy. If torn condoms are a persistent problem, use a water-based lubricant, such as K-Y jelly, or a spermicide to reduce friction.

- Do not reuse a condom.

- Keep condoms in a cool, dry, and convenient place.

- To help protect against HIV and other organisms, always use a latex rubber condom, *not* one made of animal tissue.

If you or your partner are uncomfortable with condom use, consider the following:

- *Stand your ground.* (This is mainly for women, as it is generally men who object to condoms.) Unless you want to be pregnant and are sure your partner is free of STDs, you need protection during sex. If he says no to condoms, you can say no to him. If he cares about you, he will work with you to find birth control and safer sex methods that suit you both.

- Communication is crucial. It may seem "unromantic," but planning your contraception strategy before you are sexually entangled is essential. Giving or getting a disease or worrying about pregnancy is about as unromantic as you can get. Consider visiting a family planning clinic for counseling—together. Neither partner should be forced to use a form of birth control he or she is truly unhappy with. But the issue of protection must be dealt with—by both of you.

- Don't forget your sense of humor and playfulness. Condoms can actually provide lots of laughs, and laughter and sex go well together. Fancy condoms—colored, ribbed, glow-in-the-dark, etc.—are popular for their entertainment value.

6 hours, the diaphragm should be left in place but more spermicide should be inserted with an applicator. However, a diaphragm should not be left in place for more than 24 hours.

A diaphragm should be replaced about once a year; the rubber may deteriorate and lose elasticity, thus increasing the chance of splitting. Any change in the way the diaphragm feels, as well as any dramatic gain or loss of weight, calls for a visit to a doctor or clinic to check the fit.

Effectiveness Numerous studies of diaphragm effectiveness have yielded varying results. Typical user effectiveness (actual statistical effectiveness) is in the 81–83% range. Consistent, correct use is essential to achieve maximum effectiveness. For this reason, the risk of diaphragm failure is approximately double for women who are under 30 (and therefore more fertile than older women) or who have intercourse four times weekly or more (Hatcher et al., 1990).

Advantages The diaphragm can be put in place well before the time of intercourse. For most women, there are few health problems associated with its use. It helps protect against diseases of the cervix and PID (see Chapter 16).

Possible Problems Some women dislike handling or placing diaphragms, or the mess or smell of the chemical contraceptives used with them. Some men complain of rubbing or other discomfort caused by the diaphragm. Occasionally, a woman will be allergic to rubber. Some women become more prone to urinary tract infections (see Chapter 16). As there is a small risk of toxic shock syndrome (TSS) associated with its use, a woman should not use a diaphragm under the following conditions:

- During menstruation or other vaginal bleeding.
- Following childbirth (for several months).
- During abnormal vaginal discharge.
- If she has had TSS or if *Staphylococcus aureus* bacteria are present.

She should also:

- Never wear the diaphragm for more than 24 hours.
- Learn to watch for the warning signs of TSS (see Chapter 14).

The Cervical Cap The **cervical cap** is a small rubber barrier device that fits snugly over the cervix; it is held in place by suction and can be filled with spermicidal cream or jelly. Cervical caps come in different sizes and shapes. Proper fit is extremely important, and not everyone can be fitted. Fitting must be done by a physician or a health-care practitioner.

Effectiveness There is a limited amount of research data in this country regarding the cervical cap's effectiveness. Reported user effectiveness ranges from 73–92%.

Advantages The cervical cap may be more comfortable and convenient than the diaphragm for some women. Much less spermicide is used than with the diaphragm; spermicide need not be reapplied if intercourse is repeated. The cervical cap does not interfere with the body physically or hormonally.

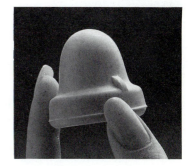

The Cervical Cap.

Possible Problems Some users are bothered by an odor that develops from the interaction of the cap's rubber with either vaginal secretions or the spermicide. There is some concern that the cap may contribute to erosion of the cervix. If a partner's penis touches the rim of the cap, it can become displaced during intercourse. Theoretically the same risk of TSS exists for the cervical cap as for the diaphragm. The precautions listed in the section on diaphragms also apply.

The Contraceptive Sponge.

The Contraceptive Sponge   In 1983, the FDA approved the **contraceptive sponge** for over-the-counter sales. When inserted into the vagina, the polyurethane sponge blocks the opening of the cervix and releases a spermicide. It must be left in place for at least 6 hours (or as long as 24 hours) following intercourse and then disposed of. Sponges are sold in boxes of three, six, and twelve. The cost of an individual sponge is between one and two dollars.

Effectiveness   The sponge has a theoretical effectiveness rate of 87–90%. It has a user effectiveness rate of about 83%. The lowest observed effectiveness rate is 72%. Higher failure rates seem to appear among women who have previously given birth (McIntyre & Higgins, 1986; Trussell, Hatcher, Cates, Stewart, & Kost, 1990).

Advantages   The sponge's advantages include convenience, safety, effectiveness, and possible prevention of some sexually transmitted diseases. (The sponge cannot be relied upon for prevention against HIV, however [Kreiss et al., 1992].) It is easy to obtain.

Possible Problems   No long-term studies of the sponge's safety have been completed. It is recommended that the sponge *not* be used during menstruation because of the risk of TSS at that time. The precautions listed in the section on diaphragms also apply to the contraceptive sponge. Some women report an unpleasant odor from the sponge; some report allergic reactions; others report inadvertently expelling the sponge during a bowel movement. Some women experience difficulty removing the sponge.

The Female Condom.

The Female Condom   There are two types of condoms newly designed for women to wear. One is a disposable, soft, loose-fitting polyurethane sheath with a diaphragmlike ring at each end. One ring is inside the sheath and is used to insert and anchor the condom against the cervix. The larger outer ring remains outside the vagina and acts as a barrier, protecting the vulva and the base of the penis (Figure 12.2). The other type of female condom, made of latex, is secured by a G-string. A condom pouch in the crotch of the G-string unfolds as the penis pushes it into the vagina. Female condoms cost about $2.50 per condom at drugstores, less at family planning clinics.

Because of the newness of these products, their effectiveness cannot accurately be determined at this time, although clinical tests of the polyurethane sheath indicate it is less likely to leak than the male latex condom. In laboratory tests, this condom was not permeated by HIV, indicating that it may be a promising alternative for both contraception and the control of STDs. Female condoms may prove advantageous for women whose partners are reluctant to use a male condom. They give women an additional way to control their fertility.

Spermicides

A **spermicide** is a substance that is toxic to sperm. The most commonly used spermicide in products sold in the United States is the chemical **nonoxynol-9**. Spermicidal preparations are available in a variety of forms: foam,

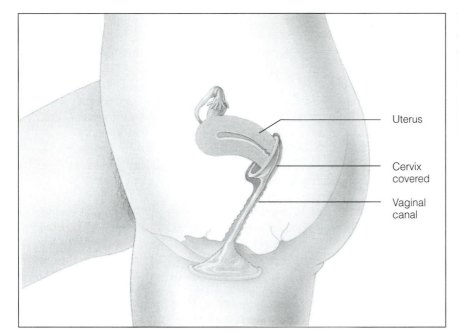

FIGURE 12.2 The Female Condom in Position. The female condom, a sheath of soft polyurethane, is anchored around the cervix with a flexible ring (much like a diaphragm). A larger ring secures the sheath outside the vagina and also helps protect the vulva.

Uterus

Cervix covered

Vaginal canal

film, jelly, cream, tablets, and suppositories. Contraceptive sponges and some condoms are also treated with spermicides. Spermicidal preparations are considered most effective when used in combination with a barrier method. Spermicidal preparations are sold in tubes, packets, or other containers which hold about 12–20 applications. The cost per use is about forty cents to one dollar.

A further benefit of spermicides is that they significantly reduce STD risk. Nonoxynol-9 has been demonstrated to have a toxic effect on a number of disease agents, including HIV (at least in laboratory experiments). Although the use of spermicides lowers the risk of contracting an STD, it does not entirely eliminate that risk. There is no way to ensure that the spermicide will kill *all* the viruses that may be present. (See Chapter 16 for further information on STD prevention.)

Contraceptive Foam **Contraceptive foam** is a chemical spermicide sold in aerosol containers. It is a practical form of spermicide for use with a condom. Methods of application vary with each brand, but foam is usually released deep in the vagina either directly from the container or with an applicator. The foam forms a physical barrier to the uterus, and its chemicals inactivate sperm in the vagina. It is most effective if inserted no more than half an hour before intercourse. Shaking the container before applying the foam increases its foaminess so that it spreads further. The foam begins to go flat after about half an hour. It must be reapplied when intercourse is repeated.

Effectiveness Foam has a theoretical effectiveness rate of 98.5%. User failure brings its effectiveness down to as low as 71%. Failure tends to result from not applying the foam every single time the couple has intercourse,

If toothpaste tasted as disgusting as spermicide, the teeth of the nation would have fallen out years ago.
Germaine Greer

from relying on foam inserted hours before intercourse, or from relying on foam placed hurriedly or not placed in deeply enough. If used properly and consistently, however, it is quite reliable. Used with a condom, foam is highly effective.

Advantages There are almost no medical problems associated with the use of foam. Foam helps provide protection against sexually transmitted diseases.

Possible Problems Some women dislike applying foam. Some complain of messiness, leakage, odor, or stinging sensations. Occasionally, a woman or man may have an allergic reaction to it.

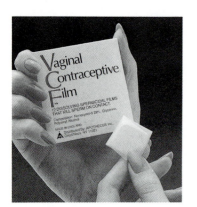

The Contraceptive Film.

Contraceptive Film **Contraceptive film** (also called vaginal contraceptive film, or VCF) is a relatively new spermicidal preparation. It is sold in packets of small (2-inch square), translucent tissues. This thin tissue contains the spermicide nonoxynol-9, which dissolves into a sticky gel when inserted into the vagina. It is placed directly over the cervix, not less than 5 minutes or more than 1.5 hours before intercourse. It remains effective for 2 hours after insertion. Contraceptive film works effectively in conjunction with the condom.

Effectiveness Extensive research has not been done on the effectiveness of film, because of its relative newness on the market. The highest effectiveness rates reported are 82–90%. Of course, proper and consistent use with a condom will highly increase the effectiveness.

Advantages Film is easy to use for many women. It is easily obtained from a drugstore. It is easy to carry in a purse, wallet, or pocket.

Possible Problems Some women may not like inserting the film into the vagina. Some women may be allergic to it. Increased vaginal discharge and temporary pain while urinating after using contraceptive film have been reported.

Creams and Jellies These chemical spermicides come in tubes and are inserted with applicators or placed inside diaphragms or cervical caps. They can be bought without prescription at most drugstores. They work in a manner similar to foams, but are considered less effective when used alone. Like foam, jellies and creams seem to provide some protection against STDs. This factor makes their use with a diaphragm even more attractive.

Suppositories and Tablets These chemical spermicides are inserted into the vagina before intercourse. Body heat and fluids dissolve the ingredients, which will inactivate sperm in the vagina after ejaculation. They must be inserted early enough to dissolve completely before intercourse.

Effectiveness of Creams, Jellies, Suppositories, and Tablets Reports on these methods vary widely. It is suspected that the variations are connected with each user's technique of application. Directions for use that come with these contraceptives are not always clear. Jellies, creams, vaginal tablets, and suppositories should be used in conjunction with a barrier method for maximum effectiveness.

Advantages The methods are simple and easily obtainable, with virtually no medical problems. They help protect against STDs, including chlamydia, trichomonas, gonorrhea, genital herpes, and HIV.

Possible Problems Some people have allergic reactions to spermicides. Some women dislike the messiness, odor, or necessity of touching their own genitals. Others experience irritation or inflammation, especially if they use any of the methods frequently. A few women lack the vaginal lubrication to dissolve the tablets in a reasonable amount of time. And a few women complain of having anxiety about the effectiveness of any of the methods during intercourse.

A 1981 study linked spermicide use with congenital birth defects in children born to women who were spermicide users (Jick, Hannon, Stergachis, Heidrich, Perera, & Rothman, 1981). Lawsuits against the manufacturers of spermicides have been filed. A clear link, however, has not been proven to the satisfaction of a number of experts, according to subsequent interviews with the authors of the study and staff members of the Centers for Disease Control (Kowal, 1981). They feel that there is not sufficient evidence to indicate a need for concern on the part of spermicide users. Some clinicians recommend that spermicides not be used when a possible pregnancy exists (Hatcher et al., 1990).

The IUD (Intrauterine Device)

The **intrauterine device,** or **IUD,** is a tiny plastic or metal device that is inserted into the uterus through the cervical os (opening) (Figure 12.3). The particular type of device determines how long it may be left in place; the range is one year to indefinitely.

Although most IUDs have been withdrawn from the U.S. market because of the proliferation of lawsuits against their manufacturers in recent years, they are still considered a major birth control method. The two IUDs currently available in the United States are the Copper T-380A, marketed as the ParaGard, and the progesterone T device, marketed as the Progestasert IUD. The Copper T-380A is made of polyethylene; the stem of the T is wrapped with fine copper wire. It is approved for 4 years of use. More than 8 million Copper T-380As have been distributed worldwide. The Progestasert is also in the form of a T. It is made of a polymer plastic with a hollow stem containing progesterone, which is continually released. The Progestasert is effective for 1 year. At the time an IUD is removed, a new one may be inserted. The cost of an IUD, including insertion, starts at about $200 at family planning clinics.

The withdrawal from the U.S. market of the major IUDs affected one in ten women who used reversible contraception in the 1980s (Forrest, 1986). In 1982, more than 2 million American women used the IUD. The number had dropped, by 1985, possibly to as low as 1.4 million ("Ortho Stops," 1985). The drop in IUD use undoubtedly reflected the anxiety women felt regarding the well-publicized risks associated with its use. And there clearly

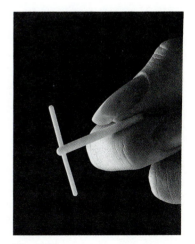

The IUD.

FIGURE 12.3 An IUD (Progestasert) in Position.

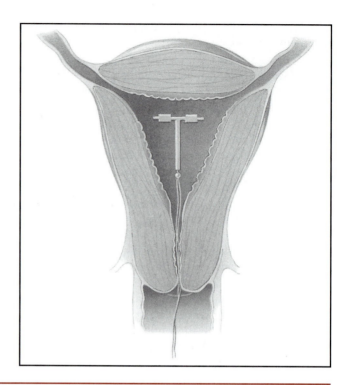

are some risks involved with the IUD, especially for certain women. Nevertheless, it remains the birth control method of about 70 million women throughout the world, including 40–45 million women in China.

The IUD apparently works in a number of ways, some of which are not yet clearly understood. Its mechanisms of action are thought to include the following (Alvarez, 1988; Ortiz & Croxatto, 1987; Treiman & Liskin, 1988):

- Immobilization of sperm and interference with their migration to the fallopian tubes.
- Speeded transport of the oocyte through the fallopian tube.
- Inhibition of fertilization.
- Inhibition of implantation.

IUDs must be inserted and removed by a trained practitioner.

Effectiveness IUDs are 97–99% effective theoretically. User effectiveness is 90–96%. The Copper T-380A has the lowest failure rate of any IUD developed to date.

Advantages Once inserted, IUDs require little care. They don't interfere with spontaneity during intercourse.

Possible Problems Insertion may be painful. Heavy cramping usually follows and sometimes persists. Menstrual flow usually increases. Up to one-third of users, especially women who have never been pregnant, expel the device within the first year. This usually happens during menstruation. The IUD can be reinserted, however, and many women retain it the second time.

The IUD is associated with increased risk of pelvic inflammatory disease (see Chapter 16). Because of the risk of sterility induced by PID, many physicians recommend that women planning to have children use alternative methods. Women who have had PID or who have multiple sex partners should be aware that an IUD will place them at significantly greater risk of PID, STDs, and other infections.

The IUD cannot be inserted in some women because of unusual uterine shape or position. Until recently, it was considered difficult to insert and less effective for teenage girls. But newer, smaller IUDs have been found to provide good protection even for young teenagers. Occasionally, the device perforates the cervix. This usually happens at the time of insertion, if it happens at all. Removal sometimes requires surgery.

Sometimes pregnancy or ectopic pregnancy (implantation within the fallopian tube) occurs and is complicated by the presence of the IUD. If the IUD is not removed, there is about a 50% chance of spontaneous abortion; if it is removed, the chance is around 25%. Furthermore, spontaneous abortions that occur when an IUD is left in place are likely to be septic (infection-bearing) and possibly life-threatening. Ectopic pregnancies have been found to occur six to ten times more frequently in users of Progestasert than in users of the Copper T-380A (Hatcher et al., 1990).

Fertility Awareness Methods

Fertility awareness methods of contraception require substantial education, training, and planning. They are based on a woman's knowledge of her body's reproductive cycle. Requiring a high degree of motivation and self-control, these methods are not for everyone. Fertility awareness is also referred to as "natural family planning." Some people make the following distinction between the two. With fertility awareness, the couple may use an alternate method (such as a diaphragm with jelly or a condom with foam) during the fertile part of the woman's cycle. Natural family planning does not include the use of any contraceptive device and is thus considered to be more natural; it is approved by the Catholic church.

Fertility awareness methods include the calendar (rhythm) method, the basal body temperature (BBT) method, the mucus (also called the Billings or ovulation) method, and the sympto-thermal method, which combines the latter two. These methods are not recommended for women who have irregular menstrual cycles, including postpartum and lactating mothers.

All women can benefit from learning to recognize their fertility signs. It is useful to know when the time of greatest likelihood of pregnancy occurs, both for women who wish to avoid pregnancy and for those who want to become pregnant.

The Calendar (Rhythm) Method The **calendar (rhythm) method** is based on calculating "safe" days based on the range of a woman's longest and shortest menstrual cycles. It may not be practical or safe for women with irregular cycles. For women with regular cycles, the calendar method is reasonably effective because the period of time when an oocyte is receptive to fertilization is only about 24 hours. As sperm generally live 2–4 days, the maximum period of time in which fertilization could be expected to occur may be calculated with the assistance of a calendar.

There are attacks on fecundity itself with means that human and Christian ethics must consider illicit. Instead of increasing the amount of bread on the table of a hungry humanity as modern means of production can do today, there are thoughts of diminishing the number of those at the table through methods that are contrary to honesty. This is not worthy of civilization.

Pope John Paul II

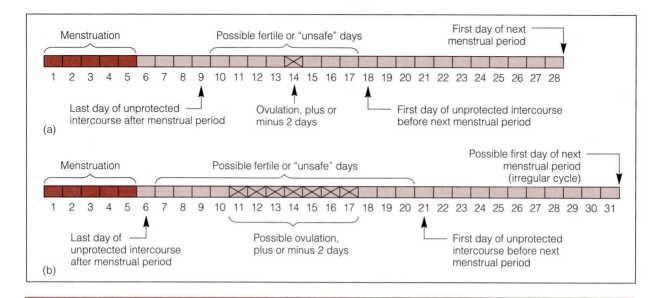

FIGURE 12.4 Fertility Awareness Calendar. To use the calendar method or other fertility awareness methods, a woman must keep track of her menstrual cycles. (a) The top chart shows probable safe and unsafe days for a woman with a regular 28-day cycle. (b) The bottom chart shows safe and unsafe days for a woman whose cycles range from 25 to 31 days. Note that the woman with an irregular cycle has significantly more unsafe days. The calendar method is most effective when combined with the BBT and mucus methods.

Ovulation generally occurs 14 (plus or minus 2) days before a woman's menstrual period. Taking this into account, and charting her menstrual cycles for a minimum of 8 months to determine the longest and shortest cycles, a woman can determine her expected fertile period. Figure 12.4 shows the interval of fertility calculated in this way. During the fertile period, a woman must abstain from sexual intercourse or use an alternative method of contraception. A woman using this method must be meticulous in her calculations, keep her calendar up to date, and be able to maintain an awareness of what day it is. Statistically, only about one-third of all women have cycles regular enough to use this method satisfactorily.

The Basal Body Temperature (BBT) Method
A woman's temperature tends to be slightly lower during menstruation and for about a week afterward. Just before ovulation, it dips; it then rises sharply (one-half to one whole degree) following ovulation. It stays high until just before the next menstrual period.

A woman practicing the **basal body temperature (BBT) method** must record her temperature every morning upon waking for 6–12 months to have an accurate idea of her temperature pattern. When she is quite sure she recognizes the rise in temperature and can predict about when in her cycle it will happen, she can begin using the method. She will abstain from intercourse or use an alternate contraceptive method for 3–4 days before the expected rise, and for 4 days after it has taken place. If she limits intercourse to only the "safe" time after her temperature has risen, the method is more effective. The method requires high motivation and control. For greater accuracy, it may be combined with the mucus method described below.

The Mucus Method (Billings or Ovulation Method)
Women who use the **mucus method** determine their point in the menstrual cycle by examining the mucous secretions of the cervix. In many women, there is a

TABLE 12.2 How to Calculate the Interval of Fertility

If Your Short-est Cycle Has Been*	Your First Fertile (Unsafe) Day Is	If Your Long-est Cycle Has Been	Your Last Fertile (Unsafe Day Is)
21 days	3rd day	21 days	10th day
22	4th	22	11th
23	5th	23	12th
24	6th	24	13th
25	7th	25	14th
26	8th	26	15th
27	9th	27	16th
28	10th	28	17th
29	11th	29	18th
30	12th	30	19th
31	13th	31	20th
32	14th	32	21st
33	15th	33	22nd
34	16th	34	23rd
35	17th	35	24th

*Cycle begins on first day of menstrual period.

noticeable change in the appearance and character of cervical mucus prior to ovulation. After menstruation, most women experience a moderate discharge of cloudy, yellowish, or white mucus. Then, for a day or two, a clear, slippery mucus is secreted. Ovulation occurs immediately after the clear, slippery mucous secretions. The preovulatory mucus is elastic in consistency, rather like raw egg white, and a drop can be stretched between two fingers into a thin strand (at least 6 cm, or 2⅜ in.). This elasticity is called *spinn-barkeit*. Following ovulation, the amount of discharge decreases markedly. The 4 days before and the 4 days after these secretions are considered the unsafe days. An alternative contraception method may be used during this time. The method requires training and a high degree of motivation to be successful. Clinics are offered in some cities. (For more information, check with your local family planning or women's health clinic.) This method may be combined with the BBT method for greater effectiveness.

The Sympto-Thermal Method When the BBT and mucus methods are used together, it is called the **sympto-thermal method.** Additional signs that may be useful in determining ovulation are mid-cycle pain in the lower abdomen on either side (*mittelschmerz*) and a very slight discharge of blood from the cervix ("spotting").

Effectiveness of Fertility Awareness Methods It is problematic to calculate the effectiveness of fertility awareness methods. With this type of contraception, in a sense, the user *is* the method: The method's success or failure rests largely upon her diligence. Women who wish to rely on fertility awareness methods of contraception should enroll in a class at a clinic. Learning to read one's own unique fertility signs is a complex process requiring one-on-one counseling and close monitoring. For those who have used fertility awareness with unfailing dedication, these methods have been demonstrated to be as much as 99% effective. Many studies, however, show fairly high failure rates. Some researchers believe that this is due to risk taking during the fertile phase. Additionally, there is always some difficulty in predicting ovulation with pinpoint accuracy; thus, there is a greater chance of pregnancy as a result of intercourse prior to ovulation than as a result of intercourse following it. Furthermore, there is recent evidence that sperm may survive as long as 5 days, suggesting that a reliably "safe" period of time prior to ovulation may be very short indeed and consequently hard to predict. All fertility awareness methods increase in effectiveness if intercourse is unprotected only during the safe period following ovulation.

Advantages Fertility awareness (or natural family planning) methods are acceptable to most religious groups. They are free and pose no health risks. If a woman wishes to become pregnant, awareness of her own fertility cycles is very useful.

Possible Problems These methods are not suitable for women with irregular menstrual cycles or couples who are not highly motivated to use them. Some couples who practice abstinence during fertile periods may begin to take risks out of frustration. These couples may benefit by exploring other forms of sexual expression, and counseling can help.

See Figure 12.5 for a comparison of the effectiveness of various contraceptive methods.

Sterilization

Among married couples in the United States, sterilization (of one or both partners) is the most popular form of birth control. **Sterilization** involves surgical intervention that makes the reproductive organs incapable of producing or delivering viable gametes (sperm and eggs). Annually, about 1 million Americans choose this method of family planning, which is also known as **voluntary surgical contraception** (Hatcher et al., 1990). Before 1975, most sterilizations in this country were performed on men, but currently, women choose to be sterilized at twice the rate of men. By 1984, 137 million people had been sterilized worldwide ("Population Crisis," 1985).

Sterilization for Women In 1988, approximately 17% of women had chosen sterilization as their form of contraception (Hatcher et al., 1990). The majority of women who choose this method are over 30. Most female sterilizations are **tubal ligations,** "tying the tubes." (See Figure 12.6.) The two most common operations are laparoscopy and minilaparotomy. Less commonly performed types of sterilization for women are culpotomy, culdoscopy, and hysterectomy. Generally, this surgery is not reversible; only women who are completely certain that they want no (or no more) children should choose this method.

Sterilization for women is quite expensive. Surgeon, anesthesiologist, and hospital fees are substantial. The newer procedures, in which the woman

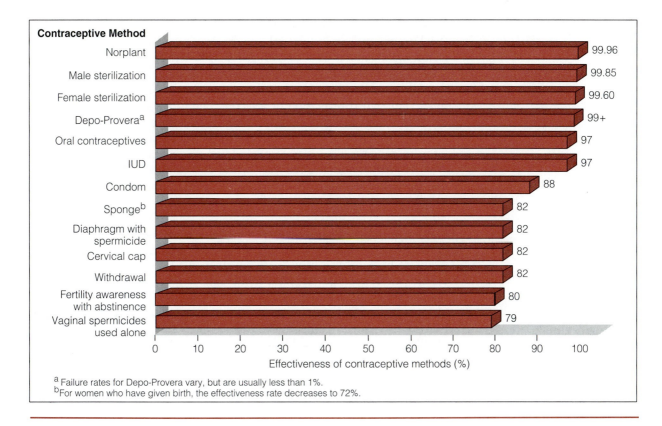

Contraceptive Method	Effectiveness (%)
Norplant	99.96
Male sterilization	99.85
Female sterilization	99.60
Depo-Provera[a]	99+
Oral contraceptives	97
IUD	97
Condom	88
Sponge[b]	82
Diaphragm with spermicide	82
Cervical cap	82
Withdrawal	82
Fertility awareness with abstinence	80
Vaginal spermicides used alone	79

Effectiveness of contraceptive methods (%)

[a] Failure rates for Depo-Provera vary, but are usually less than 1%.
[b] For women who have given birth, the effectiveness rate decreases to 72%.

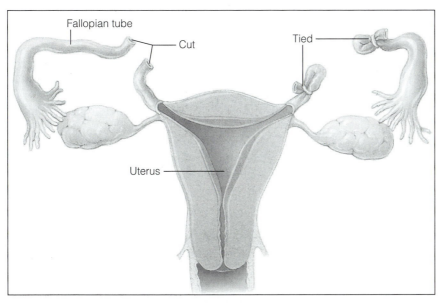

Fallopian tube — Cut — Tied

Uterus

FIGURE 12.5 (above) Effectiveness of Contraceptive Methods. This graph compares the actual effectiveness rates of various methods during the first year of use.

FIGURE 12.6 (left) Tubal Ligation.

returns home on the same day, have the advantage of being one-half to one-third as expensive as abdominal surgery, but they still may cost hundreds or even thousands of dollars. Many health insurance policies will cover all or part of the cost of sterilization for both men and women. In some states, Medicaid pays for certain patients.

Laparoscopy   Sterilization by **laparoscopy** usually requires a day or less in the hospital or clinic. General anesthesia is usually recommended. The woman's abdomen is inflated with gas to make the organs more visible. The surgeon inserts a rodlike instrument with a viewing lens (the laparoscope) through a small incision at the edge of the navel and locates the fallopian tubes. Through this incision or a second one, the surgeon inserts another instrument that closes the tubes, usually by electrocauterization (burning). Special small forceps that carry an electric current clamp the tubes and cauterize them. The tubes may also be closed off or blocked with tiny rings, clips, or plugs. There is a recovery period of several days to a week. During this time, the woman will experience some tenderness and some vaginal bleeding. Rest is important.

Minilaparotomy   Local or general anesthesia is used with **minilaparotomy.** A small incision is made in the lower abdomen, through which the fallopian tubes are brought into view. They are then tied off or sealed with electric current, clips, or rings. Recovery is the same as with laparoscopy.

Culpotomy and Culdoscopy   In these operations, an incision is made at the back of the vagina. In **culpotomy,** the tubes are viewed through the incision and then tied or otherwise blocked, then cut. **Culdoscopy** is the same procedure but uses a viewing instrument called a culdoscope. The advantage of these procedures is that they leave no visible scars. They require more expertise on the part of the surgeon, however, and have higher complication rates than laparoscopy and minilaparotomy.

Hysterectomy   Hysterectomy (surgical removal of the uterus) is not performed for sterilization except under special circumstances. Because it involves the removal of the entire uterus, it is both riskier and more costly than other methods. It involves greater recovery time and, for some women, is potentially more difficult psychologically. It may be appropriate for women who have a uterine disease or other problem that is likely to require a future hysterectomy anyway. (Hysterectomy is discussed at greater length in Chapter 14.)

Effectiveness   Surgical contraception is essentially 100% effective. In *extremely* rare instances (less than one-quarter of 1%), probably because of improperly performed surgery, a tube may reopen or grow back together, allowing an egg to pass through.

Once sterilization has been done, no other method of birth control will ever be necessary. (A woman who risks exposure to STDs, however, may wish to protect herself with a spermicide or condom.)

Sterilization does not reduce or change a woman's feminine characteristics. It is not the same as menopause and does not hasten the approach of menopause, as some people believe. A woman still has her menstrual periods until whatever age menopause naturally occurs for her. Her ovaries, uterus (except in the case of hysterectomy), and hormonal system have not been changed. The only difference is that sperm cannot now reach her eggs. (The eggs, which are released every month as before, are reabsorbed by the body.) Sexual enjoyment is not diminished. In fact, a high percentage of women report that they feel more relaxed during intercourse because anxiety about

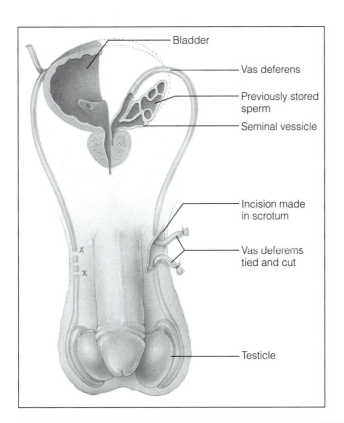

FIGURE 12.7 Vasectomy.

Bladder

Vas deferens

Previously stored
sperm

Seminal vessicle

Incision made
in scrotum

Vas deferens
tied and cut

Testicle

pregnancy has been eliminated. There do not seem to be any harmful side effects associated with female sterilization.

Sterilization should be considered irreversible. The most recently developed methods of ligation using clips, rings, or plugs may be more reversible than those employing electrocauterization, but the overall success rate for reversals is quite low; it is also very costly and not covered by most insurance plans. Only 15–25% percent of women who attempt to have their tubal ligations reversed succeed in conceiving.

The tubal ligation itself is a relatively safe procedure. With electrocauterization, there is a chance that other tissues in the abdomen may be damaged, especially if the surgeon is not highly skilled. These "bowel burns" may require further surgery but often heal on their own. Anesthesia complications are the most serious risk. The risk of death is quite low: four deaths per 100,000 operations (Peterson et al., 1983). Infection is also a possibility, and it may be treated with antibiotics.

Sterilization for Men A **vasectomy** is a minor surgical procedure that can be performed in a doctor's office under a local anesthetic. It takes approximately half an hour. In this procedure, the physician makes a small incision (or two incisions) in the skin of the scrotum. Through the incision, each vas deferens (sperm-carrying tube) is lifted, cut, tied, and often cauterized with electricity (Figure 12.7). After a brief rest, the man is able to walk out of the office; complete recuperation takes only a few days.

A man may retain some viable sperm in his system for days or weeks following a vasectomy. He should use other birth control until his semen has been checked, about 8 weeks following the operation.

Effectiveness   Vasectomies are 99.85% effective. In very rare cases, the ends of a vas deferens may rejoin. But this is virtually impossible if the operation is correctly performed.

Advantages   No birth control method will ever be needed again. But the man may still wish to use a condom to prevent getting or spreading an STD. Sexual enjoyment will not be diminished; he will still have erections and orgasms and ejaculate semen. Vasectomy is relatively inexpensive.

Possible Problems   Compared to other birth control methods, the complication rates for vasectomy are very low. Most problems occur when proper antiseptic measures are not taken during the operation, or when the man exercises too strenuously in the few days after it. Hematomas (bleeding under the skin) and granulomas (clumps of sperm) can be treated with ice packs and rest. Epididymitis (inflammation of the tiny tubes that connect the testicle and vas deferens) can be treated with heat and scrotal support.

One-half to two-thirds of men develop sperm antibodies following vasectomy. The body produces these antibodies in response to the presence of sperm that have been absorbed by body tissues. There is no evidence that this poses any threat to a man's health.

Tests on monkeys have shown some increased risks of heart disease with vasectomy, but recent studies on humans have not produced similar findings. One large study of more than 10,000 men with vasectomies found *less* cardiovascular disease than in other men (Massey et al., 1984).

A few men, those who equate fertility with virility and potency, may experience psychological problems following vasectomy. However, according to the authors of *Contraceptive Technology* (Hatcher et al., 1985), "Most well-adjusted males will experience no adverse psychological changes following their sterilization, if they understand what to expect ... and are given an opportunity to express their fears and have their questions answered."

Among men who attempt to have their vasectomies reversed, about 50% experience success. The cost is high and not covered by insurance in many cases. Vasectomy should be considered permanent.

Informed Consent   Because sterilization is irreversible, it is of paramount importance that a person who contemplates it be informed about the procedure and be sure about his or her own needs and wishes. About 10% of sterilized people later decide they want children (Cushner, 1986). Federal law requires that recipients of sterilization give informed consent prior to undergoing surgery. Requirements vary from state to state, but their intent is to protect people from making hasty or ill-informed decisions or being coerced into an act that has serious, lifelong consequences. Certain groups have been subject to abuses in this area. Among those who have been sterilized during duress or coercion or without being able to give informed consent are members of racial and ethnic minorities, especially non-English speakers. People with mental or emotional disabilities have also suffered from this abuse.

Postcoital Birth Control

Postcoital birth control (also called "morning-after birth control") is a controversial issue. **Postcoital birth control** involves the expulsion of an ovum that may have been fertilized; it can be viewed as a type of early abortion. Postcoital birth control is administered by many physicians and family planning clinics.

The Morning-After Pill and Menstrual Extraction The principal form of this type of birth control is the morning-after pill or the emergency contraceptive pill (ECP). It is generally a combined estrogen-progestin birth control pill, given in a larger-than-normal dose under medical supervision, within 72 hours after unprotected intercourse (Trussell, Stewart, Guest, & Hatcher, 1992). (Information regarding the use of birth control pills for postcoital birth control is available at many family planning clinics.)

Another method of after-the-fact birth control is **menstrual extraction,** which involves the removal of the endometrial contents by suction through a small tube attached to a vacuum pump. This procedure may be performed until an expected menstrual period is 2 weeks late. It can be done with or without a positive diagnosis of pregnancy. Another form of postcoital birth control is to have an IUD inserted within 5–7 days after unprotected intercourse. This method is not recommended for women who have not had children, have multiple sex partners, or have a history of PID.

RU-486 In 1986, a study of a new drug, mifepristone, known as **RU-486,** concluded that it is "an effective and safe method for termination of very early pregnancy but that it should be used only under close medical supervision" (Couzinet, LeStrat, Ulmann, Boulieu, & Schaison, 1986). RU-486 is an antiprogesterone steroid (or progesterone antagonist) developed by a French physician. It prevents the cells of the uterine lining from getting the progesterone they need to support a blastocyst (fertilized ovum). This "tricks" the body into thinking it's at the end of a menstrual cycle; it sheds the lining of the uterus in what appears to be "an abundant painless menstrual period" (Couzinet et al., 1986). The blastocyst or embryo is expelled, too.

RU-486 has the potential to be used in three ways. One use is as a morning-after pill, taken within a few days of unprotected intercourse. In this case, the oocyte, if present, will be expelled before fertilization or, if it has been fertilized, before implantation (Glasier, Thong, Dewar, Mackie, & Baird, 1992). Another use is as an agent to induce a very early abortion— within the first 5 or 6 weeks of pregnancy. The final use would be as a once-a-month birth control pill, taken a few days before an expected menstrual period.

Clinical trials of RU-486 have been conducted over a 5-year period in 15 countries to date. With the exception of heavy bleeding in a few women, no serious side effects have been noted (Couzinet et al., 1986; Nieman et al., 1987). The effectiveness rate for terminating pregnancy has been about 85%. The safety of the drug taken over a longer period of time is not known.

RU-486 is used in several countries, including China, Britain, France, Sweden, and Germany. Currently, RU-486 may be imported to the U.S. for individual use. As of this writing, it has been approved by the FDA for manufacture. It is expected to be available to the public in 1995.

THE FUTURE OF CONTRACEPTION

Most of us who use contraception find some drawback in whatever method we use. Hormonal methods may be costly or have unwanted side effects, or we may feel that putting on a condom or inserting a diaphragm interrupts lovemaking too much. The inconveniences, the side effects, and the lack of 100% effectiveness—all these point to the need for more effective and more diverse forms of contraception than we have now.

Obstacles to Research

High development costs, government regulations, and marketing priorities all play a part in restricting contraceptive research. The biggest barrier to developing new contraceptive techniques, however, is the fear of lawsuits, according to a 1990 report by two federal agencies, the National Research Council and the Institute of Medicine. Pharmaceutical manufacturers will not easily forget that the IUD market was virtually destroyed in the 1970s and 1980s by numerous costly lawsuits. While a number of the suits, especially against A. H. Robbins, the manufacturer of the Dalkon Shield, may have been justified, the result (in addition to the bankruptcy of Robbins) was the removal of almost all IUDs from the American market. Safety was not an issue in most cases. Indeed, due to the apparent eagerness of the American public to sue for huge amounts of money and the subsequent publicity, many people, both in this country and abroad, have acquired "rather inaccurate views about contraceptive methods, believing the risks to be much greater and the benefits to be much smaller than they actually are" (Forrest, 1986). (See Table 12.1.)

Another reason for limited contraceptive research is extensive government regulation, which requires extensive product testing. While we can all agree that we don't wish to be poisoned by the medicines we take, perhaps it wouldn't hurt to take a closer look at the process by which new drugs become available to the public. Approval from the U.S. Food and Drug Administration (FDA) takes an average of 7.5 years. Since drug patents are in effect for only 17 years, the pharmaceutical companies have less than 10 years to recover their developmental costs. Furthermore, pharmaceutical corporations are not willing to expend millions in research only to have the FDA refuse to approve the marketing of new discoveries. According to Carl Djerrasi (1979), the "father" of the birth control pill, safety is a relative, not an absolute concept. We may need to reexamine the question, "How safe is safe?" and weigh potential benefits along with possible problems.

We have seen that contraceptive research and development has become a marketing and political issue as well as a scientific one. As you read the following section on future contraceptive development, bear in mind that these projects may be aborted before they see the light of day.

Developing Technologies

Research in the area of hormonal methods of contraception is expected to continue to be a priority. The aim is to continue to make birth control pills (and implants) safer and to eliminate the undesirable side effects. Other types of hormonal birth control are also undergoing development. These include long-acting injectables, vaginal rings containing hormones, and hormone injections for men.

Injectable Hormones In addition to DMPA, which was recently approved for use in the United States, there are other injectable hormones. Norethindrone enanthate, a synthetic progesterone, is a common injectable contraceptive in use outside of this country. Its effects are similar to those of DMPA. Research on male contraception involves injections of high doses of synthetic testosterone, "fooling" the hypothalamus into shutting down production of gonadotropin-releasing hormone (GnRH). Without GnRH, no follicle-stimulating hormone (FSH) is produced, and consequently, no sperm are produced (Perkins, 1991). Another tactic involves injecting a hormone antagonist that acts directly on the hypothalamus to block GnRH production. Because of undesirable side effects, these methods are still under study. Side effects include weight gain, acne, and, unless testosterone is included as part of the treatment, a loss of sex drive (Perkins, 1991). In China, gossypol, an extract of unrefined cottonseed oil, is being extensively studied. Researchers have encountered two major problems: Gossypol is so effective in subduing sperm production that it has produced irreversible (so far) effects in some men; it has also produced serious side effects in some. Nevertheless, gossypol research continues in China ("Gossypol," 1987).

Other Developments New developments in contraceptives include drugs that can be used by both men and women. High doses of synthetic luteinizing-hormone-releasing hormone (LHRH) cause the pituitary to decrease production of luteinizing hormone (LH) and follicle-stimulating hormone (FSH); thus, ovulation is prevented in women and sperm production in men. For women, a daily pill containing LHRH is being developed. For men, a nasal spray shows promise; it is currently being used in some European countries.

Another "male method" currently being researched involves the implantation of a small silicone plug within the vas deferens (sperm duct). An advantage of this method would be its potential for complete reversibility. For women, new plugs and clips for use in tubal ligation are being developed; these could be removed later on, to reverse the sterilization.

Surgical sterilization techniques are also being refined and simplified. A "microvasectomy" method developed by a Chinese physician shows promise because it involves less tissue trauma and a low potential for infection. In this procedure, the scrotal wall is pierced, not cut, and the opening is bluntly enlarged to allow the withdrawal of the vas deferens.

ABORTION

When most people hear the word "abortion," they think of a medical procedure. But **abortion,** or expulsion of the conceptus, can happen naturally, or can be made to happen in one of several ways. Many abortions happen spontaneously—because a woman suffers a physical trauma, because the conceptus is not properly developed, or, more commonly, because physical conditions within the uterus break down and end the development of the conceptus. Approximately one-third of all abortions reported in a year in the U.S. are **spontaneous abortions;** these are commonly referred to as miscarriages (see Chapter 13). In this section, however, we examine *induced abortion,* the intentional termination of a pregnancy. Unless otherwise noted, when we refer to abortion, we mean induced abortion.

Under safe, clean, and legal conditions, abortion is a very safe medical procedure. Self-administered or under illegal, clandestine conditions, abortion can be very dangerous. The continued availability of legal abortion is considered by most physicians, psychologists, and public health professionals to be critical to the public's physical and mental well-being (Stephenson, Wagner, Badea, & Serbanescu, 1992; Susser, 1992).

Before we continue, it is important to understand that abortion is not a neutral subject in our society. As a consequence, the study of abortion is fraught with emotion, making it difficult to approach objectively. Nancy Adler (1992), a leading public-health researcher, noted:

> The scientific study of abortion has been burdened by the fact that it is a procedure about which individuals have strong feelings. Deeply held beliefs and assumptions may affect research in this area more than in others, influencing which questions are asked about abortion and the ways in which questions are framed. In addition, abortion inevitably occurs in the context of pregnancy, and assumptions about the nature of such pregnancies can also influence research.

Abortions cannot be examined as if they were all the same. Distinctions must be made, for example, between wanted, unintended, and unwanted pregnancies. It is also important to know at what stage of pregnancy an abortion occurs. Abortions occurring during the first trimester, for example, use simpler procedures, involve an embryo or less-developed fetus, and are psychologically more positive than abortions occurring later (Adler, Major, Roth, Russo, & Wyatt, 1990). Finally, it is important to know the woman's age and motivation as these vary considerably and are associated with different emotional responses.

Methods of Abortion

An abortion can be induced in several ways. Surgical methods are most common, but the use of medications is also possible. Methods for early abortions (those performed in the first 3 months of pregnancy) differ from those for late abortions (those performed after the 3rd month). RU-486, a medical (nonsurgical) method of early abortion, was discussed earlier in the chapter.

Surgical Methods Surgical methods include vacuum aspiration, dilation and curettage (D & C), dilation and evacuation (D & E), hysterotomy, and several other methods. To facilitate the dilation of the cervix prior to abortion, the health-care practitioner may insert a **laminaria,** a small stick of seaweed, into the cervical opening. The laminaria expands gradually, dilating the cervix gently in the process. It must be placed at least 6 hours prior to the abortion.

Vacuum Aspiration (First-Trimester Method) **Vacuum aspiration** is performed under local anesthesia. The cervix is dilated with a series of graduated rods (a laminaria may have been used to begin dilation). Then, a

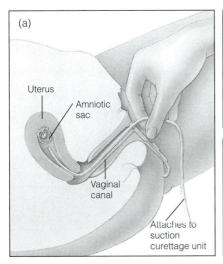
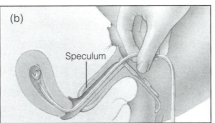

Uterus

Amniotic sac

Vaginal canal

Attaches to suction curettage unit

Speculum

Suction curette

FIGURE 12.8 Vacuum Aspiration. (a) The vagina is opened with a speculum, and a thin vacuum tube is inserted. (b) The uterus is gently vacuumed. (c) The curette end of the vacuum tube may be used to gently scrape the uterine wall; the conceptus and other contents of the uterus are suctioned out.

small tube attached to a vacuum is inserted through the cervix. The uterus is gently vacuumed, removing the conceptus, placenta, and endometrial tissue (Figure 12.8).

Curettage (see below) may follow. The patient returns home the same day. She will experience cramping, bleeding, and, possibly, emotional reactions over the following days. Serious complications are unusual for a legal, properly performed abortion.

Dilation and Curettage (D & C) (First-Trimester Method) In **dilation and curettage** the cervix is dilated under general anesthesia, and the uterine wall is scraped with a small spoon-shaped instrument (a curette). This method is generally considered less desirable than vacuum aspiration because it causes more bleeding, is more painful, and is sometimes less effective.

Dilation and Evacuation (D & E) (Second-Trimester Method) **Dilation and evacuation (D & E)** is usually performed between the 13th and 20th weeks of pregnancy. Local or general anesthesia is used. The cervix is slowly dilated, and the fetus is removed by alternating curettage and solution. The patient is given an intravenous solution of the hormone oxytocin to encourage contractions and limit blood loss. Because it is a second-trimester procedure, a D & E is somewhat riskier and often more traumatic than a first-trimester abortion.

Hysterotomy (Second-Trimester Method) In **hysterotomy,** the fetus is removed through an incision made in the woman's abdomen. This is essentially a caesarean section—major surgery requiring several days in the hospital. Its use is limited.

Other Methods of Abortion Abortion can also be induced medically with injections or suppositories. These abortions are performed during the second trimester and generally require hospitalization. Prostaglandins, saline solutions, and urea are used in this way, alone or in various combinations.

FIGURE 12.9 Attitudes Toward Abortion, by State, 1992. Legal aspects of abortion, including the rights of states to regulate it, are discussed in Perspective 3.

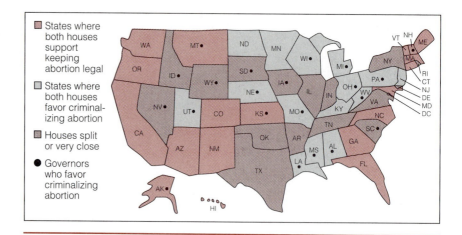

- ☐ States where both houses support keeping abortion legal
- ☐ States where both houses favor criminalizing abortion
- ☐ Houses split or very close
- ● Governors who favor criminalizing abortion

As discussed in Chapter 3, many cells of the body contain prostaglandins, fatty-acid-based hormones that are active in many body processes including reproduction. Prostaglandins are injected into the amniotic sac (which contains the fetus within the uterus) or administered as vaginal suppositories to stimulate uterine contractions and induce abortion. Some of the side effects associated with their use are gastrointestinal symptoms, cervical lacerations, and temperature elevation. Saline solutions and solutions of urea are toxic to the fetus and can be injected amniotically. These solutions are relatively inexpensive; they are generally considered more effective when used in combination with prostaglandins.

Another type of second-trimester abortion uses amniocentesis and amnioinfusion. This procedure involves the removal of amniotic fluid surrounding the fetus with a long needle—amniocentesis—followed by the replacement of that fluid with some type of medication—amnioinfusion. Solutions containing prostaglandins or urea, saline solution, or a combination may be used.

The Prevalence of Abortion

Abortion is an issue of great concern throughout the world. According to the World Health Organization (WHO), almost three-quarters of the world's people live in countries that permit abortions. Over 900,000 conceptions occur worldwide each day. Half are unplanned, and one-quarter of unplanned pregnancies are unwanted. The majority of women give birth, but between one-quarter and one-third abort their pregnancies. Worldwide, there are about 150,000 abortions performed daily. About 50,000 of them are illegal and are performed in unsafe conditions in a hostile social environment. According to WHO, these illegal abortions result in the death of 500 women every day. Each year, there are 36–53 million legal abortions; in addition, about 15 million clandestine abortions are also performed (World Health Organization, 1992). Almost 1400 women die each day as a result of pregnancy or childbirth; of the 500,000 women who die each year, 496,000 are in developing countries (Fathalla, 1992).

The latest data on abortions in the United States indicate that in 1988, there were about 6 million pregnancies and 1.5 million abortions (U.S.

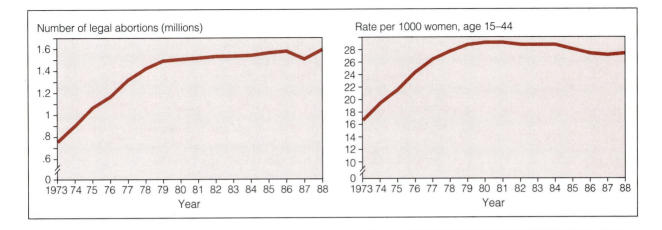

Number of legal abortions (millions)

Rate per 1000 women, age 15–44

FIGURE 12.10 Abortion in the United States, 1973–1988. (a) Number of legal abortions (in millions). (b) Abortion rate per 1000 women, age 15–44.

Bureau of the Census, 1992). Twenty-one percent of American women of reproductive age have had abortions. If current abortion rates continue, nearly half of all American women will have at least one abortion during their lifetime (Forrest, 1987). The 1988 abortion rate was 2.3% for whites and 5.6% for African Americans (U.S. Bureau of the Census, 1990). Among adolescents, Latinos have a lower abortion rate than either Anglos or African Americans (Aneshensel, Fielder, & Becerra, 1989). (Figure 12.9 illustrates attitudes toward abortion, and Figure 12.10 shows the statistics concerning the number of abortions in the U.S.)

Women and Abortion

A key research issue concerning the psychological effects of legal abortion is their prevalence, or frequency of occurrence. A report released by the American Psychological Association reviewing the scientific literature on the psychological effects of legal abortion concluded that most women felt the most distress immediately *preceding* an abortion, and felt relief following it (Adler et al., 1990). Only a small minority of women report adverse psychological effects (Major & Cozzarelli, 1992).

Characteristics of Women Having Abortions A review of various abortion studies indicates the following characteristics of women having abortions in the United States (Adler, David, Major, Roth, Russo, & Wyatt, 1992).

- *Race and ethnicity.* The majority of women (69%) having abortions are white. Although nonwhite women (age 15–44) represent 17% of the population, they have 31% of the abortions. Latinas represent 8% of all women, but 13% of women seeking abortions. The lower abortion rates of whites represent fewer unintended pregnancies rather than less acceptance of abortion.

- *Socioeconomic circumstances.* One out of every three women having an abortion is poor. The abortion rate for poor women is three times that for women with incomes over $25,000. Almost one-third attend school or college; one-third are unemployed.

- *Minors.* Nearly 12% of abortions are obtained by minors. Over 98% are unmarried. Most are white, in school, have no children, and have had no previous abortions. Typically, they avoid having children in order to remain in school and to become more mature before becoming mothers. Thirteen percent of the adolescents, however, had had prior abortions; 9% were already mothers (and one-sixth of them already had two children).

- *Adults.* Eighty percent of adult women having abortions are separated, divorced, or never married; 20% are married. Among adult women seeking abortions, almost half are already mothers. Women who are already mothers have significant family responsibilities. Of the mothers, nearly half of the single mothers and two-thirds of the married mothers already have at least two children.

Reasons for Having an Abortion There are many stereotypes about women who have an abortion: They are selfish, promiscuous, single, unwilling to accept family responsibilities, childless, nonmaternal, depressed, sinful, and immoral (Gordon, 1990; Petchesky, 1990). Furthermore, national public opinion surveys depict a "simplistic image" of women's reasons for abortion (Adler et al., 1992). Because few women openly discuss their abortion experiences, stereotypical views of abortion continue unchallenged.

Women generally have multiple reasons for wanting an abortion (Torres & Forrest, 1988; Adler et al., 1992). An important study by Aida Torres and Jacqueline Forrest (1988) came to the following conclusions:

1. *The abortion decision is complex, with several reasons at play.* It is not undertaken lightly. The multiple reasons most commonly cited by women include concern about how a child would change her life, not being able to afford a child, problems in the relationship, or wanting to avoid being a single parent.

2. *The woman's developmental life stage is important.* Eleven percent of the women stated they were "too immature" or "too young" to have a child; 21% said they were "unready for responsibility."

3. *Many reasons have to do with women's relationships with other people or educational or economic circumstances.* Decisions reflect not just the woman's personal qualities. Twenty-three percent said their husband or partner didn't want a child. Over two-thirds said they couldn't afford a child. These reasons point to women's ongoing sense of responsibility to others or outside circumstances.

Torres and Forrest (1988) found that being white, African American, or Latina had little influence in abortion decision making. Latinas were only slightly less likely than non-Latinas to say they did not want additional children.

Making an abortion decision, regardless of the ultimate outcome, raises many emotional issues for women. There is no painless way of dealing with an unwanted pregnancy. For many, such a decision requires a reevaluation of their relationships, an examination of their childbearing plans, a search to understand the role of sexuality in their lives, and an attempt to clarify their life goals. In a recent study (Lunneborg, 1992), a 47-year-old woman recalled her decision to abort 25 years earlier:

It was the biggest growth experience in my life.... It has given me a greater understanding and compassion toward society as a whole, that we are fallible and we do have to deal with a variety of crises and traumas, and we do the best we can with them and come out as stronger people.

A study of women who underwent abortions found that they and their male partners shared many common feelings: feelings of loss, anxiety, uncertainty (Black, 1991). Although they felt understood by their partners, they also felt their response was different from that of their partners. As women, they experienced a loss from within that men could not comprehend. Another study found that fewer than 5% did not voluntarily tell their husbands (Smith & Kronauge, 1990). Almost all who conferred with their husbands said that their husbands agreed with the decision. A controlled study comparing 92 pregnant women in stable relationships who had abortions with pregnant women who gave birth found no significant qualitative differences between the groups in their relationships a year later (Barnett, Freudenberg, & Wille, 1992).

Negative Consequences of Abortion   Although some pro-life activists argue that women who have abortions suffer from a "postabortion syndrome," there is little evidence that such a syndrome exists. The evidence supporting such a syndrome is anecdotal, clinical, or from pro-life organizations. Various studies suggest, however, that a small minority of women experience guilt, anxiety, depression, and regret following an abortion (Major & Cozzarelli, 1992).

Those who are distressed tend to feel coerced, have little social support from their partners or parents, and have poor coping skills. They also tend to have their abortions later in their pregnancy (Adler et al., 1990; Armsworth, 1991). Adolescents are more likely to feel ambivalent or dissatisfied about their abortion than older women. Adolescents, however, tend to be further along in their pregnancies and more likely to feel forced by circumstances to have an abortion (Franz & Reardon, 1992).

Men and Abortion

In the decision-making process, the man is often forgotten. Attention is usually focused on the woman, who is undergoing personal agony in making the decision. If the man is thought of, it is often with hostility and blame. And yet the man, like the woman, may be undergoing his own private travail, experiencing guilt and anxiety, feeling ambiguous about the possibility of parenthood.

A common feeling men experience is powerlessness. They may try to remain cool and rational, believing that if they reveal their confused feelings, they will be unable to give their partners emotional support (Wade, 1978). Since the drama is within the woman and her body, a man may feel he must not influence her decision.

There is the lure of fatherhood, all the same. A pregnancy forces a man to confront his own feelings about parenting. Parenthood for males, as for females, is a profound passage into adulthood. For young men, there is a mixture of pride and fear about the potential for being a father and an adult.

After an abortion, many men feel residual guilt, sadness, and remorse. It

In the abortion debate, both sides tend to claim moral rightness. The pro-life movement equates the abortion of an embryo with murder.

is not uncommon for some men to temporarily experience erectile or ejaculatory difficulties. It is fairly common for couples to split up after an abortion; the stress, conflict, and guilt can be overwhelming. Many abortion clinics now provide counseling for men, as well as women, involved in an abortion.

The Abortion Debate

There are few absolutes left in the age after Einstein, and the case of abortion like almost everything else is a case of relative goods and ills to be evaluated one against the other.
Germaine Greer

Those who support the prohibition of abortion generally identify themselves as "pro-life." Those who support a woman's right to choose for herself whether to have an abortion generally identify themselves as "pro-choice." But such labels often confuse rather than clarify issues. They are used as moral symbols to gain support for or against legal abortion. Indeed, the advocates of each position all too often condemn the other as malevolent, elite, and conspiratorial, leaving little room for rational discourse (Vanderford, 1989). Each side uses value-laden terms. A conceptus is called an "embryo" or "fetus" by pro-choice advocates and a "baby" or "unborn child" by pro-life advocates. Pro-choice advocates refer to pregnant women as "women" (as if they were not pregnant) and pro-life advocates refer to them as "mothers" (as if they had already given birth). For abortion workers, women having abortions are "clients"; for pro-life extremists, they are "baby killers."

The moral beliefs of those opposing abortion reinforce their desire to make it illegal. But those supporting the legal right to abortion frequently have more complex responses. Although they may have moral reservations about abortion, they nevertheless support the right of a woman to make her own personal choice.

I have noticed that all the people who favor abortion have already been born.
Ronald Reagan

The Pro-Life Argument For those who oppose abortion, there is a basic principle from which their arguments follow: The moment an egg is fertilized, it becomes a human being, with the full rights and dignity afforded

Religious groups in the pro-choice movement defend abortion as a moral choice because "tragic conflicts of life with life" may make it necessary.

other humans. An embryo is no less human than a fetus, and a fetus is no less human than a baby. Morally, aborting an embryo is the equivalent of killing a person.

Even though the majority of those opposing abortion would consider rape and incest (and sometimes a defective embryo or fetus) to be exceptions, the pro-life leadership generally opposes any justification for an abortion, except to save the life of the pregnant woman. To abort the embryo of a rape or incest survivor, they reason, is still taking an innocent human life.

In addition, pro-life advocates argue that abortion is the first step toward a society that eliminates undesirable human beings. If we allow the elimination of embryos, they argue, what is to stop the killing of the disabled, the elderly, or the merely inconvenient? Finally, pro-life advocates argue that there are thousands of couples who want to adopt children but are unable to do so because so many pregnant women choose to abort rather than give birth.

The Pro-Choice Argument Those who believe that abortion should continue to be legal present a number of arguments. First, for pro-choice men and women, the fundamental issue is who decides whether a woman will bear children: the woman or the state. Since women continue to bear the primary responsibility for rearing children, pro-choice advocates believe that women should not be forced to give birth to unwanted children. Becoming a mother alters a woman's role more profoundly than almost any other event in her life; it is more significant than getting married. When

Norma McCorvey was given the pseudonym "Jane Roe" in a 1969 legal case challenging the Texas law against abortion. In 1973, the U.S. Supreme Court guaranteed women's fundamental right to abortion. It declared that no restrictions could be placed on a woman's right to abortion during the first 3 months of pregnancy.

women have the *choice* of becoming mothers, they are able to decide the timing and direction of their lives.

Second, while pro-choice advocates support sex education and contraception to eliminate much of the need for abortion, they believe that abortion should continue to be available as birth control backup. Because no contraceptive method is 100% effective, unintended pregnancies occur even among the most conscientious contraceptive users.

Third, if abortion is made illegal, large numbers of women nevertheless will have illegal abortions, substantially increasing the likelihood of dangerous complications, infections, and death. Those who are unable to have an abortion may be forced to give birth to and raise a child they did not want. (For a discussion of *Roe v. Wade* and the legal issues surrounding abortion choice, see Perspective 3.)

If men could get pregnant, then abortion would be a sacrament.
Gloria Steinem

Abortion and Religion While the morality of abortion is often hotly debated among Christians and Jews, there are no direct statements in the Old or New Testaments regarding abortion. Neither Moses, Jesus of Nazareth, nor Paul of Tarsus addressed the question. Whatever scriptural basis for or against abortion is inferred or based on interpretation.

A key element in both pro-choice and pro-life arguments turns on when *human* life begins. Both pro-life and pro-choice supporters believe that the conceptus *is* life. They disagree as to whether or not it is *human* life in the same sense as the life of those of us who have been born. The debate, however, is theological rather than scientific. The answer as to *when* embryonic or fetal life becomes *human* life depends on one's moral or religious beliefs rather than on scientific evidence. And even among religious groups, there is no unanimity. During the Middle Ages, for example, it was believed that the soul entered a male conceptus 40 days after conception but waited 80 days before entering a female. As the conceptus did not become human

FROM *ROE* TO *CASEY*: ABORTION, THE SUPREME COURT, AND POLITICS

In 1969 in Texas, 21-year-old Norma McCorvey, a single mother, discovered she was pregnant. In hopes of obtaining a legal abortion, she lied to her doctor, saying that she had been raped. Her physician informed her, however, that Texas prohibited all abortions except those to save the life of the mother. He suggested she travel to California, where she could obtain a legal abortion. But she had no money. Two lawyers heard of her situation and took her case in order to challenge abortion restrictions as an unconstitutional invasion of the individual's right to privacy. For the case, McCorvey was given "Roe" as a pseudonym. In 1970, a court in Texas declared the law unconstitutional, but the state appealed the decision. Meanwhile, McCorvey had the baby and gave away her child for adoption. Ultimately, the case reached the Supreme Court, where the court issued its famous *Roe v. Wade* decision in 1973 (*Roe v. Wade* 410 U.S. 113 [1973]).

Under the 1973 *Roe* decision, a woman's right to abortion was guaranteed as a fundamental right, part of the constitutional right to privacy (Tribe, 1992). According to constitutional law, fundamental rights cannot be encroached upon without *compelling* reasons (which are rarely found).

The right to privacy is one of the most important rights evolved by the liberal judiciary in the twentieth century. Judicial attacks on *Roe* do not focus on the morality of abortion. Instead, they focus on whether there exists a constitutional right to privacy, which has been the basis for the protection of our sexual rights. In 1928, Justice Louis Brandeis defined the right to privacy as "the right to be left alone—the most comprehensive of rights and the right most valued by civilized men." Since then, the right to privacy has been the bulwark against government intrusion into the private affairs of individuals. It has been instrumental in protecting marital and reproductive rights. The privacy doctrine formed the basis for the "right to reproduce" (*Skinner v. Oklahoma* [1942]), protecting individuals from forced sterilization, the "right to contraceptive use" (*Griswold v. Connecticut* [1965]), allowing individuals to engage in sexual intercourse without having children, the "right to marital choice" (*Loving v. Virginia* [1967]), permitting interracial marriage. Under the privacy doctrine, the *Roe* decision extends to women "the right to choose motherhood."

The constitutional right to privacy has been strongly opposed by conservative judges, including Chief Justice Rehnquist, who argue against privacy because it is not explicitly stated in the Constitution. According to their interpretation, individual rights do not exist unless they are specifically enumerated in the Constitution. While most legal scholars and mainstream judges disagree with their interpretation, Reagan/Bush federal court appointees, who make up the majority of judges, tend to limit privacy rights when they conflict with the state.

In delivering the Court's opinion in *Roe*, Justice William Brennan stated (*Roe v. Wade* 410 U.S. 113 [1973]):

The right to privacy . . . is broad enough to encompass a woman's decision whether or not to terminate a pregnancy. The detriment that the State would impose upon the pregnant woman by denying this choice altogether is apparent. Specific and direct harm medically diagnosable even in early pregnancy may be involved. Maternity, or additional offspring, may force upon the woman a distressful life and future. Psychological harm may also be imminent. Mental and physical health may be taxed by childcare. There is also the distress, for all concerned, associated with the unwanted child, and there is the problem of bringing a child into a family already unable, psychologically or otherwise, to care for it. In other cases, as

(continued)

Perspective 3

FROM *ROE* TO *CASEY*: ABORTION, THE SUPREME COURT, AND POLITICS *(continued)*

in this one, the . . . stigma of unwed motherhood may be involved. All these are factors the woman and her responsible physician necessarily will consider in consultation.

At the time, only four states permitted abortion at the woman's discretion.

The Roe decision created a firestorm of opposition among political and religious conservatives and fueled a conservative political resurgence (Wills, 1990). In the Reagan and Bush administrations, opposition to *Roe v. Wade* became a litmus test for judicial appointments. But because abortion was determined a fundamental right by the *Roe* decision, efforts by the states to curtail it had failed.

The 1989 *Webster v. Reproductive Rights* case (109 S.CT.3040) was a turning point. In it, the pro-life campaign to alter the composition of the Supreme Court bore fruit. For the first time, the Court rejected the definition of abortion as a fundamental right. Instead, abortion became a "limited constitutional right." Under the new standard, the Court gave states the right to limit abortion access provided the limitations did not place an "undue burden" on the pregnant woman. This change from a fundamental right to a limited right effectively nullified much of *Roe v. Wade* without actually overturning it (Tribe, 1992).

States were permitted to impose extensive restrictions, as long as they did not actually prohibit abortion.

With the appointment of Clarence Thomas to the Supreme Court in 1991, it was expected that *Roe* would be overturned entirely, as the majority of justices were known to be hostile to it.

In 1992, the landmark decision of *Planned Parenthood v. Casey* (112 S.CT.279) replaced *Webster* as the reigning constitutional doctrine on abortion and government regulation (Tribe, 1992). In *Casey*, moderately conservative justices—Sandra Day O'Connor, Anthony Kennedy, and David Souter—joined liberal justices—Harry Blackmun and John Paul Stevens—to form a majority reaffirming the "essential holding" of *Roe*, "a recognition of the right of the woman to choose to have an abortion before viability, and to obtain it without undue interference from the State." Under the *Casey* ruling, a law regulating abortion is unconstitutional "if its purpose or effect is to place a substantial obstacle in the path of a woman seeking an abortion before the fetus attains viability."

In their joint opinion, Justices O'Connor, Kennedy, and Souter discussed three important points. First, they discussed morality and the Supreme Court's role in politics. They stated (*Planned Parenthood v. Casey* 112 S.CT.279 [1992]):

until it was ensouled, aborting an "unensouled" conceptus was not considered grounds for excommunication. It was not until 1869 that Pope Pius IX promulgated the doctrine that the soul entered the ovum at the time of fertilization. From this doctrine follows the belief that to abort an embryo or fetus is to kill a human being. Many Protestants accept similar beliefs about the soul and conception. As a result of such beliefs, Catholics and Christian fundamentalists are the most likely to oppose abortion as immoral (Byrnes & Segers, 1992; Wills, 1990).

Other religious groups, such as Methodists, Unitarians, and other main-

Some of us as individuals find abortion offensive to our most basic principles of morality, but that cannot control our decision. Our obligation is to define the liberty of all, not to mandate our own moral code. The underlying constitutional issue is whether the State can resolve these philosophic questions in such a definitive way that a woman lacks all choice in the matter. . . .

Second, they argued that women's ability to make reproductive decisions was critical to equality. They stated: "The ability of women to participate equally in the economic and social life of the Nation has been facilitated by their ability to control their reproductive lives."

Third, they reaffirmed the judicial principle that requires courts to follow established laws and precedents when applicable to a similar set of facts. (Attempts to overturn *Roe* had threatened to undermine this important principle.) They stated: "An entire generation has come of age free to assume *Roe's* concept of liberty in defining the capacity of women to act in society, and to make reproductive decisions."

As of 1994, it appears unlikely that abortion will be prohibited by the Supreme Court in the near future. Not only did some conservatives reaffirm the right to abortion in the *Casey* decision, but in 1993, one of the staunch opponents of *Roe* resigned and was replaced by a pro-choice justice, Ruth Bader Ginsburg.

Pro-life advocates have now focused attention on the states because the states have been granted additional powers to restrict abortion. Some states have banned abortions in public facilities, prohibited publicly employed physicians and nurses from performing abortions, imposed 24-hour waiting periods on women, required parental consent for minors, and instituted mandatory counseling about fetal development and alternatives to abortion. As of the beginning of 1994, the only restriction struck down by the Supreme Court is the requirement that women notify their husbands prior to an abortion. To date, these restrictions most severely impact adolescents and poor women (Benshoof, 1993; Field, 1993).

As states are now permitted to regulate abortion, "the will of the people" or "the tyranny of the majority" (depending on one's point of view) becomes especially important in determining abortion rights. (See Byrne & Segers, 1992; Ginsburg, 1989; Staggenborg, 1991; and Wills, 1990 for more on the politics of abortion.) Some states have become battlefields between pro-choice and pro-life advocates. For example, in 1990, over 465 abortion-related bills were introduced into state legislatures, tripling the number of the year before (Sollom, 1991). Much of the debate centers around funding for poor women (Meier & McFarlane, 1993). Abortion laws in the states have become a patchwork of rights and restrictions. (See Figure 12.9 on p. 506.)

stream Protestants, tend to support abortion choice (Wenz, 1992). While they generally believe that an embryo or fetus is life, they also believe that other human issues must be considered. The Methodist church, for example, asserts that the "sanctity of unborn human life makes us reluctant to approve abortion" but adds that "we recognize tragic conflicts of life with life that may justify abortion" (Granberg, 1991; Kallstedt & Smidt, 1991). And some Catholics support abortion rights based on the primacy of conscience, which asserts that every Catholic has the right to follow his or her conscience in matters of morals.

The Abortion Controversy and Ethnicity   Although African American and Latina women have a disproportionate number of abortions, they are not especially active in the abortion debate. There may be several reasons for this (Brotman, 1992). First, African American and Latina women are disproportionately poor, and, like the poor in general, they tend to be uninvolved in politics and social movements. They think of abortion more in personal than in social terms. Second, most black churches, as well as the Catholic church and *evangelico* Protestant churches (the two religious groups in which most church-going Latinos participate), are generally opposed to abortion. Third, members of ethnic groups are less likely to discuss sex (and especially abortion) publicly because of their tabooed nature. Fourth, there is a history of forced sterilization against ethnic minorities, especially African Americans, but also Native Americans and Latinos. Some ethnic men and women believe that abortion is a form of genocide. (Eleven percent of the members in one black women's organization thought abortion was a plot to eliminate African Americans [Brotman, 1992].)

Control over our fertility helps us control our lives as people. It also allows the human race to survive and, at least in parts of the world, to prosper. The topic of birth control provokes much emotional controversy. Individuals and institutions alike are inclined to believe in the moral rightness of their particular stance on the subject, whatever that stance may be. As each of us tries to find his or her own path through the quagmire of controversy, we can be guided by what we learn. We need to arm ourselves with knowledge—not only about the methods and mechanics of contraception and birth control but also about our own motivations, needs, weaknesses, and strengths.

SUMMARY

Risk and Responsibility

• Over the period of 1 year, a couple that does not use contraception has a 90% chance of pregnancy. Most couples do not use contraception during their first intercourse. As people become older, they tend to become more consistent users of contraceptive methods.

• Many people knowingly risk pregnancy by having unprotected intercourse. The more "successful" they are at risk taking, the more likely they are to take chances again. They begin to feel invulnerable. People also take risks because of faulty knowledge; they don't understand how conception occurs or how birth control methods work.

• People also weigh the perceived costs of contraception against the anticipated benefits of pregnancy. Some of the costs include acknowledging sexuality, obtaining contraception, and planning and continuing contraception. Benefits include proving manhood or womanhood, proving fertility, defining a commitment, and defining a relationship to one's parents.

• Because women are the ones who get pregnant, they may have greater interest than men in controlling their fertility. But it is important for men to share the responsibility. They can do this by using condoms, finding ways to be sexual and loving without intercourse, helping with the cost and routines of birth control, or, if they do not want children, having a vasectomy.

Preventing Sexually Transmitted Diseases

- Certain contraceptive methods can help prevent such STDs as genital herpes, chlamydia, gonorrhea, and HIV infection, which may lead to AIDS. The condom is the most effective; it protects the wearer and his partner. Spermicides are toxic to many disease organisms. Women's barrier methods help protect against diseases of the cervix.

Methods of Contraception and Birth Control

- *Birth control* is any means of preventing a birth from taking place. *Contraception* is birth control that works specifically by preventing the union of sperm and egg.

- The most reliable method of birth control is *abstinence*—refraining from sexual intercourse. There are many ways to show affection (and express sexuality) without penile-vaginal contact, including talking, hugging, massaging, and manual stimulation of the genitals.

- *Oral contraceptives,* "the pill," are the most widely used form of reversible birth control in the U.S. Birth control pills contain synthetic hormones: progestin and (usually) estrogen. The pill is highly effective if taken regularly. There are side effects and possible problems that affect some users. The greatest risks are to smokers, women over 35, and women with certain health disorders, such as cardiovascular problems.

- Thin capsules containing progestin that are implanted under the skin of a woman's arm protect against pregnancy for five years. When they are removed, fertility is restored. These *implants* (marketed as *Norplant*) may be the most effective reversible contraceptive ever marketed.

- The injectable hormone *Depo-Provera (DMPA)* recently became available in the U.S. Its effects last 3–6 months.

- A *condom* is a thin sheath of latex rubber (or processed animal tissue) that fits over the erect penis and prevents semen from being transmitted. It is the third most widely used birth control method in the U.S. Condoms are very effective for contraception when used correctly, especially in combination with spermicidal foam or film. Latex condoms also help provide protection against STDs.

- The diaphragm, cervical cap, contraceptive sponge, and female condom are barrier methods used by women. The *diaphragm* and *cervical cap* are made of rubber and cover the cervical opening. They are used with spermicidal jelly or cream. The diaphragm is effective if used properly (with spermicide); some people have trouble using it consistently. The effectiveness of cervical caps is not yet well established. The *contraceptive sponge* contains spermicide. It is fairly effective, although women who have previously given birth have higher failure rates than others. *Female condoms* are fairly new and have not yet been widely tested. In addition to lining the vagina, they cover much of the vulva, providing more protection against disease organisms.

- *Spermicides* are chemicals that are toxic to sperm. *Nonoxynol-9* is the most common. *Contraceptive foam* provides fairly good protection when used alone, but other preparations are more effective when combined with a barrier method. Other spermicidal products are film, cream, jelly, suppositories, and tablets. Contraceptive sponges and some condoms are treated with spermicides.

- Many types of *IUDs (intrauterine devices)* have been taken off the market in the U.S. because of the threat of lawsuits. An IUD is a tiny plastic or metal device that is inserted through the cervical os into the uterus and disrupts the fertilization and implantation processes. The most serious problem associated with the IUD is increased risk of pelvic inflammatory disease (PID); therefore, IUDs are not recommended for women who have multiple sex partners or who plan to have children in the future.

- *Fertility awareness methods* (or natural family planning) involve a woman's awareness of her body's reproductive cycles. These include the *calendar (rhythm)*, *basal body temperature (BBT)*, *mucus*, and *sympto-thermal methods*. These methods are suitable only for women with regular menstrual cycles and high motivation.

- Surgical *sterilization* (or *voluntary surgical contraception*) is the most popular form of birth control among married couples in this country. The most common form for women is *tubal ligation*, closing off the fallopian tubes. The surgical procedure that sterilizes men is a *vasectomy*, in which each vas deferens (sperm-carrying tube) is closed off. These methods of birth control are close to 100% effective. Usually, there are no serious side effects. These surgeries should be considered irreversible.

- *Postcoital* ("morning-after") *birth control* is a controversial issue. Some doctors give high doses of birth control pills to induce the shedding of the uterine lining. A new drug known as *RU-486* is used in Europe and China and should soon be available in the U.S. It can be used as a morning-after pill, a once-a-month pill, or to induce an early abortion.

The Future of Contraception

- Research and development of new contraceptive technologies is slowed by the cost of development, government regulation, and marketing considerations. Possible new directions include improved oral contraception and implants, injectable hormones for both women and men, and vaginal rings containing hormones. Other possibilities for men are hormone nasal sprays and silicone plugs that are implanted in the sperm ducts.

Abortion

- *Abortion*, the expulsion of the conceptus from the uterus, can be spontaneous or induced. Surgical methods of abortion are *vacuum aspiration, dilation and curettage (D & C), dilation and evacuation (D & E)*, and *hysterotomy*. Nonsurgical methods utilize injections of prostaglandins, saline solution, or urea solution. Abortion is generally safe if done in the first trimester. Second-trimester abortions are significantly riskier. Abortion may have profound psychological effects on both women and men.

- In the United States, there are about 6 million pregnancies and 1.5 million abortions annually. Twenty-one percent of American women of reproductive age have had abortions. Most women having abortions are white; about one-third are poor and one-third are attending school; about 80% of adult women who have abortions are separated, divorced, or have never been married; almost half are already mothers.

- For women, the abortion decision is complex; their developmental/life stage is important, and their reasons for choosing abortion have to do with relationships or educational or economic circumstances. Few women experience long-term negative consequences following abortion. Men often feel powerless and ambivalent; many men feel residual guilt and sadness following an abortion.

• In the abortion controversy, pro-life advocates argue that life begins at conception, that abortion leads to euthanasia, and that many who want to adopt are unable to because fewer babies are born as a result of abortion. Pro-choice advocates argue that women have the right to decide whether to continue a pregnancy, that abortion is needed as a birth control alternative because contraceptives are not 100% effective, and that if abortion is not legalized, women will have unsafe illegal abortions.

• Religious opinion is divided about abortion. There is no direct statement regarding abortion in the Old or New Testament. A key issue concerns when the embryo or fetus becomes human life.

KEY TERMS

birth control

conceptus

contraception

coitus interruptus

abstinence

oral contraceptive

implant

Norplant

Depo-Provera (DMPA)

condom

diaphragm

cervical cap

contraceptive sponge

spermicide

nonoxynol-9

contraceptive foam

contraceptive film

intrauterine device (IUD)

fertility awareness method

calendar (rhythm) method

basal body temperature (BBT) method

mucus method

sympto-thermal method

sterilization

voluntary surgical contraception

tubal ligation

laparoscopy

minilaparotomy

culpotomy

culdoscopy

vasectomy

postcoital birth control

menstrual extraction

RU-486

abortion

spontaneous abortion

laminaria

vacuum aspiration

dilation and curettage (D & C)

dilation and evacuation (D & E)

hysterotomy

RESOURCES

Planned Parenthood Federation of America
810 Seventh Avenue
New York, NY 10019
(212) 541-7800
Most cities have a Planned Parenthood organization listed in the telephone directory. Planned Parenthood provides information, counseling, and medical services related to reproduction and sexual health to anyone who wants them. No one is denied because of age, social group, or inability to pay. Information can also be obtained through the national office, given above.

National Abortion Rights Action League (NARAL)
1101 14th Street, NW
Washington, DC 20005
(202) 408-4600
A political organization concerned with family planning issues and dedicated to making abortion "safe, legal, and accessible" for all women. Affiliated with many state and local organizations. Newsletter and brochures available.

Birthright
686 N. Broad Street
Woodbury, NJ 08096
(800) 848-5683
An assistance and counseling service for pregnant women. Services include telephone counseling and referrals to local offices and clinics. Birthright counsels against abortion and does not give out information on birth control.

Public Health Departments

Counties throughout the United States, regardless of size, have county health clinics that will provide low-cost family planning services. Some cities also have public-health clinics. To locate their offices, look up the city or county in the telephone directory, then check under headings such as

Department of Health	*Health*
Family Planning	*Public Health Department*
Family Services	*(City or County's name) Health (or Medical) Clinic*

SUGGESTIONS FOR FURTHER READING

Chesler, Ellen. *A Woman of Valor: Margaret Sanger and the Birth Control Movement in America.* New York: Simon & Schuster, 1992. The biography of Margaret Sanger who, in the early decades of this century, fought for women's contraceptive rights, an idea as divisive then as abortion rights are today.

Ginsburg, Faye D. *Contested Lives: The Abortion Debate in an American Community.* Berkeley, CA: University of California Press, 1989. An important sociological work that explores the historical roots of the abortion controversy and the contemporary conflict between pro-life and pro-choice groups in an American community. It reveals the complex reasoning of both groups through individual stories that destroy stereotypical thinking.

Gordon, Linda. *Woman's Body, Woman's Right: A Social History of Birth Control in America*, rev. ed. New York: Penguin, 1990. A well-written, sometimes surprising history of birth control.

Greer, Germaine. *Sex and Destiny.* New York: Harper & Row, 1984. A critique of the politics of fertility that is brilliant, controversial, opinionated, passionate, and refreshing; covers a wide range of topics, including contraception, abortion, infanticide, eugenics, and population control.

Hatcher, Robert, et al. *Contraceptive Technology: 1994–1996.* New York: Irvington Publishers, 1993. The most comprehensive and technically reliable book on developments in contraceptive technology; updated regularly.

Luker, Kristin. *Taking Chances.* Berkeley, CA: University of California Press, 1975. A major work on contraceptive risk taking; one of the most influential books in the field.

Tribe, Laurence. *Abortion: The Clash of Absolutes.* New York: W. W. Norton, 1992. An incisive, balanced book on the social, medical, political, legal, religious, and moral aspects of the abortion debate.

Chapter Thirteen

CONCEPTION, PREGNANCY, AND CHILDBIRTH

PREVIEW: SELF-QUIZ

1. Infertility is increasing among American couples of all ages. True or false?

2. Miscarriage and stillbirth are major life events for parents. True or false?

3. The primary cause of infertility in women is an untreated sexually transmitted disease. True or false?

4. Fertilization generally takes place within the uterus. True or false?

5. Home pregnancy tests are about 95% accurate. True or false?

6. Even a moderate amount of alcohol consumption affects the fetus. True or false?

7. The United States ranks 24th among developed countries for low infant mortality. True or false?

8. About one-fourth of all U.S. births involve cesarean sections. True or false?

9. Circumcision, the surgical removal of the foreskin of the penis, is performed mainly for health reasons. True or false?

10. Breast-feeding is recommended by the American Academy of Pediatricians because it provides better nutrition and protection from disease than formula. True or false?

ANSWERS 1. F, 2. T, 3. T, 4. F, 5. F, 6. T, 7. T, 8. T, 9. F, 10. T

Chapter Outline

The birth of a wanted child is considered by many parents to be the happiest event of their lives. Today, however, pain and controversy surround many aspects of this completely natural process. As we struggle to balance the rights of the mother, the father, the fetus, and society itself in these matters, we find ourselves considering the quality of life as well as life's mere existence.

For most American women, pregnancy will be relatively comfortable, and the outcome predictably joyful. Yet for increasing numbers of others, especially among the poor, the prospect of having children raises the specters of drugs, disease, malnutrition, and familial chaos. And there are those couples who have dreamed of and planned for families for years, only to find that they are unable to conceive.

In this chapter, we view pregnancy and childbirth from biological, social, and psychological perspectives. We examine the process of deciding to have a child, as well as that of choosing not to have children. In addition, we consider pregnancy loss, infertility, and reproductive techniques. And we look at the challenges of the transition to parenthood.

*Creation often
needs two hearts
one to root
and one to flower*

Marilou Awiakta

CHILDREN BY CHOICE

Parenthood may now be considered a matter of choice, owing to the widespread use of birth control. If men and women want to have children, they can decide when to have them. As a result, America's birth rate has fallen to an average of two children per marriage, the number deemed ideal by 56% of the people interviewed in a 1985 Gallup poll. Just 30 years ago, 37% of those interviewed wanted a large family of four or more children. Today, only 11% want so large a family. Approximately 2% want no children at all, according to the 1985 poll, but that number is expected to increase (Nock, 1987).

Child-Free Marriage

In recent articles and discussions of marriage in which there are no children, the word "childless" is often replaced by **child-free.** This change in terminology reflects a shift of values in our culture. Couples who do not choose to have children need no longer be viewed as lacking something hitherto considered essential for personal fulfillment. Indeed, the use of the suffix "free" suggests liberation from the bonds of a potentially oppressive condition (Callan, 1985). Women who choose to be child-free are generally well educated and career-oriented. One woman, an artist who is married, explains her decision not to have children: "I'm kind of a pragmatist, and I never really believed women could do it all. I knew I couldn't be an artist and a mother and support myself too." Another, a teacher, says, "People think more about the new car they're going to buy than about whether they should have children. . . . There are challenges and responsibilities in parenthood, and I think we glorify it in America. We don't talk about the realities. . . ." (quoted in Donnelly, 1992).

Even when there is less familial and societal pressure to reproduce, the decision to remain without children is not always easily made. Although

If your parents didn't have any children, there's a good chance that you won't have any.

Clarence Day

the partners in some child-free marriages have never felt that they wanted to have children, for most the decision seems to have been gradual. Jean Veevers (1980) identified four stages of this decision process:

1. The couple decides to postpone children for a definite time period (until he gets his degree, until she gets her promotion, and so on).

2. When the time period expires, they decide to postpone children indefinitely (until they "feel like it").

3. They increasingly appreciate the positive advantages of being child-free (as opposed to the disadvantages of being childless).

4. The decision is made final, generally by the sterilization of one or both partners.

Studies of child-free marriages show the following nine basic reasons given by those who have chosen this alternative, in order of importance (Houseknecht, 1987):

1. Freedom from child-care responsibility and greater opportunity for self-fulfillment.

2. A more satisfactory marital relationship.

3. The wife's career considerations.

4. Monetary advantages.

5. Concern about population growth.

6. A general dislike of children.

7. Early socialization experiences and doubts about parenting ability.

8. Concern about the physical aspects of childbirth.

9. Concern for children in the present world conditions.

Couples usually have some idea that they will or will not have children before they marry. If the intent isn't clear from the start or if one partner's mind changes, the couple may face serious problems. Conflict and resentment may come to characterize the relationship unless one person has a change of mind or is able to concede the other's wishes without rancor. Many studies of child-free marriages indicate a higher degree of marital adjustment or satisfaction than is found among couples with children. In one study, child-free women reported more frequent exchange of stimulating ideas with their husbands, more shared projects and outside interests, and greater agreement on household tasks and career decisions (Houseknecht, 1982). These findings are not particularly surprising, if we consider the greater amount of time and energy that child rearing entails. It has also been observed that divorce is more probable in child-free marriages, perhaps because, unlike some other unhappily married couples, the child-free couples do not stay together "for the sake of the children" (Glenn & McLanahan, 1982).

Deferred Parenthood

The 1970s saw the beginning of a "baby boomlet." Births to women in their thirties more than doubled between 1970 and 1979 and continued to increase in the 1980s. In 1989, the U.S. Bureau of the Census reported a

Couples who defer parenthood until other components of their lives—such as careers—are solidified express increased satisfaction with their lives and their marital relationships.

"bumper crop" of 4 million babies (to women of all ages). This increase in births is attributed to the fact that women in their thirties (themselves products of the post-World War II baby boom) have postponed childbirth. Although most women still begin their families while in their twenties, demographers predict that the trend toward later parenthood will continue to grow, especially in middle- and upper-income groups (Price, 1982; Whitehead, 1990).

The average age at marriage has increased slowly and steadily since 1960. More career and lifestyle options are available to single women now than in the past. Marriage and reproduction are no longer economic or social necessities. People may take longer to search for the "right" mate (even if it takes more than one marriage to do it), and they may wait for the right time to have children. Increasingly, effective birth control (including safe, legal abortion) has also been a significant factor in the planned deferral of parenthood. (The abortion controversy was discussed in Chapter 12.)

Besides giving parents a chance to complete their education, build careers, and firmly establish their own relationship, delaying parenthood can also be advantageous for other reasons. Maternity and medical expenses, food, furniture and equipment, clothes, toys, babysitters, lessons, and summer camp are costly. In 1989, the annual cost of raising a child ranged from

$4100 to $9770, depending on the family's income level, age of the child, and region of residence (Lino, 1990). (These costs are based on two-parent, two-child families; with three or more children, the cost per child declines.) To raise a child through age 17 runs from $81,810 to $160,080 in current dollars. Obviously, parents who have had a chance to establish themselves financially will be better able to bear the economic burden of child rearing.

Ann Goetting's (1986) review of parental satisfaction research revealed that "those who postpone parenthood until other components of their lives—especially their careers—are solidified" express enhanced degrees of satisfaction. Older parents may also be more emotionally mature and thus more capable of dealing with parenting stresses (although age isn't necessarily indicative of emotional maturity). In addition, as Jane Price (1982) writes:

> Combating the aging process is something of a national preoccupation. . . . In our society, the power of children to revitalize and refresh is part of the host of forces encouraging men and women to become parents much later than they did in the past.

The decision-making period is an important part of the pregnancy process. Once the choice to have a child has been made, however, the theoretical part is over and the practical part begins. We now turn to practicalities, beginning with fertilization.

FERTILIZATION AND FETAL DEVELOPMENT

As you will recall from Chapter 3, once the secondary oocyte has been released from the ovary, it drifts into the fallopian tube, where it may be fertilized if live sperm are present (Figure 13.1). If the pregnancy proceeds without interruption, the birth will occur in approximately 266 days. (Traditionally, physicians count the first day of the pregnancy as the day on which the woman would have begun her menstrual period; they calculate the due date to be 280 days, which is also 10 lunar months, from that day.)

The Fertilization Process

The oocyte remains viable for 12–24 hours after ovulation; most sperm are viable in the female reproductive tract for 12–48 hours, although some "super sperm" may be viable for up to 72 hours (Marieb, 1992). Therefore, for fertilization to occur, intercourse must take place no more than 72 hours prior to or 24 hours after ovulation.

Of the millions of sperm ejaculated into the vagina, only a few thousand (or even just a few hundred) actually reach the fallopian tubes. The others leak from the vagina or are destroyed within its acidic environment. Those that make it into the cervix (which is easier during ovulation, when the cervical mucus becomes more fluid) may still be destroyed by white blood cells within the uterus. Furthermore, the sperm that actually reach the oocyte within a few minutes of ejaculation are not yet capable of getting through its outer layers. They must first undergo **capacitation,** the process by which their membranes become fragile enough to release the enzymes from their acrosomes (the helmetlike coverings of the sperm's nuclei). It

Union between man and woman is a creative act and has something divine about it. . . . The object of love is a creative union with beauty on both the spiritual and physical levels.

Plato

Ancient men knew nothing of the sperm and the ovum. This knowledge belongs to the era of the microscope. For him the seminal fluid was the substance that grew into the child—drawing sustenance from the womb of the pregnant woman, absorbing the blood that issued periodically from the womb when there was no child there. The woman's body nurtured the seed, as the soil nurtured the grain of rice. But the seed was the man's seed and the child was the man's child. It was his ongoing spirit, his continuing life.

David Mace and Vera Mace

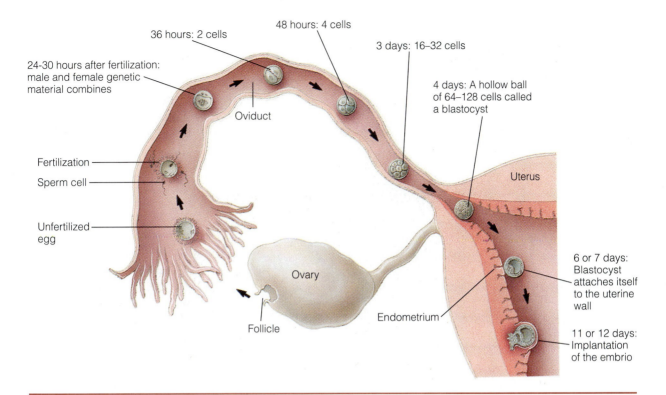

24-30 hours after fertilization: male and female genetic material combines

36 hours: 2 cells

48 hours: 4 cells

3 days: 16–32 cells

4 days: A hollow ball of 64–128 cells called a blastocyst

Oviduct

Uterus

Fertilization

Sperm cell

Unfertilized egg

Ovary

Endometrium

Follicle

6 or 7 days: Blastocyst attaches itself to the uterine wall

11 or 12 days: Implantation of the embrio

FIGURE 13.1 Ovulation, Fertilization, and Development of the Blastocyst. This drawing charts the progress of the ovulated oocyte (unfertilized egg) through fertilization and pre-embryonic development.

takes 6–8 hours for this **acrosomal reaction** to occur. Enzymes from hundreds of sperm must be released in order for the oocyte's outer layers (the corona radiata and the zona pellucida) to soften sufficiently to allow a sperm to be absorbed.

Once a single sperm is inside the oocyte cytoplasm, an electrical reaction occurs that prevents any other sperm from entering the oocyte. Immediately, the oocyte begins to swell, detaching the sperm that still cling to its outer layer. Then it completes the final stage of meiotic cell division and becomes a mature ovum by forming the ovum nucleus and casting out the second polar body. (Ovum development was discussed at length in Chapter 3.) The nuclei of sperm and ovum then release their chromosomes, which combine to form the **diploid zygote,** containing 23 pairs of chromosomes. (Each parent contributes one chromosome to each of the pairs.) Fertilization is now complete, and pre-embryonic development begins. Within 9 months, this single cell, the zygote, may become the 6000 billion cells that constitute a human being. Recall from Chapter 12 that from fertilization through birth, the developing human offspring is referred to as the *conceptus.*

Development of the Conceptus

Following fertilization, the zygote undergoes a series of mitotic divisions, during which the cells replicate themselves. After 4 or 5 days, there are about 100 cells, now called a **blastocyst.** On about the fifth day, the blastocyst arrives in the uterine cavity, where it floats for a day or two before implanting in the soft, blood-rich uterine lining (endometrium), which has

Everyone wants to know when his or her baby's going to be born. It is fairly simple to figure out the date: Add 7 days to the first day of the last menstrual period. Then subtract 3 months and add 1 year. For example, if a woman's last menstrual period began on July 17, 1994, add 7 days (July 24). Next, subtract 3 months (April 24). Then add 1 year. This gives the expected date of birth as April 24, 1995. Few births actually occur on the date predicted, but 60% of babies are born within 5 days of the predicted time.

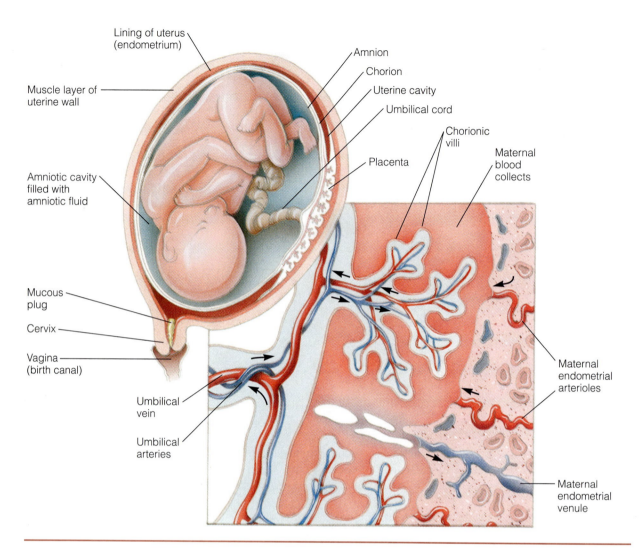

Lining of uterus (endometrium)

Muscle layer of uterine wall

Amniotic cavity filled with amniotic fluid

Mucous plug

Cervix

Vagina (birth canal)

Umbilical vein

Umbilical arteries

Amnion

Chorion

Uterine cavity

Umbilical cord

Chorionic villi

Placenta

Maternal blood collects

Maternal endometrial arterioles

Maternal endometrial venule

FIGURE 13.2 The Fetus in the Uterus and a Cross Section of the Placenta. The placenta is the organ of exchange between mother and fetus. Nutrients and oxygen pass from the mother to the fetus, and waste products pass from the fetus to the mother via blood vessels within the umbilical cord.

What was your original face before you were born?

Zen koan (riddle)

spent the past 3 weeks preparing for its arrival. The process of **implantation** takes about 1 week. Human chorionic gonadotropin (HCG) secreted by the blastocyst maintains the uterine environment in an "embryo-friendly" condition and prevents the shedding of the endometrium, which would normally occur during menstruation.

The blastocyst, or pre-embryo, rapidly grows into an **embryo,** which will, in turn, be referred to as a **fetus** around the eighth week of **gestation** (pregnancy). During the first 2 or 3 weeks of development, the **embryonic membranes** are formed. These include the **amnion** (amniotic sac), a membranous sac that will contain the embryo and **amniotic fluid;** the **yolk sac,** producer of the embryo's first blood cells and the germ cells that will develop into gonads; the **chorion,** the embryo's outermost membrane; and the **allantois,** the structural base of the umbilical cord and urinary bladder (Figure 13.2).

During the 3rd week, extensive cell migration, or **gastrulation,** occurs, and the stage is set for the development of the organs. The first body segments and the brain begin to form. The digestive and circulatory systems begin to develop in the 4th week; the heart begins to pump blood. By the end of the first month, the spinal cord and nervous system have also begun to develop. The 5th week sees the formation of arms and legs. In the 6th week, the eyes and ears form. At 7 weeks, the reproductive organs begin to differentiate in males; female reproductive organs continue to develop. At 8 weeks, the fetus is about the size of a thumb, although the head is nearly as large as the body. The brain begins to function to coordinate the development of the internal organs. Facial features begin to form, and bones begin to develop. Arms, hands, fingers, legs, feet, toes, and eyes are almost fully developed at 12 weeks. At 15 weeks, the fetus has a strong heartbeat, some digestion, and active muscles. Most bones are developed by then, and the eyebrows appear. At this stage, the fetus is covered with a fine, downy hair called **lanugo.**

Throughout its development, the fetus is nourished through the **placenta.** The placenta begins to develop from part of the blastocyst following implantation. It grows larger as the fetus does, passing nutrients from the mother's bloodstream to the fetus, to which it is attached by the **umbilical cord.** The placenta serves as a biochemical barrier; it allows dissolved substances to pass to the fetus, but blocks blood cells and large molecules.

By 5 months, the fetus is 10–12 inches long and weighs between ½ and 1 lb. The internal organs are well developed, although the lungs cannot function well outside the uterus. At 6 months, the fetus is 11–14 inches long and weighs more than 1 lb. At 7 months, it is 13–17 inches long and weighs about 3 lb. At this point, most healthy fetuses are viable—that is, capable of surviving outside the womb. (Although some fetuses are viable at 5 or 6 months, they require specialized care to survive.) The fetus spends the final 2 months of gestation growing rapidly. At term (9 months), it will be about 20 inches long and will weigh about 7 lb. (Color photographs on pages 486–487 show embryonic and fetal development, and Figure 13.3 on page 488 indicates the actual sizes of the developing embryo during the first 15 weeks following fertilization.)

Yes—the history of man for the nine months preceding his birth would probably be far more interesting, and contain events of greater moment, than all the three score and ten that follow.

Samuel Coleridge

BEING PREGNANT

Pregnancy is an important life event for both women and their partners. From the moment it is discovered, a pregnancy affects people's feelings about themselves, their relationships with their partners, and the interrelationships of other family members as well.

Pregnancy Tests

Chemical tests designed to detect the presence of human chorionic gonadotropin (HCG), secreted by the implanted blastocyst, usually determine pregnancy approximately two weeks following a missed (or spotty) menstrual period. In the **agglutination test,** a drop of the woman's urine causes a test solution to coagulate if she is not pregnant; if she is pregnant, the solution will become smooth and milky in consistency. Home pregnancy tests to detect HCG may be purchased in most drugstores. The directions

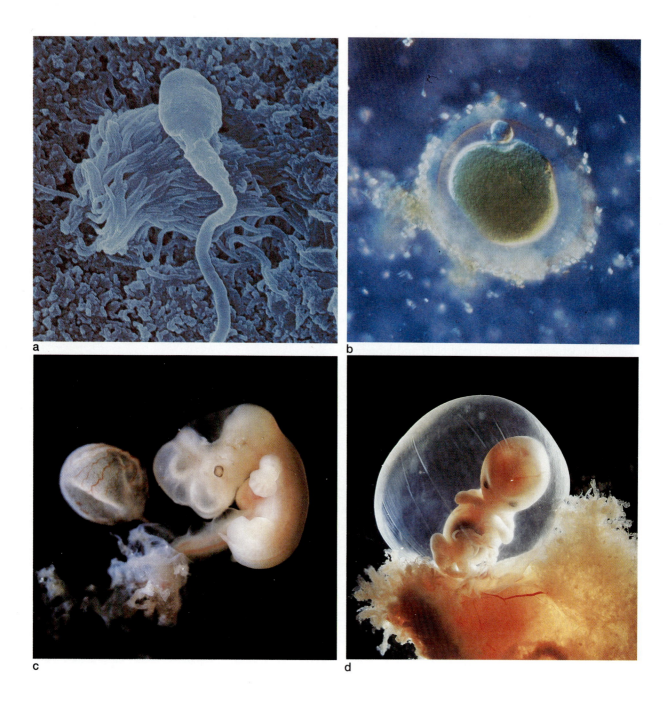

a

b

c

d

must be followed closely. Blood analysis can also be used to determine if a pregnancy exists. Although such tests diagnose pregnancy with better than 95% accuracy, no absolute certainty exists until a fetal heartbeat and movements can be detected, or ultrasound is performed.

The first reliable physical sign of pregnancy can be distinguished about 4 weeks after a woman misses her period. By this time, changes in her cervix and pelvis are apparent during a pelvic examination. At this time the

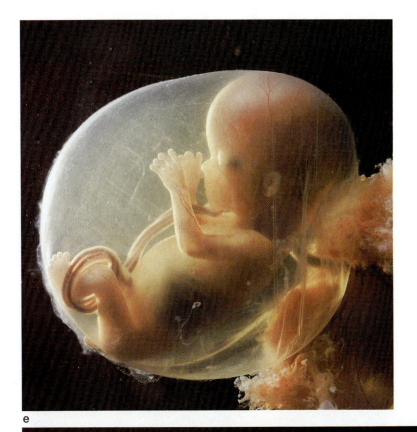

e

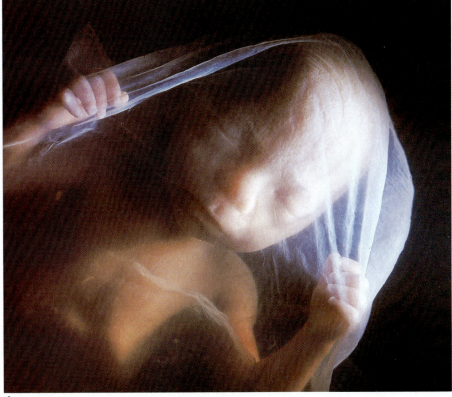

f

(a) After ejaculation, several million sperm move through the cervical mucus toward the fallopian tubes; an ovum has moved into one of the tubes. On their way to the ovum, millions of sperm are destroyed in the vagina, uterus, or fallopian tubes. Some go the wrong direction in the vagina, and others swim into the wrong tube. (b) The mother's and father's chromosomes have united, and the fertilized ovum has divided for the first time. After about 1 week, the blastocyst will implant itself in the uterine lining. (c) The embryo is 5 weeks old and is ⅖ of an inch long. It floats in the embryonic sac. The major divisions of the brain can be seen, as well as an eye, hands, arms, and a long tail. (d) The embryo is now 7 weeks old and is almost 1 inch long. Its external and internal organs are developing. It has eyes, nose, mouth, lips, and tongue. (e) At 12 weeks, the fetus is over 3 inches long and weighs almost 1 ounce. (f) At 16 weeks, the fetus is more than 6 inches long and weighs about 7 ounces. All its organs have been formed. The time that follows is now one of simple growth.

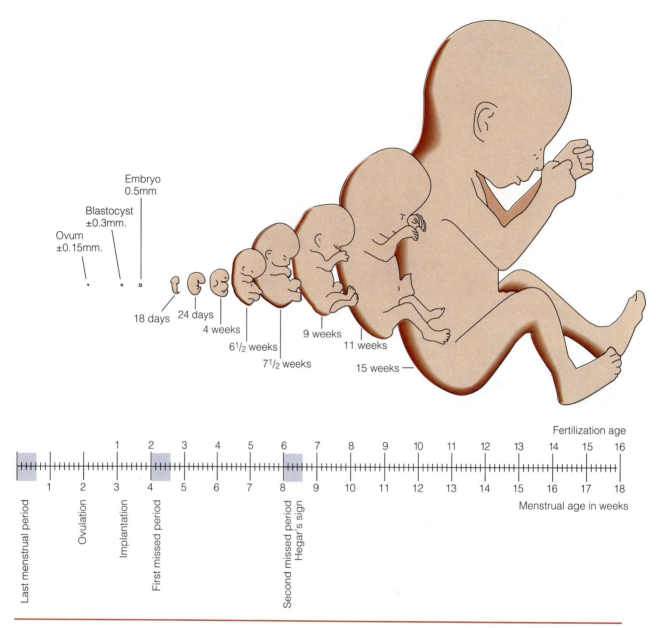

Embryo
0.5mm

Blastocyst
±0.3mm.

Ovum
±0.15mm.

18 days   24 days

4 weeks

6½ weeks

7½ weeks

9 weeks

11 weeks

15 weeks —

Fertilization age

| 1 | 2 | 3 | 4 | 5 | 6 | 7 | 8 | 9 | 10 | 11 | 12 | 13 | 14 | 15 | 16 |

| 1 | 2 | 3 | 4 | 5 | 6 | 7 | 8 | 9 | 10 | 11 | 12 | 13 | 14 | 15 | 16 | 17 | 18 |

Menstrual age in weeks

Last menstrual period

Ovulation

Implantation

First missed period

Second missed period
Hegar's sign

FIGURE 13.3 Growth of the Embryo and Fetus. In this drawing, the actual sizes of the developing embryo and fetus are shown, from conception through the first 15 weeks.

woman would be considered to be 8 weeks pregnant, according to medical terminology; physicians calculate pregnancy as beginning at the time of the woman's last menstrual period rather than at the time of actual fertilization (since that date is often difficult to determine). Another signal of pregnancy, called **Hegar's sign,** is a softening of the uterus just above the cervix, which can be felt during a vaginal examination. Additionally, a slight purple hue colors the labia minora; the vagina and cervix also take on a purplish color rather than the usual pink.

The Pregnant Woman and Her Partner

A woman's feelings during pregnancy will vary dramatically according to who she is, how she feels about pregnancy and motherhood, whether the pregnancy was planned, whether she has a secure home situation, and many other factors. Her feelings may be ambivalent; they will probably change over the course of the pregnancy.

A woman's first pregnancy is especially important because it has traditionally symbolized her transition to maturity. Even as social norms change and it becomes more common and "acceptable" for women to defer childbirth until they've established a career or for them to choose not to have children, the significance of first pregnancy should not be underestimated. It is a major developmental milestone in the lives of mothers—and of fathers as well (Notman & Lester, 1988; Snarey et al., 1987; for male procreative consciousness, see Marsiglio, 1991).

A couple's relationship is likely to undergo changes during pregnancy. It can be a stressful time, especially if the pregnancy was unanticipated. Communication is especially important during this period, because each partner may have preconceived ideas about what the other is feeling. Both partners may have fears about the baby's well-being, the approaching birth, their ability to parent, and the ways in which the baby will interfere with their own relationship. All of these concerns are normal. Sharing them, perhaps in the setting of a prenatal group, can deepen and strengthen the relationship (Kitzinger, 1989). If the pregnant woman's partner is not supportive or if she does not have a partner, it is important that she find other sources of support—family, friends, women's groups—and that she not be reluctant to ask for help.

A pregnant woman's relationship with her own mother may also undergo changes. In a certain sense, becoming a mother makes a woman the equal of her own mother. She can now lay claim to being treated as an adult. Women who have depended on their mothers tend to become more independent and assertive as their pregnancy progresses. Women who have been distant, hostile, or alienated from their own mothers may begin to identify with their mothers' experience of pregnancy. Even women who have delayed childbearing until their thirties may be surprised to find their relationships with their mothers changing and becoming more "adult." Working through these changing relationships is a kind of "psychological gestation" that accompanies the physiological gestation of the fetus (Silver & Campbell, 1988).

The first trimester (3 months) of pregnancy may be difficult physically for the expectant mother. She may experience nausea, fatigue, and painful swelling of the breasts. She may also have fears that she may miscarry or that the child will not be normal. Her sexuality may undergo changes, resulting in unfamiliar needs (for more, less, or differently expressed sexual love), which may in turn cause anxiety. (Sexuality during pregnancy is discussed further later in this section.) Education about the birth process and her own body's functioning, as well as support from partner, friends, relatives, and health-care professionals, are the best antidotes to fear.

During the second trimester, most of the nausea and fatigue disappear, and the pregnant woman can feel the fetus move within her. Worries about miscarriage will probably begin to diminish, too, for the riskiest part of fetal development has passed. The pregnant woman may look and feel radiantly happy. She will very likely feel proud of her accomplishment and be delighted as her pregnancy begins to show. She may feel in harmony with life's natural rhythms. One mother writes (quoted in C. Jones, 1988):

> I love my body when I'm pregnant. It seems round, full, complete somehow. I find that I am emotionally on an even keel throughout; no more premenstrual depression and upsets. I love the feeling that I am never alone, yet at the same time I am my own person. If I could always be five months pregnant, life would be bliss.

Some women, however, may be concerned about their increasing size. They may fear that they are becoming unattractive. A partner's attention and reassurance will ease these fears.

The third trimester may be the time of the greatest difficulties in daily living. The uterus, originally about the size of the woman's fist, has now enlarged to fill the pelvic cavity and pushes up into the abdominal cavity, exerting increasing pressure on the other internal organs (Figure 13.4). Water retention (edema) is a fairly common problem during late pregnancy. Edema may cause swelling in the face, hands, ankles, and feet, but it can often be controlled by cutting down on salt and carbohydrates. If dietary changes do not help this condition, a pregnant woman should consult her physician. Her physical abilities are limited by her size. She may be required by her employer to stop working (many public schools, for example, do not allow women to teach after their 6th month). A family dependent on the pregnant woman's income may suffer a severe financial crunch.

The woman and her partner may become increasingly concerned about the upcoming birth. Some women experience periods of depression in the month preceding their delivery; they may feel physically awkward and sexually unattractive. Many feel an exhilarating sense of excitement and anticipation marked by energetic bursts of industriousness. They feel that the fetus is a member of the family (Stanton, 1985). Both parents may begin talking to the fetus and "playing" with it by patting and rubbing the mother's belly.

The principal developmental tasks for the expectant mother and father may be summarized as follows (Valentine, 1982; also see Notman & Lester, 1988; Silver & Campbell, 1988; Snarey et al., 1987):

Tasks of an Expectant Mother

- Development of an emotional attachment to the fetus.
- Differentiation of the self from the fetus.
- Acceptance and resolution of the relationship with the woman's own mother.
- Resolution of dependency issues (generally involving parents or husband/partner).
- Evaluation of practical and financial responsibilities.

Tasks of an Expectant Father

- Acceptance of the pregnancy and attachment to the fetus.
- Evaluation of practical and financial responsibilities.
- Resolution of dependency issues (involving wife/partner).
- Acceptance and resolution of the relationship with the man's own father.

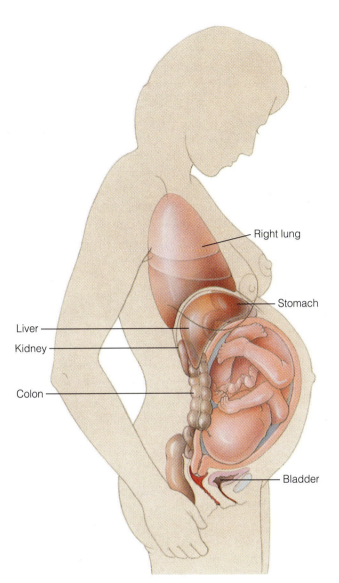

FIGURE 13.4 Mother and Fetus in Third Trimester of Pregnancy. The expanding uterus affects the mother's internal organs, causing feelings of pressure and possible discomfort.

Right lung

Stomach

Liver

Kidney

Colon

Bladder

Sexuality During Pregnancy

It is not unusual for a woman's sexual feelings and actions to change during pregnancy, although there is great variation among women in these expressions of sexuality. Some women feel beautiful, energetic, sensual, and interested in sex, whereas others feel awkward and decidedly unsexy. Some studies indicate a lessening of women's sexual interest during pregnancy and a corresponding decline in coital frequency (Stimpson & Person, 1980). A recent study of 219 pregnant women found that although libido, intercourse, and orgasm declined, the frequencies of oral and anal sex and masturbation remained at prepregnancy levels (Hart, Cohen, Gingold, & Homburg, 1991). It is also quite possible that a woman's sexual feelings will fluctuate during this time. Men may also feel confusion or conflicts about sexual activity. They, like many women, may have been conditioned to find the pregnant body unerotic. Or they may feel deep sexual attraction to their pregnant partners, yet fear their feelings are "strange" or unusual. They may also worry about hurting their partner or the baby.

Although there are no "rules" governing sexual behavior during pregnancy, a few basic precautions should be observed:

- If the woman has had a prior miscarriage, she should check with her health practitioner before having intercourse, masturbating, or engaging in other activities that might lead to orgasm. Powerful uterine contractions could induce a spontaneous abortion in some women, especially during the first trimester.

- If there is bleeding from the vagina, the woman should refrain from sexual activity and consult her physician or midwife at once.

- If the insertion of the penis into the vagina causes pain that is not easily remedied by a change of position, the couple should refrain from intercourse.

- Pressure on the woman's abdomen should be avoided, especially during the final months of pregnancy.

- Late in pregnancy, an orgasm is likely to induce uterine contractions. Generally, this is not considered harmful, but the pregnant woman may want to discuss it with her practitioner. (Occasionally, labor is begun when the waters break as the result of orgasmic contractions.)

A couple, especially if it is their first pregnancy, may be uncertain as to how to express their sexual feelings. The following guidelines may be helpful:

- Even during a normal pregnancy, sexual intercourse may be uncomfortable. The couple may want to try such positions as side-by-side or rear-entry, to avoid pressure on the woman's abdomen and to facilitate more shallow penetration. (See illustrations of different sexual positions in Chapter 10.)

- Even if intercourse is not comfortable for the woman, orgasm may still be intensely pleasurable. She may wish to consider the possibilities of masturbation (alone or with her partner) or of cunnilingus.

- Both partners should remember that there are no "rules" about sexuality during pregnancy. This is a time for relaxing, enjoying the woman's changing body, talking a lot, touching each other, and experimenting with new ways—both sexual and nonsexual—of expressing affection.

Complications of Pregnancy and Dangers to the Fetus

Usually, pregnancy proceeds without major complications. Good nutrition is one of the most important factors in having a complication-free pregnancy. However, some women experience minor to serious complications.

Effects of Teratogens Substances other than nutrients may reach the developing embryo or fetus through the placenta. Although few extensive studies have been done on the subject, toxic substances in the environment can also affect the health of the fetus. Whatever a woman breathes, eats, or drinks is eventually received by the conceptus in some proportion. A fetus's blood-alcohol level, for example, is equal to that of the mother (Rosenthal, 1990). **Teratogens,** substances that cause defects (such as brain damage or physical deformities) in developing embryos or fetuses, are directly traceable in only about 2–3% of cases of birth defects. They are thought to be linked to 25–30% of such cases; the causes of the remaining cases remain unknown (Healy, 1988).

Alcohol Studies have linked chronic ingestion of alcohol during pregnancy to fetal alcohol syndrome (FAS), which can include unusual facial characteristics, small head and body size, congenital heart defects, defective joints, poor mental capabilities, and abnormal behavior patterns. Lesser amounts of alcohol may result in fetal alcohol effect (FAE), the most common problem of which is growth retardation (Waterson & Murray-Lyon, 1990). The Centers for Disease Control (CDC) estimate that more than 8000 alcohol-affected babies are born every year in this country (2.7 babies out of every 1000). Some studies place the figure higher—as high as 50,000 alcohol-affected births per year (Getlin, 1989). The CDC also reports that FAS is six times more common in African Americans than in whites and thirty times more common in Native Americans (Rosenthal, 1990). (Studies have also found that African American women and Latinas are more likely to abstain from alcohol than white women, and that a woman's level of alcohol consumption rises with her education and income [Rosenthal, 1990]). Most experts counsel pregnant women to abstain entirely from alcohol because there is no safe dosage known at this time.

Opiates and Cocaine Mothers who regularly use opiates (heroin, morphine, codeine, and opium) are likely to have infants who are addicted at birth. Cocaine—especially in the smokable "crack" form—may be associated with devastating birth defects (Chasnoff, 1988). A study in New York of drug-exposed infants revealed that the opiate-exposed babies showed more neurological damage than the cocaine-exposed babies, and that those infants exposed to polydrug abuse (both opiates and cocaine) were worse off than those exposed to any single drug in terms of gestational age at birth, birthweight, and length of hospital stay (Kaye, Elkind, Goldberg, & Tytun, 1989). A 1989 study in Rhode Island found that 35 (7.5%) out of the 465 women in labor who were studied had drug traces in their urine (Centers for Disease Control, 1990). (The urine samples were provided to the Department of Health without names to protect the women's anonymity, although various demographic data were supplied.) It should be noted that many drug-exposed infants have been subjected to alcohol exposure as well.

Tobacco Cigarette smoking affects the unborn child. Babies born to women who smoke during pregnancy are an average of one-fourth to one-half pound lighter at birth than babies born to nonsmokers. Secondhand smoke is also considered dangerous to the developing fetus (Healy, 1988). Smoking has been implicated in sudden infant death syndrome (SIDS), respiratory disorders in children, and various adverse pregnancy outcomes.

Prescription and Over-the-Counter Drugs Prescription drugs should be used only under careful medical supervision, as some may cause serious harm to the fetus. Isotretinoin (Acutane), a popular antiacne drug, has been implicated in over 1000 cases of severe birth defects over the past several years (Kolata, 1988). Vitamins, aspirin, and other over-the-counter drugs, as well as large quantities of caffeine-containing food and drink (coffee, tea, cola, chocolate) should be avoided or used only under medical supervision. Vitamin A in large doses can cause serious birth defects.

Toxic Chemicals and Pollutants Chemicals and environmental pollutants are also potentially threatening. Continuous exposure to lead, most commonly in paint products or water from lead pipes, has been implicated in a variety of learning disorders. Mercury, from fish contaminated by industrial wastes, is a known cause of physical deformities. Solvents, pesticides, and certain chemical fertilizers should be avoided or used with extreme caution both at home and in the workplace. A recent study of pregnant women who worked with computers suggested a strong correlation between exposure to certain types of video display terminals and miscarriage. Researchers linked the tripled rate of miscarriage to high levels of a particular electromagnetic field (Lindbohm, Hietanan, Kyronen, & Sallmen, 1992).

Infectious Diseases Infectious diseases can also damage the fetus. If a woman contracts German measles (rubella) during the first 3 months of pregnancy, her child may be born with physical or mental disabilities. Immunization against rubella is available, but it must be done before the woman is pregnant; otherwise, the injection will be as harmful to the fetus as the disease itself. Group B streptococcus, a bacterium carried by 15–40% of pregnant women, is harmless to adults but can be fatal to newborns. Each year, about 12,000 infants are infected; 1600–2000 of them die. The American Academy of Pediatrics has recommended that all pregnant women be screened for strep B. Antibiotics administered to the infant during labor can greatly reduce the danger to the child ("Prenatal Tests," 1992).

Sexually Transmitted Diseases Sexually transmitted diseases may also damage the fetus. In 1988, the CDC recommended that all pregnant women be screened for hepatitis B, a virus that can be passed to the infant at birth. If the mother tests positive, her child can be immunized immediately following birth (Moore, 1988). A woman with gonorrhea may expose her child to blindness from contact with the infected vagina; the baby will need immediate antibiotic treatment. A woman with HIV or AIDS has a 30–40% chance of passing the virus to the fetus via the placenta (Cowley, 1990; Fischl, Dickinson, Segal, Flannagan, & Rodriguez, 1987). The number of infants with HIV or AIDS is increasing as more women become infected with the virus either before or during pregnancy. In 1989, there were 547 newborns who were HIV-positive, a 38% increase over the previous year (Cowley, 1990). (Not all infants who are born with a positive HIV status remain that way, however; some "reconvert" to negative status once their mother's blood is out of their system.) Nationwide, more than 4700 children have AIDS, and three times that number are estimated to be infected with HIV ("AIDS and Children," 1989, Centers for Disease Control, 1993).

The increasingly widespread incidence of genital herpes may present some hazards for newborns. The herpes simplex virus may cause brain damage and is potentially life-threatening for these infants. Careful monitoring by a physician can determine whether or not a vaginal delivery should take place. Charles Prober (1987) and colleagues at the Stanford Medical School have extensively studied births to mothers with herpes. They found that a number of infants born to infected mothers had herpes antibodies in their blood; these infants did not contract herpes during vaginal delivery. Although the harmful potential of neonatal herpes should not be underestimated, if the appropriate procedures are followed by the infected mother and her physician or midwife, the chance of infection from genital lesions is minimal (Dr. Margaret Yonekura in "Neonatal Herpes," 1984).

The current incidence of death due to neonatal herpes is about 2000 cases annually (Petit, 1992). An initial outbreak of herpes can be especially dangerous if the woman is pregnant; the virus may be passed through the placenta to the fetus. Recent research indicates that fathers may inadvertently infect their newborns (Kulhanjian, Soroush, Au, Bronzan, & Yasukawa, 1992). Infected men who have been symptomless for years and have not previously transmitted the virus to their wives may do so during pregnancy, placing their infants at great risk. In rare cases, herpes-infected infants may be born to mothers who show no symptoms themselves. This indicates that undiagnosed intrauterine herpes infections may be passed to the fetus (Stone, Brooks, Guinan, & Alexander, 1989). Testing for genital herpes is therefore recommended for both expectant parents. Once the baby is born, a mother who is experiencing an outbreak of either oral or genital herpes should wash her hands often and carefully and not permit contact between her hands, contaminated objects, and the baby's mucous membranes (inside of eyes, mouth, nose, penis, vagina, vulva, and rectum). If the father is infected, he should do likewise until the lesions have subsided.

Ectopic Pregnancy In **ectopic pregnancy** (tubal pregnancy), the incidence of which has more than quadrupled in the last 20 years, the fertilized egg implants itself in the fallopian tube. Generally, this occurs because the tube is obstructed, most often as a result of pelvic inflammatory disease (Hilts, 1990). The pregnancy will never come to term. The embryo may spontaneously abort, or the embryo and placenta will continue to expand until they rupture the fallopian tube. Salpingectomy (removal of the tube) and abortion of the conceptus may be necessary to save the mother's life.

Toxemia and Preeclampsia **Toxemia,** which may appear in the 20th to 24th week of pregnancy, is characterized by high blood pressure and edema. It can generally be treated through nutritional means. If untreated, toxemia can develop into preeclampsia after the 24th week.

Preeclampsia is characterized by increasingly high blood pressure. Toxemia and preeclampsia are also known as gestational edema-proteinuria-hypertension complex. If untreated, they can lead to eclampsia, maternal convulsions that pose a serious threat to mother and child. Eclampsia is not common; it is prevented by keeping the blood pressure down through diet, rest, and sometimes medication. It is important for a pregnant woman to have her blood pressure checked regularly.

Low Birth Weight Prematurity, or **low birth weight (LBW),** is a major complication in the third trimester of pregnancy, affecting about 7% of newborns yearly (over 284,391 in 1989) in the United States (Pear, 1992). The most fundamental problem of prematurity is that many of the infant's vital

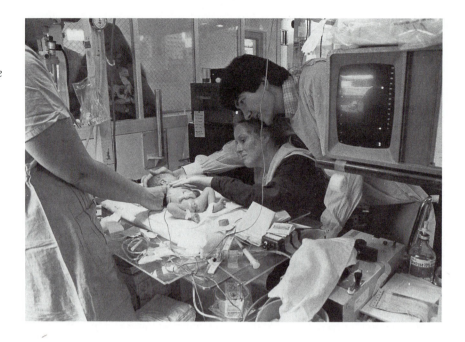

Low birth weight (prematurity) affects about 7% of newborns in the United States. Adequate prenatal care significantly reduces the risk of low birth weight.

organs are insufficiently developed. An LBW baby usually weighs less than 5.5 lb at birth. Most premature infants will grow normally, but many will experience disabilities. LBW infants are subject to various respiratory problems as well as infections. Feeding, too, is a problem because the infants may be too small to suck a breast or bottle, and their swallowing mechanisms may be too underdeveloped to permit them to drink. As premature infants get older, problems such as low intelligence, learning difficulties, poor hearing and vision, and physical awkwardness may become apparent.

Premature delivery is one of the greatest problems confronting obstetrics today. About half the cases are related to teenage pregnancy, smoking, poor nutrition, and poor health in the mother (Pear, 1992; Schneck, Sideras, Fox, & Dupuis, 1990); the causes of the other half are unknown. One study of LBW babies found a sixfold increase in the risk of low birth weight if the mother had financial problems during pregnancy (Binsacca et al., 1987). A 1987 study of 1382 women indicated that delaying childbearing until after age 35 does not increase the risk of delivering an LBW infant (Barkan & Bracken, 1987).

Prenatal care is extremely important as a means of preventing prematurity (Rush et al., 1988). One-third of all LBW births could be averted with adequate prenatal care (Scott, 1990a). We need to understand that if children's needs are not met today, we will all face the consequences of their deprivation tomorrow. The social and economic costs are bound to be very high.

Diagnosing Abnormalities of the Fetus

In addition to the desire to bear children, the desire to bear healthy children has encouraged the development of new diagnostic technologies. In cases where serious problems are suspected, these technologies may be quite helpful, but often it seems that they are used "simply because they're there."

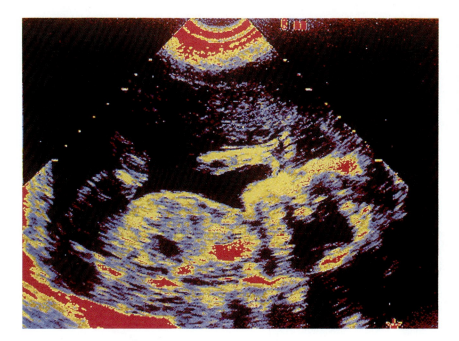

Ultrasound examinations use high-frequency sound waves to create a picture of the fetus in the uterus. The sound waves are transmitted through a quartz crystal; when they detect a change in the density, the sound waves bounce back to the crystal. The results are interpreted on a televisionlike screen; the picture is called a **sonogram.** Sonograms are used to determine fetal age and the location of the placenta; when used with amniocentesis, they help determine the fetus's position so that the needle may be inserted safely. Often, it is possible to determine the fetus's sex. More extensive ultrasound techniques can be used to gain further information if there is the possibility of a problem with fetal development. Although no problems in humans have been noted to result from ultrasound, high levels of ultrasound have created problems in animal fetuses.

In **amniocentesis,** amniotic fluid is withdrawn from the uterus with a long, thin needle inserted through the abdominal wall (the position of the fetus is determined by ultrasound). The fluid is then examined for evidence of possible birth defects such as Down syndrome, cystic fibrosis, Tay-Sachs disease, spina bifida, and conditions that are caused by chromosomal abnormalities. The sex of the fetus can also be determined. About 80–90% of amniocentesis tests are performed in cases of "advanced" maternal age, usually when the mother is over 35. The test is performed at about 16 weeks of pregnancy. Amniocentesis carries a slight risk (a ½–2% chance of fetal death, depending on how early in pregnancy the test is performed (Brandenburg, Jahoda, Pijpers, Reuss, Kleyer, & Wladmiroff, 1990; Hanson, Happ, Tennant, Hune, & Peterson, 1990).

An alternative to amniocentesis recently introduced in the United States is **chorionic villus sampling (CVS)** (Figure 13.5). This procedure involves removal through the abdomen (by needle) or through the cervix (by catheter) of tiny pieces of the membrane that encases the embryo; it can be

FIGURE 13.5 (a) Amniocentesis and (b) Chorionic Villus Sampling.

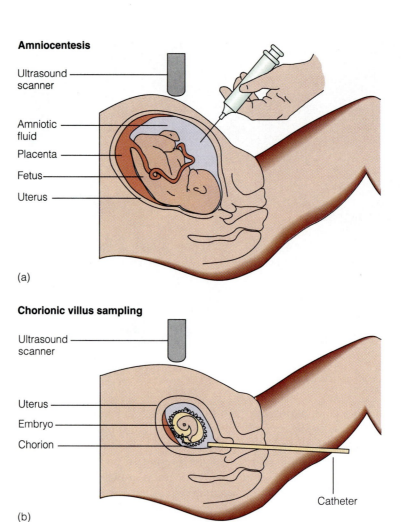

Amniocentesis

Ultrasound scanner

Amniotic fluid

Placenta

Fetus

Uterus

(a)

Chorionic villus sampling

Ultrasound scanner

Uterus

Embryo

Chorion

Catheter

(b)

performed between 9 and 11 weeks of pregnancy. There may be a somewhat greater-than-normal chance of miscarriage with CVS due to the possible introduction of infectious microorganisms at the time of the procedure (Baumann, Jovanovick, Gellert, & Rauskolb, 1991). A worldwide 1992 study of 80,000 women who had been diagnosed by CVS found no greater evidence of malformations in their children than in the general population ("Survey," 1992). An advantage of CVS is that it can yield results sooner than amniocentesis (Kolker, 1989).

Alpha-feto protein (AFP) screening is a test (or series of tests) performed on the mother's blood after 16 weeks of pregnancy. It reveals defects of the spine, spinal cord, skull, and brain, such as anencephaly and spina bifida. It is much simpler than amniocentesis but sometimes yields false positive results (Samuels & Samuels, 1986). If the results are positive, other tests, such as amniocentesis and ultrasound, will be performed to confirm or negate the AFP screening findings.

For approximately 95% of women who undergo prenatal testing, the results are negative. The results of amniocentesis and AFP screening can't be determined, however, until approximately 20 weeks of pregnancy; consequently, if the pregnancy is terminated through abortion at this stage, the process is likely to be physically and emotionally difficult. If a fetus is found to be defective, it may be carried to term, aborted, or, in rare but increasing instances, surgically treated while still in the womb (Kolata, 1990). Gene therapy, in which defective enzymes in the genes of embryos are replaced by normal ones, is considered a challenging frontier of reproductive medicine.

The 1988 National Commission to Prevent Infant Mortality stated that although "sophisticated technologies and great expense can save babies born at risk . . . , the lack of access to health care, the inability to pay for health care, poor nutrition, unsanitary living conditions, and unhealthy habits such as smoking, drinking and drug use all threatened unborn children" (cited in Armstrong & Feldman, 1990).

Pregnancy Loss

The loss of a child through miscarriage, stillbirth, or death during early infancy is often a devastating experience that has been largely ignored in our society. The statement, "You can always have another one," may be meant as consolation, but it is particularly chilling to the ears of a grieving mother. In the past few years, however, the medical community has begun to respond to the emotional needs of parents who have lost a pregnancy or an infant.

Spontaneous Abortion Spontaneous abortion, or miscarriage, is a powerful natural selective force toward bringing healthy babies into the world. About one out of four women is aware she has miscarried at least once (Beck, 1988). Studies indicate that at least 60% of all miscarriages are due to chromosomal abnormalities in the fetus (Adler, 1986). Furthermore, as many as 75% of all fertilized eggs do not mature into viable fetuses (Beck, 1988). A study found that 32% of implanting blastocysts miscarry (Wilcox et al., 1988). The first sign that a pregnant woman may miscarry is vaginal bleeding (spotting). If a woman's symptoms of pregnancy disappear and she develops pelvic cramps, she may be miscarrying; the fetus is usually expelled by uterine contractions. Most miscarriages occur between the 6th and 8th week of pregnancy (Welch & Herman, 1980). Evidence is increasing that certain occupations involving exposure to chemicals increase the likelihood of spontaneous abortions (Hemminki et al., 1983). Miscarriages may also occur from uterine abnormalities or hormonal levels that are insufficient for maintaining the uterine lining.

Infant Mortality The U.S. infant mortality rate, while at its lowest point ever, remains far higher than that of most of the developed world. The U.S. Public Health Service reported 8.9 deaths for every 1000 live births in 1991. Nevertheless, among developed nations, our country ranks 24th for low infant mortality (Pear, 1992). This means that 23 countries have *lower* infant mortality rates than the United States. In some inner-city areas, such as Detroit, Washington, DC, and parts of Oakland (California), the infant mortality rate approaches that of nonindustrialized countries, with more than 20 deaths per 1000 births (Petit, 1990). Of the more than 35,000 American babies less than 1 year old who die each year, most are victims of the poverty that often results from racial or ethnic discrimination. Up to one-third of these deaths could be prevented if mothers were given adequate health care (Scott, 1990b).

The infant mortality rate for African Americans is more than twice that for whites. Native Americans are also at high risk; for example, about one out of every 67 Navajo infants dies each year (Wilkerson, 1987). A recent study by the CDC found that mortality rates for many ethnic minorities have been severely underestimated as a result of the infants' being mistakenly classified as white ("Death Rates," 1992; Hahn, Mulinare, & Teutsch, 1992). According to this research, during the years 1983–1985, infant mortality rates were overreported for whites by 2.1% and underreported for all other groups: 8.9% for Latinos, 3.2% for blacks, 46.9% for Native Americans, 33.3% for Chinese Americans, 48.8% for Japanese Americans, and 78.7% for Filipino Americans.

In 1981, the federal government began to dramatically cut pregnancy and infant care programs such as WIC (Women, Infants, and Children) to fund its record-breaking military budget. Medicaid and Aid to Families with Dependent Children have also been cut, leaving many families without prenatal or postnatal care. On the state level also, the current trend is to cut back on medical and health care for low-income people. In countries such as France, Sweden, and Japan, for example, all pregnant women are entitled to free prenatal care. Free health care and immunizations are also provided for infants and young children. Working Swedish mothers are guaranteed one year of paid maternal leave, and French families in need are paid regular government allowances (Scott, 1990a). Although the United States has the resources to support its mothers and children in similar ways, such programs are few and far between.

Although many infants die of poverty-related conditions, others die from congenital problems (conditions appearing at birth) or from infectious diseases, accidents, or other causes. Sometimes the causes of death are not apparent; in 1985, one out of every 378 infant deaths was attributed to **sudden infant death syndrome (SIDS),** a perplexing phenomenon wherein an apparently healthy infant dies suddenly while sleeping. A recent study from Australia identified four factors that appear to increase the chances of SIDS (Ponsonby et al., 1993). These are a soft, fluffy mattress, wrapping the baby up in a blanket, the baby having a cold or other minor illness, and a room heated to over 57° Fahrenheit.

Coping with Loss The depth of shock and grief felt by many who lose an infant before or during birth is sometimes difficult to understand for those who have not had a similar experience. What they may not realize is that most women form a deep attachment to their children even before birth. At first, the attachment may be a "fantasy image of [the] future child" (Friedman & Gradstein, 1982). During the course of the pregnancy, the mother forms an actual acquaintance with her infant through the physical sensations she feels within her. Thus, the death of the fetus can also represent the death of a dream and of a hope for the future. This loss must be acknowledged and felt before psychological healing can take place (Panuthos & Romeo, 1984).

Women (and sometimes their partners) who must face the loss of a pregnancy or a young infant generally experience similar stages in their grieving process. The feelings that are experienced are influenced by many factors: supportiveness of the partner and other family members, the reaction of social contacts, life circumstances at the time of the loss, circumstances of the loss itself, whether other losses have been experienced, the prognosis for future childbearing, and the woman's unique personality (Friedman & Gradstein, 1982). Physical exhaustion and, in the case of miscarriage, hormone imbalance often compound the emotional stress of the grieving mother. The initial stage of grief is often one of shocked disbelief and numbness. This stage gives way to sadness, spells of crying, preoccupation with the loss, and perhaps loss of interest in the rest of the world. Emotional pain may be accompanied by physical sensations and symptoms, such as tightness in the chest or stomach, sleeplessness, and loss of appetite. It is not unusual for parents to feel guilty, as if they had somehow caused the loss, although this is rarely the case. Anger (toward the physician, perhaps, or God) is also a common emotion.

Experiencing the pain of loss is part of the healing process. This process takes time—months, a year, perhaps more for some. Support groups or counseling are often helpful, especially if healing does not seem to be progressing—if, for example, depression and physical symptoms don't appear to be diminishing. Keeping active is another way to deal with the pain of loss, as long as it isn't a way to avoid facing feelings. Projects, temporary or part-time work, or travel (for those who can afford it) can be ways of renewing energy and interest in life. Planning the next pregnancy may be curative, too, keeping in mind that the body and spirit need some time to heal. It is important to have a physician's input before proceeding with another pregnancy; specific considerations may need to be discussed, such as a genetic condition that may be passed to the child, or a physiological problem of the mother. If future pregnancies are ruled out, the parents need to take stock of their priorities and consider other options that may be open to them, such as adoption. Counselors and support groups can be invaluable at this stage.

Dear Auntie will come with presents and will ask, "Where is our baby, sister?" And, Mother, you will tell her softly, "He is in the pupils of my eyes. He is in my bones and in my soul."
Rabindranath Tagore

INFERTILITY

Some couples experience the pain of loss when they plan to have a child and then discover that they cannot get pregnant. **Infertility** is broadly defined as the inability to conceive a child after trying for a year or more. Until recently, the problem of infertility attracted little public attention. In the last few years, however, numerous couples, many of whom have deferred pregnancy because of career plans or later marriages, have discovered that they are unable to conceive or that the woman is unable to carry the pregnancy to live birth. Still, a recent study by the National Center for Health Statistics showed that overall, the fertility rate for American women is not declining (Cimons, 1990; Faludi, 1991). In 1988, 8.4% of women age 15–44 had an "impaired ability" to have children. This means that one out of 12 or 13 American couples is involuntarily childless. The greatest increase in infertility is found among young couples in the 20- to 24-year-old bracket. Their infertility rate rose from 3.6% in 1965 to 10.6% in 1982. Infertility among young African American couples has risen even more dramatically; it is almost twice that of white couples (Faludi, 1991). Every year, well over 1 million American couples seek help for infertility.

Female Infertility

Most cases of infertility among women are due to physical factors. Hormones, stress, immunological factors, and environmental factors may also be involved.

Physical Causes The leading cause of female infertility is blocked fallopian tubes, generally the result of pelvic inflammatory disease (PID), an infection of the fallopian tubes or uterus that is usually the result of a sexually transmitted disease. It can be caused by *gonococcus, chlamydia,* or several other organisms. About 1.7 million cases of PID were treated in 1986; doctors estimate that about half of the cases go untreated because PID is often symptomless, especially in the early stages (Hilts, 1990; Mueller, Luz-Jimenez, Daling, Moore, McKnight, & Weiss, 1992). Generally, only the woman with PID seeks treatment, and the man from whom she contracted the STD that caused it may continue to pass it on (Hilts, 1990). Surgery, including laser surgery, may restore fertility if the damage has not progressed too far. Septic abortions (where bacteria have been introduced), abdominal surgery, and certain types of older IUDs can also cause infections that lead to PID. (See Chapter 16 for information on prevention and treatment of sexually transmitted diseases.)

The second leading cause of infertility in women is endometriosis; it is sometimes called the "career woman's disease" because it is most prevalent in women age 30 and over, many of whom have postponed childbirth. In this disease, uterine tissue grows outside the uterus, often appearing on the ovaries, in the fallopian tubes (where it may also block the tubes), and in the abdominal cavity. In its most severe form it may cause painful menstruation and intercourse, but most women with endometriosis are unaware that they have it. Hormone therapy and sometimes surgery are used for treatment.

In addition, benign growths such as fibroids and polyps on the uterus, ovaries, or fallopian tubes may also affect a woman's fertility. Surgery can restore fertility in many of these cases.

Hormonal and Other Psychological Causes In addition to physical causes, there may be hormonal reasons for infertility. The pituitary gland may fail to produce sufficient hormones (follicle-stimulating hormone, or FSH, and luteinizing hormone, or LH) to stimulate ovulation, or it may release them at the wrong time. Stress, which may be increased by the anxiety of trying to achieve a pregnancy, may also contribute to lowered fertility (Menning, 1988). Occasionally, immunological causes may be present, the most important of which is the production of sperm antibodies by the woman. For an unknown reason, a woman may be allergic to her partner's sperm, and her immune system will produce antibodies to destroy them.

Environmental Factors Toxic chemicals or exposure to radiation therapy threaten a woman's reproductive capacity. Smoking appears to reduce fertility in women (Baird & Wilcox, 1985; Laurent, Thompson, Addy, Garrison, & Moore, 1992). Evidence indicates that the daughters of mothers who took diethylstilbestrol (DES), a drug once thought to increase fertility and reduce the risk of miscarriage, have a significantly higher infertility rate, although studies remain somewhat contradictory (Berger & Goldstein, 1984).

Nature also plays a part. Beginning around age 30, a woman's fertility naturally begins to decline. By age 35, about one-fourth of women are infertile (Carroll, 1990).

Male Infertility

The primary causes of male infertility are low sperm count, lack of sperm motility, and blocked passageways. Some studies show that men's sperm counts have dropped by as much as 50% over the last 30 years (Andrews, 1984; Faludi, 1991).

As with women, environmental factors may contribute to men's infertility. Increasing evidence suggests that toxic substances, such as lead or chemicals found in some solvents and herbicides, are responsible for decreased sperm counts (Andrews, 1984). Smoking may produce reduced sperm counts or abnormal sperm (Evans et al., 1981). Prescription drugs such as cimetidine (Tagamet, for ulcers), prednisone (a corticosteroid that reduces tissue inflammation), or some medications for urinary tract infections have also been shown to affect the number of sperm that a man produces (Andrews, 1984).

Large doses of marijuana cause decreased sperm counts and suppression of certain reproductive hormones. These effects are apparently reversed when marijuana smoking stops (Ehrenkranz & Hembree, 1986). Men are more at risk than women from environmental factors because they are constantly producing new sperm cells; for the same reason, men may also recover faster once the affecting factor has been removed (Menning, 1988).

Sons of mothers who took DES may have increased sperm abnormalities and fertility problems (Retik & Bauer, 1984). Too much heat may temporarily reduce a man's sperm count (the male half of a couple trying to conceive may want to stay out of the hot tub for a while). A fairly common problem is the presence of a varicose vein called a **varicocele** above the testicle. Because it impairs circulation to the testicle, the varicocele causes an elevated scrotal temperature and thus interferes in sperm development. The varicocele may be surgically removed, but unless the man has a fairly good sperm count to begin with, his fertility may not improve.

Emotional Responses to Infertility

By the time a couple seeks medical advice about their fertility problems, they may have already experienced a crisis in confronting the possibility of not being able to become biological parents. Many such couples feel they have lost control over a major area of their lives (Golombok, 1992; Olshansky, 1992). A number of studies suggest that women generally are more intensely affected than men (Andrews, Abbey, & Halman, 1991; Brand, 1989; McEwan et al., 1987; Wright, Duchesne, Sabourin, Bissonnette, Benoit, & Girard, 1991). After seeking help, childless couples typically go through three phases, according to Miriam Mazor (1979; also see Mazor & Simons, 1984):

1. The first phase revolves around the injury to the self implicit in the situation. Patients are preoccupied with the infertility study and with formulating theories about why it is happening to them, what they have done wrong, why they are so defective and bad that they are denied something the rest of the world takes for granted.

2. The second phase occurs when treatment is unsuccessful; it involves mourning the loss of the children the partner will never bear, and an intense examination of what parenthood means to them as individuals, as a couple, and as members of families and of society.

3. Finally, in the third phase, they must come to terms with the outcome of the study: they must make some kind of decision about their future, whether to pursue plans for adoption (or for donor insemination or surrogacy) or to adjust to childlessness and go on with life.

Infertility Treatment

Almost without exception, fertility problems are physical, not emotional, despite myths to the contrary, which often prevent infertile couples from seeking medical treatment. The two most popular myths are that anxiety over becoming pregnant leads to infertility, and that if an infertile couple adopts a child, the couple will then be able to conceive on their own (Kolata, 1979). Neither has any basis in medical fact, although it is true that some presumably infertile couples have conceived following an adoption. (This does not mean, however, that one should adopt a child to remedy infertility.) Approximately 10% of infertility cases are unexplained. In some of these cases, fertility is restored for no discernible reason; in others, the infertility remains a mystery (Jones, 1989). About 60% of couples with serious infertility problems will eventually achieve a pregnancy (Lord, 1987).

Couples undergoing treatment for infertility often undergo periods of depression and anxiety; they may have feelings of inadequacy, inferiority, or loss of control over their lives (Olshansky, 1992). Fertility specialists and other health-care providers can help alleviate such stress by increasing their patients' sense of control. This is done by such means as listening; offering encouragement; explaining the risks, costs, and success rates in detail; and by allowing the patients to make informed decisions about tests and procedures (Abbey, Halman, & Andrews, 1992). It has been suggested that those who are having difficulty conceiving for reasons as yet unexplained be referred to as "subfertile" instead of "infertile" and that their condition not be thought of as permanent (Marrero & Ory, 1991). (See Golombok, 1992, for a review of the literature on the psychological aspects of infertility.)

The techniques and technologies developed to achieve conception include fertility drugs, intrauterine insemination, and the establishment of sperm banks, in vitro fertilization (including embryo freezing), surrogate motherhood, and embryo transplants.

Medical Intervention In cases where infertility is a result of impaired ovulatory function in women, it may be able to be remedied with medication. Treatment may include hormones that stimulate the ovarian follicles or regulate the menstrual cycle (Toback, 1992). Hormone therapy may be used alone or in combination with the techniques discussed below. About 10–20% of the pregnancies achieved with the help of "fertility drugs" result in multiple births as the result of more than one egg being released by the ovary (Rosenthal, 1992). Multiple births pose higher risks to both mothers and infants. Twins are about ten times more likely than babies born alone to have very low birth weights (3.3 lb or less); triplets are over 30 times more likely to have very low birth weights and three times more likely to have severe disabilities than infants born alone (Dr. Barbara Luke, cited in Rosenthal, 1992).

Current medical research is focusing increasingly on "male factor infertility." Approaches for treating men include new methods of sperm evaluation and processing, and the use of medication to improve sperm velocity (Go, 1992; Meacham & Lipshultz, 1991; Ohninger & Alexander, 1991).

Intrauterine Insemination When childlessness is the result of male infertility (or low fertility) or a genetically transmitted disorder carried by the male, couples may try **intrauterine insemination (IUI),** also known as **artificial insemination (AI).** Single women who want children but who have not found an appropriate partner or who wish to avoid emotional entanglements have also made use of this technique, as have lesbian couples. The American Fertility Society estimates that there are about 30,000 births a year from intrauterine insemination (Kantrowitz & Kaplan, 1990).

During ovulation, semen is deposited by syringe near the cervical opening. The semen may come from the partner; if he has a low sperm count, several collections of semen may be taken and frozen, then collectively deposited in the woman's vagina, improving the odds of conception. If the partner had a vasectomy earlier, he may have had the semen frozen and stored in a sperm bank. If the man is sterile or has a genetically transferable disorder, **therapeutic donor insemination (TDI),** also known as artificial insemination by donor (AID), may be used. Anonymous donors—often medical students—are paid nominal amounts for their deposits of semen. Intrauterine insemination tends to produce males rather than females; in the general population, about 51% of the children born are male, but this figure reaches about 60% when conception is achieved artificially. Intrauterine insemination has a success rate of about 60% for infertile couples.

Most doctors inseminate women at least twice during the preovulatory phase of their menstrual cycle. On average, women who become pregnant have received inseminations over a period of 2–4 months (Curie-Cohen, 1979; Scott, Mortimer, Taylor, Leader, & Pattinson, 1990).

Some lesbians, especially those in committed relationships, are choosing to create families through artificial insemination. To date, there are no reliable data on the number of such births, but anecdotal information indicates that it is in the thousands. There are many questions raised when a lesbian couple contemplates having a baby in this way: Who will be the birth mother? What will the relationship of the other mother be? Will the donor be known or unknown? If known, will the child have a relationship with him? Will the child have a relationship with the donor's parents? Which, if any, of the child's grandparents will have a relationship with him or her? Will there be a legal contract between the parenting parties? There are few precedents to learn from or role models to follow in these cases (Pies, 1987).

Another issue that such couples have to face is that the nonbiological parent generally has no legal tie to the child (de la Madrid, 1991). Furthermore, society may not recognize her as a "real" parent, since children are expected to have only one real mother and one real father.

The practices of fertility clinics and sperm banks vary widely with respect to medical and genetic screening and the number of times a particular donor may be used. In a study by the Congressional Office of Technology Assessment in 1988, more than half the physicians surveyed said they did not screen donors for HIV. The commercial sperm banks surveyed did screen for HIV, however, as well as for most other sexually transmitted diseases (Gaines, 1990). There has been one reported case in the United States of a woman contracting HIV through donated semen (Chiasson, Stoneburner, & Joseph, 1990). The American Fertility Society (1992) has issued guidelines for screening semen donors for HIV. The Society has concluded that

> under present circumstances the use of fresh semen for donor insemination is no longer warranted and that all frozen specimens should be quarantined for 180 days and the donor retested and found to be seronegative for HIV before the specimen is released.

Although the viability of sperm is reduced by freezing, new techniques of cryopreservation ("superfreezing") minimize the deleterious effects (Shanis, Check, & Baker, 1989). Recent studies show that TDI with frozen semen can have a success rate comparable to that with fresh semen (Byrd, Bradshaw, Carr, Edman, Odom, & Ackerman, 1990; Scott et al., 1990).

In Vitro Fertilization and Embryo Transfer **In vitro fertilization (IVF)** entails combining sperm and oocyte in a laboratory dish and subsequently implanting the blastocyst, or pre-embryo, into the uterus of the mother or a surrogate (Figure 13.6). To help increase the chances of pregnancy, several oocytes are generally collected, fertilized, and implanted. The mother takes hormones to regulate her menstrual cycle so that the uterus will be prepared for the fertilized ovum. Sometimes the blastocysts are frozen and stored, to be implanted at a later date. The egg can come from the mother or from a donor. If it is a donor oocyte, the donor may be artificially inseminated with the father's sperm, and the embryo removed from the donor and transplanted in the mother-to-be's uterus. More commonly, donor oocytes are "harvested" from the donor's ovary, which has been hormonally stimulated to produce 12–18 eggs instead of the usual one. This procedure is done by inserting a 16-inch needle into the donor's ovary by way of the vagina and drawing out the egg cells, which are then mixed with the father's sperm. In two days, three or four blastocysts are implanted in the mother's uterus. Women who give their oocytes in "donor egg programs" may receive up to $2500, according to guidelines set by the American Fertility Society (Rafferty, 1992a, 1992b).

The first birth achieved through IVF occurred in 1978 in England. Thousands of successful pregnancies from this procedure have since come to term in the United States, Australia, the Netherlands, and several other countries. These procedures are all quite costly and must usually be repeated a number of times before a viable pregnancy results. Varying success rates—from 12% to about 20%—have been reported (Cowan, 1992; Jones, 1989; Yulsman, 1990). The number of IVF births is increasing yearly. In 1990,

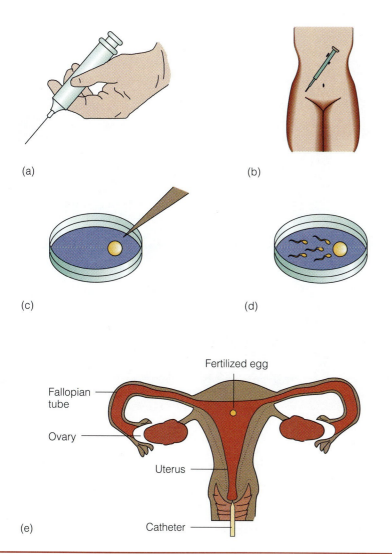

(a)

(b)

(c)

(d)

Fertilized egg

Fallopian
tube

Ovary

Uterus

Catheter

(e)

FIGURE 13.6 In Vitro Fertilization. (a) The woman is given hormone injections to stimulate oocyte production. Additional hormones (HCG) are given to stimulate ovulation and to prepare the uterus to receive the fertilized ovum. (b) The follicles are viewed through a laparoscope inserted through an incison at the navel. The oocytes are retrieved by being drawn into a long, hollow needle. (The ovary may also be viewed and the oocytes extracted through the vagina.) (c) Each egg cell is placed in a petri dish containing a culture that is chemically similar to the uterine environment. (d) Sperm are added. (e) Two days later, the fertilized ova (usually no more than three) are injected into the uterus.

there were 2345 live deliveries as a result of IVF (American Fertility Society, 1990). This figure does not represent the actual number of babies, as there is a high rate of multiple births (twins or triplets) with IVF. One study found 32% of IVF pregnancies to be multiple; the authors recommended that the number of embryos transferred be limited to a maximum of three in order to reduce the health risks to mother and fetuses (Bollen, Camus, Staessen, Tournaye, Devroey, & Van Steirteghem, 1991).

GIFT and ZIFT Another fertilization technique, **gamete intrafallopian transfer (GIFT),** may be recommended for couples who have no known reason for their infertility. In this process, sperm and eggs are collected from the parents and deposited together in the fallopian tube. In 1988, 892 live GIFT babies were delivered in the U.S., including 159 sets of twins, 34 sets of triplets, 3 sets of quadruplets, and 1 set of quintuplets (Perlman, 1990).

When in vitro procedures are used to combat infertility, there is about a one in three chance of multiple birth.

In **zygote intrafallopian transfer (ZIFT),** eggs and sperm are united in a petri dish and then transferred immediately to the fallopian tube to begin cell division. In 1988, there were 98 ZIFT babies, representing a success rate of about 20% (Perlman, 1990). As with IVF, both GIFT and ZIFT carry an increased risk of multiple pregnancy (Bollen et al., 1991).

Direct Sperm Injection A revolutionary new method of fertilization, developed by a Belgian physician, involves the direct injection of a single sperm into an oocyte in a laboratory dish (Kolata, 1993). As in IVF, the blastocyst is then implanted in the mother. It was previously believed that such a technique would not work because it bypasses both the capacitation of the sperm and the softening of the oocyte's outer layers (which requires the presence of several hundred sperm). As of August 1993, 300 pregnancies had been produced by this method and 100 babies had been born. (Most of the other pregnancies were still in progress.) Direct sperm injection holds great promise for many men who have low sperm counts or large numbers of abnormal sperm.

Surrogate Motherhood

The idea of **surrogate motherhood,** in which one woman bears a child for another, is not new. In the Old Testament (Genesis 16:1–15), Abraham's wife Sarah, finding herself unable to conceive, arranged for her husband to impregnate the servant Hagar. These days, the procedures are considerably more complex, and the issues are definitely cloudier. Some people question the motives of surrogate mothers. There have been cases of women having babies for their friends or even for their relatives. In 1991, a South Dakota woman became the first American "surrogate granny" when she was implanted with the fertilized ova of her daughter, who had been born without a uterus (Plummer & Nelson, 1991). Some women simply extend this kind of altruism to women they don't know. A study of 125 surrogate candidates found their major motivations to be money (they are usually paid $10,000–$25,000 or more), enjoying being pregnant, and unreconciled birth traumas, such as abortion or relinquishing a child for adoption (Parker, 1983).

Well-publicized court battles involving surrogacy point to the need for some kind of regulation. In the celebrated "Baby M" case, after numerous legal twists and turns, the New Jersey Supreme Court ruled in 1988 that contracts involving surrogate motherhood in exchange for money were illegal. It also ruled that a woman could volunteer to become a surrogate as long as no money was paid and she was allowed to revoke her decision to give up the child. "We . . . restore the surrogate as mother of the child. She is not only the natural mother, but also the legal mother," the court wrote (cited in Hanley, 1988). The baby in question was allowed to remain in the custody of her biological father and his wife, a situation previously determined to be in the child's best interests. A lower court subsequently awarded the surrogate mother 6 hours a week of unsupervised visitation with the child.

Although many states have laws prohibiting women from taking payment in exchange for giving a child up for adoption, most have not as yet enacted legislation specifically relating to surrogacy. Exceptions are Nevada, which has legitimized surrogacy contracts involving payment, and Arkansas, which specifies that the couple who contract with the surrogate are the legal parents. Several other states have declared such contracts to be unenforceable, while at least one state is considering making surrogacy for pay a felony (Budiansky, 1988). Proposed legislation in other states would require all parties to undergo counseling, and the surrogate and biological father to be screened for genetic and sexually transmitted diseases (Donovan, 1986). (See Andrews, 1984, for guidelines on choosing surrogacy.)

In the United States, there are thought to be several hundred births to surrogate mothers each year (Andrews, 1984; Woodward, 1987). A number of new, privately run agencies have been created to match surrogates and couples, highlighting the commercial potential of surrogate motherhood.

Modern technology has made possible numerous procedures to assist human reproduction. New technologies have raised new ethical issues, however, which are discussed in Perspective 1.

GIVING BIRTH

Throughout pregnancy, numerous physiological changes occur in order to prepare the woman's body for childbirth, or **parturition.** Hormones secreted by the placenta regulate the growth of the fetus, stimulate maturation of the breasts for lactation, and ready the uterus and other parts of the body for labor. During the later months of pregnancy, the placenta produces the hor-

THE ETHICS OF REPRODUCTIVE TECHNOLOGY

The desire to have healthy, happy, beautiful children is understandable, basic, and human. But in the face of today's reproductive technology, many of us may have to search our souls for the answers to a number of ethical questions. When faced with infertility, the possibility of birth defects, or the likelihood of a difficult labor, we need to weigh the possible benefits of a given technique against the costs and risks involved. What are your feelings about the following reproductive issues?

- *Fetal diagnosis.* If you (or your partner) were pregnant, would you choose to have ultrasound? Should ultrasound be used routinely in all pregnancies or only in selected cases, such as when the mother is over 35 or there is a suspected problem? When you would consider amniocentesis appropriate? Should all fetuses be electronically monitored during birth (entailing the attachment of electrodes to the infant's scalp in the uterus), or should this technique be reserved for problem births? Would you want your child to be routinely monitored in this way?

- *Cesarean section.* How would you determine that C-section was necessary for yourself or your partner? Should vaginal delivery be attempted first? What if it was a breech birth? What if you (or your partner) had had a previous C-section?

- *Artificial insemination and in vitro fertilization.* Should these techniques be available to anyone who wants them? Under what circumstances, if any, would you use these techniques? What are the rights of all the parties involved: parents, donors, physicians, child? What are the embryo's or fetus's rights? For example, does a frozen embryo have the "right to life" if its parents die before it is implanted in a surrogate? Can you envision a situation in which you would want to donate ova or sperm? What if your partner wanted to?

- *Surrogate motherhood.* Should a woman be allowed to "carry" a pregnancy for a couple using father-donated sperm? Does it matter if profit is involved? Should a contract involving surrogate motherhood be legally binding? Whose rights should take precedence, those of the surrogate (who is the biologi-

mone **relaxin,** which increases flexibility in the ligaments and joints of the pelvic area. In the last trimester, most women occasionally feel uterine contractions that are strong but generally not painful. These are called **Braxton Hicks contractions.** They exercise the uterus, preparing it for labor.

Labor and Delivery

During labor, contractions begin the **effacement** (thinning) and **dilation** (opening up) of the cervix. It is difficult to say exactly when labor starts, which helps explain the great differences reported in lengths of labor for different women. When the uterine contractions become regular, true labor begins. During these contractions, the lengthwise muscles of the uterus involuntarily pull open the circular muscles around the cervix. This process generally takes 2–36 hours. Its duration depends on the size of the baby, the baby's position in the uterus, the size of the mother's pelvis, and the

cal mother) or of the couple (which includes the biological father)? What are the child's rights? Who decides? Can you think of a circumstance when you might wish to have the services of a surrogate mother? Could you be a surrogate or accept your partner being one?

For all the preceding techniques, consider the following questions: Who is profiting (scientists, physicians, business people, donors, parents, children)? Who is bearing the greatest risks? How great are the costs—monetary and psychological—and who is paying them? What are the long-range goals of this technology? Are we "playing God"? How might this technology be abused? Are there certain techniques you think should be outlawed?

- *Abortion.* When do you think human life begins? Do we ever have the right to take human life? Under what conditions, if any, should abortion be permitted? Whenever the pregnant woman requests it? If there is a serious birth defect? If there is a minor birth defect (such as a shortened limb)? If

the fetus is the "wrong" sex? If rape or incest led to the pregnancy? Under what conditions, if any, would you have an abortion or want your partner to have one? If you had an unmarried pregnant teenage daughter, would you encourage her to have one?

- *Tissue donation.* Is it appropriate to use the tissues or organs of human corpses for medical purposes? Is it appropriate to use aborted fetuses for tissue donation? For research?

- *Life and death.* Is prolonging the life of an infant always the most humane choice? What if it also prolongs suffering? Should life be prolonged whenever possible, at all costs? Who decides?

- *Fertility and fulfillment.* Do you think your reproductive values and feelings about your own fertility (or lack of it) are congruent with reality, given the world's population problems? For you, are there viable alternatives to conceiving or bearing a child? What are they? Would adoption be one alternative? Why?

condition of the uterus. The length of labor tends to shorten after the first birth experience.

Labor can generally be divided into three stages. The first stage is usually the longest, lasting 4–16 hours. An early sign of first-stage labor is the expulsion of a plug of slightly bloody mucus that has blocked the opening of the cervix during pregnancy. At the same time or later on, there is a second fluid discharge from the vagina. This discharge, referred to as the "breaking of the waters," is the amniotic fluid, which comes from the ruptured amnion. (Because the baby is subject to infection after the protective membrane breaks, the woman should receive medical attention soon thereafter, if she has not already.)

The hormone **oxytocin** produced by the fetus, along with prostaglandins from the placenta, stimulates strong uterine contractions. At the end of the first stage of labor, which is called **transition,** the contractions come more quickly and are much more intense than in the early stages of labor. Many

[Power] sounds in our bodies. Contractions creep up, seizing ever stronger until they make a mockery of all the work we have done on our own. Birth can silence our ego and, for the moment, we feel ourselves overcome by a larger life pounding through our own.

Penny Armstrong and
Sheryl Feldman

During labor, uterine contractions cause the opening and thinning of the cervix. The length of labor varies from woman to woman and birth to birth; it is usually between 4 and 16 hours. During transition, the end of first-stage labor, contractions are the most intense.

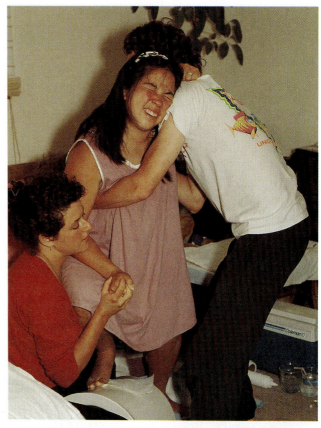

The second stage of labor is the delivery of the infant. In this photograph, the newborn exhibits the "startle reflex" at the unexpected sensations of the world outside the womb.

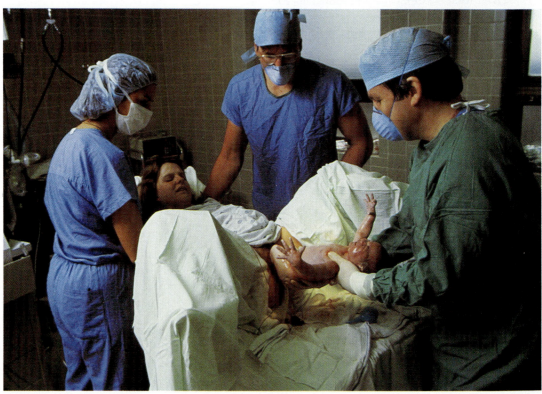

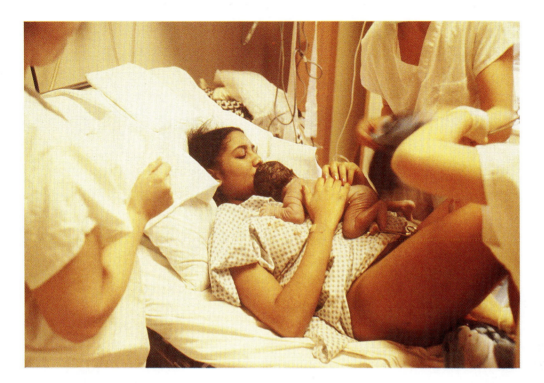

Mother and baby rest together following delivery. The umbilical cord will be cut and tied off when it stops pulsating.

women report time as the most difficult part of labor. During the last part of first-stage labor, the baby's head enters the birth canal. This marks the shift from dilation of the cervix to expulsion of the infant. The cervical opening is now almost fully dilated (about 10 cm [4 in] in diameter), but the baby is not yet completely in position to be pushed out. Some women feel despair, isolation, and anger at this point. Many appear to lose faith in those assisting in the birth. A woman may find that management of the contractions seems beyond her control; she may be afraid that something is wrong. At this time, she needs the full support and understanding of her helpers. Transition is usually, though not always, brief (half an hour to one hour).

Second-stage labor begins when the baby's head moves into the birth canal and ends when the baby is born. During this time, many women experience a great force in their bodies. Some women find this the most difficult part of labor. Others find that the contractions and bearing down bring a sense of euphoria. One father describes his wife's second-stage labor (Jones, 1986):

> When the urge to bear down swept through her, Jan felt as if she were one with all existence and connected with the vast primordial power that summons life forth from its watery depths.

The baby is usually born gradually. With each of the final few contractions, a new part of the infant emerges (Figure 13.7). The baby may even cry before he or she is completely born, especially if the mother did not have medication. Sheila Kitzinger (1985) describes the moment of birth as a sexual event:

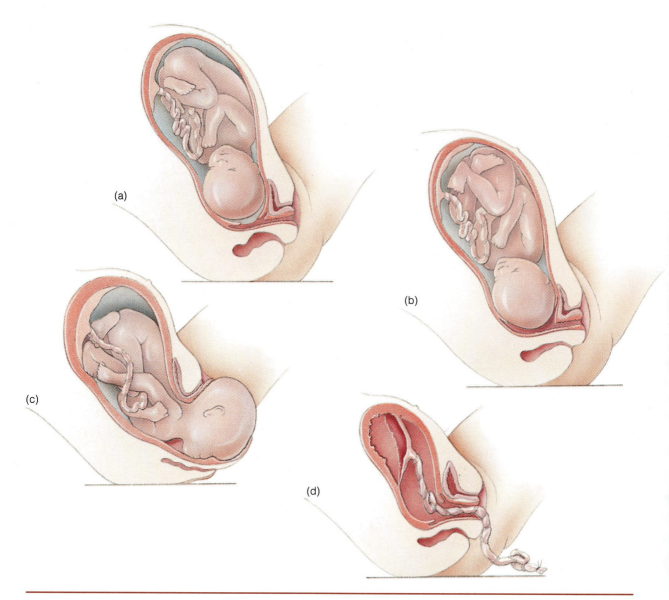

FIGURE 13.7 The Birth Process: Labor and Delivery. (a) First stage: cervix beginning to dilate. (b) Transition: cervix dilated. (c) Second stage: delivery of the infant. (d) Third stage: delivery of the placenta.

The whole body slips out in a rush of warm flesh, a fountain of water, a peak of overwhelming surprise and the little body is against her skin, kicking against her thighs or swimming up over her belly. She reaches out to hold her baby, firm, solid, with bright, bright eyes. A peak sexual experience, the birth passion, becomes the welcoming of a new person into life.

The baby will still be attached to the umbilical cord connected to the mother, which is not cut until it stops pulsating. He or she will appear wet, often covered by a milky substance called **vernix.** The head may look oddly shaped at first, from the molding of the soft plates of bone during birth. This shape is temporary, and the baby's head usually achieves a normal appearance within 24 hours.

After the baby has been delivered, the uterus will continue to contract, expelling the placenta, also called the afterbirth, and completing the third and final stage of labor. The doctor or midwife will examine the placenta to make sure it is whole. If the practitioner has any doubt that the entire placenta has been expelled, he or she may examine the uterus to make sure no parts of the placenta remain to cause adhesions or hemorrhage. Immediately following birth, the attendants assess the physical condition of the **neonate,** or newborn. Heart rate, respiration, color, reflexes, and muscle tone are individually rated with a score of 0 to 2. The total, called an **Apgar score,** will be at least 8 if the child is healthy. For a few days following labor (especially if it is a second or subsequent birth), the mother will probably feel strong contractions as the uterus begins to return to its prebirth size and shape. This process, called **involution,** takes about 6 weeks. She will also have a bloody discharge called **lochia,** which continues for several weeks.

Following birth, if the baby has not been drugged by anesthetics administered to the mother, he or she will probably be alert and ready to nurse. Breast-feeding, discussed later, provides benefits for both mother and child. If the infant is a boy, the parents will need to decide about circumcision, the surgical removal of the foreskin of the penis (discussed later).

Choices in Childbirth

Women and couples planning the birth of a child have decisions to make in a variety of areas: place of birth, birth attendant(s), medications, preparedness classes, circumcision, breast-feeding—to name just a few. The "childbirth market" is beginning to respond to consumer concerns, so it's important for prospective consumers to fully understand their options. Perspective 2 provides questions to help prospective parents plan their birth experience.

Hospital Birth The impersonal, routine quality of hospital birth (and hospital care in general) is increasingly being questioned. As anthropologist Margaret Mead observed, hospital conditions have generally been designed not for the woman who is giving birth but "primarily to facilitate the ministrations of the obstetrician" (Mead, 1975). One woman described her initial feelings in the hospital (quoted in Leifer, 1990):

> When they put that tag around my wrist and put me into that hospital gown, I felt as if I had suddenly just become a number, a medical case. All of the excitement that I was feeling on the way over to the hospital began to fade away. It felt like I was waiting for an operation, not about to have my baby. I felt alone, totally alone, as if I had just become a body to be examined and not a real person.

Another woman was shocked at the impersonal treatment (quoted in Leifer, 1990):

> And then this resident gave me an internal [examination], and it was quite painful then. And I said: "Could you wait till the contraction is over?" And he said he had to do it now, and I was really upset because he didn't even say it nicely, he just said: "You'll have to get used to this, you'll have a lot of this before the baby comes."

All is beautiful
All is beautiful
All is beautiful, yes!
Now Mother Earth
And Father Sky
Join one another and meet
forever helpmates
All is beautiful
All is beautiful
All is beautiful, yes!
Now the night of darkness
And the dawn of light
Join one another and meet
forever helpmates
All is beautiful
All is beautiful
All is beautiful, yes!
Now the white corn
And the yellow corn
Join one another and meet
forever helpmates
All is beautiful
All is beautiful
All is beautiful, yes!
Life that never ends
Happiness of all things
Join one another and meet
Forever helpmates
All is beautiful
All is beautiful
All is beautiful, yes!
Navajo Night Chant

MAKING A BIRTH PLAN

Prospective parents must make many important decisions. The more informed they are, however, the better able they will be to decide what is right for them. If you were planning a birth, how would you answer the following questions?

1. Who will be the birth attendant—a physician, a nurse-midwife? Do you already have someone in mind? If not, what criteria are important to you in choosing a birth attendant? Have you considered hiring a labor assistant, or *doula*, a professional childbirth companion employed to guide the mother during labor?

2. Who will be present at the birth—the husband or partner? Other relatives or friends? Children? How will these people participate? Will they provide emotional support and encouragement? Will they provide practical help, such as "coaching" the mother, giving massages, fetching supplies, taking photographs or videos? Can these people be sensitive to the needs of the mother?

3. Where will the birth take place—in a hospital, a birth center, at home? If in a hospital, is there a choice of rooms?

4. What kind of environment will you create in terms of lighting, room furnishings, and sounds? Is there special music you would like to hear?

5. What kinds of medication, if any, do you feel comfortable with? Do you know what the options are for pain-reducing medications? What about hormones to speed up or slow down labor? How do you feel about having an IV inserted as a precaution, even if medication is not planned? If you should change your mind about medication part of the way through labor, how will you communicate this to your attendants?

6. What about fetal monitoring? Will there be machines attached to you or the baby? What types and degree of monitoring do you feel comfortable with?

7. What is your attendant's policy regarding food and drink during labor? What kinds of foods or drinks, such as ice cream, fruit, juices, or ice chips, do you think you (or your partner) might want to have?

8. What about freedom of movement during labor? Will you (or your partner) want the option of walking around during labor? Will there be a shower or bath available? Will the baby be delivered with the mother lying on her back with her feet in stirrups, or will she be free to choose her position, such as squatting or lying on her side?

9. Do you want a routine episiotomy? Under what conditions would it be acceptable?

10. What do you wish the role of instruments or other interventions, such as forceps or vacuum extraction, to be? Who will determine if and when they are necessary?

11. Under what conditions is a cesarean section acceptable? Who will decide?

12. Who will "catch" the baby as she or he is born? Who will cut the umbilical cord, and at what point will it be cut?

13. What will be done with the baby immediately after birth? Will he or she be with the mother or the father? Who will bathe and dress the baby? What kinds of tests will be done on the baby, and when? What other kinds of procedures, such as shots and medicated eye drops, will be given, and when?

14. Will the baby stay in the nursery, or is there rooming-in? Is there a visiting schedule?

15. How will the baby be fed—by breast or bottle? Will feeding be on a schedule or "on demand"? Is there someone with breast-feeding experience available to answer questions if necessary? Will the baby have a pacifier between feedings?

16. If the baby is a boy, will he be circumcised? When?

Some hospitals are responding to the need for a family-centered child-birth. Fathers and other relatives or close friends often participate today. Some hospitals permit rooming-in, in which the baby stays with the mother rather than in the nursery, or a modified form of rooming-in. Regulations vary as to when the father and other family members and friends are allowed to visit.

But the norm is still, all too often, the impersonal birth. During one of the most profound experiences of her life, a woman may have her baby among strangers to whom birth is merely "business as usual." There are likely to be bright lights, loud noises, and people coming and going, moving her, poking at her, and asking questions when she's in the middle of a contraction. She will probably be given a routine enema and have her pubic hair shaved, even though surgery is not anticipated. She and her unborn child are likely to be attached to various types of monitoring machines. Studies have shown that while fetal monitoring is helpful in high-risk cases, it is generally not helpful in normal (low-risk) situations. The baby's heart rate can usually be detected by a stethoscope held against the mother's abdomen.

Some form of anesthetic is administered during most hospital deliveries, as well as various hormones (to intensify the contractions and to shrink the uterus after delivery). The mother isn't the only recipient of the drugs, however; they go directly through the placenta to the baby, in whom they may reduce heart and respiration rates.

During delivery, the mother will probably be given an **episiotomy,** a surgical procedure that enlarges the vaginal opening by cutting through the perineum toward the anus. Although an episiotomy may be helpful if the infant is in distress, it is usually performed for the benefit of the obstetrician—to give him or her more control over the birth, and to speed up the delivery. Recent studies show that episiotomies are performed in about 80% of first vaginal births in hospitals (Hetherington, 1990; Klein et al., 1992); yet one midwife who has assisted at over 1200 births reports a rate of less than 1% (Armstrong & Feldman, 1990). A Canadian study of 703 uncomplicated births found no advantage to routine episiotomies; the disadvantages were pain and bleeding (Klein et al., 1992). The authors recommended that "liberal or routine use of episiotomy be abandoned."

The baby is usually delivered on a table, against the force of gravity. He or she may be pulled from the womb with a vacuum extractor (which has a small suction cup that fits onto the baby's head) or forceps. (In some cases of acute fetal distress, these instruments may be crucial in order to save the infant's life, but too often they are used by physicians as a substitute for patience and skill.) In most cultures, a woman gives birth while sitting in a birthing chair, kneeling or squatting. Until the present century, most American women used birthing chairs; the delivery table was instituted for the convenience of the physician. A few hospitals use a motorized birthing chair that can be raised, lowered, or tilted according to the physician's and the woman's needs. In about one-fourth of births in this country, the baby is not delivered vaginally but is surgically removed from the uterus.

Cesarean Section

Cesarean section, or C-section, is the removal of the fetus by an incision in the mother's abdominal and uterine walls. The first reported cesarean section performed on a living woman occurred in the seventeenth century, when a butcher cut open his wife's uterus to save her and

In the nineteenth century, the possibility of eliminating "pain and travail" created a new kind of prison for women—the prison of unconsciousness, of numbed sensations, or amnesia, and complete passivity.
Adrienne Rich

their child. In 1970, 5.5% of American births were done by cesarean section. Today, cesarean births account for about 24% of all births; more than 900,000 women have C-sections each year (U.S. Bureau of the Census, 1990). This represents more than a 400% increase in 20 years.

Although there is a decreased mortality rate for infants born by C-section, the mothers' mortality rate is higher. As with all major surgeries, there are possible complications, and recovery can be slow and difficult.

Hoping to reduce the alarming number of C-sections, the National Institutes of Health (NIH) have issued the following guidelines:

1. Because a woman has had a previous cesarean delivery does not mean that subsequent deliveries must be C-sections; whenever possible, women should be given the option of a vaginal birth.

2. Abnormal labor does not mean that a C-section is necessary. Sleep or medication may resolve the problems. Only after other measures have been tried should a physician perform a cesarean, unless the infant is clearly in danger.

3. Breech babies—those who enter the birth canal buttocks-first or feet-first—do not necessarily require C-sections. A physician's experience using his or her hands to deliver the baby vaginally is crucial.

If a woman does not want a C-section unless it is absolutely necessary, she should learn about her physician's attitude about and record on performing cesareans. It is noteworthy that the greatest number of cesareans are performed in the socioeconomic group of women with the lowest medical risk (Hursh & Summey, 1984). In a study of 245,854 births, the C-section rate for middle- and upper-income women was 22.9%, whereas for lower-income women it was 3.2% (Gould, Davey, & Stafford, 1989). Therefore, it is assumed that cesareans are often performed for reasons other than medical risk. Some of the reasons offered include threat of malpractice (although such suits are apparently rare for vaginal deliveries), lack of physician training in vaginal births, and "economic incentives" for the hospital and the physician (Cohen & Estner, 1983). A 1987 international study by the U.S. Department of Health and Human Services urged the medical community to consider the appropriateness of the continued rise in C-sections (Notzon, Placek, & Taffel, 1987).

Prepared Childbirth Increasingly, Americans are choosing among such childbirth alternatives as prepared childbirth, rooming-in, birthing centers, home births, and midwives. As the chief of obstetrics at a major hospital observed (quoted in Trafford, 1980):

> It's a major upheaval in medicine, and the conflict has tended to polarize the consumer and the caregiver. The basic problem is that we have changed obstetrics with the latest medical advances and not incorporated essentially humanistic considerations.

Prepared childbirth (or natural childbirth) was popularized by Grantly Dick-Read (1972) in the first edition of his book, *Childbirth Without Fear*, in the 1930s. Dick-Read observed that fear causes muscles to tense, which in turn increases pain and stress during childbirth. He taught both partners about childbirth and gave them physical exercises to ease muscle tension.

Encouraged by Dick-Read's ideas, women began to reject anesthetics during labor and delivery, and were consequently able to take a more active role in childbirth, as well as be more aware of the whole process.

In the 1950s, Fernand Lamaze (1956, 1970) developed a method of prepared childbirth based on knowledge of conditioned reflexes. Women learn to mentally separate the physical stimulus of uterine contractions from the conditioned response of pain. With the help of a partner, women use breathing and other exercises throughout labor and delivery. Although Lamaze did much to advance the cause of prepared childbirth, he has been criticized by other childbirth educators as too controlling or even "repressive," according to Armstrong and Feldman (1990). A woman does not give birth, they write, "by direction, as if it were a flight plan."

Prepared childbirth, then, is not so much a matter of controlling the birth process as of understanding it and having confidence in nature's plan. Michael Odent, who heads a remarkable maternity clinic in Pithiviers, France, believes strongly that laboring mothers should be allowed freedom to give birth in their own ways. In *Birth Reborn* (1984), he writes:

> We encourage women in labor to give in to the experience, to lose control, to forget all they have learned—all the cultural images, all the behavioral patterns. The less a woman has learned about the "right" way to have a child, the easier it will be for her.

Clinical studies consistently show better birth outcomes for mothers who have had prepared childbirth classes (Conway, 1980). Prepared mothers (who usually attend classes with the father or other partner) handle pain more successfully, use less medication and anesthesia, express greater satis-

Women can give birth by the action of their own bodies, as animals do. Women can enjoy the process of birth and add to their dignity by being educated to follow the example set by instinctive animals.

Robert A. Bradley, MD

faction with the childbirth process, and experience less postpartum depression than women undergoing routine hospital births (Hetherington, 1990).

Birthing Rooms and Centers Birth (or maternity) centers, institutions of long standing in England and other European countries (see Odent, 1984), now are being developed in the United States. In 1990, there were 132 free-standing birth centers in this country (Armstrong & Feldman, 1990). Although they vary in size, organization, and orientation, birth centers share the view that childbirth is a normal, healthy process that can be assisted by skilled practitioners (midwives or physicians) in a homelike setting. The mother (or couple) has considerable autonomy in deciding the conditions of birth: lighting, sounds, visitors, delivery position, and so on. Some of these centers can provide some kinds of emergency care; all have procedures for transfer to a hospital if necessary.

An extensive survey of 11,814 births in birth centers in 1988 concluded that "birth centers offer a safe and acceptable alternative to hospital confinement for selected pregnant women, particularly those who have previously had children, and that such care leads to relatively few cesarean sections" (Rooks, Weatherby, Ernst, Stapleton, Rosen, & Rosenfield, 1989). Another large study showed that free-standing birth centers are associated with "a low cesarean section rate, low neonatal mortality [or] no neonatal mortality" (Eakins, 1989). Some hospitals now have their own birthing centers (or rooms) that provide for labor and birth in a comfortable setting and allow the mother or couple considerable autonomy. Hospital practices vary widely, however; prospective parents should carefully determine their needs and thoroughly investigate their options.

Home Birth Home births have increased during the last two decades, although they still constitute a small fraction of total births, amounting to not quite 2%, according to available data. Home births tend to be safer than hospital births if they are supervised by midwives or physicians. This is, in part, the result of careful medical screening and planning that eliminate all but the lowest-risk pregnancies. A couple can create their own birth environment at home, and home births cost considerably less, usually at least one-third less, than hospital delivery. With the supervision of an experienced practitioner, parents have little to worry about. But if a woman is at risk, she is wiser to give birth in a hospital where medical equipment is readily available.

Midwifery The United States has an increasing number of certified nurse-midwives who are trained not only as registered nurses but also in obstetrical techniques. They are well qualified for routine deliveries and minor medical emergencies. They also often operate as part of a total medical team that includes a backup physician, if needed. Their fees are generally considerably less than a doctor's. Nurse-midwives usually participate in both hospital and home births, although this may vary according to hospital policy, state law, and the midwife's preference. (Massachusetts, Alabama, South Dakota, and Wisconsin bar nurse-midwives—although not necessarily lay midwives—from attending home births ["Massachusetts Midwife," 1987].)

Lay midwifery, in which the midwives are not formally trained by the

The Huichol people of Mexico traditionally practiced couvade. The father squatted in the rafters above the laboring mother. When the mother experienced a contraction, she would pull the ropes that had been attached to his scrotum, so that he could "share" the experience of childbirth.

medical establishment but by other experienced midwives, has also increased in popularity during the past two decades. Many satisfactory births with lay midwives in attendance have been reported, but extensive, reliable information is not available, owing to the "underground" nature of lay midwifery, which is often practiced outside of (and without the support of) the regular practice of medicine. Many midwives belong to organized groups; a number of these groups use some form of self-certification to ensure that high professional standards are maintained (Butter & Kay, 1990).

If a woman decides she wants to give birth with the aid of a midwife outside a hospital setting, she should have a thorough medical screening to make sure she or her infant will not be at risk during delivery. She should learn about the midwife's training and experience, what type of backup services the midwife has in the event of complications or emergencies, and how the midwife will handle a transfer to a hospital if it becomes necessary.

See Perspective 3 for a reevaluation of the role of medicine in childbirth.

The Question of Circumcision

In 1975, when about 93% of newborn boys were circumcised, the American Academy of Pediatrics and the American College of Obstetricians and

THE MEDICALIZATION OF CHILDBIRTH

The Past

Prior to the nineteenth century, childbirth was a female-centered event, taking place at home under the supervision of a skilled female midwife. The pregnant woman was surrounded by friends and relatives who shared their knowledge and experiences; the younger women in attendance learned first-hand what to expect when they themselves gave birth. After the birth, the new mother began "lying-in," a period of several days to several weeks. During her lying-in, friends, neighbors, and relatives cooked, took care of the other children, and tended to her wifely duties. At the end of her lying-in, the woman gave a "groaning party" for the women who had helped her. The groaning referred to both the groaning of labor and the groaning of the guests who ritualistically over-ate.

Childbirth, however, was not viewed as an especially joyful occasion, as it is today. Rather, it was seen as a time that revealed the power of God and nature over women. Through the pain of childbirth, women were reminded of God's curse on Eve for tempting Adam and eating the forbidden fruit: "In sorrow thou shalt bring forth children" (Genesis 3:16). And because women frequently died in childbirth, it was a time of foreboding. Anne Bradstreet (1612–1672) wrote "Before the Birth of One of Her Children" for her husband:

> How soon, my Dear, death may my steps attend,
> How soon't may be thy lot to lose thy friend,
> We both are ignorant, yet love bids me
> These farewell lines to recommend to thee,
> That when that knot's untied that made us one
> I may seem thine, who in effect am none.

Before the nineteenth century, most midwives were women. Then an important device, invented in the early seventeenth century, ultimately helped replace the female midwife with the male obstetrician. It was the forceps, a device looking like two enlarged spoons that could be inserted into the birth canal to draw out the fetus in a difficult delivery.

Until the invention of the forceps by Peter Chamberlen, fetuses that could not travel through the birth canal were killed and then dismembered with sharp hooks. Chamberlen, however, did not reveal his secret instrument to anyone; the forceps were kept a family secret for over a century. When he and his brothers had to assist a difficult delivery, they took from their carriage a massive dark chest, whose contents they revealed to no one. Upon entering the birthing room, they blindfolded the mother to prevent their secret from being discovered.

Eventually, the forceps became well known. Male midwives used them, but forceps were not used by female midwives. This may have been because of a tradition that associated males with instrumental interference, because surgeon guilds refused to permit midwives to use them, or because forceps were associated with the deadly hooks that destroyed fetuses. Whatever the reason, male midwives began using forceps not only for difficult deliveries but also to speed up labor, giving them a distinct advantage over female midwives.

When the earliest medical schools were established in the United States, they included midwifery as the first medical specialty. In the nineteenth century, medicine was neither an affluent nor a highly respected profession. To increase both status and income, physicians attempted to become more scientific. In doing so, they rejected female midwives as untrained and unscientific. A medical school education, however, did not necessarily give physicians much expertise. One obstetrician recalled his first delivery in 1850 (quoted in Wertz & Wertz, 1978):

> I was left alone with a poor Irish woman and one crony, to deliver her child . . . and I thought it necessary to call before me every circumstance I had learned from books—I must examine and I did. But whether it was head or breech, hand or foot, man or monkey that was defended from my uninstructed finger by the distended membranes, I was as uncomfort-

ably ignorant, with all my learning, as the fetus itself that was making all this fuss.

In 1847, to the horror if his colleagues, a physician administered ether to a woman in labor to ease her birthing pains. Physicians had feared that anesthesia would cause the labor contractions to stop. But the labor progressed normally despite the fact that the woman was unconscious. Women now had the possibility of giving birth without pain. Before, women had accepted birthing pains as part of the natural process.

When women began to ask for anesthetics during childbirth to relieve their pain, there was an outcry from the religious community: Painless childbirth was blasphemy against God. But after England's Queen Victoria gave birth under anesthetics, the religious opposition discreetly disappeared. The Bible was reinterpreted to make the use of anesthetics acceptable during labor. The acceptance of painless labor was crucial in moving childbirth from the home to the hospital. With the introduction of anesthetics, the nineteenth century was witnessing a new attitude toward pain, especially pain affecting women. "Victorian culture," wrote historians Richard and Dorothy Wertz (1978), "encouraged women to be more sensitive to pain than men and to express openly their aches and illnesses." Pain became subjectively perceived as something women were no longer capable of enduring.

In order to meet the demand for painless childbirth, hospitals expanded their facilities to meet women's new need for anesthetics. In doing so, however, birth moved from being a female-centered, natural process taking place in the home, to one dominated by male experts, requiring medical skill, and taking place in a hospital. This transformation was completed in less than 100 years. In 1900, only 5% of all births took place in hospitals; by 1981, over 95% of all births occurred in hospitals.

The Present

Hospital practices today reflect both the wisdom and the folly of this change. Although only 5–10% of births actually require medical procedures, we seem to assume that childbirth is an inherently dangerous process. In high-risk cases, of course, the advances of technology can and do save lives. But many questions remain: Why do women accept unnecessary, uncomfortable, demeaning, and even dangerous intervention in the birth process? Why do they tolerate a 24% cesarean rate, a 61% episiotomy rate, the almost universal administration of drugs, and the use of intrusive fetal monitoring—not to mention routine enemas and the shaving of pubic hair? Why do they allow their infant boys to have their penises surgically altered? Why do they accept, often without question, the physician's opinion over their own gut feelings?

Penny Armstrong and Sheryl Feldman (1990) suggest that society's increasing dependence on technology has hampered women's ability to view birth as a natural process for which they are naturally equipped. Women have allowed themselves to be persuaded that technology can do the job better than they can on their own. Society expects birth technology to deliver a "product"—a "perfect" baby—without understanding that nature has already equipped women to deliver that product without much outside interference in the physical process (although encouragement and emotional support are paramount). Sheila Kitzinger (1989) writes:

> It is not advances in medicine but improved conditions, better food and general health which have made childbirth much safer for mothers and babies today than it was 100 years ago. The rate of stillbirths and deaths in the first week of life is directly related to a country's gross national product and to the position of the mother in the social class.

The idea that the pain of childbirth is to be avoided at all costs is a relatively new one. When Queen Victoria accepted ether, she undoubtedly had little idea of the precedent she was setting. While today's advocates of "natural" childbirth do not deny that there is pain involved, they do argue that it is a different pain from that of injury and that normally it

(continued)

THE MEDICALIZATION OF CHILDBIRTH *(continued)*

is worth experiencing. This "pain with a purpose" is an intrinsic part of the birth process (Kitzinger, 1989). To obliterate it with drugs is to obliterate the mother's awareness and the baby's as well, depressing the child's breathing, heart rate, and general responsiveness in the process.

Another aspect of dependence on technology is that we get the feeling we are omnipotent and should be able to solve any problem. Thus, if something goes wrong with a birth—if a child is stillborn or has a disability—we look around for something or someone to blame. We have become unwilling to accept that some aspects of life and death are beyond human control.

Prospective parents face a daunting array of decisions. The more informed they are, however, the better able they will be to decide what is right for them. According to Armstrong and Feldman (1990):

> Teaching women that they have a say—whether they consciously exercise it or not—is a major educational undertaking, one that requires breaking the hold obstetrical medicine has on the American imagination and helping women to rediscover their natural power at birth.

And you shall circumcise the flesh of your foreskin: and it shall be a token of the covenant between Me and you.

Genesis (17:9–14)

Gynecologists issued a statement declaring that there is "no absolute medical indication" for routine **circumcision.** This surgical operation, which involves slicing and removing the sleeve of skin (foreskin) that normally covers the glans penis, has been performed routinely on newborn boys in the United States since the 1930s (Romberg, 1985). Although it is obviously painful, circumcision is often done without anesthesia. (A 1993 study recommends using an anesthetic cream to reduce infants' pain during the procedure [Benini, Johnston, Faucher, & Aranda, 1993]). Circumcision carries medical risks in 4–28% of the cases (Samuels & Samuels, 1986). The principal risks are excessive bleeding, infection, and faulty surgery. It can be life-threatening.

In 1989, the American Academy of Pediatrics modified its stance on circumcision, stating that "newborn circumcision has potential medical benefits and advantages as well as disadvantages and risks." They recommended that "the benefits and risks should be explained to the parents and informed consent obtained." This change was at least partially in response to several studies that indicate a possible connection between lack of circumcision and urinary tract infections, penile cancer, and sexually transmitted diseases (Wiswell, 1990). Studies also indicate that more extensive research is necessary before conclusions can be drawn (Maden et al., 1993). Factors such as hygiene and number of sexual partners must also be taken into consideration.

Almost 60% of newborn boys were circumcised in 1985, according to the National Center for Health Statistics. Although this represents a substantial drop from 93% in 1975, it still places the United States far ahead of other Western countries, which circumcise less than 1% of their newborn boys. The exception is Israel. In Judaism, the ritual circumcision, the *bris*, is an important religious event. Circumcision has religious significance for Moslems as well (Bullough, 1976).

Aside from religious reasons, the other reasons given by parents for circumcising their infants are "cleanliness" and "so he'll look like his dad." A circumcised penis is not necessarily any cleaner than an intact one. Infants do not require cleaning under their foreskins (Brody, 1985); adults do, but it is no more difficult to wash under one's foreskin than behind one's ears. If reasonable cleanliness is observed, an intact penis poses no more threat of disease to a man's sexual partner than a circumcised one would. As for "looking like dad," most parents can probably find ways to keep their son's self-esteem intact along with his foreskin. There is no evidence we know of to suggest that little boys are seriously traumatized if dad's penis doesn't look exactly like theirs. We know one dad (circumcised) who says to his sons (uncircumcised), "Boy, you guys are lucky. You should've seen what they did to me!"

A recent analysis of the potential financial costs and health benefits of circumcision concluded that "there is no medical indication for or against circumcision" and that decisions "may be most reasonably made on [the basis of] nonmedical factors such as parent preference or religious convictions" (Lawler, Bisonni, & Holtgrave, 1991).

Breast-Feeding

In the case of hospital birth, the infant will generally be brought to the mother at scheduled intervals for feeding and visiting. In the last few years, some hospitals have tried to comply with mothers' wishes for "demand" feeding (when the baby feels hungry, as opposed to when the hospital wants to feed the child), but because most hospital maternity wards are busy places, they often find it difficult to meet the individual needs of many infants and mothers. If the mother is breast-feeding, a rigid hospital schedule can make it difficult for her to establish a feeding routine with her child.

About three days after childbirth, **lactation**—the production of milk—begins. Before lactation, sometimes as early as the second trimester, a yellowish liquid called **colostrum** is secreted by the nipples. It is what nourishes the newborn infant before the mother's milk comes in. Colostrum is high in protein and contains antibodies that help protect a baby from infectious diseases. Hormonal changes during labor begin the changeover from colostrum to milk, but unless a mother nurses her child, her breasts will soon stop producing milk. If she chooses not to breast-feed, she is usually given an injection of estrogen soon after delivery to stop lactation. It is not certain, however, whether estrogen is actually effective; furthermore, it may cause an increased risk of blood clotting.

Breast-feeding has declined significantly over the last few years, dropping from 63% to 52% between 1982 and 1991 (Weiss, 1992). Nutritionists are alarmed. A mother's milk—if she is healthy and has a good diet—offers the best nutrition for the baby. In addition, her milk contains antibodies that will protect her child from infectious diseases such as respiratory infections and meningitis. Finally, a breast-fed baby is less likely to become constipated, contract skin diseases, or develop respiratory infections. Low birth weight babies, similarly, do best with mothers' milk rather than formula or mature milk from a donor, since "nature adapts mothers' milk to meet

Circumcision is the surgical removal of the foreskin.

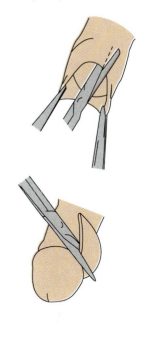

Breast-feeding provides the best nutrition for infants. It also helps protect against many infectious diseases and gives both mother and child a sense of well-being.

infants' needs" (Johnson & Goldfinger, 1981). A benefit to the mother is that hormonal changes, stimulated by breast-feeding, cause the uterus to contract and help ensure its return to a normal state. The American Academy of Pediatricians endorses total breast-feeding for a baby's first 6 months. Breast-feeding has psychological as well as physical benefits. Nursing provides a sense of emotional well-being for both mother and child through close physical contact. A woman may feel that breast-feeding affirms her body, giving her assurance that she is plentiful, capable of nourishing, able to sustain the life of another through her milk.

Many mothers who work outside the home find that they can continue breast-feeding by using a breast pump (either manual or electric) to express milk at home, which can then be refrigerated and fed to the baby later on. Mothers can also express milk at work, either to refrigerate and take home, or to discard; expressing milk regularly relieves the pressure of overfull breasts and keeps up the rate of milk production.

American mothers may worry about whether they will be able to breast-feed "properly." But what the distinguished physician Niles Newton wrote in 1955 still applies today:

> Successful breast-feeding is the type of feeding that is practiced by the vast majority of mothers all over the world. It is a simple, easy process. When the baby is hungry, it is simply given a breast to suck. There is an abundance of milk, and the milk supply naturally adjusts itself to the child's growth and intake of other foods.

See Perspective 4 for breast-feeding hints.

PRACTICAL HINTS ON BREAST-FEEDING

Some women start breast-feeding with perfect ease and hardly any discomfort. For others, it can be frustrating and sometimes painful, but it need not be. Midwife Raven Lang tells us that the following method will lead to successful breast-feeding.

- When you first put the baby to your breast, limit her to one minute per breast. Try not to nurse again for a half hour to an hour. If the baby fusses, give her the end of your little finger (or a pacifier) to suck.

- The second hour, let her nurse 2 minutes at each breast; the third hour, 3 minutes; the fourth hour, 4 minutes, and so on.

- Your baby will not want to nurse every hour of the day and night (although it may seem like it). The basic rule to follow is: Increase your nursing time by only 1 minute per breast with each subsequent feeding, until you are nursing comfortably for as long a session as you and the baby both enjoy.

- Remember that for the first three days, the baby is getting colostrum only. By the time your true milk comes in on the third day, things should be going smoothly. Also, even a slow-nursing infant gets about four-fifths of her nourishment during the first 5 minutes.

Lang says that although mothers are generally most effective when they care for their babies "by feel" rather than "by the book" (or in this case "by the clock"), the process of establishing breast-feeding is an exception to this "rule."

Most women find that a good nursing bra, one that provides good uplift and that opens easily for nursing, makes breast-feeding easier and more comfortable. Many wear such a bra day and night during the months they are nursing.

Rest and relax as much as possible during the months that you are breast-feeding, especially at the beginning. Your body is doing a tremendous amount of work and needs extra care.

While nursing, find a position that is comfortable for you and your baby: A footstool, a pillow, and a chair with arms are often helpful.

Touch the baby's cheek with the nipple to start. She will turn her head to grasp the nipple. (If you try to push her to the nipple with a finger touching her other cheek or chin, she will turn away from the nipple toward the finger.)

Allow her to grasp the entire darkly colored part of the breast in her mouth. She gets the milk by squeezing it from the nipple, not by actually sucking. Her grasp on your nipple may hurt for the first few seconds, but the pain should disappear once she is nursing in a good rhythm. When you want to remove her mouth from your breast, first break the suction by inserting your finger in the corner of her mouth. This will prevent sore nipples.

A small amount of milk may come out of your nipples between feedings. A small nursing pad or piece of sanitary napkin inserted in the bra over the nipple will absorb this milk, keeping the bra clean and preventing irritation of the nipple.

If your entire breast becomes sore, you may be able to relieve the pain simply by lifting and supporting the breast with one hand during nursing. Hot compresses between nursing sessions may further relieve soreness.

If you notice a spot of tenderness or redness on your breast or nipple that persists for more than two feedings, be sure to seek advice from your breast-feeding support group or physician promptly.

If you have difficulty beginning to breast-feed, don't give up! Ask friends, women's centers, clinics, or the local La Leche League chapter for help. Don't worry about not having enough milk; the more your baby nurses, the more you'll produce.

Many American women choose not to breast-feed. Their reasons include the inconvenience of not being able to leave the baby for more than a few hours at a time, tenderness of nipples (which generally passes within several days to two weeks), and inhibitions about nursing a baby, especially in public. If a woman works, bottle-feeding may be her only practical alternative, as American companies rarely provide leaves, part-time employment, or nursing breaks (or breast-pump breaks) for their female employees. Some women may have a physical condition that precludes breast-feeding. Some men feel jealous of the baby's intimate relationship with their partner. Others feel incompetent because they cannot contribute to nourishing their child.

Bottle-feeding an infant does make it possible for the father and other caregivers to share in the nurturing process. Some mothers (and fathers) have discovered that maximum contact and closeness can be enjoyed when the infant is held against their naked breast while nursing from a bottle.

BECOMING A PARENT

Men and women who become parents enter a new phase of their lives. Even more than marriage, parenthood signifies adulthood—the final, irreversible end of youthful roles. A person can become an ex-spouse but never an ex-parent. The irrevocable nature of parenthood may make the first-time parent doubtful and apprehensive, especially during the pregnancy. Yet, for the most part, parenthood has to be learned experientially, although ideas can modify practices. A person may receive assistance from more experienced parents, but, ultimately, each new parent has to learn on his or her own.

The Postpartum Period

Cleaning and scrubbing can wait till tomorrow.
For babies grow up we've learned to our sorrow.
So quiet down cobwebs, dust go to sleep.
I'm rocking my baby and babies don't keep.

Anonymous

The time immediately following birth is a critical period for family adjustment. No amount of reading, classes, and expert advice can prepare expectant parents for the real thing. The 3 months or so following childbirth (the "fourth trimester") constitute the **postpartum period.** This time is one of physical stabilization and emotional adjustment. The abrupt transition from being a nonparent to being a parent may create considerable stress. Parents take on parental roles literally overnight, and the job goes on without relief around the clock. Many parents express concern about their ability to meet all the responsibilities of child rearing (Klinman & Vukelich, 1985).

New mothers, who may well have lost most of their interest in sexual activity during the last weeks of pregnancy, will probably find themselves returning to prepregnancy levels of desire and coital frequency. Some women, however, may have difficult reestablishing their sexual lives because of fatigue, physiological problems such as continued vaginal bleeding, and worries about the infant (Reamy & White, 1987).

The postpartum period also may be a time of significant emotional upheaval. Even women who had easy and uneventful deliveries may experience a period of "postpartum blues," characterized by alternating periods of crying, unpredictable mood changes, fatigue, irritability, and occasionally mild confusion or lapses of memory. A woman has irregular sleep patterns because of the needs of her newborn, the discomfort of childbirth, or the strangeness of the hospital environment. Some mothers may feel lonely, isolated from their familiar world. Many women blame themselves for their fluctuating moods. They may feel that they have lost control over their lives because of the dependency of their newborns. One woman commented (Boston Women's Health Collective, 1978):

> We often feel guilty, because we think our own inadequacies are the cause of our unhappiness. We rarely question whether the roles we have are realizable. Because of social pressures surrounding motherhood, and the mystique of the maternal instinct . . . many women are unable to pinpoint their feelings of confusion and inadequacy or are unable to feel that it is legitimate to verbalize their hesitation and problems.

Biological, psychological, and social factors are all involved in postpartum depression. Biologically, during the first several days following delivery, there is an abrupt fall in certain hormone levels. The physiological stress accompanying labor, as well as dehydration, blood loss, and other physical factors, contribute to lowering the woman's stamina. Psychologically, conflicts about her ability to mother, ambiguous feelings toward or rejection of her own mother, and communication problems with the infant or partner may contribute to the new mother's feelings of depression and helplessness. Finally, the social setting into which the child is born is important, especially if the infant represents a financial or emotional burden for the family. Postpartum counseling prior to discharge from the hospital can help couples gain perspective on their situation so that they know what to expect and can evaluate their resources (Reamy & White, 1987).

Although the postpartum blues are felt by many women, they usually don't last more than a couple of weeks. Interestingly, men seem to get a form of postpartum blues as well. Dr. Martha Zaslow and colleagues (1981) at the National Institute of Child Health observed, "It looks increasingly as if a number of the things we assumed about mothers and motherhood are really typical of parenthood." When infants arrive, many fathers do not feel prepared for their new parenting and financial responsibilities. Some men are overwhelmed by the changes that take place in their marital relationship. Fatherhood is a major transition for them, but their feelings are overlooked, because most people turn their attention to the new mother.

Parental Roles and Stress

Many of the stresses felt by new parents closely reflect gender roles (Cowan & Cowan, 1988; Scott & Alwin, 1989). Overall, mothers seem to experience greater stress than fathers (Harriman, 1983).

Motherhood Many women see their destiny as motherhood. Given the choice of becoming mothers or not (made possible through birth control), most women would probably choose to become mothers at some point in their lives, and they would make this choice for very positive reasons (Cook et al., 1982; Gallup & Newport, 1990; Genevie & Margolies, 1987). But many women make no conscious choice; they become mothers without weighing their decision or considering its effect on their lives and the lives of their children and partners.

Although researchers are unable to find any instinctual motivation for

Warning! The Surgeon General has determined that trying to be a good parent can be hazardous to your health.

Art Dworken

having children among humans (which does not necessarily mean that such motivation does not exist), they recognize many social motives impelling women to become mothers. When a woman becomes a mother, she may feel that her identity as an adult is confirmed. Having a child of her own proves her womanliness because, from her earliest years, she has been trained to assume the role of mother. She has changed dolls' diapers and pretended to feed them, practicing infant care. She played house while her brother built forts. As Jessie Bernard (1982) writes:

> An inbred desire is no less potent than an instinctive one. The pain and anguish resulting from deprivation of an acquired desire for children are as real as the pain and anguish resulting from an instinctive one.

Whatever the reason, most women choose motherhood.

And most, though not all, would choose it again. Interviews with 2000 mothers found that eight out of ten would have children if they had the chance to do it again (Genevie & Margolies, 1987). Still, there remains an ambivalence that many mothers face. Liz Koch (1987) writes:

> We fear we will lose ourselves if we stay with our infants. We resist surrendering even to our newborns for fear of being swallowed up. We hear and accept both the conflicting advice that bonding with our babies is vital, and the opposite undermining message that to be a good mother, we must get away as soon and as often as possible. We hear that if we mother our own babies full time, we will have nothing to offer society, our husbands, ourselves, even our children.

Koch observes that the "job" of mother is not valued because it is associated with "menial tasks of housekeeper, cook, laundrymaid," and so on. She writes:

> If instead we looked at our mothering in and of itself, we could begin to separate the house from our role as mother. . . . It is also a way to educate our partners about the importance of caring for young children. . . . If we separate out and redefine our role as mother, it can become meaningful work, with intellectual, creative, and physical dimensions.

Fatherhood When we speak of "mothering" a child, everyone knows what we mean: nurturing, caring for, feeding, diapering, soothing, loving. Mothers generally "mother" their children almost every day of the year for at least 18 consecutive years. The meaning of "fathering" is quite different. "Fathering" a child need take no more than a few minutes, if we understand the term in its traditional sense—that is, impregnating the mother. Nurturant behavior by a father toward his child has not typically been referred to as "fathering." ("Mothering" doesn't seem appropriate either in this context.) The verb "to parent" has been coined to fill the need for a word that adequately describes the child-tending behaviors of both mothers and fathers (Verzaro-Lawrence, 1981).

As we have seen, the father's traditional roles of provider and protector are instrumental; they satisfy the family's economic and physical needs. From a developmental viewpoint, the father's importance to the family derives not only from his role as a representative of society, connecting his family and his culture, but also from his role as a developer of self-control and autonomy in his children. The mother's role in the traditional model is expressive; she gives emotional and physiological support to her family.

Since mother is not all there is to any woman, once she becomes a mother, how does a woman weave the mother into her adult self?
Andrea Eagan

It is so still in the house.
There is a calm in the house;
The snowstorm wails out there,
And the dogs are rolled up with
snouts under the tail.
My little boy is sleeping on the
ledge.
On his back he lies, breathing
through his open mouth.
His little stomach is bulging round.
Is it strange if I start to cry with
joy?
Eskimo mother's song

We learn from experience. A man never wakes up his second baby just to see it smile.
Grace Williams

However, the lines between these roles are becoming increasingly blurred because of economic pressures and new societal expectations. For example, fathers today are increasingly participating in the pregnancy and birth processes; it is not clear, however, whether or not this involvement predisposes the father to greater participation with his children later on.

Overall, it appears that the family today emphasizes the expressive qualities of all its members, including the father, much more than in the past (Lamb, 1986). The "emergent" perspective described by Robert Fein (1980) views men as psychologically capable of participating in virtually all parenting behaviors (except gestation and lactation). Further, such participation is beneficial to the development and well-being of both children and adults. The implicit contradiction between the terms "real man" and "good father" needs to be resolved if boys are to develop into fathers who feel their "manhood enlarged and not depleted by active, caring fatherhood" (Pogrebin, 1982).

In support of this emergent view of fatherhood, Dr. Benjamin Spock (1968, 1976) has made a number of changes in his *Baby and Child Care* (otherwise known as the "baby bible"). On the subject of father participation in child rearing, the original version (1945) said:

> A man can be a warm father and a real man at the same time. . . . Of course, I don't mean that the father has to give as many bottles or change just as many diapers as the mother. But it's fine for him to do these things occasionally. He might make the formula on Sunday.

The revised edition (Spock & Rothenberg, 1985) advises all fathers to take on at least half of the child management duties and participate in the housework:

> When a father does his share as a matter of course . . . it does much more than simply lighten his wife's work load and give her companionship. . . . It shows that he believes this work is crucial for the welfare of the family, that it calls for judgment and skill, and that it's his responsibility as much as it is hers. . . . This is what sons and daughters need to see in action if they are to grow up without sexist attitudes.

Research about fathers caring for infants has revealed one dramatic finding: If a man is involved in the physical care of his own or someone else's child younger than age 3, the probability that he will later be involved in the abuse of any child is greatly reduced (Parker & Parker, 1984, 1986).

Several trends are indicative of the father's changing role. More men are attending the births of their children and taking time off from work afterward, more men are taking children to day care or to the doctor, more men are enrolled in parenting classes, diaper-changing tables are appearing in the men's rooms of airports and train stations, and fathers with babies are becoming highly visible in advertising (Lawson, 1990). "The truth is leaking out," Kyle Pruett writes, "through the real lives of men and their children that the uninvited, uninvolved, unwelcomed, inept father is moving toward obsolescence" (Pruett, 1987).

Don't be the man you think you should be, be the father you wish you'd had.

Letty Cottin Pogrebin

Gay and Lesbian Parents

There may be as many as 1.5 million lesbian mothers rearing their children in the United States (Hoeffer, 1981). The number of gay fathers is estimated at 1–3 million (Bozett, 1987b). Most of

Families headed by lesbians or gay men generally experience the same joys and pains as those headed by heterosexuals—with one exception: They are likely to face insensitivity and discrimination from society.

these parents are or have been married; consequently, many children of lesbians and gay men begin their lives in "traditional" families, even though separation or divorce may occur later on. Adoption, insemination, surrogacy, and foster parenting are also options being used increasingly by both singles and couples who are lesbian or gay (Goleman, 1992; Ricketts & Achtenberg, 1989). Because of the nontraditional nature of these families, it is difficult to determine the number of gays and lesbians who choose these alternatives.

Studies of gay fathers indicate that "being gay is compatible with effective parenting" (Bozett, 1987c; Goleman, 1992; Harris & Turner, 1986). Furthermore, it appears that gays who disclose their orientation to their children and who have a stable gay relationship tend to provide better-quality parenting than those who remain married and keep their sexual orientation hidden (Barret & Robinson, 1990). One study of gay fathers (Turner, Scadden, & Harris, 1985) concluded that (1) most gay fathers have positive relationships with their children, (2) the father's sexual orientation is relatively unimportant to the relationship, and (3) gay fathers endeavor to create stable home environments for their children.

Heterosexual fears about gays and lesbians as parents center around concerns about parenting abilities, fears of sexual abuse, and worries that the children will "catch" the homosexual orientation. All of these fears are unwarranted. A review of the literature on children of gay men and lesbians found virtually no documented cases of sexual abuse by gay parents or their lovers; such exploitation appears to be disproportionately committed by heterosexuals (Barret & Robinson, 1990; Cramer, 1986).

Fears that gay and lesbian parents may reject children of the other sex also appear unfounded. Such fears reflect two common misconceptions: that being gay or lesbian is a rejection of members of the other sex, and that people are able to choose their sexual orientation. A review of about three dozen studies of children of lesbians and gays found the parents' orientation to have no impact on the children's sexual orientation or their feelings about their gender (Patterson, 1992). According to Dr. Michael Lamb, chief of the Section on Social and Emotional Development at the National Institute of Child Health and Human Development, "What evidence there is suggests there are no particular developmental or emotional deficits for children raised by gay or lesbian parents. . . . These kids look OK" (quoted in Goldman, 1992).

Coping with Parental Stress In spite of fathers' increasing participation in child rearing, and even though a couple may have an egalitarian relationship before the birth of the first child, it usually becomes more traditional once a child is born. The mother may give up her job to rear the child. Because the father is usually away at work during the day, the housework may become her full responsibility. If the mother must continue to work in addition to the father, or if the woman is single, she will have a dual role as both homemaker and provider. She will also probably have the responsibility for finding adequate child care, and it will probably be she who stays home with the child when he or she is sick.

A study by Jacqueline Ventura (1987) found multiple role demands to be the greatest source of stress for mothers. Thirty-five percent of mothers were concerned about juggling a job, parenting, housekeeping, and "taking care of husband." (A "small number of fathers also described the struggle to finish take-home work or household tasks and help with child care.") A study by Judith Myers-Walls (1984) found that mothers' adjustment to fulfilling multiple roles was made easier if they used the following coping strategies: (1) holding a positive view of the situation, (2) developing a "salient" role (deciding which role should dominate when conflict arose), (3) compartmentalizing roles, and (4) compromising standards (of household cleanliness, for example). Abner Boles and Harriet Curtis-Boles (1986) suggest that African American families' flexibility and egalitarianism may stand them in good stead during this transition to parenthood: "Black families have repeatedly demonstrated an ability to cross the boundaries of gender-linked sex roles and perform roles as needed to insure the effective functioning of the family."

Another important factor in maintaining marital quality during this time is the father's emotional and physical support (Tietjen & Bradley, 1985). Jay Belsky (1986) writes, "The more help that husbands can be induced, encouraged, or coerced to give around the home, the less dissatisfied the wife is likely to be with the union." Studies indicate that "parental similarities far outweigh differences, suggesting that beyond the biological advantage accorded the mother by virtue of her physiology, both parents are equally capable of caring for their young" (Belsky, Lerner, & Spanier, 1984). Both traditional gender roles and our traditional work structure, which does not permit men the opportunity to be at home or to work part-time, stand in the way of fathers participating equally (or replacing mothers) as the primary nurturers. Nature does not prevent men from nurturing, but societal expectations and the social structure often do.

Having a family is like having a bowling alley installed in your head.
Martin Mull

Before I got married, I had six theories about bringing up children. Now I have six children and no theories.
John Wilmot, Earl of Rochester

You can learn things from children—how much patience you have, for instance.
Franklin P. Jones

For many, the arrival of a child is one of life's most important events. It fills parents with a deep sense of accomplishment. The experience itself is profound and totally involving. A father describes his wife (Kate) giving birth to their daughter (Colleen) (Armstrong and Feldman, 1990):

> Toward the end, Kate had her arms around my neck. I was soothing her, stroking her, and holding her. I felt so close. I even whispered to her that I wanted to make love to her—It wasn't that I would have or meant to—it's just that I felt that bound up with her. Colleen was born while Kate was hanging from my neck. . . . I looked down and saw Mimi's [the midwife's] hands appearing and then, it seemed like all at once, the baby was in them. I had tears streaming down my face. I was laughing and crying at the same time. . . . Mimi handed her to me with all the goop on her and I never even thought about it. She was so pink. She opened her eyes for the first time in her life right there in my arms. I thought she was the most beautiful thing I had ever seen. There was something about that, holding her just the way she was. . . . I never felt anything like that in my life.

SUMMARY

Children by Choice

• Because of effective birth control methods, parenthood is a matter of choice. Couples who choose not to have children often think of themselves as "child-free" rather than "childless."

• Many couples defer parenthood to complete their education, build careers, gain economic security, and establish their relationship.

Fertilization and Fetal Development

• Fertilization of the oocyte by a sperm usually takes place in the fallopian tube. The chromosomes of the ovum combine with those of the sperm to form the *diploid zygote*; it divides many times to form a *blastocyst*, which implants itself in the uterine wall.

• The blastocyst becomes an *embryo*, then a *fetus*, which is nourished through the *placenta*, via the umbilical cord. From fertilization through birth, the devel- oping offspring is called the conceptus.

Being Pregnant

• The first reliable pregnancy test can be made two to four weeks after a woman misses her menstrual period by the *agglutination test*. *Hegar's sign* can be detected by a trained examiner. Pregnancy is confirmed by the detection of the fetal heartbeat and movements, or examination by ultrasound.

• A woman's feelings vary greatly during pregnancy. It is important for her to share her fears and to have support from her partner, friends, relatives, and health-care workers. Her feelings about sexuality are likely to change during pregnancy. Men may also have conflicting feelings. Sexual activity is generally safe unless there is pain, bleeding, or history of miscarriage.

• Harmful substances may be passed to the embryo or fetus through the pla- centa. Substances that cause birth defects are called *teratogens;* these include alcohol, tobacco, certain drugs, and environmental pollutants. Infectious diseases, such as rubella, may damage the fetus. Sexually transmitted diseases may be passed to the infant through the placenta or the birth canal during childbirth.

• *Ectopic pregnancy, toxemia, preeclampsia,* and *low birth weight* (prematurity) are the most common complications of pregnancy.

• Abnormalities of the fetus may be diagnosed using *ultrasound, amniocentesis, chorionic villus sampling (CVS),* or *alpha-feto protein (AFP) screening.*

• Some pregnancies end in spontaneous abortion (miscarriage); about 1 in 4 women is aware she has miscarried at least once. Infant mortality rates in the U.S. are extremely high compared to those in other industrialized nations. Loss of pregnancy or death of a young infant is recognized as a serious life event.

Infertility

• *Infertility* is the inability to conceive a child after trying for a year or more. The primary causes of female infertility are blocked fallopian tubes (often the result of pelvic inflammatory disease), endometriosis, and hormonal abnormalities. The primary causes of male infertility are low sperm count, blocked passageways, and lack of sperm motility. Couples with fertility problems often feel they have lost control over an important area of their lives.

• Techniques for combating infertility include hormonal treatments, intrauterine insemination, in vitro fertilization, GIFT, ZIFT, and direct sperm injection. *Intrauterine insemination (IUI),* or *artificial insemination (AI),* involves depositing sperm by syringe in a woman's vagina. *In vitro fertilization (IVF)* involves combining sperm and egg in the laboratory and implanting the resultant blastocyst(s) in the uterus. *Surrogate motherhood* is also an option for childless couples, but it raises many legal and ethical issues.

Giving Birth

• Throughout pregnancy, a woman feels *Braxton Hicks contractions.* These contractions also begin the *effacement* and *dilation* of the cervix to permit delivery.

• Labor can be divided into three stages. First-stage labor begins when uterine contractions become regular. When the cervix has dilated approximately 10 cm, the baby's head enters the birth canal; this is called *transition.* In second-stage labor, the baby emerges from the birth canal. In third-stage labor, the placenta (afterbirth) is expelled.

• *Cesarean section* is the removal of the fetus by an incision through the mother's abdomen into her uterus. A dramatic increase in C-sections in recent years has led to criticism that the procedure is used more often than necessary.

• *Prepared childbirth* encompasses a variety of methods that stress the importance of understanding the birth process and of relaxation and emotional support of the mother during childbirth.

• Professionally staffed birth centers and special birthing rooms in hospitals are providing attractive alternatives to impersonal hospital birth settings for normal births. Nurse-midwives and lay midwives are trained in obstetric techniques. Many women are now choosing midwives because they want home births, cannot afford physicians, or prefer the attendance of a woman.

• *Circumcision* has been performed routinely in this country for many years. There are usually no medical reasons for this painful and sometimes dangerous procedure, and the practice is being increasingly questioned. Circumcision holds religious meaning for Jews and Muslims.

• A little over 50% of American women breast-feed their babies today. Mother's milk is more nutritious than formula or cow's milk and provides immunity to many diseases. Nursing offers emotional rewards to mother and infant.

Becoming a Parent

• A critical adjustment period follows the birth of a child. The mother may experience feelings of depression (sometimes called "postpartum blues") that are a result of biological, psychological, and social factors. Participation of the father in nurturing the infant and performing household duties may help alleviate both the mother's and father's feelings of confusion and inadequacy.

• The role of mother is important for many women; nevertheless, many mothers feel ambivalent because of conflicting messages about what a "good" mother should be. Fathers may also feel conflict, because their role is changing toward being more involved in child rearing.

• Lesbian and gay parents often face additional challenges, because society tends to view them with suspicion. Gay and lesbian parenting, however, appears to differ very little from heterosexual parenting.

• The first year of child rearing is apt to be stressful, especially for the mother. Coping strategies for mothers include having a positive view, prioritizing roles, compartmentalizing, and compromising certain standards.

• Couples have less stress if they already have a strong relationship, communicate openly, agree on family planning, and originally had a strong desire for the child. The husband's involvement in child care and household tasks is important.

KEY TERMS

child-free marriage

capacitation

acrosomal reaction

diploid zygote

blastocyst

implantation

embryo

fetus

gestation

embryonic membrane

amnion

amniotic fluid

yolk sac

chorion

allantois

gastrulation

lanugo

placenta

umbilical cord

agglutination test

Hegar's sign

teratogen

ectopic pregnancy

toxemia

preeclampsia

low birth weight (LBW)

ultrasound

sonogram

amniocentesis

chorionic villus sampling (CVS)

alpha-feto protein (AFP) screening

sudden infant death syndrome (SIDS)

infertility

varicocele

intrauterine insemination (IUI)

artificial insemination (AI)

therapeutic donor insemination (TDI)

in vitro fertilization (IVF)

gamete intrafallopian transfer (GIFT)

zygote intrafallopian transfer (ZIFT)

surrogate motherhood

parturition

relaxin	vernix	prepared childbirth
Braxton Hicks contraction	neonate	circumcision
effacement	Apgar score	lactation
dilation	involution	colostrum
oxytocin	lochia	postpartum period
transition	episiotomy	
	cesarean section (C-section)	

RESOURCES

Infant Care

La Leche League International
P.O. Box 1209
Franklin Park, IL 60131
(708) 455-7730
(708) 830-8087 (24-hour counseling hotline)
Advice and support for breast-feeding mothers. Call or check the phone directory for local chapters.

National Organization of Circumcision Information Resource Centers (NOCIRC)
P.O. Box 2512
San Anselmo, CA 94979
(415) 488-9883
A nonprofit resource center that provides medical and legal information on circumcision and female genital mutilation; opposes routine hospital circumcision of newborns.

Infertility

The American Fertility Society
2140 Eleventh Avenue South, Suite 200
Birmingham, AL 35205-2800
(205) 933-8494
Up-to-date information on many aspects of infertility, reproductive biology, and conception control. Numerous publications, including ethical guidelines for reproductive technologies.

Resolve, Inc.
5 Water Street
Arlington, MA 02174
(617) 643-2424
A national nonprofit organization with local chapters that provides information, a resource list, a newsletter, and counseling.

The Center for Surrogate Parenting, Inc.
8383 Wilshire Boulevard, Suite 750
Beverly Hills, CA 90211
(213) 655-1974

A private organization that matches prospective parents and surrogate mothers for a fee.

Pregnancy Loss and Infant Death

SHARE
St. Elizabeth's Hospital
211 South Third Street
Belleville, IL 62222
(618) 234-2414
Offers support, information, and referrals to parents who have experienced miscarriage, stillbirth, or the death of an infant. Many affiliated groups throughout the country.

Sudden Infant Death Syndrome (SIDS) Alliance
10500 Little Patuxent Parkway, Suite 420
Columbia, MD 21044
(800) 221-SIDS (221-7437), (301) 964-8000 (Maryland)
Provides information, counseling, and referrals to families who have lost a child to SIDS. Local chapters and free literature.

Miscellaneous

American College of Nurse Midwives
1522 K Street NW, Suite 1000
Washington, DC 20005
(202) 289-0171
Maintains a directory of certified nurse-midwives and provides information on midwifery education programs.

The Fatherhood Project
330 7th Avenue
New York, NY 10001
(212) 268-4846
A national research project that provides information and promotes "wider options for male involvement in child rearing."

SUGGESTIONS FOR FURTHER READING

For the most current research findings in obstetrics, see Obstetrics and Gynecology, The New England Journal of Medicine, *and* JAMA: Journal of the American Medical Association.

Armstrong, Penny, and Sheryl Feldman. *A Wise Birth.* New York: William Morrow and Company, 1990. Written with intelligence and warmth, a thought-provoking book that explores the effects of medical technology and technological thinking on modern childbirth.

Boone, Margaret S. *Capital Crime: Black Infant Mortality in America.* Newbury Park, CA: Sage Publications, 1989. A sobering look at the devastating effects of discrimination and poverty on African American children.

Dorris, Michael. *The Broken Cord.* New York: Harper & Row, 1990. A moving account of the author's experience with his adopted son, who was affected by fetal alcohol syndrome.

Dunham, Carrell (The Body Shop Staff). *Mamatoto: A Celebration of Birth.* New York: Viking Penguin, 1992. Childbirth in many cultures, joyously explored through words and pictures.

Eisenberg, Arlene, Sandy Hathaway, and Heidi E. Merkoff. *What to Expect While You're Expecting,* rev. ed. New York: Workman Publishing, 1991. A thorough and thoroughly readable "encyclopedia" for expectant and new parents.

Menning, Barbara Eck. *Infertility: A Guide for the Childless Couple,* 2nd ed. New York: Prentice-Hall Press, 1988. Useful information for couples facing infertility.

Nilsson, Lennart, and Lars Hamberger. *A Child Is Born.* New York: Delacourt/Seymour Lawrence, 1990. The story of birth, beginning with fertilization, told in stunning photographs with text.

Ulrich, Laurel Thatcher. *A Midwife's Tale: The Life of Martha Ballard.* New York: Vintage Books, 1991. A beautifully written and richly detailed story based on the 200-year-old diaries of a midwife in Maine; winner of 1990 Pulitzer Prize.

Chapter Fourteen

THE SEXUAL BODY IN HEALTH AND ILLNESS

P REVIEW: SELF-QUIZ

1. Fat people are more likely than slim people to have eating disorders. True or false?

2. Sexual enjoyment tends to decline as people age because of physiological changes. True or false?

3. About half of all men over 50 experience some enlargement of the prostate gland. True or false?

4. A woman can eliminate the "hot flashes" that often accompany menopause by taking estrogen. True or false?

5. People with spinal cord injuries generally cannot have sexual relations. True or false?

6. Breast cancer affects about 1 out of 9 American women by age 85. True or false?

7. Most women over 30 should have an annual mammogram (breast X-ray) to screen for cancer. True or false?

8. Cervical cancer is the most common reproductive cancer among women. True or false?

9. Hysterectomy (removal of the uterus) is not performed unless it is an absolute medical necessity. True or false?

10. Prostate cancer is the most common cancer among men. True or false?

ANSWERS 1. F, 2. F, 3. T, 4. T, 5. F, 6. T, 7. F, 8. F, 9. F, 10. T

Chapter Outline

The interrelatedness of our physical health, our psychological well-being, and our sexuality is complex. It's not something that most of us even think about, especially as long as we remain in good health. But as we age, we are more and more likely to encounter physical problems and limitations, many of which may profoundly influence our sexual lives. Our bodies may appear to betray us in a variety of ways: They grow too much or not enough or in the wrong places, they develop aches and pains and strange symptoms, and they are subject to devastating injuries and diseases. We need to inform ourselves about these problems so that we can deal with them effectively.

In this chapter, we look at our attitudes and feelings about our bodies in addition to looking at specific health issues. We begin with a discussion of body image and eating disorders. We next discuss aging and its effects on the sexual lives of both women and men. Then we turn to issues of sexuality and disability. We discuss the physical and emotional effects of specific diseases such as arthritis, diabetes, heart disease, and cancer as they influence our sexual functioning. Other issues specific to women or men are then addressed. Finally, we look at the effects of alcohol and other drugs on our sexuality.

As we grow emotionally as well as physically, we may also develop new perceptions of what it means to be healthy. We may discover new dimensions in ourselves to lead us to a more fulfilled and healthier sexuality.

Our bodies are gardens,
To which our wills are gardeners.
William Shakespeare

LIVING IN OUR BODIES: THE QUEST FOR PHYSICAL PERFECTION

Health is more than the absence of disease, and sexual health is more than healthy sex organs. According to the World Health Organization (1992), "sexual health is the integration of the physical, emotional, intellectual, and social aspects of sexual being, in ways that are positively enriching and that enhance personality, communication, and love." Sexual health has to do with how we function biologically, but it is also a function of our behavior and our awareness and acceptance of our bodies. In terms of sexuality, health requires us to know and understand our bodies, to feel comfortable with them. It requires a woman to feel at ease with the sight, feeling, and smell of her vulva; to be comfortably aware of her breasts—their shape, size, and contours. Sexual health requires a man to accept his body, including his genitals, and to be aware of physical sensations such as lower back pain or a feeling of congestion in his bladder. It asks men to abandon the idea that masculinity means they should ignore their bodily pains, endure stress, and suffer in silence.

Our general health affects our sexual functioning. Fatigue, stress, and minor ailments all affect our sexual interactions. If we ignore these aspects of our health, we are likely to experience a decline in our sexual drive, as well as suffer physical and psychological distress. A person who always feels tired or is constantly ill or debilitated is likely to feel less sexual than a healthy person. Health and sexuality are gifts we must take care of.

Fat and Fat Phobia

Our culture worships physical perfection and religiously pursues it (Wolf, 1991). Our deities are slim, sexy, perfectly muscled actors, actresses, models, and athletes. Their images are everywhere: on billboards, magazine covers, movie screens. We spend hours every week in front of our televisions, mesmerized by their glory. As for scripture, we have volumes upon volumes of holy words: sermons and testimonies on the subjects of fitness, exercise, weight loss, diet, nutrition, health, and beauty.

In our culture avoiding fat is a moral issue.

Michael P. Levine

The above may be facetious, but it is *not* an exaggeration. Think of the energy, time, and especially money that people are willing to spend in pursuit of the "perfect" body (or face, or "image"). Think of the concern, worry, and even despair that people experience when they feel they don't measure up to society's expectations. And think of the guilt. Many of us would rather have violated one of the Ten Commandments (with the exception, possibly, of "Thou shalt not kill") than have eaten a package of Mint Milanos.

Ideal body size and shape are culturally relative concepts. In some cultures, such as that of Samoa, large body size is desirable. Fat symbolizes abundance, richness, and strength. Fat women are viewed as fruitful and nurturing, and they are admired. This is clearly not the case in our society. The cultural norm for both women and men is becoming slimmer and slimmer. Studies of *Playboy* magazine's centerfold models from 1959 to 1985 show a clear trend toward taller, leaner figures (Garner, Garfinkel, Schwartz, & Thompson, 1980; Mazur, 1986). And even though Playmates have grown taller, they have lost weight. This glorification of slimness does nothing to enhance the self-esteem of people who don't quite fit into the slender mold.

Muscles I don't care about—my husband likes me to be squishy when he hugs me.

Dixie Carter

Studies show that we perceive attractive (slim) people to be more sensitive, lovable, healthy, and desirable than unattractive (fat) people. (See Chapter 10 for a discussion of attractiveness.) Fat people are often thought of as lazy, dirty, unhealthy, and out of control. In exploring our feelings about fat (our own and other people's), we need to look at some popular misconceptions.

Misconception#1: Fat Is Unhealthy This is a source of ongoing debate in medical circles, but an emerging opinion seems to be that fat is not necessarily unhealthy per se. While obesity can certainly complicate a condition such as heart disease, for example, it does not necessarily cause the disease. Many heavy people lead long and healthy lives.

Misconception #2: Obesity Is Caused by Overeating Body weight is not necessarily related to food intake. There are other factors, such as exercise, metabolism, and genetic predisposition. Dr. William Bennett's (1982) "set point" theory posits that we each have a weight (or range of weight) at which our body will normally stay if we leave it alone—that is, if we don't attempt to change it through dieting or other means. According to this theory, some people have a higher set point than others and are, consequently, naturally heavier. Regular exercise and a healthful, balanced diet will cause the body to stabilize at the lower part of its set-point range, but this range may still be well above that of another person of the same sex, age, and height.

Contrary to popular stereotypes, people of all shapes and sizes can lead healthy and happy lives.

Misconception #3: Fat People Are Out of Control This is actually a corollary to #2 above. The idea is "If so-and-so could just *exercise* his/her will power and get *control* of him/herself, he/she would not be fat." This line of thinking is faulty for two reasons. First, as discussed above, fatness may not be the result of overeating. Second, fat people as a group show no more tendency toward compulsive eating behavior than do slim or medium-sized people. Eating disorders are found in people of *all* shapes and sizes, as we discuss in the following section. Some fat people can benefit from self-help groups such as Overeaters Anonymous (see "Resources" at the end of the chapter). But for them, as well as other large people, the first step to better health is acceptance. All of us need to learn to look a bit beyond our outer coverings so that we may better accept others—and ourselves.

Eating Disorders: Anorexia and Bulimia

Many of us are willing to pay high costs—physically, emotionally, and financially—in order to meet the expectations of our culture and to feel worthy, lovable, and sexually attractive. While having these desires is clearly a normal human characteristic, the means by which we try to fulfill them can be extreme and even self-destructive. While many American women and some men try to control their weight by dieting at some time in their lives, some people's fear and loathing of fat (often combined with fear or

We have entered an era of cultural life when everyone is preoccupied with a woman's body, but few women, whether fat or thin, feel comfortable living inside the body they possess.

Kim Chernin

disgust regarding sexual functions) impels them to extreme forms of eating behavior. Compulsive overeating (binge eating) and compulsive overdieting (purging)—and combinations thereof—are the behaviors classified as eating disorders. The eating disorders we will discuss are known as anorexia nervosa and bulimia. There may be as many as 7 million American women who suffer from anorexia and bulimia (Shute, 1992).

While most studies of eating disorders have singled out white middle-class and upper-class women, recent studies suggest these problems transcend ethnic and socioeconomic boundaries. A study of teenagers in New Mexico found the highest prevalence of "disturbed eating" among Native Americans (Smith & Krejci, 1991). Other research suggests that ethnic minority women, poor women, and lesbians have generally been excluded from such research, and that women in these groups may develop eating disorders in response to traumas arising from racism, poverty, and sexism as well as sexual abuse (Thompson, 1992).

Michael P. Levine (1987; 1993) defines **eating disorders** as eating and weight management practices that have the following characteristics:

1. They reduce a person's health and vigor and threaten his or her life.

2. They are carried out in secrecy, reducing the person's ability to fulfill obligations to self and others.

3. The person suffers from obsessions, anxiety, irritability, depression, and guilt.

4. The person becomes increasingly self-absorbed and emotionally unstable.

5. The person is out of control.

Anorexia Nervosa "Anorexia" is the medical term for loss of appetite. The term "anorexia nervosa" is a misnomer for the condition it purports to describe. Those with anorexia are, in fact, obsessively preoccupied with food; they live in a perpetual struggle with the pangs of hunger. Dr. Hilde Bruch (1978), a pioneer in the study of eating disorders, defined **anorexia nervosa** as the "relentless pursuit of excessive thinness." About 90–96% of **anorexics,** people with anorexia, are female (Levine, 1993). Most anorexia begins during the teenage years; only 10–30% of cases develop after age 20–25 (Eckert, 1985). Between 1 and 6 out of every 200 young women are estimated to be affected by anorexia (Levine, 1993).

Most anorexics share a number of characteristics. Basically, they are ruled by a desire for thinness, the conviction that their bodies are too large (even in the face of evidence to the contrary), and the "grim determination" to sustain weight loss (Levine, 1987). Typically, the anorexic loses a significant amount of weight, becomes debilitated and ill as a result, refuses help, and continues in a potentially life-threatening downward spiral. Like other eating disorders, anorexia is often the "tip of the iceberg," a symptom of an underlying psychological disturbance or set of disturbances (Zerbe, 1992).

Physiologically, anorexics suffer from amenorrhea (delay of menarche or cessation of menstrual periods); they may also suffer from hypothermia, the body's inability to maintain heat. Other symptoms include the growth of lanugo (fine body hair), insomnia, constipation, dry skin and hair, and problems with teeth and gums.

Fashion doll   "Happy To Be Me" doll

BARBIE VS. HAPPY

The Barbie doll (left) represents an unattainable ideal for American girls. In 1991, a rival, the Happy to Be Me doll, appeared on the scene. Happy's creator wanted to present a more realistic image to young, impressionable minds. Do you think the American public is ready for Happy?

Behaviorally, anorexics often exhibit hyperactivity, social withdrawal, binge eating, and purging with self-induced vomiting, laxatives, or diuretics. The accumulated physical and psychological effects of anorexia are profound. The mortality rate is higher than that for any other psychiatric illness (Bayer & Baker, 1985). Prevention and treatment of anorexia are discussed below.

Bulimia The word "bulimia" is derived from Greek roots meaning "ox hunger." **Bulimia** is characterized by episodes of uncontrolled overeating (binge eating), which the person then tries to counteract by purging—vomiting, exercising or dieting excessively, or using laxatives or diuretics. Psychologically, bulimics experience chronic depression, anxiety, and guilt. Other characteristics associated with bulimia are dramatic weight fluctuation, emotional instability, and a high need for approval. Bulimia is more prevalent than anorexia; it may occur in as many as 1 out of every 5 college women (Bayer & Baker, 1985).

A Retreat from Sexual Identity Clinicians who work with eating-disordered patients often find that they have histories of abuse, including incest or other sexual abuse (Simpson & Ramberg, 1992). They may also have been raised to be fearful of sex and to view the body as dirty or sinful. Sexual dysfunctions and inhibitions are common among those with severe eating disorders (Rothschild, Fagan, Woodall, & Andersen, 1991; Zerbe, 1992).

Eating disorders, especially anorexia, often develop during adolescence. A feminist analysis views eating disorders among teenage girls as a way of retreating from sexuality (Orbach, 1982). It is not unusual for adolescents to experience fear and feelings of powerlessness as their bodies and roles change. For some young women, manipulation of their own bodies may be the only area of life over which they feel control. The refusal of food, in spite of the intense demands of hunger, may be equated with strength.

Ambivalence toward their body and their sexual nature characterizes many people with eating disorders. An adolescent girl may feel (possibly on a subconscious level) that accepting a "curvy" woman's body means accepting a traditional gender role. Becoming asexual by becoming excessively fat or thin can be seen as a rebellion against models of feminine subservience and ineffectiveness. Acquiring an asexual body is also a means of retreating from the powerful forces of sexuality. For adolescents especially, sexuality appears dangerous and evil on the one hand, desirable and beautiful on the other. The conflict generated by these opposing views can result in sexuality's becoming "curiously disembodied from the person" (Orbach, 1982).

Sexual abuse may also be involved in rejection of the body (Young, 1992). Through self-starvation, a young woman may demonstrate her wish to simply disappear. Others may express their rejection of sexuality by insulating themselves in a protective layer of fat. Both anorexia and bulimia "express the tension about acceptance and rejection of the constraints of femininity" (Orbach, 1982).

Prevention and Treatment of Eating Disorders Parents, teachers, counselors, and even friends can help prevent eating disorders in young people. The first task in prevention may be the most difficult because it involves

When a society is urged to eat much, eat often, eat sweetly and be slender, fat people are thoroughly victimized. They are victims of the double binds of capitalism, which are sexist, racist, and class-biased.
Hillel Schwartz

combating the contradicting major cultural images and expectations having to do with weight. The basic message should be: Thinness is not an appropriate measure of the value of a human being. Goodness, desirability, and success do not increase in inverse proportion to one's waistline.

Additionally, it is important to recognize the role of low self-esteem in the development of eating disorders. People who feel they are worthy of love and respect are not likely to develop self-destructive behaviors. The causes of low self-esteem and rejection of the body may be rooted in childhood psychological or sexual abuse (Beckman & Burns, 1990; Young, 1992; Zerbe, 1991). These issues need to be dealt with in supportive therapeutic situations before healing can begin.

Dieting should not be undertaken unless one understands the motivations behind it. Feelings of inadequacy need to be dealt with in some type of therapy (counseling, or a self-help group). Once undertaken, a diet should be supervised by a qualified medical practitioner.

As we discussed at greater length in Chapter 10, studies show that most of us think attractive (which includes slim) people are more healthy, lovable, sexual, poised, and generally "better" than unattractive (which includes fat) people (Dion, Berscheid, & Walster, 1972; Hatfield & Sprecher, 1986). Before we can be of assistance to someone with an eating disorder, we need to look at ourselves to see what kind of messages we are sending (consciously or unconsciously) about our own emotional responses to fat.

Treatment strategies for eating disorders take a variety of forms. Behaviorist approaches may utilize group therapy, drug therapy, reality imaging, or hypnotherapy. Sex therapy, including the woman's partner if she has one, may be recommended. Humanistic and existential approaches focus on each anorexic's unique experience (Ditmar & Bates, 1987). As is true with many other kinds of psychiatric disorders, the role of family dynamics is significant in the development and treatment of eating disorders.

Although early intervention with psychotherapy can sometimes forestall hospitalization, many girls and women with anorexia do need to be hospitalized, especially if their body functioning has reached starvation levels. (For organizations to contact about anorexia or bulimia, see "Resources" at the end of the chapter.)

SEXUALITY AND AGING

Men and women tend to view aging differently. As men approach their fifties, they generally fear the loss of their sexual capacity but not their attractiveness; in contrast, women generally fear the loss of their attractiveness but not their sexuality.

Most older studies on aging and sexuality indicated a decline in sexual desire or interest as people age. Several recent studies seem to indicate, however, that although physiological functions such as lubrication and erection may be slowed, sexual interest, enjoyment, and satisfaction often remain strong (Garrison, 1989; Mulligan, Retchin, Chinchilli, & Bettinger, 1988; Mulligan & Moss, 1991; Schiavi, Schreiner-Engel, Mandel, Schanzer, & Cohen, 1990). In a recent longitudinal study, almost 700 middle-aged women were interviewed twice, at a 6-year interval (Hällstrom & Samuels-

Marital satisfaction and emotional health foster the desire for sexual intimacy in lasting relationships.

son, 1990). Almost two-thirds of the women studied experienced no significant change in their levels of desire after 6 years. While 27% experienced a decline, 10% actually experienced an increase. What is most notable about this study is that it shows the impact of marital satisfaction and mental health on sexual desire. Not surprisingly, many of the women whose desire decreased over 6 years felt that their marriages lacked intimacy, had spouses who were alcoholic, and were themselves depressed. Such an unhappy combination is a sure antidote to desire. Those whose desire increased had initially experienced weaker desire, had troubled marriages, and had been depressed. Six years later, as their marriages improved and their mental health improved, their desire increased, moving them closer to the average.

Because of physical changes, notes psychiatrist Herant Katchadourian (1987):

> Middle-aged couples may be misled into thinking that this change heralds a sexual decline as an accompaniment to aging. . . . Sexual partners who have been together for a long time have the benefits of trust and affection. In the younger years of marriage, sex tends to be a battleground where scores are settled and

peace is made, but if a couple has stuck together until middle age, sex should become a demilitarized zone. . . . They continue to enjoy the physical pleasures of sex but do not stop there. . . . The sensual quality of the person, rather than the body as such, becomes the main course.

For older lesbian and gay couples, as well as heterosexuals, the happiest are those with a strong commitment to the relationship. The need for intimacy, companionship, and purpose transcends issues of sexual orientation (Lipman, 1986).

Because our society tends to desexualize the old, aging people may interpret their slower responses as signaling the end of their sexuality. Education programs for older people, in which they learn about anatomy, physiology, and sexual response, have been shown to be helpful in dispelling myths, building confidence, and giving permission to be sexual (Fazio, 1987; Goldman & Carroll, 1990; Kellett, 1991).

Women's Issues

Beginning sometime in their forties, most women begin to experience a decline in fertility. The ovaries produce less and less estrogen, and ovulation becomes less regular. Over a few year's time, menstrual periods become irregular and eventually stop, usually between the ages of 45 and 55. This period of time is referred to as the **climacteric.** The average age of **menopause,** the complete cessation of menstruation, is 52, although about 10% of women complete it before age 40 (Beck, 1992). Most women experience some physiological or psychological symptoms during menopause, but for only about 5–15% of women are the effects severe enough to cause them to seek medical assistance (Brody, 1992).

Physical Effects of Menopause   The most common physical effects of menopause are hot flashes and vaginal symptoms, such as dryness, thinning of the vaginal walls, and pain or bleeding during intercourse. These effects may begin while a woman is still menstruating and may continue after menstruation has ceased. As many as 75% of women experience some degree of hot flashes, which usually diminish within 2 years following the end of menopause. A **hot flash** is a period of intense warmth, flushing, and (often) perspiration, typically lasting for a minute or two (but ranging anywhere from 15 seconds to 1 hour in length). Some women perspire so heavily that they soak through their clothing or bedclothes. A hot flash occurs when falling estrogen levels cause the body's "thermostat" in the brain to trigger dilation (expansion) of blood vessels near the skin's surface, producing a sensation of heat. Some women who are going through menopause experience insomnia (which can be related to hot flashes), mood changes, changes in sexual interest (more commonly a decrease), urinary incontinence, weakening of pelvic floor muscles, headaches, or weight gain.

When beginning menopause, women may have a higher risk of pregnancy (Miller, 1981). A woman may believe that her periods have stopped for good when they actually have not. Or she may take chances because she assumes her fertility is very low. Women in this age group also may have limited options regarding birth control. Estrogen birth control pills are not generally prescribed for women over 35, although current research indicates that combined low-dosage estrogen/progestin pills are probably safe if a woman has no risk factors, such as smoking or a family history of heart disease (Hatcher et al., 1990; Mishel, 1988). Most women in this age group choose tubal ligations, or their partners choose vasectomy, as their method of birth control. To determine that she is no longer fertile, a woman can have a simple blood test for FSH (follicle-stimulating hormone).

Long-term effects related to lowered estrogen levels may be experienced by some women. **Osteoporosis,** the loss of bone mass, leads to problems such as wrist and hip fractures in about 25% of white and Asian women and Latinas; African American women are less susceptible to osteoporosis (Greenwood, 1992). Women who are fair-skinned, thin, or who smoke are at increased risk for osteoporosis. Lowered estrogen can also contribute to diseases of the heart and arteries related to rising levels of LDL cholesterol and falling levels of HDL cholesterol. Hereditary factors also play a part in cardiovascular disease.

For many women, menopause is not viewed as a medical condition and does not require any special treatment. Others may be bothered enough by attendant symptoms to seek medical advice or assistance. Some women may be concerned about the possibility of future problems, such as osteoporosis. Others may be concerned about changes in their sexual feelings or patterns, or about the implications of fertility loss, aging, and changing standards of attractiveness. Because physicians may have a tendency to treat menopause as a medical "problem," women may find themselves subjected to treatments they don't understand or would not choose if they were better informed. It's important for women seek out practitioners who will work with them to meet their needs in the ways that are most appropriate for each individual.

Different approaches may be appropriate for treating the physical effects of menopause, depending on the individual's experience and her feelings about the alternatives. A common medical treatment for symptoms of menopause is hormone replacement therapy, which is discussed below. Other approaches include exercise and calcium supplements to reduce bone loss, low-cholesterol diets, exercise and nutritional supplements to lower cholesterol, topical lubricants to counteract vaginal dryness, and Kegel exercises to strength pelvic floor muscles (see Perspective 4). Frequent sexual stimulation (by self or partner) may help maintain vaginal moistness. For women who smoke, quitting smoking provides benefits in many areas, including reducing the risk of osteoporosis, less intense hot flashes, and an improved sense of well-being (Greenwood, 1992).

Hormone Replacement Therapy

Hormone replacement therapy **(HRT)** is the administration of estrogen—often combined with progestin—in the form of pills, vaginal cream, or a small adhesive patch. The pills are generally taken daily; progestin pills may be added for part of the cycle. The woman will often take pills for part of a month and then stop taking them, to allow the uterine lining to be shed. Some women prefer to apply estrogen directly to the vagina in the form of a cream; this may be done either daily or less frequently. The estrogen patch, worn on the back or abdomen, must be changed every few days. Additional progestin may also be prescribed.

HRT has both benefits and risks. A woman should investigate before beginning treatment. The principal benefits of HRT are that it greatly reduces the risks of osteoporosis, heart attack, and stroke; it virtually eliminates hot flashes; and it allows the vaginal walls to remain supple and moist

(Sarrel, 1988). This latter effect can have a positive impact on the sexual interactions of those women who would otherwise experience pain or bleeding with intercourse (Walling, Andersen, & Johnson, 1990). The possible risks of HRT include increased chance of cancers of the uterine lining and breast; there is also the possibility of PMS-like symptoms. Adding progestin to part of the cycle is thought to prevent endometrial cancer, but it may have unpleasant side effects for some women. The inconvenience of a menstrual-type flow at the end of the monthly HRT cycle may also discourage some women from taking progestin. The risk of breast cancer may be higher in women with a family history of the disease. Women who take HRT for less than 5 years do not appear to be at increased risk of breast cancer. Furthermore, among older women in general, the risk of heart diseases are considerably greater than the risk of breast cancer. For example, a white woman age 50–94 has a 31% chance of dying of heart disease but only a 2.8% chance of dying of breast cancer (Brody, 1992). About 15–18% of postmenopausal women use HRT (Brody, 1992). (See Perspective 1 for a discussion of assessing the risks of medical treatments. See Riley, 1991, for a general review of sexuality, menopause, and HRT.)

Psychological Aspects Many women find they feel relieved when they no longer have to worry about getting pregnant. Not having to worry about birth control may be very liberating. Most women are pleased when they no longer have to deal with a monthly menstrual flow. Some women may be bothered by the physical effects of menopause, while for others, the psychological effects are greater. Even though most women close to their fifties no longer wish to bear children, the knowledge that she is no longer capable of reproduction may be painful for a woman. In addition to grieving for the loss of her fertility, she may also feel that she is losing her sexual attractiveness. Because women in our society are often judged on the basis of their appearance and youthfulness, those who have "used their glamour and sexiness to attract men and enhance their self-esteem" may find aging particularly painful (Greenwood, 1992).

A woman's partner may also be experiencing midlife anxieties or physical problems of his or her own, which may contribute to confusion or depression. Couples or individuals may relieve their sexual difficulties by altering their sexual scripts—reordering their priorities to place less importance on frequency of intercourse and orgasm, and more on pleasuring and communication, for example (Leiblum, 1990).

Men's Issues

Changes in male sexual responsiveness begin to become apparent when men are in their forties and fifties, a period of change sometimes referred to as the **male climacteric.** For about 5% of men, these physical changes are accompanied by experiences such as fatigue, an inability to concentrate, depression, loss of appetite, and a decreased interest in sex (Kolodny, Masters, & Johnson, 1979). As a man ages, his frequency of sexual activity declines; achieving erection requires more stimulation and time, and the erection may not be as firm (Mulligan & Moss, 1991). Ejaculation takes longer and may not occur every time the penis is stimulated; the force of the ejaculation is less than before, as is the amount of ejaculate (Zilbergeld,

Perspective 1

ASSESSING MEDICAL RISKS

Headlines linking vasectomy to prostate cancer or birth control pills to breast cancer send waves of fear through the population. Each time word of a new medical risk reaches us, we are thrown into confusion and possibly even despair. What do we do if we've just had a type of surgery that supposedly had no negative side effects, and now we read that it does? Or if we've been taking a medication that is suddenly purported to cause a life-threatening disease? Health writer Jane Brody advises us: Don't panic (Brody, 1993).

In assessing newly discovered medical "risks," we need to proceed calmly and carefully. Brody offers five questions for consideration:

1. What is the source of the report? The most reliable studies appear in professional journals that are subject to peer review, such as *The New England Journal of Medicine*, *Journal of the American Medical Association*, and *Lancet*. Unpublished reports from conferences and studies done at private, nongovernment-funded institutions are probably not as reliable.

2. Are there other studies on the same subject? Even in scientific studies, results can occur by chance alone. It is therefore important that findings be replicated by independent researchers before they are used as the basis for making radical changes.

3. What is the degree of risk compared to the benefits? Even if it is doubled or tripled, a risk that was initially small still has not become a great risk (a 2% risk increasing to 4–6%, for example). A 50% risk that increases by half (to 75%), however, is much more alarming. Also, a procedure or medication may increase some risks but greatly reduce others, so it is important not to generalize but to consider risks versus benefits on a case-by-case basis.

4. Are there comparable but safer alternatives? It may take some investigation, but there may be alternatives or variations to a procedure that are less risky. Taking progestin along with estrogen, for example, is said to greatly reduce the risk of uterine cancer for women choosing HRT.

5. Is the research biologically explainable or supported by animal studies? If the study results are only theoretical and not based on actual biological findings, Brody suggests that researchers should be sent "scurrying to the laboratory." A risk that may be serious should be scientifically demonstrated as soon as possible.

1992). Sexual interest and enjoyment generally do not decrease (Schiavi et al., 1990). While some of the changes are related directly to age and a normal decrease in testosterone production, others may be the result of diseases associated with aging (Mulligan et al., 1988; Whitbourne, 1990). Poor general health, diabetes, atherosclerosis, and urinary incontinence can contribute to sexual dysfunction. (Sexual dysfunctions are discussed in Chapter 15.)

It is important for older men to understand that slower responses are a normal function of aging and are unrelated to the ability to give or receive sexual pleasure. "The senior penis," writes Bernie Zilbergeld (1992), "can still give and take pleasure, even though it's not the same as it was decades ago."

About half of men over age 50 are affected to some degree by **benign prostatic hypertropy,** an enlargement of the prostate gland. The enlarged

Health and vitality (and sexiness) are not necessarily related to age, as demonstrated by this group from the sixteenth annual Bald-Headed Men of America convention.

prostate may put pressure on the urethra, resulting in the frequent and urgent need to urinate. It does not affect sexual functioning. If the blockage of the urethra is too severe, surgery can correct the problem. The surgery may lead to **retrograde ejaculation,** in which the ejaculate is released into the bladder instead of the urethra upon orgasm. Retrograde ejaculation is not dangerous, and the sensations of orgasm are generally unchanged (Thompson, 1990).

SEXUALITY AND DISABILITY

A wide range of disabilities and physically limiting conditions affect human sexuality, yet the sexual needs and desires of those with disabilities have been generally overlooked and ignored. One physician was amazed to learn from a panel of people with paraplegia (paralysis of the lower body) that "if they had their choice between getting back their walking or their normal sexual function, they'd choose sex." He went on to say, "In the hospital we put all our effort toward walking—we were doing nothing about this other problem" (*Medical World News*, 1972).

In 1987, Ellen Stohl, a young woman who uses a wheelchair, created controversy by posing seminude for an eight-page layout in *Playboy*. Some people (including some editors at *Playboy*) felt the feature could be construed as exploitive of disabled people. Others, Stohl among them, felt that it would help normalize society's perception of people with disabilities. She said, "I realized I was still a woman. But the world didn't accept me as that. Here I am a senior in college and have a 3.5 average, and people treat me like I'm a 3-year-old" (quoted in Cummings, 1987).

Physical Limitations

Many people are subject to sexually limiting conditions for some or all of their lives. These conditions may be congenital, appearing at birth, such as cerebral palsy (a neuromuscular disorder) and Down syndrome (a developmentally disabling condition). They may be caused by a disease such as arthritis or cancer, or be the result of an accident, as in the case of spinal cord injuries. As a result of such a condition, limitations may be placed on a person's ability to move freely; he or she may not experience the range of sensations available to the able-bodied. Communication may be problematic, particularly if a person has impaired sight, hearing, or speech.

A person with a disability may have various kinds of equipment to deal with, such as an artificial limb (prosthesis), a brace, a wheelchair, an ostomy bag, crutches, or a cane.

Changing Expectations Educating people with physical limitations as to their sexual potential, and providing counseling to build self-esteem and combat negative stereotypes, are increasingly being recognized as crucial issues by the medical community (Beckmann, Gittler, Barzanky, & Beckmann, 1989; Bullard & Knight, 1981; Rieve, 1989).

To establish sexual health, the person must overcome previous sexual performance expectations and realign them with his or her actual sexual capacities. In cases where the spinal cord is completely severed, for example, there is no feeling in the genitals, but that does not eliminate sexual desires or put a stop to other possible sexual behaviors. Many men with spinal cord damage are able to have erections or partial erections; some may ejaculate, although the orgasmic feelings accompanying ejaculation are generally absent. Those who are not capable of ejaculation may be able to father a child through electroejaculation sperm retrieval and intrauterine insemination of the man's partner. In this procedure, the prostate gland is electrically stimulated through the rectum, causing erection and ejaculation. It is successful in about 45% of cases but carries some risk of internal burns (Bennett et al., 1988).

Women with spinal cord injuries generally do not experience orgasm, although they are able to experience sensuous feelings in other parts of their bodies. People with spinal cord injuries (and anyone else, for that matter) may engage in oral or manual sex—anything, in fact, they and their partners find pleasurable and acceptable. They may discover new erogenous areas of their bodies, such as their thighs, necks, ears, or underarms. Spinal cord injuries do not usually affect fertility. Many women with such injuries are able to have painless childbirth, although forceps delivery, vacuum extraction, or cesarean section may be necessary.

Overcoming Guilt A major problem for many of those with disabilities is overcoming the guilt they feel because their bodies don't meet the cultural "ideal." They often live in dread of rejection, which may or may not be realistic, depending on whom they seek as partners. Many people with dis-

You only possess what will not be lost in a shipwreck.

El-Ghazaki

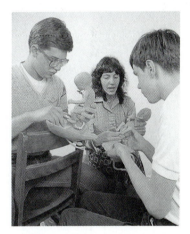

Children with physical or developmental disabilities may have special needs when it comes to sexuality education. Here, students with visual impairments take a hands-on approach to learning about pregnancy and childbirth with the help of lifelike models.

abilities have rich fantasy lives. This is fortuitous, because imagination is a key ingredient to developing a full sexual life. Robert Lenz, a consultant in the field of sexuality and disability, received a quadriplegic (paralyzed from the neck down) spinal cord injury when he was 16 (Lenz & Chaves, 1981). In the film *Active Partners*, he says:

> One thing I do know is that I'm a much better lover now than I ever was before. There are a lot of reasons for that, but one of the biggest is that I'm more relaxed. I don't have a list of do's and don'ts, a timetable or a proper sequence of moves to follow, or the need to "give" my partner an orgasm every time we make love. Sex isn't just orgasm for me; it's pleasuring, playing, laughing, and sharing.

A major function of therapists working with disabilities is to give their clients "permission" to engage in sexual activities that are appropriate to their capacities, and to suggest new activities or techniques (Kolodny, Masters, & Johnson, 1979). Clients should also be advised about the use of vibrators and artificial penises and vaginas; these devices "should be available in surgical supply stores as freely as the porno supply shops, where they are presently sold" (Diamond, 1974). (For information on obtaining aids to sexual enhancement, see "Resources" at the end of Chapter 15. See Perspective 2 regarding the sexual rights of people with disabilities.)

Communicating Needs It is important to understand that sexual satisfaction is not synonymous with orgasm. Sex is a means of communicating deeply intimate and human feelings to another person. These feelings can be communicated between lovers without elaborate nightlong bouts of lovemaking or the idealized anatomy of the able-bodied, godlike figures on television and movie screens. Satisfaction really comes from good sexual communication and intimacy, fostered by trust, sensitivity, creativity, patience, and, when indicated, a sense of humor. Lenz says:

> I learned very shortly after getting out of the rehabilitation center the difference between the proper, medical way of doing things and the practical, easy way of doing things. I've gotten very pragmatic—you might say that now she [Bernadette, his partner] drops me into bed. Now that's what I call pragmatic!

Impairment of Sight and Hearing

Loss of sight or hearing, especially if it is total and has existed from infancy, presents many difficulties in both the theoretical and the practical understanding of sexuality. A young person who has been blind from birth is unlikely to know what a person of the other sex actually "looks" (or feels) like. Children who are deaf often do not have parents who communicate well in sign language; as a result, they may not receive much instruction about sex at home, nor are they likely to understand abstract concepts such as "intimacy" (Cornelius, Chipouras, Makas, & Daniels, 1982; FitzGerald & FitzGerald, 1977). Older individuals who experience significant losses of sight or hearing may become depressed, develop low self-esteem, and withdraw from contact with others. Because they don't receive visual or auditory cues that most of us take for granted, the hearing-impaired or sight-impaired may have communication difficulties within their sexual relationships. These difficulties can often be overcome with education or counseling,

Perspective 2

depending on the circumstances. Schools and programs for visually and hearing-impaired children offer specially designed curricula for teaching about sexuality. Deaf students may receive instruction from sex educators who are also trained in signing. Blind students have "hands-on" lessons with anatomically correct dolls, contraceptive devices, tampons, and so on.

Chronic Illness

Diabetes, cardiovascular disease, and arthritis are three of the most prevalent diseases in America. While these conditions are not always described as disabilities, they may require considerable adjustments in a person's sexuality because they (or the medications or treatments given to control them) may affect libido, sexual capability or responsiveness, and body image. Many older couples find themselves dealing with issues of disease and disability in addition to aging (Power-Smith, 1991). There are many other disabling conditions, too numerous to discuss here, that may affect our lives or those of people we know. Some of the information presented here may be applicable to conditions not specifically dealt with, such as multiple sclerosis or post-polio syndrome. We encourage readers with specific questions regarding sexuality and chronic diseases to seek out networks, organizations, and self-help groups that specialize in those issues. (Other chronic illnesses that affect sexuality include cancer and HIV-related diseases. Some types of cancer are discussed later in this chapter, and HIV is discussed in Chapter 17.)

Diabetes **Diabetes mellitus,** commonly referred to simply as diabetes, is a chronic disease characterized by an excess of sugar in the blood and urine, due to a deficiency of insulin, a protein hormone. Men with diabetes are more affected sexually by their disease than are women. Almost half of men with diabetes experience erectile dysfunctions, although there is apparently little or no relationship between the severity of the diabetes and the dysfunction. In one study, 70% of men with diabetes suffered erectile dysfunction during the first year of treatment to control the diabetes (Woods, 1984). Fertility is not dramatically affected by diabetes, although in one study, the wives of men with diabetes had a significantly higher rate of miscarriage (Woods, 1984).

Women who have diabetes generally experience little or no decline in libido and are able to lubricate during sexual activity (Ellenberg, 1980). There is conflicting opinion, however, about the effects of diabetes on women's orgasmic response (Ellenberg, 1980; Kolodny, 1971). Lowered rates of orgasmic responsiveness among women may be due to factors other than the physical disease itself, such as depression, fear, and anxiety. Women with diabetes may have fertility problems; furthermore, they have a greater frequency of miscarriages, stillbirths, and birth defects (Woods, 1984). If a person has diabetes, genetic counseling is advisable before planning a pregnancy, because it is a hereditary disease.

Cardiovascular Disease   A heart attack or stroke is a major event in a person's life, affecting important aspects of daily living. Following an attack, a person often enters a period of depression in which the appetite declines, sleep habits change, and there is fatigue and a loss of libido. There is often an overwhelming fear of sex from the belief that sexual activity might provoke another heart attack or stroke. At a symposium on sexuality and heart attacks sponsored by the American Heart Association, Thomas Hackett of Harvard Medical School observed that the fear of another heart attack is enhanced "by the fact that sexual activity has long been regarded as unwholesome and a sin. Why, then," he asked, "should one not be punished for yielding to desire?" ("Special Report," 1980). One study found that out of 100 male patients, 24 never resumed sexual relations again; 10 never tried again, and 14 experienced erectile dysfunctions (Papadopoulous, 1980). Of the 76 who did resume sexual activity, 49 did so with decreased frequency. The wives of heart attack patients also expressed great concern about sexuality. They were fearful of the risks, concerned over their husbands' sexual difficulties, apprehensive during intercourse of possible symptoms of another attack. Usually, sexual activity is safe 2 to 3 weeks after the heart attack patient returns home from the hospital, but it depends on the individual's physical and psychological well-being.

A person recovering from a heart attack should resume sexual activities gradually, and only after consultation with a physician (Tardif, 1989). He or she should not engage in sexual activity (especially if directed toward orgasm) before or after vigorous exercise, after a large meal or drinking alcohol, or when anxious, tired, or angry. If the environment is especially hot or cold, sex should also be delayed, since extreme temperatures may tax the heart.

Lament of a Coronary

My doctor has made a prognosis
That intercourse fosters thrombosis,
But I'd rather expire fulfilling desire
Than abstain, and suffer neurosis.
                                    Anonymous

Arthritis   Whereas more men suffer from cardiovascular disease, the majority of people with arthritis are women. About 20 million people have symptoms of arthritis, most of them older women, but the disease may afflict and disable children and adolescents as well. Arthritis is a painful inflammation and swelling of the joints, usually of the knees, hips, and lower back, which may lead to deformity of the limbs. Sometimes the joints can be moved only with great difficulty and pain; sometimes they cannot be moved at all. The cause of arthritis is not known.

Sexual intercourse may be painful or impossible for arthritic women because they are not able to rotate their hip joints or spread their legs sufficiently for their partners to enter in the male-above ("missionary") position. Simply the pressure of their partners' bodies can cause excruciating pain. A woman with this type of arthritis may experiment to find a position that is comfortable for her. Usually, this means that her partner enters her vagina from behind, perhaps as she kneels, supported by pillows, a bed, or other furniture. For men with arthritis, the best position is the male-above position; in this position, the man experiences less pain in his hip joints and does not have to bear his partner's weight. Oral sex, as well as the pleasuring of the body, have definite advantages for those with arthritis.

Developmental Disabilities

There are about 6 million Americans with varying degrees of developmental disabilities (sometimes referred to as "mental retardation"). The sexuality of these people has only recently been widely acknowledged by those who work with them. Their sexual rights are just beginning to be recognized, although there is a great deal of debate about these issues. Developmentally disabled individuals face both prejudice and discrimination. Myths regard them as being either asexual and childlike, or "sex-crazed" and unable to control their impulses. The capabilities of the developmentally disabled vary widely. Mildly or moderately disabled people may be able to learn to behave appropriately, protect themselves from abuse, and understand the basics of reproduction. Some may manage to marry, work, and raise families with little assistance (Monat-Haller, 1982; Pincus, 1988).

Sex education is of great importance for adolescents who have developmental disabilities. Some parents may fear that this will "put ideas into their heads," but it is more likely, given the combination of explicit media presentations and the effects of increased hormonal output, that the ideas are already there. It may be difficult or impossible to teach more severely affected people how to engage in safe sexual behaviors. There is ongoing debate about the ethics of mandatory birth control devices—such as IUDs or implants—or sterilization for these people. These issues are especially salient in cases where there is the chance of passing the disability genetically to a child.

SEXUALITY AND CANCER

In ancient Greece, physicians examining the invasive tissues extending from malignant breast tumors thought these tissues looked like the jutting claws of a crab. From the Greek word for crab, *karkinos*, we have derived our word, "cancer." Cancer, however, is not a single disease; it is more than 300 distinct illnesses that can affect any organ of the body. These various cancers grow at different speeds and have different treatment success and failure rates. Most cancers, but not all (leukemia, for example), form solid tumors.

All cancers have one thing in common: They are the result of the aberrant behavior of cells. Generally, the problem lies in the cell's genes. The DNA molecules within the chromosomes of the cell's nucleus are blueprints for each cell's activities. Cancer-causing agents (carcinogens) are believed to jumble up the DNA's messages, causing the cell to abandon its normal functions. The tumors that result are either benign or malignant. **Benign tumors** usually develop slowly, remain localized, and can be removed by surgery, if necessary. **Malignant tumors,** however, are a different story. Instead of remaining localized, they invade nearby tissues and disrupt the normal functioning of vital organs. This disruption may eventually cause death.

Malignant cancers go through four stages of growth. In the first stage, the tumor remains localized at its origin. In the second stage, it begins to invade underlying tissues, but remains an intact, growing mass. In the third stage, small clusters of cancerous cells break away from the main tumor. Now the tumor is large enough to be detected, and if it is found in this third stage, it may be most easily treated. If the cancer is not treated, it enters its fourth stage. Now the malignant cancer cells circulate through the lymph system or bloodstream (or both), entering other vital organs, such as the lungs, liver, and brain. This process, in which the disease spreads from one part of the body to another unrelated part, is called **metastasis.** This metastatic process, not the original tumor, accounts for 80% of cancer deaths.

Cancer and Women

Cancers of the breasts and reproductive organs are feared by many women. Because of these fears, some women avoid having regular breast examinations or Pap tests. If a woman feels a breast lump or her doctor tells her she has a growth in her uterus, she may plunge into despair or panic. These reactions are understandable, but they are also counterproductive. Most lumps and bumps are benign (not harmful) conditions, such as uterine fibroids, ovarian cysts, and fibroadenomas of the breast.

Breast Cancer   Breast cancer is the second most prevalent form of cancer among women, following lung cancer. Each year, it strikes 150,000–175,000 American women, and each year, almost 45,000 die from it (Russell, 1991). An estimated 1 out of every 9 American women will contract it by age 85 (Kaplan, 1992). Those who survive the cancer may suffer psychologically because mastectomy (the removal of the breast and surrounding tissue) leaves them feeling sexually unattractive or deformed, and wondering if the cancer will recur in another 5, 10, or 20 years.

On a more hopeful note, the survival rate for cancer is constantly improving, especially with early detection. The 5-year survival rate for breast cancer from 1950 to 1954 was 59%; for the period 1977–1982, it was 74% (Broznan, 1986). "Five-year survival rate" refers to the percentage of patients who are living 5 years after cancer diagnosis. Because of increased success in treating cancer, more emphasis is being put on the quality of the patient's life after diagnosis. There is the aftermath of treatment (often disfiguring) and the possibility of recurrence to deal with. There are new physical and psychological concerns. This concept of "survivorship" requires a major shift in public attitudes. We can begin to think of cancer not "as a strictly acute disease that either quickly kills the victim or is cured in short order," but "as a chronic disease, more in the class of diabetes or arthritis" (Parachini, 1987). (For information on cancer survivor support groups and publications, see "Resources" at the end of the chapter.)

Breast cancer is a catch-all term for at least 15 different types of tumors. Each type has a different rate of growth and tendency to metastasize in different organs. By the time a breast tumor is large enough to be felt, it is usually at least 2 years old. A slow-growing tumor can take as long as 9 years to develop to the size of a pea. During this time, in approximately half the cases, there has already been some micrometastasis—microscopic spreading of malignant cells—to other organs. Some cancerous cells are destroyed by the body's own immune system; others continue to grow slowly. Breast cancer tends to be a multicentric disease; that is, if one malignancy has been found, there are likely to be others.

The principal risk factors connected with breast cancer are a family history of cancer, a history of breast cancer (principally mother or sister), and previous cancer (breast or other). Other possible factors include late child-bearing (starting after age 30), early menstruation, late menopause, and a history of fibrocystic disease. Diet may also play a part; a high consumption of animal fat is associated with increased risk (Boston Women's Health Book Collective, 1992). Alcohol consumption also has been implicated in the development of breast cancer, according to recent studies. Researchers at Harvard University and the National Institutes of Health (NIH) found that even moderate drinking appears to increase the risk, especially among younger women; the risk increases with the amount of alcohol consumed (Schatzin et al., 1987; Willet et al., 1987).

Detection There is considerable debate about the effectiveness of various methods in detecting breast cancer. Experts agree, however, that the key to effective treatment is early detection. The American Cancer Society (ACS) recommended in 1980 that all women over 20 perform a breast self-examination once a month (see Perspective 3), that women between 20 and 40 have a breast examination by a physician every 3 years, and that women over 40 have an examination by a physician every year. After the age of 50, a woman should have an annual **mammogram** (low-dose X-ray screening); a woman between 40 and 50 should have an annual mammogram if her physician recommends it, especially if her mother or sister has had breast cancer. Due to the cost of mammograms (about $60–$250) and doctor's visits, many women have problems affording preventive breast care. A study at the UCLA School of Medicine found that 6 out of 10 white women over age 35 had had mammograms, compared to 5 out of 10 African Americans and 3 out of 10 Latinas (Stein, Fox, & Murata, 1991).

Recent research suggests that mammography may not be helpful in detecting tumors in women under age 50 because the breast tissue is usually too dense for a tumor to be discerned (Lavecchia, Negri, Bruzzi, & Franceshi, 1993). Women under 50 should be especially diligent in examining their own breasts, especially if they are at above-average risk for breast cancer. Mammography screening reduces the chance of death from breast cancer among women over 50 by 30–50% (Boston Women's Health Book Col-

BREAST SELF-EXAMINATION

Follow the steps below to examine your breasts regularly once a month. This examination is best done after your menstrual period. If you find something you consider abnormal, contact your doctor for an examination. Most breast lumps are not serious, but all should come to the doctor's attention for an expert opinion after appropriate examination. You may have a condition that will require treatment or further study. If necessary, your doctor may recommend laboratory tests or X-rays as part of a more detailed examination. Follow your doctor's advice. Your early recognition of a change in your breast and the doctor's thoughtful investigation will determine the safest course. Keep up this important health habit even during pregnancy and after menopause.

Stand in front of a mirror. Examine your breasts with your arms raised. Look for changes in contour and shape of the breasts, color and texture of the skin and nipple, and evidence of discharge from the nipple. Repeat the visual examination with your arms at your side, with your hand on your hips, and while bending slightly forward.

While lying on your back, use your left hand to palpate the right breast, while holding your right arm at a right angle to the rib cage, with your elbows bent. Repeat the procedure on the other side. Use the pads of three or four fingers to examine every inch of your breast tissue. Move your fingers in circles about the size of a dime. Do not lift your fingers from your breast between palpations. You can use powder or lotion to help your fingers glide from one spot to the next.

Use varying levels of pressure for each palpation, from light to deep, to examine the full thickness of your breast tissue. Using pressure will not injure the breast.

Use one of the following search patterns to examine all of your breast tissue. Examine all of the shaded areas.

a. Start in the armpit and proceed downward to the lower boundary. Move a finger's width toward the middle and continue palpating upward until you reach the collarbone. Repeat this until you have covered all breast tissue.

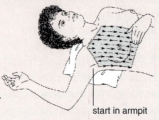

start in armpit

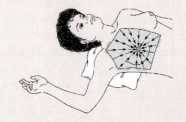

b. Examine each "wedge" of your breast, moving from the outside boundary toward the nipple.

c. Imagine your breasts as the face of a clock. Start at 12 o'clock and palpate along the boundary of each circle until you return to your starting point. Then move down a finger's width and continue palpating in ever smaller circles until you reach the nipple. Depending on the size of your breast, you may need 8 to 10 circles.

Once you have completed the pattern, perform two additional exams: (1) squeeze your nipples to check for discharge (some women have a normal discharge), and (2) examine the breast tissue that extends into your armpit while your arm is relaxed at your side.

lective, 1992). There is a slight risk that repeated exposure to radiation from mammography may actually induce breast cancer, especially if a woman has had regular mammograms beginning in her twenties or thirties. Younger women at high risk for breast cancer should inform themselves of the latest research in this area and consult with one or more practitioners before deciding for or against mammography.

It is important to recognize that most breast lumps—75–80%—are *not* cancerous. Many disappear on their own. Of lumps that are surgically removed for diagnostic purposes (biopsied), 80% prove to be benign. Most are related to **fibrocystic disease** (a common and generally harmless breast condition, not really a disease at all), or they are **fibroadenomas** (round, movable growths, also harmless, that occur in young women).

Treatment   Surgical removal of the breast is called **mastectomy.** The leading treatments for breast cancer are modified radical mastectomy and simple (or total) mastectomy. In modified radical mastectomy, the entire breast is removed, along with the lining of the underlying chest muscles and some or all of the nearby lymph nodes. Less drastic is simple mastectomy, which involves the removal of only the breast and a few lymph nodes if necessary. Another approach, increasingly popular, is known as **lumpectomy.** It involves removal of only the tumor and lymph nodes, thus sparing the breast and underlying muscle. Lumpectomy is generally followed by radiation treatments to halt the further spread of cancerous cells.

Because many women fear the loss of a breast as much as they fear the cancer itself (Kaplan, 1992), they delay seeking diagnosis for breast lumps. The possibility of being able to keep her breast even if a tumor is discovered may inspire a woman to seek early diagnosis, according to Dr. Bernard Fisher, a pioneer developer of lumpectomy (Kotulak, 1979). (Fisher's studies on alternatives to radical mastectomies led an NIH panel to recommend the abandonment of radical mastectomies as the treatment of first choice.) In 1985, a study of more than 1800 women indicated that the survival rate for lumpectomy combined with radiation is the same as for mastectomy (Fisher et al., 1985).

Other treatments for cancer are radiation alone and chemotherapy (alone or in combination with surgery). The final word on the overall effectiveness of radiation is not in, but it appears to hold promise for certain situations. Radiation therapy is time-consuming and has a number of unpleasant side effects, but for increasing numbers of women, it provides a real alternative to surgery (Spletter, 1982). Chemotherapy involves the use of powerful drugs or hormones to destroy cancerous cells. It may be used alone or in conjunction with surgery (in which case it is called adjuvant chemotherapy). Some types of breast tumors thrive on estrogen; these "estrogen-positive" tumors can be treated with tamoxifen, an antiestrogen agent. Chemotherapy appears to be more effective for premenopausal than postmenopausal women (Broznan, 1986).

A woman who undergoes a mastectomy is confronted with the loss of one or several visible parts of her body. First, she has lost her breast. Second (in the case of radical surgery), the removal of chest muscles and auxiliary lymph tissues leaves not only visible scars but also may restrict the movement and strength of her arm. Psychologically, the loss of her breast may symbolize for her the loss of sexuality; she may feel scarred and be fearful

Surviving cancer can deepen one's appreciation of life. Notice the tattoo along this woman's mastectomy scar.

of rejection, since breasts in American culture are such primary sexual symbols (Kaplan, 1992). She also may experience a definite decrease in her sexual excitability. Because the breasts play an important role in sexual arousal and foreplay for many women, their loss may prevent some women from becoming fully aroused sexually (Woods, 1984).

Adjustment to mastectomy varies among women. If a woman has based much of her self-esteem on how she appears to others, the adjustment is likely to be more difficult. Nancy Woods (1984) notes:

> The woman who perceives herself as mutilated by her surgery will probably perceive herself as less acceptable to society and especially to her sex partner. She may withdraw from her sexual relationship or either consciously or unconsciously prompt rejection from her male partner.

Therapy may help a postmastectomy patient who is experiencing these difficulties by "breaking the link between negative associations and sex . . . and modifying the tendency . . . to focus on painful issues . . . instead of the erotic and intimate pleasures of lovemaking" (Kaplan, 1992).

Much of the emotional adjustment after a mastectomy depends on how the woman's partner reacts. She is often fearful that he will reject her; the two may find themselves unable to discuss their sexuality. Some men are initially shocked and feel repulsion and confusion. Other men may be fearful of resuming intercourse lest they hurt their partners. If the relationship prior to the mastectomy was good and the couple were sexually happy, the postmastectomy adjustment will be less difficult (Woods, 1984). In general, the emotional and sexual well-being of women who have had mastectomies appears to be comparable to those who have had lumpectomies (Pozo et al., 1992; Wolberg, Romsaas, Tanner, & Malec, 1989). One study found that lumpectomy patients reported higher-quality sex lives (Pozo et al., 1992). Breast reconstruction surgery is an option women are increasingly choosing. For many, it speeds emotional recovery by restoring feelings of wholeness (see Perspective 4).

Lesbians and Breast Cancer In 1993, an epidemiologist with the National Cancer Institute reported that lesbians have a hypothetical risk of developing breast cancer that is two to three times higher than that of heterosexual women ("Lesbians' Cancer Risk," 1993). Cancer researcher Suzanne Haynes estimated that lesbians have a one-in-three lifetime chance of breast cancer based on known risk factors and information from a 1987 survey of lesbian health. Smoking, alcohol use, lack of childbearing, and poor access to health care are all factors that contribute to breast cancer risk; these are all apparently more common among lesbians (due in part to psychological and social pressures resulting from discrimination) than among heterosexual women. This study highlights the need for scientific research focusing on lesbians and breast cancer.

Cervical Cancer and CIN **Cervical intraepithelial neoplasia (CIN)** or **cervical dysplasia** is a condition of the cervical epithelium (covering membrane) that *may* lead to cancer if it is not treated. It is more common than cancer of the breast or uterus. CIN, however, is almost 100% curable; for this reason, cervical cancer is generally not even included in cancer statistics (Salsbury & Johnson, 1981).

Some health researchers consider CIN to be a sexually transmitted disease (Hatcher et al., 1990). Sexually active women do appear to be at higher risk than others. This was first suggested in studies from the 1800s. In 1842, for example, it was noted that nuns had a significantly lower cervical cancer rate than married women, presumably because they did not have sexual relations. The greatest risks are posed for women who begin sexual intercourse before age 20, women who have more than three sex partners before age 35, or women whose partners have had more than three partners (Richart, 1983). Herpes simplex virus and human papilloma virus, as well as other STD carriers, are associated with CIN (Blakeslee, 1992; Crum, Ikenberg, Richart, & Gissmann, 1984), although some researchers dispute that there is a direct causal relationship (Franco, 1991). Some evidence indicates that combination oral contraceptives (with progestin) provide some protection against cervical and uterine cancer (Kaufman et al., 1980).

The Pap Test The most reliable means of making an early detection of cervical cancer is the **Pap test** (or Pap smear). This is a simple procedure that not only can detect cancer but also can reveal changes in cells that make them precancerous. A Pap test can warn against cancer even before it begins.

The Pap test is usually done during a pelvic exam and takes about a minute or so. Cell samples are gently and usually painlessly scraped from the cervix and examined under a microscope. If any are suspicious, the physician

I had imagined that the loss of a breast would create catharsis, that I would emerge like a phoenix from the fire, reborn, with all things made new, especially the pain in my heart. . . . Not so. It all had to be begun again, the long excruciating journey through pain and rejection, through anger and understanding, toward some regained sense of myself.

May Sarton

BREAST RECONSTRUCTION

One out of every 13 women who are reading these words will develop breast cancer by age 70 (one out of 9 by age 85). As most breast cancer is treated by surgical removal of the breast, the subject of breast reconstruction—literally, building a new breast—is one of paramount interest to a number of women (and those who care about them).

In 1978, the *total* number of American women who had undergone breast reconstruction was 15,000. Today, due to sophisticated plastic surgery and the fact that most insurance companies are willing to provide coverage for it, breast reconstruction is undertaken by more than 100,000 women annually.

Women who wanted to have their breasts restored were once thought of by the medical community and society at large as vain or neurotically insecure, but current thinking is becoming more compassionate and humane. While many women do not feel the need to restore a missing breast or at least do not feel it strongly enough to go through additional surgery, many others welcome the opportunity to restore their feelings of bodily integrity and balance. For these women, reconstruction is an important step in recovering from breast cancer.

Depending on a woman's age, general health, type of tumor, and individual preference, breast reconstruction may be performed at the same time as mastectomy or several months (or longer) afterward. The reconstructive surgery itself varies according to the extent of the mastectomy and how much muscle, skin, and underlying tissue remain with which to work. For women who have undergone modified radical or total mastectomy, the operation involves inserting a breast-shaped implant under the remaining chest muscle. In cases of radical mastectomy, extra muscle and skin must be taken from another part of the body to cover the implant. This may be done by rotating a flap of the latissimus dorsi muscle and a covering piece of skin from the back to the chest. Or it may involve using skin and fatty tissue from the abdominal area, a procedure known as a "transflap."

The implants are usually pouches filled with saline solution or silicone gel; polyurethane foam forms are also used. Although the safety of silicone implants has been questioned, they are still used in some cases. It is considered safe for most women who currently have them to keep them as long as there are no problems, such as pain or swelling. During reconstructive surgery or in a subsequent operation, the surgeon may also attach a nipple fashioned out of skin from the labia, inner thigh, inside of the mouth, or other tissue. (If there are no cancerous cells in it, the woman's own nipple sometimes can be saved ["banked"] by temporarily attaching it to another part of the body, such as the inner thigh, and moving it to the new breast after reconstruction.) Common problems involve scarring, impaired arm movement, and swelling of the upper arm. Physical therapy is recommended to restore mobility in the arm and upper body. Implants occasionally "migrate" or leak; leakage from saline implants is not dangerous, however. Pain or swelling in conjunction with silicone implants should be reported to the physician at once. Additional surgeries may be required to make adjustments and repairs.

Deciding about breast reconstruction involves many issues. It is not lightly contemplated by women who have already undergone the pain and trauma of cancer and surgery. But it provides a significant option to many by filling an important need.

Mary Spletter (1982) wrote of her breast reconstruction:

Am I happier? Am I glad I did it? Has it been worth it? The answer to all these questions is a definite yes. Although the results are not perfect, there is no comparison between the before and after. . . . I feel more at peace with my body and myself. . . . I don't feel quite so victimized by a disease that not only threatened my life, but also deformed my body. . . . I enjoy not having to take part of me out of the drawer every day. . . . and, more important, I have proved that you don't have to accept everything in life that you don't like.

will make further exams. Pap smears are often graded on a scale of 1 to 5 as follows:

Class 1: No abnormalities.

Class 2: Atypical benign symptoms or early CIN.

Class 3: Advanced CIN.

Classes 4 and 5: Cancer *in situ* (CIS), or invasive cervical carcinoma.

Women should have a Pap test yearly unless their physician recommends differently. Unfortunately, the test is not as effective in detecting cancer in the body of the uterus, which occurs in women most frequently during or after menopause.

Treatment Cervical neoplasia is very responsive to treatment in its early stages. In the case of a Class 3 Pap smear, a **biopsy**—surgical removal for diagnosis—may be performed. As some abnormalities clear up on their own, the physician may wait several months and do a follow-up smear. There may be some risk in delaying treatment, however. If the cervix shows visible signs of abnormality, a biopsy should be performed at once. Cervical biopsies are done with the aid of a colposcope, an instrument that contains a magnifying lens. Sometimes **conization,** the removal of a cone of tissue from the center of the cervix, is performed. This procedure is time-consuming and requires hospitalization. A recent innovation known as loop electrosurgical excision procedure (LEEP) consists of an electrified wire loop that removes a small plug of tissue and stops bleeding at the same time. This simple office procedure is useful in both diagnosis and treatment of CIN. One physician reports a 90% cure rate with one LEEP treatment and a 98% cure rate with two treatments (Alex Ferenczy in Blakeslee, 1991). Depending on the extent and severity of the CIN and whether it has progressed to cancer, other treatment options range from electric cauterization, or cryosurgery, to laser surgery, radiotherapy, or hysterectomy.

A study of women treated for early stage cervical cancer compared the sexual satisfaction of those who had been treated with hysterectomy to those treated with radiotherapy with or without surgery (Schover, Fife, & Gershenson, 1989). In both groups, sexual satisfaction, orgasmic capacity, and frequency of masturbation remained stable, whereas frequency of sexual activities with a partner declined. After one year, however, the women who had received radiation developed dyspareunia (painful intercourse) and had more problems with desire and arousal.

Ovarian Cancer Cancers of the ovaries are relatively rare. They make up only about 5% of all gynecological cancers, yet they are among the most deadly. Ovarian cancer is hard to diagnose because there are no symptoms in the early stages; it is not usually detectable by a Pap smear. Diagnosis is done by pelvic examination and needle aspiration (removal of fluid) or biopsy. Treatment involves surgical removal of the tumor and ovary, often followed by radiation or chemotherapy. Follow-up care is especially important (Madaras & Patterson, 1984).

Uterine Cancer More than 99% of cancers of the uterus involve the endometrium, the lining of the uterus. Certain women appear more at risk of developing endometrial cancer than others. White women contract endometrial cancer at almost twice the rate of black women. The risk factors include extreme obesity, childlessness, late menopause, diabetes, hypertension, certain ovarian disorders, breast and ovarian cancer, radiation exposure, menstrual irregularity, and inherited characteristics. Estrogen is associated with endometrial cancer. The safety of hormone replacement therapy continues to be controversial; HRT may increase the risk of endometrial cancer at least four to seven times, although the administration of progestin with the estrogen is thought to greatly reduce the risk (Madaras & Patterson, 1984).

Abnormal bleeding may be the only symptom of uterine cancer. Women who are going through or have been through menopause should be especially concerned if they have vaginal bleeding. Irregular bleeding in premenopausal women usually has causes other than cancer. A woman in her menstrual years will generally be treated for abnormal bleeding with dilation and curettage (D & C), removal of the uterine lining and contents; analysis of the endometrium may well rule out cancer, and the D & C will probably have eliminated the cause of bleeding as well. A menopausal or postmenopausal woman may have an endometrial biopsy; then, if the results are negative, she will have a D & C to confirm them. If the results are positive, the uterine cancer will be treated by surgery, radiation, or both.

Hysterectomy **Hysterectomy** is the surgical removal of the uterus. It may consist of a simple hysterectomy (removing the uterus and a portion of the vagina) or a radical hysterectomy, which involves the additional removal of ovaries, tubes, vagina, and adjacent tissues. Approximately 650,000 hysterectomies are performed each year, many of which are unnecessary (Boston Women's Health Book Collective, 1992). At this rate, half the women in America will have a hysterectomy by age 65 (Allgeier, 1982). There are certain conditions, however, that make a hysterectomy necessary: (1) when a cancerous or precancerous growth cannot be treated otherwise; (2) when noncancerous growths on the uterus become so large that they interfere with other organs (such as when they hinder bladder or bowel functions), or cause pain or pressure; (3) when bleeding is so heavy that it cannot be controlled, or when it leads to anemia; (4) when severe infection cannot be controlled in any other way.

There are other problems that *may* require a hysterectomy: (1) benign tumors on the uterine wall; (2) the uterus bulging into the vagina (prolapsed uterus); and (3) tissue growth on the ovaries, outside the uterine walls, and in the pelvic cavity (endometriosis).

If a woman's physician recommends a hysterectomy, she should have the opinion confirmed by a second physician. She should inquire about the alternatives to a hysterectomy and try to determine how effective such alternatives are. It is important for her to feel that she has all the necessary information and not to make a hasty decision based on fear. She must make an informed decision about her condition, her needs, and the recommendation of her physicians.

The hysterectomy is performed by removing the uterus surgically through the vagina or through an abdominal incision. At the same time, there may be an **oophorectomy,** removal of one or both ovaries, because of endometriosis, cysts, or tumors. If both ovaries are removed from a premenopausal woman, she may begin hormone therapy to control the symptoms caused by

Her knowledge of the womb is academic: most women do not actually feel any of the activities of their ovaries or womb until they go wrong.

Germaine Greer

the lack of estrogen. But since estrogen therapy may be linked to increased cancer risk, such therapy should be undertaken with caution.

For many couples, a hysterectomy may cause a major crisis. A study of premenopausal women who had hysterectomies revealed that the uterus was an important symbol of femininity to them, and its removal influenced their perceptions of their sexuality, youthfulness, and attractiveness (Woods, 1984). For those women who wanted to have children, the loss of the uterus was a dramatic, depressing occurrence; for those who did not want more children, the hysterectomy was seen as a relief, freeing them of the burdens of contraception. Most women viewed the loss of menstrual periods with regret, including those who had basically negative feelings about menstruation. The women feared a loss of sexual desire and the ability to respond sexually.

Some of these fears may be well founded. From 33% to 46% of women report difficulties with arousal and orgasm following hysterectomy, especially if oophorectomy was also performed (Zussman et al., 1981). The absence of the cervix and uterus deprives a woman of certain sensations that may have been important for both arousal and orgasm. Removal of the ovaries can result in lowered libido because testosterone (the sex-drive hormone) is mainly produced there. Furthermore, the absence of ovarian estrogen can cause menopausal symptoms such as vaginal dryness and thinning of the vaginal walls. Therapy and self-help groups for posthysterectomy patients can be very useful for women who wish to increase sexual desire and pleasure. **Androgen replacement therapy**—testosterone administered orally, by injection, or by a slow-release pellet placed under the skin—may be helpful to some women (Boston Women's Health Book Collective, 1992).

The spouses of women who have had a hysterectomy often experience difficulties, which, in turn, affect the women's adjustment to their surgery (Kolodny et al., 1979). Some men respond to their wives' hysterectomies by divorce or by engaging in extramarital relations; some experience erectile dysfunctions. Nancy Woods (1984) wrote:

> Threatened loss of self-esteem, a disappointing life situation, or a predicament of helplessness all seemed to contribute to poor adaptation to hysterectomy, and many of these situations were precipitated by the spouse.

A study of 89 women who had undergone hysterectomy and oophorectomy found that 37% experienced deterioration of their sexual relationships after surgery, while 34% had improved sexual responsiveness (Dennerstein, Wood, & Burrows, 1977). If a woman had exhibited a high level of anxiety about her hysterectomy, she was more likely to experience difficulties afterward.

Most women recover well from hysterectomy, although fatigue and depression are not unusual during the first few weeks. It's important for a woman who has a hysterectomy to use common sense, follow the doctor's instructions, and not try to become too active too soon. It's also important for her to have the support and attention of friends and family members.

Cancer and Men

Generally speaking, men are less likely than women to get regular checkups and to seek help at the onset of symptoms. This tendency can have unfortunate consequences where reproductive cancers are concerned, because early detection can often mean the difference between life and death. Prostate and testicular cancer both appear to be increasing dramatically, so it is of paramount importance that men pay attention to what goes on in their genital and urinary organs. Just as women should regularly examine their breasts, men should regularly examine their testicles. Men over 40 should have an annual rectal examination of the prostate gland.

Prostate Cancer   Prostate cancer is the most common form of cancer among men; it is second only to lung cancer as a fatal disease in men. Since 1973, the rate of prostate cancer has increased by more than 50%. Around 122,000 new cases are diagnosed each year; approximately 34,000 men die from it annually (Angier, 1991; Centers for Disease Control, 1992). As a man gets older, his chances of developing prostate cancer increase. Before age 40, the disease is relatively rare, but in the age group 55–74, it is the third leading cause of cancer deaths among men, and after age 74, it is the second highest cause of cancer death. Prostate cancer appears to be more common in African Americans than whites, but it is suggested that this may be the result of later detection among those with limited access to health care (Centers for Disease Control, 1992).

Detection   Various signs may point to prostate cancer. Although these signs are more likely to indicate prostatic enlargement or benign tumors than cancer, they should never be ignored. They include:

- Weak or interrupted flow of urine.
- Inability to urinate or difficulty in beginning to urinate.
- Frequent need to urinate, especially at night; bed-wetting.
- Urine flow that is not easily stopped.
- Painful or burning urination.
- Continuing pain in lower back, pelvis, or upper thighs.

The first step in diagnosing prostate cancer is to have a physician conduct a digital exam. By inserting a finger into the rectum, the physician can usually feel an irregular or unusually firm area on the prostate that may indicate a tumor. If the physician discovers a suspicious area, he or she will then make a battery of tests including X-rays, urine and blood analysis, and biopsy.

Many men are reluctant to get rectal examinations. Urologist William Catalona asserts that "85% of men will not submit to a rectal exam unless they're already having problems" (quoted in Angier, 1991). A blood test, costing between $50 and $75, is also helpful in diagnosing prostate cancer, although it may not be as accurate as actually feeling the gland. Early detection is crucial and often makes the difference between life and death.

Treatment   If detected early, prostate cancer has a high cure rate. Depending on the stage of the cancer, treatment may include surgery, hormone treatment, radiation therapy, or chemotherapy. If the cancer has not spread beyond the prostate gland, all or part of the gland is removed by surgery. Modern surgical techniques can usually assure that the man's sexual functioning remains unimpaired (Angier, 1991). Men who had prostate surgery prior to the development of these techniques, or whose tumors have spread beyond the prostate gland itself, may experience sexual difficulties following surgery resulting from damage to nearby nerves. In a study conducted by the Veterans Administration and the University of California at Los Angeles, 72% of prostate cancer patients reported sexual dysfunctions following surgery. Thirty-one percent reported diminished sexual interest (Parachini, 1987).

Some men choose to have penile implants following prostate surgery so that intercourse will again be possible (see Chapter 15). In any event, sensitive sex counseling should be an integral part of treatment. Some men who retain the ability to become erect experience retrograde ejaculation and are infertile because semen does not pass out of the urethra. There are medical techniques, however, such as "washing" the man's urine following elimination, whereby viable sperm may be retrieved; insemination of his partner then follows.

If the cancer has spread beyond the prostate gland, additional treatment may be administered. Hormone therapy with estrogens may be given; this may also cause erectile dysfunctions, breast enlargement, or cardiovascular problems. Radiation therapy is used for tumors that are very small or that cannot be treated surgically. Radiation or chemotherapy is used to treat metastasized cancers. Androgens (male hormones) accelerate the growth of some types of malignant prostatic tumors; in these cases, removal of the testes—**orchiectomy**—may slow or stop the tumor's development. Sensitive psychotherapy should accompany treatment by orchiectomy.

Testicular Cancer Cancer of the testes was once one of the rarest cancers among men, but for unknown reasons, its rates have tripled since 1972. There is some evidence linking it to a man's mother's having taken DES (a drug formerly prescribed to prevent miscarriage) while pregnant (Kolodny et al., 1979). Testicular cancer is highest among young white men between ages 20 and 35. These men tend to be middle and upper class; young professionals have four times the incidence as unskilled laborers. This cancer is rare among African Americans. Approximately 3000 cases are diagnosed each year, but the actual incidence may be significantly higher. Malignancies that start in the testes spread to the lymph nodes or lungs and then are reported at the latter sites. If testicular cancer is caught early, it is curable; if it is found late, it is often deadly. Except for the rarest form of testicular cancer, the cure rate is about 95%.

Detection The first sign of testicular cancer is usually a painless lump or slight enlargement and a change in the consistency of the testicle; the right testicle is more often involved than the left. Although the tumors that grow on the testes are often painless, there is often a dull ache in the lower abdomen and groin, accompanied by a sensation of dragging and heaviness. If the tumor is growing rapidly, there may be severe pain in the testicles.

Because of the lack of symptoms and pain in the early stage, patients often do not go to a doctor for several months after discovering a slightly enlarged testicle. This delay accounts for the fact that in 88% of patients with testicular cancer, it has already metastasized by the time it is diagnosed.

A self-examination is the best line of defense against metastasis of testicular cancer (see Perspective 5). It only takes a couple of minutes and should be performed once a month. Suspicious findings should be reported to a physician at once. A doctor's exam includes palpation (feeling the testes and the surrounding area) and transillumination (exposure to strong light). X-rays are taken of the chest, urinary tract, and lymph glands to determine if metastasis has taken place. For a final diagnosis, the affected testicle is surgically removed to determine the type of cancer; this removal is also the first step in treatment.

There are two major forms of testicular cancer. **Seminomas** are the most common, comprising about 40% of testicular tumors; they are spread via the lymph system. The other type, actually a group of different cancers, are referred to collectively as **nonseminomas;** they are more malignant than seminomas and are spread through the bloodstream.

Treatment After the affected testicle is removed, an artificial one may be inserted in the scrotal sac. Radiation treatment or chemotherapy may follow. UCLA researcher David Wellisch has noted that seminoma patients have a "much easier time" recovering from treatment than do nonseminoma patients (Parachini, 1987).

Although the cure rate for all testicular cancer is over 95% (provided the disease has not widely metastasized), the aftermath of treatment is problematic for some men. Wellisch (quoted in Parachini, 1987) noted that men in their thirties wonder, "Am I going to be acceptable? Am I damaged goods? Am I going to be able to procreate?" (Since sterility is a possible side effect of testicular surgery, some physicians recommend that a man who desires to have children consider the idea of sperm-banking prior to surgery.) Dr. Wellisch and his colleagues have also found that partners of cured testicular cancer patients perceive them as neither mutilated nor undesirable (Gritz, Wellisch, Wang, Siau, Landsverk, & Cosgrove, 1989).

OTHER WOMEN'S HEALTH ISSUES

There are a number of other disorders of the female reproductive system. Those that are generally sexually transmitted are discussed in Chapter 16. Here we discuss toxic shock syndrome and endometriosis, as well as health issues that particularly concern lesbians. Perspective 6 discusses female circumcision, an important international issue in women's health.

Because most of women's sexual structures are not easily visible, even women themselves may not be familiar with their appearance. Becoming acquainted with her genitals can help a woman become more at ease with her sexuality and more aware of potential problems (see Perspective 7).

Toxic Shock Syndrome

Toxic shock syndrome (TSS) came to public awareness in 1980, when several young women died from causes that were at first undetermined. They shared similar symptoms: high fever, severe vomiting and diarrhea, and a bright rash on palms and soles. Within 48 hours, their symptoms were followed by a sharp drop in blood pressure and fatal shock. Other women were

Perspective 5

TESTICULAR SELF-EXAMINATION

Just as women practice breast self-examination each month, men should practice preventive medicine by doing testicular self-examination regularly.

The best time to discover any small lumps is right after a hot shower or bath, when the skin of the scrotum is most relaxed. Each testicle should be gently examined with the fingers of both hands, slowly and carefully. Learn what the collecting structure at the back of the testicle (the epididymis) feels like so that you won't mistake it for an abnormality. If you find any lump or growth, it most often will be on the front side of the testicle.

Any lumps or suspicious areas should be promptly reported to your urologist or other health-care practitioner.

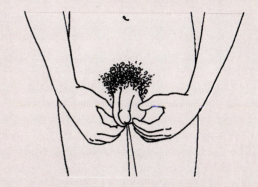

Roll each testicle between the thumb and fingers; the testicles should feel smooth, except for the epididymis at the back of each. A hard lump, enlargement, or contour changes should be reported to your health-care practitioner.

stricken, but their disease was arrested in its early stages, although some were left permanently disabled. The CDC linked TSS to the use of tampons (although a few men apparently have also suffered from it). Tampons, especially the superabsorbent type, appear to be the main culprit (Fuller et al., 1980). Contraceptive sponges, diaphragms, and cervical caps also carry a theoretical risk of TSS if they are used during the menstrual period (Hatcher et al., 1990).

Toxic shock syndrome is caused by the *Staphylococcus aureus* bacterium, a common agent of infection. Although approximately 17% of menstruating women have these bacteria in their vaginas, they do not pose a threat under normal circumstances. Tampons or other devices that block the vagina or cervix during menstruation apparently lead to the creation of an ideal culture medium for staph bacteria. Once TSS is diagnosed, it is easily treated with antibiotics. It is important to stop the infection early before it does significant damage.

The risk of developing TSS is actually quite low—about 3 out of 100,000 women develop it. The group at highest risk is 15- to 19-year-old women. According to one study, the incidence rate for this group was almost 5 out of 100,000 (Markowitz et al., 1987). If a woman has had TSS, she should not use tampons (or barrier contraception during menstruation) without first consulting her physician. The FDA advises all women who use tampons to reduce the already low risk by using sanitary napkins during part of their

OTHER WOMEN'S HEALTH ISSUES   571

Perspective 6

THE UNKINDEST CUT? FEMALE CIRCUMCISION

In over 20 African countries, some parts of Asia, and within immigrant communities elsewhere, female infants, children, or young women may have their clitorises slit or cut out entirely (**clitoridectomy**) and all or part of their labia sliced off. The sides of their vulvas or their vaginal openings may be stitched together—a process called **infibulation**—leaving only a tiny opening for the passage of urine or menstrual flow. These surgeries are generally performed with a knife, razor, or even a tin can lid or piece of broken glass, without anesthesia; conditions are often unsanitary. The effects of these devastatingly painful operations include bleeding, infections, infertility, scarring, inability to enjoy sex, and, not uncommonly, death. Upon marriage, a young woman may undergo considerable pain and bleeding as the entry to the vagina is reopened by tearing her flesh. In childbirth, the old wounds must be reopened surgically, or tearing will result. In spite of these dreadful consequences, as many as 70–100 million female infants, girls, and women alive today are estimated to have undergone this operation, known as **female circumcision** (Perlez, 1990; Simons, 1993; Walker, 1992).

This ancient custom, practiced mainly by Muslims, but also by Christians and animists, is difficult for outsiders to understand. Why would a loving mother allow this to be done to her defenseless daughter, and even hold her down during the procedure? As with many other practices (including male circumcision in our own culture), the answer is "tradition." Although the surgery undoubtedly began as a way of controlling women's sexuality (it virtually eliminates the possibility of sexual pleasure), many Muslims believe (erroneously) that it is required by the Koran, the Islamic holy book (Simons, 1993). Clitoridectomy was practiced by physicians in the nineteenth century in both England and the U.S., mainly as a cure for masturbation, which was thought to awaken women's insatiable sexual appetites (Barker-Benfield, 1976). It continued in this country until at least 1937. "Female castration"

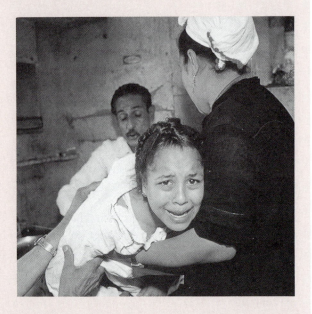

(oophorectomy) and hysterectomy were practiced as cures for a variety of psychological disorders, especially between 1880 and 1900 but continuing well into this century. (In the film *Rambling Rose,* the lively young woman played by Laura Dern narrowly escapes a hysterectomy that is prescribed for "her own good.")

In Africa, female circumcision is opposed by many national leaders and is illegal in a number of countries. African medical workers stress the health dangers and feel that education has helped curb the practice to some degree. But there is still strong social pressure for it, and the operations are often carried on in secret. Raakiya Omaar, the Somali head of Africa Watch, a human rights organization, told an interviewer (Perlez, 1990):

The older women still feel young girls are never going to get married unless they are circumcised. . . . It's such a long, embedded social tradition that if Western people say, "this is barbaric," it backfires. Emphasis must be put on the medical aspects, not the sexual issues.

GYNECOLOGICAL SELF-EXAMINATION

Self-Exam of Outer Genitals

In a space that is comfortable for you, take time to look at your outer genitals, using a mirror and a good light. The name given to female outer genitals is the vulva. The large, soft folds of skin with hair on them are the outer lips, or labia majora. The color, texture, and pattern of this hair vary widely among women. Inside the outer lips are the inner lips, or labia minora. These have no hair and vary in size from small to large and protruding. They extend from below the vagina up toward the pubic bone, where they form a hood over the clitoris. If you pull back the hood you will be able to see your clitoris. The size and shape of the clitoris, as well as the hood, vary widely among women. These variations have nothing to do with a woman's ability to respond sexually. You may also find some cheesy white matter under the hood. This is called smegma and is normal.

Below the clitoris is a smooth area and then a small hole. This is the urinary opening, or meatus. The Skene's glands are located on either side of the urinary opening but you won't be able to feel them unless they are infected. Below the urinary opening is the vaginal opening, which is surrounded by rings of tissue. One of these, which you may or may not be able to see, is the hymen. The hymen normally has some openings, and it is not unusual, even in a virgin, for this membrane to be completely open. Just inside the vagina, on both sides, are the Bartholin's glands. They may secrete a small amount of mucus during sexual excitement but little else of their function is known; if they are infected, they will be swollen, but otherwise you won't notice them. The smooth area between your vagina and anus is called the perineum.

Once you're familiar with the normal appearance of your outer genitals, you can check for unusual rashes, soreness, warts, or parasites, such as crabs. It is a good idea to keep a record of your observations, both to look back and notice your natural patterns and to help any medical people you may need to consult.

Self-Exam of Vagina and Cervix

You can also examine your inner genitals, using a speculum, flashlight, and mirror. A speculum is an instrument used to hold the vaginal walls apart, allowing a clear view of the vagina and cervix. You should be able to obtain a speculum from a clinic that specializes in women's health or family planning.

Take a few deep breaths to help you relax. You may want to put a finger in your vagina to help you locate your cervix. Aim up and toward the small of your back. Your cervix will feel firmer than the surrounding walls of your vagina. It is donut-shaped, with a slight depression in the center. Knowing the position of your cervix will make it easier to locate with a speculum.

Learn how to use the speculum before actually inserting it. The blades are closed when inserted into the vagina. They are then opened by squeezing the handles together and pushing the tab on the handle down firmly to lock them in place. Once you are familiar with the speculum, it will be easier to use it. It is helpful to urinate first. A speculum in place puts pressure on the bladder, which may be uncomfortable if your bladder is full.

Make yourself comfortable. You may want to lie down with your legs flopped open, as you do in the doctor's office, or sit propped up with pillows, or squat. Experiment to see what works best for you. Have a mirror and a flashlight or small lamp handy. If you need some kind of lubricant, use water or a water-soluble jelly such as K-Y. Vaseline and other petroleum jellies upset the natural balance of the vagina.

Using a Speculum Hold the two blades of the speculum together with one hand, and spread the inner lips of the vagina with the other. Insert the speculum with the handles to the side. Aim toward the small of your back and then up, or toward your cervix if you've checked its location, until the speculum is in as far as it will comfortably go. Then rotate the handles so that

(continued)

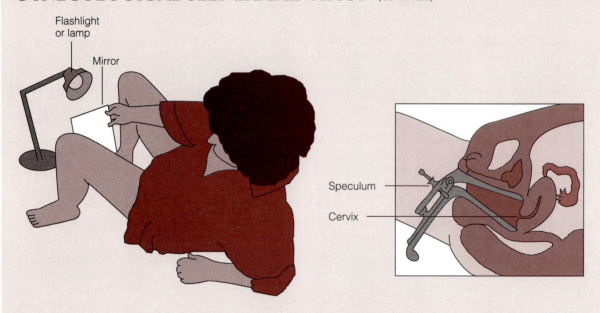

Perspective 7

GYNECOLOGICAL SELF-EXAMINATION *(continued)*

Flashlight
or lamp

Mirror

Speculum

Cervix

they are pointing up toward you. Slowly open the blades by squeezing the handles together and then pressing down on the shorter one and pulling up on the longer one until you hear them click into place. You will feel some pressure, but it shouldn't be painful. Hold the mirror between your legs and direct the light

menstrual periods (at night, for example). Tampons should also be changed frequently.

TSS *can* be treated effectively if it is detected. The warning signs are (Hatcher et al., 1990):

- Fever (101°F or higher).
- Diarrhea.
- Vomiting.
- Muscle aches.
- Sunburnlike rash.

Endometriosis

Sometimes called the "career woman's disease," **endometriosis** may affect as many as 10 million American women. Its nickname derives from its appar-

toward it so that it reflects off the mirror into the vagina. If your cervix is not in sight, or only partly visible behind your vaginal folds, try moving the speculum around a bit, or bear down with the muscles you use when you move your bowels. Usually the cervix will pop into view.

The Cervix With your speculum in place and open, you should be able to see your vaginal walls and cervix. Your vaginal walls will usually be pale pink unless infected or irritated. Notice the natural bumps and folds, and look for any abnormal sores or warts. At the end of the vagina is a donut-shaped protrusion, which is your cervix. The cervix is the end of the uterus. It varies in shape and position from woman to woman. Usually, the cervix will be centered as you look into the vagina, but sometimes it may be off to one side, viewable only from an angle. The cervix is basically pink, although if you've bumped it putting in the speculum, it may have some blood on the surface. This is nothing to worry about. Right before menstruation and in early pregnancy, the cervix may become bluish in color, from hormonal changes and buildup of blood.

The little hole in the center of the cervix is called the os. It is the entrance to the uterus. The size and shape vary from a slit to a rounded circle. It tends to be more open during ovulation and in women who have had children or abortions. If you are menstruating, you'll be able to watch your menstrual blood drip from the os.

Occasionally, a woman may have some trouble locating her cervix, although usually this is a matter of practice. If you have had a hysterectomy, your cervix probably has been removed. We encourage women to continue self-exam after having had a hysterectomy to check for any changes in the vagina.

In doing a vaginal self-exam, there often will be some initial fears or uneasiness about touching your body, as well as associations you may have with pain and pelvic exams done in doctors' offices. Don't be discouraged if your first try is unsuccessful. It may take several tries. If your cervix is especially difficult to locate, you may want to sit on the edge of the bed or use the speculum with the handles down. See what works best for you. You can also ask someone to help you, or see if there is a women's health center available to you in your community.

Source: Adapted from Santa Cruz Women's Health Center.

ent prevalence among women who have delayed childbearing, although recent studies suggest that, as Dr. Donald Chatman observed, endometriosis is "an equal-opportunity disease," available to women of all socioeconomic groups (quoted in Wallis, 1986). Endometriosis is caused by bits of endometrial tissue (uterine lining) that spread to and grow in other parts of the body. It is a major cause of infertility.

It is not known for certain how endometriosis begins. The "retrograde menstruation" theory suggests that during menstruation, a small amount of menstrual blood and endometrial tissue "back up" through the fallopian tubes and into the pelvic cavity. Instead of being absorbed, it may implant and grow on the tubes or ovaries or spread further in the body. Another theory is that dormant cells of endometrial tissues that have been scattered in the body since it developed from a fetus are "awakened" by the influx of hormones at puberty, when they begin to grow. Endometrial tissues swell, bleed, and shed during the menstrual cycle. Although endometriosis generally occurs in the pelvic cavity, it may also affect other parts of the body, including the kidneys, intestines, lungs, and even the nasal passages (Wallis, 1986).

Symptoms of endometriosis include pain (usually pelvic pain, which can be very intense), and abnormal menstrual bleeding. It is usually diagnosed by palpation (feeling) and laparoscopic examination.

Treatment is a complex issue. The woman's age, her childbearing plans, and the extent of the disease are all significant factors. Hormone therapies to interfere with ovulation can help. Sometimes birth control pills are prescribed. A synthetic male hormone, danazol, stops ovulation and thus causes shrinkage of endometrial tissues. It does have masculinizing side effects, however, and it is very expensive (Madaras & Patterson, 1984). A new synthetic hormone, nafarelin, similar to gonadotropin-releasing hormone (GRH), also shows promise. Pregnancy can help if it is feasible for a woman to arrange her childbearing plans accordingly.

Surgery is also a possibility, and it may be the only choice, if the endometriosis is severe. Radical surgery may involve a total hysterectomy or removal of the ovaries or fallopian tubes. Conservative surgery—cutting, electrocauterization, or laser therapy—may be advised, although it may not protect against recurrence as effectively as more radical treatment (Madaras & Patterson, 1984).

Prompt treatment is crucial if endometriosis is suspected. It is also important for the woman who has endometriosis to inform herself about the disease and thoroughly investigate the options, since treatment for this condition is very much an individual matter.

Lesbian Health Issues

In addition to many of the medical concerns shared among all women, lesbians face additional difficulties. Several studies have found that lesbians encounter prejudice and discrimination when seeking health care (Robertson, 1992; Stevens, 1992). First, it may be assumed that they are heterosexual, leading to the inclusion of inappropriate questions, comments, or procedures and the exclusion of appropriate measures. Second, if they do disclose their orientation, they are likely to be treated with hostility. As a result of these experiences, lesbians are less likely than heterosexuals to seek health care. Thus, they may put themselves at higher risk for diseases that should be detected early on. Older lesbians are especially vulnerable because they are not generally as willing to disclose their sexual orientation; they often feel "invisible" (Tully, 1989). Surveys of lesbians regarding health-care choices have found preferences for female practitioners, holistic approaches, preventive care and education, and woman-managed clinics (Lucas, 1992; Trippet & Bain, 1992).

MEN'S HEALTH: PROSTATITIS

Many of men's sexual health problems are related to sexually transmitted diseases, discussed in Chapter 16. One condition affecting men that is not sexually transmitted is **prostatitis,** the inflammation of the prostrate gland. It affects as many as 30–40% of American men between 20 and 40 years of age. There are two types: infectious prostatitis and congestive prostatitis.

Infectious prostatitis is generally caused by *E. coli* bacteria. *Congestive prostatitis* usually results from abstention from ejaculation or infrequent ejaculation. It is sometimes called the "priest's disease."

The prostate secretes most of the fluid portion of a man's ejaculate (semen). If a man does not ejaculate, this fluid begins to decompose, and the prostate becomes congested, causing congestive prostatitis (Roen, 1974). Congestive prostatitis can also be caused by dramatic changes in a man's sexual behavior patterns. The prostate develops its own production pattern based on the man's sexual activity; therefore, if a highly active man cuts back his sexual routine, his prostate will continue its high production and become congested with too much fluid over a period of time. Similarly, if the man goes from no orgasms a day to several, he may develop congestive prostatitis (Rowan & Gillette, 1973).

Symptoms of prostatitis include swelling in the genital area, a feeling of heat, and pain. Frequently, there is pain in the lower back. When there is infection, there may be a thin mucous discharge from the penis that may be visible in the morning before urination. Acute prostatitis often results in a loss of libido and painful ejaculations; chronic prostatitis is often associated with sexual dysfunctions (Davis & Mininberg, 1976).

Infectious prostatitis is treated with antibiotics. But treatment may be problematic, because antibiotics are unable to pass into the prostatic fluid, which acts as a reservoir for the infection (Kolodny et al., 1979). Congestive prostatitis may be treated with warm baths and prostatic massage, which is done by inserting a finger in the anus and gently massaging the prostate. If the prostatitis is especially painful, any form of sexual excitement should be avoided (Davis & Mininberg, 1976).

DES DAUGHTERS AND SONS

Between 1941 and 1971, an estimated 6 million women used **diethylstilbestrol,** or **DES,** a synthetic estrogen, to prevent miscarriages, particularly if they had a previous history of miscarriage or bleeding during pregnancy or were diabetic (Burger, 1981). The mothers who used the drug are now referred to as DES mothers. Some studies suggest that there is a possible increased risk of breast cancer, uterine cancer, and cancer of the ovaries among DES mothers. These women should have regular gynecological and breast exams. In addition, before taking any drugs containing estrogen, such as birth control pills, morning-after pills, or HRT, they should consult their doctors. Taking estrogen in any of these forms may increase their risk of cancer (DES Action, 1980).

About 3 million women whose mothers took DES were born between 1941 and 1971. They range in age now from early adulthood to middle age. Approximately 50–85% of these daughters have developed immature glandular cells in the cervix and wall of the vagina, or **adenosis.** Some DES daughters also have minor structural changes in the vagina and cervix. None of these changes interferes with their normal sexual functioning. The effects of DES on reproductive abilities are unclear, however (Barnes et al., 1980; Herbst et al., 1980). It will probably be a number of years before the effect of DES on fertility is understood.

It is well established, however, that DES daughters run a significantly higher risk of developing cancer of the vagina. Vaginal cancer is extremely rare and usually strikes women in their late fifties and older. Only three cases had been reported worldwide in women under 35 before it was linked to DES. Now the rate is 1 case of vaginal cancer in every 1000 DES daughters. Among DES daughters, the peak years for developing the cancer are ages 19–22 (Adess, 1980). The earlier it is found, the more successfully it can be treated.

DES daughters should not take oral contraceptives. A federal DES Task Force reported: "In view of the lack of information on long-term effects of estrogens in [DES daughters], the committee felt that oral contraceptives and other estrogens should be avoided" (quoted in Adess, 1980). It is important for women to determine whether they are DES daughters. (See Burger, 1981, for a DES daughter's personal account of vulvo-vaginal cancer, surgery, and recovery.)

About 1 in 4 DES sons has some problem with his reproductive system, including low sperm count, abnormal sperm, epididymal cysts, and, in some cases, genitals that do not mature during puberty (Adess, 1980). About 12% of DES sons in one study had testicular abnormalities (Kolodny et al., 1979). There may also be an increased risk of infertility. (For more information on DES daughters and sons, see "Resources" at the end of the chapter.)

ALCOHOL, DRUGS, AND SEXUALITY

In the minds of many Americans, sex and alcohol (or sex and "recreational" drugs) go together like hamburger and fries. Although experience shows us that sexual performance and enjoyment generally go down as alcohol or drug levels go up, many people persist in believing the age-old myths. One study of 125 women age 15–31 found that 65% had combined alcohol use with sex in the preceding month, and that 43% had used alcohol at the time of their first sexual experience (Flanigan, 1990). In a survey of 243 single college students, only 19% of those over 21 had never had sex as a result of intoxication (Butcher, Manning, & O'Neal, 1991).

Disinhibition: The Alcohol-and-Sex Connection

He gave the vine to mortals, easing them of pain,
And if wine ceases there will be an end of Love,
An end of every pleasure in the life of man.

Euripides, 405 B.C.

The belief that alcohol and sex go together, while not new, is certainly reinforced by popular culture. Alcohol advertising often features beautiful women, barely clothed. Beer drinkers are portrayed as young, healthy, and fun-loving. Wine drinkers are romantics, surrounded by candlelight and roses. Those who choose Scotch are the epitome of sophistication. These images reinforce long-held cultural myths associating alcohol with social prestige and sexual enhancement (Leigh, 1990; Roenrich & Kinder, 1991; Whitbeck & Hoyt, 1991). Because of the ambivalence we often have about sex ("It's good but it's bad"), many people feel more comfortable about initiating or participating in sexual activities if they have had a drink or two. This phenomenon of activating behaviors that would normally be suppressed is known as **disinhibition** (Woods & Mansfield, 1981). While a small amount of alcohol may have a small disinhibiting, or relaxing, effect, greater quantities can result in aggression, loss of judgment, poor coordination, and loss of consciousness.

The Effects of Alcohol on Sexuality

Although people may drink to give themselves "permission" to be sexual, the effects of alcohol are generally detrimental to sexual performance and enjoyment. Furthermore, large amounts of alcohol ingested by both men and women can contribute to infertility and birth defects.

Physical Effects Alcohol affects the ability of both men and women to become sexually aroused. Men may have difficulty getting or maintaining an erection, and women may not experience vaginal lubrication. Physical sensations are likely to be dulled. Chronic users of alcohol typically experience desire and arousal difficulties (O'Farrell, Choquette, & Birchler, 1991; Schiavi, 1990). This may be due in part to poor general health and also to lowered production of reproductive hormones. Alcohol has been demonstrated to affect RNA in male rats, suppressing its function in testosterone and sperm production (Emanuele, Tentler, Emanuele, & Kelley, 1991). Researchers have determined that drinking a six-pack of beer in less than 2 hours can halt a man's RNA activity for up to 12 hours. (This does not mean, however, that no sperm are present; production is slowed, but most men will remain fertile.)

High-Risk Behaviors There is abundant evidence that alcohol use puts people at high risk for numerous unwanted or dangerous consequences. These include unwanted intercourse, sexual violence, pregnancy, and sex-

Macduff: What . . . things does drink especially provoke?
Porter: . . . Lechery, sir, it provokes and unprovokes; it provokes the desire, but it takes away the performance; therefore, much drink may be said to be an equivocator with lechery: it makes him, and it mars him; it sets him on, and it takes him off; it persuades him, and disheartens him; makes him stand to, and not stand to. . . .

William Shakespeare

ually transmitted diseases. A study of 332 male college students found that risky sexual behaviors, such as unprotected intercourse, were associated with alcohol use (Clapper & Lipsitt, 1991). Another study of 243 college students found that 47% of the men and 57% of the women had had intercourse from one to five times *primarily* because they were intoxicated (Butcher et al., 1991). Nineteen percent of the men and 33% of the women said they had had intercourse because they felt awkward about refusing.

The disinhibiting effect of alcohol allows some men to justify acts of sexual violence they would not otherwise commit (Abbey, 1991; Roenrich & Kinder, 1991). Men may expect that alcohol will make them sexually aggressive and act accordingly; they may believe that if a woman drinks, she is consenting to have sex. Additionally, a woman who has been drinking may have difficulty in sending and receiving cues about expected behavior and in resisting assault (Abbey, 1991). Alcohol use is often a significant factor in sexual violence of all types (Benson et al., 1992).

Gay and Lesbian Issues

A larger percentage of alcoholism is found among gay men and lesbians than among the population as a whole (Ratner, 1988). A number of reasons are given for this, including socializing behaviors (gay and lesbian bars are almost the only social institutions where they can freely meet) and psychological stress (due to isolation and conflicting feelings about being gay) (Glaus, 1988). The particular needs of gays and lesbians who have problems with alcohol or drugs are not generally well met (Israelstam, 1986). Therapies, peer support groups, and intervention techniques that are sensitive to the particular needs of lesbians and gay men need to be developed and expanded (Israelstam, 1986; Ratner, 1988).

Drug Use and Sexuality

The effects of drugs on sexuality are myriad and far too complex to cover here in great detail. Many medications have a negative effect on sexual desire and functioning. Most "recreational" drugs, although they may be perceived to increase sexual enjoyment (Bills & Duncan, 1991), actually have the opposite effect. Marijuana, however, appears to enhance the sexual experiences of some users. General positive expectations for marijuana use include relaxation, tension reduction, and social and sexual facilitation (Schafer & Brown, 1991). In sexual encounters, marijuana users report greater sensitivity to touch and awareness of physical closeness (Halikas, Weller, & Morse, 1982).

Amphetamines and cocaine both have reputations as sexual stimulants. While small doses may temporarily increase responsiveness, most studies show that high doses or habitual use have a negative effect on sexual functioning. Cocaine can produce either erectile failure or *priapism*—painful, persistent erections—in men (Kolodny, 1983). Heavy use nearly always leads to sexual dysfunction, such as an inability to achieve erection or orgasm (Washton, 1989). A study of 228 heavy cocaine users found a variety of responses to the same dosage (Macdonald, Waldorf, Reinarman, & Murphy, 1988). Men reported more sexual enhancement than women. The same levels of sexual impairment were found among those who sniffed the drug and those who smoked it as "freebase." Those who injected cocaine experienced the greatest dysfunction.

Aside from the adverse physical effects of drugs themselves, a major negative consequence of substance abuse is that it puts many people at significant risk of sexually transmitted diseases, including HIV infection (Cottler, Helzer, & Tipp, 1990). Addiction to cocaine, especially in the smokable form known as "crack," has led to the widespread practice of bartering sex for cocaine (Fullilove, Fullilove, Bowser, & Gross, 1990). This practice, as well as the practice of injecting cocaine or heroin, and the low rate of condom usage, has led to epidemics of STDs, including AIDS, in some urban areas. (Chapters 16 and 17 contain more information on STDs and HIV transmission.)

We've explored issues of self-image and sexual well-being as they affect our feelings about beauty, weight, aging, and physical limitations or disabilities. We've covered territory from menopause to cancer, and looked at the effects of alcohol and certain drugs on our sexuality. Our intent is to give you information to assist you in personal health issues and to stimulate thinking about how society deals with certain aspects of sexual health. We encourage you to learn more about your own body and your own sexual functioning. If things don't seem to work right, if you don't feel well, if you have questions, see your physician or other health-care practitioner. If you're not satisfied, get a second opinion. Read about health issues that apply to you and the people you're close to. Because we live in our bodies, we need to appreciate and respect them. By taking care of ourselves physically, we can maximize our pleasures in sexuality and in life.

SUMMARY

Living in Our Bodies: The Quest for Physical Perfection

• Our society is preoccupied with bodily perfection. Slim people are considered to be "better" than fat people. As a result, *eating disorders* have become common, especially among young women. Eating disorders reduce a person's health and vigor; are carried out in secrecy; are accompanied by obsessions, depression, anxiety, and guilt; lead to self-absorption and emotional instability; and are characterized by a lack of control. Those with eating disorders may have a history of psychological or sexual abuse in childhood.

• *Anorexia nervosa* is characterized by an all-controlling desire for thinness. Anorexics, usually female teenagers, are convinced that their bodies are too large, no matter how thin they actually are. Sexual dysfunction often accompanies anorexia. Anorexics diet (and often exercise) obsessively. Anorexia is potentially fatal.

• *Bulimia* is characterized by episodes of uncontrolled overeating (binge eating), counteracted by purging—vomiting, dieting, exercising excessively, or taking laxatives or diuretics. Bulimia may occur in as many as 1 out of every 5 college women.

Sexuality and Aging

• Although some physical functions may be slowed by aging, sexual interest, enjoyment, and satisfaction remain high for many older people. Women tend to be more concerned about the loss of attractiveness, whereas men tend to worry about their sexual capacity.

• In their forties, women's fertility begins to decline. Generally, between ages 45 and 55, *menopause*, the cessation of menstrual periods, occurs. Other physical changes occur, which may or may not present problems. The most common are hot flashes, changes in the vagina, and a gradual loss of bone mass. *Hormone replacement therapy (HRT)* is sometimes used to treat these symptoms. Women need to weigh the risks and benefits.

• Men need to understand that slower sexual responses are a normal part of aging and are not related to the ability to give or receive sexual pleasure. About half of men experience some degree of prostate enlargement after age 50. If it is severe, surgery can be performed.

Sexuality and Disability

• A wide range of disabilities and physical limitations can affect sexuality. People with these limitations need support and education so that they may enjoy their full sexual potential. Society as a whole needs to be aware of the concerns of the disabled and to allow them the same sexual rights as others.

• Chronic illnesses, such as diabetes, cardiovascular disease, and arthritis, pose special problems for a sexual life. People with these diseases (and their partners) can learn what to expect of themselves sexually and how to best cope with their particular conditions.

Sexuality and Cancer

• Cancer (in its many forms) occurs when cells begin to grow aberrantly. Most cancers form tumors. *Benign tumors* grow slowly and remain localized. *Malignant tumors* can spread throughout the body. When malignant cells are released into the blood or lymph system, they begin to grow away from the original tumor; this process is called *metastasis*.

• Breast cancer strikes 1 in 9 American women by age 85. Although the survival rate is improving, those who survive it may still suffer psychologically. Breast self-examination and *mammograms* (low-dose X-ray screenings) are the principal methods of detection. Surgical removal of the breast is called *mastectomy*. Radiation and chemotherapy are also used to fight breast cancer.

• *Cervical intraepithelial neoplasia (CIN)*, the appearance of certain abnormal cells on the cervix, can be diagnosed by a *Pap test*. It may then be treated by biopsy, cauterization, cryosurgery, or other surgery. If untreated, it may lead to cervical cancer.

• The most common gynecological cancer that poses a serious threat is uterine cancer; over 99% of these cancers affect the endometrium, the uterine lining. Abnormal bleeding is often the only symptom. It is treated with surgery (hysterectomy), radiation, or both.

• *Hysterectomy* is the surgical removal of the uterus. Many of these operations are performed unnecessarily. Conditions requiring hysterectomy are: (1) when cancerous or precancerous growth cannot be treated otherwise, (2) when non-cancerous growths interfere with other organs, (3) when heavy bleeding cannot be otherwise controlled, and (4) when severe infection cannot be otherwise controlled. Other problems may sometimes require hysterectomy. The removal of the ovaries (*oophorectomy*) will precipitate menopausal symptoms because the estrogen supply stops. For many women, hysterectomy may be a major psychological crisis; support and sensitivity from family, friends, and physicians are needed.

• Prostate cancer is the most common form of cancer among men. If detected early, it has a high cure rate. Surgery, radiation, hormone therapy, and chemotherapy are possible treatments. If the entire prostate is removed, sterility results, and erectile difficulties may occur.

• Testicular cancer rates are increasing. If caught early, it is curable; if not, it may be deadly. Self-examination is the key to detection; even slight symptoms should be reported at once. *Seminomas* are the most common type of testicular cancer. Treatment consists of surgery, sometimes followed by radiation and chemotherapy. Because of lowered fertility following the removal of a testicle, some men experience psychological distress and feelings of inadequacy.

Other Women's Health Issues

• *Toxic shock syndrome (TSS)* is a potentially fatal disease caused by *Staphylococcus aureus* bacteria. Tampons, especially "superabsorbent" ones, can lead to TSS by creating ideal conditions for staph germs to multiply in a menstruating woman's vagina. Theoretically, contraceptive sponges, diaphragms, and cervical caps also pose a risk of TSS. Women who use tampons should do so with appropriate caution. TSS is easily cured with antibiotics if caught early.

• *Endometriosis* is the growth of endometrial tissue outside the uterus. It is a major cause of infertility. Symptoms include intense pelvic pain and abnormal menstrual bleeding. Treatment depends on a number of factors. Various hormone treatments and types of surgery are employed.

• Lesbians tend to have poorer health care than heterosexual women, partly because they face hostility from health-care practitioners. Fear of discrimination may keep them from getting early diagnosis of serious diseases, such as breast cancer.

Men's Health

• *Prostatitis* is the inflammation of the prostate gland. *Congestive prostatitis* is usually the result of abstention from ejaculation or infrequent ejaculation. It is treated with warm baths and digital massage. *Infectious prostatitis* is difficult to treat, although antibiotics are prescribed for it; chronic prostatitis is painful and can lead to sexual dysfunctions.

DES Daughters and Sons

• *DES* (*diethylstilbestrol*) is a synthetic estrogen that was widely prescribed between 1941 and 1971 to prevent miscarriages. Women who took DES, and their children, are subject to various cancers and other problems at a far higher rate than the general population. DES sons and daughters need to be aware of their special health risks and seek treatment accordingly.

Alcohol, Drugs, and Sexuality

- Drugs and alcohol are commonly perceived as enhancers of sexuality, although in reality this is rarely the case. These substances have the effect of *disinhibition*, activating behaviors that would otherwise be suppressed.

- Some people use alcohol to give themselves permission to be sexual. Some men may use alcohol to justify sexual violence. People under the influence of alcohol or drugs tend to place themselves in risky sexual situations, such as exposing themselves to sexually transmitted diseases.

KEY TERMS

eating disorder	benign tumor	oophorectomy
anorexia nervosa	malignant tumor	androgen replacement therapy
anorexic	metastasis	orchiectomy
bulimia	mammogram	seminoma
climacteric	fibrocystic disease	nonseminoma
menopause	fibroadenoma	toxic shock syndrome (TSS)
hot flash	mastectomy	endometriosis
osteoporosis	lumpectomy	prostatitis
hormone replacement therapy (HRT)	cervical intraepithelial neoplasia (CIN)	diethylstilbestrol (DES)
male climacteric	cervical dysplasia	adenosis
benign prostatic hypertrophy	Pap test	disinhibition
retrograde ejaculation	biopsy	
diabetes mellitus	conization	
	hysterectomy	

RESOURCES

Alcohol and Drugs

Alcoholics Anonymous
P.O. Box 549, Grand Central Station
New York, NY 10163
(212) 683-3900
A voluntary, worldwide fellowship of men and women who support each other in obtaining and maintaining sobriety. See your telephone directory for local chapters.

Narcotics Anonymous
Support for those who wish to get off or stay off drugs of all types. Check your local directory or call information for your nearest support group.

National Association of Gay and Lesbian Alcoholism Professionals
204 W. 20th Street
New York, NY 10011
(212) 713-5074
Offers support for gay men and lesbians dealing with alcoholism.

Rational Recovery
P.O. Box 8000
Lotus, CA 95651
(916) 621-2667
An alternative to Alcoholics Anonymous.

Cancer

American Cancer Society and Reach for Recovery
1599 Clifton Road NE
Atlanta, GA, 30329
(404) 320-3333
Information and support for people with cancer; many local offices. Reach for Recovery is a group for breast cancer survivors.

National Cancer Institute
9000 Rockville Pike, Room 340
Bethesda, MD 20892
(800) 4-CANCER (422-6237)
Provides information on cancer treatment. Call the hotline for referrals.

Breast Cancer Action
P.O. Box 460185
San Francisco, CA 94146
(415) 922-8279
Information and political action for women with breast cancer.

Encore
Contact your local YWCA for information on Encore, a support organization for women with breast cancer.

Chronic Illness

American Diabetes Association
1660 Duke Street
P.O. Box 25757
Alexandria, VA 22313
(703) 549-1500
Information and referrals concerning diabetes.

American Heart Association
7320 Greenville Avenue
Dallas, TX 75231
(214) 373-6300
Information and referrals concerning heart disease prevention and treatment.

Arthritis Information Clearinghouse
P.O. Box 34427
Bethesda, MD 20034
(301) 495-4484
Information and referrals concerning arthritis and other rheumatic diseases.

Eating Disorders

The American Anorexia-Bulimia Association
133 Cedar Lane

Teaneck, NJ 07666
(201) 836-1800
Information and referrals for people with anorexia or bulimia and their families.

Overeaters Anonymous
P.O. Box 92870
Los Angeles, CA 90009
(213) 542-8363
Support group for compulsive overeaters. Your telephone directory lists local groups.

Miscellaneous
DES Action USA
1615 Broadway
Oakland, CA 94612
(415) 465-4011
Information for those who believe they may have been exposed to DES in utero.

The Endometriosis Association
8585 N. 76th Place
Milwaukee, WI 53223
(800) 992-3636
Information and referrals for women with endometriosis.

SUGGESTIONS FOR FURTHER READING

Journals with articles relevant to sexual health include Journal of the American Medical Association (JAMA), The New England Journal of Medicine, Women and Health, *and the British journal* Lancet.

Boston Women's Health Book Collective. *The New Our Bodies, Ourselves.* New York: Simon & Schuster, 1992. A gold mine of information on many aspects of women's health, including sexuality, aging, and medical problems, such as cancer.

Greenwood, Sadja. *Menopause, Naturally: Preparing for the Second Half of Life.* Volcano, CA: Volcano Press, 1992. A compassionate and comprehensive guide through menopause by a female physician.

Hepburn, Cuca, and Bonnie Gutierrez. *Alive and Well: A Lesbian Health Guide.* Freedom, CA: Crossing Press, 1988. A comprehensive guide addressing the health needs of lesbians, who are often excluded from sensitive medical care.

Love, Susan. *Dr. Susan Love's Breast Book.* Reading, MA: Addison-Wesley, 1990. Breast care and information on cancer from a leading authority.

Schover, Leslie, and Soren Jensen. *Sexuality and Chronic Illness.* New York: Guilford Press, 1988. How people living with chronic disease can have a healthy sex life.

Shute, Jenefer. *Life-Size.* Boston: Houghton Mifflin, 1992. A fascinating look inside the mind of a young anorexic woman.

White, Evelyn C., ed. *The Black Women's Health Book: Speaking for Ourselves.* Seattle, WA: Seal Press, 1990. Addresses issues typically faced by African American women in seeking competent and compassionate health care.

Wolf, Naomi. *The Beauty Myth: How Images of Beauty Are Used Against Women.* New York: William Morrow, 1991. How our culture and its media images cause women to judge their worth in terms of physical appearance.

Chapter Fifteen

SEXUAL ENHANCEMENT AND THERAPY

PREVIEW: SELF-QUIZ

1. Normal men and women do not experience erectile or orgasmic difficulties. True or false?

2. Communication and intimacy are important to maintaining sexual functioning in relationships. True or false?

3. Ethnicity affects the definition of what is a sexual problem. True or false?

4. Most sexual difficulties originate from physical problems. True or false?

5. Premature ejaculation is the most difficult sexual problem to treat. True or false?

6. Conflict between partners may lead to the disappearance of sexual desire. True or false?

7. Some sexual problems experienced by gay men and lesbians are the result of psychological conflicts they feel about their homosexuality. True or false?

8. Sexual problems are considered signs of neurosis by most sex therapists. True or false?

9. Evaluating one's performance during sexual activities often leads to improvement. True or false?

10. Smaller proportions of women than men experience arousal difficulties. True or false?

ANSWERS 1. F, 2. T, 3. T, 4. F, 5. F, 6. T, 7. T, 8. F, 9. F, 10. T

Chapter Outline

The quality of our sexuality is intimately connected to the quality of our lives and relationships. Because our sexuality is an integral part of ourselves, it reflects our excitement and boredom, intimacy and distance, emotional well-being and distress, health and illness. As a consequence, our sexual desires and activities ebb and flow. Sometimes they are highly erotic; at other times, they may be boring. Furthermore, many of us who are sexually active may sometimes experience sexual difficulties or problems. A study of college students, for example, found that 13% reported sexual problems of one kind or another (Spencer & Zeiss, 1987). A review of 23 studies on sexual problems found that nearly half the men and women reported occasional or frequent lack of desire, problems in arousal or orgasm, and painful intercourse (Spector & Carey, 1990). The widespread variability in our sexual functioning, however, suggests how "normal" at least occasional sexual difficulties are. Bernie Zilbergeld (1992) writes:

> Sex problems are normal and typical. I know, I know, all of your buddies are functioning perfectly and never have a problem. If you really believe that, I have a nice piece of oceanfront property in Kansas I'd like to talk to you about.

In this chapter, we examine some ways to enhance your sexuality to bring you greater pleasure and intimacy. Then we look at several common sexual problems and their causes. Finally, we see how those problems are treated.

SEXUAL ENHANCEMENT

Sexual enhancement refers to improving the quality of one's sexual relationship. There are a number of sexual-enhancement programs for people who function well sexually, but who nevertheless feel they can improve the quality of their sexual interactions and relationships. The programs generally aim at providing accurate information about sexuality, developing communication skills, fostering positive attitudes, and increasing self-awareness (Cooper, 1985). In some ways, your study of human sexuality examines many of the same cognitive, attitudinal, and communication themes explored in sexual-enrichment programs.

Zilbergeld (1992) suggests that there are six requirements for what he calls "great sex." They form the basis of many sexual-enhancement programs:

1. Accurate information about sexuality, especially your own and your partner's.
2. An orientation toward sex based on pleasure, such as arousal, fun, love, and lust, rather than performance and orgasm.
3. Being involved in a relationship that allows each person's sexuality to flourish.
4. An ability to communicate verbally and nonverbally about sex, feelings, and relationships.
5. Being equally assertive and sensitive about your own sexual needs and those of your partner.
6. Accepting, understanding, and appreciating differences between partners.

Although research is sketchy, those who participate in sexual-enhancement programs generally rate their relationship and sexual satisfaction levels higher than nonparticipants. The difficulty with such studies, however, is that those involved in such programs may be more highly motivated than others. Furthermore, it is also not clear how long the positive effects last.

Vivez, si m'en croyez, n'attendez à demain.
Cueillez dès aujourd'hui les roses de la vie.
Live, if you believe me, don't wait for tomorrow.
Gather today the roses of life.
Pierre de Ronsard

Good sex involves the ability to communicate nonverbally—through laughter and good times—as well as verbally.

Nevertheless, sexual-enhancement programs may be very helpful for couples in enriching their relationships. One study of couples who completed a sexual-enhancement program, for example, found that they felt they improved the affectional quality of their relationship; wives, in particular, felt their sexual relationships significantly improved (Cooper & Stoltenberg, 1987). And a 3-year follow-up of a divorce-prevention program emphasizing communication and sensual/sexual enhancement found that the couples completing the program had higher levels of marital and sexual satisfaction than a control group (Markman, Floyd, Stanley, & Storaasli, 1988).

In the following sections, we illustrate some of the approaches used in sexual-enhancement programs.

Self-Awareness

Being aware of your own sexual needs is often critical to enhancing your sexuality. Because of gender-role stereotypes and negative learning about sexuality, we often lose sight of our own sexual needs.

Conditions for Good Sex Sexual stereotypes present us with images of how we are supposed to behave sexually. Images of the "sexually in charge" man and the "sexual, but not too sexual" woman may interfere with our ability to express our own individual sexual feelings, needs, and desires. We follow the scripts and stereotypes we have been socialized to accept, rather than our own unique responses. Following these cultural images may impede our ability to have what therapist Carol Ellison calls "good sex." In an essay about intimacy-based sex therapy, Ellison (1985) writes that you will know you are having good sex if you feel good about yourself, your partner, your relationship, and what you're doing. It's good sex if, after a while, you still feel good about yourself, your partner, your relationship, and what you did. Good sex does not necessarily include orgasm or intercourse. It can be kissing, holding, masturbating, oral sex, anal sex, and so on. It can be heterosexual, gay, lesbian, or bisexual.

Zilbergeld (1992) suggests that to fully enjoy our sexuality, we need to explore our "conditions for good sex." There is nothing unusual about requiring conditions for any activity. For a good night's sleep, for example, each of us has certain conditions. We may need absolute quiet, no light, a feather pillow, an open window. Others, however, can sleep during a loud dormitory party, curled up in the corner of a stuffy room. Of conditions for good sex, Zilbergeld writes:

> In a sexual situation, a condition is anything that makes you more relaxed, more comfortable, more confident, more excited, more open to your experience. Put differently, a condition is something that clears your nervous system of unnecessary clutter, leaving it open to receive and transmit sexual messages in ways that will result in a good time for you.

Different individuals report different conditions for good sex. Some common conditions, according to Zilbergeld (1992), include:

- *Feeling intimate with your partner.* This is often important for both men and women, despite stereotypes of men wanting only sex. If the partners are feeling distant from each other, they may need to talk about their feelings before becoming sexual. Emotional distance can take the heart out of sex.

- *Feeling sexually capable.* Generally, this relates to an absence of anxieties about sexual performance. For men, this includes anxiety about becoming erect or ejaculating too soon. For women, it includes worry about painful intercourse or lack of orgasm. For both men and women, it includes worry about whether one is a good lover.

- *Feeling trust.* Both men and women may need to know they are emotionally safe with their partner. They need to feel confident that they will not be judged, ridiculed, or talked about.

- *Feeling aroused.* A person does not need to be sexual unless he or she is sexually aroused or excited. Simply because one's partner wants to be sexual does not mean that you have to be.

- *Feeling physically and mentally alert.* This condition requires a person not to feel particularly tired, ill, stressed, or preoccupied. It requires one not to be under the influence of excessive alcohol or drugs.

- *Feeling positive about the environment and situation.* A person may need privacy, to be in a place where he or she feels protected from intrusion. Each needs to feel that the other is sexually interested and wants to be sexually involved.

Happiness is a butterfly which, when pursued, is always beyond our grasp, but which, if you will sit down quiet, may alight upon you.
Nathaniel Hawthorne

Each individual has his or her own unique conditions for good sex. If you are or have been sexually active, to discover your conditions for good sex, think about the last few times you were sexual and were highly aroused. Compare those times to other times when you were much less aroused (Zilbergeld, 1992). Make a list of the factors that were different between the two. Consider the following areas: your feelings about your partner at the time, such as intimate, distant, indifferent, or angry; how interested you were in being sexual; anxieties about sexual performance; the surroundings; preoccupation, worry, or stress about nonsexual matters; your health; whether you were using alcohol or other drugs.

Put the list away for a few days, then see if there is anything you want to add or change. Reword the list so that each of the conditions is specific. For example, if you wrote "Felt pressured to have sex," rewrite as "Need to feel unpressured." When you rewrite these conditions, you can get a clearer sense of what your conditions for good sex are. If you feel comfortable, you should communicate your needs with your partner.

Homework Exercises We are often unaware of our body and our erotic responses. Sexual-enhancement programs often give us specific exercises to undertake in privacy. Such "homework" exercises require individuals to make a time commitment to themselves or their partner to carry out homework assignments. Typical assignments include the exercises below. If you feel comfortable with any of the assignments, you might want to try one or more. (For additional exercises for men, see Zilbergeld, 1992; for exercises for women, see Barbach, 1982).

- *Mirror examination.* Use a full-length mirror to examine your body while nude. Use a hand mirror to view your genitals. Look at all your features in an uncritical manner; view yourself with a feeling of acceptance.

- *Body relaxation and exploration.* Take 30 minutes to an hour to fully relax. Begin with a leisurely shower or bath; then, remaining nude, find a comfortable place to touch and explore your body and genitals.

- *Masturbation.* In a relaxed situation, with body oils or lotions to enhance your sensations, explore ways of touching your body and genitals that bring you pleasure. Do this exercise for several sessions without having an orgasm; experience erotic pleasure without orgasm as its goal. If you are about to have an orgasm, decrease stimulation. After several sessions without having an orgasm, continue pleasuring yourself until you have an orgasm.

- *Erotic aids.* **Erotic aids** are devices, such as vibrators and dildos, or oils and lotions, designed to enhance erotic responsiveness. Erotic devices are also called **sex toys,** emphasizing their playfulness. You may wish to try using a sex toy or shower massage as you masturbate, with your partner or by yourself. You may also want to view videos at home or read erotic poetry or stories to yourself or partner (Neidigh & Kinder, 1987). (See "Resources" at the end of the chapter for sources of erotic enhancement.)

Many of these exercises can be also done with a partner; each takes turn in erotically exploring the other.

Full nakedness, all joys are due to thee,
As souls unbodied, bodies unclothed must be . . .

John Donne

Communication

We have already discussed communication in Chapter 9. As you will recall, we communicate both verbally and nonverbally. In this section, we apply some of what we know about verbal and nonverbal communication to specific situations.

Verbal Communication Verbal communication has the advantage in being more direct and less ambiguous than nonverbal communication. Let's take the example of verbally communicating your conditions for good sex. Look at your conditions for good sex. How would you communicate with your partner to get these conditions met? Effective communication requires you to (1) bring up the subject at an appropriate time, (2) say what your *specific* conditions for good sex are, (3) offer suggestions or alternatives for achieving them, and (4) ask for your partner's feedback.

Imagine that Adriana listed "Not feeling pressured" as one of her conditions for good sex. She decided to talk with her boyfriend Philip about it. (The scenario could also be reversed.) Here is their conversation.

ADRIANA: I need to feel unpressured about having sex so that I can enjoy it more. (Statement of the problem using "I-message.")

PHILIP: What do you mean? (Clarification seeking.)

ADRIANA: Last night I said I didn't feel like it. (Factual statement.)

PHILIP: I know, but I thought once we started, you'd enjoy it. (Justification.)

ADRIANA: I enjoy making love with you. (Affirmation.) But when I'm pressured, I get uptight. I feel used. (Statement of feelings.)

PHILIP: You're always uptight. It's your problem, not mine. ("You-message"; blaming and escalating.)

ADRIANA: I didn't say it was your problem. I'm not blaming you. (Clarifying and deescalating.) I said *I* need to feel unpressured about sex. (Restatement of problem using "I-message.")

PHILIP: We may as well break up if you feel that way. Obviously you don't love me. (Defensiveness.)

ADRIANA: Let me see if I understand what you're saying. You believe we should break up because I need to feel unpressured about sex. You don't believe I love you. (Paraphrasing and deescalating.)

PHILIP: Well, I don't really want to break up. I feel badly because you don't want to have sex with me. (Statement of feelings.)

ADRIANA: I do want to have sex with you. (Reaffirmation.) I just don't want to feel pressured. (Restatement of problem.) There is a big difference.

PHILIP: I guess that's right, there is a big difference. But I'm confused. I don't exactly know what to do. (Statement of feelings.)

ADRIANA: You could ask me. Or you could let me initiate. (Offering solutions.) Does that sound OK to you? (Requesting feedback.)

PHILIP: I feel a little uncomfortable about asking you if it's OK. (Statement of feelings.)

Talking is the major way we establish, maintain, monitor, and adjust our relationships.

Deborah Tannen

Some individuals and couples use erotic aids such as vibrators, dildos, oils, and lotions to enhance their sexual responsiveness.

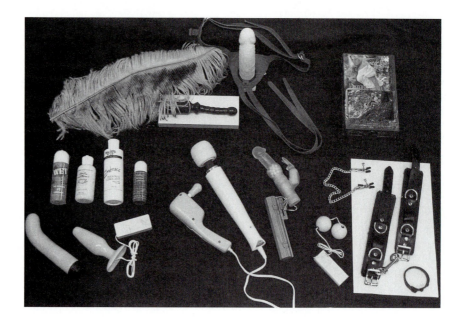

ADRIANA: Do you know what it is that makes you uncomfortable? (Request for more information.)

PHILIP: I don't know. It's kind of like I don't exactly know what words to say. I feel embarrassed. (Statement of feelings.)

ADRIANA: I understand it might be embarrassing. (Paraphrasing.) Well, what about letting me initiate sex for a while? See how that works out. What do you think? (Offering alternative; seeking feedback.)

PHILIP: OK, let's try it to see what happens. (Agreement.)

ADRIANA: It means a lot to me that you'll try this. (Appreciation.) Let's talk about how this seems to be working a little later. (Keeping communication open.)

In this exchange, the couple came to an agreement that may enhance their sexual relationship. The exchange points out that enhancement often has nothing to do with the mechanics of sex. Instead, the quality of the communication and the willingness of partners to change are critical. (If you would like to learn the rules for having *bad* sex, see Perspective 1.)

Nonverbal Communication Nonverbal communication can sometimes be misunderstood. We often do for our partner what we would like to have done for us. Imagine that a man who wants to be kissed on the neck kisses his partner's neck, hoping she will return the pleasure. But the more he kisses her neck, the less she kisses his. Finally, he asks why she stopped kissing his neck the more he increased kissing hers. It turns out she did not like being kissed on the neck. She hoped that by decreasing her neck kissing, he would stop kissing her neck. Once the couple discussed the situation, they agreed that he would stop kissing her neck, and she would increase kissing his. Verbal communication was necessary to resolve the confusion caused by what turned out to be nonverbal miscommunication.

TEN RULES FOR HAVING BAD SEX

You don't have to follow all the rules listed below to have bad sex. Often just one is sufficient.

1. *Do it like they do in the movies.* Movies show you how to have great sex. If you do it like the stars, with lots of acrobatics and orgasms (and maybe a little force), you'll have great sex, too. And remember, just like in the movies, don't use a condom, because no one ever gets pregnant or infected.

2. *Pressure your partner into having sex.* If your partner doesn't want to, you can always accuse him or her of being uptight. Tell your partner he or she will enjoy it once you start. If necessary, tell your partner you love him or her. In fact, tell your partner anything, but get him or her into bed.

3. *Make your partner a sex object.* Remember, your partner is not a person but a body. Your partner is there to satisfy *your* needs, not his or hers (that would be selfish). If his or her needs happen to get satisfied along with yours, it's because you're a great lover. If they're not satisfied, it's your partner's problem because *you* are a great lover.

4. *Don't touch.* Grabbing's OK, though. And forget kissing, that's for teenagers. The point of sex is intercourse, so why bother with anything else? (Unless, of course, your partner wants to give *you* oral sex.)

5. *Make orgasm your goal.* What's the point of having sex if you don't have an orgasm? And if your partner's taking too long, tell him or her to hurry up. You haven't got all day. You've got more important things to do.

6. *Ask: Did you come?* If the answer is no, ask why not.

7. *Tell your partner that he or she is a bad lover.* This will make him or her feel bad and you feel good because it tells your partner that you know what *real* sex is. If your partner gets hurt, you can say you were just trying to be honest. While you're at it, give your partner a few pointers about what he or she is doing wrong. Be sure to do this repeatedly until he or she learns—or leaves.

8. *Don't use condoms or birth control.* If you don't practice safer sex, think how much fun you'll have worrying about whether you might have become infected with an STD. In addition, both you and your partner will get to worry about pregnancy.

9. *Don't bathe.* This may not sound like much, but watch how your partner squirms to get out of your reach (or smell, to be more precise). Not brushing your teeth for a few days, smoking a pack of cigarettes, or exhaling beer breath is just as effective.

10. *Get drunk or stoned out of your mind.* This may give you some of the worst sex you've ever had. You may not even have had sex at all, but you won't know for sure.

Other times, however, nonverbal communication may be very helpful (Barbach, 1982). A woman, for example, may want her partner to use his hand to stimulate her clitoris for her to have an orgasm. She might tell her partner what she needs, how to move his hand, and where to touch her vulva. Unfortunately, verbal instructions alone may not work. Show and tell may be more effective. The woman could take her partner's hand in hers and place it on her vulva and guide him to the motion, rhythm, and places that are most exciting to her. In the same manner, a man could take his partner's hand in his and show how he likes to be stimulated.

Intensifying Erotic Pleasure

One of the most significant elements in enhancing one's physical experience of sex is intensifying arousal. Intensifying arousal centers sexual experience on erotic pleasure rather than on sexual performance. This can be done in many ways, some of which are described below.

Sexual Arousal Sexual arousal refers to the physiological responses, fantasies, and desires associated with sexual anticipation and sexual activity. We have different levels of arousal. These levels are not necessarily associated with particular types of sexual activities. Sometimes we feel more sexually aroused when we kiss than when we have sexual intercourse or oral sex. Masturbation may sometimes be more exciting than oral sex or coitus.

The first element in increasing sexual arousal is having your conditions for good sex met. If you need privacy, find a place in which to be alone; if you need a romantic setting, go for a walk at the beach by moonlight, or listen to music with candlelight; if you want limits on your sexual activities, tell your partner; if you need a certain kind of physical stimulation, show or tell your partner what you like.

A second element in increasing arousal is focusing on the sensations you are experiencing. Once you begin an erotic activity, such as massaging or kissing, do not let yourself be distracted. When you're kissing, don't think about what you're going to do next or about an upcoming test in your human sexuality class. Instead, focus on the sensual experience of your lips and heart. Zilbergeld (1992) writes:

> Focusing on sensations means exactly that. You put your attention in your body where the action is. When you're kissing, keep your mind on your lips. This is *not* the same as thinking about your lips or the kiss; just put your attention in your lips. As you focus on your sensations, you may want to convey your pleasure to your partner. Let him or her know through your sounds and movements that you are excited.

A Ban on Intercourse Waiting, delays, and obstacles may intensify arousal. This is one of the pleasures of sexual abstinence that may get lost soon after one begins coitus. Lonnie Barbach (1982) suggests that sexually active people may intensify arousal by placing a ban on sexual intercourse for a period of time. If you are gay or lesbian, you may place a comparable ban on your preferred activity. Barbach writes:

> If you . . . place a ban on intercourse, it is important to maintain other forms of sexual activity during that period. Holding, kissing, and manual and oral stimulation can be substituted for intercourse. In addition, although intercourse may be off limits for a while, you may also want to agree not to have orgasms either alone or together as a means of building up anticipation and excitement.

During this time, you may explore other ways of being erotic or sexual.

My beloved is white and ruddy, the chiefest among ten thousand. His head is as the most fine gold; his locks are bushy, and black as a raven. His eyes are as the eyes of doves by the rivers of waters, washed with milk, and fitly set: His cheeks are as a bed of spices, as sweet flowers: his lips like lilies, dropping sweet smelling myrrh: His hands are as gold rings set with the beryl: his belly is as bright ivory overlaid with sapphires: His legs are as pillars of marble, set upon sockets of fine gold: his countenance is as Lebanon, excellent as the cedars: His mouth is most sweet: yea, he is altogether lovely. This is my beloved, and this is my friend, O daughters of Jerusalem.

Song of Solomon 5:10–16

Impulse arrested spills over, and the flood is feeling, the flood is passion, the flood is even madness: it depends on the force of the current, the height and strength of the barrier. . . . Feeling lurks in that interval of time between desire and its consummation.

Aldous Huxley

Barbach (1982), JoAnn Loulan (1984), and Zilbergeld (1992), suggest the following activities, among others:

- Sit or lie down close to each other. Gaze into each other's eyes to establish an intimate connection. Gently caress each other's face and hair as you continue gazing. Tell each other what fantasies you have about the other.

- Bathe or shower with your partner, soaping his or her body slowly and sensually but not touching the genitals. At another time, you may want to include genital stimulation.

- Give and receive a sensual, erotic massage. Do not touch the genitals, but massage around them teasingly. Use body oils and lotions to increase tactile sensitivity. Later, you may want to include genital stimulation.

- Use your lips, tongue, and mouth to explore your partner's body, especially the neck, ears, nipples, inner thighs, palms, fingers, feet, and toes. Take your time.

- "Dirty dance" together, feeling the curves and textures of your partner's body; put your hands under your partner's clothes, and caress him or her. Kiss and caress each other as you slowly remove each other's clothing. Then hold each other close, kiss and massage each other, explore each other's body with your mouth, tongue, and lips.

How beautiful are thy feet with shoes, O prince's daughter! The joints of thy thighs are like jewels, the work of the hands of a cunning workman. Thy navel is like a round goblet, which wanteth not liquor: thy belly is like a heap of wheat set about with lilies. Thy two breasts are like two young roes that are twins. Thy neck is as a tower of ivory; thine eyes like the fishpools in Heshbon, by the gate of Bath-rabbim: thy nose is as the tower of Lebanon which looketh toward Damascus. Thine head upon thee is like Carmel, and the hair of thine head like purple: the King is held in the galleries. How fair and how pleasant art thou, O love, for delights! This thy stature is like to a palm tree, and thy breasts to clusters of grapes. I said, I will go up to the palm tree, I will take hold of the boughs thereof: now also thy breasts shall be as clusters of the vine, and the smell of thy nose like apples. And the root of thy mouth like the best wine for my beloved, that goeth down sweetly, causing the lips of those that are asleep to speak.

Song of Solomon 7:1–9

SEXUAL DISORDERS AND DYSFUNCTIONS

Sexual disorders and dysfunctions refer to difficulties individuals experience in their sexual functioning. Heterosexuals, gay men, and lesbians experience similar kinds of sexual problems (Margolies, Becher, & Jackson-Brewer, 1987; Nichols, 1987; Reece, 1988).

Sexual dysfunctions are generally defined as impaired physiological responses that prevent individuals from functioning sexually, such as erectile difficulties or absence of orgasm. Common sexual dysfunctions among men include erectile dysfunction, the inability to have or maintain erection; premature ejaculation, the inability to delay ejaculation; inhibited ejaculation, the inability to ejaculate; and delayed ejaculation, prolonged delay in ejaculating. Common dysfunctions among women include anorgasmia, the absence of orgasm; vaginismus, the tightening of the vaginal muscles, prohibiting penetration; and dyspareunia, painful intercourse.

Recently, researchers and therapists have become interested in defining and treating sexual disorders as well as dysfunctions. **Sexual disorders** include such problems as hypoactive sexual desire, low or absent sexual desire, and sexual aversion, a consistently phobic response to sexual activities or the idea of such activities. Disorders are similar to sexual dysfunctions insofar as they limit an individual's ability to be sexual. But properly speaking, disorders affect the brain's arousal capabilities rather than physiological responses. Individuals with sexual disorders retain their ability to respond physically; the problem is that they have no desire to be sexual. They have shut down their brains' erotic centers.

In examining sexual disorders and dysfunctions, many contemporary researchers and therapists use the triphasic model developed by Helen Singer Kaplan (1979) to describe the sexual response cycle (see Chapter 3). The triphasic model divides the sexual response cycle into three stages: (1) desire, (2) excitement, and (3) orgasm. The most common disorders or dysfunctions for each stage are as follows:

Desire. Hypoactive sexual desire (HSD) and sexual aversion.

Excitement. Erectile dysfunction, painful intercourse, and vaginismus.

Orgasm. Anorgasmia, premature ejaculation, and inhibited or delayed ejaculation.

Sexual Disorders

Hypoactive sexual desire and sexual aversion may be deeply rooted psychological problems; they are difficult to treat (Hawton, Catalan, & Fagg, 1991; Kaplan, 1987; Levine, 1987). Therapists became aware of them during the 1980s as a result of Kaplan's work (Kaplan, 1979, 1987).

Hypoactive Sexual Desire Hypoactive sexual desire (HSD), or low or absent sexual desire, is a widespread problem. Kaplan (1979) described the characteristics of a person experiencing hypoactive sexual desire, also known as **inhibited sexual desire:**

> [He] behaves as though his sexual circuits have been "shut down." He loses interest in sexual matters, will not pursue sexual gratification, and if a sexual situation presents itself, is not moved to avail himself of the opportunity.

HSD is fairly common to both men and women (Spector & Carey, 1990). One study found that a third of 365 couples ceased having sexual intercourse for long periods; the median time of abstinence was 8 weeks (Edwards & Booth, 1977). Some therapists and psychiatrists state that HSD is the primary complaint of men in therapy (Botwin, 1979).

Hypoactive sexual desire is related to other sexual dysfunctions insofar as it is rooted in anxieties. Usually, however, it stems from deeper, more intense sexual anxieties, greater hostility toward the partner, and more pervasive defenses than found in people with erectile and orgasmic difficulties (Hawton, Catalan, & Fagg, 1991; Kaplan, 1987). Sometimes, however, HSD is a means of coping with other sexual dysfunctions that precede it. Kolodny, Masters, and Johnson (1979) observe: "By developing a low interest in sexual activity, the person avoids the unpleasant consequences of sexual failure such as embarrassment, loss of self-esteem, and frustration."

There appear to be a number of causes of HSD (Hawton et al., 1991; Kaplan, 1979). Depression is probably the most common cause. Anger toward the partner also may be significant. Over a period of time, if anger is not resolved, it may develop into resentment or hatred that colors every aspect of the relationship. Most people cannot experience sexual desire for someone with whom they are angry or deeply resentful. "Anger and sex act as mutual inhibitants," noted Kaplan (1979).

In addition, stress, traumatic marital separation or divorce, loss of work, or forced retirement are frequently associated with HSD. When a person is under stress, energies and resources are directed toward dealing with emotional problems. When the stress ends, the person usually reexperiences his or her sexual desires. Drugs, hormone deficiency, and illness also decrease desire.

There are also more remote causes of HSD. Some men or women may feel mild anxiety over possible performance, guilt, or anticipated lack of pleasure. Others are fearful of romantic success and intimacy and consequently avoid sexual activities. Still others experience deep anxieties resulting from childhood sexual abuse, fear of pleasure, or suppressed anger toward the partner.

Psychological causes of hypoactive sexual desire are often difficult to pinpoint and treat. People with HSD may have a "turn-off" mechanism, notes Kaplan (1979):

> Most of the patients I have studied tend to suppress their desire by evoking negative thoughts or by allowing spontaneously emerging negative thoughts to intrude when they have a sexual opportunity. They have learned to put themselves into negative emotional states. . . . In this manner they make themselves angry, fearful, or distracted, and so tap into the natural physiologic inhibitory mechanisms which suppress sexual desire when this is appropriate and in the person's best interest.

Gay men and lesbians may experience hypoactive sexual desire if they are unable to accept their sexual orientation (Margolies et al., 1988; Reece, 1988). Because of HIV and AIDS, some gay men have become especially depressed and have lost their sexual desire (Reece, 1988; Shannon & Woods, 1991).

The treatment for most sexual dysfunctions involves some form of behavior modification, but such therapies do not work well for HSD (Kaplan,

1979; Kolodny, Masters, & Johnson, 1979). Treatment requires psychosexual therapy to gain insight into the underlying motives that inhibit sexual desire.

Sexual Aversion **Sexual aversion** is a consistently phobic response to sexual activities or the idea of such activities (Kaplan, 1987). It is often confused with hypoactive desire because avoidance often manifests itself as a lack of interest in sexual matters. Closer examination, however, may show that the lack of desire is a defense against anxiety-causing situations, such as intimacy or touch (Ponticas, 1992).

More women than men experience sexual aversion. There is some debate, however, about how extensive this disorder is. Kaplan (1987) believes that it is widespread. She feels it has been underreported because it is frequently misdiagnosed as hypoactive sexual desire or as an excitement-phase disorder. Masters and Johnson, however, consider sexual aversion "an infrequently encountered disorder"; they report having seen only 164 cases at their institute between 1972 and 1985 (Masters, Johnson, & Kolodny, 1990).

In cases of sexual aversion, the frequency of intercourse typically falls to once or twice a year (or less). While it is not uncommon for some people to be uninterested or to dislike various forms of noncoital sexual activity, they nevertheless enjoy (or tolerate) sexual intercourse. A person experiencing sexual aversion, however, feels overwhelming anxieties about *any* kind of sexual contact. A mere kiss, touch, or caress may cause a phobic response out of fear that it might lead to something sexual. Sometimes these responses are internalized, but at other times, they can lead to physical responses such as sweating, nausea, vomiting, or diarrhea. Anticipating sex often provokes greater anxiety than the sexual activity itself.

Sexual aversion often results from severely negative parental attitudes during childhood, sexual trauma, such as rape or sexual abuse, consistent sexual pressure from a long-term partner, and gender identity confusion (Masters et al., 1990). Many cases of sexual aversion appear to be linked to adolescent difficulty with body image or self-esteem. Adolescent boys with gynecomastia (transitory breast enlargement), girls with excessive body or facial hair, and adolescents of both sexes with acne or obesity problems often avoid the sexual experimentation and activity typical for their age.

As with heterosexuals, gay men and lesbians may enjoy certain activities, such as kissing or mutual masturbation, but feel aversive to other activities. For gay men, sexual aversion often focuses on issues of anal eroticism (Reece, 1988). For lesbians, aversion frequently focuses on cunnilingus (Nichols, 1988). Although cunnilingus is often the preferred activity among lesbians for reaching orgasm, as many as 25% rarely or never engage in it (Blumstein & Schwartz, 1983).

A study of 382 college students found that there was considerable fear about sexual activity, especially because of AIDS (Katz, Gipson, Kearl, & Kriskovich, 1989). Almost half expressed skepticism about "safe sex." Because of their anxieties, almost one-third had repeatedly avoided all or almost all genital contact; women were especially likely to avoid such sexual interactions. Approximately 10% believed their fears about sexuality warranted treatment. The researchers expressed concern that sexual aversion may increase because of fears linked to HIV.

Male Sexual Dysfunctions

Both males and females may experience desire disorders. They may also experience dyspareunia, painful intercourse, but it is relatively uncommon among men (Lazarus, 1989). Most specifically, male sexual problems focus on the excitement stages of the response cycle: the ability to have or maintain an erection, and premature or delayed ejaculation.

Erectile Dysfunctions **Erectile dysfunction** is the inability to have or maintain an erection during intercourse. (Erectile dysfunctions were previously known as "impotence.") Such dysfunctions are common; as many as 3–9% of American men experience erectile difficulties (Spector & Carey, 1990). They affect as many as half the men in America at one time or another, according to one estimate (Kaplan, 1974). Erectile dysfunctions are divided into primary and secondary dysfunctions. Those men with primary erectile dysfunction have never had an erection, and those with secondary erectile dysfunction have had erections in the past. Secondary erectile dysfunctions are more common than primary dysfunctions and are easier to treat, since they are often situational in origin.

Erectile difficulties may occur because of fatigue, too much alcohol, depression, conflict, or a host of other transitory reasons. Despite their common and usually transitory occurrence, erectile difficulties deeply affect a man's masculine self-concept.

Premature Ejaculation In **premature ejaculation,** a man, with minimal stimulation, is unable to control or delay his ejaculation as long as he wishes, resulting in personal or interpersonal distress. It is estimated that 36–38% of American men experience premature ejaculation (Spector & Carey, 1990). Although it is one of the most common sexual dysfunctions of heterosexual men in sex therapy, women more than men complain of it (Masters & Johnson, 1970). Often, couples are confused, bewildered, and unhappy when the man consistently ejaculates too early. The woman may be sexually dissatisfied, while her partner may feel that she is too demanding. He may also feel considerable guilt and anxiety. They may begin to avoid sexual contact with each other. The man may experience erectile problems because of his anxieties over premature ejaculation; he may withdraw from sex completely. Heterosexual men go into therapy more often for premature ejaculation than do gay men (Reece, 1988). (For a discussion of the relativity of the concept of premature ejaculation, see Perspective 2.)

Inhibited and Delayed Ejaculation In **inhibited ejaculation,** the penis is erect, but the man is unable to ejaculate. Because ejaculation and orgasm are separate phenomena, the man may nevertheless be able to have an orgasm. In mild forms, it occurs with some frequency. About 4–9% of men have experienced this difficulty (Spector & Carey, 1990). In **delayed ejaculation,** the man is not able to ejaculate easily in intercourse; it may take 40 minutes of concentrated thrusting before ejaculation occurs.

Anxiety-provoking situations can interfere with a man's ejaculatory reflex. He may not be able to have an orgasm in certain situations in which he feels guilt or conflict. He may only experience orgasm from masturbation.

Perspective 2

SEXUAL DYSFUNCTIONS: A RELATIVE CONCEPT?

The idea of a sexual dysfunction implies a model of an effectively working, "functional" sexual system to which it may be compared. Unfortunately, the major sex therapists have never explicitly described their model of a "functional" sexual system. As a result, their ideas concerning what is dysfunctional can sometimes be imprecise and confusing. Carol Tavris (1992) writes:

> Scientific efforts to categorize and label sexual disorders are, by definition, subjective decisions because they depend on criteria for sexual normalcy, which change with the times. . . . A century ago, most Victorian doctors believed that masturbation was a practice that could cause "masturbatory insanity"; terrible treatments were devised to keep people from masturbating. Now masturbation is advocated as a healthy activity and a treatment in its own right.

We can obtain a sense of our contemporary beliefs about proper sexual "functioning" by briefly examining some of the underlying ideas about premature ejaculation and anorgasmia. Although premature ejaculation is a male dysfunction, both it and anorgasmia reflect ideas about the nature of female sexuality. (For a critique on the classification of sexual dysfunctions, see Tavris, 1992, and Tiefer, 1992; for a new classification system, see Schmidt, 1992).

From Rapid Ejaculation to Premature Ejaculation

Over the last several decades, premature ejaculation has emerged as a major sexual dysfunction. As long as procreation was the primary aim of sexual intercourse and male satisfaction was more important than female satisfaction, however, rapid ejaculation did not represent a sexual problem. Even as late as 1948, Kinsey argued that rapid ejaculation was a sign of sexual health and vigor. "It would be difficult to find another situation in which an individual who was quick and intense in his responses was labeled anything but su-

perior . . . however inconvenient and unfortunate . . . from the standpoint of the wife" (Kinsey et al., 1948). The rise of a more egalitarian view of sexual interactions changed this opinion.

When female sexual arousal and satisfaction were recognized as legitimate goals in America, rapid ejaculation was transformed into a dysfunction known as premature ejaculation. The shift in our cultural definition of female sexuality formed the basis for this change. In fact, Masters and Johnson (1970) argued that a realistic definition of premature ejaculation "should reflect sociocultural orientation together with the consideration of the prevailing requirements of sexual partners." They wrote:

> The Foundation considers a man a premature ejaculator if he cannot control his ejaculatory process for a sufficient length of time during intra-vaginal containment to *satisfy his partner in at least 50 percent of their coital connections* [italics ours]. If the woman is persistently nonorgasmic for reasons other than rapidity of the male's ejaculatory process, there is no validity to the definition.

Such a definition presents several difficulties, however. First, in this definition, the person who defines rapid ejaculation as a problem is not the man who experiences it, but his partner. The question is then, "For whom is ejaculation premature?" Second, the criterion for diagnosing the *male* as dysfunctional is based on whether the *female* received sufficient penile stimulation to have an orgasm. Third, if the *woman* is not orgasmic in intercourse, by definition the man is not a premature ejaculator; premature ejaculation exists only in relation to an orgasmic partner. If the woman is not orgasmic in intercourse, according to Masters and Johnson's definition, it does not even matter whether the man ejaculates rapidly. This overlooks the fact that even if a woman is not orgasmic in intercourse, both she and her partner might enjoy prolonged intercourse. Fourth, Masters and Johnson appear to assume that female orgasms derived from penile thrusting are superior to orgasms derived from manual or oral stimulation.

Anorgasmia: A Modern Dysfunction

In the nineteenth century, the model of a healthily functioning female was one in which women experienced little or no sexual desire (Tavris, 1992). Women were not expected to be orgasmic. Those who experienced strong desires were described by physicians as suffering from "furor uterinus"; on occasion, clitoridectomies, the surgical removal of the clitoris, were performed to "cure" young girls and women of their "excessive" desires and "unhealthy" masturbatory activities. (One hundred years later, by contrast, Masters and Johnson [1970] created a category of sexual dysfunction called "masturbatory orgasmic inadequacy" to describe women who were unable to have an orgasm through masturbation.)

Some therapists, including Masters and Johnson, transform the absence of female orgasm during intercourse into anorgasmia, a sexual dysfunction (Masters & Johnson, 1970; Masters et al., 1985). Making the absence of orgasm a dysfunction, however, assumes that orgasm is a natural phenomenon in women. There is considerable debate as to whether female orgasm is an innate or a culturally learned response. Various studies suggest that 8–12% of women who have had intercourse have never experienced orgasm. Those who are orgasmic are often not consistently orgasmic. About one-third to one-half of women who are orgasmic in intercourse require manual stimulation of the clitoris (Hite, 1976; Kaplan, 1974). Kaplan (1974) believes that the research on female orgasms during intercourse is so controversial and inconsistent that "all opinions, including my own, about the prevalence and normalcy of coital orgasm . . . must be regarded as hypothetical until systematic studies have been conducted."

If we do not know whether female orgasm during intercourse is biologically based we have no scientific basis for classifying the absence of female orgasm as a dysfunction. In fact, most sex therapists do not regard the absence of coital orgasm a sexual problem if the woman enjoys intercourse and is orgasmic in other ways, such as by masturbation, manual stimulation by her partner, or oral-genital sex. Many couples experience little or no impact on their sexual satisfaction if the woman is not orgasmic during intercourse (Heiman, 1986; Raboch & Raboch, 1992).

Models of Functional Sexuality

The underlying model for defining rapid ejaculation and absence of orgasm as dysfunctions includes the belief (1) that both partners *should* have orgasms in intercourse through penile thrusting, and (2) that orgasm rather than erotic pleasure, intimacy, or reproduction is the goal of intercourse.

There are alternative ways of looking at sexual interactions, however, that would not transform rapid ejaculation or absence of orgasm into sexual dysfunctions. One way, for example, is to make intimacy and pleasure—rather than orgasm—the goals of intercourse. Another way is to make orgasms achieved through manual or oral stimulation of a partner as valid as those achieved through penile thrusting.

Thomas Szasz (1990) approaches the ideas and practices of sex therapy with some caution:

> Today, it is dogmatically asserted—by the medical profession and the official opinion-makers of our society—that it is healthy or normal for people to enjoy sex, that the lack of such enjoyment is the symptom of a sexual disorder, that such disorders can be relieved by appropriate medical (sex-therapeutic) interventions, and that they ought, whenever possible, to be treated. This view, though it pretends to be scientific, is, in fact, moral or religious: it is an expression of the medical ideology we have substituted for traditional religious creeds.

Because something is not "functioning" according to therapy's hidden models does not necessarily mean that something is wrong with us. We need to evaluate our sexuality in terms of our own and our partner's satisfaction and the meanings we give to our sexuality.

Often this inhibition is overcome when the situation or partner changes or when the man engages in a fantasy, receives additional stimulation, or is distracted. Inhibited ejaculation is more common among gay men than heterosexuals (Reece, 1988).

Female Sexual Dysfunctions

Most female sexual difficulties center on the orgasmic phase, although occasionally women experience vaginismus during the excitement phase.

Vaginismus In **vaginismus,** the muscles around the vaginal entrance go into involuntary spasmodic contractions, preventing the insertion of the penis. During the nineteenth century, vaginismus was one of the most common complaints among women, who were taught to dread intercourse or to perform it perfunctorily. Today, about 2% of women are estimated to experience vaginismus (Renshaw, 1988). Vaginismus is essentially a conditioned response that reflects fear, anxiety, or pain. It may result from negative attitudes about sexuality, harsh early sexual experiences, sexual abuse or rape, or painful pelvic examinations (Vandeweil, Jaspers, & Schultz, 1990). Lesbians rarely enter therapy for vaginismus, because if penetration is problematic, they eliminate it from their repertoire of sexual activities (Nichols, 1988).

Dyspareunia **Dyspareunia,** painful intercourse, often occurs because a woman is not entirely aroused before her partner attempts intercourse (Lazarus, 1989). About 8–23% of women have reported dyspareunia (Spector & Carey, 1990). Men may attempt intercourse too early, either because they are in a rush or because they mistake lubrication alone as a sign that their partner is ready for intercourse. Sexual inhibitions, a poor relationship with her partner, or hormonal imbalances may contribute to dyspareunia. Women past menopause have decreased vaginal lubrication and lose much of the elasticity of the vagina from a decrease in estrogen production. The use of lubricating jelly or estrogen therapy may help. Vaginitis, endometriosis, or pelvic inflammatory disease may make intercourse painful. If longer stimulation or the use of lubricants does not relieve the dyspareunia, a woman should consult her physician or health-care practitioner to determine the cause. As with vaginismus, lesbians infrequently report dyspareunia as a problem. If the insertion of sex toys is painful, they eliminate them from their sexual repertoire (Nichols, 1988).

Anorgasmia **Anorgasmia** is the condition of not being orgasmic. (Anorgasmia is also known as orgasmic dysfunction, inorgasmia, and preorgasmia.) It is the most common female dysfunction seen by sex therapists; 18–76% of women in therapy are anorgasmic (Spector & Carey, 1990). (Previously, anorgasmia was known as "frigidity," a pejorative term connoting emotional coldness.) There are several types of anorgasmia.

In *primary anorgasmia*, a woman has never experienced an orgasm. Various studies suggest that approximately 5–10% of American women have never experienced orgasm (Spector & Carey, 1990). In *secondary anorgasmia*, a woman has previously experienced orgasm in sexual intercourse but no longer does so. In *situational anorgasmia*, a woman has had orgasms in certain situations, such as when masturbating, but not when being sexually stimulated by her partner.

Absence of orgasm may occur for any number of reasons, such as lack of effective penile stimulation during intercourse, insufficient manual stimulation of the clitoris by the woman or her partner, or insufficient duration of intercourse. Not being orgasmic, however, does not mean a woman is not sexual; many anorgasmic women rate their sexual experiences positively (Raboch & Raboch, 1992). Among lesbians, orgasm problems are not as frequently seen by therapists as is hypoactive desire (Nichols, 1988).

PHYSICAL CAUSES OF SEXUAL DYSFUNCTIONS

Most sexual dysfunctions are psychological in origin, but some may have physical or hormonal causes. It is generally believed that 10–20% of sexual dysfunctions are organic (structural) in nature. Organic causes may partially contribute to another 10–15% (Kaplan, 1983; LoPiccolo, 1991). Even individuals whose disorders are organic in origin, however, may develop psychological problems as they try to cope with their difficulties (Krauss et al., 1990).

Our vascular, neurological, and endocrine systems are sensitive to changes and disruptions. As a result, various illnesses may have an adverse effect on our sexuality (Wise, Epstein, & Ross, 1992). Some prescription drugs, such as medication for hypertension, may affect sexual responsiveness (Buffum, 1992; "Drugs That Cause Sexual Dysfunction," 1992). Chemotherapy and radiation treatment for cancer affect sexual desire and responsiveness (Ofman & Auchincloss, 1992).

Physical Causes in Men

Diabetes and alcoholism are the two leading causes of erectile dysfunctions; together they account for several million cases. Alcoholism is widely associated with sexual dysfunctions (Schiavi, 1990). Diabetes, which causes impotence in as many as 1 million men, damages blood vessels and nerves, including those within the penis. Other causes of sexual difficulties include lumbar-disc disease and multiple sclerosis, which interfere with the nerve impulses regulating erection (Weiss, 1992). Atherosclerosis is another major physical problem causing blockage of the arteries, including the blood flow necessary for erection. Spinal cord injuries may affect erectile abilities (Stein, 1992). Smoking may also contribute to sexual difficulties (Rosen et al., 1991).

While sexual dysfunctions often reflect or cause disruptions in relationships, if the dysfunction is due to cancer, paraplegia, or diabetes, there may be less relationship strain. If the relationship was stable before the onset of the illness, a couple may have a satisfactory relationship without sexual intercourse. Other forms of sexual interaction may also provide sexual intimacy and pleasure. "When the bond between the mates is love and intimacy," observes Peter Martin (1981), "the loss of sex due to physical illness does not make the marriage an unhappy one." In part this is true because sexual dysfunctions often reflect conflict and discord within a relationship.

Physical Causes in Women

Organic causes are linked to about 5% of anorgasmia cases in women. These include medical conditions such as diabetes and heart disease, hormone deficiencies, and neurological disorders, as well as drug use and alcoholism. Spinal cord injuries may affect sexual responsiveness (Stein, 1992). Multiple sclerosis can decrease vaginal lubrication and sexual response (Weiss, 1992).

Dyspareunia may result from an obstructed or thick hymen, clitoral adhesions, a constrictive clitoral hood, or a weak **pubococcygeus,** the pelvic floor muscle surrounding the urethra and, in women, the vagina. Antihistamines used to treat colds and allergies, as well as marijuana, may reduce vaginal lubrication. Endometriosis and ovarian and uterine tumors and cysts may affect a woman's sexual response. A poor episiotomy can lead to sexual dysfunctions.

The skin covering the clitoris can become infected. Women who masturbate too vigorously can irritate their clitoris, making intercourse painful. Men can stimulate their partners too roughly, causing soreness in the vagina, urethra, or clitoral area. If their hands are dirty, they may cause a vaginal or urinary tract infection.

Treatment of Physical Problems

Sexual dysfunctions are often a combination of physical and psychological problems (LoPiccolo, 1991). Even people whose disorders are physical may develop psychological or relationship problems as they try to cope with their difficulties (Krauss et al., 1990). Thus, treatment for organically based dysfunctions may need to include psychological counseling.

Coital pain caused by inadequate lubrication and thinning vaginal walls often occurs as a result of decreased estrogen associated with menopause. Lubricants or hormone replacement therapy, discussed in Chapter 14, often resolve the difficulties. There are no other widely used medical treatments for organic female sexual difficulties.

Most medical and surgical treatment for men centers on erectile dysfunctions. Often these problems are due to illnesses or injuries that impair the vascular system, affecting penile vasocongestion. Microsurgery may correct the blood-flow problem, but it is not always successful (Mohr & Beutler, 1990; Puech-Leao, 1992; Weidner, Weiske, Rudnick, Becker, Schroeder-Printzen, & Brahler, 1992).

Medications may also be injected into the penis to dilate the blood vessels (Althof & Turner, 1992). Once the vessels are enlarged, the penis can become engorged with blood, allowing an erection. The man may inject the medication himself a few minutes prior to intercourse. The resulting erection may last as long as 4 hours. One study of this treatment found that 85% of the respondents reported that their sex lives had improved (Hollander, Gonzalez, & Norman, 1992). Another study found their wives quite happy with the treatment (Althof, Turner, Levine, Bodner, Kursh, & Resnick, 1992). Unfortunately, some complications may exist, including soreness caused by the injection, prolonged erections, and possible liver damage (Gregoire, 1992).

Suction devices may also be used to induce and maintain an erection. A vacuum chamber is placed over the flaccid penis and the air suctioned out,

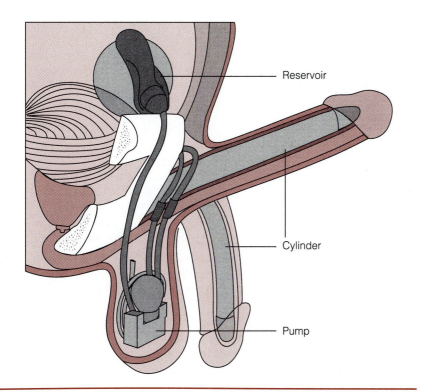

FIGURE 15.1 An inflatable penile prosthesis enables men with physical difficulties to have and maintain erections.

causing blood to be drawn into the penis. When the penis is erect, an elastic ring is placed around the base of the penis to prevent the blood from exiting. The chamber is removed, and the penis stays erect as long as the band is intact. As there are no reports of major complications, vacuum suction may be an important method for inducing erection (Aloni et al., 1992). A study of paraplegics found that over half the men purchasing a suction device were still using it after 21 months. The frequency of intercourse increased from 0.3 to 1.5 times per week (Heller, Keren, Aloni, & Davidoff, 1992).

Erections may also be assisted by implanting a penile prosthesis in the penis and testicles (Gregoire, 1992). There are two types of penile implants. One type consists of a pair of semirigid rods imbedded in the cavernous bodies of the penis. They are relatively easy to implant, but the penis remains permanently semierect. The second type is an inflatable implant that permits the penis to be either erect or flaccid. A pair of inflatable tubes is implanted in the penis' cavernous bodies, a fluid-filled reservoir is inserted near the bladder, and a pump is placed in the scrotum (Figure 15.1). To get an erection, the man or his partner squeezes the scrotal pump, and fluid fills the empty tubes, causing an erection. A release valve is triggered to empty the fluid from the tubes back into the reservoir.

Relatively little research has examined the value of implants, although one recent study of wives whose husbands used the implants found general satisfaction (Althof et al., 1992). They reported significant increase in sexual arousal, intercourse, and orgasm; they felt more at ease in their relationship. Their primary negative response was the lack of spontaneity.

PSYCHOLOGICAL CAUSES OF SEXUAL DYSFUNCTIONS

Sexual dysfunctions may have their origin in any number of psychological causes. Some dysfunctions originate from immediate causes, others from conflict within the self, and still others from a particular sexual relationship. Gay men and lesbians often have unique issues affecting their sexual functioning.

Immediate Causes

The immediate causes of sexual dysfunctions lie in the current situation, including fatigue and stress, ineffective sexual behavior, and sexual anxieties.

Fatigue and Stress Many dysfunctions have fairly simple causes. Men and women may find themselves physically exhausted from the demands of work or child rearing. They may bring their fatigue into the bedroom in the form of sexual apathy or disinterest. "I'm too tired to make love tonight" may be a truthful description of a person's feelings. What these couples may need is not therapy or counseling but a vacation, relief from their daily routines. Without such relief, one partner may begin to blame the other for their diminished sex life. If the fatigue continues, each partner adjusts to the lowered level of desire or activity. The man may no longer approach his partner, or the woman may not expect her partner to be responsive. Silence, frustration, and anger may replace a once tender and erotic relationship. A pattern that has become independent of fatigue is now set. Then, even if both partners change their lifestyle to end the source of fatigue, its legacy may remain in an unhappy pattern of sexual unresponsiveness and frustration.

Long-term stress can also contribute to lowered sexual drive and less responsiveness. A man or woman preoccupied with making ends meet, with an unruly child, or with prolonged illness can temporarily lose his or her sexual desire.

Ineffective Sexual Behavior Kaplan (1974) found that there is a surprising amount of ignorance and misinformation that prevents couples from being effectively sexual with each other. Ineffective sexual behavior appears to be especially relevant in explaining why many women do not experience orgasm in sexual interactions. The couple may not be aware of the significance of the clitoris or the necessity for direct stimulation.

Some gay men and lesbians have not learned effective sexual behaviors because they are inexperienced. They have grown up without easily accessible sexual information or positive role models (Reece, 1988).

Sexual Anxieties A number of anxieties, such as performance anxiety, can lead to sexual problems. If a man fails to experience an erection or a woman is not orgasmic, he or she may feel anxious and fearful. The anxiety may block the very response the man or woman desires.

Performance anxieties may give rise to **spectatoring,** the process in which a person becomes a spectator of his or her sexual performance (Masters &

Daughter: *I am frightened, mother. Tonight's my wedding night. What shall I do?*
Mother: *Shut your eyes and think of the British Empire.*
 Nineteenth-century English joke

Johnson, 1970). When people become spectators of their sexual activities, they critically evaluate and judge whether they are "performing" well or whether they are doing everything "right" for having orgasms. Kaplan (1983) believes spectatoring is involved in most orgasmic dysfunctions.

Performance anxiety may be even more widespread among gay men. Rex Reece (1988) writes: "Many gay men move in a social, sexual milieu where sexual arousal is expected immediately or soon after meeting someone. If response is not rapidly forthcoming, rejection is very likely."

Excessive Need to Please a Partner Another source of anxiety is an excessive need to please a partner (Kaplan, 1974). A man who experiences this anxiety may want a speedy erection to please (or impress) his partner. He may feel he must always delay his orgasm until after his partner's. A woman who experiences this anxiety may want to have an orgasm quickly to please her partner. She may worry that she is not sufficiently attractive to her partner.

One result of the need to please is that men and women may pretend to have orgasms. One study found that two-thirds of the women and one-third of the men reported faking orgasm (Darling & Davidson, 1986). Women fake orgasm most often to avoid disappointing their partner or hurting his feelings. Both also fake orgasm to present a false image of their sexual performance. Unfortunately, faking orgasm miscommunicates to the partner that each is equally satisfied. Because the orgasmic problem is not addressed, resentment and anger may simmer.

Conflict Within the Self

Our religious traditions tend to view sex as inherently dangerous, as lust and fornication. Sexual intercourse within marriage is the only sexual behavior and context endorsed by *all* Christian and Jewish denominations. Premarital intercourse, oral sex, cohabitation, and gay and lesbian relationships are condemned to various degrees. As a consequence, religious background may contribute to sexual problems (Simpson & Ramberg, 1992). Masters, Johnson & Kolodny (1992) note that rigid religious upbringing is associated with vaginismus, primary anorgasmia, and erectile dysfunction. Ideas of the inherent sinfulness of sexuality are not as culturally pervasive as they once were, but they are still powerful forces that form notions of sexuality as we mature. Much of the process of growing up is a casting off of the sexual guilt and negativity instilled from childhood. And among gay men and lesbians, internalized homophobia, self-hatred because of one's homosexuality, is a major source of conflict traced to a conservative religious upbringing (Nichols, 1988; Reece, 1988).

Guilt and conflict do not usually eliminate a partner's sexual drive; rather, they inhibit the drive and alienate a person from his or her sexuality. A person may come to see sexuality as something bad or "dirty," rather than a force to happily affirm. Sexual expression is forced, Kaplan (1974) writes, "to assume an infinite variety of distorted, inhibited, diverted, sublimated, alienated and variable forms to accommodate the conflict." These conflicts are usually much more deeply rooted than the kinds of anxieties described earlier. They exist within the person rather than in situations. Because they are part of the personality, they cannot be as easily changed.

Relationship Causes

Sexual problems do not exist in a vacuum, but usually within the context of a relationship. Most frequently, married couples go into therapy because they have a greater investment in the relationship than couples who are dating or living together. Sexual difficulties in a dating or cohabiting relationship often do not rise to the surface. It is often easier for unmarried couples to break up than to change the patterns that contribute to their sexual problems.

The recognition that sexual problems often originate in the difficulties of a relationship is one of the most important advances in the behavioral sciences, according to Kaplan (1974). She writes:

> The system, or the model, which governs the relationship, rather than the problems of the individual spouses, is often the major source of a sexual dysfunction and the optimum site of intervention. In treating a sexual dysfunction, modification of the sexual and marital system is the basic aim.

If left unresolved, rage, anger, disappointment, and hostility often become a permanent part of couple interaction. Desire discrepancies become sources of conflict rather than acceptance. Underlying fears of rejection or abandonment may help form the relationship structure. But these factors vastly influence the nature and quality of the relationship between partners. Nonsexual problems, such as power and control issues, often manifest themselves in inhibited sexual desire (Hawton et al., 1991). People unconsciously turn themselves off from their partners as a result of their hostility.

TREATING SEXUAL PROBLEMS

There are several approaches to sex therapy, the most important ones being behavior modification and psychosexual therapy. William Masters and Virginia Johnson were the pioneers in the cognitive-behavioral approach, while the most influential psychosexual therapist is Helen Singer Kaplan. The cognitive-behavioral approach works well with sexual dysfunctions, such as erectile and orgasmic problems. Psychosexual therapy is more effective in treating sexual disorders, such as hypoactive desire and sexual aversion (Atwood & Dershowitz, 1992).

Masters and Johnson: A Cognitive-Behavioral Approach

Whatever endures can be created only gradually by long-continued work and careful reflections. . . . He who demands too much at once. . . . succeeds at nothing.
I Ching

In this section, we examine the program developed by Masters and Johnson in the treatment of sexual dysfunctions. Their work has been the starting point for contemporary sex therapy. First, not only did they reject the Freudian model of tracing sexual problems to childhood, they relabeled sexual problems as sexual dysfunctions rather than aspects of neuroses. Masters and Johnson (1970) argued that the majority of sexual dysfunctions are the result of sexual ignorance, faulty techniques, or relationship problems. Second, they treated dysfunctions using a combination of cognitive and behavioral techniques. Third, they treated couples rather than individuals.

Dysfunctional Couples Cognitive-behavioral therapists approach the problems of erectile and orgasmic difficulties by dealing with the couple rather than the individual. They regard sexuality as an interpersonal phenomenon rather than an individual one. In fact, they tell their clients that there are no dysfunctional individuals, only dysfunctional couples, and that faulty sexual interaction is at the root of sexual problems. Neither individual is to blame; rather, it is their mutual interaction that sustains a dysfunction.

Therapists using this approach attempt to take into therapy only those couples genuinely committed to their relationship. Each partner must be willing to give the other emotional support during the therapy for it to be successful. Some couples who come to the clinic may be so alienated from each other that they are told to see a divorce lawyer instead. Divorce in these cases may be the best therapy. Often, sexual dysfunctions are simply situational, reflecting distrust, anger, fear, or indifference toward the partner.

Treatment lasts 12 days on the average. During this time, couples are seen daily by the therapists. The couple is told not to attempt sexual intercourse until they are given permission by their therapist team, a man and a woman. In this way, each partner is immediately relieved of any pressure to perform, thus easing anxieties and allowing the development of a more relaxed attitude toward sex.

Case Histories The first morning, each individual is interviewed separately by the therapist of the same sex; in the afternoon, the interview is repeated by the therapist of the other sex. The therapists are careful not to assign blame to either partner, for it is the couple, rather than the individual, that is being treated. They ask whether the couple is demonstrative with each other; whether each appears to like sex; what their best sexual experiences were, their worst, and with whom they occurred. The therapists constantly remind the couple that they are not seeking to assign blame. The therapists are aware that many of their clients' responses may be evasive, unclear, erroneous, or even false, because the topic is often painful or embarrassing.

After the interviews and the case histories have been taken, the couple meets with both therapists to discuss what has been learned so far. The therapists explain what they have learned about the couple's personal and sexual interaction, encouraging the man and woman to expand or correct what they are saying. Then the therapists discuss the sexual myths and fallacies that the couple holds that may interfere with their sexual interaction.

If there appear to be significantly different views about the couple's sexual history, the therapists point out the importance of honest communication between the partners. The therapists stress openness and directness, the ability of a partner to say, "I don't like fellatio" or "I like cunnilingus."

Sensate Focus At the end of the third day, the therapists introduce **sensate focus,** focusing on touch and the giving and receiving of pleasure. The other senses—smell, sight, hearing, and taste—are worked on indirectly as a means of reinforcing the touch experience. To increase their sensate focus, the couple is given "homework" assignments. In the privacy of their own room, they are to take off their clothes so that nothing will restrict their sensations. One partner must give pleasure and the other receive it. The

License my roving hands, and let them go,
Behind, before, above, between, below.

John Donne

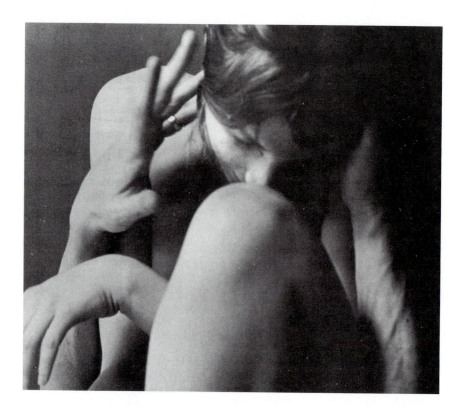

giver touches, caresses, massages, strokes his or her partner's body everywhere except the genitals and the breasts. The purpose is not sexual arousal but simply sense awareness. The receiver simply tries to relax and receive pleasure, which may be more difficult than it might seem. Masters and Johnson point out that this may be the first time a couple has touched and caressed without a sexual aim, "without the demand for personal reassurance, or without a sense of need to return the favor." Later, the partners change roles, and each guides the other to nongenital pleasure spots. After the fourth day, the couple is given permission to touch each other's genitals and the woman's breasts. They are still not permitted to try intercourse. At this time, the couple is given a lesson on sexual anatomy, especially the female genitals, which may have been a mystery to both of them.

Through the fourth day, therapy is basically the same for any type of sexual dysfunction. Thereafter the therapists begin to focus on the particular dysfunction affecting the couple. (For a discussion of cultural/ethnic differences in sex therapy, see Perspective 3.)

Male Dysfunctions The therapists use different techniques for treating the specific dysfunction.

Erectile Dysfunctions When dealing with erectile difficulties, the couple is taught that fears and anxieties are largely responsible, and that the removal of these fears is the first step in therapy. Once the fear is removed, the man is less likely to be an observer of his sexuality; he can become an actor rather than a spectator or judge.

CULTURAL/ETHNIC DIFFERENCES AND SEX THERAPY

Sex therapy assumes a Western middle-class model of sexuality. While this model may be effective in explaining and treating sexual difficulties among white middle-class Americans, it may be ineffective in treating members of other cultures and ethnic groups. As Yoav Lavee (1991) notes, the dominant Western model makes four assumptions about sexuality:

1. Sex is primarily a means of exchanging pleasure.
2. Both partners are equally involved.
3. People need and want information about sex.
4. Communication is important for good sexual relationships.

These assumptions about sexuality are not universal. There is considerable variation among different cultural and ethnic groups in the United States, as well as among those in non-Western cultures, such as Native American, Asian, Middle Eastern, and East Indian (Lavee, 1991; McGoldrick et al., 1982).

Among non-Western clients, the issues focus on men's obtaining sexual pleasure; there is little concern about women's pleasure. In treating Arab, North African, and Asian Jews in Israel, Lavee (1991) found that his clients were primarily men who complained about erectile difficulties. Premature ejaculation was problematical only when it interfered with the man's pleasure. When both husband and wife were invited to attend therapy, usually only the man attended. Finally, individuals and couples alike resisted suggestions of sensate focus exercises. Even if they did agree to do them, most did not follow through; many dropped out of therapy.

While middle-class white Americans tend to utilize the services of medical and mental-health professionals, including sex and family therapists, members of various ethnic groups consult such professionals considerably less often. Two reasons may explain this. First, as ethnic minorities tend to be poorer than whites, they do not have the financial resources. Second, physical and mental health have often been de-

fined in terms of white middle-class standards of physical and psychological functioning and behavior. As a consequence, members of ethnic minorities have been stereotypically misdiagnosed. For decades, for example, it was asserted that African American men had weak masculine identities because of the absence of fathers in families; the presence of strong, independent women was thought to be emasculating. African American males allegedly overcompensated by being obsessed with sex and "promiscuous." Such misdiagnosis has a long history. During slavery times, for example, some blacks were diagnosed as suffering from "drapetomania," a disease that caused them to run away (Wilkinson & Spurlock, 1986).

For Latinos, the myth of the supermasculine "macho" male dominated the mental-health profession and continues to have influence (Guerrero Pavich, 1988). Because of the prevalence of stereotypes masquerading as diagnoses, many members of ethnic groups are suspicious of the mental-health professions (Wilkinson, 1986; Wilson, 1986).

Many issues must be considered when treating members of diverse cultural and ethnic groups. First, there are differing cultural definitions of what is a problem. If the purpose of sex is male pleasure or reproduction, then most female "problems" disappear as long as they do not interfere with sexual intercourse. Low sexual desire and lack of orgasm in women are deemed irrelevant. Vaginismus or painful intercourse are perceived as problems only if they prevent sexual intercourse. These beliefs are consistent with cultural beliefs that women are not supposed to seek or experience sexual pleasure. Emma Guerrero Pavich (1986) notes that traditional Latinas often "deny any sexual feelings toward their male partners." She writes:

The good woman is not erotic; she tolerates her sexual needs and does not develop her own sensuality. Sexual relations are for procreation and are tolerated only because of the rewards of having children. *(continued)*

Perspective 3

CULTURAL/ETHNIC DIFFERENCES AND SEX THERAPY (continued)

Female sexual problems in male-centered cultures are usually viewed as reproductive ones, especially infertility.

We do not know whether women's perceptions necessarily support some or all of these cultural views. In male-centered societies, it is difficult for women to speak out. Furthermore, tradition and socialization, as well as the fear of being labeled immoral, lead many women to accept and embrace beliefs that appear highly alien to us. As we saw in our discussion of female circumcision in Chapter 14, for example, many women support the removal of the clitoris despite the fact that such practices eliminate a woman's sexual pleasure.

Second, there are different "explanations" as to what causes sexual problems. In many rural areas in the world, erectile and infertility problems are blamed on sorcery or supernatural causes. In American history, barrenness has been blamed on witches; in seventeenth-century Massachusetts, for example, women were hanged for their alleged sorcery. At other times, the causes of sexual problems are believed to be dietary. In some cultures, including our own, erectile problems are often thought to be medical in origin. Within our own culture, we tend to view sexual difficulties as sometimes having medical causes, but more often having psychological ones.

Third, there are cultural differences concerning whom to consult for problems. If the problem is thought to be caused by supernatural forces, *curanderos*, curers, are called in Latin America to furnish the victim with charms or medicines to ward off the evil. Sometimes priests are called in to pray for deliverance (Lavee, 1991).

In American society, there is considerable variation as to whom to call for treatment. Among individualistic, white, working-class and middle-class American men, no one is called. The man is supposed to solve the problem by himself; talking to others is a sign of weakness (Rubin, 1976). African Americans tend to use the extended family network, although women are more willing than males to initiate therapy (Hines & Boyd-Franklin, 1982). Among Asian Americans, sexual problems are expected to be worked out within the family, especially between the spouses. Traditional Irish Americans and Latinos are more likely to turn to priests (Espin, 1984; McGoldrick, 1982).

Because there is considerable cultural and ethnic variation, Lavee (1991) writes:

If the client's sexual values are different, we ought to remember that a well-integrated life philosophy, that has proven effective for many generations, stands behind them. It may therefore be easier and wiser to fit the treatment to the client's values than to attempt to "teach" them what healthy sex is.

After the sensate focus exercises have been integrated into the couple's behavior, they are told to play with each other's genitals, but not to attempt an erection. Often, erections may occur because there is no demand on the man; but he is encouraged to let his penis become soft again, then erect, then soft, as reassurance that he can successfully have erections. This builds his confidence and his partner's by letting her know that she can excite him.

During this time, the couple is counseled on other aspects of their relationship that contribute to their sexual difficulties: the feelings of resentment or hostility they have toward each other, how they feel unfulfilled or cheated, what they can do to change their behaviors and end resentment.

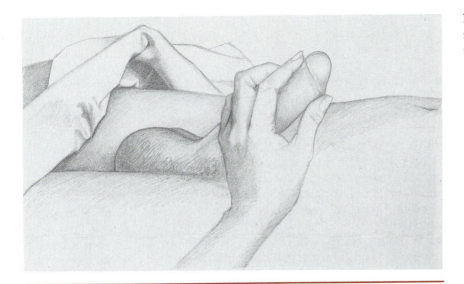

They also talk about their practice sessions and are encouraged to discuss their "mistakes" in a lighthearted manner. These discussions are aimed at further reducing the anxieties that the couple may experience during their practice sessions.

Then, about the tenth day, the couple attempts their first intercourse, if the man has had erections with some success. The woman initiates the attempt, using the woman-above position. She manipulates his penis, bringing it to erection, and then she inserts it into her vagina, moving slowly. There is no attempt at orgasm. They repeat this exercise several times, so the man can gain confidence in his ability to sustain an erection within his partner. If he loses his erection, she gets off him and begins to fondle him until he becomes erect again. If he does not become erect again, the session ends. After the couple completes this exercise successfully, she again mounts him, but this time he thrusts, and she does not move. Then they move together, still with no attempt at orgasm; the only object is sensual pleasure. Eventually, in the final session, the man will have an orgasm.

Premature Ejaculation Cognitive-behavioral therapists treat premature ejaculation by using initially the same pattern they use in treating erectile dysfunctions. They concentrate especially on reducing fears and anxieties and increasing sensate focus and communication. Then they use a simple exercise called the **squeeze technique** (Figure 15.2). (This technique was developed in the 1950s and remains the most effective treatment to date [St. Lawrence & Madakasira, 1992].) The man is brought manually to a full erection. Just before he is about to ejaculate, his partner squeezes his penis with her thumb and forefinger just below the corona. She squeezes with considerable pressure for 10–30 seconds and reduces his erection by 10–30%, causing him to lose his urge to ejaculate. After 30 seconds of inactivity, she arouses him again and, just before he ejaculates, she squeezes again. Using this technique, the couple can go 15–20 minutes before the man ejaculates. After several days of therapy, in the woman-above position, she inserts his penis.

Inhibited Ejaculation Inhibited ejaculation is treated by having the man's partner manipulate his penis. The partner asks for verbal and physical direction to bring him the most pleasure possible. It may take a few sessions before the man reaches his first orgasm. The idea is to identify his partner with sexual pleasure and desire. He is encouraged to feel stimulated not only by his partner, but also by her erotic responses to him. After the man has reached orgasm through manual stimulation, he then proceeds to vaginal intercourse. First, his partner brings him to a high level of sexual excitement manually. When he is excited, she gets on top of him and inserts his penis into her vagina. She immediately begins strong pelvic thrusts. Generally, this technique brings ejaculation quickly. If it does not, the woman gets off and begins manual stimulation again. As the man reaches the point when he is about to ejaculate involuntarily, he motions to her. She quickly tries to insert his penis before orgasm. Sometimes he will ejaculate before she has his penis entirely in her vagina. Nevertheless, even if he ejaculates only a drop into her vagina, this usually assists him in overcoming his sense of incompetence. After a few more such sessions, he usually begins to establish a certain confidence in himself. The therapists then suggest that the woman insert his penis at lower levels of sexual excitement. Finally, the man is able to function sexually without fear of ejaculatory inhibition.

Female Dysfunctions Each female dysfunction is treated differently in behavior modification therapy.

Anorgasmia After the sensate focus sessions, the woman's partner begins to touch and caress her vulva; she guides his hand to show him what she likes. The man is told, however, not to stimulate the clitoris directly because it may be extremely sensitive, and that may cause pain instead of pleasure. Instead, he caresses and stimulates the area around the clitoris, the labia, and the upper thighs. During this time, the couple is told not to attempt orgasm, since it would place undue performance pressure on the woman. They are simply to explore the woman's erotic potential and discover what brings her the greatest pleasure.

After the couple has learned to arouse the woman to a high erotic level, the next step is to begin intercourse in the woman-above position. When both are sexually excited, the woman inserts the penis into her vagina and remains motionless, simply being aware of the penis inside her. Then she begins to move slowly. Once she is aroused, she signals her partner to begin moving and thrusting. They continue as long as it is pleasurable to them both. The next time they begin intercourse, they lie side by side, which permits both to move with the greatest flexibility and freedom. It is especially effective for the woman, because she can move in whatever manner is the most stimulating for her at any time. As Kaplan (1974) notes: "The main principle of achieving orgasm is simple: maximize the stimulation and minimize the inhibition." (A woman may increase her erotic sensations through the use of Kegel exercises, as discussed in Perspective 4.)

KEGEL EXERCISES

These exercises were originally developed by Dr. Arnold Kegel (*KAY-gul*) to help women with problems controlling urination. They are designed to strengthen and give you voluntary control of a muscle called pubococcygeus (*pew-bo-kawk-SEE-gee-us*), or P.C. for short. The P.C. muscle is part of the sling of muscle stretching from your pubic bone in front to your tail bone in back. Since the muscle encircles not only the urinary opening but also the outside of the vagina, some of Dr. Kegel's patients discovered a pleasant side effect—increased sexual awareness. (Men may also benefit from doing Kegels!)

Why Do Kegel Exercises?

Learning Kegel exercises:

- Can help you be more aware of feelings in your genital area.
- Can increase circulation in the genital area.
- May help increase sexual arousal started by other kind(s) of stimulation.
- Can be helpful after childbirth to restore muscle tone in the vagina.

Identifying the P.C. Muscle Sit on the toilet. Spread your legs apart. See if you can stop and start the flow of urine without moving your legs. That's your P.C. muscle, the one that turns the flow on and off. If you don't find it the first time, don't give up; try again the next time you have to urinate.

The Exercises

Slow Kegels Tighten the P.C. muscle as you did to stop the urine. Hold it for a slow count of three. Relax it.

Quick Kegels Tighten and relax the P.C. muscle as rapidly as you can.

Pull in—Push out Pull up the entire pelvic floor as though trying to suck water into your vagina. Then push or bear down as if trying to push the imaginary water out. (This exercise will use a number of "stomach" or "abdominal" muscles as well as the P.C. muscle.)

At first, do ten of each of these exercises (one "set") five times every day. Each week, increase the number of times you do each exercise by five (15, 20, 25, etc.). Keep doing five "sets" each day.

- You can do these exercises any time during daily activities that don't require a lot of moving around: driving your car, watching television, doing dishes, sitting in school or at your desk or lying in bed.
- When you start, you will probably notice that the muscle doesn't want to stay "contracted" during "Slow Kegels" and that you can't do "Quick Kegels" very fast or evenly. Keep at it. In a week or two you will probably notice that you can control it quite well.
- Sometimes the muscle will start to feel a little tired. Not surprising. You probably haven't used it very much before. Take a few seconds' rest and start again.
- A good way to check on how you are doing is to insert one or two lubricated fingers into your vagina.
- Remember to keep breathing naturally and evenly while doing your Kegels!

Vaginismus Vaginismus is one of the easiest sexual dysfunctions to eliminate, using vaginal dilators, plastic penile-shaped rods. The woman uses a set of dilators graduated in diameter. She inserts one before going to bed at night, taking it out in the morning. As soon as the woman is able to receive a dilator of one size without having vaginal spasms, a larger one is used. In most cases, the vaginismus disappears.

Helen Singer Kaplan: Psychosexual Therapy

Helen Singer Kaplan (1974, 1979, 1983) modified Masters and Johnson's behavioral treatment program to include psychosexual therapy. The cognitive-behavioral approach works well for excitement and orgasmic dysfunctions resulting from mild to mid-level sexual anxieties. But if the individual experiences severe anxieties resulting from intense relationship or psychic conflicts, or from childhood sexual abuse or rape, a behavioral approach alone frequently does not work. Such severe anxieties usually manifest themselves in sexual aversion or hypoactive sexual desire.

The role of the therapist in such instances is to provide clients with insight into the origins of the dysfunction. Individuals with desire disorders, for example, often resist behavioral exercises such as sensate focus and pleasuring. They may respond to these exercises with boredom, anxiety, or discomfort; they resist experiencing pleasure. The therapist can intervene by pointing out that they are actively (consciously or unconsciously) creating inhibitions by focusing on negative feelings ("She makes strange sounds"; "His arms are too hairy"), by distracting themselves with thoughts of work or household matters, or by calling up performance fears ("I won't be able to come").

The therapist creates a crisis by confronting individuals with their resistances, then pointing out that they are in control of their resistances and that they can change if they want to. Some individuals will improve as a result of the crisis. Others, however, feel powerless to change. They require additional psychosexual therapy to gain insight into their disorders. They need to discover and resolve the unconscious roots of their disorders, in order to permit themselves to experience desire once again for their partners.

Other Therapeutic Approaches

Both cognitive-behavioral and psychosexual therapy are expensive. Psychosexual therapy takes a considerable amount of time, often a year or more. In response to these limitations, brief sex therapy, self-help, and group therapy have developed.

PLISSIT Model of Therapy One of the most widespread models used by sex therapists is the **PLISSIT model** (Annon, 1974, 1976). PLISSIT is an acronym for the four progressive levels of sex therapy: Permission, Limited Information, Specific Suggestions, and Intensive Therapy.

The first level in the PLISSIT model is *permission giving*. At one time or another, most sexual behaviors were prohibited by important figures in our lives. When we were children, our parents forbade most, if not all, sexual behaviors. We may have heard religious, educational, and political figures denounce many heterosexual and homosexual behaviors as unnatural or sinful. As we grew older, few significant figures gave us permission to explore our sexuality. Few of our feelings and desires (most of which are probably shared by the majority of Americans) were validated.

Because desires and activities such as fantasies or masturbation were not validated, we often questioned their "normality" or "morality." We shrouded them in secrecy or covered them with shame. Without permission to be sexual, we may experience sexual disorders and dysfunctions.

Sex therapists act as "permission givers" for us to be sexual. They become authority figures who validate our sexuality by helping us accept our sexual feelings and behaviors. They reassure us and help us clarify our sexual values. They also validate our ability to say no to activities in which we are uncomfortable.

The second level is giving *limited information*. This information is limited to the specific area of difficulties. If a woman is anorgasmic in intercourse, for example, the therapist might explain that not all women are orgasmic in coitus without additional manual stimulation before, during, or after penetration. The therapist might discuss the effects of drugs such as alcohol, marijuana, and cocaine on sexual responsiveness.

The third level is *specific suggestions*. If permission giving and limited information are not sufficient, the therapist next suggests specific "homework" exercises. If a man experiences premature ejaculation, the therapist may suggest that he and his partner try the squeeze technique. An anorgasmic woman might be instructed to masturbate with or without her partner to discover the best way for her partner to assist her to experience orgasm. A man experiencing inhibited sexual desire might be instructed to engage in pleasuring activities with his partner over a period of several weeks.

The fourth level is *intensive therapy*. If the individual still continues to experience a sexual problem, he or she will need to enter intensive therapy, such as psychosexual therapy. About 1 out of 10 people with sexual problems requires sex therapy (Annon, 1974).

Self-Help and Group Therapy   The PLISSIT model provides a sound basis for understanding how partners, friends, books, self-help exercises, and group therapy may be useful in helping us deal with the first three levels of therapy: permission, limited information, and specific suggestions. Partners, friends, books, and group therapy sessions under a therapist's guidance, for example, may provide permission for us to engage in sexual exploration and discovery. From these sources, we may learn that many of our sexual fantasies and behaviors are very common. Such methods are most effective when the dysfunctions arise from a lack of knowledge or mild sexual anxieties. They also are considerably less expensive than most other types of sex therapies.

Perhaps the first step in dealing with a sexual problem is to turn to your own immediate resources. Begin by discussing the problem with your partner; find out what he or she thinks. Discuss specific strategies that might be useful. Sometimes simply communicating your feelings and thoughts will resolve the difficulty. Seek out friends with whom you can share your feelings and anxieties. Find out what they think. Ask them whether they have had similar experiences, and how they handled them. Try to keep your perspective—and your sense of humor.

Group therapy may be particularly valuable for providing us with an open, safe forum in which we can discuss our sexual feelings and experience and discover our commonalities with others. The presence of a therapist in these sessions can provide valuable insight and direction.

Gay and Lesbian Sex Therapy

Until recently, sex therapy treated sexual dysfunctions and disorders as implicitly heterosexual. The model for sexual functioning, in fact, is generally orgasmic heterosexual intercourse. There was virtually no mention of gay or lesbian sexual concerns (Margolies et al., 1988; Reece, 1988).

For gay men and lesbians, sexual issues differ from those of heterosexuals in several ways. First, while gay men and lesbians may have desire, erectile, or orgasmic difficulties, the context in which they occur may differ significantly from that of heterosexuals. Problems among heterosexuals most often focus on sexual intercourse, while gay and lesbian sexual difficulties focus on other behaviors. Gay men in sex therapy, for example, most often experience aversion toward anal eroticism (Reece, 1988). Lesbians in sex therapy frequently complain about aversive feelings toward cunnilingus. Anorgasmia, however, is not frequently viewed as a problem (Margolies, 1988). Heterosexual women, by contrast, frequently complain about lack of orgasm.

Second, lesbians and gay men must deal with both societal homophobia and internalized homophobia (Friedman, 1991; Margolies et al., 1988). Fear of violence makes it difficult for gay men and lesbians to openly express their affection in the same manner as heterosexuals. While no one takes note of a man and woman kissing in the mall, for example, if two men or two women kissed in the same place, they might be accused of "flaunting" their homosexuality. They might be jeered at or even assaulted. As a consequence, lesbians and gay men learn to repress their expressions of feelings in public; this repression may carry over into private as well. Internalized homophobia may result in diminished sexual desire, creating sexual aversion, and fostering guilt and negative feelings about sexual activity.

Third, gay men must deal with the association between sex and HIV infection that has cut a deadly swath through the gay community. Although HIV infects men and women, regardless of their orientation, gay men feel especially vulnerable because they have suffered the greatest losses in recent years. Grieving over the death of friends, lovers, and partners has left many depressed. In turn, this affects their sexual desire and creates high levels of sexual anxiety. Many are fearful of contracting HIV even if they practice safer sex. And HIV-positive men, even if they are practicing safer sex, are often afraid of transmitting the infection to their loved ones (Friedman, 1991; Rudolph, 1989; Shannon & Woods, 1991).

These unique lesbian and gay concerns require that sex therapists expand their understanding and treatment of sexual problems. If the therapist is not gay or lesbian, he or she needs to have a thorough knowledge of homosexuality and the gay and lesbian world. Therapists further need to be aware of their own assumptions and feelings about homosexuality. Some therapists continue to believe that homosexuality is morally wrong and convey their beliefs to their clients under the guise of therapy (Coleman, Rosser, &

It is important for gay men and lesbians with sexual difficulties to choose a therapist who affirms their orientation and understands the special issues confronting them.

Strapko, 1992). Therapists working with gay or lesbian clients need to develop inclusive models of sexual treatment that are "gay-positive."

Seeking Professional Assistance

If you are unable to resolve your sexual difficulties yourself, seek professional assistance. It is important to realize that seeking such assistance is not a sign of personal weakness or failure. Rather, it is a sign of strength, for it demonstrates an ability to reach out and a willingness to change. It is a sign that you care for your partner, your relationship, and yourself. As you think about therapy, consider the following points:

- What are your goals in therapy? Are you willing to make changes in your relationship to achieve your goals?

- Do you want individual, couple, or group therapy? If you are in a relationship, is your partner willing to attend therapy?

- What characteristics are important for you in a therapist? Do you prefer a female or male therapist? Is the therapist's age, religion, or ethnic background important to you?

- What are the therapist's professional qualifications? There are few certified sex therapy programs; most therapists who treat sexual difficulties come from various professional backgrounds, such as psychiatry, clinical psychology, psychoanalysis, marriage and family counseling, and social work.

- What is the therapist's approach? Is it behavioral, psychosexual, psychoanalytic, religious, spiritual, feminist, or something else? What is the therapist's attitude toward gender roles? Do you feel comfortable with the approach?

- If you are lesbian or gay, does the therapist affirm your sexual orientation? Does the therapist understand the special problems gays and lesbians face?
- After a session or two with the therapist, do you have confidence in him or her? If not, discuss your feelings with the therapist. If you believe your dissatisfaction is not a defense mechanism, change therapists.

While therapy is often successful, it is not magical. Much depends on your willingness to confront painful feelings and to change. This entails time and effort and often considerable amounts of money as well, unless the therapist has a sliding payment scale (usually ranging from $10 to $100 or more an hour, depending on your income) or you are covered by a good health insurance plan. But ultimately, the difficult work may reward you with greater satisfaction and a deeper relationship. (See "Resources" at the end of the chapter for information on finding a sex therapist.)

As we consider our sexuality, it is important to realize that sexual difficulties and problems are commonplace. But sex is more than orgasms or certain kinds of activities. Even if we have difficulties in some areas, there are other areas in which we may be fully sexual. If we have erectile or orgasmic problems, we can use our imagination to expand our repertoire of erotic activities. We can touch each other sensually, masturbate alone or with our partner, caress, kiss, eroticize and explore our bodies with fingers and tongues. We can enhance our sexuality if we look at sex as the mutual giving and receiving of erotic pleasure, rather than a command performance. By paying attention to our conditions for good sex, maintaining intimacy, and focusing on our erotic sensations and those of our partner, we can transform our sexual relationships.

SUMMARY

Sexual Enhancement

- Many people sometimes experience sexual difficulties or problems. Nearly half of the men and women in various surveys report occasional or frequent lack of desire, problems in arousal or orgasm, and painful intercourse. The widespread variability of sexual functioning suggests the "normality" of at least occasional sexual difficulties.

- *Sexual enhancement* refers to improving the quality of one's sexual relationship. Sexual-enhancement programs generally aim at providing accurate information about sexuality, developing communication skills, fostering positive attitudes, and increasing self-awareness. Awareness of your own sexual needs is often critical to enhancing your sexuality. Verbal and nonverbal communication are both important. Enhancing sex includes the intensification of arousal.

Sexual Disorders and Dysfunctions

- *Sexual dysfunctions* are impaired physiological responses. *Sexual disorders* are problems affecting the brain's arousal capabilities. The triphasic sexual response cycle divides responses into three stages. The most common dysfunctions for each stage are as follows: (1) desire—hypoactive sexual desire (HSD) and sexual aversion; (2) excitement—erectile dysfunction, painful intercourse, and vaginismus; and (3) orgasm—anorgasmia, premature ejaculation, and inhibited or delayed ejaculation.

• *Hypoactive sexual desire (HSD)* is low sexual desire. Depression is probably the most common cause. Anger toward the partner, stress, traumatic marital separation or divorce, loss of work, anxiety, and guilt are frequently associated with HSD. *Sexual aversion* is a consistently phobic response to sexual activities or the idea of such activities.

• Male sexual problems focus on the excitement stage. *Erectile dysfunction* is the inability to have or maintain an erection during intercourse. Erectile difficulties may occur because of fatigue, too much alcohol, depression, conflict, or a host of other transitory reasons.

• *Premature ejaculation* is the inability to control or delay ejaculation as long as desired, causing personal or interpersonal distress. In *inhibited ejaculation*, the penis is erect but the man is unable to ejaculate. In *delayed ejaculation*, the man is not able to ejaculate easily in intercourse.

• In *vaginismus*, the muscles around the vaginal entrance go into spasmodic contractions. Vaginismus is essentially a conditioned response that reflects fear, anxiety, or pain. *Dyspareunia*, painful intercourse, often occurs because a woman is not entirely aroused before her partner attempts intercourse. Sexual inhibitions, a poor relationship with her partner, or hormonal imbalances may contribute to dyspareunia.

• *Anorgasmia* refers to the condition of not being orgasmic. Absence of orgasm may occur from a lack of effective penile stimulation during intercourse, insufficient manual stimulation of the clitoris by the woman or her partner, or insufficient duration of intercourse. Not being orgasmic, however, does not mean a woman is not sexual; many anorgasmic women rate their sexual experiences positively.

Physical Causes of Sexual Dysfunctions

• About 10–20% of sexual dysfunctions are organic (structural); organic problems may contribute to an additional 10–15% of dysfunctions. Diabetes and alcoholism are the two leading causes of erectile dysfunctions. Prescription drugs may affect sexual responsiveness.

• Coital pain caused by inadequate lubrication and thinning vaginal walls often occurs as a result of decreased estrogen associated with menopause. Lubricants or hormone replacement therapy often resolve the difficulties.

• Illnesses or injuries may impair the vascular system, affecting penile vasocongestion. Microsurgery may correct the blood-flow problem, but it is not always successful. Medications may be injected into the penis to dilate the blood vessels. Suction devices may be used to induce and maintain an erection. Erections may also be assisted by implanting a penile prosthesis.

Psychological Causes of Sexual Dysfunctions

• Sexual dysfunctions may have their origin in any number of psychological causes. The immediate causes of sexual dysfunctions lie in the current situation, including fatigue and stress, ineffective sexual behavior, sexual anxieties, and an excessive need to please one's partner. Conflict within the self, including religious teachings, guilt, negative learning, and internalized homophobia may contribute to dysfunctions. Relationship conflicts may lead to sexual dysfunctions.

Treating Sexual Problems

• Masters and Johnson developed a cognitive-behavioral approach to sexual difficulties. They relabeled sexual problems as dysfunctions rather than neuroses or diseases, used direct behavior modification practices, and treated couples rather than individuals. Treatment begins with interviews and case histories by a male and female therapist team; next, the couple begins *sensate focus* exercises without intercourse; then, therapists begin treating the specific dysfunctions with different "homework" exercises. Finally, at the end of the treatment period, the couple is given "permission" to engage in sexual intercourse. Kaplan's psychosexual therapy program combines behavioral exercises with insight therapy.

• The *PLISSIT model* of sex therapy refers to four progressive levels: Permission, Limited Information, Specific Suggestions, and Intensive Therapy. Individuals and couples can often resolve their difficulties by talking over their problems with their partners or friends, reading self-help books, and attending sex therapy groups. If they are unable to resolve their difficulties in these ways, they should consider intensive sex therapy.

• There are three significant concerns for gay men and lesbians in sex therapy. (1) The context in which problems occur may differ significantly from that of heterosexuals, such as issues revolving around anal eroticism and cunnilingus. (2) They must deal with both societal homophobia and internalized homophobia. (3) Gay men must deal with the association between sex and HIV/AIDS.

KEY TERMS

sexual enhancement	sexual aversion	dyspareunia
erotic aid	erectile dysfunction	anorgasmia
sex toy	premature ejaculation	pubococcygeus
sexual dysfunction	inhibited ejaculation	spectatoring
sexual disorder	delayed ejaculation	sensate focus
hypoactive sexual desire (HSD)	vaginismus	squeeze technique
inhibited sexual desire		PLISSIT model

RESOURCES

Sex Therapy

American Association of Sex Educators, Counselors and Therapists (AASECT)
435 North Michigan Avenue, Suite 1717
Chicago, IL 60611
(312) 644-0828
AASECT certifies therapists and will send you a list of therapists in your area dealing with sexual problems. Your instructor, school psychologist, or health-care practitioner may also be able to recommend a sex therapist.

Sexual Enhancement

For those without easy access to stores with erotic products, such products may be mail-ordered from various distributors. One well-respected source is The Sexuality Library (938 Howard Street, San Francisco, CA 94103, [415] 974-8990), which distributes erotic toys, books, magazines, art, and videos through its catalog. Others may be found in advertisements found in some women's and men's magazines, as well as erotic magazines and journals.

SUGGESTIONS FOR FURTHER READING

Barbach, Lonnie. *For Each Other: Sharing Sexual Intimacy.* New York: Doubleday, 1982. A thoughtful book for exploring women's sexuality; includes exercises.

Heiman, Julia, and Joseph LoPiccolo. *Becoming Orgasmic: A Sexual Growth Program for Women.* Englewood Cliffs, NJ: Prentice-Hall, 1988. Suggestions on how to develop one's orgasmic responsiveness.

Isensee, Rik. *Love Between Men: Enhancing Intimacy and Keeping Your Relationship Alive.* New York: Prentice-Hall Press, 1990. Enhancing gay relationships through communication, problem-solving, and, if needed, therapy.

Leiblum, Sandra, and Raymond Rosen, eds. *Principles and Practice of Sex Therapy: Update for the 1990s.* New York: Guilford Press, 1989. A collection of essays on various aspects of sex therapy designed for professionals.

Loulan, JoAnn. *Lesbian Sex.* San Francisco: Spinsters Ink, 1984. A thoughtful examination of the various aspects of lesbian sexuality, including ways of enhancing sexuality and relationships.

Szaz, Thomas. *Sex by Prescription: The Startling Truth About Today's Sex Therapy.* Syracuse, NY: Syracuse University Press, 1990. A searing indictment of the medicalization of sex and sexual problems by the gadfly of psychiatry.

Zilbergeld, Bernie. *The New Male Sexuality.* New York: Bantam Books, 1992. The most widely recommended book by therapists for men on enhancing sexual relationships. Women can equally profit from it, not only for themselves but also for understanding male sexuality.

Chapter Sixteen

SEXUALLY TRANSMITTED DISEASES

PREVIEW: SELF-QUIZ

1. A person can have a sexually transmitted disease (STD) and not even know it. True or false?

2. By law, doctors must report all cases of sexually transmitted diseases to the Public Health Service. True or false?

3. Being poor and living in an urban area are risk factors leading to STDs. True or false?

4. Because of penicillin, syphilis is no longer considered a major health problem. True or false?

5. About 1 out of every 6 or 7 Americans carries the herpes virus. True or false?

6. A vaccination against hepatitis B is widely available. True or false?

7. In general, men experience more severe consequences of STDs than women do. True or false?

8. You can often tell by looking at someone whether or not he or she is the type to have an STD. True or false?

9. Condoms have been demonstrated to help protect against many STDs, including chlamydia, gonorrhea, syphilis, and HIV/AIDS. True or false?

10. Government public-health policy has established that 2 to 3 million cases of gonorrhea a year is acceptable. True or false?

ANSWERS 1. T, 2. F, 3. F, 4. F, 5. T, 6. T, 7. F, 8. F, 9. T, 10. T

Chapter Outline

The consequences of sexually transmitted diseases (STDs) are felt on both personal and societal levels. Personal costs range from inconvenience and discomfort to severe pain, serious illness, infertility, and even death. STDs, primarily syphilis, gonorrhea, and chlamydia, cause almost one-third of all reproductive deaths of mothers or infants (Grimes, 1986). Society as a whole pays for the damage caused by STDs. In 1984, the cost of PID (pelvic inflammatory disease, caused principally by chlamydia and gonorrhea) was estimated at $2.6 billion in the United States. In 1992, the CDC projected that the cost of HIV and AIDS would be $11.8 billion in 1993 and $14.5 billion in 1994 (cited in Krieger, 1992).

In this chapter and the next one, we discuss the factors that contribute to the "STD epidemic" in this country. We explore the particular issues affecting women and the urban poor. This chapter contains an overview of the incidence, symptoms, and treatment of the principal STDs that affect Americans, with the exception of HIV/AIDS, which is the subject of Chapter 17. Much of this chapter is devoted to the prevention of STDs, including positive health behaviors, safer sex practices, and communication skills. Finally, we discuss how public-health policies affect the course of STDs.

O rose, thou art sick!
The invisible worm
That flies in the night,
In the howling storm,

Has found out thy bed
Of crimson joy,
And his dark secret love
Does thy life destroy.

William Blake

X-RATED DISEASES: THE PSYCHOLOGICAL IMPACT OF STDS

If you missed school or work because of strep throat or chickenpox, you probably wouldn't mind telling people why you were gone. But if you were absent because of chlamydia or gonorrhea, chances are you would hesitate to reveal the actual nature of your illness. And what would you tell your girlfriend, boyfriend, wife, or husband?

Ambivalence About Sexuality

The deep ambivalence our society feels about sexuality is clearly brought to light by the way in which we deal with sexually transmitted diseases. If we think we have strep throat, we waste no time getting ourselves to a health center or doctor to obtain the appropriate medication. We probably take precautions not to spread the germs to those around us, and we have no hesitation about calling a friend or our boss and croaking, "Guess what? I've got strep throat!"

But let's say we're experiencing some discomfort when we urinate, and there's a sort of unusual discharge. We will likely try to ignore the symptoms at first. We hope they'll go away if we just don't think about them. But they don't. Pretty soon, we're feeling some actual pain, and we know something is definitely not right. With fear and trepidation, we slink into the clinic or doctor's office, hoping we don't see anyone we know so we don't have to explain why we're there. The doctor or clinician examines our "private parts," which makes us very uncomfortable, and he or she asks us a lot of embarrassing questions. When we pick up our prescription, we can't look the pharmacist in the eye. And then there's the whole problem of telling our partner—or, worse yet, partners—about our predicament. Sound familiar? We hope not! But for millions of Americans, at least part of this scenario will ring true.

STD ATTITUDE SCALE

This scale was developed by William Yarber, Mohammad Torabi, and C. Harold Veenker to measure the attitudes of young adults in terms of high or low risk for sexually transmitted diseases. Follow the directions, and mark your responses to the statements below. Then calculate your risk as indicated.

Read each statement carefully. Indicate your first reaction by writing the letter that corresponds to your answer.

Key

SA = Strongly Agree   D = Disagree
 A = Agree   SD = Strongly Disagree
 U = Undecided

1. How one uses his/her sexuality has nothing to do with STDs.

2. It is easy to use the prevention methods that reduce one's chances of getting an STD.

3. Responsible sex is one of the best ways of reducing the risk of STDs.

4. Getting early medical care is the main key to preventing the harmful effects of STDs.

5. Choosing the right sex partner is important in reducing the risk of getting an STD.

6. A high frequency of STDs should be a concern for all people.

7. People with an STD have a duty to get their sex partners to seek medical treatment.

8. The best way to get a sex partner to STD treatment is to take him/her to the doctor with you.

9. Changing one's sex habits is necessary once the presence of an STD is known.

10. I would dislike having to follow the medical steps for treating an STD.

11. If I were sexually active, I would feel uneasy doing things before and after sex to prevent getting an STD.

Source: Adapted from Yarber, Torabi, & Veenker, 1988.

My boy, if there were no disease in the world, there would be no decency. The fear of God. Our illness is a sign of the disapproval of God for what we did.

John Horne Burns, 1947

Why all this emotion over chlamydia but not over strep throat? Where do all the fear, hesitation, denial, embarrassment, guilt, shame, and humiliation come from? Why are STDs the only class of illnesses we categorize by their *mode of transmission* rather than by the type of organism that causes them? All these questions stem from a common source: Americans are confused about sex! And because we, as a society, are so ambivalent and anxious, we don't deal with STDs rationally. We pretend we won't get them and ignore them when we do. We lie to ourselves and our partners. And even if we feel *we* wouldn't put someone down or think badly of him or her

12. If I were sexually active, it would be insulting if a sex partner suggested we use a condom to avoid getting an STD.

13. I dislike talking about STDs with my peers.

14. I would be uncertain about going to the doctor unless I was sure I really had an STD.

15. I would feel that I should take my sex partner with me to a clinic if I thought I had an STD.

16. It would be embarrassing to discuss STD with one's partner if one were sexually active.

17. If I were to have sex, the chance of getting an STD makes me uneasy about having sex with more than one partner.

18. I like the idea of sexual abstinence (not having sex) as the best way of avoiding STDs.

19. If I had an STD, I would cooperate with public-health people to find the sources of STDs.

20. If I had an STD, I would avoid exposing others while I was being treated.

21. I would have regular STD checkups if I were having sex with more than one partner.

22. I intend to look for STD signs before deciding to have sex with anyone.

23. I will limit my sexual activity to just one partner because of the chances of getting an STD.

24. I will avoid sexual contact anytime I think there is even a slight chance of getting an STD.

25. The chance of getting an STD would not stop me from having sex.

26. If I had a chance, I would support community efforts toward controlling STDs.

27. I would be willing to work with others to make people aware of STD problems in my town.

Scoring
Calculate points as follows: Items 1, 10–14, 16, and 25: Strongly Agree = 5, Agree = 4, Undecided = 3, Disagree = 2, Strongly Disagree = 1. Items 2–9, 15, 17–24, 26, and 27: Strongly Agree = 1, Agree = 2, Undecided = 3. Disagree = 4, Strongly Disagree = 5.

The higher the score, the stronger the attitude that predisposes a person toward risky sexual behaviors. You may also calculate your points within three subscales: items 1–9 represent the "belief subscale," items 10–18 the "feeling subscale," and items 19–27 the "intention to act" subscale.

for having an STD, if we get one ourselves, we feel embarrassed, ashamed, and guilty. We may even feel (or others may tell us) we are being punished by God or fate for being sinful or bad. Meanwhile, our culture continues to extol the attractions of uninhibited sexual activity (during which no one ever uses a condom or contracts a sexually transmitted disease) through movies, music, television programs, and advertising. The great gap between our behavior and our ideals is clearly demonstrated by the widespread occurrence of sexually transmitted diseases (Brandt, 1987; Nilsson Schonnesson, 1990).

What's in a Name? VD and STDs

The term STD (sexually transmitted disease) has replaced the traditional VD (venereal disease). (The root of "venereal" is Venus, the Roman goddess of love.) The term that once associated diseases with love has been replaced with a more impersonal one, linking disease only to the act of sex, with love or without it. In current terminology, VD refers only to the "old-fashioned" sexually transmitted diseases, such as syphilis and gonorrhea, which are spread solely by sexual contact. The term "STD" includes diseases such as hepatitis B and HIV, which may be transmitted by means other than sexual ones. STDs have also been euphemistically referred to as "social diseases," as if all communicable diseases were not spread in a social context. The common cold, transmitted by sneezes, coughs, and unwashed hands, is arguably the most "social" disease of all. We have all been both the recipients and the donors of these very sociable cold viruses, and while we may have felt miserable physically, psychologically we've been just fine.

THE STD EPIDEMIC

Since the late 1950s, STDs have increased dramatically in the United States. In addition to the ambivalence about being sexual that leads to risk taking, there are a number of other reasons for this increase. These factors include changes in society, the particular biological characteristics of the disease organism, and the way in which diseases are spread within groups of people.

Social Factors

Social and cultural factors contributing to the spread of STDs are listed below.

- Changes in sexual mores have led to the widespread acceptance of sexual activity outside of marriage, for both women and men.
- Beginning in the 1960s with the advent of the pill and IUD, condom use declined dramatically, removing a very effective method of **prophylaxis,** or protection, from mainstream use. Condom use began to increase, however, in recent years because of the serious nature of a relatively new STD known as AIDS. Still, it is obvious from the prevalence of STDs today that a large portion of the population remains unconvinced about the efficacy of condoms in STD prevention (Cates & Stone, 1992).
- Educational efforts regarding STDs (and sexuality in general) are often hampered by vocal minorities who feel that knowledge about sex is what causes people to engage in it.
- The confusion of moral and medical issues also hampers funding for research and treatment of illnesses that are seen as somehow "deserved." For example, significant funding for AIDS research did not begin until it was clear that heterosexuals as well as gay men were threatened (Altman, 1986; Shilts, 1987).
- The health-care system cannot meet our needs. STDs are rampant in low-income urban areas where health services are limited and health-care

Social factors contributing to the spread of STDs include acceptance of sexual activity outside of marriage and the excessive consumption of alcohol.

workers may not be responsive to the community's needs. Racism, or at least an insensitivity to ethnic issues, may be partly responsible. Funds for public-health programs—to provide education, diagnosis, treatment, partner tracing, and follow-up—are limited, to say the least. Health-care agencies often find themselves vying with one another for funding.

- Alcohol and drug abuse contribute indirectly to the spread of STDs by impairing people's ability to make rational decisions about sexual conduct (Hibbs & Gunn, 1991; Romanowski & Piper, 1988). The exchange of sex for drugs may contribute to the spread of STDs such as syphilis (Hibbs & Gunn, 1991).

Biological Factors

The characteristics of certain organisms and the diseases they produce also contribute to STD transmission (Alexander, 1992).

- Many STDs are **asymptomatic;** they produce no symptoms, especially in the first stages. A person may have an STD and infect others without knowing that he or she is affected.

- Because resistant strains of viruses, bacteria, and other pathogens are continuously developing, antibiotics that have worked in the past may no longer be effective. Infected people may continue to transmit the disease, either because they believe they have been cured or because they were asymptomatic to begin with. The clinician or the patient may underrate the value of a follow-up examination to ensure that the initial treatment has worked, or to try an alternative medication if necessary.

- Some STDs, such as herpes, genital warts, and HIV, cannot be cured. A person who carries any of these viruses is always theoretically able to transmit them to others.

STD Prevalence

An estimated 12–13 million Americans, including 3 million teenagers, are affected by STDs every year (Figure 16.1) (Cowley, 1991; Hatcher et al., 1990; Kassler & Cates, 1992). Based on reports of publicly funded clinics and private practitioners, public-health officials can only estimate the number of STD cases. Reporting regulations vary. For example, reports of syphilis are thought to be the most accurate because of the strict laws regarding both screening (testing) and reporting. Gonorrhea reporting, however, is less complete. Although public clinics are required to report gonorrhea cases, private physicians are not, and many, in fact, do not (Moran, Aral, Jenkins, Peterman, & Alexander, 1989). Therefore, officials must calculate the numbers as best they can. The same is true for other STDs. Furthermore, a large number of STD cases may go entirely undiagnosed and untreated, especially among people with limited access to health care. It is quite likely that the **prevalence,** or frequency of occurrence, of STDs is greater rather than smaller than the current estimates.

The Epidemiology of STDs

Most STDs are preventable. Almost all are curable. Yet many of them are on the rise, especially among groups with certain characteristics in common. The study of diseases, how they spread within a population, and how they may be controlled is called **epidemiology.** Epidemiologists look at groups of people—in a college community or inner-city area, for example—to see who is getting a particular disease. They try to trace the path of the disease—who had it before and who gets it next—and find the patterns involved with its transmission.

Risk Factors Versus Risk Markers In STD epidemiology, it is important to distinguish between risk factors and risk markers. A **risk factor** implies a causal relationship between certain individual characteristics and the likelihood of exposure to disease. Certain health-care behaviors (or lack of them), or certain sexual behaviors, may be considered true risk factors—ones that increase the chance of contracting an STD (Aral & Holmes, 1990). Having a large number of sex partners appears to be a significant risk factor (Joffe et al., 1992). Others include having sexual contact with gay or bisexual men who have not been tested to ensure they do not have HIV, having sexual contact with IV (intravenous) drug users, not using condoms, and delaying or not seeking treatment when symptoms appear.

   Risk markers, while often coincidentally correlated with the prevalence of STDs, are not *causally* related. Risk markers often include demographic characteristics, such as marital status, socioeconomic status, place of residence, and ethnicity. Thus, while the highest rates of gonorrhea are found in black, female teenagers living in urban areas characterized by poverty, there is nothing inherent in being black, female, a teenager, urban, or poor that predisposes a person to contract an STD (Moran et al., 1989). We can see, however, that low socioeconomic status is highly correlated with poorer health in general, including higher infant mortality and shorter life expectancy. Presumably, limited access to health education, screening and diagnostic facilities, preventive health care, health insurance, and treatment

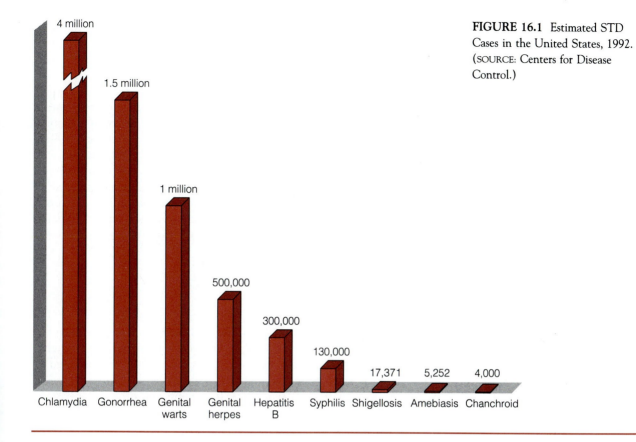

FIGURE 16.1 Estimated STD Cases in the United States, 1992. (SOURCE: Centers for Disease Control.)

facilities all contribute to poorer health outcomes among groups with low socioeconomic status. There is no research to suggest any correlation between the sexual behaviors of any particular ethnic or cultural group and the incidence of STD within that group.

A recent study of 4342 women identified age at first intercourse as a useful risk marker for STDs. Women who became sexually active between ages 10 to 14 were almost four times more likely to have had five or more sex partners during the past year than women who became sexually active after age 16. They were three times more likely to have had sex with bisexual men, IV drug users, and HIV-infected men (Greenberg, Magder, & Aral, 1993).

Core Groups A number of epidemiologists use the "core group model" to explain how certain diseases are transmitted within a population. **Core groups** are small, definable, stable groups with a consistently high prevalence of a particular disease (Rothenberg & Potterat, 1990). A number of studies of gonorrhea have demonstrated the apparent validity of this model (Hethcote & Yorke, 1984; Potterat, Rothenberg, Woodhouse, Muth, Pratts, & Fogle, 1985; Rothenberg, 1983; Yorke, 1978). A study in upstate New York, for example, showed that within each of 12 metropolitan areas, there was a central core area where 50% of the cases were located, surrounded by an adjacent area containing 30% of the cases, and a peripheral area containing the remaining cases (Rothenberg, 1983). The incidence of gonorrhea decreased in a gradient from the core outward; in some cities, the risk of contracting gonorrhea was estimated to be 20 times higher in the core area than in the peripheral area. This risk is due to the existence of a group of individuals who "serve as a pool of high-frequency transmitters of infection and play an important role in maintaining the incidence of infection in the general population" (Rice, Roberts, Handsfield, & Holmes, 1991). (Figure 16.2 shows distribution patterns for gonorrhea and chlamydia in Colorado Springs in 1988.) Researchers suggest that the role of cultural factors in STD transmission is not currently understood. Core groups need to be studied with care and sensitivity, so that effective screening, diagnosis, and treatment of STDs in these groups can occur (Moran et al., 1989; Rice et al., 1991).

PRINCIPAL STDS

The following STDs are discussed in order of their prevalence, based on the number of estimated new cases per year. The actual numbers may be higher because of unreported or untreated cases. HIV and AIDS are discussed in Chapter 17. For quick reference, Table 16.1 (pp. 650–651) lists the principal STDs, along with their symptoms, treatment, and other information.

Chlamydia

The most common STD in the United States, affecting over 4 million people each year, is caused by an organism called *Chlamydia trachomatis*, which has properties of both a bacterium and a virus (Hatcher et al., 1990). It affects the urinary tract and reproductive organs of both women and men. Although *C. trachomatis* has undoubtedly been around for centuries, it is only within the last 15 years that large-scale screening has been possible. Chlamydial infection, commonly referred to as simply **chlamydia,** appears to be distributed diffusely throughout the general population, unlike other STDs, which tend to be more highly concentrated in core groups (Zimmerman et al., 1990). Chlamydia has been responsible for hundreds of thousands of cases of pelvic inflammatory disease (PID), a leading cause of infertility and ectopic pregnancy (Washington, Cates, & Zaidi, 1984). (PID is discussed at length later in this chapter.) Also, untreated chlamydia can be quite painful and can lead to conditions requiring hospitalization, including acute arthritis. Infants of mothers infected with chlamydia may develop dangerous eye, ear, and lung infections.

About 80% of women with chlamydia show no symptoms until serious complications have arisen (Ault & Faro, 1993; Keim, Woodard, & Anderson, 1992). When early symptoms do occur, they are likely to include:

- Unusual vaginal discharge.
- Burning sensation with urination.
- Unexplained vaginal bleeding between menstrual periods (Krettek, Arkin, Chaisilwattana, & Monif, 1993).

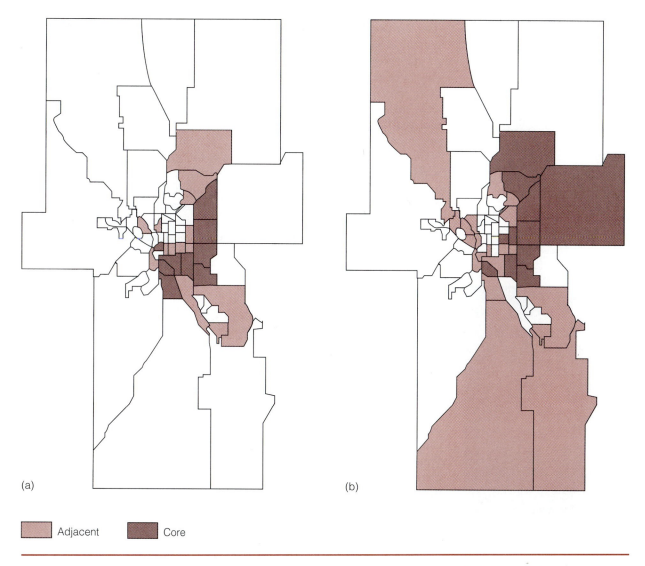

(a)

(b)

▨ Adjacent   ▨ Core

Later symptoms, occurring up to several months after exposure, are:

- Low abdominal pain.
- Bleeding between menstrual periods.
- Low-grade fever.

One-third to one-half of men are asymptomatic when first infected. Men's symptoms may include:

- Unusual discharge from the penis.
- Burning sensation when urinating.
- Itching and burning around the urethral opening (urethritis).
- Pain and swelling of the testicles.
- Low-grade fever.

FIGURE 16.2 Distribution Patterns for Gonorrhea and Chlamydia, Colorado Springs, 1988. Core areas with high distribution and adjacent areas with moderate distribution are identified on census tract maps. (a) Gonorrhea distribution. (b) Chlamydia distribution. Notice that some chlamydia core areas and gonorrhea core areas overlap; also notice that chlamydia is more widespread. (SOURCE: AJPH November 1990, Vol. 80, No. 11.)

The last two symptoms may indicate the presence of chlamydia-related **epididymitis,** inflammation of the epididymis. Untreated epididymitis can lead to infertility. For both women and men, early symptoms will appear 7–21 days after exposure, if they appear at all. Chlamydia responds well to antibiotic therapy, generally with doxycycline.

In many instances, chlamydia is not detected unless the affected person is tested for it in the process of being treated for something else, or unless he or she has been named as a partner, or "contact," of someone diagnosed with chlamydial infection (Zimmerman et al., 1990). Since so many people with chlamydial infections are asymptomatic, it is a sound health practice for those who are sexually active—especially if they have numerous partners—to be checked for it regularly (every 3–6 months). Routine screening (by culturing discharge from the vagina or penis) and nationwide reporting of chlamydia will be necessary if it is to be controlled (Rothenberg, 1991; Zimmerman et al., 1990).

Gonorrhea

The second most prevalent STD affects 1.1 to 1.5 million Americans yearly (Rice, Aral, Blount, & Zaidi, 1987). **Gonorrhea,** popularly referred to as "the clap" or "drip," is caused by the *Neisseria gonorrhoeae* bacterium. ("Clap" is derived from the Middle English word for brothel.) Although the overall incidence of gonorrhea declined in the 1980s, the rate of new infections among whites has decreased much more dramatically than that of inner-city African Americans (Gershman & Rolfs, 1991). Some research indicates that gonorrhea rates are continuing to rise among blacks, especially female teenagers (Rice et al., 1991). A decade ago, blacks were infected at about 12 times the rate of whites. In 1991, the rate was reported to have increased to 39 times higher among African Americans than among whites (Cowley, 1991).

Although the rate of gonorrhea occurrence appears to have declined among Native Americans in recent years, it remains substantially higher than the rate for non-Native Americans. A study from 1984 to 1988 found the gonorrhea rate to be 501 per 100,000 in the 13 states studied (Toomey, Oberschelp, & Greenspan, 1989). The rate among African Americans was 2045 per 100,000; among Latinos, it was 279 per 100,000; and among whites, it was 97 per 100,000. As discussed earlier, there is nothing inherent in demographic characteristics such as place of residence or ethnicity that causes people with those characteristics to be at greater risk.

The bacterium *N. gonorrhoeae* thrives in the warm, moist environment provided by the mucous membranes lining the mouth, throat, vagina, cervix, urethra, and rectum. Symptoms of gonorrhea, if they occur, appear within 2–21 days after exposure. Men tend to experience the symptoms of gonorrhea more readily than women, notably as a watery discharge ("drip") from the penis, the first sign of urethritis. ("Gonorrhea" is from the Greek, meaning "flow of seed.") Other symptoms in men may include:

- Itching or burning at the urethral opening.
- Pain when urinating.

If untreated, the disease will soon produce these other symptoms:

Gonorrhea infection in men is often characterized by a discharge from the penis.

I had the honor
To receive, worse luck!
From a certain empress
A boiling hot piss.
Frederick the Great of Prussia
(1712–1786)

- Thick yellow or greenish discharge.
- Increasing discomfort or pain with urination.

Although most men seek treatment by this stage, some do not. Even if the symptoms diminish, the bacteria are still present. Those who do not get treatment can still infect their partners and may develop serious complications, such as abscesses of the prostate gland and epididymitis.

About 50–80% of women with gonorrhea show no symptoms or very mild symptoms, which they tend to ignore (Hook & Holmes, 1985). Since untreated gonorrhea, like untreated chlamydia, can lead to PID, it is important for a woman to be on guard for symptoms and to be treated if she thinks she may have been exposed to gonorrhea (if she has had multiple sex partners, for example). Symptoms a woman may experience include:

- Thick yellow or white vaginal discharge.
- Burning sensation when urinating.
- Unusual pain during menstruation.
- Severe lower abdominal pain.

Gonorrhea may be passed to an infant during childbirth, causing conjunctivitis (an eye infection) and even blindness if not treated. (Most states require that all newborn infants have their eyes treated with antibiotics in the event that they may have been exposed to gonorrhea in the birth canal.) Penicillin and related antibiotics are effective against most strains of gonorrhea; tetracycline may be used in the case of allergy to penicillin. Because *N. gonorrhoeae* can evolve rapidly into penicillin-resistant strains, a variety of antibiotics may need to be tried before the infection is eliminated.

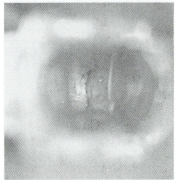

Genital warts appear in a variety of forms. In women, genital warts may appear on the vaginal wall.

Genital Warts

About one half to 1 million Americans develop **genital warts** every year. The virus responsible for these warts, **human papilloma virus (HPV),** exists in numerous different strains; one of the most prevalent types is *condyloma acuminatum.* An estimated two-thirds of the partners of people with HPV contract the infection (Cowley, 1991). Many cases may be passed along by people who are asymptomatic or haven't noticed the warts. Studies of people with genital warts show that HPV is correlated with earlier onset of sexual activity, more sexual partners, and less regular contraceptive use than among controls (Schneider, Sawada, Gissmann, & Shaw, 1987). Although genital warts are generally considered more of a nuisance than a danger, HPV has been shown to be linked with CIN and cervical cancer in a number of studies (Crum et al., 1984; Reeves et al., 1989). The nature of the relationship is disputed, however; HPV may be a contributing factor but may not actually cause cancer (Franco, 1991). (The development of CIN was discussed in Chapter 14.)

Genital warts usually appear within 3 months of exposure. They generally range in size from a pencil point to a quarter of an inch in diameter. They may be flat, bumpy, round, or smooth; white, gray, pink, or brown. Some look like miniature cauliflowers, others like tiny fingers. In men, genital warts usually develop on the shaft or glans of the penis or around the anus. In women, they are found on the cervix, vaginal wall, vulva, or anus. Warts inside the cervix, vagina, or rectum are difficult to detect without examination. The warts are removed by freezing (cryosurgery), laser therapy, cutting, or a chemical solution such as podophyllin. Removal of the warts is done for cosmetic reasons or for comfort; it does not eliminate HPV from the person's system. The extent to which a person can still transmit HPV after the visible warts have been removed is unknown. In 80% of cases, the warts eventually reappear (Hatcher et al., 1990).

Genital Herpes

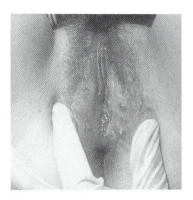

Women may develop herpes lesions on the vulva, perineum, anus, or within the vagina.

Genital herpes, caused by the **herpes simplex virus (HSV),** is carried by an estimated 31 million Americans. The number of cases are increasing at the rate of 200,000–500,000 per year (Cowley, 1991; Hatcher et al., 1990). HSV exists in two strains: HSV type 1, which is usually responsible for cold sores and fever blisters around the mouth; and HSV type 2, which is usually associated with genital lesions. Both types of HSV, however, can and do develop equally well on the mouth or genitals (Buchman et al., 1980). Serious complications from HSV are rare in adults but may result if the individual's general health is not good or the immune system is depressed. Such complications include urethral blockages and meningitis, inflammation of the membranes surrounding the brain and spinal cord. In women there appears to be some association between HSV and CIN or cervical cancer (Hatcher et al., 1990), although the nature of the connection is debated (Franco, 1991). Newborns may contract HSV if they come into contact with active lesions during birth. This may result in infections of the eyes, skin, or mucous membranes; infections of the central nervous system; or even death. (Managing childbirth for women with HSV was discussed in Chapter 13.)

For many people with HSV, the initial infection is the most severe. Sometimes it is the only outbreak a person experiences. Within 3–20 days after exposure, small bumps called **vesicles** or **papules** appear on the genitals: penis, anus, perineum, vulva, or within the vagina. The papules may itch at first; they then form blisters or pustules that rupture, forming small, often painful, ulcers. These sores may be further irritated by tight clothing, moisture, or urine. In addition, an affected person may experience:

- Swollen lymph nodes in the groin.
- Flulike symptoms.

The first outbreak lasts an average of 12 days. Subsequent outbreaks last an average of 5 days. They may begin with feelings of itchiness or tingling at the site where the lesions will appear, and along the neural pathways traveled by the virus from the lower spinal cord, where it lies dormant (inactive), to the genital region. Just prior to the outbreak is a period of a few days known as the **prodrome.** During this time, and while there are actual lesions, the virus is active; live viruses are shed from the affected areas and are spread upon contact. Some people with HSV may shed the virus without experiencing symptoms (Maccato & Kaufmann, 1992; Mertz, Benedetti, Ashley, Selke, & Corey, 1992). People who experience recurrent herpes outbreaks note they are often preceded by stress, fatigue, overexposure to cold or sun, or certain foods, such as nuts or citrus fruits.

Herpes Hysteria Although most people with HSV experience little or no discomfort from it after the initial outbreak, they may experience intense psychological pain and distress from the knowledge that they are carrying an incurable STD. Even though 1 out of every 6 or 7 Americans over the age of 15 carries HSV (Hatcher et al., 1990), society as a whole still tends to regard people with STDs as deviant, immoral, or otherwise suspect. This attitude, so indicative of our national ambivalence about sexuality, does little to help us deal realistically with STDs, especially the "incurable" herpes.

Most people who experience symptoms of HSV find them manageable, if sometimes uncomfortable. Drug therapy may be helpful for those with persistent symptoms. With reasonable caution (abstinence during outbreaks, condoms if one is unsure) and candor (disclosure of risks to one's partner), the likelihood of spreading HSV is significantly reduced. Fear of stigmatization is one of the principal factors responsible for the spread of herpes because it keeps people from dealing rationally with the issue.

Managing HSV The antiviral drug acyclovir (brand name Zovirax) is often helpful in reducing or suppressing HSV symptoms (Goldberg et al., 1993). It can be administered either orally (as a pill) or topically (as an ointment). Acyclovir is especially effective during initial infections, but some people with recurrent episodes find taking the oral medication helpful, either at a low "maintenance" dosage to ward off outbreaks, or at a higher dosage when they feel an outbreak coming on (American Social Health Association, 1992). Other methods reported to be useful in preventing, shortening, or lessening the severity of recurrent outbreaks are:

- Plenty of rest. This allows the immune system to work at its best capacity.
- A balanced diet. This also fosters a healthy immune system. Observing foods that appear to trigger outbreaks may be helpful.
- L-lysine. The amino acid L-lysine, taken orally, is reportedly helpful to a number of people.
- No tight clothes. Tight jeans, tight or nylon underwear, and nylon pantyhose create an ideal, warm, moist environment for HSV. Loose-fitting, cotton clothing is preferable.
- Keeping the area cool and dry. If lesions do appear, an icepack may provide temporary relief and may also discourage the viruses from remaining at the site of the lesion. The icepack should have a dry surface that is either disposable or washable.

Reasonable Precautions HSV can be spread by hand—to another person, or even to a different location on one's own body. A person experiencing an outbreak should wash his or her hands frequently with soap. Caution should also be taken not to touch one's eyes (or another's) if one has touched a lesion. Serious eye infection may result. Pregnant women or their partners who have HSV should be sure to discuss precautionary procedures with their medical practitioners.

A Final Caution HSV is pretty tough as viruses go. Although it cannot live long in chlorinated pools or hot tubs, it has been noted to survive for several hours in tap water or on surfaces such as towels, cups, toilet seats, sauna benches, and plastic patio chairs (Nerurkar et al., 1983). If you are experiencing a herpes outbreak, be considerate of others so that they do not come into contact with viruses that may be shedding. If you do not believe you have HSV, take reasonable steps to avoid exposure.

Syphilis

When **syphilis** first appeared in Europe in the late 1490s, its early manifestations were considerably more horrible than they appear today. One observer (cited in Quétel, 1990) reported:

> These [pustules] looked rather like grains of millet, and usually appeared on the outer surface of the foreskin, or on the glans, accompanied by a mild pruritus [itching]. Sometimes the first sign would be a single "pustule" looking like a painless cyst, but the scratching provoked by the pruritus subsequently produced a gnawing ulceration. Some days later the sufferers were driven to distraction by the pains they experienced in their arms, legs and feet, and by an eruption of large "pustules" (which) lasted . . . for a year or more, if left untreated.

Whether syphilis was introduced to Europe from the New World by Spanish explorers or from Africa by those who plied the slave trade is debated by historians. Its legacy of suffering, however, is debated by no one.

In the 1800s, physicians began to make the connection between late-stage syphilis and madness. The symptoms of "general paralysis" (caused by lesions on the meninges of the brain) were noted to include impaired speech and locomotion and "delusions of wealth and grandeur" (Quétel, 1990). "The pox" was the subject of much literature and art, and a number of great literary figures and artists were said to be afflicted (or inspired) by it. These included Johann von Goethe, Charles Baudelaire, Guy de Maupassant, Gustave Flaubert, Friedrich Nietzsche, John Keats, and Isaak Dinesen.

In the 1940s, it was found that penicillin very effectively killed *Treponema pallidum*, the bacterium that causes syphilis. At last the disease that had caused widespread pain, anguish, and death for centuries began to fade from view in most parts of the developed world. In the United States, strict control measures were instituted, requiring the testing of many citizens for syphilis, including those in the armed services and couples seeking marriage licenses. Health departments and medical laboratories were (and are) required to report all cases of syphilis to the government. Beginning in the 1980s, however, the number of cases began increasing dramatically, especially within inner cities. In 1986, the syphilis rate was the highest it had been since 1948 (Rothenberg, 1991); it has continued to climb to an estimated 120,000–130,000 cases annually (Cowley, 1991). The current epidemic appears to be concentrated mainly in young, heterosexual, minority populations. In some instances it appears to be correlated with crack cocaine use, possibly related to the practice of exchanging sex (principally fellatio) for the drug (Gershman & Rolfs, 1991; Greenberg, Schnell, & Conlon, 1992).

T. pallidum is a spiral-shaped bacterium (a **spirochete**) that requires a warm, moist environment, such as the genitals or the mucous membranes inside the mouth, to survive. It is spread through vaginal, anal, and oral sexual contact. A mother infected with syphilis can pass it to the fetus through the placenta. Since neonatal syphilis can lead to brain damage and

The microbe of the terrible disease, the treponema . . . is as much the power behind genius and talent, heroism and wit as that behind general paralysis . . . and almost all forms of degenerescence.

Leon Daudet, 1915

death, it is imperative for pregnant women to be screened for it within the first trimester. If they are treated during this period, the newborn will not be affected. Untreated syphilis in adults may lead to brain damage, heart disease, blindness, or death.

The course of syphilis as it appears today progresses through four discrete stages, although it is most often treated during the first two.

Primary Syphilis The first symptom of syphilis appears 1–12 weeks after contact with an infected partner. It is a small, red, pea-sized bump that soon develops into a round, painless sore called a **chancre** (*SHANK-er*). The chancre may be covered by a crusty scab; it may be hard around the edges and ringed by a pink border. It appears at the site where the bacteria initially entered the body, usually within the vagina or on the cervix in women, or on the glans of the penis in men. The chancre may also appear on the labia, the shaft of the penis, the testicles, rectum, within the mouth, or on the lips. Unless it is in a visible area, it may not be noticed. Without treatment, it will disappear in 1–5 weeks, but the bacteria remain in the body, and the person is still highly contagious.

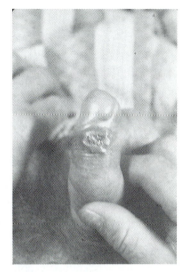

The first symptom of syphilis is a red, pea-sized bump called a chancre at the site where the bacteria originally entered the body.

Secondary Syphilis Untreated primary syphilis develops into secondary syphilis about 6 weeks after the chancre has disappeared. The principal symptom at this stage is a skin rash that neither itches nor hurts. The rash is likely to occur on the palms of the hands and the soles of the feet, as well as on other areas of the body. The individual may also experience flulike symptoms. The rash or other symptoms may be very mild or may pass unnoticed. The person is still contagious.

Latency If secondary syphilis is not treated, the symptoms disappear within 2–6 weeks, beginning the latent stage. The infected person may feel no further symptoms for years, or perhaps will never experience any. Or he or she may have symptoms that are vague or difficult to diagnose without a blood test to screen for *T. pallidum*. After about a year, the bacteria can no longer be spread to sexual partners, although a pregnant women can still transmit the disease to the fetus.

Tertiary Syphilis In the United States, syphilis is rarely seen in its tertiary stage because treatment usually prevents the disease from progressing that far. (But see Perspective 1 on the Tuskegee experiment, in which treatment with penicillin was intentionally withheld in order to observe the effects of tertiary syphilis on African American men.) The symptoms of tertiary syphilis may appear years after the initial infection. Possible effects include:

- Gummas (large ulcers) within the muscles, liver, lungs, eyes, or endocrine glands.
- Heart disease.
- Neurosyphilis (leading to "general paralysis" or "paresis,") involving the brain and spinal cord, and leading to muscular paralysis, psychosis, and death.

Hamlet: How long will a man lie in the earth ere he rot?
Gravedigger: Faith, if he be not rotten before he die (as we have many pocky corpses nowadays that will scarce hold the laying in), he will last you some eight year or nine year.

William Shakespeare

And he died in the year fourteen-twenty,
Of the syphilis, which he had a-plenty.
François Rabelais (1490–1553)

THE TUSKEGEE SYPHILIS STUDY: "A Tragedy of Race and Medicine"

In 1932 in Macon County, Alabama, the U.S. Public Health Service, with the assistance of the Tuskegee Institute, a prestigious black college, recruited 600 African American men to participate in an experiment involving the effects of untreated syphilis on blacks. Of this group, 399 men had been diagnosed with syphilis, and 201 were controls. The study was originally meant to last 6 to 9 months, but "the drive to satisfy scientific curiosity resulted in a 40-year experiment that followed the men to 'end point' (autopsy)" (Thomas & Quinn, 1991). The history of this experiment—the racial biases that created it, the cynicism that fueled it, and the callousness that allowed it to continue—is chillingly chronicled by James Jones (1993) in *Bad Blood: The Tuskegee Experiment—A Tragedy of Race and Medicine*.

The purpose of the study was to determine if there were racial differences in the developmental course of syphilis. There was speculation in the (white) medical world that tertiary syphilis affected the cardiovascular systems of blacks, whereas it affected whites neurologically. The racial prejudice behind this motivation may seem hard to fathom today, yet, as we shall see, the repercussions still reverberate strongly through African American communities.

Although much of the original funding for the study came from the Julius Rosenwald Foundation (a philanthropic organization dedicated to improving conditions within African American communities) with the understanding that treatment was to be a part of the study, and although Alabama law required prompt treatment of diagnosed venereal diseases, the Public Health Service managed to ensure that treatment was withheld from the participants. In the 1940s, the Public Health Service kept draft boards from ordering treatment for 250 A-1 registrants who were part of the experiment. It involved health departments across the country in a conspiracy to withhold treatment from subjects who had moved from Macon County. Even after 1951, when penicillin became the standard treatment for syphilis, the Public Health Service refused to treat the Tuskegee "subjects" on the grounds that the experiment was a "never-again-to-be-repeated opportunity" (Jones, 1993).

The Tuskegee participants were never informed that they had syphilis. The Public Health Service, assuming they would not understand medical terminology, referred to it as "bad blood," a term used to describe a variety of ailments in the rural South. The participants were not told their disease was sexually transmitted, nor were they told it could be passed from mother to fetus. We can only speculate on the extent to which this wanton disregard for human life allowed the disease to spread and wreak its misery and death in the black South and beyond.

It was not until 1966 that anyone within the public-health system expressed any moral concern over the study. Peter Buxtun, an investigator for the Public Health Service, wrote a concerned letter to the director of the Division of Venereal Diseases, William Brown. Nothing changed. In 1968, Buxtun wrote a second letter, questioning the study's ramifications in light of the current climate of racial unrest in the nation. Dr. Brown showed the letter to the Centers for Disease Control (CDC), which convened a panel to discuss the issue. Having reviewed the study, the panel decided to allow it to continue until "end point." In 1972, Peter Buxtun told his story to Edith Lederer, a friend who was an international reporter for the Associated Press. Ultimately the story was assigned to Jean Heller, who broke it in the *Washington Post* on July 25, 1972, whereupon it became front-page news across the country. A congressional subcommittee headed by Senator Edward Kennedy began hearings in 1973. The results included the rewriting of the Department of Health, Education, and Welfare's regulations on the use of human subjects in scientific exper-

'NOW can we give him penicillin?'

Editorial cartoon by Tony Auth, *Philadelphia Inquirer*, July 1972. (*Courtesy Tony Auth*)

iments. A $1.8 billion class-action suit was filed on behalf of the Tuskegee participants and their heirs. A settlement for $10 million was made out of court.

Since the original disclosure and outcry, there has been little discussion of the Tuskegee experiment within the public-health system or the public media. (David Feldman's powerful 1989 play, *Miss Evers' Boys,* and an hour-long 1992 PBS documentary are the exceptions.) Stephen Thomas and Sandra Crouse Quinn (1991) of the Minority Health Research Laboratory at the University of Maryland's Department of Health cite the "failure of public health professionals to comprehensively discuss the Tuskegee experiment" as an ongoing "source of misinformation [that] helps to maintain a barrier between the Black community and health care service providers." Current public-health efforts to control the spread of HIV, AIDS, and other STDs raise the specter of genocide among many members of the African American community. For ex-

ample, in 1990, as part of an HIV education program conducted by the Southern Christian Leadership Conference with CDC funding, a survey of 1056 black church members found that 35% of them believed AIDS to be a form of genocide and another 30% were unsure. Thirty-four percent thought the virus was manmade, and an additional 44% were unsure.

A tremendous gap exists in this country between the health-care needs of minority-status families and the beliefs within those communities. In order to begin to close the gap, we must, as stated by Thomas and Quinn (1991), "recognize that Blacks' belief in AIDS as a form of genocide is a legitimate attitudinal barrier rooted in the history of the Tuskegee Syphilis study." On both physiological and psychological levels, there is much healing to be done.

(For reflections on the legacy of the Tuskegee study, see Caplan, 1992; Edgar, 1992; King, 1992; and Jones, 1992.)

In the primary, secondary, and early latent stages, syphilis is easily treated with penicillin (Goldmeier & Hay, 1993). Later stages may require additional injections. Other antibiotics can be used if the infected person is allergic to penicillin.

Hepatitis

Hepatitis is a viral disease affecting the liver. There are two types of the virus that may be sexually transmitted, hepatitis A and hepatitis B. Hepatitis A is most often contracted through unsanitary conditions, in contaminated food or water. It is believed to be transmitted sexually mainly via infected fecal matter—for example, during oral-anal sex ("rimming"). Immune serum globulin injections provide some immunity to hepatitis A. Although the symptoms of hepatitis A are similar to those of hepatitis B, the disease is not considered as dangerous. Affected individuals usually recover within 6 weeks and develop immunity against reinfection. Hepatitis B is commonly spread through sexual contact, in blood, semen, saliva, vaginal secretions, and urine. It affects an estimated 300,000 Americans annually and leads to about 5000 deaths (Cowley, 1991). The incidence of hepatitis B is declining among gay men (probably due to safer sex practices) and increasing among heterosexuals.

The symptoms of hepatitis include:

- Fatigue.
- Diarrhea.
- Nausea.
- Abdominal pain.
- Jaundice (caused by accumulating blood pigments not destroyed by the liver).
- Darkened urine.

There is no medical treatment for hepatitis. Rest and fluids are recommended until the disease runs its course, generally in a few weeks. Occasionally, serious liver damage or death results.

Hepatitis B can be prevented by a simple, widely available vaccination. Many health authorities recommend routine vaccination for those most at risk, including people with more than one sexual partner, teenagers, gay men, IV drug users, and health-care workers who come into contact with blood. Relatively few people, however, take advantage of the hepatitis B vaccine. Screening for hepatitis B is also recommended for pregnant women so that their newborns can be immediately vaccinated if necessary.

Urinary Tract Infections (NGU/NSU)

Both women and men are subject to sexually transmitted infections of the urinary tract. Most of these infections are caused by either C. *trachomatis* or N. *gonorrhoeae*, but others are caused by different organisms, such as *Ureaplasma urealyticum*. These urinary tract infections are sometimes referred to as **nongonococcal urethritis (NGU)** or **nonspecific urethritis (NSU).** In men **urethritis,** inflammation of the urethra, produces:

- Painful urination.

- Urinary frequency.
- White or yellowish discharge from the penis.

Women are likely to be asymptomatic. They may not realize they are infected until a male partner is diagnosed. If a woman does have symptoms, they are likely to include:

- Itching or burning while urinating.
- Unusual vaginal discharge.

If urethritis is not a result of gonorrhea, it will probably not respond to penicillin. It is important to have a laboratory test for an unusual discharge from the penis or vagina so that the appropriate antibiotic can be prescribed. Tetracycline and erythromycin are usually effective against NGU. Untreated NGU may result in the consequences described for chlamydia. The most common urinary tract infection among women, cystitis, is discussed later in this chapter.

Vaginal Infections

Vaginal infections, or **vaginitis,** affect 3 out of 4 women at least once in their lives. These infections are often, although not always, sexually transmitted. They may also be induced by an upset in the normal balance of vaginal organisms by such things as stress, birth control pills, antibiotics, nylon underwear, and douching. The three principal types of vaginitis are bacterial vaginosis, candidiasis, and trichomonal infection. See Perspective 2 for suggestions on the prevention of vaginitis.

Bacterial Vaginosis Bacterial vaginal infections, referred to as **bacterial vaginosis,** may be caused by a number of different organisms, most commonly *Gardnerella vaginalis*, often a normal inhabitant of the healthy vagina. An overabundance of *Gardnerella*, however, produces:

- Vaginal itching.
- Whitish discharge, with a fishy odor that is more pronounced when the discharge is combined with semen.

Most men who carry *Gardnerella* are asymptomatic; some may experience inflammation of the urethra or glans. Bacterial vaginosis in women is commonly treated with metronidazole (Flagyl), unless the woman is pregnant or breast-feeding; then clindamycin may be prescribed. Some people experience unpleasant side effects, such as nausea, with metronidazole. There is disagreement as to the usefulness of treating men unless they actually have symptoms (Hatcher et al., 1990; Mengel et al., 1989). If a man has symptoms, then treating him is necessary to prevent infection or reinfection of his partner.

Candidiasis The fungus *Candida albicans* is normally present in the healthy vagina of many women. Various conditions may cause *C. albicans* to multiply rapidly, producing the condition known as **candidiasis** *(can-di-DYE-a-sis)*, moniliasis, or, more commonly, yeast infection. Symptoms include:

MAINTAINING VAGINAL HEALTH

Here are some simple guidelines that may help a woman avoid getting vaginitis:

- Do not use vaginal deodorants, especially deodorant suppositories or tampons. They upset the natural chemical balance of the vagina. Despite what pharmaceutical companies may advertise, the healthy vagina does not have a bad odor. If the vagina does have an unpleasant smell, then something is wrong, and you should check with your doctor or clinic.

- For the same reason, do not use douches, except medicated douches that have been recommended by a clinician, or vinegar solutions for yeast infections (see below).

- Maintain good genital hygiene by washing regularly (about once a day is fine) with mild soap. Bubble baths and strongly perfumed soaps may cause irritation to the vulva.

- After a bowel movement, wipe the anus from front to back, away from the vagina, to prevent contamination with fecal bacteria.

- Wear cotton underpants and pantyhose with a cotton crotch. Nylon does not "breathe," and it allows heat and moisture to build up and create an ideal environment for infectious organisms to reproduce.

- If you use a vaginal lubricant, be sure it is water-soluble. Oil-based lubricants such as Vaseline encourage bacterial growth.

- If you have candidiasis (yeast infection), try douching every 2 or 3 days with a mild vinegar solution (2 tablespoons of vinegar to 1 quart of water). You can also try applying plain yogurt twice a day to the vulva and vagina. (It must be yogurt that contains live lactobacillus culture.) Adding yogurt to your diet and avoiding foods with a high sugar content may also help.

- If you are diagnosed with a vaginal infection, particularly trichomoniasis, be sure to have your male partner treated also, to avoid being reinfected.

- Intense itching of the vagina and vulva.
- A lumpy, cottage cheese-like discharge.

C. albicans may be transmitted sexually, although this does not necessarily lead to symptoms. Conditions that may induce candidiasis include dietary imbalances, antibiotics, birth control pills, and pregnancy. Clotrimazole (Gyne-Lotrimin) and miconazole (Monostat) are available over the counter as vaginal creams or suppositories for the treatment of yeast infections. A woman who is uncertain about the symptoms should be diagnosed by a clinic or physician. (See Perspective 2 for suggestions on treating yeast infections.)

Trichomoniasis *Trichomonas vaginalis* is a single-celled protozoan responsible for about one-quarter of all cases of **trichomoniasis,** commonly referred to simply as trichomonas, or "trich" (pronounced "trick"). It is a hardy parasite that may survive for several hours on damp items such as towels and toilet seats. Its principal mode of transmission, however, is sexual intercourse. Even though they are often asymptomatic, men may carry *Tricho-*

monas. If men do exhibit symptoms, they tend to be those associated with urethritis (Krieger et al., 1993). The symptoms of trichomoniasis can be very unpleasant for women. They include:

- Intense itching of the vagina and vulva.
- A frothy, unpleasant-smelling vaginal discharge.
- Painful intercourse.

Metronidazole (Flagyl) is effective in treating trichomoniasis. To prevent reinfection, both partners must be treated.

Parasites

Although they are not diseases per se, parasites such as scabies and pubic lice can be spread by sexual contact.

Scabies The red, intensely itchy rash caused by the barely visible mite *Sarcoptes scabiei* is called **scabies.** It usually appears on the genitals, buttocks, feet, wrists, knuckles, abdomen, armpits, or scalp as a result of the mites' tunneling beneath the skin to lay their eggs and the baby mites' making their way back to the surface. It is highly contagious and spreads quickly among people who have close contact, both sexual and nonsexual. The mites can also be transferred on clothes, towels, and bedding. Scabies is usually treated with a prescribed lotion containing lindane, applied at bedtime and washed off in the morning. Young children and pregnant or nursing women should obtain an alternate prescription to lindane, because it can be toxic to infants and young children. Clothing, towels, and bedding of people who have scabies should be disinfected by washing in hot water and drying in high heat, or dry cleaning.

Pubic Lice The tiny *Phthirus pubis*, commonly known as a "crab," moves easily from the pubic hair of one person to that of another (probably along with several of its relatives). When **pubic lice** mate, the male and female each grasp an adjacent hair; the female soon begins producing eggs (nits), which she attaches to the hairs at the rate of about three eggs a day for 7–10 days. The nits hatch within 7–9 days and begin reproducing in about 2 weeks, creating a very ticklish (or itchy) situation. Pubic lice can be transmitted nonsexually. They may fall into underwear, sheets, or towels, where they can survive up to a day *and* lay eggs that hatch in about a week. Thus, it is possible to get crabs simply by sleeping in someone else's bed, wearing his or her clothes, or sharing a towel.

A person can usually tell when he or she has pubic lice. There is intense itching, and upon inspection, one discovers a tiny, pale, crablike louse or its minuscule, pearly nits attached near the base of a pubic hair. There are both prescription and over-the-counter treatments for pubic lice. A Gamma-benzene solution sold as Kwell may be prescribed. Other preparations such as Nix (permethrin) and RID (A-200 pyrinate) do not require a prescription. In addition to killing all the lice and nits on the body, the person must wash all infected linen and clothing in hot water and dry it on high heat, or the crabs may still be around, waiting and hungry.

See Table 16.1 for the symptoms and treatments of the principal STDs.

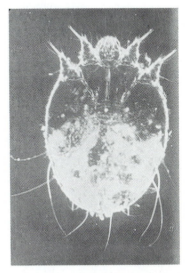

Pubic lice, or "crabs," are easily spread during intimate contact; they may also be transmitted on bedclothes, towels, or underwear.

TABLE 16.1 Principal Sexually Transmitted Diseases

STD and Infecting Organism	Symptoms	Time from Exposure to Occurrence	Medical Treatment	Comments
Chlamydia (*Chlamydia trachomatis*)	Women: 80% asymptomatic; others may have vaginal discharge or pain with urination. Men: 30–50% asymptomatic; others may have discharge from penis, burning urination, pain and swelling in testicles, or persistent low fever.	7–21 days	Doxycycline, tetracycline, erythromycin	If untreated, may lead to pelvic inflammatory disease (PID) and subsequent infertility in women.
Gonorrhea (*Neisseria gonorrhoeae*)	Women: 50–80% asymptomatic; others may have symptoms similar to chlamydia. Men: itching, burning or pain with urination, discharge from penis ("drip").	2–21 days	Penicillin, tetracycline, or other antibiotics	If untreated, may lead to pelvic inflammatory disease (PID) and subsequent infertility in women.
Genital warts (Human papilloma virus)	Variously appearing bumps (smooth, flat, round, clustered, fingerlike, white, pink, brown, etc.) on genitals, usually penis, anus, vulva, vagina, or cervix.	1–6 months (usually within 3 months)	Surgical removal by freezing, cutting, or laser therapy. Chemical treatment with podophyllin (80% of warts eventually reappear).	Virus remains in the body after warts are removed.
Genital herpes (Herpes simplex virus)	Small, itchy bumps on genitals, becoming blisters that may rupture, forming painful sores; possibly swollen lymph nodes; flulike symptoms with first outbreak.	3–20 days	No cure although acyclovir may relieve symptoms. Nonmedical treatments may help relieve symptoms.	Virus remains in the body, and outbreaks of contagious sores may recur. Many people have no symptoms after the first outbreak.
Syphilis (*Treponema pallidum*)	Stage 1: Red, painless sore (chancre) at bacteria's point of entry. Stage 2: Skin rash over body, including palms of hands and soles of feet.	Stage 1: 1–12 weeks Stage 2: 6 weeks to 6 months after chancre appears	Penicillin or other antibiotics	Easily cured, but untreated syphilis can lead to ulcers of internal organs and eyes, heart disease, neurological disorders, and insanity.

(continued)

TABLE 16.1 *continued*

STD and Infecting Organism	Symptoms	Time from Exposure to Occurrence	Medical Treatment	Comments
Hepatitis (Hepatitis A or B virus)	Fatigue, diarrhea, nausea, abdominal pain, jaundice, darkened urine due to impaired liver function.	1–4 months	No medical treatment available; rest and fluids are prescribed until the disease runs its course.	Hepatitis B more commonly spread through sexual contact; can be prevented by vaccination.
Urethritis (various organisms)	Painful and/or frequent urination; discharge from penis; women may be asymptomatic.	1–3 weeks	Penicillin, tetracycline, or erythromycin, depending on organism.	Laboratory testing is important to determine appropriate treatment.
Vaginitis (*Gardnerella vaginalis*, *Trichomonas vaginalis*, or *Candida albicans*)	Intense itching of vagina and/or vulva, unusual discharge with foul or fishy odor, painful intercourse. Men who carry organisms may be asymptomatic.	2–21 days	Depends on organism; oral medications include metronidazole and clindamycin. Vaginal medications include clotrimazole and miconazole.	Not always acquired sexually. Other causes include stress, oral contraceptives, pregnancy, tight pants or underwear, antibiotics, douching, and dietary imbalance.
HIV infection and AIDS (Human immunodeficiency virus)	Possible flulike symptoms but often no symptoms during early phase. Variety of later symptoms including weight loss, persistent fever, night sweats, diarrhea, swollen lymph nodes, bruiselike rash, persistent cough.	Several months to several years	No cure available, although many symptoms and opportunistic infections can be treated with a variety of medications. Good general health practices can delay or reduce the severity of symptoms.	Cannot be self-diagnosed; a blood test must be performed to determine the presence of the virus.
Pelvic inflammatory disease (PID) (women only)	Low abdominal pain, bleeding between menstrual periods, persistent low fever.	Several weeks or months after exposure to chlamydia or gonorrhea (if untreated)	Penicillin or other antibiotics; surgery.	Caused by untreated chlamydia or gonorrhea; may lead to chronic problems such as arthritis and infertility.

Other STDs

A number of other sexually transmitted diseases appear in the United States but with less frequency than they do in some developing countries.

- *Chancroid* is a painful sore or group of sores on the penis, caused by the bacterium *Hemophilus ducreyi*. Women may carry the bacteria but are generally asymptomatic for chancroid.

- *Cytomegalovirus (CMV)* is a virus of the herpes group that affects people with depressed immune systems. A fetus may be infected with CMV in the uterus.

- *Enteric infections* are intestinal infections caused by bacteria, viruses, protozoans, or other organisms that are normally carried in the intestinal tract. Amebiasis, giardiasis, and shigellosis are typical enteric infections. They often result from anal sex or oral-anal contact.

- *Granuloma inguinale* appears as single or multiple nodules, usually on the genitals, that become lumpy but painless ulcers that bleed on contact.

- *Lymphogranuloma venereum (LGV)* begins as a small, painless lesion at the site of infection, then develops into a painful abscess, accompanied by pain and swelling in the groin.

- *Molluscum contagiosum*, caused by a relatively large virus, is characterized by smooth, rounded, shiny lesions, appearing on the trunk, the genitals, or around the anus.

STDS AND WOMEN

STDs affect men and women similarly in some ways and differently in others. Overall, the consequences for women appear to be more serious than those for men. Generally speaking, heterosexual women contract STDs more readily than men and risk greater damage to their health and reproductive functioning. As a group, lesbians are at the lowest risk for STDs; they are not immune, however, and can still benefit by observing safer sex guidelines and basic hygiene to avoid transmitting organisms such as HSV by hand.

Biological Sexism

Where STDs are concerned, there is a kind of "biological sexism" working to the disadvantage of women. According to Robert Hatcher and colleagues (1990), this is partly a result of the "fluid dynamics of intercourse," wherein "women are apparently more likely than men to acquire a sexually transmitted infection from any single sexual encounter." For example, the risk of acquiring gonorrhea from a single "coital event" when one partner is infectious is approximately 25% for men and 50% for women (Figure 16.3). Long-term effects of STDs for women include pelvic inflammatory disease, ectopic pregnancy, infertility, and cervical cancer.

A woman's anatomy may increase her susceptibility to STDs. The warm, moist interiors of the vagina and uterus are ideal environments for many organisms. The thin, sensitive skin inside the labia and the mucous membranes lining the vagina may also be more permeable to infecting organisms than the skin covering a man's genitals. Additionally, menstruation may cause a woman to be more vulnerable. As the endometrium sloughs off the uterine walls, tiny blood vessels rupture, causing bleeding and incidentally providing a pathway for infecting organisms directly into the woman's bloodstream. (If a woman has a bloodborne disease such as hepatitis, or HIV/AIDS, it may also be passed to her partner in menstrual blood.)

Women who use barrier methods of contraception, such as the sponge,

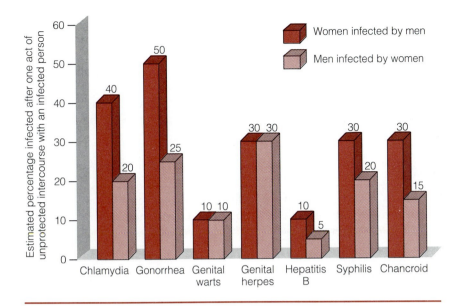

FIGURE 16.3 STD Risks for Women and Men Compared. This graph shows the estimated percentage of women and men infected with each STD after a single act of intercourse with an infected partner. Who is at greater risk? (SOURCE: *Health & Sexuality* 2(2):3, 1991.)

diaphragm, or female condom, tend to be better protected against STDs than women who rely on men to use a condom (Rosenberg, Davidson, Chen, Judson, & Douglas, 1992).

Pelvic Inflammatory Disease (PID)

Pelvic inflammatory disease (PID), also known as **salpingitis,** is one of the leading causes of female infertility. Over 800,000 cases of PID occur annually, resulting in about 200,000 hospitalizations (McNeeley, 1992). PID begins with an initial infection of the fallopian tube (or tubes) by an organism such as *C. trachomatis* or *N. gonorrhoeae,* which makes it possible for bacteria to invade and develop (Ault & Faro, 1993). As the infection spreads, the tubes swell and fester, often causing acute pain. Scar tissue begins to form within the tubes and may block the passage of eggs en route to the uterus, or cause a fertilized egg to implant within the tube itself—an ectopic pregnancy. PID occurs more commonly in women who have had a number of sex partners, women with a previous history of PID, and very young women. Adolescent females run a 1-in-8 risk of contracting PID, whereas women 24 years or older run a 1-in-80 risk (Sweet, 1986). A woman may be more susceptible to PID during the first few days of her period, or if she uses an IUD.

Symptoms of PID include:

- Lower abdominal pain.
- Cervical discharge.
- Cervical tenderness.
- Fever.

Because definitive diagnosis of PID usually requires laparoscopy (an expensive examination involving minor surgery to insert the viewing instrument), physicians may go ahead and prescribe antibiotics once such conditions as appendicitis and ectopic pregnancy have been ruled out. Untreated PID can lead to life-threatening conditions such as pelvic abscesses and ectopic pregnancy. Once the infection is under control, further examination and treatment may be necessary to prevent infertility, ectopic pregnancy, or chronic abdominal pain, all of which may result from scar tissue buildup. To prevent reinfection, women with PID should be sure their partners are examined for STDs.

Cystitis

Cystitis, a bladder infection that affects mainly women, is often related to sexual activity, although it is not transmitted from one partner to another. Cystitis is characterized by:

- Painful, burning urination.
- Urinary frequency.

It occurs when bacteria such as *Escherichia coli*, normally present in the lower intestine and in fecal material, are introduced into the urinary tract. This can occur when continuous friction (from intercourse or manual stimulation) in the area of the urethra traumatizes the tissue and allows nearby bacteria to easily enter the urinary tract. It often occurs at the beginning of a sexual relationship, when sexual activity is high (hence the nickname "honeymoon cystitis"). If cystitis is not treated promptly, more serious symptoms will occur:

- Lower abdominal pain.
- Fever.
- Kidney pain.

Damage to the kidneys may occur. (For measures to prevent cystitis or steps to treat it if it occurs, see Perspective 3.)

PREVENTING STDS

He had a mania for washing and disinfecting himself. . . . For him the only danger came from microbes which attacked the body. He had not studied the microbe of conscience which eats into the soul.

Anaïs Nin

It seems that STDs should be easy to prevent, at least in theory. But in reality, STD prevention involves a subtle interplay of knowledge, psychological factors, and behaviors. In other words, STD prevention *is* easy, *if* you know the facts, *if* you believe in it, and *if* you act in accordance with your knowledge and belief. In the earlier part of this chapter, we gave you the facts. Now let's think about the psychological and behavioral components of preventing STDs.

Risk Taking

The psychology of risk taking where STDs are concerned is similar in many ways to the psychology of contraceptive risk taking (see Chapter 12). Our ambivalence about sexuality may cause us to deny that we are sexual creatures, while at the same time we are engaging in sexual behaviors that put us at risk. Thus, we may not use a condom because our partner "doesn't

PREVENTING AND TREATING CYSTITIS

The following precautions may help a woman avoid cystitis:

- Urinate frequently, to avoid the buildup of highly acidic urine.
- Urinate before sexual activity and immediately afterward, to flush bacteria from the urethra.
- Drink plenty of fluids (water is best), especially just before and just after intercourse.
- Eat a well-balanced diet and get plenty of rest, especially if your resistance is low.
- If you use a diaphragm and are troubled by cystitis, have it checked for proper fit. You may need a smaller size, or you may need to consider another form of contraception.

If you have cystitis:

- Drink copious amounts of water (at least 16 glasses a day). It won't hurt you, as long as you urinate frequently. A pinch of baking soda in a glass of water may help neutralize the urine's acidity. Some women find that drinking cranberry juice provides relief. Coffee, tea, colas, and alcohol are not advisable as they may irritate the urinary tract.
- Pain and itching may be relieved by spraying or sponging water on the urethral opening. If urination is very painful, try urinating while sitting in a few inches of warm water (in the bathtub or a large pan).
- If symptoms persist or in the case of fever, see your doctor or clinic. Sulfa drugs or other antibiotics will usually clear up the symptoms within a few days. (A caution about sulfa drugs: 10–14% of African Americans have an inherited deficiency of a blood enzyme called glucose-6-phosphate-dehydrogenase [G6PD]; sulfa drugs may cause a serious anemic reaction in these people.)

look like the type to have an STD," or we may be monogamous "except for once in a while." Denying our sexuality in this way is not just psychologically unhealthy—it is physically dangerous. Epidemics such as smallpox and polio were halted because vaccinations were given to everyone, not just those who were considered to be at high risk. Although vaccinations are not available for most STDs, the same principle can still be applied. If precautions to prevent STD transmission were taken by everyone, regardless of whether or not they were perceived by themselves or others to be at risk, STDs would virtually be stopped dead in their tracks.

Abstinence

The most absolutely foolproof method of STD prevention is to abstain from intimate sexual contact, specifically penile-vaginal intercourse, anal intercourse, and oral sex. Hugging, massaging, kissing, petting, and mutual masturbation are all ways of sharing intimacy that are extremely unlikely to transmit STDs. (But watch out for colds!)

"Abstinence has never looked better," writes health educator Felicia

Guest (in Hatcher et al., 1990). It may be an especially useful strategy for people who are casually dating, giving them time to get to know a partner before engaging in intercourse. It is the only reliable course of action for a person who has an STD or whose partner has an STD (or a suspected STD). Freely chosen abstinence is a legitimate personal choice regarding sexuality. People who wish to be abstinent need to communicate their preferences clearly and unambiguously to their dates or partners. They also need to learn to avoid high-pressure sexual situations and to stay away from alcohol and drugs, which can impair their judgment. Abstainers also need to be informed about safer sex practices, including condom use, in the event that they decide to engage in sex after all.

Good Health, Safer Sex

When we value ourselves, our bodies, and our lives, we are likely to practice good health behaviors, such as eating well, exercising, getting enough rest, and seeking medical care when we need it. When we become sexual, we need to develop particular habits and patterns to promote our continuing good health. Specific health behaviors that help protect us from STDs include:

- Good genital hygiene (simply washing with mild soap and warm water, especially under the foreskin for uncircumcised males, before and after sex).
- Practicing safer sex. (See Perspective 4.)
- Knowing the signs and symptoms of STDs.
- Talking to a partner about past and current exposure, or possible exposure, to an STD.
- Examining self and partner for genital sores or unusual discharge.
- Seeking medical care at the onset of symptoms.
- Following treatment instructions.

People who are sexually active with more than one partner should have a medical examination to screen for STDs every 3–6 months (Hatcher et al., 1990). This is especially important for women because they are often asymptomatic.

The Health Belief Model

We doe delightfully our selves allow
To that consumption; and profusely
 blinde,
We kill our selves, to propagate our
 kinde.

John Donne

Although we are aware of STDs and their consequences, many of us do not take steps to prevent them unless we perceive the disease as a specific threat to ourselves. The **health belief model** helps explain the psychology behind our sexual health behaviors (Darrow & Siegel, 1990; Rosenstock, 1974). According to this model, four factors must be present in order for an individual to take action to avoid a disease:

1. The person must believe that he or she is personally susceptible to it.
2. The individual must believe that the disease would have at least a moderately severe effect on his or her life.

Perspective 4

SAFER AND UNSAFE SEXUAL PRACTICES

Safer sex practices are an integral part of good health practices. (Many people prefer the term "safer sex" to "safe sex," since all sexual contact carries at least a slight risk—a condom slipping off, perhaps—no matter how careful we try to be.) For detailed information on condom use, see Chapter 12; see Chapter 17 for information on using various types of latex barriers.

Safer Practices

- Hugging.
- Kissing (but possibly not deep, French kissing).
- Massaging.
- Petting.
- Masturbation (solo or mutual, unless there are sores or abrasions on the genitals or hands).
- Erotic videos, books, etc.

Possibly Safe Practices

- Deep, French kissing, unless there are sores in the mouth.
- Vaginal intercourse with a latex condom and spermicide.

- Fellatio with a latex condom.
- Cunnilingus, if the woman does not have her period or a vaginal infection (a latex dental dam or a square of plastic wrap provides extra protection).
- Anal intercourse with a latex condom and spermicide (authorities disagree as to whether this should be considered "safer" even with a condom, because it is the riskiest sexual behavior without one).

Unsafe Practices

- Vaginal or anal intercourse without a latex condom.
- Fellatio without a latex condom.
- Cunnilingus, if the woman has her period or a vaginal infection and a dental dam is not used.
- Oral-anal contact.
- Contact with blood, including menstrual blood.
- Semen in the mouth.
- Sharing vibrators, dildos, etc., without washing them between uses.

3. He or she must believe that taking a particular action will reduce the susceptibility to or the severity of the disease.

4. He or she must believe that the costs of prevention (or treatment) are worth the benefits.

Let's take a closer look at each of these factors.

Susceptibility People tend to underestimate their risk of getting STDs. They may not understand that the risk of STD infection goes up exponentially with each new sex partner (Figure 16.4). This is because when we have sex with someone, we are potentially in contact with all the sexually transmittable organisms of every person our partner has ever had sex with, which include (potentially) all the organisms of those with whom each of our partner's former partners have had sex, and so on. Furthermore, people

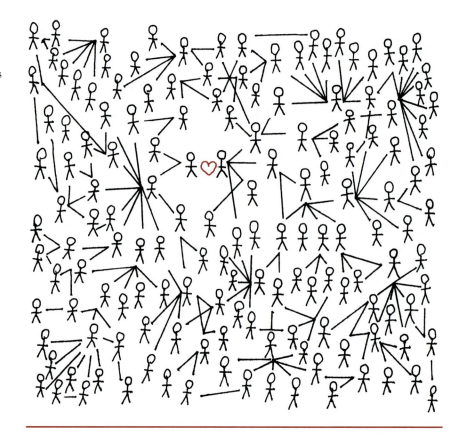

FIGURE 16.4 The Exponential Risk of Contracting an STD. When we have sex with someone, we are potentially putting ourselves in contact with all the sexually transmittable organisms of every person with whom our partner has had sex, which include all the organisms of those with whom our partner's former partners have had sex, and so (and on).

persist in believing that they can distinguish a person who has an STD simply by looking at her or him (Balshem, Oxman, van Rooyen, & Girod, 1992).

Severity In the "Age of AIDS," we can hardly afford to be blasé about the consequences of getting an STD. Moreover, the consequences (especially for women) of STDs such as chlamydia, gonorrhea, and genital warts may be painful, expensive, and heartbreaking, even if they are not usually life-threatening.

Appropriate Action Knowledge about ways to prevent, recognize, and treat STDs enables us to act in ways that benefit our health. For example, we are more likely to use a condom if we believe it will actually help us avoid getting an STD. If we don't understand how condoms work or if we are unaware of their proven effectiveness, we may not use them or may use them only grudgingly at our partner's insistence.

Benefits Versus Costs People may not act to prevent STDs because they perceive the costs as being too high. The costs could include the embarrassment of talking to a partner about STDs, the actual monetary expense of treatment, the inconvenience of buying or putting on a condom, or the change of lifestyle from many partners to a single, monogamous rela-

A key element in avoiding sexual risk taking is the willingness to communicate about sex and safer sex practices.

tionship. A person has to determine if these kinds of costs are worth the benefits of preventive action or treatment, such as feeling healthy, being pain-free, not having to worry about getting infected, and not passing an STD to a partner.

The health belief model can help us understand the role of denial in the transmission of sexually related diseases. Denial can be bolstered by the belief systems of people who experience fear, guilt, and shame in association with their sexual activities:

- "I won't get that disease because I don't go out with those kinds of people." (Denial of susceptibility.)
- "Well, it's no big deal if I get a little discharge. It'll go away." (Denial of severity.)
- "I don't need to see a doctor; the rash will clear up by itself." (Denial of appropriate action.)
- "It's just too embarrassing to talk about these kinds of things." (Denial of benefits, exaggeration of costs.)

STDs and Communication

We may catch the flu in a crowded bus or subway, but we won't be intimate enough (presumably) to give or get a sexually transmitted disease. Acquiring an STD requires that we get intimately close to another person. Just as getting STDs requires intimacy, so does preventing them. Avoiding an STD may even require more intimacy than getting one, because very often it means we have to talk. Learning to communicate isn't always easy. It can be embarrassing, especially if we are unaccustomed to sharing personal and sexual feelings. But it gets easier with practice. And anyway, when you come right down to it, embarrassment is not as bad as herpes, gonorrhea, or AIDS.

A man, on entering the waiting room of a veterinarian's office with his sick dog, sat next to a lady with a beautiful wolfhound. The wolfhound was extremely high spirited and happily gamboled around the waiting room as the man's own dog lay limply on the floor. Finally, curious as to why such an apparently healthy dog should be in a veterinarian's office, he turned to the lady and said: "You certainly have a beautiful dog."

"Oh, thank you," she replied.

"He looks so healthy," said he, "that I am surprised to see him in a veterinarian's office. What is wrong with him?"

"Oh," she said with some embarrassment, "he has syphilis."

"Syphilis!" he said. "How did he get syphilis?"

"Well," she said, "he claims he got it from a tree."

Dorothy Parker

Elements of Communication   The key elements in communicating about sexual issues in general were discussed in Chapter 9. Important elements in communicating about STDs include initiating the discussion, mutual disclosure of relevant information, and joint decision making.

Initiating the Discussion   In some situations, we may be able to use nonverbal communication regarding STD prevention. While it may lack the depth and intimacy that words can produce, it is certainly preferable to no communication at all. For example, if you thought you were going to have sex with someone, you could be sure you had a condom with you, and, if you are a man, you could simply put it on at the appropriate time. If you are a woman, you could offer it to your partner when the moment was right. If your partner agreed, all would be well with this very minimal amount of communicating. But if your partner were to recoil in horror and say, "Yuck, I never use those," it's likely that you would need to begin verbal communication if you were serious about protection.

It is preferable to initiate a discussion of safer sex before you are entangled in a passionate embrace. In the "heat of the moment," we are all subject to suspension of our rational faculties. "Oh well, just this once won't matter," we may think. And it may matter very much indeed. When sexual intimacy appears on the horizon of a relationship, we need to be prepared with strategies for introducing the topics of contraception and STD prevention. Some people are able to state their concerns simply and directly: "Do you have condoms, or shall I get some?" Others may need to broach the subject more indirectly: "What do you think about safer sex?" or "It's not easy for me to talk about this, but I think we should decide about protection." Once the ice has been broken, the other person will usually be receptive and responsive to a discussion. There's a good chance he or she has been trying to get the courage to say the same thing.

Mutual Disclosure   When we embark on a relationship that includes sexual activity, it is important to have some information about our partner's sexual health. While it would be nice if our partner simply volunteered the relevant information, this is probably not going to occur. We are most likely going to have to ask some very personal questions. One of the best ways to get someone to disclose personal information is to reveal important personal information about ourselves. There is always some risk involved in self-disclosure. For example, you may say, "Before we go any further, you should know that I had an outbreak of herpes two years ago. It hasn't recurred so there's very little chance that I'm contagious at this time, but I wanted you to know." If your partner does not know the facts about herpes, he or she may freak out. But it is more likely that your honesty will be appreciated. (Besides, there's a 1 in 6 chance your partner has HSV, too!)

The information potential sexual partners should disclose to each other includes:

- Present STD or symptoms that might indicate an STD.
- Possible recent exposure to an STD.
- Past history of STDs.
- Present lifestyle, including multiple sexual partners and IV drug use.

- Past history of many sex partners, gay or bisexual male partners, or partners with a history of IV drug use.
- HIV serostatus (positive or negative result, as determined by an HIV blood test). This is especially important for gay or bisexual men, IV drug users, and their sex partners.

If both partners are sincerely concerned about the other's well-being, they will probably be able to overcome any feelings of embarrassment, guilt, or shame and share this important information. For this reason, relationships that develop over time and are founded on mutual caring and trust are likely to be safer sexually than one-night stands. Unfortunately, a person with no emotional investment in a relationship may not always be motivated to tell the truth. In one study, 35% of the men surveyed reported that they had lied to a woman in order to have sex with her (Goleman, 1988). Twenty percent said that if a woman asked if they had been tested for HIV, they would lie, saying that they had had the test and the results were negative. Taking some time to get to know your partner is a good way to help ensure your own sexual good health.

Joint Decision Making If partners use a condom during intercourse, they probably have done so by mutual consent. Either they have both agreed it is important to use a condom, or one of them has proposed condom use and the other has tacitly agreed by going along with it. What may not be clear is that if two people have sex without using a condom, they have mutually agreed that protection is unimportant or unnecessary. Perhaps they have not discussed their decision with each other, but it is a decision nonetheless. Perhaps one (or even both) of the partners would rather be using a condom but hasn't said anything from embarrassment or fear of rejection. In choosing not to discuss the subject, the person has made the decision to risk getting an STD. In order to have safer sex, both partners need to agree on what practices they will engage in and under what circumstances they will or will not use condoms. Otherwise, "one partner who is not motivated to practice safer sex may not cooperate with the other partner, may undercut the other partner's resolve, or may refuse to use condoms properly" (Darrow & Siegel, 1990). (See Perspective 5 to find out what to expect at an STD clinic if you think you have contracted an STD.)

STDS AND PUBLIC POLICY

Most people can protect themselves from STDs armed with little more than knowledge, condoms, and the motivation to use them. Still, STDs continue to spread, especially within impoverished inner-city communities. Most of us are probably disturbed, if not appalled, by this situation. We may be further distressed by the words of Edward Richards and Donald Bross, specialists in both law and medicine (Richards & Bross, 1990):

Gonorrhea is under control, in the sense that the United States has chosen to allocate only enough resources to gonorrhea control programs to set the equilibrium point at approximately 2 to 3 million cases a year. Assuming that this resource allocation has been rationally determined, it reflects the amount of

This disease is like other diseases: it is one of our afflictions. There is no shame in being wretched—even if one deserves to be so. Come, come, let us have a little plain speaking! I should like to know how many of these rigid moralists, who are so choked with their middle-class prudery that they dare not mention the name syphilis, or when they bring themselves to speak of it do so with expressions of every sort of disgust, and treat its victims as criminals, have never run the risk of contracting it themselves?

Eugène Brieux, 1901

A VISIT TO AN STD CLINIC

Let's say you think you may have an STD. Perhaps you've noticed a peculiar discharge from your vagina or penis, and it hurts when you urinate. Or maybe you noticed some unusual little bumps on your partner's genitals—*after* you'd made love. So you decide that a visit to your local STD clinic or your college health clinic is in order. You call first to see if you need an appointment. (Check the yellow pages of your telephone directory under Clinics, Family Planning, or Health Services if you don't know the number.)

After an uncomfortable, semisleepless night, you find yourself at the clinic at 10:00 the next morning. Here's a version of what might happen next:

- The receptionist gives you a clipboard with a bunch of papers to fill out. The most important of these is a medical/sexual history. Take your time filling it out, and include any information you think might be helpful to the clinician who will see you and recommend treatment. You return the papers to the receptionist.

- You wait. Most clinics are working within a limited budget. They may have a small staff and a large clientele. Bring your patience (and a book).

- Your name or number is called. You go into another room and sit down to talk with a counselor or social worker. (This may happen after your medical exam, or be combined with it.) She or he is there to give you information and to answer your questions, in addition to getting more specific details about the reason for your visit. The more honest and straightforward you are about your sexual activities, the more help you will be able to receive. Health-care workers are not interested in passing judgment on you; they are there to help you get well. Your records will be kept confidential.

- Depending on your symptoms, you may next be asked for a urine sample or a blood sample. The health-care worker should explain the reasons for any test or procedure.

- Next, you go to an examination room. If you are a woman, you will probably be instructed to remove your clothes from the waist down and cover yourself with a paper gown or drape. You will probably lie down on an examining table with your feet in stirrups so that the clinician can have a clear view of your genital area and give you a vaginal examination. If you are a man, you will probably be asked to remove your pants or simply to lower them. The clinician who examines you may be a physician, intern, public-health nurse, nurse practitioner, or other medically trained person. Depending on your symptoms, the clinician may use a cotton swab to take a small sample of the affected tissue or discharge for microscopic evaluation or culturing. For men, this may involve squeezing the glans to produce the discharge. For women, it may involve the insertion of a speculum to open the vagina and then a gentle swabbing of the cervix. (A note for women: If you are examined by a man, the law requires that a female assistant be present.) Be sure to tell the clinician about any discomfort or pain you experience during the exam. After the examination, you dress and go back to the waiting room or to a conference room.

- The clinician, counselor, or another health-care worker discusses your diagnosis with you. In some cases, treatment will be started right away. In others, you may have to wait several days for lab results. In any event, it is imperative to follow the clinic's instructions exactly. If you have questions, be sure to ask.

- You get your medication from the clinic or pharmacy, and begin taking it.

- You inform your partner (or partners) of your diagnosis and insist that he or she (or they) seek immediate treatment. This is crucially important for halting the spread of an STD and preventing your own possible reinfection.

- You refrain from sexual activity until the clinician tells you it is safe. You return for a follow-up visit if required.

- You decide that next time, you'll use a condom.

An important part of controlling the spread of STDs is having free access to condoms and relevant information. Here, peer educator Kevin Turner, also known as Mr. Condom, distributes condoms and STD facts in Seattle.

money that the United States is willing to invest in a disease that poses the [amount of] risk to society [that gonorrhea does].

In other words, the incidence of STDs is largely determined by public policy. Cases not only of gonorrhea, but of other STDs as well, could be significantly reduced by government funding of appropriate policies and programs. Our country needs to develop "the political will to develop national STD program priorities, goals, and strategies, and also to allocate sufficient resources to implement those strategies needed to achieve the program goals" (Holmes et al., 1990; also see Alexander, 1992).

Public policies and programs to prevent and treat STDs exist throughout the country. Most programs are woefully underfunded, however, and in the position of having to vie with each other for operating expenses. A multifaceted approach to STD prevention and treatment includes:

- Development of curricula to provide accurate and relevant information to elementary and secondary students.

- Free distribution of condoms and information regarding STDs.

- Adequately trained clinicians and adequately staffed clinics to diagnose and treat STDs and provide counseling.

- Outreach programs to high-risk or core transmission group members, who might not ordinarily seek treatment.

- Screening programs to detect curable STDs such as gonorrhea, chlamydia, syphilis, and hepatitis.

- Free, voluntary testing for HIV.

- Free or low-cost treatment programs for affected individuals and their children.

- Contact tracing and partner notification of individuals known to have an STD (a controversial but highly effective method of STD reduction; see Richards & Bross, 1990).

- Research projects to develop new diagnostic techniques, treatments, and vaccines.

- Improved reporting of STDs by private physicians.

- Training of physicians and medical students in all aspects of STD diagnosis and management.

As individuals, we have the knowledge and means to protect ourselves from STDs. As a society, we should have a larger goal. In the words of King Holmes and the other editors of *Sexually Transmitted Diseases* (1990), "We must acknowledge and correct the failure of society and of politicians to support the basic needs for public health in general and for STD control in particular."

SUMMARY

X-Rated Diseases: The Psychological Impact of STDs

- Although the media and popular culture encourage us to express ourselves sexually, Americans continue to experience a great deal of embarrassment, guilt, and shame over their sexuality. This deep ambivalence discourages us from dealing realistically with sexually transmitted disease (STDs).

The STD Epidemic

- The incidence of STDs has increased dramatically since the 1950s for a number of reasons. Social factors include changes in sexual mores, decreased condom use due to the advent of the pill and IUD, obstruction of educational efforts and research by vocal minorities who confuse medical issues with moral ones, inadequate health-care facilities, and the misuse of alcohol and drugs. Biological factors include the fact that many STDs are *asymptomatic*, and the evolution of strains of viruses and bacteria that are resistant to prescribed antibiotics.

- *Epidemiology* is the study of diseases—how they spread, and how they may be controlled. In STD epidemiology, it is important to understand the difference between *risk factors*, which may cause individuals to actually be at risk for STDs (such as having many sex partners or not using condoms) and *risk markers*, which are coincidentally associated with an STD (such as low socioeconomic status and urban residence) but are not causally related.

- The core group model is used to explain how certain STDs, such as gonorrhea, are transmitted within a population. *Core groups* are small, stable groups with a consistently high prevalence of a particular disease that continuously introduce the infection into the general population.

Principal STDs

- The principal STDs affecting Americans are *chlamydia, gonorrhea, genital warts, genital herpes, syphilis, hepatitis, urinary tract infections (NGU or NSU), vaginitis,* and *HIV/AIDS* (see Table 16.1 for a summary). Parasites that may be sexually transmitted include *scabies* and *pubic lice.*

STDs and Women

- There is a kind of "biological sexism" where STDs are concerned. Women tend to be more susceptible to STDs than men and to experience graver consequences, such as *pelvic inflammatory disease (PID)*, an infection of the fallopian tubes that can lead to infertility and *ectopic pregnancy*. Intense stimulation of the vulva can irritate the urethra, leading to *cystitis* (bladder infection).

Preventing STDs

- STD prevention involves the interaction of knowledge, psychological factors, and behaviors to avoid taking risks. Abstinence is a legitimate personal strategy for avoiding STDs. Good health behaviors, including safer sex, are very effective in protecting against STDs. Consistent condom use is an important component of safer sex.

- The *health belief model* is used to help explain the psychology behind our sexual health behaviors. In order to take action to avoid a disease, according to this model, a person must believe that he or she is personally susceptible to it, the disease would have at least a moderately severe affect on his or her life, taking a particular action would reduce the susceptibility to or severity of the disease, and the costs are worth the benefits.

- Communication is an important factor in STD prevention. Important elements of communication are initiating the discussion, mutual disclosure of relevant information, and joint decision making.

STDs and Public Policy

- The course of STDs in this country is greatly affected by public health policies and programs. We need to expand and develop programs in research, education, screening, and treatment of STDs so that all Americans may enjoy the benefits of our nation's wealth and medical expertise.

KEY TERMS

prophylaxis

asymptomatic

prevalence

epidemiology

risk factor

risk marker

core group

chlamydia

epididymitis

gonorrhea

genital warts

human papilloma
   virus (HPV)

genital herpes

herpes simplex
   virus (HSV)

vesicle

papule

prodrome

syphilis

spirochete

chancre

hepatitis

nongonococcal
   urethritis (NGU)

nonspecific
   urethritis (NSU)

urethritis

vaginitis

bacterial vaginosis

candidiasis

trichomoniasis

scabies

pubic lice

pelvic inflammatory
   disease (PID)

salpingitis

cystitis

health belief model

RESOURCES

American Social Health Association
P.O. Box 13827
Research Triangle Park, NC 27709
(919) 361-8400, STD Hotline: (800) 227-8922
The Hotline provides information and referrals on all aspects of STDs. Call the main number for a wide variety of publications.

Herpes Resource Center
P.O. Box 13827
RT Park, NC 27709
(919) 361-8488 (NC), (415) 328-7710 (CA)
Confidential referrals and information.

Planned Parenthood
Planned Parenthood provides information, counseling, and medical services related to sexual health to anyone regardless of age, social group, or ability to pay. Check local listings for the clinic nearest you.

Public Health Departments
Many health departments have clinics that treat STDs; check local listings.

U.S. Centers for Disease Control (CDC)
Division of STD/HIV Prevention
1600 Clifton Road NE
Atlanta, GA 30333
(404) 639-3286
The CDC conducts research and collects data from nationwide sources. Many publications, including the Morbidity and Mortality Weekly Report (MMWR), *which contains the latest STD information, are put out by the CDC.*

SUGGESTIONS FOR FURTHER READING

Brandt, Allan M. *No Magic Bullet: A Social History of Venereal Disease in the United States Since 1880.* New York: Oxford University Press, 1985. An informative and very readable history of the social and political aspects of STDs.

Hatcher, Robert. *Safely Sexual.* New York: Irvington Publishers, 1991. A practical and sensitive guide to safer sex and pregnancy prevention.

Holmes, King K., et al., eds. *Sexually Transmitted Diseases,* 2nd ed. New York: McGraw-Hill, 1990. The definitive collection of recent research by leading authorities on STDs in the U.S. and Europe (95 chapters, over 1000 pages).

Ibsen, Henrik. *Ghosts.* A tragic play by one of the world's great playwrights, centering around the life of a young man with congenital syphilis.

Jones, James. *Bad Blood: The Tuskegee Syphilis Experiment—A Tragedy of Race and Medicine.* Rev. ed. New York: Free Press, 1981, 1993. A fascinating—and chilling—account of a 40-year experiment by the Public Health Service, using African Americans in the rural South as human guinea pigs. Discusses the experiment's impact on current HIV/AIDS prevention efforts in the black community.

Quétel, Claude. *A History of Syphilis.* Cambridge, England: Polity Press, 1990. A fascinating social and scientific journey across 500 years with *T. pallidum.*

Chapter Seventeen

HIV AND AIDS

PREVIEW: SELF-QUIZ

1. Acquired immune deficiency syndrome (AIDS) is caused by the human immunodeficiency virus (HIV). True or false?

2. The virus that causes AIDS can get through microscopic holes that naturally occur in latex condoms. True or false?

3. Scientists have not actually seen a human immunodeficiency virus. True or false?

4. Women are more likely than men to acquire HIV during sexual intercourse with an infected partner. True or false?

5. Viruses can "crawl" from one surface to another. True or false?

6. Today the chance of being exposed to HIV during a blood transfusion is between 1 in 40,000 and 1 in 225,000. True or false?

7. It is expected that in the U.S. by the year 2000, the number of men and women affected by HIV will be equal. True or false?

8. If a pregnant woman has HIV, her child is sure to have it also. True or false?

9. If you receive an HIV-positive blood test, it means you definitely have AIDS. True or false?

10. HIV is *not* transmitted through normal household or social activities. True or false?

ANSWERS 1. T, 2. F, 3. F, 4. T, 5. F, 6. T, 7. T, 8. F, 9. F, 10. T

Chapter Outline

In the past decade, there has been no single phenomenon that has changed the face of sexuality as much as the appearance of the minuscule virus known as **HIV,** or **human immunodeficiency virus.** In the early 1980s, physicians in San Francisco, New York, and Los Angeles began noticing repeated occurrences of formerly rare diseases among young and relatively healthy men. Kaposi's sarcoma, a cancer of the blood vessels, and pneumocystis carinii pneumonia, a lung infection that is usually not dangerous, had become killer diseases resulting from the breakdown of the immune system of the affected men (Centers for Disease Control, 1982). Even before the virus responsible for the breakdown was discovered, the disease was given a name: acquired immune deficiency syndrome, or AIDS. At first, AIDS within the United States seemed to be confined principally to three groups: gay men, Haitians, and people with hemophilia. Soon, however, it became apparent that no particular group could afford to be complacent, as the disease spread into communities with high rates of intravenous drug use and into the general population, including heterosexual men and women (and their children) at all socioeconomic levels. The far-reaching consequences of the AIDS epidemic, in addition to the pain and loss directly caused by the illness, have included widespread fear, superstition, and hatred. Ignorance of its modes of transmission has fueled the flames of homophobia among some people. Among other people, it has kindled a general fear of sexual expression. In many communities, however, it has engendered compassion and solidarity as people have come together to care for those who are living with HIV or AIDS, and to educate themselves and others.

Although researchers know a great deal about the virus and the way it works, among the general public, misinformation abounds. By now most of us know how HIV is spread. And yet, for a variety of reasons, people continue engaging in behaviors that put them at risk. Our goal in this chapter is to give a solid grounding in the biological aspects of the disease and in its psychological and sociological aspects as well. Because it is not likely that a cure for AIDS will be found in the near future, we must develop the attitudes and behaviors that will stop its deadly progression. AIDS *is* preventable. We hope that the material in this chapter will assist you in making healthy, informed choices for yourself and in becoming a force for education and positive change in the community.

We begin this chapter by exploding some common myths about AIDS (see Perspective 1), then go on to describe the disease, the virus itself, and the workings of the immune system. We next discuss modes of transmission, the effects of HIV and AIDS on certain groups of people, current treatments, education, prevention, and HIV testing. Then we deal with the demographic aspects of the epidemic—its effect on various communities and groups: the gay community, teenagers, women, children, ethnic minorities, and the poor. Public policy, research issues, and the impact of AIDS worldwide are also discussed. The final section of the chapter is about living with HIV or AIDS. We offer practical advice for those who have the virus or whose friends or loved ones do. Also included is a resource guide for those who wish to obtain further information.

Ring around the rosey,
Pocket full of posies.
Ashes! Ashes!
We all fall down.

Nursery Rhyme

Most of all I fear the effects of the AIDS virus on the social compact that has held American society together through periods of profound turmoil as well as tranquility. The epidemic of AIDS may force on us one of the most serious tests of social and political will that our society has ever undergone.

C. Everett Koop,
former Surgeon General

AIDS MYTHS, AIDS FACTS

Myths and rumors about HIV and AIDS abound. Many are kept alive by the media, especially the tabloid newspapers, read by millions, and certain talk-show hosts and newspaper columnists. Some politicians and religious leaders, especially those with "anti-sex" agendas, are also responsible for the spread of misinformation. We briefly discuss some common myths below. As you read the chapter, you will understand more about the issues that are raised.

- *Myth:* If you're not in a high-risk group, you don't have to worry about AIDS. In other words, "low risk means no risk."

  Fact: This is one of the most deadly myths about AIDS. Statistics don't seem very relevant when the "one out of 100" (or whatever the number) happens to be you. Protecting ourselves or our children from potentially deadly diseases such as diphtheria or whooping cough is something most of us take for granted. We get the vaccinations even if we are not in a high-risk area or group. But it is precisely because virtually everyone takes these precautions that these diseases no longer threaten the general public. Admittedly, it is easier to get a shot than to use a condom each time you have sex, but that doesn't change the principle: If everyone assumes responsibility, together we can stop the transmission of most diseases, including AIDS.

- *Myth:* Scientists have not actually seen an AIDS virus.

  Fact: Researchers have seen countless AIDS viruses (through a microscope, of course) and understand a great deal about them. Because the presence of the virus is determined by testing for the antibodies that the immune system develops to

fight HIV, people may erroneously assume that the virus itself cannot be found. It can be, but the tests would be prohibitively expensive and involve unnecessary pain and risk.

- *Myth:* HIV was developed in the laboratory as germ warfare against gays or blacks, or it was spread through contaminated vaccines, such as that for polio.

  Fact: There have been many theories as to the origin of HIV. Some are grounded in science, whereas others have sprung solely from fear or paranoia. The pattern of HIV's spread does not ultimately support any of these theories. There is not a shred of evidence that the virus is manmade, nor have any traces of it been found in samples of frozen early vaccines. The most promising work in the search for HIV's origin is based on the obvious— but not yet well-understood—relationship of HIV (especially HIV-2) to SIV (simian immunodeficiency virus) (Essex & Kanki, 1988). SIV is widely prevalent among African green monkeys, but it is not deadly to them. Scientists hope that by studying SIV they will discover mechanisms by which HIV can be weakened or disabled.

- *Myth:* The AIDS virus is easy to "catch."

  Fact: The virus is only easy to catch in intimate situations when infected blood, semen, vaginal secretions, or breast milk have a direct pathway into the bloodstream of an uninfected person. The virus is delicate and dies quickly when exposed to spermicide, bleach, and a variety of other disinfectants. It can't survive in the open air. It is not spread by handshakes, hugs, or kisses where blood is not present.

- *Myth:* Latex condoms have naturally occurring holes that are 50 times bigger than the human immunodeficiency virus, so condoms do not really provide protection.

  Fact: Good quality latex condoms do not have such holes. Laboratory tests have shown that virus-sized particles do not normally leak from the better brands (Voeller et al., 1988). While poorer brands have been shown to leak minute amounts of virus-sized particles, in laboratory studies, researchers nevertheless conclude that "worst-case condom barrier effectiveness" is "at least 10,000 times better than not using a condom at all" (Carey, Herman, Retta, Rinaldi, & Athey, 1992). Numerous studies of couples in which one person is HIV-positive and one is not have shown extremely low rates of transmission when condoms are consistently used (CDC, 1993; de Vincenzi et al., 1992; Fischl et al., 1987; Padian, 1990).

- *Myth:* HIV doesn't cause AIDS.

  Fact: Most AIDS researchers are appalled at well-publicized claims (by another researcher) that the connection between HIV and AIDS is coincidental rather than causative. It is dangerous to publicize this sort of conclusion, as it may cause people infected with HIV, or those who are involved with them, to engage in unsafe practices. While the exact way (or ways) in which HIV destroys the immune system is still under investigation, there is no reason to doubt that it is the "first cause" of AIDS (Delaney, 1992). Factors that may combine with HIV to lead to the development of AIDS are discussed in this chapter.

- *Myth:* You can have AIDS without HIV.

  Fact: Some people are discouraged from being tested for HIV because they believe they can have AIDS without having the virus. While it is true that "false negative" results occasionally appear in HIV testing, retesting at a later date (recommended for those who think they may be at risk) should determine if the virus is present. However, between mid-1982 and mid-1993, the CDC confirmed reports of 113 cases of AIDS-like infections without the presence of HIV (CDC, 1993). This condition, called ideopathic CD4+T-lymphocytopenia (ICL), does not appear to be concentrated in any particular population or geographical area (as AIDS was at first), but the CDC has set up a national surveillance system to determine how (or if) it progresses (CDC, 1992). There are numerous other well-known diseases and conditions affecting the immune system, but these are generally not infectious.

- *Myth:* If you are HIV-positive, it means you have AIDS.

  Fact: Although it currently appears that people who test positive for HIV will go on to develop AIDS eventually, having the virus is not the same as having AIDS. Many people who are HIV-positive feel perfectly normal and healthy. If they maintain a healthful lifestyle, their immune system may continue to function well for a number of years. It is important to remember, though, that anyone who is HIV-positive can transmit the virus regardless of how healthy he or she may look or feel.

WHAT IS AIDS?

AIDS is an acronym for **acquired immune deficiency syndrome.** This condition is so named for the following reasons:

A   Acquired, because it is not inherited.

I   Immune, because it affects the immune system, which protects the body against foreign organisms.

D   Deficiency, because the body lacks immunity.

S   Syndrome, because the symptoms occur as a group.

To receive an AIDS diagnosis according to the CDC classification system (and thus be eligible for treatments, programs, and insurance funds that would not otherwise be available), a person must, in most cases, have a positive blood test indicating the presence of HIV antibodies and a T-cell count (discussed later) below 200 (CDC, 1992). If the T-cell count is higher, the person must have one or more of the diseases or conditions listed in the following section. At the beginning of 1993, T-cell count, along with cervical cancer/CIN, pulmonary tuberculosis, and recurrent bacterial pneumonia, were added to the CDC definition of AIDS. These additions led to a dramatic increase in the number of people who "officially" have AIDS. If a person has HIV antibodies but does not meet the other criteria, he or she is said to "have HIV" or be "living with HIV."

Conditions Associated with AIDS

The CDC currently lists 26 clinical conditions to be used in diagnosing AIDS along with HIV-positive status (CDC, 1992). These conditions fall into several categories: opportunistic infections, cancers, conditions associated specifically with AIDS, and conditions that *may* be diagnostic for AIDS under certain circumstances. The most commonly occurring diseases and conditions within these categories are listed below.

Opportunistic Infections Opportunistic infections (OIs) are diseases that take advantage of a weakened immune system; normally they do not develop in healthy people or are not life-threatening. Common OIs associated with HIV are:

- **Pneumocystis carinii pneumonia (PCP).** The most common opportunistic infection of people with AIDS; a lung disease caused by a common organism (probably a protozoan or fungus) that is not usually harmful. The organisms multiply, resulting in the accumulation of a fluid in the lungs (pneumonia).

- *Mycobacterium avium intracellulare (MAI)*. An atypical tuberculosis, usually affecting the lungs; also may affect the liver, spleen, lymph system, bone marrow, gastrointestinal tract, skin, or brain. MAI is the most common form of TB among people with AIDS. It is resistant to most antibiotics.

- *Mycobacterium tuberculosis (TB)*. An infection that generally occurs in the lungs and may appear in other sites such as the lymph nodes. This "old-fashioned" form of TB is infectious but treatable with common antibiotics.

- *Bacterial pneumonia.* Accumulation of fluid in the lungs due to the presence of any of several common bacteria. Multiple episodes of bacterial pneumonia may occur in people with AIDS.
- *Toxoplasmosis.* A disease of the brain and central nervous system caused by a parasite frequently present in cat feces.

Cancers Certain types of cancer are commonly associated with AIDS, including the following:

- **Kaposi's sarcoma.** A cancer of the blood vessels, causing red or purple blotches to appear under the skin; rare except in older men of central African or Mediterranean descent. Among people with AIDS, it is more common in gay or bisexual men than in women or heterosexual men.
- *Lymphomas.* Cancers of the lymphatic system. Lymphoma may also affect the brain.
- *Invasive cervical cancer.* Cancer or dysplasia (CIN) that can lead to cancer. Cervical cancer and CIN are more common in women who are HIV-positive than in other women. Cervical cancer can lead to uterine cancer if untreated.

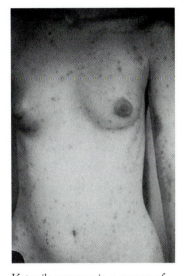

Kaposi's sarcoma is a cancer of the blood vessels commonly associated with AIDS. It causes red or purple blotches to appear under the skin's surface.

Clinical Conditions Associated with AIDS Conditions that are specifically linked to AIDS include:

- **Wasting syndrome.** Severe weight loss, usually accompanied by weakness and persistent diarrhea.
- *HIV encephalopathy (AIDS dementia).* Impairment of mental functioning, changes in mood or behavior, or impaired movement caused by direct infection of the brain with HIV.

Other Infections Infections listed by the CDC that may lead to an AIDS diagnosis under certain circumstances include:

- *Candidiasis (thrush).* A fungal (yeast) infection affecting the mouth, throat, esophagus, trachea, lungs, or vagina. Recurring candidiasis is especially common in women with AIDS.
- *Herpes simplex.* A common viral STD. Persistent lesions (lasting a month or more) or lesions on the lungs or esophagus may be diagnostic for AIDS.
- *Cytomegalovirus (CMV).* A virus of the herpes family, often sexually transmitted. In people with AIDS, it can lead to encephalitis (a brain infection), retinitis (infection of the retina that can lead to blindness), pneumonia, or hepatitis.

Because the immune systems of people with HIV may not be functioning well (and those of people with advanced AIDS certainly are not), they may be subject to numerous other infections that would not normally be much of a problem, such as colds, flus, and intestinal infections. Health precautions for people living with HIV are discussed later in the chapter.

Symptoms of HIV Infection and AIDS A person with HIV may feel fine, or he or she may experience one or more of the symptoms that follow.

A person who has received an AIDS diagnosis is more likely to experience at least some of them. It is important to remember, however, that all of these are also common symptoms of conditions that are not related to HIV or AIDS. *AIDS cannot be self-diagnosed.* A person who is experiencing persistent discomfort or illness should be checked out by a medical practitioner. Symptoms that may be associated with HIV or AIDS include:

- Unexplained persistent fatigue.
- Unexplained fever, chills, or night sweats for a period of several weeks or more.
- Unexplained weight loss greater than 10 lb or 10% of body weight in less than 2 months.
- Swollen lymph nodes in the neck, armpits, or groin that are unexplained and last more than 2 months. This condition is called *lymphadenopathy.*
- Pink, purple, or brown blotches on or under the skin, inside the mouth, nose, eyelids, or rectum that do not disappear.
- Persistent, fuzzy, white spots or other sores in the mouth (indicative of either *hairy leukoplakia* or candidiasis).
- Persistent dry cough and shortness of breath.
- Persistent diarrhea.

In addition, women may experience the following:

- Abnormal Pap smears.
- Persistent vaginal candidiasis.
- Abdominal cramping (due to PID).

The Immune System

The principal ingredients in blood are plasma (the fluid base), red blood cells, white blood cells, and platelets. The normal human body contains about 25 trillion red blood cells, which account for about 4 lb of body weight and circulate throughout the body carrying oxygen to the tissues.

Leukocytes Around 1 trillion white blood cells, or **leukocytes,** account for 2–3 lb of body weight. Whereas there are 20–50 million white cells in the blood of a healthy adult, billions more are distributed throughout the body in the lymph nodes (located mainly in the neck, face, armpits, and groin), spleen, and other lymphatic tissues (within connective tissue, throughout the small intestine, in the tonsils). There are several kinds of leukocytes, all of which play major roles in defending the body against invading organisms or mutant (cancerous) cells. Because HIV invades and eventually kills some kinds of leukocytes, it impairs the body's ability to ward off infections and other harmful conditions that ordinarily would not be threatening. The principal type of leukocyte we will be discussing is the lymphocyte.

Macrophages, Antigens, and Antibodies **Macrophages,** literally "big eaters," are formed from monocytes (another type of leukocyte) within the bone marrow. Although some circulate in the blood, most migrate to lymph nodes or lymphatic tissues, where they wait for foreign particles to be brought to them. The macrophage engulfs the foreign particle and displays the invader's antigen (*antibody generator*) like a signal flag on its own surface. **Antigens** are large molecules that are capable of stimulating the immune system and then reacting with the antibodies that are released to fight them. **Antibodies** bind to antigens, inactivate them, and mark them for destruction by killer cells. If the body has been previously exposed to the organism (by fighting it off or being vaccinated), the response is much quicker because memory cells are already biochemically programmed to respond.

B Cells and T Cells The **lymphocytes** crucial to the immune system's functioning are **B Cells** and several types of **T cells.** Like macrophages, **helper T cells** are programmed to "read" the antigens and then begin directing the immune system's response. They send chemical signals to B cells, which begin making antibodies specific to the presented antigen. Helper T cells also stimulate the proliferation of B cells and T cells (which are genetically programmed to replicate, or make copies of themselves) and activate both macrophages and **killer T cells,** transforming them into Ramboesque agents of destruction whose only purpose is to attack and obliterate the enemy. Suppressor T cells are activated when an antigen has been successfully destroyed. They slow and finally stop the immune response. T cells are also identified by the type of protein receptor (called CD4 or CD8) they display on their surface. Helper T cells display CD4, while killer T cells and suppressor T cells display CD8. The number of helper T cells in an individual's body is an important indicator of how well the immune system is functioning, as we will discuss later.

The Virus

In some ways, viruses are really very primitive entities. They have no life on their own. They can't propel themselves independently, and they can't reproduce unless they are inside a host cell. They are basically just minute capsules of protein containing a bit of genetic material and a few enzymes. It would take 16,000 human immunodeficiency viruses to cover the head of a pin in a single layer. Under strong magnification, HIV resembles a spherical pincushion, bristling with tiny pinheadlike knobs (Figure 17.1). These knobs are the antigens, which contain a protein called gp120; the CD4 receptors on a helper T cell are attracted (fatally, as it turns out) to gp120 (Redfield & Burke, 1988). Within the virus's protein core is the genetic material (RNA) that carries the information the virus needs to replicate itself. Also in the core is an enzyme called **reverse transcriptase.** When a cell is functioning normally, its DNA (genetic material) manufactures RNA, programming it to run the cell's "machinery." Reverse transcriptase enables the virus to "write" its RNA (the genetic software or program) into a cell's DNA. Viruses with this ability to reverse the normal genetic writing process are known as **retroviruses.** There are numerous variant strains of HIV-1 resulting from mutations (Jean-Claude Chermann, cited in Challice, 1992). The virus begins undergoing genetic variation as soon as it has infected a person, even before antibodies are developed (Pang, Shlesinger, Daar,

FIGURE 17.1 The Structure of HIV (Cross Section). Notice the knoblike antigens on the virus's surface, which contain gp120. Also notice RNA and reverse transcriptase within the core.

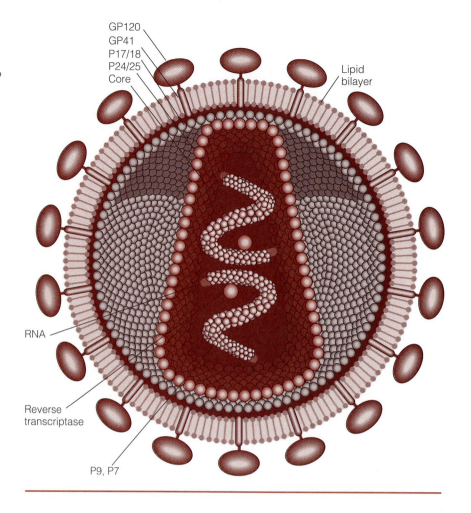

GP120
GP41
P17/18
P24/25
Core
Lipid bilayer
RNA
Reverse transcriptase
P9, P7

Moudgil, Ho, & Chen, 1992). This tendency to mutate is one factor that makes HIV difficult to destroy.

T-Cell Destruction When HIV enters the bloodstream, helper T cells rush to the invading viruses, whose antigen knobs plug neatly into their CD4 receptors, as if they were specifically designed for them. Normally at this stage a T cell reads the antigen, stimulating antibody production in the B cells and beginning the process of eliminating the invading organism. Although antibody production does begin, the immune process starts to break down almost at once. The virus injects its contents into the host T cell and, using the reverse transcriptase, copies its own genetic code into the cell's genetic material (DNA). As a result, when the immune system is activated, the T cell begins producing HIV instead of replicating itself. The T cell is killed in the process. HIV also targets other types of cells, including macrophages, dendritic cells (leukocytes found in the skin and intestinal mucous membranes), and brain cells.

HIV-1 and HIV-2 Almost all cases of HIV in the U.S. involve the subtype of the virus known as HIV-1. Another subtype, HIV-2, has been found to exist mainly in West Africa (Essex & Kanki, 1988). HIV-2 has a 60–90% chance of being detected in the standard HIV test, although more extensive testing will reveal its presence. Most people in the U.S. are not likely to have HIV-2 unless they are from West Africa or have had intimate contact with a West African. There were 30 confirmed cases of HIV-2 in this country as of 1993; 6 of those had progressed to AIDS (CDC, 1993). Overall, it appears that HIV-2 takes longer than HIV-1 to damage the immune system; it may not always develop into AIDS (Essex & Kanki, 1988).

AIDS Pathogenesis: How the Disease Progresses

As discussed earlier, when viruses are introduced into the body, they are immediately snatched up by helper T cells and whisked off to the lymph nodes. Although HIV begins replication right away within the host cells, the virus itself may not be detectable in the blood for some time. HIV antibodies, however, are generally detectable in the blood within 2–6 months (the testing process is discussed later). The process in which a person develops antibodies is called **seroconversion.** A person's **serostatus** is HIV-negative if antibodies are not detected and HIV-positive if antibodies are detected.

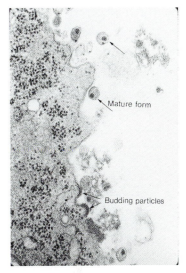

A T cell infected with HIV begins to replicate the viruses, which bud from the cell wall, eventually killing the host cell.

T-Cell (CD4) Count T-cell count or CD4 count refers to the number of helper T cells that are present in a cubic milliliter of blood. A healthy person's T-cell count averages about 1000, but it can range from 500 to 1600. The number of T cells may vary, depending on a person's general health and whether or not they are fighting off an illness.

Early Phase of Infection When a person is first infected with HIV, he or she may experience severe flulike symptoms as the immune system goes into high gear to fight off the invader. The person's T cell count may temporarily plunge as the virus begins rapid replication; it generally stabilizes at about 500 or higher during this phase. During this period, the virus is dispersed throughout the lymph nodes where it replicates, a process called "seeding" (Kolata, 1992). HIV may also be trapped within **dendritic cells**— certain leukocytes inside the lymph nodes, intestinal mucous membranes, and inner layers of the skin (Langhoff & Haseltine, 1992). The virus may stay localized in these areas for years, but it continues to replicate and destroy T cells. Most researchers agree that it does not have an actual "dormant" period, as previously believed (Kolata, 1992).

Intermediate Phase As time goes by, the T cells gradually diminish in number. One theory about why this occurs is that infected dendritic cells, which are easily invaded but not destroyed by the virus, begin to produce large quantities of HIV (Langhoff & Haseltine, 1992). These newly created viruses quickly destroy the T cells. Another theory is that HIV directs the cells to produce "superantigens," which are supertoxic to certain subgroups

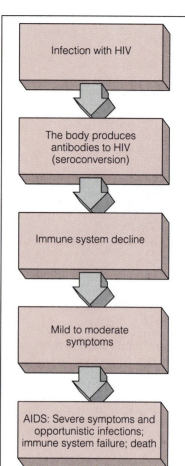

Infection with HIV	HIV is transmitted through intimate contact with body fluids: blood, blood products, semen, or vaginal secretions. The primary means of transmission are sexual contact, direct exposure to blood through transfusions (prior to 1985) or injection drug use, and from an infected mother to her child during pregnancy, childbirth, or breast-feeding.
The body produces antibodies to HIV (seroconversion)	Antibodies usually appear 2 to 12 weeks after the initial infection, a process known as seroconversion. Once antibodies appear, an infected person tests positive if given an HIV antibody test. About 30% of people experience flulike symptoms during this period, lasting for a few days to a few weeks.
Immune system decline	Though the individual has no symptoms, the virus is infecting and destroying cells of the immune system. Many people remain asymptomatic for 3 to 10 or more years. About half of all people infected with HIV develop AIDS within 10 years.
Mild to moderate symptoms	Once the immune system is damaged, many people begin to experience symptoms such as skin rashes, fatigue, weight loss, night sweats, and so on. When the damage is more severe, people are vulnerable to opportunistic infections. Treatments may allow recovery, but infections often recur.
AIDS: Severe symptoms and opportunistic infections; immune system failure; death	People are diagnosed with AIDS if they develop one of the conditions defined as a marker for AIDS or if their CD4 T-cell count drops below 200/mm³. Chronic or recurrent illnesses continue until the immune system fails, and death results.

Note: The pattern of HIV infection is different for every patient, and not everyone infected with HIV will go through all these stages.

FIGURE 17.2 The General Pattern of HIV Infection.

of CD4 cells (Inberti, Sottini, Bettinardi, Puoti, & Primi, 1991). During this phase, as the number of infected cells goes up, the number of T cells goes down, generally to between 200 and 500 per milliliter of blood.

Advanced Phase When AIDS is in the advanced phase, the lymph nodes appear "burned out" (Israelski, 1992). The T cells and other fighter cells of the immune system are no longer able to trap foreign invaders. Infected cells continue to increase, and the T-cell count drops to under 200. The virus is detectable in the blood. At this point, the person is fairly ill to very ill. The T-cell count may continue to plummet to zero. Figure 17.2 diagrams the general pattern of HIV infections.

EPIDEMIOLOGY AND TRANSMISSION OF HIV

An *epidemic* is the rapid and wide spreading of a contagious disease. In this country over about the past 12 years, the number of people known to have

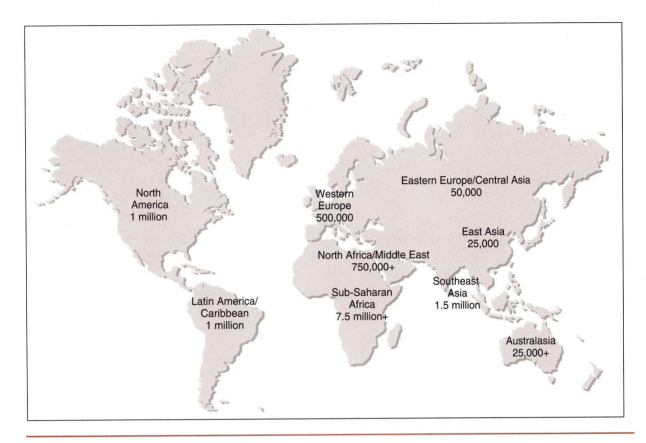

FIGURE 17.3 Worldwide HIV Distribution, 1992. (SOURCE: Data from WHO.)

Labels on map:

North America 1 million

Western Europe 500,000

Eastern Europe/Central Asia 50,000

East Asia 25,000

North Africa/Middle East 750,000+

Southeast Asia 1.5 million

Sub-Saharan Africa 7.5 million+

Latin America/ Caribbean 1 million

Australasia 25,000+

HIV or AIDS has grown from a few dozen to well over 1 million (about 1 in 250). Worldwide, over 14 million people are infected with HIV (Figure 17.3). Rates of infection are rising in the Caribbean, North Africa, the Middle East, eastern Europe, and central Asia. The steepest rises are occurring in southern and Southeast Asia (Merson, 1993). These numbers suggest it is not unreasonable to refer to HIV/AIDS as an epidemic.

A great deal has been discovered about AIDS since it first perplexed physicians and scientists in 1981. Much of what we now know regarding HIV transmission is due to the work of epidemiologists who track the progress of the disease in the U.S. and throughout the world.

Epidemiology of HIV/AIDS

At this book's publication, the latest figures from the CDC indicated that 121,046 people were currently diagnosed with AIDS in the U.S. Total deaths attributed to AIDS through mid-1993 were 194,344 (CDC, 1993). Approximately 1 million people were estimated to be infected with HIV (Figure 17.4). About 56% of total reported U.S. AIDS cases involved gay or bisexual men, and 23% involved heterosexual IV drug users (both men and women). Men who have sex with men *and* use IV drugs accounted for about 6% of cases. About 1.5% of AIDS cases involved children (CDC, 1993). These percentages represent total AIDS cases since 1981, including those who have died. Currently, the face of HIV/AIDS is changing, as gays

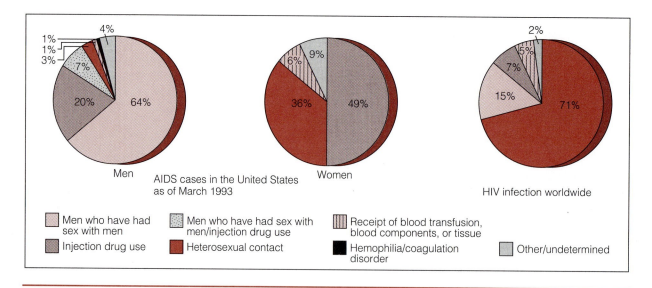

FIGURE 17.4 Transmission Routes of HIV for Adults and Adolescents. (SOURCE: Data from Centers for Disease Control and Prevention, 1993; *HIV/AIDS Surveillance Report*, May, p. 7–8; Mann, J., D.J.M. Tarantola and T.W. Netter, eds. 1992. *AIDS in the World*. Cambridge, Mass.: Harvard University Press, p. 33.)

have tended to modify their sexual behaviors, whereas heterosexuals have not. As we discussed earlier, heterosexual transmission is becoming more common and is expected to continue to increase (CDC, 1993; Holmes et al., 1990). The role of IV and injection drug use in the spread of HIV is also increasing as HIV-infected drug users pass the virus to each other in blood and to female partners during sexual activity (Koziol & Henderson, 1992). Pregnant women may also infect the fetus in utero. HIV rates are now growing fastest among women, teenagers, and young adult heterosexuals. One model epidemiologists use to understand the spread of HIV views the infection as a "traveling wave" that moves at a fixed rate outward from core areas of infection, such as middle-class gay communities and inner-city ghettoes (Wallace, 1991). The role of education in changing behaviors has been demonstrated in some populations, notably the gay community, which has slowed the rate of new infection markedly (Koziol & Henderson, 1992).

Myths and Modes of Transmission

Before we further discuss the ways in which HIV has been shown to be transmitted, we should mention some of the ways in which it is *not* transmitted. You *cannot* get HIV from:

- *Casual contact.* Normal household or social contact does not transmit HIV. Shaking hands, hugging, kissing, playing, and providing personal care such as bathing, feeding, and dressing are extremely unlikely to transmit HIV. Extensive studies of households with an HIV-infected member have shown no evidence of transmission through casual contact (Fischl, Dickinson, Segal, Flanagan, & Rodriguez, 1987; Friedland et al., 1986; Mann et al., 1986; Rogers et al., 1990).

- *Inanimate objects.* HIV cannot live outside the body fluids in which it is normally found. It cannot survive on countertops, toilet seats, drinking fountains, telephones, eating utensils, and so on. If a surface or object is contaminated by infected blood or semen, it can be disinfected with bleach, alcohol, hydrogen peroxide, Lysol, or other household cleaners (Martin, Gresenguet, Massanga, Georges, & Testa, 1985).

- *Blood donation.* In the U.S., it is not possible to get HIV from donating blood. Sterilized needles are used to draw the blood; they are disposed of afterward; they are never reused.

- *Animals.* Household pets and farm animals can neither get HIV nor pass it on. Laboratory chimpanzees may be intentionally infected with HIV, but there are no known cases of transmission from chimps to humans.

- *Insect bites.* Extensive research has shown that HIV is not transmitted by biting insects such as mosquitoes. The virus has been demonstrated not to replicate in flies, ticks, and mosquitoes. Surveillance of areas with large mosquito populations, such as Florida, Haiti, and parts of Africa, has shown no evidence of HIV antibodies in preadolescents, at least some of whom would be expected to contract a mosquito-borne illness (CDC, 1986; Lifson, 1988).

- *Saliva.* About 1% of people with HIV have detectable virus in their saliva (Ho et al., 1985). The amounts are very small, and enzymes in the saliva are hostile to the virus (Levy, 1988). There are no known cases of transmission from saliva, although theoretically there could be a slight risk if the saliva from a person with advanced AIDS were to enter another's bloodstream or if a person with HIV had blood in the mouth. There is no evidence of HIV transmission from biting (Tsoukas, Hadjis, Shuster, Theberge, Feorino, & O'Shaughnessy, 1988) or mouth-to-mouth resuscitation (Saviteer, White, & Cohen, 1985).

- *Tears or sweat.* HIV exists in minute quantities in the tears of some infected people, but researchers have found no evidence of transmission via tears (Tsoukas et al., 1988). Researchers have been unable to find the virus in the sweat of HIV-infected people (Wormser et al., 1992).

- *Vaccines.* The processes by which vaccines are manufactured effectively remove or inactivate HIV (CDC, 1984, 1987). In the U.S., sterile, fresh needles are used to give the vaccinations, and they are destroyed afterward.

- *Water.* HIV cannot live or replicate in water. It is not transmitted in drinking water, nor in hot tubs or swimming pools.

In order for HIV to replicate in the body, it must have a path of entry into the bloodstream. The most common modes of transmission involve HIV-infected semen, blood, or vaginal secretions. Activities or situations that may promote transmission include:

- Vaginal or anal intercourse without a latex condom, fellatio without a latex condom, cunnilingus without latex or other barrier.

- Sharing needles contaminated with HIV-infected blood during IV drug use, tattooing, home injections of medications, or self-administered steroid injections.

- Passing the virus from mother to fetus in the uterus (20–50% chance) or in blood during delivery.

- Breast-feeding, if the mother is HIV-positive.

- Sharing sex toys such as dildos or vibrators without disinfecting them.
- Accidental contamination with infected blood entering the body through the mucous membranes of the eyes or mouth, or through cuts, abrasions, or punctures in the skin.
- Before April 1, 1985, from contaminated blood (transfusions) or organs (transplants).

The first three modes are the most common. We will discuss each of these in greater detail in the following sections.

Sexual Transmission

Semen and vaginal secretions of people with HIV may contain infected cells, especially in the later phases of AIDS. Latex barriers, condoms, dental dams, and surgical gloves can provide good protection against the transmission of HIV if used properly.

Anal Intercourse The riskiest form of sexual interaction for both men and women is receiving anal sex (de Vincenzi et al., 1992; Voeller, 1991). The membrane lining the rectum is delicate and ruptures easily, exposing tiny blood vessels to infection from virus-carrying semen. Infected blood from the rectum may also enter the penis through the mucous membrane at the urethral opening. Heterosexual anal intercourse is more common than many people realize; studies show that at least 10% of heterosexual couples regularly practice it (Voeller, 1991). Some couples rely on it as a way to avoid pregnancy.

Vaginal Intercourse Vaginal sex is also quite risky, especially for women. Women are at higher risk if they already have a vaginal infection because HIV will attract white blood cells that are present and infect them (Anderson, 1989). Women with **cervical ectopy** are also at higher risk because the epithelium (covering tissue of the cervix) is unusually thin (Moss et al., 1991). Cervical ectopy is often present in adolescents, pregnant women, women who use birth control pills, and women over 45. Men contract HIV during intercourse at 1/10–1/20 the rate that women contract it from men. Menstrual blood in which there is HIV can facilitate transmission of the virus to a sex partner (de Vincenzi et al., 1992), as can infected vaginal secretions containing abundant leukocytes.

Oral Sex HIV may be transmitted through oral sex between heterosexuals, gay men, or lesbians (Lifson et al., 1990; UCSF, 1991). Infection can occur when semen or vaginal secretions from a person with HIV gets into an uninfected person's body via sores or cuts in or around a person's mouth, such as cold sores (herpes) or lesions from gum disease.

Sex Toys HIV can be transmitted in vaginal secretions on such objects as dildos and vibrators; therefore, it is very important that these objects not be shared or be washed thoroughly before use.

Male and Female Transmission Rates As we discussed in Chapter 16, women are more likely than men to contract an STD when exposed to

it during intercourse. HIV provides no exception to this rule. Researcher Nancy Padian and colleagues studied 379 heterosexual couples in which only one person of each pair was infected, and found that the rate of transmission from man to woman (in unprotected intercourse) was 20 times greater than from woman to man (Padian, Shiboski, & Jewel, 1991).

IV Drug Use

Sharing needles or other paraphernalia (including cotton pieces) used to inject drugs provides an ideal pathway for HIV (Celentano, Vlahov, Cohn, Anthony, Solomon, & Nelson, 1991; National Commission, 1991). Infection via the bloodstream is called **parenteral transmission.** An intravenous drug user (IVDU) or injection drug user (IDU) may already have an immune system weakened by poor health, poor nutrition, or an STD. A study in Baltimore of 2921 IV drug users found a significant association between a history of syphilis and HIV seropositivity (Nelson et al., 1991). IVDUs who become infected often pass the virus sexually to their partners (Ross, Wodak, Gold, & Miller, 1992). A survey of women partners of male IVDUs in New York City led researchers to estimate that between 876 and 1668 women in the city were infected in this way in 1988 (Fordyce, Blum, Balanon, & Stoneburner, 1991). The researchers estimated that in New York City, a total of 5390–10,230 women between the ages of 15 and 40 were already infected by their IVDU partners.

When we think of injection drug use, we usually think in terms of psychotropic (mind-affecting) drugs such as heroin or cocaine. We may conjure up images of run-down tenement rooms or "shooting galleries," where needles are passed around. But these are not the only settings for sharing drugs.

HIV transmission in connection with the recreational use of injection drugs also occurs among people who are of middle or upper socioeconomic status (Glaser, Strange, & Rosati, 1989). Moreover, injection drug use exists among athletes who may share needles for steroids to increase muscle mass. HIV can be transmitted just as easily in a brightly lit locker room or upscale living room, as in a dark alley.

Mother-to-Child Transmission

Passing a disease from mother to child in the womb is known as **perinatal transmission.** Infants whose mothers are HIV-positive will have HIV anti-bodies at birth. This does not necessarily mean they will become infected with the virus. There is a range of risk for perinatal HIV transmission of 20% to 35–50% for each pregnancy (Smeltzer & Whipple, 1991). The risk increases to 65% if the woman has previously had an infected child (Min-koff, 1989). Although the standard HIV antibody test may not be useful in these cases (because the antibodies may be the mother's, not the infant's), a *PCR (polymerase chain reaction) test* may be performed. This test can deter-mine the presence of HIV antigen, which will appear before the child's own antibodies develop.

It is not known exactly how HIV is passed from mother to fetus, although it is generally accepted that HIV manages to cross the placental barrier (Minkoff, 1989). Factors such as whether the HIV infection or the preg-nancy occurred first, the timing of the initial infection relative to the stage of pregnancy (if the woman was already pregnant when infected), the effect of pregnancy hormones, and the phase of the mother's infection need further investigation if physicians are going to be able to help HIV-positive women achieve the best possible pregnancy outcomes.

Uncommon Modes of Transmission

Although the great majority of HIV infections are acquired in the ways just discussed, many people still worry about getting the virus through casual (nonsexual) contact or accidents. There is also concern about transmission through blood transfusions, although this mode is very unlikely today in countries that routinely test donated blood for HIV.

Nonsexual Contact Nonsexual, casual contact that typically occurs with health-care workers, family members, and in school and day-care settings is highly unlikely to transmit HIV under ordinary circumstances. Many studies have shown the risk of transmission within families (excluding sexual part-ners) to be extremely low. For example, a study of 89 household members caring for 25 HIV-positive children showed no seroconversion to HIV-positive status. Close personal contact—bathing, cleaning up blood and bodily fluids, sharing dishes and utensils, and hugging and kissing—was common. After 4 months or longer, no indication of HIV was found in other family members (Rogers et al., 1990). Numerous other studies have had sim-ilar findings (Fischl et al., 1987; Friedland et al., 1986; Mann et al., 1986).

Much media attention has been focused on the possibility of transmission in health-care situations, either from infected providers (doctors, dentists, nurses, and so on) to their patients or from infected patients to their care

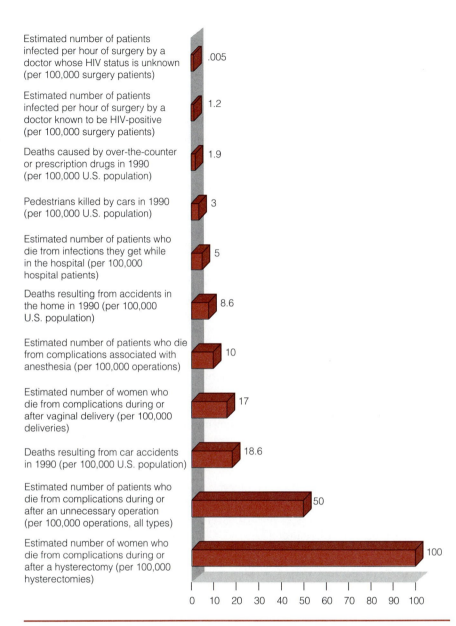

Estimated number of patients infected per hour of surgery by a doctor whose HIV status is unknown (per 100,000 surgery patients) .005

Estimated number of patients infected per hour of surgery by a doctor known to be HIV-positive (per 100,000 surgery patients) 1.2

Deaths caused by over-the-counter or prescription drugs in 1990 (per 100,000 U.S. population) 1.9

Pedestrians killed by cars in 1990 (per 100,000 U.S. population) 3

Estimated number of patients who die from infections they get while in the hospital (per 100,000 hospital patients) 5

Deaths resulting from accidents in the home in 1990 (per 100,000 U.S. population) 8.6

Estimated number of patients who die from complications associated with anesthesia (per 100,000 operations) 10

Estimated number of women who die from complications during or after vaginal delivery (per 100,000 deliveries) 17

Deaths resulting from car accidents in 1990 (per 100,000 U.S. population) 18.6

Estimated number of patients who die from complications during or after an unnecessary operation (per 100,000 operations, all types) 50

Estimated number of women who die from complications during or after a hysterectomy (per 100,000 hysterectomies) 100

0 10 20 30 40 50 60 70 80 90 100

FIGURE 17.5 Relative Risks. Although people may worry about contracting HIV in health-care settings, the actual risks are very low. This graph compares various medical risks: the chance of contracting HIV from a surgeon of unknown HIV status and from an HIV-infected surgeon, and chances of death from several other sources including car accidents and childbirth. There are no known cases of HIV transmission by a surgeon; however, by the time you finish this chapter, at least three people in the U.S. will be killed in car accidents. (SOURCE: Data from *Health* Magazine, Sept. 1992.)

providers. All studies of these situations show that the risk of transmission is very low, especially if standard infection control precautions and common sense are observed (see Figure 17.5) (Klein et al., 1988; Koziol & Henderson, 1992). Fewer than 5% of health-care workers are HIV-positive; of these, 94% have risk factors not related to their profession, such as homosexual activity or previous blood transfusion (CDC, 1991). They are unlikely to have become infected during professional activity.

Frightened parents have taken their children out of school or day-care centers where there is a child with HIV. They express fear that the virus could be transmitted through saliva, which, as we have discussed, is extremely unlikely. They also are concerned about the possibility of accidents, which we discuss in the following section.

Right now, mid-course in the epidemic, we have a society that has indulged itself in the right to hate sick people and the right to panic in the face of that.

June Osborn, MD

Accidents People sometimes express concern about the possibility of accidental blood exchange—during children's play, or contact sports, for example. While it is theoretically possible that blood could be passed in this way, it is highly unlikely that the blood of one person could spill into another person's open wound and from there into the bloodstream. (It was this kind of fear, expressed by professional basketball players, that led HIV-positive basketball superstar Magic Johnson to retire once and for all.) Children with HIV have been barred from schools and day-care centers because of the fear that they might be hurt while playing and somehow get their blood into another child. There are no known cases of HIV being transmitted in this way, however.

Medical and dental accidents are also feared, although the chance of transmission in these situations is slight. A CDC surveillance project of 870 health-care workers who had been accidentally injected with HIV-positive blood found a very small incidence of transmission: less than 1% (CDC, 1988). Currently, the CDC reports that 32 health-care workers have been documented as seroconverting to HIV-positive status after occupational exposure to the virus. Seven of them have developed AIDS. Most were infected as a result of punctures or cuts sustained while working with HIV-positive blood (CDC, 1993). Although these types of cases are few, they nonetheless point to the need for observing appropriate precautions when dealing with needles and sharp instruments.

Blood is too precious a thing in these times.

Count Dracula

Blood Transfusions and Organ Donations Theoretically, donated blood, plasma, body organs, and semen are all capable of sustaining HIV. Because of this, today these medical procedures include either screening out HIV or destroying it. Since April 1, 1985, blood has been screened for HIV. Plasma is treated to inactivate any virus that may be present. The chance of being infected with HIV via blood transfusion is estimated at 1 per 40,000–225,000 units (Dodd, 1992). Donated organs must be screened for HIV, and there are guidelines regarding semen donation for artificial insemination (discussed in Chapter 13).

Factors Contributing to Infection

Although most researchers agree that HIV is responsible for AIDS, many believe there may be additional factors that need to come into play before the immune system is seriously impaired. There are certain actions or conditions that appear to put some people at higher risk than others for HIV. Other conditions, known as cofactors, may make a person with HIV more prone to developing AIDS.

Risk Factors Researchers have found that there are certain physiological or behavioral factors that increase the risk of contracting HIV. For people of both sexes, these include behaviors already discussed such as anal intercourse, multiple sex partners, and IV drug use. Other factors are having an STD, especially if genital ulcers are present (Chirgwin, DeHovitz, Dillon, & McCormack, 1991; Hook et al., 1992; Martin, Gresenguet, Massanga, Georges, & Testa, 1992). Herpes lesions and syphilitic chancres, for example, provide a pathway for HIV into the body. Throat inflammation due to gonorrhea, syphilis, or herpes may also increase susceptibility during oral sex

(UCSF AIDS Health Project, 1991). Multiple exposure to HIV also increases the risk of contracting it, although it can also be transmitted in a single encounter. Moreover, a person in the advance phase of AIDS is likely to pass on greater quantities of the virus (de Vincenzi et al., 1992). Non-IV "recreational" drug use is also considered a risk factor for HIV. In part this is because drug use is associated with risk taking in general (Doll et al., 1991). There is also a connection between crack cocaine use and STDs, including HIV (Bowser, 1988; Carlson & Seigel, 1991; Chirgwin et al., 1991). The exchange of sex (especially fellatio) for crack is commonplace.

Factors that may tend to place women at higher risk include cervical ectopy, which may be associated with adolescence, pregnancy, use of oral contraceptives (Moss et al., 1991), IUD use, or being over age 45. Possible risk factors for men include contact with HIV-infected menstrual blood (de Vincenzi et al., 1992) and, possibly, lack of circumcision. Studies done in Africa suggest that circumcision *may* help protect against HIV (Marx, 1989). This may be because genital lesions related to STDs are more likely to form under the foreskin than on an exposed glans, especially in the absence of good hygiene. These studies are not considered conclusive.

Cofactor Theory **Cofactors,** conditions that *may* make a person who is HIV-positive more likely to develop AIDS, include a history of STDs, drug use, alcohol use, poor nutrition, stress, smoking, pregnancy, and repeated exposure to HIV. Individual genetic conditions that predispose some people toward AIDS may exist, as well as genetic elements that provide resistance to HIV or the development of AIDS (Johnson, 1993). There is a need for considerably more research concerning possible cofactors for AIDS development.

AIDS DEMOGRAPHICS

The statistical characteristics of populations are called **demographics.** Public-health researchers often look at groups of people in terms of age, socio-economic status, living area, ethnicity, or sex in order to understand the dynamics of disease transmission and prevention. In instances where sexually transmitted diseases are involved, they also look at sexual behaviors. This may entail studying groups based on sexual orientation as well as other characteristics that may be considered risk markers. No one is exempt from HIV exposure by virtue of belonging or not belonging to a specific group. Certain groups, however, appear *as a whole* to be at greater risk than others, or to face special difficulties where HIV is concerned. Many individuals within these groups may not be at risk, however, because they do not engage in risky behaviors.

The Gay Community

"AIDS has given a human face to an invisible minority," says Robert Bray of the National Gay and Lesbian Task Force. As of 1993, 172,085 gay men had been diagnosed with AIDS. Over 100,000 had died. Another several hundred thousand are estimated to be infected with HIV. Although epidemiologists do not know for certain how HIV first arrived in the gay com-

Members of Act Up focus public attention on issues affecting people with HIV and AIDS.

The poor homosexuals—they have declared war upon nature and now nature is exacting an awful retribution.

Pat Buchanan

I think God did send AIDS for a reason. It was to show how mean and sinful a healthy man can be toward a sick man.

Joe Bob Briggs

munity (one speculation is that men vacationing in Haiti contracted it there and brought it back), they do know that it spread like wildfire mainly because anal sex is such an efficient mode of transmission. Furthermore, initial research, education, and prevention efforts were severely hampered by a lack of government and public interest in what was perceived to be a "gay disease" (Shilts, 1987). Now, more than 12 years after the virus first appeared, the gay community continues to reel under the repeated blows dealt by AIDS. Overall, sexual practices have become much safer, and the rate of new infection has fallen dramatically. But men who were infected years ago continue to sicken and die.

Many members of the gay community have lost dozens of their friends. They may be coping with **multiple-loss syndrome,** a psychological condition that may be characterized by depression, hypochondria, feelings of guilt, sexual dysfunction, or self-destructive behavior. One man from New York expressed these feelings (quoted in Navarro, 1992): "Half my friends are dead. For a gay man friends are everything; it's not like we have kids and families." A man from San Francisco said, "I've had unsafe sex." Then he asked, "Why was I spared while my friends and lovers test positive?" (quoted in Navarro, 1992). According to psychotherapist Thomas Moon (quoted in Navarro, 1992):

> The bottom line is that this is a terrible tragedy, and that can't be changed by psychotherapy. The choice people can make is to live as best they can in the middle of mass death, but there's a great deal of suffering they'll have to go through.

In spite of the initial lack of public support for the fight against AIDS, or perhaps at least partly because of it, the gay and lesbian communities rallied together in a variety of ways to support each other, educate them-

selves and the public, and influence government policies. Grass-roots projects such as clinics, self-help groups, and information clearinghouses were created by people from both the gay and the straight communities whose lives were affected by HIV. The role of volunteers remains a crucial component of many AIDS organizations. Many people have devoted themselves to supporting the HIV/AIDS community or educating the public. Playwright and social activist Larry Kramer was instrumental in founding the AIDS Coalition to Unleash Power (Act Up) to focus public attention on the crisis (sometimes by unorthodox methods). Under the direction of Cleve Jones, the Names Project began creating a giant quilt, each square of which has been lovingly created by friends and families of people who have died as a result of AIDS. The AIDS quilt now contains over 24,000 squares. It is too large to be exhibited in one place, but sections of it are displayed at various locations around the country. A visit to the Names Project quilt not only commemorates those we have lost but also reminds us of the work that remains to be done. Allan Bérubé (1988) writes:

> Visiting the quilt is a ritual that allows many of us to remember and grieve together in the face of incomprehensible loss. Each panel holds unique meanings for the survivors that are intensely personal. But sewn together into a patchwork quilt, they create a work of folk art that has no center, no limit, no one meaning, and no easy answers. . . . We can walk inside this quilt, by ourselves or holding each other, as we do each day inside this epidemic. . . . AIDS did not empower us to do this; we empowered ourselves.

There is recent speculation that despair within the gay community may be leading some men to abandon safer sex practices (Navarro, 1993). When people feel there is no hope, they may intentionally put themselves at risk. But members of the gay community not only empower themselves to face

Fear = Silence
Silence = Death
Knowledge = Power
    AIDS Coalition to Unleash
              Power (Act-Up)

AIDS has changed us forever. It has brought out the best in us, and the worst.
              Michael Gottlieb, MD

the AIDS epidemic, they inspire and empower many outside the community to lend their voices and support to the cause of AIDS prevention. Nonetheless, there is still the perception of AIDS as a gay disease rather than a viral disease, and those who have moral objections to homosexual behavior still blame AIDS on gays (Lawrence, Husfeldt, Kelly, Hood, & Smith, 1990).

Women and Children

Over 37,000 women are currently diagnosed with AIDS in this country; several hundred thousand are estimated to be infected with HIV (CDC, 1993). Almost 75% of affected women are African American or Latina. Heterosexual transmission is rapidly increasing (Osborn, 1991). Among women, heterosexually transmitted HIV increased 42% from 1990 to 1992 (Detailed U.S. AIDS Report, 1993). Public health officials expect that by the year 2000, the numbers of women and men with HIV will be equal (NIAID/CDC, 1991). Although women as a group are not at special risk for HIV, there are activities that put certain women at high risk. These include IV or injection drug use, being a sex partner of a gay or bisexual man, being a sex partner of an IV or injection drug user, or having multiple sex partners.

Women are often diagnosed with HIV at a later stage than men (Diaz, 1991; Perez, 1991; Smeltzer & Whipple, 1991). There are two principal reasons for this. First, most women are not generally perceived to be at risk for HIV, so neither they nor their physicians will be alert to signs of HIV infection. Second, women generally serve in caregiving roles for their children, partners, and older relatives. They may also be breadwinners. Consequently, they may not seek care for themselves until they are quite ill. "By the time a woman discharges all her family and economic responsibilities," comments AIDS researcher Dr. Anthony Fauci, "she [may be] far advanced in her HIV infection" (quoted in NIAID/CDC, 1991).

Transmission to Women Currently, most women with HIV acquired it from IV drug use. Most of the others acquired it sexually from a partner who used IV drugs. A survey of 137 female partners of IV drug users found that most of them understood the basics of HIV transmission and prevention and believed there was at least some chance they would contract HIV (Corby, Wolitski, Thornton, Johnson, & Tanner, 1991). Even so, 95% of them engaged in unprotected vaginal intercourse; 6.6% reported anal intercourse without a condom. The most frequent reason for the nonuse of condoms was dislike by the partner, followed by personal dislike.

A study of 3555 women with heterosexually acquired AIDS reported that 11% had sex with a bisexual man as their only risk factor; in some areas, however, the rate of contact with bisexual men was close to 50% (Chu, Peterman, Doll, Buehler, & Curran, 1992). Bisexual men tend to be secretive with their female partners regarding their male contacts; although they may use condoms during anal sex with male partners, they are less likely to use them with female partners (Boulton, Hart, & Fitzpatrick, 1992).

Issues of Women with HIV Among the most pressing needs of women with HIV is their inclusion in clinical trials for HIV and AIDS treatments.

The faces of HIV: Doris and Her Son.

Women have generally been excluded from such trials, partly because AIDS has not been perceived to affect women. But as women's physiology is different from men's, especially in regard to hormones, it is imperative that they have access to new and experimental therapies, in order to discover not only what works for them but what does not (Minkoff & Dehovitz, 1991; Williams, 1992).

Issues of poverty, racism, and sexism also need to be addressed if all women are to receive the care they need (Williams, 1992). Not only are HIV-positive women of color largely excluded from quality medical care, lesbians with HIV are practically invisible. Although as a group they are not at high risk for HIV, lesbians can and do contract the virus in the same ways as heterosexuals. (Health-care issues of lesbians were discussed in Chapter 14.)

Pregnancy is a particularly painful dilemma for a woman with HIV. Issues that must be considered include the chance of the child's being HIV-infected (20–50%), the desire of the woman to have a child, the probability that the child will be orphaned, the effect of HIV on the pregnancy, and the effect of pregnancy on the course of HIV (Smeltzer & Whipple, 1991).

Children and HIV As of June 30, 1993, there had been 2510 deaths to children under 13 attributable to AIDS (CDC, 1993). There are about 4700 children with diagnosed AIDS at this time, and thousands more with HIV. Most children with HIV were infected perinatally. Some older children were infected from blood transfusions prior to 1985. The impact of HIV is greatest among 1- to 4-year-olds, particularly African American and Latino children. Of children in this age group in New York state, AIDS is the leading cause of death among Latino children and the second leading cause of death among African American children. In the U.S., an estimated 1500–2000 children infected with HIV were born in 1989 alone. As the number of infected women rises, the number of infected children is also expected to rise, putting an increasing burden on families and society who must care for hundreds (or possibly thousands) of orphans, many of whom have HIV or AIDS (Chu et al., 1991).

The devastation wrought upon families by AIDS is described here by June Osborn, who is the chair of the National Commission on AIDS (Osborn, 1991):

> There have been stories—growing more frequent all the time—of older children who have been left standing, like sole surviving trees in a burned-out forest, after their mother, father, and younger siblings have died around them. In one such poignant anecdote, a 13-year-old was quoted as saying how happy she was to be pregnant because at last she would have someone she could *keep*!

Teenagers

HIV cases are increasing rapidly among young people (Mangasarian, 1993). Between 1990 and 1992, the number of AIDS cases among 13- to 24-year-olds rose by 77% (Select Committee, 1992). (We should bear in mind that most of those in their twenties were probably infected in their teens.) Young gays, blacks, Latinos, and runaways are among those most affected, but others are also at increasing risk, including whites, heterosexuals, and rural teens.

As we discussed in Chapter 6, adolescence and risk taking often seem to go together like peanut butter and jelly. Because teenagers often have a sense of invulnerability, they may put themselves at great risk without really understanding what it means. In a telephone survey of 1773 Massachusetts 16- to 19-year-olds, 31% of those who were sexually active reported always using condoms. Certain attitudes and behaviors were 2–3 times more prevalent among condom users than nonusers (Hingson, Strunin, Berlin, & Heeren, 1990). These included belief that condoms are effective in preventing HIV transmission and that they do not reduce sexual pleasure, lack of embarrassment about using them, and the habit of carrying condoms. Recalling the health belief model, we can see how beliefs about effectiveness and riskiness influence teenage behavior in these cases. The same study and others have found that use of alcohol and drugs tends to reduce condom use (Keller et al., 1991). Public health officials, including Surgeon General Joycelyn Elders, support education about condoms for sexually active teenagers (Roper, Peterson, & Curran, 1993). (AIDS education is discussed later in the chapter.)

I have never shared needles. And obviously I'm not a gay man. The only thing I did was something every single one of you has already done or will do.

Krista Blake,
infected with HIV as a teenager

Poverty, Ethnicity, and HIV

HIV and AIDS, like many of society's ills, are often linked with poverty that is enforced by racism and discrimination. The disease is a significant presence among the homeless. Despair often fosters unsafe behaviors, and poverty and prejudice limit access to health care. Poor people in ethnic communities plagued with crime and violence may find themselves trapped in a vicious downward spiral. Until there is social and economic justice, even education and health care may not be sufficient to stem the rising tide of HIV. In 1990, HIV was the eighth leading cause of death for all Americans, but the sixth leading cause for African Americans. It is the leading cause of death for black men between the ages of 35 and 44, the second leading cause for black men and women between 25 and 35, and the eighth leading cause among children under 15 (Smith, 1992). While white AIDS patients live an average of 3 years after diagnosis, African American and Latino men survive 2 years or less. Following diagnosis, African American women's average survival time is 18 months to 2 years; that of Latinas is a mere 3 months.

Ethnic communities are often suspicious of outsiders, whom they may perceive to be interfering or threatening. In Chapter 16, we discussed the infamous Tuskegee syphilis study and its effects on African Americans' perceptions of the health-care establishment. In 1988, the CDC began to respond to the need for ethnically sensitive programs by establishing grants for 32 ongoing HIV prevention programs targeting specific racial and ethnic groups, including African Americans, Latinos, Native Americans, and Alaskan natives. One group targeted Asian Americans and Pacific Islanders (Holman et al., 1991). Until the health issues of ethnic communities are consistently approached with sensitivity, it will be difficult to ascertain the best means of providing optimum assistance and care (Doll et al., 1991; Mays & Jackson, 1991; Schinke et al., 1990; Wyatt, 1991).

EDUCATION AND PREVENTION

As a whole, our society remains in denial about the realities of HIV risk. A sample of 574 clients attending an STD clinic found that among heterosexuals who reported having sex with people other than their regular partner, 79% did not consider themselves at risk for HIV (James et al., 1991). Among heterosexuals, 66% of the men and 44% of the women reported having multiple sex partners. This apparent lack of self-perception is not unusual. Studies of college students generally indicate inconsistent condom use as well as frequent high-risk behaviors, such as alcohol intoxication (Bruce, Shrum, Trefethen, & Slovik, 1990; Butcher, Manning, & O'Neal, 1991).

Fear of the pox is the beginning of wisdom.
Anonymous physician, 1918

Protecting Ourselves

In order to protect ourselves and those we care about from HIV, there are some things we should know in addition to the basic facts about transmission and prevention.

Self-Assessment

HIV PREVENTION ATTITUDE SCALE

Read each statement carefully. Record your immediate reaction to each statement by writing the letter that corresponds to your answer. There is no right or wrong answer for each statement, so mark your own response.

Key
A = Strongly agree   D = Disagree
B = Agree   E = Strongly disagree
C = Undecided

1. I am certain that I could be supportive of a friend with HIV.
2. I feel that people with HIV got what they deserve.
3. I am comfortable with the idea of using condoms for sex.
4. I would dislike the idea of limiting sex to just one partner to avoid HIV infection.
5. It would be embarrassing to get the HIV antibody test.
6. It is meant for some people to get HIV.
7. Using condoms to avoid HIV is too much trouble.
8. I believe that AIDS is a preventable disease.
9. The chance of getting HIV makes using IV drugs stupid.
10. People can influence their friends to practice safe behavior.
11. I would shake hands with a person having HIV.
12. I will avoid sex if there is a slight chance that the partner might have HIV.
13. If I were to have sex, I would insist that a condom be used.
14. If I used IV drugs, I would not share the needles.
15. I intend to share HIV facts with my friends.

Scoring
Calculate the total points for each form using the following point values.
Items 1, 3, 8–15: Strongly agree = 5, Agree = 4, Undecided = 3, Disagree = 2, Strongly disagree = 1. For the remaining items: Strongly agree = 1, Agree = 2, Undecided = 3, Disagree = 4, Strongly disagree = 5.

The higher the score, the more positive the prevention attitude.

Source: William L. Yarber, Professor of Health Education, Indiana University, Bloomington; Mohammad Torabi, Professor of Health Education, Indiana University, Bloomington; L. Harold Veenker, Professor Emeritus of Health Education, Purdue University, Lafayette, IN.

What We Need to Know First, we should be aware that alcohol and drug use significantly increase risky behaviors. If we are serious about protecting ourselves, we need to assess our risks when we are clearheaded and act to protect ourselves. Second, we need to develop our communication skills so that we can discuss risks and prevention with our partner or potential partner. If we want our partner to disclose information about past high-risk behavior, we have to be willing to do the same (Shtarkshall & Awerbuch, 1992). Third, we may need to have information on HIV testing. If we have engaged in high-risk behavior, we may want to be tested for our own peace of mind and that of our partner. If we test positive for HIV, we need to make important decisions regarding our health, sexual behavior, and lifestyle. Fourth, if we are sexually active with more than one long-term, monogamous partner, we need to become very familiar with condoms.

Condoms   Although America has responded to the threat of AIDS by increased purchasing of condoms, condom use remains low among many segments of the population (Catania et al., 1992; CDC, 1992). Following Surgeon General Koop's 1987 report endorsing condoms for safer sex, sales soared from 240 million to 299 million the following year (Moran, Janes, Peterman, & Stone, 1990). While increased sales imply increased use, it is clear that many people remain unconvinced regarding either their own vulnerability to HIV or the usefulness of condoms in preventing its spread.

Although any sexual activity involving semen, vaginal fluid, or blood carries some degree of risk, condoms have repeatedly been demonstrated to effectively reduce risk (CDC, 1993; Conant, Hardy, Sernatinger, Spicer, & Levy, 1986; Fischl et al., 1987; Van de Perre, Jacobs, & Sprecher-Goldberger, 1987). In a major study that took place in nine countries over a 4-year period, there were 472 couples in which only one partner was HIV-positive at the beginning of the study. Three men and seven women seroconverted during the study; however, none of the couples who had used condoms regularly passed the infection to the uninfected partner (de Vincenzi et al., 1992). As we have stressed before, condoms do not guarantee 100% safety from HIV. Abstinence is safer. But if we choose to have sex, using a condom significantly reduces the risk (just as putting on a seat belt improves your safety when riding in a car). (You may want to refer to Chapter 12 for more information on condoms and Chapter 16 for safer sex guidelines. For information regarding latex, see Perspective 2.)

Getting the Word Out

Education is the key to AIDS prevention. Yet, despite widespread public educational efforts on the part of public-health officials and AIDS organizations, many people remain uninformed about and unsympathetic to people with AIDS and HIV (at least until it strikes someone they care for).

Obstacles to Education: Blame and Denial   HIV/AIDS is still seen by many people as a disease of "marginalized" groups—those who are outside the mainstream of American life as seen on reruns of "Leave It to Beaver" and "The Brady Bunch." (Robert Reed, who played the role of the Brady dad, died of AIDS-related causes in 1992.) People who are not white, not middle class, and not heterosexual are often viewed with suspicion by people who are. People who are gay or lesbian are often ignored or reviled even within their own ethnic communities. People who use drugs are written off as useless, worthless, and criminal. Prostitutes are frequently blamed for spreading STDs, even though they undoubtedly contract the disease from men, who more than likely have or will spread it to their partner or partners.

Some of this intolerance stems from conservative religious beliefs that

Perspective 2

LEARNING TO LOVE LATEX

"It's like taking a shower in a raincoat!" goes the old (male) complaint about wearing a condom. Many of the complainers, however, have not actually tried using condoms or have only tried one or two kinds. Becoming a virtuoso of safer sex requires becoming experienced with different varieties of condoms and other latex products. While the idea of using a piece of rubber as part of normal sexual activity may appear clinical to the uninitiated, experienced safer-sex practitioners have found ways to turn latex protective devices into sexual enhancers.

Latex Care

Latex products that are used in safer sex include condoms, dental dams, gloves (for sex and cleanup), and finger covers. Proper care of these products helps assure their effectiveness as barriers to disease-causing organisms. Here are some guidelines for latex care:

1. Check the expiration date on the package of your latex product. Latex deteriorates with age; its shelf life averages 2½–5 years.

2. Keep your latex away from heat. For example, don't leave condom packets in the sun or in your glove compartment. It's all right to carry condoms in your wallet, but don't leave them there for more than 2 weeks or so.

3. Handle latex with care. Be especially careful not to tear your latex product when you open the package. Be careful with long fingernails.

4. Keep all oil-based products away from your latex. These include oil-based lubricants (such as Vaseline), massage oils, cocoa butter, and vaginal medications such as estrogen preparations and antifungal creams. To see what oil does to latex, try this experiment: Rub a little massage oil, cooking oil, or Vaseline into a condom. Wait a minute or so, then stretch the latex and see what happens.

Dental Dams, Etc.

Because HIV and other STDs can be transmitted in vaginal fluids (including menstrual blood), it's important to know how to practice cunnilingus safely. Organisms from genital sores or lesions, such as herpes, also can be spread during oral or manual sexual contact. There are several products that can provide barrier protection during these activities.

Dental dams are squares of latex used by dentists to isolate a particular tooth during dental procedures. They can usually be obtained at family planning clinics, women's clinics, or AIDS organizations. During sex, dams can be used over the vulva or anus while it is being orally or manually stimulated. The following suggestions may help you with your dental dam:

1. Before you try using a dam with a partner, experiment with it yourself. Try stretching it, tasting it, and rubbing it against your skin.

2. You may want to wash the dam before use to improve its flavor. Use a mild soap, and rinse it well.

3. For increased sensitivity, consider using a water-based lubricant on the genital side of the dam.

4. Because the dam may slip during use, keep track of which side is which. (You may want to mark one side with a pen.) Consider keeping several

view sexuality in general and homosexuality in particular as sinful. People with these views often tend to blame those with HIV for their own illness. But it isn't just religious conservatives who have these kinds of attitudes. A study of college students' attitudes toward people with HIV found they blamed gay men more than heterosexuals for getting AIDS when sexual

dams handy in case one slips off and you lose track of which side is which. Partners may wish to take turns holding the dam in place, or you can purchase a beltlike dam holder.

5. Although you can wash dams thoroughly and reuse them once or twice, it is safer to discard them and use a fresh one each time.

Some people have found an alternative to dental dams that is more comfortable for them—plastic wrap! Although no tests have been performed on the efficacy of plastic wrap as a barrier against disease organisms, it is thought to provide protection equivalent to that of latex dams when used according to similar guidelines. You can cut it to any size (the more area it covers, the better). Don't expose it to heat (including hot water), however, and don't reuse it.

Another alternative for cunnilingus is a condom that has been cut open and flattened. You can snip the condom on one side before unrolling it. Use sharp scissors, and cut from the rolled edge to the center of the tip, then simply unroll it. You'll find the thin latex to be an excellent transmitter of heat and touch. A condom can also be slipped over the fingers for clitoral, vaginal, or anal stimulation. Latex gloves and finger covers (cots) also provide protection during manual sexual activities where there are sores, cuts, or abrasions.

Condom Sense

Basic guidelines for condom use are given in Chapter 12. Here are a few further suggestions to assist you in using condoms safely and pleasurably.

1. Some brands are more highly rated for safety than others. A study funded by the NIH rated Ramses Non-Lube, Ramses Sensitol, Gold Circle Coin, Gold Circle, and Sheik Elite the highest (Nakamura et al., 1988, Voeller et al., 1988). A *Consumer Reports* study found the most effective condoms to be Gold Circle Coin, LifeStyles Extra-Strength Lubricated, Saxon Wet Lube, Ramses Non-Lube, and Sheik Non-Lube ("Can You Rely on Condoms?" 1989). The best-selling brand, Trojan, was generally rated low by both studies. Many Japanese condoms are also considered to be of high quality because they are individually tested, rather than randomly tested, as American condoms are. For up-to-date studies, check your library, family planning clinic, or AIDS resource center.

2. To maximize your pleasure, try different kinds of condoms. Some brands and styles may fit more comfortably than others. Some, including the Japanese brands, are quite thin and allow a lot of sensitivity. Some brands of thinner condoms may be more prone to tearing than others. In cases of tears or slippage, apply spermicide or lubricant with nonoxynol-9 to reduce the chance of infection. If one brand consistently tears, try a different one.

3. If breakage is a problem no matter what kind of condom you use (some people are just friskier than others), consider "double bagging"—using two condoms! Some folks swear by this.

There is no product or practice (except abstinence) that can guarantee 100% safety from HIV and other STDs, but with a little latex and common sense, we can provide a lot of protection for ourselves and those we care about.

contact was the mode of transmission. They also believed that a person who got HIV through a blood transfusion was less responsible for getting it than one who got it sexually or through IV drugs. Men were more apt than women to blame the person for getting AIDS (Dowell, LoPresto, & Sherman, 1991).

Such blaming has consequences that are both ugly and dangerous. While one effect of AIDS has been to make gay men more visible and less suspect, another has been to attract hate-motivated violence against them. Men who have been victims of vicious attacks of gay bashing report that their attackers accuse them of causing AIDS (Webb, 1992). Projecting the blame for AIDS onto certain groups not only stigmatizes people in those groups; it also keeps the blamer from looking into his or her own behavior. This denial is one of the biggest obstacles AIDS educators face. And it affects not only adults, but their children, too.

We are, as a society, uncomfortable with our bodies, with sex, with sexuality. We're in denial about a lot of issues associated with these subjects. We like to pretend they don't exist. That denial is now killing our kids.

Gabe Kruks, Gay and Lesbian Community Services Center

Teaching Children About HIV and AIDS It is difficult to know at this time what effect public education is having on the spread of AIDS. Some elementary and secondary schools have some sort of teaching about it, but it remains controversial (Calamidas, 1990). "Teens are at the mercy of adults," writes Barbara Kantrowitz (1992), "—parents, teachers, politicians—who often won't give young people the information they desperately need to make the right choices about their sexual behavior." Fear abounds among adults: fear that sex education will lead to sex, that teaching about homosexuality will lead to being gay, that discussion of sexuality is immoral. Some conservative groups feel that sex education should be done by parents (unfortunately, these same parents may also be the least informed). Most parents want AIDS education for their children, especially those of high school age ("How the Public Feels," 1986). However, there is good evidence that younger adolescents are becoming sexually active, and they are notoriously the least informed and least likely to use protection (Sonenstein et al., 1991). Current sex educators believe that focus should be on self-esteem, communication, critical thinking, and building refusal skills. They believe abstinence should be stressed as a positive, healthy, mature, and socially acceptable choice. For those who are sexually active, which seems inevitable for most older teens, the facts about risks and prevention, including the effectiveness of properly used condoms, need to be taught and reinforced (Mangasarian, 1993; O'Reilly & Aral, 1985; Roper, Peterson, & Curran, 1993).

One effective way for young people (and old people) to learn about HIV and AIDS is having people who are living with HIV talk to them about their lives. Project First Hand in Santa Cruz, California, provides such an opportunity (Mota, 1991). Trained volunteers who are HIV-positive speak to students of all grade levels, and to health-care workers and people in diverse settings such as rehabilitation centers, migrant camps, churches, and businesses. Their goals are to personalize the HIV epidemic and to encourage people to look at the ways in which they deny their own risk taking. They also work toward increasing the understanding of people with HIV and reducing homophobia. This type of program is valuable not only for what it can give a community but also for the purpose and meaning it adds to the lives of the participants.

Outreach Programs Outreach programs to groups who are at particularly high risk for HIV can be very effective if they are sensitive to the unique cultural, ethnic, and social issues that apply to these groups. Education about risk, prevention, and testing is often most effective when given by peers from the community in question (Kantrowitz, 1992). Examples of programs that are used to reach specific groups of people include:

The Faces of HIV: Krista, who contracted HIV as a teenager.

- Trained teen peer-counselors who talk to teenagers in clinics or classrooms; young people who are living with HIV can be especially effective by simply telling their stories (Mota, 1991). Peer-group support and reinforcement have been shown to reduce risky behaviors among adolescents (Babouri, 1985; Jemmott, Jemmott, & Fong, 1992).

- Gay men who distribute condoms and safer sex information in "public sex environments," such as parks, roadside rest stops, and public restrooms (Beckstein, 1990).

- Young African American or Latino men who distribute clean needles, bleach kits, and condoms in ethnic neighborhoods where there is high drug use.

- Latina women who counsel other women in their neighborhoods about risks, safer sex, health care, and communication.

- Former prostitutes or other sex workers and IV drug users who can talk about their own lives to members of these risk groups; if they are HIV-positive, it can be especially effective.

Community-based clinics, staffed by community members, can provide a variety of services, including examinations and treatment for STDs, HIV testing, and counseling. But many communities simply do not have the funds for such programs. IV needle-exchange programs, especially when they include information about risks and HIV prevention, also have an important role in AIDS prevention. These programs have been controversial because some people believe they are endorsing or encouraging drug use. Others feel that since the drug use already exists, saving lives should be the first priority. Needle-exchange programs are illegal in some areas, although they are often allowed to continue as long as the workers keep a low profile.

HIV Testing

Free or low-cost and anonymous or confidential HIV testing is available in many areas, although in some places, people are turned away from test sites because of a lack of funding. Many kinds of people choose to be tested. Data from one test site showed 184 people, ages 18–78. Of these, there were 112 men and 72 women; 173 were white, 11 were people of color; 53 were gay or bisexual men; 46 were heterosexuals with multiple partners; 33 were transfusion recipients. Of the whole group, 179 (97%) tested negative; 5 (3%) tested positive (Duncan, 1991).

Types of Tests Almost everyone who has the HIV virus will develop antibodies within 2–6 months after exposure. The most common tests look for these antibodies. Occasionally, a person with HIV will not have discernible antibodies when tested; if there is reason to suspect HIV, other tests can be performed that will be definitive (Pan et al., 1991).

The most common test for HIV is called the **ELISA,** an acronym for enzyme-linked immunosorbent assay. This simple blood test screens for the antibodies to HIV that are usually present 2 months after infection with the virus. A negative test result—meaning no antibodies are found—is considered highly (99.7%) accurate if received 6 months after the date of last possible exposure (Damon Clinical Laboratories, 1990). In the event of a positive or inconclusive test result, a person should be retested; in ELISA tests on the general population, only about 20–30% of seropositive results will be true positives indicating HIV infection. The test used to recheck positive ELISA results is called the **Western blot.** In the Western blot procedure, the antibodies are tested to determine whether they are specific to HIV or not. Usually, Western blot results are clearly either positive or negative; if there is an inconclusive result, the person should be tested again in 6 months; a few people who are HIV-negative will repeatedly get inconclusive results. If necessary more complex tests can be performed, including HIV-antigen (polymerase chain reaction [PRC] tests) (Wolinsky, Shepard, Winkelstein, & Levy, 1988), recombinant DNA-HIV tests, and CD4+ T-cell counts.

Getting Tested Most people who go for an HIV test are anxious. They are there because they think there is at least a small chance that they've been exposed to HIV. Even though the vast majority of test results are negative, there is still the understandable fear that one has drawn the short straw. For many people, there are probably also feelings of ambivalence, anxiety, or guilt about the risky behaviors that led them to the test site. Because of these kinds of responses, which are perfectly normal, counseling is an important part of the testing process. It is important for people being tested to understand what their risks for HIV actually are and to know what the results mean. It is also important for everyone, no matter how they test, to understand the facts of transmission and prevention (Wenger, Linn, Epstein, & Shapiro, 1991). For the majority who test negative, practicing abstinence or safer sex, remaining monogamous, avoiding IV drugs, and other preventive measures can eliminate much of the anxiety associated with HIV. (These measures reduce the risk of other diseases as well.)

Counseling is vitally important for those who are HIV-positive. Early treatment and positive health behaviors are essential to retaining good health and prolonging life. Pregnancy counseling should be made available for women. It is also important for a person to know that he or she can pass the virus to others.

Partner Notification Theoretically, both current and past partners should be notified so that they can be tested and receive counseling. There is considerable controversy surrounding the issues of disclosure of HIV serostatus and partner notification. The rights of the individual to privacy may be in direct conflict with the public's right to know. From a public-health standpoint, mandatory contact tracing would be a helpful way to slow down the spread of HIV. But from a civil rights standpoint, it would be a gross violation. Moreover, in some instances it would be impossible to track down all contacts, such as in cases involving prostitution or anonymous sexual contacts. AIDS counselors and health-care practitioners currently encourage those with HIV to make all possible efforts to contact past and current partners. In some cases, counselors try to make such contacts, with their clients' permission.

YOU CAN'T LIVE ON HOPE.

NO SE PUEDE VIVIR DE ESPERANZAS.

TREATMENT AND RESEARCH

The issues concerning treatment and research of HIV and AIDS are multifaceted. Many kinds of questions, some of which have no easy answers, are brought to light. These issues often involve an interplay of medicine, ethics, economics, and law. Ultimately, it is government policy that determines the direction of most AIDS research, treatment, and services.

The major issues that will influence the future direction of government policy in regard to HIV and AIDS include (1) how provisions for health care for the uninsured and underinsured will be made on state and national levels, (2) the effectiveness of policies designed to change risky sexual behaviors, (3) the effectiveness of programs to change behaviors of IV and injection drug users, and (4) the development of the disease itself (Fox, 1991). It is hoped that President Clinton's 1993 appointment of an AIDS Policy Coordinator (Kristine Gebbie) will be useful in organizing and guiding government policy in directions that support AIDS education, research, and health care.

Existing Treatments

There are three basic types of medical treatment for HIV and AIDS. One type consists of therapies to treat the symptoms and infections; these include antibiotics, pain medications, and so on. Another type consists of drugs that affect the virus in some way. This category includes newly formulated antiretroviral drugs that act directly on the virus to change or delay the way in which it progresses. A third category includes treatments designed to bolster the immune system's natural responses. Most physicians agree that early detection of HIV is essential for deriving optimum benefits from medical care and healthy lifestyle choices. Those who seek testing and early treatment tend to be white, educated, middle-class gay men with good health insurance and access to doctors who work with HIV (Lambert, 1990). Most of the medicines used to treat HIV are very costly.

AZT (zidovudine or azidothymidine) has been used to increase CD4+ T cells or prevent their decrease. It does this by slowing the production of reverse transcriptase, the enzyme HIV uses to replicate. Its effectiveness declines with time, however, and there can be negative side effects such as nausea, headaches, and anemia. A number of researchers believe AZT therapy should begin in the early (asymptomatic) phase of HIV infection (Graham et al., 1992; Gruters et al., 1991). The drawback to early use of AZT may be that AZT-resistant HIV strains develop, so other researchers advocate saving it until the immune system has been weakened (Fauci, cited in Kolata, 1992). A recent French and English study of 1700 asymptomatic people with HIV indicated that AZT only helped them for about a year and did not prevent the development of AIDS or extend life (Aboulker & Swart, 1993; Cohen, 1993). There are other antiretroviral drugs, however, that can be used if resistance develops. These include ddI (didanosine) and ddC (dideoxycytidine).

Like AZT, ddI interferes with HIV replication and slows the onset of AIDS symptoms. It has proved most useful for people with resistance to AZT and generally has fewer negative side effects. There is recent evidence that the combination of AZT and ddI is more effective than either drug used alone, but the long-term effectiveness is still unknown (Project Inform, 1990). Especially in cases where AZT alone has not proven effective, ddC appears to be most useful in combination with AZT. It can have unpleasant side effects, the most common of which is peripheral neuropathy—tingling, numbness, or pain, usually in the hands and feet (Project Inform, 1990).

Among the most common drugs used to treat the opportunistic infections associated with AIDS are preventive antibiotics such as Septra and Bactrim, dapsone, and aerosolized pentamidine, all of which can be very effective against pneumocystis (PCP). Pentamidine is generally administered once a month by a physician or a respiratory therapist; it is forcibly sprayed into the lungs. The antiviral drug acyclovir is used to treat herpes, shingles, hairy leukoplakia, Epstein-Barr virus, and cytomegalovirus.

Alternative and Experimental Therapies   Several different kinds of treatments are currently being tested in ongoing clinical trials. These include both preventive vaccines to inhibit HIV development and therapeutic vaccines to strengthen the immune system. Among the treatments being explored are:

- gp120 vaccine: a vaccine created from the HIV protein to stimulate HIV antibody production. Initial testing of this vaccine has yielded encouraging results.

- d4T: an antiviral drug.

- Protease inhibitors: drugs that inhibit the production of an enzyme critical to HIV replication.

- Alpha interferon: a human protein that has been used in cancer therapy.

- HIV immunogen: a therapeutic vaccine made from killed HIV.
- "Naked DNA" vaccine: a vaccine made of HIV from which the protein coating has been removed.
- "Compound Q": a drug derived from the Chinese root *Trichosanthes kirilowii* that appears to selectively kill HIV-infected macrophages.
- N-acetylcysteine: a compound containing the essential amino acid cysteine that appears to decrease HIV replication.

There are also other classes of drugs that may be developed, but, as we discuss in the following section, political and financial constraints limit the scope of AIDS research.

AIDS Research

The U.S. government spent $1.3 billion on AIDS research in 1992, yet most experts in the field say it is not nearly enough (Pear, 1993). Private foundations also contribute to AIDS research. For 1991, the Foundation Center reported $5.2 million from private foundations. Additionally, $8.6 million was contributed by the private foundation Amfar in 1991 and $10.5 million in 1992 (Cronin, 1993). Public charities and corporations have also donated to AIDS research. Still, there are many other life-threatening diseases that require attention. The result is that dollars for health research must be spread out over numerous areas. In 1992, for example, the Public Health Service spent almost $1.9 billion on cancer research, $726 million on heart disease, and $282 million on diabetes (Cronin, 1993). Although these figures are large, in 1992 the federal government spent $37 *billion* for military research and development (Pear, 1993). The doling-out process often tends to be more political than rational. AIDS research involving children, for example, is more likely to be funded than that involving gay men or drug users, even though children are a very small portion of AIDS patients (Pear, 1993). Arguments in favor of increased AIDS spending include the following (Project Inform, 1992):

- Unlike cancer, heart disease, and diabetes, AIDS is an infectious disease.
- The number of people infected is growing rapidly.
- AIDS is primarily a disease of the young (diseases such as cancer and heart disease are often associated with aging).
- Major progress has already been made against diseases such as heart disease and cancer.
- A significantly greater amount needs to be spent on testing new treatments; the current figure is only about $150 million per year.

Drug Testing

The Federal Drug Administration (FDA) requires lengthy and extensive testing before drugs can be made available to the public. These measures are designed to protect people from unanticipated negative effects, but for people who feel they are going to die anyway unless they find a treatment, the process can appear unnecessarily lengthy—if not cruel. The standard practice of giving one group an experimental drug and giving the control

The problem is that the government spends far too little on health research overall, including AIDS, heart disease and cancer. . . . People fighting for all those afflicted with life-threatening illnesses must band together and seek a larger pie for all and resist the pressure to fight each other over the meager scraps falling from the Federal table.

Project Inform

group a placebo hardly seems fair when lives are at stake. In the case of aerosolized pentamidine, the drug now commonly used to prevent PCP, frustrated community groups ran their own trials in 1984. When it became clear that the drug worked, the FDA reluctantly approved it (Arno & Feiden, 1992).

The AIDS Clinical Trial Group, a chain of centers that tests new drugs, has now been established, but critics say it is not responsive to the needs of many groups. "More people need to be brought into the trials," says Anthony Fauci, who was largely responsible for getting the government to set up the Trial Group, "and more of them should be black, Hispanic, women and children" (quoted in Hilts, 1990). Progress in developing new drugs is also slowed by lack of cooperation among drug companies and lack of funding to develop new avenues of inquiry (Israelski, 1992). In 1990, the National Institutes of Health (NIH) granted funding to 401 HIV-related research projects; funding was turned down for 1141 (Cronin, 1993).

LIVING WITH HIV OR AIDS

People who discover they are facing a life-threatening disease often find that they are suddenly treated differently by their family, friends, and associates. We need to realize that a diagnosis does not mark the end of life. While it may be a cause for sadness and grieving, it also may be a time for reevaluation and growth. In times of crisis, families and friends often find renewed strength and closeness.

Those of us whose friends or family members are living with HIV, or who are ourselves HIV-positive, need information, practical support, and emotional support. We must understand the health issues that are involved and become aware of the resources that are available—from both outside and inside ourselves.

Discrimination and HIV

The Faces of HIV: Brad. We note with regret that Brad died in 1993.

People with HIV and AIDS often face discrimination and intolerance at work, in their living arrangements, and among medical caregivers, including nurses (Scherer, Wu, & Haughey, 1991), psychotherapists (Rudolph, 1989), and physicians. One study of U.S. doctors found that 23% said they wouldn't care for AIDS patients if they had a choice (Shapiro, Hayward, Guillemot, & Jayle, 1992). Thirty-nine percent of the physicians surveyed said a surgeon had refused to provide services to at least one HIV-positive patient under their care. Workplace discrimination, in addition to being fueled by unreasonable fear of infection, is increasingly based on economic considerations: the rising costs of health insurance. Some companies and organizations, however, such as the United Auto Workers, General Motors, BankAmerica, Levi Strauss, Pacific Telesis, and Digital Equipment Corporation have taken proactive stances (Pomice, 1990). They have instituted programs to educate workers and assist employees who have HIV; some actively support AIDS-related causes.

Courts and government agencies often discriminate against people with AIDS. Judges may reinforce stereotypes and fears about HIV and AIDS rather than being guided by scientific evidence (Gostin, 1992). For example,

The Faces of HIV: Kevin and Cyndi. Kevin and Cyndi are a couple living with HIV.

courts have given harsh sentences to people with HIV for spitting at other people, even though there is virtually no risk of transmission via saliva. Others have been charged with attempted murder for transmitting HIV during consensual sexual activity (Nossiter, 1992).

If You Are HIV-Positive

People with AIDS, sometimes referred to as **PWAs,** and people with HIV, **PWHs,** have the same needs as every one else—and a few more. In addition to dealing with the special issues of loss and grief, you will need to pay special attention to maintaining good health. (See Perspective 3.)

Taking Care of Your Health   As we have discussed already, early detection of HIV can greatly enhance both the quality and the quantity of life. It is important to find a physician who has experience working with HIV and AIDS, and—even more important, perhaps—who is sensitive to the issues confronted by PWHs and PWAs. In addition to appropriate medical treatment, factors that can help promote your continuing good health include good nutrition, plenty of rest, appropriate exercise, limited (or no) alcohol use, and stress reduction. People with HIV or AIDS should stop smoking tobacco because it increases susceptibility to PCP. Also, you need to reduce your chances of exposure to infectious organisms. This doesn't mean shutting yourself up in a room and never coming out. It simply means you need to take a little more than ordinary care not to expose yourself to infectious organisms—for example, in spoiled or improperly cooked foods, on unwashed glasses or utensils used by sick household members, or from

Thinking about illness!—To calm the imagination of the invalid, so that at least he should not, as hitherto, have to suffer more from thinking about his illness than from the illness itself—that, I think, would be something! It would be a great deal!

Friedrich Nietzsche

certain kinds of pets. Your doctor or nearest HIV/AIDS resource group should have more information on these measures.

Additionally, if you have decided to have sexual relations, it means practicing safer sex—even if your partner is also HIV-positive. Researchers caution that one can become reinfected with different HIV strains—definitely not a pleasant thought (Chermann in Challice, 1992). Moreover, STDs of all kinds can be much worse for people with an impaired immune system. HIV doesn't mean an end to being sexual—but it does suggest that different ways of expressing love and lust may be explored.

It is recommended that women who are HIV-positive have Pap tests every 6 months to a year. Cervical biopsies may also be necessary to determine if CIN or cancer is present.

As a black gay man, I've always felt I had to choose: Am I gay or am I black?

Reggie Williams, National Task Force on AIDS Prevention

Other Needs Besides taking care of one's physical health, a person who is living with HIV needs to take care of psychological and emotional needs. The stigma and fear surrounding HIV and AIDS often make it difficult to just get on with the business of living. Suicide is the leading cause of non-HIV related death among people who are HIV-positive (Israelski, 1992). Among gays and bisexual men, social support is generally better for whites than for blacks; in black communities, there tends to be less affirmation from primary social support networks and less openness about orientation (Ostrow et al., 1991). Women, who usually concern themselves with caring for others, may not be inclined to seek out supportive groups and networks (Kline, Kline, & Oken, 1992). But people who live with HIV and AIDS say that it's important not to feel isolated. If you are HIV-positive, we encourage you to seek support from AIDS organizations in your area. (See "Resources" at the end of the chapter for referrals to groups in your area, or check your local telephone directory.)

Being involved in meaningful work is important to everyone, but it is especially important for people who cope day-to-day with a life-threatening disease. Many people need to work for the income or health benefits the job provides. Others may be able to take time off to pursue other interests, to travel; or, they may seek a less stressful type of work. For most people, some kind of work is important because it helps give meaning to life and provides a sense of camaraderie with others (Navarro, 1992). Some PWHs find volunteer work quite rewarding, especially in the area of HIV education and outreach.

Those who love and care for people with HIV and AIDS need support, too. If you are a caregiver, you may need to actively seek information and support from the appropriate resources. There is a great deal of information available on practical matters of living with and caring for people with HIV. There are hotlines and support networks to help deal with the emotional aspects. Or you may want to start your own support group. Reaching out and sharing empower us to meet the challenges we face today and will undoubtedly continue to face in the future.

"Education is going to be the vaccine for AIDS," says June Osborn, who is Dean of the University of Michigan's School of Public Health and was chair of the National Commission on AIDS. As we have seen, there are many public misperceptions concerning HIV and AIDS, and the denial of risk appears to be epidemic in many areas. But AIDS can be prevented. We hope that this chapter has provided you with information that will serve as your vaccine.

What we learn in times of pestilence [is] that there are more things to admire in men than to despise.
Albert Camus

SUMMARY

What Is AIDS?

- *AIDS* is an acronym for *acquired immune deficiency syndrome*. In order for a person to receive an AIDS diagnosis, he or she must have a positive blood test indicating the presence of *HIV (human immunodeficiency virus)* antibodies and have a T-cell count below 200; if the T-cell count is higher, the person must have one or more of the 26 diseases or conditions associated with AIDS. These include *opportunistic infections*, such as *Pneumocystis carinii pneumonia* and tuberculosis; cancers, such as *Kaposi's sarcoma*, lymphomas, and cervical cancer; and conditions associated with AIDS, such as *wasting syndrome* and AIDS dementia. Other conditions may lead to an AIDS diagnosis, including persistent candidiasis and outbreaks of herpes.

- Symptoms that may be associated with HIV/AIDS include unexplained persistent fatigue; unexplained fever; persistent chills or night sweats; unexplained weight loss; persistent, unexplained swollen lymph nodes; pink, purple, or brown blotches on or under the skin that do not disappear; persistent white spots or other sores in the mouth; persistent dry cough and shortness of breath; and persistent diarrhea. Additionally, women may experience abnormal Pap smears, persistent vaginal candidiasis, or persistent abdominal cramping. Because these symptoms may be indicative of many other diseases and conditions, HIV and AIDS cannot be self-diagnosed; testing by a clinician or physician is necessary.

- *Leukocytes*, or white blood cells, play major roles in defending the body against invading organisms and cancerous cells. One type, the *macrophage*, engulfs foreign particles and displays the invader's *antigen* on its own surface. *Antibodies* bind to antigens, inactivate them, and mark them for destruction by killer cells. Other white blood cells called *lymphocytes* include *helper T cells*, which are programmed to "read" the antigens and then begin directing the immune system's response. T cells are also identified by the type of protein receptor (called CD4 or CD8) they display on their surface. The number of helper T cells in an individual's body is an important indicator of how well the immune system is functioning.

• Viruses are minute capsules of protein and enzymes; they can't propel themselves independently, and they can't reproduce unless they are inside a host cell. Within the human immunodeficiency virus's protein core is the genetic material (RNA) that carries the information the virus needs to replicate itself. Also in the core is an enzyme called *reverse transcriptase*, which enables the *retrovirus* to "write" its RNA (the genetic program) into a host cell's DNA.

• Although HIV begins replication right away within the host cells, it is not detectable in the blood for some time—often years. HIV antibodies, however, are generally detectable in the blood within 2–6 months. A person's *serostatus* is HIV negative if antibodies are not present and HIV positive if antibodies are detected. "T-cell count" or "CD4 count" refers to the number of helper T cells that are present in a cubic milliliter of blood. A healthy person has a T-cell count in the range of 500–1600.

• When a person is first infected with HIV, he or she may experience severe flu-like symptoms. During this period, the virus is dispersed throughout the lymph nodes and other tissues. The virus may stay localized in these areas for years, but it continues to replicate and to destroy T cells. As the number of infected cells goes up, the number of T cells goes down. In advanced AIDS, the T-cell count drops to under 200, and the virus itself is detectable in the blood.

Epidemiology and Transmission of HIV

• Over 121,000 people are currently diagnosed with AIDS in the U.S. Another 1 million are estimated to be infected with HIV; worldwide, over 14 million people are infected with HIV. As of 1993, about 56% of U.S. AIDS cases had involved gay or bisexual men and 23% involved heterosexual IV drug users (both men and women). Heterosexual transmission is becoming more common and is expected to continue to increase. The role of IV drug use in the spread of HIV is increasing as HIV-infected drug users pass the virus to each other in blood and to women partners during sexual activity. Women may then infect their children in utero or through breast-feeding.

• Ways in which HIV is *not* transmitted include normal household or social contact, such as shaking hands, hugging, kissing, playing, and providing personal care such as bathing and feeding; via surfaces or inanimate objects, such as countertops, toilet seats, drinking fountains, telephones, and eating utensils; blood donation; pets; insect bites; tears; sweat; vaccines; and water. Saliva is unlikely to transmit HIV.

• Activities or situations that may promote transmission include sexual transmission through vaginal or anal intercourse without a condom; fellatio without a condom; cunnilingus without a latex or other barrier; sharing needles contaminated with infected blood; in utero infection from mother to fetus (20–50% chance), from blood during delivery, or in breast milk; sharing sex toys without disinfecting them; accidental contamination with infected blood entering the body through mucous membranes (eyes or mouth) or cuts, abrasions, or punctures in the skin (relatively rare); or blood transfusions administered prior to April 1, 1985.

• Certain physiological or behavioral factors increase the risk of contracting HIV. In addition to anal intercourse, multiple sex partners, and IV drug use, these factors include having an STD (especially if genital ulcers are present), multiple exposure to HIV, and drug and alcohol use. *Cofactors*, conditions that may make a person more likely to develop AIDS if HIV is already present, include a history of STD, drug abuse, alcohol abuse, poor nutrition, stress, smoking, pregnancy, and repeated exposure to HIV.

AIDS Demographics

• Studying *demographics*, such as age, socioeconomic status, living area, ethnicity, or sex, can help researchers understand the dynamics of disease transmission and prevention. In instances where sexually transmitted diseases are involved, they also look at sexual behaviors. Certain groups appear as a whole to be a greater risk than others, or to face special difficulties where HIV is concerned, including gay men, women, teenagers, and young inner-city African Americans.

• The gay and lesbian communities, along with other concerned individuals, have rallied together in a variety of ways to support people with HIV and AIDS, to educate themselves and the public, and to influence government policies. There remains, however, the perceptions of AIDS as a gay disease rather than a viral disease, and those who have "moral" objections to homosexual behaviors still blame AIDS on gays.

• It is expected that by the year 2000, the numbers of women and men with HIV will be equal. Women face unique issues where HIV is concerned, including later diagnosis, lack of inclusion in clinical trials, and issues tied in with poverty, racism, and sexism. As the number of infected women rises, the number of infected children is also expected to rise. Because teenagers often have a sense of invulnerability, they may put themselves at great risk without really understanding what it means.

• HIV/AIDS, like many of society's ills, is often linked with poverty that is enforced by racism and discrimination. AIDS is a leading cause of death in many communities.

Education and Prevention

• To protect ourselves and those we care about from HIV, we need to be aware that alcohol and drug use significantly increases risky behaviors, develop communication skills so that we can talk with our partner, and get information on HIV testing. If we are sexually active with more than one long-term, monogamous partner, we need to use condoms consistently.

• Projecting the blame for AIDS onto certain groups, such as gays, not only stigmatizes people in those groups, it also keeps the blamer from looking into his or her own behavior. This denial is one of the biggest obstacles AIDS educators face.

• Outreach programs by peers to groups who are at particularly high risk for HIV can be very effective if they are sensitive to the unique cultural, ethnic, and social issues that apply to these groups. Community-based clinics provide a variety of services, including examinations and treatment for STDs, HIV testing, and counseling.

• Free or low-cost, anonymous or confidential HIV testing is available in many areas, although in some places people are turned away from test sites because of a lack of funding. The most common test, *ELISA*, looks for antibodies for the virus.

Treatment and Research

• There are three basic types of medical treatments for HIV and AIDS: therapies to treat the symptoms and infections, such as antibodies and pain medications; drugs that affect the virus in some way, such as AZT; and therapies that boost the immune system. A number of treatments and preventive therapies are currently being researched. Political and financial constraints often limit the scope of AIDS research.

Living with HIV/AIDS

• An HIV or AIDS diagnosis may be a cause for sadness and grieving, but it also may be a time for reevaluation and growth. Those whose friends or family members are living with HIV, or who are themselves HIV-positive, need information, practical support, and emotional support. People with HIV or AIDS often face discrimination in society.

• Early detection of HIV can greatly enhance both the quality and quantity of life. Appropriate medical treatment, good nutrition, plenty of rest, appropriate exercise, limited (or no) alcohol use, and stress reduction are important. People with HIV or AIDS should stop smoking tobacco and take precautions to reduce their exposure to infectious organisms. They also need to practice safer sex and consider seeking support from AIDS organizations. AIDS caregivers need support, too.

KEY TERMS

human immuno-
    deficiency virus
    (HIV)

acquired immune
    deficiency syn-
    drome (AIDS)

opportunistic
    infection (OI)

pneumocystis
    carinii pneumonia
    (PCP)

Kaposi's sarcoma

wasting syndrome

leukocyte

macrophage

antigen

antibody

lymphocyte

B cell

T cell

helper T cell

killer T cell

reverse transcriptase

retrovirus

seroconversion

serostatus

dendritic cell

cervical ectopy

parenteral trans-
    mission

perinatal trans-
    mission

cofactor

demographics

multiple-loss
    syndrome

ELISA

Western blot

PWA

PWH

RESOURCES

CDC National AIDS Hotline
(800) 342-2437 (342-AIDS); TTY/TDD Hotline, (800) 243-7889

Linea Nacional de SIDA (Spanish)
(800) 344-7432 (344-SIDA)
24-hour services provide information and referrals regarding HIV and AIDS.

CDC National AIDS Clearinghouse
(800) 458-5231
Provides information on services and educational resources. Also provides copies of Public Health Service publications.

National Technical Information Service
5285 Port Royal Road
Springfield, VA 22161
(703) 487-4650
Distributes CDC publications for a charge.

Project Inform
347 Dolores Street, Suite 301
San Francisco, CA 94110
(415) 558-9051
(800) 822-7422
Conducts research and collects data for educators, health-care practitioners, PWHs, and PWAs. Treatment information, newsletter, and other publications are available.

You can also contact your local state or county health department, AIDS resource organization, or the American Red Cross for assistance in your area.

SUGGESTIONS FOR FURTHER READING

Altman, Dennis. *AIDS in the Mind of America.* Garden City, NY: Anchor Press/ Doubleday, 1986. The social, political, and psychological aspects of AIDS in the first half of the 1980s.

Arno, Peter S., and Karyn L. Feiden. *Against the Odds: The Story of AIDS Drug Development, Politics and Profits.* New York: HarperCollins, 1992. A fascinating and frustrating story of what can occur when human medical needs conflict with those of business and government.

DiClemente, Ralph J. *Adolescents and AIDS.* Newbury Park, CA: Sage Publications, 1992. A well-researched and sobering report on the risks teenagers face (and take) today.

Huber, Jeffrey T. *How to Find Information About AIDS.* New York: Haworth Press, 1992. An important resource guide.

Monette, Paul. *Half a Life.* The National Book Award winner about the author's coming of age in the age of AIDS; Monette also wrote *On Borrowed Time* and *Afterlife.*

Pizzi, Michael. *Productive Living Strategies for People with AIDS.* New York: Haworth Press, 1990. Practical advice for people with HIV and AIDS.

Shilts, Randy. *And the Band Played On: People, Politics and the AIDS Epidemic.* New York: St. Martin's Press, 1987. The fascinating story behind the "discovery" of AIDS, complete with real heroes and, unfortunately, real villains.

Chapter Eighteen

SEXUAL COERCION: HARASSMENT, AGGRESSION, AND ABUSE

PREVIEW: SELF-QUIZ

1. Most rapes are committed by acquaintances or dates. True or false?

2. Sexual harassment is considered illegal only when a superior requests sexual favors from a subordinate in exchange for keeping his or her job. True or false?

3. Men and women often have differing perceptions of what constitutes sexual harassment. True or false?

4. Historically, there were few if any penalties for a master raping his slave. True or false?

5. Evidence indicates that relatively few gay men and lesbians have been physically attacked because of their sexual orientation. True or false?

6. Prejudices based on race and on sexual orientation share many characteristics. True or false?

7. Sexually abusive men tend to hold nontraditional beliefs about women and women's roles. True or false?

8. The majority of sexually victimized children are prepubescent girls. True or false?

9. Lack of sexual desire is common among rape survivors. True or false?

10. The least common form of sexual abuse within the family is uncle-niece abuse. True or false?

ANSWERS 1. T, 2. F, 3. T, 4. T, 5. F, 6. T, 7. F, 8. T, 9. T, 10. F

Chapter Outline

While sexuality permits us to form and sustain deep bonds and intimate relationships, it may also have a darker side. For some people, sex is linked with coercion, degradation, aggression, and abuse. In these cases, sex becomes a weapon. Sex can be a means to exploit, humiliate, or harm others. In this chapter, we first examine the various aspects of sexual harassment, including the distinction between flirting and harassment and sexual harassment in schools, colleges, and the workplace. Next we look at harassment, prejudice, and discrimination directed against gay men and lesbians. Then we examine sexual aggression, including date rape and stranger rape, the motivations for rape, and the consequences of rape. Finally, we discuss child sexual abuse, examining the factors contributing to abuse, the types of sexual abuse and their consequences, and programs for preventing child sexual abuse.

Undismayed, he plucks the rose,
In the hedgerow blooming.
Vainly, she laments her woes;
Vainly doth her thorns oppose,
Gone her sweet perfuming. . . .
German Art Song

SEXUAL HARASSMENT

Sexual harassment refers to two distinct types of behavior: the abuse of power for sexual ends, and the creation of a hostile environment. In abuse of power, sexual harassment consists of unwelcome sexual advances, requests for sexual favors, or other verbal or physical conduct of a sexual nature as a condition of instruction or employment. Only a person with power over another can commit the first kind of harassment. In the Supreme Court's 1986 *Meritor Savings Bank v. Vinson* decision, sexual harassment was extended to include a hostile environment. In a **hostile environment,** someone acts in sexual ways that interfere with a person's performance at school or in the workplace. Such harassment is illegal. The 1964 Civil Rights Act prohibits discrimination and harassment based on race or gender. And the 1991 Civil Rights Act reinforced laws against sexual harassment, including awarding increased damages beyond lost wages.

Sexual harassment is a mixture of sex and power; power may often be the dominant element. In school and in the workplace, men devalue women by calling attention to their sexuality. Sexual harassment may be a way to keep women "in their place" and make them feel vulnerable.

There are other forms of behavior that, although not illegal, are considered by many to be sexual harassment. These include unwelcomed whistles, taunts, and obscenities directed from a man or group of men to a woman walking past them. They also include a man "talking to" a woman's breasts or body during conversation, or persistently giving her "the once over" as she walks past him, sits down, or enters or leaves a room. Such incidents may make women feel uncomfortable and vulnerable. (They have been described, in fact, as "little rapes.") The cumulative effect of these behaviors is to lead women to limit their activities, to avoid walking past groups of men, and to stay away from beaches, concerts, parties, and sports events unless they are accompanied by others (Bowman, 1993).

Flirtation Versus Harassment

There is nothing wrong with flirtation per se. A certain smile, look, or compliment can give zest and pleasure to both people. But persistent and unwelcomed flirtation can be sexual harassment if the flirtatious person holds power over the other, or if the flirtation creates a hostile school or work environment. Whether flirtation is sexual harassment depends on three factors. These apply to male-female, male-male, and female-female interactions.

1. *Whether you have equal power.* A person's having power over you limits your ability to refuse, for fear of reprisal. For example, if a professor or teaching assistant in your class asks you for a date, you are placed in an awkward position. If you say no, will your grade suffer? Will you be

ignored in class? What other consequences might occur? If your boss at work asks for dates, you may be similarly concerned about losing your job, being demoted, or having your work environment become hostile.

2. *Whether you are approached appropriately.* "Hi babe, nice tits, wanna screw?" or "Hey stud, love your buns, wanna do it?" are patently offensive. But approaches that are complimentary ("You look really nice today"), indirect ("What do you think of the course?"), or direct ("Would you like to have some coffee?") are acceptable because they do not pressure you. You have the opportunity to let the overture pass, respond positively, or politely decline.

3. *Whether you wish to continue contact.* If you find the other person appealing, you may want to continue the flirtation. You can express interest or flirt back. But if you do not, you may want to stop the interaction by not responding or by responding in a neutral or discouraging manner.

The issue is complicated by several factors related to culture and gender. Differing cultural expectations may lead to misinterpretation. For example, when a Latino, whose culture encourages mutual flirting, says *"muy guapa"* (good looking) to a Latina woman walking by, the words may be meant *and* received as a compliment. But when a Latino says the same to a non-Latina woman, he may be dismayed to find the woman insulted. While he perceives her as uptight and she perceives him as rude, both are misinterpreting each other because of cultural differences. (See Perspective 1 for a discussion of the impact of the Thomas/Hill hearings on sexual harassment awareness and on the African American community.)

There are three significant gender differences that may contribute to sexual harassment. First, men are generally less likely to perceive activities as harassing than are women (Jones & Remland, 1992; Popovich et al., 1992). Second, men tend to misperceive women's friendliness as sexual interest (Johnson, Stockdale, & Saal, 1991; Stockdale, 1993). Third, men are more likely than women to perceive male-female relationships as adversarial (Reilly, Lott, Caldwell, & Deluca, 1992).

Power differences also affect perception (Popovich et al., 1986). Personal questions asked by an instructor or supervisor, for example, are more likely to be perceived as sexual harassment than they would be if a student or co-worker asked them. People sometimes experience confusion as to what constitutes appropriate behavior in social situations involving employers and employees or instructors and students. There is nothing inappropriate per se in professors and students or employers and employees meeting together for lunch, coffee, and so on; they can socialize at parties or other functions. Friendly interactions are quite appropriate. What needs to be clear, however, is that the relationship has an educational, business, or professional basis rather than a romantic or sexual one. Flirtatious or sexual ways of relating are inappropriate in these contexts.

Harassment in School and College

Sexual harassment in various forms is widespread. It does not necessarily begin in adulthood; it may begin as early as middle childhood.

THE CLARENCE THOMAS / ANITA HILL HEARINGS: DIFFERING WHITE AND AFRICAN AMERICAN PERCEPTIONS

In 1991, Clarence Thomas was nominated by President George Bush to succeed Thurgood Marshall as a U.S. Supreme Court justice. As the Senate Judiciary Committee was about to recommend Thomas's nomination, it learned that a former Thomas employee, Anita Hill, a conservative black Republican, had accused him of sexual harassment (Phelps & Winternitz, 1992). The committee called a special public session to hear and evaluate Hill's charges. Americans were riveted to their TV screens as they watched Thomas and Hill testify about the alleged harassment. In intimate detail, the charges were broadcast and denied. It was not a simple matter, however, of who was telling the truth. Instead, it was a complex drama that had different meanings for white and black Americans. For white Americans, the drama was one of sexual harassment that laid out its dynamics in painful detail. Thomas supporters accused Hill of making up her story out of revenge; some accused her of being a spurned woman. For many white Americans, the issue was *who* was telling the truth. But some African Americans believed white Americans were enthralled by the chance to glimpse into black life and sexuality. These blacks doubted that white Americans would have focused so intently on the hearings if Thomas and Hill had been white (Chrisman, 1992; Karenga, 1992).

For black Americans, the hearings were a painful public discussion of African American sexuality and male-female relationships before a largely white audience. African Americans feared that the intimate but public discussion would fuel white America's prejudices and stereotypes about black sexuality. "White Americans will hear this story not just as a lesson about the ubiquity of sexual harassment in the workplace," wrote Charles Lawrence III (1992), "they will hear it as a story of an oversexed black man." Maulana Karenga (1992) wrote that the hearings reinforced the

"stereotype of the black man ever perversely concerned with the size, length, and place to put his penis, even on his way to the solemn and hallowed halls of the Supreme Court." The hearings also reinforced the myth of the "unchaste" black woman and, as a consequence, argued Lawrence (1992), most white Americans would not believe Anita Hill. Finally, the hearings brought up the African American stereotype of "black-woman-as-traitor-to-the-race." This stereotype, well known among African Americans, portrays women who stand up to men as undermining blacks as a race. For black Americans, the sexual harassment issue became secondary to the issue of "washing dirty linen in public" (Burnham, 1992).

While the hearings had different meanings for whites and blacks, the ultimate impact of the Thomas/Hill hearings was to bring the issue of sexual harassment into the foreground. The number of complaints filed with the Equal Employment Opportunities Commission (EEOC) increased 69%, from 3329 in 1991 to 5629 in 1992. It mobilized women voters and candidates who were indignant because the majority of American males did not believe that Anita Hill was sexually harassed.

Elementary and High School Harassment It's a "time-honored" practice for boys to "tease" girls: flipping up their skirts, calling them names, poking them with pencils, touching their breasts, spreading sexual gossip, and so on. If such behavior is defined as teasing, its impact is discounted; it is just "fun." But if the behavior is thought of as sexual harassment, then the acts may be evaluated in a new light. Such behavior, researcher Carrie Herbert (1989) found, leads girls to "become more subordinated, less autonomous, and less capable of resisting. This behavior controls the girls through intimidation, embarrassment, or humiliation." Psychologist Ann Reynolds states (quoted in Carr, 1992):

> A young girl, at age 11, doesn't have a firm self-concept yet. Young girls being treated that way in their adolescence leads to women feeling estranged from their own bodies, which . . . damages the ability to see oneself in a positive light.

Sexual harassment can be initiated by teachers or peers. In 1992, the Supreme Court expanded its interpretation of sex discrimination in Title IX of the 1972 Education Act to include sexual harassment in schools. It applies to both teachers and students (Adler, 1992). Harassment by teachers is believed to be underreported (Wishnietsky, 1991). Among students, sexual harassment occurs most often when boys are in groups. Their motives may often be homosocial—heightening their group status by denigrating girls rather than any specific animosity toward a particular girl (Carr, 1992). Girls are often troubled by the boys' behaviors but rarely protest. An eighth-grade girl said, "It's so bad you want to ignore it. It might be you don't know what to do so you act like it never happened" (Gross, 1992). In most cases, boys are unaware of their impact on girls; they are ignorant rather than malicious. They misunderstand the difference between a teasing compliment and a crude remark.

Herbert (1989) found that "sexual harassment was accepted as part of the hidden curriculum for female students." Harassment was either ignored or regarded as normal or typical behavior among boys—"Boys will be boys." Girls were frequently blamed for the harassment because they did not "stand up for themselves," or else they took the incidents "too seriously."

Many parents and educators are becoming increasingly aware that the roots of sexual harassment are found in what children learn from their peers at school. In 1992, Minnesota became the first state to institute a law prohibiting sexual harassment in schools. In 1993, California made sexual harassment grounds for suspension or expulsion from the public schools.

College Harassment Sexual harassment on college and university campuses has become a major concern in recent years (Bursik, 1992; Paludi, 1990; for a review of the literature, see Hotelling, 1991). Various studies suggest that 15–35% of women college students have experienced some form of harassment from other students, faculty members, or administrators (Bursik, 1992; Kenig & Ryan, 1986; Paludi, 1990). A random sample of undergraduate women at the University of California, Berkeley, found that almost one-third had received unwanted sexual attention from a male instructor while in college (Benson & Thompson, 1982).

Two major problems in dealing with issues of sexual harassment are gender differences in levels of tolerance and attribution of blame. Women are often blamed for not taking a "compliment" and for provoking unwanted

Sexual harassment has become an important but often divisive issue on many college campuses. Exactly what acts constitute sexual harassment are unclear to many.

sexual attention by what they wear or how they look. These attitudes also seem to be widely held in college settings, especially among men. In one study of sexual harassment in college, students, faculty, and staff were asked whether they would define a behavior as sexual harassment (1) if it was perpetrated by someone in an authority position and (2) if it was perpetrated by someone not in authority (Kenig & Ryan, 1986). The behaviors were:

Gender-stereotyped jokes or depictions.

Teasing sexual remarks.

Unwanted suggestive looks or gestures.

Unwanted letters or telephone calls.

Unwanted leaning or cornering.

Unwanted pressure for dates.

Unwanted touching.

Unwanted pressure for sexual activity.

The study found that women defined more of these behaviors as sexual harassment than men did (also see Jones & Remland, 1992). While both men and women respondents were more likely to judge a behavior as sexual harassment if done by a person in authority, there was a significant gender difference if the person was without authority. In that case, men were less likely to identify seven out of eight types of behavior as harassment. Men and women generally agreed only about unwanted touching. Gender-related differences appeared most frequently for circumstances or behaviors that were most ambiguous.

The study also found significant gender differences in attributing responsibility for sexual harassment (Kenig & Ryan, 1986). Men were significantly more likely than women to believe that attractive women had to expect sexual advances and needed to know how to handle them, that it was only natural for men to make sexual advances to attractive women, and that people who received annoying sexual attention had usually provoked it. Other studies reinforce the widespread "blaming-the-victim" attitude (Summers, 1991). If a woman wears "provocative" clothing, her dress is deemed to provoke the harassment (Pryor & Day, 1988). Heavy makeup also "justifies" harassment (Workman & Johnson, 1991). The more personally involved the harassed person is with the harasser, the more he or she is likely to be blamed (Williams & Cyr, 1992).

As a consequence of sexual harassment, students may find it difficult to study; others worry about their grades. If the harasser is an instructor controlling grades, students fear reporting the harassment. They may use strategies such as avoiding courses taught by the harasser. In extreme cases, the emotional consequences may sometimes be as severe as for those who are raped (Paludi, 1990).

Most universities and colleges have developed sexual harassment policies. Such policies help make students aware of harassment issues, but their effectiveness depends on educating students about what constitutes harassment (Gressman et al., 1992; Williams, Lam, & Shively, 1992). Younger female students, in particular, are often unable to define clearly harassing situations as harassment, despite feelings of discomfort (Bremer, Moore, & Bildersee, 1991; Jaschick & Fretz, 1991). With the exception of coercive or highly intrusive behaviors, many students are uncertain about what behaviors constitute sexual harassment (Fitzgerald & Ormerod, 1991).

If a student finds himself or herself sexually harassed, the first step is to request the harasser to stop. The person may not be aware of the impact of his or her behavior. If he or she does not stop, the student should consult an advisor, resident assistant, counselor, or dean.

Sexual Harassment in the Workplace

Issues of sexual harassment are complicated in the workplace because work, like college, is one of the most important places where adults meet potential partners. As a consequence, sexual undercurrents or interactions often take place. Flirtations, romances, and affairs are common in the work environment. Drawing the line between flirtation and harassment can be filled with ambiguity—especially for men.

Furthermore, sexuality and power issues can become intertwined. Power can manifest itself in sexual coercion or harassment. Sexual harassment tends to be most pervasive in formerly all-male occupations. In these occupations, sexual harassment is a means of exerting control over women and asserting male dominance. Such male bastions as the building trades, the trucking industry, law enforcement, and the military have been especially resistant to women entering (Niebhuhr & Boyles, 1991; Schmitt, 1990).

Sexual harassment can be perpetuated by fellow employees as well as by supervisors. In fact, the Merit Systems Protection Board (1981) study of 20,000 federal employees found that co-workers sexually harassed both women and men more than did their supervisors. Furthermore, harassers frequently bothered more than just one person at work. The Merit Systems study concluded that "some individuals are more likely to harass than others and that sexual harassment is not necessarily normal interaction among men and women on the job, [nor do] all men and women engage in it."

While most victims are females, males are also subject to sexual harassment. The Merit Systems study found that in a 2-year period, 42% of the female and 15% of the male employees had been sexually harassed. It was not clear, however, if the men defined sexual harassment in the same way as the women did.

In the military, sexual harassment, especially of women, is rampant. At the 1991 naval Tailhook convention, a gauntlet of drunk officers lined a corridor while several dozen men hurled women down the hallway. There they were groped, grabbed, pawed, and drenched in alcohol. After it was over, a captain delivered the women to the elevator, saying, "It's been a pleasure, ladies" (Salholz, 1992).

The Tailhook scandal was just the tip of the iceberg. In 1990, the Pentagon conducted its first major study of sexual harassment. It was found that 64% of the women in the military had been sexually harassed (Schmitt, 1990). This is a significantly higher rate than found in civilian life. (Among civilians, 30–40% of women typically report sexual harassment.) Seventy-one percent of the military women who reported incidents indicated they had experienced three or more forms of harassment. These included offensive teasing or jokes, looks, gestures, touching, cornering, pressure for sex, or attempted or completed sexual assault or rape. Seventeen percent of the men reported sexual harassment from men and women. (There was no breakdown of harassment by gender of the harassers, however.) The power differentials and the expectation of obedience within the military provide fertile ground for sexual harassment (Niebhuhr & Boyles, 1991).

Sexual harassment can have a variety of consequences. One study of the workplace found that about 9% of the women and 1% of the men quit their jobs because of harassment; almost 7% of the women and 2% of the men were dismissed from their jobs as part of the harassment (Gutek, 1985). Victims often report depression, anxiety, shame, humiliation, and anger (Paludi, 1990).

ANTI-GAY/LESBIAN HARASSMENT, PREJUDICE, AND DISCRIMINATION

Americans feel profoundly ambivalent about gay men and lesbians. A large-scale survey conducted by *The New York Times* in 1993 found that 55% believed sexual behavior between adult gay men or lesbians is morally wrong (Schmalz, 1993). At the same time, 78% believed gay men and lesbians should have equal job opportunities. Forty-three percent supported gay men and lesbians in the military, while an equal number opposed it. And 42% believed laws should be passed to guarantee equal rights for gay men and lesbians. (While whites and African Americans more or less agreed on other issues, regarding equal rights protection, 53% of African Americans believed legal protection was necessary, whereas 40% of whites so believed.)

Researchers have identified two forms of discrimination or bias against gay men and lesbians: heterosexual bias and anti-gay prejudice. We discuss these below.

Heterosexual Bias

Heterosexual bias, also known as **heterosexism,** is the tendency to see the world in heterosexual terms and to ignore or devalue homosexuality (Herek, Kimmel, Amaro, & Melton, 1991; Rich, 1983). Heterosexual bias may take numerous forms, including ignoring, segregating, and submerging. Examples of this type of bias include the following:

- *Ignoring the existence of lesbians and gay men.* Discussions of various aspects of human sexuality may ignore gay men and lesbians, assuming that such individuals do not exist, are not significant, or are not worthy of inclusion. Without such inclusion, discussions of human sexuality are really discussions of *heterosexual* sexuality.

- *Segregating lesbians and gay men from heterosexuals.* Where sexual orientation is irrelevant, separating gay men and lesbians from others is a form of segregation, as in military proposals to provide separate housing.

- *Submerging gay men and lesbians into a larger category.* Sometimes it is appropriate to make sexual orientation a category in data analysis, as in studies of adolescent suicide rates. If orientation is not included, findings may be distorted (Herek et al., 1991).

Anti-Gay Prejudice

Anti-gay prejudice is a strong dislike, fear, or hatred of gay men and lesbians because of their homosexuality. *Homophobia* is an irrational or phobic fear of gay men and lesbians. Not all anti-gay feelings are phobic in the clinical sense of being excessive and irrational. They may be unreasonable or biased. (They may be, however, within the norms of a biased culture.) Because prejudice may not be clinically phobic, "homophobia" is being increasingly replaced by the nonclinical phrase "anti-gay prejudice" (Haaga, 1991).

As a belief system, anti-gay prejudice justifies discrimination based on sexual orientation. In his classic work on prejudice, Gordon Allport (1958) states that social prejudice is acted out in three stages: offensive language, discrimination, and violence. Gay men and lesbians experience each stage. They are called "faggot," "dyke," "queer," and "homo." They are discriminated against in terms of housing, employment opportunities, adoption, parental rights, family acceptance, and so on. And they are the victims of violence, known as **gay-bashing** or **queer-bashing.** Among college students, anti-gay prejudice often extends to those heterosexuals who voluntarily choose to room with a lesbian or gay man. They are assumed to have "homosexual tendencies" and to have many of the negative stereotypical traits of gay men and lesbians, such as poor mental health (Sigelman et al., 1991).

Effects on Heterosexuals Anti-gay prejudice adversely affects heterosexuals as well. First, it creates fear and hatred, negative emotions that cause distress and anxiety. Second, it alienates them from their gay family members, friends, neighbors, or co-workers (Holtzen & Agresti, 1990). Third, it limits their range of behaviors and feelings, such as hugging or being emotionally intimate with same-sex friends, for fear that such intimacy may be "homosexual" (Britton, 1990). Heterosexuals may also restrict displays of affection with their same-sex friends, for fear it could be misinterpreted and lead to violence (Garnets et al., 1990). Fourth, it may lead to exaggerated displays of masculinity to prove that one is not gay, that is, effeminate (Mosher & Tompkins, 1988).

Antidiscrimination Laws Gay men and lesbians have been seeking legislation to protect themselves from discrimination based on sexual orientation. Such legislation guarantees lesbians and gay men equal protection under the law; it is not affirmative action or quota programs, as opponents often maintain. Public opinion supports equal employment opportunities for gay men and lesbians. Over half the respondents in a representative nationwide poll viewed homosexuality as no threat to the family. Twenty-one states and 130 municipalities offer some form of legal protection against discrimination (Turque, 1992).

The movement toward antidiscrimination laws has helped propel a conservative reaction. "Radical homosexuals are on the march," Rev. Louis Sheldon writes. "In the war for the hearts and minds of America, this will be a crucial battle" (Ewell, 1993). Columnist Patrick Buchanan contends that offering protection from discrimination based on sexual orientation is a restraint on freedom. He writes (Buchanan, 1993):

> The gay rights movement is not about expanding freedom, it is about circumscribing freedom. What, after all, does the gay rights agenda demand of those who believe homosexuality is unnatural and morally wrong? It demands that any employer, landlord, or homeseller who acts on his belief be exposed, prosecuted, punished, branded a bigot.

In 1992, Colorado passed a referendum overturning local laws prohibiting discrimination against gay men and lesbians. The Colorado Supreme Court, however, placed an injunction against its enforcement because it was unconstitutional. Gay rights legislation will be a battlefield throughout the 1990s.

Violence Against Gay Men and Lesbians Violence against gay men and lesbians has a long history. At times, such violence has been sanctioned by religion. During the Renaissance, the Inquisition burned "sodomites." In the sixteenth century, England's King Henry VIII made sodomy punishable by death. In our own times, homosexuals were among the first victims of the Nazis, who killed 50,000 in concentration camps. Because of worldwide violence and persecution against lesbians and gay men, the Netherlands, Germany, and Canada in 1992 granted asylum to men and women based on their homosexuality (Farnsworth, 1992).

Today, gay men and lesbians continue to be the targets of violence. Over 90% have been subjected to anti-gay verbal abuse or threats. Almost one-quarter reported they had been physically attacked (Herek, 1989).

During the Middle Ages, gay men (called sodomites) were burned at the stake as heretics (above). In Germany in 1933, the Nazis burned Magnus Hirschfeld's library and forced him to flee the country (above, right). Gay men and lesbians were among the first Germans the Nazis forced into concentration camps, where over 50,000 people were killed. Today, violence against gay men and lesbians, known as gay-bashing, continues (right). The pink triangle recalls the symbol the Nazis required lesbians and gay men to wear, just as they required Jews to wear the star of David.

Personal Sources of Anti-Gay Prejudice Anti-gay prejudice in people may be derived from several sources (Marmor, 1980): (1) a deeply rooted insecurity concerning a person's own sexuality and gender identity, (2) a strong fundamentalist religious orientation, and (3) simple ignorance concerning homosexuality. A review of empirical studies on attitudes toward gay men and lesbians found that people with negative attitudes differ from those with more favorable attitudes in several ways (Herek, 1984). Those with negative attitudes tend to be:

- Less likely to have had personal contact with gay men or lesbians.
- Less likely to have engaged in same-sex behaviors.
- More likely to perceive their peers as having negative attitudes toward homosexuality.
- More likely to reside in the Midwest, the South, small towns, or rural areas where negative attitudes toward homosexuality are the norm.
- More likely to be older and less educated.
- More likely to be religious, attend church regularly, and subscribe to a conservative religious ideology.
- More likely to be nonpermissive about sexuality or to manifest more guilt or negative attitudes about sexuality.
- More likely to manifest high levels of authoritarianism and related personality characteristics.

The literature also indicates fairly consistent gender differences in attitudes toward lesbians and gay men (Herek, 1984). Heterosexuals tend to have more negative attitudes toward gays of their own sex than of the other sex. Heterosexual men tend to be less tolerant than heterosexual women.

As a result of anti-gay prejudice, gay men and lesbians are discriminated against in employment, insurance, housing, and parental rights. They face imprisonment for engaging in oral and anal sex, for which heterosexuals are seldom prosecuted. Medical and public-health efforts against HIV/AIDS were inhibited initially because AIDS was perceived as "the gay plague" and was considered "punishment" against gay men for their "unnatural" sexual practices (Altman, 1985). The fear of HIV/AIDS has contributed to increased anti-gay prejudice among some heterosexuals (Lewes, 1992). Anti-gay prejudice influences parental reactions to their gay and lesbian children, often leading to estrangement (Holtzen & Agresti, 1990). And in some cases, a gay man's advances toward a homophobic male have led to manslaughter. Although such sexual advances have been used as grounds for acquittal, in California they are considered insufficient provocation (Mison, 1992). (The bias in such a defense can be seen if one imagines a woman being allowed to kill a man for making an advance.)

Institutional Sources of Anti-Gay Prejudice Institutions are enduring social structures, such as family, religion, education, law, and government, built around distinct social values. Much anti-gay prejudice is conveyed through some of our institutions, especially conservative religious groups and the military.

Religion and Homosexuality Christianity and Judaism have been particularly important in reinforcing negative views of homosexuality. According to researcher Bruce Voeller (1980): "Among societal institutions, the church is the primal source of intolerance of homosexuality. . . . This has created particularly severe problems for gays and lesbians who are religious." The spectrum of religious opinion runs from full equality for lesbians and gay men among Quakers and other groups that value tolerance to total rejection in Catholic and many fundamentalist teachings. Today, a vigorous debate continues in all churches and among religious Jews about the nature and position of homosexuality in Christianity and Judaism (Nugent & Gramick, 1989). (For a discussion of major studies and policy statements in Christian denominations, see Nugent & Gramick, 1989; for Judaism, see Kahn, 1989).

In considering homosexuality from a religious perspective, individuals have two important tasks to undertake. The first is to separate core religious beliefs from peripheral ones. Consider the two biblical passages below. Which message is central in Christianity, and which is secondary?

> You shall love your neighbor as yourself. (Matthew 22:39)

> If a man lies with another man as he lies with a woman, both of them have committed an abomination and they shall be put to death. (Leviticus 20:13)

They shall come up with acceptance to my altar.

Isaiah 60:7

If Christianity's central message is love, it is argued, then "love's justice requires a single standard for homosexual and heterosexual people alike" (Nugent & Gramick, 1989). The single standard argument is reinforced by the assertion that homosexuality is "part of the divine plan of creation, that homosexual people are present as a sign of the rich diversity of creation, and that homosexual expression is as natural and good in every way as heterosexuality" (Nugent & Gramick, 1989). If there is a single standard (Nugent & Gramick, 1989):

> homosexual expressions are neutral in themselves; they become moral or immoral to the extent that they are expressive of self-giving love, capable of grounding friendship and fostering mutuality, or generating friendship that enables the partners to grow and become more fully human.

The second task is to separate religious beliefs from prejudice. Prejudice can masquerade as belief. During the nineteenth century, for example, the Bible was quoted extensively to justify slavery (Wood, 1990). As John Boswell (1980) writes:

> Religious beliefs may cloak or incorporate intolerance, especially among adherents of revealed religions which specifically reject rationality as an ultimate criterion of judgment. . . . But careful analysis can almost always differentiate between conscientious application of religious ethics and the use of religious precepts as justification for personal animosity or prejudice. If religious strictures are used to justify oppression by people who regularly disregard precepts of equal gravity from the same moral code, or if prohibitions which restrain a disliked minority are upheld in their most literal sense as absolutely inviolable while comparable precepts affecting the majority are relaxed or reinterpreted, one must suspect something other than religious belief as the motivating cause of the oppression.

Consider the two passages on the following page on premarital virginity and extramarital sex from Deuteronomy:

[If] the tokens of virginity were not found in the young woman, then they shall bring out the young woman to the door of her father's house, and the men of her city shall stone her to death. (Deuteronomy 22:20–21)

If a man is found lying with the wife of another man, both of them shall die. (Deuteronomy 22:22)

Although the penalties in these passages are as severe as those found against homosexuals in Leviticus, many Americans are far more tolerant of premarital and extramarital sex than they are of homosexuality.

Boswell points out that the Bible consistently condemns hypocrisy, the pursuit of wealth, adultery, and prostitution, but Western culture does not consider hypocrites, greedy people, adulterers, or prostitutes unnatural, nor does it persecute them. As Boswell (1980) writes, "Biblical strictures have been employed with great selectivity by all Christian states, and in a historical context *what* determines the selection is clearly the crucial issue."

Despite hostility, religious lesbians and gay men have formed their own churches and synagogues, such as the Metropolitan Community Church. Denominational caucuses, including the Catholic group Dignity, Affirmation, Lutherans Concerned, and Presbyterians for Lesbian and Gay Concerns, have emerged to advocate tolerance within the churches.

As Robert Nugent and Jeannine Gramick (1989) observe, for Christianity, homosexuality is like "a 'fishbone' caught in the church's throat that the church can neither eject nor swallow entirely."

The Military and Homosexuality   Gay men serve without restriction in the military in Canada, Israel, Japan, Sweden, and several other European countries. When Canada ended its military ban on gays in 1992, there was little opposition or trouble. In 1993, by contrast, when President Clinton announced his intention to end discrimination against gay men and lesbians in the U.S. military, a firestorm of protest ensued. Many military men opposed it. "We're all crammed together in the showers, and I don't want to worry that some gay guy is staring at me," complained one man. Another asked, "Now how am I going to feel if I walk into a dormitory and see pictures on the wall from *Playgirl* magazine?" Still another said, "I couldn't sleep at night. I'd be worried that some homosexual is going to sneak over and make a pass at me" (Applebome, 1993).

Some women find it ironic that many military men are fearful of being sexually harassed by gay men. "Welcome to the club, boys" was one woman's response to male anxiety. Columnist Joanne Jacobs (1993) asks, "Why so much concern for the comfort level of men, who fear they might be looked at with lust by another man, and so little concern for the actual victims of heterosexual predators?"

What accounts for the military's strong reaction to gay men *openly* serving in the armed forces? Writer Randy Shilts (1993) believes the official prohibition on gay men in the military has served to reinforce what he calls "the ideology of masculinity." During basic training, male recruits are taunted with both homophobic ("Don't be a fag") and sexist ("Don't be a pussy") epithets. The primary definition of being a man is being *not* gay and *not* female. The military's underlying logic, asserts Shilts, has been that gays must be banned so that the uniform is proof of heterosexuality. Although gay men and lesbians have served honorably for generations, anti-gay reg-

When I was in the military they gave me a medal for killing two men—and a discharge for loving one.

Leonard Matlovich

If we could have a city or army composed of lovers and their favorites (as in Thebes) . . . such men as these, when fighting side by side, one might almost consider able to make a small band victorious over all the world. For a man in love would surely choose to have all the rest rather than his favorite see him abandoning his post or flinging away his arms. He would sooner die many deaths.

Plato

ulations "allow[ed] the military to say they ejected all gays." The regulations, he says, had "little to do with military goals and everything to do with a culture enforcing millennia-old taboos." The military's new 1993 policy of "Don't ask, don't tell, don't pursue" permits gay men and lesbians to serve in the military as long as they do not reveal their homosexuality, and preserves the myth that the military is a fortress of masculinity and heterosexuality.

In female branches of the military, "lesbian baiting," the accusation of being lesbian, has been a powerful undercurrent since World War II, when women began serving in large numbers. Because the military is fundamentally a male institution, women's authority and careers have been undermined sharply by such accusations. As Shilts (1993) writes:

> Sexual harassment ran rampant throughout the military in the 1980s, to an extent barely imaginable to the civilian world. . . . All women suffered from the discrimination and harassment meted out by confused and insecure men, but no group suffered as much as lesbians, because no group so embodied male fears.

A disproportionate number of those discharged because of homosexuality are women. In 1992, 708 military personnel were discharged for being gay. Of these, 23% were women, despite the fact that they make up only 11.5% of the force (Wood, 1993). Furthermore, some heterosexual women in the military report being accused of being lesbian if they don't respond to male approaches. Because of military prohibitions against homosexuality, such lesbian baiting places additional pressure on women (Shilts, 1993).

Ending Anti-Gay Prejudice

While legislation to prohibit discrimination is important for ending prejudice, education and positive social interactions are also important vehicles for change. Two researchers studied the impact of including a unit on homosexuality in their human sexuality course (Serdahely & Ziemba, 1984). They found that students who, at the beginning of the course, scored above the class mean on anti-gay attitudes, by the end had a significant decrease in their scores. Other researchers report increased tolerance following human sexuality courses (Stevenson, 1990). Gregory Herek (1984) suggests that those holding negative attitudes based on biblical teachings be exposed to other biblical interpretations of homosexuality (such as Hasbany, 1990). Herek also suggests that negative attitudes about homosexuality may be reduced by arranging positive interactions between heterosexuals and gay men and lesbians. These interactions should be in settings of equal status, common goals, cooperation, and a moderate degree of intimacy. Such interactions may occur when family members or close friends come out. Other interactions should emphasize common group membership (such as religious, social, ethnic, or political) on a one-to-one basis (Herek, 1984). Religious volunteers working with people with HIV or AIDS often decrease their prejudice as they give care and comfort (Kayal, 1992).

SEXUAL AGGRESSION

In recent years, we have increasingly expanded our knowledge about sexually aggressive acts and their consequences. We have expanded our focus beyond stranger rape and examined the consequences of sexually aggressive acts on survivors. Earlier, researchers had focused primarily on **rape,** penile-vaginal penetration performed against a *woman's* will through the use or threat of force. They assumed rape was committed by strangers for the purpose of sexual gratification. In their work, researchers generally examined the sexual psychopathology of male offenders and the characteristics of women that "precipitated" rapes, such as acting docile, living alone, and dressing in a certain way (White & Farmer, 1992).

In the 1970s, feminists challenged the belief that rape was an act of sexual deviance. Instead, they believed that rape was an act of violence and aggression against women. The principal motive was power, not sex (Brownmiller, 1975). As a result of feminist influence, research focus shifted. Today, much research focuses on cultural attitudes and myths that may encourage rape (Donat & D'Emilio, 1992). In the 1980s, rape research broadened to include date rape and marital rape.

Contemporary research now views rape as a category of sexual aggression. **Sexual aggression** refers to sexual activity, including petting, oral-genital sex, anal intercourse, and sexual intercourse, performed against a person's will through the use of force, argument, pressure, alcohol or drugs, or authority (Cate & Lloyd, 1992; Muehlenhard, Powch, Phelps, & Giusti, 1992). Unlike rape, which by definition excludes men as victims, sexual aggression includes both women *and* men as victims. It also includes gay men and lesbians, who have been excluded from such research because of rape's heterosexual definition (Muehlenhard et al., 1992). **Sexual coercion** is a broader term than rape or sexual aggression. It includes arguing, pleading, and cajoling, as well as force and the threat of force.

In studying sexual aggression, it is important to keep in mind the type of sexual activity that is being discussed. Not long ago, for example, the news media reported a Stanford University survey that found a high incidence of rape on campus. The report caused considerable alarm among students. But the survey did not study rape; it studied sexual coercion. The study, in fact, did not even use the word "rape" (Greensite, 1991). Such confusion of terms can be seriously misleading.

Being forced is poison for the soul.
Ludwig Borne (1786–1837)

Rape

In rape, sex is a means of achieving power or releasing anger and hatred. Rape *forces* its victim into an intimate physical relationship with the rapist against her or his will. The victim does not experience pleasure; she or he experiences terror. In most cases, the victim is a woman; sometimes the victim is a man. In almost every case, however, the assailant is a man. The weapon in rape is the penis (which may be supplemented by a knife or a gun); the penis is used to attack, subordinate, and humiliate the victim.

Rape is not only an act but also a threat. As small girls, women are warned against taking candy from strangers, walking alone down dark streets, and leaving doors and windows unlocked. Men may fear assault, but women fear assault *and* rape. As a result, many women live with the possibility of being raped as a part of their consciousness. Rape, and the fear of rape, are facts of life for women; this is not true for men.

Incidence As many as 683,000 adult women were raped in 1990, according to a report sponsored by the Department of Health and Human Services (National Victim Center, 1992). In a telephone survey of 4008 women, the National Victim Center found that 0.7% had been forcibly raped in the previous year. Of those who were raped, only 22% reported they were raped by strangers. But 29% were raped by acquaintances, 16% by a relative not in the immediate family, 11% by a father or stepfather, 9% by a boyfriend or ex-boyfriend, and 9% by a husband or ex-husband (Figure 18.1).

The researchers did not interview female children or adolescents; nor did they include males. If these groups had been included, the estimated number of rapes might have doubled. Altogether, the survey estimated that 12.1 million women had been raped at least once; 61% were raped as adolescents.

Using a different methodology, the National Crime Survey (NCS), by contrast, estimated there were 130,236 rapes in 1990 and 207,610 in 1991 (Johnston, 1992). The NCS has been repeatedly criticized for seriously underestimating rapes (Johnston, 1992; Koss, 1992). Rape researcher Mary Koss believes the National Victim Center study more accurately reflects the actual number of rapes.

While earlier estimates of rape suggested that African American women were more likely to be sexually assaulted than white women, newer estimates do not find significant ethnic differences (Wyatt, 1992). A recent community study comparing Latino and Anglo rape rates found a significantly lower incidence among Latinos. The researchers speculate that the lower rate may be attributed to *machismo,* which requires men to be protective of women (Sorenson & Siegal, 1992). The lower rate, however, may also be attributed to Latinas' greater reluctance to report rape because of the strong emphasis on female virginity and purity in Latino culture.

There are several reasons why there are often discrepancies in rape estimates (George, Winfield, & Blazer, 1992; Koss, 1992; White & Farmer, 1992). First, definitions of rape may vary from one survey to another. Second, different sample sizes and methodologies may account for different estimates. Third, rape survivors are often reluctant to disclose their assault to interviewers. They fear being blamed or denigrated. As a result, figures may underestimate the actual number of rapes.

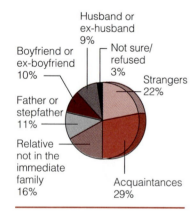

FIGURE 18.1 Types of Rape. (SOURCE: Data from National Victim Center, 1992.)

Sexual assault peer educators at Brown University dramatize date rape to make students aware of its dynamics.

Forms of Rape

Rapists may be acquaintances, dates, husbands, fathers or other family members, as well as strangers.

Date Rape **Date rape,** sexual intercourse with a dating partner that occurs against his/her will with force or the threat of force, is the most common form of rape. Date rape is also known as **acquaintance rape.** (For an overview of current research, see Benson, Charlton, & Goodhart, 1992, and Berkowitz, 1992).

Date rapes are usually not planned. Two researchers (Bechhofer & Parrot, 1991) describe a typical date rape:

> He plans the evening with the intent of sex, but if the date does not progress as planned and his date does not comply, he becomes angry and takes what he feels is his right—sex. Afterward, the victim feels raped while the assailant believes that he has done nothing wrong. He may even ask the woman out on another date.

Alcohol and/or drugs are often involved. One study found that 79% of women who had been date raped had been drinking or taking drugs prior to the rape. Seventy-one percent said their assailant had been drinking or taking drugs (Copenhaver & Grauerholz, 1991). There are often high levels of alcohol and drug use among middle school and high school students who have unwanted sex (Rapkin & Rapkin, 1991).

Incidence Lifetime experience of date rape ranges from 15%–28% for women, according to various studies. If the definition is expanded to include attempted intercourse as a result of verbal pressure or the misuse of authority, then women's lifetime incidence increases significantly. When all types of unwanted sexual activity are included, ranging from kissing to sexual

The effect of women's greater fear of crime is to produce social constraints upon them; women not heeding those constraints may be punished not only by direct victimization, but also by being blamed for their own victimization.

Stephanie Riger

SEXUAL AGGRESSION   731

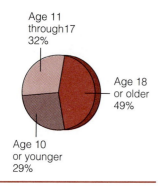

Age 11 through 17
32%

Age 18 or older
49%

Age 10 or younger
29%

FIGURE 18.2 Ages of Rape Victims. (SOURCE: Data from National Victim Center, 1992.)

intercourse, 25–50% of college women report sexual aggression in dating (Cate & Lloyd, 1992). There is also considerable sexual coercion in gay male relationships. Coercion also exists in lesbian relationships, though less than in gay male and heterosexual ones (Waterman, Dawson, & Bologna, 1989).

In a large-scale study on sexual aggression, Koss (1988) surveyed over 6100 students in 32 colleges. Her findings indicated the following:

- 54% of the women surveyed had been sexually victimized in some form; 15% had been raped.

- 25% of the women surveyed had been the victims of rape or attempted rape; 84% knew their assailants.

- 47% of the rapes were by first dates, casual dates, or romantic acquaintances.

- 25% of the men had perpetuated sexual aggression, 37% had attempted rape, and 4% had actually committed rape.

- 75% of the raped women did not identify their experiences as rapes.

A study of 140 sorority women found that a high proportion of them had been sexually coerced or raped (Copenhaver & Grauerholz, 1991). Almost half experienced some form of sexual coercion; 24% experienced attempted rape, and 17% completed rape. Over half the incidents occurred within the context of fraternal life. Half the rapes occurred within a fraternity house. The researchers concluded that fraternities tolerate, perhaps even encourage, sexual coercion.

Physical violence often goes hand in hand with sexual aggression. In a study of acquaintance rape victims, 75% of the women sustained bruises, cuts, black eyes, and internal injuries; some had been knocked unconscious (Belknap, 1989).

When No Is No   There is considerable confusion and argument about consent. As we saw in Chapter 9, much sexual communication is done nonverbally and ambiguously. Charlene Muehlenhard and colleagues (1992) note:

> Most sexual scripts do not involve verbal consent. One such script involves two people who are overcome with passion. Another such script involves a male seducing a hesitant female, who, according to the sexual double standard, must not acknowledge her desire for sex lest she be labeled "loose" or "easy." Neither of these scripts involves explicit verbal consent from both persons.

The fact that we don't usually give verbal consent for sex indicates the significance of nonverbal clues. Nonverbal communication is imprecise. It can be misinterpreted easily if not reinforced verbally. For example, men frequently mistake a woman's friendliness for sexual interest (Johnson et al., 1991; Stockdale, 1993). They often misinterpret a woman's cuddling, kissing, and fondling as interest in engaging in sexual intercourse (Muehlenhard, 1988; Muehlenhard & Linton, 1987). A woman needs to verbally make her boundaries clear, and men need to avoid misinterpreting clues.

Our sexual scripts often assume "yes" unless a "no" is directly stated (Muehlenhard et al., 1992). This makes individuals "fair game" unless a person explicitly says "no." The assumption of consent puts women at a disadvantage. Because men traditionally initiate sex, a man can initiate sex whenever he desires without the woman explicitly consenting. A woman's withdrawal can be considered "insincere" because consent is always assumed. Such thinking reinforces a common sexual script in which men initiate and women refuse so as not to appear "promiscuous." In this script, the man continues believing that her refusal is "token." Some common reasons for offering "token" refusals include not wanting to appear "loose," unsureness of how the partner feels, inappropriate surroundings, and game playing (Muehlenhard & Hollabaugh, 1989; Muehlenhard & McCoy, 1991). One study found that almost 40% of the women had offered a "token" no at least once (Muehlenhard & Hollabaugh, 1989). Because some women sometimes say "no" when they mean "coax me," male-female communication may be especially unclear regarding consent (Muehlenhard & Cook, 1991). Furthermore, men are more likely than women to think of male-female relationships as a "battle of the sexes" (Reilly et al., 1992). Because relationships are conflictual, refusals are to be expected as part of the battle. A man, however, may feel he "should" persist since his role is to conquer, even if he's not interested in sex (Muehlenhard & Schrag, 1991; Muehlenhard & McCoy, 1991). (For a discussion of rape myths, see Perspective 2.)

Profile A review of the current literature (Cate & Lloyd, 1992) found that sexually coercive men, in contrast to noncoercive ones, tend to:

- Hold traditional beliefs about women and women's roles.
- Display hostility toward women.
- Believe in rape-supportive myths.
- Accept general physical violence.
- Express anger and dominance sexually.
- Report high levels of sexual activity.
- Use exploitative techniques.

Women involved in sexually coercive dating relationships do not differ significantly from those in noncoercive relationships (Cate & Lloyd, 1992). They have more or less the same levels of self-esteem, assertiveness, feminist ideology, and belief in rape-supportive myths. A significant factor that researchers are now investigating is the possible link with childhood sexual abuse (Koss & Dinero, 1989; Lundberg-Love & Geffner, 1989). It may be that women who were abused in childhood discount signs of aggression because they fear they may be overreacting. As the aggression proceeds, such women may become paralyzed because the situations reenact their original abuse situation (Lundberg-Love & Geffner, 1989).

Stranger Rape The majority of rapes *reported* to the police are stranger rapes. A typical stranger rape scenario does not necessarily involve an unknown assailant hiding in the bushes or a stairwell on a dark night. Rather, it is likely to involve a chance meeting with a man at school, on the street, at a bus stop, at the beach or park, in a restaurant, bar, music club, or other such location. The man often seems friendly and congenial. The woman relaxes her guard because the man seems nice, even protective.

If a man seizes a betrothed virgin in the city and lies with her, then you shall bring them both out to the gate of the city, and you shall stone them to death, the young woman because she did not cry for help, though others could have heard her, and the man because he violated his neighbor's wife.

Deuteronomy 22:23–24

If a man seizes a virgin who is not betrothed and lies with her and they are discovered, then the man shall give the young woman's father 50 silver shekels and he shall have her as his wife because he has violated her.

Deuteronomy 22:28–29

Perspective 2

RAPE MYTHS

Our society has a number of myths about rape, which serve to encourage rather than discourage rape (Burt, 1980). Such myths blame women for their own rapes as if they somehow "deserved" them or were responsible for them. In fact, in a large national sample, two-thirds of the women who were raped worried they might be blamed for their assaults (National Victim Center, 1992).

According to Martha Burt (1980), belief in rape myths is part of a larger belief structure that includes gender-role stereotypes, sexual conservatism, acceptance of interpersonal violence, and acceptance of a "battle of the sexes" philosophy of male-female relationships. Men are more likely than women to believe rape myths (Brady et al., 1991; Reilly et al., 1992; Quakenbush, 1991). A recent survey found that men who tended to be tolerant of rape myths, who believed that relationships were adversarial, and who stated they would rape if they would not be detected, were more likely than other men to have victimized women sexually (Reilly et al., 1992). Sandra Byers and Raymond Eno (1991) found that acceptance of rape-supportive myths among college men was associated with the use of physical force, verbal coercion, and belief in "uncontrollable physical arousal." In contrasting age groups, another study found that high school boys were more likely than college men to accept rape myths (Blumberg & Lester, 1991).

Myth #1: Women Want to Be Raped

It is popularly believed that women have an unconscious wish to be raped (Burt, 1980). The fact that many women have rape fantasies is cited as proof. But as Molly Haskell (1976) points out:

> The world of difference between "rape fantasy" and rape can be expressed in one word: control. The point of a fantasy is that a woman . . . orders the reality within it, ordains its terms, and censors it according to her needs; the point of rape is that a woman is violated against her will.

This myth supports the misconception that a woman enjoys being raped because she sexually "surrenders." The myth perpetuates the belief that rape is a sexual act rather than a violent one.

Myth #2: Women Ask for It

Many people believe that women "ask for it" by their behavior. One-quarter of the men believed this, according to one study (Holcomb, Holcomb, Sondag, & Williams, 1991). In another study, a woman going home with a man on their first date suggested to over half the respondents that she was inviting sex (Burt, 1980). Almost half believed that a woman wearing a short skirt or no bra was asking to be raped. In fact, in a notorious 1989 Florida rape case, the foreman of the jury told a woman who was raped that she "asked for it" because she was wearing a white lace miniskirt without underwear when she was assaulted. The jury acquitted the man. He was subsequently tried for raping another woman in Georgia and sentenced to life imprisonment. Despite some attempts to reform rape laws, women continue to bear the brunt in proving their accusations (Goldberg-Ambrose, 1992).

He casually maneuvers her to an isolated place—an alley, park, apartment, or house—where the rape occurs.

A study of women age 57–82 who were raped found that they were more likely to have been raped by strangers and to have been raped in their homes than younger rape victims (Muram, Miller, & Cutler, 1992). Stranger rapes

Myth #3: Women Are Only Raped by Strangers

Women are warned to avoid or distrust strangers as a means of avoiding rape; such advice, however, isolates them from normal social interactions. Furthermore, studies indicate that half or more of all rapes are committed by nonstrangers such as acquaintances, friends, dates, husbands, or relatives (Russell, 1984).

Myth #4: Women Could Really Avoid Rape If They Wanted

This myth reinforces the stereotype that women "really" want to be raped or that they should curtail their movements. In one study, 25% of male students believed this myth (Holcomb et al., 1991). Women are often warned not to be out after dark alone, but few of the rapes in one study could have been avoided this way (Groth, 1979). Furthermore, a substantial number of rapes take place in the home or nearby, when a woman is going about her regular routine, according to one study of 320 victims of rape and attempted rape (McIntyre, 1980). Women are also approached at work, on their way to or from work, at church, or kidnapped from shopping centers or parking lots at midday. Restricting women's activities does not seem to have an appreciable impact on rape. (In reaction to a number of rapes in Israel some time ago, lawmakers proposed a 10:00 P.M. curfew for women. Golda Meier, then prime minister, replied that it would make more sense to impose the curfew on men, since they were the rapists. The proposal was promptly dropped.)

Myth #5: Women Cry Rape for Revenge

This myth suggests that women who are left by men accuse them of rape as a means of revenge. About 25% of the men in one study believed this (Holcomb et al., 1991). FBI crime statistics show that only about 2% of rape reports are false; this rate is lower than the rate for most other crimes. False reporting is unlikely because of the many obstacles that women face before an assailant is brought to trial and convicted.

Myth #6: Rapists Are Crazy or Psychotic

Very few men who rape are clinically psychotic. The vast majority are psychologically indistinguishable from other men, except that rapists appear to have more difficulty handling hostile feelings (Rodabaugh & Austin, 1981). In fact, studies on date rape find little psychological difference between rapists and nonrapists; they differ primarily in such ways as greater hostility toward women, acceptance of traditional gender roles, and greater willingness to use force (Cate & Lloyd, 1992).

Myth #7: Most Rapists Are Black Men

Most rapists and their victims are members of the same race or ethnic group. But the black rapist myth reinforces racism by calling up the sexual stereotype of the "oversexed" black man. It conjures images of African American men preying on white women. Following the Civil War, the specter of black men ravishing southern white women became the rationale for lynchings, which were used to instill terror in the black community (D'Emilio & Freeman, 1988). There is no evidence to suggest that black rapists prefer white women. Rapists appear to attack women on the basis of opportunity, not ethnicity (South & Felson, 1990).

are more likely to involve guns or knives than date rapes. Almost one-third of stranger rapes involve weapons (Harlow, 1991). A stranger rape is more likely to be taken seriously by the police because it reflects the rape stereotype better than date or marital rape (Russell, 1990). (For a discussion of preventing sexual assault, see Perspective 3.)

Perspective 3

PREVENTING SEXUAL ASSAULT

There are no guaranteed ways to prevent sexual assault or coercion. Each situation, assailant, and targeted woman or man is different (Fischhoff, 1992). But rape education courses may be effective in reducing the rape myths that provide support for sexual aggression (Fonow, Richardson, & Wemmerus, 1992).

To reduce the risk of date rape, consider these guidelines:

- When dating someone for the first time, go to a public place, such as a restaurant, movie, or sports event.

- Share expenses. A common scenario is a date expecting you to exchange sex for his or her paying for dinner, the movie, drinks, and so on (Muehlenhard & Schrag, 1991; Muehlenhard et al., 1991).

- Avoid using drugs or alcohol if you do not want to be sexual with your date. Such use is associated with date rape (Abbey, 1991).

- Avoid ambiguous verbal or nonverbal behavior. Make sure your verbal and nonverbal messages are identical. If you only want to cuddle or kiss, for example, tell your partner that those are your limits. Tell him or her that if you say no, you mean no. If necessary, reinforce your statement emphatically, both verbally and physically (pushing him or her away) (Muehlenhard & Linton, 1987).

To reduce the risk of stranger rape, consider the guidelines below. But try to avoid becoming paranoid; use reasonable judgment. Do not let fear control your life.

- Do not identify yourself as a person living alone, especially if you are a woman. Use initials on the mailbox and in the telephone directory.

- Don't open your door to strangers; keep your house and car doors locked. Have your keys ready when you unlock your doors. Look in the back seat before getting into your car.

- Avoid dark and isolated areas. Carry a whistle or airhorn. Let people know where you are going.

- If someone approaches you threateningly, turn and run. If you can't run, resist. Studies indicate that resisting an attack by shouting, causing a scene, or fighting back can deter the assailant. Fighting and screaming may reduce the level of the abuse without increasing the level of physical injury. Most women who are injured during a rape appear to have been injured *prior* to resisting (Ullman & Knight, 1992).

- Take self-defense training. It will raise your level of confidence and your fighting abilities. It may scare off the assailant or give you the opportunity to escape (Cummings, 1992). Many women take self-defense training following sexual aggression to reaffirm their sense of control.

There may be special needs for women in some ethnic groups. For African American women, it is impor-

---

Marital Rape Throughout the United States, a husband can be prosecuted for raping his wife, although 26 states limit the conditions, such as requiring extraordinary violence. Only 17 states offer full legal protection to wives (Muehlenhard et al., 1991). Laws against marital rape, however, have not been widely enforced. In the few cases in which husbands have been convicted of marital rape, they were separated and living apart from their wives.

Many people discount rape in marriage as a "marital tiff" that has little

Self-defense classes help raise women's confidence and their ability to protect themselves.

tant that they recognize the efforts of enslaved women, such as Celia, who killed her master as he attempted to rape her, and other black women, past and present, in fighting rape (McLaurin, 1991; Wyatt, 1992). Rape prevention requires acknowledging the discrediting of African American women through the perpetuation of stereotypes, disbelief in their rapes, and the consequent underreporting of rapes (Wyatt, 1992). Asian American women, whose culture encourages reticence and restraint, may need to develop their abilities to make a scene or develop effective strategies consistent with their values (Del Carmen, 1991).

If you are sexually assaulted (or the victim of an attempted assault), report the assault as soon as possible. You are probably not the assailant's first victim. As much as you might want to, do not change clothes or shower. Semen and hair or other materials on your body or clothing may be very important in arresting and convicting a rapist. You may also want to contact a rape crisis center; its staff members are knowledgeable about dealing with the police and the traumatic aftermath of rape. But most importantly, remember that you are not to blame for the rape. Don't blame yourself for doing something "stupid" or not doing something "right." The rapist is the only one to blame.

to do with "real" rape (Finkelhor & Yllo, 1985). When college students were asked to describe marital rape, they created "sanitized" images: "He wants to and she doesn't, so he does anyway." "They are separated but he really loves her, so when he comes back to visit, he forces her because he misses her." The realities are very different.

In Diana Russell's 1982 study on marital rape, 930 randomly selected women in San Francisco were interviewed. Eighty-seven out of the 644 women who had ever been married (about 13%) had been raped by their husbands. Russell found that force was used in 84% of the rapes and the threat of force in 9%. (The remaining victims were asleep, intoxicated, or surprised and not able to resist.) Of the wives who were raped, thirty-one percent reported their rapes as isolated events that occurred only once. But another 31% reported that they had been raped more than 20 times. Other studies of wives who had been raped by their husbands reported that 59–87% were raped multiple times (cited in Russell, 1990).

Marital rape victims experience betrayal, anger, humiliation, and guilt (Finkelhor & Yllo, 1985). One woman described her feelings of betrayal after her husband first raped her:

> I feel if I'd been raped by a stranger, I could have dealt with it a whole lot better. . . . When a stranger does it, he doesn't know me, I don't know him. He's not doing it to me as a person, personally. With your husband it becomes personal. You say, This man knows me. He knows my feelings. He knows me intimately, and then to do this to me—it's such personal abuse.

Following their rape, many wives feel intense anger toward their husbands. A minority feel guilt and blame themselves for not being better wives. Others develop negative self-images and view their lack of sexual desire as a reflection of their own inadequacies rather than as a consequence of abuse.

Gang Rape Gang rape may be perpetrated by strangers or acquaintances. It may be motivated not only by power but also by male-bonding factors (Sanday, 1990). It is a common form of adolescent rape, most often occurring with strangers (Holmes, 1991). Among adults, gang rape disproportionately occurs in tightly knit groups, such as fraternities, athletic teams, or military units. When gang rape takes place on campus, the attackers may often know the woman, who may have been invited to a party or apartment. Alcohol is often involved. In gang rape, the woman is raped by a series of attackers who take turns; the mean number of attackers is five (O'Sullivan, 1991). The assailants demonstrate their masculinity and "share" a sexual experience with their friends. The assault may sometimes last for hours.

A recent study compared 44 college women who experienced gang sexual assault to 44 who were individually assaulted (Gidyez & Koss, 1990). In general, gang sexual assaults were more violent. Their victims offered greater resistance and were more likely to report the attack to the police. Gang assault victims were also more traumatized. As a result, they were more likely to contemplate suicide and seek psychotherapy.

People who would not rape alone may rape in groups for several reasons (O'Sullivan, 1991). Responsibility is diffused in a group; no single individual is to blame. A person may lose his sense of individuality and merge with the group's standards. He might model his behavior on the sexual aggressiveness of the others.

Statutory Rape **Statutory rape** is consensual sexual intercourse with a girl beneath a state's **age of consent,** the age at which a person is legally deemed capable of giving informed consent. It may not matter whether the male is the same age, older, or younger. If a female is younger than a certain age—varying from age 7 in Delaware to age 21 in Kansas—the court ignores her consent. The enforcement of statutory rape laws, however, is generally sporadic, accidental, or arbitrary.

Sexual Assault Against Males   Sexual assault against males may be perpetrated by other men or by women. (For men we use the term "sexual assault" rather than rape because most rape definitions specify vaginal penetration by the penis.) Most sexual assaults on men are by other men. Female assaults on males are significantly less common. While some gay men are sexually assaulted by other gays, we know very little about such assaults; crime statistics are not kept on such victimization (Duncan, 1990). But it is important to note that men who sexually assault other men are not necessarily gay. Because the motive in sexual assaults is power and domination, sexual orientation is often irrelevant (Gagnon, 1977).

Based on police reports, in 1991 about 1 man in 1000 was sexually assaulted; many were forced to perform fellatio or were anally penetrated (U.S. Department of Justice, 1991). A study of Anglo and Latino residents in Los Angeles found that 16% of the men had been sexually assaulted. The highest proportion were college educated, age 18–39 (Sorenson & Siegal, 1992). In the aftermath of an assault, men attempt to restrain their emotions. They are significantly less likely than women to report specific emotional and behavioral reactions to their assault. Instead of saying they feel sad or feel their stomach muscles constricting, they are likely to say only that they are upset; they hesitate going into detail (Sorenson & Siegal, 1992).

Prison Sexual Assault   In 1990, the United States had the second largest prison incarceration rate in the world: 2.9 prisoners per 1000 population. There were over 774,000 men and women incarcerated, mostly men (U.S. Bureau of the Census, 1992). Despite our immense prison population, we know very little about prison sex. What we do know, however, is that male-male prison sex is often devoid of affection. Sexual assault is common, and it is an important means by which domination is established. Most assailants and victims are heterosexual. John Gagnon (1977), one of the few researchers to investigate prison sex, writes:

> Sex occurs, but it is often without choice and in degrading and violent circumstances. . . . It is usually motivated by aggression, violence, and control, and it is often less important in terms of the ejaculation it produces than the way it enhances the dominant partner's masculinity. The ability to dominate and control, to make someone else do what you want is extremely important in male status ranking.

According to Gagnon, some of the men who are coerced drift into same-sex sexual relations because they are afraid. They need the protection of the dominant male. They comply because they fear sexual assault from others.

It is important to note that affectionate relationships do occur in prisons. For both men and women, sex and love with another inmate may become the means by which they resist dehumanization. Once they leave prison, most resume the heterosexual or gay/lesbian style of relationships in which they had previously participated.

Female-Male Sexual Assault   Although uncommon, there are some instances of women sexually assaulting men. Philip Sarrel and William Masters (1982) reported 11 cases in which men were assaulted by women. These include a medical student who was sexually assaulted while the woman threatened him with his scalpel, and a burly truck driver who was blind-folded, tied to a bed, and sexually assaulted by four women. All the victims reported feelings of terror and helplessness.

Although threatened with knives and guns, the men were able to have erections (Sarrel & Masters, 1982). After the assaults, the men suffered rape trauma syndrome similar to that experienced by women (discussed later). They experienced sexual difficulties, depression, and anxiety. Most felt abnormal because they did respond sexually during the assault. Because they were sexually assaulted by women, they doubted their masculinity.

Motivations for Rape

Most stranger rapes and some acquaintance or marital rapes can be characterized as *anger rapes, power rapes,* or *sadistic rapes* (Groth, Burgess, & Holmstrom, 1977). This typology has been very influential, but it is based on interviews with incarcerated stranger rapists. As a result, it may not reflect the motivations of the majority of rapists who are acquaintances, boyfriends, and husbands.

Anger Rapes Anger rapists are physically brutal; the consequences of their extreme violence often require hospitalization of the victim. These rapes account for approximately 40% of stranger rapes (Groth & Birnbaum, 1979). Groth (1979) described anger rapes:

> The assault is characterized by physical brutality. Far more actual force is used . . . than would be necessary if the intent were simply to overpower the victim and achieve sexual penetration. Instead, this type of offender attacks his victim, grabbing her, striking her, knocking her to the ground, beating her, tearing her clothes and raping her. His aim is to hurt and debase his victim, and he expresses contempt for her through abusive and profane language. . . . Often this type of offender forces the victim to submit to or perform additional sexual acts that he may regard as particularly degrading, such as sodomy or fellatio.

Power Rapes Power rapes, representing about 55% of stranger rapes in Nicholas Groth and Jean Birnbaum's study, are acts of dominance. Typically, the rapist does not want to hurt the woman but to dominate her sexually. The rape may be triggered by what the rapist regards as a slight to his masculinity. He attempts to restore his sense of power, control, and identity by raping. He uses sex to compensate for his sense of inadequacy. He uses only as much force as necessary to rape his victim.

Sadistic Rapes Sadistic rapes, in which sex and aggression are violently fused, are by far the most brutal. A sadistic rapist finds "intentional maltreatment of his victim intensely gratifying and takes pleasure in her torment, anguish, distress, helplessness and suffering" (Groth & Birnbaum, 1979). There is often bondage and a ritualistic quality. The victim is often severely injured and may not survive the attack. While sadistic rapes are overwhelmingly the most brutal, they are also the least frequent. About 5% of the stranger rapes in Groth and Birnbaum's study were sadistic.

While I was in the boat I captured a very beautiful Carib woman, whom the Lord Admiral [Christopher Columbus] gave to me. When I had taken her to my cabin she was naked—as was their custom. I was filled with desire to take my pleasure with her and attempted to satisfy my desires. She was unwilling, and so treated me with her nails that I wished I had never begun. . . . I then took a piece of rope and whipped her soundly, and she let forth such incredible screams that you would not have believed your ears. Eventually we came to such terms, I assure you, that you would have thought she had been brought up in a school for whores.

Michael Cuneo, 1493

The Aftermath of Rape

According to the National Victim Center (1992), more than two-thirds of the women who were raped in 1990 were not physically injured. Twenty percent received minor injuries, and 4% sustained serious injuries (Figure 18.3).

It is important that rape victims gain a sense of control over their lives to counteract the helplessness they experienced during their rape (Robertson, 1990). They need to cope with the depression and other symptoms resulting from their trauma. Although white and African American women experience rape in more or less the same proportion, the African American woman's experience may be somewhat different. As Gail Wyatt (1992) writes, "In American culture, rape and sexual vulnerability have a unique history because of the sexual exploitation of slaves for over 250 years." Historically, there were no penalties for the rape of black women by whites. Because whites believed African American women were promiscuous by nature, they believed black women could not actually be raped. Contemporary white stereotypes continue to view black women as promiscuous. There are two important consequences of this stereotype. First, African American women who are raped assume that they are less likely to be believed than white women, especially if the rapist is white. Second, African American women are less likely to report the rape to the police, whom they view as unsympathetic to blacks in general and to raped black women in particular. Third, African American women are less likely to seek treatment and support to help the healing process.

Rape Trauma Syndrome   Rape is a traumatic event, to which a woman may have a number of responses. The emotional changes she undergoes as a result of rape are collectively known as **rape trauma syndrome.** Rape survivors are likely to experience depression, anxiety, restlessness, and guilt. These responses are consistent with **post-traumatic stress disorder (PTSD),** a group of characteristic symptoms that follow an intensely distressing event outside a person's normal life experience (Bownes, O'Gorman, & Sayers, 1991a, 1991b; Nadelson, 1990; Resnick, Kilpatrick, & Lipousky, 1991). Both whites and African Americans experience similar symptoms (Wyatt, 1992).

Rape trauma syndrome consists of two phases: an acute phase, and a long-term reorganization phase.

Acute Phase   The acute phase begins immediately following the rape. It may last for several weeks or more. In the first few hours after a rape, the woman's responses are characterized by feelings of self-blame and fear. She may believe that she was somehow responsible for the rape: she was wearing something provocative, she should have kept her doors locked, she should have been suspicious of her attacker. Self-blame, however, leads to higher rates of depression (Frazier, 1991) (Figure 18.4).

The woman is shaken by fears: that the attacker will return, that she may be killed, that others will react negatively. She may act out these feelings through expressive, controlled, or combined reactions. An expressive response leaves the woman crying, expressing signs and feelings of fear,

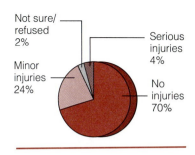

FIGURE 18.3 Injuries from Rape. (SOURCE: Data from National Victim Center, 1992.)

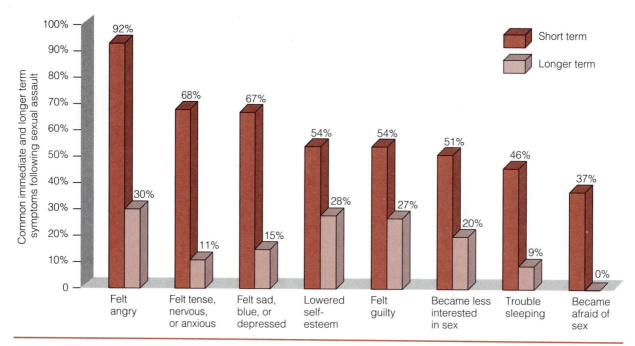

FIGURE 18.4 Short-Term and Long-Term Symptoms Following Sexual Assault. (SOURCE: George, L. K., Windfield, I., and Blazer, D. G. [1992]. Sociocultural Factors in Sexual Assault. *Journal of Social Issues*, 48(1), 115.)

anger, rage, anxiety, and tension. If she controls her responses, she hides her feelings and tries to appear calm. Nevertheless, there are often signs of tension: headaches, irritability, sleeplessness, restlessness, and jumpiness. Women may also feel humiliated, angry, embarrassed, vengeful, and fearful. Women are more likely than men to express these varied symptoms following rape (Sorenson & Siegel, 1992).

Long-Term Reorganization Phase Following the acute phase, the rape survivor enters the long-term reorganization phase. The rape is a crisis in a woman's life and relationships (Nadelson, 1990). If the rape took place at home, she may move, fearing that the rapist will return. Some women develop fears of being indoors if the rape occurred indoors, while those raped outside sometimes fear being outdoors. About 3 months after their rapes, 60% of the women in one study reported depression. Forty percent rated their depressions as severe (Mackey et al., 1992).

Response by Family Members A rape is not only a crisis in the woman's life, but a family crisis as well (White & Rollins, 1981). If the woman has children, the children may be considerably upset by the rape (Mio & Foster, 1991).

The way a family responds to rape is influenced by our cultural stereotypes. Some men may respond to their partners' rapes by blaming them. Unsupportive behavior has a severe impact on the woman's readjustment (Davis, Brickman, & Baker, 1991). Our culture also expects the man to be protective of the woman. If a woman is raped, her partner may blame himself for not protecting her: he should not have left her alone, he should have insisted that she use a car instead of walking, he should have accompanied her shopping. If the woman and her partner are able to place blame where

Rape crisis centers help sexual assault survivors cope with the effects of rape trauma.

it belongs—on the rapist—they will be more able to deal with the consequences of rape. Finally, the belief that rape is primarily a sexual act rather than a violent one affects a partner's response to rape.

The situation is somewhat different in adolescent rapes. Adolescents, who make up a significant proportion of rape victims, often fear telling their parents (Ageton, 1983). They experience ambivalence. At the same time that they desire support, they are fearful of being blamed. Susan Ageton's study (1983) found that more than three-quarters of the adolescents did not inform their parents. (When they did, however, their parents were overwhelmingly supportive.) Instead of seeking support from parents, they sought it from their peers. More than two-thirds told their friends, who offered significant support; 60% who told their friends found that their friendship deepened as a result.

Effect on Sexuality Typically, women find that their sexuality is severely affected for a short time or longer after a rape (Nadelson, 1990). Some begin avoiding sexual interactions, because sex reminds them of the rape. Those who are less depressed, however, have fewer sexual difficulties (Mackey et al., 1992). The two most common sexual problems are fear of sex and a lack of sexual desire (Howard, 1980). Both white and African American women report similar sexual problems (Wyatt, 1992).

In a 3-year study of 100 rape victims, women who did not develop sexual problems as a result of the rape had explained their rapes to their partners, who were warm, empathetic, and responsive to them (Howard, 1980). Recovery from the rape trauma was accelerated by letting the woman determine when sex with her partner would take place. A number of women who did not develop sexual problems had refrained from sexual activities with their partners for a while.

A therapist helps a child deal with her sexual abuse.

CHILD SEXUAL ABUSE

Child sexual abuse is a widespread occurrence, whether by relatives or non-relatives. **Child sexual abuse** is *any* sexual interaction (including fondling, sexual kissing, and oral sex, as well as vaginal or anal penetration) between an adult and a prepubertal child. It does not matter whether the child is perceived by the adult to be freely engaging in the sexual activity. Because of the child's age, he or she cannot give informed consent; the activity can only be considered as self-serving to the adult.

There is considerable variation in estimates of the prevalence of child abuse. A review of small-scale studies found prevalence estimates ranging from 6–62% for females and 3–31% for males (Peters et al., 1986). The first national survey found that 27% of the women and 16% of the men surveyed had experienced sexual abuse as children (Finkelhor, Hotaling, Lewis, & Smith, 1990). Different definitions of abuse, methodologies, samples, and interviewing techniques account for the varied estimates (Gelles & Conte, 1991).

Child sexual abuse is generally categorized in terms of kin relationship. **Extrafamilial abuse** is sexual abuse by unrelated people. **Intrafamilial abuse** is sexual abuse by biologically related people and step relatives. The abuse may be pedophilic or nonpedophilic. (As you recall from Chapter 11, pedophilia refers to an adult's sexual attraction to children.) **Nonpedophilic sexual abuse** refers to an adult's sexual interaction with a child that is not sexually motivated; the most important nonsexual motives are power and affection (Groth, 1978). (For sexual abuse from an anthropological perspective, see Konker, 1992.)

The victimization may include force or the threat of force, pressure, or the taking advantage of trust or innocence. The most serious or harmful forms of child sexual abuse include actual or attempted penile-vaginal pen-

Perspective 4

CHILD SEXUAL ABUSE MYTHS

Despite the high rates of sexual abuse within the family, when we think of child sexual abuse we tend to think that the perpetrators are strangers. In the majority of instances, the sexual abuser is known to the victim: He is a father, brother, uncle, neighbor, friend, or acquaintance. Diana Russell (1984) found that in extrafamilial sexual abuse, 41% of the perpetrators were intimately connected to the victim (friend, family friend, and so on), and 42% were acquaintances.

Another common misconception is that most sexual abusers are gay men; instead, the overwhelming majority are heterosexuals. Even males who sexually abuse boys are not necessarily gay (Groth & Gray, 1982). The child's age, more than his or her sex, appears to be important for most male pedophiles.

The most dangerous stereotype, however, is that the offender is responding to the sexual advances of a precocious child. In this stereotype, "the offender himself is the victim of a provocative and seductive child, for here the victim is blamed for being abused, and the actual offender is not held fully responsible for his behavior" (Groth, 1980).

In Genesis 19:30–36, the biblical story of Lot gives religious reinforcement to this myth:

Lot went out of Zo'ar, and dwelled in the hills with his two daughters for he was afraid to dwell in Zo'ar. So he dwelled in a cave with his two daughters. Then the first-born said to the other, "Our father is old, and there is not a man on earth to come into us in the manner of men. Let us make our father drink wine and we will lie with him that we may have offspring through our father." So they made their father drink wine that night and his older daughter went in and lay with her father. He did not know when she lay down or when she arose. And then on the next day, the older daughter said to the younger one, "Behold, I lay last night with our father. Let us make him drink wine again tonight, then you go in and lie with him that we may have children by our father." So they gave their father wine that night, and the younger daughter slept with him. He did not know when she lay down or when she arose. Thus both Lot's daughters became great with child by their father.

Other misconceptions include that the sexual abuser is an old man, someone who is insane or developmentally disabled, an alcoholic or drug addict, or a sexually deprived or oversexed individual.

etration, fellatio, cunnilingus, and analingus, with or without the use of force. Other serious forms range from forced digital penetration of the vagina to fondling of the breasts (unclothed), or simulated intercourse without force. The least serious forms of sexual abuse range from kissing to intentional sexual touching of the clothed genitals or breasts or other body parts, with or without the use of force (Russell, 1984).

Most victimized children are between 8 and 12 years of age; the majority are girls (Finkelhor, 1984). Russell's study (1984), which divided abusive acts into very serious, serious, and least serious (described earlier), found that in cases of nonfamilial abuse, 53% of the abuse was very serious, 27% serious, and 20% less serious. Intrafamilial abuse generally tended to be of the less serious form. (For a discussion of child sexual abuse myths, see Perspective 4.)

TABLE 18.1 Preconditions for Sexual Abuse

	Level of Explanation	
	Individual	Social/Cultural
Precondition I: Factors Related to Motivation to Sexually Abuse		
Emotional congruence	Arrested emotional development Need to feel powerful and controlling Reenactment of childhood trauma to undo the hurt Narcissistic identification with self as a young child	Masculine requirement to be dominant and powerful in sexual relationships
Sexual arousal	Childhood sexual experience that was traumatic or strongly conditioning Modeling of sexual interest in children by someone else Misattribution of arousal cues Biological abnormality	Child pornography Erotic portrayal of children in advertising Male tendency to sexualize all emotional needs
Blockage	Oedipal conflict Castration anxiety Fear of adult females Traumatic sexual experience with adult Inadequate social skills Marital problems	Repressive norms about masturbation and extramarital sex

(continued)

SOURCE: Reprinted with permission of the Free Press, a division of MacMillan, Inc. from *Child Sexual Abuse: New Theory and Research* by David Finkelhor. Copyright © 1984 by David Finkelhor.

We have only recently recognized the sexual abuse of boys; this neglect has been part of the more general neglect of all sexual victimization of males (Russell, 1984). A review of the literature shows that boys are estimated to be victims of about one-third of all pedophilic abuse committed by males (Groth & Gray, 1982). Finkelhor (1979) found in his study of 796 college students that more than 8% of the men reported sexual victimization. He speculates that men tend to underreport sexual abuse because they experience greater shame; they feel their masculinity has been undermined. Boys tend to be blamed more than girls for their victimization, especially if they did not forcibly resist: "A real boy would never let someone do *that* without fighting back" (Rogers & Terry, 1984).

TABLE 18.1 *continued*

	Level of Explanation	
	Individual	**Social/Cultural**
Precondition II: Factors Predisposing to Overcoming Internal Inhibitors	Alcohol Psychosis Impulse disorder Senility Failure of incest inhibition mechanism in family dynamics	Social toleration of sexual interest in children Weak criminal sanctions against offenders Ideology of patriarchal prerogatives for fathers Social toleration for deviance committed while intoxicated Child pornography Male inability to identify with needs of children
Precondition III: Factors Predisposing to Overcoming External Inhibitors	Mother who is absent or ill Mother who is not close to or protective of child Mother who is dominated or abused by father Social isolation of family Unusual opportunities to be alone with child Lack of supervision of child Unusual sleeping or rooming conditions	Lack of social supports for mother Barriers to women's equality Erosion of social networks Ideology of family sanctity
Precondition IV: Factors Predisposing to Overcoming Child's Resistance	Child who is emotionally insecure or deprived Child who lacks knowledge about sexual abuse Situation of unusual trust between child and offender Coercion	Unavailability of sex education for children Social powerlessness of children

General Preconditions for Sexual Abuse

Researchers have found that intrafamilial and extrafamilial sexual abuse share many common elements. Because there are so many variables—such as the age and sex of the victims and perpetrators, their relationship, the type of acts involved, and whether there was force—one cannot automatically say that abuse within the family is more harmful than extrafamilial abuse.

David Finkelhor (1984) believes there are four preconditions that need to be met by the offender for sexual abuse to occur (see Table 18.1). These preconditions apply to pedophilic, nonpedophilic, incestuous, and nonincestuous abuse.

1. *Motivation to sexually abuse a child.* This consists of three components: (1) emotional congruence, in which relating sexually to a child fulfills some important emotional need; (2) sexual arousal toward the child; and (3) blockage, in which alternative sources of sexual gratification are not available or are less satisfying.

2. *Overcoming internal inhibitions against acting on motivation.* Inhibitions may be overcome by the use of alcohol or poor impulse control.

3. *Overcoming external obstacles to committing sexual abuse.* The most important obstacle appears to be the supervision and protection a child receives from others, such as family members, neighbors, and the child's peers. The mother is especially significant in protecting children. Growing evidence suggests that children are more vulnerable to abuse when the mother is absent, neglectful, or incapacitated in some way through illness, marital abuse, or emotional problems.

4. *Undermining or overcoming a child's potential resistance to the abuse.* The abuser may use outright force or select psychologically vulnerable targets. Certain children may be more vulnerable because they feel insecure, needy, or unsupported and will respond to the abuser's offers of attention, affection, or bribes. Children's ability to resist may be undercut because they are young, naive, or have a special relationship to the abuser as friend, neighbor, or family member.

According to Finkelhor (1984), *all* four factors must come into play for sexual abuse to occur. Each factor acts as a filter for the previous one. Some people have strong motivation to sexually abuse a child. Of these, however, only some are able to overcome their internal inhibitions; fewer can overcome the external obstacles, and still fewer can overcome the child's resistance.

Forms of Intrafamilial Sexual Abuse

The incest taboo is nearly universal in human societies. **Incest** is generally defined as sexual intercourse between people too closely related to legally marry (usually interpreted to mean father-daughter, mother-son, or brother-sister). (There are only a few exceptions to the incest taboo, and these concern brother-sister marriages in the royal families of ancient Egypt, Peru, and Hawaii.) Sexual abuse in families can involve blood relatives, most commonly uncles and grandfathers, and step relatives, most often stepfathers and stepbrothers. In grandfather-granddaughter abuse, the grandfathers frequently have sexually abused their children as well. Stepgranddaughters are at greater risk than granddaughters (Margolin, 1992). (For a review of assessment and treatment of incest perpetrators, see Cole, 1992.)

It is not clear what type of familial sexual abuse is the most frequent (Peters et al., 1986; Russell, 1986). Some researchers believe that father-daughter (including stepfather-daughter) abuse is the most common; others think that brother-sister abuse is most common. Still other researchers believe that incest committed by uncles is the most common (Russell, 1986). Mother-son sexual relations are considered to be rare (or are underreported).

There is concerted family resistance to discovering what is going on, and there are complicated stratagems to keep everyone in the dark. . . . We would know more of what is going on if we were not forbidden to do so, and forbidden to realize that we are forbidden to do so.

R. D. Laing

Father-Daughter Sexual Abuse There is general agreement that the most traumatic form of sexual victimization is father-daughter abuse, including that committed by stepfathers. One study indicated that 54% of the girls sexually abused by their fathers were extremely upset (Russell, 1986). In contrast, 25% who were abused by other family members reported the same degree of emotional upset. Over twice as many abused daughters reported serious long-term consequences. Some factors contributing to the severity of father-daughter sexual relations include the following:

- Fathers were more likely to have engaged in penile-vaginal penetration than other relatives (18% versus 6%).

- Fathers sexually abused their daughters more frequently than other perpetrators abused their victims (38% of the fathers sexually abused their daughters 11 or more times, compared to a 12% abuse rate for other abusing relatives).

- Fathers were more likely to use force or violence than others (although the numbers for both fathers and others were extremely low).

In the past, many have discounted the seriousness of sexual abuse by a stepfather because there is no *biological* relationship. The emotional consequences are just as serious, however. Sexual abuse by a stepfather still represents a violation of the basic parent-child relationship. As Judith Herman (1981) notes, psychologically it does not matter if the father and child are related by blood. "What matters is the relationship that exists by virtue of the adult's parental power and the child's dependency." In fact, sexual abuse committed by stepfathers is often greater in severity. Forty-one percent of the abusing stepfathers in Russell's study (1986) abused their daughters more than 20 times. Only 17% of biological fathers abused their daughters that frequently. In 47% of the cases involving stepfathers, the abuse continued for a year or more. In contrast, only 28% of incest committed by biological fathers continued that long.

Brother-Sister Sexual Abuse There are contrasting views concerning the consequences of brother-sister incest. Researchers generally have expressed little interest in it. Most have intended to view it as harmless sex play, or sexual exploration between mutually involved siblings. The research, however, has generally failed to distinguish between exploitative and nonexploitative brother-sister sexual activity. One study found that brother-sister incest can be a devastating invasion of individual boundaries (Canavan, Myers, & Higgs, 1992). Russell (1986) suggests that the idea that brother-sister incest is usually harmless and mutual may be a myth. In her study, the average age difference between the brother (age 17.9 years) and sister (10.7 years) is so great that the siblings can hardly be considered peers. The age difference represents a significant power difference. Furthermore, not all brother-sister sexual activity is "consenting"; considerable physical force may be involved. Russell writes:

> So strong is the myth of mutuality that many victims themselves internalize the discounting of their experiences, particularly if their brothers did not use force, if they themselves did not forcefully resist the abuse at the time, if they still continued to care about their brothers, or if they did not consider it abuse when

it occurred. And sisters are even more likely than daughters to be seen as responsible for their own abuse.

Russell discovered that 2% of the women in her random sample had at least one sexually abusive experience with a brother.

Uncle-Niece Sexual Abuse Both Alfred Kinsey (1953) and Diane Russell (1986) found the most common form of intrafamilial sexual abuse to involve uncles and nieces. Russell reported that almost 5% of the women in her study had been molested by their uncles, slightly more than the percentage abused by their fathers. The level of severity of the abuse was generally less in terms of the type of sexual act and the use of force. Although such abuse does not take place within the nuclear family, many victims found it quite upsetting. One-quarter of the respondents indicated long-term emotional effects (Russell, 1986).

Children at Risk

Not all children are equally at risk for sexual abuse. Although any child can be sexually abused, some groups of children are more likely to be victimized than others. A review (Finkelhor & Baron, 1986) of the literature indicates that those children at higher risk for sexual abuse are the following:

- Female children.
- Preadolescent children.
- Children with absent or unavailable parents.
- Children whose relationships with parents are poor.
- Children whose parents are in conflict.
- Children who live with a stepfather.

Children between 10 and 12 appear to be the most vulnerable, while those under 6 or 7 seem to be less vulnerable (Finkelhor & Baron, 1986). Children who have poor relationships with their parents (especially mothers) or whose parents are absent or unavailable and have high levels of marital conflict appear to be at higher risk. A child in such a family may be less well supervised and, as a result, more vulnerable to manipulation and exploitation by an adult. In this type of family, the child may be unhappy, deprived, or emotionally needy; the child may be more responsive to the offers of friendship, time, and material rewards promised by the abuser.

Finally, children with stepfathers are at greater risk for sexual abuse. Russell (1986) found that only 2.3% of the daughters studied were sexually abused by their biological fathers. In contrast, 17% were abused by their stepfathers. The higher risk may result from the incest taboos not being as strong in step relationships, and because stepfathers have not built up inhibitions resulting from parent-child bonding beginning in infancy. As a result, stepfathers may be more likely to view the child sexually. In addition, stepparents may also bring into the family step relatives—their own parents, siblings, or children—who may feel no incest-related prohibition about becoming sexually involved with stepchildren.

Effects of Child Sexual Abuse

Until recently, much of the literature on child sexual abuse has been anecdotal, case studies, or small-scale surveys of nonrepresentative groups. More recently, researchers have used control groups to compare psychological and behavioral differences between sexually abused and nonabused children (Briere, 1992; Gelles & Conte, 1991). There are numerous well-documented consequences of child sexual abuse that hold true for both intrafamilial and extrafamilial abuse (see Kendall-Tackett, Williams, & Finkelhor, 1993, for a review of the literature). These include both initial and long-term consequences. Many child sexual abuse survivors experience symptoms of post-traumatic stress disorder (McLeer, Deblinger, Henry, & Ovraschel, 1992).

Initial Effects The initial consequences of sexual abuse occur within the first 2 years. The proportion of victimized children who experience these disturbances ranges from one-quarter to almost two-thirds, depending on the study. (For a review of the short-term effects of sexual abuse, see Beitchman et al., 1991.) Some of the typical effects are:

- *Emotional disturbances*, including fear, anger, hostility, guilt, and shame.
- *Physical consequences*, including difficulty in sleeping, changes in eating patterns, and pregnancy.
- *Sexual disturbances*, including significantly higher rates of open masturbation, sexual preoccupation, and exposure of the genitals (Hibbard & Hartman, 1992).
- *Social disturbances*, including difficulties at school, truancy, running away from home, and early marriages by abused adolescents. (A large proportion of homeless youth are fleeing parental sexual abuse [Athey, 1991].)

Ethnicity appears to influence how a child responds to sexual abuse. A recent study compared sexually abused Asian American children with a random sample of abused white, African American, and Latino children (Rao, Diclemente, & Pouton, 1992). The researchers found that Asian American children suffered less sexually invasive forms of abuse. They tended to be more suicidal and to receive less support from their parents than non-Asians. They were also less likely to express anger or to sexually act out. These different responses point to the importance of understanding cultural context when treating ethnic victims. (For a discussion of child sexual abuse histories among African American college students, see Priest, 1992.)

Long-Term Effects Although there can be some healing of the initial effects, child sexual abuse may leave lasting scars on the adult survivor (Beitchman et al., 1992). These adults often have significantly higher incidences of psychological, physical, and sexual problems than the general population. Abuse may predispose some women to sexually abusive dating relationships (Cate & Lloyd, 1992).

Long-term effects include the following (Beitchman et al., 1992; Browne & Finkelhor, 1986; Elliott & Briere, 1992; Wyatt, Gutherie, & Notgass, 1992):

- Depression, the most frequently reported symptom of adults sexually abused as children.
- Self-destructive tendencies, including suicide attempts and thoughts of suicide (Jeffrey & Jeffrey, 1992).
- Somatic disturbances and dissociation, including anxiety and nervousness, eating disorders (anorexia and bulimia), feelings of "spaciness," out-of-body experiences, and feelings that things are "unreal" (DeGroot, Kennedy, Rodin, & McVey, 1992; Walker et al., 1992; Young, 1992).
- Negative self-concept, including feelings of low self-esteem, isolation, and alienation.
- Interpersonal relationship difficulties, including difficulties in relating to both sexes, parental conflict, problems in responding to their own children, and difficulty in trusting others.
- Revictimization, in which women abused as children are more vulnerable to rape and marital violence.
- Sexual problems, in which survivors find it difficult to relax and enjoy sexual activities, or avoid sex and experience hypoactive (inhibited) sexual desire and lack of orgasm.

Sexual Abuse Trauma The consequences of child sexual abuse may create a traumatic dynamic that affects the child's ability to deal with the world. Angela Browne and David Finkelhor (1986) suggest a model of **sexual abuse trauma** that contains four components: traumatic sexualization, betrayal, powerlessness, and stigmatization. When these factors converge as a result of sexual abuse, they affect the child's cognitive and emotional orientation to the world. They create trauma by distorting a child's self-concept, world view, and emotional development. These consequences affect abuse survivors not only as children but also as adults.

Traumatic Sexualization Traumatic sexualization refers to the process in which the sexually abused child's sexuality develops inappropriately and becomes interpersonally dysfunctional. Browne and Finkelhor (1986) note:

> It occurs through the exchange of affection, attention, privileges, and gifts for sexual behavior, so that the child learns sexual behavior as a strategy for manipulating others to get his or her other developmentally appropriate needs met. It occurs when certain parts of the child's anatomy are fetishized and given distorted importance and meaning. It occurs through the misconceptions and confusions about sexual behavior and morality that are transmitted to the child from the offender. And it occurs when very frightening memories and events become associated in the child's mind with sexual activity.

Sexually traumatized children learn inappropriate sexual behaviors (such as manipulating an adult's genitals for affection), are confused about their sexuality, and inappropriately associate certain emotions—such as loving and caring—with sexual activities. Childhood sexual abuse may be associated with the reasons some women later become prostitutes (Simons & Whitbeck, 1991).

As adults, sexual issues may become especially important. Survivors may suffer flashbacks, sexual dysfunctions, and negative feelings about their bodies. They may also be confused about sexual norms and standards. A fairly common confusion is the belief that sex may be traded for affection. Some women label themselves as "promiscuous," but this label may be more a result of their negative self-image than their actual behavior. There seems to be a history of childhood sexual abuse among many prostitutes.

Betrayal Children feel betrayed when they discover that someone on whom they have been dependent has manipulated, used, or harmed them. Children may also feel betrayed by other family members, especially mothers, for not protecting them from abuse.

As adults, survivors may experience depression as a manifestation, in part, of extended grief over the loss of trusted figures. Some may find it difficult to trust others. Other survivors may feel a deep need to regain a sense of trust and become extremely dependent. Distrust may manifest itself in hostility and anger. In adolescents, antisocial or delinquent behavior may be a means of protecting themselves from further betrayal. Anger may express a need for revenge or retaliation. At other times, distrust may manifest itself in social isolation and avoidance of intimate relationships.

Powerlessness Children experience a basic kind of powerlessness when their bodies and personal space are invaded against their will. A child's powerlessness is reinforced as the abuse is repeated.

In adulthood, powerlessness may be experienced as fear or anxiety; a person feels unable to control events. Adults survivors often believe that they have impaired coping abilities. This feeling of ineffectiveness may be related to the high incidence of depression and despair among survivors. Powerlessness may also be related to increased vulnerability or revictimization by rape or marital violence; survivors feel unable to prevent subsequent victimization. Other survivors, however, may attempt to cope with their earlier powerlessness by an excessive need to control or dominate others.

Stigmatization Stigmatization refers to guilt and shame about sexual abuse that are transmitted to abused children and then internalized by them. Stigmatization is communicated in numerous ways. The abuser conveys it by blaming the child or, through his secrecy, communicates a sense of shame. If the abuser pressures the child for secrecy, the child may also internalize feelings of shame and guilt. Children's prior knowledge that their family or community considers such activities deviant may contribute to their feelings of stigmatization.

As adults, survivors may feel extreme guilt or shame about having been sexually abused. They may have low-self-esteem because they feel that the abuse had made them "damaged merchandise." They also feel different from others, because they mistakenly believe that they alone have been abused.

Treatment Programs

There is a growing trend toward dealing with child sexual abuse, especially father-daughter sexual abuse, through therapy programs working in conjunction with the judicial system, rather than breaking up the family by removing the child or the offender (Nadelson & Sauzier, 1986). Because the offender is often also the breadwinner, incarcerating him may greatly increase the family's emotional distress. The district attorney's office may work with clinicians in evaluating the existing threat to the child and deciding whether to prosecute or refer the offender to therapy (or both). The goal is not simply to punish the offender, but to try to assist the victim and the family in coming to terms with the abuse.

Many of these clinical programs work on several levels at once: They treat the individual, the father-daughter relationship, the mother-daughter relationship, and the family as a whole. They work on developing self-esteem and improving the family and marital relationships. If appropriate, they refer individuals to alcohol- or drug-abuse treatment programs.

A crucial ingredient of many treatment programs is individual and family attendance at self-help group meetings. These self-help groups are composed of incest survivors, offenders, mothers, and other family members. Self-help groups such as Parents United and Daughters and Sons United assist the offender in acknowledging his responsibility and in understanding the impact of the abuse on all those involved.

Preventing Sexual Abuse

The idea of preventing sexual abuse is relatively new (Berrick & Barth, 1992). Prevention programs began about a decade ago, a few years after programs were started to identify and help child or adult survivors of sexual abuse. (For an evaluation of commercially available materials for preventing child abuse, see Roberts et al., 1990.) Such prevention programs have been hindered, however, by three factors (Finkelhor, 1986a, 1986b):

- Sexual abuse is complicated by differing concepts of what constitutes appropriate sexual behaviors and partners, which are not easily understood by children.

- Sexual abuse, especially incest, is a difficult and scary topic for adults to discuss with children. Children who are frightened by their parents, however, may be less able to resist abuse than those who are given strategies of resistance.

- Sex education is controversial. Even where it is taught, instruction often does not go beyond physiology and reproduction. The topic of incest is especially opposed.

In confronting these problems, child abuse prevention (CAP) programs have been very creative. These programs typically aim at three audiences: children, parents, and professionals, especially teachers. CAP programs aimed at children include plays, puppet shows, filmstrips, videotapes, books, and comic books to teach children that they have rights. Children have the right to control their own bodies (including their genitals) and to feel "safe," and they have the right not to be touched in ways that feel confusing or wrong. The CAP programs stress that the child is not at fault when such abuse does occur. These programs generally teach three strategies (Gelles & Conte, 1991). First, children are taught to say "no." Second, they are told to get away from the assailant or situation. Third, they are instructed to tell a trusted adult about what happened (and to keep telling until they are believed). It is not known how well these strategies work, because assessment studies cannot ethically duplicate the various situations. In particular,

Touch Talk!

What to do if someone touches you and you don't like it.

written and illustrated by Eric Berg

One objective of child-abuse prevention programs is to teach children the difference between "good" touching and "bad" touching.

it is difficult to replicate the most common sexual abuse situation: abuse by a parent, relative, or friend.

Other programs focus on educating parents who, it is hoped, will in turn educate their children. These programs aim at helping parents discover abuse or abusers by identifying warning signs. Such programs, however, need to be culturally sensitive, as Latinos and Asians may be reluctant to discuss these matters with their children (Ahn & Gilbert, 1992). Parents seem reluctant in general to deal with sexual abuse issues with their children, according to David Finkelhor (1986a). Many do not feel that their children are at risk. And parents are fearful of unnecessarily frightening their children. Parents also feel uncomfortable about taking with their children about sex in general, much less about such tabooed subjects as incest. In addition, parents may not believe their own children, or may feel uncomfortable confronting a suspected abuser, who may be a partner, uncle, friend, or neighbor.

CAP programs also seek to educate professionals, especially teachers, physicians, mental-health professionals, and police officers. Because of their close contact with children and their role in teaching children about the world, teachers are especially important. Professionals are encouraged to be watchful for signs of sexual abuse and to investigate children's reports of such abuse. A number of schools have instituted programs to educate students and their parents as well. (For a research review of child sexual abuse prevention, see Berrick & Barth, 1992.)

Sexual harassment, anti-gay harassment and discrimination, sexual aggression, and sexual abuse of children represent the darker side of human sexuality. Their common thread is the humiliation, subordination, or victimization of others. But we need not be victims. We can educate ourselves and others about these activities; we can work toward changing attitudes and institutions that support these destructive and dehumanizing behaviors.

SUMMARY

Sexual Harassment

• *Sexual harassment* includes two distinct types of illegal harassment: the abuse of power for sexual ends, and the creation of a *hostile environment*. Sexual harassment may begin as early as middle childhood. In college, 15–35% of women students have experienced some form of sexual harassment from other students, faculty members, or administrators. Major problems in dealing with harassment are male and female differences in levels of tolerance, and attributing blame for the harassment.

• In the workplace, fellow employees as well as supervisors may engage in sexual harassment. In many instances, harassment may not represent sexual attraction as much as an exercise of power. While most victims of sexual harassment are females, males are also subject to harassment.

Anti-Gay/Lesbian Harassment, Prejudice, and Discrimination

• Researchers have identified two forms of discrimination or bias against gay men and lesbians: heterosexual bias and anti-gay prejudice. *Heterosexual bias* includes ignoring, segregating, and submerging gay men and lesbians into larger categories that make them invisible.

- *Anti-gay prejudice* is a strong dislike, fear, or hatred of gay men and lesbians. Social prejudice is acted out through offensive language, discrimination, and violence. Anti-gay prejudice is derived from a deeply rooted insecurity concerning a person's own sexuality and gender identity, a strong fundamentalist religious orientation, or simple ignorance concerning homosexuality.

- Much anti-gay prejudice is supported by conservative religious institutions and the military. In considering homosexuality from a religious perspective, individuals need to separate core religious beliefs from peripheral ones and to separate religious beliefs from prejudice. The military ban on lesbians and gay men has been replaced by a "Don't ask, don't tell" policy that tolerates homosexuality as long as it is discrete.

Sexual Aggression

- *Rape* is penile-vaginal penetration performed against a woman's will. *Sexual aggression* refers to any sexual activity against a person's will through the use of force, argument, pressure, use of alcohol/drugs, or authority. *Sexual coercion*, a broader term than rape or sexual aggression, includes arguing, pleading, and cajoling as well as force or the threat of force.

- *Date rape* is the most common form of rape. Date rapes are usually not planned. Alcohol or drugs are often involved. There is also considerable sexual coercion in gay male relationships; there is less coercion in lesbian relationships. Physical violence often goes hand-in-hand with sexual aggression. There is considerable confusion and argument about consent, especially because much sexual communication is nonverbal and ambiguous.

- The majority of *reported* rapes are by strangers. Stranger rapes are more likely to involve guns or knives than date rapes. A stranger rape is more likely to be taken seriously by the police because it reflects the rape stereotype better than date or marital rape.

- In most states, a husband can be prosecuted for raping his wife. Many people discount rape in marriage as a "marital tiff" that has little to do with "real" rape. Marital rape victims experience feelings of betrayal, anger, humiliation, and guilt.

- Gang rape may be perpetrated by strangers or acquaintances. It may be motivated by power and by male-bonding factors.

- Most sexual assaults on men are male against male; female-against-male assaults are significantly less common. Because the motive in sexual assaults is power and domination, sexual orientation is often irrelevant. In prison, sexual assault is common as a means of establishing dominance.

- Most stranger rapes (and some acquaintance or marital rapes) can be characterized as anger rapes, power rapes, or sadistic rapes. This typology, however, may not reflect the motivations of the majority of rapists who are acquaintances, boyfriends, and husbands.

- The emotional changes women undergo as a result of rape are collectively known as *rape trauma syndrome*. Women develop depression, anxiety, restlessness, and guilt. The symptoms following rape are consistent with *post-traumatic stress disorder (PTSD)*. Rape trauma syndrome consists of the acute phase and long-term reorganization phase. Women find their sexuality severely affected for a short time or longer.

Child Sexual Abuse

• *Child sexual abuse* is *any* sexual interaction between an adult and a prepubertal child. *Incest* is sexual intercourse between individuals too closely related to legally marry. The child's victimization may include force or the threat of force, pressure, or the taking advantage of trust or innocence.

• The preconditions for sexual abuse include motivation to sexually abuse a child, overcoming internal inhibitions against acting on the motivation, overcoming external obstacles, and undermining or overcoming a child's potential resistance. All four factors must come into play for sexual abuse to occur.

• Initial consequences of abuse include physical consequences and emotional, social, and sexual disturbances. Child sexual abuse may leave lasting scars on the adult survivor, including depression, self-destructive tendencies, somatic disturbances, and dissociation. Symptoms may include anxiety and nervousness, negative self-concept, relationship difficulties, revictimization, and sexual problems.

• *Sexual abuse trauma* includes traumatic sexualization, betrayal, powerlessness, and stigmatization. Treatment programs simultaneously treat the individual, the father-child relationship, the mother-child relationship, and the family as a whole.

• Child abuse prevention (CAP) programs have been hindered by different concepts of appropriate sexual behavior, adult fear of discussion, and controversy over sex education. Prevention programs generally teach children to say "no," to get away from the assailant or situation, and to tell a trusted adult about what happened.

Rape Myths

• Rape myths serve to encourage rape by blaming women. Men are more likely than women to believe rape myths. Rape myths include beliefs that women want to be raped, women ask for it, women are only raped by strangers, women could really avoid rape if they wanted, women "cry rape" for revenge, rapists are crazy or psychotic, and most rapists are black.

Preventing Sexual Assault

• To reduce the risk of date rape, go to a public place on a first date, share expenses, avoid using drugs or alcohol, and avoid ambiguous verbal or nonverbal behavior. To reduce the risk of stranger rape, don't identify yourself as a person living alone, don't open your door to strangers, and avoid dark and isolated areas. If someone approaches you threateningly, turn and run. Take self-defense training. If you are sexually assaulted (or in case of an attempted assault), report the assault as soon as possible.

Child Sexual Abuse Myths

• Sexual abuse myths include the belief that abusers are strangers; in most cases, however, the sexual abuser is known to the victim. Another common misconception is that most sexual abusers are gay men; instead, the overwhelming majority are heterosexuals. Men who abuse boys are not necessarily gay; the child's age is more important than gender for most male pedophiles. The most dangerous stereotype is that the offender is responding to the sexual advances of a precocious child.

KEY TERMS

sexual harassment	sexual coercion	child sexual abuse
hostile environment	date rape	extrafamilial abuse
heterosexual bias	acquaintance rape	intrafamilial abuse
heterosexism	statutory rape	nonpedophilic
anti-gay prejudice	age of consent	sexual abuse
gay-bashing	rape trauma	incest
queer-bashing	syndrome	sexual abuse trauma
rape	post-traumatic	
sexual aggression	stress disorder (PTSD)	

SUGGESTIONS FOR FURTHER READING

Draucker, Claire Burke. *Counseling Survivors of Childhood Sexual Abuse*. Newbury Park, CA: Sage Publications, 1992. A comprehensive examination of treating adult survivors of childhood sexual abuse, using case studies.

Dziech, Billie Wright. *The Lecherous Professor: Sexual Harassment on Campus*. 2nd ed. Urbana: University of Illinois Press, 1990. The dynamics of sexual harassment in the college environment.

Hasbany, Richard, ed. *Homosexuality and Religion*. New York: Haworth Press, 1990. A survey of recent Christian and Jewish positions on homosexuality, current biblical and theological scholarship, gay and lesbian ministers, priests, and rabbis, and pastoral counseling for gay men and lesbians.

Herek, Gregory, and Kevin Benl, eds. *Hate Crimes: Confronting Violence Against Lesbians and Gay Men*. Newbury Park, CA: Sage Publications, 1991. An overview of violence against gay men and lesbians: the context, the perpetrators, and responses.

Koss, Mary, and Mary Harvey. *The Rape Victim: Clinical and Community Intervention*. Newbury Park, CA: Sage Publications, 1991. A study of rape incidence, the impact on survivors, and societal attitudes; deals with rape crisis centers and ways of helping rape survivors cope.

McLaurin, Melton. *Celia: A Slave*. Athens, GA: University of Georgia Press, 1991. The moving portrait of a young enslaved woman who was raped and sexually abused by her master until she killed him.

Parrot, Andrea, and Laurie Bechhofer, eds. *Acquaintance Rape: The Hidden Crime*. New York: John Wiley, 1991. A collection of scholarly essays on date rape.

Chapter Nineteen

COMMERCIAL SEX: SEXUALLY ORIENTED MATERIAL AND PROSTITUTION

P REVIEW: SELF-QUIZ

1. Nonviolent, sexually explicit material does not appear to be linked with violence against women. True or false?

2. Sexually oriented material is obscene by definition. True or false?

3. Almost all adult Americans have read or viewed sexually explicit material. True or false?

4. Most Americans believe that sexually explicit material depicting consensual sexual activity between adults should be accessible to adults. True or false?

5. Sexually explicit films tend to be less violent than PG- and R-rated mainstream films. True or false?

6. Written materials on sexual subjects are no longer censored in America. True or false?

7. Prostitution is illegal everywhere in the United States. True or false?

8. Adolescents who enter prostitution often have a history of childhood sexual abuse. True or false?

9. Most women who work in prostitution are call girls. True or false?

10. With few exceptions, male prostitutes are gay. True or false?

ANSWERS 1. T, 2. F, 3. T, 4. T, 5. T, 6. F, 7. F, 8. T, 9. F, 10. F

M oney and sex are bound together in the production and sale of sexually oriented material and in prostitution. Money is exchanged for sexual images or descriptions portrayed by videos, films, magazines, books, music, and photographs that depict people in explicit or suggestive sexual activities. Money is also exchanged for sexual services provided by streetwalkers, call girls, massage parlor workers, and other sex workers. The sex industry is a multibillion-dollar industry with countless millions of consumers and customers. As a nation, however, we feel profoundly ambivalent about sexually oriented material and prostitution. Many condemn it as immoral and exploitative and wish to censor or eliminate it. Others find it harmless, an erotic diversion, or an aspect of society that cannot (or should not) be regulated; they believe censorship and police action do greater harm than good.

In this chapter, we examine sexually oriented material, including depictions of sex in popular culture, the role of technology in developing new forms of sexually oriented material, the effects of sexually oriented material, and censorship issues. Then we examine prostitution, focusing on females and males working in prostitution and the legal issues involved.

SEXUALLY ORIENTED MATERIAL IN CONTEMPORARY AMERICA

Studying sexually oriented material objectively is difficult because it touches deep and often conflicting feelings we have about sexuality. Some enjoy it,

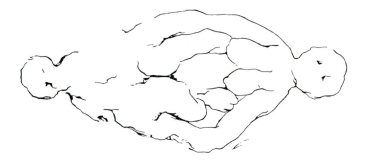

Human beings have always been interested in depicting sexual activities. The oldest existing depiction of sexual intercourse was found in a cave in France and is over 20,000 years old.

others feel it is degrading, and still others believe it may lead to violence or moral chaos.

Is It Pornography or Erotica?

Much of the discussion about sexually oriented material concerns the question of whether such material is erotic or pornographic. Unfortunately, there is a lack of agreement about what constitutes erotica or pornography. Part of the problem is that erotica and pornography are subjective terms. **Erotica** describes a positive evaluation of sexually oriented material. (The word "erotica" is derived from the Greek *erotikos,* meaning a love poem.) **Pornography** represents a negative evaluation of sexually oriented material. ("Pornography" is a nineteenth-century word derived from the Greek *porne,* meaning prostitute, and *graphos,* meaning depicting.)

The same sexually oriented material may evoke a variety of responses in different people (Fisher, 1986; Reiss, 1990). Some people may enjoy the material, others may be repulsed, and still others may simultaneously feel aroused and guilty. "What I like is erotica, but what you like is pornography," may be a facetious statement, but one that's not entirely untrue. Judgments about sexually explicit material tend to be relative historically and according to individuals.

Because of the tendency to use "erotica" as a positive term and "pornography" as a negative term, we will use the neutral term "sexually oriented material" whenever possible. **Sexually oriented material** is material such as photographs, videos, films, magazines, or books whose primary themes, topics, or depictions involve sexuality or cause sexual arousal. **Sexually explicit material** is material that intimately depicts sexual activities, the vulva, the erect penis, or the anus. This material is also considered **hardcore.** Other sexually oriented material may be considered **softcore** if it is not explicit, such as the depiction of nudes in *Playboy.* Sometimes, however, the context may require us to use either "erotica" or "pornography." This is especially true if studies we are citing are clearly making a positive or negative evaluation. (For a discussion of changing views on sexually oriented material, see Perspective 1.)

And is there any moral shut
Within the bosom of the rose?
Alfred, Lord Tennyson

How can you accuse me of liking
pornography when I don't even
have a pornograph?
Groucho Marx

Sexually Oriented Material and Popular Culture

Over the last few decades, sexually oriented material, especially softcore, has become an integral part of popular culture. *Playboy* and *Penthouse* are among

CHANGING PERSPECTIVES ON OBSCENITY

Why does one generation condemn something—such as a book, painting, or photograph—as obscene while another generation calls it literature or art, or ignores it entirely as a subject of moral evaluation?

Society and Moral Outrage

One possible explanation of changing definitions may be found in the writing of sociologist Emile Durkheim (1858–1917). In *The Division of Labor in Society*, Durkheim wrote that there is behavior regarded as deviant in all societies. In fact, Durkheim argued, a society requires deviance as a means of uniting its average citizens through moral outrage.

Moral outrage reaffirms basic values and creates solidarity. Deviance and outrage establish the outer boundaries of acceptable behavior. These boundaries are repeatedly tested by individuals on the fringe, and they are repeatedly defended.

Using Durkheim's approach, obscenity may be viewed as society's way of defining its limits of acceptable sexual behavior. It is necessary to describe various behaviors or depictions as deviant or obscene in order to validate society's sexual standards. Thus, as the boundaries of acceptability expand, what one generation identified as obscene, the next may not. In a less permissive era, for example, the depiction of women in bathing suits was acceptable, but depictions of nude women were considered obscene. Such pictures were limited to underground "girlie" magazines, calendars, glossy photos, and postcards. Today, however, the boundaries have changed. The use of nudes is found in advertising, mass-circulation magazines such as *Vogue* and *Redbook*, and movies. Nudity in itself is no longer regarded as obscene. Today's main areas of dispute are depictions suggesting violence and degradation, and depictions of homoeroticism.

Variability in Personal Responses

Why does one person evaluate sexually explicit material negatively and another positively? The answer seems to lie in his or her emotional response to the material. A person's erotophobic/erotophilic attitudes (discussed in Chapter 10) affect his or her response to sexually oriented material. Erotophilic people tend to respond positively to such material while erotophobic people do not (Fisher, 1986). Ira Reiss (1990) writes:

> Our reactions to sexually arousing films or books provide insight into our personal sexual attitudes. What we really are reacting to is not the objective material but rather a projection of our own innermost feelings concerning the type of sexuality presented. We may feel that sexuality being portrayed is too revealing, too embarrassing, too suggestive, or too private.

An experiment conducted by Donn Byrne and colleagues (1974) found that whether participants identified material as pornographic depended on whether they had positive or negative *feelings* about the material. Byrne noted that "decisions about pornography are made simply on the basis of how such stimuli make one feel." He continues:

> It seems difficult for most people to indicate that someone or something makes them feel good or bad and . . . that they simply respond with like or dislike. Instead, the individual's own reactions are attributed to the object itself in terms of its intrinsic qualities. Thus, an erotic depiction is not just pleasing or displeasing to oneself; the depiction itself is good or bad.

Byrne noted an additional tendency: People attempt to justify their feelings and evaluations in general terms rather than personal ones. They tend to say that the sexually explicit material is beneficial or harmful, instead of saying that they personally prefer or don't prefer the material.

Crotch-grabbing has become a feature of rock performances, emphasizing the sexual nature of much popular music (left). As a sign of modesty, it is an artistic convention to cover the genitals with the hand (or fig leaf), as in Botticelli's fifteenth-century masterpiece, The Birth of Venus *(and the photograph of the Red Hot Chili Peppers on p. 17). Such obvious concealment, however, also calls attention to the genitals and their forbidden nature. Paradoxically, both Venus's modesty and Madonna's crotch-grabbing convey the same message: The genitals are tabooed.*

the most widely circulated magazines in America. In fact, one researcher found that 100% of males of high school age or older had read or looked at *Playboy*, *Playgirl*, or similar magazines (Bryant & Brown, 1985). Ninety-seven percent of high school girls and 93% of adult women had viewed similar magazines. Among junior high students, 92% of the boys and 84% of the girls had seen such magazines.

The depiction of sexual activities is not restricted to books, magazines, and videos. There are various establishments that offer live adult entertainment. Bars, for example, feature topless dancers. Some clubs or adult entertainment establishments employ erotic dancers who expose themselves and simulate sexual acts before their audience. Furthermore, studies of numerous cities and states indicate that the majority supports the right of adults to possess sexually explicit material. In reviewing a number of public-opinion studies, two researchers concluded that there is a consensus in the United States that adults should have access to "sexually explicit material depicting adults in consensual activity" (Diamond & Dannemiller, 1989).

As sexual themes, ideas, images, and music continue to expand in art, literature, and popular culture, the boundaries increasingly blur between what is socially acceptable and what is considered obscene. Thus, we are confronted with such questions as: Is Madonna's book *Sex* obscene, artistic, or in bad taste? Are Michael Jackson's and Marky Mark's crotch-clutchings obscene or expressive? Are the explicit talk shows of Geraldo Rivera and Howard Stern prurient or informative?

Why are softcore sexual depictions more acceptable than hardcore? Why are drawings of sexual interactions in a human sexuality textbook considered educational, while photographs of similar activities in a sex magazine considered obscene? Why is Peter Paul Ruben's seventeenth-century painting *The Rape of the Daughters of Leucippus* considered great art (and worth millions of dollars) rather than the glorification of sexual assault? Why do some people accept softcore sexual depictions of heterosexuals but condemn the same activities between gay or lesbian couples as obscene? There are no easy answers in trying to identify what is obscene and what is not.

As we have seen throughout our study of human sexuality, sexuality is an integral part of popular culture. Looking at beauty pageants, for example, we can see how essentially sexual portrayals of women may be defined as either legitimate or illegitimate. Women walking down a runway in bathing suits while their beauty and grace are judged is an all-American tradition. To some people, however, such pageants exploit women as sex objects. Consider the ironies involved in Vanessa Williams's becoming Miss America. In 1985, Williams was forced to give up her crown when nude photographs of her were made public in *Penthouse* magazine. When Williams appeared in *Penthouse,* she crossed the boundary that separates legitimate from illegitimate portrayals of sex. Miss America, according to Ellen Goodman (1985), is "a virginal sex object" who projects feelings of availability and innocence, allure but inexperience. *Penthouse* projects images of sexuality and experience; there are no "virgins" in *Penthouse.* Both Miss America and *Penthouse,* however, sell fantasy sex. Goodman wrote:

> Pageants and penthouses are both in the flesh biz. A beauty contest displays a woman solely as a body; a pornographer subdivides that body into parts. Both make their subject into an object, both offer her up for the pleasure of the devouring public.

The Miss America pageant and *Penthouse* illustrate some of the problems involved in labeling material obscene. Both the pageant and the magazine essentially transform women into sex objects, yet one is acceptable by society and the other is not.

Technology and Sexually Oriented Material

In the nineteenth century, technology transformed the production of sexually oriented material. Cheap paper and large-scale printing, combined with mass literacy, created an enormous market for books and drawings. In the mid-nineteenth century, with the invention of photography, sexually oriented photographs began to be produced. (Nudes were among the earliest photographs made.) With the ability to reprint photographs on paper, photographic images were mass produced and mass distributed.

Today, technology is once again extending the forms in which sexually oriented material is conveyed. A New York cable TV program called "Voyeurvision" features a lingerie-clad woman on a bed who takes phone calls on the air (at $5 per minute) and acts out sexual fantasies as the caller (and hundreds of thousands of others) watches (Kaplan, 1992). Computer-directed "virtual reality" programs promise "simulated" sexual experiences, in which you can "experience" your fantasies.

Sex and Computers

There are hundreds of computer software programs, such as "Leisure Suit Larry," that are animated and X-rated (Markoff, 1992). Computer bulletin boards may specialize in various sexual interests, ranging from "talking dirty" to dominance and submission. Some computer users change their age or assume cross-gender identities when they sign on.

In 1992, one of the largest computer game companies began a network that allows subscribers to interact with computer-animated graphic sex games. Users configure the appearance of their cartoonlike characters and engage in a variety of situations with characters controlled by other subscribers. When the characters have sex, only their faces will be visible on the screen. The users, however, can see the face of their partner, and they are able to control the expression on their own character's face (Markoff, 1992).

Dial-a-Porn

Millions of people have called 900-number telephone sex lines. One sex line in New York City receives over 500,000 calls daily (Matek, 1988). Advertisements for phone sex appear in most sexually oriented magazines; they depict nude or seminude women and men in sexually suggestive poses. The caller can either charge his or her call to a credit card or call a 900-number, in which case the charges are billed to the person's telephone number. For fees generally ranging from $3 to $15 a minute, a person can have a woman or man "talk dirty" with him or her. Fantasy phone sex also caters to "specialty" interests, such as bondage and submission, transvestism, and transsexuality.

Anonymous telephone sex provides the caller with pseudo-intimacy. Through the voice, the caller receives a sense of physical closeness. Because the phone worker is paid to respond to the caller's fantasies, the caller can move the conversation in the direction desired. The worker gives the caller the illusion that his or her fantasies are being fulfilled (Matek, 1988).

Although the ads depict the fantasy phone worker as highly erotic, often these calls are forwarded to their homes or apartments. There, the workers who answer the calls are probably going about more mundane tasks, such as washing dishes, cleaning the bathroom, or studying for an accounting exam. Sometimes the workers become involved in the fantasy, but more often they only half-listen while going about other tasks.

X-Rated Videocassettes

Videocassettes and VCRs have revolutionized both movies and television. Television sets are increasingly being used not only to receive TV broadcasts but also to screen films recorded on videotape. Homes and dormitories provide an alternative to movie theaters for viewing films. One study of college students found that, on average, males viewed 6 hours and females viewed 2 hours of sexually explicit material a month (Padgett, Brislutz, & Neal, 1989).

The VCR revolution has been so great that sexually oriented videos have replaced films, and bedrooms have supplanted adult theaters, or "porno" movie houses. The number of adult theaters in the U.S. plummeted from 750 in 1983 to 250 in 1987. In fact, sexually oriented videos account for 15–25% of all videocassettes sold. Three-quarters of all video stores rent erotic videotapes; 200 million X-rated videos were rented in 1989. Mainstream X-rated videos generally depict stereotypical gender roles, but sexual

Dial-a-Porn is a multi-million dollar business. Despite attempts to censor or regulate it, it continues to flourish. Those favoring it argue that dial-a-porn is a form of safe sex and is protected by freedom of speech laws. Those opposed argue that it is obscene and easily accessible to people under 18 years of age, including young children.

The VCR revolution drove "porno" movie houses out of business as individuals became able to view x-rated videos in the privacy of their own homes. Over 200 million x-rated videos are rented annually.

aggression is not typical. When it does occur, the victim is rarely depicted as enjoying it (Garcia & Milano, 1990).

Videocassettes have had a profound effect on *who* views erotic films. Adult movie houses were the domain of men; relatively few women entered them. But with erotic videos available in the privacy of the bedroom, women also have become consumers of sexually oriented films and videos. By 1986, video stores reported that they rented the majority of sexually oriented videos to women or couples.

The inclusion of women in the audience has led to **femme porn,** erotic films catering to women or couples. Femme porn avoids violence, is less male-centered, and is more sensitive to women's erotic fantasies. Candida Royalle, a former "porno" actress, started Femme Productions to create nonsexist, woman-centered sexually explicit videos. Royalle says that "what angers me about traditional porn is it's always these little nymphets there to please men's fantasies" (quoted in Fraser, 1990). The women in her videos play strong, autonomous, and *sexual* roles. The women are attractive, she says, but they are ordinary women who may have small breasts, stretch marks, or cellulite thighs so as not to intimidate women viewers. The men, by contrast, appear more like "Ken dolls"—good-looking but without much personality.

The Effects of Sexually Oriented Material

Look but don't touch! You can show but you can't sell! Sublimate! Stimulate! This isn't really reality. Fantasy is legal, reality is not.
Alene Smith

There are a number of concerns about the effects of sexually oriented material. Does it cause people to engage in deviant acts? Is it a form of sex discrimination against women? And, finally, does it cause violence against women?

Sexual Expression People who read or view sexually explicit material recognize it as fantasy; they use it as a release from their everyday world (Davis, 1983). Exposure to sexually oriented material temporarily encourages sexual expression and may activate a person's *typical* sexual behavior pattern.

Sexually oriented materials deal with fantasy sex, not sex as we know it in the context of human relationships. Sexually explicit sex usually takes place in a world in which people and situations are defined in exclusively sexual terms. People are stripped of their nonsexual connections, note John Gagnon and William Simon (1973):

> This process of simplification . . . is perhaps one of the major sources of potency of pornography itself. Everything is grist for the mill of sexual fantasy because the process of that fantasy strips away the hulls of reality, seeking only those kernels that fit its needs.

People are interested in sexually oriented material for a number of reasons (Bryant & Brown, 1989). First, people enjoy the sexual sensations erotica arouses. It can be a source of pleasure. Masturbation or other sexual activities, pleasurable in themselves, may accompany the use of sexually oriented material or follow it. Second, since the nineteenth century, sexually oriented material has been a source of sexual information and knowledge (Marcus, 1966). Eroticism generally is hidden from view and discussion. When sexuality is discussed in the family, schools, or in public, it is discussed moralistically, rationally, or objectively. Most discussions are limited to sexual intercourse; other activities are avoided. Because the erotic aspects of sex are rarely talked about, sexually oriented material fills the void. In fact, several studies of college students have found that sexually oriented material is an important source of sex information, especially concerning oral sex (Duncan, 1990; Duncan & Nicholson, 1991; Duncan & Donnelly, 1991). Third, sexually oriented material, like fantasy, may provide an opportunity for people to rehearse sexual activities. Fourth, reading or viewing sexually oriented material for pleasure or for enhancing one's fantasies or masturbatory experiences may be regarded as safe sex.

Sexually oriented material may perform an additional function for gay men by allowing safe sex and reaffirmation. According to one writer, the HIV/AIDS crisis has threatened to deeroticize gay sexuality because of fear (Preston, 1991). Being HIV-positive or a person with AIDS creates anxieties about HIV transmission to others. But gay sexually oriented material permits those with HIV or AIDS to explore their own sexuality with masturbatory images and scenes while refraining from sexual relationships.

Men tend to react more positively to sexually explicit material than women (Thompson, Chaffe, & Oshagan, 1990). Men more than women believe sexually explicit material has positive effects, such as sexual release and a lowering of inhibitions. Both believe, however, that sexually explicit material may have negative effects, such as dehumanizing women and causing a loss of respect between men and women.

Sexually Oriented Material and Sexual Aggression: What Do We Know?
In 1970, the President's Commission on Pornography and Obscenity concluded that pornography did not cause harm or violence. It recommended that all legislation restricting adult access to it be repealed as incon-

sistent with the First Amendment. A member of the commission, Charles Keating, Jr., a prominent antipornography crusader (later imprisoned for savings-and-loan fraud) dissented: "Such an advocacy of moral anarchy. . . . Such a bold advocacy of a libertine philosophy! . . . The defenders of pornography are guilty of degrading sex." He argued that the report should be rejected as immoral.

In the 1980s, President Ronald Reagan established a new pornography commission under Attorney General Edwin Meese. (Six of the eleven members were on record as opposing pornography prior to their appointments [Noble, 1990].) In 1986, the Attorney General's Commission on Pornography stated that "the most prevalent forms of pornography" were violent; it offered no evidence, however, to substantiate its assertion (U.S. Attorney General's Commission on Pornography [AGCOP], 1986). There is no evidence, in fact, to indicate that the majority of sexually explicit material is violent. One researcher noted that in random viewings of sexually explicit films, about 16% of the movies depicted elements of violence (mostly relatively mild forms of aggression, such as pushing a woman down onto the bed or yelling at her) (Slade, 1984). The researcher also noted that a sample of 300 videotapes and film loops exhibited between 1979 and 1984 in sex arcades showed that violent films never accounted for more than 10% of them.

There is some evidence that violent sexually oriented material is increasing. A study of cartoons in *Playboy* and *Penthouse* over a 5-year period found that there was an increase in violent cartoons over that period, but violent cartoons accounted for only about 5% of all cartoons (Malamuth & Spinner, 1980). If there is more violence in sexually oriented material than before, the increase may be a reflection of the trend toward violence in movies and television in general, according to researcher Joseph Slade (1984). A study conducted by Joseph Scott (1985) of violence in the movies found that X-rated movies were less violent than G-, PG-, or R-rated movies. The average number of violent acts per movie were 20.3 for R-rated movies, 16.2 for G-rated movies, 15.3 for PG movies, and 4.4 for X-rated movies. Slade (1984) notes that "pornographic features thus far have rarely reached levels of violence equivalent to those in *Indiana Jones and the Temple of Doom*, a film rated PG." He points out, however, that the degree of violence in films of the 1970s and 1980s rose markedly, in contrast to the classic stag films of the 1950s. Regarding depictions of "brutal force," Slade writes:

> Where the classic stage might allow a performer to whack his lover with a hairbrush, the new loops permitted an aggressor to raise welts or draw blood. After brief flirtations with such fetishes, producers and consumers seemed to agree that brutal force really belonged off to the side of mainstream eroticism, and that is where it has been shunted for the present.

In the 1970s, feminists and others who worked to increase rape awareness began to call attention to the violence against women portrayed in the media. They found rape themes in sexually explicit material especially disturbing. They believed these images reinforced rape myths. Many feminists believe that pornography depicting women being raped or submitting to men legitimizes and encourages rape (Morgan, 1977). (The issue of sexually oriented material and sex discrimination is discussed later in the chapter.)

There is no evidence, however, that nonviolent sexually oriented material is associated with actual sexual aggression against women. Even the conservative Commission on Pornography agreed that nonviolent sexually oriented material had no such effect (AGCOP, 1986). But it did assert that "some forms of sexually explicit materials bear a causal relationship . . . to sexual violence." It presented no scientific evidence as proof, however.

The case concerning the relationship between violent sexually oriented material and sexual aggression against women has not been substantiated. The Society for the Scientific Study of Sex responded to the Meese Commission in a policy statement: "The evidence for a direct causal link between exposure to sexually explicit material, pornography, or violent pornography to consequences such as sexual violence, sexual coercion, or rape is incomplete and inadequate" (Board of Directors, 1987).

The most important studies *suggesting* a link between sexually oriented material and violence have been experimental ones published in the 1980s. A report by Neil Malamuth (1981) demonstrates both the strengths and the weaknesses of such studies. Malamuth divided 29 males into groups that were either sexually force-oriented or nonforce-oriented based on their willingness to use force to obtain sex. Both groups were shown a rape or a mutually consenting sexual act in an audio slide show; all were then exposed to an audio rape read by a female. They were then asked to create their own sexual fantasy. The study found that there were no differences in arousal when men were exposed to the different stimuli. But when asked to create a fantasy, the force-oriented group created more sexually arousing fantasies if they were exposed to the rape audiovisual. The nonforce-oriented group created more arousing fantasies of mutual consent if they were exposed to mutually consenting audiovisuals. The most significant finding, however, was that both groups created more violent sexual fantasies if they were exposed to the audiovisual rape than to the mutually consenting version.

Such experimental studies permit researchers to examine the different variables in laboratory settings. But the fundamental problem of such studies is whether conclusions derived in laboratory settings can be generalized to the outside world. Do attitudes translate into behavior? Does the creation of more violent sexual fantasies lead to rape? None of the leading researchers makes such claims.

Pornography is not contagious. . . . The eleven members of the Meese Commission on Pornography exposed themselves to vast amounts of pornography. . . . None has admitted to having been turned into a maurading and predatory paraphilic practitioner of sexual violence.

John Money

Sexually Oriented Material and Sex Discrimination

Since the 1980s, feminists have been divided about sexually explicit material. One segment of the feminist movement, which identifies itself as antipornography, views sexually explicit material as inherently degrading and dehumanizing to women. Activists such as Andrea Dworkin (1989) and Catharine MacKinnon believe that sexually explicit material provides the social basis for women's subordination by turning them into sex objects (Dworkin & MacKinnon, 1988). In the 1980s, Minneapolis passed legislation declaring sexually explicit material a form of sexual discrimination. The law provided that individuals could sue the makers, distributors, or exhibitors of sexually explicit material that depicted the subordination of women. Dworkin and MacKinnon, who were influential in passing the ordinance, argued that sexually explicit material inhibited women's equal rights by encouraging exploitation and subordination of women. The ordinance was subsequently overturned as unconstitutional. In Canada, however, a similar ordinance has been upheld as constitutional by the Canadian Supreme Court.

Feminists and other critics of this approach point out that it has an anti-sexual bias that associates sex with exploitation. Sexually explicit images, rather than specifically sexist images, are singled out. Further, discrimination and the subordination of women in Western culture have existed since ancient times, long before the rise of sexually oriented material. The roots of subordination lie far deeper. The elimination of sexual depictions of women would not alter discrimination of women significantly, if at all. Finally, some feminists believe that the approach represents a double standard. Writes feminist Carol Vance (1988): "It reasserts that women are sexually different from men and in need of special protection. Yet special protection inadvertently reinforces the ways in which women are legally and socially said to be different from men."

Feminist Muriel Dimen (1984) notes that feminists have been divided about sexuality, especially what is "politically correct sexuality." She writes:

> Feminists have made judgments about political correctness, particularly in the area of sexual behavior. This is because of the special cultural tension between sexuality and feminism. . . . On the one hand, because women have been traditionally defined as sex objects, feminism demands that society no longer focus on their erotic attributes, which, in turn, feminism downplays. On the other hand, because women have been traditionally defined as being uninterested in sex, they have been deprived of pleasure. . . . Feminism therefore demands sexual freedom for women.

This tension within feminism, Dimen believes, accounts for the efforts by some to suppress sexually explicit images of women, while others believe such images are liberating for women.

Child Pornography Child pornography is a form of child sexual exploitation. Children involved in pornography, who are usually between ages 8 and 16, are motivated by friendship, interest in sexuality, offers of money, or threats. Younger children may be unaware that their photographs are being used sexually. Many of these children are related to the photographer (Burgess, Hartman, McCausland, & Powers, 1984). Many children who have been exploited in this way report distress and poor adjustment; they may suffer from depression, anxiety, and guilt. Many engage in destructive and antisocial behavior, according to Ann Burgess and colleagues (1984).

While the courts have generally continued to oppose censoring sexually explicit material and to affirm the individual's right to possess such material, a major exception is child pornography. In 1990, the Supreme Court affirmed the right to prosecute individuals for the possession of child pornography (*Osborne v. Ohio*, No. 88-5986). But the Court did not argue that the possession of child pornography would "poison the minds of its viewers." It rejected such a view as "paternalistic." Instead, it hoped to "protect the victims of child pornography" by destroying the "market for the exploitative use of children." In an earlier (1982) child pornography decision, the Court similarly reasoned that prohibiting the distribution of child pornography would protect children from exploitation.

In 1977, the United States passed the Protection of Children Against Sexual Exploitation Act. (Unfortunately, this legislation does not address the widespread exploitation and victimization of adolescent prostitutes.) Since then, those involved in child pornography have been vigorously prosecuted. In 1993, for example, federal, state, and local law-enforcement officials served warrants on 30 individuals in 15 states involved in a Danish computer bulletin board that trafficked in obscene photographs of children (Foo, 1993). A problem with child pornography laws, however, is that they are often so broadly written that, in the words of Justice William Brennan, photographs of "teenagers in revealing dresses" or "toddlers romping unclothed" may lead to unjust arrests (*Osborne v. Ohio*, No. 88-5986). Such arrests of innocent parents or legitimate professional photographers have, in fact, occurred.

Fortunately, child pornography is not widespread, although it is commonly perceived as being so. Child pornography accounts for a tiny fraction of sexually explicit material, but it is often made to appear as representative of sexually explicit material in general. Feminist writer Florence Rush (1980), for example, erroneously reported that child pornography accounted for 40% of the sales of sexually explicit material (Rush, 1980). She further stated: "There is little doubt that men are sexually attracted to children, and entrepreneurs and advertisers attempt to capture this market." But as John Money (1986) points out, "This kind of pornography is erotically useless to people who do not have the particular kind of paraphilia that it depicts." Child pornography, in reality, appears to have a very limited audience.

Censorship, Sexually Oriented Material, and the Law

To censor means to examine in order to suppress or delete anything considered objectionable. **Censorship** occurs when the government, private groups, or individuals impose their moral or political values on others by suppressing words, ideas, or images they deem offensive.

There has been a dramatic shift in what is censored over the last generation. While overt censorship of books has declined significantly since the 1960s (except in schools and public libraries), it continues to assert itself in films, on TV, in photographic images, and in popular music. Indeed, the Meese Commission virtually ignored the written word (Vance, 1992); instead, it focused on visual images. What it said of the written word is important, however. The commission (AGCOP, 1986) noted:

> There remains a difference between reading a book and looking at pictures. . . . The absence of photographs necessarily produces a message that seems to necessitate for its assimilation more real thought and less reflexive action than does the more typical pornographic item.

Simply put, printed words are no longer considered dangerous. The change of censorship targets from the written word to visual and aural media, suggest some critics, reflects the shift from a literate culture based on words to a postliterate culture based on images and sounds. Books are no longer considered dangerous because they have lost their power in a culture dominated by television, movies, videos, and radio (Kendrick, 1987, 1992). Indeed, as English professor William Kendrick suggests, the acceptance of the written word as harmless and visual representations as harmful indicates that America has split into two cultures: a top-tier reading culture and a bottom-tier nonreading culture. It is the nonreading public that needs "protection" from sexual images. Furthermore, Carole Vance (1992) suggests

To slurp or not to slurp at the fountain of filth is a decision to which each of us is entitled.
Stephen Kessler

Two of the most heavily censored books in America are Leslea Newman's Heather Has Two Mommies, *about a lesbian family,* and Michael Willhoite's Daddy's Roommate, *about a child who visits his gay father and roommate. These books are opposed because they depict loving gay and lesbian families.*

that, in recent years, the written word has become legally protected as an established art form and means of expression. Popular art forms, such as photography, film, videos, and pop music, by contrast, are not widely considered "real" art. As such, they lack the cultural protection given to art and, consequently, are more likely to be censored.

Censorship and Obscenity **Obscenity** is the state of being contrary to generally accepted moral standards. In 1711, the first American obscenity law was enacted by the Massachusetts legislature in response to the Puritan clergy's being taunted with anticlerical pamphlets (President's Commission on Pornography and Obscenity, 1972). The law condemned

> evil communications, wicked, profane, impure, filthy and obscene songs, compsures [compositions], writings or prints [that] do corrupt the mind and are incentives to all manner of impieties and debaucheries, more especially when digested, composed, or uttered in imitation of preaching, or any other style of divine worship.

I may disagree with what you say but I will defend to the death your right to say it.

Voltaire

Obscenity was originally an offense against religion, often because it contained a sexual innuendo or reference. (It had been a time-honored practice to mock the clergy with sexual humor since at least the early Renaissance, with the writings of Chaucer and Bocaccio.) The first American obscenity trial took place in 1815, when a man was arrested in Pennsylvania for showing for profit a picture of a man and woman in an "indecent posture." Obscenity laws were sporadically enforced until the 1870s, when the Committee for the Suppression of Vice, under the leadership of Anthony Comstock, a young grocer, undertook a campaign to root out vice and filth (including masturbation). In 1873, the United States passed legislation to prohibit the distribution of obscene material. It appointed Comstock a special agent in charge of enforcement. During his zealous activities, he con-

We are condemned to avoid half the life that passes us by.

Robert Louis Stevenson

fiscated and destroyed tens of millions of condoms (as contributing to vice). D. M. Bennett, a nineteenth-century publisher, asked, "Why should priests and magistrates supervise the sexual organs of citizens any more than the brains and stomach?" He was arrested and sentenced to 17 months of hard labor for his views. Comstock banned Walt Whitman's *Leaves of Grass* in Boston and attacked Voltaire for blasphemy. In 1912, he personally arrested Margaret Sanger, the founder of the American birth control movement, for distributing obscene devices and literature—condoms and birth control pamphlets. His pursuit of sexual censorship gave rise to the term "Comstockery."

During the first half of this century, under American obscenity laws, James Joyce's *Ulysses* and the works of D. H. Lawrence were prohibited, Havelock Ellis's *Studies in the Psychology of Sex* was banned, nude paintings

A book whose sale is forbidden,
all men rush to see.
And prohibition turns
one reader into three.

Italian proverb

ROCK, RAP, AND RIGHTEOUSNESS: CENSORSHIP AND POPULAR MUSIC

From its beginning, rock and roll music, with its overt sexual themes, has attracted censors. In the 1950s, sociology writer Vance Packard testified before the U.S. Senate that rock and roll stirred "the animal instinct in modern teenagers" by its "raw savage tone." When Elvis ("The Pelvis") Presley appeared on "The Ed Sullivan Show," he was filmed only from the waist up. When the Rolling Stones appeared on the show several years later, words from the song "Satisfaction" were bleeped out; Mick Jagger had to change the words of "Let's Spend the Night Together" to "let's spend some time together" (Heins, 1993).

The current cycle of music censorship began in 1985 when Tipper Gore (whose husband is Vice President Al Gore) heard Prince's "Darling Nikki," a song about masturbation. She organized Parents Music Resource Center (PMRC) to focus public attention on the explicitness of rock music. Senate hearings were called to pressure record companies to label offensive music. Frank Zappa, one of America's foremost rock innovators and composers, defended rockers' artistic freedom. "Masturbation is not illegal. If it is not illegal, why should it be illegal to sing about?" (Chapple & Talbot, 1990). "There should be warning labels on politicians," complained the bass guitarist of the satirical rock group Spinal Tap (Heins, 1993).

Because the hearings intimidated the record companies, they began labeling potentially offensive music. Charles Krauthammer (1985) writes of labeling:

> Labels offer parental guidance, sure. But how many kids shop for records with their parents? . . . Labeling is useful in one way only. Many, perhaps most, stores and malls will ban X-rated music, creating enormous economic pressure on artists and studios to produce non-X music. That's how music ratings work. It amounts to an elegant form of censorship—elegant because it is censorship made to look like consumer information.

Shortly afterward, televangelist Jimmy Swaggart (since disgraced for his involvement in a sex scandal) denounced rock music as "degenerate filth which denigrates all the values we hold sacred." He held a meeting with Wal-Mart officials, and soon thereafter the giant discount chain stopped stocking rock and teen magazines deemed offensive.

In 1990, the major record companies adopted a "sexually explicit lyrics" label (Heins, 1993). Although the label was not meant to suggest that record stores should refuse to sell labeled recordings to minors, police in some areas warned music stores that such records were considered obscene. Major retailers, such as Sears and J.C. Penney, announced that they would not carry labeled recordings.

were ripped from gallery and museum walls, and everything but tender kisses was banned from the movies for years.

U.S. Supreme Court decisions in the 1950s and 1960s eliminated much of the legal framework supporting literary censorship on the national level. But censorship continues to flourish on the state and local levels, especially among schools and libraries. The women's health book *Our Bodies, Ourselves* has been a frequent object of attack because of its feminist perspective and descriptions of lesbian sexuality. More recently, two children's books have

Since the late 1980s, local officials have attempted to shut down shows by the Beastie Boys, Run-DMC, and LL Cool J. LL Cool J was arrested for making lewd movements on stage (Chapple & Talbot, 1990). In 1990, 2 Live Crew's album "Nasty as They Wanna Be" was declared obscene by a Florida judge. The judge maintained that the music and explicit sexual lyrics were "utterly without any redeeming social value." In 1992, the decision was reversed. In its reversal, the appellate court stated "because music possesses inherent artistic value, no work of music alone can be declared obscene." Later that year, Washington became the first state to ban the sale of music with explicit sexual lyrics to minors.

Marjorie Heins (1993) writes:

Creative works are constitutionally protected in large part because of the critical role they play in a society that values individual autonomy, dignity, and growth; it also expresses, defines, and nourishes the human personality. Art speaks to our emotions, our intellects, our spiritual lives, and also our physical and sexual lives. Artists celebrate joy and abandon, but they also confront death, depression, and despair. For some of us, rock 'n' roll or rap artists may play these roles and provide these connections; for others, classical composers, sculptors, or playwrights may elicit the most powerful responses.

By the early 1990s, it became common practice to "censor by suggestion." Police departments or district attorneys warned retailers to remove certain music, especially rap or rock (never opera) because, they *suggested*, it might be obscene. Since obscenity could only be tested in court, many stores withdrew the material because they could not bear the expense of a costly court trial. While the police denied this was censorship, it short-circuited the legal process. As Justice William Brennan observed, "People do not lightly disregard public officers' thinly veiled threats to institute criminal proceedings against them if they do not come around" (quoted in Heins, 1993).

Many critics complain about the themes of sex, violence, suicide, incest, and sexism found in contemporary music. While these themes may be objectionable, they are not unique to rock and rap. Wolfgang Amadeus Mozart's opera *Don Giovanni* begins with a famous aria enumerating the hundreds of women he has seduced. The Greek tragedy *Oedipus Rex* is about incest. Some of the works of such great artists as Bruegel, Rembrandt, Goya, and Picasso (to name but a few) deal with seduction, incest, bestiality, rape, and sadism.

There is no doubt that some popular music is repugnant, tasteless, vulgar, puerile, degrading, racist, sexist, homophobic, offensive, lewd, and stupid. But Supreme Court decisions have long demonstrated our inability to create objective criteria for determining what is obscene. When we consider popular music, it is important to remember that the purpose of the Constitution's First Amendment is not to judge art but to protect our freedom of expression. As the Supreme Court stated in *Cohen v. California* (1971): "One man's lyric may be another's vulgarity."

been added to the list of most censored books: Leslea Newman's *Heather Has Two Mommies* and Michael Willhoite's *Daddy's Roommate*. Both books have come under attack because they describe children in healthy lesbian and gay families. Judy Blume's books for teenagers, J. D. Salinger's *The Catcher in the Rye*, and the *Sports Illustrated* swimsuit issue are regular items on banned-book lists. Exhibits of the photographs taken by the late Robert Mapplethorpe have been strenuously attacked for "promoting" homoeroticism. (For a discussion of art, morals, and politics, see Hughes, 1992.) The

If America persists in the way it's going, and the Lord doesn't strike us down, He ought to apologize to Sodom and Gomorrah.

Jesse Helms

director of a Cincinnati museum was arrested for violating local obscenity ordinances when he hung the Mapplethorpe show (Mansneurus, 1990). (The director was acquitted because the prosecution could find no credible witnesses to support its contention of obscenity [Hughes, 1992].) (For a discussion of rock and rap censorship, see Perspective 2.)

Obscenity Laws It is difficult to arrive at a legal definition of obscenity for determining whether a specific illustration, photograph, novel, or movie is obscene. Traditionally, American courts considered material obscene if it tended to corrupt or deprave its user. This common-law tradition was challenged in *Roth v. United States* in 1957, which overturned a lower court's decision that D. H. Lawrence's *Lady Chatterley's Lover* was obscene. According to the *Roth* decision, material is obscene if, and only if, "the average person, applying contemporary community standards, would find that the work, taken as a whole, appeals to the prurient [lustful or lewd] interest." In 1973, the Supreme Court in *Miller v. California* supplemented the *Roth* decision by arguing that the state had to prove that the work, "taken as a whole, did not have serious literary, artistic, political, or scientific value." In 1987, in *Pope v. Illinois,* the Supreme Court rejected the application of contemporary community standards when judging a work's social value. Instead, social value was to be judged from the standpoint of a "reasonable person." Together, the *Roth, Miller,* and *Pope* decisions present the main guidelines for determining whether a work is obscene. Their main points are as follows:

1. The dominant theme of the work must appeal to prurient sexual interests and portray sexual conduct in a patently offensive way.

2. Taken as a whole, the work must be without serious literary, artistic, political, or scientific value.

3. A "reasonable" person must find the work, when taken as a whole, to possess no social value.

The problem with these criteria, as well as the earlier standards, is that they are highly subjective. Who is a reasonable person? You or I, the local minister, priest, or rabbi, Pat Robertson, Hugh Hefner, Gloria Steinem, or Phyllis Schlafly? Moreover, there are many instances in which reasonable people disagree about whether material has social value. In his dissent, Justice John Paul Stevens (*Pope v. Illinois*) cautioned that the reasonable person doctrine might once again endanger *Ulysses* and *Lady Chatterley's Lover,* for juries "might well believe that the majority of the population who find no value in such a book are more reasonable than the minority who do find value." Most of us would probably find that a reasonable person has opinions regarding obscenity that closely resemble our own. (Otherwise, we would think that he or she was unreasonable.)

As we saw earlier, our evaluation of sexually explicit material is closely related to how we feel about such material (Byrne, Fisher, Lambreth, & Mitchell, 1974). Our judgments are not based on reason but on emotion. Justice Potter Stewart's exasperation in *Jacobelis v. Ohio* (1965) reveals a reasonable person's frustration in trying to define pornography: "But I know it when I see it." Our inability to find criteria for objectively defining obscenity makes it potentially dangerous to censor such material. We may

There is no such thing as a moral or immoral book. Books are well written or badly written.

Oscar Wilde

The American impulse is to turn morality into law.

John Garvey

Congress shall make no law respecting an establishment of religion, or prohibiting the free exercise thereof; or abridging the freedom of speech, or of the press, or the right of the people peaceably to assemble, and to petition the Government for a redress of grievances.

First Amendment to the Constitution

end up using our own *personal* standards for restricting freedom of speech guaranteed by the First Amendment. By enforcing our own biases, we endanger the freedom of others. To date, the law has been unable to distinguish between such recognized literary classics as *Lady Chatterley's Lover* and *Ulysses* (both of which had once been suppressed in the United States as obscene) and books such as *Snuff, Women in Bondage,* and *Sisters of de Sade.* When the classics are accepted, so are the others; when the others are suppressed, so are the classics. To outlaw *Snuff* is to endanger *Ulysses.*

Ira Reiss (1990) writes:

> If we viewed sexuality in a more positive light, would we be so concerned about movies or books that arouse people sexually? It is time for us to get rid of this incoherent legal concept of obscenity. By this time in American history, grown-ups ought to be pluralistic enough to accept portrayals of sexuality for others even though personally they do not like them. Many Americans see sexuality as very dangerous, and therefore they think that sexual arousal is likely to lead people to do all kinds of harmful things. Such a fearful view of sex implies that minimizing sexual stimulation will help in achieving greater good for everyone. Accordingly, we have restricted the First Amendment rights to free speech in the area of sex and virtually nowhere else!

PROSTITUTION

Prostitution is the exchange of sexual acts, such as sexual intercourse, fellatio, anal intercourse, discipline and bondage, and obscene insults, for money. Both men and women, including transvestites and transsexuals, work as prostitutes.

Females Working in Prostitution

During the 1980s, an estimated 80,000 women worked in prostitution (Potterat et al., 1990). This estimate may be considerably smaller than the actual number because many women engage in it occasionally or drift in and out. Many women who accept money or drugs for sexual activities do not consider themselves prostitutes. According to Janus and Janus (1993), 4% of the women in their representative study reported exchanging sex for money.

The Subculture of Prostitution Prostitution forms its own subculture. It has its own hierarchy, code of conduct, and vocabulary. When a woman accepts money as payment for sexual activity, she is labeled a prostitute, a label that defines her exclusively in sexual terms. Whether she was previously identified as a student, mother, secretary, or executive, her primary social identity becomes prostitute after she accepts money for sex. But the degradation associated with prostitution also tells us, maintains researcher and social worker Richie McMullen (1987), how we as individuals and a society feel about sexuality. "All too often," he notes, "it is the person, 'prostitute,' who receives a morally projected identification, which says more about the projecting person or society than it does about the 'prostitute' in question."

To the Censorious Ones
I'm coming up out of the tomb,
  Men Of War
Just when you thought you had me
  down, in place, hidden
I'm coming up now
Can you feel the ground rumble
  under your feet?
It's breaking apart, it's turning over,
  it's pushing up
It's thrusting into your point of
  view, your private property
O Men of War, Censorious Ones!
GET READY BIG BOYS GET
  READY
I'm coming up now
I'm coming up with all that was
  hidden
Get ready, Big Boys, get ready
I'm coming up with all you wanted
  buried,
All the hermetic texts with stories in
  them of
Hot & dangerous women
Women with lascivious tongues,
  sharp eyes & claws
I've been working out, my muscles
  are strong
I'm pushing up the earth with all
  you try to censor
All the iconoclasm & bravado you
  scorn
All the taunts against your banner
  & salute
I'm coming up from Hell with all
  you ever suppressed
All the dark fantasies, all the dregs
  are coming back
I'm leading them back up now
They're going to bark & bite
I'm opening the box
BOO!

                    Anne Waldman

The prostitute identity is fundamentally a criminal one. Therefore, once women are identified as prostitutes, they may begin to withdraw from the conventional world and move into the subculture of prostitution known as "the life." They may avoid contact with their families and move to different cities. Their new world is populated by pimps, petty thieves, mobsters, and patrons. Eventually, prostitution becomes their only world. It is difficult for women to leave prostitution because the conventional world continues to stigmatize them as prostitutes or ex-prostitutes.

Women working in prostitution begin using the subculture's language. They call themselves "working girls," "hookers," or "hoes" rather than prostitutes. Their customers are "dates," "johns," or "tricks." A sexual transaction is known as "turning a trick" or "catching a date" (Zausner, 1986). Such terminology acts as a psychological shield that helps protect prostitutes from viewing themselves as sinful, immoral, or deviant (McMullen, 1987).

Sex as Work Prostitutes often identify themselves as "working girls" or "sex workers," probably an accurate description of how they perceive themselves in relationship to sex. They are usually not prostitutes because they like anonymous sex and multiple partners per se, but because they perceive it as good-paying work. They generally do not expect to enjoy sex with their customers. They separate sex as a physical act for which they are paid from sex as an expression of intimacy and pleasure. One prostitute (quoted in Zausner, 1986) describes her feelings about sex:

> I don't think about sex when I'm working. You have to be a good actress to make men think that you like it when you don't. I only enjoy sex if I'm with someone I care about.

Another study, however, found that many of the prostitutes interviewed enjoyed their sexual activities (Savitz & Rosen, 1989). Thirty-nine percent stated they enjoyed sexual intercourse with their clients most or all of the time. Fifty-seven percent reported they enjoyed fellatio most or all of the time; 70% said they enjoyed cunnilingus most or all of the time.

Although prostitutes may be willing to perform various sexual acts, many will not kiss; they regard kissing as a particular form of intimacy which they reserve for men they care about. Another prostitute (quoted in Perkins & Bennett, 1985) says:

> I won't kiss a client, and the guys won't attempt it. Oh, some will try it, and some girls do it too. Those girls think they will give them a bit more, but the area where I work they're not supposed to. It goes with cutting prices or giving specials. I won't kiss under any circumstances because to me kissing is special and reserved for pleasure only.

Entrance into Prostitution A major study of adolescent prostitution found that the majority of prostitutes under age 18 were less than 16 when they first began. The average age for the first act of prostitution was 14 (Weisberg, 1985).

Childhood sexual abuse, discussed in Chapter 18, is often a factor in adolescent girls' and boys' entrance into prostitution, for two reasons (Earls & David, 1990; Simons & Whitbeck, 1991). First, sexual abuse increases the likelihood that a preadolescent or adolescent will become involved in the deviant street culture and activities. Physically and sexually abused youths are more likely to be rejected by their conventional peers and become involved in delinquent activities. Second, one of their primary reasons for fleeing home is parental abuse—generally physical abuse for boys, sexual abuse for girls.

Some researchers believe that sexual abuse at home creates psychological defenses that facilitate prostitution on the streets. One researcher (Miller, 1986) observes:

> The experience of emotional distancing during sexual contact that incest victims often describe is too like the psychological state described by prostitutes when they are servicing a trick for one not to be a sort of rehearsal for the other. In those cases, sexual exploitation on the street seems but an extension of sexual exploitation in the family.

Furthermore, childhood sexual abuse may have severely affected the young woman's self-concept. Not only can abuse separate a woman's emotions from her sexuality, it also may serve to reinforce her perception of herself as a sexual object and as a sexually debased person (James & Meyerding, 1977). These factors may combine to encourage a person's entrance into prostitution.

Girls are generally introduced into prostitution by pimps, men upon whom prostitutes are emotionally and financially dependent. Prostitutes give their pimps the money they earn. In turn, pimps provide housing, buy them clothes and jewelry, and offer them protection on the streets. One woman describes her pimp (quoted in Zausner, 1986):

> I don't really think of him as a pimp because he treats me like a woman and not like a hoe. I do give him all of the money that I make working the streets but he doesn't force me to do anything and he never hits me like other pimps do. He's a lot nicer than a pimp. He's my friend and lover. . . . He's going to let me go to college. . . . I give all my money to my man. That's the way the game goes. It's our money. We survive together. If I want to be with him, I have to play by the rules. He puts the money in the bank and invests some of it in cars, clothes for me and him, and jewelry.

Although girls meet their pimps in various ways, pimps most frequently initiate the contact. They use both psychological and physical coercion. Many girls and young women are "sweet-talked" into prostitution by promises of money, protection, and companionship. Adolescent prostitutes are more likely than adults to have pimps.

Once involved with pimps, women are frequently abused by them. Physical abuse most often occurs when the woman acts "disrespectful" to the pimp. Other factors include violating the rules of prostitution, failing to earn sufficient money, or leaving or threatening to leave the pimp. Kelly Weisberg (1985) notes of adolescent prostitutes:

> Most prostitutes accept the violence as a way of life or feel they deserve it. Some are even flattered by it or accept it as evidence that the pimp cares for them. Many juveniles accept the abuse with passivity because they are convinced that violence is the acceptable standard by which men and women relate. Since they

grew up in families in which violence is a way of life, the prostitutes accept physical abuse as an intrinsic aspect of close personal relationships.

The women also run the risk of abuse and violence from their customers. Streetwalkers are especially vulnerable.

Personal Background and Motivation Adult prostitutes are often women who were targets of early male sexual aggression, had extensive sexual experience in adolescence, were rejected by peers because of sexual activities, and were not given adequate emotional support by their parents. There are high rates of physical and sexual abuse (including intrafamilial abuse) in their childhoods (Silbert & Pines, 1981; Zausner, 1986). Their parents failed to provide their daughters with a model of affectionate interaction. As a result, as the girls grew up, they tended to be anxious, to feel lonely and isolated, and to be unsure of their own identity (Greenwald, 1970; Simon & Gagnon, 1973).

Adolescent prostitutes describe their general psychological state of mind as very negative, depressed, unhappy, or insecure at the time they first entered prostitution. There were high levels of drug use, including alcohol, marijuana, cocaine, and/or heroin (Weisberg, 1985). Their emotional state makes them particularly vulnerable to pimps.

Because these women had already had extensive but impersonal sexual experiences, their main emotional conflict resulted not from the performance of the act but from accepting money for it. They could justify a consistent pattern of impersonal sexual relations in terms of affection, romance, pleasure, or desire, but these justifications disappear when payment becomes the motive. A small nonrepresentative sample of prostitutes and nonprostitutes found that the most important distinguishing characteristic of nonprostitutes was their aversion to accepting money for sex (Potterat et al., 1985). Sex was equated with their own pleasure rather than someone else's.

Prostitutes report various motives for entering prostitution. One study reported that 5 out of 14 prostitutes were interested in earning quick and easy money; 2 were attracted by the prostitution subculture; and 7 were attracted by the "thrills and adventures of the life" (Potterat et al., 1985).

When women describe the most attractive things about their lives in the prostitution subculture, they describe them in monetary and material terms. One prostitute notes (Weisberg, 1985), "I said to myself how can I do these horrible things and I said money, money, money." Compared to minimum-wage jobs, which may be the only alternative, prostitution appears to be an economically rational decision. But prostitutes also are aware of the psychological and physical costs. They fear the dangers of physical and sexual abuse, AIDS and other sexually transmitted diseases, harassment, jail, and legal expenses. They are also aware of the damage done to their self-esteem from stigmatization and rejection by family and society, negative feelings toward men and sex, bad working conditions, lack of a future, and control by pimps (Weisberg, 1985).

Prostitutes may justify their deviant behavior in terms of the cultural values accepted by the conventional world. They may take pride in financial success, their high earnings, easy life, beautiful clothes, expensive cars. Women who live two lives—mother and wife by day, prostitute by night—are likely to hold conventional middle-class values and to explain their

Erotic dancing in bars, clubs, and peep shows led to the end of strip-tease in burlesque shows in the 1970s (left). Americans tend to romanticize prostitution on TV and in movies, as demonstrated by the movie "Pretty Woman" (above).

prostitution in terms of family responsibilities: They need the money for their children, sick parents, unemployed husbands, or other reasons.

Prostitutes exhibit a range of feelings toward their customers. Some may project onto others their feelings of being deviant. If customers regard prostitutes as bad, the women feel that the so-called respectable people who come to them are worse—hypocrites, freaks, weirdos, and perverts who ask them to perform sexual acts which the women often consider degrading. Prostitutes frequently encounter such people, and may generalize from these experiences (Greenwald, 1970). Other prostitutes, however, are accepting and nonjudgmental of their customers. "My customers are people like everyone else," reports one prostitute (Zausner, 1986). "If they're nice to me and don't try to fuck with me, then I like them."

Forms of Female Prostitution There are four major types of female prostitutes: those who work as streetwalkers, in brothels, in massage parlors, and as call girls.

Streetwalkers Streetwalkers are by far the most numerous. Streetwalking is usually the first type of prostitution in which adolescents become involved; it is also the type they prefer (Weisberg, 1985). Women working as streetwalkers are often high school dropouts or runaways who fled abusive homes. Since streetwalkers make their contacts through public solicitation, they are more visible and more likely to be arrested. Without the ability to easily screen her customers, the streetwalker is more likely to be victimized, beaten, robbed, or raped. She is also more likely to have a pimp.

Streetwalkers in one study worked an average of 5 days a week and had 4 or 5 clients a day, half of whom were repeats (Freund et al., 1989). Fellatio was their most common activity; less than one-quarter of their contacts involved sexual intercourse.

Brothels Before the early part of the twentieth century, brothels were widespread throughout the United States. They performed many of the social functions of a bar, pool hall, or club for men; they were places to drink, socialize, make friends, and talk with women. Food and liquor were served downstairs; upstairs were the rooms where sex took place for money. The moral reformers of the progressive era (1900–1920) effectively destroyed the American brothel culture. The reformers, however, did not end prostitution; instead, they ended an important social aspect of it and drove women into the streets where they were more likely to be victimized (Rosen, 1982).

While greatly diminished in numbers, brothels can be found in most large cities. They are legal in some counties in Nevada. A major attraction of brothels is their comfortable and personable atmosphere. In brothels, men can sit and have a cup of coffee or a drink, watch television, or casually converse with the women. Many customers are regulars. Sometimes they go to the brothel simply to talk or relax rather than to engage in sex (Perkins & Bennett, 1985).

Some brothels, such as B&D dungeons, which cater to bondage and discipline customers, specialize in different types of sex (Perkins & Bennett, 1985). These "dungeons" are equipped with whips, racks, leg irons; they replicate a gothic atmosphere. Women in such brothels adopt pseudonyms such as "Madam Lash" or add the prefix "Mistress" to their first names. They dress in black, studded leather and make themselves up as forbidding dominatrices (plural of dominatrix, a woman who dominates) (Delacoste & Alexander, 1987).

Masseuses There are relatively few brothels any longer; most have been replaced by massage parlors. The major difference between brothels and massage parlors is that brothels present themselves as places of prostitution, while massage parlors try to disguise their intent. There are basically four types of massage parlors (Bryant & Palmer, 1975). First, genuine massage parlors actually provide exercise and physical therapy instead of sex. Second, there are "rip-off joints" that entice customers with sexual advertising, women dressed as harem slaves, and brothel-like decor. The customers get a massage but no sex. Since most massage parlors depend on transient customers, they are not concerned that the customer will never return. A third type of massage parlor is little more than a brothel in disguise. The customer is able to get any type of sexual service he desires for a fee, which is negotiated with the masseuses. The fourth type is the "massage and masturbation only" parlor. These so-called M-and-M parlors are probably the most widespread; their primary service is the "local" or "relief" massage in which there is only masturbation. By limiting sex to masturbation, these parlors are able to avoid legal difficulties, because most criminal sex statutes require genital penetration, oral sex, discussion of fees, and explicit solicitation for criminal prosecution. Women who work M-and-M parlors are frequently referred to as "hand whores"; these women, however, often do not consider themselves

Prostitution

- *Prostitution* is the exchange of sexual acts for money. Both men and women work as prostitutes. Prostitution forms its own subculture. When a woman accepts money as payment for sexual activity, she is labeled a prostitute, a deviant label that defines her exclusively in sexual terms. Prostitutes often identify themselves as "working girls" or "sex workers."

- Women are generally introduced into prostitution by pimps. Adolescent prostitutes describe their general psychological state of mind as very negative, depressed, unhappy, or insecure at the time they first entered prostitution. The women, especially streetwalkers, also run the risk of abuse and violence from their customers. Prostitutes report various motives for entering prostitution, including earning quick and easy money, the prostitution subculture, and the excitement of "the life." Their main emotional conflict results not from having sex but from accepting money for it.

- Streetwalkers are the most numerous prostitutes. Streetwalking is usually the first type of prostitution in which adolescents become involved. Others work in brothels; a major attraction is their comfortable and personable atmosphere. Massage parlors are more widespread. Some masseuses have intercourse with clients, while others provide only masturbation. Call girls have the highest status among prostitutes.

- Most research on male prostitution focuses on street hustlers. Male prostitution is shaped by the peer delinquent, gay, and transvestite subcultures. The three most important reasons given for engaging in prostitution are money, sex, and fun/adventure.

- Arrests for prostitution are symbols of community disapproval; they are not effective in ending prostitution. Female prostitution is the only sexual offense for which women are extensively prosecuted; the male patron is seldom arrested. Decriminalization of prostitution is often urged because it is a victimless crime, or because prostitutes are victimized by their pimps, customers, police, and the legal system. Other people advocate regulation by police and health departments.

- Prostitutes are at higher risk for HIV/AIDS than the general population because many are IV drug users, have multiple partners, and do not always require their customers to use condoms. Female and male prostitutes and their customers may provide a pathway for HIV into the general heterosexual community.

KEY TERMS

erotica	hardcore	obscenity
pornography	softcore	peer delinquent subculture
sexually oriented material	femme porn	solicitation
sexually explicit material	censorship	

SUGGESTIONS FOR FURTHER READING

Davis, Murray S. *Smut: Erotic Reality/Obscene Ideology*. Chicago: University of Chicago Press, 1983. An excellent sociological analysis of the interrelatedness of sexuality, erotica/pornography, society, and religion.

Delacoste, Frédérique, and Priscilla Alexander, eds. *Sex Work: Writing by Women in the Sex Industry*. Pittsburgh, PA: Cleis Press, 1987. A collection of short, personal stories by women who work as prostitutes, masseuses, topless dancers, models, and actresses, many of who regard themselves as feminists.

Donnerstein, Edward, et al., eds. *The Question of Pornography*. New York: Free Press, 1987. A review of the scientific research on sexually oriented material, their effects, and the legal issues involved.

Heins, Marjorie. *Sex, Sin, and Blasphemy: A Guide to America's Censorship Wars*. New York: The New Press, 1993. Recent censorship battles—and what's at stake—in art, music, dance, and the mass media by the director of the American Civil Liberties Union's Art Censorship Project.

Rosen, Ruth. *The Lost Sisterhood: Prostitution in America, 1890–1918*. Baltimore: Johns Hopkins University Press, 1982. An examination of women who chose prostitution, as well as the middle-class reformers who sought to end it. A sympathetic exploration of their lives and feelings at a time when American attitudes toward prostitution radically changed.

Steward, Samuel M. *Understanding the Male Hustler*. New York: Haworth Press, 1992. A look at the world of male prostitution from the hustler's point of view.

Steinberg, David, ed. *The Erotic Impulse: Honoring the Sensual Self*. New York: Jeremy Tarcher, 1992. An outstanding collection of essays and poems by writers, poets, teachers, and psychologists.

Weisberg, Kelly D. *Children of the Night: A Study of Adolescent Prostitution*. Lexington, MA: Lexington Books, 1984. An outstanding scholarly work on the world of adolescent prostitution.

abortion The expulsion of the conceptus, either spontaneously or by induction.

abstinence Refraining from sexual intercourse.

acculturation The process of an ethnic group's adaptation to the attitudes, behaviors, and values of the dominant culture.

acquired immune deficiency syndrome (AIDS) A disease caused by the human immunodeficiency virus (HIV) in which the immune system is weakened and unable to fight opportunistic infections, such as pneumocystis carinii pneumonia (PCP) and Kaposi's sarcoma.

acrosomal reaction The release of enzymes from a sperm's acrosome.

acrosome The covering of the head of the sperm containing enzymes that will assist in the penetration of an oocyte's wall.

adenosis A condition involving immature glandular cells in the cervix and wall of the vagina, common among women whose mothers took DES.

adolescence The social and psychological state occurring during puberty.

adrenogenital syndrome *See* congenital adrenal hyperplasia.

agape In John Lee's typology of love, altruistic love.

age of consent The age at which a person is legally deemed capable of giving consent.

agglutination test A pregnancy test using the woman's urine.

AI Artificial insemination. *See* intrauterine insemination.

AIDS *See* acquired immune deficiency syndrome.

AIDS dementia Impairment of mental functioning, changes in mood or behavior, and impaired movement caused by direct infection of the brain with HIV. Also known as HIV encephalopathy.

allantois The embryonic membrane that is the structural base of the umbilical cord and urinary bladder.

alpha-feto protein (AFP) screening A blood test of a pregnant woman's blood to determine the existence of neural tube defects.

alveoli (singular, *alveolus*) Small glands within the female breast that begin producing milk following childbirth.

amenorrhea The absence of menstruation, unrelated to aging.

amniocentesis A process in which amniotic fluid is withdrawn by needle from the uterus and then examined for evidence of possible birth defects.

amnioinfusion An abortion method involving the replacement of amniotic fluid with some type of medication.

amnion An embryonic membranous sac containing the embryo and amniotic fluid.

amniotic fluid The fluid within the amniotic sac that surrounds the embryo or fetus.

ampulla The widened part of the fallopian tube or the vas deferens.

analingus The licking of the anal region.

anal intercourse The insertion of the erect penis into the partner's anus.

anal stage In Freudian theory, the period from age 1 to 3, during which the child's erotic activities center on the anus.

anatomical sex Identification as male or female based on physical sex characteristics, such as gonads, uterus, vulva, vagina, or penis.

androgen Any of the male hormones, including testosterone.

androgen-insensitivity syndrome A hereditary condition passed through X chromosomes in which a genetic male is born with testes but is unable to absorb testosterone; as a result, the estrogen influence prevails, and his body tends toward a female appearance, failing to develop male internal and external sex organs. Also known as testicular feminization.

androgen replacement therapy The administration of testosterone to increase sex drive.

androgyny The unique and flexible combination of instrumental and expressive traits in accordance with individual differences, situations, and stages in the life cycle.

anorexia nervosa An eating disorder characterized by the pursuit of excessive thinness.

anorexic A person with anorexia.

anorgasmia A sexual dysfunction characterized by the absence of orgasm.

antibody A cell that binds to the antigen of an invading cell, inactivating it and marking it for destruction by killer cells.

anti-gay prejudice A strong dislike, fear, or hatred of gay men and lesbians because of their homosexuality. *See also* heterosexual bias; homophobia.

antigen A molecular structure on the wall of a cell capable of stimulating the immune system and then reacting with the antibodies that are released to fight it.

anus The opening of the rectum, consisting of two sphincters, circular muscles that open and close like valves.

anxious/ambivalent attachment A style of infant attachment characterized by separation anxiety and insecurity when the infant's primary caregiver goes out of sight.

Apgar score The cumulative rating of the newborn's heart rate, respiration, color, reflexes, and muscle tone.

areola A ring of darkened skin around the nipple.

artificial insemination (AI) *See* intrauterine insemination.

assigned gender The gender ascribed by others, usually at birth.

asymptomatic Without symptoms.

attitude The predisposition to act, think, or feel in certain ways toward particular things.

atypical sexual behavior Consensual sexual activity that is not statistically typical of American sexual behavior.

atypical sexuality Sexuality that differs from the more common forms of sexual behavior.

autoerotic asphyxia A form of sexual masochism linking strangulation with masturbation.

autoeroticism Sexual self-stimulation or behavior involving only the self; usually refers to masturbation but also includes sexual fantasies and dreams.

avoidant attachment A style of infant attachment characterized by the infant's avoidance of its primary caregiver as a defense against rejection.

bacterial vaginosis   A vaginal infection commonly caused by the bacterium *Gardnerella vaginalis*.

Barnum effect   The tendency to believe that general statements, which apply more or less to everyone, apply specifically to oneself.

Bartholin's gland   One of two small ducts on either side of the vaginal opening that secretes a small amount of moisture during sexual arousal. Also known as vestibular gland.

basal body temperature (BBT) method   A contraceptive method based on a woman's temperature in the morning upon waking; when the temperature rises, the woman is fertile.

B cell   A type of lymphocyte involved in antibody production.

B&D   *See* bondage and discipline.

behavior   The way a person acts.

benign prostatic hypertrophy   Enlargement of the prostate gland, affecting over half of men over age 50.

benign tumor   A tumor that is slow-growing, localized, and may be surgically removed if necessary.

berdache   A male who assumes female dress, gender role, and status; regarded in some cultures as a third gender.

bias   A personal leaning or inclination.

biased sample   A nonrepresentative sample.

biopsy   The surgical removal of tissue for diagnosis.

birth canal   The passageway through which an infant is born; the vagina.

birth control   Any means of preventing a birth from taking place, including contraception and abortion.

bisexuality   A sexual orientation in which one is equally and consistently attracted to members of both sexes.

blastocyst   A collection of about 100 human cells that develops from the zygote.

blood-testis barrier   A barrier that prevents a sperm's antigens from entering the bloodstream and provoking an immune response.

bondage and discipline (B&D)   Activities in which a person is bound while another simulates or engages in light or moderate discipline activities, such as spanking and whipping.

brain-testicular axis   A complex feedback system, involving the hypothalamus, the pituitary gland, and the testes, that regulates spermatogenesis.

Braxton Hicks contractions   Uterine contractions during the last trimester of pregnancy that exercise the uterus, preparing it for labor.

bris   In Judaism, ritual circumcision.

bulbourethral glands   *See* Cowper's glands.

bulimia   An eating disorder characterized by episodes of uncontrolled overeating followed by purging (vomiting).

butch   A lesbian who dresses and acts in a stylized masculine manner. *See also* femme.

calendar method   A contraceptive method based on calculating "safe" days depending on the range of a woman's longest and shortest menstrual cycles.

camp   A form of satire based on the affectionate exaggeration or parody of social conventions, often including cross-dressing.

Candida albicans   The fungus that causes candidiasis or yeast infection.

candidiasis   A yeast infection caused by the fungus *Candida albicans*. Also known as moniliasis.

capacitation   The process by which a sperm's membranes become fragile enough to release the enzymes from its acrosomes.

castration anxiety   In Freudian theory, the belief that the father will cut off the child's penis because of rivalry for the mother/wife.

cervical cap   A small, rubber, contraceptive barrier device that fits snugly over the cervix.

cervical dysplasia   *See* cervical intraepithelial neoplasia.

cervical ectopy   A condition of the cervix in which the epithelium (covering tissue) is unusually thin.

cervical intraepithelial neoplasia (CIN)   A condition of the cervical epithelium (covering membrane) that may lead to cancer if not treated. Also known as cervical dysplasia.

cervix   The tapered end of the uterus, opening toward the vagina.

chancre   A round, pea-sized, painless sore symptomatic of the first stage of syphilis.

chancroid   A painful sore or group of sores on the penis, caused by the bacterium *Hemophilus ducreyi*; women may carry the bacterium but are generally asymptomatic.

chemical castration   Reducing or eliminating sexual impulses by chemically reducing the testosterone level.

child-free marriage   A marriage in which the couple have chosen not to have children.

child sexual abuse   Any sexual interaction (including fondling, erotic kissing, oral sex, and genital penetration) between an adult and a prepubertal child.

chlamydia   An STD caused by the *Chlamydia trachomatis* organism. Also known as chlamydial infection.

chorion   The embryo's outermost membrane.

chorionic villus sampling (CVS)   A procedure in which tiny pieces of the membrane that encases the embryo are removed and examined for evidence of possible birth defects.

cilia (singular, *cilium*)   Tiny, hairlike fibers on fimbriae whose waving motion conducts the oocyte into the fallopian tube.

CIN   *See* cervical intraepithelial neoplasia.

circumcision   The surgical removal of the foreskin that normally covers the glans penis.

clap   A colloquial word for gonorrhea.

climacteric   The time during which a woman's menstrual periods become increasingly irregular prior to menopause.

clinical research   The in-depth examination of an individual or group by a clinician who assists with psychological or medical problems.

clitoral hood   A fold of skin covering the glans of the clitoris.

clitoridectomy   The surgical removal of the clitoris and all or part of the labia. Also known as female circumcision.

clitoris   An external sexual structure that is the center of arousal in the female, located above the vagina at the meeting of the labia minora.

CMV   *See* cytomegalovirus.

cofactor   A condition that may make a person more likely to develop an infection.

cognition   Mental processes that intervene between stimulus and response, such as evaluation and reflection.

cognitive development theory   A child development theory that views growth as the mastery of specific ways of perceiving, thinking, and doing that occur at discrete stages.

cognitive social learning theory A child development theory that emphasizes the learning of behavior from others, based on the belief that consequences control behavior.

coitus Sexual intercourse.

coitus interruptus The removal of the penis from the vagina prior to ejaculation.

colostrum A yellowish substance containing nutrients and antibodies that is secreted by the breast 2 or 3 days prior to actual milk production.

coming out The public acknowledgment of one's gay, lesbian, or bisexual orientation.

commitment The determination to continue a relationship.

communication A transactional process in which symbols, such as words, gestures, and movements, are used to establish human contact, exchange information, and reinforce or change attitudes and behaviors.

conceptus In medical terminology, the developing human offspring from fertilization through birth.

condom A thin sheath of latex rubber (or processed animal tissue) that fits over the erect penis to prevent semen from being transmitted. Latex condoms also help protect against many sexually transmitted diseases.

conflict A communication process in which people perceive incompatible goals and interference from others in achieving those goals.

congenital adrenal hyperplasia A condition in which a genetic female with ovaries and vagina develops externally as a male as a result of a malfunctioning adrenal gland. Previously known as adrenogenital syndrome.

congestive prostatitis An inflammation of the prostate gland usually caused by abstaining from ejaculation or infrequent ejaculation.

conization The removal of a cone of tissue from the center of the cervix.

contraception The prevention of conception.

contraceptive film A small, translucent tissue that contains spermicide and dissolves into a sticky gel when inserted into the vagina.

contraceptive foam A chemical spermicide dispensed in an aerosol container.

contraceptive sponge A polyurethane sponge inserted inside the vagina that blocks the opening of the cervix and releases a spermicide.

control group A group that is not being treated nor the subject of an experiment.

core group A small, definable, stable group with a consistently high prevalence of a particular disease.

corona The rim of tissue between the glans and the penile shaft.

corona radiata The outer layer of cells surrounding an oocyte.

corpora cavernosa The hollow chambers in the shaft of the clitoris or penis that fill with blood and swell during arousal.

corpus albicans The deteriorated corpus luteum that exists in the absence of fertilization.

corpus luteum The tissue formed from a ruptured ovarian follicle that produces important hormones after the oocyte emerges.

corpus spongiosum A column of erectile tissue within the penis enclosing the urethra.

correlational study The measurement of two or more naturally occurring variables to determine their relationship to each other.

covert sensitization A form of aversion therapy in which negative fantasies are used as punishment for acting out unacceptable fantasies.

Cowper's glands Two small structures below the prostate gland that secrete a clear mucus into the urethra prior to ejaculation. Also known as bulbourethral glands.

crabs A colloquial word for an infestation of pubic lice.

cremaster A muscle within the scrotal sac that causes the testes to elevate.

cross-dressing Wearing the clothing of a member of the other sex.

crura (singular, *crus*) The internal branches of the clitoral or penile shaft.

cryptorchidism A condition in which one or both testes has not descended.

culdoscopy A form of tubal ligation in which an incision is made at the back of the vagina and the tubes are viewed with a culdoscope.

culpotomy A form of tubal ligation in which an incision is made at the back of the vagina.

cultural equivalency perspective The view that attitudes, behaviors, and values of diverse ethnic groups are basically similar, with differences resulting from adaption to historical and social forces, such as slavery, discrimination, or poverty.

cultural relativity The perspective that the appropriateness of any custom or activity must be evaluated in terms of how it fits within the culture as a whole.

cunnilingus Oral stimulation of the female genitals.

cystitis A bladder infection affecting mainly women that is often related to sexual activity, although it is not transmitted from one partner to another.

cytomegalovirus (CMV) A virus of the herpes group that affects people with depressed immune systems; infants may be infected with CMV in utero.

dartos A smooth muscle under the skin of the scrotum that causes the surface to wrinkle when it contracts.

date rape Sexual intercourse with a dating partner that occurs against his or her will with force or the threat of force. Also known as acquaintance rape.

D & C *See* dilation and curettage.

D & E *See* dilation and evacuation.

delayed ejaculation A sexual dysfunction characterized by the male's inability to easily ejaculate during intercourse.

demographics The statistical characteristics of human populations.

dendritic cell A type of leukocyte inside the lymph nodes, intestinal mucous membranes, and inner layers of the skin.

dependent variable In an experiment, a factor that is affected by changes in the independent variable. *See also* independent variable; variable.

Depo-Provera An injectable contraceptive containing medroxyprogesterone acetate (DMPA).

DES Diethylstilbestrol, a synthetic estrogen once used to prevent miscarriages, associated with a possible increased cancer risk among the women who took it and their children.

deviant sexual behavior Sexual behavior that diverges from the norm.

DHT deficiency   A genetic disorder in which some males are unable to convert testosterone into the hormone dihydrotestosterone (DHT), required for the normal development of external male genitals. They are usually identified as girls at birth, but at adolescence they begin to develop male genitals.

diabetes mellitus   A chronic disease characterized by excess sugar in the blood and urine due to a deficiency of insulin.

diaphragm   A rubber cup with a flexible rim that is placed deeply inside the vagina, blocking the cervix, to prevent sperm from entering the uterus.

diethylstilbestrol   *See* DES.

dilation   Opening up of the cervix during labor.

dilation and curettage (D & C)   A first-trimester abortion method using a small spoon-shaped instrument (curette) to remove the conceptus.

dilation and evaluation (D & E)   A second-trimester abortion method in which the cervix is slowly dilated and the fetus removed by alternating solution and curettage.

diploid cell   A cell formed by the union of two gametes.

diploid zygote   A zygote (fertilized ovum) containing 23 pairs of chromosomes.

disinhibition   The phenomenon of activating behaviors that would normally be suppressed.

DMPA   Medroxyprogesterone acetate, used in Depo-Provera.

domestic partnership   A legal category granting some rights ordinarily reserved to married couples, such as insurance coverage, to committed, cohabiting heterosexual, gay, and lesbian couples.

domination and submission (D/S)   Sexual arousal derived from the consensual acting out of sexual scenes in which one person dominates and the other submits.

dominatrix   In bondage and discipline, a woman who specializes in "disciplining" a submissive partner.

douching   The flushing of the vagina with water or a medicated liquid.

doula   A professional childbirth companion employed to guide the mother during labor.

drag   Cross-dressing, often with comic intent.

drag queen   A gay man who dresses outrageously as a woman.

drip   A colloquial word for gonorrhea.

dyke   In the butch-femme subculture, a nonpejorative term referring to a lesbian who dresses and acts in a stylized masculine manner. Outside the butch-femme subculture, a pejorative term for a "nonfeminine" woman, whether lesbian or heterosexual.

dysmenorrhea   Pelvic cramping and pain experienced by some women during menstruation.

eating disorder   Eating and weight-management practices that endanger a person's physical and emotional health.

ectopic pregnancy   A pregnancy in which the fertilized egg implants in a fallopian tube instead of in the uterus. Also known as tubal pregnancy.

effacement   Thinning of the cervix during labor.

effeminacy   Having feminine qualities.

ego   In Freudian theory, the self.

egocentric fallacy   An erroneous belief that one's own personal experience and values are held by others in general. *See also* ethnocentrism.

ejaculation   The process by which semen is forcefully expelled from the penis.

ejaculatory duct   One of two structures within the prostate gland connecting with the vasa deferentia.

ejaculatory inevitability   The point at which ejaculation *must* occur.

Electra complex   In Freudian theory, the female child's erotic desire for the father and simultaneous fear of the mother. *See also* Oedipal complex.

ELISA   A simple blood test that screens for HIV antibodies; the most common test for HIV.

embryo   The early form of life in the uterus between the stages of blastocyst and fetus.

embryonic membranes   The embryo's membranes, including the amnion, yolk sac, chorion, and allantois.

emission   The first stage of ejaculation, in which sperm and semen are propelled into the urethral bulb.

endometriosis   A disease caused by bits of endometrial tissue (uterine lining) spreading and growing in other parts of the body; a major cause of infertility.

endometrium   The lining of the uterine walls.

enteric infection   One of several intestinal infections caused by bacteria, viruses, protozoa, or other organisms that are normally carried in the intestinal tract; examples are amebiasis, giardiasis, and shigellosis.

epidemic   The rapid and wide spreading of a contagious infection.

epidemiology   The study of diseases, how they spread within a population, and how they may be controlled.

epididymis   The coiled tube formed by the merging of the seminiferous tubules, where sperm mature.

epididymitis   Inflammation of the epididymis.

episiotomy   A surgical procedure during childbirth that enlarges the vaginal opening by cutting through the perineum toward the anus.

erectile dysfunction   A sexual dysfunction characterized by the inability to have or maintain an erection during intercourse. Commonly referred to as impotence.

erection   The process of the penis becoming rigid through vasocongestion; an erect penis.

erection reflex   The response to arousal in which the penis becomes erect; may be triggered by a variety of stimuli.

erogenous zone   Any area of the body that is highly sensitive to touch and associated with sexual arousal.

eros   In John Lee's typology of love, the love of beauty.

erotica   Sexually oriented material that is positively evaluated. *See also* pornography; sexually oriented material.

erotic aid   A device, such as a vibrator or dildo, or oils and lotions, designed to enhance erotic responsiveness.

erotophilia   A positive emotional response to sexuality.

erotophobia   A negative emotional response to sexuality.

estrogen   The principal female hormone, regulating reproductive functions and the development of secondary sex characteristics.

ethnic group   A group of people distinct from other groups because of cultural characteristics transmitted from one generation to the next.

ethnicity   Ethnic affiliation or identity.

ethnocentrism   The belief that one's own ethnic group, nation, or culture is innately superior to others. *See also* ethnocentric fallacy.

exhibitionism   A paraphilia characterized by an intense urge to display one's genitals to another person without the intent of forming a relationship with the person.

experimental research   The systematic manipulation of an individual or the environment to learn the effect of such manipulation on behavior.

expressiveness   Revealing or demonstrating one's emotions. *See also* instrumentality.

expulsion   The second stage of ejaculation, characterized by rapid, rhythmic contractions of the urethra, prostate, and muscles at the base of the penis, causing semen to spurt from the urethral opening.

extrafamilial abuse   Child sexual abuse by unrelated individuals. *See also* intrafamilial abuse.

fallacy   An error in reasoning that affects our understanding of a subject.

fallopian tube   One of two uterine tubes extending toward an ovary.

feedback   The ongoing process in which participants and their messages create a given result and are subsequently modified by that result.

fellatio   Oral stimulation of the penis.

female circumcision   *See* clitoridectomy.

female impersonator   A man who impersonates a woman as part of a performance.

femme porn   Sexually oriented material catering to women and heterosexual couples.

femme   A feminine lesbian with a butch partner. *See also* butch.

fertility awareness method   One of several contraceptive methods based on a woman's knowledge of her body's reproductive cycle, including calendar (rhythm), basal body temperature (BBT), mucus, and symptothermal methods.

fetishism   A paraphilia in which a person is sexually attracted to certain objects. *See also* partialism.

fetishistic transvestism   A paraphilia in which a man becomes sexually excited by cross-dressing.

fibroadenoma   A harmless round, movable growth in the breast in young women.

fibrocystic disease   A common and generally harmless breast condition.

fimbriae   The fingerlike ends of the fallopian tubes, extending toward the ovary.

flagellum   The tail that propels a sperm.

follicle-stimulating hormone (FSH)   A hormone that regulates ovulation.

follicular phase   The phase of the ovarian cycle during which a follicle matures.

foreskin   The sleevelike skin covering the shaft of the penis and extending over the glan penis. Also known as prepuce.

frenulum   The triangular area of sensitive skin on the underside of the penis, attaching the glans to the foreskin.

frotteurism   A paraphilia characterized by recurrent, intense urges or fantasies to sexually touch another person without consent.

FSH   *See* follicle-stimulating hormone.

gamete   A sex cell, containing the genetic material necessary for reproduction; an oocyte (ovum) or sperm.

gamete intrafallopian transfer (GIFT)   A means of achieving pregnancy by collecting oocyte and sperm and depositing them in the fallopian tube.

Gardnerella vaginalis   The bacterium that is the most common cause of bacterial vaginosis.

gastrulation   The process of extensive cell migration during early embryonic development.

gay-bashing   Violence directed against gay men or lesbians because of their orientation. Also known as queer-bashing.

gender   The social and cultural characteristics associated with being male or female.

gender dysphoria   Dissatisfaction with one's gender.

gender identity   The gender one feels himself or herself to be.

gender role   The role a person is expected to perform as a result of being male or female in a particular culture. Preferred over the term *sex role*.

gender schema   The cognitive organization of information by gender.

gender-role attitude   Beliefs about appropriate male and female personality traits and activities.

gender-role behaviors   The activities in which individuals engage in accordance with their gender.

gender-role stereotype   A rigidly held, oversimplified, and overgeneralized belief that all males and all females possess distinct psychological and behavioral traits.

genetic sex   Identification as male or female according to chromosomal and hormonal sex characteristics.

genital herpes   An STD caused by the herpes simplex virus (HSV).

genitalia   *See* genitals.

genitals   The reproductive and sexual organs of males and females. Also known as genitalia.

genital stage   In Freudian theory, the period in which adolescents become interested in genital sexual activities, especially sexual intercourse.

genital warts   An STD caused by the human papilloma virus (HPV).

gestation   Pregnancy.

GIFT   *See* gamete intrafallopian transfer.

glans clitoridis   The erotically sensitive tip of the clitoris.

glans penis   The head of the penile shaft.

gonad   An organ (ovary or testis) that produces gametes, the sex cells containing the genetic material for reproduction.

gonadotropin   A hormone that acts directly on the gonads.

gonorrhea   An STD caused by the *Neisseria gonorrhoeae* bacterium.

Grafenberg spot   According to some researchers, an erotically sensitive area on the front wall of the vagina midway between the introitus and the cervix. Also known as G spot.

Graffian folllicle   A fully ripened ovarian follicle. Also known as vesicular follicle.

granuloma inguinale   An STD consisting of single or multiple nodules, usually on the genitals, that become lumpy, painless ulcers that bleed on contact.

G spot   *See* Grafenberg spot.

hairy leukoplakia   Persistent, fuzzy white spots appearing in the mouth.

halo effect   The assumption that attractive people possess more desirable social characteristics than unattractive people.

haploid cell   A gamete.

hardcore   Sexually explicit material that intimately depicts sexual activities, the vulva, the erect penis, or the anus. *See also* softcore.

health belief model   A health behavior model arguing that four factors must be present for an individual to take action to avoid a disease: belief in personal susceptibility, belief that the disease would have at least a moderately severe effect on one's life, belief that taking a particular action will reduce the susceptibility to or the severity of the disease, and belief that the costs of prevention or treatment are worth the benefits.

Hegar's sign   The softening of the uterus above the cervix, indicating pregnancy.

helper T cell   A lymphocyte that "reads" antigens and directs the immune system's response.

hepatitis   A viral disease affecting the liver; two types of virus may be sexually transmitted: hepatitis A and hepatitis B.

hermaphrodite   A person with both male and female gonads: either one of each, two of each, or two ovotestes (gonads that have both ovarian and testicular tissue in the same gland). Also known as true hermaphrodite.

herpes simplex virus (HSV)   The virus that causes genital herpes.

hetaera (plural, *hetaerae*)   In ancient Greece, a courtesan, usually an educated slave.

heterosexism   *See* heterosexual bias.

heterosexual bias   The tendency to see the world in heterosexual terms and to ignore or devalue homosexuality. Also known as heterosexism.

heterosexuality   Sexual relationships between females and males.

heterosociality   Relationships with the other sex that are based on respect and friendship.

HIV   *See* human immunodeficiency virus.

HIV encephalopathy.   *See* AIDS dementia.

homoeroticism   Sexual attraction, desire, or impulses directed toward members of the same sex; homosexuality.

homophobia   An irrational or phobic fear of gay men and lesbians. *See also* anti-gay prejudice; heterosexual bias.

homosexuality   Sexual relationships between members of the same sex.

homosociality   Relationships in which self-esteem and status are more closely linked to evaluations from people of the same sex than of the other sex.

hormone   A chemical substance that acts as a messenger within the body, regulating various functions.

hormone replacement therapy (HRT)   The administration of estrogen, often with progestin, in the form of pills, vaginal cream, or a small adhesive patch.

hostile environment   As related to sexuality, a work or educational atmosphere that interferes with a person's performance because of sexual harassment.

hot flash   An effect of menopause consisting of a period of intense warmth, flushing, and perspiration, typically lasting 1–2 minutes.

HPV   *See* human papilloma virus.

HSV   *See* herpes simplex virus.

human immunodeficiency virus (HIV)   The virus that causes AIDS.

human papilloma virus (HPV)   The virus that causes genital warts.

hymen   A thin membrane partially covering the introitus prior to first intercourse or other breakage.

hypoactive sexual desire   A sexual disorder characterized by low or absent sexual desire.

hysterectomy   The surgical removal of the uterus.

hysterotomy   A late abortion method in which the fetus is removed through an incision made in the woman's abdomen; used only in emergencies.

id   In Freudian theory, the instinct.

implant   A contraceptive method using thin, matchstick-sized capsules inserted under the skin of a woman's arm.

implantation   The process by which a blastocyst becomes embedded in the uterine wall.

impotence   *See* erectile dysfunction.

incest   Sexual intercourse between individuals too closely related to legally marry, usually interpreted to mean father-daughter, mother-son, or brother-sister.

incidence   The degree of occurrence; the number of cases of a disease or condition within a given time period.

independent variable   A factor that can be manipulated or changed by the experimenter. *See also* dependent variable; variable.

induced abortion   The intentional termination of a pregnancy.

induction   A type of reasoning in which arguments are formed from a premise to provide support for its conclusion.

infectious prostatitis   Inflammation of the prostate gland generally caused by *E. coli* bacteria.

infertility   The inability to conceive a child after trying for a year or more.

infibulation   The stitching together of the sides of the vulva or vaginal opening; a part of female circumcision.

informed consent   Assent given by a mentally competent individual at least 18 years old with full knowledge of the purpose and potential risks and benefits of participation.

infundibulum   The funnel-shaped end of a fallopian tube.

inhibin   A hormone involved in spermatogenesis.

inhibited ejaculation   A sexual dysfunction characterized by the male's inability to ejaculate despite an erection and stimulation.

inhibited sexual desire   *See* hypoactive sexual desire.

instrumentality   Being oriented toward tasks and problem solving. *See also* expressiveness.

internalized homophobia   Self-hatred because of one's homosexuality.

interstitial cells   *See* Leydig cells.

intrafamilial abuse   Child sexual abuse by biologically and step-related individuals. *See also* incest.

intrauterine device   *See* IUD.

intrauterine insemination (IUI)   A means of achieving pregnancy by depositing semen by syringe near the cervical opening during ovulation. Also known as artificial insemination (AI).

introitus   The opening of the vagina.

in vitro fertilization (IVF)   A means of achieving pregnancy by combining sperm and oocyte in a laboratory dish and implanting the blastocyst in the mother's uterus.

involution   Contractions of the uterus that return it to its prebirth size and shape.

IUD   Intrauterine device, a T-shaped device inserted into the uterus through the cervical os to prevent conception or implantation of the fertilized egg.

IUI *See* intrauterine insemination.

IVF *See* in vitro fertilization.

jealousy An aversive response that occurs because of a partner's real, imagined, or likely involvement with a third person.

Kaplan tri-phasic model A model that divides sexual response into three phases: desire, excitement, and orgasm.

Kaposi's sarcoma A rare cancer of the blood vessels that is common among people with AIDS.

Kegel exercises A set of exercises designed to strengthen and give voluntary control over the pubococcygeus and to increase sexual pleasure and awareness.

killer T cell A lymphocyte that attacks foreign cells.

Klinefelter syndrome A condition in which a male has one or more extra X chromosomes, causing the development of female secondary sex characteristics.

koro A Japanese term referring to the conviction that one's penis is shrinking and is going to disappear.

labia majora (singular, *labium majus*) Two folds of spongy flesh extending from the mons pubis and enclosing the labia minora, clitoris, urethral opening, and vaginal entrance. Also known as major lips.

labia minora (singular, *labium minus*) Two small folds of skin within the labia majora that meet above the clitoris to form the clitoral hood. Also known as minor lips.

lactation The production of milk in the breasts (mammary glands).

laminaria A small stick of seaweed placed into the cervical opening about 6 hours prior to an abortion to dilate the cervix.

lanugo The fine, downy hair covering the fetus.

laparoscopy A form of tubal ligation using a viewing lens (the laparoscope) to locate the fallopian tubes and another instrument to cut and close them.

latency stage In Freudian theory, the period from age 6 to puberty in which sexual impulses are no longer active.

LBW *See* low birth weight.

lesbian separatist A lesbian desiring to create a separate "womyn's" subculture distinct from that of heterosexuals and gay men.

leukocyte White blood cell.

Leydig cells Cells within the testes that secrete androgrens. Also known as interstitial cells.

LGV *See* lymphogranuloma venereum.

LH *See* luteinizing hormone.

libido The sex drive.

lochia A bloody vaginal discharge following childbirth.

low birth weight (LBW) Prematurity; a condition in which the newborn weighs less than 5.5 lb; a major complication in the third trimester of pregnancy.

ludus In John Lee's typology of love, playful love.

lumpectomy Breast surgery that removes only the malignant tumor and surrounding lymph nodes.

luteal phase The phase of the ovarian cycle during which a follicle becomes a corpus luteum and then degenerates.

luteinizing hormone (LH) A hormone involved in ovulation.

lymphocyte A type of leukocyte active in the immune response.

lymphogranuloma venereum (LGV) An STD that begins as a small, painless lesion at the site of infection, then develops into a painful abscess, accompanied by pain and swelling in the groin.

lymphoma Cancer of the lymphatic system; commonly affects the brain.

machismo In Latino culture, highly prized masculine traits. The term is used derisively in Anglo culture.

macrophage A type of white blood cell that destroys foreign cells.

MAI *See* mycobaterium avium intracellulare.

male climacteric Physical changes in the middle-aged male.

malignant tumor A tumor that invades nearby tissues and disrupts the normal functioning of vital organs.

mammary gland A mature female breast.

mammogram A low-dose X-ray of the breast.

mania In John Lee's typology of love, obsessive love.

masochism *See* sadomasochism; sexual masochism.

mastectomy The surgical removal of the breast.

Masters and Johnson four-phase model A model that divides sexual response into four phases: excitement, plateau, orgasm, and resolution.

masturbation Stimulation of the genitals for pleasure.

meiosis A form of cell division in which the cell's nucleus undergoes two consecutive divisions.

menarche The onset of menstruation.

menopause The complete cessation of menstruation.

menses The menstrual flow, in which the endometrium is discharged.

menstrual cycle The more-or-less monthly process during which the uterus is readied for implantation of a fertilized ovum. Also known as uterine cycle.

menstrual extraction The removal of the endometrial contents by suction; sometimes used as a form of postcoital birth control.

menstrual phase The shedding of the endometrium during the menstrual cycle.

metastasis The process in which cancer spreads from one part of the body to another unrelated part via the bloodstream or lymphatic system.

mifepristone *See* RU-486.

mikvah In Orthodox Judaism, a ritual bath undertaken by females following menstruation.

minilaparotomy A form of tubal ligation in which a small incision is made in the lower abdomen.

miscarriage A spontaneous abortion.

mittelschmerz A midcycle pain in the lower abdomen on either side accompanied by a very slight discharge of blood from the cervix due to ovulation.

model A hypothetical description used to study or explain a phenomenon.

modeling The process by which learning takes place by imitating others.

molluscum contagiosum A viral STD characterized by smooth, rounded, shiny lesions, appearing on the trunk, on the genitals, or around the anus.

moniliasis An infection caused by the fungus *Candida albicans*; usually affects the vagina but can also affect the mouth or throat (thrush), esophagus, or lungs. Also known as candidiasis or yeast infection.

mons pubis In the female, the mound of fatty tissue covering the pubic bone; the pubic mound. Also known as mons veneris.

mons veneris The pubic mound; literally, mountain of Venus. Also known as mons pubis.

mucous method A contraceptive method using a woman's cervical mucus to determine ovulation.

multiple-loss syndrome A psychological condition associated with the loss (through death) of large numbers of loved ones.

mycobacterium avium intracellulare (MAI) An atypical form of tuberculosis, the most common form of TB among people with AIDS.

myotonia Increased muscle tension.

necrophilia A nonspecified paraphilia characterized by sexual interaction with a corpse.

neonate A newborn.

neurosis A psychological disorder characterized by anxiety or tension.

NGU *See* nongonococcal urethritis.

nonfetishistic transvestism A nonparaphilic behavior by a person who cross-dresses to relieve the tensions associated with the male gender role.

nongonococcal urethritis (NGU) Urethral information caused by something other than the gonococcus bacterium.

nonmarital sex Sexual activities occurring primarily among single adults over 30 and widowed men and women.

nonoxynol-9 The sperm-killing chemical in spermicide.

nonpedophilic sexual abuse An adult's sexual interaction with a child that is not motivated as much by sexual desire as by nonsexual motives, such as power or affection.

nonseminoma A group of testicular cancers spread through the bloodstream.

nonspecific urethritis (NSU) Inflammation of the urethra with an unspecified, nongonococcal cause.

nonspecified paraphilia A paraphilia that does not meet the criteria of any of the major paraphilias, such as exhibitionism, voyeurism, or pedophilia; includes telephone scatalogia, partialism, zoophilia, and necrophilia.

norm A cultural rule or standard.

normal sexual behavior Behavior that conforms to a group's average or median patterns of behavior.

Norplant The trade name of a contraceptive implant that is inserted under the skin of a woman's arm.

NSU *See* nonspecific urethritis.

nymphomania A pejorative, unscientific, and often moralistic term referring to "excessive" or "abnormal" sexual desire in women. *See also* satyriasis.

objectivity The observation of things as they exist in reality as opposed to our feelings or beliefs about them.

obscenity That which is deemed offensive to "accepted" standards of decency or morality. *See also* erotica; pornography; sexually explicit material.

observational research A method of gathering information in which a researcher systematically and unobtrusively observes behavior.

Oedipal complex In Freudian theory, the male child's erotic desire for his mother and simultaneous fear of his father. *See also* Electra complex.

OI *See* opportunistic infection.

oocyte The female gamete, commonly referred to as an egg or ovum.

oogenesis The production of oocytes; the ovarian cycle.

oophorectomy The surgical removal of one or both ovaries.

open marriage A marriage in which both partners agree to allow each other to have openly acknowledged and independent relationships with others, including sexual ones.

opinion An unsubstantiated belief or conclusion about what seems to be true according to an individual's personal thoughts.

opportunistic infection (OI) An infection that normally does not occur or is not life-threatening, that takes advantage of a weakened immune system.

oral contraceptive A series of pills containing synthetic estrogen and/or progesterone, which regulates egg production and the menstrual cycle. Commonly known as "the pill."

oral stage In Freudian theory, the period lasting from birth to age 1 in which infant eroticism is focused on the mouth.

orchiectomy The removal of the testes.

orgasm The climax of sexual excitement, including rhythmic contractions of muscles in the genital area and intensely pleasurable sensations; usually accompanied by ejaculation in males beginning in puberty.

orgasmic platform A portion of the vagina that undergoes vasocongestion during sexual arousal.

os The cervical opening.

osteoporosis The loss of bone mass.

ovarian cycle The more-or-less monthly process during which oocytes are produced.

ovarian follicle A saclike structure in which an oocyte develops.

ovary One of a pair of organs that produces oocytes, female gametes.

ovulation The release of an oocyte from the ovary during the ovarian cycle.

ovulatory phase The phase of the ovarian cycle during which ovulation occurs.

ovum (plural, *ova*) An egg; an oocyte; the female gamete.

oxytocin A hormone produced by the fetus that stimulates strong uterine contractions.

papule A small bump appearing on the skin.

paraphilia A sexual behavior characterized by intense recurrent sexual urges and sexually arousing fantasies lasting at least 6 months and involving nonhuman objects, the suffering or humiliation of oneself or one's partner (not merely simulated), or children or other nonconsenting individuals. The person has acted on these urges or is markedly distressed by them.

paraphiliac A person who has a paraphilia.

parenteral transmission Infection via the bloodstream.

partialism A nonspecified paraphilia in which a person is sexually attracted to body parts. *See also* fetishism.

parturition Childbirth.

pathological behavior Behavior deemed diseased by current medical standards.

PCP *See* pneumocystis carinii pneumonia.

pedophile An individual who is sexually attracted to prepubescent children. *See also* pedophilia.

pedophilia A paraphilia characterized by intense, recurring sexual urges or fantasies involving sexual activities with a prepubescent child.

peer An age-mate.

peer delinquent subculture An antisocial youth subculture.

pelvic floor The underside of the pelvic area extending from the top of the pubic bone to the anus.

pelvic inflammatory disease (PID) An infection of the fallopian tube (or tubes) caused by an organism, such as *C. trachomatis* or *N. gonorroehae*, in which scar tissue may form within the tubes and block the passage of eggs or cause an ectopic pregnancy; a leading cause of female infertility.

penis The male organ through which semen and urine pass.

penis envy In Freudian theory, female desire to have a penis.

perinatal transmission The passing of a disease from mother to fetus.

perineum An area of soft tissue between the genitals and the anus that covers the muscles and ligaments of the pelvic floor.

phallic stage In Freudian theory, the period from age 3 to 6, during which both male and female children exhibit interest in the genitals.

pheromone A sexually arousing chemical substance secreted into the air by many kinds of animals.

Phthirus pubis A pubic louse, colloquially known as a crab.

PID *See* pelvic inflammatory disease.

placenta The organ of exchange between the mother and the fetus.

pleasure principle In Freudian theory, the principle that organisms (including people) seek pleasure and avoid pain.

pleasuring Erotic, nongenital touching.

plethysmograph A device attached to the genitals to measure physiological response.

PLISSIT A model for sex therapy consisting of four progressive levels: Permission, Limited Information, Specific Suggestions, and Intensive Therapy.

PMS *See* premenstrual syndrome.

pneumocystis carinii pneumonia (PCP) An opportunistic lung infection caused by a common, usually harmless organism; the most common opportunistic infection among people with AIDS.

polar body In oogenesis, the smaller of two cells produced during meiosis I.

pornography Sexually oriented material that is negatively evaluated. *See also* erotica; sexually oriented material.

POSSLQ A census category referring to a "person of the opposite sex sharing living quarters"; an unmarried cohabiting heterosexual male or female.

postcoital birth control A form of birth control involving the early expulsion of an ovum that may have been fertilized. Also known as morning-after birth control.

postpartum period The period (about 3 months) following childbirth, characterized by physical stabilization and emotional adjustment.

post-traumatic stress disorder (PTSD) A characteristic group of symptoms, such as depression, that follow an intensely distressing event outside a person's normal life experience. *See also* rape trauma syndrome.

power The ability or potential ability to influence another person or group.

pragma In John Lee's typology of love, practical love.

preeclampsia A condition in pregnancy characterized by increasingly high blood pressure.

premarital sex Sexual activities, especially sexual intercourse, taking place prior to marriage or among adolescents or young adults.

premature ejaculation A sexual dysfunction characterized by the inability to control or delay ejaculation as long as desired, causing distress.

premenstrual syndrome (PMS) A set of severe symptoms associated with menstruation.

prepuce *See* foreskin.

prevalence Overall occurrence; the total number of cases of a disease.

priapism Painful, persistent erections.

primary spermatocyte The cell that undergoes meiosis to form four spermatids.

principle of least interest A principle governing a situation in which the partner with the least interest in continuing a relationship has the most power in it.

prodrome A period prior to a viral outbreak when live viruses are shed from the affected areas.

progesterone A female hormone that helps regulate the menstrual cycle and sustain pregnancy.

proliferative phase The building up of the endometrium in response to increased estrogen during the menstrual cycle.

prophylaxis Protection from disease.

prostaglandins A type of hormone with a fatty acid base that stimulates muscle contractions.

prostate gland A muscular gland encircling the urethra that produces about one-third of the seminal fluid.

prostatitis Inflammation of the prostrate gland.

prototype In psychology, a mental model.

proximity Nearness in terms of physical space and time.

pseudohermaphrodite A person with two testes or two ovaries but an ambiguous genital appearance. *See also* hermaphrodite.

pseudohermaphroditism The condition in which an individual's chromosomes and gonads are of one sex but the external genitals resemble those of the other sex. *See also* androgen-insensitivity syndrome; congenital adrenal hyperplasia.

psychoanalysis A psychological system developed by Sigmund Freud that traces behavior to unconscious motivations.

psychosexual development Development of the psychological components of sexuality.

puberty The stage of human development when the body becomes capable of reproduction.

pubic louse *Phthirus pubis*, colloquially known as a crab, a tiny louse that infests the pubic hair.

pubococcygeus A part of the muscle sling stretching from the pubic bone in front to the tailbone in back.

PWA A person with AIDS.

PWH A person with HIV.

queer-bashing *See* gay-bashing.

random sample A portion of a larger group collected in an unbiased way.

rape Penile-vaginal penetration against a woman's will through the use or threat of force. *See also* sexual aggression; sexual coercion; date rape; statutory rape.

rape trauma syndrome   The emotional changes an individual undergoes as a result of rape.

reactive jealousy   A type of jealousy that occurs because of a partner's current, past, or anticipated relationship with another person.

reality principle   In Freudian theory, the principle by which the external world exerts influence on the organism.

refactory period   For men, a period following orgasm during which they are not capable of becoming erect or having an orgasm again.

relative love and need theory   A theory that explains power in terms of the individual's involvement and needs in the relationship.

relaxin   A hormone produced by the placenta in the later months of pregnancy that increases flexibility in the ligaments and joints of the pelvic area. In men, relaxin is contained in semen, where it assists in sperm motility.

representative sample   A small group representing a larger group in terms of age, sex, ethnicity, socioeconomic class, orientation, and so on.

repression   A psychological mechanism that keeps people from becoming aware of hidden memories and motives because they arouse guilt or pain.

retrograde ejaculation   The backward expulsion of semen into the bladder rather than out of the urethral opening.

retrovirus   A virus capable of reversing the normal genetic writing process, causing the host cell to replicate the virus instead of itself.

reverse transcriptase   An enzyme in the cone of a retrovirus enabling it to write its own genetic program into a host cell's DNA.

risk factor   An implied causal relationship between certain individual characteristics and the likelihood of exposure to disease.

risk marker   A characteristic, such as a demographic characteristic, correlated but not causally related with disease prevalence.

role testing   The trying out of different roles.

root   The portion of the penis attached to the pelvic cavity.

RU-486   An effective oral, postcoital birth control method containing mifepristone.

sadism   *See* sadomasochism; sexual sadism.

sadomasochism (S&M)   A popular, nonclinical term for domination and submission.

salpingitis   Infection of the fallopian tubes.

Sarcoptes scabiei   The barely visible mite that causes scabies.

satyriasis   A pejorative and unscientific term referring to "uncontrollable" or "excessive" sexual desire in men. *See also* nymphomania.

scabies   A red, intensely itchy rash appearing on the genitals, buttocks, feet, wrists, knuckles, abdomen, armpits, or scalp, caused by the barely visible mite *Sarcoptes scabiei*.

schema (plural, *schemata*)   A set of interrelated ideas that helps us process information by categorizing it in useful ways. *See also* gender schema.

scientific method   The systematic collecting of data, forming a hypothesis, testing it empirically, and observing the results.

script   In sociology, the acts, rules, and expectations associated with a particular role.

scrotum   A pouch of skin that holds the two testicles.

secretory phase   The phase of the menstrual cycle during which the endometrium begins to prepare for the arrival of a fertilized ovum; without fertilization, the corpus luteum begins to degenerate.

secure attachment   A style of infant attachment characterized by the infant's feeling of security and confidence with its primary caregiver.

self-disclosure   The revelation of personal information that others would not ordinarily know because of its riskiness.

semen   The ejaculated fluid, containing sperm. Also known as seminal fluid.

seminal fluid   *See* semen.

seminal vesicle   One of two glands at the back of the bladder that secrete about 60% of the seminal fluid.

seminiferous tubules   Tiny, tightly compressed tubes in which spermatogenesis takes place.

seminoma   A form of testicular cancer spread via the lymph system.

sensate focus   The focusing on touch and the giving and receiving of pleasure as part of the treatment of sexual difficulties.

serial monogamy   A succession of monogamous marriages.

seroconversion   The process by which a person develops antibodies.

serostatus   The absence or presence of antibodies for a particular antigen.

sex   Identification as male or female based on genetic and anatomical sex characteristics.

sex flush   A rash that temporarily appears as a result of blood rushing to the skin's surface during sexual excitation.

sex information/advice genre   A media genre that transmits information and norms about sexuality to a mass audience, to both inform and entertain.

sex reassignment surgery (SRS)   The surgical process by which the reproductive organs are surgically altered from one sex to the other.

sex role   *See* gender role.

sex toy   A device, such as a vibrator or dildo, designed to enhance erotic responsiveness. Also known as erotic aid.

sex typing   Following gender-role stereotypes.

sexual abuse trauma   The distressing emotional results of child sexual abuse that include traumatic sexualization, a sense of betrayal, feelings of powerlessness, and stigmatization.

sexual aggression   Any kind of sexual activity against a person's will gained through the use of force, pressure, alcohol or drugs, or authority. *See also* rape; sexual coercion.

sexual aversion   A sexual disorder characterized by a consistently phobic response to sexual activities or the idea of such activities.

sexual coercion   A broad term referring to any kind of sexual activity initiated with another person through the use of argument, pressure, pleading, and cajoling, as well as force, pressure, alcohol or drugs, or authority. *See also* rape; sexual aggression.

sexual disorder   An impairment of an individual's sexual responsiveness caused by interference with the brain's arousal capacity.

sexual dysfunction   An impaired physiological response that prevents an individual from functioning sexually, such as erectile difficulties or absence of orgasm.

sexual enhancement Improvement of the quality of one's sexual relationship.

sexual harassment The abuse of power for sexual ends; the creation of a hostile work or educational environment because of unwelcomed conduct or conditions of a sexual nature.

sexual impulse The incitement or inclination to act sexually.

sexually explicit material Material that intimately depicts sexual activities, the vulva, the erect penis, or the anus. Also known as hardcore. *See also* erotica; pornography.

sexually oriented material Material such as photographs, videos, films, magazines, or books whose primary themes, topics, or depictions involve sexuality or sexual arousal. *See also* erotica; pornography.

sexual masochism A paraphilia in which a person experiences intense, recurring sexual urges or fantasies involving real acts of being humiliated, beaten, harmed, or otherwise made to suffer for purposes of sexual arousal.

sexual orientation The pattern of sexual and emotional attraction based on the gender of one's partner.

sexual outlet A sexual activity that ordinarily leads to orgasm.

sexual sadism A paraphilia in which a person experiences intense, recurring sexual urges or fantasies involving real acts in which physical or psychological harm is inflicted upon a victim.

sexual variation A departure from the sexual norms and dominant patterns in a culture; atypical sexuality.

shaft The body of the penis.

S&M *See* sadomasochism.

smegma An oily substance produced by several small glands beneath the foreskin of the penis and hood of the clitoris.

social construction Society's assignment of categories, such as masculinity, femininity, heterosexuality, and homosexuality.

sociobiology A theory based in evolutionary biology asserting that nature has structured us with the basic desire to pass on our individual genes to future generations and that this desire motivates much, if not all, of our behavior.

socioeconomic status Ranking in society based on a combination of occupational, educational, and income levels.

softcore Nonexplicit sexually oriented material. *See also* hardcore.

solicitation In terms of prostitution, a word, gesture, or action that implies an offer of sex for sale.

sonogram A visual image created by ultrasound.

spectatoring The process in which a person becomes a spectator of his or her sexual activities, thereby causing sexual dysfunctions or disorders.

sperm The male gamete. Also known as spermatozoon.

spermatic cord A tube suspending the testicle within the scrotal sac, containing nerves, blood vessels, and a vas deferens.

spermatid The early form of a spermatozoon, prior to spermiogenesis.

spermatogenesis The production of sperm.

spermatogonia (singular, *spermatogonium*) Primitive cells from which spermatazoa develop.

spermatozoon (plural, *spermatazoa*) *See* sperm.

spermicide A substance that is toxic to sperm.

spermiogenesis The process by which a sperm develops from a spermatid.

spinnbarkeit The elasticity of preovulatory cervical mucus.

spirochete A spiral-shaped bacterium.

spontaneous abortion The natural expulsion of the conceptus; commonly referred to as miscarriage.

squeeze technique A technique for the treatment of premature ejaculation in which the partner squeezes the man's erect penis below the glans immediately prior to ejaculation.

status An individual's position in a group.

statutory rape Consensual sexual intercourse with a female under the age of consent.

stereotype A set of simplistic, rigidly held, overgeneralized beliefs about a person or group of people; ideas that are resistant to change.

sterilization A surgical procedure that makes the reproductive organs incapable of producing or "delivering" viable gametes (sperm and eggs). Also known as voluntary surgical contraception.

storage In John Lee's typology of love, companionate love.

strain gauge A rubber-bandlike device placed over the penis to measure physiological responses. *See also* plethysmograph.

sudden infant death syndrome (SIDS) A phenomenon in which an apparently healthy infant dies suddenly while sleeping.

superego In Freudian theory, the conscience.

survey research A method of gathering information from a small group to make inferences about a larger group.

suspicious jealousy A type of jealousy that is groundless or that arises from ambiguous evidence.

sweating The moistening of the vagina by secretions from its walls.

symbol In communication, a word or gesture that stands for something else.

sympto-thermal method A fertility awareness method combining the BBT and mucous methods.

syphilis An STD caused by the *Treponema pallidum* bacterium.

TB *See* tuberculosis.

T cell Any of several types of lymphocytes involved in the immune response.

TDI *See* therapeutic donor insemination.

telephone scatalogia A nonspecified paraphilia characterized by a recurrent, intense urge or fantasy to make obscene telephone calls.

tenting The expansion of the inner two-thirds of the vagina during sexual arousal.

teratogen A toxic substance that causes birth defects.

testicle One of the paired male gonads inside the scrotum. Also called testis.

testicular feminization *See* androgen-insensitivity syndrome.

testis (plural, *testes*) *See* testicle.

testosterone A steroid hormone associated with sperm production, the development of secondary sex characteristics in males, and the sex drive in both males and females.

therapeutic donor insemination (TDI) Intrauterine insemination in which the semen is from a donor rather than from the woman's husband.

toxemia High blood pressure and edema that may occur between the 20th and 24th weeks of a pregnancy.

toxic shock syndrome (TSS) A potentially life-threatening condition caused by the *Staphylococcus aureus* bacterium and linked to the use of superabsorbent tampons.

toxoplasmosis An opportunistic infection that affects the brain and nervous system.

transition The end of the first stage of labor, when the infant's head enters the birth canal.

transsexual A person whose genitals and gender identity as male or female are discordant. Postsurgical transsexuals have surgically altered their genitals to fit their gender identity.

transvestism A clinical term referring to the wearing of clothes of the other gender, usually for sexual arousal.

trich *See* trichomoniasis.

Trichomonas vaginalis A single-celled protozoan responsible for about one-fourth of all cases of vaginitis; men may carry it asymptomatically.

trichomoniasis A vaginal infection caused by *Trichomonas vaginalis*. Also known as trich.

trust Belief in the reliability and integrity of another person, process, thing, or institution.

TSS *See* toxic shock syndrome.

tubal ligation The cutting and tying off (or other method of closure) of the fallopian tubes so that ova cannot be fertilized.

tubal pregnancy *See* ectopic pregnancy.

tuberculosis (TB) A lung disease caused by the bacterium *Mycobacterium tuberculosis*.

tumescense Swelling, such as that caused by vasocongestion.

Turner syndrome A chromosomal error affecting females born lacking an X chromosome, resulting in the failure to develop ovaries.

ultrasound The use of high-frequency sound waves to create a visual image of the fetus in utero.

umbilical cord The cord connecting the placenta and fetus, through which nutrients pass.

urethra The tube through which urine passes.

urethral bulb The expanded portion of the urethra.

urethral opening The opening in the urethra through which urine is expelled.

urethritis Inflammation of the urethra.

uterine cycle *See* menstrual cycle.

uterus A hollow, thick-walled, muscular organ held in the pelvic cavity by flexible ligaments and supported by several muscles. Also known as womb.

vacuum aspiration A first-trimester form of abortion using vacuum suction to remove the conceptus and other tissue from the uterus.

vagina In females, a flexible, muscular organ opening between the legs and extending diagonally toward the small of the back. It encompasses the penis during sexual intercourse and is the pathway (birth canal) through which an infant is born.

vaginismus A sexual dysfunction characterized by muscle spasms around the vaginal entrance, preventing the insertion of a penis.

vaginitis Any of several kinds of vaginal infection.

value judgment An evaluation as "good" or "bad" based on moral or ethical standards rather than objective ones.

variable An aspect or factor that can be manipulated in an experiment. *See also* dependent variable; independent variable.

varicocele A varicose vein above the testicle that may cause lowered fertility in men.

vas deferens (plural, *vasa deferentia*) One of two tubes that transport sperm from the epididymis to the ejaculatory duct within the prostate gland.

vasectomy A form of surgical sterilization in which each vas deferens is severed, thereby preventing sperm from entering the seminal fluid.

vasocongestion Blood engorgement of body tissues.

vernix The milky substance that sometimes covers an infant at birth.

vesicle A small bump appearing on the skin; a blister.

vesicular follicle *See* Graffian follicle.

vestibular gland *See* Bartholin's gland.

vestibule The area enclosed by the labia minora.

voluntary surgical contraception *See* sterilization.

voyeurism A paraphilia characterized by recurring, intense sexual urges and fantasies to secretly observe another person who is nude, disrobing, or engaging in sexual activity.

vulva The collective term for the external female genitals.

wasting syndrome Severe weight loss, usually accompanied by weakness and persistent diarrhea.

Western blot A test to determine whether antibodies are specific to HIV.

womb *See* uterus.

yeast infection A vaginal infection caused by the fungus Candida albicans. Also known as candidiasis or moniliasis.

yolk sac The producer of the embryo's first blood cells and germ cells, which will develop into gonads.

ZIFT *See* zygote intrafallopian transfer.

zona pellucida The gel-like membrane encasing an oocyte.

zoophilia A nonspecified paraphilia referring to sexual excitement derived from sexual interactions with animals.

zygote intrafallopian transfer (ZIFT) A means of achieving pregnancy in which oocyte and sperm are combined in a laboratory dish and immediately transferred to the fallopian tube.

Bibliography

Abbey, A. (1991). Acquaintance Rape and Alcohol Consumption on College Campuses: How Are They Linked? *Journal of the American College Health, 39*(4), 165–169.

Abbey, A., Halman, L. J., & Andrews, F. M. (1992). "Psychosocial, Treatment, and Demographic Predictors of the Stress Associated with Infertility." *Fertility and Sterility, 57*(1), 122–128.

Abel, G. (1989). "Paraphilias." In H. I. Kaplan & B. Sadock (Eds.), *Comprehensive Textbook of Psychiatry, Vol. 1* (5th ed.), Baltimore, MD: Williams & Wilkins.

Aboukler, J. P., & Swart, A. M. (1993). "Preliminary Analysis of the Concorde Trial." *Lancet, 341*(8849), 889–890.

Ackerman, D. (1990). *A Natural History of the Senses.* New York: Random House.

Adams, D. (1986). "Instruction and Course Content in Sex Knowledge and Attitudes and Internal Locus of Control." *Psychological Reports, 58*(1), 91–94.

Adams, D. (1990). "Identifying the Assaultive Husband in Court: You Be the Judge." *Response to the Victimization of Women and Children, 13*(1), 13–16.

Adelman, M. B. (1992). "Sustaining Passion: Eroticism and Safe-Sex Talk." *Archives of Sexual Behavior, 21*, 481–494.

Adess, N. (1980). "DES Update." *Family Planning and Reproductive Health*, 11–12.

Adler, J. (1986, March 24). "Learning from the Loss." *Newsweek*, pp. 66–67.

Adler, J. (1992, October 19). "Must Boys Always Be Boys?" *Newsweek*, p. 7.

Adler, N. E. (1992). "Unwanted Pregnancy and Abortion: Definitional and Research Issues." *Journal of Social Issues, 48*(3), 19–35.

Adler, N. E., David, H. P., Major, B. N., Roth, S. H., Russo, N. F., & Wyatt, G. E. (1990). "Psychological Responses After Abortion." *Science, 246*, 41–44.

Adler, N. E., David, H. P., Major, B. N., Roth, S. H., Russo, N. F., & Wyatt, G. E. (1992). "Psychological Factors in Abortion: A Review." *American Psychologist, 47*(10), 1194–2204.

Adler, N., Hendrick, S., & Hendrick, C. (1989). "Male Sexual Preference and Attitudes Toward Love and Sexuality." *Journal of Sex Education and Therapy, 12*(2), 27–30.

Ageton, S. (1983). *Sexual Assault Among Adolescents.* Lexington, MA: Lexington Books.

Agnew, J. (1986). "Problems Associated with Anal Erotic Activity." *Archives of Sexual Behavior, 15*(4), 307–314.

Ahn, H. N., & Gilbert, N. (1992). "Cultural Diversity and Sexual Abuse Prevention." *Social Service Review, 66*(3), 410–428.

"AIDS and Children: A Family Disease." (1989, November). *World AIDS Magazine*, pp. 12–14.

Ainsworth, M., et al. (1978). *Patterns of Attachment: A Psychological Study of the Strange Situation.* Hillsdale, NJ: Erlbaum.

Alan Guttmacher Institute (1986). *Teenage Pregnancy in Developed Countries.* New Haven, CT: Yale University Press.

Alapack, R. (1991). "The Adolescent First Kiss." *Humanistic Psychologist, 19*(1), 48–67.

Alcott, W. (1868). *The Physiology of Marriage.* Boston: J. P. Jewett.

Alexander, L. L. (1992). "Sexually Transmitted Diseases: Perspectives on This Growing Epidemic." *Nurse Practitioner, 17*(10), 31 ff.

Alexander, W., & Judd, B. (1986). "Differences in Attitudes toward Nudity in Advertising." *Psychology: A Quarterly Journal of Human Behavior, 23*(1), 26–29.

Allgeier, A. R. (1982). "Sexuality and Gender Roles in Middle-Aged and Elderly Persons." In E. Allgeier & N. McCormick (Eds.), *Gender Roles and Sexual Behavior.* Mountain View, CA: Mayfield.

Allport, G. (1958). *The Nature of Prejudice.* Garden City, NY: Doubleday.

Aloni, R., Heller, L., Keren, O., Mendelson, E., & Davidoff, G. (1992). "Noninvasive Treatment for Erectile Dysfunction in the Neurologically Disabled Population." *Journal of Sex & Marital Therapy, 18*(3), 243–249.

Althof, S., & Turner, I. (1992). "Self-Injection Therapy and External Vacuum Devices in the Treatment of Erectile Dysfunction: Methods and Outcome." In R. Rosen & S. Leiblum (Eds.), *Erectile Disorders.* New York: Guilford Press.

Althof, S. E., Turner, L. A., Levine, S. B., Bodner, J., Kursh, E. D., & Resnick, M. I. (1992). "Through the Eyes of Women: The Sexual and Psychological Responses of Women to Their Partner's Treatment with Self-Injection or External Vacuum Therapy." *Journal of Urology, 147*(4), 1024–1027.

Altman, D. (1982). *The Homosexualization of America, the Americanization of the Homosexual.* New York: St. Martin's Press.

Altman, D. (1985). *AIDS in the Mind of America.* Garden City, NY: Doubleday.

Alvarez, F., et al. (1988). "New Insights on the Mode of Action of Intrauterine Devices in Women." *Fertility and Sterility, 49*, 768–773.

American Fertility Society. (1992). "In Vitro Fertilization–Embryo Transfer (IVF–ET) in the United States: 1990 Results from the IVF–ET Registry." *Fertility and Sterility, 57*(1), 15–24.

American Psychiatric Association. *Diagnostic and Statistical Manual of Mental Disorders* (4th ed.). Washington, DC: American Psychiatric Association, 1994.

Ames, M. A., & Houston, D. (1990). "Legal, Social, and Biological Definitions of Pedophilia." *Archives of Sexual Behavior, 19*(4), 333–342.

Andersen, D. A., Lustig, M. W., & Andersen, J. F. (1987). "Regional Patterns of Communication in the United States: A Theoretical Perspective." *Communication Monographs, 54*, 128–144.

Anderson, J. R. (1989). "Gynecologic Manifestations of AIDS and HIV Disease." *The Female Patient, 14*, 57ff.

Andrews, F. M., Abbey, A., & Halman, L. J. (1991). "Stress from Infertility, Marriage, Factors, and Subjective Well-Being of Wives and Husbands." *Journal of Health and Social Behavior, 32*(3), 238–253.

Andrews, L. (1984). *New Conceptions: A Consumer's Guide to the Newest Infertility Treatments.* New York: St. Martin's Press.

Andrews, S. (1992, November 2). "The Naked Truth." *San Jose Mercury News*, pp. 1, 4.

Aneshensel, C., Fielder, E., & Becerra, R. (1989). "Fertility and Fertility-Related Behavior Among Mexican-American and Non-Hispanic White Females." *Journal of Health and Social Behavior, 30*(1), 56–78.

Angier, N. (1991, November 13). "Prostate Cancer Gets Spotlight as Major Threat." *The New York Times*, p. B8.

Annon, J. (1974). *The Behavioral Treatment of Sexual Problems.* Honolulu, HI: Enabling Systems.

Annon, J. (1976). *Behavioral Treatment of Sexual Problems: Brief Therapy.* New York: Harper & Row.

Applebome, P. (1993, January 28). "Military People Split Over Ban on Homosexuals." *The New York Times*, p. A10.

Applebome, P. (1993, February 1). "Homosexual Issues Galvanizes Conservative Foes of Clinton." *The New York Times*, pp. A1, A8.

Aral, S., & Holmes, K. K. (1990). "Epidemiology of Sexual Behavior and Sexually Transmitted Diseases." In K. K. Holmes et al. (Eds.), *Sexually Transmitted Diseases* (2nd ed.). New York: McGraw-Hill.

Armstrong, P., & Feldman, S. (1990). *A Wise Birth*. New York: William Morrow.

Armsworth, M. W. (1991). "Psychological Responses to Abortion." *Journal of Counseling and Development, 69*, 377–379.

Arndt, W. B., Jr. (1991). *Gender Disorders and the Paraphilias*. Madison, CT: International Universities Press.

Arno, P. S., & Feiden, K. L. (1992). *Against the Odds: The Story of AIDS Drug Development*. New York: HarperCollins.

Aron, A., & Aron, E. (1991). "Love and Sexuality." In K. McKinney & S. Sprecher (Eds.), *Sexuality in Close Relationships*. Hillsdale, NJ: Erlbaum.

Aron, A., & Strong, B. "Prototypes of Love and Sexuality." Forthcoming.

Ash, M. (1980). "The Misnamed Female Sex Organ." In M. Kirkpatrick (Ed.), *Women's Sexual Development*. New York: Plenum Press.

Athey, J. L. (1991). "HIV Infection and Homeless Adolescents." *Child Welfare, 70*(5), 517–528.

Atwood, J. D., & Gagnon, J. (1987). "Masturbatory Behavior in College Youth." *Journal of Sex Education and Therapy, 13*, 35–42.

Atwood, J. D., & Dershowitz, S. (1992). "Constructing a Sex and Marital Therapy Frame: Ways to Help Couples Deconstruct Sexual Problems." *Journal of Sex and Marital Therapy, 18*(3), 196–218.

Babouri, E. M. (1985). "Use of the Group Modality in the Prevention of Sexually Transmitted Diseases Among Adolescent Girls." *International Journal of Adolescent Medicine and Health*, July–December 1985 (1), 3–4.

Bachrach, C. (1984). "Contraceptive Practice Among American Women, 1973–1982." *Family Planning Perspectives, 16*(6), 253–258.

Bailey, J. M., & Pillard, R. C. (1991). "A Genetic Study of Male Sexual Orientation." *Archives of General Psychiatry, 48*(12), 1089–1096.

Bailey, J. M., Pillard, R. C., Neale, M. C., & Agyei, Y. (1993). "Heritable Factors Influence Sexual Orientation in Women." *Archives of General Psychiatry, 50*(3), 217–223.

Bailey, J. M., Willerman, L., & Parks, C. (1991). "A Test of the Maternal Stress Theory of Human Male Homosexuality." *Archives of Sexual Behavior, 20*, 277–293.

Baird, D. D., & Wilcox, A. J. (1985). "Cigarette Smoking Associated with Delayed Conception." *JAMA: Journal of the American Medical Association, 253*(20), 2979–2983.

Baldwin, J. D., Whitely, S., & Baldwin, J. I. (1992). "The Effect of Ethnic Group on Sexual Activities Related to Contraception and STDs." *Journal of Sex Research, 29*(2), 189–206.

Balshem, N., Oxman, G., Van Rooven, D., & Girod, K. (1992). "Syphilis, Sex and Crack Cocaine: Images of Risk and Morality." *Social Science and Medicine, 35*(2), 147–160.

Bancroft, J. (1984). "Hormones and Human Sexual Behavior." *Journal of Sex and Marital Therapy, 10*, 3–21.

Barbach, L. (1982). *For Each Other: Sharing Sexual Intimacy*. Garden City, NY: Doubleday.

Barclay, A. (1980). "Changes in Sexual Fantasy with Age." *Medical Aspects of Human Sexuality*, 15ff.

Barkan, S., & Bracken, M. (1987). "Delayed Childbearing: No Evidence for Increased Low Risk of Low Birth Weight and Preterm Delivery." *American Journal of Epidemiology, 125*(1), 101–109.

Barker-Benfield, G. J. (1976). *The Horrors of the Half-Known Life: Male Attitudes toward Women and Sexuality in Nineteenth-Century America*. New York: Harper & Row.

Barnes, A. B., et al. (1980). "Fertility and Pregnancy Outcomes in Women Exposed in Utero to Diethylstilbestrol." *New England Journal of Medicine, 302*(11), 609–613.

Barnes-Kedar, I., Amiel, A., Maor, O., & Fejgin, M. (1993). "Elevated Human Chorionic Gonadotropin Levels in Pregnancies with Sex Chromosome Abnormalities." *American Journal of Medical Genetics, 45*(3), 356–357.

Barnett, W., Freudenberg, N., & Wille, R. (1992). "Partnership after Induced Abortion—A Prospective Controlled Study." *Archives of Sexual Behavior, 21*(5), 443–455.

Baron, L. (1983). "Sex Differences in Attitudes and Experiences of Romantic Love." *Dissertation Abstracts International, 43*, 372A.

Barret, R. L., & Robinson, B. E. (1990). *Gay Fathers*. Lexington, MA: Lexington Books.

Barron, J. (1987, June 3). "In Ads for Condoms a Focus on Women." *The New York Times*, p. 14.

Barrow, G., & Smith (1992). *Aging, Ageism, and Society*. St. Paul, MI: West.

Barrows, S. (1986). *Mayflower Madam*. New York: Arbor House.

Bartell, G. D. (1970). "Group Sex Among the Mid-Americans." *Journal of Sex Research, 6*, 113–130.

Barth, R., & Kinder, B. (1987). "The Mislabeling of Sexual Impulsivity." *Journal of Sex and Marital Therapy, 13*(1), 15–23.

Basow, S. A. (1986). *Gender Stereotypes: Traditions and Alternatives*. (2nd ed.) Pacific Grove, CA: Brooks/Cole.

Basow, S. A. (1992). *Gender: Stereotyping and Roles*. Pacific Grove, CA: Brooks/Cole.

Basow, S. A., & Campanile, F. (1990). "Attitudes Toward Prostitution as a Function of Attitudes Toward Feminism in College Students." *Psychology of Women, 14*(1), 135–141.

Baumann, P., Jovanovic, V., Gellert, G., & Rauskolb, R. (1991). "Risk of Miscarriage After Transcervical and Transabdominal CVS in Relation to Bacterial Colonization of the Cervix." *Prenatal Diagnosis, 11*(8), 551–557.

Baumeister, R. F. (1988a). "Gender Differences in Masochistic Scripts." *Journal of Sex Research, 25*, 478–499.

Baumeister, R. F. (1988b). "Masochism as an Escape from Self." *Journal of Sex Research, 25*(1), 28–59.

Bauserman, R. (1990). "Objectivity and Ideology: Criticism of Theo Sandfort's Research on Man-Boy Sexual Relations." *Journal of Homosexuality, 20*(1–2), 297–312.

Baxter, L. A. (1987). "Cognition and Communication in Relationship Process." In R. Burnett, P. McGhee, & D. Clarke (Eds.), *Accounting for Relationships: Explanation, Representation, and Knowledge*. London: Methuen.

Baxter, R. L., De Riemer, C., Landini, A., & Leslie, L. (1985). "A Content Analysis of Music Videos." *Journal of Broadcasting and Electronic Media, 29*(3), 333–340.

Bayer, A., & Baker, D. (1985). *Eating Disorders: Anorexia and Bulimia*. Santa Cruz, CA: Network Publications.

Bayer, R. (1981). *Homosexuality and American Psychiatry: The Politics of Diagnosis*. New York: Basic Books.

Bean, F., & Tienda, M. (1987). *The Hispanic Population of the United States*. New York: Russell Sage Foundation.

Becerra, R. (1988). "The Mexican American Family." In C. Mindel et al. (Eds.), *Ethnic Families in America: Patterns and Variations* (3rd ed.). New York: Elsevier North Holland.

Bechhofer, L., & Parrot, L. (1991). "What Is Acquaintance Rape?" In A. Parrot & L. Bechhofer (Eds.), *Acquaintance Rape: The Hidden Crime*. New York: John Wiley.

Beck, M. (1988, August 15). "Miscarriages." *Newsweek*, pp. 46–49.

Beck, M. (1992, May 25). "Menopause." *Newsweek*, pp. 71–79.

Beck, S. H., Cole, B. S., & Hammond, J. A. (1991). "Religious Heritage and Premarital Sex: Evidence from a National Sample of Young Adults." *Journal for the Scientific Study of Religion, 30*(2), 173–180.

Beckman, K. A., & Burns, G. L. (1990). "Relation of Sexual Abuse and Bulimia in College Women." *International Journal of Eating Disorders, 9*, 487–492.

Beckmann, C. R., Gittler, M., Barzansky, B. M., & Beckmann, C. A. (1989). "Gynecologic Health Care of Women with Disabilities." *Obstetrics and Gynecology, 74*(1), 75–79.

Beckstein, D. (1990). *AIDS Prevention in Public Sex Environments*. Santa Cruz, CA: Santa Cruz AIDS Project.

Behar, R. (1989). "Sexual Witchcraft, Colonialism, and Women's Powers: Views from the Spanish Inquisition." In A. Lavrin (Ed.), *Sexuality and Marriage in Colonial Latin America*. Lincoln, NE: University of Nebraska Press.

Behr, A. (1986, July 21). "Gay Teens Often Turn to Suicide." *San Jose Mercury News*, pp. 1, 6.

Beier, E., & Sternberg, D. (1977). "Marital Communication." *Journal of Communication*, 27(3), 92–97.

Beitchman, J. H., et al. (1992). "A Review of the Long-Term Effects of Child Sexual Abuse." *Child Abuse and Neglect*, 16(1), 101–128.

Belcastro, P. (1985). "Sexual Behavior Differences Between Black and White Students." *Journal of Sex Research*, 21(1), 56–67.

Belk, R. (1991). "The Ineluctable Mysteries of Possessions." *Journal of Social Behavior and Personality*, 6(6), 17–55.

Belknap, J. (1989). "The Sexual Victimization of Unmarried Women by Non-Relative Acquaintances." In M. Pirog-Good & J. Stets (Eds.), *Violence in Dating Relationships*. New York: Praeger.

Bell, A. (1974). "Homosexualities: Their Range and Character." In J. K. Cole & R. Dienstbier (Eds.), *Nebraska Symposium on Motivation*. Lincoln, NE: University of Nebraska Press.

Bell, A., & Weinberg, M. (1978). *Homosexualities: A Study of Diversities Among Men*. New York: Simon & Schuster.

Bell, A., Weinberg, M., & Hammersmith, S. (1981). *Sexual Preference: Its Development in Men and Women*. Bloomington, IN: Indiana University Press.

Bello, D., Pitts, R., & Etzel, M. (1983). "The Communication Effects of Controversial Sexual Content in Television Programs and Commercials." *Journal of Advertising*, 12(3), 32–43.

Belsky, J., et al. (1984). *The Child in the Family*. Reading, MA: Addison-Wesley.

Belsky, J. (1986, September). "Transition to Parenthood." *Medical Aspects of Human Sexuality*, 20, 56–59.

Bem, S. L. (1975). "Androgyny vs. the Tight Little Lives of Fluffy Women and Chesty Men." *Psychology Today*, 9(4), 58–59ff.

Bem, S. L. (1983). "Gender Schema Theory and Its Implications for Child Development: Raising Gender-Aschematic Children in a Gender Schematic Society." *Signs*, 8(4), 598–616.

Bem, S. L. (1989). "Genital Knowledge and Gender Constancy in Preschool Children." *Child Development*, 60(3), 649–662.

Bem, S. L., & Lewis, S. A. (1975). "Sex Role Adaptability: One Consequence of Psychological Androgyny." *Journal of Personality and Social Psychology*, 31(4), 634–643.

Bem, S. L., Martyna, W., & Watson, C. (1976). "Sex Typing and Androgyny: Further Explorations of the Expressive Domain." *Journal of Personality and Social Psychology*, 34, 1016–1023.

Bennett, C. J., et al. (1988). "Sexual Dysfunction and Electroejaculation in Men with Spinal Cord Injury." *Journal of Urology*, 139, 453–457.

Bennett, W. (1982). *The Dieter's Dilemma: Eating Less and Weighing More*. New York: Basic Books.

Benshoof, J. (1993). "Planned Parenthood v. Cases: The Impact of the Undue Burden Standard on Reproductive Health Care." *JAMA: Journal of the American Medical Association*, 269(17), 2249–2257.

Benson, D., Charlton, C., & Goodhart, F. (1992). "Acquaintance Rape on Campus: A Literature Review." *Journal of American College Health*, 40, 157–165.

Benson, D., & Thompson, G. (1982). "Sexual Harassment on a University Campus: The Confluence of Authority Relations, Sexual Interest, and Gender Stratification." *Social Problems*, 29, 236–251.

Benson, R. (1980). *Handbook of Obstetrics and Gynecology* (7th ed.). Los Altos, CA: Lane Medical Publications.

Bera, W., et al. (1991). *Male Adolescent Sexual Abuse*. Newbury Park, CA: Sage Publications.

Bergen, D. J., & Williams, J. E. (1991). "Sex Stereotypes in the United States Revisited: 1972–1988." *Sex Roles*, 24(7/8), 413–423.

Berger, A. A. (1991). "Of Mice and Men: An Introduction to Mouseology; or Anal Eroticism and Disney." *Journal of Homosexuality*, 21(1–2), 155–165.

Berger, M. J., & Goldstein, D. P. (1984). "Infertility Related to Exposure to DES in Utero: Reproductive Problems in the Female." In M. Mazor & H. Simons (Eds.), *Infertility: Medical, Emotional, and Social Considerations*. New York: Human Sciences Press.

Berger, R. M. (1982). "The Unseen Minority: Older Gays and Lesbians." *Social Work*, 27, 236–242.

Berkowitz, A. (1992). "College Men as Perpetrators of Acquaintance Rape and Sexual Assault: A Review of Recent Research." *Journal of American College Health*, 40(4), 175–181.

Bernard, J. (1982). *The Future of Marriage*. (2nd ed.). New York: Columbia University Press.

Bernstein, H. (1991, February 5). "Ruling May Curb Harassment." *Los Angeles Times*, p. 3.

Berrick, J. D., & Barth, R. P. (1992). "Child Sexual Abuse Prevention—Research Review and Recommendations." *Social Work Research and Abstracts*, 28, 6–15.

Berscheid, E. (1983). "Emotion." In H. H. Kelley et al. (Eds.), *Close Relationships*. New York: W. H. Freeman.

Berscheid, E., & Frei, J. (1977). "Romantic Love and Sexual Jealousy." In G. Clanton & L. Smith (Eds.), *Jealousy*. Englewood Cliffs, NJ: Prentice-Hall.

Berscheid, E., & Walster, E. H. (1974). "A Little Bit About Love." In T. L. Huston (Ed.), *Foundations of Interpersonal Attraction*. New York: Academic Press.

Bérubé, A. (1988, September). "Caught in the Storm: AIDS and the Meaning of Natural Disaster." *Out/Look*, 8–19.

Betchen, S. (1991). "Male Masturbation as a Vehicle for the Pursuer/Distancer Relationship in Marriage." *Journal of Sex and Marital Therapy*, 17(4), 269–278.

Beyette, B. (1986, October 17). "Teen Sex-Education Campaign Launched." *Los Angeles Times*, pp. 20, 22.

Bieber, I. (1962). *Homosexuality: A Psychoanalytic Study*. New York: Basic Books.

Bills, S. A., & Duncan, D. F. (1991). "Drugs and Sex: A Survey of College Students' Beliefs." *Perceptual and Motor Skills*, 72, 1293–1294.

Billy, J. O., Tanfer, K., Grady, W. R., & Klepinger, D. H. (1993). "The Sexual Behavior of Men in the United States." *Family Planning Perspectives*, 25(2), 52–60.

Billy, J. O., & Udry, J. R. (1985). "The Influence of Male and Female Best Friends on Adolescent Sexual Behavior." *Adolescence*, 20(77), 21–32.

Binion, V. (1990). "Psychological Androgyny: A Black Female Perspective." *Sex Roles*, 22(7–8), 487–507.

Binsacca, B. D., et al. (1987). "Factors Associated with Low Birth Weight in an Inner-City Population." *American Journal of Public Health*, 77(4), 505–506.

Black, R. D. (1991). "Women's Voices After Pregnancy Loss: Couples' Patterns." *Social Work in Health Care*, 16(2), 19–36.

Blackwood, E. (1984). "Sexuality and Gender in Certain Native American Tribes: The Case of Cross-Gender Females." *Signs*, 10, 27–42.

Blakeslee, S. (1991, October 30). "Simplifying the Surgical Removal of Precancerous Cervical Lesions." *The New York Times*, p. B9.

Blakeslee, S. (1992, January 21). "Wart Virus Tied to Cervix Cancer." *The New York Times*, p. B6.

Blanchard, R., Steiner, B. W., Clemmensen, L. H., & Dickey, R. (1989). "Prediction of Regrets in Postoperative Transsexuals." *Canadian Journal of Psychiatry*, 34(1), 43–45.

Blanchard, R., Clemmensen, L., & Steiner, B. (1986). "Phallometric Detection of Fetishistic Arousal in Heterosexual Male Cross-Dressers." *Journal of Sex Research, 22*(4), 452–462.

Blanchard, R., & Hucker, S. (1991). "Age, Transvestism, Bondage, and Concurrent Paraphilic Activities in 117 Fatal Cases of Autoerotic Asphyxia." *British Journal of Psychiatry, 159*, 371–377.

Blatch, H. (Ed.). (1922). *Elizabeth Cady Stanton*. New York: Harper & Row.

Block, J. (1983). "Differential Premises Arising from Differential Socialization of the Sexes: Some Conjectures." *Child Development, 54*, 1335–1354.

Blum, R., et al. (1992). "American Indian–Alaska Native Youth Health." *Journal of the American Medical Association, 267*, 1637.

Blumberg, M. L., & Lester, D. (1991). "High School and College Students' Attitude Toward Rape." *Adolescence, 26*(103), 727–729.

Blumenfeld, W., & Raymond, D. (1989). *Looking at Gay and Lesbian Life*. Boston: Beacon Press.

Blumstein, P., & Schwartz, P. (1983). *American Couples*. New York: McGraw-Hill.

Board of Directors of the Society for the Scientific Study of Sex. (1987). "SSSS Responds to the U.S. Attorney General's Commission on Pornography." *Journal of Sex Research, 23*(2), 284–285.

Boland, J., & Follingstad, D. (1987). "The Relationship Between Communication and Marital Satisfaction: A Review." *Journal of Sex and Marital Therapy, 13*(4), 286–313.

Boland, R. (1992). "Selected Legal Developments in Reproductive Health in 1991." *Family Planning Perspectives, 24*(4), 178–185.

Boles, A. J., & Curtis-Boles, H. (1986). "Black Couples and the Transition to Parenthood." *The American Journal of Social Psychiatry, 6*(1), 27–31.

Bollen, N., Camus, M., Staessen, C., Tournaye, H., Devroey, P., & VanSteirteghem, A. C. (1991). "The Incidence of Multiple Pregnancy After In Vitro Fertilization and Embryo Transfer, Gamete, or Zygote Intrafallopian Transfer." *Fertility and Sterility, 55*(2), 314–318.

Bonilla, L., & Porter, J. (1990). "A Comparison of Latino, Black, and Non-Hispanic White Attitudes Toward Homosexuality." *Hispanic Journal of Behavioral Sciences, 12*, 437–452.

Borhek, M. (1988). "Helping Gay and Lesbian Adolescents and Their Families: A Mother's Perspective." *Journal of Adolescent Health Care, 9*(2), 123–128.

Borneman, E. (1983). "Progress in Empirical Research on Children's Sexuality." *SIECUS Report*, 1–5.

Borrello, G., & Thompson, B. (1990). "A Note Regarding the Validity of Lee's Typology of Love." *Journal of Psychology, 124*(6), 639–644.

Boston Women's Health Book Collective. (1992). *The New Our Bodies, Ourselves*. New York: Simon and Schuster.

Boston Women's Health Collective (1978). *Our Bodies, Ourselves*. Boston: Little, Brown.

Bostwick, H. (1860). *A Treatise on the Nature and Treatment of Seminal Disease, Impotency, and Other Kindred Afflictions*. (12th ed.). New York: Burgess, Stringer.

Boswell, J. (1980). *Christianity, Social Tolerance, and Homosexuality*. Chicago: University of Chicago Press.

Botwin, C. (1979, September 16). "Is There Sex After Marriage?" *The New York Times Magazine*, pp. 108–112.

Boulton, M., Hart, G., & Fitzpatrick, R. (1992). "The Sexual Behavior of Bisexual Men in Relation to HIV Transmission." *AIDS Care, 4*(2), 165–175.

Bouman, P. G. (1988). "Sex Reassignment Surgery in Male-to-Female Transsexuals." *Annals of Plastic Surgery, 21*(6), 526–531.

Bowlby, J. (1969, 1973, 1980). *Attachment and Loss, Vols. I–III*. New York: Basic Books.

Bowman, C. G. (1993). "Street Harassment and the Informal Ghettoization of Women." *Harvard Law Review, 106*(3), 517–580.

Bownes, I. T., O'Gorman, E. C., & Sayers, A. (1991a). "Assault Characteristics and Post-Traumatic Stress Disorder in Rape Victims." *Acta Psychiatrica Scandinavica, 83*, 27–30.

Bownes, I. T., O'Gorman, E. C., & Sayers, A. (1991b). "Psychiatric Symptoms, Behaviorial Responses and Post-Traumatic Stress Disorder in Rape Victims." Division of Criminological and Legal Psychology First Annual Conference. *Issues in Criminological and Legal Psychology, 1*, 25–33.

Bowser, B. (1988). "Crack and AIDS: An Ethnographic Impression." *MIRA: Multicultural Inquiry and Research on AIDS, 2*(2), 1–3.

Bowser, B. P., Fullilove, M. T., & Fullilove, R. E. (1990). "African-American Youth and AIDS High-Risk Behavior: The Social Context and Barriers to Prevention." *Youth and Society, 22*(1), 54–66.

Bozett, F. W. (1987a). "Children of Gay Fathers." In F. W. Bozett (Ed.), *Gay and Lesbian Parents*. New York: Praeger.

Bozett, F. W. (Ed.). (1987a). *Gay and Lesbian Parents*. New York: Praeger.

Bozett, F. W. (1987b). "Gay Fathers." In F. W. Bozett (Ed.), *Gay and Lesbian Parents*. New York: Praeger.

Brady, E. C., et al. (1991). "Date Rape: Expectations, Avoidance, Strategies, and Attitudes Toward Victims." *Journal of Social Psychology, 131*(3), 427–429.

Brand, H. J. (1989). "The Influence of Sex Differences on the Acceptance of Infertility." *Journal of Reproductive and Infant Psychology, 7*(2), 129–131.

Brandenburg, H., et al. (1990). "Fetal Loss Rate After Chorionic Villus Sampling and Subsequent Amniocentesis." *American Journal of Medical Genetics, 35*(2), 178–180.

Brandt, A. M. (1987). *No Magic Bullet: A Social History of Venereal Disease in the United States Since 1880*. New York: Oxford University Press.

Brauer, A. P., Brauer, D., & Rhodes, R. (1991). *The ESO Ecstacy Program*. New York: Warner Books.

Braunthal, H. (1981). "Working with Transsexuals." *International Journal of Social Psychology, 27*(1), 3–12.

Brecher, E. (1984). *Love, Sex and Aging*. Boston: Little, Brown.

Bremer, B. A., et al. (1991). "Do You Have to Call It 'Sexual Harassment' to Feel Harassed?" *College Student Journal, 25*(3), 258–268.

Breslow, N. (1989). "Sources of Confusion in the Study and Treatment of Sadomasochism." *Journal of Social Behavior and Personality, 4*(3), 263–274.

Breslow, N., Evans, L., & Langley, J. (1985). "On the Prevalence and Roles of Females in the Sadomasochistic Subculture: Report on an Empirical Investigation." *Archives of Sexual Behavior, 14*, 303–317.

Bretschneider, J., & McCoy, N. (1988). "Sexual Interest and Behavior in Healthy 80- to 102-Year-Olds." *Archives of Sexual Behavior, 17*(2), 109–128.

Briere, J. (1992). "Methodological Issues in the Study of Sexual Abuse Effects." *Journal of Consulting and Clinical Psychology, 60*(2), 196–204.

Briere, J., & Runtz, M. (1989). "University Male's Sexual Interest in Children: Predicting Potential Indices of 'Pedophilia' in a Nonforensic Sample." *Child Abuse and Neglect, 13*(1), 65–75.

Brierly, H. (1979). *Transvestism*. New York: Pergamon Press.

Bringle, R., & Buunk, B. (1985). "Jealousy and Social Behavior: A Review of Personal, Relationship, and Situational Determinants." In P. Shaver (Ed.), *Review of Personality and Social Psychology, Vol. 6: Self, Situation, and Social Behavior*. Newbury Park, CA: Sage Publications.

Bringle, R., & Buunk, B. (1991). "Extradyadic Relationships and Sexual Jealousy." In K. McKinney & Susan Sprecher (Eds.), *Sexuality in Close Relationships*. Hillsdale, NJ: Erlbaum.

Brinton, L. A., et al. (1986). "Long-Term Use of Oral Contraceptives and Risk of Invasive Cervical Cancer." *International Journal of Cancer, 38*, 339ff.

Britton, D. M. (1990). "Homophobia and Homosociality: An Analysis of Boundary Maintenance." *Sociological Quarterly*, 31(3), 423–439.

Brody, E. (1985). "Parent Care as a Normative Family Stress." *Gerontologist*, 25, 19–29.

Brody, J. E. (1985, August 14). "Assessing the Question of Male Circumcision." *The New York Times*, p. 18.

Brody, J. E. (1986, July 6). "Teens and the Rush to Have Sex." *San Jose Mercury News*, p. 5.

Brody, J. E. (1992). "Estrogen Is Found to Improve Mood, Not Just Menopause Symptoms." *The New York Times*, p. 141.

Brody, J. E. (1993, February 24). "Don't Panic. Before Worrying About All the Medical Studies, Take a Close Look at the Evidence." *The New York Times*, p. B7.

Brotman, B. (1992, July 19). "Why Abortion Rights Is a White Fight." *San Jose Mercury News*, p. A4.

Brown, G. (1980). *The New Celibacy*. New York: McGraw-Hill.

Brown, G. R., & Collier, Z. (1989). "Transvestites' Women Revisted: A Nonpatient Sample." *Archives of Sexual Behavior*, 18, 73–83.

Brown, J. D., & Campbell, K. (1986). "Race and Gender in Music Videos: The Same Beat but a Different Drummer." *Journal of Communication*, 36(1), 94–106.

Brown, J. D., & Newcomer, S. F. (1991). "Television Viewing and Adolescents' Sexual Behavior." *Journal of Homosexuality*, 21(1-2), 77–91.

Brown, J. D., & Schulze, L. (1990). "The Effects of Race, Gender, and Fandom on Audience Interpretations of Madonna's Music Videos." *Journal of Communication*, 40, 88–102.

Brown, P. L. (1990, October 4). "Where to Put the TV Set?" *The New York Times*, p. 4.

Browne, A., & Finkelhor, D. (1986). "Initial and Long-Term Effects: A Review of the Research." In D. Finkelhor (Ed.), *Sourcebook on Child Sexual Abuse*. Beverly Hills, CA: Sage Publications.

Brownmiller, S. (1975). *Against Our Will: Men, Women, and Rape*. New York: Simon & Schuster.

Brozan, N. (1986, June 21). "Early Detection Is Key in Breast Cancer." *The New York Times*, pp. 19, 20.

Bruce, K. E., Shrum, J. C., Trefethen, C., & Slovik, L. F. (1990). "Students' Attitudes About AIDS, Homosexuality, and Condoms." *AIDS Education and Prevention*, 2(3), 220–234.

Bruch, H. (1978). *The Golden Cage: The Enigma of Anorexia Nervosa*. Cambridge, MA: Harvard University Press.

Bryant, C. (1982). *Social Deviancy and Social Proscription*. New York: Human Sciences Press.

Bryant, C., & Palmer, C. E. (1975). "Massage Parlors and 'Hand Whores'." *Journal of Sex Research*, 11, 227–241.

Bryant, J., & Brown, D. (1989). "Uses of Pornography." In Z. Dolf & B. Jennings (Eds.), *Pornography: Research Advances and Policy Considerations*. Hillsdale, NJ: Erlbaum.

Bryant, Z. L., & Coleman, M. (1988). "The Black Family as Portrayed in Introductory Marriage and Family Textbooks." *Family Relations*, 37(3), 255–259.

Buchanan, P. (1993, February 15). "Is the GOP Falling into Humpty Dumpty Country?" *San Jose Mercury News*, p. A12.

Buchholz, E., & Gol, B. (1986). "More Than Playing House: A Developmental Perspective on the Strengths in Teenage Motherhood." *American Journal of Orthopsychology*, 56(3), 347–359.

Buchman, T., et al. (1980). "The Structure of Herpes Simplex Virus DNA and Its Application to Molecular Epidemiology." *Annals of the New York Academy of Science*, 354, 279–290.

Budiansky, S. (1988, April 18). "The New Rules of Reproduction." *U.S. News and World Report*, pp. 66–69.

Buffum, J. (1992). "Prescription Drugs and Sexual Function." *Psychiatric Medicine*, 10(2), 181–198.

Bullard, D., & Knight, S. (Eds.). (1981). *Sexuality and Disability: Personal Perspectives*. St. Louis, MO: Mosby.

Bullough, V. (1976). *Sexual Variance in Society and History*. New York: John Wiley.

Bullough, V. (Ed.) (1979). *The Frontiers of Sex Research*. Buffalo, NY: Prometheus.

Bullough, V. (1991). "Transvestism: A Reexamination." *Journal of Psychology and Human Sexuality*, 4(2), 53–67.

Bullough, V., & Weinberg, J. S. (1988). "Women Married to Transvestites: Problems and Adjustments." *Journal of Psychology and Human Sexuality*, 1, 83–104.

Burch, B. (1987). "Barriers to Intimacy: Conflicts Over Power, Dependency, and Nurturing in Lesbian Relationships." In Boston Lesbian Psychologies Collective (Ed.), *Lesbian Psychology: Explorations and Challenges*. Urbana, IL: University of Chicago Press.

Burcky, W., Reuterman, N., & Kopsky, S. (1988). "Dating Violence Among High School Students." *School Counselor*, 35(5), 353–358.

Burger, E. (1981). "Radical Hysterectomy and Vaginectomy for Cancer." In D. Bullard & S. Knight (Eds.), *Sexuality and Disability: Personal Perspectives*. St. Louis, MO: Mosby.

Burgess, A., Harman, C., McCausland, M., & Powers, P. (1984). "Response Patterns in Children and Adolescents Exploited Through Sex Rings and Pornography." *American Journal of Psychiatry*, 141, 656–662.

Burnett, R., McGhee, P., & Clarke, D. (Eds.). *Accounting for Relationships: Explanation, Representation and Knowledge*. London: Methuen.

Burnham, M. (1992). "The Supreme Court Appointment Process and the Politics of Sex and Gender." In T. Morrison (Ed.), *Racing Justice, En-Gendering Power*. New York: Pantheon.

Burns, A., Farrell, M., & Christie-Brown, J. (1990). "Clinical Features of Patients Attending a Gender-Identity Clinic." *British Journal of Psychiatry*, 157, 265–268.

Bursik, K. (1992). "Perceptions of Sexual Harassment in an Academic Context." *Sex Roles*, 27(7–8), 401–412.

Burt, M. (1980). "Cultural Myths and Supports for Rape." *Journal of Personality and Social Psychology*, 38, 217–230.

Bush, C. R., Bush, J. P., & Jennings, J. (1988). "Effects of Jealousy Threats on Relationship Perceptions and Emotions." *Journal of Social and Personal Relationships*, 5(3), 285–303.

Butcher, A. H., Manning, D. T., & O'Neal, E. C. (1991). "HIV-Related Sexual Behaviors of College Students." *Journal of American College Health*, 40(3), 115–118.

Butter, I. H., & Kay, B. J. (1990). "Self-Certification in Law Midwives Organizations—A Vehicle for Professional Autonomy." *Social Science and Medicine*, 30(12), 1329–1339.

Butts, J. D. (1981). "Adolescent Sexuality and Teenage Pregnancy from a Black Perspective." In T. Ooms (Ed.), *Teenage Pregnancy in a Family Context*. Philadelphia: Temple University Press.

Buunk, B., & Hupka, R. (1987). "Cross-Cultural Differences in the Elicitation of Sexual Jealousy." *Journal of Sex Research*, 23(1), 12–22.

Buunk, B., & van Driel, B. (1989). *Variant Lifestyles and Relationships*. Newbury Park, CA: Sage Publications.

Buxton, R. (1991). "Dr. Ruth Westheimer: Upsetting the Normalcy of the Late-Night Talk Show." *Journal of Homosexuality*, 21(1-2), 139–153.

Byers, E. S., & Eno, R. J. (1991). "Predicting Men's Sexual Coercion and Aggression from Attitudes, Dating History, and Sexual Response." *Journal of Psychology and Human Sexuality*, 4(3), 55–70.

Byers, E. S., & Heinlein, L. (1989). "Predicting Initiations and Refusals of Sexual Activities in Married and Cohabiting Heterosexual Couples." *Journal of Sex Research*, 26, 210–231.

Bygdeman, M., Swahn, M. L., Gemzell-Danielsson, K., & Svalander, P. (1993). "Mode of Action of RU 486." *Annals of Medicine*, 25(1), 61–64.

Byrd, W., et al. (1990). "A Prospective Randomized Study of Pregnancy Rates Following Intrauterine and Intracervical Insemination Using Frozen Donor Sperm." *Fertility and Sterility, 53*(3), 521–527.

Byrne, D., et al. (1977). "Negative Sexual Attitudes and Contraception." In D. Byrne & L. A. Byrne (Eds.), *Exploring Human Sexuality*. New York: Harper & Row.

Byrne, D., Fisher, W. A., Lambreth, J., & Mitchell, H. E. (1974). "Evaluations of Erotica: Facts or Feelings." *Journal of Personality and Social Psychology, 29*, 111–116.

Byrne, D., & Murnen, K. (1988). "Maintaining Love Relationships." In R. Sternberg & M. Barnes (Eds.), *The Psychology of Love*. New Haven, CT: Yale University Press.

Cado, S., & Leitenberg, H. (1990). "Guilt Reactions to Sexual Fantasies During Intercourse." *Archives of Sexual Behavior, 19*(1), 49–63.

Calamidas, E. G. (1990). "AIDS and STD Education: What's Really Happening in Our Schools?" *Journal of Sex Education and Therapy, 16*(1), 54–63.

Calderone, M. (1983). "Fetal Erection and Its Message to Us." *SIECUS Report, 11*(5-6), 9–10.

Calderone, M. S. (1983). "Childhood Sexuality: Approaching the Prevention of Sexual Disease." In G. Albee et al. (Eds.), *Promoting Sexual Responsibility and Preventing Sexual Problems*. Hanover, NH: University Press of New England.

Califia, P. (1979). "Lesbian Sexuality." *Journal of Homosexuality, 4*, 255–266.

Callan, V. (1985). "Perceptions of Parents, the Voluntarily and Involuntarily Childless: A Multidimensional Scaling Analysis." *Journal of Marriage and the Family, 47*(4), 1045–1050.

Callendar, C., & Kochems, L. (1985). "Men and Not-Men: Male Gender-Mixing Statuses and Homosexuality." Special issue: Anthropology and Homosexual Behavior. *Journal of Homosexuality, 11*, 165–178.

Callender, C., et al. (1983). "The North American Berdache." *Current Anthropology, 24*(4), 443–456.

"Can You Rely on Condoms?" (1989, March). *Consumer Reports*, p. 135.

Canavan, M. M., et al. (1992). "The Female Experience of Sibling Incest." *Journal of Marital and Family Therapy, 18*, 129–142.

Cantor, M. (1987). "Popular Culture and the Portrayal of Women: Content and Control." In M. Beth & M. M. Ferree (Eds.), *Analyzing Gender*. Newbury Park, CA: Sage Publications.

Cantor, M. (1991). "The American Family on Television: From Molly Goldberg to Bill Cosby." *Journal of Comparative Family Studies, 22*(2), 205–216.

Caplan, A. L. (1992). "Twenty Years After: The Legacy of the Tuskegee Syphilis Study. When Evil Intrudes." *Hastings Center Report, 22*(6), 29–32.

Carey, R. F., Herman, W. A., Retta, S. M., Rinaldi, J. E., Herman, B. A., & Athey, T. W. (1992). "Effectiveness of Latex Condoms as a Barrier to Human Immunodeficiency Virus-Sized Particles under Conditions of Simulated Use." *Sexually Transmitted Diseases, 19*(4), 230–234.

Cargan, L., & Melko, M. (1982). *Singles: Myths and Realities*. Beverly Hills, CA: Sage Publications.

Carl, D. (1986). "Acquired Immune Deficiency Syndrome: A Preliminary Examination of the Effects on Gay Couples and Coupling." *Journal of Marital and Family Therapy, 12*(3), 241–247.

Carlson, R. G., & Siegal, H. A. (1991). "The Crack Life: An Ethnographic Overview of Crack Use and Sexual Behavior Among African-Americans in a Midwest Metropolitan City." *Journal of Psychoactive Drugs, 23*(1), 11–20.

Carmen, A., & Moody, H. (1985). *Working Women: The Subterranean World of Street Prostitution*. New York: Harper & Row.

Carnes, P. (1983). *Out of Shadows*. Minneapolis, MN: CompCare Publications.

Carr, P. (1992, February 16). "Sexual Harassment Pushes Its Way into the Schoolyard." *San Jose Mercury News*, pp. 1L, 8L.

Carrera, M. (1980). "Sexual Learning in the Elementary School." In E. Roberts (Ed.), *Childhood Sexual Learning: The Unwritten Curriculum*. Cambridge, MA: Ballinger.

Carrera, M. (1981). *Sex: The Facts, the Acts, and Your Feelings*. New York: Crown.

Carrier, J. (1992). "Miguel: Sexual Life History of a Gay Mexican American." In G. Herdt (Ed.), *Gay Culture in America: Essays from the Field*. Boston: Beacon Press.

Carrier, J., Joseph, C., Nguyen, B., & Su, S. (1992). "Vietnamese American Sexual Behaviors and the HIV Infection." *Journal of Sex Research, 29*(4), 547–560.

Carroll, J. (1990, March 5). "Tracing the Causes of Infertility." *San Francisco Chronicle*, pp. 3ff.

Carroll, J., Volk, K. D., & Hyde, J. J. (1985). "Differences in Males and Females in Motives for Engaging in Sexual Intercourse." *Archives of Sexual Behavior, 14*, 131–139.

Carter, B., & McGoldrick, M. (Eds.). (1989). *The Changing Family Life Cycle* (2nd ed.). Boston: Allyn & Bacon.

Carter, D. B. (Ed.). (1987). *Current Conceptions of Sex Roles and Sex Typing*. New York: Praeger.

Cary, A. (1992, April 18). "Big Fans on Campus." *TV Guide*, pp. 26–31.

Cass, V. C. (1983). "Homosexual Identity: A Concept in Need of Definition." *Journal of Homosexuality, 9*(2-3), 105–126.

Cassell, C. (1984). *Swept Away*. New York: Simon & Schuster.

Catania, J. A., et al. (1992). "Prevalence of AIDS-Related Risk Factors and Condom Use in the United States." *Science, 258*(5085), 1101–1106.

Catchpole, T. (1992, November). "A Short History of Political Tricks." *Playboy*, pp. 86–87, 169.

Cate, R. M., & Lloyd, S. A. (1992). *Courtship*. Newbury Park, CA: Sage Publications.

Cates, W. J., & Stone, K. M. (1992). "Family Planning, Sexually Transmitted Diseases and Contraceptive Choices: A Literature Update. Part I." *Family Planning Perspectives, 24*(2), 75–84.

Cautela, J. E. (1986). "Behavioral Analysis of a Fetish: First Interview." *Journal of Behavior Therapy and Experimental Psychiatry, 17*(3), 161–165.

CDC. See Centers for Disease for Control or Centers for Disease Control and Prevention.

Celentano, D. D., Vlahov, D., Cohn, S., Anthony, J. C., Solomon, L., & Nelson, K. E. (1991). "Risk Factors for Shooting Gallery Use and Cessation Among Intravenous Drug Users." *American Journal of Public Health, 81*(10), 1291–1295.

Center for Population Options. (1992). *Teenage Pregnancy and Too-Early Childbearing: Public Costs, Personal Consequences*.

Centers for Disease Control. (1982). "Update on Acquired Immune Deficiency Syndrome (AIDS)—United States." *Morbidity and Mortality Weekly Report, 31*(37).

Centers for Disease Control. (1984). "Hepatitis B Vaccine Evidence Confirming the Lack of AIDS Transmission." *Morbidity and Mortality Weekly Report, 33*, 685–687.

Centers for Disease Control. (1985). "Recommendation for Assisting in the Prevention of Perinatal Transmission of Human T-lymphotrophic Virus Type III." *Morbidity and Mortality Weekly Report, 34*, 721–726, 731–732.

Centers for Disease Control. (1986a). "Acquired Immunodeficiency Syndrome in Western Palm Beach County, Florida." *Morbidity and Mortality Weekly Report, 35*, 609–613.

Centers for Disease Control. (1986b). "The Cancer and Steroid Hormone (CASH) Study of the Centers for Disease Control and the National Institute of Child Health and Human Development: Oral Contraceptive Use and the Risk of Breast Cancer." *New England Journal of Medicine, 315*, 405–411.

Centers for Disease Control. (1986c). "Positive HTLV-III/LAV Antibody Results for Sexually Active Members of Social/Sexual Clubs." *Morbidity and Mortality Weekly Report*, 1–2.

Centers for Disease Control. (1987). "Lack of Transmission of Human Immunodeficiency Virus Through RHo(D) Immune Globulin." *Morbidity and Mortality Weekly Report*, 36,728.

Centers for Disease Control. (1990). "Statewide Prevalence of Illicit Drug Use by Pregnant Women—Rhode Island." *Morbidity and Mortality Weekly Report*, 39(14), 225–227.

Centers for Disease Control. (1992a). "1993 Revised Classification System for HIV Infection and Expanded Surveillance Case Definition for AIDS Among Adolescents and Adults. *Morbidity and Mortality Weekly Report*, 41(RR-17), 1–19.

Centers for Disease Control. (1992a). "Update: CD4+ T-lymphocetopenia in Persons Without Evident Symptoms." *Morbidity and Mortality Weekly Report*, 41(31), 578–579.

Centers for Disease Control and Prevention. (1993a). "Update: Barrier Protection Against HIV Infection and Other Sexually Transmitted Diseases." *Morbidity and Mortality Weekly Report*, 42(30), 589–596.

Centers for Disease Control and Prevention. (1993b). Division of STD/HIV Prevention: *Annual Report, 1992*.

Centers for Disease Control and Prevention. (1993c). "Facts About Condoms and Their Use in Preventing HIV Infection and Other STDs." *HIV/AIDS Prevention*, 1–3.

Centers for Disease Control and Prevention. (1993d). "Surveillance Report: U.S. AIDS Cases Reported Through December 1992." *HIV/AIDS Surveillance Report*, 1–23.

Centers for Disease Control and Prevention. (1993e). "Surveillance Report: U.S. AIDS Cases Reported Through March 1993." *HIV/AIDS Surveillance Report*, 5(1), 1–19.

Centers for Disease Control and Prevention. (1993f). "Surveillance Report: U.S. AIDS Cases Reported through June 30, 1993." *HIV/AIDS Surveillance Report*, 5(2), 1–19.

Challice, J. (1992, May). "AIDS Research." *PAACNotes*, 121–124.

Chapman, A. (1988). "Male-Female Relations: How the Past Affects the Present." In H. McAdoo (Ed.), *Black Families* (2nd ed.). Beverly Hills, CA: Sage Publications.

Chasnoff, I. J. (1988). "Drug Use in Pregnancy: Parameters of Risk." *Pediatric Clinics of North America*, 35(6), 1403–1412.

Chiasson, M. A., Stoneburner, R. L., & Joseph, S. C. (1990). "Human Immunodeficiency Virus Transmission Through Artificial Insemination." *Journal of Acquired Immune Deficiency Syndromes*, 3(1), 69–72.

Chirgwin, K., DeHovitz, J. A., D. S., & McCormack, W. M. (1991). "HIV Infection, Genital Ulcer Disease, and Crack Cocaine Use Among Patients Attending a Clinic for Sexually Transmitted Diseases." *American Journal of Public Health*, 81(12), 1576–1579.

Chong, J. M. (1990). "Social Assessment of Transsexuals Who Apply for Sex Reassignment Therapy." *Social Work in Health Care*, 14(3), 87–105.

Chow, W. H., et al. (1985). "Vaginal Douching as a Potential Risk Factor for Tubal Ectopic Pregnancy." *Family Planning Perspectives*, 153, 727ff.

Chrisman, R., & Allen, R. (Eds.). (1992). *Court of Appeal: The Black Community Speaks Out on the Racial and Sexual Politics of Clarence Thomas vs. Anita Hill*. New York: Ballantine.

Christian-Smith, L. K. (1990). *Becoming a Woman Through Romance*. New York: Routledge.

Christopher, F., & Cate, R. (1984). "Factors Involved in Premarital Decision-Making." *Journal of Sex Research*, 20, 363–376.

Christopher, F. S., & Frandsen, M. M. (1990). "Strategies of Influence in Sex and Dating." *Journal of Social and Personal Relationships*, 7, 89–105.

Chu, S. Y., Buehler, J. W., Oxtoby, M. J., & Kilbourne, B. W. (1991). "Impact of the Human Immunodeficiency Virus Epidemic on Mortality in Children, United States." *Pediatrics*, 87(6), 806–810.

Chu, S. Y., Peterman, T. A., Doll, L. S., Buehler, J. W., & Curran, J. W. (1992). "AIDS in Bisexual Men in the United States: Epidemiology and Transmission to Women." *American Journal of Public Health*, 82(2), 220–224.

Chung, W., & Choi, H. (1990). "Erotic Erection Versus Nocturnal Erection." *The Journal of Urology*, 143, 294–297.

Cimons, M. (1990, December 7). "American Infertility Rate Not Growing, Study Finds." *The New York Times*, p. 3.

Clanton, G., & Smith, L. (1977). *Jealousy*. Englewood Cliffs, NJ: Prentice-Hall.

Clapper, R. L., & Lipsitt, L. P. (1991). "A Retrospective Study of Risk-Taking and Alcohol-Mediated Unprotected Intercourse." *Journal of Substance Abuse*, 3(1), 91–96.

Clark, D. (1992). "Cagney & Lacey: Feminist Strategies of Detection." In M. E. Brown (Ed.), *Television and Women's Culture: The Politics of the Popular*. Newbury Park, CA: Sage Publications.

Clift, E. (1990, July 2). "The Right Wing's Cultural Warrior." *Newsweek*, p. 51.

Cochran, J. K., & Beeghley, L. (1991). "The Influence of Religion on Attitudes Toward Nonmarital Sexuality: A Preliminary Assessment of Reference Group Theory." *Journal of the Scientific Study of Religion*, 30(1), 45–63.

Cochran, S. D., Mays, V. M., & Leung, L. (1991). "Sexual Practices of Heterosexual Asian-American Young Adults: Implications for Risk of HIV Infection." *Archives of Sexual Behavior*, 20(4), 381–394.

Cogen, R., & Steinman, W. (1990). "Sexual Function and Practice in Elderly Men of Lower Socioeconomic Status." *Journal of Family Practice*, 31(2), 162–166.

Cohen, B. (1992, September 14). "Discrimination: The Limits of the Law." *Newsweek*, pp. 35–40.

Cohen, J. (1993). "Early AZT Takes a Pounding in French-British 'Concorde' Trial." *Science*, 260(5105), 157.

Cohen, N. W., & Estner, L. J. (1983). "Silent Knife: Cesarean Section in the United States." *Society*, 21(1), 95–111.

Colditz, G. A., et al. (1993). "Family History, Age, and Risk of Breast Cancer—Prospective Data from the Nurses Health Study." *Journal of the American Medical Association*, 270(3), 338–343.

Cole, E., & Rothblum, E. (1990). "Commentary on 'Sexuality and the Midlife Woman'." Special Issue: Women at Midlife and Beyond. *Psychology of Women Quarterly*, 14(4), 509–512.

Cole, W. (1992). "Incest Perpetrators: Their Assessment and Treatment." *Psychiatric Clinics of North America*, 15(3), 689–701.

Coleman, E. (1986). "Sexual Compulsion vs. Sexual Addiction: The Debate Continues." *SIECUS Report*, 14, 7–10.

Coleman, E., Colgan, P., & Gooren, L. (1992). "Male Cross-Gender Behavior in Myanmar (Burma): A Description of the Acault." *Archives of Sexual Behavior*, 21(3), 313–321.

Coleman, E., Rosser, B. R., & Strapko, N. (1992). "Sexual and Intimacy Dysfunction Among Homosexual Men and Women." *Psychiatric Medicine*, 10(2), 257–271.

Coleman, M., & Ganong, L. (1991). "Remarriage and Stepfamily Research in the 1980s: Increased Interest in an Old Form." In A. Booth (Ed.), *Contemporary Families: Looking Forward, Looking Back*. Minneapolis, MN: National Council on Family Relations.

Collier, M. J. (1991). "Conflict Competence Within African, Mexican, and Anglo American Friendships." In S. Ting-Toomey & Felipe Korzenny (Eds.), *Cross-Cultural Interpersonal Communication*. Newbury Park, CA: Sage Publications.

Collins, P. H. (1991). "The Meaning of Motherhood in Black Culture." In R. Staples (Ed.), *The Black Family* (4th ed.). Belmont, CA: Wadsworth.

Conant, M., Hardy, D., Sernatinger, J., Spicer, D., & Levy, J. A. (1986). "Condoms Prevent Transmission of AIDS-Associated Retrovirus." *JAMA: Journal of the American Medical Association, 255*(13), 1702–1712.

Condry, J., & Condry, S. (1976). "The Development of Sex Differences: A Study of the Eye of the Beholder." *Child Development, 47*(4), 812–819.

Condy, S., Templer, D. E., Brown, R., & Veaco, L. (1987). "Parameters of Sexual Contact of Boys with Women." *Archives of Sexual Behavior, 16*(5), 379–394.

Conrad, P., & Schneider, J. (1980). *Deviance and Medicalization: From Badness to Sickness.* St. Louis, MO: Mosby.

Constantine, L., & Martinson, F. (Eds.). (1981). *Children and Sex.* Boston: Little, Brown.

Conway, C. (1980). "Psychophysical Preparations for Childbirth." In L. McNall (Ed.), *Contemporary Obstetric and Gynecological Nursing.* St. Louis, MO: Mosby.

Cook, A., et al. (1982). "Changes in Attitudes Toward Parenting Among College Women: 1972 and 1979 Samples." *Family Relations, 31,* 109–113.

Cooper, A. (1985). "Sexual Enhancement Programs: An Examination of Their Current Status and Directions for Future Research." *Archives of Sexual Behavior, 21*(4), 387–404.

Cooper, A., & Stoltenberg, C. D. (1987). "Comparison of a Sexual Enhancement and a Communication Training Program on Sexual and Marital Satisfaction." *Journal of Counseling Psychology, 34,* 309–314.

Cooper, A. J., Swaminath, S., Baxter, D., & Poulin, C. (1990). "A Female Sex Offender with Multiple Paraphilias." *Canadian Journal of Psychiatry, 35*(4), 334–337.

Copenhaver, S., & Gauerholz, E. (1991). "Sexual Victimization Among Sorority Women: Exploring the Link Between Sexual Violence and Institutional Practices." *Sex Roles, 24,* 31–41.

Corby, N., & Zarit, J. (1983). "Old and Alone: The Unmarried in Later Life." In R. Weg (Ed.), *Sexuality in the Later Years: Roles and Behavior.* New York: Academic Press.

Corby, N. H., Wolitski, R. J., Thornton-Johnson, S., & Tanner, W. M. (1991). "AIDS Knowledge, Perception of Risk, and Behaviors among Female Sex Partners of Injection Drug Users." *AIDS Education and Prevention, 3*(4), 353–366.

Corea, G. (1985). *The Mother Machine: Reproductive Technology from Artificial Insemination to Artificial Wombs.* New York: Harper & Row.

Cornelius, D., et al. (1982). *Who Cares? A Handbook on Sex Education and Counseling Services for Disabled People.* Baltimore, MD: University Park Press.

Cornett, C., & Hudson, R. (1985). "Psychoanalytic Theory and Affirmation of the Gay Lifestyle: Are They Necessarily Antithetical?" *Journal of Homosexuality, 12*(1), 97–108.

Cornog, M. (1986). "Naming Sexual Body Parts: Preliminary Patterns and Implications." *Journal of Sex Research, 22*(3), 399–408.

Cortese, A. (1989). "Subcultural Differences in Human Sexuality: Race, Ethnicity, and Social Class." In K. McKinney & S. Sprecher (Eds.), *Human Sexuality: The Societal and Interpersonal Context.* Norwood, NJ: Ablex.

Cosby, B. (1968, December). "The Regular Way." *Playboy,* pp. 288–289.

Cosgray, R. E., Hanna, V., Fawley, R., & Money, M. (1991). "Death from Auto-Erotic Asphyxiation in Long-Term Psychiatric Setting." *Perspectives in Psychiatric Care, 27*(1), 21–24.

Cottler, L. B., Helzer, J. E., & Tipp, J. E. (1990). "Lifetime Patterns of Substance Use Among General Population Subjects Engaging in High-Risk Sexual Behaviors; Implications for HIV Risk." *American Journal of Drug and Alcohol Abuse, 16*(3-4), 207–222.

Courtright, J., & Baran, S. (1980). "The Acquisition of Sexual Information by Young People." *Journalism Quarterly, 57*(1), 107–114.

Couzinet, B., et al. (1986). "Termination of Early Pregnancy by the Progesterone Antagonist RU 486 (Mifepristone)." *New England Journal of Medicine, 315*(25), 1565–1570.

Cowan, A. L. (1992, June 1). "Can a Baby-Making Venture Deliver?" *The New York Times,* pp. C1, C4.

Cowan, C. P., & Cowan, P. A. (1988). "Who Does What When Partners Become Parents: Implications for Men, Women, and Marriage." *Marriage and Family Review, 12*(3-4), 105–131.

Cowley, G. (1991, December 9). "Sleeping with the Enemy." *Newsweek,* pp. 58–59.

Cramer, D. (1986). "Gay Parents and Their Children: A Review of Research and Practical Implications." *Journal of Counseling and Development, 64,* 504–507.

Cramer, D., & Roach, A. (1987). "Coming Out to Mom and Dad: A Study of Gay Males and Their Relationships with Their Parents." *Journal of Homosexuality, 14*(1-2), 77–88.

Cramer, R. E., Dragna, M., Cupp, R. G., & Stewart, P. (1991). "Contrast Effects in the Evaluation of the Male Sex Role." *Sex Roles, 24*(3-4), 181–193.

Crepault, C., & Couture, M. (1980). "Men's Erotic Fantasies." *Archives of Sexual Behavior, 9,* 565–581.

Creti, L., & Libman, E. (1989). "Cognition and Sexual Expression in the Aging." *Journal of Sex and Marital Therapy, 15*(2), 83–101.

Crisp, Q. (1982). *The Naked Civil Servant.* New York: New American Library.

Crosby, J. (Ed.). (1985). *Reply to Myth: Perspectives on Intimacy.* New York: John Wiley.

Cruikshank, M. (1992). *The Gay and Lesbian Liberation Movement.* New York: Routledge.

Crum, C. P., et al. (1984). "Human Papillomavirus Type 16 and Early Cervical Neoplasm." *New England Journal of Medicine, 310,* 880–883.

Cuber, J. (1969). "Adultery: Reality vs. Stereotype." In G. Newbeck (Ed.), *Extramarital Relations.* Englewood Cliffs, NJ: Prentice-Hall.

Culp, R. E., Cook, A. S., & Housley, P. C. (1983). "A Comparison of Observed and Reported Adult-Infant Interactions: Effects of Perceived Sex." *Sex Roles, 9,* 475–479.

Cummings, J. (1987, June 8). "Disabled Model Defies Sexual Stereotypes." *The New York Times,* p. 17.

Cummings, N. (1992). "Self-Defense Training for College Women." *Journal of American College Health, 40*(4), 183–188.

Cupach, W. R., & Comstock, J. (1990). "Satisfaction with Sexual Communication in Marriage." *Journal of Social and Personal Relationships, 7,* 179–186.

Cupach, W. R., & Metts, S. (1991). "Sexuality and Communication in Close Relationships." In K. McKinney & Susan Sprecher (Eds.), *Sexuality in Close Relationships.* Hillsdale, NJ: Erlbaum.

Curie-Cohen, M., et al. (1979). "Current Practice of Artificial Insemination by Donor in the United States." *New England Journal of Medicine, 300*(11), 585–590.

Cushner, I. M. (1986). "Reproductive Technologies: New Choices, New Hopes, New Dilemmas." *Family Planning Perspectives, 18*(3), 129–132.

Dailey, D. (Ed.). (1988). *The Sexually Unusual.* New York: Harrington Press.

Dalton, K. (1984). *The Premenstrual Syndrome and Progesterone Therapy.* London: William Heinemann Medical Books.

Damon Clinical Laboratories. (1990). *Clinical Insight: AIDS Profiles.* Needham Heights, MA: Damon Clinical Laboratories.

Dancey, C. (1992). "The Relationship of Instrumentality and Expressivity to Sexual Orientation in Women." *Journal of Homosexuality, 23*(4), 73–82.

Darling, C. A., & Davidson, J. K. (1986). "Enhancing Relationships: Understanding the Feminine Mystique of Pretending Orgasm." *Journal of Sex and Marital Therapy, 12*, 182–196.

Darling, C. A., Davidson, J. K., & Conway-Welch, C. (1990). "Female Ejaculation: Perceived Origins, The Grafenberg Spot/Area, and Sexual Responsiveness." *Archives of Sexual Behavior, 19*, 29–47.

Darling, C. A., Davidson, J. K., & Cox, R. P. (1991). "Female Sexual Response and the Timing of Partner Orgasm." *Journal of Sex and Marital Therapy, 17*(1), 3–21.

Darling, C. A., Davidson, J. K., & Jennings, D. A. (1991). "The Female Sexual Response Revisited: Understanding the Multiorgasmic Experience in Women." *Archives of Sexual Behavior, 20*, 527–540.

Darling-Fisher, C., & Tiedje, L. (1990). "The Impact of Maternal Employment Characteristics on Fathers' Participation in Child Care." *Family Relations, 39*(1), 20–26.

Darrow, W. W., & Siegel, K. (1990). "Preventive Health Behavior and STDs." In K. K. Holmes et al. (Eds.), *Sexually Transmitted Diseases*. (2nd ed.). New York: McGraw-Hill.

Davenport, W. (1987). "An Anthropological Approach." In James Geer & W. O'Donohue (Eds.), *Theories of Human Sexuality*. New York: Plenun Press.

Davidson, J. K., & Darling, C. A. (1986). "The Impact of College-Level Sex Education on Sexual Knowledge, Attitudes, and Practices: The Knowledge/Sexual Experimentation Myth Revisited." *Deviant Behavior, 7*, 13–30.

Davidson, J. K., Darling, C. A., & Conway-Welch, C. (1989). "The Role of the Grafenberg Spot and Female Ejaculation in the Female Orgasmic Response: An Empirical Analysis." *Journal of Sex and Marital Therapy, 15*(2), 102–120.

Davidson, J. K., & Hoffman, L. (1986). "Sexual Fantasies and Sexual Satisfaction: An Empirical Investigation of Erotic Thought." *Journal of Sex Research, 22*, 184–205.

Davis, J. E., & Mininberg, D. T. (1976, August). "Prostatitis and Sexual Function." *Medical Aspects of Human Sexuality, 10*, 32–40.

Davis, M. S. (1983). *Smut: Erotic Reality/Obscene Ideology*. Chicago: University of Chicago Press.

Davis, R. C., et al. (1991). "Supportive and Unsupportive Responses of Others to Rape Victims: Effects on Concurrent Victim Adjustment." *American Journal of Community Psychology, 19*(3), 443–451.

Davis, S. (1990). "Men as Success Objects and Women as Sex Objects: A Study of Personal Advertisements." *Sex Roles, 23*, 43–50.

Davis, S. M., & Harris, M. B. (1982). "Sexual Knowledge, Sexual Interest, and Sources of Sexual Information of Rural and Urban Adolescents from Three Cultures." *Adolescence, 17*(66), 471–492.

Davitz, J. R. (1969). *The Language of Emotion*. New York: Academic Press.

Dawson, D. (1986). "The Effects of Sex Education on Adolescent Behavior." *Family Planning Perspectives, 18*(4), 162ff.

De Armand, C. (1983). "Let's Listen to What the Kids Are Saying." *SIECUS Report*, 3–4.

"Death Rates for Minority Infants Were Underestimated, Study Says." (1992, January 8). *The New York Times*, p. A10.

De Vincenzi, I., et al. (1992). "Comparison of Female to Male and Male to Female Transmission of HIV in 563 Stable Couples." *British Medical Journal, 304*(6830), 809–813.

Deaux, K. (1984). "From Individual Differences to Social Categories: Analysis of a Decade's Research on Gender." *American Psychologist, 39*(2), 105–116.

Deaux, K., & Lewis, L. L. (1983). "Components of Gender Role Stereotypes." *Psychological Documents, 13* (Ms. No. 2583), 25.

De Cecco, J. P. (Ed.). (1988). *Gay Relationships*. New York: Haworth Press.

De Cecco, J. P., & Elia, J. P. (1993). "A Critique and Synthesis of Biological Essentialism and Social Constructionist Views of Sexuality and Gender. Introduction." *Journal of Homosexuality, 24*(3-4), 1–26.

De Cecco, J. P., & Elia, J. P. (1993). "If You Seduce a Straight Person, Can You Make Them Gay—Issues in Biological Essentialism Versus Social Constructionism in Gay and Lesbian Identities. Preface." *Journal of Homosexuality, 24*(3-4), R23–R24.

De Cecco, J. P., & Shively, M. (1983). "From Sexual Identity to Sexual Relationships: A Conceptual Shift." *Journal of Homosexuality, 9*(2-3), 1–26.

Degler, C. (1980). *At Odds*. New York: Oxford University Press.

De Groot, J. M., et al. (1992). "Correlates of Sexual Abuse in Women with Anorexia Nervosa and Bulimia Nervosa." *Canadian Journal of Psychiatry, 37*(7), 516–581.

De La Chappelle, A. (1983). "Sex Chromosome Abnormalities." In A. F. Emery & D. L. Rimarin (Eds.), *Principles and Practices of Medical Genetics*. New York: Churchill Livingstone.

Delacoste, F., & Alexander, P. (Eds.). (1987). *Sex Work: Writings by Women in the Sex Industry*. Pittsburgh, PA: Cleis Press.

Delamater, J. D., & MacCorquodale, P. (1979). *Premarital Sexuality: Attitudes, Relationships, Behavior*. Madison, WI: University of Wisconsin Press.

Delaney, J., et al. (1976). *The Curse: A Cultural History of Menstruation*. New York: Dutton.

Delaney, M. (1992, September 4). "Evidence Does Not Back Duesberg's AIDS Views." *San Francisco Chronicle*, p. A14.

Del Carmen, R. (1990). "Assessment of Asian-Americans for Family Therapy." In F. Serafica et al. (Eds.), *Mental Health of Ethnic Minorities*. New York: Praeger.

Demb, J. M. (1991). "Abortion in Inner-City Adolescents: What the Girls Say." *Family Systems Medicine, 9*, 93–102.

Demb, J. M. (1992). "Are Gay Men Artistic? A Review of the Literature." *Journal of Homosexuality, 23*(4), 83–92.

D'Emilio, J., & Freedman, E. (1988). *Intimate Matters: A History of Sexuality in America*. New York: Harper & Row.

Derlega, V. J., Metts, S., Petronio, S., & Margulis, S. (1993). *Self-Disclosure*. Newbury Park, CA: Sage Publications.

DES Action. (1980). *You May Be a DES Daughter*. San Francisco: DES Action/California.

De Salvo, S. (1985, December 22). "Teen Parents." *San Jose Mercury*, pp. 1, 2.

"Detailed U.S. AIDS Report Offers Hints, Warnings." (1993, June 11). *Baltimore Sun*, p. 3A.

Dewaraja, R., & Money, J. (1986). "Transcultural Sexology: Formicophilia, a Newly Named Paraphilia in a Young Buddhist Male." *Journal of Sex and Marital Therapy, 12*(2), 139–145.

De Young, M. (1988). "The Indignant Page: Techniques of Neutralization in the Publications of Pedophile Organizations." *Child Abuse and Neglect, 12*(4), 583–591.

De Young, M. (1989). "The World According to NAMBLA." *Journal of Sociology and Social Welfare, 16*(1), 111–126.

Diamond, M. (1974). "Sexuality and the Handicapped." *Rehabilitation Literature, 35*, 34–40.

Diamond, M., & Dannemiller, J. E. (1989). "Pornography and Community Standards in Hawaii: Comparisons with Other States." *Archives of Sexual Behavior, 18*, 6.

Diaz, E. (1990). "Public Policy, Women, and HIV Disease." *SIECUS Report, 19*, 4–5.

Di Blasio, F. A., & Benda, B. B. (1992). "Gender Differences in Theories of Adolescent Sexual Activity." *Sex Roles, 27*(5-6), 221–236.

Dick-Read, G. (1972). *Childbirth Without Fear*. (4th ed.). New York: Harper & Row.

Dimen, M. (1984). "Politically Correct? Politically Incorrect?" In C. S. Vance (Ed.), *Pleasure and Danger: Exploring Female Sexuality*. New York: Routledge & Kegan Paul.

Dion, K. K., Berscheid, E., & Walster, E. (1972). "What Is Beautiful Is Good." *Journal of Personality and Social Psychology, 24,* 285–290.

Diop, C. A. (1987). *Precolonial Black Africa.* Trenton, NJ: Africa World.

Dittmar, H., & Bates, B. (1987). "Humanistic Approaches to the Understanding and Treatment of Anorexia Nervosa." *Journal of Adolescence, 10,* 57–69.

Djerrasi, C. (1979). *The Politics of Contraception.* New York: Norton.

Dodd, R. Y. (1992). "The Risk of Transfusion-Transmitted Infection." *New England Journal of Medicine, 327*(6), 419–421.

Doll, L. S., et al. (1991). "Homosexual Men Who Engage in High-Risk Sexual Behavior. A Multicenter Comparison." *Sexually Transmitted Diseases, 18*(3), 170–175.

Donat, P. L., & D'Emilio, J. (1992). "A Feminist Redefinition of Rape and Sexual Assault: Historical Foundations and Change." *Journal of Social Issues, 48*(1), 9–22.

Donovan, P. (1986). "New Reproductive Technologies: Some Legal Dilemmas." *Family Planning Perspectives, 18,* 57ff.

Dowell, K. A., Lo Presto, C. T., & Sherman, M. F. (1991). "When Are AIDS Patients to Blame for Their Disease? Effects of Patients' Sexual Orientation and Mode of Transmission." *Psychological Reports, 69*(1), 211–219.

Downey, J., Elkin, E. J., Erhard, A. A., Meyer, B. H. F., Bell, J. J., & Morishima, K. J. (1991). "Cognitive Ability and Everyday Functioning in Women with Turner Syndrome." *Journal of Learning Disabilities, 24*(1), 32–39.

Drugger, K. (1988). "Social Location and Gender-Role Attitudes: A Comparison of Black and White Women." *Gender and Society, 2*(4), 425–448.

"Drugs That Cause Sexual Dysfunction: An Update." (1992, August 7). *Medical Letter on Drugs and Therapeutics, 34*(876), 73–78.

Dryfoos, J. (1985). "What the United States Can Learn About Prevention of Teenage Pregnancy from Other Developed Countries." *SIECUS Report, 14*(2), 1–7.

Duncan, D. F. (1990). "Prevalence of Sexual Assault Victimization Among Heterosexual and Gay/Lesbian University Students." *Psychological Reports, 66*(1), 65–67.

Duncan, D. F. (1991). "Who Does Have a Test for AIDS?" *Psychological Reports, 68*(1), 138.

Duncan, D. F., & Donnelly, J. W. (1991). "Pornography as a Source of Sex Information for Students at a Private Northeastern University." *Psychological Reports, 68*(3, Pt. 1), 782.

Duncan, D. F., & Nicholson, T. (1991). "Pornography as a Source of Sex Information for Students at a Southeastern State University." *Psychological Reports, 68*(3, Pt. 1), 802.

Dunkle, J. H., & Francis, P. L. (1990). "The Role of Facial Masculinity/Femininity in the Attribution of Homosexuality." *Sex Roles, 23*(3-4), 157–167.

Durant, R., Pendergast, R., & Seymore, C. (1990). "Contraceptive Behavior Among Sexually Active Hispanic Adolescents." *Journal of Adolescent Health, 11*(6), 490–496.

Dworkin, A. (1989). *Pornography: Men Possessing Women.* New York: Dutton.

Dwyer, S. M., & Myers, S. (1990). "Sex Offender Treatment: A Six-Month to Ten-Year Follow-Up Study." *Annals of Sex Research, 3*(3), 305–318.

Eagly, A. H. (1987). *Sex Differences in Social Behavior: A Social-Role Interpretation.* Hillsdale, NJ: Erlbaum.

Eakins, P. S. (1989). "Free-Standing Birth Centers in California." *Journal of Reproductive Medicine, 34*(12), 960–970.

Earls, C. M., & David, H. (1990). "Early Family and Sexual Experiences of Male and Female Prostitutes." *Canada's Mental Health, 38,* 7–11.

Eber, M., & Wetli, C. (1985). "A Case of Autoerotic Asphyxia." *Psychotherapy, 22*(3), 662–668.

Eckert, E. D. (1985). "Characteristics of Anorexia Nervosa." In J. E. Mitchell (Ed.), *Anorexia Nervosa and Bulimia: Diagnosis and Treatment.* Minneapolis, MN: University of Minnesota Press.

Edelman, R. (1986). "Adaptive Training for Existing Male Transsexual Gender Role: A Case History." *Journal of Sex Research, 22*(4), 514–519.

Edwards, J., & Booth, A. (1977). "The Cessation of Marital Intercourse." *American Journal of Psychiatry, 133,* 1333–1336.

Ehrenkranz, J. R., & Hembree, W. C. (1986). "Effects of Marijuana on Male Reproductive Function." *Psychiatric Annals, 16*(4), 243–248.

Eichler, M. (1989). "Reflections on Motherhood, Apple Pie, the New Reproductive Technologies and the Role of Sociologists in Society." *Society-Societe, 13*(1), 1–5.

Eldh, J. (1993). "Construction of a Neovagina with Preservation of the Glans Penis as a Clitoris in Male Transsexuals." *Plastic and Reconstructive Surgery, 91*(5), 895–903.

Elkind, D. (1984). *All Grown Up and No Place to Go.* Reading, MA: Addison-Wesley.

Ellenberg, M. (1980). "Vaginal Lubrication in Diabetic Women." *Medical Aspects of Human Sexuality, 14,* 66.

Elliott, D. M., & Briere, J. (1992). "Sexual Abuse Trauma Among Professional Women: Validating the Trauma Symptom Checklist (TSC-40)." *Child Abuse and Neglect, 16*(3), 391ff.

Ellis, H. (1900). *Studies in the Psychology of Sex.* Philadelphia: F. A. Davis.

Ellis, H. (1938). *Psychology of Sex: A Manual for Students.* New York: Harcourt Brace Jovanovich.

Ellison, C. (1985). "Intimacy-Based Sex Therapy." In W. Eicher & G. Kockott (Eds.), *Sexology.* New York: Springer-Verlag.

Emanuele, M. A., Tentler, J., Emanuele, N. V., & Kelley, M. R. (1991). "In Vivo Effects of Acute ETOH on Rat Alpha-Luteinizing and Beta-Luteinizing Hormone Gene Expression." *Alcohol, 8*(5), 345–348.

Emery, A. F., & Rimarin, D. L. (Eds.).(1983). *Principles and Practices of Medical Genetics.* New York: Churchill Livingstone.

Emmanuel, N. P., Lydiard, R. B., & Ballenger, J. C. (1991). "Fluoxetine Treatment of Voyeurism." *American Journal of Psychiatry, 148,* 950.

Ephron, N. (1975). *Crazy Salad.* New York: Alfred Knopf.

Erikson, E. (1986). *Vital Improvements in Old Age: The Experience of Old Age in Our Time.* New York: Norton.

Erickson, P. I., & Rapkin, A. I. (1991). "Unwanted Sexual Experiences Among Middle and High School Youth." *Journal of Adolescent Youth, 12,* 319–325.

Ernster, V. L. (1975). "American Menstrual Slang." *Sex Roles, 5,* 1–13.

Espín, O. M. (1984). "Cultural and Historical Influences on Sexuality in Hispanic/Latin Women: Implications for Psychotherapy." In C. Vance (Ed.), *Pleasure and Danger: Exploring Female Sexuality.* New York: Routledge & Kegan Paul.

Essex, M., & Kanki, P. J. (1988, October). "The Origins of the AIDS Virus." *Scientific American, 259*(4), 64–71.

Evans, H. L., et al. (1981). "Sperm Abnormalities and Cigarette Smoking." *Lancet, 1*(8221), 627–629.

Ewell, M. (1993, January 9). "Anti-Gay Push in the Works." *San Jose Mercury News,* p. 3B.

Faderman, L. (1991). *Odd Girls and Twilight Lovers.* New York: Penguin Books.

Fagot, B., & Leinbach, M. (1987). "Socialization of Sex Roles Within the Family." In D. B. Carter (Ed.), *Current Conceptions of Sex Roles and Sex Typing.* New York: Praeger.

Falbo, T., & Peplau, L. A. (1980). "Power Strategies in Intimate Relationships." *Journal of Personality and Social Psychology, 38,* 618–628.

Falicov, C. (1982). "Mexican Families." In M. McGoldrick et al. (Eds.), *Ethnicity and Family Therapy.* New York: Guilford Press.

Falk, K. (1984). *How to Write a Romance and Get It Published*. New York: New American Library.

Faludi, S. (1991). *Backlash: The Undeclared War Against American Women*. New York: Crown.

Fang, R. H., Chen, C. F., & Imperato-McGinley, M. S. (1992). "A New Method for Clitoroplasty in Male-to-Female Sex Reassignment Surgery." *Plastic and Reconstructive Surgery, 89*(4), 179–182.

Farnsworth, C. H. (1992, January 14). "Homosexual Is Granted Refugee Status in Canada." *The New York Times*, p. A5.

Fathalla, M. F. (1992). "Reproductive Health in the World: Two Decades of Progress and the Challenge Ahead." In World Health Organization, *Reproductive Health*. Biennial Report 1990–1991. Geneva, Switzerland: World Health Organization.

Fausto-Sterling, A. (1985). *Myths of Gender: Biological Theories About Women and Men*. New York: Basic Books.

Fay, R., Turner, C., Klassen, A., & Gagnon, J. (1989). "Prevalence and Patterns of Same-Gender Sexual Contact Among Men." *Science, 243*(4889), 338–348.

Fazio, L. (1987). "Sexuality and Aging: A Community Wellness Program." Special Issue: Community Programs for the Health Impaired Elderly. *Physical and Occupational Therapy in Geriatrics, 6*(1), 59–69.

Fedora, O., Reddon, J. R., Morrison, J. W., & Fedora, S. T. (1992). "Sadism and Other Paraphilias in Normal Controls and Aggressive and Nonaggressive Sex Offenders." *Archives of Sexual Behavior, 21*(1), 1–15.

Fedora, O., Reddon, J. R., & Yendall, L. T. (1986). "Stimuli Eliciting Sexual Arousal in Genital Exhibitionists: A Possible Clinical Application." *Archives of Sexual Behavior, 15*(5), 417–427.

Fehr, B. (1988). "Prototype Analysis of the Concepts of Love and Commitment." *Journal of Personality and Social Psychology, 55*(4), 557–579.

Fein, R. (1980). "Research on Fathering." In A. Skolnick & J. Skolnick (Eds.), *The Family in Transition*. Boston: Little, Brown.

Feirstein, B. (1982). *Real Men Don't Eat Quiche*. New York: Pocket Books.

Feitl, L. F. (1990, April). "My Body, My Self." *Sesame Street Magazine Parents' Guide*, pp. 20–25.

Feray, J. C., & Herzer, M. (1990). "Homosexual Studies and Politics in the 19th Century: Karl Maria Kertbeny." *Journal of Homosexuality, 19*(1), 23–47.

Ferree, M. M. (1991). "Beyond Separate Spheres: Feminism and Family Research." In A. Booth (Ed.), *Contemporary Families: Looking Forward, Looking Back*. Minneapolis, MN: National Council on Family Relations.

Field, M. A. (1993). "Abortion Law Today." *Journal of Legal Medicine, 14*(1), 3–24.

Findlay, H. (1992). "Freud, Fetishism, and the Lesbian Dildo Debates." *Feminist Studies, 18*(3), 563–579.

Fine, M. (1988). "Sexuality, Schooling, and Adolescent Females: The Missing Discourse of Desire." *Harvard Education Review, 58*, 29–53.

Finkelhor, D. (1979). *Sexually Victimized Children*. New York: Free Press.

Finkelhor, D. (1984). *Child Sexual Abuse: New Theory and Research*. New York: Free Press.

Finkelhor, D. (1986a). "Prevention Approaches to Child Sexual Abuse." In M. Lystad (Ed.), *Violence in the Home: Interdisciplinary Perspectives*. New York: Brunner/Mazel.

Finkelhor, D. (1986b). "Sexual Abuse: Beyond the Family Systems Approach." *Journal of Psychotherapy and the Family, 2*, 53–65.

Finkelhor, D., et al. (1990). "Sexual Abuse in a National Survey of Adult Men and Women." *Child Abuse and Neglect, 14*(1), 19–28.

Finkelhor, D., & Baron, L. (1986). "High-Risk Children." In D. Finkelhor (Ed.), *Sourcebook on Child Sexual Abuse*. Beverly Hills, CA: Sage Publications.

Finkelhor, D., Hotaling, G., Lewis, I. A., & Smith C. (1990). *Missing, Abducted, Runaway, and Throwaway Children in America*. Washington, DC: U.S. Department of Justice.

Finkelhor, D., Williams, L. M., & Burns, B. (1988). *Sexual Abuse in Day Care: A National Study*. Durham, NH: University of New Hampshire, Family Research Laboratory.

Finkelhor, D., & Yllo, K. (1985). *License to Rape: The Sexual Abuse of Wives*. New York: Holt Rinehart.

Fischhoff, B. (1992). "Giving Advice: Decision Theory Perspectives on Sexual Assault." *American Psychologist, 47*, 577–588.

Fischl, M. A., et al. (1987). "The Efficacy of Azidothymidine (AZT) in the Treatment of Patients with AIDS and AIDS-Related Complex." *Journal of Sex Research, 317*, 185–188.

Fischl, M. A., Dickinson, D. M., Scott, G. B., Klimas, N., Fletcher, M. A., & Parks, W. (1987). "Evaluation of Heterosexual Partners, Children, and Household Contacts of Adults with AIDS." *JAMA: Journal of the American Medical Association 257*(5), 640–644.

Fisher, B., et al. (1985). "Five-Year Results of a Randomized Clinical Trial Comparing Total Mastectomy and Segmental Mastectomy with or without Radiation in the Treatment of Breast Cancer." *New England Journal of Medicine, 312*(11), 665–673.

Fisher, B., et al. (1985). "Ten-Year Results of a Randomized Clinical Trial Comparing Radical Mastectomy and Total Mastectomy with or without Radiation in the Treatment of Breast Cancer." *New England Journal of Medicine, 312*(11), 674–681.

Fisher, W. (1983, March). "Why Teenagers Get Pregnant." *Psychology Today*, 70–71.

Fisher, W. (1986). "A Psychological Approach to Human Sexuality." In D. Byrne & K. K. Kelley (Eds.), *Alternate Approaches to Human Sexuality*. Hillsdale, NJ: Erlbaum.

Fisher, W., et al. (1988). "Erotophobia-Erotophilia as a Dimension of Personality." *Journal of Sex Research, 25*(1), 123–151.

Fisher, W., & Gray, J. (1988). "Erotophobia-Erotophilia and Sexual Behavior During Pregnancy and Postpartum." *Journal of Sex Research, 25*(3), 379–396.

Fitzgerald, L. F., & Ormerod, A. J. (1991). "Perceptions of Sexual Harassment: The Influence of Gender and Academic Context." *Psychology of Women Quarterly, 15*(2), 281–294.

FitzGerald, M., & FitzGerald, D. (1977). "Deaf People Are Sexual Too!" *SIECUS Report, 6*(2), 1, 13–15.

Flanigan, B. J. (1990). "The Social Context of Alcohol Consumption Prior to Female Sexual Intercourse." *Journal of Alcohol and Drug Education, 36*(1), 97–113.

Flor-Henry, P., Lang, R. A., Koles, Z. J., & Frenzel, R. R. (1991). "Quantitative EEG Studies of Pedophilia." *International Journal of Psychophysiology, 10*(3), 253–258.

Foa, U. G., Anderson, B., Converse, J., & Urbansky, W. A. (1987). "Gender-Related Sexual Attitudes: Some Cross-Cultural Similarities and Differences." *Sex Roles, 16*(19-20), 511–519.

Focus on the Family. (1993, February 11). "In Defense of a Little Virginity." *Good Times*, Santa Cruz, CA, pp. 30–31.

Follingstad, D. R., Rutledge, L. L., Berg, B. J., & Haure, E. S. (1990). "The Role of Emotional Abuse in Physically Abusive Relationships." *Journal of Family Violence, 5*(2), 107–120.

Fonow, M. M., et al. (1992). "Feminist Rape Education: Does It Work?" *Gender and Society, 6*(1), 108–121.

Foo, R. (1993, March 5). "U.S. Cracks Child Porn Ring." *San Jose Mercury News*, pp. 1A, 20A.

Ford, C., & Beach, F. (1972). *Patterns of Sexual Behavior*. New York: Harper & Row.

Fordyce, E. J., Blum, S., Balanon, A., & Stoneburner, R. L. (1991). "A Method for Estimating HIV Transmission Rates Among Female Sex Partners of Male Intravenous Drug Users." *American Journal of Epidemiology, 133*(6), 590–598.

Forgey, D. G. (1975). "The Institution of Berdache Among the North American Plains Indians." *Journal of Sex Research, 11*, 1–15.

Forrest, J. (1986). "The End of IUD Marketing in the United States: What Does It Mean for American Women?" *Family Planning Perspectives, 18*(2), 52–57.

Forrest, J. (1987). "Unintended Pregnancy Among American Women." *Family Planning Perspectives, 19*(2), 76–77.

Forrest, J. D., & Singh, S. (1990). "The Sexual and Reproductive Behavior of American Women, 1982–1988." *Family Planning Perspectives, 22*(5), 206–214.

Foucault, M. (1980). *The History of Sexuality: An Introduction. Vol. I.* New York: Pantheon Books.

Fowler, O. S. (1878). *Amativeness: or, Evils and the Remedies of Excessive Perverted Sexuality.* New York: Fowler & Wells.

Fox, B., & Joyce, C. (1991). "Americans Compete for Control Over Sex." *New Scientist, 12,* 23.

Fox, S. I. (1987). *Human Physiology.* Dubuque, Iowa: W. C. Brown.

Frable, D. E., & Bem, S. L. (1985). "If You Are Gender Schematic, All Members of the Opposite Sex Look Alike." *Journal of Personality and Social Psychology, 49*(2), 459–468.

Franco, E. L. (1991). "The Sexually Transmitted Disease Model for Cervical Cancer: Incoherent Epidemiologic Findings and the Role of Misclassification of Human Papillomavirus Infection." *Epidemiology, 2*(2), 98–106.

Franklin, D. L. (1988). "The Impact of Early Childbearing on Development Outcomes: The Case of Black Adolescent Parenting." *Family Relations, 37,* 268–274.

Franz, W., & Readon, D. (1992). "Differential Impact of Abortion on Adolescents and Adults." *Adolescence, 27*(105), 161–172.

Fraser, L. (1990, February). "Nasty Girls." *Mother Jones,* pp. 32–35, 48–50.

Frazier, P. A. (1991). "Self-Blame as a Mediator of Postrape Depressive Symptoms." *Journal of Social and Clinical Psychology, 10*(1), 47–57.

Freeman, E. (1980). "Adolescent Contraceptive Use." *American Journal of Public Health, 70,* 790–797.

French, J. P., & Bertram Raven. (1959). "The Bases of Social Power." In I. Cartwright (Ed.), *Studies in Social Power.* Ann Arbor, MI: University of Michigan Press.

Freud, S. (1938). "Three Contributions to the Theory of Sex." A. A. Brill (Ed.), *The Basic Writings of Sigmund Freud.* New York: Modern Library.

Freund, K., & Kuban, W. (1993). "Toward a Testable Developmental Model of Pedophilia: The Development of Erotic Age Preference." *Child Abuse and Neglect, 17*(2), 315–324.

Freund, K. (1988). "Courtship Disorder: Is This Hypothesis Valid?" In R. A. Prentky et al. (Eds.), *Human Sexual Aggression: Current Perspectives.* New York: New York Academy of Science.

Freund, K., & Blanchard, R. (1993). "Erotic Target Location Errors in Male Gender Dysphorics, Paedophiles, and Fetishists." *British Journal of Psychiatry, 162,* 558–563.

Freund, M., Leonard, T. L., & Lee, N. (1989). "Sexual Behavior of Resident Street Prostitutes with Their Clients in Camden, New Jersey." *Journal of Sex Research, 26,* 460–478.

Freund, K., Sher, H., & Hucker, S. (1983). "The Courtship Disorders." *Archives of Sexual Behavior, 12,* (369–379).

Freund, K., & Watson, R. J. (1993). "Gender Identity Disorder and Courtship Disorder." *Archives of Sexual Behavior, 22*(1), 13–21.

Freund, K., Watson, R., & Dickey, R. (1990). "Does Sexual Abuse in Childhood Cause Pedophilia: An Exploratory Study." *Archives of Sexual Behavior, 19*(6), 557–568.

Freund, K., Watson, R., Dickey, R., & Rienzo, D. (1991). "Erotic Gender Differentiation in Pedophilia." *Archives of Sexual Behavior, 20*(6), 555–566.

Freund, K., Watson, R., & Rienzo, D. (1988). "The Value of Self-Reports in the Study of Voyeurism and Exhibitionism." *Annals of Sex Research, 1*(2), 243–262.

Friday, N. *Men in Love.* (1980). New York: Delacorte Press.

Friedland, G. H. (1986). "Lack of Transmission of HTLV-III Infection to Household Contacts of Patients with AIDS or AIDS-Related Complex with Oral Candidiasis." *New England Journal of Medicine, 314,* 344–349.

Friedman, R., & Gradstein, B. (1982). *Surviving Pregnancy Loss.* Boston: Little, Brown.

Friedman, R. C. (1991). "Couple Therapy with Gay Couples." *Psychiatric Annals, 21*(8), 485–490.

Friend, R. (1980). "GAYging: Adjustment and the Older Gay Male." *Alternative Lifestyles, 3*(2), 231–248.

Fritz, G. S., Stoll, K., & Wagner, N. N. (1981). "A Comparison of Males and Females Who Were Sexually Molested as Children." *Journal of Sex and Marital Therapy, 7,* 54–58.

Fromm, E. (1974). *The Art of Loving.* New York: Perennial Library.

Frost, P. (1992, December 7). "Artichoke." *The New Yorker,* p. 66.

Fuller, A., Jr., et al. (1980). "Toxic-Shock Syndrome." *New England Journal of Medicine, 303*(15), 880.

Fullilove, R. E., Fullilove, M. T., Bowser, B. P., & Gross, S. (1990). "Risk of Sexually Transmitted Disease Among Black Adolescent Crack Users in Oakland and San Francisco, Calif." *JAMA: Journal of the American Medical Association, 263*(6), 851–855.

Furstenberg, F. K., Jr., et al. (1985). "Sex Education and Sexual Experience Among Adolescents." *American Journal of Public Health, 75*(11), 1331–1332.

Furstenberg, F. K., Jr., & Cherlin, A. (1991). *Divided Families.* Cambridge, MA: Harvard University Press.

Furstenberg, F. K., Jr., Lincoln, R., & Menken, J. (Eds.). (1981). *Teenage Sexuality, Pregnancy, and Childbearing.* Philadelphia: University of Pennsylvania Press.

Furstenberg, F. K., Jr., & Nord, C. (1985). "Parenting Apart: Patterns in Childrearing After Marital Disruption." *Journal of Marriage and the Family, 47*(4), 893–904.

Furstenberg, F. K., Jr., & Spanier, G. (1987). *Recycling the Family: Remarriage After Divorce* (rev. ed.). Newbury Park, CA: Sage Publications.

Gagnon, J. (1977). *Human Sexualities.* New York: Scott, Foresman.

Gagnon, J. (1985). "Attitudes and Responses of Parents to Pre-Adolescent Masturbation." *Archives of Sexual Behavior, 14*(5), 451–466.

Gagnon, J. (1986). "Sexual Scripts: Permanence and Change." *Archives of Sexual Behavior, 15*(2), 97–120.

Gagnon, J., & Simon, W. (1973). "Perspectives on the Sexual Scene." In J. Gagnon & W. Simon (Eds.), *The Sexual Scene* (2nd ed.). New Brunswick, NJ: Transaction Books.

Gagnon, J., & Simon, W. (1973). *Sexual Conduct: The Social Sources of Human Sexuality.* Chicago: Aldine.

Gagnon, J., & Simon, W. (1987). "The Sexual Scripting of Oral Genital Contacts." *Archives of Sexual Behavior, 16*(1), 1–25.

Gaines, J. (1990, October 7). "A Scandal of Artificial Insemination." *The Good Health Magazine/The New York Times Magazine,* p. 23ff.

Gallup, G. H., Jr., & Newport, F. (1990, June 4). "Parenthood: A Nearly Universal Desire." *San Francisco Chronicle,* p. 3.

Ganong, L., & Coleman, M. (1987). "Sex, Sex Roles, and Family Love." *Journal of Genetic Psychology, 148,* 45–52.

Gao, G. (1991). "Stability of Romantic Relationships in China and the United States." In S. Ting-Toomey & Felipe Korzenny (Eds.), *Cross-Cultural Interpersonal Communication.* Newbury Park, CA: Sage Publications.

Garber, L. (1991). *Vested Interests.* Boston: Little, Brown.

Garcia, L. T., & Milano, L. (1990). "A Content Analysis of Erotic Videos." *Journal of Psychology and Human Sexuality, 3*(2), 95–103.

Garner, D. M., Garfinkel, P. E., Schwartz, D., & Thompson, M. (1980). "Cultural Expectations of Thinness in Women." *Psychological Reports, 11,* 483–491.

Garnets, L., et al. (1990). "Violence and Victimization of Lesbians and Gay Men: Mental Health Consequences." *Journal of Interpersonal Violence, 5*, 366–383.

Garrison, J. E. (1989). "Sexual Dysfunction in the Elderly: Causes and Effects." *Journal of Psychotherapy and the Family, 5*(1-2), 149–162.

Garza-Leal, J., & Landron, F. (1991). "Autoerotic Asphyxial Death Initially Misinterpreted as Suicide and Review of the Literature." *Journal of Forensic Science, 36*(6), 1753–1759.

Gay, P. (1986). *The Bourgeois Experience: The Tender Passion.* New York: Oxford University Press.

Gebhard, P. (1976). "Fetishism and Sadomasochism." In P. Gebhard (Ed.), *Sex Research: Studies from the Kinsey Institute.* New York: Oxford University Press.

Gebhard, P. (Ed.). (1976). *Sex Research: Studies from the Kinsey Institute.* New York: Oxford University Press.

Gebhard, P., Pomeroy, W. B., & Christensen, C. V. (1965). "Situational Factors Affecting Human Sexual Behavior." In F. Beach (Ed.), *Sex and Behavior.* New York: John Wiley.

Gecas, V., & Seff, M. (1991). "Families and Adolescents." In A. Booth (Ed.), *Contemporary Families: Looking Forward, Looking Back.* Minneapolis, MN: National Council on Family Relations.

Geist, C. (1980). "Violence, Passion, and Sexual Racism: The Plantation Novel." *Southern Quarterly, 18*(2), 60–72.

Gelles, R. J., & Conte, J. R. (1991). "Domestic Violence and Sexual Abuse of Children: A Review of Research in the Eighties." In A. Booth (Ed.), *Contemporary Families: Looking Forward, Looking Back.* Minneapolis, MN: National Council on Family Relations.

Genevie, L., & Margolies, E. (1987). *The Motherhood Report: How Women Feel About Being Mothers.* New York: MacMillan.

George, L. K., Windfield, I., & Blazer, D. G. (1992). "Sociocultural Factors in Sexual Assault—Comparison of Two Representative Samples of Women." *Journal of Social Issues, 48*(1), 105–125.

Geraghty, C. (1990). *Women and Soap Opera: A Study of Prime Time Soaps.* London: Polity Press.

Gershman, K. A., & Rolfs, R. T. (1991). "Diverging Gonorrhea and Syphilis Trends in the 1980s: Are They Real?" *American Journal of Public Health, 81*(10), 1263–1267.

Getlin, J. (1989, July 24). "Legacy of a Mother's Drinking." *Los Angeles Times,* p. 1ff.

Gidyez, C. A., & Koss, M. P. (1990). "A Comparison of Group and Individual Sexual Assault Victims." *Psychology of Women Quarterly, 14*(3), 325–342.

Ginsburg, F. (1989). *Contested Lives: The Abortion Debate in an American Community.* Berkeley: University of California Press.

Glaser, J. B., Strange, T. J., & Rosati, D. (1989). "Heterosexual Human Immunodeficiency Virus Transmission Among the Middle Class." *Archives of Internal Medicine, 149*(3), 645–649.

Glasier, A., Thong, K. J., Dewar, M., Mackie, M., & Baird, D. T. (1992). "Mifepristone (RU-486) Compared with High-Dose Estrogen and Progesterone for Emergency Postcoital Contraception." *New England Journal of Medicine, 327*(15), 1041–1044.

Glass, R. H., & Ericsson, R. J. (1982). *Getting Pregnant in the 1980s.* Berkeley: University of California Press.

Glaus, K. O. (1988). "Alcoholism, Chemical Dependency and the Lesbian Client." Special Issue: Lesbianism: Affirming Nontraditional Roles. *Women and Therapy, 8*(1-2), 131–144.

Glazer-Malbin, N. (Ed.). (1975). *Old Family/New Family.* New York: Van Nostrand.

Glenn, J. (1981). "Penis Enlargement." *Medical Aspects of Human Sexuality, 15*(3), 23.

Glenn, N. (1991). "Quantitative Research on Marital Quality in the 1980s: A Critical Review." In A. Booth (Ed.), *Contemporary Families: Looking Forward, Looking Back.* Minneapolis, MN: National Council on Family Relations.

Glenn, N., & McLanahan, S. (1982). "Children and Marital Happiness: A Further Specification of the Relationship." *Journal of Marriage and the Family, 43*(1), 63–72.

Go, K. J. (1992). "Recent Advances in the Treatment of Male Infertility." *Naacogs Clinical Issues in Perinatal and Women's Health Nursing, 3*(2), 320–327.

Gochoros, J. S. (1989). *When Husbands Come Out of the Closet.* New York: Harrington Park Press.

Goetting, A. (1986). "The Developmental Tasks of Siblingship Over the Life Cycle." *Journal of Marriage and the Family, 48*(4), 703–714.

Goldberg, L. H., Kaufman, R., Kurtz, T. O., Conant, M. A., & Eron, L. J. (1993). "Long-Term Suppression of Recurrent Genital Herpes with Acyclovir." *Archives of Dermatology, 129*(5), 582–587.

Goldberg-Ambrose, C. (1992). "Unfinished Business in Rape Law Reform." *Journal of Social Issues, 48*(1), 173–175.

Golden, G. (1989, May). "Parental Attitudes to Infant's Sex Play Determine Child's Later Attitude to Sex." *Medical Aspects of Human Sexuality,* 73–97.

Goldman, A., & Carroll, J. L. (1990). "Educational Intervention as an Adjunct to Treatment in Erectile Dysfunction of Older Couples." *Journal of Sex and Marital Therapy, 16*(3), 127–141.

Goldmeier, D., & Hay, P. (1993). "A Review and Update on Adult Syphilis, with Particular Emphasis on Its Treatment." *International Journal of STD and AIDS, 4*(2), 70–82.

Golombok, S. (1992). "Psychological Functioning of Infertility Patients." *Human Reproduction, 7*(2), 208–212.

Gonzalez, E. R. (1981). "Premenstrual Syndrome: An Ancient Woe Deserving of Modern Scrutiny." *JAMA: Journal of the American Medical Association, 245*(14), 1393–1396.

Gonzalez, E. R. (1980). "New Era in Treatment of Dysmenorrhea." *JAMA: Journal of the American Medical Association, 244,* 1885–1886.

Goodman, E. (1985). *Keeping in Touch.* New York: Summit Books.

Goodman, W. (1992, August 4). "TV's Sexual Circus Has a Purpose." *The New York Times,* p. 2.

Gooren, L., & Cohen-Kettenis, P. T. (1991). "Development of Male Gender Identity/Role and a Sexual Orientation Towards Women in a 46,XY Subject with Incomplete Form of the Androgen Insensitivity Syndrome." *Archives of Sexual Behavior, 20*(5), 459–470.

Gordon, E. B. (1991). "Transsexual Healing: Medicaid Funding for Sex Reassignment Surgery." *Archives of Sexual Behavior, 20*(1), 61–74.

Gordon, S. (1984, March). "Parents as Sexuality Educators." *SIECUS Report,* 10–11.

Gordon, S. (1986, October). "What Kids Need to Know." *Psychology Today,* pp 46ff.

Gorman, C. (1992, January 20). "Sizing Up the Sexes." *Time,* pp. 42–51.

Gosselin, C., & Wilson, G. (1980). *Sexual Variations.* New York: Simon & Schuster.

"Gossypol: Effective Contraceptive, But Can Side Effects Be Overcome?" (1987, January). *Contraceptive Technology Update, 8*(1), 5–6.

Gostin, L. O. (1992). "Health Law." *JAMA: Journal of the American Medical Association, 268*(3), 364–366.

Gouchie, C., & Kimura, D. (1991). "The Relationship Between Testosterone Levels and Cognitive Ability Patterns." *Psychoneuroendocrinology, 16,* 323–334.

Gould, J. B., Davey, B., & Stafford, R. S. (1989). "Socioeconomic Differences in Rates of Cesarean Section." *New England Journal of Medicine, 321*(4), 233–239.

Grady, D. (1992, June). "Sex Test of Champions: Olympic Officials Struggle to Define What Should Be Obvious—Just Who Is a Female Athlete." *Discover,* pp. 78–82.

Grafenberg, E. (1950). "The Role of Urethra in Female Orgasm." *International Journal of Sexology, 3*, 145–148.

Graham, N. M., et al. (1992). "The Effects on Survival of Early Treatment of Human Immunodeficiency Virus Infection." *New England Journal of Medicine, 326*(16), 1032–1042.

Granberg, D. (1991). "Conformity to Religious Norms Regarding Abortion." *Sociological Quarterly, 32*(2), 267–275.

Green, R. (1987). *The "Sissy-Boy Syndrome" and the Development of Homosexuality.* New Haven, CT: Yale University Press.

Greenberg, B. S., & D'Alessio, D. D. (1985). "Quantity and Quality of Sex in the Soaps." *Broadcasting and Electronic Media, 29*, 309–321.

Greenberg, J., Magder, L., & Aral, S. (1992). "Age at First Coitus: A Marker for Risky Sexual Behavior in Women." *Sexually Transmitted Diseases, 19*(6), 331–334.

Greenberg, J., Schnell, D., & Conlon, R. (1992). "Behaviors of Crack Cocaine Users and Their Impact on Early Syphilis Intervention." *Sexually Transmitted Diseases, 19*(6), 346–350.

Greenburg, D., & Jacobs, M. (1966). *How to Make Yourself Miserable.* New York: Random House.

Greensite, G. (1991). "Acquaintance Rape Clarified." *Student Guide,* Santa Cruz, CA, pp. 15, 68.

Greenwald, H. (1970). *The Elegant Prostitutes: A Social and Psychoanalytic Study.* New York: Walker.

Greenwood, S. (1992). *Menopause Naturally: Preparing for the Second Half of Life.* Volcano, CA: Volcano Press.

Gregersen, E. (1986). "Human Sexuality in Cross-Cultural Perspective." In D. Byrne & K. Kelley (Eds.), *Alternative Approaches to the Study of Sexual Behavior.* Hillsdale, NJ: Erlbaum.

Gregoire, A. (1992). "New Treatments for Erectile Impotence." *British Journal of Psychiatry, 160*, 315–326.

Gregor, T. (1985). *Anxious Pleasures: The Sexual Lives of an Amazonian People.* Chicago: University of Chicago Press.

Gressman, G. D., et al. (1992). "Female Awareness of University Sexual Harassment Policy." *Journal of College Student Development, 33*(4), 370–371.

Grimes, D. (1983). "Reversible Contraception for the 1980's." *Journal of the American Medical Association, 250*, 3081–3083.

Griswold Del Castillo, Richard (1984). *La Familia: Chicano Families in the Urban Southwest, 1848 to the Present.* Notre Dame, IN: University of Notre Dame.

Gritz, E. R., Wellisch, D. K., Wang, H. J., Siau, J., Landsverk, J. A., & Cosgrove, M. D. (1989). "Long-Term Effects of Testicular Cancer on Sexual Functioning in Married Couples." *Cancer, 64*(7), 1560–1567.

Gross, J. (1992, March 11). "Schools Are Newest Arena for Sex-Harassment Cases." *The New York Times,* pp. 1, 18.

Groth, A. N. (1979). *Men Who Rape: The Psychology of the Offender.* New York: Plenum Press.

Groth, A. N., & Birnbaum, H. J. (1978). "Adult Sexual Orientation and Attraction to Underage Persons." *Archives of Sexual Behavior, 7*(3), 175–181.

Groth, A. N., Burgess, A. W., & Holmstrom, L. L. (1977). "Rape: Power, Anger, and Sexuality." *American Journal of Psychiatry, 104*(11), 1239–1243.

Groth, A. N., Hobson, W. F., & Gary, T. (1982). "Heterosexuality, Homosexuality, and Pedophilia: Sexual Offenses Against Children." In A. Scacco (Ed.), *Male Rape: A Casebook of Sexual Aggression.* New York: AMS Press.

Gruters, R. A., et al. (1991). "Differences in Clinical Course in Zidovudine-Treated Asymptomatic HIV-Infected Men Associated with T-Cell Function at Intake." *AIDS, 5*(1), 43–47.

Gudjonsson, G. (1990). "Cognitive Distortions and Blame Attribution Among Paedophiles." *Sexual and Marital Therapy, 5*(2), 183–185.

Guerrero Pavich, Emma. (1986). "A Chicana Perspective on Mexican Culture and Sexuality." In L. Lister (Ed.), *Human Sexuality, Ethnoculture, and Social Work.* New York: Haworth Press.

Gump, J. (1980). "Reality and Myth: Employment and Sex Role Ideology in Black Women." In F. Denmark & J. Sherman (Eds.), *The Psychology of Women.* New York: Psychological Dimensions.

Gutek, B. (1985). *Sex and the Workplace.* San Francisco: Jossey-Bass.

Gutin, J. C. (1992, June). "Why Bother?" *Discover,* pp. 32–39.

Gutman, H. (1976). *The Black Family: From Slavery to Freedom.* New York: Pantheon.

Guttentag, M., & Secord, P. (1983). *Too Many Women.* Newbury Park, CA: Sage Publications.

Gwartney-Gibbs, P. (1986). "The Institutionalization of Premarital Cohabitation: Estimates from Marriage License Applications." *Journal of Marriage and the Family, 48*, 423–434.

Haaga, D. A. (1991). "Homophobia?" *Journal of Behavior and Personality, 6*, 171–174.

Hafner, D. W. (1992). "From Where I Sit." *Family Life Educator, 11*(2), 14–15.

Hage, J. J., Bout, C. A., Bloem, J. J., & Megens, J. A. (1993). "Phalloplasty in Female-to-Male Transsexuals: What Do Our Patients Ask For?" *Annals of Plastic Surgery, 30*(4), 323–326.

Hahn, R. A. (1992). "The State of Federal Health Statistics on Racial and Ethnic Groups." *JAMA: Journal of the American Medical Association, 267*(2), 268–271.

Halikas, J. A., Weller, R. A., & Morse, C. (1982). "Effects of Regular Marijuana Use on Sexual Performance." *Journal of Psychoactive Drugs, 14*, 59–70.

Hall, C. (1980). *A Primer of Freudian Psychology.* New York: New American Library.

Hall, G. J. (1991). "Sexual Arousal as a Function of Physiological and Cognitive Variables in a Sexual Offender Population." *Archives of Sexual Behavior, 20*(4), 359–369.

Hall, J. G., & Gilchrist, D. M. (1990). "Turner Syndrome and Its Variants." *Pediatric Clinics of North America, 37*(6), 1421–1440.

Hallstrom, T., & Samuelsson, S. (1990). "Changes in Women's Sexual Desire in Middle Life: The Longitudinal Study of Women in Gothenburg [Sweden]." *Archives of Sexual Behavior, 19*(3), 259–267.

Hamer, D. H., et al. (1993). "A Linkage Between DNA Markers on the X-Chromosome and Male Sexual Orientation." *Science, 261*(5119), 321–327.

Hamilton, D. L. (1979). "A Cognitive-Attributional Analysis of Stereotyping." *Advances in Experimental Psychology, 12*, 53–81.

Hankinson, S. E., Colditz, G. A., Hunter, D. J., Spencer, T. L., Rosner, B., & Stampfau, M. J. (1992). "A Quantitative Assessment of Oral Contraceptive Use and Risk of Ovarian Cancer." *Obstetrics and Gynecology, 80*(4), 708–714.

Hanley, R. (1988, February 4). "Surrogate Deals for Mothers Held Illegal in New Jersey." *The New York Times,* p. 1ff.

Hansen, G. (1985). "Dating Jealousy Among College Students." *Sex Roles, 12*(7-8), 713–721.

Hansen, G. (1987). "Extradyadic Relations During Courtship." *Journal of Sex Research, 23*(3), 383–390.

Hansen, W. B., Wolkenstein, B. H., & Hahn, G. L. (1992). "Young Adult Behavior: Issues in Programming and Evaluation." *Health Education Research, 7*, 305–312.

Hanson, F. W., et al. (1990). "Ultrasonography—Guided Early Amniocentesis in Singleton Pregnancies." *American Journal of Obstetrics and Gynecology, 162*(6), 1381–1383.

Hanson, S. L., Myers, D. E., & Ginsburg, A. L. (1987). "The Role of Responsibility and Knowledge in Reducing Teenage Out-of-Wedlock Childbearing." *Journal of Marriage and the Family, 49*(2), 241–256.

Hare-Mustin, R. T., & Marecek, J. (1990a). "Beyond Difference." In R. T. Hare-Mustin & J. Marecek (Eds.), *Making a Difference: Psychology and the Construction of Gender.* New Haven, CT: Yale University Press.

Hare-Mustin, R. T., & Marecek, J. (1990b). "Gender and the Meaning of Difference." In R. T. Hare-Mustin & J. Marecek (Eds.), *Making a Difference: Psychology and the Construction of Gender*. New Haven, CT: Yale University Press.

Hare-Mustin, R. T., & Marecek, J. (Eds.). (1990c). *Making a Difference: Psychology and the Construction of Gender*. New Haven, CT: Yale University Press.

Hare-Mustin, R. T., & Marecek, J. (1990d). "On Making a Difference." In R. T. Hare-Mustin & J. Marecek (Eds.), *Making a Difference: Psychology and the Construction of Gender*. New Haven, CT: Yale University Press.

Hariton, E. B., & Singer, J. I. (1974). "Women's Fantasies During Sexual Intercourse." *Journal of Consulting and Clinical Psychology, 42*, 313–322.

Harlow, C. W. (1991). *Female Victims of Violent Crime*. Washington, DC: U.S. Department of Justice. (NCJ-126826).

Harriman, L. (1983). "Personal and Marital Changes Accompanying Parenthood." *Family Relations, 32*, 387–394.

Harris, M. B., & Turner, P. H. (1985). "Gay and Lesbian Parents." *Journal of Homosexuality, 12*(2), 101–113.

Harry, J. (1986). "Sampling Gay Men." *Journal of Homosexuality, 22*(1), 21–34.

Harry, J. (1988). "Decision Making and Age Differences Among Gay Male Couples." In J. De Cecco (Ed.), *Gay Relationships*. New York: Haworth Press.

Hart, J., Cohen, E., Gingold, A., & Homburg, R. (1991). "Sexual Behavior in Pregnancy: A Study of 219 Women." *Journal of Sex Education and Therapy, 17*(2), 88–90.

Harvard Law Review. (1991). "Constitutional Barriers to Civil and Criminal Restrictions on Premarital and Extramarital Sex." *Harvard Law Review, 104*(7), 1660–1680.

Harvey, S. (1987). "Female Sexual Behavior: Fluctuations During the Menstrual Cycle." *Journal of Psychosomatic Research, 31*, 101–110.

Haskell, M. (1976, November). "2000-Year-Old Misunderstanding: Rape Fantasy." *Ms.*, pp. 84–86ff.

Haskell, M. (1987). *From Reverence to Rape*. (2nd ed.). Chicago: University of Chicago Press.

Hass, A. (1979). *Teenage Sexuality: A Survey of Teenage Sexual Behavior*. New York: Macmillan.

Hassold, T., Arnovitz, K., Jacobs, P. A., May, K., & Robinson, D. (1990). "The Parental Origin of the Missing or Additional Chromosome in 45,X and 47,XXX Females." *Birth Defects Original Article Series, 26*(4), 297–304.

Hatcher, R., et al. (1986). *Contraceptive Technology: 1986–1988*. New York: Irvington.

Hatcher, R., et al. (1990). *Contraceptive Technology: 1990–1992*. New York: Irvington.

Hatcher, R., et al. (1993). *Contraceptive Technology: 1992–1994*. New York: Irvington.

Hatchett, S. J. (1991). "Women and Men." In J. S. Jackson (Ed.), *Life in Black America*. Newbury Park, CA: Sage Publications.

Hatfield, E., & Sprecher, S. (1986). *Mirror, Mirror: The Importance of Looks in Everyday Life*. New York: State University of New York.

Hatfield, E., & Walster, G. W. (1981). *A New Look at Love*. Reading, MA: Addison-Wesley.

Hausman, B. L. (1993). "Demanding Subjectivity: Transsexualism, Medicine, and the Technologies of Gender." *Journal of the History of Sexuality, 3*(2), 270–302.

Hawkins, R. O. (1990). "The Relationship Between Culture, Personality, and Sexual Jealousy in Men in Heterosexual and Homosexual Relationships." *Journal of Homosexuality, 19*(3), 67–84.

Hawton, K., Catalan, J., & Fagg, J. (1991). "Low Sexual Desire: Sex Therapy Results and Prognostic Factors." *Behavior Research and Therapy, 29*(3), 217–224.

Hayden, N. (1991). *How to Satisfy a Woman Every Time*. New York: Dutton.

Hays, D., & Samuels, A. (1989). "Heterosexual Women's Perceptions of Their Marriages to Bisexual or Homosexual Men." *Journal of Homosexuality, 18*, 81–100.

Hazan, C., & Shaver, P. (1987). "Romantic Love Conceptualized as an Attachment Process." *Journal of Personality and Social Psychology, 52*(3), 511–524.

Healy, J. M. (1988, November). "Preventing Birth Defects of the Mind." *Parents' Magazine*, p. 176ff.

Heath, D. (1984). "An Investigation of the Origins of a Copious Vaginal Discharge During Intercourse." *Journal of Sex Research, 20*, 194–215.

Heath, R. (1972). "Pleasure and Brain Activity in Man." *Journal of Nervous and Mental Disorders, 154*, 3–18.

Hefner, R., Rebecca, M., & Oleshansky. (1975). "Development of Sex-Role Transcendence." *Human Development, 18*, 143–158.

Heider, K. (1979). *Grand Valley Dani: Peaceful Warriors*. New York: Holt, Rinehart & Winston.

Heilbrun, C. (1982). *Toward a Recognition of Androgyny*. New York: Norton.

Heiman, J., LoPiccolo, L., & LoPiccolo, J. (1976). *Becoming Orgasmic: A Sexual Growth Program for Women*. Englewood Cliffs, NJ: Prentice-Hall.

Heiman, J., et al. (1986). "Historical and Current Factors Discriminating Sexually Functional from Sexually Dysfunctional Married Couples." *Journal of Marital and Family Therapy, 12*(2), 163–174.

Heiman, J., & LoPiccolo, J. (1988). *Becoming Orgasmic: A Sexual and Personal Growth Program for Women*. Englewood Cliffs, NJ: Prentice-Hall.

Heller, L., Keren, O., Aloni, R., & Davidoff, G. (1992). "An Open Trial of Vacuum Penile Tumescence: Constriction Therapy for Neurological Impotence." *Paraplegia, 30*(8), 550–553.

Hemminki, K., et al. (1983). "Spontaneous Abortion in an Industrialized Community in Finland." *American Journal of Public Health, 73*(1), 32–37.

Hendrick, C., & Hendrick, S. S. (1986). "A Theory and Method of Love." *Journal of Personality and Social Psychology, 50*, 392–402.

Hendrick, C., & Hendrick, S. S. (1988, May). "Lovers Wear Rose-Colored Glasses." *Journal of Social and Personal Relationships, 5*(2), 161–183.

Hendrick, S. S. (1981). "Self-Disclosure and Marital Satisfaction." *Journal of Personality and Social Psychology, 40*, 1150–1159.

Hendrick, S. S., & Hendrick, C. (1987). "Multidimensionality of Sexual Attitudes." *Journal of Sex Research, 23*(4), 502–526.

Hendrick, S. S., Hendrick, C., & Adler, N. L. (1988). "Romantic Relationships: Love, Satisfaction, and Staying Together." *Journal of Personality and Social Psychology, 54*, 980–988.

Henley, N. (1977). *Body Politics: Power, Sex, and Nonverbal Communication*. Englewood Cliffs, NJ: Prentice-Hall.

Herbert, C. M. H. (1989). *Talking of Silence: The Sexual Harassment of Schoolgirls*. London: The Falmer Press.

Herbst, A. L., et al. (1980). "A Comparison of Pregnancy Experience in DES-Exposed and DES-Unexposed Daughters." *Journal of Reproductive Medicine, 24*, 62–68.

Herdt, G. (1984). "A Comment on Cultural Attributes and Fluidity of Bisexuality." *Journal of Homosexuality, 10*(3-4), 53–61.

Herdt, G. (1987). "Transitional Objects in Sambia Initiation." Special Issue: Interpretation in Psychoanalytic Anthropology. *Ethos, 15*, 40–57.

Herdt, G., & Boxer, A. (1992). "Introduction: Culture, History, and Life Course of Gay Men." In G. Herdt (Ed.), *Gay Culture in America: Essays from the Field*. Boston: Beacon Press.

Herek, G. M. (1984). "Beyond Homophobia: A Social Psychological Perspective on Attitudes Toward Lesbians and Gay Men." *Journal of Homosexuality, 10*(1-2), 1–21.

Herek, G. M. (1985). "On Doing, Being, and Not Being: Prejudice and the Social Construction of Sexuality." *Journal of Homosexuality, 12*(1), 135–151.

Herek, G. M. (1989). "Hate Crimes Against Lesbians and Gay Men: Issues for Research and Policy." *American Psychologist, 44,* 948–955.

Herek, G. M., Kimmel, D. C., Am ro, H., & Melton, G. B. (1991). "Avoiding Heterosexist Bias in Psychological Research." *American Psychologist, 46*(9), 957–963.

Herman, J. (1981). *Father-Daughter Incest.* Cambridge, MA: Harvard University Press.

Herold, E. E., Mantle, D., & Zemitis, D. (1979). "A Study of Sexual Offenses Against Females." *Adolescence, 14,* 65–72.

Herold, E. E., & Way, L. (1983). "Oral-Genital Sexual Behavior in a Sample of University Females." *Journal of Sex Research, 19*(4), 327–338.

Herzer, M. (1985). "Kertbeny and the Nameless Love." *Journal of Homosexuality, 12*(1), 1–26.

Hetherington, S. E. (1990). "A Controlled Study of the Effect of Prepared Childbirth Classes on Obstetric Outcomes." *Birth, 17*(2), 86–90.

Hewitt, J. (1987). "Preconceptional Sex Selection." *British Journal of Hospital Medicine, 37*(2), 149ff.

Heyl, B. (1989). "Homosexuality: A Social Phenomenon." In K. McKinney & S. Sprecher (Eds.), *Human Sexuality: The Societal and Interpersonal Context.* Norwood, NJ: Ablex.

Hibbard, R. A., & Hartman, G. L. (1992). "Behavioral Problems in Alleged Sexual Abuse Victims." *Child Abuse and Neglect, 16*(5), 755–762.

Hibbs, J. R., & Gunn, R. A. (1991). "Public Health Intervention in a Cocaine-Related Syphilis Outbreak." *American Journal of Public Health, 8*(10), 1259–1262.

Hill, I. (1987). *The Bisexual Spouse.* McLean, VA: Barlina Books.

Hilts, P. (1991, October 11). "Growing Concern Over Pelvic Infection in Women." *The New York Times,* p. B7.

Hilts, P. J. (1990, June 13). "Poorer Countries Are Hit Hardest by Spread of AIDS, U.N. Reports." *The New York Times,* p. A6.

Hines, M. (1982). "Prenatal Gonadal Hormones and Sex Differences in Human Behavior." *Psychological Bulletin, 92,* 56–80.

Hines, P. M., & Boyd-Franklin, N. (1982). "Black Families." In M. McGoldrick et al. (Eds.), *Ethnicity and Family Therapy.* New York: Guilford Press.

Hingson, R. W., Strunin, L., Berlin, B. M., & Heeren, T. (1990). "Beliefs About AIDS, Use of Alcohol and Drugs, and Unprotected Sex Among Massachusetts Adolescents." *American Journal of Public Health, 80*(3), 295–299.

Hirschfeld, M. (1978). *Research on Love Between Men.* Los Angeles: Urania Manuscripts.

Hirschfeld, M. (1991). *Transvestites: The Erotic Drive to Cross Dress.* Buffalo, NY: Prometheus Press.

Hite, S. (1976). *The Hite Report.* New York: Macmillan.

Ho, D. D., et al. (1985). "Infrequency of Isolation of HTLV-III Virus from Saliva in AIDS." *New England Journal of Medicine, 313,* 1606.

Ho, D. D., Bredesen, D. E., Vinters, H. V., & Daar, E. S. (1989). "The Acquired Immunodeficiency Syndrome (AIDS) Dementia Complex." *Annals of Internal Medicine, 111*(5), 400–410.

Hobart, C., & Griegel, F. (1992). "Cohabitation Among Canadian Students at the End of the Eighties." *Journal of Comparative Family Studies, 23*(3), 311–338.

Hochhauser, M. (1992). "Moral Development and HIV Prevention Among Adolescents." *Family Life Educator, 10*(3), 9–12.

Hockenberry, S. L., & Billingham, R. E. (1987). "Sexual Orientation and Boyhood Gender Conformity: Development of the Boyhood Gender Conformity Scale (BGCS)." *Archives of Sexual Behavior, 16,* 475–492.

Hoeffer, B. (1981). "Children's Acquisition of Sex-Role Behavior in Lesbian-Mother Families." *American Journal of Orthopsychiatry, 51,* 536–544.

Holcomb, D. R., et al. (1991). "Gender Differences Among College Students." *College Student Journal, 25*(4), 434–439.

Hollander, J. B., Gonzalez, J., & Norman, T. (1992). "Patient Satisfaction with Pharmacologic Erection Program." *Urology, 39*(5), 439–441.

Holman, P. B., Jenkins, W. C., Gayle, J. A., Duncan, C., & Lindsey, B. K. (1991). "Increasing the Involvement of National and Regional Racial and Ethnic Minority Organizations in HIV Information and Education." *Public Health Reports, 106*(6), 687–694.

Holmes, K. K., et al. (1990). "Future Directions." In K. K. Holmes et al. (Eds.), *Sexually Transmitted Diseases* (2nd ed.). New York: McGraw-Hill.

Holmes, K. K., et al. (Eds.). (1990). *Sexually Transmitted Diseases* (2nd ed.). New York: McGraw-Hill.

Holmes, R. M. (1991). *Sex Crimes.* Newbury Park, CA: Sage Publications.

Holtzen, D. W., & Agresti, A. A. (1990). "Parental Responses to Gay and Lesbian Children." *Journal of Social and Clinical Psychology, 9*(3), 390–399.

Hook, E. W., III, et al. (1992). "Herpes Simplex Virus Infection as a Risk Factor for Human Immunodeficiency Virus Infection in Heterosexuals." *Journal of Infectious Diseases, 165*(2), 251–255.

Hooker, E. (1957). "The Adjustment of the Overt Male Homosexual." *Journal of Projective Psychology, 21,* 18–31.

Hopson, J., & Rosenfeld, A. (1984, August). "PMS: Puzzling Monthly Symptoms." *Psychology Today,* 30–35.

Hort, B. E., Leinbach, M. D., & Fagot, B. I. (1991). "Is There Coherence Among the Cognitive Components of Gender Acquisition?" *Sex Roles, 24*(3-4), 195–207.

Hotelling, K. (1991). "Sexual Harassment: A Problem Shielded by Silence." *Journal of Counseling and Development, 69*(6), 497–501.

Houlberg, R. (1991). "The Magazine of a Sadomasochism Club—The Tie That Binds." *Journal of Homosexuality, 21*(1-2), 167–183.

Houseknecht, S. K. (1982). "Childlessness and Marital Adjustment." In J. Rosenfeld (Eds.), *Relationships: The Marriage and Family Reader.* Glencoe, IL: Scott, Foresman.

Houseknecht, S. K. (1987). "Voluntary Childlessness." In M. B. Sussman & S. K. Steinmetz (Eds.), *Handbook of Marriage and the Family.* New York: Plenum Press.

"How the Public Feels." (1986, November 24). *Time,* p. 58.

Howard, E. (1980, November). "Overcoming Rape Trauma." *Ms.,* p. 35.

Howard, J. (1988). "A Structural Approach to Interracial Patterns in Adolescent Judgments About Sexual Intimacy." *Sociological Perspectives, 31*(1), 88–121.

Howard, J. A., Blumstein, P., & Schwartz, P. (1986). "Sex, Power, and Influence Tactics in Intimate Relationships." *Journal of Personality and Social Psychology, 51*(1), 102–109.

Howard, L., et al. (1986). "Evaluation of Chlamydiazyme for the Detection of Genital Infection Caused by Chlamydia Trachomatis." *Journal of Clinical Microbiology, 23,* 329–332.

Humm, A. J. (1992). "Homosexuality: The New Frontier in Sexuality Education." *Family Life Educator, 10*(3), 13–18.

Humphreys, L. (1975). *Tearoom Trade: Impersonal Sex in Public Places.* Chicago: Aldine.

Hunt, M. (1974). *Sexual Behavior in the 1970s.* Chicago: Playboy Press.

Hunt, M., & Hunt, B. (1977). *The Divorce Experience.* New York: McGraw-Hill.

Hunter, A. G., & Davis, J. E. (1992). "Constructing Gender: An Exploration of Afro-American Men's Conceptualization of Manhood." *Gender and Society, 6*(3), 464–479.

Hupka, R. B. (1981). "Cultural Determinants of Jealousy." *Alternative Lifestyles, 4*(3), 310–356.

Hurst, M., & Summey, P. S. (1984). "Childbirth and Social Class: The Case of Cesarean Delivery." *Social Science and Medicine, 18*(8), 621–631.

Imberti, L., Sottini, A., Bettinardi, A., Puoti, M., & Primi, D. (1991). "Selective Depletion in HIV Infection of T Cells That Bear Specific T Cell Receptor V Beta Sequences." *Science, 254*(5033), 860–862.

Imperato-McGinley, J. (1974). "Steroid 5'-reductase Deficiency in Man: An Inherited Form of Male Pseudohermaphroditism." *Science, 186,* 1213–1215.

Imperato-McGinley, J. (1979). "Androgens and the Evolution of Male Gender Identity Among Male Pseudohermaphrodites with 5'-reductase Deficiency." *New England Journal of Medicine, 300,* 1233–1237.

Imperato-McGinley, J., et al. (1991). "Cognitive Abilities in Androgen-Insensitive Subjects." *Clinical Endocrinology, 34*(5), 341–347.

Irvine, J. M. (1990). *Disorders of Desire.* Philadelphia: Temple University Press.

Isensee, R. (1990). *Love Between Men: Enhancing Intimacy and Keeping Your Relationship Alive.* New York: Prentice-Hall.

Israelski, D. (1992). "Current Issues in HIV/AIDS Research: A Report from the Amsterdam Conference." Talk given at Dominican Hospital, Santa Cruz, CA.

Israelstam, S. (1986). "Alcohol and Drug Problems of Gay Males and Lesbians: Therapy, Counseling and Prevention Issues." *Journal of Drug Issues, 16*(3), 443–461.

Jackson, J. S. (Ed.). (1991). *Life in Black America.* Newbury Park, CA: Sage Publications.

Jacobs, J. (1993, February 4). "Male GIs as Sexual Prey: Welcome to the Club." *San Jose Mercury News,* p. 7b.

Jacobs, S. E., & Cromwell, J. (1992). "Visions and Revisions of Reality: Reflections on Sex, Sexuality, Gender and Gender Variance." *Journal of Homosexuality, 23*(4), 43–70.

Jacoby, A., & Williams, J. (1985). "Effects of Premarital Sexual Standards and Behavior on Dating and Marriage Desirability." *Journal of Marriage and the Family, 47*(4), 1059–1065.

Jacques, J., & Chason, K. (1979). "Cohabitation: Its Impact on Marital Success." *Family Coordinator, 28*(1), 35–39.

James, C. (1992, November 22). "Dangerous Liaisons Are All the Rage." *The New York Times,* p. 13.

James, J., & Myerdling, J. (1977). "Early Sexual Experiences as a Factor in Prostitution." *American Journal of Psychiatry, 134,* 1381–1385.

James, N. J., Gillies, P. A., & Bignell, C. J. (1991). "AIDS-Related Risk Perception and Sexual Behaviour Among Sexually Transmitted Disease Clinic Attenders." *International Journal of STD and AIDS, 2*(4), 264–271.

Jaschik, M. L., & Fretz, B. R. (1991). "Women's Perceptions and Labeling of Sexual Harassment." *Sex Roles, 25*(1-2), 19–23.

Jeffrey, T. B., & Jeffrey, L. K. (1991). "Psychologic Aspects of Sexual Abuse in Adolescence." *Current Opinion in Obstetrics and Gynecology, 3*(6), 825–831.

Jemmott, J. B. I., Jemmott, L. S., & Fong, G. T. (1992). "Reductions in HIV Risk-Associated Sexual Behaviors Among Black Male Adolescents: Effects of an AIDS Prevention Intervention." *American Journal of Public Health, 82*(3), 372–377.

Jenks, R. (1985). "Swinging: A Replication and Test of a Theory." *Journal of Sex Research, 21*(2), 199–210.

Jensen, M. A. (1984). *Love's Sweet Return: The Harlequin Story.* Toronto: Women's Press.

Jick, H., et al. (1981). "Vaginal Spermicides and Congenital Disorders." *JAMA: Journal of the American Medical Association, 243*(13), 1329–1332.

Joffe, G. P., et al. (1992). "Multiple Partners and Partner Choice as Risk Factors for Sexually Transmitted Disease Among Female College Students." *Sexually Transmitted Diseases, 19*(5), 272–278.

Johnson, C. (1993, June 5). "More Women-Controlled AIDS Prevention Methods Needed—WHO." *San Jose Mercury News,* p. 6.

Johnson, C. B., Stockdale, M. S., & Saal, F. E. (1991). "Persistence of Men's Misperceptions of Friendly Cues Across a Variety of Interpersonal Encounters." *Psychology of Women Quarterly, 15*(3), 463–475.

Johnson, G. T., & Goldfinger, S. (Eds.). (1981). *The Harvard Medical School Health Letter Book.* Cambridge, MA: Harvard University Press.

Johnston, D. (1992, April 24). "Survey Shows Number of Rapes Far Higher Than Official Figures." *The New York Times,* p. A9.

Jones, C. (1986, June). "Sharing the Childbearing Miracle." *Nurturing News, 8*(2), pp. 5, 18ff.

Jones, C. (1988). *Mind Over Labor.* New York: Penguin.

Jones, E. F., et al. (1985). "Teenage Pregnancy in Developed Countries: Determinants and Policy Implications." *Family Planning Perspectives, 17*(2), 53–63.

Jones, J. H. (1992). "Twenty Years After. The Legacy of the Tuskegee Syphilis Study. AIDS and the Black Community." *Hastings Center Report, 22*(6), 38–40.

Jones, J. H. (1993). *Bad Blood: The Tuskegee Syphilis Experiment* (rev. ed.). New York: Free Press.

Jones, M. (1989). *A Child by Any Means.* London: Piatkus.

Jones, R. W., & Bates, J. E. (1988). "Satisfaction in Male Homosexual Couples." In J. De Cecco (Ed.), *Gay Relationships.* New York: Haworth Press.

Jones, T. S., & Remland, M. S. (1992). "Sources of Variability in Perceptions of and Responses to Sexual Harassment." *Sex Roles, 27*(3-4), 121–142.

Jordan, W. (1968). *White Over Black: American Attitudes Toward the Negro.* Chapel Hill, NC: University of North Carolina Press.

Jorgensen, S., & Adams, R. (1988). "Predicting Mexican-American Family Planning Intentions: An Application and Test of a Social Psychological Model." *Journal of Marriage and the Family, 50,* 107–119.

Jurich, A., & Polson, C. (1985). "Nonverbal Assessment of Anxiety as a Function of Intimacy of Sexual Attitude Questions." *Psychological Reports, 57*(3, Pt. 2), 1247–1243.

Kagan, J. (1976). "The Psychological Requirements for Human Development." In N. Talbot (Ed.), *Raising Children in Modern America.* Boston: Little, Brown.

Kahn, Y. (1989). "Judaism and Homosexuality: The Traditionalist/Progressive Debate." *Journal of Homosexuality, 18*(3-4), 47–82.

Kalin, T. (1992, August). "Gays in Film: No Way Out." Special Issue: The Sexual Revolution in Movie, Music and TV. *US,* pp. 68–70.

Kalis, P., & Neuendorf, K. (1989). "Aggressive Cue-Prominence and Gender Participation in MTV." *Journalism Quarterly, 66*(1), 148–154, 229.

Kantor, L. M. (1992). "Scared Chaste? Fear-Based Educational Curricula." *SIECUS Report, 21*(3), 1–13.

Kantrowitz, B. (1990, February 12). "The Crack Children." *Newsweek,* pp. 62–63.

Kantrowitz, B. (1992, August 3). "Teenagers and AIDS." *Newsweek,* pp. 44–49.

Kantrowitz, B., & Kaplan, D. A. (1990, March 19). "Not the Right Family." *Newsweek,* pp. 50–51.

Kaplan, A. (1979). "Clarifying the Concept of Androgyny: Implications for Therapy." *Psychology of Women, 3,* 223–230.

Kaplan, A., & Bean, J. P. (Eds.). (1979). *Beyond Sex-Role Stereotypes.* Boston: Little, Brown.

Kaplan, E. H. (1988). "Crisis? A Brief Critique of Masters, Johnson, and Kolodny." *Journal of Sex Research, 25,* 317–322.

Kaplan, G. T., & Rogers, L. J. (1984). "Breaking Out of the Dominant Paradigm." *Journal of Homosexuality, 10*(3-4), 71–75.

Kaplan, H. S. (1974). *The New Sex Therapy.* New York: Brunner/Mazel.

Kaplan, H. S. (1979). *Disorders of Desire.* New York: Brunner/Mazel.

Kaplan, H. S. (1983). *The Evaluation of Sexual Disorders: Psychological and Medical Aspects.* New York: Brunner/Mazel.

Kaplan, H. S. (1987). *Sexual Aversion, Sexual Phobias, and Panic Disorders.* New York: Brunner/Mazel.

Kaplan, H. S. (1992). "A Neglected Issue: The Sexual Side Effects of Current Treatment for Breast Cancer." *Journal of Sex and Marital Therapy, 18*(1), 3–19.

Kaplan, H. S., & Owett, T. (1993). "The Female Androgen Deficiency Syndrome." *Journal of Sex and Marital Therapy, 19*(1), 3–24.

Kaplan, M. (1992, August). "You Get What You Pay For: Cable TV and Sex." Special Issue: The Sexual Revolution in Movie, Music and TV. *US*, pp. 78–80.

Karenga, M. (1992). "Under the Camouflage of Color and Gender: The Dread and Drama of Thomas-Hill." In R. Chrisman & R. Allen (Eds.), *Court of Appeal: The Black Community Speaks Out on the Racial and Sexual Politics of Clarence Thomas vs. Anita Hill.* New York: Ballantine.

Kasl, C. D. (1989). *Women, Sex, and Addiction.* New York: Ticknor & Fields.

Kassler, W. J., & Cates, W. J. (1992). "The Epidemiology and Prevention of Sexually Transmitted Diseases." *Urological Clinics of North America, 19*(1), 1–12.

Katchadourian, H. (1987). *Midlife in Perspective.* New York: W. H. Freeman.

Katz, R., Gipson, M. J., Kearl, A., & Kriskovich, M. (1989). "Assessing Sexual Aversion in College Students: The Sexual Aversion Scale." *Journal of Sex and Marital Therapy, 15*(2), 135–140.

Kaufman, D., et al. (1980). "Decreased Risk of Endometrial Cancer Among Oral Contraceptive Users." *New England Journal of Medicine, 303*, 1045–1047.

Kayal, P. M. (1992). "Healing Homophobia: Volunteerism and Sacredness in AIDS." *Journal of Religion and Health, 31*(2), 113–128.

Kaye, K., et al. (1989). "Birth Outcomes for Infants of Drug Abusing Mothers." *New York State Journal of Medicine, 144*(7), 256–261.

Kehoe, M. (1988). "Lesbians Over 60 Speak for Themselves." *Journal of Homosexuality, 16*, 1–111.

Keim, J., Woodard, M. P., & Anderson, M. K. (1992). "Screening for Chlamydia Trachomatis in College Women in Routine Gynecological Exams." *Journal of American College Health, 41*(1), 17–19, 22–23.

Keller, D., & Rosen, H. (1988). "Treating the Gay Couple Within the Context of Their Families of Origin." *Family Therapy Collections, 25*, 105–119.

Keller, S. E., Bartlett, J. A., Schleifer, S. J., Johnson, R. L., Pinner, E., & Delaney, B. (1991). "HIV-Relevant Sexual Behavior Among a Healthy Inner-City Heterosexual Adolescent Population in an Endemic Area of HIV." *Journal of Adolescent Health, 12*(1), 44–48.

Kellett, J. M. (1991). "Sexuality of the Elderly." *Sexual and Marital Therapy, 6*(2), 147–155.

Kelley, H. (1983). "Love and Commitment." In H. Kelley et al. (Eds.), *Close Relationships.* New York: W. H. Freeman.

Kelly, M. P., Strassberg, D. S., & Kircher, J. R. (1990). "Attitudinal and Experiential Correlates of Anorgasmia." *Archives of Sexual Behavior, 19*(2), 165–167.

Kelly, T. E., et al. (1992). "Survival of Fetuses with 45,X: An Instructive Case and Hypothesis." *American Journal of Medical Genetics, 42*(6), 825–826.

Kelly, T. E., Ferguson, J. E., & Golden, W. (1992). "Survival of Fetuses with 45,X: An Instructive Case and Hypothesis." *American Journal of Medical Genetics, 42*(6), 825–826.

Kendall-Tackett, K., Williams, L. M., & Finkelhor, D. (1993). "Impact of Sexual Abuse on Children: A Review and Synthesis of Recent Empirical Studies." *Psychological Bulletin, 113*(1), 164 (17 pages).

Kendrick, W. (1987). *The Secret Museum: Pornography in Modern Culture.* New York: Viking Press.

Kendrick, W. (1992, May 31). "Increasing Our Dirty-Word Power: Why Yesterday's Smut Is Today's Erotica." *The New York Times Book Review*, pp. 3, 36.

Kenig, S., & Ryan, J. (1986). "Sex Differences of Tolerance and Attribution of Blame for Sexual Harassment on a University Campus." *Sex Roles, 15*(9-10), 535–549.

Kennedy, H. (1988). *Ulrichs: The Life and Works of Karl Heinrich Ulrichs, Pioneer of the Modern Gay Movement.* Boston: Alyson Publications.

Kensington, C. (1991). *Elise.* San Francisco: Spinsters Ink.

Kenyon, E. B. (1989). "The Management of Exhibitionism in the Elderly: A Case Study." *Sexual and Marital Therapy, 4*(1), 93–100.

Keuls, E. (1985). *The Reign of the Phallus: Sexual Politics in Ancient Greece.* New York: Harper & Row.

King, M. B. (1990). "Sneezing as a Fetishistic Stimulus." *Sexual and Marital Therapy, 5*(1), 69–72.

King, P. A. (1992). "Twenty Years After. The Legacy of the Tuskegee Syphilis Study. The Dangers of Difference." *Hastings Center Report, 22*(6), 35–38.

Kinsey, A., Pomeroy, W., & Martin, C. (1948). "Sexual Behavior in the Human Male." Philadelphia: Saunders.

Kinsey, A., Pomeroy, W., Martin, C., & Gebhard, P. (1953). *Sexual Behavior in the Human Female.* Philadelphia: Saunders.

Kisker, E. (1984). "The Effectiveness of Family Planning Clinics in Serving Adolescents." *Family Planning Perspectives, 16*(5), 212ff.

Kisker, E. (1985). "Teenagers Talk About Sex, Pregnancy and Contraception." *Family Planning Perspectives, 17*(2), 83–89.

Kissman, K., & Allen, J. A. (1993). *Single-Parent Families.* Newbury Park, CA: Sage Publications.

Kite, M. (1984). "Sex Differences in Attitudes Toward Homosexuals: A Meta-Analytic Review." *Journal of Homosexuality, 10*(1-2), 69–82.

Kitzinger, S. (1989). *The Complete Book of Pregnancy and Childbirth.* New York: Knopf.

Kleczkowska, A., et al. (1990). "Turner Syndrome: The Leuven Experience (1965–1980) in 478 Patients." *Genetic Counseling, 1*(3-4), 235–240.

Klein, R. S., et al. (1988). "Low Occupational Risk of Human Immunodeficiency Infection Among Dental Professionals." *New England Journal of Medicine, 318*, 86–90.

Kline, A., Kline, E., & Oken, E. (1992). "Minority Women and Sexual Choice in the Age of AIDS." *Social Science and Medicine, 34*(4), 447–457.

Klinman, D., & Vukelich, C. (1985). "Mothers and Fathers: Expectations for Infants." *Family Relations, 34*(3), 305–313.

Knafo, D., & Jaffe, Y. (1984). "Sexual Fantasizing in Males and Females." *Journal of Research in Personality, 18*, 451–462.

Knapp, J., & Whitehurst, R. (1977). "Sexually Open Marriage and Relationships: Issues and Prospects." In R. Libby & R. Whitehurst (Eds.), *Marriage and Alternatives: Exploring Intimate Relationships.* Glenview, IL: Scott, Foresman.

Knopp, F. H. (1984). *Retraining Sex Offenders: Methods and Models.* Syracuse, NY: Safer Society Press.

Koblinsky, S. A., & Sugawara, A. I. (1984). "Nonsexist Curricula, Sex of Teacher and Children's Sex-Role Learning." *Sex Roles, 10*, 357–367.

Kockott, G., & Fahrner, E. M. (1988). "Male-to-Female and Female-to-Male Transsexuals: A Comparison." *Archives of Sexual Behavior, 17*(6), 539–546.

Kohen, J. A., et al. (1979). "Divorced Mothers: The Costs and Benefits of Female Family Control." In G. Levinger & O. C. Moles (Eds.), *Separation and Divorce*. New York: Basic Books.

Kohlberg, L. (1969). "The Cognitive-Development Approach to Socialization." In A. Goslin (Ed.), *Handbook of Socialization Theory and Research*. Chicago: Rand McNally.

Kolata, G. (1979, May). "Early Warnings and Latent Cures for Infertility." *Ms.*, pp. 86–89.

Kolata, G. (1988, April 22). "Anti-Acne Drug Faulted in Birth Defects." *The New York Times*, p. 1ff.

Kolata, G. (1990, May 31). "A Major Operation on a Fetus Works for the First Time." *The New York Times*, p. 1ff.

Kolata, G. (1992, March 17). "How AIDS Smolders: Immune System Studies Follow the Tracks of H.I.V." *The New York Times*, pp. B5, 8.

Kolker, A. (1989). "Advances in Prenatal Diagnosis: Social-Psychological and Policy Issues." *International Journal of Technology Assessment in Health Care, 5*(4), 601–617.

Kolodny, R., Masters, W., & Johnson, V. (1979). *Textbook of Sexual Medicine*. Boston: Little, Brown.

Komarovsky, M. (1985). *Women in College*. New York: Basic Books.

Konker, C. (1992). "Rethinking Child Sexual Abuse: An Anthropological Perspective." *American Journal of Orthopsychiatry, 62*(1), 147–153.

Koss, M. P. (1988). "Hidden Rape: Sexual Aggression and Victimization in a National Sample of Students in Higher Education." In A. W. Burgess (Ed.), *Rape and Sexual Assault II*. New York: Garland Press.

Koss, M. P. (1992). "The Underdetection of Rape: Methodological Choices Influence Incidence Estimates." *Journal of Social Issues, 48*, 61–75.

Koss, M. P., & Dinero, T. E. (1989). "Discriminant Analysis of Risk Factors for Sexual Victimization Among a National Sample of College Women." *Journal of Consulting and Clinical Psychology, 57*, 242–250.

Kotlowitz, A. (1991). *There Are No Children Here*. New York: Doubleday.

Kotulak, R. (1979, November 4). "Hopeful Forecast for Cancer Surgery." *San Francisco Chronicle*, p. 18.

Koziol, D. E., & Henderson, D. K. (1992). "Evolving Epidemiology of HIV Infection Among Adults." *Annals of Allergy, 68*(5), 375–385.

Krames, L., England, R., & Flett, G. (1988). "The Role of Masculinity and Femininity in Depression and Social Satisfaction in Elderly Years." *Sex Roles, 19*(11-12), 713–721.

Krauss, D. J., et al. (1990). "In Treating Impotence, Urology and Sex Therapy Are Complimentary." *Urology, 36*(5), 467–470.

Kreiss, J., et al. (1992). "Efficacy of Nonoxynol-9 Contraceptive Sponge Use in Preventing Heterosexual Acquisition of HIV in Nairobi Prostitutes." *JAMA: Journal of the American Medical Association 268*(4), 477–482.

Krettek, J. E., Arkin, S. I., Chaisilwattana, P., & Monif, G. R. (1993). "Chlamydia Trachomatis in Patients Who Used Oral Contraceptives and Had Intermenstrual Spotting." *Obstetrics and Gynecology, 81*(5, Pt. 1), 728–731.

Krieger, J. N., et al. (1993). "Clinical Manifestations of Trichomoniasis in Men." *Annals of Internal Medicine, 118*(11), 844–889.

Krieger, L. M. (1992, July 19). "Global Attack on AIDS." *San Francisco Examiner*, pp. A1, 10.

Kruesi, M. J., Fine, S., Valladares, L., & Philips, R. A. (1992). "Paraphilias: A Double-Blind Crossover Comparison of Clomipramine Versus Despipramine." *Archives of Sexual Behavior, 21*(6), 587–593.

Kruks, G. (1991). "Gay and Lesbian Homeless/Street Youth: Special Issues and Concerns." Special Issue: Homeless Youth. *Journal of Adolescent Health, 12*(7), 515–518.

Kulhanjian, J. A., et al. (1992). "Identification of Women at Unsuspected Risk of Primary Infection with Herpes Simplex Virus Type 2 During Pregnancy." *New England Journal of Medicine, 326*(14), 916–920.

Kupersmid, J., & Wonderly, D. (1980). "Moral Maturity and Behavior: Failure to Find a Link." *Journal of Youth and Adolescence, 9*, 249–261.

Kurdek, L. (1988). "Relationship Quality of Gay and Lesbian Cohabiting Couples." *Journal of Homosexuality, 15*(3-4), 93–118.

Kurdek, L. (1991). "Sexuality in Homosexual and Heterosexual Couples." In K. McKinney & Susan Sprecher (Eds.), *Sexuality in Close Relationships*. Hillsdale, NJ: Erlbaum.

Kurdek, L., & Schmitt, P. (1988). "Relationship Quality of Gay Men in Closed and Open Relationships." In J. De Cecco (Ed.), *Gay Relationships*. New York: Haworth Press.

Ladas, A., Whipple, B., & Perry, J. (1982). *The G Spot*. New York: Holt, Rinehart & Winston.

La Franchi, S. (1992). "Human Growth Hormone: Who Is a Candidate for Treatment?" *Postgraduate Medicine, 91*(5), 373–374, 380–382 passim.

Lamaze, F. (1970). *Painless Childbirth*. (1st ed., 1956). Chicago: H. Regnery.

Lamb, M. (1986). *The Father's Role: Cross-Cultural Perspectives*. Hillsdale, NJ: Erlbaum.

Lambert, B. (1990, September 6). "Despite Advice, Few Are Taking Drugs for AIDS." *The New York Times*, pp. A1, A18.

Lamontagne, Y., & Lesage, A. (1986). "Private Exposure and Covert Sensitization in the Treatment of Exhibitionism." *Journal of Behavior Therapy and Experimental Psychiatry, 17*(3), 197–201.

Landau, R. (1989). "Affect and Attachment: Kissing, Hugging, and Patting as Attachment Behaviors." *Infant Mental Health Journal, 10*(1), 59–69.

Landis, S. E., et al. (1992). "Results of a Randomized Trial of Partner Notification in Cases of HIV Infection in North Carolina." *New England Journal of Medicine, 326*(2), 101–106.

Laner, M. R. (1990). "Violence or Its Precipitators: Which Is More Likely to Be Identified as a Dating Problem?" *Deviant Behavior, 11*(4), 319–329.

Lang, R., Checkley, K. L., & Pugh, G. (1987). "Genital Exhibitionism: Courtship Disorder or Narcissism?" *Canadian Journal of Behavioural Science, 19*(2), 216–232.

Lang, R., & Frenzel, R. (1988). "How Sex Offenders Lure Children." *Annals of Sex Research, 1*(2), 303–317.

Langevin, R., Wright, P., & Handy, L. (1988). "Empathy, Assertiveness, and Defensiveness Among Sex Offenders." *Annals of Sex Research, 1*, 533–547.

Langevin, R., Wright, P., & Handy, L. (1989). "Studies of Brain Damage and Dysfunction in Sex Offenders." *Annals of Sex Research, 2*(2), 163–179.

Langhoff, E., & Haseltine, W. A. (1992). "Infection of Accessory Dendritic Cells by Human Immunodeficiency Virus Type 1." *Journal of Investigative Dermatology, 99*(5), 89S–94S.

Lantz, H. (1980). "Family and Kin as Revealed in the Narratives of Ex-Slaves." *Social Science Quarterly, 60*(4), 667–674.

La Torre, R., & Wendenburg, K. (1983). "Psychological Characteristics of Bisexual, Heterosexual, and Homosexual Women." *Journal of Homosexuality, 9*(1), 87–97.

Laube, D. (1985). "Premenstrual Syndrome." *The Female Patient, 6*, 50–61.

Laurent, S. L., Thompson, S. J., Addy, C., Garrison, C. Z., & Moore, E. E. (1992). "An Epidemiologic Study of Smoking and Primary Infertility in Women." *Fertility and Sterility, 57*(3), 565–572.

Lavecchia, C., Negri, E., Bruzzi, P., & Franceschi, S. (1993). "The Impact of Mammography on Breast Cancer Detection." *Annals of Oncology, 4*(1), 41–44.

Lavee, Y. (1991). "Western and Non-Western Human Sexuality: Implications for Clinical Practice." *Journal of Sex and Marital Therapy*, 17(5), 203–213.

Lavrakas, P. (1975). "Female Preferences for Male Physiques." *Journal of Research in Personality*, 9, 324–334.

Lawrence III, C. (1992). "Cringing at the Myths of Black Sexuality." In R. Chrisman & R. Allen (Eds.), *Court of Appeal: The Black Community Speaks Out on the Racial and Sexual Politics of Clarence Thomas vs. Anita Hill*. New York: Ballantine.

Lawson, C. (1990, April 12). "Fathers, Too, Are Seeking a Balance Between Their Families and Careers." *The New York Times*, p. 1ff.

Lazarus, A. A. (1989). "Dyspareunia: A Multimodel Psychotherapeutic Perspective." In S. R. Lieblum & R. C. Rosen (Eds.), *Principles and Practice of Sex Therapy* (2nd ed.). New York: Guilford Press.

Leavitt, F., & Berger, J. C. (1990). "Clinical Patterns Among Male Transsexual Candidates with Erotic Interest in Males." *Archives of Sexual Behavior*, 19(5), 491–505.

Ledwitz-Rigby, F. (1980). "Biochemical and Neurophysiological Influences on Human Sexual Development." In J. E. Parsons (Ed.), *The Psychobiology of Sex Differences and Sex Roles*. Washington, DC: Hemisphere.

Lee, J. A. (1973). *The Color of Love*. Toronto: New Press.

Lee, J. A. (1988). "Love Styles." In R. Sternberg & M. Barnes (Eds.), *The Psychology of Love*. New Haven, CT: Yale University Press.

Leiblum, S. R. (1990). "Sexuality and the Midlife Woman." Special Issue: Women at Midlife and Beyond. *Psychology of Women Quarterly*, 14(4), 495–508.

Leifer, M. (1990). *Psychological Effects of Motherhood: A Study of First Pregnancy*. New York: Praeger.

Leigh, B. C. (1990). "Alcohol Expectancies and Reasons for Drinking: Comments from a Study of Sexuality." *Psychology of Addictive Behaviors*, 4(2), 91–96.

Leitenberg, H., Detzer, M. J., & Srebnik, D. (1993). "Gender Differences in Masturbation and the Relation of Masturbation Experience in Preadolescence and Early Adolescence to Sexual Behavior and Sexual Adjustment in Young Adulthood." *Archives of Sexual Behavior*, 22(2), 87–98.

Lemkau, J. P. (1988). "Emotional Sequelae of Abortion: Implications for Clinical Practice." Special Issue: Women's Health: Our Minds, Our Bodies. *Psychology of Women Quarterly*, 12, 461–472.

Lenz, R., & Chaves, B. (1981). "Becoming Active Partners: A Couple's Perspective." In D. Bullard & S. Knight (Eds.), *Sexuality and Disability: Personal Perspectives*. St. Louis, MO: Mosby.

Leo, J. (1986, November 26). "Sex and Schools." *Time*, pp. 54–63.

Leonard, A. S. (1991). "From Law: Homophobia, Heterosexism and Judicial Decision Making." *Journal of Gay and Lesbian Psychotherapy*, 1, 65–91.

Lerner, H. E. (1976). "Parental Mislabeling of Female Genitals as a Determinant of Penis Envy and Learning Inhibitions in Women." *Journal of the American Psychoanalytic Association*, 24, 269–283.

"Lesbians' Cancer Risk Estimated to Be High." (1993, February 5). *San Jose Mercury News*, p. 8.

Lester, J. (1973, July). "Men: Being a Boy." *Ms.*, pp. 112–113.

Le Vay, S. (1991). "A Difference in Hypothalamic Structure Between Heterosexual and Homosexual Men." *Science*, 253, 1034–1037.

Levin, R. J. (1975). "The Redbook Report on Premarital and Extramarital Sex: The End of the Double Standard?" *Redbook*, 38–44, 190–192.

Levine, L., & Barbach, L. (1983). *The Intimate Male*. New York: Signet Books.

Levine, M. P., & Troiden, R. (1988). "The Myth of Sexual Compulsivity." *Journal of Sex Research*, 25(3), 347–363.

Levine, M. P. (1987). *How Schools Can Help Combat Student Eating Disorders: Anorexia Nervosa and Bulimia*. Washington, DC: National Education Association.

Levine, M. P. (1992). "The Life and Death of Gay Clones." In G. Herdt (Ed.), *Gay Culture in America: Essays from the Field*. Boston: Beacon Press.

Levine, M. P. (1993). "The Role of Culture in Eating Disorders." In D. N. Suggs & A. W. Miracle (Eds.), *Culture and Human Sexuality*. Pacific Grove, CA: Brooks/Cole.

Levine, S. (1987). "More on the Nature of Desire." *Journal of Sex and Marital Therapy*, 13(1), 35–44.

Levine, S. B., Risen, C. B., & Althof, A. E. (1990). "Essay on the Diagnosis and Nature of Paraphilia." *Journal of Sex and Marital Therapy*, 16(2), 89–102.

Levy, J. A. (1988). "Transmission of AIDS: The Case of the Infected Cell." *JAMA: Journal of the American Medical Association*, 259, 3037–3038.

Lewes, K. (1992). "Homophobia and the Heterosexual Fear of AIDS." *American Imago*, 49(3), 343–356.

Lewis, D. (1890). *Chastity: or, Our Secret Sins*. Philadelphia: G. Maclean.

Lewis, L. (1992). "Consumer Girl Culture: How Music Video Appeals to Girls." In M. E. Brown (Ed.), *Television and Women's Culture: The Politics of the Popular*. Newbury Park, CA: Sage Publications.

Li, C. K. (1990). "'The Main Thing Is Being Wanted': Some Case Studies in Adult Sexual Experiences with Children." *Journal of Homosexuality*, 20(1-2), 129–143.

Libman, E. (1989, July). "Sociocultural and Cognitive Factors in Aging and Sexual Expression: Conceptual and Research Issues." *Canadian Psychology*, 30(3), 560–567.

Lieberman, B. (1988). "Extrapremarital Intercourse: Attitudes Toward a Neglected Sexual Behavior." *Journal of Sex Research*, 24, 291–299.

Lieberson, S., & Waters, M. (1988). *From Many Strands: Ethnic and Racial Groups in Contemporary America*. New York: Russell Sage Foundation.

Lief, H. I., & Hubschman, L. (1993). "Orgasm in the Postoperative Transsexual." *Archives of Sexual Behavior*, 22(2), 145–155.

Lifson, A. R. (1988). "Do Alternative Modes for Transmission of Human Immunodeficiency Virus Exist?" *JAMA: Journal of the American Medical Association*, 152, 1353–1357.

Lifson, A. R., et al. (1990). "HIV Seroconversion in Two Homosexual Men After Receptive Oral Intercourse with Ejaculation: Implications for Counseling Concerning Safe Sex Practices." *American Journal of Public Health*, 80(12), 1509–1511.

Lindbohm, M. L., Hietanan, M., Kyronen, P., & Sallmen, M. (1992). "Magnetic Fields of Video Display Terminals and Spontaneous Abortion." *American Journal of Epidemiology*, 136, 1041–1051.

Lindemalm, G., Korlin, D., & Uddenberg, N. (1986). "Long-Term Follow-Up of 'Sex Change' in 13 Male-to-Female Transsexuals." *Archives of Sexual Behavior*, 15(3), 187–210.

Lino, M. (1990). "Expenditures on a Child by Husband-Wife Families." *Family Economics Review*, 3(3), 2–12.

Lipman, A. (1986). "Homosexual Relationships." *Generations*, 10, 51–54.

Lips, H. (1992). *Sex and Gender*. Mountain View, CA: Mayfield.

Longo, R. E., & Groth, A. N. (1983). "Juvenile Sexual Offenses in the Histories of Adult Rapists and Child Molesters." *International Journal of Offender Therapy & Comparative Criminology*, 27, 150–155.

Lont, C. (1990). "The Roles Assigned to Females and Males in Non-Music Programming." *Sex Roles*, 22(9-10), 661–668.

LoPiccolo, J. (1991). "Counseling and Therapy for Sexual Problems in the Elderly." *Clinics in Geriatric Medicine*, 7, 161–179.

LoPresto, C., Sherman, M., & Sherman, N. (1985). "The Effects of a Masturbation Seminar on High School Males' Attitudes, False Beliefs, Guilt, and Behavior." *Journal of Sex Research*, 21, 142–156.

Lord, L. (1985, December 9). "Mortality." *U.S. News and World Report*, pp. 52–59.

Lord, L., et al. (1987, November 30). "Coming to Grips with Alcoholism." *U.S. News and World Report*, pp. 56–62.

Lorefice, L. (1991). "Fluoxitine Treatment of a Fetish." *Journal of Clinical Psychiatry, 52*(1), 41.

Losh-Hesselbart, S. (1987). "Development of Gender Roles." In M. Sussman & S. Steinmetz (Eds.), *Handbook of Marriage and the Family*. New York: Plenum Press.

Lott, B. (1990). "Dual Natures or Learned Behavior: The Challenge to Feminist Psychology." In R. T. Hare-Mustin & J. Marecek (Eds.), *Making a Difference: Psychology and the Construction of Gender*. New Haven, CT: Yale University Press.

Loulan, J. (1984). *Lesbian Sex*. San Francisco: Spinsters Book Company.

Lowry, D., & Towles, D. (1989). "Prime-Time TV Portrayals of Sex, Contraception, and Venereal Disease." *Journalism Quarterly, 66*(2), 347–352.

Lucas, V. A. (1992). "An Investigation of the Health Care Preferences of the Lesbian Population." *Health Care for Women International, 13*(2), 221–228.

Luker, K. (1975). *Taking Chances*. Berkeley: University of California Press.

Lunneborg, P. (1992). *Abortion: The Positive Decision*. New York: Bergin & Garvy.

Luria, Z., et al. (1987). *Human Sexuality*. New York: John Wiley.

Lynch, F. R. (1992). "Nonghetto Gays: An Ethnography of Suburban Homosexuals." In G. Herdt (Ed.), *Gay Culture in America: Essays from the Field*. Boston: Beacon Press.

Lyon, J. (1985). *Playing God in the Nursery*. New York: Norton.

Maccato, M. L., & Kaufman, R. H. (1992). "Herpes Genitalis." *Dermatologic Clinics, 10*(2), 415–422.

MacDonald, A., Jr. (1981). "Bisexuality: Some Comments on Research and Theory." *Journal of Homosexuality, 6*, 9–27.

Macdonald, P. T., Waldorf, D., Reinarman, C., & Murphy, S. (1988). "Heavy Cocaine Use and Sexual Behavior." *Journal of Drug Issues, 18*(3), 437–455.

Mackey, T., et al. (1992). "Factors Associated with Long-term Depressive Symptoms of Sexual Assault Victims." *Archives of Psychiatric Nursing, 6*(1), 10–25.

Macklin, E. (1987). "Nontraditional Family Forms." In M. Sussman & S. Steinmetz (Eds.), *Handbook of Marriage and the Family*. New York: Plenum Press.

Madaras, L., & Patterson, J. (1984). *Womancare: A Gynecological Guide to Your Body*. New York: Avon.

Maddock, J. W., et al. (1983). "Human Sexuality and the Family." New York: Haworth Press.

Madsen, W. (1973). *Mexican-American Youth of South Texas*. (2nd ed.). New York: Holt, Rinehart & Winston.

Major, B., & Cozzarelli, C. (1992). "Psychosocial Predictors of Adjustment to Abortion." *Journal of Social Issues, 48*(3), 121–142.

Malamuth, N. (1981). "Rape Fantasies as a Function of Exposure to Violent Sexual Stimuli." *Archives of Sexual Behavior, 10*(1), 33–47.

Malamuth, N., & Spinner, B. (1980). "A Longitudinal Content Analysis of Sexual Violence in Best-Selling Erotic Magazines." *Journal of Sex Research, 16*(3), 226–237.

Malatesta, V., Chambless, D., Pollack, M., & Cantor, A. (1989). "Widowhood, Sexuality, and Aging: A Life Span Analysis." *Journal of Sex and Marital Therapy, 14*(1), 49–62.

Mancini, J., & Bliezner, R. (1991). "Aging Parents and Adult Children Research Themes in Intergenerational Relations." In A. Booth (Ed.), *Contemporary Families: Looking Forward, Looking Back*. Minneapolis, MN: National Council on Family Relations.

Mancini, J. A., & Blieszner, R. (1992). "Social Provisions in Adulthood: Concept and Measurement in Close Relationships." *Journal of Gerontology, 47*(1), P14–P20.

Mandoki, M. W., Sumner, G. S., Hoffman, R. P., & Riconda, D. L. (1991). "A Review of Klinefelter's Syndrome in Children and Adolescents." *Journal of the American Academy of Child and Adolescence Psychiatry, 30*(2), 167–172.

Mangasarian, L. (1993, June 5). "Experts Say AIDS Spreading into Adolescent Population." *San Jose Mercury News*, p. 6A.

Mann, J. M., et al. (1986). "Prevalence of HTLV-III/LAV in Household Contacts of Patients with Confirmed AIDS and Controls in Kinshasa, Zaire." *JAMA: Journal of the American Medical Association, 256*, 721–724.

Mansnerus, L. (1990, April 24). "The Cincinnati Case: What Are the Issues? What Is at Stake?" *The New York Times*, pp. B1, B3.

Marcus, S. (1964). *The Other Victorians*. New York: Basic Books.

Marecek, J., et al. (1988). "Gender Roles in the Relationships of Lesbians and Gay Men." In J. De Cecco (Ed.), *Gay Relationships*. New York: Haworth Press.

Margiglio, W. (1991). "Male Procreative Consciousness and Responsibility: A Conceptual Analysis and Research Agenda." *Journal of Family Issues, 12*, 268–290.

Margiglio, W., & Donnelly, D. (1991). "Sexual Relations in Later Life: A National Study of Married Persons." *Journal of Gerontology, 46*, S338–S344.

Margolies, L., Becher, M., & Jackson-Brewer, K. (1988). "Internalized Homophobia: Identifying and Treating the Oppressor Within." In Boston Lesbian Psychologies Collective (Eds.), *Lesbian Psychologies*. Urbana, IL: University of Illinois Press.

Margolin, L. (1992). "Sexual Abuse by Grandparents." *Child Abuse and Neglect, 16*(5), 735–742.

Margolin, L., & White, L. (1987). "The Continuing Role of Physical Attractiveness in Marriage." *Journal of Marriage and the Family, 49*, 21–27.

Margolin, M. (1978). *The Ohlone Way*. Berkeley, CA: Heyday Books.

Marieb, E. N. (1992). *Human Anatomy and Physiology*. (2nd ed.). Redwood City, CA: Benjamin/Cummings.

Marin, G., & Marin, B. V. (1989). "A Comparison of Three Interviewing Approaches for Studying Sensitive Topics with Hispanics." *Hispanic Journal of the Behavioral Sciences, 11*(4), 330–340.

Marin, G., & Marin, B. (1991). *Research with Hispanic Populations*. Newbury Park, CA: Sage Publications.

Markman, H. (1981). "Prediction of Marital Distress: A Five-Year Follow-Up." *Journal of Consulting and Clinical Psychology, 49*, 760–761.

Markman, H., Duncan, W., Storaasli, R. D., & Howes, P. W. (1987). "The Prediction and Prevention of Marital Distress: A Longitudinal Investigation." In K. Hahlweg & M. Goldstein (Eds.), *Understanding Major Mental Disorders: The Contribution of Family Interaction Research*. New York: Family Process Press.

Markman, H., Floyd, F. J., Stanley, S. M., & Storaasli, R. D. (1988). "Prevention of Marital Distress: A Longitudinal Investigation." *Journal of Consulting and Clinical Psychology, 56*(2), 210–217.

Markowitz, L., et al. (1987). "Toxic Shock Syndrome: Evaluation of National Surveillance Data Using a Hospital Discharge Survey." *JAMA: Journal of the American Medical Association, 258*(1), 75–78.

Marmor, J. (1980). "Homosexuality and the Issue of Mental Illness." In J. Marmor (Ed.), *Homosexual Behavior*. New York: Basic Books.

Marmor, J. (Ed.). (1980). *Homosexual Behavior*. New York: Basic Books.

Marmor, J. (1980). "The Multiple Roots of Homosexual Behavior." In J. Marmor (Ed.), *Homosexual Behavior*. New York: Basic Books.

Marrero, M. A., & Ory, S. J. (1991). "Unexplained Infertility." *Current Opinion in Obstetrics and Gynecology, 3*(2), 211–218.

Marshall, D. (1971). "Sexual Behavior on Mangaia." In D. Marshall & R. Suggs (Eds.), *Human Sexual Behavior*. New York: Basic Books.

Marshall, P., et al. (1981). "The Role of Nocturnal Penile Tumescence in Differentiating Between Organic and Psychogenic Impotence." *Archives of Sexual Behavior*, 10(1), 1–10.

Marshall, W. L. (1988). "The Use of Sexually Explicit Material by Rapists, Child Molesters, and Non-Offenders." *Journal of Sex Research*, 25, 267–268.

Marshall, W. L., Eccles, A., & Barabee, H. E. (1991). "The Treatment of Exhibitionism: A Focus on Sexual Deviance Versus Cognitive and Relationship Features." *Behaviour Research and Therapy*, 29(2), 129–135.

Marshall, W. L., Payne, K., Barabee, H. E., & Eccles, A. (1991). "Exhibitionism: Sexual Preference for Exposing." *Behaviour Research and Therapy*, 29(1), 37–40.

Marsiglio, W., & Donnelly, D. (1991). "Sexual Relations in Later Life: A National Study of Married Persons." *Journal of Gerontology*, 46(6), S338–S344.

Marsiglio, W., & Mott, F. (1986). "The Impact of Sex Education on Sexual Activity, Contraceptive Use and Premarital Pregnancy Among American Teenagers." *Family Planning Perspectives*, 18(4), 215ff.

Martin, G. (1989). "Relationship, Romance, and Sexual Addiction in Extramarital Affairs." *Journal of Psychology and Christianity*, 8(4), 5–25.

Martin, G. (1992, October 16). "Justify Her Love." *San Jose Mercury News*, pp. 1, 4.

Martin, P. (1981). "Happy Sexless Marriages." *Medical Aspects of Human Sexuality*, 15(1), 25.

Martin, P. M., Gresenguet, G., Massanga, M., Georges, A., & Testa, J. (1992). "Association Between HIV1 Infection and Sexually Transmitted Disease Among Men in Central Africa." *Research in Virology*, 143(3), 205–209.

Martin, T. C., & Bumpass, L. L. (1989). "Recent Trends in Marital Disruption." *Demography*, 26, 37–51.

Marx, J. L. (1989). "Circumcision May Protect Against the AIDS Virus." *Science*, 245, 470–471.

Mason, K., & Lu, Y. H. (1988). "Attitudes Toward Women's Familial Roles: Changes in the United States, 1977–1985." *Gender and Society*, 2(1), 39–57.

Massa, G., Maes, M., Heinrichs, C., Vandeweghe, M., Craen, M., & Vanderschueren-Lodeweyckx, M. (1993). "Influence of Spontaneous or Induced Puberty on the Growth Promoting Effect of Treatment with Growth Hormone in Girls with Turner's Syndrome." *Clinical Endocrinology*, 38(3), 253–260.

"Massachusetts Midwife Curb Upheld." (1987, May 25). *The New York Times*, p. 5.

Masse, M., & Rosenblum, K. (1988). "Male and Female Created They Them: The Depiction of Gender in the Advertising of Traditional Women's and Men's Magazines." *Women's Studies International Forum*, 11(2), 127–144.

Massey, F. J., et al. (1984). "Vasectomy and Health: Results from a Large Cohort Study." *JAMA: Journal of the American Medical Association*, 252, 1023–1029.

Masters, W. H., & Johnson, V. E. (1966). *Human Sexual Response*. Boston: Little, Brown.

Masters, W. H., & Johnson, V. E. (1970). *Human Sexual Inadequacy*. Boston: Little, Brown.

Masters, W. H., & Johnson, V. E. (1974). *The Pleasure Bond*. Boston: Little, Brown.

Masters, W. H., & Johnson, V. E. (1979). *Homosexuality in Perspective*. Boston: Little, Brown.

Masters, W. H., Johnson, V. E., & Kolodny, R. C. (1985). *Human Sexuality* (2nd ed.). New York: Little, Brown.

Masters, W. H., Johnson, V. E., & Kolodny, R. C. (1986). *Masters and Johnson on Sex and Human Loving*. Boston: Little, Brown.

Masters, W. H., Johnson, V. E., & Kolodny, R. C. (1988). *Crisis: AIDS and Heterosexual Behavior*. New York: Grove Press.

Masters, W. H., Johnson, V., & Kolodny, R. C. (1992). *Human Sexuality* (3rd ed.). New York: HarperCollins.

Matek, O. (1988). "Obscene Phone Callers." In D. Dailey (Ed.), *The Sexually Unusual*. New York: Harrington Park Press.

Mathur, A., Stetol, L., Schatz, D., Maclaren, N. K., Scott, M. L., & Lippe, B. (1991). "The Parental Origin of the Single X Chromosome in Turner Syndrome: Lack of Correlation with Parental Age or Clinical Phenotype." *American Journal of Human Genetics*, 48(4), 682–686.

Matteo, S., & Rissman, E. (1984). "Increased Sexual Activity During Midcycle Portion of the Human Menstrual Cycle." *Hormones and Behavior*, 18, 249–255.

Mays, V. M., Cochran, S. D., Bellinger, G., & Smith, R. G. (1992). "The Language of Black Gay Men's Sexual Behavior: Implications for AIDS Risk Reduction." *Journal of Sex Research*, 29(3), 425–434.

Mays, V. M., & Jackson, J. S. (1991). "AIDS Survey Methodology with Black Americans." *Social Science and Medicine*, 33(1), 47–54.

Mazor, M., & Simons, H. (Eds.). (1984). *Infertility: Medical, Emotional and Social Considerations*. New York: Human Sciences Press.

Mazur, A. (1986). "U.S. Trends in Feminine Beauty and Overadaptation." *Journal of Sex Research*, 22(3), 281–303.

McAnich, J. (1989). "Editorial Comment on the Report of the Task Force on Circumcision." *Pediatrics*, 84, 667.

McCabe, M. P., & Collins, J. K. (1984). "Measurement of Depth of Desired and Experienced Sexual Involvement at Different Stages of Dating." *Journal of Sex Research*, 20, 377–390.

McCauley, E., & Ehrhardt, A. (1980). "Female Sexual Response." In D. Youngs & A. Ehrhardt (Eds.), *Psychosomatic Obstetrics and Gynecology*. New York: Appleton-Century-Crofts.

McClure, D. (1988, May). "Men with One Testicle." *Medical Aspects of Human Sexuality*, 22–32.

McClary, S. (1990). "Living to Tell: Madonna's Resurrection of the Fleshy." *Genders*, 7, 1–21.

McCormack, M. J., et al. (1990). "Patient's Attitudes Following Chorionic Villus Sampling." *Prenatal Diagnosis*, 10(4), 253–255.

McEwan, K. L., Costello, C. G., & Taylor, P. J. (1987). "Adjustment to Infertility." *Journal of Abnormal Psychology*, 96(2), 108–116.

McGoldrick, M. (1982). "Normal Families: An Ethnic Perspective." In F. Walsh (Ed.), *Normal Family Processes*. New York: Guilford Press.

McGoldrick, M., Pearce, J. K., & Giordano, J. (Eds.). (1982). *Ethnicity and Family Therapy*. New York: Guilford Press.

McIntosh, E. (1989). "An Investigation of Romantic Jealousy Among Black Undergraduates." *Social Behavior and Personality*, 17(2), 135–141.

McIntosh, E., & Tate, D. T. (1990). "Correlates of Jealous Behaviors." *Psychological Reports*, 66(2), 601–602.

McIntyre, I. (1980). "Victim Response to Rape: Alternative Outcomes." *Final Report to the National Institute of Mental Health* R01MH 29043, Rockville, MD: National Institute of Mental Health.

McIntyre, S. L., & Higgins, J. E. (1986). "Parity and Use-Effectiveness with the Contraceptive Sponge." *American Journal of Obstetrics and Gynecology*, 155, 796–801.

McKusick, L., Contes, T. J., Morin, S. F., & Pollack, L. (1990). "Longitudinal Predictors of Reductions in Unprotected Anal Intercourse Among Gay Men in San Francisco: The AIDS Behavioral Research Project." *American Journal of Public Health*, 80(8), 978–973.

McLaurin, M. (1991). *Celia: A Slave*. Athens, GA: University of Georgia Press.

McLeer, S. V., et al. (1992). "Sexually Abused Children at High Risk for Post-Traumatic Stress Disorder." *Journal of the American Academy of Child and Adolescent Psychiatry*, 31(5), 875–879.

McMahon, K. (1990). "The Cosmopolitan Ideology and the Management of Desire." *Journal of Sex Research*, 27(3), 381–396.

McMullen, R. (1987). "Youth Prostitution: A Balance of Power." *Journal of Adolescence*, 10, 35–43.

McNeeley, S. G., Jr. (1992). "Pelvic Inflammatory Disease." *Current Opinion in Obstetrics and Gynecology*, 4(5), 682–686.

McWhirter, D. (1990). "Prologue." In D. McWhirter, S. A. Sanders, & J. M. Reinisch (Eds.), *Homosexuality/Heterosexuality: Concepts of Sexual Orientation*. New York: Oxford University Press.

McWhirter, D., Sanders, S. A., & Reinisch, J. M. (Eds.). (1990). *Homosexuality/Heterosexuality: Concepts of Sexual Orientation*. New York: Oxford University Press.

Meacham, R. E., & Lipshultz, L. I. (1991). "Assisted Reproductive Technologies for Male Factor Infertility." *Current Opinion in Obstetrics and Gynecology*, 3(5), 656–661.

Mead, M. (1975). *Male and Female*. New York: William Morrow.

Meek, T. D., et al. (1990). "Inhibition of HIV-1 Protease in Infected T-lymphocytes by Synthetic Peptide Analogues." *Nature*, 343(6253), 90–92.

Meier, K. J., & McFarlane, D. R. (1993). "The Politics of Funding Abortion: State Responses to the Political Environment." *American Politics Quarterly*, 21(1), 81–101.

Mengel, M. B. (1989). "Diagnostic Criteria for Bacterial Vaginosis." *Journal of Family Practice*, 29, 359–360.

Menning, B. E. (1988). *Infertility: A Guide for Childless Couples*. Englewood Cliffs, NJ: Prentice-Hall.

Merson, M. H. (1993). "Slowing the Spread of HIV: Agenda for the 1990s." *Science*, 260(5112), 1266–1268.

Mertz, G. J., Benedetti, J., Ashley, R., Selke, S. A., & Corey, L. (1992). "Risk Factors for the Sexual Transmission of Genital Herpes." *Annals of Internal Medicine*, 116(3), 197–202.

Metts, S., & Cupach, W. (1989). "The Role of Communication in Human Sexuality." In K. McKinney & S. Sprecher (Eds.), *Human Sexuality: The Social and Interpersonal Context*. Norwood, NJ: Ablex.

Meuwissen, I., & Over, R. (1992). "Sexual Arousal Across Phases of the Human Menstrual Cycle." *Archives of Sexual Behavior*, 21, 101–119.

Milan, R., Jr., & Kilmann, P. (1987). "Interpersonal Factors in Premarital Contraception." *Journal of Sex Research*, 23(3), 321–389.

Miller, B. (1986). *Family Research Methods*. Newbury Park, CA: Sage Publications.

Miller, B. C., Christopherson, C. R., & King, P. K. (1993). "Sexual Behavior in Adolescence." In T. P. Gullotta et al. (Eds.), *Adolescent Sexuality*. Newbury Park, CA: Sage Publications.

Miller, B. C., & Dyk, P. A. (1990). "Adolescent Fertility-Related Behavior in the 1990s: Risking the Future Continued." *Journal of Family Issues*, 11(3), 235–238.

Miller, B. C., & Fox, G. L. (1987). "Theories of Adolescent Heterosexual Behavior." *Adolescent Research*, 2, 269–282.

Miller, E. M. (1986). *Street Women*. Philadelphia: Temple University Press.

Miller, W. (1981). "Psychological Vulnerability to Unwanted Pregnancy." In F. Furstenberg et al. (Eds.), *Teenage Sexuality, Pregnancy, and Childbearing*. Philadelphia: University of Pennsylvania Press.

Mindel, C. H., Haberstein, R. W., & Wright, Roosevelt, Jr. (Eds.). (1988). *Ethnic Families in America: Patterns and Variations* (3rd ed.). New York: Elsevier North Holland.

Minkoff, H. L. (1989). "AIDS in Pregnancy." *Current Problems in Obstetrics, Gynecology and Fertility*, 12, 205–228.

Minkoff, H. L., & Dehovitz, J. A. (1991). "Care of Women Infected with the Human Immunodeficiency Virus." *JAMA: Journal of the American Medical Association*, 266(16), 2253–2258.

Mio, J. S., & Foster, J. D. (1991). "The Effects of Rape Upon Victims and Families: Implications for a Comprehensive Family Therapy." *American Journal of Family Therapy*, 19(2), 147–159.

Mison, R. B. (1992). "Homophobia in Manslaughter: The Homosexual Advance as Provocation." *California Law Review*, 80(1), 133–178.

Moergen, S., Merkel, W. T., & Brown, S. (1990). "The Use of Covert Sensitization and Social Skills Training in Treatment of an Obscene Phone Caller." *Journal of Behavior Therapy and Experimental Psychology*, 21(4), 269–275.

Moffatt, M. (1989). *Coming of Age in New Jersey: College and American Culture*. New Brunswick, NJ: Rutgers University Press.

Mohr, J., & Beutler, I. (1990). "Erectile Dysfunction: A Review of Diagnostic and and Treatment Procedures." *Clinical Psychology Review*, 10, 123–150.

Moller, L. C., Hymel, S., & Rubin, K. H. (1992). "Sex Typing in Play and Popularity in Middle Childhood." *Sex Roles*, 26(7-8), 331–335.

Monat-Haller, R. K. (1982). *Sexuality and the Mentally Retarded: A Clinical and Therapeutic Guidebook*. San Diego, CA: College Hill Press.

Money, J. (1980). *Love and Lovesickness*. Baltimore: Johns Hopkins University Press.

Money, J. (1986). "Statements of the Shadow Commissioners." In P. Nobile (Ed.), *United States of America vs. Sex: How the Meese Commission Lied About Pornography*. New York: Minotaur Press.

Money, J. (1988). "Commentary: Current Status of Sex Research." *Journal of Psychology and Human Sexuality*, 1(1), 5–16.

Money, J. (1988). *Gay, Straight, and In-Between*. New York: Oxford University Press.

Money, J. (1990). "Forensic Sexology: Paraphilic Serial Rape (Biastophilia) and Lust Murder (Erotophonophilia)." *American Journal of Psychotherapy*, 44(1), 26–37.

Money, J., & Tucker, P. (1976). *Sexual Signatures: On Being a Man or a Woman*. London: Harrap.

Montagu, A. (1986). *Touching* (3rd ed.). New York: Columbia University Press.

Montauk, S., & Clasen, M. (1989, January). "Sex Education in Primary Care: Infancy to Puberty." *Medical Aspects of Human Sexuality*, 22–36.

Moore, L. J. (1988, May 9). "Protecting Babies from Hepatitis-B." *U.S. News & World Report*, p. 85.

Moore, M. M. (1985). "Nonverbal Courtship Patterns in Women: Context and Consequences." *Ethology and Sociobiology*, 6(2), 237–247.

Moran, J. S., et al. (1989). "The Impact of Sexually Transmitted Diseases on Minority Populations." *Public Health Reports*, 104(6), 560–564.

Moran, J. S., Janes, H. R., Peterman, T. A., & Stone, K. M. (1990). "Increase in Condom Sales Following AIDS Education and Publicity, United States." *American Journal of Public Health*, 80(5), 607–608.

Morawski, J. G. (1990). "Toward the Unimagined: Feminism and Epistemology in Psychology." In R. T. Hare-Mustin & J. Marecek (Eds.), *Making a Difference: Psychology and the Construction of Gender*. New Haven, CT: Yale University Press.

Morgenthaler, E. (1992, January 23). "These Thieves Are Partial to Sequins, and Pretty in Pink: Gangs of Florida Transvestites Steal Millions in Dresses." *The Wall Street Journal*, p. 1.

Morin, J. (1986). *Anal Pleasure and Health: A Guide for Men and Women*. Burlingame, CA: Yes Press.

Morokoff, P. (1986). "Volunteer Bias in the Psychophysiological Study of Female Sexuality." *Journal of Sex Research*, 22(1), 35–51.

Morse, E. V., et al. (1991). "The Male Street Prostitute: A Vector for Transmission of HIV Infection into the Heterosexual World." *Social Science and Medicine*, 32(5), 535–539.

Moser, C. (1988). "Sadomasochism." In D. Dailey (Ed.), *The Sexually Unusual*. New York: Harrington Park Press.

Mosher, D. L., & Tomkins, S. S. (1988). "Scripting the Macho Man: Hypermasculine Socialization and Enculturation." *Journal of Sex Research, 25*, 60–84.

Moss, G. B., et al. (1991). "Association of Cervical Ectopy with Heterosexual Transmission of Human Immunodeficiency Virus: Results of a Study of Couples in Nairobi, Kenya." *Journal of Infectious Diseases, 164*(3), 588–591.

Mota, R. G. (1991). "Project First Hand: The Power of HIV-Infected Educators in AIDS Prevention." *Exchange: World Health Organization Global Program on AIDS, 1*, 1–12.

Mota, R. G. (1992, July). "Breast-Feeding and HIV Transmission." *I.H.P.: International Health Programs Newsletter, 1*, 1ff.

Moultrup, D. J. (1990). *Husbands, Wives, and Lovers: The Emotional System of the Extramarital Affair*. New York: Guilford Press.

Muehlenhard, C. L. (1988). "Misinterpreted Dating Behaviors and the Risk of Date Rape." *Journal of Social and Clinical Psychology, 9*(1), 20–37.

Muehlenhard, C. L., & Cook, S. W. (1988). "Mens' Self-Reports of Unwanted Sexual Activity." *Journal of Sex Research, 24*, 58–72.

Muehlenhard, C. L., & Hollabaugh, L. C. (1988). "Do Women Sometimes Say No When They Mean Yes? The Prevalence and Correlates of Women's Token Resistance to Sex." *Journal of Personality and Social Psychology, 54*, 872–879.

Muehlenhard, C. L., & Linton, M. (1987). "Date Rape and Sexual Aggression in Dating Situations." *Journal of Consulting Psychology, 34*, 186–196.

Muehlenhard, C. L., & McCoy, M. L. (1991). "Double Standard/Double Bind." *Psychology of Women Quarterly, 15*, 447–461.

Muehlenhard, C. L., Ponch, I. G., Phelps, J. L., & Giusti, L. M. (1992). "Definitions of Rape: Scientific and Political Implications." *Journal of Social Issues, 48*(1), 23–44.

Muehlenhard, C. L., & Schrag, J. (1991). "Nonviolent Sexual Coercion." In A. Parrot & L. Bechhofer (Eds.), *Acquaintance Rape: The Hidden Crime*. New York: John Wiley.

Mueller, B. A., et al. (1992). "Risk Factors for Tubal Infertility: Influence of History of Prior Pelvic Inflammatory Disease." *Sexually Transmitted Diseases, 19*(1), 28–34.

Mulligan, T., & Moss, C. R. (1991). "Sexuality and Aging in Male Veterans: A Cross-Sectional Study of Interest, Ability, and Activity." *Archives of Sexual Behavior, 20*(1), 17–25.

Mulligan, T., & Palguta, R. (1991). "Sexual Interest, Activity, and Satisfaction Among Male Nursing Home Residents." *Archives of Sexual Behavior, 20*(2), 199–204.

Mulligan, T., Retchin, S. M., Chinchilli, V. M., & Bettinger, C. B. (1988). "The Role of Aging and Chronic Disease in Sexual Dysfunction." *Journal of the American Geriatrics Society, 36*(6), 520–524.

Mullins, L. L., Lynch, J., Orten, J., Youll, L. K., Verschraegen-Spae, Dypere, H., Speleman, F., Dhoult, M., & DePaepe, A. (1991). "Developing a Program to Assist Turner's Syndrome Patients and Families." *Social Work in Health Care, 16*(2), 69–79.

Muram, D., Miller, K., & Cutler, A. (1992). "Sexual Assault of the Elderly Victim." *Journal of Interpersonal Violence, 7*(1), 70–76.

Murnen, S. K., Perot, A., & Byrne, D. (1989). "Coping with Unwanted Sexual Activity: Normative Responses, Situational Determinants, and Individual Differences." *Journal of Sex Research, 26*, 85–106.

Murray, T. E. (1989). *The Language of Sadomasochism*. New York: Greenwood Press.

Murry, V. M. (1991). "Socio-Historical Study of Black Female Sexuality: Transition to First Coitus." In R. Staples (Ed.), *The Black Family* (4th ed.). Belmont, CA: Wadsworth.

Murstein, B. (1976). *Who Will Marry Whom: Theories and Research in Marital Choice*. New York: Springer.

Murstein, B. (1987). "A Clarification and Extension of the SVR Theory of Dyadic Pairing." *Journal of Marriage and the Family, 49*, 929–933.

Mydans, S. (1992, November 21). "Christian Conservatives Counting Hundreds of Gains in Local Votes." *The New York Times*, p. A1ff.

Nadelson, C. C. (1990). "Consequences of Rape: Clinical and Treatment Aspects." *Psychotherapy and Psychosomatics, 51*(4), 187–192.

Nadelson, C., & Sauzier, M. (1986). "Intervention Programs for Individual Victims and Their Families." In M. Lystad (Ed.), *Violence in the Home: Interdisciplinary Perspectives*. New York: Brunner/Mazel.

Nakamura, R. M., et al. (1988). "In Vitro Condom Testing." *IV International Conference on AIDS*, Stockholm, #6510.

National Victim Center. (1992). *Rape in America: A Report to the Nation*. Charleston, SC: Crime Victims Research and Treatment Center.

Nava, M. (1990). *How Town*. New York: Ballantine Books.

Navarro, M. (1992, November 23). "Trials and Triumphs Emerge for HIV-Infected Workers." *The New York Times*, pp. A1, A12.

Navarro, M. (1993, January 11). "Healthy, Gay, Guilt-Striken: AIDS' Toll on the Virus-Free." *The New York Times*, pp. A1, A16.

Neidigh, L., & Kinder, B. (1987). "The Use of Audiovisual Materials in Sex Therapy: A Critical Overview." *Journal of Sex and Marital Therapy, 13*(1), 64–72.

Nelson, K. E., Vlahov, D., Cohn, S., Odunmbaku, M., Lindsay, A., Antohony, J. C., & Hook, E. W. (1991). "Sexually Transmitted Diseases in a Population of Intravenous Drug Users: Association with Seropositivity to the Human Immunodeficiency Virus (HIV)." *Journal of Infectious Diseases, 164*(3), 457–463.

"Neonatal Herpes Is Preventable." (1984, February). *U.S.A. Today*, pp. 8–9.

Nestle, J. (1983). "The Fem Question." In C. Vance (Ed.), *Pleasure and Danger*. New York: Routledge & Kegan Paul.

Newcomb, M. (1979). "Cohabitation in America: An Assessment of Consequences." *Journal of Marriage and the Family*, 597–603.

Newcomb, M., & Bentler, P. (1980). "Assessment of Personality and Demographics Aspects of Cohabitation and Marital Success." *Journal of Personality Development, 4*(1), 11–24.

Newcomer, S., & Udry, R. (1985). "Oral Sex in an Adolescent Population." *Archives of Sexual Behavior, 14*(1), 41–46.

Newton, N. (1955). *Maternal Emotions*. New York: Basic Books.

NIAID/CDC. (1991). "U.S. Public Health Service National Conference: Women and HIV Infection." *Clinical Courier, 9*(6), 1–7.

Nichols, M. (1987). "Lesbian Sexuality: Issues and Developing Theory." In Boston Lesbian Psychologies Collective (Ed.), *Lesbian Psychologies: Explorations and Challenges*. Urbana, IL: University of Illinois Press.

Nichols, M. (1988). "Bisexuality in Women: Myths, Realities, and Implications for Therapy." Special Issue: Women and Sex Therapy. *Women and Therapy, 7*, 235–252.

Niebuhr, R. E., & Boyles, W. R. (1991). "Sexual Harassment of Military Personnel: An Examination of Power Differentials." Special Issue: Racial, Ethnic, and Gender Issues in the Military. *International Journal of Intercultural Relations, 15*, 445–457.

Nielson, J., & Wohlert, M. (1991). "Chromosome Abnormalities Found Among 34,910 Newborn Children: Results from a 13-Year Incidence Study in Arhus, Denmark." *Human Genetics, 87*(1), 81–83.

Nieman, L., et al. (1987). "The Progesterone Antagonist RU-486: A Potential New Contraceptive Agent." *New England Journal of Medicine, 316*(4), 187–191.

Nilsson Schonnesson, L. (1990). "Educational Requirements of Human Sexuality in the Counseling for and Prevention of Sexually Transmitted Diseases." *Seminars in Dermatology, 9*(2), 185–189.

Nock, S. (1987). "The Symbolic Meaning of Childbearing." *Journal of Family Issues*, 8(4), 373–393.

Noller, P. (1984). *Nonverbal Communication and Marital Interaction*. Oxford, England: Pergamon Press.

Noller, P., & Fitzpatrick, M. A. (1991). "Marital Communication." In A. Booth (Ed.), *Contemporary Families: Looking Forward, Looking Back*. Minneapolis, MN: National Council on Family Relations.

Norton, A. J. (1983). "Family Life Cycle: 1980." *Journal of Marriage and the Family*, 45, 267–275.

Nossiter, A. (1992, November 28). "Some Legal Experts See Intolerance as HIV and Sex are Linked to Crime." *The New York Times*, p. 6.

Notarius, C., & Johnson, J. (1982). "Emotional Expression in Husbands and Wives." *Journal of Marriage and the Family*, 44(2), 483–489.

Notman, M. T., & Lester, E. P. (1988). "Pregnancy: Theoretical Considerations." *Psychoanalytic Inquiry*, 8(2), 139–159.

Notzon, F. C., et al. (1987). "Comparisons of National Cesarean-Section Rates." *New England Journal of Medicine*, 316(7), 386–389.

Nugent, R., & Gramick, J. (1989). "Homosexuality: Protestant, Catholic, and Jewish Issues: A Fishbone Tale." *Journal of Homosexuality*, 18, 7–46.

Oakley, A. (1985). *Sex, Gender, and Society* (rev. ed.). New York: Harper & Row.

O'Carroll, R. (1989). "The Difficulty in Dealing with Deviance: An Illustrative Case Study." *Journal of Sex and Marital Therapy*, 4(2), 177–186.

Odent, M. (1984). *Birth Reborn*. New York: Pantheon.

Oehninger, S., & Alexander, N. J. (1991). "Male Infertility: The Focus Shifts to Sperm Manipulation." *Current Opinion in Obstetrics and Gynecology*, 3(2), 182–190.

O'Farrell, T. J., Choquette, K. A., & Birchler, G. R. (1991). "Sexual Satisfaction and Dissatisfaction in the Marital Relationships of Male Alcoholics Seeking Marital Therapy." *Journal of Studies on Alcohol*, 52(5), 441–447.

Ofman, U. S., & Auchincloss, S. S. (1992, August). "Sexual Dysfunction in Cancer Patients." *Current Opinion in Oncology*, 4(4), 605–613.

Okami, P. (1991). "Self-Reports of 'Positive' Childhood and Adolescent Sexual Contacts with Older Persons: An Exploratory Study." *Archives of Sexual Behavior*, 20(5), 437–457.

Olds, J. (1956). "Pleasure Centers in the Brain." *Scientific American*, 193, 105–116.

Olds, S. W. (1985). *The Eternal Garden: Seasons of Our Sexuality*. New York: Times Books.

Olshansky, E. F. (1992). "Redefining the Concepts of Success and Failure in Infertility Treatment." *Naacogs Clinical Issues in Perinatal and Women's Health Nursing*, 3(2), 343–346.

Olson, T., & Wallace, C. (1987). "Families, Decision-Making and Human Development." *Concerned Women of America*. Washington, DC.

Orbach, S. (1982). *Fat Is a Feminist Issue II: A Program to Conquer Compulsive Eating*. New York: Berkley Books.

O'Reilly, K. R., & Aral, S. O. (1985). "Adolescence and Sexual Behavior: Trends and Implications for STDs." *Journal of Adolescent Health Care*, 6(4), 262–270.

Orlofsky, J., & O'Heron, C. (1987). "Stereotypic and Nonstereotypic Sex Role Trait and Behavior Orientations: Implications for Personal Adjustment." *Journal of Personality and Social Psychology*, 52, 1034–1042.

Orten, J. L. (1990). "Coming Up Short: The Physical, Cognitive, and Social Effects of Turner's Syndrome." *Health and Social Work*, 15(2), 100–106.

Ortiz, M. E., & Croxatto, H. B. (1987). "The Mode of Action of IUDs." *Contraception*, 36(1), 37–53.

Ortiz, S., & Casas, J. M. (1990). "Birth Control and Low-Income Mexican-American Women: The Impact of Three Values." *Hispanic Journal of the Behavioral Sciences*, 12(1), 83–92.

Osborn, J. E. (1990). "Women and HIV/AIDS: The Silent Epidemic?" *SIECUS Report*, 19(2), 1–4.

Ostrow, D. G., Whitaker, R. E., Frasier, K., Cohen, C., Wan, J., Frank, C., & Fisher, E. (1991). "Racial Differences in Social Support and Mental Health in Men with HIV Infection: A Pilot Study." *AIDS Care*, 3(1), 55–62.

O'Sullivan, C. S. (1991). "Acquaintance Gang Rape on Campus." In A. Parrot & L. Bechhofer (Eds.), *Acquaintance Rape: The Hidden Crime*. New York: John Wiley.

O'Sullivan, L., & Byers, E. S. (1992). "College Students' Incorporation of Initiator and Restrictor Roles in Sexual Dating Interactions." *Journal of Sex Research*, 29(3), 435–446.

Padgett, V. R., Brislutz, J. A., & Neal, J. A. (1989). "Pornography, Erotica, and Attitudes Toward Women: The Effects of Repeated Exposure." *Journal of Sex Research*, 26, 479–491.

Padian, N. S., Shiboski, S. C., & Jewell, N. P. (1991). "Female-to-Male Transmission of Human Immunodeficiency Virus." *JAMA: Journal of the American Medical Association*, 266(12), 1664–1667.

Padilla, E. R., & O'Grady, K. E. (1987). "Sexuality among Mexican Americans: A Case of Sexual Stereotyping." *Journal of Personality and Social Psychology*, 52, 5–10.

Paludi, M. A. (1990). "Sociopsychological and Structural Factors Related to Women's Vocational Development." *Annals of the New York Academy of Sciences*, 602, 157–168.

Pan, L. Z., Sheppard, H. W., Winkelstein, W., & Levy, J. A. (1991). "Lack of Detection of Human Immunodeficiency Virus in Persistently Seronegative Homosexual Men with High or Medium Risk for Infection." *Journal of Infectious Diseases*, 164(5), 962–964.

Pang, S., Shlesinger, Y., Daar, E. S., Moudgil T., Ho, D. D., & Chen, I. S. (1992). "Rapid Generation of Sequence Variation During Primary HIV-1 Infection." *AIDS*, 6(5), 453–460.

Panuthos, C., & Romeo, C. (1984). *Ended Beginnings: Healing Childbearing Losses*. New York: Warner Books.

Panzarine, S., & Elster, A. B. (1983). "Coping in a Group of Expectant Adolescent Fathers: An Exploratory Study." *Journal of Adolescent Health Care*, 4, 117–120.

Parachini, A. (1987, February 3). "Survivorship: A New Movement Among Cancer Patients." *Los Angeles Times*, pp. 1, 2.

Parker, H., & Parker, S. (1984). "Cultural Rules, Rituals and Behavior Regulation." *American Anthropologist*, 86(3), 584–600.

Parker, H., & Parker, S. (1986). "Father-Daughter Sexual Child Abuse: An Emerging Perspective." *American Journal of Orthopsychiatry*, 56(4), 531–549.

Parker, P. (1983). "Motivation of Surrogate Mothers—Initial Findings." *American Journal of Psychiatry*, 140(1), 117–118.

Parker, R. G. (1991). *Bodies, Pleasures, and Passions*. Boston: Beacon Press.

Parrinder, G. (1980). *Sex in the World's Religions*. New York: Oxford University Press.

Parsons, T. (1955). "Family Structure and the Socialization of the Child." In T. Parsons & R. F. Bales (Eds.), *Family Socialization and Interaction Process*. Glencoe, IL: Free Press.

Patterson, C. J. (1992). "Children of Lesbian and Gay Parents." *Child Development*, 63, 1025–1042.

Patton, M. (1986). "Twentieth-Century Attitudes Toward Masturbation." *Journal of Religion and Health*, 25(4), 291–302.

Paul, J. P. (1984). "The Bisexual Identity: An Idea Without Social Recognition." *Journal of Homosexuality*, 9, 45–63.

Paul, J. P. (1993). "Childhood Cross-Gender Behavior and Adult Homosexuality: The Resurgence of Biological Models of Sexuality." *Journal of Homosexuality*, 24(3-4), 41–54.

Pauly, I., & Edgarton, M. (1986). "The Gender Identity Movement: A Growing Surgical-Psychiatric Liaison." *Archives of Sexual Behavior, 15*(4), 315–327.

Pauly, J. (1990). "Gender Identity Disorders: Evaluation and Treatment." *Journal of Sex Education and Therapy, 16*(1), 2–24.

Peacock, N. (1982). "Contraceptive Decision-Making Among Adolescent Girls." *Journal of Sex Education and Therapy, 8*, 31–34.

Pear, R. (1992, April 22). "U.S. Reports Rise in Low-Weight Births." *The New York Times*, p. A18.

Pear, R. (1993, February 7). "As AIDS Money Is Parceled Out, Political Questions." *The New York Times*, p. E3.

Pelz, L., Sager, G., Hinkel, G. K., Kirchner, M., Kruger, C., & Verron, G. (1991). "Delayed Spontaneous Pubertal Growth Spurt in Girls with the Ullrich-Turner Syndrome." *American Journal of Medical Genetics, 40*(4), 401–405.

Peo, R. (1988). "Transvestism." In D. Dailey (Ed.), *The Sexually Unusual*. New York: Harrington Park Press.

Peplau, L. (1981). "What Homosexuals Want." *Psychology Today, 15*(3), 28–38.

Peplau, L. (1988). "Research on Homosexual Couples." In J. De Cecco (Ed.), *Gay Relationships*. New York: Haworth Press.

Peplau, L., et al. (1977). "Sexual Intimacy in Dating Relationships." *Journal of Social Issues, 33*(2), 86–109.

Peplau, L., & Cochran, S. (1988). "Value Orientations in the Intimate Relationships of Gay Men." In J. De Cecco (Ed.), *Gay Relationships*. New York: Haworth Press.

Peplau, L., & Gordon, S. (1982). "The Intimate Relationships of Lesbians and Gay Men." In E. Allgeier & N. McCormick (Eds.), *Gender Roles and Sexual Behavior*. Mountain View, CA: Mayfield.

Perez, E. (1990). "Why Women Wait to Be Tested for HIV Infection." *SIECUS Report, 19*, 6–7.

Perilstein, R., Lipper, S., & Friedman, L. J. (1991). "Three Cases of Paraphilias Responsive to Fluoxetine Treatment." *Journal of Clinical Psychology, 52*(4), 169–170.

Perkins, B., & Bennet, G. (1985). *Being a Prostitute: Prostitute Women and Prostitute Men*. Sydney, Australia: Allen & Unwin.

Perkins, J. L. (1991). "Primary Prevention of Adolescent Pregnancy." *Birth Defects Original Article Series, 27*, 9–28.

Perlez, J. (1990, January 15). "Puberty Rite for Girls Is Bitter Issue Across Africa." *The New York Times*, p. A4.

Perlman, D. (1990, March 5). "Brave New Babies." *San Francisco Chronicle*, p. 3ff.

Perry, J. D., & Whipple, B. (1981). "Pelvic Muscle Strength of Female Ejaculators: Evidence in Support of a New Theory of Orgasm." *Journal of Sex Research, 17*(1), 22–39.

Persky, H., et al. (1982). "The Relation of Plasma Androgen Levels to Sexual Behavior and Attitudes of Women." *Psychosomatic Medicine, 44*, 157–173.

Person, E. S., Terestman, N., Myers, W. A., & Goldberg, E. L. (1989). "Gender Differences in Sexual Behaviors and Fantasies in a College Population." *Journal of Sex and Marital Therapy, 15*(3), 187–214.

Petchesky, R. P. (1990). *Abortion and Woman's Choice: The State, Sexuality, and Reproductive Freedom*. (rev. ed.). Boston: Northeastern University Press.

Peters, K. (1992, October 15). "Gay Activists Denounce NAMBLA, Attempt to Highlight Differences." *Spartan Daily*, p. 1.

Peters, S., et al. (1986). "Prevalence of Child Sexual Abuse." In D. Finkelhor (Ed.), *Sourcebook on Child Sexual Abuse*. Newbury Park, CA: Sage Publications.

Peterson, H., et al. (1983). "Deaths Attributable to Tubal Sterilization in the United States, 1977–1981." *American Journal of Obstetrics and Gynecology, 146*, 131ff.

Peterson, J., Kretchmer, A., Nellis, B., Lever, J., & Hertz, R. (1983, March). "The *Playboy* Readers Sex Survey, Part 2." *Playboy*, 90–92, 178–184.

Peterson, J. L. (1992). "Black Men and Their Same-Sex Desires and Behaviors." In G. Herdt (Ed.), *Gay Culture in America: Essays from the Field*. Boston: Beacon Press.

Petit, C. (1990, May 9). "New Study to Ask Why So Many Infants Die." *San Francisco Chronicle*, p. 3.

Petit, C. (1992, April 2). "Why Both Parents Should Be Tested for Herpes." *San Francisco Chronicle*, p. D7.

Pfaus, J., Myronuk, & Jacobs. (1986). "Soundtrack Contents and Depicted Sexual Violence." *Archives of Sexual Behavior, 15*(3), 231–237.

Phelps, T. M., & Winternitz, H. (1992). *Capitol Games*. New York: Hyperion Books.

Phillips, G., & Over, R. (1992). "Adult Sexual Orientation in Relation to Memories of Childhood Gender Conforming and Gender Nonconforming Behaviors." *Archives of Sexual Behavior, 21*(6), 543–558.

Pies, C. (1987). "Considering Parenthood: Psychological Issues for Gay Men and Lesbians Choosing Alternative Fertilization." In F. W. Bozett (Ed.), *Gay and Lesbian Parents*. New York: Praeger.

Pincus, S. (1988). "Sexuality in the Mentally Retarded Patient." *American Family Physician, 37*(2), 319–323.

Pines, A., & Aronson, E. (1983). "Antecedents, Correlates, and Consequences of Sexual Jealousy." *Journal of Personality, 51*(1), 108–136.

Plato. (1961). "Protagoras." In E. Hamilton & H. Cairns (Eds.), *The Collected Dialogues of Plato*. New York: Bollengen Foundation.

Plummer, W., & Nelson, M. (1991, August 26). "A Mother's Priceless Gift." *People*, p. 18.

Pogrebin, L. C. (1982, February). "Are Men Discovering the Joys of Fatherhood?" *Ms.*, pp. 41–46.

Pogrebin, L. C. (1983). *Family Politics*. New York: McGraw-Hill.

Polit-O'Hara, D., & Kahn, J. (1985). "Communication and Contraceptive Practices in Adolescent Couples." *Adolescence, 20*(77), 33–43.

Pomeroy, W. (1972). *Dr. Kinsey and the Kinsey Institute*. New York: Harper & Row.

Pomice, E. (1990, April 2). "A Businesslike Approach to AIDS." *U.S. News & World Report*, p. 4.

Ponticas, Y. (1992). "Sexual Aversion Versus Hypoactive Sexual Desire: A Diagnostic Challenge." *Psychiatric Medicine, 10*(2), 273–281.

Popovich, P. M., et al. (1986). "Assessing the Incidence and Perceptions of Sexual Harassment Behaviors Among American Undergraduates." *Journal of Psychology, 120*, 387–396.

Popovich, P. M., et al. (1992). "Perceptions of Sexual Harassment as a Function of Sex of Rater and Incident Form and Consequence." *Sex Roles, 27*(11-1), 609–625.

Population Crisis Committee. (1985). "Issues in Contraceptive Development." *Population, 15*(3), 456ff.

Potterat, J. J., et al. (1985). "Gonorrhea as a Social Disease." *Sexually Transmitted Diseases, 12*, 25–32.

Potterat, J. J., Phillips, L., Rothenberg, R. B., & Darrow, W. V. (1985). "On Becoming a Prostitute: An Exploratory Case-Comparison Study." *Journal of Sex Research, 21*(3), 329–335.

Potterat, J. J., Woodhouse, D. E., Muth, J. B., & Muth, S. Q. (1990). "Estimating the Prevalence and Career Longevity of Prostitute Women." *Journal of Sex Research, 27*, 233–243.

Pozo, C., et al. (1992). "Effects of Mastectomy Versus Lumpectomy on Emotional Adjustment to Breast Cancer: A Prospective Study of the First Year Postsurgery." *Journal of Clinical Oncology, 10*(8), 1292–1298.

PPFA [Planned Parenthood Federation of America]. (1985, November). "They Did It 9000 Times on Television Last Year, How Come Nobody Got Pregnant?" *San Francisco Chronicle*, p. 14.

Pratt, C., & Schmall, V. (1989). "College Students' Attitudes Toward Elderly Sexual Behavior: Implications for Family Life Education." *Family Relations, 38*, 137–141.

Press, A. (1992). "Class, Gender, and the Female Viewer: Women's Responses to "Dynasty"." In *Television and Women's Culture: The Politics of the Popular.* Newbury Park, CA: Sage Publications.

Price, D. (1993, January 14). "Twin Study Links Genetics, Gayness Closer." *San Jose Mercury News*, p. 2.

Price, J. (1982). "Who Wants to Have Children? And Why?" In J. Rosenfeld (Ed.), *Relationships: The Marriage and Family Reader.* Glenview, IL: Scott, Foresman.

Price, J. H., & Miller, P. A. (1984). "Sexual Fantasies of Black and White College Students." *Psychological Reports, 54*, 1007–1014.

Priest, R. (1992). "Child Sexual Abuse Histories Among African-American College Students: A Preliminary Study." *American Journal of Orthopsychiatry, 62*(3), 475–477.

Prober, C., et al. (1987). "Low Risk of Herpes Simplex Virus Infections in Neonates Exposed to the Virus at the Time of Vaginal Delivery to Mothers with Recurrent Genital Herpes Simplex Virus Infections." *New England Journal of Medicine, 316*, 129–138.

Project Inform. (1990, March 27). "AZT—Retrovir." *Project Inform Fact Sheet*, 1–4.

Project Inform. (1990, June 14). "ddl—Dideoxyinosine (VIDEX)." *Project Inform Fact Sheet*, 1–2.

Project Inform. (1991, May 1). "ddC—Dideocyctidine—HIVID." *Project Inform Fact Sheet*, 1–2.

Project Inform. (1992). "The Myth of 'Too Much Spending on AIDS'." *Project Inform Fact Sheet*, 1–2.

Pruett, K. (1987). *The Nurturing Father: Journey Toward the Complete Man.* New York: Warner Books.

Pryor, J. B., & Day, J. D. (1988). "Interpretations of Sexual Harassment: An Attributional Analysis." *Sex Roles, 18*(7-8), 405–417.

Puech-Leao, P. (1992). "Venous Surgery in Erectile Dysfunction." *Urologia Internationalis, 49*(1), 29–32.

Puglisi, J. T., & Jackson, D. W. (1981). "Sex Role Identity and Self-Esteem in Adulthood." *Journal of Aging and Human Development, 12*, 129–138.

Quackenbush, R. L. (1991). "Attitudes of College Men Toward Women and Rape." *Journal of College Students Development, 32*, 376–377.

Quadagno, D., et al. (1991). "Women at Risk for Human Immunodeficiency Virus." *Journal of Psychology and Human Sexuality, 4*(3), 97–110.

Quétel, C. (1990). *History of Syphilis.* Cambridge, England: Polity Press.

Raboch, J., & Raboch, J. (1992). "Infrequent Orgasms in Women." *Journal of Sex and Marital Therapy, 18*(3), 114–120.

Radway, J. A. (1984). *Reading the Romance.* Chapel Hill, NC: University of North Carolina Press.

Raisbaum, H. (1986). "El Rol Sexual Femenino en los Medios Comunicacion Masiva: Un Estudio Comparativo de Telenovelas Mexicanas y Estadounidenses." *Revista Mexicana de Psicología, 3*(2), 188–196.

Ramey, E. (1972). "Men's Cycles." *Ms.*, pp. 8ff.

Randolph, E. (1988, March 9). "Critics Say Medical Journals Would Have Rejected AIDS Study." *Washington Post*, p. A7.

Rangaswamy, K. (1987). "Treatment of Voyeurism by Behavior Therapy." *Child Psychiatry Quarterly, 20*, 3–4.

Rao, K., et al. (1992). "Child Sexual Abuse of Asians Compared with Other Populations." *Journal of the American Academy of Child and Adolescent Psychiatry, 31*(5), 880–887.

Ratner, E. (1988). "A Model for the Treatment of Lesbian and Gay Alcohol Abusers." *Alcoholism Treatment Quarterly, 5*(1-2), 25–46.

Raven, B., et al. (1975). "The Bases of Conjugal Power." In R. Cromwell & D. Olson (Eds.), *Power in Families.* New York: Halstead Press.

Ravinder, S. (1987). "Androgyny: Is It Really the Product of Educated Middle-Class Western Societies?" *Journal of Cross-Cultural Psychology, 18*(2), 208–220.

Reamy, K., & White, S. (1987). "Sexuality in the Puerperium: A Review." *Archives of Sexual Behavior, 16*(2), 165–187.

Redfield, R. R., & Burke, D. S. (1988). "HIV Infection: The Clinical Picture." *Scientific American*, 90ff.

Reece, R. (1988). "Special Issues in the Etiologies and Treatments of Sexual Problems Among Gay Men." *Journal of Homosexuality, 15*, 43–57.

Reed, D., & Weinberg, M. (1984). "Premarital Coitus: Developing and Established Sexual Scripts." *Social Psychology Quarterly, 47*(2), 129–138.

Reeves, W. C., et al. (1989). "Human Papillomavirus Infection and Cervical Cancer in Latin America." *New England Journal of Medicine, 320*, 1437.

Reichel-Dolmatoff, G. (1971). *Amazonian Cosmos.* Chicago: University of Chicago Press.

Reid, P., & Comas-Diaz, L. (1990). "Gender and Ethnicity: Perspectives on Dual Status." *Sex Roles, 22*(7), 397–408.

Reid, R. (1986). "Premenstrual Syndrome: A Time for Introspection." *American Journal of Obstetrics and Gynecology, 155*(5), 921–926.

Reilly, M. E., et al. (1992). "Tolerance for Sexual Harassment Related to Self-Reported Sexual Victimization." *Gender and Society, 6*(1), 122–138.

Reinisch, J. (1986, August 26). "The Kinsey Report." *San Francisco Chronicle*, p. 16.

Reinisch, J., Ziemba-Davis, M., & Sanders, S. (1991). "Hormonal Contributions to Sexually Dimorphic Behavioral Development in Humans." *Psychoneuroendocrinology, 16*, 213–278.

Reiss, I. (1967). *The Social Context of Premarital Sexual Permissiveness.* New York: Irvington.

Reiss, I. (1980). "A Multivariate Model of the Determinants of Extramarital Sexual Permissiveness." *Journal of Marriage and the Family, 42*, 395–411.

Reiss, I. (1986). *Journey into Sexuality: An Exploratory Voyage.* Englewood Cliffs, NJ: Prentice-Hall.

Reiss, I. (1989). "Society and Sexuality: A Sociological Explanation." In K. McKinney & S. Sprecher (Eds.), *Human Sexuality: The Societal and Interpersonal Context.* Norwood, NJ: Ablex.

Reiss, I. (1990). *An End to Shame: Shaping Our Next Sexual Revolution.* Buffalo, NY: Prometheus Books.

Renshaw, D. (1988). "Short-Term Therapy for Sexual Dysfunction: Brief Counseling to Manage Vaginismus." *Clinical Practice in Sexuality, 6*(5), 23–29.

Renshaw, D. C. (1988). "Young Children's Sex Play: Counseling the Parents." *Medical Aspects of Human Sexuality, 22*(12), 68–72.

Resnick, H. S., et al. (1991). "Assessment of Rape-Related Post-traumatic Stress Disorder: Stressor and Symptom Dimensions." *Psychological Assessment, 3*(4), 561–572.

Retik, A. B., & Bauer, S. B. (1984). "Infertility Related to DES Exposure in Utero: Reproductive Problems in the Male." In M. Mazor & H. Simons (Eds.), *Infertility: Medical, Emotional, and Social Considerations.* New York: Human Sciences Press.

Reuben, D. (1969). *Everything You Ever Wanted to Know About Sex—But Were Afraid to Ask.* New York: David McKay.

Rice, R. J., Roberts, P. L., Handsfield, H. H., & Holmes, K. K. (1991). "Sociodemographic Distribution of Gonorrhea Incidence: Implications for Prevention and Behavioral Research." *American Journal of Public Health, 81*(10), 1252–1258.

Rice, S. (1989). "Sexuality and Intimacy for Aging Women: A Changing Perspective." *Journal of Women and Aging, 1*(1-3), 245–264.

Rich, A. (1983). "Compulsory Heterosexuality and Lesbian Existence." In A. Snitow et al. (Eds.), *Powers of Desire: The Politics of Sexuality*. New York: Monthly Review Press.

Richards, E. P., & Bross, D. C. (1990). "Legal Aspects of STD Control: Public Duties and Private Rights." In K. K. Holmes et al. (Eds.), *Sexually Transmitted Diseases* (2nd ed.). New York: McGraw-Hill.

Richardson, D. (1983). "The Dilemma of Essentiality in Homosexual Theory." *Journal of Homosexuality*, 9(2-3), 79–90.

Ricketts, W., & Actenberg, R. (1989). "Adoption and Foster Parenting for Lesbians and Gay Men: Creating New Traditions in Family." *Marriage and Family Review*, 14, 83–118.

Rieff, P. (1979). *Freud: The Mind of a Moralist*. Chicago: University of Chicago Press.

Rieve, J. E. (1989). "Sexuality and the Adult with Acquired Physical Disability." *Nursing Clinics of North America*, 24(1), 265–276.

Riley, A. J. (1991). "Sexuality and the Menopause." *Sexual and Marital Therapy*, 6(2), 135–146.

Rio, L. M. (1991). "Psychological and Sociological Research and the Decriminalization or Legalization of Prostitution." *Archives of Sexual Behavior*, 20(2), 205–218.

Riseden, A. D., & Hort, B. E. (1992). "A Preliminary Investigation of the Sexual Component of the Male Stereotype." Unpublished manuscript.

Roberts, E. (1980). (Ed.). *Childhood Sexual Learning: The Unwritten Curriculum*. Cambridge, MA: Ballinger.

Roberts, E. (1982). "Television and Sexual Learning in Childhood." In *National Institute of Mental Health, Television and Behavior*. Washington, DC: U.S. Government Printing Office.

Roberts, E. (1983). "Childhood Sexual Learning: The Unwritten Curriculum." In C. Davis (Ed.), *Challenges in Sexual Science*. Philadelphia: Society for the Scientific Study of Sex.

Roberts, L., & Krokoff, L. (1990). "A Time Series Analysis of Withdrawal, Hostility, and Displeasure in Satisfied and Dissatisfied Marriages." *Journal of Marriage and the Family*, 52(1), 95–105.

Roberts, M. C., Alexander, K., & Fanurik, D. (1990). "Evaluation of Commercially Available Materials to Prevent Child Sexual Abuse." *American Psychologist*, 45(6), 782–783.

Robertson, D. (1990). "Counseling Women Who Have Been Sexually Assaulted." *Issues in Criminological and Legal Psychology*, 19, 46–53.

Robertson, M. M. (1992, April). "Lesbians as an Invisible Minority in the Health Services Arena." *Health Care for Women International*, 13(2), 155–163.

Robinson, B. (1987). *Teenage Fathers*. Lexington, MA: Lexington Books.

Robinson, B. (1988). "Teenage Pregnancy from the Father's Perspective." *American Journal of Orthopsychiatry*, 58(1), 46–51.

Robinson, H. (1992, December 14). "Sex, Marriage, and Divorce." *Christianity Today*, 36(15), 29–33.

Robinson, P. (1976). *The Modernization of Sex*. New York: Harper & Row.

Robinson, P. (1983). "The Sociological Perspective." In R. Weg (Ed.), *Sexuality in the Later Years: Roles and Behavior*. New York: Academic Press.

Rodabaugh, B., & Austin, M. (1981). *Sexual Assault*. New York: Garland Press.

Roen, P. (1974). *Male Sexual Health*. New York: William Morrow.

Roenrich, L., & Kinder, B. N. (1991). "Alcohol Expectancies and Male Sexuality: Review and Implications for Sex Therapy." *Journal of Sex and Marital Therapy*, 17, 45–54.

Rogers, M. F., et al. (1990). "Lack of Transmission of Human Immunodeficiency Virus from Infected Children to Their Household Contacts." *Pediatrics*, 85(2), 210–214.

Rogers, P. A., Murphy, C. R., Leeton, J., Hoise, M. J., & Beaton, L. (1992). "Turner's Syndrome Patients Lack Tight Junctions Between Uterine Epithelial Cells." *Human Reproduction*, 7(6), 883–885.

Rogers, S. M., & Turner, C. F. (1991). "Male-Male Sexual Contact in the U.S.A.: Findings from Five Sample Surveys, 1970–1990." *Journal of Sex Research*, 28(4), 491–519.

Romanowski, B., & Piper, G. (1988). "Sexually Transmitted Diseases: An Overview." Special Issue: Sociopsychological Aspects of Sexually Transmitted Diseases. *Journal of Social Work and Human Sexuality*, 6(2), 7–20.

Romberg, R. (1985). *Circumcision: The Painful Dilemma*. South Hadley, MA: Bergin and Garvey.

Rome, E. (1992). "Anatomy and Physiology of Sexuality and Reproduction." In Boston Women's Health Book Collective, *The New Our Bodies, Ourselves*. New York: Simon & Schuster.

Rongen-Westelaken, C., Vanes, A., Wit, J., Otten, B. J., & Demuink Keizer-Schrama, C. (1992). "Growth Hormone Therapy in Turner's Syndrome." *American Journal of Diseases of Children*, 146(7), 817–820.

Rooks, J., et al. (1989). "Outcomes of Care in Birth Centers." *New England Journal of Medicine*, 321, 1804–1811.

Roopnarine, J. L., & Mounts, N. S. (1987). "Current Theoretical Issues in Sex Roles and Sex Typing." In D. B. Carter (Ed.), *Current Conceptions of Sex Roles and Sex Typing: Theory and Research*. New York: Praeger.

Roos, P., & Cohen, L. (1987). "Sex Roles and Social Support as Moderates of Life Stress Adjustment." *Journal of Personality and Social Psychology*, 52(3), 576–585.

Roper, W. L., Petersen, H. B., & Curran, J. W. (1993). "Commentary: Condoms and HIV/STD Prevention—Clarifying the Message." *American Journal of Public Health*, 83(4), 501–503.

Roscoe, W. (1991). *The Zuni Man/Woman*. Albuquerque, NM: University of New Mexico Press.

Rosegrant, J. (1986). "Contributions to Psychohistory: Fetish Symbols in *Playboy* Centerfolds." *Psychological Reports*, 59(2, Part 1), 623–631.

Rosen, M. P., et al. (1991). "Cigarette Smoking: An Independent Risk Factor for Artherosclerosis in the Hypogastric-Cavernous Arterial Bed of Men with Arteriogenic Impotence." *Journal of Urology*, 145(4), 759–776.

Rosen, R. (1982). *The Lost Sisterhood: Prostitution in America, 1900–1918*. Baltimore, MD: Johns Hopkins University Press.

Rosenberg, M. J., Davidson, A. J., Chen, J. H., Judson, F. N., & Douglas, J. M. (1992). "Barrier Contraceptives and Sexually Transmitted Diseases in Women: A Comparison of Female-Dependent Methods and Condoms." *American Journal of Public Health*, 82(5), 669–674.

Rosenfeld, R. G., Frane, J., Attie, L. M., Brasel, J. A., Bursten, S., & Clarer. (1992). "Six-Year Results of a Randomized, Prospective Trial of Human Growth Hormone and Oxandrolone in Turner Syndrome." *Journal of Pediatrics*, 121(1), 49–55.

Rosenstock, I. (1974). "Historical Origins of the Health Belief Model." *Health Education Monographs*, 2, 328–335.

Rosenthal, E. (1990, February 4). "When a Pregnant Woman Drinks." *The New York Times Magazine*, pp. 30ff.

Rosenthal, E. (1990, August 28). "The Spread of AIDS: A Mystery Unravels." *The New York Times*, pp. B5–6.

Rosenthal, E. (1992, May 26). "Cost of High-Tech Fertility: Too Many Tiny Babies." *The New York Times*, pp. B5, B7.

Rosenzweig, J. M., & Dailey, D. M. (1989). "Dyadic Adjustment/Sexual Satisfaction in Women and Men as a Function of Psychological Sex Role Self-Perception." *Journal of Sex and Marital Therapy*, 15, 42–56.

Rosman, J., & Resnick, P. J. (1989). "Sexual Attraction to Corpses: A Psychiatric Review of Necrophilia." *Bulletin of the American Academy of Psychiatry and the Law*, 17(2), 153–163.

Ross, M. (1983a). "Femininity, Masculinity, and Sexual Orientation." *Journal of Homosexuality, 9*(1), 27–36.

Ross, M. (1983b). "Homosexuality and Sex Roles: A Re-Evaluation." *Journal of Homosexuality, 9*(1), 1–6.

Ross, M. W., & Need, J. A. (1989). "Effects of Adequacy of Gender Reassignment Surgery on Psychological Adjustment: A Follow-Up of Fourteen Male-to-Female Patients." *Archives of Sexual Behavior, 18*(2), 145–153.

Ross, M. W., Wodak, A., Gold, J., & Miller, M. E. (1992). "Differences Across Sexual Orientation on HIV Risk Behaviors in Injecting Drug Users." *AIDS Care, 4*(2), 139–148.

Rossignol, A. M., et al. (1989). "Tea and Premenstrual Syndrome in the People's Republic of China." *American Journal of Public Health, 79*, 67–69.

Roth, P. (1969). *Portnoy's Complaint.* New York: Random House.

Rothenberg, R. (1983). "The Geography of Gonorrhea." *American Journal of Epidemiology, 117*(6), 688–694.

Rothenberg, R. B. (1991). "These Other SIDS." *American Journal of Public Health, 81*, 1250–1251.

Rothenberg, R. B., & Potterat, J. J. (1990). "Strategies for Management of Sex Partners." In K. K. Holmes et al. (Eds.), *Sexually Transmitted Diseases* (2nd ed.). New York: McGraw-Hill.

Rothschild, B. S., Fagan, P. J., & Woodall, C. (1991). "Sexual Functioning of Female Eating-Disordered Patients." *International Journal of Eating Disorders, 10*, 389–394.

Rotolo, J., & Lynch, J. (1991). "Penile Cancer: Curable with Early Detection." *Hospital Practice, 131*–138.

Rowan, E. L. (1988). "Pedophilia." In D. Dailey (Ed.), *The Sexually Unusual.* New York: Harrington Park Press.

Rowan, E. L. (1989). "Masturbation According to the Boy Scout Handbook." *Journal of Sex Education and Therapy, 15*(2), 77–81.

Rowan, R., & Gillette, P. (1973). *Your Prostate.* New York: Doubleday.

Rowland, R. (1987). "Technology and Motherhood: Reproductive Choice Reconsidered." *Signs: Journal of Women in Culture and Society, 12*(3), 512–528.

Rubenstein, C., & Tavris, C. (1987, September). "Special Survey Results: 26,000 Women Reveal the Secrets of Intimacy." *Redbook,* pp. 147–149ff.

Rubin, A. M., & Adams, J. R. (1986). "Outcomes of Sexually Open Marriages." *Journal of Sex Research, 22*, 311–319.

Rubin, L. (1976). *Worlds of Pain.* New York: Basic Books.

Rubin, L. (1990). *Erotic Wars.* New York: Farrar, Straus, & Giroux.

Rubin, R. T., Reinisch, J. M., & Haskett, R. F. (1981). "Postnatal Gonadal Steroid Effects on Human Behavior." *Science, 211*, 1318–1324.

Rubin, Z., Provenzano, F., & Luria, Z. (1974). "The Eye of the Beholder: Parents' View of Sex of Newborn." *American Journal of Orthopsychiatry, 44*, 512–519.

Ruble, D. N. (1977). "Premenstrual Syndrome: A Reinterpretation." *Science, 197*, 291–292.

Rudolph, J. (1989). "Effects of a Workshop on Mental Health Practitioners' Attitudes Toward Homosexuality and Counseling Effectiveness." *Journal of Counseling and Development, 68*(1), 81–85.

Rudolph, J. (1989). "The Impact of Contemporary Ideology and AIDS on the Counseling of Gay Clients." *Counseling and Values, 33*, 96–108.

Rush, D., et al. (1988). "The National WIC Evaluation." *American Journal of Clinical Nutrition, 48*(2), 439–483.

Rush, F. (1980). "Child Pornography." In L. Lederer (Ed.), *Take Back the Night: Women on Pornography.* New York: William Morrow.

Russell, D. (1984). *Sexual Exploitation: Rape, Child Sexual Abuse, and Workplace Harassment.* Newbury Park, CA: Sage Publications.

Russell, D. E. H. (1986). *The Secret Trauma: Incest in the Lives of Girls and Women.* New York: Basic Books.

Russell, D. E. H. (1990). *Rape in Marriage* (rev. ed.). Bloomington, IN: Indiana University Press.

Russell, S. (1991, December 3). "Women Fight Breast Cancer and the Health Care System." *San Francisco Chronicle,* pp. A1, A10.

Russo, N. F., Horn, J. D., & Schwartz, R. (1992). "U.S. Abortions in Context: Selected Characteristics." *Journal of Social Issues, 48*(3), 183–202.

Russo, V. (1987). *The Celluloid Closet.* New York: Harper & Row.

Safilios-Rothschild, C. (1970). "The Study of the Family Power Structure." *Journal of Marriage and the Family, 32*, 539–543.

Safilios-Rothschild, C. (1976). "Family Sociology or Wives' Sociology? A Cross-Cultural Examination of Decision-Making." *Journal of Marriage and the Family, 38*, 355–362.

Salgado de Snyder, V. N., Cervantes, R., & Padilla, A. (1990). "Gender and Ethnic Differences in Psychosocial Stress and Generalized Distress Among Hispanics." *Sex Roles, 22*(7), 441–453.

Salholz, E. (1992, August 10). "Deepening Shame." *Newsweek,* pp. 30–36.

Salovey, P., & Rodin, J. (1991). "Provoking Jealousy and Envy: Domain Relevance and Self-Esteem Threat." *Journal of Social and Clinical Psychology, 10*(4), 395–413.

Salsbury, K., & Johnson, E. (1981). *The Indispensable Cancer Handbook.* New York: Seaview Books.

Sampson, R. (1966). *The Problem of Power.* New York: Pantheon.

Samuels, M., & Samuels, N. (1986). *The Well Pregnancy Book.* New York: Summit Books.

Sanday, P. (1990). *Fraternity Gang Rape: Sex, Brotherhood and Privilege on Campus.* New York: New York University Press.

Sanders, J., & Robinson, W. (1979). "Talking and Not Talking About Sex: Male and Female Vocabulary." *Journal of Communication, 29*(2), 22–30.

Sanders, S. A., Reinisch, J. M., & McWhirter, D. P. (1990). "Homosexuality/Heterosexuality: An Overview." In D. P. McWhirter, S. A. Sanders, & J. M. Reinisch (Eds.), *Homosexuality/Heterosexuality: Concepts of Sexual Orientation.* New York: Oxford University Press.

Santrock, J. (1983). *Life-Span Development.* Dubuque, IA. W. C. Brown.

Sarrel, L., & Sarrel, P. (1984). *Sexual Turning Points: The Seven Stages of Adult Sexuality.* New York: Macmillan.

Sarrel, P. M. (1990). "Sexuality and Menopause." *Obstetrics and Gynecology, 75* (4 Suppl.), 26S–30S.

Sarrell, P. M., & Johnson, W. H. (1982). "Sexual Molestation of Men by Women." *Archives of Sexual Behavior, 11*, 117–131.

Sarrel, P. M., Rousseau, M., Mazure, C., & Glazer, W. (1990). "Ovarian Steroids and the Capacity to Function at Home and in the Workplace. Multidisciplinary Perspectives on Menopause." *Annals of the New York Academy of Sciences, 592*, 156–161, 185–192.

Sarton, M. (1980). *Recovering: A Journal.* New York: Norton.

Satterfield, S. (1988). "Transsexualism." In D. Dailey (Ed.), *The Sexually Unusual.* New York: Harrington Park Press.

Saunders, E. (1989). "Life-Threatening Autoerotic Behavior: A Challenge for Sex Educators and Therapists." *Journal of Sex Education and Therapy, 15*(2), 77–81.

Saunders, E. B., & Awad, G. (1991). "Male Adolescent Sexual Offenders: Exhibitionism and Obscene Phone Calls." *Child Psychiatry and Human Development, 21*(3), 169–178.

Savin-Williams, R., & Rodriguez, R. G. (1993). "A Developmental, Clinical Perspective on Lesbian, Gay Male, and Bisexual Youths." In T. P. Gullotta et al. (Eds.), *Adolescent Sexuality.* Newbury Park, CA: Sage Publications.

Saviteer, S. M., White, G. C., & Cohen, M. S. (1985). "HTLV-III Exposure During Cardiopulmonary Resuscitation." *New England Journal of Medicine, 313*, 1607.

Savitz, L., & Rosen, L. (1988). "The Sexuality of Prostitutes: Sexual Enjoyment Reported by 'Streetwalkers'." *Journal of Sex Research, 24,* 200–208.

Sayers, J. (1991). *Mothers of Psychoanalysis.* New York: Norton.

Scanzoni, J. (1979). "Social Processes and Power in Families." In W. Burr et al. (Eds.), *Contemporary Theories About the Family, Vol. I.* New York: Free Press.

Schaap, C., Buunk, B., & Kerkstra, A. (1988). "Marital Conflict Resolutions." In P. Noller & M. A. Fitzpatrick (Eds.), *Perspectives on Marital Interaction.* Philadelphia: Multilingual Matters.

Schafer, J., & Brown, S. A. (1991). "Marijuana and Cocaine Effect Expectancies and Drug Use Patterns." *Journal of Consulting and Clinical Psychology, 59*(4), 558–565.

Schatzin, A., et al. (1987). "Alcohol Consumption and Breast Cancer in the Epidemiologic Follow-Up Study of the First National Health and Nutrition Examination Survey." *New England Journal of Medicine, 316*(19), 1169–1173.

Scherer, Y. K., Wu, Y. W., & Haughey, B. P. (1991). "AIDS and Homophobia Among Nurses." *Journal of Homosexuality, 21*(4), 17–27.

Schiavi, R. C., Schreiner-Engle, P., Mandeli, J., Schanzer, J., & Cohen, E. (1990). "Chronic Alcoholism and Male Sexual Dysfunction." *Journal of Sex and Marital Therapy, 16*(1), 23–33.

Schinke, S. P., Botvin, G. J., Orlandi, M. A., Schilling, R. F., & Gordon, A. N. (1990). "African-American and Hispanic-American Adolescents, HIV Infection, and Preventative Intervention." *AIDS Education and Prevention, 2*(4), 305–312.

Schlesselman, J. J. (1990). "Oral Contraception and Breast Cancer." *American Journal of Obstetrics and Gynecology, 163*(4:2), 1379–1387.

Schlesselman, J. J., et al. (1988). "Breast Cancer in Relation to Early Use of Oral Contraceptives: No Evidence of a Latent Effect." *JAMA: Journal of the American Medical Association, 259,* 1828–1833.

Schmalz, J. (1993, January 31). "Homosexuals Wake to See a Referendum: It's on Them." *The New York Times,* p. E1.

Schmidt, C. W. (1992). "Changes in Terminology for Sexual Disorders in DSM-IV." *Psychiatric Medicine, 10*(2), 247–255.

Schmitt, E. (1990, September 12). "2 Out of 3 Women in Military Study Report Sexual Harassment Incidents." *The New York Times,* p. A12.

Schneck, M. E., et al. (1990). "Low-Income Adolescents and Their Infants: Dietary Findings and Health Outcomes." *Journal of the American Dietetic Association, 90*(4), 555–558.

Schover, L. R., Fife, M., & Gershenson, D. M. (1989). "Sexual Dysfunction and Treatment for Early Stage Cervical Cancer." *Cancer, 63*(1), 204–212.

Schur, E. (1980). *The Politics of Deviance: Stigma Contests and the Uses of Power.* Englewood Cliffs, NJ: Prentice-Hall.

Schwanberg, S. (1985). "Changes in Labeling Homosexuality in Health Sciences: A Preliminary Investigation." *Journal of Homosexuality, 12*(1), 51–73.

Schwartz, I. D., & Root, A. W. (1991). "The Klinefelter Syndrome of Testicular Dysgenesis." *Endocrinology and Metabolism Clinics of North America, 20*(1), 153–163.

Schwarz, P. Interview with Bryan Strong, December 20, 1992.

Scott, J. (1986). "Gender: A Useful Category of Historical Analysis." *American Historical Review, 91,* 1053–1075.

Scott, J. (1986). "An Updated Longitudinal Content Analysis of Sex References in Mass Circulation Magazines." *Journal of Sex Research, 22*(3), 385–392.

Scott, J. (1990a, December 24). "Trying to Save the Babies." *Los Angeles Times,* pp. 1, 18ff.

Scott, J. (1990b, December 31). "Low Birth Weight's High Cost." *Los Angeles Times,* p. 1.

Scott, J., & Alwin, D. F. (1989). "Gender Differences in Parental Strain: Parental Role or Gender Role." *Journal of Family Issues, 10*(4), 482–503.

Scott, S. G., et al. (1990). "Therapeutic Donor Insemination with Frozen Semen." *Canadian Medical Association Journal, 143*(4), 273–278.

Seidman, S. (1989). "Constructing Sex as a Domain of Pleasure and Self-Expression: Sexual Ideology in the Sixties." *Theory, Culture, and Society, 6*(2), 293–315.

Senn, C., & Radtke, H. L. (1990). "Women's Evaluations of and Affective Reactions to Mainstream Violent Pornography, Nonviolent Pornography, and Erotica." *Violence and Victims, 5*(3), 143–155.

Serdahely, W., & Ziemba, G. (1984). "Changing Homophobic Attitudes through College Sexuality Education." *Journal of Homosexuality, 10*(1), 148ff.

Severn, J., Belch, G. E., & Belch, M. A. (1990). "The Effects of Sexual and Nonsexual Advertising Appeals and Information Level on Cognitive Processing and Communication Effectiveness." *Journal of Advertising, 19,* 14–22.

Shah, R., Woolley, M. M., & Costin, G. (1992). "Testicular Feminization: The Androgen Insensitivity Syndrome." *Journal of Pediatric Surgery, 27*(6), 757–760.

Shanis, B. S., et al. (1989). "Transmission of Sexually Transmitted Diseases by Donor Semen." *Archives of Andrology, 23*(3), 249–257.

Shannon, J. W., & Woods, W. J. (1991). "Affirmative Psychotherapy for Gay Men." *Counseling Psychologist, 19*(2), 197–215.

Shapiro, M. F., Hayward, R. A., Guillemot, D., & Jayle, D. (1992). "Residents' Experiences in, and Attitudes Toward, the Care of Persons with AIDS in Canada, France, and the United States." *JAMA: Journal of the American Medical Association, 268*(4), 510–515.

Shaver, P. (1984). *Emotions, Relationships, and Health.* Newbury Park, CA: Sage Publications.

Shaver, P., Hazan, C., & Bradshaw, D. (1988). "Love as Attachment: The Integration of Three Behavioral Systems." In R. Sternberg & M. Barnes (Eds.), *The Psychology of Love.* New Haven, CT: Yale University Press.

Shedler, J., & Block, J. (1990). "Adolescent Drug Use and Psychological Health: A Longitudinal Inquiry." *American Psychologist, 45,* 612–630.

Shelp, E. (1986). *Born to Die?* New York: Free Press.

Shepard, C. (1989). *Forgiven: The Rise and Fall of Jim Bakker and the PTL Ministry.* Boston: Atlantic Monthly Press.

Sherman, B., & Dominick, J. (1986). "Violence and Sex in Music Videos: TV and Rock 'n' Roll." *Journal of Communication, 36*(1), 79–93.

Shilts, R. (1987). *And the Band Played On: Politics, People, and the AIDS Epidemic.* New York: St. Martin's Press.

Shilts, R. (1993). *Conduct Unbecoming: Lesbians and Gays in the Military, Vietnam to the Persian Gulf.* New York: St. Martin's Press.

Shipp, E. R. (1985, December 18). "Curtailing Teen-Age Pregnancy." *The New York Times,* pp. 19, 22.

Shon, S., & Ja, D. (1982). "Asian Families." In M. McGoldrick et al. (Eds.), *Ethnicity and Family Therapy.* New York: Guilford Press.

Shostak, A. B. (1987). "Singlehood." In M. Sussman & S. Steinmetz (Eds.), *Handbook of Marriage and the Family.* New York: Plenum Press.

Shtarkshall, R. A., & Awerbuch, T. E. (1992). "It Takes Two to Tango but One to Infect (On the Underestimation of the Calculated Risk for Infection with HIV in Sexual Encounters, Arising from Nondisclosure of Previous Risk Behavior or Seropositivity)." *Journal of Sex and Marital Therapy, 18*(2), 121–127.

Shute, J. (1992). *Life-Size*. Boston: Houghton Mifflin.

Sigelman, C. K., et al. (1991). "Courteousy Stigma: The Social Implications of Associating with a Gay Person." *Journal of Social Psychology, 131,* 45–56.

Silbert, M., & Pines, A. (1981). "Child Sexual Abuse as an Antecedent to Prostitution." *Child Abuse and Neglect, 5*(4), 407–411.

Silver, D., & Campbell, B. K. (1988). "Failure of Psychological Gestation." *Psychoanalytic Inquiry,* 8(2), 222–223.

Simon, P. M., et al. (1992). "Psychological Characteristics of a Sample of Male Street Prostitutes." *Archives of Sexual Behavior, 21*(1), 33–44.

Simon, W. (1992). "Letters to the Editor: Reply to Muir and Eichel." *Archives of Sexual Behavior, 21*(6), 595–597.

Simon, W., & Gagnon, J. (1986). "Sexual Scripts: Permanence and Change." *Archives of Sexual Behavior, 15*(3), 97–120.

Simon, W., & Gagnon, J. (1987). "A Sexual Scripts Approach." J. H. Geer & W. O'Donohue (Eds.), *Theories of Human Sexuality.* New York: Plenum Press.

Simons, M. (1993, January 11). "France Jails a Gambian Woman Who Had Daughters Circumcised." *The New York Times,* p. A5.

Simons, R. L., & Whitbeck, L. B. (1991). "Sexual Abuse as a Precursor to Prostitution and Victimization Among Adolescent and Adult Homeless Women." *Journal of Family Issues, 12*(3), 361–380.

Simpson, J., Campbell, B., & Berscheid, E. (1986). "The Association Between Romantic Love and Marriage: Kephart (1967) Twice Revisited." *Personality and Social Psychology Bulletin, 12,* 363–372.

Simpson, W. S., & Ramberg, J. A. (1992). "Sexual Dysfunction in Married Female Patients with Anorexia and Bulimia Nervosa." *Journal of Sex and Marital Therapy, 18*(1), 44–54.

Singh, S. (1986). "Adolescent Pregnancy in the United States: An Interstate Analysis." *Family Planning Perspectives, 18*(5), 210–220.

Sinnott, J. (1986). *Sex Roles and Aging: Theory and Research from a Systems Perspective.* New York: Karger.

Skitka, L. J., & Maslach, C. (1990). "Gender Roles and the Categorization of Gender-Relevant Information." *Sex Roles, 22,* 3–4.

Slade, J. (1984). "Violence in the Hard-Core Pornographic Film: A Historical Survey." *Journal of Communication, 34*(3), 148–163.

Slater, P. (1974). *The Pursuit of Loneliness.* Boston: Beacon Press.

Sluzki, C. (1982). "The Latin Lover Revisited." In M. McGoldrick et al. (Eds.), *Ethnicity and Family Therapy.* New York: Guilford Press.

Smeltzer, S. C., & Whipple, B. (1991). "Women and HIV Infection." *IMAGE: Journal of Nursing Scholarship, 23*(4), 249–256.

Smith, D. K. (1992). "HIV Disease as a Cause of Death for African Americans in 1987 and 1990." *Journal of the National Medical Association, 84*(6), 481–487.

Smith, E. A., & Udry, J. R. (1985). "Coital and Non-Coital Sexual Behaviors of White and Black Adolescents." *American Journal of Public Health, 75,* 1200–1203.

Smith, E. J. (1982). "The Black Female Adolescent: A Review of the Educational, Career, and Psychological Literature." *Psychology of Women Quarterly, 6,* 261–288.

Smith, F. (1986, June 25). "Experimental AIDS Drug May Have Led to 3 Patients' Death." *San Jose Mercury News,* pp. 1, 6.

Smith, H., & Cox, C. (1983). "Dialogue with a Dominatrix." In T. Weinberg & G. W. L. Kamel (Eds.), *S and M: Studies in Sadomasochism.* Buffalo, NY: Prometheus Books.

Smith, J. E., & Krejci, J. (1991). "Minorities Join the Majority: Eating Disturbances Among Hispanic and Native American Youth." *International Journal of Eating Disorders, 10,* 179–186.

Smith, M. W., & Kronauge, C. (1990). "The Politics of Abortion: Husband Notification Legislation." *Sociological Quarterly, 31*(4), 585–598.

Smith, R. W. (1979). "What Kind of Sex Is Natural?" In V. Bullough (Ed.), *The Frontiers of Sex Research.* Buffalo, NY: Prometheus Books.

Snarey, J., et al. (1987). "The Role of Parenting in Men's Psychosocial Development." *Developmental Psychology, 23*(4), 593–603.

Snitow, A. (1983). "Mass Market Romance: Pornography for Women Is Different." In A. Snitow et al. (Ed.), *Powers of Desire: The Politics of Sexuality.* New York: Monthly Review Press.

Snitow, A., Stansells, C., & Thompson, S. (Eds.). (1983). *Powers of Desire: The Politics of Sexuality.* New York: Monthly Review Press.

Snyder, P. (1974). "Prostitution in Asia." *Journal of Sex Research, 10,* 119–127.

Soley, L., & Reid, L. (1986). "Taking It Off: Are Models in Magazine Ads Wearing Less?" *Journalism Quarterly, 85*(4), 960–966.

Sollom, T. (1991). "State Legislation on Reproductive Health in 1990: What Was Proposed and Enacted." *Family Planning Perspectives, 23,* 82–94.

Sonenstein, F. L. (1986). "Rising Paternity: Sex and Contraception Among Adolescent Males." In A. B. Elster & M. E. Lamb (Eds.), *Adolescent Fatherhood.* Hillsdale, NJ: Erlbaum.

Sonenstein, F. L., et al. (1991). "Levels of Sexual Activity Among Adolescent Males in the United States." *Family Planning Perspectives, 23*(4), 162–167.

Sonenstein, F. L., Pleck, J. H., & Ku, L. C. (1989). "Sexual Activity, Condom Use, and AIDS Awareness Among Adolescent Males." *Family Planning Perspectives, 21*(4), 152–158.

Sorenson, S. B., & Siegel, J. M. (1992). "Gender, Ethnicity, and Sexual Assault: Findings from a Los Angeles Study." *Journal of Social Issues, 48*(1), 93–104.

South, S., & Felson, R. (1990). "The Racial Patterning of Rape." *Social Forces, 69*(1), 71–93.

Spallone, P., & Steinberg, D. L. (1987). *Made to Order: The Myth of Reproductive and Genetic Progress.* New York: Pergamon Press.

Spanier, G. B., & Thompson, L. (1987). *Parting: The Aftermath of Separation and Divorce.* Newbury Park, CA: Sage Publications.

"Special Report: Sexuality and the Cardiovascular Patient." (1980, February). *The Female Patient,* 48–54.

Specter, M. (1988, March 8). "Heterosexual AIDS Study Denounced." *The Washington Post,* p. A3.

Spector, I. P., & Carey, M. P. (1990). "Incidence and Prevalence of the Sexual Dysfunctions: A Critical Review of the Empirical Literature." *Archives of Sexual Behavior, 19*(4), 389–408.

Spence, J., et al. (1985). "Sex Roles in Contemporary Society." In G. Lindzey & E. Aronson (Eds.), *Handbook of Social Psychology.* New York: Random House.

Spence, J., & Sawin, L. L. (1985). "Images of Masculinity and Femininity." In V. O'Leary et al. (Eds.), *Sex, Gender, and Social Psychology.* Hillsdale, NJ: Erlbaum.

Spencer, S. L., & Zeiss, A. M. (1987). "Sex Roles and Sexual Dysfunction in College Students." *Journal of Sex Research, 23,* 338–347.

Speroff, L., Glass, R. H., & Kase, N. G. (1989). *Clinical Gynecologic Endocrinology and Infertility.* (4th ed.). Baltimore, MD: Williams & Wilkins.

Spletter, M. (1982). *A Woman's Choice: New Options in the Treatment of Breast Cancer.* Boston: Beacon Press.

Spock, B., & Rothenberg, M. (1985). *Dr. Spock's Baby and Child Care.* New York: Pocket Books.

Sprecher, S. (1989). "Influences on Choice of a Partner and on Sexual Decision Making in the Relationship." In K. McKinney & S. Sprecher (Eds.), *Human Sexuality: The Social and Interpersonal Context.* Norwood, NJ: Ablex.

Sprecher, S., et al. (1989). "Sexual Relationships." In K. McKinney & S. Sprecher (Eds.), *Human Sexuality: The Societal and Interpersonal Context.* Norwood, NJ: Ablex.

Sprecher, S., & McKinney, K. (1993). *Sexuality.* Newbury Park, CA: Sage Publications.

Sprecher, S., McKinney, K., Walsh, R., & Anderson, C. (1988). "A Revision of the Reiss Premarital Sexual Permissiveness Scale." *Journal of Marriage and the Family, 50*(3), 821–828.

St. Lawrence, J. S., Husfeldt, B. A., Kelly, J. A., Hood, H. V., & Smith, Jr., S. (1990). "The Stigma of AIDS: Fear of Disease and Prejudice Toward Gay Men." *Journal of Homosexuality, 19*(3), 85–101.

St. Lawrence, J., & Joyner, D. (1991). "The Effects of Sexually Violent Rock Music on Male's Acceptance of Violence Against Women. *Psychology of Women Quarterly, 15*(1), 49–63.

St. Lawrence, J. S., & Madakasira, S. (1992). "Evaluation and Treatment of Premature Ejaculation: A Critical Review." *International Journal of Psychiatry in Medicine, 22*(1), 77–97.

Stack, C. B. (1974). *All Our Kin: Strategies for Survival in a Black Community.* New York: Harper & Row.

Stack, S., & Gundlach, J. H. (1992). "Divorce and Sex." *Archives of Sexual Behavior, 21*(4), 359–368.

Staggenborg, S. (1991). *The Pro-Choice Movement: Organization and Activism in the Abortion Conflict.* New York: Oxford University Press.

Stanton, M. C. (1985). "The Fetus: A Growing Member of the Family." *Family Relations, 34*(3), 321–326.

Staples, R. (1988). "The Black American Family." In C. Mindel et al. (Eds.), *Ethnic Families in America: Patterns and Variations* (3rd ed.). New York: Elsevier North Holland.

Staples, R. (1991). "The Sexual Revolution and the Black Middle Class." In R. Staples (Ed.), *The Black Family* (4th ed.). Belmont, CA: Wadsworth.

Staples, R., & Johnson, L. B. (1993). *Black Families at the Crossroads: Challenges and Prospects.* San Francisco: Jossey-Bass.

Steck, L., Levitan, D., McLane, D., & Kelley, H. H. (1982). "Care, Need, and Conceptions of Love." *Journal of Personality and Social Psychology, 43*, 481–491.

Stein, J. A., Fox, S. A., & Murata, P. J. (1991). "The Influence of Ethnicity, Socioeconomic Status, and Psychological Barriers on Use of Mammography." *Journal of Health and Social Behavior, 32*(2), 101–113.

Stein, P. (1983). "Singlehood." In E. Macklin & R. Rubin (Eds.), *Contemporary Families and Alternative Lifestyles.* Newbury Park, CA: Sage Publications.

Steinberg, D. (Ed.). (1992). *The Erotic Impulse.* New York: Tarcher/Perigee.

Stelzer, C., Desmond, S. M., & Price, J. H. (1987). "Physical Attractiveness and Sexual Activity of College Students." *Psychological Reports, 60*, 567–573.

Stengel, R. (1985, December 9). "The Missing-Father Myth." *Time,* p. 90.

Stephen, T. D., & Harrison, T. M. (1985). "A Longitudinal Comparison of Couples with Sex-Typical and Non-Sex-Typical Orientation to Intimacy." *Sex Roles, 12*(1-2), 195–206.

Stephenson, P., Wagner, M., Badea, M., & Serbanescu, F. (1992). "Commentary: The Public Health Consequences of Restricted Induced Abortion—Lessons from Romania." *American Journal of Public Health, 82*(10), 1328–1331.

Stermac, L., Blanchard, R., Clemmensen, C. H., & Dickey, R. (1991). "Group Therapy for Gender-Dysphoric Heterosexual Men." *Journal of Sex and Marital Therapy, 17*(4), 252–258.

Stern, M., & Karraker, K. H. (1989). "Sex Stereotyping in Infants: A Review of Gender Labelling." *Sex Roles, 20*, 501–522.

Sternberg, R. (1986). "A Triangular Theory of Love." *Psychological Review, 93*, 119–135.

Sternberg, R. (1988). "Triangulating Love." In R. Sternberg & M. Barnes (Eds.), *The Psychology of Love.* New Haven, CT: Yale University Press.

Sternberg, R., & Barnes, M. (1985). "Real and Ideal Others in Romantic Relationships: Is Four a Crowd?" *Journal of Personality and Social Psychology, 49*, 1589–1596.

Sternberg, R., & Grajek, S. (1984). "The Nature of Love." *Journal of Personality and Social Psychology, 47*, 312–327.

Stets, J., & Pirog-Good, M. (1987). "Violence in Dating Relationships." *Social Psychology Quarterly, 50*(3), 237–246.

Stevens, P. E. (1992). "Lesbian Health Care Research: A Review of the Literature from 1970 to 1990." *Health Care for Women International, 13*(2), 91–120.

Stevenson, M. (1990). "Tolerance for Homosexuality and Interest in Sexuality Education." *Journal of Sex Education and Therapy, 16*, 194–197.

Stevens-Simon, C., & Beach, R. K. (1992). "School-Based Prenatal and Postpartum Care: Strategies for Meeting the Medical and Educational Needs of Pregnant and Parenting Students." *Journal of School Health, 62*(7), 304–309.

Stockdale, M. S. (1993). "The Role of Sexual Misperceptions of Women's Friendliness in an Emerging Theory of Sexual Harassment." *Journal of Vocational Behavior, 42*(1), 84–101.

Stoller, R. J. (1975). *Perversion: The Erotic Form of Hatred.* New York: Pantheon.

Stoller, R. J. (1977). "Sexual Deviations." In F. Beach (Ed.), *Human Sexuality in Four Perspectives.* Baltimore, MD: Johns Hopkins University Press.

Stoller, R. J. (1991). *Pain & Passion: A Psychoanalyst Explores the World of S & M.* New York: Plenum Press.

Stone, K. M., et al. (1989). "National Surveillance for Neonatal Herpes Simplex Virus Infections." *Sexually Transmitted Diseases, 16*(3), 152–160.

Straayer, C. (1992). "Redressing the Natural—The Temporary Transvestite Film." *Wide Angle: A Quarterly Journal of Film History, Theory, and Criticism, 14*(1), 36–55.

Strage, M. (1980). *The Durable Fig Leaf.* New York: William Morrow.

Strong, B. (1973, June). "Origins of the Sex Education Movement." *History of Education Quarterly,* 1–18.

Strong, B. (1973). "Toward a History of the Experiential Family: Sex and Incest in the 19th Century." *Journal of Marriage and the Family, 34*, 457–466.

Struckman-Johnson, D., & Struckman-Johnson, C. (1991). "Men and Women's Acceptance of Coercive Sexual Strategies Varied by Initiator Gender and Couple Intimacy." *Sex Roles, 25*, 661–676.

Studer, M., & Thornton, A. (1987). "Adolescent Religiosity and Contraceptive Use." *Journal of Marriage and the Family, 49*, 117–128.

Sue, D. (1979). "Erotic Fantasies of College Students During Coitus." *Journal of Sex Research, 15*, 299–305.

Suggs, D. N., & Miracle, A. W. (1993). (Eds.). *Culture and Human Sexuality.* Pacific Grove, CA: Brooks/Cole.

Summers, R. (1991). "Determinants of Judgments of and Responses to a Complaint of Sexual Harassment." *Sex Roles, 25*(7-8), 379–392.

Surra, C. (1991). "Research and Theory on Mate Selection and Premarital Relationship in the 1980s." In A. Booth (Ed.), *Contemporary Families: Looking Forward, Looking Back.* Minneapolis, MN: National Council on Family Relations.

"Survey of 80,000 Cases Calls Birth-defect Test Safe." (1992, August 4). *San Jose Mercury News,* p. 3F.

Susser, M. (1992). "Induced Abortion and Health as a Value." *American Journal of Public Health, 82*(10), 1323–1324.

Sweet, J. A., & Bumpass, L. L. (1987). *American Families and Households.* New York: Russell Sage Foundation.

Sweet, R. (1986). "Pelvic Inflammatory Disease." *Sexually Transmitted Diseases, 13*(3), 192–198.

Swensen, C. H., Jr. (1972). "The Behavior of Love." In H. A. Otto (Ed.), *Love Today: A New Exploration*. New York: Association Press.

Symons, D. (1979). *The Evolution of Human Sexuality*. New York: Oxford University Press.

Szaz, T. (1990). *Sex by Prescription: The Startling Truth About Today's Sex Therapy*. Syracuse, NY: Syracuse University Press.

Szinovacz, M. (1987). "Family Power." In M. Sussman & S. Steinmetz (Eds.), *Handbook of Marriage and the Family*. New York: Plenum Press.

Talamini, J. T. (1982). *Boys Will Be Girls*. Washington, DC: University Press of America.

Tanfer, K. (1987). "Patterns of Premarital Cohabitation Among Never-Married Women in the United States." *Journal of Marriage and the Family, 49*, 683–697.

Tanfer, K., & Cubbins, L. A. (1992). "Coital Frequency Among Single Women: Normative Constraints and Situational Opportunities." *Journal of Sex Research, 29*(2), 221–250.

Tanfer, K., & Schoorl, J. J. (1992). "Premarital Sexual Careers and Partner Change." *Archives of Sexual Behavior, 21*, 45–68.

Tanke, E. D. (1982). "Dimensions of the Physical Attractiveness Stereotype: A Factor/Analytic Study." *Journal of Psychology, 110*, 63–74.

Tardif, G. S. (1989). "Sexual Activity After a Myocardial Infarction." *Archives of Physical Medicine and Rehabilitation, 70*(10), 763–766.

Tavris, C. (1992). *The Mismeasure of Woman*. New York: Norton.

Tavris, C., & Sadd, S. (1977). *The Redbook Report on Female Sexuality*. New York: Dell.

Tavris, C., & Wade, C. (1984). *The Longest War: Sex Differences in Perspective* (2nd ed.). New York: Harcourt Brace Jovanovich.

Taylor, E. (1989). *Prime-Time Families*. Berkeley, CA: University of California Press.

Taylor, R. J., Chatters, L. M., Tucker, B., & Lewis, E. (1991). "Developments in Research on Black Families." In A. Booth (Ed.), *Contemporary Families: Looking Forward, Looking Back*. Minneapolis, MN: National Council on Family Relations.

Teachman, J. D., & Polonko, K. A. (1990). "Cohabitation and Marital Stability in the United States." *Social Forces, 69*(1), 207–220.

"Teen-Age Fathers Now Getting Help." (1986, August 21). *The New York Times*, p. 24.

Templeman, T., & Stinnett, R. (1991). "Patterns of Sexual Arousal and History in a 'Normal' Sample of Young Men." *Archives of Sexual Behavior, 20*(2), 137–150.

Tessina, T. (1989). *Gay Relationships: For Men and Women. How to Find Them, How to Improve Them, How to Make Them Last*. Los Angeles: Tarcher.

Testa, R. J., Kinder, B. N., & Ironson, G. (1987). "Heterosexual Bias in the Perception of Loving Relationships of Gay Males and Lesbians." *Journal of Sex Research, 23*(2), 163–172.

Tharp, J. (1991). "The Transvestite as Monster: Gender Horror in 'The Silence of the Lambs' and 'Psycho'." *Journal of Popular Film and Television, 19*(3), 106–113.

Thayer, L. (1986). *On Communication*. Norwood, NJ: Ablex.

Thomas, S. B., & Quinn, S. C. (1991). "The Tuskegee Syphilis Study, 1932 to 1972: Implications for HIV Education and AIDS Risk Education Programs in the Black Community." *American Journal of Public Health, 81*(11), 1498–1504.

Thompson, A. (1983). "Extramarital Sex: A Review of the Research Literature." *Journal of Sex Research, 19*(1), 1–22.

Thompson, A. (1984). "Emotional and Sexual Components of Extramarital Relations." *Journal of Marriage and the Family, 46*(1), 35–42.

Thompson, B. W. (1992). "'A Way Outa No Way': Eating Problems Among African-American, Latina, and White Women." *Gender and Society, 6*(4), 546–561.

Thompson, C. E. (1990). "Transition of the Disabled Adolescent to Adulthood." *Pediatrician, 17*(4), 308–313.

Thompson, L., & Walker, A. J. (1989). "Gender in Families: Women and Men in Marriage, Work, and Parenthood." *Journal of Marriage and the Family, 51*, 845–871.

Thompson, M. E., Chaffee, S. H., & Oshagan, H. H. (1990). "Regulating Pornography: A Public Dilemma." *Journal of Communication, 40*(3), 73–83.

Thompson, S. (1986, December 23). "Pregnant on Purpose." *The Village Voice*, p. 28ff.

Thornton, A. (1989). "Changing Attitudes Toward Family Issues in the United States." *Journal of Marriage and the Family, 51*(4), 873–893.

Thornton, A. (1990). "The Courtship Process and Adolescent Sexuality." *Journal of Family Issues, 11*(3), 239–273.

Thornton, A., & Camburn, D. (1987). "The Influence of the Family on Premarital Sexual Attitudes and Behavior." *Demography, 24*, 323–340.

Tiefer, L. (1992). "Critique of the DSM-III-R Nosology of Sexual Dysfunctions." *Psychiatric Medicine, 10*(2), 227–245.

Tietjen, A., & Bradley, C. F. (1985). "Social Support and Maternal Psychosocial Adjustment During the Transition to Parenthood." *Canadian Journal of Behavioural Science, 17*(2), 109–121.

Ting-Toomey, S. (1983). "An Analysis of Verbal Communication Patterns in High and Low Marital Adjustment Groups." *Human Communications Research, 9*(4), 306–319.

Ting-Toomey, S., & Korzenny, Felipe. (1991). (Eds.). *Cross-Cultural Interpersonal Communication*. Newbury Park, CA: Sage Publications.

Toback, B. M. (1992). "Recent Advances in Female Infertility Care." *Naacogs Clinical Issues in Perinatal and Women's Health Nursing, 3*(2), 313–319.

Toback, J. (1992, August). "James Toback on 'The Hunger'." Special Issue: The Sexual Revolution in Movie, Music & TV. *US*, pp. 56–58.

Toomey, K. E., Oberschelp, A. G., & Greenspan, J. R. (1989). "Sexually Transmitted Diseases and Native Americans: Trends in Reported Gonorrhea and Syphilis Morbidity, 1984–1988." *Public Health Reports, 104*(6), 566–572.

Torres, A., & Forrest, J. D. (1988). "Why Do Women Have Abortions?" *Family Planning Perspectives, 20*, 7–9.

Torres, A., & Singh, S. (1986). "Contraceptive Practice Among Hispanic Adolescents." *Family Planning Perspectives, 18*(4), 193–194.

Trafford, A. (1980, November 10). "Medical Science Discovers the Baby." *U.S. News & World Report*, pp. 59–62.

Trall, R. T. (1853). *Home Treatment of Sexual Abuse*. New York: M. L. Holbrook.

Treiman, K., & Liskin, L. (1988). "IUDs: A New Look." *Population Reports*, Series B (No. 5), 1–31.

Tribe, L. (1992). *Abortion: The Clash of Absolutes*. New York: Norton.

Trippet, S. E., & Bain, J. (1992, April). "Reasons American Lesbians Fail to Seek Traditional Health Care." *Health Care for Women International, 13*(2), 145–153.

Troiden, R. (1988). *Gay and Lesbian Identity: A Sociological Analysis*. New York: General Hall.

True, R. H. (1990). "Psychotherapeutic Issues with Asian American Women." *Sex Roles, 22*(7), 477–485.

Trussell, J., Hatcher, R. A., Cates, W., Stewart, F. H., & Kost, K. (1990). "Contraceptive Failure in the United States: An Update." *Studies in Family Planning, 21*(1), Table 1.

Trussell, J., & Kost, K. (1987). "Contraceptive Failure in the United States: A Critical Review of the Literature." *Studies in Family Planning, 18*, 237–283.

Trussell, J., Stewart, F., Guest, F., & Hatcher, R. A. (1992). "Emergency Contraceptive Pills: A Simple Proposal to Reduce Unintended Pregnancies." *Family Planning Perspectives*, 24, 269–273.

Tsoi, W. F. (1990). "Developmental Profile of 200 Male and 100 Female Transsexuals in Singapore." *Archives of Sexual Behavior*, 19, 595–605.

Tsoukas, C., et al. (1986, June 23). "Risk of Transmission of HTLV-III/LAV from Human Bites." Paper presented at the Second International Conference on AIDS, Paris.

Tucker, M. B., & Taylor, R. J. (1989). "Demographic Correlates of Relationship Status Among Black Americans." *Journal of Marriage and the Family*, 51, 655–665.

Tucker, R. K., Marvin, M. G., & Vivian, B. (1991). "What Constitutes a Romantic Act?" *Psychological Reports*, 89(2), 651–654.

Tuleja, T. (1987). *Curious Customs*. New York: Harmony Books.

Tuller, N. R. (1988). "Couples: The Hidden Segment of the Gay World." In J. De Cecco (Ed.), *Gay Relationships*. New York: Haworth Press.

Tully, C. T. (1989). "Caregiving: What Do Midlife Lesbians View as Important?" *Journal of Gay and Lesbian Psychotherapy*, 1(1), 87–103.

Turner, P. H., et al. (1985, March). "Parenting in Gay and Lesbian Families." Paper presented at the first meeting of the Future of Parenting Symposium, Chicago.

Turner, R. J., & Avison, W. R. (1985). "Assessing Risk Factors for Problem Parenting: The Significance of Social Support." *Journal of Marriage and the Family*, 47(4), 881–892.

Turque, P. (1992, September 14). "Gays Under Fire." *Newsweek*, pp. 35–40.

Tuttle, G. E., & Pillard, R. C. (1991). "Sexual Orientation and Cognitive Abilities." *Archives of Sexual Behavior*, 20(3), 307–318.

Twinam, A. (1989). "Honor, Sexuality, and Illegitimacy in Colonial Spanish America." In A. Lavrin (Ed.), *Sexuality and Marriage in Colonial Latin America*. Lincoln, NE: University of Nebraska Press.

UCSF AIDS Health Project. (1991). "Risks of Oral Sex." *HIV Counselor Perspectives* (California Department of Health Services), 1(2), 1–8.

Ullman, S. E., & Knight, R. A. (1991). "A Multivariate Model for Predicting Rape and Physical Injury Outcomes During Sexual Assaults." *Journal of Consulting and Clinical Psychology*, 59(5), 724–731.

Unger, R. K. (1979). "Toward a Redefinition of Sex and Gender." *American Psychologist*, 34, 1085–1094.

Uribe, V., & Harbeck, K. M. (1991). "Addressing the Needs of Lesbian, Gay, and Bisexual Youth: The Origins of Project 10 and School Based Intervention." *Journal of Homosexuality*, 22, 9–28.

U.S. Bureau of the Census. (1990). *Statistical Abstract of the United States* (110th ed.). Washington, DC: U.S. Government Printing Office.

U.S. Bureau of the Census. (1991). "The Hispanic Population in the United States." *Current Population Reports*, Series P-20. Washington, DC: U.S. Government Printing Office.

U.S. Bureau of the Census. (1991). "Marital Status and Living Arrangements, 1990." *Current Population Reports*, Series P-20. Washington, DC: U.S. Government Printing Office.

U.S. Bureau of the Census. (1992). *Statistical Abstract of the United States* (112th ed.). Washington, DC: U.S. Government Printing Office.

U.S. Bureau of the Census. (1993). *Statistical Abstract of the United States* (113th ed.). Washington, DC: U.S. Government Printing Office.

U.S. Department of Justice. (1991). *Sourcebook of Criminal Justice Statistics*. Washington, DC: U.S. Government Printing Office.

Uslander, A., et al. (1973). *Their Universe: The Story of a Unique Educational Program*. New York: Delacorte Press.

Valentine, D. (1982). "The Experience of Pregnancy: A Developmental Process." *Family Relations*, 31, 243–248.

Van Buskirk. (1992, August). "Soap Opera Sex: Tuning In, Tuning Out." Special Issue: The Sexual Revolution in Movie, Music & TV. *US.*, pp. 64–67.

Vance, C. S. (1988). "Ordinances Restricting Pornography Could Damage Women." In R. T. Francoeur (Ed.), *Taking Sides: Clashing Views on Controversial Issues in Human Sexuality*. Guilford, CT: Dushkin Publishing Group.

Vance, C. S., & Pollis, C. (1990). "Introduction: Special Issue on Feminist Perspectives on Sexuality." *Journal of Sex Research*, 27(1), 1–5.

Van-de-Perre, P., Jacobs, D., & Sprecher-Goldberger, S. (1987). "The Latex Condom: An Efficient Barrier Against Sexual Transmission of AIDS-Related Viruses." *AIDS*, 1, 49–52.

Vanderford, M. (1989). "Vilification and Social Movements: A Case Study of Pro-Life and Pro-Choice Rhetoric." *Quarterly Journal of Speech*, 75(2), 166–182.

Vandewiel, H. B. M., Jaspers, J. P. M., Schultz, W. C. M. W., & Gal, J. (1990). "Treatment of Vaginismus: A Review of Concepts and Treatment Modalities." *Journal of Psychosomatic Obstetrics and Gynecology*, 11, 1–18.

Van Wyk, P. H., & Geist, C. S. (1984). "Psychosocial Development of Heterosexual, Bisexual, and Homosexual Behavior." *Archives of Sexual Behavior*, 13, 505–544.

Vasquez-Nuthall, E., et al. (1987). "Sex Roles and Perceptions of Femininity and Masculinity of Hispanic Women: A Review of the Literature." *Psychology of Women Quarterly*, 11, 409–426.

Vaughan, D. (1986). *Uncoupling: Turning Points in Intimate Relationships*. New York: Oxford University Press.

Vaughter, R. M. (1976). "Psychology." *Signs*, 2(1), 120–146.

Veevers, J. (1980). *Childless by Choice*. Toronto, Canada: Buttersworth.

Vega, W. (1991). "Hispanic Families." In A. Booth (Ed.), *Contemporary Families: Looking Forward, Looking Back*. Minneapolis, MN: National Council on Family Relations.

Ventura, J. N. (1987). "The Stresses of Parenthood Reexamined." *Family Relations*, 36, 26–29.

Verschraegen-Spae, M. R. (1992). "Familial Turner Syndrome." *Clinical Genetics*, 41(4), 218–220.

Verwoerdt, A., et al. (1969). "Sexual Behavior in Senescence." *Geriatrics*, 24, 137–157.

Verzaro-Lawrence, M. (1981, May). "Shared Childrearing: A Challenging Alternative Lifestyle." *Alternative Lifestyles*, 4 (2), 205–217.

Vessey, M. P., et al. (1983). "Neoplasia of the Cervix Uteri and Contraception: A Possible Adverse Effect of the Pill." *Lancet*, 2, 930–934.

Vessey, M. P., Lawless, M., Yeates, D., & McPherson, K. (1985). "Progestin-Only Oral Contraception: Findings in a Large Prospective Study with Special Reference to Effectiveness." *British Journal of Family Planning*, 10, 117–121.

Vincent, R., et al. (1987). "Sexism on MTV: The Portrayal of Women in Rock Video." *Journalism Quarterly*, 64(4), 750–755, 941.

Virga, V. (1980). *Gaywyck*. New York: Avon.

Voeller, B. (1980). "Society and the Gay Movement." In J. Marmor (Ed.), *Homosexual Behavior*. New York: Basic Books.

Voeller, B. (1991). "AIDS and Heterosexual Anal Intercourse." *Archives of Sexual Behavior*, 20(3), 233–276.

Vogel, D. A., Lake, M. A., & Evans, S. (1991). "Children's and Adults' Sex-Stereotyped Perceptions of Infants." *Sex Roles*, 24, 605–616.

Voydanoff, P., & Donnelly, B. (1990). *Adolescent Sexuality and Pregnancy*. Newbury Park, CA: Sage Publications.

Wade, R. C. (1978). *For Men About Abortion*. Boulder, CO: R. C. Wade.

Walker, A. (1992). *Possessing the Secret of Joy*. New York: Harcourt Brace Jovanovich.

Walker, E. A., et al. (1992). "Medical and Psychiatric Symptoms in Women with Childhood Sexual Abuse." *Psychosomatic Medicine, 54*(6), 658–664.

Wallace, R. (1991). "Traveling Waves of HIV Infection on a Low Dimensional 'Socio-Geographic' Network." *Social Science and Medicine, 32*(7), 847–852.

Waller, W., & Hill, R. (1951). *The Family: A Dynamic Interpretation*. New York: Dryden Press.

Walling, M., Andersen, B. L., & Johnson, S. R. (1990). "Hormonal Replacement Therapy for Postmenopausal Women: A Review of Sexual Outcomes and Related Gynecologic Effects." *Archives of Sexual Behavior, 19*(2), 119–127.

Wallis, C. (1985, December 9). "Children Having Children." *Time*, pp. 78–79.

Wallis, C. (1986, April 28). "The Career Woman's Disease." *Time*, p. 62.

Wardle, F. (1989, December). "Helping Children Respect Differences." *PTA Today*, pp. 5–6.

Washton, A. M. (1989). *Cocaine Addiction: Treatment, Recovery, and Relapse Prevention*. New York: Norton.

Waterman, C. K., et al. (1989). "Sexual Coercion in Gay Male and Lesbian Relationships: Predictors and Implications for Support Services." *Journal of Sex Research, 26*(1), 118–125.

Waterson, E. J., & Murray-Lyon, I. M. (1990). "Preventing Alcohol-Related Birth Damage: A Review." *Social Science and Medicine, 30*(3), 349–364.

Watson, R. (1983). "Premarital Cohabitation vs. Traditional Courtship: Their Effects on Subsequent Marital Adjustment." *Family Relations, 32*(1), 139–147.

Webb, P. (1983). *The Erotic Arts*. New York: Farrar, Straus & Giroux.

Webb, T. (1992 August 2). "Rural Teen Who Got AIDS Warns Others They're at Risk." *San Jose Mercury News*, A2.

Weeks, J. (1985). *Sexuality and Its Discontents*. London: Routledge & Kegan Paul.

Weeks, J. (1986). *Sexuality*. New York: Tavistock Publications and Ellis Horwood, Ltd.

Weeks, J. (1993, February 11). "Someone Wicked This Way Comes." *San Jose Mercury News*, pp. 1C, 6C.

Weg, R. (1983b). "Introduction: Beyond Intercourse and Orgasm." In R. Weg (Ed.), *Sexuality in the Later Years: Roles and Behavior*. New York: Academic Press.

Weg, R. (1983). "The Physiological Perspective." In R. Weg (Ed.), *Sexuality in the Later Years: Roles and Behavior*. New York: Academic Press.

Weidner, W., Weiske, W. H., Rudnick, J., Becker, H. C., Schroeder-Printzen, J., & Brahler, E. (1992). "Venous Surgery in Veno-Occlusive Dysfunction: Long-time Results after Dorsal Vein Resection." *Urologia Internationalis, 49*(1), 24–28.

Weinberg, M. S., & Williams, C. J. (1974). *Male Homosexuals: Their Problems and Adaptations*. New York: Oxford University Press.

Weinberg, M. S., & Williams, C. J. (1988). "Black Sexuality: A Test of Two Theories." *Journal of Sex Research, 25*(2), 197–218.

Weinberg, M. S., Williams, C. J., & Moser, C. (1984). "The Social Constituents of Sadomasochism." *Social Problems, 31*, 379–389.

Weinberg, T. S. (1987). "Sadomasochism in the United States: A Review of Recent Sociological Literature." *Journal of Sex Research, 23*, 50–69.

Weinberg, T. S., & Kamel, G. W. L. (Eds.). (1983). *S and M: Studies in Sadomasochism*. Buffalo, NY: Prometheus Books.

Weir, J. (1992, March 29). "Gay-Bashing, Villany and the Oscars." *The New York Times*, p. 17.

Weis, D. (1985). "The Experience of Pain During Women's First Sexual Intercourse: Cultural Mythology About Female Sexual Initiation." *Archives of Sexual Behavior, 14*, 421–428.

Weisberg, D. K. (1985). *Children of the Night: A Study of Adolescent Prostitution*. Lexington, MA: Lexington Books.

Weiss, D. (1983). "Open Marriage and Multilateral Relationships: The Emergence of Nonexclusive Models of the Marital Relationship." In E. Macklin & R. Rubin (Eds.), *Contemporary Families and Alternative Lifestyles*. Newbury Park, CA: Sage Publications.

Weiss, D., & Jurich, J. (1985). "Size of Community as a Predictor of Attitudes Toward Extramarital Sexual Relations." *Journal of Marriage and the Family, 47*(1), 173–178.

Weiss, J. (1992). "Multiple Sclerosis: Will It Come Between Us? Sexual Concerns of Clients and Their Partners." *Journal of Neuroscience Nursing, 24*(4), 190–193.

Weiss, P. (1992, August 18). "The Bond of Mother's Milk." *San Jose Mercury News*, pp. 1–2E.

Weiss, R. (1975). *Marital Separation*. New York: Basic Books.

Weissbach, T. A., & Zagon, G. (1975). "The Effect of Deviant Group Membership Upon Impression of Personality." *Journal of Social Psychology, 95*, 263–266.

Weizman, R., & Hart, J. (1987). "Sexual Behavior in Healthy Married Elderly Men." *Archives of Sexual Behavior, 16*(1), 39–44.

Welch, M., & Herman, D. (1980, February). "Why Miscarriage Is So Misunderstood." *Ms.*, pp. 14–22.

Wenger, N. S., Linn, L. S., Epstein, M., & Shapiro, M. F. (1991). "Reduction of High-Risk Sexual Behavior Among Heterosexuals Undergoing HIV Antibody Testing: A Randomized Clinical Trial." *American Journal of Public Health, 81*(12), 1580–1585.

Wenz, P. S. (1992). *Abortion Rights as Religious Freedom*. Philadelphia: Temple University Press.

Wertz, R., & Wertz, D. (1977). *Lying-In: A History of Childbirth in America*. New York: Free Press.

Wheeless, L. R., Wheeless, V. E., & Baus, R. (1984). "Sexual Communication, Communication Satisfaction, and Solidarity in the Developmental Stages of Intimate Relationships." *Western Journal of Speech Communication, 48*, 217–230.

Whelan, E. (1986). *Boy or Girl?* New York: Pocket Books.

Whitam, F. L. (1977). "Childhood Indicators of Male Homosexuality." *Archives of Sexual Behavior, 6*, 89–96.

Whitbeck, L. B., & Hoyt, D. R. (1991). "Campus Prestige and Dating Behaviors." *College Student Journal, 25*(4), 457–469.

Whitbourne, S. K. (1990). "Sexuality in the Aging Male." *Generations, 14*(3), 28–30.

Whitbourne, S., & Ebmeyer, J. (1990). *Identity and Intimacy in Marriage: A Study of Couples*. New York: Springer-Verlag.

White, C. (1982). "Sexual Interest, Attitudes, Knowledge, and Sexual History in Relation to Sexual Behavior of the Institutionalized Aged." *Archives of Sexual Behavior, 11*, 11–21.

White, G. (1980a). "Inducing Jealousy: A Power Perspective." *Personality and Social Psychology Bulletin, 6*(2), 222–227.

White, G. (1980b, October). "Physical Attractiveness and Courtship Progress." *Journal of Personality and Social Psychology, 39*(4), 660–668.

White, G. (1981a). "Jealousy and Partner's Perceived Motives for Attraction to a Rival." *Social Psychology Quarterly, 44*(1), 24–30.

White, G. (1981b). "A Model of Romantic Jealousy." *Motivation and Education, 5*, 600–668.

White, J. W., & Farmer, R. (1992). "Research Methods: How They Shape Views of Sexual Violence." *Journal of Social Issues, 48*, 45–59.

White, J., & Parham, T. (1990). *The Psychology of Blacks: An African-American Perspective* (2nd ed.). Englewood Cliffs, NJ: Prentice-Hall.

White, P., & Rollins, J. (1981). "Rape: A Family Crisis." *Family Relations,* 103–109.

Whitehead, B. D. (1990, October 7). "How to Rebuild a 'Family Friendly' Society." *Des Moines Sunday Register,* p. 3.

Whiting, B. (1979). "Contributions of Anthropology to the Study of Gender Identity, Gender Role, and Sexual Behavior." In H. Katchadourian (Ed.), *Human Sexuality: A Comparative and Developmental Perspective.* Berkeley, CA: University of California Press.

"WHO Collaborative Study of Neoplasia and Steroid Contraceptives, Breast Cancer, Cervical Cancer, and Depot Medroxyprogesterone Acetate." (1984, November 24). *Lancet,* 2(8413) 1207–1208.

Why Gal. (1992, April 17). "Male Nipples Are Good for Something." *Seattle Times,* p. 6.

Wilcox, A., et al. (1988). "Incidents of Early Loss of Pregnancy." *New England Journal of Medicine,* 319(4), 189–194.

Wilkerson, I. (1987, June 26). "Infant Mortality: Frightful Odds in Inner City." *The New York Times,* p. 1ff.

Wilkinson, C. B. (1986). (Ed.). *Ethnic Psychiatry.* New York: Plenum Medical Book Company.

Wilkinson, C. B., & Spurlock, J. (1986). "The Mental Health of Black Americans: Psychiatric Diagnosis and Treatment." In C. B. Wilkinson (Ed.), *Ethnic Psychiatry.* New York: Plenum Medical Book Company.

Wilkinson, D., et al. (Eds.). (1992). "Transforming Social Knowledge: The Interlocking of Race, Class, and Gender." *Gender and Society.* Special issue.

Wilkinson, D., Zinn, M. B., & Chow, E. N. L. (1992). "Race, Class, and Gender: Introduction." *Gender and Society,* 6(3), 341–345.

Wilkinson, S., & Kitzinger, C. (Eds.). (1993). *Heterosexuality.* Newbury Park, CA: Sage Publications.

Willemsen, T. M. (1993). "On the Bipolarity of Androgyny: A Critical Comment on Kottke (1988)." *Psychological Reports,* 72(1), 327–332.

Willet, W. C., et al. (1987). "Moderate Alcohol Consumption and the Risk of Breast Cancer." *New England Journal of Medicine,* 316(19), 1174–1180.

Williams, D. M., Patterson, M. N., & Hughes, I. A. (1993). "Androgen Insensitivity Syndrome." *Archives of Disease in Childhood,* 68(3), 343–344.

Williams, E. A., et al. (1992). "The Impact of a University Policy on the Sexual Harassment of Female Students." *Journal of Higher Education,* 63(1), 50–64.

Williams, J. K. (1992). "School-Aged Children with Turner's Syndrome." *Journal of Pediatric Nursing,* 7(1), 14–19.

Williams, J. K., et al. (1991). "A Comparison of Memory and Attention in Turner Syndrome and Learning Disability." *Journal of Pediatric Psychology,* 16(5), 585–593.

Williams, J. K., Richman, L. C., & Yarbrough, D. B. (1992). "Comparison of Visual-Spatial Performance Strategy Training in Children with Turner Syndrome and Learning Disabilities." *Journal of Learning Disabilities,* 25(10), 658–664.

Williams, J., & Jacoby, A. (1989). "The Effects of Premarital Heterosexual and Homosexual Experience on Dating and Marriage Desirability." *Journal of Marriage and the Family,* 51, 489–497.

Williams, K. B., & Cyr, R. R. (1992). "Escalating Commitment to a Relationship: The Sexual Harassment Trap." *Sex Roles,* 27(1-2), 47–72.

Williams, W. L. (1985). "Persistence and Change in the Berdache Tradition Among Contemporary Lakota Indians." *Journal of Homosexuality,* 11(3-4), 191–200.

Wills, G. (1989, December 21). "The Phallic Pulpit." *The New York Review of Books,* pp. 20–26.

Wills, G. (1990). *Under God.* New York: Simon & Schuster.

Wilson, G. (1978). *The Secrets of Sexual Fantasy.* London: J. M. Dent.

Wilson, M. N., et al. (1990). "Flexibility and Sharing of Childcare Duties in Black Families." *Sex Roles,* 22(7-8), 409–425.

Wilson, P. (1986). "Black Culture and Sexuality." *Journal of Social Work and Human Sexuality,* 4(3), 29–46.

Wilson, S. M., & Medora, N. P. (1990). "Gender Comparisons of College Students' Attitudes Toward Sexual Behavior." *Adolescence,* 25(99), 615–627.

Wilson, W. (1988). "Rape as Entertainment." *Psychological Reports,* 63(2), 607–610.

Wise, T. N., et al. (1991). "Personality and Sexual Functioning of Transvestitic Fetishists and Other Paraphilics." *Journal of Nervous and Mental Disease,* 179(11), 694–698.

Wise, T. N., et al. (1992). "Sexual Issues in the Medically Ill and Aging." *Psychiatric Medicine,* 10(2), 169–180.

Wise, T. N., & Meyer, J. K. (1980). "The Border Area Between Transvestism and Gender Dysphoria: Transvestitic Applicants for Sex Reassignment." *Archives of Sexual Behavior,* 9, 327–342.

Wishnietsky, D. H. (1991). "Reported and Unreported Teacher-Student Sexual Harassment." *Journal of Educational Research,* 84(3), 164–169.

Wolberg, W. H., Romsaas, E. P., Tanner, M. A., & Malec, J. F. (1989). "Psychosexual Adaptation to Breast Cancer Surgery." *Cancer,* 63(8), 1645–1655.

Wolf, D. (1980). *The Lesbian Community.* Berkeley, CA: University of California Press.

Wolf, M., & Kielwasser, A. (1991). "Introduction: The Body Electric: Human Sexuality and the Mass Media." *Journal of Homosexuality,* 21(1-2), 7–18.

Wolf, N. (1991). *The Beauty Myth: How Images of Beauty Are Used Against Women.* New York: Morrow.

Wolfe, L. (1981). *The Cosmos Report.* New York: Bantam.

Wolff, C. (1986). *Magnus Hirschfeld: A Portrait of a Pioneer in Sexology.* London: Quartet Books.

Wolinksy, S., et al. (1988, June 12). "Polymerase Chain Reaction (PCR) Detection of HIV Provirus Before HIV Seroconversion." Paper presented at the Fourth International Conference on AIDS, Stockholm, Sweden.

Wood, D. (1993, January 29). "Military Women Say Anti-Gay Rule Harms Heterosexuals' Careers, Too." *San Jose Mercury News,* p. 17.

Wood, F. G. (1990). *The Arrogance of Faith: Christianity and Race in America from the Colonial Era to the Twentieth Century.* New York: Knopf.

Woodhouse, A. (1985). "Forgotten Women: Transvestism and Marriage." *Women's Studies International Forum,* 8(6), 583–592.

Woodhouse, A. (1989). "Breaking the Rules or Bending Them: Transvestism, Femininity, and Feminism." *Women's Studies International Forum,* 12(4), 417–423.

Woods, N. F. *Human Sexuality in Health and Illness.* (1984). (3rd ed.). St. Louis, MO: Mosby.

Woods, S. C., & Mansfield, J. G. (1981, February 11). "Ethanol and Disinhibition: Physiological and Behavioral Links." In R. Room & Collins (Eds.), *Proceedings of Alcoholism and Drug Abuse Conference, Berkeley/Oakland* (pp. 4–22). Washington, DC: U.S. Department of Health and Human Services.

Woodward, K. (1987, March 23). "New Rules for Making Love and Babies." *Newsweek,* pp. 42–43.

Workman, J. E., & Johnson, K. K. (1991). "The Role of Cosmetics in Attributions About Sexual Harassment." *Sex Roles,* 24(11-12), 759–769.

World Health Organization. (1992). *Reproductive Health: A Key to a Brighter Future.* Biennial Report, 1990–1991. Geneva, Switzerland: World Health Organization.

Wormser, G. P., et al. (1992). "Absence of Infectious Human Immunodeficiency Virus Type 1 in 'Natural' Eccrine Sweat." *Journal of Infectious Diseases,* 165(1), 155–158.

Wright, J., Duchesne, C., Sabourin, S., Bissonnette, F., Benoit, J., & Girard, Y. (1991). "Psychosocial Distress and Infertility: Men and Women Respond Differently." *Fertility and Sterility, 55*(1), 100–108.

Wright, P., Nobrega, J., Langevin, R., & Wortzman, G. (1990). "Brain Density and Symmetry in Pedophilic and Sexually Aggressive Offenders." *Annals of Sex Research, 3*(3), 319–328.

Wyatt, G. E. (1991). "Examining Ethnicity Versus Race in AIDS Related Sex Research." *Social Science and Medicine, 33*(1), 37–45.

Wyatt, G. E. (1992). "The Sociocultural Context of African American and White American Women's Rape." *Journal of Social Issues, 48*(1), 77–91.

Wyatt, G. E., et al. (1988). "Kinsey Revisited II: Comparisons of the Sexual Socialization and Sexual Behavior of Black Women Over 33 Years." *Archives of Sexual Behavior, 17*(4), 289–332.

Wyatt, G. E., et al. (1992). "Differential Effects of Women's Child Sexual Abuse and Subsequent Sexual Revictimization." *Journal of Consulting and Clinical Psychology, 60*(2), 167–174.

Wyatt, G. E., & Lyons-Rowe, S. (1990). "African American Women's Sexual Satisfaction as a Dimension of Their Sex Roles." *Sex Roles, 22*(7–8), 509–524.

Wynn, R., & Fletcher, C. (1987). "Sex Role Development and Early Educational Experiences." In D. B. Carter (Ed.), *Current Conceptions of Sex Roles and Sex Typing.* New York: Praeger.

Yap, P. M. (1993). "Koro—A Culture-Bound Depersonalization." In D. N. Suggs & A. W. Miracle (Eds.), *Culture and Human Sexuality.* Pacific Grove, CA: Brooks/Cole.

Yarber, W. L., Torabi, M. R., & Veenker, C. H. (1989). "Development of a Three-Component Sexually Transmitted Diseases Attitude Scale." *Journal of Sex Education and Therapy, 15,* 36–49.

Yorke, J. A., et al. (1978). "Dynamics and Control of the Transmission of Gonorrhea." *Sexually Transmitted Diseases, 5,* 51–56.

Young, L. (1992). "Sexual Abuse and the Problem of Embodiment." *Child Abuse and Neglect, 16*(1), 89–100.

Yulsman, T. (1990, October 7). "A Little Help for Creation. The Good Health Magazine." *The New York Times,* p. 22ff.

Zabin, L. S., et al. (1986). "Evaluation of a Pregnancy Prevention Program for Urban Teenagers." *Family Planning Perspectives, 18,* 119ff.

Zabin, L. S., & Clark, S. D. (1981). "Why They Delay: A Study of Teenage Family Planning Clinic Patients." *Family Planning Perspectives, 13,* 205–217.

Zabin, L. S., Hardy, J. B., Smith, E. A., & Hirsch, M. B. (1986). "Substance Use and Its Relation to Sexual Activity Among Inner-City Adolescents." *Journal of Adolescent Health Care, 7*(5), 320–331.

Zacharias, L., et al. (1976). *Obstetrical and Gynecological Survey, 31*(4).

Zaslow, M., et al. (1981, April). "Depressed Mood in New Fathers." Unpublished manuscript, Society for Research in Child Development.

Zausner, M. (1986). *The Streets: A Factual Portrait of Sex Prostitutes as Told in Their Own Words.* New York: St. Martin's Press.

Zaviacic, M., et al. (1988). "Concentrations of Fructose in Female Ejaculate and Urine." *Journal of Sex Research, 24,* 319–325.

Zelnik, M. (1981). *Sex and Pregnancy in Adolescence.* Newbury Park, CA: Sage Publications.

Zelnik, M., & Kantner, J. F. (1972). "Probability of Premarital Intercourse." *Social Science Research, 1,* 335–341.

Zelnik, M., & Shaw, F. (1983). "First Intercourse Among Young Adults." *Family Planning Perspectives, 15,* 64–70.

Zerbe, K. J. (1992). "Why Eating-Disordered Patients Resist Sex Therapy: A Response to Simpson and Ramberg." *Journal of Sex and Marital Therapy, 18*(1), 55–64.

Zevin, D. (1992, August). "The Pleasure Principle." Special Issue: The Sexual Revolution in Movies, Music & TV. *US.,* pp. 32–36.

Zilbergeld, B. (1992). *Male Sexuality.* Boston: Little, Brown.

Zimmerman, H. L., et al. (1990). "Epidemiological Differences Between Chlamydia and Gonorrhea." *American Journal of Public Health, 80*(11), 1338–1342.

Zinn, M. B. (1990). "Family, Feminism, and Race." *Gender and Society, 4,* 68–82.

Zinn, M. B., & Eitzen, D. S. (1990). *Diversity in Families* (2nd ed.). New York: HarperCollins.

Photo Credits

Index

Boldface numbers indicate pages on which key terms appear.

Herpes simplex virus (HSV), 563,
    640–642, 673
Hetaerae, **31**
Heterosexism, **722**
Heterosexual bias, **722**
Heterosexuality
    anti-gay prejudice and, 723
    bisexuality and, 237–238
    definition of, **29**
    fear of gays and lesbians as parents and,
        532
    Kinsey's research on, 71
    pedophilia and, 412
    power and, 340
    premature ejaculation and, 601
    sexual orientation of, 29
Heterosociality, **206**
Hill, Anita, 717
Hirschfeld, Magnus, 76
Hispanics. *See* Latinos
HIV-1, 676
HIV-2, 676
HIV encephalopathy, 673
HIV (human immunodeficiency virus). *See
    also* AIDS
    accidents and, 686
    adolescence and, 692
    African Americans and, 693
    AIDS and, 669, 672
    Alaskan natives and, 693
    anal intercourse and, 98, 382, 682
    artificial insemination and, 506
    Asian Americans and, 693
    bisexuality and, 706
    blood transfusions and, 686
    childhood and, 692
    as complication of pregnancy, 494, 680,
        684, 691
    condoms and, 212–213, 428, 483–484,
        695
    contraception and, 428
    as danger to fetus, 494, 684
    dental accidents and, 686, 696
    discrimination and, 704–705
    drug abuse and, 680, 683–684
    epidemic of, 678–679
    epidemiology of, 679–680
    ethnicity and, 693
    fellatio and, 376
    first appearance of, **669**
    gay men and, 706
    gay subculture and, 246
    HIV-1 and, 676
    HIV-2 and, 676
    hypoactive sexual desire and, 599
    intercourse and, 682
    Latinos and, 693
    living with, 704–707
    men and, 683
    myths about, 670–671
    nonsexual contact and, 684–685
    oral-genital sex and, 682
    organ donations and, 686
    Pacific Islanders and, 693
    popular culture and, 670–671
    positive testing for, 705–706
    poverty and, 693

prevention of
    condoms and, 695
    protection and, 693–695
    self-assessment of attitude and, 694
    sex education and, 695–700
prostitution and, 785
research on, 669
risk factors and, 686–687
sex therapy for fears of, 620
sex toys and, 682
sexual expression and, 767
spermicides and, 445
spread of, 680
symptoms of, 673–674
tests, 700–701
transmission of
    IV drug use, 683–684
    modes of, 681–682
    mother-to-child, 684
    myths of, 680–681
    sexual, 682–683
    uncommon, 684–686
    women and, 690
treatment, 701–703
virus causing, 675–676
whites and, 693, 706
women and, 683, 690–691, 706
Hollywood films. *See* Films
Home birth, 520
Home pregnancy tests, 485–486
Homoerotic, **238**
Homophobia, 620, 722, 727. *See also* Anti-
    gay prejudice
Homosexuality. *See also* Gay men; Lesbians
    biological theories of, 198–199
    definition of, **29**
    DSM-III and, 77
    Ellis's research on, 68, 69
    fear of, 620, 722, 727
    Kinsey's research on, 70–71
    military and, 727–728
    misconceptions about, 247
    pedophilia and, 412–413
    psychological theories of, 199
    religion and, 726–727
    sex education and, 217
    sexual orientation of, 29
    situational, 237
Homosociality, **206**
Hooker, Evelyn, 76
Hormonal methods of contraception
    implants, 437–438
    oral contraceptives, 433–436
Hormone replacement therapy (HRT),
    549–550, 577
Hormones
    definition of, **100**
    estrogen, 14, 100, 135, 433, 549–550,
        577
    follicle-stimulating hormone, 104, 105,
        135, 136, 459
    gonadotropin-releasing hormone, 104,
        135, 136, 459, 576
    hermaphroditism and, 184–185
    human chorionic gonadotropin, 105,
        484, 485
    ICSH, 135, 137

infertility and
    cause of, 502
    treatment of, 504–505
inhibin, 135, 136, 137
luteinizing hormone, 104, 135, 136, 459
luteinizing-hormone-releasing hormone,
    459
oxytocin, 511
progesterone, 105, 433
relaxin, 141, 510
reproductive, 100, 135–137
in sex reassignment surgery, 188
sexual desire and, 117
Hormone therapy
    androgen replacement therapy, 567
    infertility and, 504–505
    menopause and, 549–550
Hospital childbirth, 515, 517
Hostile environment, **715**
Hot flash, **548**
HPV (human papilloma virus), 563,
    639–640
HRT (hormone replacement therapy),
    549–550, 577
HSD (hypoactive sexual desire),
    598–600
HSV (herpes simplex virus), 563,
    640–642, 673
Human chorionic gonadotropin (HCG),
    105, 484, 485
Human immunodeficiency virus. *See* HIV
Human papilloma virus (HPV), 563,
    639–640
Humiliation, 397
Hustlers, 783
Hymen, **95**, 203
Hypoactive sexual desire (HSD),
    598–600
Hypothalamus, 199, 459
Hysterectomy, 454, **566**–567
Hysterotomy, **561**

ICSH, 135, 137
Id, **65**
Immune system, 674–675
Implantation, **484**
Implants, **437**–438
Incest, 23, **748**
Independent variables, **62**
Induced abortion, 460
Induction, **55**
Infants
    breast-feeding and, 525–528
    circumcision of, 521, 524–525
    gender-role learning by, 196
    low birth weight, 495–496
    mortality rate of, 499–500
    premature delivery of, 496
    sexual arousal in, 194
    sexuality and, 194, 195–196
    touching and, 317–318
Infatuation, 289, 290
Infections. *See also* AIDS; HIV; STDs
    AIDS and, 672–673
    as complications of pregnancy, 494
    condoms and, 134
    enteric, 652

of sexual attitudes, 26–28
of sexual communication, 314
of STD attitude, 630–631
Self-awareness, 330, 590–592
Self-conflict, 609
Self-disclosure, **281**, 304, 332, 334, 660–661
Self-exams, 560, 571, 573–575
Self-help, 619–620
Semen, **141**, 204
Seminal fluid, 141, 204
Seminal vesicles, **133**
Seminiferous tubules, **132**
Seminomas, **570**
Sensate focus, **611**–612
Senses, 116
Separation, marital, 261
Septa, 702
Serial monogamy, **249**
Seroconversion, **677**
Serostatus, **677**
Servilism, 397
Sex, **150**–152, 497. *See also* Gender
Sex determination, 140–141
Sex discrimination, 769–770
Sex education
    advice columnists and, 45–50
    AIDS and, 216, 698
    contemporary, 216–218
    developmental disabilities and, 557
    fear-based, 214
    HIV and, 216, 645
        prevention of, 695–700
    homosexuality and, 217
    pop psychology and, 45–50
    sexual activity and, 217
    of STDs, 216
Sex flush, **118**
Sex information/advice genre, **45**–50
Sex Information and Education Council of the United States (SIECUS), 216
Sex knowledge, self-assessment of, 59–61
Sex organs. *See also* specific names
    female
        breasts, 98–99, 203
        external structures, 92, 94
        function of, 91–92
        internal structures, 94–95
        other structures, 98
    male
        breasts, 134, 204
        external structures, 126–131
        function of, 126
        internal structures, 131–134
        other structures, 134
    self-exam of, 573–575
Sex play, 196–199
Sex reassignment surgery (SRS), **187**–189
Sex research
    approaches to, 56
    clinical research and, 58
    of Ellis, 64, 67–68
    ethics in, 56–57
    ethnicity and sexuality and, 77–78

experimental research and, 62–63
on female sexual response, 112
feminist scholarship and, 73–74
of Freud (Sigmund), 64, 65–67
gay men and, 75–77
induction and, 55
of Johnson, 64, 72–73
of Kinsey, 64, 69–72
lesbians and, 75–77
of Masters, 64, 72–73, 610
media and, 48–49
observational research and, 61–62
sampling and, 57, 63
scientific method and, 55
survey research and, 58, 60
of von Krafft-Ebing, 64–65
Sex researchers. *See* specific names
Sex therapy
    African Americans and, 614
    eating disorders and, 546
    ethnicity and, 613–614
    gay men and, 620–621
    HIV fears and, 620
    Latinos and, 613
    lesbians and, 620–621
    PLISSIT model and, 618–619
    as sexual dysfunction treatment, 618–621
    whites and, 613
Sex toys, **592**, 682
Sex-typed, **180**. *See also* Gender-role stereotypes
Sexual abuse, 545. *See also* Child sexual abuse; Rape
Sexual abuse trauma, **752**
Sexual activity. *See also* Extramarital sexual activity; Premarital sexual activity; specific types
    after age 75, 266
    bad, conditions for, 595
    conflict about, 341–342
    critical thinking about, 50–55
    divorce and, 261, 262–263
    exploitation and, 714–715
    extrarelational, 256–257
    gay men and, 326–328
    good, conditions for, 590–592
    lesbians and, 326–328
    love and, 274–275, 277–281
    marriage and, 255
    menopause and, 549
    nonmarital, 232
    nonperipheral aspects of, 280–281
    popular culture and, 631
    pregnancy and, 492
    problems with, 588–589
    prototypes of, 278–280
    refusal of, 342, 732–733
    in romance novels, 22
    safe, 656, 657
    sex education and, 217
    sexual communication and, 324–325, 330–331
    without love, 277
Sexual addiction, 388–389

Sexual aggression, **729**, 767–769. *See also* Rape; sexual assault
Sexual anxieties, 608–609
Sexual arousal. *See also* Sexual response
    in childhood, 194
    in infants, 194
    intensifying, 596
    of men, 141–144
    sexual desire and, 115
    of women, 117–119
Sexual assault, 739–740. *See also* Child sexual abuse; Rape
Sexual attitudes, 11, 26–28, 84, 85
Sexual attraction, 351–355
Sexual aversion, **600**
Sexual behavior. *See also* Atypical sexual behavior; Paraphilic sexual behavior; specific behaviors
    adolescent
        contraception and, 212–218
        first intercourse and, 211–212
        kissing and, 210
        masturbation and, 209, 365–368
        oral-genital sex and, 210–211, 373
        sequence of, 209–211
        virginity and, 211–212
    deviant, 38, 64–65
    Ellis's research on, 67–69
    emotions and, 350
    explicit, 12, 20
    Freud's (Sigmund) research on, 65–67
    ineffective, 608
    judging, 40
    Kinsey's research on, 69–72
    labeling and, 386–387
    Masters and Johnson's research on, 72–73
    natural, 34–35
    normal, 35–38, 68–69
    sexual scripts and, 355
    touching and, 318–319
    typical, 38–39
    von Krafft-Ebing's research on, 64–65
Sexual coercion, **729**. *See also* Child sexual abuse; Rape
Sexual communication
    in beginning relationships, 320–326
    development of, 329–334
    in established relationships, 326–328
    gay men and, 325–326
    importance of, 319
    in intimate relationships, 328–329
    lesbians and, 325–326
    in marriage, 329
    men and, 322–325
    satisfaction, 314, 328–329
    self-assessment of, 314
    sexual activity and, 324–325, 330–331
    sexual vocabulary and, 331
    women and, 322–325
Sexual conflicts, 341–342
Sexual desire
    brain and, 115–116
    erotophilia and, 354–355
    erotophobia and, 354–355